John P. C

4 C

150 Idora Avenue

San Francisco, 27

La. 4- 0287

∪ – : iambic
– ∪ : trochaic
∪ ∪ – : anapestic
– ∪ ∪ : dactyllic
– – : spondi

Prose and Poetry of England

St. Thomas More Series

PROSE AND POETRY
OF ENGLAND

SECOND EDITION

Julian L. Maline, Ph.D.

PROFESSOR OF EDUCATION, WEST BADEN COLLEGE OF LOYOLA UNIVERSITY

John J. Divine, A.M.

INSTRUCTOR IN ENGLISH, ST. LOUIS UNIVERSITY HIGH SCHOOL, ST. LOUIS, MISSOURI

JOHN J. KILLOREN, A.M

RICHARD F. SMITH, A.M.

JOHN J. WALSH, PH.D.

SYRACUSE, NEW YORK

The L. W. Singer Company, Inc.

THE COVER DESIGN:

"Entry into Jerusalem" is an outstanding example of the work of Fra Angelico (1387–1455), a Florentine painter of the early Renaissance period who is famous for his religious art. The painting is now in Florence, Italy. (Reproduced from a color reproduction by Fratelli Alinari, Florence, Italy. Permission from Art Reference Bureau, Inc., Ancram, N. Y.)

THE FRONTISPIECE:

A stained glass window in a 14th century church which combines symbols of Christianity with the realism of the early Renaissance.

IMPRIMATUR:

✠ *Paul C. Schulte, Archbishop of Indianapolis.*

THE DESIGN:

Stefan Salter

THE ILLUSTRATIONS:

Fritz Kredel

PREFACE

In this completely revised edition of PROSE AND POETRY OF ENGLAND, ST. THOMAS MORE SERIES, the editors have necessarily kept in mind the viewpoint of both the student and the teacher.

In editing the text from the viewpoint of the student, the editors presuppose that the superior as well as the average and sub-average student will use the text. For that reason, some of the selections and study aids have been chosen for the superior student alone. The entire text need not (and should not) be studied by every student. On the other hand, more than sufficient materials for the intellectual capacity of the average 12th grade student have been included.

By offering challenging as well as easily comprehended selections and study materials, the editors have consciously attempted to avoid any intimation of "the canonization of mediocrity," so increasingly apparent in American secondary school education. From long years of actual classroom experience, the editors are convinced that too many teachers underestimate the capacity of our American youth for intellectual and cultural development. The Christian teacher should help the student acquire an intellectual maturity befitting an intelligent Christian citizen, rather than allow him to seek and find the level of the mass mind.

The ST. THOMAS MORE SERIES makes the honest claim that all the selections have been completely edited from a totally Catholic viewpoint. This does not mean that Catholic writing alone is represented. The editors feel that it is more valuable for the young Catholic student to study critically the great masterpieces of the English literary tradition, although at times they may be at variance with Catholic tradition, than for him to devote himself exclusively to Catholic literary art. A critical evaluation of all philosophies is a very effective way for the student to see the truth in Catholic thought and criticism, since he must live his life in a world which reflects pagan and heretical as well as Christian influences.

With proper teacher motivation, the student should attain from the study of this text a fairly high level of (a) mastery of the various types of prose and poetry; (b) a realistic and practical Catholic application of what is read and studied to contemporary social, cultural, and religious life; (c) an introduction to the cultural past as integrated with the present; (d) an extension of vocabulary and reading skills; (e) a critical appreciation and personal cultural enrichment.

For many teachers, the study aids accompanying each selection will serve only as suggestions to be used as they fit individual teacher plans. However, the editors do feel that the detailed analyses of the abundant selections in this book should provide useful material for both the experienced and inexperienced teacher.

It is hoped that, in teaching a selection, the primary emphasis will be placed upon the explanation of the text both for understanding and literary and critical appreciation. For that reason, larger selections of a specific type of prose and poetry have been included in this revision. Thus, for example, one-third of the epic *Beowulf* and almost one-half of the metrical romance *Sir Gawain and the Green Knight* have been printed in the text. In this way, the selection can be studied as representative of an entire epic or metrical romance.

Other objectives in teaching a selection should be the evaluation of an individual piece for its (a) technique and (b) the application of its thought content to life as the student lives it and will live it. Minimal emphasis should be placed on historical background and biographical material.

For those teachers who follow the type rather than the chronological approach to literature, there will be found throughout the book detailed treatment of each type of prose and poetry. A table of contents by types is also included.

The editors sincerely hope that the end result of the teaching of this text will be a more mature enrichment of the Catholic adolescent mind, a deeper appreciation of his place in society, and a glimpse, at least, of the contemporary world as a part of Western culture—a culture which has been bequeathed to him by the Catholic literary giants from the age of *Beowulf* and Chaucer and Thomas More down to Chesterton and the other twentieth century Christian writers.

CONTENTS

CONTENTS

CONTENTS

IV   THE SEVENTEENTH AND EIGHTEENTH CENTURIES

(1603–1780)

HISTORICAL AND LITERARY BACKGROUND

The Stuart Interval (1603–1625) — The Puritan Age (1625–1660) — Protestants Divided — King Charles I Put to Death

CAVALIER POETS

METAPHYSICAL POETRY

CONTENTS

The Defeat of Napoleon — The Rediscovery of Old Ballads — Romanticism and Exaggerated Romanticism — Revolt Against Artificiality — Nature and the Eternal

CONTENTS

VI THE VICTORIAN ERA

(1840–1900)

HISTORICAL AND LITERARY BACKGROUND

Changing England — Democracy on the March — Victorian Writers — Outstanding Poets — The Short Story Appears in England — Victorian Drama

CONTENTS

THE OXFORD MOVEMENT AND THE CATHOLIC REVIVAL

VII THE TWENTIETH CENTURY

HISTORICAL AND LITERARY BACKGROUND 483

Political and Social Changes — The Rise of the Labor Party — England Suffered from World Wars — Literature Reflects Complexity of the Age — The Catholic Revival — The Short Story — Short Stories of Today

CONTENTS

CONTENTS

CONTENTS BY TYPES

CONTENTS BY TYPES

CONTENTS BY TYPES

CONTENTS BY TYPES

CONTENTS BY TYPES

One of the earliest known maps of England and Scotland.

ANGLO-SAXON ENGLAND

BEGINNINGS TO 1066

The student who would appreciate the richness and variety of English expression should know something of the soil in which the English language and English literature grew. And for a Catholic, it is important to note that much of English thought is associated with Catholic traditions centuries old.

The dark-haired, blue-eyed Iberians were the first inhabitants of Britain. Of them we know little, since they left no written literature or history. They did leave behind them, however, their impressive stone structures, ruins of which still survive at Stonehenge and Avebury.

Several centuries before the birth of Christ, successive waves of Britons or Brythonic Celts swept across the east of England, subjugating and absorbing, to a large extent, the Iberians. Rude and primitive as the Britons were, their literature shows that they were both fierce in battle and keenly appreciative of the beauties of nature and the charm of womanhood, which they held in great respect. In their thatched huts, before the peat fires, their poets sang of the great warrior Cuchulainn [1] and of Deirdre [2] the beautiful.

In 55 B.C. Caesar, with his temporary expedition, made the British Isles a part of Roman History. Very shortly after the death of the British King, Cymbeline, in the first century after Christ, the Roman legions made a
ROMAN
permanent invasion and for four centuries the Roman
OCCUPATION
eagles soared over the British Isles. The Romans brought with them the elements of order, culture, and stability. Strong stone roads, high walls, lighthouses, elaborate villas, baths, and coins stamped the land with civilization. The Latin language now made possible exchange of ideas with the continent. Soon, by ways unknown to us, Christianity came to the Romanized Britons.

With Christianity came literature. The earliest book known to have been written on British soil was the *Commentary of St. Paul* by the heretic Pelagius.[3] The British Church had an established hierarchy by the late third century. At the Council of Arles in 314, she was represented by three bishops. Many of the sons of the British Church suffered martyrdom under Diocletian. Even while the Roman empire was tottering and crying out for assistance from her British legions, Fastidious, a British bishop, was calmly writing a Latin book on "The Christian Life." He wrote: "He is a Christian who follows the life of Christ, who imitates Christ in all things."

[1] CUCHULAINN (kōō·kŭl'ĭn)—Irish legendary hero who appears in many of the great tales of early Celtic literature.

[2] DEIRDRE (dēr'drē)—Tragic heroine of early Celtic literature.

[3] PELAGIUS (pē·lā'jĭ·ŭs)—Early Christian heretic against whom St. Augustine wrote. Pelagius denied original sin and Christian grace.

When the Roman legions were recalled to help save a hopelessly collapsing Empire in the beginning of the fifth century, the British people found themselves without protection from their savage border neighbors, the Picts and the Scots. About

THE ANGLO-SAXON

INVASION

449 A.D. the Angles, Saxons, and Jutes—tribes from the woods of northern Germany and the marshy shores of the North Sea and the Baltic—drove their swift, shallow boats onto the defenseless beachheads of Britain's eastern coast. From the coast they swarmed westward in raid after raid, tearing down the Roman towers, burning fields and dwellings, stealing and enslaving the helpless Celts. The Britons, who had become used to letting the Romans do their fighting for them, fell easy victims to the Anglo-Saxon invaders. The British survivors were driven back into the mountainous districts of Wales, Devonshire, and Cornwall.[4] The new invaders were little interested in learning the British language and adopted only a few words from the Celtic tongue or from the Latin language as spoken by the Britons.

But we must not think of these Germanic tribes as pirates by nature or trade. They were a hardy, powerful, determined race, who found the struggle for existence

[4] CORNWALL—There is a tradition that the British King Arthur dwelt in Tintagel in Cornwall and that Cornwall is the original setting of Arthur and his Round Table.

a bloody affair. A warlike people in need of more land for wives and children, impatient of government, fiercely jealous of their personal liberty, they fought their bloody way into British territory. It was these Angles, Saxons and Jutes who were eventually to determine the basic language and culture of the English race. After their wild spell of pillaging and looting, they settled down into numerous kingdoms, the most important of which were Northumbria in the north, Mercia in the Midlands, and Wessex in the south. The Angles occupied Northumbria, and from them Britain came to be called "Angle-lond."

The Anglo-Saxons lived, not in towns built and walled with stone as the Romans had done, but in groups of wooden houses surrounded by a wooden stockade. The words for such communities were *tun* or *ham*, words which still remain in modern English as *town* and *home*. Each chieftain was surrounded by a band of freemen, called thanes, who ate at their lord's table and defended him with their lives. These warriors wore shirts of mail called *byrnies*; their helmets were crowned with boars' heads and other decorations; their arms were swords, spears, bows and arrows. Generosity was the quality most admired in their leader. Thus he was referred to as "the ring giver."

The peasants lived in their tiny huts around the great halls of their lords. The mead halls, so graphically described in *Beowulf*, were designed to serve as emergency stockades and were powerfully constructed. High and drafty, their stone masonry and massive beams were smoke-blackened and gaunt. Around the walls, heavy oaken tables, hacked by the trencher knives of roistering guests, supported enormous piles of roasted venison, fish, and many fowls. Ale and mead—a potent beverage brewed from honey—were their drinks. And as the drinking horn made the rounds, the delight of the men was to listen to the scop [5] or the bard recalling the blood-curdling adventures of some hero whose exploits became more wonderful and more fraught with danger as the legend of his fame was unfolded from generation to generation. It was undoubtedly through such retelling that the historical figure of King Arthur and his brave defense of Celtic liberty against the invading Saxon tribes grew into the golden legend that we know.

The Anglo-Saxon invaders were heathens, worshipping the old German gods, Odin and Thor, and believing in charms, man-eating monsters, and in Wyrd, the iron fate that determines all. The world of their songs was an heroic world of warriors who were supermen, of fabulous exploits on land and sea. They told their tales and sang their songs from memory.

To these hearty thanes, Christianity came about 600 A.D. Missionaries arrived in Britain almost simultaneously from two directions; and, as might be expected, the challenge of Christ captured the wild enthusiasm and restless imagination of this spirited people. Catholicism was spread through the north by some of those vigorous Irish monks who at this period were carrying the light of the Gospel and secular learning to every part of the world. Oswald, king of Northumbria, had been converted while in exile by St. Columba, the Irish poet, scholar,

COMING OF

CHRISTIANITY

[5] scop—An Anglo-Saxon court poet.

statesman, ruler, and saint. From Columba's school, Oswald brought back Aidan, to establish a similar school at Lindisfarne. It was this school which became the fountain of culture and learning for northern England.

Meanwhile, some years before Aidan's arrival, Christianity had entered England by another door. St. Augustine, sent by Pope Gregory the Great, landed with his fellow missionaries at Kent in 597. They sang a *Te Deum* in the ruins of an old pre-Saxon church and made this spot the wellspring of Christianity for the southern kingdoms of England. Though Augustine and his men had remarkable success, the work of conversion was carried on against heavy odds. There was many a turning back to the worship of Odin and Thor before Christian victory was finally complete.

The eighth century marked the golden summit of Anglo-Saxon culture and learning. The Celtic warmth and feeling which Irish monks had given to Northumbria, and the Roman organization which Augustine and his missionaries brought to the south, joined hands and ushered in the first dawn of English learning and literature. It was the Christian missioners who brought the Anglo-Saxons into contact with the literature of Greece and Rome. Theodore from distant Tarsus, and Hadrian from Africa, wandered up and down the length and breadth of the Island, setting up schools, preaching and teaching everywhere, dispensing their knowledge of Greek and Latin as well as divine literature.

THE GOLDEN AGE OF ANGLO-SAXON LITERATURE

Monasteries were founded which became the haven of literature and arts. In these monasteries, great libraries were built up; in them was taught the rhythm of the liturgical chant, which worked itself into the very fiber of English verse; in fact, practically all the poetry that has come down to us from this period of English history was written in the monasteries and by the monks.

It was the monks who gathered up the ancient folk tales and preserved them in writing. It was a monk who composed *Beowulf*, the folk epic which gives us a splendid picture of Anglo-Saxon life and character. It was the monks, too, who taught these war-like folk new songs in which the heroes were Christ and His Apostles. Evidence of this can be seen in the sublimely beautiful and genuinely Christian poetry of Cynewulf whose *Christ*, *The Dream of the Rood*, and *Elene* mark the highest level to which Old English poetry attained.

In Saint Bede (673–735), a native Anglo-Saxon, who even in his life won the title of Venerable, we have one of the greatest scholars of all time. He wrote almost one hundred books, among which is his *Ecclesiastical History of England*. This most important primary source book of English history was originally written in Latin but was later translated into Anglo-Saxon prose by King Alfred. It is in his *History* that Bede tells the story of Caedmon, the ignorant cowherd at the monastery of Whitby, who received in a vision the gift of song. The fragment of Caedmon's song quoted by Bede is the earliest recorded piece of Old English poetry.

Unfortunately, these buds of culture, which gave such promise of great things to be, were destroyed by the invasion of a new enemy, the Danes. In the ninth century legions of Vikings swept silently up the British rivers in their black, dragon-prowed ships; and from them the blond giants stormed across the north country, leveling the monasteries and mead halls, burning and destroying until the land became desolate. Then they pushed southward across the Thames, and within a century would likely have devastated the whole Island had not their steadily advancing masses met Alfred in the great battle of Edington. Elsewhere the natives had huddled together like sheep without a shepherd, but now at last England had a leader—and a great one. At battle's close, the Danes had been routed; and Alfred, the noble Christian of the West Saxons, rolled back the tide of conquest. It is this routing of the new pagan invasion by Alfred which Gilbert K. Chesterton makes the theme of his ringing *Ballad of the White Horse.*

DANISH INVADERS

AND THE AGE

OF ALFRED

But in the long struggle with the Danes, Anglo-Saxon culture had lost its vitality. Alfred had no sooner forced the Danes to peace than he turned his attention to the problems of reconstruction. All that was left of the great monasteries of the north was uncleared rubble. Alfred set about to attract scholars to him and to establish schools where "every free born youth who possessed the means should abide at his book until he could well understand English writing." In his educational program Alfred chose to emphasize the importance of a native language and literature as a means for developing a national spirit. Even the old warriors of the court were put to school, and there are amusing stories of how many of them insisted that they much preferred struggling with the Danes to struggling with the alphabet!

In order that there might be English writings for his people to read, Alfred, together with his scholars, translated many books from the Latin into Anglo-Saxon. Among others, he selected four outstanding works of the previous century: Orosius' *History of the World,* Boethius' *Consolations of Philosophy,* Bede's *Ecclesiastical History of England,* and Pope Gregory's *Pastoral Care.* Alfred wrote *Prefaces* to all these works, one of the most famous being that to the *Pastoral Care* in which he points out to the clergy both the glorious heritage and tradition that is theirs, and their obligation to pass on this heritage to the faithful. He also revived the old *Anglo-Saxon Chronicle,* which before his time had been a memorandum of English events of unequal importance. He was to make this *Chronicle* a valuable source book for English historians. Alfred's work is remarkable to this day for its compelling power of thought and expression, and he well deserves the title of "Father of English Prose."

THE FIRST

ANGLO-SAXON

PROSE

In spite of all his efforts, Alfred did not succeed during his lifetime in re-educating his people to the degree of culture they had obtained in the days of Venerable Bede. After his death, however, disorder and invasion slowly gave way to peace. Christianity gained a solid foothold. The monasteries were restored under Benedictine rule and became once again centers of learning and refinement. The court,

the church, the monastery, the school, the farm, and the marketplace became the pivotal points in English life.

Old English prose reached its golden summit in the late tenth and early eleventh centuries. The most important development was the homily, a sermon with a moral lesson that became a thing of art under the polished pens of the learned monks and bishops. In the history of English prose the Old English homily is important since it began a prose tradition which has lasted to modern times. The manner and style of the homily with its narrative illustrations, its varied use of allegory, its appeal to the will rather than to the intellect, can be traced through the thirteenth and fourteenth century devotional literature to the prose of the fifteenth century. Its influence was felt in the Renaissance in the prose of St. Thomas More and even in such literary forms as the Elizabethan drama. We find it in the allegories of John Bunyan, whose *Pilgrim's Progress* introduced the Puritan homily to American literature.

Outstanding among the Old English sermons of the tenth and eleventh centuries were the *Blickling Homilies*; the sermons of Bishop Wulfstan, Archbishop of York; and the sermons of the greatest writer of his day, Aelfric. He it was who carried

Old English prose to its height in the generation before the Norman conquest. In life, character, and love of books and learning, Aelfric greatly resembles Bede. No other Old English prose writer had such a marked influence on the English people of his own time and a greater molding power over English literature to come.

In the last days of the Saxon dominion, poetic forms disappeared, and the primitive majesty and simple grandeur of the earlier poetry died away. Yet in the British genius there still lives an energy and endurance born of these early poets. Now and again through the centuries there flash glimpses of the ships and swords, the plough-shares, and the jeweled crosses of those early days. And though the heroes and the monsters disappeared, English poetry still shows a closeness to nature, a devotion to family, a fierce defending of liberty, a thread of brooding melancholy, an abiding love of the sea—heritages all of its Anglo-Saxon ancestry.

OLD ENGLISH POETRY

The Anglo-Saxons loved their books with a passionate reverence. The great Bede tells us that he took delight in reading and writing, and placed books first when naming the treasures brought home by monks from their journeys to Rome. And it was Alfred who wrote: "Through learning is belief held, and every man who loves wisdom is happy." The unknown author of the strange poem known as *Salamon and Saturn* sums up what the first writers of English literature thought of books:

> Books are glorious; they give in earnest
> a wise will to him who wonders.
> They heal the heart's mood of every man,
> heal the distress of daily life;
> they found and make firm the strong thought.
> Strong is he who tastes of book lore;
> He is ever wiser in wielding power.
> Books bring triumph to true-hearted men,
> health of mind to him who loves them.[6]

Of the vast storehouse of Old English literary writings which must have existed, comparatively few manuscripts have come down to us. And little wonder, when we recall how often the priceless treasuries of the monastery libraries were ravaged by invasion and raid; how many thousands of manuscripts were burnt and destroyed by the persecutors of the Church under Henry VIII and Elizabeth. Among the old English records, four are outstanding and contain the greater number of poems written before the eleventh century: the *Junius Manuscript*, now in Bodleian Library, Oxford University, which contains the poems at one time attributed to Caedmon; *The Exeter Book*, which contains the largest collection of Old English Poetry which has come down to us; *The Vercelli Manuscript*; and the *Cotton Vitellius A 15*, which was almost destroyed by fire in 1731. This precious manuscript contains the only surviving handwritten copy of *Beowulf*.

[6] "Salamon and Saturn" from *Word Hoard*—Passages from Old English Literature from the Sixth to the Eleventh Centuries, translated and arranged by Margaret Williams, M.A., copyright, 1940, by Sheed and Ward, Inc., New York.

The language found in the greater number of these manuscripts is the Wessex dialect of the tenth century. Much of the poetry was originally composed in the earlier forms of the Northumbrian and Mercian dialects; but the original copies perished in the Danish invasions. When the Wessex scribes made copies of the earlier manuscripts in the tenth century, they transformed the Northumbrian and Mercian dialects into their own West Saxon, which was then known as the "King's English."

We must not think that Old English poetry was primitive or crude. Its poetic rules were highly technical. Each line contained four accents with a pause in the middle of the line. The strongest word in each half-line, or hemistich, alliterated with the strongest accent in the second half-line. Each half-line had two strong accents and one or several light syllables. This rise and fall of accented and light beats in each line could be varied into five distinct accent patterns. The result was a strong rhythm, without rhyme, and without stanza form—and very suggestive of modern free verse. In Old English poetry nouns were considered the strongest parts of speech, then adjectives, then verbs. Sometimes the alliteration was double in one or both half-lines.

Here are two typical lines from *Beowulf*:

> Gren´del gong´an. God´es yr´re baer
> (Grendel going. God's ire (he) bore.)

> Flo´ta fam´ ig-heals   fu´ gel geli´ cost.
> (Foamy-neck floaters, like unto fowls.)

The translation which you will read has imitated the important features of the original poem. Again notice that each line had four major accents, and that every line is marked by alliteration:

> Grendel, fated, fled to the fens
>
> or
>
> The stranger from far, the stalwart and strong.

The influence of Anglo-Saxon poetic technique is felt in our day, especially in the versification of Gerard Manley Hopkins. Hopkins admitted that he found the movement of his "new rhythm" in *Piers Plowman*, the great poem of the fourteenth century, which was written according to the rules of Old English poetry.

The Anglo-Saxon people spoke a form of Low German dialect which eventually became the root from which our English language sprang. Although it is true that many of the Old English words have disappeared, it is also

ANGLO-SAXON

LANGUAGE

true that most of the short, everyday words are direct descendants of this early English speech. Examples of such basic words are *day, father, mother, man, wife, drink, sleep, fight,* the personal pronouns and the numerals. Old English had its own pronunciation and spelling, and its own grammar with many inflectional forms, which show its kinship to Greek and Latin.

XXth CENTURY   Vth CENTURY

The resemblances and the differences between the Anglo-Saxon and Modern English are easily illustrated in the Old English version of the Our Father:

> Faeder ūre, thū the eart on heofunum,
> Sī thīn nama gehālgod.
> Tobecume thīn rīce.
> Gewurthe thīn willa on earthan swā swā on heofunum.
> Ure gehaeghwāmlican hlāf syle ūs tō daeg.
> And forgyf ūs ūre gyltas, swā swā wē forgyfath ūrum gyltendum.
> And ne gelāēd thū ūs on costnunge,
> Ac ālys ūs of yfele. Sōthlīce.

An important characteristic of the Germanic languages is that they form new words by joining two or more old words. The Anglo-Saxon word for *vocabulary* was *word-hoard*; for *drowning* was *sea-death*. Modern English has kept this capacity for forming compounds; but it is usually more convenient for us to make new words by using Latin and Greek stems, prefixes, and suffixes. And so though we have expressions like *schoolhouse, railroad,* and *playwright,* we also say *depend* (not *under-hang*) and *submarine* (not *under-sea-boat*).

The Anglo-Saxons had an amazing poetic vocabulary—vivid, singing words. They had as many as twenty synonyms for such words as *sea, horse, warriors.* Adjectives had a double richness, like *thought-hard, winter-weary, battle-bright*. Their love for compounds often gave us such imaginative expressions as *World-father* for *Creator*, and *foamy-necked floaters* for *boats*. They had a real fondness for figures of speech, especially for metaphor and personification. The sun was a *sky-candle*, the sea, *the whale's road*, the ship, the *sea-horse*, the shield was the *linden-wood*. The use of these metaphorical compounds is so characteristic of their poetry that it is recognized as a particular figure of speech and called a *kenning*.

Old English prose first followed the Latin pattern, since it had been translated from the Latin. Its sentence structure was awkward and its grammar was inadequate. If the poetic vocabulary was complete, its vocabulary for the more abstract ideas required in prose was very limited. But as learning progressed and the Danes stopped pillaging the monasteries, prose developed. The spade work of Alfred gave growth to the rich flowering of the writing of Aelfric, the cultured teacher of the eleventh century.

NARRATIVE POETRY

In almost every language, the earliest literature is poetry rather than prose. The reasons for this are, perhaps, that the first literature was oral rather than written, and that it was sung or chanted in connection with some religious or tribal celebration; hence, poetry was a more natural medium of communication.

Poetry is generally classified as narrative, lyric, or dramatic. Why the earliest form of poetry should be narrative or story-telling poetry is easy to understand. Just like the child, all simple and primitive peoples are naturally interested in the common things they know, and the fantastic things they do not know and sometimes fear. So the blind Homer sang of Circe and the Enchantress, the singing Sirens, and one-eyed giants, as well as the banquet feast, the funeral pyres, and the tenderness of love. Scops and troubadours wandered from castle to castle in Saxon and Norman times, with their tales of fiery dragons, magic swords, and ladies in distress. And in our own time the American cowboy riding under the stars, the lumberjack around his camp fire, and the hill dweller in his mountain home have added to the wealth of American folklore the simple, naive, and sometimes violent tales which represent in part the life they know, and in part the life they hunger for.

Perhaps we have taken stories for granted, like our food and friends; but why do stories fascinate people? The most interesting adventure in the world is life; and stories give us a large or small cross-section of life, lived by *someone, somewhere, somehow*. An analysis of the simplest story, as well as of the most complex novel, will invariably reveal that *someone* (the character), *somewhere* (the setting), came up against some odds, some decision, the outcome of which *somehow* (sequence, story or plot) influences his life and the lives of others. A story is then interesting because it portrays life. Life is interesting because it is a vital activity, often a clash of opposing forces, external to man, or within his soul. And since the

THE CLASSIFICATION OF POETRY

outcome of such a clash is never certain because of man's free will, there will be inevitably *interest* and *suspense*.

Narrative poetry is generally divided into four types: (1) the epic, (2) the ballad, (3) the metrical romance, (4) the metrical tale. This book includes examples of all of these forms.

An epic is a long narrative poem, the highest, the most dignified, and the most sublime form of narrative poetry. It has been defined by the Greek, Aristotle, who said that an epic is an "imitation of life which is narrative in form and poetic in meter . . . it has for its subject a single action, whole and complete . . . The characters celebrated should be of lofty type." The essential story is usually quite simple, and progress is made throughout towards a definite goal. But the path taken is seldom the shortest one. Numerous episodes and "flash backs" lead to detours. In other words, the epic moves slowly, developing (in detail) the characteristics of greatness of its leading man, the epic hero.

THE EPIC

There is always one central heroic character who embodies, to some extent, the outstanding characteristics of his race. He is usually involved in a struggle against opposing forces of nature, of men and supermen; it is through his deeds and by his efforts as a *representative* of his people that the episodes, each one of which is often complete in itself, are linked together and unified in a continuous narrative. As Professor Kerr points out in his *Epic and Romance*, "the grandeur and magnitude of the epic lies not so much in the elevated language, nor in the greatness of theme, nor in the length of the poem as in the greatness of soul of the hero." It is because of his "king-size" manner that the words, rhythm, and subordinate characters of the poem must take on suitable and like proportions.

There are two types of epic, the *folk epic*, and the literary epic. The folk epic originated among the people, and passed through a long period of telling before it reached its written form. The poet who finally made it a unified poem is usually unknown. *The Iliad* and *The Odyssey* of Homer, which tell of the last days of the Trojan War and the struggle of Ulysses to reach and save his own kingdom of Ithaca, after the fall of Troy, are the finest examples of the folk epic in the literature of the world. *The Nibelungenlied*, the German folk epic, tells the stories of the Germanic characters of the sixth and seventh centuries, Brunhild, Siegfried, and Hagen, later commemorated in the operas of Wagner. *The Song of Roland*, the great epic of France, recounts how Roland, one of Charlemagne's Twelve Peers, dies bravely because of the treachery of his own stepfather in betraying the cause of Charlemagne in his fight against the Saracens. *Beowulf* is the only folk epic in the English language.

The literary epic is the conscious product of one known writer. But the poet chooses his materials from respected traditions. To some extent, the literary epic also reflects the thought and opinions of the age in which it was written. The greatest literary epic in the English language is Milton's *Paradise Lost*. Other epics are Vergil's *Aeneid* and Dante's *Divine Comedy*, the latter perhaps the greatest piece of writing of all time, whose vast theme is the salvation of the human soul.

We may briefly summarize the essential elements of the epic as follows: The plot is a unified story whose direct action is short, but whose implied action is on a sweeping scale. There is one central, heroic character, plus some other superhuman and lesser characters. The setting is in the distant past, either legendary or supernatural. The mood is noble and dignified; religious and sublime. The poetic form often employs certain devices such as a formal introduction called "the invocation"; a *roll-call of important characters*; and *lofty speeches* descriptive of persons, places, and events.

Beowulf is the oldest epic in any modern European language. Written in the eighth century by an unknown monk, the poem gives us a splendid example of the epic tradition. Although its material is Scandinavian in background, its structure is in the tradition of the literary epic, and there is no doubt of the Christian influence in its spirit. Much of the subject matter of the poem was originally collected through oral transmission; and the poem itself may have been developed from an earlier series of epic tales, though none of these has survived. But *Beowulf*, in the form in which it has come to us, is a single, unified poem.

THE EPIC

BEOWULF

The Christian author of *Beowulf* took the primitive material derived from pagan folk-lore and legend and infused into it a Christian spirit which colors the entire poem. The thoughts and judgments, the actions and the motives of the noble characters are Christian. Pagan elements still remain, however. For example, side by side we find references to the blind power of Wyrd, or Fate, and to the omnipotence and providence of the true God. But just as often it is implied that Fate is controlled by the Christian God. Again, the origin of Grendel and his dam or mother from the Scandinavian water troll is lost in the poet's identification of these monsters as the adversaries of God. Reference to the Old Testament runs throughout the poem in unmistakably Christian terms.

The character of Beowulf is suffused with the Christian spirit. Again and again he asks for divine guidance and acknowledges the assistance of God in his heroic deeds. The Christian way of life motivates the conduct of the noble characters. No more beautiful expression of Christian wisdom can be found than that of the advice of Hrothgar to Beowulf at the height of his triumphs.

Beowulf is a story of the pagan past of the ancestors of the eighth century Anglo-Saxon, retold in the light of Christian teachings of the Golden Age of Anglo-Saxon literature. It is a tale in which the endurance, loyalty, and courage of the heroic age are tempered with Christian virtues and graced with the courtly manners which were to characterize all subsequent English medieval literature.

There can be little doubt that the epic *Beowulf* was composed under the influence of the Vergilian epic. In general form and movement it manifests a literary quality of form and movement, an epic dignity of speech and action, a well-developed theme not derived from the Scandinavian tale. Vergil's *Aeneid* was well known in the early Middle Ages. Venerable Bede and Alcuin were lovers of Vergil. Surely the educated poet of the Age of Bede who fashioned *Beowulf* must have had in mind the *Aeneid* as the model of the classical epic.

Was the epic composed by a Christian monk to give an example of a noble king and the Christian ideal? Edmund Spenser, who wrote the *Faerie Queene*, said that the purpose of his book "is to fashion a gentleman or noble person in vertuous and gentle discipline." Although we have no such statement of the purpose of the author of *Beowulf*, many passages in the poem suggest that he wrote the poem not merely to retell an heroic pagan story, but to give his age a narrative of an heroic Christian king who would serve as a model for noble living.

The spirit of the poem is the spirit of England, and its poetic ideal is the Christian ideal. It is a poem suited to the Christian court. Its English strain is felt in its tone of pondering sadness and lament, as well as its moral temper. Both the youthful and the aged Beowulf illustrate that chivalrous spirit which gave birth to the knight errant of the medieval courtly romance.

"Beyond the call of duty" was the theme of Beowulf's life. Courage, strength united to gentleness, solicitude for the needs and dangers of others, a sense of honor and valor ennobled by unselfish service, faith and trust in God—these are some of the lessons of life that come to the modern world from the pages of *Beowulf*.

Beowulf

TRANSLATED BY CHARLES W. KENNEDY

The story begins in the land of the Danes in the reign of King Hrothgar. The glory of his rule was symbolized in the great hall which he built and called Heorot¹ or Hall of the Hart.² But in time disaster came to the land in the form of two monsters: Grendel and his dam or mother, both of hideous shape and superhuman size.

To Hrothgar was granted glory in war,
Success in battle; retainers bold
Obeyed him gladly; his band increased
To a mighty host. Then his mind was
 moved   4
To have men fashion a high-built hall,
A mightier mead-hall than man had
 known,
Wherein to portion to old and young
All goodly treasure that God had given,
Save only the folk-land, and lives of
 men.
His word was published to many a peo-
 ple   10
Far and wide o'er the ways of the earth
To rear a folk-stead richly adorned;
The task was speeded, the time soon
 came
That the famous mead-hall was finished
 and done.
To distant nations its name was known,
The Hall of the Hart; and the king kept
 well   16
His pledge and promise to deal out gifts,
Rings at the banquet. The great hall
 rose

High and horn-gabled, holding its place
Till the battle-surge of consuming flame
Should swallow it up. . . .   21
Then an evil spirit who dwelt in the
 darkness
Endured it ill that he heard each day
The din of revelry ring through the hall,
The sound of the harp, and the scop's
 sweet song.   25
A skillful bard sang the ancient story
Of man's creation; how the Maker
 wrought
The shining earth with its circling wa-
 ters;
In splendor established the sun and
 moon   29
As lights to illumine the land of men;
Fairly adorning the fields of earth
With leaves and branches; creating life
In every creature that breathes and
 moves.
So the lordly warriors lived in gladness,
At ease and happy, till a fiend from hell
Began a series of savage crimes. 36
They called him Grendel, a demon grim
Haunting the fen-lands, holding the
 moors,
Ranging the wastes, where the wretched
 wight

¹ HEOROT (hā′ō·rŏt).
² HART—Deer.

38. FEN-LANDS—Marshes.
39. WIGHT—A creature, a living being, from the Anglo-Saxon.

Made his lair with the monster kin;   40
He bore the curse of the seed of Cain
Whereby God punished the grievous
  guilt
Of Abel's murder. Nor ever had Cain
Cause to boast of that deed of blood;
God banished him far from the fields of
  men;   45
Of his blood was begotten an evil brood,
Marauding monsters and menacing
  trolls,
Goblins and giants who battled with
  God
A long time. Grimly He gave them re-
  ward!

*[Night raids by Grendel gradually di-
minished the number of Hrothgar's warriors and turned the hall into a place of
fear and dread. For twelve years this
terror lay upon the land.*

*But news of this dire calamity which
was afflicting the Danes reached the
land of the Geats in southern Sweden,
where it came to the knowledge of the
hero Beowulf. Against the advice of
his uncle, Hygelac, and eager for fame
and adventure, Beowulf with a small
band of followers sailed for Denmark to
match his strength against Grendel.]*

Then tales of the terrible deeds of
  Grendel   50
Reached Hygelac's thane in his home
  with the Geats;
Of living strong men he was the strong-
  est,
Fearless and gallant and great of heart.
He gave command for a goodly vessel
Fitted and furnished; he fain would sail

47. TROLLS—A troll is a preternatural being, celebrated in Scandinavian folk-lore. It
is sometimes referred to as a dwarf, sometimes
as a giant, which inhabits caves, hills and the
sea. The myth of the trolls has been woven
into the story of *The Song of Norway*, the
modern light opera.

Over the swan-road to seek the king   56
Who suffered so sorely for need of men.
And his bold retainers found little to
  blame
In his daring venture, dear though he
  was;
They viewed the omens, and urged him
  on.   60
Brave was the band he had gathered
  about him,
Fourteen stalwarts seasoned and bold,
Seeking the shore where the ship lay
  waiting,
A sea-skilled mariner sighting the land-
  marks.
Came the hour of boarding; the boat
  was riding   65
The waves of the harbor under the hill.
The eager mariners mounted the prow;
Billows were breaking, sea against sand.
In the ship's hold snugly they stowed
  their trappings,
Gleaming armor and battle-gear;   70
Launched the vessel, the well-braced
  bark,
Seaward bound on a joyous journey.
Over breaking billows, with bellying sail
And foamy beak, like a flying bird   74
The ship sped on, till the next day's sun
Showed sea-cliffs shining, towering hills
And stretching headlands. The sea was
  crossed,
The voyage ended, the vessel moored.
And the Weder people waded ashore
With clatter of trappings and coats of
  mail;   80
Gave thanks to God that His grace had
  granted
Sea-paths safe for their ocean-journey.

*[Beowulf and his company landed and
were challenged by the Danish coast-
guard, who noted the princely form and
bearing of Beowulf. After learning his
name and his mission, the coast-guard
led the company over the stone-paved*

*streets where the Hall of the Hart
gleamed in its glory. They piled their
war-gear and boar-crested helmets outside the hall. A warrior bore the news
of their coming to Hrothgar. Beowulf
entered proudly.*]

Then the bold one rose with his band
    around him,
A splendid massing of mighty thanes;
A few stood guard as the Geat gave bid-
    ding   85
Over the weapons stacked by the wall.
They followed in haste on the heels of
    their leader
Under Heorot's roof. Full ready and
    bold
The helmeted warrior strode to the
    hearth;
Beowulf spoke; his byrny glittered, 90
His war-net woven by cunning of smith:
"Hail! King Hrothgar! I am Hygelac's
    thane,
Hygelac's kinsman. Many a deed
Of honor and daring I've done in my
    youth.
This business of Grendel was brought to
    my ears   95
On my native soil. The sea-farers say
This best of buildings, this boasted hall,
Stands dark and deserted when sun is
    set,
When darkening shadows gather with
    dusk.
The best of my people, prudent and
    brave,   100
Urged me, King Hrothgar, to seek you
    out;

They had in remembrance my courage
    and might.
Many had seen me come safe from the
    conflict,
Bloody from battle; five foes I bound
Of the giant kindred, and crushed their
    clan.   105
Hard-driven in danger and darkness of
    night
I slew the nicors that swam the sea,
Avenged the woe they had caused the
    Weders,
And ended their evil—they needed the
    lesson!
And now with Grendel, the fearful
    fiend,   110
Single-handed I'll settle the strife!
Lord of nations, and leader of men,
I beg one favor—refuse me not,
Since I come thus faring from far-off
    lands—   114
That I may alone with my loyal earls,
With this hardy company, cleanse Hart-
    Hall.
I have heard that the demon in proud
    disdain
Spurns all weapons; and I too scorn—
May Hygelac's heart have joy of the
    deed—   119
To bear my sword, or sheltering shield,
Or yellow buckler, to battle the fiend.
With hand-grip only I'll grapple with
    Grendel;
Foe against foe I'll fight to the death,
And the one who is taken must trust to
    God's grace!"

107. NICOR—A water monster.

ᛞᴘᵹah ſẏð þan hie þæſ laðan laſꞇ ſcea
·ᴘeðon ᴘeꞃꝼan ꝫaſꞇeſ þæſ þ ꝫe·ᴘin ꞇo

[*Hrothgar gratefully welcomed Beowulf amid royal entertainment and entrusted to Beowulf and his band the task of freeing Heorot from the scourge of Grendel. At the height of the celebration the jealous and proud Danish courtier, Unferth, alluded to a swimming match between Beowulf and Breca in which Unferth claimed that Breca had bested Beowulf. Unferth predicted an evil fate for Beowulf if he dared to encounter Grendel. But Beowulf replied:*]

"My good friend Unferth, addled with
    beer   125
Much have you made of the deeds of
    Breca!
I count it true that I had more courage,
More strength in swimming than any
    other man.
In our youth we boasted—we were both
    of us boys—
We would risk our lives in the raging
    sea.   130
And we made it good! We gripped in
    our hands
Naked swords, as we swam in the waves,
Guarding us well from the whales' assault.
In the breaking seas he could not outstrip me,
Nor would I leave him. For five nights
    long   135
Side by side we strove in the waters
Till racing combers wrenched us apart,
Freezing squalls, and the falling night,
And a bitter north wind's icy blast.
Rough were the waves; the wrath of the
    sea-fish   140
Was fiercely roused; but my firm-linked
    byrny,
The gold-adorned corselet that covered
    my breast,
Gave firm defense from the clutching
    foe.

Down to the bottom a savage sea-beast
Fiercely dragged me and held me fast
In a deadly grip; nonetheless it was
    granted me   146
To pierce the monster with a point of
    steel.
Death swept it away with the swing of
    my sword.
The grisly sea-beasts again and again
Beset me sore; but I served them home
With my faithful blade as was wellbefitting.   151
Bloody with wounds, at the break of
    day,
They lay on the sea-beach slain with the
    sword.
No more would they cumber the mariner's course
On the ocean deep. From the east came
    the sun,   155
Bright beacon of God, and the seas subsided;
I beheld the headlands, the windy
    walls.
Fate often delivers an undoomed earl
If his spirit be gallant! And so I was
    granted
To slay with the sword-edge nine of the
    nicors.   160
I have never heard tell of more terrible
    strife
Under dome of heaven in darkness of
    night,
Nor of man harder pressed on the paths
    of ocean.
But I freed my life from the grip of the
    foe
Though spent with the struggle. The
    billows bore me,   165
The swirling currents and surging seas,
To the land of the Finns. And little
    I've heard
Of any such valiant adventures from
    you!
Neither Breca nor you in the press of
    battle

Ever showed such daring with dripping
    swords—   170
Though I boast not of it! But you
    stained your blade
With blood of your brothers, your clos-
    est of kin;
And for that you'll endure damnation in
    hell,
Sharp as you are! I say for a truth,
Son of Ecglaf, never had Grendel   175
Wrought such havoc and woe in the
    hall,
That horrid demon so harried your king,
If your heart were as brave as you'd have
    men think!
But Grendel has found that he never
    need fear
Revenge from your people, or valiant
    attack   180
From the Victor-Scyldings; he takes his
    toll,
Sparing none of the Danish stock.
But soon will I show him the stuff of the
    Geats,
Their courage in battle and strength in
    the strife."

[*Hrothgar's hopes were high as he listened to Beowulf's bold resolve. At
nightfall, Beowulf and his men took
over the hall, sleeping with their weapons at hand. Then suddenly out of the
mist and darkness, Grendel burst in
upon them.*]

From the stretching moors, from the
    misty hollows,   185
Grendel came creeping, accursed of
    God,
A murderous ravager minded to snare
Spoils of heroes in high-built hall.
Under clouded heavens he held his way
Till there rose before him the high-
    roofed house,   190

181. VICTOR-SCYLDINGS (shǐl′dǐngz)—Descendants of Scyld. Danes.

Wine-hall of warriors gleaming with
    gold.
Storming the building he burst the por-
    tal,
Though fastened of iron, with fiendish
    strength;
Forced open the entrance in savage fury
And rushed in rage o'er the shining
    floor.   195
A baleful glare from his eyes was gleam-
    ing
Most like to a flame. He found in the
    hall
Many a warrior sealed in slumber,
A host of kinsmen. His heart rejoiced;
The savage monster was minded to
    sever   200
Lives from bodies ere break of day,
To feast his fill of the flesh of men.
But he was not fated to glut his greed
With more of mankind when night was
    ended!
    The hardy kinsman of Hygelac waited
To see how the monster would make his
    attack.   206
The demon delayed not, but quickly
    clutched
A sleeping thane in his swift assault,
Tore him in pieces, bit through the
    bones,
Gulped the blood, and gobbled the
    flesh,   210
Greedily gorged on the lifeless corpse,
The hands and the feet. Then the fiend
    stepped nearer,
Sprang on the Sea-Geat lying out-
    stretched,
Clasping him close with his monstrous
    claw.
But Beowulf grappled and gripped him
    hard,   215
Struggled up on his elbow; the shepherd
    of sins
Soon found that never before had he
    felt
In any man other in all the earth

A mightier hand-grip; his mood was
    humbled,
His courage fled; but he found no
    escape! 220
He was fain to be gone; he would flee to
    the darkness,
The fellowship of devils. Far different
    his fate
From that which befell him in former
    days!
The hardy hero, Hygelac's kinsman,
Remembered the boast he had made at
    the banquet; 225
He sprang to his feet, clutched Grendel
    fast,
Though fingers were cracking, the fiend
    pulled free.
The earl pressed after; the monster was
    minded
To win his freedom and flee to the fens.
He knew that his fingers were fast in the
    grip 230

Of a savage foe. Sorry the venture,
The raid that the ravager made on the
    hall.
    There was din in Heorot. For all the
    Danes,
The city-dwellers, the stalwart Scyldings,
That was a bitter spilling of beer! 235
The walls resounded, the fight was fierce,
Savage the strife as the warriors strug-
    gled.
The wonder was that the lofty wine-hall
Withstood the struggle, nor crashed to
    earth, 239
The house so fair; it was firmly fastened
Within and without with iron bands
Cunningly smithied; though men have
    said
That many a mead-bench gleaming with
    gold
Sprang from its sill as the warriors strove.
The Scylding wise men had never
    weened 245

That any ravage could wreck the build-
ing
Till the time when the swelter and surge
of fire
Should swallow it up in a swirl of
flame.
   Continuous tumult filled the hall;
A terror fell on the Danish folk   250
As they heard through the wall the hor-
rible wailing,
The groans of Grendel, the foe of God
Howling his hideous hymn of pain,
The hell-thane shrieking in sore defeat.
He was fast in the grip of the man who
was greatest   255
Of mortal men in the strength of his
might,
Who would never rest while the wretch
was living,
Counting his life-days a menace to man.
   Many an earl of Beowulf brandished
His ancient iron to guard his lord,   260
To shelter safely the peerless prince.
They had no knowledge, these daring
thanes,
When they drew their weapons to hack
and hew,
To thrust to the heart, that the sharpest
sword,
The choicest iron in all the world,   265
Could work no harm to the hideous foe.
On every sword he had laid a spell,
On every blade; but a bitter death
Was to be his fate; far was the journey
The monster made to the home of
fiends.   270
   Then he who had wrought such
wrong to men,
With grim delight as he warred with
God,
Soon found that his strength was feeble
and failing
In the crushing hold of Hygelac's thane.
Each loathed the other while life should
last!   275
There Grendel suffered a grievous hurt,

A wound in the shoulder, gaping and
wide;
Sinews snapped and bone-joints broke,
And Beowulf gained the glory of battle.
Grendel, fated, fled to the fens,   280
To his joyless dwelling, sick unto death.
He knew in his heart that his hours were
numbered,
His days at an end. For all the Danes
Their wish was fulfilled in the fall of
Grendel.
The lord of the Geats made good to the
East-Danes   285
The boast he had uttered; he ended their
ill.
The token was clear when the bold in
battle
Laid down the shoulder and dripping
claw—
Grendel's arm—in the gabled hall!

[*With morning came joy as the Danes
gathered in the Hall to view the huge
claw of Grendel. They traced the
bloody steps of the monster to the edge
of the dark pool. As they returned from
the fen to Heorot, with horses proudly
prancing, a minstrel sang a song in praise
of Beowulf. A great feast was prepared
at which Hrothgar honored Beowulf and
his men with many gifts in the banquet
hall. Hour after hour the revelry continued.*

   *But the coming of night brought new
horror in the person of Grendel's mother
who came to avenge her son's death.
She entered among the sleeping Danish
thanes, woke them to struggle, and carried off Aeschere, the beloved comrade
of Hrothgar. The Danes were filled
with despair. In the morning, the aged
Hrothgar speedily summoned Beowulf,
who had no knowledge of the new attack.*]

The hero came tramping into the hall
With his chosen band—the boards re-
    sounded—   291
Greeted the leader, the Ingwine lord,
And asked if the night had been peace-
    ful and pleasant.

    Hrothgar spoke, the lord of the Scyld-
    ings:
"Ask not of pleasure; pain is renewed
For the Danish people. Aeschere is
    dead!   296
He was my comrade, closest of counsel-
    lors,
My shoulder-companion as side by side
We fought for our lives in the welter of
    war,
As an earl should be, a prince without
    peer,   300
Such was Aeschere, slain in the hall
By the wandering demon! I know not
    whither
She fled to shelter, proud of her spoil,
Gorged to the full . . .

    Oft in the hall I have heard my peo-
    ple,   305
Comrades and counsellors, telling a tale
Of evil spirits their eyes have sighted,
Two mighty marauders who haunt the
    moors.
One shape, as clearly as men could see,
Seemed woman's likeness, and one
    seemed man,   310
An outcast wretch of another world,
And huger far than a human form.
Grendel my countrymen called him, not
    knowing
What monster-brood spawned him,
    what sire begot.   314
Wild and lonely the land they live in,
Wind-swept ridges and wolf-retreats.
Dread tracts of fen where the falling
    torrent
Downward dips into gloom and shadow
Under the dusk of the darkening cliff.

292. INGWINE (ĭng'wĭ·nă)—Danes.

Not far in miles lies the lonely mere
Where trees firm-rooted and hung with
    frost   321
Overshroud the wave with shadowing
    gloom.
And there a portent appears each night,
A flame in the water; no man so wise
Who knows the bounds of its bottom-
    less depth.   325
The heather-stepper, the horned stag,
The antlered hart hard driven by
    hounds,
Invading that forest in flight from afar
Will turn at bay and die on the brink
Ere ever he'll plunge in that haunted
    pool.   330
'Tis an eerie spot! Its tossing spray
Mounts dark to heaven when high winds
    stir
The driving storm, and the sky is murky,
And with foul weather the heavens
    weep.
On your arm only rests all our hope!
Not yet have you tempted those terrible
    reaches   336
The region that shelters that sinful
    wight.
Go if you dare! I will give requital
With ancient treasure and twisted gold.
As I formerly gave in guerdon of bat-
    tle,   340
If out of that combat you come alive."

    Beowulf spoke, the son of Ecgtheow:
"Sorrow not, brave one! Better for man
To avenge a friend than much to mourn.
All men must die; let him who may   345
Win glory ere death. That guerdon is
    best
For a noble man when his name survives
    him.
Then let us rise up, O ward of the
    realm,

320. MERE—A lake or pool.
340. GUERDON (gûr'dŭn)—A reward.
342. ECGTHEOW (ĕj'thĕ·ō)—Father of Beowulf.

And haste us forth to behold the track
Of Grendel's dam."   350

[*Hrothgar leaped up and thanked
God for the hero's words. Then the
Danes and the Geats journeyed together over the moorlands to the watery
depths. Beowulf girded himself with
his war-gear and Unferth gave him his
sword, Hrunting. Beowulf accepted the
sword and asked that all his treasure be
sent to Hygelac if he died in the combat.*]

After these words the prince of the
    Weders
Awaited no answer, but turned to the
    task,
Straightway plunged in the swirling
    pool.
Nigh unto a day he endured the depths
Ere he first had view of the vast sea-
    bottom.   355
Soon she found, who had haunted the
    flood,
A ravening hag, for a hundred half-years,
Greedy and grim, that a man was grop-
    ing
In daring search through the sea-troll's
    home.
Swift she grappled and grasped the war-
    rior   360
With horrid grip, but could work no
    harm,
No hurt to his body; the ring-locked
    byrny
Cloaked his life from her clutching claw;
Nor could she tear through the tem-
    pered mail
With her savage fingers. The she-wolf
    bore   365
The ring-prince down through the wa-
    tery depths
To her den at the bottom; nor could
    Beowulf draw

His blade for battle, though brave his
    mood.
Many a sea-beast, strange sea-monsters,
Tasked him hard with their menacing
    tusks,   370
Broke his byrny and smote him sore.
    Then he found himself in a fearsome
        hall
Where water came not to work him
    hurt,
But the flood was stayed by the shelter-
    ing roof.
There in the glow of the firelight gleam-
    ing   375
The hero had view of the huge sea-troll.
He swung his war-sword with all his
    strength,
Withheld not the blow, and the savage
    blade
Sang on her head its hymn of hate.
But the bold one found that the battle-
    flasher   380
Would bite no longer, nor harm her life.
The sword-edge failed at his sorest need.
But fixed of purpose and firm of mood
Hygelac's earl was mindful of honor;
In wrath, undaunted, he dashed to
    earth   385
The jewelled sword with its scrolled de-
    sign,
The blade of steel; staked all on
    strength,
On the might of his hand, as a man
    must do
Who thinks to win in the welter of bat-
    tle   389
Enduring glory; he fears not death.

[*Beowulf gripped the shoulder of
Grendel's dam and hurled her to the
ground. In the tussle, she staggered
Beowulf, knelt upon him and drew her
dagger, but the steel of his corslet
shielded his breast. Swiftly he sprang to
his feet, seized a heavy sword from
her war-gear, and struck with fury.*]

Thrust at the throat, broke through the bone-rings;
The stout blade stabbed through her fated flesh.
She sank in death; the sword was bloody;
The hero joyed in the work of his hand.
The gleaming radiance shimmered and shone   395
As the candle of heaven shines clear from the sky.

[*The Danes who had watched at the edge of the pool believed Beowulf had been killed when they saw the water suddenly stained with blood. In despair they returned to Heorot. But the loyal Geats waited until at last Beowulf swam up from the depths bearing Grendel's head and the hilt of the sword whose blade had melted. Joyfully his companions accompanied him to the Hall of the Hart. Here again Hrothgar celebrated with an elaborate feast and giving of gifts. When all were silent Hrothgar praised the young hero who had been strong and loyal, and bade young Beowulf to strive for virtue, as the ancient Danish King Heremod did not.*]

"Strive for virtue! I speak for your good.
'Tis a wondrous marvel how mighty God
In gracious spirit bestows on men   399
The gift of wisdom, and goodly lands,
And princely power! He rules over all!
He suffers a man of lordly line
To set his heart on his own desires,
Awards him fullness of worldly joy,
A fair home-land, and the sway of cities,   405
The wide dominion of many a realm,

An ample kingdom, till, cursed with folly,
The thoughts of his heart take no heed of his end.
He lives in luxury, knowing not want,
Knowing no shadow of sickness or age; 410
No haunting sorrow darkens his spirit,
No hatred or discord deepens to war;
The world is sweet to his every desire,
And evil assails not—until in his heart
Pride overpowering gathers and grows.
  Then is his heart pierced, under his helm, 416
His soul in his bosom, with bitter dart.
He has no defense for the fierce assaults
Of the loathsome Fiend. What he long has cherished 419
Seems all too little! In anger and greed
He gives no guerdon of plated rings.
Since God has granted him glory and wealth
He forgets the future, unmindful of Fate.
But it comes to pass in the day appointed
His feeble body withers and fails; 425
Death descends, and another seizes
His hoarded riches and rashly spends
The princely treasure, imprudent of heart.
Beloved Beowulf, best of warriors,
Avoid such evil and seek the good, 430
The heavenly wisdom. Beware of pride!"

[*With the morning light Beowulf came to take his leave. He returned Hrunting with thanks to Unferth, and with his companions triumphantly took sail for home.*]

   The ship was launched.
Cleaving the combers of open sea
They dropped the shoreline of Denmark astern.

A stretching sea-cloth, a bellying sail,
Was bent on the mast; there was groaning of timbers; 436
A gale was blowing; the boat drove on.
The foamy-necked plunger plowed through the billows,
The ring-stemmed ship through the breaking seas,
Till at last they sighted the sea-cliffs of Geatland. 440
The well-known headlands; and, whipped by the wind,
The boat drove shoreward and beached on the sand.

[*Upon their arrival in the land of the Geats, they were royally welcomed and feasted by Hygelac and his court. Beowulf recounted his wonderful adventures and shared with Hygelac and the queen the gifts which Hrothgar had given him. Hygelac, in turn, gave Beowulf a gift of a costly sword, and a stately hall with a large estate. So ends the first section of the narrative.*

Years went by and at last Beowulf ruled the kingdom of the Geats. During his old age a fire dragon ravaged his land after one of his men stole a golden flagon from a huge treasure which the dragon had guarded for three hundred years. With fire and flame the dragon burned dwellings and filled all hearts with terror. Beowulf prepared for battle against this menace to his people. Armed with his sword, Naegling, and an iron shield, the king, with eleven comrades, was guided by the thief to the dragon's fen.]

The thirteenth man in the hurrying throng
Was the sorrowful captive who caused the feud.

[*Standing near the stone entrance from which hot steam poured forth, Beowulf and the dragon entered into mortal combat. His sword, Naegling, broke. All of his companions turned and fled into the forest to save their lives except the youthful Wiglaf.*]

        he saw his king   445
Under his helmet smitten with heat.
He thought of the gifts which his lord
    had given,
The wealth and the land of the Waeg-
    munding line
And all the folk-rights his father had
    owned;
  Wiglaf spoke in sorrow of soul,   450
With bitter reproach rebuking his com-
    rades:
"I remember the time, as we drank in
    the mead-hall,
When we swore to our lord who be-
    stowed these rings
That we would repay for the war-gear
    and armor,
The hard swords and helmets, if need
    like this   455
Should ever befall him.
Now is the day that our lord has need
Of the strength and the courage of stal-
    wart men.
Let us haste to succor his sore distress
In the horrible heat and merciless flame.
God knows I had rather the fire should
    enfold   461
My body and limbs with my gold-friend
    and lord."

[*Finally the dragon fastened his fangs in Beowulf's throat and the hero suffered a deadly wound. Wiglaf thrust his sword into the dragon's body and Beowulf with dying strength cut the beast in two with his dagger. Now dying Beowulf spoke:*]

448. WAEGMUNDING (wăg'mŭn·dĭng)—The family to which Wiglaf and Beowulf belonged.

"My armor and sword I would leave to
    my son
Had Fate but granted, born of my body,
An heir to follow me after I'm
    gone.   465
For fifty winters I've ruled this realm,
And never a lord of a neighboring land
Dared strike with terror or seek with
    sword.
In my life I abode by the lot assigned,
Kept well what was mine, courted no
    quarrels,   470
Swore no false oaths. And now for all
    this
Though my hurt is grievous, my heart is
    glad.
When life leaves body, the Lord of man-
    kind
Cannot lay to my charge the killing of
    kinsmen!"

[*Beowulf asked Wiglaf to gaze on the gold of dragon's loot. Wiglaf returned to his dying lord with heaps of the treasure. As he looked upon the spoils, Beowulf gave thanks to God who gave the grace to win these riches for his people. He spoke again to young Wiglaf:*]

"Heed well the wants, the need of my
    people;   475
My hour is come, and my end is near.
Bid warriors build, when they burn my
    body,
A stately barrow on the headland's
    height.
It shall be for remembrance among my
    people
As it towers high on the Cape of the
    Whale,   480
And sailors shall know it as Beowulf's
    Barrow,
Sea-faring mariners driving their ships
Through fogs of ocean from far coun-
    tries."

478. BARROW—A grave covered by an earthen mound.

Then the great-hearted king unclasped
   from his throat   484
A collar of gold, and gave to his thane;
Gave the young hero his gold-decked
   helmet,
His ring and his byrny, and wished him
   well.
"You are the last of the Waegmunding
   line.
All my kinsmen, earls in their glory,
Fate has sent to their final doom,   490
And I must follow."   These words were
   the last
The old king spoke ere the pyre received
   him,
The leaping flames of the funeral blaze,
And his breath went forth from his
   bosom, his soul
Went forth from the flesh, to the joys
   of the just.   495

[*The cowardly thanes crept back and
looked at Wiglaf as he sat by the king's
body. Wiglaf again upbraided them
and told of the contempt with which
the cowardly deed would be spoken of
in future years. A messenger rode along
the cliffs relating the sad news of Beowulf's people and prophesying the fall of
the nation. The body of the dead
dragon was tumbled over the cliff into
the sea. In accordance with Beowulf's
dying wish, a funeral pyre was built on
the headland and a barrow constructed
in which was buried the dragon's treasure. The funeral pyre was kindled, and
round the pyre wound the mourning
warriors as they proclaimed his virtue
and fame.*]

They sang their dirge and spoke of the
   hero
Vaunting his valor and venturous deeds.
So is it proper a man should praise

His friendly lord with a loving heart,
When his soul must forth from the fleet-
   ing flesh.   500
So the folk of the Geats, the friends of
   his hearth,
Bemoaned the fall of their mighty lord;
Said he was the kindest of worldly kings,
Mildest, most gentle, most eager for
   fame.

WORD STUDY

1. Give several synonyms for the following words: *addled, harried, baleful, marauding, murky, swelter, eerie, wrought.*
2. Show how the word *ominous* is related to *omen.* What does *portent* mean?
What is the difference between *cumber*
and *combers?* What is the connection
between the word *mere* and the Latin
word *mare?*
3. In translating Beowulf into modern
English, Professor Kennedy has kept the
strong action verbs, the epithets or vivid
picture adjectives, and the compound
words of the Anglo-Saxons. Carefully select several examples of such verbs and
adjectives.

FOR DISCUSSION

1. What information in the first 36
lines is given us to indicate that Hrothgar
was a successful Christian king?
2. What details are we given about
Grendel in lines 37–49?
3. Briefly describe the journey of Beowulf from the land of the Geats to Denmark.
4. Discuss the contents of Beowulf's
first speech before Hrothgar in lines 90–
124. How did Hrothgar receive Beowulf?
5. How did Beowulf refute the charge
of Unferth that Beowulf had been bested
in the swimming match with Breca? Is
there any irony or sarcasm in his reply?
Explain.

6. Briefly describe the encounter of Beowulf with Grendel. Was Grendel slain by a sword? Explain.

7. Was Beowulf present in the mead-hall when Grendel's dam slew Aeschere?

8. Briefly describe Beowulf's encounter with Grendel's dam. Was Unferth's sword, Hrunting, effective in slaying her? Explain. What did Beowulf carry with him when he arose to the surface of the pool?

9. What and who provoked the Fire Dragon to lay waste the land of the Geats during the last years of Beowulf's reign?

10. Contrast the actions of Wiglaf with those of the other thanes in Beowulf's tragic combat with the Fire Dragon. How did Beowulf suffer his mortal wound? How was the fire dragon killed?

11. What were Beowulf's parting requests as spoken to Wiglaf?

12. Enumerate the details which conclude the epic.

◇◇◇◇◇◇◇◇◇◇◇◇◇◇◇◇◇◇◇◇◇◇◇◇◇◇◇◇◇◇◇

FOR APPRECIATION

1. The selection from *Beowulf* which you have read is filled with many beautiful *kennings* like *swan-road*, *heather-stepper*, and *foamy-necked plunger*. Select at least ten *kennings* from the text.

2. Choose from the text at least ten lines in which the translator was particularly successful in imitating the alliterative form of the original Anglo-Saxon verse.

3. The hero of an epic sums up in himself the characteristics of the ideal man of the country in which the epic was written. Write a character sketch of Beowulf pointing out the virtues portrayed in him which the Christian Anglo-Saxon of the eighth century admired.

4. Reread and study carefully lines 397–431, which contain the advice of Hrothgar to Beowulf. Could the modern ruler as well as the average man profit from such advice? Discuss. Is this advice of Hrothgar solid spiritual advice? Explain.

5. An interesting study for those who have studied the *Aeneid* would be to 1) compare the *Aeneid* and *Beowulf* as examples of epic poetry; 2) compare the descriptions of the seas and the storms in *Beowulf* with some of those in the *Aeneid*; 3) analyze the similarities of setting and imagery in lines 315–334 of *Beowulf* with lines 479–591 of the Seventh Book of the *Aeneid*.

6. Do you find any evidence that the author of *Beowulf* would have his hero stand for Christ and his companions for the Apostles? Discuss.

PROJECTS

1. Write one or more brief prose descriptions modeled after the descriptions in lines 65–82; lines 315–338; lines 432–442.

2. Reread the treatment of the epic as a form of narrative poetry and show how *Beowulf* conforms to the epic tradition.

RELATED READING

Every student will want to read the entire poem in the translation by Professor Kennedy.

The *Seafarer* is one of the earliest English poems of the sea. This poem as well as excerpts from Cynewulf's majestically beautiful poems, *The Christ*, *Elene*, and *The Dream of the Rood*, may be found in modern translation in Margaret Williams' *Word-Hoard*.

You are urged to read the thrilling *Song of Roland* in the excellent modern English translation by Frederick Bliss Luquiens.

THE ECCLESIASTICAL HISTORY OF ENGLAND

THE VENERABLE BEDE

Translated by Alfred

The famous passage below, taken from Bede's Ecclesiastical History, tells the story of the first English Christian poet and of how he acquired his miraculous gift of song while living at the monastery of the Abbess Hilda. The selection also gives us a fine example of the rough, alliterative rhythm of early English prose.

In the monastery of this Abbess (Saint Hilda) was a certain brother wonderfully gifted and honoured with God's grace, because he was in the habit of putting into song the things that tended to piety and virtue, so that whatever he learned through scribes of holy lore, that he adorned after a little while with song-speech, with the greatest sweetness and zeal, and always put it in the English tongue, and through his songs the hearts of many men were often set burning with scorn of the world and with attraction to the heavenly life. And thus many others after him among the English began to make holy songs, but no other could do it like to him, because he learned songcraft not at all from men but was helped divinely, and through God's gift received songcraft.

"The Ecclesiastical History of England" by Bede and translated by Alfred from *Word Hoard*—Passages from Old English Literature from the Sixth to the Eleventh Centuries, translated and arranged by Margaret Williams, M.A., copyright, 1940, by Sheed and Ward, Inc., New York.

And for this he could not work a lie nor an idle song, but only those which led to piety and which it became a godly tongue to sing.

He was a man living in the worldly state until the time when he was advanced in years, and he had never learned any song, and for this often at the beer drinking, when it was deemed for the sake of bliss that they all, each in turn, should sing to the harp, then arose he for shame from the feasting, and went home to his house. When he had done that one time, left the house of the beer drinking and was going out to the cattleshed (the care of them was given to him that night), and when he there at the fitting time laid his limbs on the bed and slept, then stood by him a man in a dream, and hailed him and greeted him and named him by name: "Caedmon, sing me somewhat." Then answered he and said: "I cannot sing, for that I came out of the beer drinking and came hither, because I could not." Then he said that was speaking with him: "But thou canst sing to me." Said he: "What shall I sing?" Said he: "Sing me the first shaping." When he received this answer, then began he straight to sing in praise of God the Shaper verses and words he had never heard, and they went thus:

Now must we praise   heaven's keeper,
the might of the ruler   and His heart's thought,
the work of glory-father   of every wonder
He made the beginning   everlasting Lord.
He first shaped   for the children of men
the skies for a roof,   holy maker.
then afterwards   mankind's keeper
made the earth,   the soil for man,
almighty ruler   and endless Lord.

Then arose he from sleep, and he had fast in mind all that he sang sleeping, and to those words straightway added he many words in the same measure to the song worthy of God. Then came he in the morning to the town-reeve who was the ealdorman, and told him what gift he had received, and he straightway led him to the Abbess, and said it and told it to her. Then she bade be gathered the most learned men, and the disciples, and bade him tell the dream before them, and sing that song, that it might be decided by the judgment of all of them, what and whence it was. Then it was plain to them all what it was, that it was a heavenly gift given by the Lord himself. Then they related and told to him a holy story and words of godly lore. They bade him, then, if he could, change it into song, and into the harmony of verse. When he had heard it, then went he home to his house, and came again in the morning and sang to them a well-wrought poem, and gave to them what they had bidden.

Then began the Abbess to embrace and love God's gift in the man, and she advised and taught him that he should leave his worldly state and enter monkhood, and he liked it well, and she received him into the monastery with his goods and added him to the company of God's servants, and bade him be taught the account of the holy story and tale, and all that he could learn with his hearing, that he turned in his mind, and as a clean beast ruminating [1] he turned it into the sweetest song, and his

[1] RUMINATING—Meditating; also, chewing the cud.

verses were so winsome to hear that his teachers themselves learned and wrote from his mouth. He sang first the shaping of earth and the beginning of mankind, and all the story of Genesis, that is the First Book of Moses, and then the outgoing of Israel's folk from the Egyptians' land, and the ingoing into the promised land, and about many others of the holy writing of the Canonical Books, and about Christ's manhood and His suffering, and His rising into Heaven, and about the coming of the Holy Ghost, and the teaching of the Apostles, and then about the terror of the Doom to come, and the fear of the pain full of torments, and about the sweetness of the Kingdom of heaven he made many songs; and also many others about God's benefits and dooms he wrought. In all these he earnestly tried to draw men from the love of sin and of evil deeds, for he was a very godly man and humbly subject to the discipline of the rule, and against those who

would do otherwise he burned with zeal, and for this he finished and ended his life in a fair wise.

◇◇◇◇◇◇◇◇◇◇◇◇◇◇◇◇◇◇◇◇◇◇◇◇◇◇◇◇◇◇◇

FOR DISCUSSION

1. What special significance does the story of Caedmon have for a Catholic writer? Discuss.

2. Compare the sentence structure of the passage with that of modern prose. In what ways do they differ? In three or four well chosen adjectives, sum up the qualities of Bede's style as seen in Alfred's translation.

WORD STUDY

Discuss the meaning of these early English words: *songspeech, holy lore, songcraft, first shaping, town-reeve.*

PROJECTS

Write a brief sketch of the life, works, and importance of Bede.

◇◇◇◇◇

AELFRIC'S HOMILY
FOR ST. EDMUND'S DAY

Translated into Modern English by Margaret Williams

Aelfric, the most learned man of his age, wrote three series of sermons, with each series containing forty homilies. Aelfric had a special devotion to "those saints whom the English nation honors with feast days." One of these great saints was St. Edmund, King of the East Anglians, who was slain by the Danes when they invaded East Anglia in 870.

In his story of St. Edmund, Aelfric employs a style of alliterative prose closely akin to poetry.

Edmund, the blessed King of East Anglia, was wise and worthy, and ever honoured Almighty God with noble virtues. He was humble and good, and so thoroughly steadfast that he would not bend to shameful evil; not on any side did he hide his virtues, but was always mindful of true belief. If thou art set to be a head-man, do not lift thyself up, but be among men as a man of them. He was kind to the poor and to widows, as a father, and with well-willingness guided his folk ever to righteousness, and checked the mighty, and lived happily. It happened soon after that the Danish tribes came with ships, harrying and slaying wide round the land, as their way is. Among the sea-men were the first head-men, Hinguar and Hubba, in league with the devil, and they landed in Northumbria with ships, and wasted the land and slew the people. Then went Hinguar east with his ships, and Hubba stayed in Northumbria, winning victory with cruelty. Then Hinguar came rowing to East Anglia, in the year in which Alfred the King was twenty-one years old, who was the great king of the West Saxons. And the fore-said Hinguar suddenly, like a wolf, stalked the land and slew the people, men and women and unknowing children, and treated shamefully all the innocent Christians. Then straightway he sent to the king a boasting message, that he should bend to do homage to him if he cared for his life. The errand-bearer came to King Edmund and harshly gave him his message: "Hinguar our king, keen and victory-fast on sea and land, has power over many peoples, and comes now with

forces suddenly to land, that he may here have a winter-place with his army. Now he bids thee show thy secret gold-hoards and thy old treasure generously to him, that thou be his underking if thou wouldst be alive, for thou hast not the might that thou mayest withstand him."

Lo then, King Edmund called a Bishop, who was closest to him, and consulted with him how he might escape the cruel Hinguar. Then the Bishop feared in this sudden happening, and for the King's life, and said that it seemed wise to him for him to bend, as Hinguar bade. Then the King was silent and looked to the earth, and then spoke keenly to him: "Lo, thou Bishop, too shameful would it seem to the wretched people of the land; and I would rather fall in the fight, that my folk might enjoy their land." And the Bishop said "Lo, thou dear King, thy folk lies slain, and thou hast no help that thou mayest fight, and the seamen will come and will bind thee alive, unless thou with flight save thy life, or that thou so guard thee that thou bend to him." Then said King Edmund, full keen as he was: "This I will, and wish with my heart, that I alone should not live after my loved thanes, who in their beds with their wives and children were fiercely slain by these seamen. It was never my way to seek flight, but I would rather die if I must for my own land, and Almighty God knows that I will not bend from His bidding ever, nor from His true love, die I, live I." After these words he turned to the errand-bearer whom Hinguar sent to him, and said to him unafraid: "Thou wert now indeed slain, but I would not foul my clean hands in thy foul blood, for I follow Christ who gave us an example; but I blithely will be slain by you, if

"Aelfric's Homily for St. Edmund's Day" from *Word Hoard*—Passages from Old English Literature from the Sixth to the Eleventh Centuries, translated and arranged by Margaret Williams, M.A., copyright, 1940, by Sheed and Ward, Inc., New York.

God so wills. Go now swiftly and say to thy cruel lord that Edmund will never bow to Hinguar the heathen leader in his life, unless he first bows with belief to the Healer Christ in this land." Then went the errand-bearer sternly away, and met the fierce Hinguar with all his army hastening to Edmund, and he told the wicked one how he had been answered. Hinguar angrily bade his ship-army that they should take all that belonged to the King that they saw, and straightway bind him.

Lo then, Edmund the King stood in his hall when Hinguar came to him, mindful of the Healer, and threw away his weapons; he would follow Christ's example who forbade Peter with weapons to fight against the wicked Jews. Lo then, they bound the blameless Edmund, and greatly shamed him, and beat him with clubs; and then led the believing King to an earth-fast tree, and tied him thereto with hard bonds, and afterwards beat him long with whips, and he ever called out between the strokes, with true belief, to the Healer Christ. And the heathens then, for his belief, were very ireful, because he called

on Christ to help him. They shot with javelins against him until he was set all over with their darts like the quills of a porcupine, as Sebastian [1] was. When Hinguar saw, the wicked seaman, that the noble king would not forsake Christ, but with steady belief ever called upon Him, then he ordered him to be beheaded, and the heathen so did. While he called upon Christ, the heathen took the holy one to slay him, and with one blow struck off his head, and the happy soul journeyed to Christ.

There was a certain man near by, through God hidden from the heathen, who saw all this and said it afterwards, as we have said it here. Lo then, the seamen went back to their ships, and hid the head of the holy Edmund in the thick brambles, that it might not be buried. And after a time, when they had gone away, came the land-folk there where the remains were, where their lord's body lay without a head, and they were sorry in their hearts for his slaying, and especially that they had

[1] SEBASTIAN—Roman martyr who, according to the popular story, was shot to death with arrows about the year 288.

not the head to the body. Then said the witness, who had seen it before, that the seamen had the head with them, and it seemed to him, as it was in truth, that they had hidden it somewhere in the woods. Wherefore at last they went all to the woods, seeking everywhere, around bushes and brambles, if they might meet with the head. It was also a great wonder that a wolf was sent, through God's guiding, to watch over the head against the other wild beasts, day and night. They went then seeking and calling, as is the way when one goes oft into the woods: "Where art thou now, comrade?" And the head answered them: "Here, here, here." And they again called answering, until they all came to it, through the calling. There lay the grey wolf who watched the head, and with his two feet he clasped the head, greedy and hungry, and for God he durst not taste the head, but held it against wild beasts. Then were they wondering at the guarding of the wolf, and they took the holy head with them, thanking the Almighty for all His wonders. But the wolf followed them forth with the head till they came

to the town, as if he were tame, and then went back to the woods again.

◇◇◇◇◇◇◇◇◇◇◇◇◇◇◇◇◇◇◇◇◇◇◇◇◇◇◇◇◇◇

WORD STUDY

1. Note the many Anglo-Saxon compound words found in Aelfric's prose. *Well-willingness, ship-army, earth-fast* are some examples. Select at least five other compound words and give a modern English synonym for each.

2. Note also the simplicity of the diction: the many monosyllabic words; the absence of words of Latin origin. Can you explain why there are so few words with Latin roots in Anglo-Saxon writings?

3. Give several modern English synonyms for *steadfast, head-man, stalked, bidding, errand-bearer, ship-army.*

FOR DISCUSSION

1. Did Edmund follow the advice of the Bishop concerning the demand of the Danes for the East Anglian treasure? Explain.

2. Was Edmund's reply to the Danish leader a kingly one? Explain.

3. How was Edmund martyred? Briefly explain how the head of St. Edmund was preserved.

Further Readings—Pre-Saxon and Anglo-Saxon England

* CHESTERTON, G. K., *The Ballad of the White Horse* (poem)

BOWRA, C. M., *From Vergil to Milton,* Chapter 1 on "The Literary Epic."

GUMMERE, FRANCIS B., *The Oldest English Epic*

LANIER, SIDNEY, *The Boys' King Arthur*

QUENNELL, MARJORIE AND CHARLES

H. B., *Every Day Life in Roman Britain; Every Day Life in Anglo-Saxon Times*

SHAKESPEARE, WILLIAM, *King Lear* and *Cymbeline* (dramas)

TAPPAN, E. M., *In the Days of Alfred the Great*

* WARD, MAISIE, *The English Way.* Chapters on Bede, Alcuin, and Alfred.

* WAUGH, EVELYN, *Helena* (novel)

* WILLIAMS, MARGARET, *Word-Hoard.* (anthology of Anglo-Saxon writings)

Note: Books marked with an asterisk (*) throughout this volume are works by Catholic authors.

A Medieval tournament. Knights and their ladies.

THE MIDDLE ENGLISH
PERIOD

1 0 6 6 – 1 5 0 0

In the eleventh century England's peace was threatened from across the Channel. Edward the Confessor, a Saxon King who spent his youth in France, disastrously welcomed influential Norman leaders to his court. This mistake paid off when Edward's successor, Harold, came to the throne. The Normans prepared to invade England and waited for the Danes to break out in one of their perennial uprisings in the north. Then the Normans landed on the beaches of the south of England in great on-rushing waves. Harold, "the last of the Saxons," moved his poorly equipped troops to meet this unexpected terror. On October 12, 1066, Harold's forces faced the troops of William the Conqueror at Hastings. As the *Anglo-Saxon Chronicle* relates: "Then beginning the *Song of Roland*, the standard was raised and waved, the trumpets and bugles sounded, and, invoking the aid of heavenly powers, they (the Normans) began the battle." From dawn to sunset the Saxon stood against the long-range bows of the French. Harold fell wounded, the army buckled, and William of Normandy became William the Conqueror of England.

The road to London now lay open to the Normans. Tersely does the *Anglo-Saxon Chronicle* tell of William's conquest and crowning: "William over-ran the land, and came to Westminster, and Ealdred the Archbishop hallowed him King, and men paid him tribute, and gave him hostages, and after bought their land."

The new conquerors were of a different cut from the Angles, Saxons, and Danes. The Normans were both Christian and civilized. They were descendants of Scandinavian Vikings who had seeped into northern France and so ravaged Christendom that a new invocation was added to the Litany of the Saints: "From the peril of Northmen, O Lord, deliver us." Soon they changed their Germanic tongue for the French of the conquered people. With their conversion to Christianity, they absorbed the Christian culture. This new people became an integral part of the French kingdom; and it was in Normandy that the French genius was best expressed in literature, in architecture, in chivalry.

CHARACTER OF THE NORMANS

Under the new regime, most of the great estates passed into the hands of William's followers, and the English bishops and abbots were supplanted by Norman churchmen. The new Norman nobility built thick-walled strongholds in which to defend themselves from the hostile Saxons; but as time went on and the opposition between Saxon and Norman lessened, these cumbersome structures were replaced by beautiful Norman castles which formed the background for a richer, gayer life than the rough Saxons had known. The Norman bishops likewise brought a new grandeur to cathedral and monastery. Durham, Ely, and the older parts of Canterbury still bear witness to the beauty of Norman architecture. At the hands of the conquerors, the government was gradually feudalized and centralized in the court. There was also a great increase in growth and importance of town and city life. Many businesses moved to England from the Continent and laid the foundations for modern English towns as commercial centers. In the century that followed the Conquest, French language and French laughter were heard at the court. Norman chroniclers told in rich Latin how William bent England to his will. But that century was a century of silence for native English literature.

The Normans, especially under Henry I (1100–1135) and Henry II (1154–1189) introduced the notions of chivalry and knighthood. This was the time of the Crusades, and with the Crusaders came back new ideas, new mannerisms, and new luxuries from the Orient. The two universities of Oxford and Cambridge, founded during this period, helped to increase learning and to spread many new ideas that were appearing.

The assimilation of Norman culture by the native Saxons came about only after much bloodshed, cruelty, and hard feeling. But different in so many respects, these two peoples knelt at the same altar. Religion was UNION OF SAXONS a common denominator that made an ultimate fusion of the two cultures possible. The Anglo-Saxons did gradu- AND NORMANS ally absorb the refinements of the Normans, so that by the year 1300, two centuries after the Conquest, there was a new culture and a new language which was neither entirely Norman nor strictly Anglo-Saxon.

The Magna Charta, wrung from King John in 1215, was to prove potent in welding the minds and hearts of the people together. It was the first important step in the long journey towards democracy. A free man could no longer be imprisoned or tortured except after lawful trial. Fines were fixed by law. No taxes could be levied without the consent of the Council. The Church was granted freedom from royal interference.

The march of equality advanced another step in 1265, when for the first time Parliament sat, not just as agents of the clergy and nobility, but with representatives of the common people—an assembly which was to become the English House of Commons.

England by the thirteenth century was "Merrie England." Exhilaration was in the air. Men explored the whole world of adventure and romance with a vigor which still holds us spellbound. Knights went bravely riding off to the Crusades; gay companies of ladies, squires, and monks made pilgrimages to distant shrines; scholars hastened to Rome. It was an age when the miraculous and supernatural were taken for granted. Men lived on intimate, easy terms with their patron saints and saw God as the center of their lives and heaven as their ultimate home. It was an age of merriment—because men realized they were children of God.

However, in the fourteenth century a series of misfortunes worked widespread havoc not only to Catholicism, the soul of medieval England, but to England at large. These unfortunate events began with another war —this time over holdings which the Norman kings still retained in France. Before it terminated, the Hundred Years' War cost England all her French territory and in 1349 brought the Black Death to the Island. This terrible plague destroyed one-third of the population and swept away two-thirds of the clergy and the monks who had been the teachers of England through the centuries. Unprepared, and in some cases, even unworthy men were ordained to take their places, with the result that not only religion but culture in general suffered.

A TIME OF

UPHEAVAL

With the Battle of Crécy, the cannon replaced the traditional bow as an instrument of war, and spelt doom for the armored knight and the age of chivalry. The Black Death brought hunger in its wake, and hunger led to revolt. As weaving developed into an industry of primary importance, peasants left the manors to find work in the crowded towns. Boroughs and cities grew boisterous. Tax collectors were stoned off the streets and hardly a day passed without some dignitary being burned in effigy. People flocked to the country fairs, spending days and nights on the highways crowded with merchants and packmen. There were mountebanks and magicians to entice the country bumpkins, and pastry stalls that did a furious business. There were wines and silks and trinkets to be had after endless heckling. These were nervous, turbulent times when almost anything could happen—and usually did.

The great social contribution of the age was the system of guilds among the tradesmen and craftsmen, similar in many respects to our modern trade unions. As we shall see later, the guilds played a tremendous part in the development and sponsoring of the medieval drama.

As we have seen, it took more than a century for the Anglo-Saxon and Norman cultures to unite. During the first century after the Conquest, French became the language of the court and society. What literature there was, was written in either French or Latin. Anglo-Saxon was outlawed from the schools and was considered a mark of social inferiority. But in the country and among the simple people the Old English tongue persisted. It gradually assimilated Norman words and turns of expression, until by the end of the thirteenth century Old English had become Middle English, a language much closer to our modern tongue than was the old Anglo-Saxon. The new language retained much of the Anglo-Saxon vigor, but through the Norman influence gained considerably in lightness and flexibility.

CHANGES IN THE

LANGUAGE

The first effect of this fusion was a tremendous increase in the English vocabulary. Words were multiplied both numerically and expressively.

In our language today, we often have a choice of Saxon or Norman words to express a particular meaning for what we want to say. For example, *house* from the Saxon indicates an ordinary dwelling; but *mansion* and *manse* from the French

maison indicate special kinds of houses. Usually the Anglo-Saxon words are the ones with the humble or common meaning, and the Norman-French have become the dressed-up or specialized words.

The Norman-French was a *Romance* language—that is, it was a modification of the Latin which had been spoken by the Roman soldiers who conquered Gaul. Thus English received through the Norman-French a great store of Latin derivatives. Today, we make use not only of the Anglo-Saxon word *red*, but also of words like *rouge*, *ruby*, and *rubicund* derived from the Latin through the Norman-French. Another fund of Latin words kept coming into English use directly, through the studies of churchmen and scholars.

The absorption of French and Latin words into English gave our language the capacity to make thousands of new words by using prefixes and suffixes. At the same time it retained the picturesque, though sometimes cumbersome, knack of making compounds. The blend of Teutonic and Romance characteristics has resulted in giving modern English the most flexible and expressive vocabulary of all the living languages.

The second change that took place was a remarkable simplification of English grammar. Both Latin and Anglo-Saxon were highly inflected languages—that is, the various uses of words were indicated by changes in form of the words themselves. In learning a new language these inflections are the most difficult to master. And so when Saxon and Norman got to talking together, they picked up each other's words and let the inflected endings go. The resulting simplification of inflections was further aided by the adoption of a simple or normal sentence order and by the substitution of natural gender for the confusing system of grammatical gender.

With a greatly increased vocabulary and a greatly simplified grammatical structure, a vital, flexible language emerged during the Middle English period.

It was this language that was to be the raw material which Chaucer, Shakespeare, Milton, and the other great English authors were to use in creating the masterpieces of English literature.

MIDDLE ENGLISH LITERATURE

Although Middle English literature reached its high water mark with Chaucer, Langland, the Pearl Poet, and Malory in the fourteenth and fifteenth centuries, we must not suppose that there was no literary activity in the English tongue during the two previous centuries. We shall mention but a few of the less known but important contributions to later English literature before studying in detail the ballad, the metrical romance, and the metrical tale—all distinct products of medieval literature.

The Beastiary, composed of allegorical tales of the animal kingdom, and punch-packed with moral lessons, was translated into English by an unknown poet of East Anglia in the thirteenth century. Both medieval preacher and poet drew upon these tales for their sermons and their literary writings.

The Owl and the Nightingale is one of the greatest of the medieval debate poems. It was developed according to the art form of the contentio (debate) of the *Eclogues* of Vergil and made popular in England by such scholars as Alcuin. The allegory in the poem has the owl sing of what is serious and traditional in life, while the nightingale sings of what is joyous, daring, and new. The influence of this debate poetry can be seen both in the metaphysical poets of the seventeenth century and in Dryden's famous allegorical satire, *The Hind and the Panther*.

RELIGIOUS LITERATURE

Much of the literature of the Middle Ages reflects the close connection between the monastic cloister and the world. Outstanding among the religious poetry and prose of this period are the *Ancren Riwle* by the Dominican Friar Robert Bacon; and *The Form of Perfect Living* and the religious lyrics by Richard Rolle. Hundreds of other religious lyrics still survive whose authorship is unknown and whose poetic themes are the love of Franciscan poverty, love of Our Lady, and love of Christ, the ideal Knight. As a piece of prose literature, the *Ancren Riwle* molded the style of medieval English prose for centuries.

SECULAR LYRICS

The origins of the lyrics of Shakespeare as well as the moderns can be found not only in the Renaissance writers but also in the outpourings of the medieval wandering scholar and of the professional troubadour. The overcrowded universities of the time were unable to house the thousands of boys, for the most part irresponsible young clerics, who attended these seats of learning but were forced to sing for their livelihood. Unconsciously these wandering young poets accomplished for literature what no professional poet could have done. With the hymns of the Church and the poetry of Horace ringing in their ears, they created a vernacular lyric of their own. The stanza forms and especially the rhymes were derived from the Church's liturgy. Often the Latin and the English languages were woven together into what is called macaronic verse. Of Our Lady they could sing:

> Of one that is so fayr and bright
> *Velut maris stella*
> Brighter than the day is light,
> *Parens et puella.*

Their love songs and nature songs were bright and gay, echoing the happy sounds of children on the village green.

> Springtime is come with love to earth,
> With blossoms and with bird's mirth
> That all this bliss bringeth.
> Day's-eyes in the dales,
> Notes sweet of nightingales,
> Every bird singeth.[1]

MEDIEVAL STORY TELLING

With no television or radio to fill up their leisure hours, the people of the Middle Ages welcomed a good story from any source. The author of the *Gesta Romanorum* tells us that "on stormy winter nights after supper the family gathers around the fireplace to tell old stories."

John Mandeville's *Travels* is the best known of these collections of stories. Originally written in French, they were translated into Middle English. In the *Gesta Romanorum*, a collection of 380 stories whose subject matter ranged from classical mythology to the realm of the preternatural, we have a storehouse of pointed narratives from which Shakespeare and many others drew heavily. For example, we find in it the tale of the bond concerning the pound of flesh and the story of "Androcles and the Lion," so popular with children of all ages.

By the end of the fourteenth century, writing came to be looked upon as an art to be developed for its own sake, and for the first time story collections were

---

[1] "Old English Lyric" from *Glee Wood*—Passages from Middle English Literature from the Eleventh Century to the Fifteenth, translated and arranged by Margaret Williams, M.A., copyright, 1949, by Sheed and Ward, Inc., New York.

written by men who might be called our first professional writers. Outstanding among these collections were Chaucer's *Canterbury Tales* and John Gower's poetic allegory, *Confessio Amantis*.

THE BALLAD

The ballad may be defined as a comparatively short narrative poem originally composed to be sung. Most of the ballads were composed between the twelfth and sixteenth centuries. Handed down from generation to generation through oral transmission, they acquired many additions and variations and were finally written down for permanent record in the eighteenth century.

The popular or folk ballad resembles the folk epic in its origins, but differs in other respects. The composers of both types of narrative poetry are unknown, and their subject matter comes from tradition. But whereas the epic deals with an heroic theme in an heroic manner, the ballad is simple in theme, and, often, crude in form, employing commonplace words and country dialects. Ballads vary in length from a simple episode like that of "The Wife of Usher's Well" to several episodes strung together into a long loose narrative, like those of the *Robin Hood* cycle. They treat of themes which stir the imagination of the common folk. Love, jealousy, war, revenge, death, and the preternatural are the staple subjects; and the treatment is usually tragic.

Like all primitive poetry which tells a story for its own sake, the ballad is strictly objective. It contains no suggestion of how the author has been moved by the event, and it therein resembles a modern news report in which the reactions of the reporter are carefully omitted.

In the ballad, the action is generally not presented as a straight narrative. The first two stanzas give us an identification of the hero and the next two stanzas a bit of narrative. In the remaining stanzas the action is given by a succession of little scenes. Much of the action is presented through dialogue, and the characters generally speak for themselves. The motives of the characters are suggested and implied rather than directly expressed. To appreciate the complete story of the ballad, there must be much reading between the lines. As in most poetry, the concrete is preferred to the abstract. The theme of the ballad is expressed in vivid and concrete details. Its moral is generally suggested and very rarely directly expressed.

The ballads are composed in stanzas of one of two kinds; either in couplets of iambic pentameter or in the *ballad stanza*, a quatrain rhyming *a b c b*, with alternating iambic tetrameter and iambic trimeter lines. Often the ballad has a refrain with what is known as "incremental repetition," that is, a stanza that repeats the preceding stanza with the variations necessary to continue the story. The ballad "Edward, Edward" illustrates both the refrain and the repetition.

A distinction is often made between the more crude form of the folk ballad and the more polished ballads composed by the minstrels, and hence called *minstrel* ballads. These ballads were sung before the courtly assemblage, and this accounts both for the more polished language and the more romantic theme. Fine examples of the *minstrel* ballads are "The Boy and the Mantle" and "King Arthur and King Cornwall."

Versions of the old English and Scottish ballads may be heard today in the mountains of Kentucky, Tennessee and West Virginia. Yet most of our present day ballad singers have no idea that these songs were brought to America from England two or three centuries ago.

◇◇◇◇◇

Sir Patrick Spens

Artistically speaking, "Sir Patrick Spens" is one of the best, if not the best, of the old ballads. It is usually classified as an historical ballad, because it so closely parallels the story of the daughter of Alexander III, Margaret. She was married to the King of Norway, Eric; and all the knights and nobles who had accompanied her to Norway perished on the voyage home. Sir Patrick Spens is not an historical figure. Shipwrecks were of frequent occurrence off the coast of Scotland; and since ballad singers mixed fact and fiction, the details of this ballad are probably the result of a combination of several different stories.

The king sits in Dumferling toune,
  Drinking the blude-reid wine:
"O whar will I get guid sailor,
  To sail this schip of mine?"

Up and spak an eldern knicht,   5
  Sat at the kings richt kne:
"Sir Patrick Spens is the best sailor
  That sails upon the se."

The king has written a braid letter,
  And signd it wi his hand,   10
And sent it to Sir Patrick Spens,
  Was walking on the sand.

The first line that Sir Patrick red,
  A loud lauch lauched he;
The next line that Sir Patrick red,   15
  The teir blinded his ee.

"O wha is this has don this deid,
  This ill deid don to me,
To send me out this time o' the yeir,
  To sail upon the se!   20

"Mak haste, mak haste, my mirry men all,
  Our guid schip sails the morne:"
"O say na sae, my master deir,
  For I feir a deadlie storme.

    5. ELDERN KNICHT—An older knight.
    9. BRAID LETTER—A long letter.

    14. LOUD LAUCH—A loud laugh laughed he.
    16. EE—Eye.

"Late late yestreen I saw the new
    moone,   25
  Wi the auld moone in hir arme,
And I feir, I feir, my deir master,
    That we will cum to harme."

O our Scots nobles wer richt laith
  To wet their cork-heild schoone;   30
Bot lang owre a' the play wer played,
    Thair hats they swam aboone.

25–26—It is still a superstition among sailors that when the dark part of the moon can be seen inside the horn of the new moon, a storm will follow.

29. RICHT LAITH—Right loath, very unwilling.

30. SCHOONE—Shoes.

31. LANG OWRE—Long before.

32. THAIR HATS THEY SWAM ABOONE—Their hats swam above them, that is, they drowned.

O lang, lang may their ladies sit,
  Wi thair fans into their hand,
Or eir they se Sir Patrick Spens   35
    Cum sailing to the land.

O lang, lang may the ladies stand,
  Wi thair gold kems in their hair,
Waiting for thair ain deir lords,
    For they'll se thame na mair.   40

Haf owre, haf owre to Aberdour,
  It's fiftie fadom deip,
And thair lies guid Sir Patrick Spens,
  Wi the Scots lords at his feit.

38. KEMS—Combs.

41. HAF OWRE, TO ABERDOUR—Half. over, half over to Aberdour, a small town near Edinburgh.

FOR APPRECIATION

1. The calamity of the shipwreck which brought death to Sir Patrick and his men, together with the loneliness of the fair ladies who wait for their lords' return—these constitute the tragedy of the ballad. More than half the lines of the ballad are devoted to emphasizing this theme. Less than half of the lines treat of the external framework of events which are responsible for the tragedy. Select the lines in the ballad which simply tell the story. Select those lines which emphasize the tragedy.

2. Note the implied actions and motives which can be read between the lines. Why does the king drink blood-red wine in line 2? Why does the king want someone to sail his ship? Has he lost many good sailors before? What is the character of the eldern knight? Do you think he has some personal grudge against Sir Patrick?

3. Stanzas five, six and seven contain a climactic undertone of the tragedy to come. How are these fears confirmed in stanza eight? Explain.

4. In line 30, why does the poet use the word "cork-heeled"? Is there any connection between drowning and cork?

5. Does line 41 suggest that Sir Patrick and his men were drowned on the *return* voyage? Explain.

6. Reread paragraph 4 of the introduction to the ballads; then show how "Sir Patrick Spens" follows the typical ballad organization and development.

The use of the fan and the comb is a typical ballad convention. The poor, who delighted in these stories, equally disliked long descriptions, so certain details were chosen to suggest the type of characters. To the poor, golden combs and fans stood for all that they longed for and never had. They suggested luxury, nobility, and wealth.

The final stanza of a ballad usually contains a "punch line." We are prepared for the tragedy; but when it comes, we are nonetheless affected by the scene in the final two lines.

Edward, Edward

"Edward, Edward" is a famous ballad of domestic tragedy. It gives, dramatically, by a series of seven questions and answers, the dialogue between a son, guilty of patricide, and his mother who persuaded him to do the deed.

"Why dois your brand sae drap wi bluid,
  Edward, Edward,
Why dois your brand sae drap wi bluid,
  And why sae sad gang yee O?"
"O I hae killed my hauke sae guid,   5
  Mither, mither,
O I hae killed my hauke sae guid,
  And I had nae mair bot hee O."

"Your haukis bluid was nevir sae reid,
  Edward, Edward,   10
Your haukis bluid was nevir sae reid,
  My deir son I tell thee O."
"O I hae killed my reid-roan steid,
  Mither, mither,
O I hae killed my reid-roan steid,   15
  That erst was sae fair and frie O."

"Your steid was auld, and ye hae gat
  mair,
  Edward, Edward,
Your steid was auld, and ye hae gat
  mair,
  Sum other dule ye drie O."   20
"O I hae killed my fadir deir,
  Mither, mither,
O I hae killed my fadir deir,
  Alas, and wae is mee O!"

"And whatten penance wul ye drie for
  that,   25
  Edward, Edward?
And whatten penance will ye drie for
  that?
  My deir son, now tell me O."
"Ile set my feit in yonder boat,
  Mither, mither,   30
Ile set my feit in yonder boat,
  And Ile fare ovir the sea O."

"And what wul ye doe wi your towirs
  and your ha,
  Edward, Edward?
And what wul you doe wi your towirs
  and your ha,   35
  That were sae fair to see O?"
"Ile let thame stand tul they doun fa,
  Mither, mither,
Ile let thame stand tul they doun fa,
  For here nevir mair maun I bee O."

"And what wul ye leive to your bairns
  and your wife,   41
  Edward, Edward?
And what wul ye leive to your bairns
  and your wife,
  Whan ye gang ovir the sea O?"
"The warld is room, late them beg thrae
  life,   45
  Mither, mither,
The warld is room, late them beg thrae
  life,
  For thame nevir mair wul I see O."

"Edward, Edward" (Old English Ballad) from *English and Scottish Popular Ballads* edited by Sargent & Kittredge, copyright, 1904, 1932, by George Lyman Kittredge, used by permission of Houghton Mifflin Company.

1. BRAND—Sword.
4. GANG—Go.
5. HAUKE—Hawk, falcon.
16. THAT ERST . . . FRIE—That once was fair and spirited.
20. DULE . . . DRIE—Grief . . . suffer, undergo.

33. HA—Hall.
39. TUL—Till.
41. BAIRNS—Children.

"And what wul ye leive to your ain
    mither deir,
  Edward, Edward?   50
And what wul ye leive to your ain
    mither deir?

  My deir son, now tell me O."
"The curse of hell frae me sall ye beir,
  Mither, mither,
The curse of hell frae me sall ye beir,
  Sic counseils ye gave to me O."   56

◇◇◇

FOR APPRECIATION

1. Explain in detail how the action of the ballad is expressed indirectly rather than directly.

2. What details in the ballad indicate that Edward is a knight? What is the relationship between the mother and the son? How would you sum up the mother's character? Why did not Edward come out immediately and say that he murdered his father? Where is the climax of the story?

3. Show how the ballad is a good example of the use of refrain and incremental repetition.

Get Up and Bar the Door

After a rather steady diet of old ballad tragedy, it is delightful to discover an occasional burst of good humor. "Get Up and Bar the Door" is a good example both of ballad humor and of the traditional medieval friendly feud between husband and wife. In this instance, the wife comes out victorious.

It fell about the Martinmas time,
    And a gay time it was then,
When our good wife got puddings to
    make,
    And she's boild them in the pan.

The wind sae cauld blew south and
    north,   5
    And blew into the floor;
Quoth our goodman to our goodwife,
    "Gae out and bar the door."

"My hand is in my hussyfskap,
    Goodman, as ye may see;   10
An it should nae be barrd this hundred
    year,
    It's no be barrd for me."

They made a paction tween them twa,
    They made it firm and sure,
That the first word whaeer should speak,
    Shoud rise and bar the door.   16

Then there came two gentlemen,
    At twelve o clock at night,
And they could see neither house nor
    hall,
    Nor coal nor candle-light.   20

"Now whether is this a rich man's
    house,
    Or whether is it a poor?"
But neer a word wad ane o them speak,
    For barring of the door.

And first they ate the white puddings
    And then they ate the black;   26
Tho muckle thought the goodwife to
    hersel,
    Yet neer a word she spake.

Then said the one unto the other,
    "Here, man, tak ye my knife;   30
Do ye tak off the auld man's beard,
    And I'll kiss the goodwife."

"But there's nae water in the house,
    And what shall we do than?"
"What ails ye at the pudding-broo,   35
    That boils into the pan?"

"Get Up and Bar the Door" (Old English Ballad) from *English and Scottish Popular Ballads* edited by Sargent & Kittredge, copyright, 1904, 1932, by George Lyman Kittredge, used by permission of Houghton Mifflin Company.

    1. MARTINMAS—The feast of St. Martin on November 11, a religious festival in the Middle Ages.
    7. GOODMAN—It was the custom in the Middle Ages to call the husband "goodman."
    9. HUSSYFSKAP—The chores of a housewife.
    12. FOR ME—So far as I am concerned.
    13. PACTION—Agreement.

    27. MUCKLE—Much.
    35. "What is the matter with the pudding broth?" The sauce of the pudding was made from liquor.

O up then started our goodman,
  An angry man was he:
"Will ye kiss my wife before my een,
  And scad me wi' pudding-bree?" 40

40. SCAD—Scald.

Then up and started our goodwife,
  Gied three skips on the floor:
"Goodman, you've spoken the foremost
    word,
  Get up and bar the door."

FOR APPRECIATION

1. In your own words supply the action in the ballad which is implied.

2. What was the pact between husband and wife? Did the wife have to exercise a great amount of restraint during the midnight visit of the strangers? Explain. What caused the husband to lose his bet?

3. Is the stanza form and meter used in the ballad the traditional *ballad* stanza and meter? Explain.

The Wife of Usher's Well

In reading this very famous ballad, we should be not so much concerned with the few simple facts of the story, but rather with the undertones of grief and horror which are suggested through a series of vivid and concrete little scenes.

There lived a wife at Usher's Well,
  And a wealthy wife was she;
She had three stout and stalwart sons,
  And sent them oer the sea.

They hadna been a week from her   5
  A week but barely ane,
Whan word came to the carline wife
  That her three sons were gane.

They hadna been a week from her,
  A week but barely three,   10
Whan word came to the carlin wife
  That her sons she'd never see.

"I wish the wind may never cease,
  Nor fashes in the flood,
Till my three sons come hame to me,
  In earthly flesh and blood."   16

It fell about the Martinmass,
  When nights are lang and mirk,
The carlin wife's three sons came hame,
  And their hats were o the birk.   20

It neither grew in syke nor ditch
  Nor yet in ony sheugh;
But at the gates o Paradise,
  That birk grew fair eneugh.

"The Wife of Usher's Well" (Old English Ballad) from *English and Scottish Popular Ballads* edited by Sargent & Kittredge, copyright, 1904, 1932, by George Lyman Kittredge, used by permission of Houghton Mifflin Company.

7. CARLINE—Old woman.

14. FASHES—Troubles.
18. MIRK—Dark, gloomy.
20. BIRK—Birch.
21. SYKE—Trench.
22. SHEUGH—Furrow.

"Blow up the fire, my maidens,   25
  Bring water from the well;
For a' my house shall feast this night,
  Since my three sons are well."

And she has made to them a bed,
  She's made it large and wide,   30
And she's taen her mantle her about,
  Sat down at the bed-side.

Up then crew the red, red cock,
  And up and crew the gray;
The eldest to the youngest said,   35
  " 'T is time we were away."

27. A'—All.

The cock he hadna crawd but once,
  And clappd his wings at a',
When the youngest to the eldest said,
  "Brother, we must awa.   40

"The cock doth craw, the day doth daw,
  The channerin worm doth chide;
Gin we be mist out o our place,
  A sair pain we maun bide;

"Fare ye weel, my mother dear!   45
  Fareweel to barn and byre!
And fare ye weel, the bonny lass
  That kindles my mother's fire!"

42. CHANNERIN—Devouring.
44. SAIR . . . MAUN—Sore . . . must.
46. BYRE—Cow shed.

FOR APPRECIATION

1. Two popular superstitions are found in this poem. The first is that if a person wishes hard enough, even the dead must come back from their graves. The second is that all ghosts must vanish at the crowing of the cock. Discuss the application of these superstitions in the ballad.

2. In stanzas five and six how are we told that the sons are coming home as spirits and not in flesh and blood? Is this an example of an abstract fact expressed poetically? Explain. How would you state the simple fact of their return in prose? Do these stanzas give us the key to the ending of the poem? Explain.

3. Analyze stanzas seven and eight. What emotions of the mother are expressed? Are these emotions expressed directly or implied from the action? Discuss.

4. In the last four stanzas how are the emotions of fear and dread expressed? Does the simple understatement in the lines: " 'T is time we were away," and "Brother, we must awa," heighten the terror? Discuss.

5. Discuss how effectively the ballad poet contrasts life and death, the warmth of the living and the horror of the grave, in stanzas 11 and 12. What precise, concrete details did the poet select to show this contrast?

6. Do lines 46 and 47 imply that there might have been a friendship between the youngest brother and "the bonnie lass"? Note the strong contrast between the secure atmosphere of the home, the love of mother, the rustic life of the country, sig-nified by the "barn and byre," and the desolation of the grave. Discuss the poetic art as shown in these details.

7. Scan the first stanza of the poem. Would you say that this ballad literally sings?

◇◇◇◇◇

Lord Thomas and Fair Annet

Many ballad critics have called this poem the most beautiful of all the ballads. The age-old conflict between a marriage for love and a marriage of convenience ends tragically for both Lord Thomas and Fair Annet. Note again in this ballad how the story is suggested by a series of dramatic incidents, with much of the action to be read into the lines. The concluding stanzas contain the oft-repeated legend of intertwining birch and briar, as the symbol of the close union of two departed lovers.

Lord Thomas and Fair Annet
  Sate a' day on a hill;
When night was cum and sun was sett,
  They had not talkt their fill.

Lord Thomas said a word in jest,   5
  Fair Annet took it ill:
"A, I will nevir wed a wife
  Against my ain friends' will."

"Gif ye wull nevir wed a wife,
  A wife wull neir wed yee."   10
Sae he is hame to tell his mither,
  And knelt upon his knee.

"O rede, O rede, mither," he says,
  "A gude rede gie to mee;

O sall I tak the nut-browne bride,   15
  And let Faire Annet bee?"

"The nut-browne bride haes gowd and gear,
  Fair Annet she has gat nane;
And the little beauty Fair Annet haes
  O it wull soon be gane."   20

And he has till his brother gane:
  "Now, brother, rede ye mee;
A, sall I marrie the nut-browne bride,
  And let Fair Annet bee?"

"The nut-browne bride has oxen, brother,   25
  The nut-browne bride has kye;

"Lord Thomas and Fair Annet" (Old English Bal-lad) from *English and Scottish Popular Ballads* edited by Sargent & Kittredge, copyright, 1904, 1932, by George Lyman Kittredge, used by permission of Houghton Mifflin Company.

  9. GIF—if.
  13. REDE—Counsel, advice.

  17. GOWD AND GEAR—Gold and goods or property.
  21. TILL—To.
  26. KYE—Cows, cattle.

I wad hae ye marrie the nut-browne
    bride,
    And cast Fair Annet bye."

"Her oxen may dye in the house, billie,
    And her kye into the byre,   30
And I sall hae nothing to mysell
    But a fat fadge by the fyre."

And he has till his sister gane:
    "Now, sister, rede ye mee;
O sall I marrie the nut-browne bride,
    And set Fair Annet free?"   36

"I'se rede ye tak Fair Annet, Thomas,
    And let the browne bride alane;
Lest ye sould sigh, and say, Alace,
    What is this we brought hame!"   40

"No, I will tak my mither's counsel,
    And marrie me owt o hand;
And I will tak the nut-browne bride,
    Fair Annet may leive the land."

Up then rose Fair Annet's father,   45
    Twa hours or it wer day,
And he is gane into the bower
    Wherein Fair Annet lay.

"Rise up, rise up, Fair Annet," he says,
    "Put on your silken sheene;   50
Let us gae to St. Marie's kirke,
    And see that rich weddeen."

"My maides, gae to my dressing-roome,
    And dress to me my hair;
Whaireir yee laid a plait before,   55
    See yee lay ten times mair.

"My maides, gae to my dressing-room,
    And dress to me my smock;
The one half is o holland fine,
    The other o needle-work."   60

29. BILLIE—Comrade; used as a term of affection. In Middle English, "bully" also meant a fellow or a mate.
32. FADGE—A clumsy woman.
42. OWT O HAND—Forthwith, at once.
50. SHEENE—Shoes.

The horse Fair Annet rade upon,
    He amblit like the wind;
Wi siller he was shod before,
    Wi burning gowd behind.

Four and twenty siller bells   65
    Wer a' tyed to his mane,
And yae tift o the norland wind,
    They tinkled ane by ane.

Four and twenty gay gude knichts
    Rade by Fair Annet's side,   70
And four and twenty fair ladies,
    As gin she had bin a bride.

And whan she cam to Marie's kirk,
    She sat on Marie's stean:
The cleading that Fair Annet had on,
    It skinkled in their een.   76

And whan she cam into the kirk,
    She shimmered like the sun;
The belt that was about her waist,
    Was a' wi pearles bedone.   80

She sat her by the nut-browne bride,
    And her een they were sae clear,
Lord Thomas he clean forgat the bride,
    Whan Fair Annet drew near.

He had a rose into his hand,   85
    He gae it kisses three,
And reaching by the nut-browne bride,
    Laid it on Fair Annet's knee.

Up than spak the nut-browne bride,
    She spak with meikle spite: 90
"And whair gat ye that rose-water,
    That does mak yee sae white?"

63. SILLER—Silver.
67. YAE TIFT—One puff.
72. AS GIN—As if.
74. STEAN—A stone seat at the door of St. Mary's Church.
75. CLEADING—The clothing.
76. SKINKLED . . . EEN—It sparkled in their eyes.
80. BEDONE—Ornamented.
90. MEIKLE—Much.

"O I did get the rose-water
 Whair ye wull neir get nane,
For I did get that very rose-water   95
 Into my mither's wame."

The bride she drew a long bodkin
 Frae out her gay head-gear,
And strake Fair Annet unto the heart,
 That word spak nevir mair.   100

Lord Thomas he saw Fair Annet wex
 pale,
 And marvelit what mote bee;
But when he saw her dear heart's blude,
 A' wood-wroth wexed hee.

He drew his dagger, that was sae sharp,
 That was sae sharp and meet,   106

And drave it into the nut-browne bride,
 That fell deid at his feit.

"Now stay for me, dear Annet," he sed,
 "Now stay, my dear," he cry'd;   110
Then strake the dagger untill his heart,
 And fell deid by her side.

Lord Thomas was buried without
 kirk-wa,
 Fair Annet within the quiere;
And o the tane thair grew a birk,   115
 The other a bonny briere.

And ay they grew, and ay they threw,
 As they wad faine be neare;
And by this ye may ken right weil
 They were twa luvers deare.   120

96. WAME—Womb.
104. A' WOOD-WROTH—In Middle English
"wood" (wod) meant mad. He became so
mad that he lost his head.
106. MEET—Even.

114. QUIERE—Choir. A part of the church.
115. TANE . . . BIRK—And of the one
there grew a birch.
117. THREW—Intertwined.

FOR APPRECIATION

1. Do lines 7 and 8 indicate that the "jest" which provoked the lovers' quarrel might have had a serious undertone? Discuss. Who might be the "friends" in line 8?

2. Did the advice given by the mother and brother differ from that of the sister? Explain. What does the advice tell us of the three characters? Is the emotional conflict of Lord Thomas a universal one, still experienced by young people today? Discuss.

3. What action is implied between stanzas 11 and 12? State what might have happened in your own words.

4. Do lines 61–72 indicate that Annet was not so poor after all, or might Annet's father have borrowed to pay for the finery and the escorts? Discuss.

5. Discuss the motives of Fair Annet in displaying her beauty at the wedding. Can you justify the action of Lord Thomas in neglecting the nut-browne maid to pay attention to Fair Annet?

6. What motive prompted the nut-browne maid to kill Annet? What immediately provoked the murder? Is the "bodkin" in line 97 just a long hat-pin or was it a weapon deliberately concealed?

7. Was the killing of the nut-browne maid and himself murder and suicide on the part of Lord Thomas? Discuss. Why was Lord Thomas buried outside the church wall?

8. Discuss the ballad in the light of Christian moral principles. Is the ballad a real tragedy or a melodrama? Explain.

PROJECTS

1. Give a written or an oral report on the famous "Gest of Robin Hood."

2. Read and report on one of the following ballads: "Chevy Chase or The Hunting of the Cheviot," "The Douglas Tragedy," "St. Stephen and Herod," "The Boy and the Mantle," and "The Gay Goshawk."

3. Write a ballad, using the old ballad form, upon some modern theme.

4. Some musically inclined students could present a program of ballad music. Words and tunes of many of the old popular ballads can be found in *English Folk-Songs for Schools*, edited by S. Baring Gould and Cecil J. Sharp; and *One Hundred English Folk Songs*, edited by Cecil J. Sharp.

THE METRICAL ROMANCE

Metrical romances were the medieval people's entertainment—their movies and television programs. The metrical romance was a long love story in verse, whose subject matter was chivalry, romantic love, and religion. The principal characters were knights, kings, and noble ladies. Impelled by the ideals of religious faith, the sacred vows of knighthood, or the pure love of adventure, the heroes of these tales worked noble deeds and righted wrongs. Spectacular events, gorgeous court scenes, and colorful pageantry were woven into the tapestry of the story. The magical and preternatural elements are often found in the form of monsters and evil magicians. The events related in the romances were usually not true to life, but they were given the appearance of reality.

FORERUNNERS OF THE ROMANCE

The early Middle English tales celebrated northern heroes like Havelock the Dane and King Horn, men renowned for their physical strength and endurance. There is little or nothing of chivalry or courtly love in these stories; but, like their Anglo-Saxon ancestor, *Beowulf*, they deal with jousts, contests of endurance, and swordplay.

By the twelfth century the romances were classified into three great cycles: the matter of France, the matter of Britain, and the matter of Rome. The matter of France included the legends surrounding Charlemagne and his twelve peers in their fight against the Moors. The matter of Rome dealt with the stories of Troy, Rome, and the conquests of Alexander and Caesar. The matter of Britain centered around King Arthur and his court.

THE ARTHURIAN CYCLE

The Arthurian cycle, as we know it today, is a mixture of Celtic, French, and English elements. All that we know of Arthur historically is that he was a British chieftain who fought against the invasion of the Saxons in the sixth century. He owes his immortality to the fact that he lived in Wales, where a hero-worshipping people with a vivid imagination invested him with the aura of a mythological and Christian hero.

In the twelfth century Geoffrey of Monmouth wrote a Latin chronicle, *The History of the Kings of Britain*, in which Arthur was portrayed in all the trappings of medieval chivalry recently imported from France with the Norman regime. Toward the close of the twelfth century the first account in the English language of King Arthur and His Table appeared with Layamon's *Brut*. During the next two centuries, when the chivalric spirit was at its highest, many stories of new heroes crept into the Arthurian cycle.

The notion of courtly love, an insidiously poisonous, pagan thing, was transplanted from southern France, and with it Lancelot with his guilty love was introduced into the cycle. Later Lancelot was supplanted by Percival, a favorite with the German people. When the idea of the quest of the Holy Grail was blended into the cycle, Sir Galahad, of the pure heart, overshadowed both Lancelot and Percival. But Sir Gawain was ever the favorite knight of the English people.

The Arthurian stories became so popular in the fourteenth century that French writers gathered them into collections for private reading rather than for public recitation. From such French prose collections came the most famous Middle English account of the Arthur cycle. In 1469 appeared Sir Thomas Malory's *Le Morte d'Arthur*, a brilliant summation or synthesis of the entire Arthurian cycle. Malory's classic has been the primary source for all the many versions of the story of King Arthur which have been written since his day. Outstanding among the more modern stories of Arthur and the Round Table is Tennyson's *Idylls of the King*.

It was Sir Gawain who inspired the unknown Pearl Poet to write the most finished metrical romance of the Middle English period—*Sir Gawain and the Green Knight*. The Pearl Poet, so called because of his frequent allegorical use of pearls

SIR GAWAIN

AND THE

GREEN KNIGHT

and other jewels, ranks equally with Chaucer and Langland as a great English writer of the fourteenth century. He not only wrote the brilliant *Sir Gawain* but also the most beautiful spiritual dream-allegory, *Pearl*, and two verse homilies, *Patience* and *Cleanness*. A master craftsman, he composed in the northwestern dialect, much different from the Midland dialect of Chaucer. The dialect which he used, plus the fact that he lived not in London but in northern Lancashire, help to explain why he was unknown for many generations, while Chaucer became the literary darling of his own and future periods.

Sir Gawain is a detached episode of the Arthurian cycle. In this romance, we find a blend of the best elements of medieval chivalry, an artistic unity of plot, a delineation of character portrayal that rivals Chaucer's *Canterbury Tales*, and a clarity of pictorial detail which could only come from the pen of a courtly poet of great skill. The Pearl Poet must have been thoroughly acquainted not only with the psychology of human nature but also with the domestic life of the upper-classes—their households, foods, sports, and occupations.

This is a beautiful allegory on the knightly virtue of courtesy, in which purity and chastity triumph over sensuality despite superhuman obstacles. The Pearl Poet has successfully blended mysticism and realism in a poem which many critics have called the greatest romance of the Middle Ages.

Sir Gawain and the Green Knight is written in long alliterative lines arranged in groups of from fifteen to thirty lines in length. Each group is concluded by what is known as a "bob in wheel"; that is, a quatrain of three stresses is tied to the group of alliterative lines by rhyming with the last line of the alliterative group.

◇◇◇◇◇

Sir Gawain and the Green Knight

Translated by Theodore Howard Banks, Jr.

I

The poem opens with mention of the founding of Britain by Felix Brutus. But of all the British kings, Arthur was the most celebrated, "whose renown was next to the Savior's." It was at the court of Camelot where Arthur was celebrating the Christmas festival with his "peerless lords" that the strangest of marvels occurred. Arthur, Queen Guinevere, Sir Gawain [1] and others are gathered at the high table. An elaborate meal is spread before them, but Arthur will not eat until all are served and some marvelous tale is told; or until some stranger knight seeks permission to joust with one of his court. His desire is soon granted.

And scarcely the music had ceased for a moment,
The first course been suitably served in the court,
When a being most dreadful burst through the hall-door,
Among the most mighty of men in his measure.
From his throat to his thighs so thick were his sinews,   5
His loins and his limbs so large and so long,
That I hold him half-giant, the hugest of men,
And the handsomest, too, in his height, upon horseback.
Though stalwart in breast and in back was his body,

"Sir Gawain and the Green Knight," translated by Theodore H. Banks, Jr., copyright, 1929, Appleton-Century-Crofts, Inc.

[1] GAWAIN (gä′wân)—According to the Arthurian legend, Gawain was the son of Lot, a Scottish king, and Arthur's half-sister, Anna.

His waist and his belly were worthily small;   10
Fashioned fairly he was in his form, and in features

> Cut clean.
> Men wondered at the hue
> That in his face was seen.
> A splendid man to view   15
> He came, entirely green.

All green was the man, and green were his garments:
A coat, straight and close, that clung to his sides,
A bright mantle on top of this, trimmed on the inside
With closely-cut fur, right fair, that showed clearly,   20
The lining with white fur most lovely, and hood too,
Caught back from his locks, and laid on his shoulders,
Neat stockings that clung to his calves, tightly stretched,
Of the same green, and under them spurs of gold shining
Brightly on bands of fine silk, richly barred;   25
And under his legs, where he rides, guards of leather.
His vesture was verily color of verdure:
Both bars of his belt and other stones, beautiful,
Richly arranged in his splendid array
On himself and his saddle, on silken designs.   30
'T would be truly too hard to tell half the trifles
Embroidered about it with birds and with flies
In gay, verdant green with gold in the middle;
The bit-studs, the crupper, the breast-trappings' pendants,
And everything metal enamelled in emerald.   35
The stirrups he stood on the same way were colored,
His saddle-bows too, and the studded nails splendid,
That all with green gems ever glimmered and glinted.
The horse he bestrode was in hue still the same,

> Indeed; 40
> Green, thick, and of great height,
> And hard to curb, a steed
> In broidered bridle bright
> That such a man would need.

[*In the midst of this silence caused by this vision, King Arthur welcomes the stranger and asks him to linger. But the stranger replies that he will need but a moment to state his errand. He is not seeking a quarrel but a Christmas jest.*]

"Nay, I ask for no fight; in faith, now I tell thee   45
But beardless babes are about on this bench.
Were I hasped in my armor, and high on a horse,

27. VERDURE—Green growth; greenness.
34. CRUPPER—A leather loop passing under a horse's tail and buckled to the saddle.
47. HASPED—Dressed securely.

58

Here is no man to match me, your might is so feeble.
So I crave but a Christmas game in this court;
Yule and New Year are come, and here men have courage;   50
If one in this house himself holds so hardy,
So bold in his blood, in his brain so unbalanced
To dare stiffly strike one stroke for another,
I give this gisarme, this rich axe, as a gift to him,
Heavy enough, to handle as pleases him;   55
Bare as I sit, I shall bide the first blow.
If a knight be so tough as to try what I tell,
Let him leap to me lightly; I leave him this weapon,
Quitclaim it forever, to keep as his own;
And his stroke here, firm on this floor, I shall suffer,   60
This boon if thou grant'st me, the blow with another

         To pay
     Yet let his respite be
     A twelvemonth and a day.
     Come, let us quickly see 65
     If one here aught dare say."

[*When no knight responds to the challenge, Arthur steps forward to defend the court's honor; but then Gawain begs the favor "to let this fray be mine."*]

 With speed then the Green Knight took up his stand,
Inclined his head forward, uncovering the flesh,
And laid o'er his crown his locks long and lovely,
And bare left the nape of his neck for the business.   70
His axe Gawain seized, and swung it on high;
On the floor his left foot he planted before him,
And swiftly the naked flesh smote with his weapon.
The sharp edge severed the bones of the stranger,
Cut through the clear flesh and cleft it in twain,   75
So the blade of the brown steel bit the ground deeply.
The fair head fell from the neck to the floor,
So that where it rolled forth with their feet many spurned it.
The blood on the green glistened, burst from the body;
And yet neither fell nor faltered the hero,   80
But stoutly he started forth, strong in his stride;
Fiercely he rushed 'mid the ranks of the Round Table,
Seized and uplifted his lovely head straightway;
Then back to his horse went, laid hold of the bridle,
Stepped into the stirrup and strode up aloft,   85
His head holding fast in his hand by the hair.

54. GISARME—A battle axe with the shaft ending in a spike.
59. QUITCLAIM—To give up any claim to it.
63. RESPITE—Here used as intermission, interval in which to pay the debt.

And the man as soberly sat in his saddle
As if he unharmed were, although now headless,

Instead.

His trunk around he spun,   90
That ugly body that bled.
Frightened was many a one
When he his words had said.

For upright he holds the head in his hand,
And confronts with the face the fine folk on the dais.   95
It lifted its lids, and looked forth directly,
Speaking this much with its mouth, as ye hear:
"Gawain, look, that to go as agree you are ready,
And seek for me faithfully, sir, till you find me,
As, heard by these heroes, you vowed in this hall.   100
To the Green Chapel go you, I charge you, to get
Such a stroke as you struck. You are surely deserving,
Sir knight, to be promptly repaid at the New Year.
As Knight of the Green Chapel many men know me;
If therefore to find me you try, you will fail not;   105
Then come, or be recreant called as befits thee."
With furious wrench of the reins he turned round,
And rushed from the hall-door, his head in his hands.

II

[*The seasons pass and autumn arrives. Gawain prepares to seek out the Green Knight. He is clad in his most magnificent armor and mounts his great horse Gringolet.*]

When in arms he was clasped, his costume was costly;
The least of the lacings or loops gleamed with gold.   110
And armed in this manner, the man heard Mass,
At the altar adored and made offering, and afterward
Came to the King and all of his courtiers,
Gently took leave of the ladies and lords;
Him they kissed and escorted, to Christ him commending.   115
Then was Gringolet ready, girt with a saddle
That gaily with many a gold fringe was gleaming,
With nails studded newly, prepared for the nonce.
Then they showed him his shield, sheer gules, whereon shone
The pentangle painted in pure golden hue.   120

95. DAIS (dā′ĭs)—A raised platform or table where guests of honor are seated.
106. RECREANT—Cowardly, unfaithful.
118. NONCE—For the occasion.
119. GULES—In heraldry, gules is a term used for the color red.
120. PENTANGLE—A five-pointed star with interlacing lines. It was an ancient symbol of perfection. In the Middle Ages it became endowed with supernatural qualities. It was an appropriate emblem for Gawain, whose five-fold virtues were symbolized in its five sides.

On his baldric he caught, and about his neck cast it;
And fairly the hero's form it befitted.
And why that great prince the pentangle suited
Intend I to tell, in my tale though I tarry.
'T is a sign that Solomon formerly set   125
As a token, for so it doth symbol, of truth.
A figure it is that with five points is furnished;
Each line overlaps and locks in another,
Nor comes to an end; and Englishmen call it
Everywhere, hear I, the endless knot.   130
It became then the knight and his noble arms also,
In five ways, and five times each way still faithful.
Sir Gawain was known as the good, refined gold,
Graced with virtues of castle, of villainy void,

                                         Made clean.
                         So the pentangle new   136
                         On shield and coat was seen,
                         As man of speech most true,
                         And gentlest knight of mien.

121. BALDRIC—A belt worn diagonally across the breast and used to support a sword.
139. MIEN (mēn)—Appearance, bearing.

61

First, in his five wits he faultless was found; 140
In his five fingers too the man never failed;
And on earth all his faith was fixed on the five wounds
That Christ, as the creed tells, endured on the cross.
Wheresoever this man was midmost in battle,
His thought above everything else was in this, 145
To draw all his fire from the fivefold joys
That the fair Queen of Heaven felt in her child.
And because of this fitly he carried her image
Displayed on his shield, on its larger part,
That whenever he saw it his spirit should sink not. 150
The fifth five the hero made use of, I find,
More than all were his liberalness, love of his fellows,
His courtesy, chasteness, unchangeable ever,
And pity, all further traits passing. These five
In this hero more surely were set than in any. 155
In truth now, fivefold they were fixed in the knight,
Linked each to the other without any end,
And all of them fastened on five points unfailing;
Each side they neither united nor sundered,
Evermore endless at every angle, 160
Where equally either they ended or started.
And so his fair shield was adorned with this symbol,
Thus richly with red gold wrought on red gules,
So by people the pentangle perfect 't was called,

As it ought.
Gawain in arms is gay; 166
Right there his lance he caught,
And gave them all good-day
For ever, as he thought.

[*Sir Gawain journeys through North Wales into Cumberland in the wintry cold,
struggling against serpents, wolves, wood-sprites, and giants, until he comes to wild
dense wood.*]

By a mount on the morn he merrily rides 170
To a wood dense and deep that was wondrously wild;
High hills on each hand, with forests of hoar oaks
Beneath them most huge, a hundred together.
Thickly the hazel and hawthorn were tangled,
Everywhere mantled with moss rough and ragged, 175
With many a bird on the bare twigs, mournful,
That piteously piped for pain of the cold.
Sir Gawain on Gringolet goes underneath them
Through many a march and many a mire,

172. HOAR—From the Anglo-Saxon *har* meaning gray or old; white or gray with age.

Unfriended, fearing to fail in devotion,   180
And see not His Service, that Sire's, on that very night
Born of a Virgin to vanquish our pain.
And so sighing he said: "Lord, I beseech Thee,
And Mary, the mildest mother so dear,
For some lodging wherein to hear Mass full lowly,   185
And Matins, meekly I ask it, to-morrow;
So promptly I pray my Pater and Ave

                                                And Creed,"
                      Thus rode he as he prayed,
                      Lamenting each misdeed;   190
                      Often the sign he made,
                      And said, "Christ's cross me speed."
He scarcely had signed himself thrice ere he saw
In the wood on the mound a moated mansion,
Above a fair field, enfolded in branches   195
Of many a huge tree hard by the ditches:
The comeliest castle that knight ever kept.
In a meadow 't was placed, with a park all about,
And a palisade, spiked and pointed, set stoutly
Round many a tree for more than two miles.   200
The lord on that one side looked at the stronghold
That shimmered and shone through the shapely oak trees;
Then duly his helm doffed, and gave his thanks humbly
To Jesus and Julian, both of them gentle,
For showing him courtesy, hearing his cry.   205
"Now good lodging," quoth Gawain, "I beg you to grant me."
Then with spurs in his gilt heels he Gringolet strikes,
Who chooses the chief path by chance that conducted
The man to the bridge-end.

[*Gawain crosses the drawbridge and is welcomed by the lord of the castle.*]

    Gawain gazed at the man who so graciously greeted him;   210
Doughty he looked, the lord of that dwelling,
A hero indeed huge, hale, in his prime;
His beard broad and bright, its hue all of beaver;
Stern, and on stalwart shanks steadily standing;
Fell faced as the fire, in speech fair and free.   215
In sooth, well suited he seemed, thought Gawain,
To govern as prince of a goodly people.

186. MATINS—A part of the Divine Office. In the monasteries it was sung in the early morning.
199. PALISADE—A fence of stakes used for defense.
204. JULIAN—Juliana of Norwich, an anchoress, much venerated in the Middle Ages.
211. DOUGHTY—Strong, valiant.
215. FELL FACED—Fierce.

[*The lord's servants lead Gawain to richly adorned chambers where he is dressed in costly raiment. An elaborate banquet is prepared during the course of which Gawain identifies himself. After dinner, Gawain attends Vespers in the chapel, where the ladies of the castle see him for the first time.*]

Then longed the lady to look on the knight,
And emerged from her pew with many fair maidens;
In face she was fairest of all, and in figure,   220
In skin and in color, all bodily qualities;
Lovelier, Gawain thought, even than Guinevere.
He goes through the chancel to greet her, so gracious.
By the left hand another was leading her, older
Than she, a lady who looked as if aged,   225
By heroes around her reverenced highly.
The ladies, however, unlike were to look on;
If fresh was the younger, the other was yellow;
Rich red on the one was rioting everywhere,
Rough wrinkled cheeks hung in rolls on the other;   230
One's kerchiefs, with clear pearls covered and many,
Displayed both her breast and her bright throat all bare,
Shining fairer than snow on the hillsides falling;
The second her neck in a neck-cloth enswathed,
That enveloped in chalk-white veils her black chin;   235
Her forehead in silk was wrapped and enfolded
Adorned and tricked with trifles about it
Till nothing was bare but the lady's black brows,
Her two eyes, her nose, and her lips, all naked,
And those were bleared strangely, and ugly to see.   240
A goodly lady, so men before God
                                            Might decide!
                              Her body thick, and short,
                              Her hips were round and wide;
                              One of more pleasant sort   245
                              She led there by her side.

[*From Christmas Day to St. John's Day mirth and joy fill the household. Gawain is pleasantly feasted and royally entertained. On the next morning Gawain informs his host of his mission and asks the lord if, perhaps, he knows where the Green Knight dwells. The lord answers that the Chapel of the Green Knight is only two miles distant and can be easily reached in a few hours. He urges Gawain to remain as his guest until New Year's morning.*]

Then was Gawain right glad, and gleefully laughed.
"Now for this more than anything else, sir, I thank you.
I have come to the end of my quest; at your will
I shall bide, and in all things act as you bid me."   250

231. KERCHIEFS—Cloth worn by women as a covering or for ornament.

The lord then seized him, and set him beside him,
And sent for the ladies to better delight him.
Seemly the pleasure among them in private.
So gay were the speeches he spoke, and so friendly,
The host seemed a man well-nigh mad in behavior.   255
He called to the knight there, crying aloud:
"Ye have bound you to do the deed that I bid you.
Here, and at once, will you hold to your word sir?"
"Yes, certainly sir," the true hero said;
"While I bide in your house I obey your behest."   260
"You have toiled," said the lord; "from afar have travelled,
And here have caroused, nor are wholly recovered
In sleep or in nourishment, know I for certain.
In your room you shall linger, and lie at your ease
To-morrow till Mass-time, and go to your meat   265
When you will, and with you my wife to amuse you
With company, till to the court I return.

                                                You stay
                            And I shall early rise,
                            And hunting go my way."   270
                            Bowing in courteous wise,
                            Gawain grants all this play.

"And more," said the man, "let us make an agreement:
Whatever I win the wood shall be yours;
And what chance you shall meet shall be mine in exchange.   275
Sir, let's so strike our bargain and swear to tell truly
Whate'er fortune brings, whether bad, sir, or better."
Quoth Gawain the good: "By God, I do grant it.
What pastime you please appears to me pleasant."

                                III

[*At dawn the next day the lord of the castle is off to the deer hunt. He spends
the whole day in an exciting and successful chase. Meanwhile at home, while
Gawain is slumbering late in the morning, the lady comes to his chamber and attempts to make love to him. Gawain treats her with perfect courtesy and reserve
and allows her to give him one kiss. In the evening, the lord returns with his catch
of deer which he gives to Gawain; and in return the lord receives a kiss.*

   *The next day the lord hunts a wild boar. The lady again tries to make love to
Gawain.*]

Thus the fair lady tempted and tested him often   280
To make the man sin—whate'er more she'd in mind;
But so fair his defence was, no fault was apparent,
Nor evil on either side; each knew but joy

                                                On that day.

   260. BEHEST—Command.
   262. CAROUSED—Feasted.

———

[*In the evening the lord graciously receives two kisses from Gawain and gives the boar's head to him.*

After Mass on the next morning, the lord and his men go fox hunting:]

Wondrous fair were the fields, for the frost was clinging;
Bright red in the cloud-rack rises the sun, 285
And full clear sails close past the clouds in the sky.
The hunters unleashed all the hounds by a woodside:
The rocks with the blast of their bugles were ringing.
Some dogs there fall on the scent where the fox is,
And trail oft a traitoress using her tricks. 290

[*Meanwhile, at home, the lady once more visits Gawain and tempts him with her love. Courteously, without offending her in any way, Gawain refuses her attentions. He is determined not to betray the hero, the head of the house.*

The lady then gives him three kisses and begs him to receive a red gold ring. This he refuses, but she presses him to receive as a token a lace belt, "fashioned with silk, and made fair with gold."]

285. CLOUD-RACK—Collection of broken clouds drifting across the sky.
290. TRAITORESS—The she-fox who crossed and confused the trail of the male fox.

"Refuse ye this silk," the lady then said,
"As slight in itself? Truly it seems so,
Lo! it is little, and less is its worth;
But one knowing the nature knit up within it,
Would give a value more great, peradventure; 295
For no man girt with this belting of green,
And bearing it fairly made fast about him,
Might ever be cut down by any on earth,
For his life in no way in the world could be taken."
Then mused the man, and it came to his mind 300
In the peril appointed him precious 't would prove,
When he'd found the chapel, to face there his fortune.
The device, might he slaying evade, would be splendid.
Her suit then he suffered, and let her speak;
And the belt she offered him, earnestly urging it 305
(And Gawain consented), and gave it with good will,
And prayed him for her sake ne'er to display it,
But, true, from her husband to hide it. The hero
Agreed that no one should know of it ever.

[*In the evening the lord gives Gawain the skin of a fox. Gawain gives him three kisses but says nothing of the green belt.*]

IV

[*In the cold dawn of New Year's Day, Gawain arises, clads himself in knightly armor, fastens the green belt about his waist, and accompanied by one of the lord's servants, rides off on Gringolet to find the Green Knight.*]

By hillsides where branches were bare they both journeyed; 310
They climbed over cliffs where the cold was clinging.
The clouds hung aloft, but 't was lowering beneath them.
On the moor dripped the mist, on the mountains melted;
Each hill had a hat, a mist-cloak right huge.
The brooks foamed and bubbled on hillsides about them, 315
And brightly broke on their banks as they rushed down.

[*The lord's servant tries to persuade Gawain from going further, warning him that he will certainly meet his doom. Gawain refuses to heed his advice and begins his descent of the hill.*]

Rides down the rugged slope right to the dale.
Then about him he looks, and the land seems wild,
And nowhere he sees any sign of a shelter,
But slopes on each side of him, high and steep, 320

295. PERADVENTURE—Perhaps, possibly.

And rocks, gnarled and rough, and stones right rugged.
The clouds there seemed to him scraped by the crags.

[*He soon finds a mound with three openings and in it discovers the Green Chapel. Loudly he calls out:*]

"He who craves aught of me let him come hither quickly;
'T is now or never; he needs to make haste."
Said somebody, "Stop," from the slope up above him,   325
"And promptly you'll get what I promised to give you."
Then he came by a crag, from a cavern emerging,
Whirled out of the den with a dreadful weapon,
A new Danish axe to answer the blow with.
  Said the green man, "Gawain, may God give you guard!   330
You are welcome indeed, sir knight, at my dwelling.
Your travel you've timed as a true man should,
And you know the compact we came to between us;
A twelvemonth ago you took what chance gave,
And I promptly at New Year was pledged to repay you.   335
"Nay," quoth Gawain, "by God who gave me my spirit,
I'll harbor no grudge whatever harm happens.
Exceed not one stroke and still I shall stand;
You may do as you please, I'll in no way oppose   339
                                                          The blow."
                              He left the flesh all bare,
                              Bending his neck down low
                              As if he feared naught there,
                              For fear he would not show.

[*The Green Knight raises his axe and brings it down, only to draw it back. Gawain has winced. A second time he lifts the great blade but withdraws it just before it enters Gawain's neck.*]

And Gawain full fiercely said in a fury,   345
"Come! lay on, thou dread man; too long thou art threatening.
I think that afraid of your own self you feel."
"In sooth," said the other, "thy speech is so savage
No more will I hinder thy mission nor have it   349
                                                          Delayed."
                              With puckered lips and brow
                              He stands with ready blade.
He lifts his axe lightly, and lets it down deftly,
The blade's edge next to the naked neck.
Though he mightily hammered he hurt him no more   355
Than to give him a slight nick that severed the skin there.

329. DANISH AXE—A long-bladed battle-axe, so called because it was a weapon used by the Vikings.
348. SOOTH—Truth.

[When Gawain sees his blood on the snow, he pulls out his sword to defend him-
self against a possible second stroke by the Green Knight.]

Then gaily the Green Knight spoke in a great voice,
And said to the man in speech that resounded,
"Now be not so savage, bold sir, for towards you
None here has acted unhandsomely, save   360
In accord with the pact arranged in the King's court.
I promised the stroke you've received, so hold you
Well payed. I free you from all duties further.
If brisk I had been, peradventure a buffet
I'd harshly have dealt that harm would have done you.   365
In mirth, with a feint I menaced you first,
With no direful wound rent you; right was my deed,
By the bargain that bound us both on the first night,
When faithful and true, you fulfilled our agreement,
And gave me your gain as a good man ought to.   370
The second I struck at you, sir, for the morning
You kissed my wife fair and the kisses accorded me.
Two mere feints for both times I made at you, man,

                      Without woe.
            True men restore by right,   375
            One fears no danger so;
            You failed the third time, knight,
            And therefore took that blow.

" 'Tis my garment you're wearing, that woven belting,
Bestowed by my wife, as in truth I know well.   380
I know also your kisses and all of your acts
And my wife's advances; myself, I devised them.
I sent her to try you, and truly you seem
The most faultless of men that e'er fared on his feet.
As a pearl compared to white peas is more precious   385
So next to the other gay knights is Sir Gawain.
But a little you lacked, and loyalty wanted,
Yet truly 't was not for intrigue or for wooing,
But love of your life; the less do I blame you."

[Gawain bows his head in shame and fiercely hurls at the Green Knight the green
girdle which has caused him to forsake the knightly virtue of loyalty. The Green
Knight assures him that his offense has been purged and that he is spotless. He
urges Gawain to come back to the castle and be his guest. Gawain refuses, but
accepts the gift of the green girdle as a reminder of his failing.]

"When in glory I move, with remorse I'll remember   390
The frailty and fault of the stubborn flesh,

How soon 't is infected with stains of defilement;
And thus when I'm proud of my prowess in arms,
The sight of this sash shall humble my spirit."

[*The Green Knight then informs him that he is Bercilak de Hautdesert,*[2] *Lord of the castle. The whole adventure has been planned by the old woman, who is in reality Morgan le Fay,*[3] *"well versed in the crafts and cunning of magic."*]

"I was sent in this way to your splendid hall   395
To make trial of your pride, and see if the people's
Tales were true of the Table's great glory.
This wonder she sent to unsettle your wits,
And to daunt so the Queen as to cause her to die
From fear at the sight of that phantom speaker   400
Holding his head in his hand at the high table.
Lives she at home there, that ancient lady;
She's even thine aunt, King Arthur's half-sister."

[*Gawain rides back to Arthur's court, where, amid a royal welcome, he tells of his adventures and of his unknightly deed. But Arthur comforts the knight, and the ladies and lords of the court make this agreement:*]

That ladies and lords to the Table belonging,
All of the brotherhood, baldrics should bear   405
Obliquely about them, bands of bright green,
Thus following suit for the sake of the hero.
For the Round Table's glory was granted that lace,
And he held himself honored who had it thereafter,
As told in the book, the best of romances.   410
     Hony Soyt Qui Mal Pence.[4]

[2] BERCILAK DE HAUTDESERT—In many of the romances Bercilak occurs, but not as the Green Knight. Hautdesert means hermitage in the mountains and refers to the Green Chapel.
[3] MORGAN LE FAY—King Arthur's half-sister. Their mother was Igren, the Duchess of Tintagel. Gawain's mother, Anna, was another of Arthur's half-sisters. "Le Fay" means a preternatural being. In calling the old woman "le Fay," the poet gives her preternatural powers traditionally associated with Morgan; thus the old woman is linked with Celtic mythology.
[4] HONY SOYT QUI MAL PENCE—This is Middle French for the motto, "Honi soit qui mal y pense," which means "Shame to him who evil thinks." This is the motto of the Order of the Garter, England's oldest chivalric order. This episode of Sir Gawain and the green girdle may be connected with the foundation of the Order of the Garter in the fourteenth century.

◇◇◇

WORD STUDY

1. Note the simple but strong, vivid words which are used in the romance. Very few words are Latin derivatives, but many are from the French. However, the diction, like the alliterative verse form, is in the Anglo-Saxon tradition. Can you explain these facts?

2. Refresh your memory on the definitions of *connotation* and *denotation*. Ex-

plain why the following words are *connotative*: *gnarled, shimmered, unleashed, bleared, girt.* Give *denotative* synonyms for these words.

3. What is the connection between *verdure* and *verdant*? Give the meaning of the following: *recreant, mien, doughty, fare* (verb), *void.* Look up the meaning and origin of *quitclaim.*

FOR DISCUSSION

1. Briefly describe in your own words the physical characteristics of the Green Knight and his horse as he entered the banquet hall.

2. How was the challenge of the Green Knight first received? Who saved the honor of the court? What was the nature of the compact made between the Green Knight and Sir Gawain?

3. How did Gawain prepare for the journey to the Chapel of the Green Knight? Describe his travels until he arrived at the lord's mansion.

4. How was Gawain received? Where did he meet the ladies for the first time? How did the older lady and the younger lady differ in looks, dress, and age? What was the nature of the bargain struck between the lord of the house and Gawain? Was it carried out completely? Discuss.

5. Why did not Gawain succumb to the temptations of the lady? Was it difficult for him to be pure and at the same time not give offense? Explain.

6. Is there any connection between line 290, the lady, and the temptations? Discuss.

7. Who accompanied Gawain part way to the Green Chapel? Why did Gawain receive three blows instead of one? Why was he slightly injured by the last blow?

8. Why did Gawain keep the green belt? Did it have any future significance among the lords and ladies of Arthur's court? Discuss.

9. At the end of the story, we learn the identity of the person who had planned both the visit of the Green Knight to Arthur's court and Gawain's adventure. Who was that person, and what were the motives of that person as given in the romance? What was the relationship between that person and Sir Gawain? Discuss.

FOR APPRECIATION

1. There are several beautiful nature descriptions in the story. Reread lines 170–176; 193–205; 284–290; 333–345. Study the detailed imagery of these descriptions. Rewrite one of them in prose.

2. It has been said that the Pearl Poet rivals Chaucer in the art of the pen-portrait. Analyze lines 210–216 and 220–245. Discuss how effectively the poet portrays the physical characteristics of his characters.

3. Discuss in detail the symbolism of the pentangle in lines 119–165. Explain how the ideal knight is portrayed here.

4. What precise elements of the metrical romance do you find in the story? Explain.

5. Color was never used indiscriminately in the medieval romance. Each color symbolized some specific virtue, vice, or abstract quality. Green was used to symbolize the preternatural; blue the supernatural life of grace; gold stood for integrity; red symbolized charity, courage, and courtesy. Discuss in detail the symbolic use of color in the romance.

6. What precise elements of the Catholic religion are included in the story? What place does Our Lady hold? Is this consistent with the medieval tradition? Discuss.

7. Select at least ten lines in which the alliterative verse form is highly effective.

PROJECT

Discuss the allegorical significance of the entire romance. Show how the triumph of chastity is the theme of the story.

RELATED READING

The entire romance can be read in Professor Banks' splendid translation, *Sir Gawain and the Green Knight*.

Margaret Williams' *Glee-Wood* is an excellent anthology of Middle English writings. You may wish to read selections from the *Pearl* or other stories which will be found there.

Read some selections from Malory's *Le Morte d'Arthur*.

THE METRICAL TALE

The metrical tale is a narrative poem in which a story is told as simply and realistically as possible. It may deal with any phase of life, and its theme may be either allegorical or literal. In many ways, the metrical tale may be compared to the modern short-story, especially in its relative brevity and its unity of impression. As we shall see, Chaucer, in his *Canterbury Tales*, was a master of the metrical tale.

CHAUCER AND ENGLAND

The ordinary man of the fourteenth century was apt to view his world as being old, sophisticated, and corrupt. New developments in the government and organization of society were replacing the crumbling feudal system. Kings and royalty were being supplanted by the new rich who had made vast fortunes out of the commercialism of trade and finance. The common people were beginning to stir and revolt. Corruption in the Church, the state, and in individual lives was the frequent target of satirical writers. Chief among these satirists were two outstanding English poets: William Langland and Geoffrey Chaucer.

VISION OF PIERS PLOWMAN

Both Chaucer and Langland were citizens of London. But, unlike Chaucer, the court poet, the gaunt and hungry Langland lived his nights and days among the underprivileged, making a sparse living by singing psalms for the souls of the wealthy departed. The restless man burned with pity and indignation at the evils of his world. He wrote his thoughts and dreams into his *Vision of Piers Plowman*. With a sharp and angry pen, he cried out against social injustice, challenged both churchmen and the wealthy to reform, and stingingly satirized the unworthy clergy, monks, and friars. But he differed radically from the early reformer, Wycliff, who would have overthrown the Church and existing society. Langland wanted to reconstruct and revitalize society with a new spiritual vigor.

Piers Plowman is like a rough pageant of his century, in which we brush shoulders with the common man as he wears the smell of the streets on his tattered clothing. We hear the laughter and the cries of the poor as they act and talk, sometimes raucously and rowdily, sometimes gravely and profoundly. But throughout the poem there is the quest of Piers, the common Englishman, for Truth which is God and for Christ who can solve man's problems.

The poem is written in the south-Midland dialect and in the old alliterative meter of the Anglo-Saxons, which was revived in the fourteenth century.

The Vision of Piers Plowman is a long allegory composed of twenty sections, with Long Will, the author, as the dreamer. In sections one to seven, the world is seen as a field of folk between the Tower of Heaven and the Pit of Hell. The folk seem to be unmindful of everything except the making of money. Holy Church warns that a reasonable care for the business of the world is good, but that the real vocation of man is to follow Truth and Love. In this section Langland satirizes the corruption and injustices both of the secular government and the common man. The poet represents Penance, Contrition, Confession and Reparation as fighting against these abuses. The reparation imposed upon all men is to seek Saint Truth. To Piers Plowman is entrusted a pardon sent from Truth which states that whoever lives according to Truth, Love, Conscience, Reason, Penance, and Labor is in a State of Grace and will win Salvation. This is to "Do Well."

In sections eight to fifteen, Piers meets the characters Thought, Study, Clergy, Scripture, and Imagination. To each he puts the question, "What is Do Well?" Each supplies an answer not only to that question but to the question, "What are Do Better and Do Best?" In brief, the answer to Do Well is: be honest, God-fearing, neighborly, hard working and obedient to the Church. In addition to these, Do Better should teach the ignorant, heal the suffering, and practice what you teach. Do Best should be outstanding in all these virtues and should also guide and administer the Church. In each of these three vocations we have an allegorical interpretation of the life of the good layman, the good priest, and the good bishop.

In sections sixteen to twenty the poet explains how Do Better is exemplified in the teaching, healing, and suffering of the true priest, as these were exemplified in Christ. He further shows that the triple vocation of Do Well, Do Better, and Do Best is found perfectly in Christ.

After Christ's Ascension and the coming of the Holy Ghost, Christ taught Piers to build a great Barn of Unity or "Holy Church in English." But the Barn built by Piers (who is now a symbol of papal authority) is stormed by forces of evil amassed against it. In the final battle Piers vanishes, as the Pope seemed to have vanished in the great Western Schism.

Langland ends the poem in a black hour; but in the last line, we are reminded that Christ, triumphant on Easter Day, cannot fail.

CHAUCER AND THE CANTERBURY TALES

Geoffrey Chaucer was a polished courtier, statesman, professional man of letters, and man of the world. He, too, was well aware of the problems of his day; but his satire was more artistic and certainly more detached than Langland's. Chaucer never directly argues or preaches. He merely presents the corruption, the exaggerated pomp, the foolishness and rascality of the men and women of his age, and allows his readers to draw their own conclusions. His is the indirect dramatic method of the modern novelists. Langland employed the tactics of the medieval preacher. Chaucer's satire is softened throughout by his humor, his awareness of beauty, his rich love of life, and his international outlook.

In common with the Pearl Poet, Chaucer was a conscious artist. In his early years he wrote in the traditional allegorical manner and gave us such masterpieces as *The Parliament of Fowls* and *Troilus and Criseyde*. But he did not use the alliterative meter nor the Old English poetic diction of the romances. His meter and verse forms he borrowed from the French schools, and the diction he used was that of cultivated people of London.

GEOFFREY CHAUCER

In the *Canterbury Tales*, Chaucer becomes the story teller *par excellence*. With his emphasis on realism, he gives the whole work the character of a novel. Chaucer's greatness lies in his ability to portray character. For the most part, the stories which he tells are not original. There are legends, love stories, adventures, satires, allegories, and fables; all are borrowed from Italian, French, and English story collections, and from oral tradition. Chaucer's originality stems from his ability to tell the tales in masterly, brilliant versification; the idea of the pilgrimage as a framework and a source of unity for his tales; and the vitality, vividness, and satiric humor that permeate both the stories and the characters of the story tellers.

In Chaucer's day, pilgrimages to various shrines were common. One of the journeys most frequently undertaken was that to the shrine of Thomas à Becket, Archbishop of Canterbury, who had been murdered during the reign of Henry II. It was the custom of the pilgrims desiring to visit this shrine to gather at the Tabard Inn across the Thames River from London. Here they waited until a sufficient number came to make the journey pleasant and safe. Chaucer presents a group of these pilgrims in his *Canterbury Tales* and in the "Prologue" gives a description of each of them.

THE MURDER OF

THOMAS À BECKET

As a result of a suggestion of Harry Bailly, the jovial host of the Inn, who proposed to ride with the company to Canterbury as its guide, each pilgrim was to tell four tales, two during the ride to Canterbury and two during the return. Whoever was judged to be the best story-teller would be given a fine supper by all the rest when they returned.

This plan, of course, was but a device enabling Chaucer to tell a great number of stories. Had he carried out his plan there would have been more than one hundred tales, for there were twenty-nine pilgrims. Only twenty-four were written, but they cover a wide range of subject matter.

In the "Prologue," Chaucer's characterization is at its best, and the "Prologue" has been called "one of the most perfect pieces of composition in the English language." In it we have clear-cut pictures with sharp details of dress and mannerisms, and a shrewd appraisal of character. It has been called an album of medieval England and her people. Although Chaucer has given us a fairly representative cross section of medieval characters, selected from the various social levels, professions, and occupations, we must not suppose that he is sketching for us representative types. Chaucer, like the nineteenth century Dickens, was a master of caricature. All his characters were exaggerated for literary reasons. Just as it is the custom of the story-teller to make his characters larger than life, so Chaucer consciously and artistically overdrew his characters to make them interesting. Many of the people he included in the "Prologue" had a foundation in fact in his own personal life or personal prejudices. In his days, there were certainly too large a number of worldly nuns, immoral friars, wealthy monks, rowdy millers, covetous doctors, and women of the world like the Wife of Bath. These and others Chaucer satirized, but certainly not as typical of their class. For he knew too well that despite the large number of citizens in all walks of life who followed the primrose path of ease and luxury, there were abundantly more who followed the Ten Commandments.

◇◇◇◇◇

The Canterbury Tales

TRANSLATED BY THEODORE MORRISON

The following selections include a portion of the "Prologue" and THE NUN'S PRIEST'S TALE. As the portraits of the characters in the "Prologue" unfold, it is as if the reader were living for a while in the "Merrie England" of the fourteenth century.

To get the feel of Chaucer's verse, one should read it in the original. However, six hundred years have made enough changes in spelling and pronunciation to puzzle the general reader; and so first acquaintance should come through a modern translation. As a sample of the original, the first eighteen lines are presented in Middle English, with a parallel reading in modern English. To get the effect of Chaucer's pronunciation, the final e's should be pronounced and the vowels should be given the sounds they have in most European languages. Long Ā is AH; Ē is Ā; Ī is ĒĒ; ŌŌ is Ō; ĒĒ is Ā; OU or OW is ŌŌ. Final Ë is pronounced like the final A in VIRGINIA.

PROLOGUE

MIDDLE ENGLISH VERSION	A MODERN ENGLISH TRANSLATION
Whan that Aprillë with his shourës sōōtë	As soon as April pierces to the root
The droghte of Marche hath percëd to the rōōtë,	The drought of March, and bathes each bud and shoot
And bathëd every veyne in swich licour,	Through every vein of sap with gentle showers
Of which vertu engendrëd is the flour;	From whose engendering liquor spring the flowers;
Whan Zephirus eek with his swetë brēēth　　　5	When zephyrs have breathed softly all about　　　5
Inspirëd hath in every holt and hēēth	Inspiring every wood and field to sprout,
The tendrë croppës, and the yongë sonnë	And in the zodiac the youthful sun
Hath in the Ram his halfë course y-ronnë,	His journey halfway through the Ram has run;
And smalë fowlës maken melodyë,　　9	When little birds are busy with their song
That slepen al the nyght with open yë,	Who sleep with open eyes the whole night long　　　10
So priketh hem nature in hir coragës:	Life stirs their hearts and tingles in them so,
Than longen folk to goon on pilgrymagës,	On pilgrimages people long to go

8. HALFWAY THOUGH THE RAM HAS RUN —People of the Middle Ages were familiar with all the signs of the zodiac. This was a common way of indicating early April.

4. ENGENDERING—Life producing.

Condensations of "Prologue" and "The Nun's Priest's Tale" from *The Portable Chaucer*, translated and edited by Theodore Morrison, copyright, 1949, by Theodore Morrison, reprinted by permission of The Viking Press, Inc., N. Y.

And palmers for to seken straungë
strondës,
To fernë halwës couthe in sondry londës:

And specially, from every shirës endë
Of Engelond, to Caunterbury they
wendë,   16
The holy, blisful martir for to sckë,
That hem hath holpen whan that they
were seeke.

13. PALMERS—Pilgrims returned from the
Holy Land, carrying palm leaves as evidence of
their journey.

And palmers to set out for distant
strands
And foreign shrines renowned in many
lands.   14
And specially in England people ride
To Canterbury from every countryside

To visit there the blessed martyred saint
Who gave them strength when they
were sick and faint.

17. MARTYRED SAINT—St. Thomas à
Becket

In Southwark at the Tabard one
spring day
It happened, as I stopped there on my
way,   20
Myself a pilgrim with a heart devout
Ready for Canterbury to set out,

19. THE TABARD—The name of a real inn
in a suburb of London.

At night came all of twenty-nine as-
sorted
Travelers, and to that same inn resorted,
Who by a turn of fortune chanced to
fall   25
In fellowship together, and they were
all

Pilgrims who had it in their minds to ride
Toward Canterbury. The stable doors were wide,
The rooms were large, and we enjoyed the best,
And shortly, when the sun had gone to rest,   30
I had so talked with each that presently
I was a member of their company
And promised to rise early the next day
To start, as I shall show, upon our way.
　But none the less, while I have time and space,   35
Before this tale has gone a further pace,
I should in reason tell you the condition
Of each of them, his rank and his position,
And also what array they all were in;
And so then, with a knight I will begin.

　A KNIGHT was with us, and an excellent man,   41
Who from the earliest moment he began
To follow his career loved chivalry,
Truth, openhandedness, and courtesy.
He was a stout man in the king's campaigns   45
And in that cause had gripped his horse's reins
In Christian lands and pagan through the earth,
None farther, and always honored for his worth.
Meek as a girl and gentle in his ways.
He had never spoken ignobly all his days   50
To any man by even a rude inflection.
He was a knight in all things to perfection.
He rode a good horse, but his gear was plain,
For he had lately served on a campaign.

His tunic was still spattered by the rust   55
Left by his coat of mail, for he had just
Returned and set out on his pilgrimage.

　His son was with him, a young SQUIRE, in age
Some twenty years as near as I could guess.
His hair curled as if taken from a press.
He was a lover and would become a knight.   61
In stature he was of a moderate height
But powerful and wonderfully quick.
He had been in Flanders, riding in the thick
Of forays in Artois and Picardy,   65
And bore up well for one so young as he,
Still hoping by his exploits in such places
To stand the better in his lady's graces.
He wore embroidered flowers, red and white,
And blazed like a spring meadow to the sight.   70
He sang or played his flute the livelong day.
He was as lusty as the month of May.
His coat was short, its sleeves were long and wide.
He sat his horse well, and knew how to ride,
And how to make a song and use his lance,   75
And he could write and draw well, too, and dance.
So hot his love that when the moon rose pale
He got no more sleep than a nightingale.
He was modest, and helped whomever he was able,

60. AS IF TAKEN FROM A PRESS—Men as well as women used various devices for putting a curl in naturally straight hair. Older men curled and waved their beards.

51. INFLECTION—Tone of voice.

And carved as his father's squire at the
table.   80

There was also a NUN, A PRIORESS,
Whose smile was gentle and full of
guilelessness.
"By St. Loy!" was the worst oath she
would say.
She sang mass well, in a becoming way,
Intoning through her nose the words
divine,   85
And she was known as Madame Eglan-
tine.
She spoke good French, as taught at
Stratford-Bow,
For the Parisian French she did not
know.
She was schooled to eat so primly and
so well   89
That from her lips no morsel ever fell.
She wet her fingers lightly in the dish
Of sauce, for courtesy was her first wish.
With every bite she did her skillful best
To see that no drop fell upon her breast.
She always wiped her upper lip so
clean   95
That in her cup was never to be seen
A hint of grease when she had drunk
her share.
She reached out for her meat with
comely air.
She was a great delight, and always tried
To imitate court ways, and had her
pride,   100
Both amiable and gracious in her deal-
ings.
As for her charity and tender feelings,
She melted at whatever was piteous.
She would weep if she but came upon a
mouse
Caught in a trap, if it were dead or
bleeding.   105

83. "BY ST. LOY"—An oath by St. Loy
was the mildest kind of swearing.
87. STRATFORD-BOW—A Benedictine convent near London. The French taught here
was Anglo-Norman French, not the pure
French of Paris.

Some little dogs that she took pleasure
feeding
On roasted meat or milk or good wheat
bread
She had, but how she wept to find one
dead
Or yelping from a blow that made it
smart,   109
And all was sympathy and loving heart.
Neat was her wimple in its every plait,
Her nose well formed, her eyes as gray
as slate.
Her mouth was very small and soft and
red.
She had so wide a brow I think her head
Was nearly a span broad, for certainly
She was not undergrown, as all could
see.   116
She wore her cloak with dignity and
charm,
And had her rosary about her arm,
The small beads coral and the larger
green,
And from them hung a brooch of
golden sheen,   120
On it a large A and a crown above;
Beneath, "All things are subject unto
love."
A Priest accompanied her toward
Canterbury,
And an attendant Nun, her secretary.

There was a MONK, and nowhere was
his peer,   125
A hunter, and a roving overseer.
He was a manly man, and fully able
To be an abbot. He kept a hunting
stable,
And when he rode the neighborhood
could hear   129
His bridle jingling in the wind as clear
And loud as if it were a chapel bell.
Wherever he was master of a cell

111. HER WIMPLE—The veil of her habit,
worn over the head and around the neck and
chin.

The principles of good St. Benedict,
For being a little old and somewhat
    strict,
Were honored in the breach, as past
    their prime.   135
He lived by the fashion of a newer time.
He would have swapped that text for a
    plucked hen
Which says that hunters are not holy
    men,
Or a monk outside his discipline and
    rule
Is too much like a fish outside his pool;
That is to say, a monk outside his
    cloister.   141
But such a text he deemed not worth an
    oyster.
I told him his opinion made me glad.
Why should he study always and go
    mad,
Mewed in his cell with only a book for
    neighbor?   145
Or why, as Augustine commanded, la-
    bor
And sweat his hands? How shall the
    world be served?
To Augustine be all such toil reserved!
And so he hunted, as was only right.
He had greyhounds as swift as birds in
    flight.   150
His taste was all for tracking down the
    hare,
And what his sport might cost he did
    not care.

133. ST. BENEDICT—St. Benedict established
the Order of Benedictine monks in 529 at
Monte Cassino, Italy. The Order was introduced into England about 600.

143. This line is obvious satire. Here
Chaucer, the Catholic poet, is indulging in
irony at the expense of the worldly monk.

145. MEWED—To be enclosed or confined
in a cage.

146. AUGUSTINE—The great St. Augustine
of Hippo who founded the Canons Regular of
St. Augustine. The Rule of St. Augustine was
and still is the Rule of many religious congre-
gations.

His sleeves I noticed, where they met
    his hand,
Trimmed with gray fur, the finest in the
    land.
His hood was fastened with a curious
    pin   155
Made of wrought gold and clasped be-
    neath his chin,
A love knot at the tip. His head might
    pass,
Bald as it was, for a lump of shining
    glass,
And his face was glistening as if
    anointed.
Fat as a lord he was, and well ap-
    pointed.   160
His eyes were large, and rolled inside his
    head
As if they gleamed from a furnace of
    hot lead.
His boots were supple, his horse su-
    perbly kept.
He was a prelate to dream of while you
    slept.
He was not pale nor peaked like a ghost.
He relished a plump swan as his favorite
    roast.   166
He rode a palfrey brown as a ripe berry.

There was an OXFORD STUDENT too, it
    chanced,
Already in his logic well advanced.
He rode a mount as skinny as a rake,
And he was hardly fat. For learning's
    sake   171
He let himself look hollow and sober
    enough.
He wore an outer coat of threadbare
    stuff,
For he had no benefice for his enjoy-
    ment
And was too unworldly for some lay em-
    ployment.   175

167. PALFREY—A saddle horse.

174. BENEFICE—The Oxford student was a
cleric in Minor Orders who did not receive
revenue from any endowed church.

He much preferred to have beside his
    bed
His twenty volumes bound in black or
    red
All packed with Aristotle from end to
    middle
Than a sumptuous wardrobe or a merry
    fiddle.
For though he knew what learning had
    to offer   180
There was little coin to jingle in his
    coffer.
Whatever he got by touching up a
    friend
On books and learning he would
    promptly spend
And busily pray for the soul of anybody
Who furnished him the wherewithal for
    study.   185
His scholarship was what he truly
    heeded.
He never spoke a word more than was
    needed,
And that was said with dignity and
    force,
And quick and brief. He was of grave
    discourse,
Giving new weight to virtue by his
    speech,   190
And gladly would he learn and gladly
    teach.

There were five Guildsmen, in the
    livery
Of one august and great fraternity,
A WEAVER, a DYER, and a CARPENTER,
A TAPESTRY-MAKER and a HABERDASHER.
Their gear was furbished new and clean
    as glass.   196
The mountings of their knives were not
    of brass
But silver. Their pouches were well
    made and neat,

And each of them, it seemed, deserved
    a seat
On the platform at the Guildhall, for
    each one   200
Was likely timber to make an alderman.
They had goods enough, and money to
    be spent,
Also their wives would willingly consent
And would have been at fault if they
    had not.
For to be "Madamed" is a pleasant lot,
And to march in first at feasts for being
    well married,   206
And royally to have their mantles car-
    ried.

For the pilgrimage these Guildsmen
    brought their own
COOK to boil their chicken and marrow
    bone
With seasoning powder and capers and
    sharp spice.   210
In judging London ale his taste was
    nice.
He well knew how to roast and broil
    and fry,
To mix a stew, and bake a good meat
    pie,
Or capon creamed with almond, rice,
    and egg.
Pity he had an ulcer on his leg!   215

A worthy WOMAN there was from near
    the city
Of Bath, but somewhat deaf, and
    more's the pity.
For weaving she possessed so great a
    bent
She outdid the people of Ypres and of
    Ghent.
No other woman dreamed of such a
    thing   220
As to precede her at the offering,

178. ARISTOTLE—Greek philosopher of the
fourth century B.C. His works throughout the
Middle Ages and even today are considered the
ground-work of all philosophical knowledge.

219. YPRES AND GHENT—Two cities in West
Flanders famous for their fine weaving.

Or if any did, she fell in such a wrath
She dried up all the charity in Bath.
She wore fine kerchiefs of old-fashioned
    air,
And on a Sunday morning, I could
    swear,   225
She had ten pounds of linen on her
    head.
Her stockings were of finest scarlet-red,
Laced tightly, and her shoes were soft
    and new.
Bold was her face, and fair, and red in
    hue.
She had been an excellent woman all
    her life.   230
Five men in turn had taken her to wife,
Omitting other youthful company—
But let that pass for now! Over the sea
She had traveled freely; many a distant
    stream
She crossed, and visited Jerusalem   235
Three times. She had been at Rome
    and at Boulogne,
At the shrine of Compostella, and at
    Cologne.
She had wandered by the way through
    many a scene.
Her teeth were set with little gaps be-
    tween.
Easily on her ambling horse she sat.
She was well wimpled, and she wore a
    hat   241
As wide in circuit as a shield or targe.
A skirt swathed up her hips, and they
    were large.
Upon her feet she wore sharp-roweled
    spurs.
She was a good fellow; a ready tongue
    was hers.   245
All remedies of love she knew by name,
For she had all the tricks of that old
    game.

    There was a good man of the priest's
    vocation,

244. SHARP-ROWELED—A rowel is a little
wheel with sharp points attached to spurs.

A poor town PARSON of true consecra-
    tion,
But he was rich in holy thought and
    work.   250
Learned he was, in the truest sense a
    clerk
Who meant Christ's gospel faithfully to
    preach
And truly his parishioners to teach.
He was a kind man, full of industry,
Many times tested by adversity   255
And always patient. If tithes were in
    arrears,
He was loth to threaten any man with
    fears
Of excommunication; past a doubt
He would rather spread his offering
    about
To his poor flock, or spend his property.
To him a little meant sufficiency.   261
Wide was his parish, with houses far
    asunder,
But he would not be kept by rain or
    thunder,
If any had suffered a sickness or a blow,
From visiting the farthest, high or low,
Plodding his way on foot, his staff in
    hand.   266
He was a model his flock could under-
    stand,
For first he did and afterward he taught.
That precept from the Gospel he had
    caught,

248. In the following lines, Chaucer gives
us a picture of the ideal parish priest and the
one sincere religious man in the pilgrimage.
In Langland's *Piers Plowman*, the parish priest
comes in for his share of censure, along with
the monks and the friars.

258. EXCOMMUNICATION — According to
Church Law, the faithful were bound to pay
tithes or Church taxes, as commanded by God
in the Old Testament. Stubborn refusal on
the part of those who could afford to pay could
result in their being deprived of the spiritual
benefits of the Church. Abuses, of course,
crept in when unworthy churchmen demanded
such payment from the poor.

And he added as a metaphor thereto,
"If the gold rusts, what will the iron
  do?"   271
For if a priest is foul, in whom we trust,
No wonder a layman shows a little rust.
A priest should take to heart the shame-
  ful scene
Of shepherds filthy while the sheep are
  clean.   275
By his own purity a priest should give
The example to his sheep, how they
  should live.
He did not rent his benefice for hire,
Leaving his flock to flounder in the
  mire,
And run to London, happiest of goals,
To sing paid masses in St. Paul's for
  souls,   281
Or as chaplain from some rich guild
  take his keep,
But dwelt at home and guarded well his
  sheep
So that no wolf should make his flock
  miscarry.
He was a shepherd, and not a mer-
  cenary.   285
And though himself a man of strict vo-
  cation
He was not harsh to weak souls in temp-
  tation,
Not overbearing nor haughty in his
  speech,
But wise and kind in all he tried to
  teach.
By good example and just words to turn
Sinners to heaven was his whole con-
  cern.   291
But should a man in truth prove obsti-
  nate,
Whoever he was, of rich or mean estate,

278–281. The meaning of these lines is
this: The Parish priest did not hire someone
to discharge his own local parish duties, which
brought little monetary return, and leave for
the gayer life of London to live an easy life
singing Masses in St. Paul's great church, where
he would receive larger stipends from the rich
Mass foundations.

The Parson would give him a snub to
  meet the case.   294
I doubt there was a priest in any place
His better. He did not stand on dignity
Nor affect in conscience too much
  nicety,
But Christ's and his disciples' word he
  sought
To teach, and first he followed what he
  taught.

*[The other characters introduced in
the "Prologue" include a Yeoman (who
rode with the Knight), a Friar, a Merchant, a Lawyer, a Franklin (or Country
Squire), a Sailor, a Physician, a Plowman (brother of the Poor Parson), a
Bailiff, a Steward for a group of lawyers,
a Miller, and a Summoner to Ecclesiastical Courts. The last 144 lines introduce the jolly host of the Tabard Inn,
who proposes the story-telling contest
and who decides to join the pilgrims and
act as master of ceremonies on the journey.]*

WORD STUDY

1. *Spattered, peaked, swathed,* and *ambled* are picturesque words. Why?
2. Explain the meaning of *sumptuous,
deemed, furbished.* Give antonyms for
ignoble and *prim.*

FOR APPRECIATION

1. Enumerate the signs of spring which
Chaucer details in the first fifteen lines
of the "Prologue."
2. Briefly compare or contrast Chaucer's Knight with Sir Gawain.
3. Would you say that Chaucer is pok-
ing fun at the dress of the Squire? Explain. Have the Squire and the modern
"young man about town" anything in
common? Explain.

4. What precise details in Chaucer's description of the Nun would make you conclude that she was a rather worldly woman? What was Chaucer's attitude toward her? What is your reaction?

5. Discuss in detail the satire contained in the description of the Monk. What is the difference between a Monk and a Friar? If you read Chaucer's description of his Friar in the "Prologue," you will find he is much harder on the Friar than on the Monk. What may be the reason for this?

6. In your own words give a brief sketch of the Wife of Bath.

7. What was Chaucer's attitude toward the Parish priest? Discuss. Give at least five characteristics of the good parish priest as described for us by Chaucer.

8. Which characters of the "Prologue" do you think are the most effectively sketched? Give your reasons. Chaucer purposely employed caricature as a literary device. Point out lines in which caricature is employed.

9. What precise details of medieval dress, manners, customs, and attitude could you learn from reading the "Prologue"?

10. From your knowledge of history, what evidence can you give that Chaucer's characters are not completely typical of the men and women whom he portrays?

THE NUN'S PRIEST'S TALE

During the Middle Ages, the tale of the Rooster and Fox appeared in numerous fables and in several versions of the beast-epic, the romance of Reynard. In the twelfth and thirteenth centuries, these stories in which beasts and birds could speak took on a literary form, and served as a medium of satire on court and clergy as well as sermon material for the medieval preacher.

In the tale told by Sir John, the nun's confessor, Chaucer uses this fable to show some of the weaknesses of humanity thinly guised in the feathered costumes of rooster and hens. It is a masterpiece of mock-heroic verse, enriched by Chaucer's knowledge of human nature, philosophy, religion, learning, and medieval science.

The rooster, Chanticleer, and the hen, Partlet, represent man and woman, lord and lady. As the medieval lady, Partlet reviews the qualities that should be found in an ideal husband. Chanticleer refutes her learned arguments with the skill of a medieval scholar. Sir Russell Fox ranks with the most infamous traitors in history.

As you read the tale, look for the humor and the satire.

Once a poor widow, aging year by year,
Lived in a tiny cottage that stood near
A clump of shade trees rising in a dale.
This widow, of whom I tell you in my
    tale,
Since the last day that she had been a
    wife   5
Had led a very patient, simple life.
She had but few possessions to content
    her.
By thrift and husbandry of what God
    sent her
She and two daughters found the means
    to dine.
She had no more than three well-
    fattened swine,   10
As many cows, and one sheep, Moll by
    name.
Her bower and hall were black from the
    hearth-flame
Where she had eaten many a slender
    meal.
No dainty morsel did her palate feel
And no sharp sauce was needed with
    her pottage.   15
Her table was in keeping with her cot-
    tage.
Excess had never given her disquiet.
Her only doctor was a moderate diet,
And exercise, and a heart that was con-
    tented.
If she did not dance, at least no gout
    prevented;   20
No apoplexy had destroyed her head.
She never drank wine, whether white or
    red.
She served brown bread and milk, loaves
    white or black,
Singed bacon, all this with no sense of
    lack,
And now and then an egg or two. In
    short,   25
She was a dairy woman of a sort.
    She had a yard, on the inside fenced
      about

8. HUSBANDRY—Wise management.

With hedges, and an empty ditch with-
    out,
In which she kept a cock, called Chanti-
    cleer.
In all the realm of crowing he had no
    peer.   30
His voice was merrier than the merry
    sound
Of the church organ grumbling out its
    ground
Upon a saint's day. Stouter was this
    cock
In crowing than the loudest abbey
    clock.
Of astronomy instinctively aware,   35
He kept the sun's hours with celestial
    care,
For when through each fifteen degrees
    it moved,
He crowed so that it couldn't be im-
    proved.
His comb, like a crenelated castle wall,
Red as fine coral, stood up proud and
    tall.   40
His bill was black; like polished jet it
    glowed,
And he was azure-legged and azure-toed.
As lilies were his nails, they were so
    white;
Like burnished gold his hue, it shone so
    bright.
This cock had in his princely sway and
    measure   45
Seven hens to satisfy his every pleasure,
Who were his sisters and his sweethearts
    true,
Each wonderfully like him in her hue,
Of whom the fairest-feathered throat to
    see
Was fair Dame Partlet. Courteous was
    she,   50
Discreet, and always acted debonairly.

39. CRENELATED—Furnished with battlements. A battlement was a decorative device
used in medieval architecture; an elevated wall
with open spaces surrounding the medieval
castle.

She was sociable, and bore herself so
fairly,
Since the very time that she was seven
nights old,
The heart of Chanticleer was in her
hold
As if she had him locked up, every limb.
He loved her so that all was well with
him.   56
It was a joy, when up the sun would
spring,
To hear them both together sweetly
sing,
"My love has gone to the country, far
away!"
For as I understand it, in that day   60
The animals and birds could sing and
speak.
  Now as this cock, one morning at day-
break,
With each of the seven hens that he
called spouse,
Sat on his perch inside the widow's
house,
And next him fair Dame Partlet, in his
throat   65
This Chanticleer produced a hideous
note
And groaned like a man who is having
a bad dream;
And Partlet, when she heard her husband scream,
Was all aghast, and said, "Soul of my
passion,
What ails you that you groan in such a
fashion?   70
You are always a sound sleeper. Fie, for
shame!"
  And Chanticleer awoke and answered, "Dame,
Take no offense, I beg you, on this
score.
I dreamt, by God, I was in a plight so
sore
Just now, my heart still quivers from the
fright.   75

Now God see that my dream turns out
all right
And keep my flesh and body from foul
seizure!
I dreamed I was strutting in our yard at
leisure
When there I saw, among the weeds
and vines,
A beast, he was like a hound, and had
designs   80
Upon my person, and would have killed
me dead.
His coat was not quite yellow, not quite
red,
And both his ears and tail were tipped
with black
Unlike the fur along his sides and back.
He had a small snout and a fiery eye.
His look for fear still makes me almost
die.   86
This is what made me groan, I have no
doubt."
  "For shame! Fie on you, faint
heart!" she burst out.
"Alas," she said, "by the great God
above,
Now you have lost my heart and all my
love!   90
I cannot love a coward, as I'm blest!
Whatever any woman may protest,
We all want, could it be so, for our part,
Husbands who are wise and stout of
heart,
No blabber, and no niggard, and no
fool,   95
Nor afraid of every weapon or sharp
tool,
No braggart either, by the God above!
How dare you say, for shame, to your
true love
That there is anything you ever feared?
Have you no man's heart, when you
have a beard?   100
Alas, and can a nightmare set you
screaming?
95. NIGGARD—Miser.

God knows there's only vanity in dream-
ing!
Dreams are produced by such unseemly
capers
As overeating; they come from stomach
vapors
When a man's humors aren't behaving
right   105
From some excess. This dream you had
tonight,
It comes straight from the superfluity
Of your red choler, certain as can be.
  "Cato, that has been thought so wise
a man,
Didn't he tell us, 'Put no stock in
dreams'?"   110
  "Madame," he answered, "thanks for
all your lore.
But still, to speak of Cato, though his
name
For wisdom has enjoyed so great a fame,
And though he counseled us there was
no need
To be afraid of dreams, by God, men
read   115
Of many a man of more authority
Than this Don Cato could pretend to
be
Who in old books declare the opposite,
And by experience they have settled it,
That dreams are omens and prefigura-
tions   120
Both of good fortune and of tribulations
That life and its vicissitudes present.
This question leaves no room for argu-
ment.
The very upshot makes it plain, indeed.

"Yes, in St. Kenelm's life I have also
read—   125
He was the son of Cynewulf, the king
Of Mercia—how this Kenelm dreamed
a thing.
One day, as the time when he was killed
drew near,
He saw his murder in a dream appear.
His nurse explained his dream in each
detail,   130
And warned him to be wary without fail
Of treason; yet he was but seven years
old,
And therefore any dream he could but
hold
Of little weight, in heart he was so pure.
I'd give my shirt, by God, you may be
sure,   135
If you had read his story through like
me!
  "Moreover, Partlet, I tell you truth-
fully,
Macrobius writes—and by his book we
know
The African vision of great Scipio—
Confirming dreams, and holds that they
may be   140
Forewarnings of events that men shall
see.
Again, I beg, look well at what is meant
By the Book of Daniel in the Old Testa-
ment,

103–106. According to medieval science, too
much food or drink caused vapors to arise
from the stomach to the brain.
109. CATO—Dionysius Cato, who composed
a book of sayings in the fourth century.
119. In the following lines, Chaucer has
Chanticleer argue like a medieval scholar by
quoting other authorities to prove his point.
His aim is to give more and better authorities
than Partlet can. The stories are *exempla*,
found in medieval sermon books.

125. ST. KENELM'S LIFE—When Kenulphus,
King of Mercia, died in 821, he left his throne
to his son Kenelm, aged 7. Kenelm dreamed
that he saw a tree with wax lights upon it, and
that he climbed to the top. When one of his
friends cut it down, he was turned into a little
bird and flew to heaven. The bird was his
soul, the flight his death. Shortly afterwards
his ambitious aunt had him murdered and
buried under a tree; a heavenly light over the
tree discovered the place of his burial.
138. MACROBIUS—About the year 400,
Macrobius wrote a commentary on Cicero's
Somnium Scipionis (The Dreams of Scipio).
This work had a great influence on medieval
literature, especially upon Chaucer.
143. Read the story of Daniel's dream in
the *Book of Daniel*, Chapter 4.

Whether *he* held that dreams are
    vanity!
Read also about Joseph. You shall see
That dreams, or some of them—I don't
    say all—   146
Warn us of things that afterward befall.
Think of the king of Egypt, Don Phar-
    aoh;
Of his butler and his baker think also,
Whether they found that dreams have
    no result.   150
Whoever will search through kingdoms
    and consult
Their histories reads many a wondrous
    thing
Of dreams. What about Croesus, Lyd-
    ian king—
Didn't he dream he was sitting on a tree,
Which meant he would be hanged?
    Andromache,   155
The woman who was once great Hec-
    tor's wife,
On the day that Hector was to lose his
    life,
The very night before his blood was
    spilled
She dreamed of how her husband would
    be killed
If he went out to battle on that day.
She warned him; but he would not heed
    nor stay.   161
In spite of her he rode out on the plain,
And by Achilles he was promptly slain.
But all that story is too long to tell,
And it is nearly day. I must not dwell
Upon this matter. Briefly, in conclu-
    sion,   166

145. The story of Joseph is contained in the
Book of Genesis.
153. The dream of Croesus is related in the
"Monk's Tale."
155. ANDROMACHE (ăn·drŏm′á·kê)—Chaucer's knowledge of the story of Andromache
was not taken from Homer (Greek was little
known in the Middle Ages), but from Dares
Phrygius.
156. Both Hector and Achilles were heroes
of the Trojan War.

I say this dream will bring me to con-
    fusion
And mischief of some sort. And fur-
    thermore,
On laxatives, I say, I set no store,   169
For they are poisonous, I'm sure of it.
I do not trust them! I like them not
    one bit!
    "Now let's talk cheerfully, and forget
    all this.
My pretty Partlet, by my hope of bliss,
In one thing God has sent me ample
    grace,   174
For when I see the beauty of your face,
You are so scarlet-red about the eye,
It is enough to make my terrors die.
For just as true as *In principio*
Mulier est hominis confusio—
And Madame, what this Latin means is
    this: 180
'Woman is man's whole comfort and
    true bliss'—
I am then so full of pure felicity
That I defy whatever sort of dream!"
    And day being come, he flew down
    from the beam
And with him his hens fluttered, one
    and all;   185
And with a "cluck, cluck" he began to
    call
His wives to where a kernel had been
    tossed.
He was a prince, his fears entirely lost.
Grim as a lion he strolled to and fro,
And strutted only on his either toe.   190
He would not deign to set foot on the
    ground.
"Cluck, cluck," he said, whenever he
    had found
A kernel, and his wives came running
    all.
Thus royal as a monarch in his hall   194

178–179. The translation of this Latin medieval proverb is: "From the very beginning
woman is the confusion of man." Note that
Chanticleer's false translation is not detected
by Partlet.

I leave to his delights this Chanticleer,
And presently the sequel you shall hear.
   After the month in which the world
    began,
The month of March, when God cre-
   ated man,
Had passed, and when the season had
   run through
Since March began just thirty days and
   two,   200
It happened that Chanticleer, in all his
   pride,
While his seven hens were walking by
   his side,
Lifted his eyes, beholding the bright sun,
Which in the sign of Taurus had then
   run
Twenty and one degrees and somewhat
   more,   205
And knew by instinct, not by learned
   lore,
It was the hour of prime. He raised his
   head
And crowed with lordly voice. "The
   sun," he said,
"Forty and one degrees and more in
   height
Has climbed the sky. Partlet, my
   world's delight,   210
Hear all these birds, how happily they
   sing,
And see the pretty flowers, how they
   spring
With solace and with joy my spirits
   dance!"
But suddenly he met a sore mischance,
For in the end joys ever turn to woes.
Quickly the joys of earth are gone, God
   knows.   216
   A sly iniquitous fox, with black-tipped
    ears,
Who had lived in the neighboring wood
    for some three years,

His fated fancy swollen to a height,
Had broken through the hedges that
   same night   220
Into the yard where in his pride sublime
Chanticleer with his seven wives passed
   the time.
Quietly in a bed of herbs he lay
Till it was past the middle of the day,
Waiting his hour on Chanticleer to
   fall   225
As gladly do these murderers, one and
   all,
Who lie in wait, concealed, to murder
   men.
O murderer, lurking traitorous in your
   den!
O new Iscariot, second Ganelon,
False hypocrite, Greek Sinon, who
   brought on   230
The utter woe of Troy and all her sor-
   row!
O Chanticleer, accursed be that morrow
When to the yard you flew down from
   the beams!
That day, as you were well warned in
   your dreams,
Would threaten you with dire catastro-
   phe.   235
Women have many times, as wise men
   hold,
Offered advice that left men in the cold.
A woman's counsel brought us first to
   woe
And out of Paradise made Adam go
Where he lived a merry life and one of
   ease.   240
But since I don't know whom I may dis-
   please
By giving women's words an ill report,
Pass over it; I only spoke in sport.

198. THE MONTH OF MARCH—According to
the ancient tradition, the world was created at
the time of the vernal equinox.

229. GANELON—Ganelon betrayed Roland,
the hero of *The Song of Roland*.

230. GREEK SINON—Sinon invented the Trojan horse which was responsible for the fall of
Troy.

There are books about it you can read or
    skim in,
And you'll discover what they say of
    women. 245
I'm telling you the cock's words, and not
    mine.
Harm in no woman at all can I divine.
  Merrily bathing where the sand was
    dry
Lay Partlet, with her sisters all near by,
And Chanticleer, as regal as could be,
Sang merrily as the mermaid in the
    sea; 251
For the *Physiologus* itself declares
That they know how to sing the merriest
    airs.
And so it happened that as he fixed his
    eye
Among the herbs upon a butterfly, 255
He caught sight of this fox who
    crouched there low.
He felt no impulse then to strut or crow,
But cried "cucock!" and gave a fearful
    start
Like a man who has been frightened to
    the heart.
For instinctively, if he should chance to
    see 260
His opposite, a beast desires to flee,
Even the first time that it meets his eye.
  This Chanticleer, no sooner did he
    spy
The fox than promptly enough he
    would have fled.
But "Where are you going, kind sir?"
    the fox said. 265
"Are you afraid of me, who am your
    friend?
Truly, I'd be a devil from end to end
If I meant you any harm or villainy.
I have not come to invade your privacy.
In truth, the only reason that could
    bring 270

This visit of mine was just to hear you
    sing.
Beyond a doubt, you have as fine a voice
As any angel who makes heaven rejoice.
Also you have more feeling in your note
Than Boëthius, or any tuneful throat.
Milord your father once—and may God
    bless 276
His soul—your noble mother too, no
    less,
Have been inside my house, to my great
    ease.
And verily sir, I should be glad to please
You also. But for singing, I declare,
As I enjoy my eyes, that precious
    pair, 281
Save you, I never heard a man so sing
As your father did when night was on
    the wing.
Straight from the heart, in truth, came
    all his song,
And to make his voice more resonant
    and strong 285
He would strain until he shut his either
    eye,
So loud and lordly would he make his
    cry,
And stand up on his tiptoes therewithal
And stretch his neck till it grew long
    and small.
He had such excellent discretion, too,
That whether his singing, all the region
    through, 291
Or his wisdom, there was no one to sur-
    pass."
  Blind to all treachery, Chanticleer be-
    gan
To beat his wings, like one who cannot
    see
The traitor, ravished by his flattery.

252. *Physiologus* (fĭz′ĭ·ŏl′ŏ·jŭs)—The reference is to a Latin beastiary. There is a chapter in the book on sirens and mermaids.

275. BOËTHIUS (bŏ·ē′thĭ·ŭs)—(470–525)
was the author of *De Consolatione Philoso-
phiae* which was translated into Anglo-Saxon
by Alfred's scholars and later into Middle English by Chaucer. Boethius was admired not
only as a philosopher but also as a musician.

This Chanticleer stood tiptoe at full
    height.   296
He stretched his neck, he shut his eye-
    lids tight,
And he began to crow a lordly note.
The fox, Don Russell, seized him by the
    throat
At once, and on his back bore Chanti-
    cleer   300
Off toward his den that in the grove
    stood near,
For no one yet had threatened to pursue.
O destiny, that no man may eschew!
Alas, that he left his safe perch on the
    beams!
Alas, that Partlet took no stock in
    dreams!   305
In truth, no lamentation ever rose,
No shriek of ladies when before its foes
Ilium fell, and Pyrrhus with drawn blade
Had seized King Priam by the beard and
    made
An end of him—the *Aeneid* tells the
    tale—   310
Such as the hens made with their pite-
    ous wail
In their enclosure, seeing the dread sight
Of Chanticleer. But at the shrillest
    height
Shrieked Partlet. She shrieked louder
    than the wife
Of Hasdrubal, when her husband lost
    his life   315
And the Romans burned down Car-
    thage; for her state
Of torment and of frenzy was so great
She willfully chose the fire for her part,
Leaped in, and burned herself with
    steadfast heart.

308–310. Priam, the last King of Troy, was
slain by Pyrrhus, when the Greeks conquered
that city. The story is told in the Second Book
of Vergil's *Aeneid*.
  315. HASDRUBAL (hăz'droo·băl)—King of
Carthage. When the Romans burned the city
in 146 B.C., he slew himself, and his wife and
sons burned themselves.

Unhappy hens, you shrieked as when
    for pity,   320
While the tyrant Nero put to flames
    the city
Of Rome, rang out the shriek of sena-
    tors' wives
Because their husbands had all lost their
    lives;
This Nero put to death these innocent
    men.
But I will come back to my tale again.
Now this good widow and her two
    daughters heard   326
These woeful hens shriek when the
    crime occurred,
And sprang outdoors as quickly as they
    could
And saw the fox, who was making for
    the wood
Bearing this Chanticleer across his back.
"Help, help!" they cried. They cried,
    "Alas! Alack!   331
The fox, the fox!" and after him they
    ran,
And armed with clubs came running
    many a man.
Ran Coll the dog, and led a yelping
    band;
Ran Malkyn, with a distaff in her
    hand;
Ran cow and calf, and even the very
    hogs,   336
By the yelping and the barking of the
    dogs
And men's and women's shouts so ter-
    rified
They ran till it seemed their hearts
    would burst inside;
They squealed like fiends in the pit, with
    none to still them.   340
The ducks quacked as if men were going
    to kill them.
The geese for very fear flew over the
    trees.
Out of the beehive came the swarm of
    bees.

Now hear me, you good people, one
    and all! 344
Fortune, I say, will suddenly override
Her enemy in his very hope and pride!
This cock, as on the fox's back he lay,
Plucked up his courage to speak to him
    and say.
"God be my help, sir, but I'd tell them
    all,
That is, if I were you, 'Plague on you
    fall! 350
Go back, proud fools! Now that I've
    reached the wood,
I'll eat the cock at once, for all the good
Your noise can do. Here Chanticleer
    shall stay.'"
    "Fine!" said the fox. "I'll do just
    what you say."
But the cock, as he was speaking, sud-
    denly 355
Out of his jaws lurched expeditiously,
And flew at once high up into a tree.
And when the fox saw that the cock was
    free,
"Alas," he said, "alas, O Chanticleer!
Inasmuch as I have given you cause for
    fear 360
By seizing you and bearing you away,
I have done you wrong, I am prepared
    to say.
But, sir, I did it with no ill intent.

Come down, and I shall tell you what I
    meant.
So help me God, it's truth I'll offer
    you!" 365
    "No, no," said he. "We're both fools,
    through and through.
But curse my blood and bones for the
    chief dunce
If you deceive me oftener than once!
You shall never again by flattery per-
    suade me
To sing and wink my eyes, by him that
    made me. 370
For he that willfully winks when he
    should see,
God never bless him with prosperity!"
    "Ah," said the fox, "with mischief
    may God greet
The man ungoverned, rash, and indis-
    creet
Who babbles when to hold his tongue
    were needful!" 375
    Such is it to be reckless and unheedful
And trust in flattery. But you who hold
That this is a mere trifle I have told,
Concerning only a fox, or a cock and
    hen,
Think twice, and take the moral, my
    good men! 380
For truly, of whatever is written, all
Is written for our doctrine, says St. Paul.

Then take the fruit, and let the chaff lie
    still.
Now, gracious God, if it should be your
    will,
As my Lord teaches, make us all good
    men   385
And bring us to your holy bliss! Amen.

381–382. The reference here is to St. Paul's
Epistle to the Romans, Chapter 15, verse 4.

◇◇◇◇◇◇◇◇◇◇◇◇◇◇◇◇◇◇◇◇◇◇◇◇◇

WORD STUDY

1. Write original phrases in which the following words are used: *azure, burnished, lurking, debonair, wary.* What is the color of *jet?*

2. Is there a difference in meaning between *superfluous* and *abundant?* What is the relationship between *discreet* and *cautious? iniquitous* and *evil? vicissitude* and *burden?* Explain.

FOR APPRECIATION

1. Why does Chaucer begin the tale by contrasting the poverty of the widow with the splendor of the rooster? Is there any social satire implied here? Discuss. Is it possible that Chanticleer and the hens with their fine airs may symbolize the Norman culture? Discuss.

2. Study in detail the imagery which Chaucer employs in his description of Chanticleer in lines 39–44; and of the fox in lines 79–86. Is there any connection between Chanticleer's physical beauty, his vanity, and his future fall? Discuss.

3. What artistic device is contained in lines 60–61?

4. Enumerate and discuss the details of the ideal husband as given by Partlet in lines 91–99.

5. Does Chanticleer's dream in lines 74–87 prepare us for his later misfortune? Explain.

6. What kind of arguments does Chanticleer use to refute Partlet's conviction that dreams are of no account? Enumerate these arguments. What type of human being might be symbolized in the learned Chanticleer? Discuss.

7. By what trickery was Chanticleer taken captive by the fox? Explain. How did he ultimately outfox the fox?

8. Select and discuss those lines which contain the medieval attitude towards women as found in many of the writings of that age. Note lines 246–247; is this a common artistic device?

9. Discuss the satire of the entire Tale, especially in lines 100; 178–181; 267–292.

10. What is the moral of the Tale as given by Chaucer at the conclusion of the story?

11. Chaucer wrote in what is known as the "heroic couplet." Explain this verse form and scan several of the lines.

RELATED READING

Chaucer's *The Pardoner's Tale* and *The Nun's Tale* should be required reading. In addition to these literary classics, you should read at least one of the following: *The Knight's Tale* or *The Clerk's Tale* or *The Man of Law's Tale.* These and other works of Chaucer may be read in the excellent modern translations by Nevill Coghill in the Penguin Books edition; in the *Portable Chaucer,* edited by Theodore Morrison in the Viking Portable Library; or in the translation of J. U. Nicholson.

Read at least one Passus or section of Langland's *Vision of Piers Plowman.* This has been translated into modern English by Henry W. Wells.

THE DRAMA IN MEDIEVAL ENGLAND

In modern times Church and stage have been uneasy bedfellows. The same was true in the first centuries of Christianity when the Church and the early Fathers had no use for actors. In Saint Augustine's time, a pagan actor who was converted to Christianity had to give up his profession. There was reason for such action, for drama had degenerated from the high level of the ancient Grecian tragedy which had its origin in religious worship. The only survivals of the drama left to the people of the Early Middle Ages were low forms of Roman comedy.

But like their modern counterparts, the common people had to be entertained. The ancient *mime*, a form of popular comedy, was taken over by the minstrels to satisfy the appetite of the populace for buffoonery. Rope walkers, monkey trainers, tumblers, and dancers often joined these troupers and performed wherever an open space and an audience could be found. Many of these folk-plays were pagan and frankly immoral.

Classic drama, on the other hand, withdrew to the quiet of the monasteries during the hectic centuries following the fall of Rome. In one such monastery, Roswitha, a Benedictine nun, wrote six plays in the classical tradition. Although composed against the background of the iron tenth century, they showed marvelous literary powers. But Roswitha was a literary personage born out of time, and her tenth century plays had little if any influence on the candle-lit drama that was rising in England.

THE MYSTERY AND MIRACLE PLAYS

The new medieval drama like that of the Greeks had its germ in religious worship. Born at the base of the altar, at the foot of the pulpit, it was, in its simpler form, merely illustrative of incidents in the life of Christ. The earliest preserved text, the *Quem-quaeritis*[1] trope[2] found at St. Gall, has divided a chorus at the Easter Mass into two antiphonal groups,[3] with the angels standing guard over Christ's sepulchre on one side and the women seeking Christ's Body on the other. The angels chant: "Whom seek ye in the sepulchre, O followers of Christ?" and the women respond that they have come in search of Jesus of Nazareth. Then the angels proclaim joyously that He has risen. The news is greeted with a glorious *Te Deum* sung by the whole congregation. Out of the episode of the three Marys at the tomb developed the Easter cycle; out of the Shepherds' quest came the Christmas cycle. Still later the day of doom was added, so that in the full-grown mystery cycle we have the sublime panoramic view extending from the creation of the world to the Last Judgment.

By gradual transition, the strictly Biblical subject matter was supplemented by stories from the lives of the great saints and martyrs of the Church. These saint-

[1] *Quem-Quaeritis*—Whom do you seek.
[2] TROPE—A trope is a further development of a passage in the Liturgy of the Church. Thus the "Whom do you seek" of the Easter angel was amplified into an Easter play.
[3] ANTIPHONAL GROUPS—Groups which alternately sing or chant a musical response.

plays were called *miracles* in contradistinction to the *mysteries* which dealt with the life of Christ. About 1250, however, many bishops were inclined to prohibit the clergy from taking part in these plays and to forbid the use of the church for their presentation. This attitude was not really intolerant, since in the momentum of dramatic development the performances were tending to take on the nature of comedy. Noah's wife stubbornly refused to leave dry land; always she made Noah's life miserable by her garrulous scolding. The devils, too, were a problem, jabbing the cherubs with their pitchforks. So the whole hilarious business was thrown out of church, bag and baggage.

Once outside, holiday crowds swarmed over the church yards and into the fields; and to accommodate their audience, the Guilds developed a system of high-wheeled carts that moved from one street to another, each stopping to present its scene of

THEATERS

ON WHEELS

the cycle. By the year 1400 in most of the leading English towns such as York, Chester, and Coventry, the Guilds had taken over these plays. In York, for example, there was developed a series of forty-eight plays. In this cycle an attempt was made to dramatize the Biblical story from the creation of the world to the Resurrection of Christ and the Harrowing of Hell. The various scenes were divided among the different Guilds with a naive appropriateness. In the York

95

Cycle, for example, the creation of the earth was presented by the plasterers' guild, the building of the Ark by the shipwrights, the turning of water into wine at Cana by the vintners, the Last Supper by the bakers; and at Chester the Harrowing of Hell was presented by the cooks and innkeepers. The expense list for one production included such items as "a pair of gloves for God—four pair of angels' wings—a pound of hemp to mend the angels' heads—and a torch for setting the world on fire."

In the fifteenth century there developed another type of play known as the *morality*. Allegorical figures were introduced to explain the point, the moral of the tale. Finally, the stories departed entirely from their Biblical foundation and told of ordinary man and his struggle for salvation. Saintly characters wore gilt hair and beards; souls were dressed in black or white coats depending on their destination; angels won admiring gasps from the audience with skins of gold and wings that flapped. But by popular acclaim the "star" was still the Devil. As stormy a villain as ever, he strode the boards, dressed in black or red, sometimes breathing smoke from his mouth, and often endowed with a long and agile tail. At his heels came Vice, in fool's clothes, whose duty it was to tease audience and Devil alike. Ultimately both were swept back by the Virtues into a gaping hell-mouth—smoky and sulphurous and, if it was an elaborate production, belching red flames at intervals.

◇◇◇◇◇

Everyman

A MORALITY PLAY

The greatest of all moralities is the famous fifteenth-century EVERYMAN. This morality is the story of how Everyman on his journey is abandoned by all but his Good Deeds, who alone will accompany him to the judgment seat of God and plead for him. Death hovers convincingly in the background like one of Holbein's spectral skeletons. The following selection will give a fair idea of the pathos, humanity, and exaltation of the play.

Here beginneth a treatise how the High Father of Heaven sendeth Death to summon every creature to come and give account of their lives in this world and is in manner of a moral play.

MESSENGER. I pray you all give your
  audience,
And hear this matter with reverence,
By figure a moral play—
  3. BY FIGURE—In form.

96

The *Summoning of Everyman* called
   it is,
That of our lives and ending shows   5
How transitory we be all day.
The story saith,—Man, in the begin-
   ning,
Look well, and take good heed to the
   ending,
Be you never so gay!
Ye think sin in the beginning full sweet,
Which in the end causeth thy soul to
   weep,   11
When the body lieth in clay.
Here shall you see how Fellowship and
   Jollity,
Both Strength, Pleasure, and Beauty 14
Will fade from thee as flower in May.
For ye shall hear, how our heaven king
Calleth Everyman to a general reckon-
   ing:
Give audience, and hear what he doth
   say.
   GOD. I perceive here in my majesty,
How that all creatures be to me unkind,
Living without dread in worldly pros-
   perity: 21
Of ghostly sight the people be so blind,
Drowned in sin, they know me not for
   their God;
In worldly riches is all their mind,
They fear not my rightwiseness, the
   sharp rod;   25
My law that I shewed, when I for them
   died,
They forget clean, and shedding of my
   blood red;
I hanged between two, it cannot be de-
   nied;
To get them life I suffered to be dead;
I healed their feet, with thorns hurt was
   my head: 30
I could do no more than I did truly,
And now I see the people do clean for-
   sake me.

22. GHOSTLY—Spiritual.
26. SHEWED—Showed.

They thank me not for the pleasure that
   I to them meant,
Nor yet for their being that I them have
   lent;
I proffered the people great multitude of
   mercy,   35
And few there be that asketh it heartily;
They be so cumbered with worldly
   riches,
That needs on them I must do justice,
On Everyman living without fear.
Where art thou, Death, thou mighty
   messenger?   40
   DEATH. Almighty God, I am here at
   your will,
Your commandment to fulfil.
   GOD. Go thou to Everyman.
And show him in my name
A pilgrimage he must on him take,   45
Which he in no wise may escape;
And that he bring with him a sure reck-
   oning
Without delay or any tarrying.
   DEATH. Lord, I will in the world go
   run over all,
And cruelly outsearch both great and
   small;   50
Every man will I beset that liveth beastly
Out of God's laws, and dreadeth not
   fully:
He that loveth riches I will strike with
   my dart,
His sight to blind, and from heaven to
   depart,   54
Except that alms be his good friend,
In hell for to dwell, world without end.
Lo, yonder I see Everyman walking;
Full little he thinketh on my coming;
His mind is on fleshly lusts and his treas-
   ure,
And great pain it shall cause him to en-
   dure   60
Before the Lord Heaven King.
Everyman, stand still; whither art thou
   going

50. OUTSEARCH—Seek out.

Thus gaily? Hast thou thy Maker forget?

EVERYMAN. Why askst thou?
Wouldest thou wete? 65

DEATH. Yea, sir, I will show you;
In great haste I am sent to thee
From God out of his majesty.

EVERYMAN. What, sent to me?

DEATH. Yea, certainly. 70
Though thou have forget him here,
He thinketh on thee in the heavenly sphere,
As, or we depart, thou shalt know.

EVERYMAN. What desireth God of me?

DEATH. That shall I show thee; 75
A reckoning he will needs have
Without any longer respite.

EVERYMAN. To give a reckoning longer leisure I crave;
This blind matter troubleth my wit.

DEATH. On thee thou must take a long journey: 80
Therefore thy book of count with thee thou bring;
For turn again thou cannot by no way,
And look thou be sure of thy reckoning:
For before God thou shalt answer, and show
Thy many bad deeds and good but a few; 85
How thou hast spent thy life, and in what wise,
Before the chief lord of paradise.

EVERYMAN. Full unready I am such reckoning to give.
I know thee not: what messenger art thou?

DEATH. I am Death, that no man dreadeth. 90
For every man I rest and no man spareth;

65. WETE—Know.
73. OR—Before.
79. WIT—Mind.
88. FULL—Most.
91. REST—Arrest.

For it is God's commandment
That all to me should be obedient.

EVERYMAN. O Death, thou comest when I had thee least in mind;
In thy power it lieth me to save, 95
Yet of my good will I give thee, if ye will be kind,
Yea, a thousand pound shalt thou have,
And defer this matter till another day.

DEATH. Everyman, it may not be by no way;
I set not by gold, silver, nor riches, 100
Ne by pope, emperor, king, duke, ne princes.
For and I would receive gifts great,
All the world I might get;
But my custom is clean contrary.
I give thee no respite: come hence, and not tarry. 105

EVERYMAN. Alas, shall I have no longer respite?
I may say Death giveth no warning:
To think on thee, it maketh my heart sick,
For all unready is my book of reckoning.
Wherefore, Death, I pray thee, for God's mercy, 110
Spare me till I be provided of remedy.

DEATH. Thee availeth not to cry, weep, and pray:
But haste thee lightly that you were gone the journey,
And prove thy friends if thou can.

EVERYMAN. Death, if I should this pilgrimage take, 115
And my reckoning surely make,
Show me, for saint charity,
Should I not come again shortly?

DEATH. No, Everyman; and thou be once there,
Thou mayst never more come here,
Trust me verily. 121

96. GOOD—Goods.
101. NE—Not.
117. SAINT—Holy.

EVERYMAN. O gracious God, in the
    high seat celestial,
Have mercy on me in this most need;
Shall I have no company from this vale
    terrestrial
Of mine acquaintance that way me to
    lead?   125
DEATH. Yea, if any be so hardy,
That would go with thee and bear thee
    company.
And now out of thy sight I will me hie;
See thou make thee ready shortly,
For thou mayst say this is the day   130
That no man living may scape away.
EVERYMAN. Alas, I may well weep
    with sighs deep;
Now have I no manner of company
To help me in my journey, and me to
    keep;   134
I would to God I had never be gete!
128. HIE—Betake.
131. SCAPE—Escape.
135. GETE—Born.

To my soul a full great profit it had be;
For now I fear pains huge and great.
The time passeth; Lord, help that all
    wrought;
For though I mourn it availeth nought.
To whom were I best my complaint to
    make?   140
What, and I to Fellowship thereof
    spake?
We have in the world so many a day
Be on good friends in sport and play.
I see him yonder, certainly;   144
I trust that he will bear me company;
Therefore to him will I speak to ease my
    sorrow.
Well met, good Fellowship, and good
    morrow!
FELLOWSHIP SPEAKETH. Everyman,
    good morrow by this day,

141. WHAT, AND I TO FELLOWSHIP THEREOF
SPAKE?—What if I should speak of this matter to *Fellowship*?

Sir, why lookest thou so piteously?
If any thing be amiss, I pray thee, me
   say,   150
That I may help to remedy.
   EVERYMAN. Yea, good Fellowship,
   yea,
I am in great jeopardy.
   FELLOWSHIP. Sir, I must needs know
   your heaviness;
I have pity to see you in any distress;
If any have you wronged ye shall re-
   venged be,   156
Though I on the ground be slain for
   thee,—
Though that I know before that I
   should die.
   EVERYMAN. Verily, Fellowship, gra-
   mercy.
   FELLOWSHIP. Tush! by thy thank I
   set not a straw.   160
Show me your grief, and say no more.
   EVERYMAN. I shall show you how
   it is;
Commanded I am to go a journey,
A long way, hard and dangerous,
And give a strait count without delay
Before the high judge Adonai.   166
Wherefore I pray you, bear me company
As ye have promised, in this journey.
   FELLOWSHIP. That is matter indeed!
   Promise is duty,
But, and I should take such a voyage
   on me,   170
I know it well, it should be to my pain:
Also it make me afeard, certain.
But let us take counsel here as well as
   we can,
For your words would fear a strong man.
   EVERYMAN. Why, ye said, If I had
   need,   175

159. GRAMERCY—Thanks.
165. STRAIT—Strict.
166. ADONAI—God.
170. AND—If.
170. VOYAGE—Journey.
174. FEAR—Frighten.

Ye would me never forsake, quick nor
   dead,
Though it were to hell truly.
   FELLOWSHIP. So I said, certainly,
And yet if thou wilt eat, and drink, and
   make good cheer,
Or haunt to women, the lusty com-
   pany,   180
I would not forsake you, while the day
   is clear,
Trust me verily!
   EVERYMAN. Yea, thereto ye would be
   ready;
To go to mirth, solace, and play,
Your mind will sooner apply   185
Than to bear me company in my long
   journey.
   FELLOWSHIP. Now, in good faith, I
   will not that way.
But and thou wilt murder, or any man
   kill,
In that I will help thee with a good will!
   EVERYMAN. O that is a simple advice
   indeed!   190
Gentle fellow, help me in my necessity;
We have loved long, and now I need,
And now, gentle Fellowship, remember
   me.
   FELLOWSHIP. Whether ye have loved
   me or no,   194
By Saint John, I will not with thee go.
   EVERYMAN. Yet I pray thee, take the
   labour, and do so much for me
To bring me forward, for saint charity,
And comfort me till I come without the
   town.
   FELLOWSHIP. Nay, and thou would
   give me a new gown,
I will not a foot with thee go;   200
But and you had tarried I would not
   have left thee so.
And as now, God speed thee in thy
   journey,

176. QUICK—Living.
187. WILL NOT—Have no desire.
190. A SIMPLE ADVICE—A silly idea.

For from thee I will depart as fast as I may.

EVERYMAN. Whither away, Fellowship? Will you forsake me?

FELLOWSHIP. Yea, by my fay, to God I betake thee.   205

EVERYMAN. Farewell, good Fellowship; for this my heart is sore;

Adieu for ever, I shall see thee no more.

FELLOWSHIP. In faith, Everyman, farewell now at the end;

For you I will remember that parting is mourning.

EVERYMAN. Alack! shall we thus depart indeed?   210

Lo, Fellowship forsaketh me in my most need:

Yet in my mind a thing there is;—

All my life I have loved riches;

If that my good now help me might,

He would make my heart full light.   215

I will speak to him in this distress.—

Where art thou, my Goods and riches?

GOODS. Who calleth me? Everyman? What haste thou hast!

I lie here in corners, trussed and piled so high,

And in chests I am locked so fast,   220

Also sacked in bags, thou mayst see with thine eye,

I cannot stir; in packs low I lie.

What would ye have, lightly me say.

EVERYMAN. Come hither, Goods, in all the haste thou may,

For of counsel I must desire thee.   225

GOODS. Sir, and ye in the world have trouble or adversity,

That can I help you to remedy shortly.

EVERYMAN. It is another disease that grieveth me;

In this world it is not, I tell thee so.

I am sent for another way to go,   230

To give a straight account general

Before the highest Jupiter of all;

And all my life I have had joy and pleasure in thee.

Therefore I pray thee go with me,

For, peradventure, thou mayst before God Almighty   235

My reckoning help to clean and purify;

For it is said ever among,

That money maketh all right that is wrong.

GOODS. Nay, Everyman, I sing another song,

I follow no man in such voyages;   240

For and I went with thee

Thou shouldst fare much the worse for me;

For because on me thou did set thy mind,

Thy reckoning I have made blotted and blind,

My condition is man's soul to kill;   245

If I save one, a thousand I do spill;

Weenest thou that I will follow thee?

Nay, from this world, not verily.

EVERYMAN. I had wend otherwise.

GOODS. Therefore to thy soul Good is a thief;   250

For when thou art dead, this is my guise

Another to deceive in the same wise

As I have done thee, and all to his soul's reprief.

EVERYMAN. O false Good, cursed thou be!

Thou traitor to God, that hast deceived me,   255

And caught me in thy snare.

GOODS. Marry, thou brought thyself in care,

Whereof I am glad,

I must needs laugh, I can not be sad.

EVERYMAN. Ah, Good, thou hast had long my heartly love   260

I gave thee that which should be the Lord's above.

235. PERADVENTURE—Perchance.
246. SPILL—Destroy.
251. GUISE—Practice.
253. REPRIEF—Reproof, shame.

205. FAY—Faith.
210. DEPART—Separate.

But wilt thou not go with me in deed?
I pray thee truth to say.
    GOODS. No, so God me speed,   264
Therefore farewell, and have good day.
    EVERYMAN. Of whom shall I now
    counsel take?
I think that I shall never speed
Till that I go to my Good-Deed,
But alas, she is so weak,
That she can neither go nor speak;   270
Yet will I venture on her now.—
My Good-Deeds, where be you?
    GOOD-DEEDS. Here I lie cold in the
    ground;
Thy sins hath me sore bound.
    EVERYMAN. Good-Deeds, I pray you,
    help me in this need,   275
Or else I am for ever damned indeed;
Therefore help me to make reckoning
Before the redeemer of all thing,
That king is, and was, and ever shall.
    GOOD-DEEDS. Everyman, I am sorry of
    your fall,   280
And fain would I help you, and I were
    able.
    EVERYMAN. Good-Deeds, your coun-
    sel I pray you give me.
    GOOD-DEEDS. That shall I do verily;
Though that on my feet I may not go,
I have a sister, that shall with you also,
Called Knowledge, which shall with you
    abide,   286
To help you to make that dreadful reck-
    oning.
    KNOWLEDGE. Everyman, I will go
    with thee, and be thy guide,
In thy most need to go by thy side.
    EVERYMAN. My Good-Deeds, gra-
    mercy;   290
I am well content, certainly,
With your words sweet.
    KNOWLEDGE. Now go we together
    lovingly,
To Confession, that cleansing river.

273. IN—On.

    EVERYMAN. For joy I weep; I would
    we were there;   295
But, I pray you, give me cognition
Where dwelleth that holy man, Confes-
    sion.
    KNOWLEDGE. In the house of salva-
    tion:
We shall find him in that place,
That shall us comfort by God's grace.
Lo, this is Confession; kneel down and
    ask mercy,   301
For he is in good conceit with God al-
    mighty.
    EVERYMAN. O glorious fountain that
    all uncleanness doth clarify,
Wash from me the spots of vices un-
    clean,
That on me no sin may be seen;   305
I come with Knowledge for my redemp-
    tion,
Repent with hearty and full contrition;
For I am commanded a pilgrimage to
    take,
And great accounts before God to make.
Now, I pray you, Shrift, mother of sal-
    vation,   310
Help my good deeds for my piteous ex-
    clamation.
    CONFESSION. I know your sorrow well,
    Everyman;
Because with Knowledge ye come to me,
I will you comfort as well as I can,
And a precious jewel I will give thee,
Called penance, wise voider of adver-
    sity;   316
Therewith shall your body chastised be,
With abstinence and perseverance in
    God's service:
Here shall you receive that scourge of
    me,
Which is penance strong, that ye must
    endure,   320
To remember thy Saviour was scouraged
    for thee

296. COGNITION—Information.
302. CONCEIT—Favor.
310. SHRIFT—Absolution.

With sharp scourages, and suffered it
  patiently;
So must thou, or thou scape that painful
  pilgrimage;
Knowledge, keep him in this voyage,
And by that time Good-Deeds will be
  with thee.   325
But in any wise, be sure of mercy,
For your time draweth fast, and ye will
  saved be;
Ask God mercy, and He will grant truly,
When with the scourage of penance
  man doth him bind,
The oil of forgiveness then shall he
  find.   330
  EVERYMAN. O eternal God, O heav-
  enly figure,
O way of rightwiseness, O goodly vision,
Which descended down in a virgin pure
Because he would Everyman redeem,
Which Adam forfeited by his disobedi-
  ence: 335
O blessed Godhead, elect and high-
  divine,
Forgive my grievous offence;
Here I cry thee mercy in this presence.
O ghostly treasure, O ransomer and re-
  deemer   339
Of all the world, hope and conductor,
Mirror of joy, and founder of mercy,
Which illumineth heaven and earth
  thereby,
Hear my clamorous complaint, though
  it late be;
Receive my prayers; unworthy in this
  heavy life,
Though I be, a sinner most abominable,
Yet let my name be written in Moses'
  table;   346
O Mary, pray to the Maker of all thing,
Me for to help at my ending,
And save me from the power of my
  enemy,
For Death assaileth me strongly;   350
And, Lady, that I may by means of thy
  prayer

Of your Son's glory to be partaker,
By means of his passion I it crave,
I beseech you, help my soul to save.—
Knowledge, give me the scourage of
  penance;   355
My flesh therewith shall give a quit-
  tance:
I will now begin, if God give me grace.
  KNOWLEDGE. Now, Everyman, be
  merry and glad;
Your Good-Deeds cometh now; ye may
  not be sad;
Now is your Good-Deeds whole and
  sound,   360
Going upright upon the ground.
  GOOD-DEEDS. Everyman, pilgrim, my
  special friend,
Blessed be thou without end;
For thee is prepared the eternal glory.
Ye have me made whole and sound,
Therefore I will abide by thee in every
  stound.   366
  EVERYMAN. Gramercy, Good-Deeds:
  now may I true friends see;
They have forsaken me every one;
I loved them better than my Good-
  Deeds alone.
Knowledge, will ye forsake me also?
  KNOWLEDGE. Yea, Everyman, when
  ye to death do go: 371
But not yet for no manner of danger.
  EVERYMAN. Gramercy, Knowledge,
  with all my heart.
  KNOWLEDGE. Nay, yet I will not from
  hence depart,
Till I see where ye shall be come.   375
  EVERYMAN. Methinketh, alas, that I
  must be gone,
To make my reckoning and my debts
  pay,
For I see my time is nigh spent away.
Take example, all ye that this do hear
  or see,
How they that I loved best do forsake
  me,   380
366. STOUND—Season.

Except my Good-Deeds that bideth
  truly.
  GOOD-DEEDS. All earthly things is but
    vanity:
Beauty, Strength, and Discretion, do
  man forsake,
Foolish friends and kinsmen, that fair
  spake,
All fleeth save Good-Deeds, and that
  am I.   385
  EVERYMAN. Have mercy on me, God
    most mighty;
And stand by me, thou Mother and
  Maid, holy Mary.
  GOOD-DEEDS. Fear not, I will speak
    for thee.

  EVERYMAN. Here I cry God mercy.
  GOOD-DEEDS. Short our end, and min-
    ish our pain;   390
Let us go and never come again.
  EVERYMAN. Into thy hands, Lord, my
    soul I commend;
Receive it, Lord, that it be not lost;
As thou me boughtest, so me defend,
And save me from the fiend's boast,
That I may appear with that blessed
  host   396
That shall be saved at the day of doom.
In manus tuas—of might's most
For ever—*commendo spiritum meum.*

398. *In manus tuas* . . . —"Into Thy
hands I commend my spirit."

FOR DISCUSSION

1. What is the reaction of Everyman to the summons which he receives? What companions does he wish to bring with him on his journey? Which companions can accompany him, and which cannot? Explain.

2. What does Knowledge do for him? Enumerate in detail what Confession does for him.

3. Explain the meaning of lines 245–253.

4. Explain just why the play is an allegory.

5. How does a Catholic sense of values help in the appreciation of the play? Discuss.

6. What qualities in this play give it as much appeal to a twentieth-century audience as it gave to a fifteenth-century one?

7. It has been said that there is no tragedy in medieval drama. Why is this true of *Everyman*, even though the protagonist or leading character descends to the grave?

RELATED READING

Read at least one of the following mystery plays: *Noah, Abraham and Isaac, The Second Shepherd's Play.* They can be found in C. G. Child's edition of Early English Plays.

Further Readings—Middle English Period

* BELLOC, HILAIRE, *William the Conqueror* (biography)
* CERVANTES, MIGUEL DE, *Don Quixote* (fiction)
* CHESTERTON, G. K. *Chaucer* (biographical study)
  CHUTE, MARCHETTE, *Geoffrey Chaucer of England* (biographical study)
  DAVIS, WILLIAM STEARNS, *Life on a Medieval Barony*
* DINNIS, ENID, *The Anchorhold* (fiction)
  DOYLE, SIR ARTHUR CONAN, *The White Company* (fiction)
  ELIOT, THOMAS S., *Murder in the Cathedral* (drama)

* MADELEVA, SISTER M., *Chaucer's Nuns and Other Essays; The Pearl*
  MALONE, KEMP, *Chapters on Chaucer* (critical study)
* NOYES, ALFRED, *Sherwood* (poetry)
  PORTER, JANE, *Scottish Chiefs* (fiction)
* PRESTON, RAYMOND, *Chaucer* (critical study)
  SALZMAN, L. F., *English Life in the Middle Ages*
  SCOTT, WALTER, *Ivanhoe, The Talisman* (fiction)
  SHAKESPEARE, WILLIAM, *King John, Richard II* (drama)
  TENNYSON, ALFRED, *Idylls of the King* (poetry)

St. Thomas More (1478–1535).

THE RENAISSANCE AND
THE ELIZABETHAN AGE

1 5 0 0 – 1 6 0 3

The century after Chaucer's death was one of political confusion, of civil and foreign wars, and of economic disasters. In 1485, Henry Tudor brought the civil War of the Roses to an end with his victory over Richard III on Bosworth Field. Henry VII was officially recognized as King by Parliament, and thus began the reign of the Tudors which was to have such a devastating effect on English Catholic history.

During the early hectic years of the fifteenth century, there was little literary activity. In the last quarter of the century, however, William Caxton took up the new art of printing and began publishing English books. An enthusiastic admirer of both Chaucer and Malory, he edited the *Canterbury Tales* and *Morte d'Arthur* and wrote an introduction to both.

Renaissance means "rebirth" and is intended to describe a renewed interest in the classics and the Graeco-Roman culture which took fire in Italy and swept over the rest of Europe in the fifteenth and sixteenth centuries. Unfortunately in Italy this "new learning" with its emphasis on the natural man led to rank paganism. Many Italians not only highly esteemed the beauty of Homer, Aristotle, Plato, the Greek tragedians, Vergil, and Cicero, but they also made the pagan ideal of life their own. Italian writers like Boccaccio and Petrarch portrayed the Kingdom of Man as more desirable than the Kingdom of God. In their enthusiasm for the natural beauty of the pagan ideal, they exaggerated man's importance as the center of the universe to the neglect of his highest dignity—his relationship to God and his supernatural destiny. Thus, in contrast to the spirit of the Middle Ages, the universe of man's thoughts and actions became *homocentric* (man-centered) rather than *theocentric* (God-centered).

THE EARLY

RENAISSANCE

It would be a mistake, however, to consider the Renaissance as a complete reaction against the teachings and culture of the Middle Ages. In fact, modern scholars are now beginning to see that the Renaissance was a natural outgrowth of the Middle Ages in many respects. Classical literature had been known and studied throughout the Middle Ages. It was the medieval monks who copied the ancient classics before the time of the printing press and preserved them for future generations. The whole culture of the Middle Ages was built upon ancient Latin and Greek thought that had been Christianized. The interest which men had taken in philosophy and theology for centuries led to a natural reaction in favor of the humanities—the literature of Greece and Rome. The emphasis shifted from a search for truth to a search for beauty. But the greatest beauty of the Renaissance was in the Cathedral, the religious painting and sculpture of men like Michelangelo and Raphael, men working in the great Catholic tradition of St. Augustine of Hippo, St. Bernard, St. Thomas Aquinas, Dante, and Chaucer.

The intoxication that was found in the beauty of art and literature, as contrasted with the more sober discipline of logic and philosophy, led many men to condemn philosophy and theology and even to replace religion by an adoration of human beauty. It must be admitted that a great many of these excesses could have been avoided if the great philosophy of St. Thomas Aquinas had not fallen into disrepute during the late fourteenth and fifteenth centuries.

There were, then, two currents of Renaissance thinking. One carried on the Catholic tradition and incorporated it into art, letters, Christian philosophy, religion, the sacredness of love, and the supernatural dignity of man. The other emphasized the material, the carnal, and the pagan pursuit of beauty and natural perfection. It stood for freedom from law and the shackles of the Catholic Church, and for the "infinite desire" to perfect the natural capacities of man as an individual.

SAINT THOMAS MORE

The beginnings of the Renaissance in England were a much more balanced affair simply because its early leaders and scholars were Catholic humanists. Men like Colet, Linacre, Grocyn, St. Thomas More, and St. John Fisher brought to the love of the classics and the humanistic ideal the spirit of Christian humility and the total understanding of man's natural and supernatural relationship to God—his final end and ultimate source of wisdom and beauty.

In St. Thomas More we have one of the greatest of all great Englishmen. From his birth in 1478 until his execution by his old friend Henry VIII in 1535, he gave England and posterity an example of Christian sanity, sanctity, statesmanship, and scholarship perhaps never before nor since combined in one man.

More rose rapidly in his profession as a lawyer and at twenty-six was sent to Parliament. He successively and successfully became Under-Sheriff of London, a member of the King's Council, Under-Treasurer of England, Speaker of the House of Commons, and finally at fifty-one Lord Chancellor of the Realm—the first layman ever to hold that position. As a statesman and trusted adviser of Henry VIII, he represented that monarch on the most difficult diplomatic missions. A devoted husband and father, he was a friend of the poor, a champion of peace, an ardent apologist against the new heresies, and a defender of the Papacy. A man of the world who daily brushed shoulders with the high and mighty as well as with the outcast, a man whose sense of laughter made him live "for the next world but was merry withal," an heroic saint, who daily wore a hair-shirt, "whose soul was more pure than snow"—this is but a brief etching of More, the man of letters, who stands as the bridge which spans the medieval and the modern world. He is "one of the founders of modern literature," and he is the connecting link in the continuity of English Catholic thought from Bede and Chaucer to Chesterton.

Thomas More was undoubtedly a man of the Renaissance. In the field of the humanities he was as much a pioneer as his distinguished teacher, Colet, and his intimate friend Erasmus, the Dutch humanist, who had been invited to teach Greek at Oxford at the request of that other great humanist, St. John Fisher. More's *Utopia*, a delightful satire on government, society, and economic repression was England's first significant contribution to Renaissance literature. In it we see the influence of Plato's *Republic*, Plutarch's *Lives*, St. Augustine's *City of God*, and Amerigo Vespucci's *Voyages*. But the Christian humanist is at work in the *Utopia*, where More artistically portrays a dream world in which pagans guided by reason only seem to regard Christian values more highly than Christians do.

It is unfortunate that More is known only for his *Utopia* which, because of its apparently revolutionary ideas on society's and man's mode of living, has had an appeal for the radical in every century. Very few realize that More wrote controversy in English prose and that his *Richard III*, *Four Last Things*, and *Dialogue of Comfort* were recognized by both his contemporaries and later critics as outstanding examples of literary composition. In the preface to More's collected *Works*, published in 1557, William Rastell wrote that More had written "books so many and so well, as no one Englishman ever wrote the like, whereby his works be worthy to be had and read of every English man that is desirous to know and learn, not only the eloquence and property of the English tongue, but also the true doctrine of Christ's Catholic Church."

MORE'S PLACE IN

LITERATURE

It may surprise us to learn that during the Age of Elizabeth *Richard III* was printed five times within a space of twenty years. It formed the basis of Shakespeare's play and was called by an Elizabethan critic "the best written part of all our Chronicles." In the days of the Stuarts, More was regarded as among the half dozen English writers who "speak the best and purest English," and Ben Jonson, in his *English Grammar*, quotes More more frequently than any other prose work.

In his last official act as Chancellor, More wrote a long defense of liberal education and the study of Greek, which he sent to the faculty of Oxford University. This was done to thwart some of the more conservative clergy who were attempting to make a seminary out of Oxford. It is ironic that the same Henry who approved this course of action was very shortly to condemn More to the executioner's axe. It is also ironic and tragic that Henry turned from More's book *Utopia*, which he had admired so much for its gentle philosophy of government, to the infamous *Il Principe* (*The Prince*) by the Italian, Machiavelli. Encouraged by Thomas Cromwell to study Machiavelli, Henry was transformed from a Defender of the Faith, a lover of the arts, and the great friend of Thomas More into being his own pope, the destroyer of the culture of the ages, and executioner of his dearest friend. Since Henry's day *The Prince* has been the guide of many another ruthless dictator and tyrant.

With the beheading of Sir Thomas More and John Fisher, the early bloom of a truly Christian Renaissance in England was blighted, if not entirely killed; for More and Fisher gave an example of what a Christian Renaissance could have been and, perhaps, in our own day, may yet be.

The death of these two martyrs indicates another phase of Henry VIII's reign which had a tremendous effect on England's future history and literature. These men died because they refused to acknowledge Henry as supreme head of the Church of England. Henry had cut himself, and would soon cut his realm, from the Church. He ordered the devastation of the monasteries and the filling of the royal coffers with their wealth and property. Not since the invasion of the Danes had there been such pillaging and wanton destruction of priceless relics and manuscripts. The glass of Lincoln Cathedral was used as a mark for crossbow practice, and few remonstrated.

The revolt from the ancient Catholic Faith grew under Henry's daughter, Elizabeth. From that time on England was gradually Protestantized, but the culture which several centuries of Catholicism had given her lived on in her literature.

◇◇◇◇◇

RICHARD III

THOMAS MORE

The historical piece, RICHARD III, is a fragment of what Sir Thomas More had planned to be a complete history of his own times. However, engaged as he was with his controversial works and with the completion of UTOPIA, the history was never finished. Nevertheless, the fragment holds a high place in English historical prose. Shakespeare was heavily indebted to it for his play, RICHARD III. It can be said truly that with his dramatic narrative power, More initiated the art of modern historical writing in England.

The selection which appears below is a short passage from the history. More has shown how the Duke of Gloucester, appointed protector to the boy-king, Edward V, has had himself declared King Richard III and has determined to rid himself of his nephews, Edward and the younger brother, Richard. The King entrusted the job to his henchman, Sir James Tyrell, who in turn employed assassins to murder the princes in the Tower. In the passage below, More depicts the murder, and then relates the tragic end of the King and his assassins. When Henry VII defeated Richard on the field of Bosworth in 1485, he brought to an end the Civil War of the Roses and inaugurated the Tudor dynasty.

For Sir James Tyrell [1] devised that they should be murdered in their beds. To the execution whereof he appointed Miles Forest, one of the four that kept them, a fellow fleshed in murder beforetime. To him he joined one John Dighton, his own horsekeeper, a big broad square strong knave. Then all the others being removed from them, this Miles Forest and John Dighton about midnight (the sely [2] children lying their beds) came into the chamber, and suddenly lapped them up among the clothes, so bewrapped them and entangled them, keeping down by force the featherbed and pillows hard unto their mouths, that within a while smored [3] and stifled, their breath failing, they gave up to God their innocent souls into the joys of heaven, leaving to the tormentors their bodies dead in the bed. Which after that the wretches perceived, first by the struggling with the pains of death, and after long lying still to be thoroughly dead, they laid their bodies naked out upon the bed, and fetched Sir James to see them. Which upon the sight of them, caused those murderers to bury them at the stair foot, meetly [4] deep in the ground under a great heap of stones. Then rode Sir James in great haste to King Richard, and showed him all the manner of the murder; who gave him great thanks and, as some say, there made him knight. But he allowed not, as I have heard, the burying in so vile a corner, saying that he would have them buried in a better place, because they were a King's sons.

Lo, the honourable courage of a King! Whereupon, they say that a priest of Sir Robert Brakenbery [5] took up the bodies again, and secretly interred them in such a place as, by the occasion of his death which only knew it, [6] could never since come to light. Very truth is it and well knowen, that at such time as Sir James Tyrell was in the Tower for treason committed against the most famous prince King Henry the seventh, [7] both Dighton and he were examined and confessed the murder in manner above written; but whither the bodies were removed they could nothing tell.

And thus as I have learned of them that much knew and little cause had to lie, were these two noble princes, these innocent tender children, born of most royal blood, brought up in great wealth, likely long to live to reign and rule in the realm, by traitorous tyranny taken, deprived of their estate, shortly shut up in prison, and privily slain and murdered, their bodies cast God wot [8] where, by the cruel ambition of their unnatural uncle and his dispiteous [9] tormentors. Which things on every part well pondered, God never gave this world a more notable example, neither in what unsurety standeth this worldly weal, or what mischief worketh the proud enterprise of an high heart, or finally what wretched end ensueth such dispiteous

[1] SIR JAMES TYRELL—Tyrell was a strong supporter of the Yorkists and became Richard's Master of the Horse. He was later taken into favor by Henry VII but was ultimately beheaded for conspiracy against Henry in 1502.

[2] SELY—Innocent.

[3] SMORED—Smothered.

[4] MEETLY—Here the word means "moderately."

[5] SIR ROBERT BRAKENBERY—Keeper of London Tower to whom the Duke of Clarence related his horrible dream. See Shakespeare's *Richard III*, Sc. 4.

[6] BY THE OCCASION OF HIS DEATH WHICH ONLY KNEW IT—"when he—the only one who knew it—died." That is, the priest of Sir Robert of Brakenbery was the only one who knew where the princes were reburied, and when he died the secret died with him.

[7] KING HENRY THE SEVENTH—Henry defeated Richard III at Bosworth.

[8] WOT—To know, the present tense of "wit."

[9] DISPITEOUS—Pitiless, merciless.

cruelty. For first, to begin with the ministers, Miles Forest at Saint Martin's piecemeal rotted away. Dighton indeed yet walketh on alive, in good possibility to be hanged ere he die. But Sir James Tyrell died at Tower Hill, beheaded for treason. King Richard himself, as ye shall hereafter hear, slain in the field, hacked and hewed of his enemies' hands, harried on horseback dead, his hair in despite torn and togged [10] like a cur dog: and the mischief that he took, within less than three years of the mischief that he did. And yet all the mean time spent in much pain and trouble outward, much fear, anguish, and sorrow within. For I have heard by credible report of such as were secret with his chamberers, that after this abominable deed done, he never had quiet in his mind, he never thought himself sure. Where he went abroad, his eyen whirled about, his body privily fenced, his hand ever on his dagger, his countenance and manner like one alway ready to strike again; he took ill rest a nights, lay long waking and musing, sore wearied with care and watch, rather slumbered than slept, troubled with fearful dreams, suddenly sometime sterte up, leape out of his bed

[10] TOGGED—Pulled about, mauled.

and runne [11] about the chamber, so was his restless heart continually tossed and tumbled with the tedious impression and stormy remembrance of his abominable deed.

[11] STERTE, LEAPE, RUNNE—These are old past tenses of "start," "leap," "run."

FOR DISCUSSION

1. Study the balance and rhythm of More's sentences, his use of alliteration, his colorful and graphic action words. Choose several sentences in the passage and analyze them for the above qualities.

2. Explain the satire in More's remark: "Lo, the honourable courage of a King!" Is there something almost prophetic in this statement? What happened to More?

3. Note how dramatically More describes Richard's reaction to the murder. Mention several other tyrants in history and literature who suffered similar fates.

PROJECTS

1. Compare More's description of the murder with that in Shakespeare's Richard III, Act IV, Sc. 3.

2. Give the historical background of the War of the Roses.

3. Write a description of the tragic end of some tyrant. Be as graphic and dramatic as possible.

ST. THOMAS MORE'S
DEFENSE AND EXECUTION

WILLIAM ROPER

Here we are interested in More the man and the saint, whom Swift called "the person of the greatest virtue this Kingdom ever produced." Since his canonization in 1935, many books have been written about him; but all of them must rely upon his first biographer, his son-in-law, William Roper. Roper has the distinction not only of having written an excellent life of St. Thomas More, but also of having written the first biography in the English language.

The selections which we shall read have been re-written in modern English. A few lines of the original will be quoted at the end of the passage.

The Jury found him guilty. And immediately upon their verdict the Lord Chancellor, beginning to proceed in judgment against him, Sir Thomas More said to him: "My Lord, when I practiced Law, the manner in such case was to ask the prisoner before judgment why judgment should not be given against him." Whereupon the Lord Chancellor, staying his judgment, wherein he had partly proceeded, demanded of him what he was able to say to the contrary. More then most humbly made answer as follows:

"For as much, my Lord," said he, "this indictment is grounded upon an Act of Parliament [1] directly repugnant to the laws of God and His holy Church, the supreme government of which, or any part thereof, may no temporal prince presume by any law to take upon him, as rightfully belonging to the See of Rome, a spiritual pre-eminence specially granted by special prerogative by the mouth of our Savior Himself, personally present on earth, only to St. Peter and his successors, Bishops of the same See. It is therefore in law among Christian men insufficient to charge any Christian man." And for proof thereof, he declared that this Realm, being but one member and a small part of the Church, might not make a particular law disagreeable with the general law of

[1] ACT OF PARLIAMENT—On March 30, 1534, an Act of Parliament was passed requiring from all subjects an oath limiting the succession of the crown to the children of Henry VIII and Anne Boleyn. Parliament prescribed no definite form of the oath but Henry's commissioners drafted a form which not only insured Elizabeth's right to succession but invalidated Henry's marriage to Catherine, made valid Henry's marriage to Anne, and repudiated any oath that had been taken "to any foreign authority, prince, or potentate."

Christ's universal Catholic Church. No more than the city of London, being but one poor member in respect of the whole realm, might make a law against an Act of Parliament to bind the whole realm. He further showed that it was contrary both to the laws and statutes of our own Land yet unrepealed, as they might easily perceive in the *Magna Charta:* [2] *Quod ecclesia Anglicana libera sit, et habeat omnia jura sua integra et libertates suas illaesas.* [3] It was also contrary to that sacred oath which the King's Highness himself and every other Christian prince always with great solemnity received at the coronations. He alleged moreover that no more might this Realm of England refuse obedience to the See of Rome than might the child refuse obedience to his own natural father. For as St. Paul said of the Corinthians: "I have regenerated you, my children, in Christ." So might St. Gregory, Pope of Rome, of whom, by St. Augustine,[4] his messenger, we first received the Christian faith, of us Englishmen truly say: "You are my children, because I have given to you everlasting salvation, a far higher and better inheritance than any carnal father can leave to his child, and by regeneration made you my spiritual children in Christ."

[The Lord Chancellor then accused More of "stiffly sticking" contrary to the Bishops and learned men of the Realm. More claimed the support of the Clergy and learned men of the past and affirmed that he was not bound to "conform my conscience to the Council of One Realm against the general Council of Christendom." The Lord Chancellor, not desiring to have the burden of judgment entirely upon himself asked the advice of Lord FitzJames, Chief Justice of the King's Bench. The Chief Justice replied that "if the Act of Parliament be lawful, then the Indictment is good enough." Sentence was then passed against More and he returned to the Tower led by Sir William Kingston, Constable of the Tower and a dear friend of More. More comforts Kingston by saying: "Trouble not yourself but be of good cheer; for I will pray for you, and my good Lady, your wife, that we may meet in heaven together, where we shall be merry for ever and ever." We now continue in Roper's own words.]

When Sir Thomas More came to Westminster to the Tower[5] again, his daughter, my wife, desirous to see her father, whom she thought she would never see in this world again, and also to have his final blessing, watched at the Tower Wharf, where she knew he would pass by, before he could enter the Tower. As soon as she saw him, after reverently receiving his blessing on her knees she hastened towards him, without consideration or care of herself, pressed into the midst of the throng and company of the guard that were round about him, hastily ran to him, and there openly in the sight of them all embraced him and took him about the neck and kissed him. . . .

So remained Sir Thomas More in the Tower, more than a week after his trial.

[2] MAGNA CHARTA—The Great Charter which the English barons forced King John to sign at Runnymede in 1215. It laid the foundation for English religious, political, and personal freedom.

[3] *Quod ecclesia . . . suas illaesas.*—An article of the Magna Charta which gave autonomy or self-government to the English Church: "That the English Church should be free, that all its rights should be held inviolate, and that its liberties should be unimpaired."

[4] ST. AUGUSTINE—St. Augustine was sent by St. Gregory to convert the Anglo-Saxons in 597.

[5] TOWER—The Tower was the official prison of London.

Whence, the day before he suffered, he sent his shirt of hair,[6] not willing to have it seen, to my wife, his dearly beloved daughter, and a letter written with a piece of charcoal, plainly expressing the fervent desire he had to be executed on the morrow. The letter said: "I cumber you, good Margaret, much, but I would be sorry if it should be any longer than tomorrow. For tomorrow is St. Thomas' even, the sixth of July; and therefore to-morrow I long to go to God. It is a day very meet and convenient for me. I never liked your manner better towards me than when you kissed me last. For I like when daughterly love and dear charity hath no leisure to look to worldly courtesy."

And so on the next morning, being Tuesday, St. Thomas' even, in the year of our Lord 1535, according as he in his letter the day before had wished, early in the morning came to him Sir Thomas Pope, his very good friend, with a message from the King and the Council, that he should before nine of the clock of the same morning suffer death; and that therefore he should forthwith prepare himself thereto.

"Master Pope," said he, "for your tidings I heartily thank you. I have been always much bounden to the King's Highness for the benefits and honors that he has from time to time most bountifully heaped upon me; and yet I am more bound to His Grace for putting me into this place, where I have had convenient time and space to think about my end. And so help me God, most of all, Master Pope, am I bound to His Highness, because it pleases him so shortly to rid me out of the miseries of this wretched world; and therefore I will not fail earnestly to pray for His

[6] SHIRT OF HAIR—A shirt made of horse hair, used as an instrument of penance.

Grace, both here, and also in the world to come."

"The King's pleasure is further," said Master Pope, "that at your execution you shall not use many words."

"Master Pope," More replied, "you do well to give me warning of His Grace's pleasure; for other wise, at that time I purposed to have spoken at some length; but of no matter wherewith His Grace or any other should have cause to be offended. Nevertheless, whatsoever I had intended to say I am ready obediently to conform myself to His Grace's commandment; and I beseech you, Master Pope, to arrange with His Highness that my daughter Margaret may be at my burial."

"The King has consented already," said Master Pope, "that your wife, children, and other friends shall have liberty to be present thereat."

"O how much beholden, then," said Thomas More, "am I unto His Grace, who permits me to have so gracious consideration at my poor burial!"

Wherewithal, Master Pope, taking his leave of him, could not refrain from weeping. Sir Thomas More perceiving this, comforted him in this wise: "Quiet yourself, good Master Pope, and be not discomforted, for I trust that we shall some time see each other in heaven full merrily, where we shall be sure to live and love together, in joyful bliss eternally."

Upon this departure, Sir Thomas More, as one that has been invited to some solemn feast, changed himself into his best apparel. Master Lieutenant observing, advised him to put it off, saying that he who should have it was but a rascal.

"What, Master Lieutenant?" quoth he, "shall I account him a rascal that shall do me this day so singular a bene-

fit? Nay, I assure you, were it cloth of gold, I think it well bestowed on him, as St. Cyprian [7] did, who gave his executioner thirty pieces of gold." And although at length through Master Lieutenant's importunate persuasion, he altered his apparel; yet, after the example of the holy martyr St. Cyprian, he gave of the little money that was left him a coin of gold to his executioner.

And so he was brought by Master Lieutenant out of the Tower, and from thence led towards the place of execution. Going up to the scaffold, which was so weak that it was ready to fall, he said merrily to the Lieutenant, "I pray you, Master Lieutenant, see me safe up: and for my coming down let me shift for myself."

And then he desired all the people

[7] ST. CYPRIAN—Bishop of Carthage and martyr. Famous apologist of the third century.

thereabout to pray for him, and to bear witness with him, that he should suffer death in and for the faith of the holy Catholic Church. Which done, he kneeled down, and after his prayers were said, turned to the executioner with a cheerful countenance, and said to him, "Pluck up thy spirits, man, and be not afraid to do your office. My neck is very short. Take heed, therefore, that you do not strike awry."

So passed Sir Thomas More out of this world to God, upon the very same day which he most desired.

[The following is a brief selection from Roper's original. It is a good example of English prose in transition from Middle English. Note the difference in spelling.]

And so was he by master Leiuetenaunte brought out of the Tower, and from thence led to [wardes] the place of execution. Where, goinge uppe the scaffold, which was so weake that it was ready to fall, he saide merilye to master Leiuetenaunte: "I pray you, master Leiuetenaunte, see me salf uppe, and for my cominge downe let me shifte for my self."

Then desired he all the people thereaboute to pray for him, and to beare witness with him that he should (nowe there) suffer death in and for the faith of the holy chatholik churche. Whiche done, he kneled downe, and after his prayers said, turned to the executioner; and with a cheerefull countenaunce spake (thus) to him: "Plucke upp thy spirites, man, and be not afrayde to do thine office; my necke is very shortc; take heede therefore thow strike not awrye, for savinge of thine honestye."

So passed Sir Thomas More out of this world to god uppon the very same daye in which himself had most desired.

◇◇◇◇◇◇◇◇◇◇◇◇◇◇◇◇◇◇◇◇◇◇◇◇◇◇

FOR DISCUSSION

1. Note the simplicity of Roper's style. Judging from the selection you have just read, do you think Roper is a good biographer? Explain.
2. Was Margaret More's public display of affection for her father dangerous? Explain.
3. Outline the arguments which More used to show that the Act of Parliament was against the laws of God and His Church.
4. Why did More wish to die on July 6?
5. What evidence of heroic sanctity is found in the selection?
6. Discuss this comment of Addison written two centuries after More's death: "The innocent mirth which had been so conspicuous in his life, did not forsake him to the last."

WORD STUDY

What does *knave* mean today? What did it mean in More's day? Look up the definition of *weal* and *cumber*. What is the connection between *weal* and *commonwealth*? Explain the meaning of the expression a *fellow fleshed in murder*. Make sure you know the meaning of *prerogative, allege, interred*.

PROJECTS

1. Read and be prepared to discuss More's defense of a liberal education as quoted in Charles A. Brady's *Stage of Fools*, pp. 230-235.
2. More's *Utopia* is a widely discussed book. Class members may take certain chapters from the book for special reports and class discussion. Basis for discussion: Why does *Utopia* interest the twentieth century world?
3. In his epilogue to his *Life of More*, Christopher Hollis writes that four things were killed when More was killed: learning, justice, laughter, and holiness. Read the two page epilogue and make an oral or written report on it.
4. St. Thomas More was executed at Tyburn, a place sacred in the history of English Catholicism. Mention several other English martyrs who were executed there.
5. Write a brief biographical sketch of "More, the Ideal Family Man."

RELATED READING

Read the article on Thomas More in *Jubilee*, July, 1954.

You must read Charles A. Brady's *Stage of Fools*, an excellent dramatic and historical presentation of the life and times of Thomas More, written in the form of a novel.

A great scholar's estimate of More may be found in R. W. Chambers' *Thomas More* and in his *The Place of St. Thomas More in English Literature and History*.

THE ELIZABETHAN AGE

1 5 5 8 – 1 6 0 3

When the daughter of Henry VIII and Anne Boleyn took the throne, England's future looked rather meager. The treasury was empty, the army disbanded, the navy second-rate. But Elizabeth, whatever else she may have been, was no fool. And along with a red wig and a sharp tongue, she possessed a will of iron.

Forty-five years she reigned successfully. Under her rule the monarchy was established, and England attained great material prestige and prosperity. It was a swaggering, swashbuckling age given to exalting itself, its wealth, its achievements. And the people were persuaded to associate all this with her whom her subjects called their "virgin queen."

Mary, Queen of Scotland, one-time Queen of France and now claimant to the English throne through her grandmother, the daughter of Henry VII, threatened Elizabeth's security. Graciously lovely at nineteen, Catholic, and rich in foreign influence, Mary was unwelcome at Elizabeth's court where she had fled from Scotland. Political expediency favored her death, but Elizabeth kept her prisoner for twenty years before she sent her to the guillotine on a charge of plotting against the Queen's life. The tragic Queen of Scots moved all who met her to pity, but her death brought unity and strength to England. Under condemnation of death Mary had appealed to Philip of Spain to avenge her and to secure the throne for her son. At her death, Philip assembled a large fleet and army, which set out in 1588. Elizabeth made hasty preparations to meet the invasion, and the smaller English fleet under Sir Francis Drake attacked the enemy spread out in a seven-mile crescent across the English Channel. Of the hundred and fifty vessels in the Spanish Armada, less than a third escaped. Although the victory was due as much to weather conditions favoring the English as to their skill and daring, the victory was none the less a tremendous one. It marked England's emergence as a world power, and patriotic enthusiasm ran high. Pride in the British navy has ever since been traditional.

MARY, QUEEN

OF SCOTS

Elizabeth's reign was distinguished for her policy of colonization. We who live in a world that has shrunk to a neighborhood, whose farthest point—the air-line advertisements tell us—is at most forty hours from our doorstep, can hardly realize what an impact the discovery of the vast new continent of America in 1492 had on people's minds. Men set out to hunt fabulous silver mines and rivers whose waters rolled over precious stones. The expeditions were manned by "apt young men" from the West country, and financed in part by the great Queen herself. And as the ships swung down the tide, untold wealth seemed to be had only for the questing. Large merchant companies such as the Hudson Bay Company and the East India Company were chartered to trade with Russia and the Far East. And there were freebooters like Drake, Hawkins, and Sir Walter Raleigh who came back to England with hoards of gold pirated from Spanish vessels. The new attitude, whereby man was willing to undergo very great risks in the hope of exorbitant gains,

was likewise responsible for a multitude of get-rich-quick schemes. Everything from alchemy [1] to the retrieving of drowned lands was attempted.

Manufacturing received promotion and encouragement. Agriculture was studied and improved. The bourgeoisie came into economic and political power. The capitalist system was taking shape. From within, the feudal system had been dissipated by the general breakdown of medieval civilization, and from without by the economic and social policies of Henry VIII and Elizabeth. It was an age of production for profit and self-aggrandizement, of exploitation of the dispossessed, of new methods of "mass-production" and tenant-farming.

As far back as the time of Chaucer, educated Englishmen had been traveling abroad and had been gradually assimilating the Italian Renaissance ideal with its emphasis on the individual. The wide accomplishments of such universal geniuses as Michelangelo and Leonardo da Vinci stirred men's ambition. The gradual advance in the sciences and arts of the continent coupled with the discoveries of new lands made the possibility of human progress seem limitless. The whole political and economic structure was undergoing a change. With all these new ideas in the air, together with the introduction of the printing press, it is not to be wondered at that this was one of the most productive eras of English literature.

Elizabeth's chief contributions to England were these: she gave it fifty years of comparative peace, she brought it wealth, and above all she developed a sense of nationalism by playing up the Spanish threat and by building up the English navy.

PATRIOTISM, PEACE, AND PROSPERITY   The poets and prose writers alike wrote long flattering works on "the bountiful good Queen Bess." With their tongues in their cheeks, they traced her lineage back to the great King Arthur. She encouraged the flattery but did very little in a material way to aid the flatterers. She herself was fairly well versed in literature and the arts. We are familiar with the picture which represents her, during one of her visits to Oxford, listening to the handsome young Edmund Campion addressing her eloquently in Greek. (She later had him hanged, drawn, and quartered for giving a no less eloquent defense of the Catholic Faith.) Spenser, who paid her exaggerated homage in *The Faerie Queene*, hoping thereby to obtain preferment at court, learned in his Irish exile how cheaply she bought her flattery.

[1] ALCHEMY (ăl′kê·mĭ)—A combination of science and magic practiced in medieval times; one objective was to change cheap metals into gold.

Like travelers today, nearly everybody who took a voyage or made an expedition came home and wrote a book about it. Richard Hakluyt published his *Principal Navigations*, which gives accounts of the voyages of all of the great Elizabethans and their predecessors. Sidney's *Arcadia* is full of the charm that hangs about distant lands; Spenser speaks of the colony which his friend Sir Walter Raleigh attempted to found in Virginia; and Shakespeare's *Tempest* pictures the conflict between civilization and savagery on a romantic island.

But more than anything else, the new spirit of nationalism was like heady wine to the writers and poets. All the historical plays of Shakespeare surge with pride in England. There is the same patriotic rapture in Spenser's *Faerie Queene* with its glorification of Elizabeth and its vilification of Mary Stuart, Queen of Scots, and of his Catholic Majesty, Philip II of Spain. Besides these, a great number of chronicles and histories were written exalting England and the Tudor dynasty.

The Renaissance emphasis on the individual, the notion of courtly love, and the general enthusiasm of the age gave rise to a wealth of lyric poetry. Almost every Elizabethan writer tried his hand at writing sonnets. A profusion of pure lyrical songs saturated the plays of Shakespeare, Ben Jonson, Beaumont and Fletcher. Marlowe, Raleigh, and Spenser wrote in the popular pastoral form. The lyrics of Thomas Campion were as well known by the Elizabethan populace as are the outpourings of the modern tunesmith.

But by far the greatest literary achievement of the age was the flowering of the drama in the hands of Marlowe, Shakespeare, Ben Jonson, and other lesser known writers like Greene and Dekker. With Shakespeare the summits were reached. As Carlton Hayes says of Shakespeare's plays, "they are individual and nationalist, medieval and modern, Italian and classical, and above all, English."

Time out of mind there have been debates and disputes over whether or not Shakespeare was a Catholic. Even though the latest scholarship seems to indicate that he was, the point is not too important. What is important is that his plays are Catholic—as Carlyle puts it, "the outflowering of the Catholic middle ages."

No single period ever again produced such names as Marlowe, Ben Jonson, Shakespeare, Sidney, Spenser, and Francis Bacon. This was the age of literary giants who wrote their works "to last until the stars are out."

THE POETRY OF EDMUND SPENSER

We might compare the poetical works of Edmund Spenser to a mirror in which are reflected the various influences of the Renaissance on Elizabethan life and letters, the political and religious turmoil of the period, and the growing national consciousness of England, with her pride in her ancestry and her position as a rising international power. From his knowledge of the classics and the Renaissance emphasis on the courtly ideal, Spenser attempted to portray what he conceived to be the ideal commonwealth and the ideal courtier or private man.

In his *Shepherd's Calendar*, a book of twelve poems, Spenser followed a fashion, made popular by the Italian Renaissance writers, of imitating the pastoral poems of Theocritus and Vergil. Pastoral poetry treats of rural life not in a realistic but in an idealistic and allegorical manner. It is an artificial form of poetry in which the setting is always some form of Arcadia or never-never-land where men live an ideal existence, free from the strife of civilization; where nature is always kind and men live very simple lives. The characters in a pastoral poem are represented as shepherds. Sheep and cattle represent wealth. In some form or other, almost all the Elizabethan writers attempted the pastoral style.

EDMUND SPENSER

Spenser added satire to the pastoral with his many references in the *Shepherd's Calendar* to the religious conditions of his time. He further used it as a medium for flattering Elizabeth, the queen of the shepherds, and for praising poetry and its place in the life of the courtier.

It was Spenser's great ambition to write an epic of his age in which he would "imitate earlier epic poets in showing how a noble person should be fashioned."

THE FAERIE

QUEENE

During the Renaissance, epic poetry was regarded as idealized history to which were added the ideal ruler and the ideal courtier or private citizen.

The Faerie Queene is Spenser's attempt to attain these purposes. Although it is not an epic, it is a great metrical romance and places its author among the five highest ranking English poets.

Just as Vergil traced the origin of Rome to Troy, so Spenser, in the *Faerie Queene*, makes his theme the origin of the English nation. In Elizabeth, Spenser saw the return of Arthur, the fulfillment of the prophecy of the legend that Arthur would return to rule England. The Tudors were Welsh and belonged to ancient British stock like Arthur of Britain. The "glorious reign" of Elizabeth was the return of England through the Tudors to the race of Arthur. As the theme of each of the twelve books of the *Faerie Queene*, Spenser treats of those basic virtues which he considers to constitute the national and individual character. Each book is devoted to the adventures of a Knight who represents these virtues.

Prince Arthur is supposed to represent the virtue of *Magnificence* which the Greek philosopher Aristotle taught represented the sum total of all other virtues. Other virtues symbolized in the romance are *Holiness* represented by the Red Cross Knight; *Temperance* symbolized by Sir Guyon; *Chastity*, GENERAL PLAN by Britomartis; and *Courtesy*, by Calidore. Prince Arthur sees in a vision Glorianna, the Faerie Queene, and is so captivated by her beauty that he resolves to seek her out in fairy land. The adventures that befall him on the way constitute the main plot and serve as the connecting link in the story. It is the custom of the Faerie Queene to hold an annual feast which lasts twelve days. On each day she sends forth a Knight to aid some distressed person who has begged her aid. To right each separate wrong calls for the exercise of a special virtue on the part of the Knight.

The allegorical references employed in the poem are drawn from the vast fount of Spenser's knowledge of the Bible, Greek and Latin poets, writers of the Italian and French Renaissance, and medieval literature. His debt both to Chaucer and the medieval romance is very large. In keeping with the contemporary conviction that the purpose of poetry was to teach, the *Faerie Queene* has moral significance; it is not the morality of the Catholic medieval tradition, however, but rather that of the good pagan and the new Protestantism of his day.

Moreover, the poem contains a great fund of historical references and political and religious satire under the guise of the allegory. Dryden tells us that every one of the Knights of Spenser's poem was then living at the court of Elizabeth, among them Sidney and Leicester. Religious satire abounds in the secondary or implied allegory. In the first book, Duessa symbolizes Roman Catholicism and Una the Anglican religion. Archimago stands for the Pope; and the Jesuit plots are hinted at in the flattery and designs of Duessa and Archimago.

As a narrative poet, Spenser can be tedious, and very few read the entire poem today. His allegories are too involved and the later books lack unity and consistency. His greatness lies in his mastery of color, of imagery, of melodic cadence, his use of assonance and alliteration, and the unique nine-line stanza which he invented. The *Faerie Queene* is a magnificent picture book which no poet has ever successfully imitated.

The Spenserian stanza is composed of nine lines, eight of which are written in iambic pentameter and the ninth in iambic hexameter. This last line is called an *Alexandrine*. The ninth line is a conclusion to the preceding eight; in it the musical cadence of the preceding lines comes to a triumphant or quiet close. The rhyme scheme of the stanza is: *ab ab bc bc c*.

In Book I, Holiness, the Red Cross Knight, sets forth as champion of Una, Truth, to slay the Dragon that is ravaging her father's country. In her company, he fights successfully against Error, but is soon led by the deceiver Archimago, Guile and Fraud, to distrust the integrity of his Lady and to take

SYNOPSIS OF

BOOKS I AND II

Duessa in her stead. The Red Cross Knight is able to defeat the pagan Knights Sans Foy and Sans Joy, but falls an easy victim to the Giant of Pride, Orgoglio. Una brings to his aid the divine strength of Arthur. Though rescued from the sin of pride, the Red Cross Knight is weakened by suffering and remorse, and narrowly escapes the clutches of Despayre. It is only after dwelling in the House of Holiness and there learning the full way of the Christian faith that he gains strength to overcome the Dragon and becomes worthy to marry Una.

In Book II, Sir Guyon represents Temperance. In the Castle of Medina he learns that the secret of virtue is moderation. Sent out to destroy a wicked enchantress who enslaves men through base desires, Guyon overcomes Furor (Anger) and Atin (Malignity) but is seduced temporarily by Phaedria (Idleness). In the Cave of Mammon (Wealth) he overcomes Avarice and Ambition. When Guyon is reduced to exhaustion as a result of his sojourn in the Underworld, Arthur comes to his rescue. In the final canto of the Book, Guyon rejects the supreme temptation of the sensuous life in the Bower of Bliss.

(FROM) *The Faerie Queene*

EDMUND SPENSER

The setting of the following passage is the Underworld, where Guyon meets Mammon (Wealth and Worldliness). In the previous adventures of Book II, Sir Guyon was accompanied by "his trustie guyde," the palmer, who represents the virtue of temperance. His very last adventure ended with his rescue from the "Ydle lake" into which he had plunged to escape from an enchanted island where Phaedria (Idle Mirth) tempted him to spend his life in self-gratification.

> So Guyon having lost his trustie guyde,
> Late left beyond that Ydle lake, proceedes
> Yet on his way, of none accompanyde;
> And evermore himselfe with comfort feedes
> Of his own vertues and praise-worthie dedes,   5

Selections from "The Faerie Queene" by Edmund Spenser from *Spenser's Poetical Works* edited by J. C. Smith and E. De Selincourt, reprinted by permission of The Clarendon Press, England.

So long he yode, yet no adventure found,
Which fame of her shrill trompet worthy reedes;
For still he traveild through wide, wastefull ground,
That nought but desert wildernesse shewed all around.
At last he came unto a gloomy glade,   10
Covered with boughes and shrubs from heavens light,
Whereas he sitting found in secret shade
An uncouth, salvage, and uncivile wight,
Of griesly hew, and fowle ill favoured sight;
His face with smoke was tand, and eies were bleard,   15
His head and beard with sout were ill bedight,
His cole-blacke hands did seeme to have ben seard
In smithes fire-spitting forge, and nayles like clawes appeared.

His yron coate, all overgrowne with rust,
Was underneath envelopéd with gold;   20
Whose glistring glosse, darkned with filthy dust,
Well yet appearéd to have beene of old
A worke of rich entayle, and curious mould,
Woven with antickes and wyld ymagery;
And in his lap a masse of coyne he told,   25
And turned upside downe, to feede his eye
And covetous desire with his huge threasury.
And round about him lay on every side
Great heapes of gold that never could be spent:
Of which some were rude owre, not purifide   30
Of Mulcibers devouring element;
Some others were new driven, and distent
Into great ingowes and to wedges square;
Some in round plates withouten moniment;
But most were stampt, and in their metal bare   35
The antique shapes of kings and kesars straunge and rare.

6. YODE—Went.
7. REEDES—Judges.
11. HEAVENS LIGHT—Here and throughout the poem, no apostrophe indicates the possessive case.
13. UNCOUTH, SALVAGE, AND UNCIVILE WIGHT—Strange, wild, and ill-mannered creature.
14. GRIESLY—Grisly, horrible, ghastly.
15. TAND—Tanned.
16. SOUT—Soot.
16. BEDIGHT—Disfigured.
21. GLISTRING—Glittering, shining.
23. ENTAYLE—Carving.
24. ANTICKES—Ancient or strange designs.
31. MULCIBER—Vulcan, god of fire.
32. DISTENT—Stretched.
33. INGOWES—Ingot.
34. MONIMENT—Identifying mark.
36. KESARS—Emperors, from Caesar. Note the connection with modern Kaiser.

[As soon as he saw Sir Guyon, he hastily arose in fright and began to pour all the
metal into a vast open hole. But Guyon withheld his arm and spoke:]

"What art thou man—(if man at all thou art)
That here in desert hast thine habitaunce,
And these rich heapes of wealth doest hide apart
From the worldes eye, and from her right usaunce?"   40
Thereat with staring eyes fixed askaunce,
In great disdaine, he answered: "Hardy Elfe,
That darest vew my direfull countenaunce,
I read thee rash and heedlesse of thy selfe,
To trouble my still seate, and heapes of pretious pelfe.   45

"God of the world and worldlings I me call
Great Mammon, greatest god below the skye,
That of my plenty poure out unto all,
And unto none my graces do envye:
Riches, renowne, and principality,   50
Honour, estate, and all this worldes good,
For which men swinck and sweat incessantly,
Fro me do flow into an ample flood,
And in the hollow earth have their eternall brood.

"Wherefore, if me thou deigne to serve and sew,   55
At thy command lo all these mountaines bee;
Or if to thy great mind, or greedy vew,
All these may not suffise, there shall to thee
Ten times so much be numbred francke and free."
"Mammon," said he, "thy godheads vaunt is vaine,   60
And idle offers of thy golden fee;

40. USAUNCE—Usage.
41. ASKAUNCE—Sideways; the word connotes disfavor.
44. READ—Perceive.
45. PELFE—Wealth.
52. SWINCK—Toil.
55. SEW—Follow.
59. FRANCKE—Generously.
60. GODHEADS VAUNT—Godlike exhibition; your attempt at being a god.

To them that covet such eye-glutting gaine
Proffer thy giftes, and fitter servaunts entertaine."

[Guyon continues to reject Mammon's offer by saying that knightly deeds and not riches are becoming his vocation. To this Mammon replies:]

"Vaine glorious Elfe," said he, "doest not thou weet,
That money can thy wantes at will supply?   65
Sheilds, steeds, and armes, and all things for thee meet
It can purvay in twinckling of an eye;

And crownes and kingdomes to thee multiply.
Do not I kings create, and throw the crowne
Sometimes to him, that low in dust doth ly?   70
And him that raigned, into his rowme thrust downe,
And whom I lust, do heape with glory and renowne?"

[Guyon answers:]

"All otherwise," said he, "I riches read,
And deeme them roote of all disquietnesse;
First got with guile, and then preserv'd with dread,   75
And after spent with pride and lavishnesse,
Leaving behind them griefe and heavinesse.
Infinite mischiefes of them do arize,
Strife, and debate, bloodshed, and bitternesse,
Outrageous wrong, and hellish covetize,   80
That noble heart as great dishonour doth despize.

"Ne thine be kingdomes, ne the scepters thine;
But realmes and rulers thou doest both confound,
And loyall truth to treason doest incline;
Witnessese the guiltlesse bloud pourd oft on ground,   85
The crownéd often slaine, the slayer cround;
The sacred Diademe in peeces rent,
And purple robe goréd with many a wound;
Castles surprizd, great cities sackt and brent;
So mak'st thou kings, and gaynest wrongfull government."   90

64. WEET—Know.
67. PURVAY—Provide.
71. ROWME—Place, region.
72. LUST—Desire, choose.
73. READ—Regard.
80. COVETIZE—Covetousness.
82. NE . . . NE—Neither . . . Nor.
89. BRENT—Burned.

WORD STUDY

Spenser deliberately used words which were obsolete in his day, and even coined new words for metrical effect. He chose words which though still in use in his day were passing out of fashion. Hence such words as *ne, uncouth, wight, eke, whilome,* infrequently used by Shakespeare, were constantly used by Spenser. Yet his vocabulary is basically composed of simple English words. He deliberately avoided the involved mannerisms so popular in many of the Elizabethan writers.

1. Spenser used such words as *francke* (generous, free), *bayt* (deceit), *sleight* (trick), and *pelfe* (pelf). Are these words still used today in such expressions as "a Congressman's franking privileges," "fish-bait," and "sleight-of-hand"? Explain.

2. Look up the origin and give the meaning of: *grisly* and *uncouth.* Has the common meaning of the word *lust* changed from Spenser's day? How do the words *subtile* and *subtle* differ in meaning?

FOR DISCUSSION

1. Describe Mammon as Spenser pictures him in lines 13–27. Explain the meaning of lines 46–54. What was Guyon's answer to the temptation of Mammon expressed in lines 55–59? What arguments does Mammon use to further state his case in lines 64–72? Discuss in detail Guyon's further reply in lines 73–90. Do past and present history prove that Guyon was correct? Explain.

FOR APPRECIATION

1. Study the meter and the rhyme scheme, as well as the imagery in the stanza beginning with line 64.

2. Select several lines which impressed you with their musical cadence, their assonance and alliteration.

LYRIC POETRY

The distinguishing feature of narrative poems is their *objectivity.* By that is meant that a narrative poem tells a story for its own sake—that the reader is interested in the story told and not in the author's personal feelings, emotions, or views of life.

Lyric poetry, on the contrary, is highly *subjective*; that is, a lyric poem is the expression of some personal feeling, emotion, or point of view of the author. It is chiefly concerned with a definite experience of the author, in which he portrays his personal moods and reflections. Lyric poetry may tell a story, but not for its own sake. The story serves as a medium only for the expression of the author's attitude and philosophy of life.

Besides its subjectivity, a lyric poem is characterized by a definite unity, relative brevity, and an intense emotional expression. Its unity is secured by its expression of one single thought, feeling, or situation. Since the lyric is generally short, the emotion is necessarily compressed and intensified.

The chief value of the lyrical poem for us may be summarized as follows: endowed by nature and training to express the feelings of the human heart more deeply and the beauty of the universe more perfectly than the ordinary man, the poet can produce an experience which the ordinary man can feel but vaguely and express inadequately. By means of his poem the poet interprets for us the worlds within and without us in terms of truth and beauty.

The most majestic type of lyric poetry is the ode, characterized by an elevated thought and an intense intellectual and emotional seriousness. Other types of lyrics are the sonnet; the elegy, a poem written to honor someone who has died; the simple lyric; the descriptive lyric; and the meditative lyric, which is solemn, serious, and philosophical in tone.

Since the lyric is highly individualistic, it is little wonder that the Elizabethan poets, steeped in the atmosphere of the Renaissance with its emphasis on the individual, produced a profusion of lyrics.

◇◇◇◇◇

The Passionate Shepherd
to His Love

CHRISTOPHER MARLOWE

Although Marlowe was primarily a dramatist, he wrote many flawless lyrics, the best known of which is "The Passionate Shepherd to His Love." The poem was so popular in his own day that many replies were written to it, the most famous being Raleigh's. In this poem Marlowe employs the typical pastoral style of the Renaissance and gives us the Elizabethan notion of perfect love or the ideal courtship.

Come live with me and be my love,
And we will all the pleasures prove
That hills and valleys, dales and fields,
Woods or steepy mountain yields.

And we will sit upon the rocks,   5
Seeing the shepherds feed their flocks,
By shallow rivers, to whose falls
Melodious birds sing madrigals.

And I will make thee beds of roses,
And a thousand fragrant posies,   10
A cap of flowers, and a kirtle
Embroidered all with leaves of myrtle;

A gown made of the finest wool,
Which from our pretty lambs we pull;
Fair linèd slippers for the cold,   15
With buckles of the purest gold;

A belt of straw and ivy buds
With coral clasps and amber studs;
And if these pleasures may thee move,
Come live with me and be my love.   20

Thy silver dishes for thy meat
As precious as the gods do eat,
Shall on an ivory table be
Prepared each day for thee and me.

8. MADRIGALS—Love songs.

11. KIRTLE—Gown.

The shepherd swains shall dance and
   sing   25
For thy delight each May morning;
If these delights thy mind may move,
Then live with me and be my love.

◇◇

FOR APPRECIATION

1. Select the particular and concrete details which the poet chose to convey to his love the assurance that she will want for nothing.

2. What particular joys does the poet paint as being of the essence of happiness?

Has he omitted some important ones? Discuss.

3. Is there any similarity between this type of love song and the modern love song? Discuss. Is there any harmful effect in both, if taken too seriously? Explain.

4. Analyze the poem for its melodic cadence. Scan at least one stanza.

◇◇◇◇◇

The Nymph's Reply to the Shepherd

SIR WALTER RALEIGH

Raleigh's poetry is more realistic than that of his contemporaries. Humor, satire, and sometimes bitterness will be found in it. Note the acidity of his reply and the deftness with which he pierces the golden bubble of Marlowe's idyll.

If all the world and love were young,
And truth in every shepherd's tongue,
These pretty pleasures might me move
To live with thee and be thy love.   4

Time drives the flocks from field to fold,
Where rivers rage, and rocks grow cold;
And Philomel becometh dumb;
The rest complains of cares to come.

The flowers do fade, and wanton fields
To wayward Winter reckoning yields;
A honey tongue, a heart of gall,   11
Is fancy's spring, but sorrow's fall.

7. PHILOMEL—The nightingale.
22. NO DATE—No end.

Thy gowns, thy shoes, thy beds of roses,
Thy cap, thy kirtle, and thy posies,
Soon break, soon wither, soon forgotten,
In folly ripe, in reason rotten.   16

Thy belt of straw and ivy buds,
Thy coral clasps and amber studs,
All these in me no means can move
To come to thee and be thy love.   20

But could youth last, and love still
   breed,
Had joys no date, nor age no need,
Then these delights my mind might
   move
To live with thee and be thy love.

FOR APPRECIATION

1. Discuss in detail how Raleigh answers Marlowe. Is his reply effective? Why? Does he write in the pastoral form?

2. Select lines which may be satirical and ironic. Discuss their effectiveness.

3. Which of the two poems do you consider to be the more artistic by reason of meter, cadence, imagery, etc.? Discuss. Which of the two do you prefer? Why?

4. Explain the meaning of lines 11–12; line 16; lines 21–22.

5. Does Raleigh give the complete Catholic answer to the problem of love and courtship? Why or why not?

◇◇◇◇◇

The Burning Babe

ROBERT SOUTHWELL

Like Thomas More and Edmund Campion, Robert Southwell, S.J. suffered the usual fate of literary oblivion simply because he was a Catholic and a martyr. It is strange that poetry which was highly praised by both Shakespeare and Ben Jonson should have been neglected until our own day. But Southwell has been rediscovered, and critics are again giving him his rightful place as one of the better minor Elizabethan poets.

"The Burning Babe" is his most popular poem, and as a Christmas poem it is unique. Written in the cold cell of London Tower, where he was imprisoned by the priest-hunters of Elizabeth, it realistically paints the Infant Christ not in the sweet simplicity of the Babe of Bethlehem, but as the Infant Redeemer on fire with a love which men have scorned. Here we have the martyr's insight into the Sacred Heart of Christ.

As I in hoary winter's night
  Stood shivering in the snow,
Surprised I was with sudden heat,
  Which made my heart to glow;

And lifting up a fearful eye   5
  To view what fire was near,
A pretty Babe, all burning bright,
  Did in the air appear;

Who, scorchèd with excessive heat,
  Such floods of tears did shed,   10
As though His floods should quench His
    flames,
  Which with His tears were bred.

"Alas!" quoth He, "but newly born,
  In fiery heats, I fry,
Yet none approach to warm their hearts
  Or feel my heart, but I;   16

14. FRY—To burn, the regular meaning of this word in Elizabethan times.

"My faultless breast the furnace is,
  The fuel, wounding thorns;
Love is the fire, and sighs the smoke,
  The ashes, shame and scorns.   20

"The fuel Justice layeth on,
  And Mercy blows the coals,
The metal in this furnace wrought
  Are men's defilèd souls.

"For which, as now on fire I am,   25
  To work them to their good,
So will I melt into a bath,
  To wash them in My blood."

With this He vanished out of sight,
  And swiftly shrunk away,   30
And straight I called unto my mind
  That it was Christmas Day.

◇◇

FOR APPRECIATION

1. Precisely how does this poem differ from the usual Christmas theme? Discuss.

2. The poem is developed by a series of comparisons. Select several of these. Do you think them overdone?

3. Interpret the words spoken by the Infant in the vision. Explain the meaning of *fiery heats; wounding thorns; the fuel; the coals*.

4. Analyze lines 11–12. This is an example of an Elizabethan conceit which you will discuss when you study Donne's sonnet.

5. What is the meaning of *hoary*?

6. Can you find the underlying doctrine of devotion to the Sacred Heart in this poem? Discuss.

◇◇◇◇◇

To Celia

BEN JONSON

Probably no finer compliment can be paid to a woman than to have a beautiful poem written to her. When the poem can be set to music, the compliment is doubly enhanced. Such a poem is the following—a poem which the world has been singing for over three centuries.

Drink to me only with thine eyes,
  And I will pledge with mine;
Or leave a kiss but in the cup
  And I'll not look for wine.
The thirst that from the soul doth rise
  Doth ask a drink divine;   6
But might I of Jove's nectar sup,
  I would not change for thine.

I sent thee late a rosy wreath,
  Not so much honoring thee   10
As giving it a hope that there
  It could not withered be;
But thou thereon didst only breathe
  And sent'st it back to me;
Since when it grows, and smells, I swear
  Not of itself, but thee!   16

  7. JOVE—Father of the gods.   7. NECTAR—A drink prepared for the gods.

131

FOR APPRECIATION

1. In the old days it was customary, whenever the occasion offered, to drink a toast to the fair ladies present. In the opening line the poet substitutes something in the place of the wine. What is it?

2. In line 3 the poet says that if the fair lady will but touch her lips to the cup, it will suffice for him and the wine will be unnecessary. What further compliment is paid Celia in the first stanza?

3. What is the theme? What is the central thought?

◇◇◇◇◇

To the Memory of My Beloved Master, William Shakespeare

BEN JONSON

There were but ten years between the birth dates of Shakespeare and Jonson. We are told they were great friends. "I loved the man," said Jonson, "and do honor his memory, on this side idolatry." In this light, we can understand the beauty of his poem.

To draw no envy, Shakespeare, on thy name,
Am I thus ample to thy book and fame;
While I confess thy writings to be such
As neither man nor muse can praise too much.
'Tis true, and all men's suffrage. But these ways   5
Were not the paths I meant unto thy praise;
For silliest ignorance on these may light,
Which, when it sounds at best, but echoes right;
Or blind affection, which doth ne'er advance
The truth, but gropes, and urgeth all by chance;   10
Or crafty malice might pretend this praise,
And think to ruin, where it seemed to raise. . . .
But thou art proof against them, and, indeed,
Above the ill fortune of them, or the need.
I therefore will begin. Soul of the age,
The applause, delight, the wonder of our stage,   16
My Shakespeare, rise! I will not lodge thee by
Chaucer, or Spenser, or bid Beaumont lie
A little further, to make thee a room:

2. AMPLE—Abundant in praise.
4. MUSE—The Muses were goddesses of song, poetry, and the arts.
5. SUFFRAGE—Opinion, decision.

18. CHAUCER, SPENSER, BEAUMONT—Chaucer was an earlier English poet, sometimes called the "father of English literature." Spenser and Beaumont were Shakespeare's contemporaries.

Thou art a monument without a tomb,
And art alive still while thy book doth
live, 21
And we have wits to read and praise to
give.
That I not mix thee so my brain ex-
cuses—
I mean with great, but disproportioned
Muses;
For if I thought my judgment were of
years, 25
I should commit thee surely with thy
peers,
And tell how far thou didst our Lyly
outshine,
Or sporting Kyd, or Marlowe's mighty
line.
And though thou hadst small Latin and
less Greek,
From thence to honor thee, I would not
seek 30
For names, but call forth thundering
Æschylus,
Euripides, and Sophocles to us,
Pacuvius, Accius, him of Cordova dead,
To life again, to hear thy buskin tread,
And shake a stage; or when thy socks
were on, 35
Leave thee alone for the comparison
Of all that insolent Greece or haughty
Rome
Sent forth, or since did from their ashes
come.
Triumph, my Britain, thou hast one to
show

To whom all scenes of Europe homage
owe. 40
He was not of an age, but for all time!
And all the Muses still were in their
prime,
When, like Apollo, he came forth to
warm
Our ears, or like a Mercury to charm.
Nature herself was proud of his designs
And joyed to wear the dressing of his
lines, 46
Which were so richly spun, and woven
so fit,
As, since, she will vouchsafe no other
wit.
The merry Greek, tart Aristophanes,
Neat Terence, witty Plautus, now not
please, 50
But antiquated and deserted lie,
As they were not of Nature's family.
Yet must I not give Nature all; thy art,
My gentle Shakespeare, must enjoy a
part;
For though the poet's matter nature be,
His art doth give the fashion; and that
he 56
Who casts to write a living line must
sweat,
(Such as thine are) and strike the sec-
ond heat
Upon the Muses' anvil, turn the same
(And himself with it) that he thinks to
frame, 60
Or, for the laurel, he may gain a scorn;
For a good poet's made, as well as born.
And such wert thou; look how the
father's face
Lives in his issue, even so the race

25. OF YEARS—That is, mature.
26. COMMIT—Compare.
27–28. LYLY, KYD, MARLOWE—Dramatists
of Shakespeare's day.
31–32. AESCHYLUS, EURIPIDES, SOPHOCLES
—Dramatists of ancient Greece.
33. PACUVIUS, ACCIUS—Dramatists of ancient Rome.
33. HIM OF CORDOVA—Seneca, a Roman
dramatist.
34. BUSKIN—A very thick-soled high boot
worn by actors of tragedy.
35. SOCKS—Thin-soled low slippers worn
by actors of comedy.

43. APOLLO—God of the sun.
44. MERCURY—Messenger of the gods.
49. ARISTOPHANES—A writer of ancient
Greek comedy.
50. TERENCE, PLAUTUS—Writers of Roman comedy.
57. CASTS—Attempts.
61. LAUREL—A symbol of victory or
achievement.

Of Shakespeare's mind and manners
brightly shines   65
In his well turnèd and filèd lines,
In each of which he seems to shake a
lance,
As brandished at the eyes of ignorance.
Sweet Swan of Avon! what a sight it
were
To see thee in our waters yet appear,
And make those flights upon the banks
of Thames,   71
That so did take Eliza and our James!
But stay, I see thee in the hemisphere
Advanced, and made a constellation
there!
Shine forth, thou Star of poets, and with
rage   75
Or influence chide or cheer the droop-
ing stage,
Which, since thy flight from hence,
hath mourned like night,
And despairs day, but for thy volume's
light.

72. ELIZA AND OUR JAMES—Queen Elizabeth, and her successor, King James I.

❖◇❖◇❖◇❖◇❖◇❖◇❖◇❖◇❖◇❖◇❖◇❖◇❖◇

FOR APPRECIATION

1. What are the theme and the central
thought of the poem? Break down the
poem into at least five distinct thought
divisions. Give a heading for each.

2. Explain the meaning of the following lines. Line 20: *Thou art a monument without a tomb*; lines 34–35: *thy
buskin tread; when thy socks were on.*

3. Describe the art of writing as Jonson
sees it in lines 55–63.

4. Summarize in one or two paragraphs
Jonson's tribute to Shakespeare. Include
his opinions of Shakespeare's writings, the
opinions of others, the immortality of his
verse, the men whom Shakespeare sur-
passes.

5. Select several lines which you consider memorable. What are the meter
and the stanza form of the poem?

WORD STUDY

1. Describe the color of *coral, amber,
orient pearl.* Describe the taste suggested
by *nectar, gall, tart.* Is *nectar* a word used
frequently today? Explain. What is the
connotation of the word *gall* in the slang
expression "He has his gall"?

2. What kind of ideas are suggested by
laurel and *myrtle*? What is the origin of
their figurative meaning?

3. Give synonyms for *tread, ample,
chide, brandished.* What is the difference
between a *peer* and a *swain*? What does
peerless mean? Is the word *swain* used
today? Why or why not? Explain the
complete meaning of *suffrage* in the phrase
"the right of suffrage."

THE SONNET

The sonnet is a specialized type of lyric poetry which was popular in the Elizabethan period. It is a poem of fourteen lines, written in iambic pentameter, with a definite rhyme scheme. Two forms of the sonnet have been used in English poetry: the Italian, and the English or Shakespearean. The Italian form consists of an *octave*, the first eight lines which present the subject matter of the poem; and the *sestet*, the last six lines which contain the poet's reflections on that subject matter. The rhyme-scheme of the octave is *a b b a, a b b a.* In the sestet the rhyme-scheme may be *c d e, c d e* or *c d, c d, c d.*

The English or the Shakespearean sonnet consists of three quatrains and a couplet, rhyming *a b a b, c d c d, e f e f, g g.* Like the Italian sonnet it contains two waves of thought. In the English sonnet, however, the first wave of twelve lines expresses the problem, and the couplet contains the poet's reflections or solution of that problem.

The sonnet had its origin in Italy in the thirteenth century and was popular with Dante, Petrarch, and Tasso. It was introduced into England during the reign of Henry VIII by Thomas Wyatt and became very popular when the Earl of Surrey experimented with a new sonnet form. Richard Tottel's *Miscellany*, the first English anthology of poetry, printed in 1557, contained 271 "Songs and Sonnettes," written for the most part by Wyatt and Surrey.

As a result of their experimentation with the Italian sonnet, Wyatt and Surrey produced the English sonnet form employed by the great Elizabethan sonnet writers, Sidney, Spenser, and Shakespeare.

Sonnets may be written as single, independent pieces, or may be grouped together in sequences. They may express the development of an emotional experience in the life of the poet, or may actually tell a story. During the Elizabethan Period it was fashionable to write sonnet cycles, the most famous of which are *The Amoretti* of Spenser, *Astrophel and Stella* of Sidney, and Shakespeare's immortal sequence which remained unnamed.

❖❖❖❖❖

Sonnet From the Amoretti

EDMUND SPENSER

Like the sonnets of Shakespeare and Sidney, love is the theme of Spenser's Amoretti *or "Little Loves." But unlike many other Elizabethan sonnets they are sincere; for they are the sonnets of a real courtship, inspired by*

Spenser's future wife, Mary Boyle. Sonnet LXI is a glowing tribute to the woman who embodied for Spenser the ideal of pure and chaste love.

LXI

The glorious image of the Maker's beauty,
My sovereign saint, the idol of my thought,
Dare not henceforth, above the bounds of duty,
T' accuse of pride, or rashly blame for ought.
For being, as she is, divinely wrought,   5
And of the brood of angels heavenly born,
And with the crew of blessed saints upbrought,
Each of which did her with their gifts adorn—
The bud of joy, the blossom of the morn,
The beam of light, whom mortal eyes admire;   10
What reason is it then but she should scorn
Base things that to her love too bold aspire!
Such heavenly forms ought rather worship be
Than dare be loved by men of mean degree.

1. IMAGE OF THE MAKER'S BEAUTY—See Genesis, 1:26. Is Spenser here speaking of material or spiritual beauty? Or both?
14. MEAN—Low degree.

FOR APPRECIATION

1. Elizabethan love poetry was greatly influenced by the Renaissance concept of love as expressed in Castiglione's *Courtier.* According to this concept, love is a yearning of the soul after true beauty. "True love of beauty is good, holy, and brings forth fruit in the souls of them that with the bridle of reason restrain the ill disposition of sense."

The subject of the sonnet is Spenser's wife-to-be. Analyze the sonnet carefully and show that "idealized love" is the theme of the sonnet. Select the particular and concrete details which develop this theme.

2. Explain the meaning of lines 11 and 12. Do lines 13 and 14 restate the theme of the poem? Discuss. May lines 13 and 14 also imply that the poet is fortunate in having such a being for his betrothed? Discuss.

3. Give the rhyme scheme of the sonnet. Does it differ from the Shakespearean form? Explain.

WILLIAM SHAKESPEARE

Sonnets

WILLIAM SHAKESPEARE

For purely poetic expression of thoughts, nothing can quite equal Shakespeare's sonnets. Lyrics by other poets of his day sparkled with conceits (artificial expressions), and glittering extravagances. Shakespeare's sonnets are rich and deep with unforgettable beauty. We do not know who inspired them; but their affection survives "death's dateless night" in immortal lines.

XXIX

When in disgrace with fortune and men's eyes
I all alone beweep my outcast state,
And trouble deaf heaven with my bootless cries,
And look upon myself, and curse my fate,

1. FORTUNE—The Elizabethan writers frequently used the Greek and Roman notion of *fortune*. In that sense it means, not chance or luck, but destiny.
1. MEN'S EYES—Shakespeare may have been out of favor with his literary patron. Again we must remember he was an actor and a playwright. He may refer here to the changing popularity of actors and plays.
3. BOOTLESS—Useless; unavailing. It would be interesting to trace the meaning of this word from the Old English.

Wishing me like to one more rich in hope,   5
Featured like him, like him with friends possessed,
Desiring this man's art, and that man's scope,
With what I most enjoy contented least;
Yet in these thoughts myself almost despising,
Haply I think on thee,—and then my state,   10
(Like to the lark at break of day arising
From sullen earth,) sings hymns at heaven's gate;
   For thy sweet love remembered, such wealth brings
   That then I scorn to change my state with kings.

7. DESIRING THIS MAN'S ART . . . SCOPE—Jealous of this man's ability to get things done
or his skill in writing and acting. Scope can mean here his broad outlook on life, his universal
interest.

XXX

When to the sessions of sweet silent thought
I summon up remembrance of things past,
I sigh the lack of many a thing I sought,
And with old woes new wail my dear time's waste;
Then can I drown an eye, unused to flow,   5
For precious friends hid in death's dateless night,
And weep afresh love's long-since-canceled woe,
And moan the expense of many a vanished sight.
Then can I grieve at grievances foregone,
And heavily from woe to woe tell o'er   10
The sad account of fore-bemoanèd moan
Which I new pay as if not paid before;
   But if the while I think on thee, dear friend,
   All losses are restored, and sorrows end.

LV

Not marble, nor the gilded monuments
Of princes, shall outlive this powerful rhyme;
But you shall shine more bright in these contents
Than unswept stone, besmeared with sluttish time.
When wasteful war shall statues overturn,   5
And broils root out the work of masonry,
Nor Mars his sword nor war's quick fire shall burn
The living record of your memory.
'Gainst death and all-oblivious enmity
Shall you pace forth; your praise shall still find room   10
Even in the eyes of all posterity
That wear this world out to the ending doom.
   So, till the judgment that yourself arise
   You live in this, and dwell in lovers' eyes.

7. NOR MARS HIS SWORD . . . BURN—Here we have an example of the Elizabethan possessive. We would say "the sword of Mars and the fire of war."

CXVI

Let me not to the marriage of true minds
Admit impediments. Love is not love
Which alters when it alteration finds,
Or bends with the remover to remove:
O, no! it is an ever-fixèd mark,   5
That looks on tempests and is never shaken;
It is the star to every wand'ring bark,
Whose worth's unknown, although his height be taken.
Love's not Time's fool, though rosy lips and cheeks
Within his bending sickle's compass come;   10
Love alters not with his brief hours and weeks,
But bears it out even to the edge of doom.
     If this be error and upon me proved,
     I never writ, nor no man ever loved.

9. LOVE'S NOT TIME'S FOOL—Love does not vanish as the beloved grows older.

LXXIII

That time of year thou may'st in me behold
When yellow leaves, or none, or few, do hang
Upon those boughs which shake against the cold,
Bare ruined choirs, where late the sweet birds sang.

4. BARE RUINED CHOIRS—Could it be that Shakespeare is here referring to the destruction of
the monasteries and the sweet birds (the monks) who chanted the Divine Office?

In me thou see'st the twilight of such day   5
As after sunset fadeth in the west;
Which by and by black night doth take away,
Death's second self, that seals up all in rest.
In me thou see'st the glowing of such fire
That on the ashes of his youth doth lie,   10
As the death-bed whereon it must expire,
Consumed with that which it was nourished by.
    This thou perceiv'st, which makes thy love more strong
    To love that well which thou must leave ere long.

8. DEATH'S SECOND SELF—This notion of sleep occurs frequently in Shakespeare's poetry. Compare with the metaphor in *Macbeth*, Act II, Sc. 2, line 37.

12. CONSUMED—A fire is finally choked by the ashes of the fuel which fed it. Compare this fire with that in Southwell's "Burning Babe," stanza 3.

◇◇

FOR APPRECIATION

SONNET XXIX:

1. What universal experience is expressed in lines 3–8? In a few words describe this experience.

2. What thought has the power to break the mood described in the first eight lines? Find lines in the first part of the sonnet that are in exact contrast to lines 12, 13, 14.

3. What poetic devices does the poet employ to attain the weighty, solemn, and heavy movement in the first 8 lines and the rapid, light, and gay movement in the last 6 lines? Discuss. Do the two movements express the different moods of the poem? Study the rich contrast in imagery between *lark at break of day arising* with *sullen earth*. Does *sullen earth* restate the mood of the first 8 lines? Explain.

4. Scan the sonnet. Is the rhyme scheme Shakespearean or Italian?

5. The lark is famous in English literature. List several poems in which it is commemorated.

SONNET XXX:

1. In the sonnet Shakespeare uses the figure of a summons to a court session. What experiences are summoned?

2. Note the use of constant alliteration. Select the lines which illustrate this figure.

3. Shakespeare employs many Elizabethan conceits. Here is one: "old woes new wail my dear time's waste." Can you choose another?

4. Explain the meaning of lines 10–12.

5. In a simple phrase express the figure, "drown an eye."

6. Which sonnet do you prefer, 29 or 30? Discuss.

SONNET LV:

1. This poem could be used as a splendid introduction to the study of literature. Why? Shakespeare is not only immortalizing love but poetry. Select the lines which express the author's conviction that this poem would be immortal.

2. Horace wrote in one of his odes: "I have built a monument more lasting than bronze." The same idea is expressed in this sonnet. Explain how the things of the mind, the great thoughts of great men outlast wars and conflagrations, death and "all-oblivious enmity."

3. What are the qualities in literature which make it immortal? Here you are in a twentieth-century classroom studying a sonnet written almost four hundred years ago. Why has Shakespeare's prophecy in the sonnet been fulfilled?

4. Apply lines 5–8 to the wars of the modern world.

5. Let each member of the class de-

scribe the mental picture that lines 11 and 12 awaken in him. If you were an artist, how would you portray the idea contained there?

6. Give the rhyme scheme of the sonnet. Is this a true Shakespearean sonnet?

7. Compare the thought content of this with Shelley's "Ozymandias."

SONNET CXVI:

1. Work out in detail the images in the poem. Is the imagery in the sonnet consistent or confused? Explain.

2. What might be some other "impediments" to the marriage of true minds? Is Shakespeare speaking of real love or infatuation? Discuss. Discuss the place of self-sacrifice in love.

3. Explain the meaning of "Love's not Time's fool." What is the connection between "Time" and "bending sickle's compass"?

SONNET LXXIII:

1. Shakespeare uses three figures taken from three manifestations of nature to tell us his age. Explain these figures. Which do you consider the most suitable and most poetically expressed?

2. Was Shakespeare really an old man when he wrote this sonnet, or was he looking at old age from afar off?

3. Discuss in detail the choice of his diction to develop the movement and mood of the poem.

4. Is the sonnet developed in two waves of 12 and 2 lines or in two waves of 8 and 6 lines?

5. Explain the meaning of lines 13 and 14. Discuss some popular songs which have the same theme. Compare the thought content of this sonnet with that of Burns' poem "John Anderson, My Jo."

PROJECT

As a class project, try composing a Shakespearean sonnet. Agree on a topic, perhaps some humorous subject, and have one person write the lines on the blackboard as they are suggested by the class. Or, plan the content of each of the three quatrains and the final couplet, and divide the class into committees for the actual writing. Remember to use the right rhyme scheme and iambic pentameter lines.

Sonnet Forty One

PHILIP SIDNEY

*Human nature changes little from age to age. Sidney, a skilled horse-
man, wins the tourney prize and attributes his success to the inspiration
of his Stella watching in the stands. Today the hero of the gridiron or
the hardwood court outdoes himself because the twentieth-century counterpart of Stella is cheering for her athlete as she "sends forth her beams"
of approval from the sidelines.*

Having this day my horse, my hand, my lance
Guided so well that I obtained the prize,
Both by the judgment of the English eyes
And of some sent from that sweet enemy France,
Horsemen my skill in horsemanship advance,　　　　　　　　5
Town folks my strength; a daintier judge applies
His praise to sleight which from good use doth rise;
Some lucky wits impute it but to chance;
Others, because of both sides I do take
My blood from them who did excel in this,　　　　　　　　10
Think Nature me a man-at-arms did make.
How far they shot awry! the true cause is,
Stella looked on, and from her heavenly face
Sent forth the beams which made so fair my race.

1. HAVING—This word goes with "guided" in line 2.
5. ADVANCE—Speak well of.
7. SLEIGHT—Cunning.
9–10. OTHERS . . . THIS—Others say I won the prize because my ancestors on both sides
were skilled in tournament play.
12. AWRY—Missed the mark.
13. STELLA—The poetic name, meaning "a star," which Sidney used in his lyrics for Miss
Penelope Devereaux.

◇◇

FOR APPRECIATION

1. To the Elizabethan, Philip Sidney
was the typical Renaissance courtier. Select those details in the poem which might
portray such a picture.

2. Does the first wave of thought end
with the eighth or the twelfth line? Scan
the sonnet carefully and give the rhyme
scheme.

WORD STUDY: SONNETS

The effectiveness of the poetic image in
poetry is secured by the choice of the
exact connotative adjective, called an epithet. Find epithets in the preceding sonnets; give their literal and denotative
meanings, for example: *deaf heaven, sluttish time, gilded monuments, bare ruined
choirs.*

THE BIBLE

IMPORTANCE AND INFLUENCE

Will it surprise you to know that THE best-seller of the past four hundred years has been the Bible? Did you know that the book which has influenced English literature more than any other book is the Bible?

Old English literature owed its heaviest literary debt to the Bible. Throughout the Middle Ages the layman was well versed in Bible stories. And in the works of Shakespeare, Milton, Dryden, Browning, and Tennyson there are found Biblical characters, Biblical events, Biblical allusions and turns of expression. To the present day, writers have been influenced, consciously or not, by the Bible's imagery, its noble cadences and rhythms. The Bible's proverbs, more than the colorful aphorisms of Shakespeare and the epigrams of Pope, have woven themselves into the very texture of our ordinary speech. The terse and expressive figures of Biblical writers, such as "idol with feet of clay," and "handwriting on the wall," are so commonplace to us that we never question their origin. In the Bible we find models for every literary type developed in English writing: simple narrative, graphic descriptions, lucid explanations, and logical arguments. For the study of English literature, for the writing of English prose and poetry, a real knowledge of the Bible is the best possible preparation.

HISTORY

We know the Bible as one book. In reality it is a complete library, for it is a collection of seventy-three books whose composition spanned fifteen hundred years. These books—forty-six in the Old Testament, twenty-seven in the New Testament —have been gathered and guarded by the Church's "Canon of Sacred Scriptures" —books containing the inspired Word of God.

Broadly speaking, the original language of the Old Testament was Hebrew; that of the New Testament was Greek. When the Jews were scattered throughout the known world after the exile, in what is historically known as the "Dispersion," it was necessary to translate the Sacred Books into other languages. When Christianity rapidly spread in the first century, the New Testament was also translated into other languages. Before the time of Christ, the Jews at Alexandria made their Septuagint translation into Greek. For the early Christians, there were the translations into Armenian, Syriac, Arabic, Ethiopic, and Latin. At the close of the fourth century, the great scholar St. Jerome made his famous Vulgate translation. It is this Latin translation that has been held as the official text by the Catholic Church. In the Middle Ages the people who could read at all could read Latin. Thus there was little need for the Church to issue Scriptures in another language. Yet in many lands (and in England), there were translations into the native tongue before the days of printing.

The Protestant reformers of the sixteenth century have charged Catholicism with keeping the Bible as a closed book. They venerate Wyclif (d. 1384) and Tyndale (d. 1536) as "morning stars of the Reformation" for their work in bringing out the Bible. Protestantism accepted the Bible from the Church, but with important changes: seven of the books were dropped from the Canon; the Scriptures alone were regarded as "the only safe guide for faith." Tradition as a second source of Revelation was rejected; and the Church's authority was denied in the "liberalism of private and individual interpretation."

ATTITUDE OF THE

REFORMERS

It is a too common fallacy to believe that John Wyclif was the first to make an English translation of the Scriptures in 1382. In the seventh century there was the *Poem on Genesis*; in the eighth, the translations of Bede, of Eadhelm, of Guthlac, of Egbert. All of these were in the Saxon language understood and spoken by the Christians of the time. There were the free translations of King Alfred and his scholars; and of Aelfric, Archbishop of Canterbury. There were popular renderings like the *Book of Durham*, the *Rushworth Gloss*, and others which have survived.

Consequent upon the Norman Conquest (1066), Anglo-Norman became the language of England; and several specimens are still known of translations into this intermediate language—the *Paraphrases of Orm*, *Salus Animae*, and the translations of William Shoreman and Richard Rolle. Saint Thomas More in his arguments against the Tyndale edition points out that "the whole Bible long before Wyclif's day was by virtuous and well-learned men translated into the English tongue, and by good and godly people with devotion and soberness well and reverently read. . . . The Clergy keep no Bibles from the laity but such translations as be either not yet approved for good, or such as be already reproved for naught as Wyclif's was." (*Dialogues*, III). Cranmer, the Archbishop of Canterbury, who more than any other (as Belloc shows in his historical study, *Cranmer*), was responsible for the theft of Roman Catholicism from the English people, substantiates More's arguments in his preface to the Great Bible of 1540: "The Holy Bible was translated and read in the Saxon tongue, which at that time was our mother tongue, whereof there remaineth yet divers copies found in old Abbeys, of such antique manner of writing and speaking that few men now be able to read and understand them." And Protestant Foxe offers this strong testimony: "If histories be well examined, both before the conquest and after, as well before John Wyclif was born, as since, the whole body of Scripture by sundry men [was] translated into our native tongue."

But it is the authentic Bible alone that contains the inspired word. And it is the Bible correctly interpreted that the Church desires the faithful to read; for St. Peter's words still ring true: "In which are certain things hard to be understood, which the learned and unstable wrest, as they do also the other scriptures, to their own destruction." (II Peter 3:6.) As the Guardian of the Scriptures, the Church's authorization and acceptance are necessary for an acceptable translation or edition of any of the Sacred Books.

THE AUTHORITY

OF THE CHURCH

Thus the translation of Wyclif, shot through as it was with the heretical teachings of the Lollards, was condemned by the Church. In 1408 the Synod of Bishops at Oxford prohibited the translation of any part of the Bible into English by any unauthorized person, and the reading of any version before it was formally approved. Thus, too, the first Bible printed in English, the anti-Catholic version of the New Testament published by William Tyndale in 1525, was rejected. Tyndale had embodied in his version Luther's notes and explanations of texts, which were full of hatred against Rome. The learned Thomas More attacked Tyndale in his *Defence Against Heretics*, stating that "to find errors in Tyndale's book were like studying to find water in the sea." King Henry VIII, who was to wear for a few years the Roman title of "Defender of the Faith," published an edict that "the translation of the Scripture corrupted by William Tyndale should be utterly expelled, rejected, and put away out of the hands of the people. . . ."

But after Henry's break with the Church of Rome, there came a whole flood of versions and translations. Coverdale completed Tyndale's work in 1536. The Great Bible, sometimes called Cranmer's, was published in 1539. By Royal Proclamation this volume was ordered to be put in every Church in England. In 1557 William Wittingham edited another translation. The Geneva Bible with marginal notes that were fiercely Calvinistic appeared in 1560. This version became so popular with the English people that the Elizabethan bishops hastened to get out the Bishops' Bible under Matthew Parker, Archbishop of Canterbury, in 1568. With none of these, however, were the various factions in the English Church satisfied. Under James I, a group of fifty-four scholars was assigned to bring out another edition. This, the King James or Authorized Version, was published in 1611. It proved to be the best Protestant version that ever appeared; and it is this version that has had the greatest influence on subsequent English prose.

In very recent years a thoroughly modern version of the King James Bible has been written by Protestant Biblical scholars.

The persecuted Catholics in England were under a great disadvantage. The exiled Cardinal Allen had erected at Douai, France, a college for the training of priests for the English mission. Huguenot riots forced the WORK OF removal of the College to Rheims. It was at Rheims in CATHOLICS 1582 that Gregory Martin and Robert Bristow, working under Cardinal Allen, brought out the Catholic translation of the New Testament from St. Jerome's Vulgate. In 1593 the College returned to Douai. There in 1609 the translation of the Old Testament was added, and the entire version was called the Douai-Rheims edition. It is Bishop Challoner's revision (1749–50) of the Douai Rheims with which we are most familiar.

A revival of Biblical interest and studies in the late nineteenth century has led to new Catholic versions and translations. The Westminster Version, a translation of the New Testament from the original Greek and Hebrew Texts, was completed by English and American scholars in 1935. In 1937 was published the second edition of the Reverend F. A. Spencer's translation of the New Testament from the Greek. The Confraternity New Testament, revision of the Challoner-Rheims version based on the Latin Vulgate, was published in 1941, under the patronage of the Episcopal Committee of the Confraternity of Christian Doctrine. Monsignor Ronald A. Knox published his translation of the New Testament from the Latin Vulgate in 1944. He completed the translation of the Old Testament in 1948. Monsignor Knox has remarkably succeeded in presenting the New Testament in the attractive garb of the modern English idiom.

The most recent Catholic translation of the New Testament into contemporary prose appeared in 1954, the work of Father James A. Kleist, S.J., and Father Joseph L. Lilly, C.M.

◇◇◇◇◇

THE SACRIFICE OF ISAAC

(Genesis 22:1–19)

Genesis, the first book of the Old Testament, contains the story of the creation, the fall of our first parents, and the call of the fathers of the Hebrew race.

Abram of Ur has been called by God and has been blessed by the priestly King Melchisedech. God has changed his name to Abraham and has made a solemn pact whereby He promised Abraham, "I will make nations of thee, and kings shall come out of thee." To Abraham's barren wife, Sara, was born Isaac; and in him and through him rests the fulfillment of God's promise. And now Abraham's loyalty and obedience are thus tested by God.

This selection is from the Douai-Rheims version.

1 After these things, God tempted Abraham, and said to him: Abraham, Abraham. And he answered: Here I am.

2 He said to him: Take thy only begotten son Isaac, whom thou lovest, and go into the land of vision: and there thou shalt offer him for an holocaust upon one of the mountains which I will shew thee.

3 So Abraham rising up in the night, saddled his ass: and took with him two young men, and Isaac his son: and when he had cut wood for the holocaust he went his way to the place which God had commanded him.

4 And on the third day, lifting his eyes, he saw the place afar off.

5 And he said to his young men: Stay you here with the ass: I and the boy will go with speed as far as yonder, and after we have worshipped, will return to you.

6 And he took the wood for the

holocaust, and laid it upon Isaac his son: and he himself carried in his hands fire and a sword. And as they two went on together,

7 Isaac said to his father: My father. And he answered: What wilt thou, son? Behold, saith he, fire and wood: where is the victim for the holocaust?

8 And Abraham said: God will provide himself a victim for an holocaust, my son. So they went on together.

9 And they came to the place which God had shewn him, where he built an altar, and laid the wood in order upon it: and when he had bound Isaac his son, he laid him on the altar upon the pile of wood.

10 And he put forth his hand and took the sword, to sacrifice his son.

11 And behold an angel of the Lord from heaven called to him, saying: Abraham, Abraham. And he answered: Here I am.

12 And he said to him: Lay not thy hand upon the boy, neither do thou anything to him: now I know that thou fearest God, and hast not spared thy only begotten son for my sake.

13 Abraham lifted up his eyes, and saw behind his back a ram amongst the briers sticking fast by the horns, which he took and offered for a holocaust instead of his son.

14 And he called the name of that place, The Lord Seeth. Whereupon even to this day it is said: In the mountain the Lord will see.

15 And the angel of the Lord called to Abraham a second time from heaven, saying:

16 By my own self have I sworn, saith the Lord: because thou hast done this thing, and hast not spared thy only begotten son for my sake:

17 I will bless thee, and I will multiply thy seed as the stars of heaven, and as the sand that is by the sea shore: thy seed shall possess the gates of their enemies.

18 And in thy seed shall all the nations of the earth be blessed, because thou hast obeyed my voice.

◇◇◇

WORDS

Give a complete history of the word, *holocaust*.

FOR DISCUSSION

1. Give a thumb-nail sketch of Abraham's character as it is implicitly portrayed in the narrative.
2. What important spiritual lessons can be learned from this story?
3. What figures of speech are contained in verse 17?
4. What is the complete meaning of verse 18?

5. Explain why this selection is a fine example of the simple narrative. Note the absolute simplicity of the style, intelligible to any child.

A PROJECT

Discuss orally or in a written paper the relationships between the sacrifice of Isaac and the Sacrifice of the Mass.

RELATED READING

Read chapter 14 of the Book of Exodus.

◇◇◇◇◇

Poem on Wisdom

THE BOOK OF JOB

The Book of Job is a discussion in dialogue form of the problem of retribution. Is there a contradiction between the doctrine of the justice of God and the facts of human experience? We must remember that the Jewish concept of the future life did not have the fullness of our Christian Revelation. The reader is informed at the beginning that Job's sufferings are merely a test of his fidelity. But the solution expressed by Job (and endorsed by God's final speeches) is not more than negative: suffering is not always the result of sin, nor is there a necessary connection between happiness and virtue. This negative solution was a preparation for the fuller revelation of the new dispensation—the true reward of the just is eternal life in the presence of God. The "Poem on Wisdom" which now forms the twenty-eighth chapter of the Book is regarded by most critics as an independent poem set within the dialogue between Job and his friends.

The basis of Hebrew versification is thought-arrangement and not word-arrangement. In Hebrew poetry the meter is given in the balance of thought or parallelism that exists between the two parts of each verse. This thought-contrast will be more noticeable in the translation of the Psalms.

Nothing is known of the writer, except what can be deduced from this work. The thoughts are those of a Palestinian Jew of the post-Exilic period. The date of composition cannot be fixed more exactly than the fifth to third century before Christ.

This selection is taken from Reverend Edward J. Kissane's work, THE BOOK OF JOB.

1 When there is a mine for silver,
  And a place where gold is refined,
2 Iron is taken out of the earth,
  And stone is melted into copper,
3 Man putteth an end to darkness,
  And to the uttermost bound he searcheth.
4 The stone of darkness and death-shade
  Is pierced with channels by man's agency;
  Those which were forgotten of the foot
  Diminish, they are diverted by man.
5 The earth out of which cometh bread,
  Underneath is turned up by fire;

6 The stones thereof are the place of sapphires,
  That have dust of gold;
7 Man putteth forth his hand to the flint,
  He overturneth mountains by the roots;
8 In the rocks he cleaveth canals,
  Whatever is precious his eye seeth;
9 The beds of rivers he searcheth,
  And what was hidden he bringeth to light.

10 But Wisdom, where can it be found?
  And where is the place of understanding?
11 Man knoweth not the way thereto,
  And it is not found in the land of the living;

VERSES 1–4: In his search for precious metals, man labors unceasingly. He is undeterred by darkness or distance; he tunnels through rock; he changes the course of rivers.

"Poem on Wisdom" from *The Book of Job*, translation by Monsignor Edward J. Kissane, reprinted by permission of Browne & Nolan Limited, Dublin.

VERSES 5–11: The earth's surface gives food to man; from its interior he tears precious stones. Overcoming all obstacles he searches the beds of rivers and the depths of the earth, and he finds his desire.

12 The path no bird of prey knoweth,
    And the vulture's eye hath, not
        seen it;
13 The proud beasts have not trodden
        it,
    The lion hath not passed thereby;
14 The Abyss saith: 'It is not in me,'
    And the Sea saith: 'It is not with
        me.'
15 Gold cannot be given in exchange
        for it,
    Nor silver weighed as the price
        thereof;
16 It cannot be valued with the gold
        of Ophir,
    With the precious onyx or the
        sapphire;
17 Gold and glass cannot equal it,
    Nor can the exchange thereof be
        vessels of fine gold.
18 Coral and crystal need not be men-
        tioned.
    The excellence of wisdom is
        above pearls;
19 The topaz of Ethiopia cannot equal
        it,
    Neither can it be valued with fine
        gold.
20 But Wisdom, whence cometh it?
    And where is the place of under-
        standing?
21 It is hidden from the eyes of all liv-
        ing,
    And from the fowls of the air it
        is concealed;
22 Abaddon and Death say:
    With our ears we have heard a
        rumour thereof:

23 God understandeth the way there-
        of,
    And He knoweth the place
        thereof;
24 For he looketh to the ends of the
        earth,
    And seeth what is under the
        whole heavens.
25 When He made a weight for the
        wind,
    And meted out the waters by
        measure,
26 When He made an ordinance for
        the rain,
    And a way for the thunder-
        storm;
27 Then He saw and reckoned it,
    He had established it, yea, He
        had searched it out;
28 And he said unto man:
    Lo, the fear of the Lord is wisdom,
    And to depart from evil is under-
        standing.

destruction; or the place of the lost—the bottomless pit.
    VERSES 20–24: Whence Wisdom, no crea-
ture can tell. God alone knows, He who
knows all things.
    VERSES 25–28: God is the Creator and the
Orderer; His plan is Wisdom. Man's task is
to fulfill his appointed place in that plan.

◇◇◇◇◇◇◇◇◇◇◇◇◇◇◇◇◇◇◇◇◇◇◇◇◇◇◇◇

FOR APPRECIATION

1. Note the relationship in structure
between Anglo-Saxon poetry and the balance of thought of Scriptural poetry.
Compare this passage with the Anglo-
Saxon translation of Genesis.
    2. How is this poem significant in the
light of the Atomic Age? Discuss man's
material progress and his spiritual retrogres-
sion. May it be said that verses 1–11 contain the history of scientific research?
    3. Is there an implicit argument against
pantheism in the poem? Explain.
    4. Choose at least three significant fig-
ures of speech from the poem.

VERSES 12–14: But man cannot attain the
abode of Wisdom; not even if like the wild
beasts he sweeps the ends of the earth. For
Wisdom is not to be found in the surroundings
of the earth nor in the sea.
    VERSES 15–19: Man's precious stones can
buy many things, but not Wisdom.
    22. ABADDON—A Hebrew word meaning

PROJECTS

1. "Lo, the fear of the Lord is Wisdom,
    And to repent from evil is under-
    standing."

Write an editorial taking as your theme
the above text, with practical applications
to the modern world. Show how repentance and humility can improve mankind.

2. See the *Catholic Encyclopedia* for
the story of Job.

3. Explain what you mean by "the patience of Job."

RELATED READING

Read chapters 24 and 28 from the Book
of Job in the Douai-Rheims version.

THE BOOK OF PSALMS

The book which is poetic above all others in the Old Testament is the
Book of Psalms. The Psalms are a collection of the lyric poetry of ancient
Israel, a storehouse of pure and lofty song. Most of the Psalms were
composed in the days of King David, about a thousand years before Christ.
Perhaps half of the poems were made by David himself; of the other au-
thors, we know almost nothing.

But the Book of Psalms is not merely an anthology of Hebrew poetry.
It is a collection of the Sacred Chants meant to be used in the worship
of God. They are great poetry, poetry that is for all time; for they express
man as man. But more, they breathe the very essence of true religion:
they are God's inspired word concerning the never-changing relations of
the soul with God.

In the Old Dispensation, they were used in the liturgy of the Hebrew
worship. From earliest times the Psalms always have been cherished by
the Church. By far the greater part of the Office of the Breviary daily
recited or chanted by priests and religious is composed of the Psalms.
Psalms are recited in the Mass; and they so enter into every liturgical function that they have been called "the prayer-book of the liturgy."

Of the Psalms and their variety of subject matter, St. Athanasius wrote:
"They seem to be a kind of mirror for everyone who sings them, in which
he may observe the motions of the soul, and as he observes them give to
them in words. . . . Methinks that in the words of this book you may
find·an exact survey and delineation of the whole life of man, the dispo-
sitions of the soul and the movements of the mind. If a man has need

of patience and confession, if affliction or temptation has overtaken him, if he has been persecuted or has been delivered from the plots of his enemies, if he is in sorrow or trouble, or if he wishes to praise and give thanks and bless the Lord, he finds instruction in the Psalms."

The following selections from the Psalms are based on the new Latin translation made by the professors of the Pontifical Biblical Institute. This new translation has removed many of the inaccuracies which obscured the meaning of the original Hebrew text.

◇◇◇◇◇

Psalm 22

A PSALM OF DAVID

1 The Lord is my shepherd: I want for nothing; he makes me to lie in green pastures,

2 He leads me to waters where I may rest; he restores my soul.

3 He guides me along the right paths for his name's sake.

4 Although I walk in a darksome valley, I shall fear no evil, for thou art with me.

Thy crook and thy staff: these comfort me.

5 Thou preparest a table for me before the eyes of my foes;

Thou anointest my head with oil; my cup brims over.

6 Goodness and kindness will follow me all the days of my life,

And I shall dwell in the house of the Lord days without end.

◇◇

FOR DISCUSSION

1. The Oriental mind prefers the concrete, the individual picture to a general discussion of the abstract. What attribute of God has the Psalmist here portrayed from his experience?

2. Why is enumeration of deeds more effective than straight description of the Good Shepherd?

3. How is the Lord pictured in verses 5 and 6? What individual details of ancient Jewish hospitality are depicted?

4. What is the general attitude towards God on the part of the Psalmist?

PROJECTS

1. You should be acquainted with Marc Connolly's famous play, *The Green Pas-*

tures. Why is his title a good one? Would you say this play is a comedy? Why or why not?

2. Explain the place of the "crook and staff" in the Church's liturgy.

Read the parable of the Good Shepherd in Luke 15 and the bestowal of the Primacy on St. Peter in John 21.

Psalm 72

A PSALM OF ASAPH

1 How good is God to the upright; the Lord, to them that are pure of heart.

2 But my feet almost wavered, my steps almost slipped,

3 For I was envious of the ungodly, seeing the prosperity of sinners.

4 For they have no torments, healthy and fat is their body.

5 In the hardships of mortals they have no part, and they are not scourged like other men.

6 Therefore pride encircles them like a necklace, and violence covers them like a robe.

7 Their iniquity comes forth from a gross heart, the thoughts of their mind break forth.

8 They jeer and they speak spitefully, they threaten proudly.

9 They set their mouth against heaven, and their tongue ranges over the earth.

10 Therefore my people turns to them, and they gulp down great draughts of water.

11 And they say: "How does God know and is there knowledge in the Most High?"

12 Behold, the wicked are like that, and, always untroubled, they increase their power.

13 Have I, then, in vain kept my heart clean, and washed my hands in innocence?

14 For I suffer scourges all the time, and chastisement every day.

15 If I were to think: I will talk like them, I should abandon the generation of thy children.

16 Therefore I took thought that I might know this thing: but it seemed hard to me,

17 Until I went into the sanctuary of God, and considered their end.

18 Truly thou dost set them on a slippery way; thou castest them down in ruins.

19 How they fell in a moment, they have ceased to be, they are utterly consumed by a great terror.

20 Like a dream, when one awakes, O Lord, so, when thou risest up, thou shalt despise their image.

21 When my mind was being provoked, and my heart was being striken,

22 I was foolish and without understanding: I was like a brute beast before thee.

23 But I will be with thee always: thou hast taken my right hand;

24 By thy counsel thou wilt lead me, and at length thou wilt receive me into glory.

25 Whom have I in heaven but thee? and earth does not delight me if I am with thee.

26 My flesh and my heart melt away, the Rock of my heart and my portion, God forever.

27 For, behold, they that go away from thee shall perish, thou destroyest all that are unfaithful to thee.

28 But it is good for me to be near God, to put my refuge in the Lord God.
   I will declare all thy works in the gates of the daughter of Sion.

FOR DISCUSSION

1. Here is another treatment (as in the Book of Job) of the great question: Why do the wicked prosper and the good suffer? What is the attitude of the Psalmist in verses 1–12? What has brought on the temptation?

2. Is there any change of mood in verses 13–17? Explain.

3. Verses 18–22 and 23–28 portray the final lot of the wicked and the just man; how does the Psalmist develop the contrast between the two states? Is the technique effective?

4. The solution here offered is outstanding in the Old Testament. How does it compare with the teaching on immortality in our Christian Revelation? Do the two have much in common?

WORDS

Explain the phrases: *gross heart* in verse 7 and *my mind was being provoked* in verse 21.

PROJECTS

1. Choose at least five figures of speech from the Psalm and explain the meaning of each.

2. Explain the famous figure in verse 28. The "daughter of Sion" referred to is Jerusalem.

RELATED READING

Read and study Psalms 1 and 120. They are rich in meaning.

The Suffering Messias

(Isaias 52:13–53:12)

Isaias, the most literary of the prophets, has been called the Evangelist of the Old Testament. Here is his well-known prophecy of the atonement of the Messias and His exaltation. This is one of the most famous passages of the Old Testament. The translation was made by Reverend Michael J. Gruenthaner, S.J.

52:13 Behold, the Wise One, my Servant, shall be exalted,
He shall be raised up and be high exceedingly.
Just as many were appalled at him—

14 So marred from that of man was his appearance,
And his form from that of the children of men—
So shall he cause many nations to rise up;
Kings shall hold their mouths because of him.
For they shall see things of which they had not been told;
They shall understand things of which they had not heard.

53:1 Who could have believed what we have heard?
And to whom was the Lord's might revealed?

2 And he grew up as a slender shoot before Him,
And as a root out of the dry ground.
He had no form nor charm that we should gaze upon him,
No beauty that we should admire him.

3 He was despised and forsaken of men,
A man of sorrows, acquainted with pain,
Like one from whom men hide their faces.
He was despised and we esteemed him not.

4 Nevertheless, it was our pains that he bore,
And our sorrows that he carried,
While we accounted him stricken,
Smitten by God and afflicted.

5 But he was wounded for our transgressions,
Crushed for our iniquities;
The chastisement that brought us peace was upon him,
And by his stripes we were healed.

6 Like sheep, we all had gone astray:
We had turned each one his own way,
But the Lord laid upon him the punishment of us all.

7 When tortured, he submitted and opened not his mouth.
Like a lamb that is led to the slaughter,

155

Like a ewe before her shearers,
He was mute and opened not
his mouth.

8 Through oppression in judgment he was taken away.
As for his contemporaries, who considered
That he was cut off from the land of the living
Smitten for the sin of my people.

9 They appointed his grave with transgressors
And with criminals when he should die,
Although he had done no violence,
And there was no deceit in his mouth.

10 But the Lord saw fit to afflict him with suffering.
When his life shall have

offered atonement for sin
He shall see posterity, prolong his days,
And the Lord's design will prosper in his hands.

11 He shall see the fruit of his mortal travail;
He shall be content with what he shall perceive
The Just One, my Servant, shall bring justice to many,
And he shall carry their sins.

12 Therefore, I will assign him a multitude as his portion
And great numbers as his spoil,
Because he poured out his life into death,
And was numbered with transgressors.
Yea, he bore the sin of many and interposed for transgressors.

OUTLINE OF ARGUMENT

(The Poet speaks in the name of God)

52:13-14 Exaltation of the Servant emphasized by repetition, by contrast, and by enumeration of those offering homage and their reactions.

(The Poet speaks in the name of the Hearers)

53:1-2 Amazement at this revelation: that God's power should be revealed in this extraordinary way in this Servant. For this Servant grew up in humble circumstances.

2-3 Yes, this Servant — without beauty, despised, full of sorrows —like a leper was shunned and scorned.

4-9 But all His suffering was for us; all His pains, the price of our sins. This notion of vicarious suffering is driven home by many repetitions.

10-12 God allowed this suffering—as atonement for sin; the reward to this Servant, and to the redeemed.

FOR DISCUSSION

1. This prophecy concerning the sufferings of Christ is presented simply yet with great appeal. Can you give a few reasons for its literary worth?

2. Point out the strength of the contrast in 52:13-14.

3. List the attributes of Christ as given in 53:2-3. How many times is our guilt assigned as the cause of Christ's sufferings?

4. Is sadness the final effect, or does the prophet see God's goodness and generosity as the over-all view?

PROJECTS

1. Prepare explanations of the references to this prophecy in Luke 22:37, Matthew 8:17, and I Peter 2:22.

2. Discuss why Christ's atonement should have been necessary.

RELATED READING

Note the points of similarity in Psalm 21.

Read the accounts of the Passion in Matthew 27, Mark 15, and Luke 23; and, to understand Christ's motivation in these sufferings, John 14-17.

PAUL'S SPEECH AT ATHENS

(Acts 17:15–34)

The Acts of the Apostles is St. Luke's partial account of the earliest days of the Church, from Our Lord's Ascension until St. Paul's first imprisonment at Rome. Luke's concern is with the beginnings, the spread of the gospel into new territory. Naturally the dominating character is St. Paul and his labors throughout the Roman Empire.

Paul's second missionary journey has taken him on another long trip through the Roman provinces. The vision of the Macedonian has led Paul into Greece; Philippi, Thessalonica, Beroea, have heard the "good news." Now Paul waits at Athens for disciples Silas and Timothy to rejoin him. The Athens Paul saw was still the center of Greek culture; but decay had long since followed upon the Golden Age. The Epicureans, materialists, had set up pleasure as the highest good; the Stoics, pantheists, esteemed devotion to duty.

This selection from the Acts is taken from Monsignor Ronald A. Knox's translation of the New Testament. Notice how thoroughly modern is the English used by Father Knox.

Those who were escorting Paul on his journey saw him as far as Athens, and then left him, with instructions for Silas and Timothy to rejoin him as soon as possible. And while Paul was waiting for them in Athens, his heart was moved within him to find the city so much given over to idolatry, and he reasoned, not only in the synagogue with Jews and worshippers of the true God, but in the market place, with all he met. He encountered philosophers, Stoics and Epicureans, some of whom asked, What can his drift be, this dabbler? while others said, He would appear to be proclaiming strange gods; because he had preached to them about Jesus and Resurrection. So they took him by the sleeve and led him up to the Areopagus;[1] May we ask, they said, what this new teaching is thou art delivering? Thou dost introduce terms which are strange to our ears; pray let us know what may be the meaning of it. (No townsman of Athens, or stranger visiting it, has time for anything else than

[1] AREOPAGUS (ăr′ê·ŏp′·à·gŭs)—A high court of Athens which met on a hill west of the Acropolis.

saying something new, or hearing it said.)

So Paul stood up in full view of the Areopagus, and said, Men of Athens, wherever I look I find you scrupulously religious. Why, in examining your monuments as I passed by them, I found among others an altar which bore the inscription, To the unknown God. And it is this unknown object of your devotion that I am revealing to you. The God who made the world and all that is in it, that God who is Lord of heaven and earth, does not dwell in temples that our hands have made; no human handicraft can do him service, as if he stood in need of anything, he, who gives to all of us life and breath and all we have. It is he who has made, of one single stock, all the nations that were to dwell over the whole face of the earth. And he has given to each the cycles it was to pass through and the fixed limits of its habitation, leaving them to search for God; would they somehow grope their way towards him? Would they find him? And yet, after all, he is not far from any one of us; it is in him that we live, and move, and have our being; thus, some of your own poets have told us, For indeed, we are his children. Why then, if we are the children of God, we must not imagine that the divine nature can be represented in gold, or silver, or stone, carved by man's art and thought. God has shut his eyes to these passing follies of ours; now, he calls upon all men, everywhere, to repent, because he has fixed a day when he will pronounce just judgement on the whole world. And the man whom he has appointed for that end he has accredited to all of us, by raising him up from the dead.

When resurrection from the dead was mentioned, some mocked, while others said, We must hear more from thee about this. So Paul went away from among them. But there were men who attached themselves to him and learned to believe, among them Dionysius the Areopagite; and so did a woman called Damaris, and others with them.

<><><><><><><><><><><><><><><><><><><><><><>

FOR DISCUSSION

1. What evidence have you from the text that St. Paul was familiar with Grecian philosophy and art?

2. If St. Paul stood in Times Square, New York, today and spoke before a representative gathering of the citizens of that city, what might be the contents of his speech?

3. Is the resurrection of the dead still denied by modern thinkers? Why? What is the Communist's philosophy of life?

4. How many converts did St. Paul make on this occasion? Is the modern preacher any more successful?

WORDS

What kind of person is a *dabbler?* What does "to dabble in politics" mean? Give the etymology of the words: *handicraft, cycle, habitation.* What is the relation between *habitation* and *habitat?*

PROJECTS

1. Describe the Athenian market place which met Paul's eyes. Explain the presence of the philosophers there.

2. Compare this passage with that in the Douai-Rheims Version and tell specifically how Monsignor Knox has brought the translation up to date.

3. Compare it also with the Kleist-Lilly rendition and discuss which of the two translations more closely catches the tone of English as spoken today.

ELIZABETHAN PROSE

We have already seen that English prose, in its transition from Middle English, developed richly under the masterful pen of Saint Thomas More. The great modern scholar, R. W. Chambers, has written that we must "think of him [More] first in connection with the continuity of English speech, English prose, English literature. . . . To the student of English prose his work is the great link which connects modern prose with the medieval prose of Nicholas Love, Walter Hilton, and Richard Rolle."

Continuing in the scholarly tradition of More and the Christian Humanism of Oxford of which he was a part, Edmund Campion has given us in his *History of Ireland* what Evelyn Waugh has called "a superb piece of literature, comparable in vigour and rhythm to anything written in his day." We know that Campion's future as a man of English letters was cut short by his submission to Rome, his life as a Jesuit priest, and his death as an English martyr. But there is no doubt in the mind of Waugh, the great stylist of our own day, that had Campion continued the life of learning he had planned for himself "he would have come down in history as one of the great masters of English prose."

Although prose writing lagged far behind the lyrical expression of the period, scores of writers set down in simple English the results of their search in fields of history, travel, navigation, biography, and the like. In spite of the fact that many scholars continued to present their studies in the classic tongue, so many good books in the vernacular appeared that we can only glance at some representative titles.

Two English clergymen, Richard Hakluyt and Samuel Purchas, became interested in England's achievements in exploration. They made careful study of the records of men like Drake and Frobisher, checking dates and names and places. Hakluyt published his findings in a three-volume work, *Principal Navigations, Voyages and Discoveries of the English Nation*, issued in 1589, 1598, and 1600. Purchas continued the undertaking after Hakluyt's death with two volumes, *Purchas, His Pilgrimage* in 1616 and *Hakluytus Posthumous, or Purchas, His Pilgrims* in 1625. The books are of interest because they have furnished later writers with accurate information about early English "sea-dogs."

GEOGRAPHERS AND EXPLORERS

Sir Walter Raleigh and Captain John Smith wrote first-hand accounts of their experiences in the New World, but they were so eager to dazzle the reader with American splendors that their pages were misleading. For some generations certain Englishmen entertained visions of an American paradise drawn from the accounts in Raleigh's *Discovery of Guiana* or Smith's *Virginia, New England, and the Summer Isles*. While he was in prison, awaiting execution, Sir Walter wrote an ambitious but also untrustworthy *History of the World*. It concludes with a courageous and moving address to Death.

The fervent patriotism of the times aroused an interest in British history. As early as 1578 Holinshed published his *Chronicles of England, Ireland and Scotland,* an important work because it gave Shakespeare some material for *Macbeth* and for his English historical plays. William Camden did a careful piece of historical research which resulted in *Britannia*—an orderly chronicle of English history —and in the *Annals of Queen Elizabeth.* Foxe's *Book of Martyrs* was a favorite of the early Puritans and one of the first books brought to America. John Knox wrote *The History of the Reformation in Scotland.*

The period manifested an interest in the lives of great men of all times. One exceedingly popular book was Thomas North's excellent translation of Plutarch's *Parallel Lives of Greek and Roman Heroes.* This work also furnished Shakespeare with material for some of his tragedies—notably for *Julius Caesar* and *Antony and Cleopatra.*

The books noted above were written, on the whole, in a simple, direct style. Another fashion of prose writing, however, was developed by such men as John Lyly and Sir Philip Sidney. In his *Euphues,* a fictitious account of the experiences of a young Athenian visiting England, Lyly wrote in a bombastic, highly artificial style which later led to the coining of the word *euphuism* to indicate an artificially elegant mode of literary expression. In an attempt to imitate the pastoral romances of the writers of the Italian Renaissance, Sidney wrote his prose romance, *Arcadia.* The work was intended also to react against the euphuistic style of Lyly; however it, too, shows a courtly, artificial style, foreign to the direct simplicity of the main stream of English prose.

◇◇◇◇◇

THE BRAG

EDMUND CAMPION

We are at a country hostelry in England during the midsummer of 1580. It is the time of Queen Elizabeth, of Catholic persecution, and of great personal heroism. Several "gentlemen" are preparing to ride out on horseback for their day's journey. Saddlebags are being packed and horses made ready. At one side stand three "gentlemen" chatting pleasantly, we presume, about last evening's cock fight or yesterday's great spectacle in London where three "Romish" priests were hanged, cut down alive, and butchered into four parts before the approving mob of ten thousand Britons who roared their enjoyment at the scene. But let us draw nearer. The "gentlemen" quietly conversing disclose their identity to us. "Fathers," the pale, thin gentleman says, "six years I have spent in the prisons of London for the 'crime' of hearing Mass. I have come to know the judicial department of this realm too well. You have but lately come from Douai; [1] you are Jesuits; your work here is misunderstood and hated; your persecutors are crafty, unscrupulous men. Once captured, you may be killed at a blow. Black, treasonous, forged confessions will appear over your names to the shame of the Catholics. I beg you, now, to write down and sign a true confession of your state in life, your mission in England, and our Holy Faith. I shall preserve it until you are taken captive; then I will release it and show it to the whole world as a testimony of your lives."

Within five minutes the two "gentlemen," Fathers Persons and Campion, have secured paper, and are writing their manifesto. It is the work of but half an hour. Written almost without a pause, on rough paper over packed saddlebags, this document carries the words that condemn Father Edmund Campion as a priest in England, but proclaim him a hero forever. Back in Marshalsea prison, Mr. Thomas Pound gathers the prisoners of the Faith around him and reads to them the words of England's newest hero:

TO THE RIGHT HONOURABLE,
THE LORDS OF HER MAJESTIE'S
PRIVY COUNCIL [2]

Right Honourable:

Whereas I have come out of Germane and Boëmeland,[3] being sent by my Superiours, and adventured myself into this noble Realm, my deare Countrie, for the glorie of God and benefit of souls, I thought it like enough that, in this busie, watchful and suspicious worlde, I should either sooner or later be intercepted and stopped of my course. Wherefore, providing for all events, and uncertaine what may become of me, when God shall haply deliver my body into durance,[4] I supposed it needful to put this writing into readiness, desiringe your good Lordships to give it your reading, for to know my cause. This doing, I trust I shall ease you of some labour. For that which otherwise you must have sought for by practice of wit, I do now lay into your hands by plaine confession. And to the intent that the whole matter may be conceived in order, and so the better

---

[1] DOUAI—The great College of Douai, in France, had been founded by Cardinal William Allen in 1568 and was yearly attracting dozens of English youths to the noble vocation of leaving their homes, studying for the priesthood, and returning to England to be martyred for their Faith. One hundred and sixty of these Douai seminary priests were executed upon the scaffold during Elizabeth's reign alone. At Douai also was written the English translation of the Catholic Bible.

[2] The grammar and spelling of England in the sixteenth century are retained here just as Father Campion wrote them.

[3] BOËMELAND—Bohemia. Father Campion joined the Jesuit order in Rome and was then sent to Prague, in Bohemia, for six years.

[4] DURANCE—Custody, captivity.

both understood and remembered, I make thereof these nine points or articles, directly, truly, and resolutely opening my full enterprise and purpose.

i. I confess that I am (albeit [5] unworthie) a priest of the Catholike Church, and through the great mercie of God vowed now these viii years into the Religion [6] of the Societie of Jhesus. Hereby I have taken upon me a special kind of warfare under the banner of obedience, and eke [7] resigned all my interest or possibilitie of wealth, honour, pleasure, and other worldlie felicitie.

ii. At the voice of our General Provost,[8] which is to me a warrant from heaven, and Oracle of Christ, I tooke my voyage from Prage to Rome (where our said General Father is always resi-

dent) and from Rome to England, as I might and would have done joyously into any part of Christendome or Heathenesse, had I been thereto assigned.

iii. My charge [9] is, of free cost to preach the Gospel, to minister the Sacraments, to instruct the simple, to reforme sinners, to confute errors—in brief, to crie alarm spiritual against foul vice and proud ignorance, wherewith many [10] my dear Countrymen are abused.[11]

iv. I never had mind, and am strictly forbidden by our Father that sent me, to deal in any respect with matter of State or Policy of this realm, as things which appertain not to my vocation, and from which I do gladly restrain and sequester my thoughts.

v. I do ask, to the glory of God, with

---

[5] ALBEIT—Although.
[6] RELIGION—Religious order.
[7] EKE—Also.
[8] PROVOST—Superior.

[9] CHARGE—Purpose, or work.
[10] MANY—Many of.
[11] ABUSED—Afflicted, tainted.

all humility, and under your correction, iii sortes of indifferent and quiet [12] audiences: *the first* before your Honours, wherein I will discourse of religion, so far as it toucheth the common weale and your nobilities: *the second*, whereof I make more account, before the Doctors and Masters and chosen men of both Universities,[13] wherein I undertake to avow the faith of our Catholike Church by proofs innumerable, Scriptures, Councils, Fathers, History, natural and moral reasons: *the third* before the lawyers, spiritual and temporal, wherein I will justify the said faith by the common wisdom of the laws standing yet in force and practice.

vi. I would be loth to speak anything that might sound of any insolent brag or challenge, especially being now as a dead man to this world and willing to put my head under every man's foot, and to kiss the ground they tread upon. Yet have I such a courage in avouching [14] the Majesty of Jhesus my King, and such affiance [15] in his gracious favour, and such assurance in my quarrel, and my evidence so impregnable, and because I know perfectly that no one Protestant, nor all the Protestants living, nor any sect of our adversaries (howsoever they face men down in pulpits, and overrule us [16] in their kingdom of grammarians and unlearned ears) can maintain their doctrine in disputation. I am to sue most humbly and instantly for the combat with all and every of them, and the most principal that may be found: protesting that in

this trial the better furnished [17] they come, the better welcome they shall be.

vii. And because it hath pleased God to enrich the Queen my Sovrein Ladye with notable gifts [18] of nature, learning, and princely education, I do verily trust that if her Highness would vouchsafe her royal person and good attention to such a conference as, in the second part of my fifth article I have mentioned, or to a few sermons, which in her or your hearing I am to utter,—such manifest and fair light by good method and plain dealing may be cast upon these controversies, that possibly her zeal of truth and love of her people shall incline her noble Grace to disfavour some proceedings hurtful to the Realm, and procure towards us oppressed [19] more equitie.

viii. Moreover I doubt not but you her Highness' Council being of such wisdom and discreet in cases most important, when you shall have heard these questions of religion opened faithfully, which many times by our adversaries are huddled up and confounded, will see upon what substantial grounds our Catholike Faith is builded, how feeble that side is which by sway of the time prevaileth against us, and so at last for your own souls, and for many thousand souls that depend upon your government, will discountenance error when it is bewrayed,[20] and hearken to those who would spend the best blood in their bodies for your salvation.

[17] BETTER FURNISHED—More learned.

[18] NOTABLE GIFTS—To understand Queen Elizabeth's reputation for learning you should read Hilaire Belloc's *Queen Elizabeth*.

[19] US OPPRESSED—Father Campion was compelled to travel disguised as a merchant because priests found in England were killed; to hear Mass in England was a crime punishable by a year's imprisonment and a fine of 100 marks (over $1000 in modern money); to be reconciled to the Church was high treason, punishable by death.

[20] BEWRAYED—Disclosed.

[12] INDIFFERENT AND QUIET—Unprejudiced and attentive.

[13] UNIVERSITIES—Oxford and Cambridge.

[14] AVOUCHING—Declaring.

[15] AFFIANCE—Trust, confidence.

[16] Father Campion satirizes the fiery but unlearned preachers.

Many innocent hands are lifted up to heaven for you daily by those English students, whose posteritie shall never die, which beyond seas, gathering virtue and sufficient knowledge for the purpose, are determined never to give you over, but either to win you to heaven, or to die upon your pikes. And touching our Societie, be it known to you that we have made a league—all the Jesuits in the world, whose succession and multitude must overreach all the practices [21] of England—cheerfully to carry the cross you shall lay upon us, and never to despair your recovery, while we have a man left to enjoy your Tyburn [22] or to be racked with your torments, or consumed with your prisons. The expense is reckoned, the enterprise is begun; it is of God; it cannot be withstood. So the faith was planted: so it must be restored.

ix. If these my offers be refused, and my endeavours can take no place, and I, having run thousands of miles to do you good, shall be rewarded with rigour, I have no more to say but to recommend your case and mine to Almightie God, the Searcher of Hearts, who send us His

[21] PRACTICES—Death was the punishment for being convicted of belonging to the Jesuit order in England.

[22] Father Campion himself "enjoyed" Tyburn and the hangman's noose on December 1, 1581, after having been in captivity five months, and tortured on the rack at least three times.

grace, and set us at accord before the day of payment, to the end that we may at last be friends in heaven, when all injuries shall be forgotten.

FOR DISCUSSION

1. It is said that this letter was "intoxicating" to the Catholic prisoners in the Marshalsea as it was read to them after months of silence, of ruinous fines, and false reports of the failure and betrayal of the Catholic Faith in England. Explain what qualities in Father Campion's "Brag" might produce such joy in the hearts of these men.

2. Pick out words and passages showing the gentle humor and satire for which Father Campion is noted.

3. Read again the eighth and ninth points, with an attempt to capture the spirit and courage of this man who was to die for his Faith,—and who seemed to know it in advance.

PROJECTS

1. Translate into good modern idiom the first point in this work.

2. Father Campion was one of the finest scholars in Elizabethan England. See if you can imitate the clear logic, the balanced phrasing, and the vividness of his words in this exercise: You have been suddenly halted by an officer of the law and accused of treason to the United States; your answer states your views on democracy, your innocence of plots against it, and your love of American independence.

THE ENGLISH ESSAY MAKES ITS BOW

The most important development in literary prose was the appearance of a form new to English writers—the *essay*. It was Francis Bacon who made the introduction. Over in France a brilliant writer, Michel de Montaigne, who died in 1592, had been writing down brief impressions of men and human affairs and publishing them as "Essais." Five years later, Bacon, who knew and admired the work of the Frenchman, published ten short prose reflections and called them "Essays." And so the English term was born. Bacon had not rated his papers highly, and he was surprised at their success. His long, serious studies had all been written in Latin; but the essays proved he had a brilliant command of English and an almost poetic prose style. In 1612 he released a second edition, containing twenty-eight additional papers; and in 1625 his final edition, numbering fifty-eight.

Bacon's English is marked by short, pithy sentences; or by longer sentences that break easily into parallel parts. He never loses his way grammatically; and his fondness for balanced structure—phrase with phrase or clause with clause—gives his prose a definite rhythm. It reads well aloud, and it is packed with thought. The best known of all the essays, "Of Studies," appeared in the first edition of his papers. It shows forth his wit, his eloquence, and his intellectual interests. The essays added to the second edition, while he was rising rapidly to power, have a wordly-wise point of view and are coldly calculating in thought. The last twenty, written during retirement after his public disgrace, have a sober moral tone.

The essays reflect to some extent the thoughts and attitudes of the days of Elizabeth and of her successor, James I. More particularly they reflect the man who wrote them—a man described by a later poet as "the wisest, brightest, meanest of all time."

It is not generally known that another writer of the age added to the store of English essays. We are well acquainted with Ben Jonson the poet and Jonson the dramatist; but Jonson the essayist is less familiar. In the last years of his life, this lusty writer pondered much on men, on books, on learning; and from time to time he jotted down his meditations. Some, like the reminiscence on Bacon, are very short; some are much longer. He grouped them under the name *Timbers*, but they were not published until 1641, four years after his death. Most interesting are his comments on the famous men he has known, such as the one on Shakespeare in which he criticizes the dramatist for writing too much; but in which he also pays a splendid tribute to the man and his work.

OF STUDIES

FRANCIS BACON

"Why do I have to go to school?" is a question that comes up every so often in the average American home. "What good are these things?"—with a contemptuous gesture toward a stack of textbooks—"what good is studying going to do me anyway?"

Well, Francis Bacon, who lived in the days of Shakespeare, has an answer to such questions. Even though it was written three centuries ago, it is still a good answer. Briefly, he says that studies add to our profit, to our appearance or personality, and to our fun. Of course, it doesn't take much talking to prove the first point. Some studies are necessary to prepare us to earn a living. And yes, studies do help one "shine" in society. But the high school boy who feels "fed up" with school may balk a bit at the third reason. Yet Bacon considered it so important that he named it first. And isn't he right? Suppose for a moment that you had never gone to school. Suppose you could not read or write. Think of the pleasures you would have to miss. Yes, Bacon is wise to begin by saying, "Studies serve for delight." He is right about most of the other things, too.

Studies serve for delight, for ornament, and for ability. Their chief use for delight is in privateness and retiring; for ornament, is in discourse; and for ability, is in the judgment and disposition of business. For expert men [1] can execute and perhaps judge of particulars, one by one; but the general counsels, and the plots and marshaling of affairs, come best from those that are learned. To spend too much time in studies is sloth; to use them too much for ornament is affectation; to make judgment wholly by their rules is the humor [2] of a scholar. They perfect nature, and are perfected by experience; for natural abilities are like natural plants, that need proyning [3] by study; and studies themselves do give forth directions too much at large, except they be bounded in by experience. Crafty men [4] contemn studies; simple men admire them; and wise men use them: for they teach not their own use; but that [5]

[1] EXPERT MEN—Specialists who lack general information or culture.

[2] HUMOR—Peculiarity or tendency.
[3] PROYNING—Pruning.
[4] CRAFTY MEN—Laborers; workmen of various crafts or guilds.
[5] THAT—The knowledge of how to use one's learning.

is a wisdom without them and above them, won by observation. Read not to contradict and confute; nor to believe and take for granted; nor to find talk and discourse; but to weigh and consider. Some books are to be tasted, others to be swallowed, and some few to be chewed and digested: that is, some books are to be read only in parts; others to be read, but not curiously;[6] and some few to be read wholly, and with diligence and attention. Some books also may be read by deputy,[7] and extracts made of them by others; but that would be only in the less important arguments, and the meaner sort of books; else distilled books are like common distilled waters, flashy[8] things. Reading maketh a full man; conference a ready man;[9] and writing an exact man. And therefore, if a man write little, he had need have a great memory; if he confer[10] little, he had need have a present wit; and if he read little, he had need have much cunning, to seem to know that he doth not. Histories make men wise; poets witty; the mathematics subtile; natural philosophy deep; moral grave; logic and rhetoric able to contend. *Abeunt studia in mores*.[11] Nay, there is no stond or impediment in the wit, but may be wrought out by fit studies:[12] like as diseases of the body may have appropriate exercises. Bowling is good for the stone and reins;[13] shooting for the lungs and breast; gentle walking for the stomach; riding for the head; and the like. So if a man's wit be wandering, let him study the mathematics; for in demonstrations, if his wit be called away never so little, he must begin again: if his wit be not apt to distinguish or find differences, let him study the Schoolmen;[14] for they are *cymini sectores*:[15] if he be not apt to beat over matters, and to call one thing to prove and illustrate another, let him study the lawyers' case: so every defect of the mind may have a special receipt.

[14] SCHOOLMEN—Theologians or philosophers.
[15] *Cymini sectores*—Hairsplitters or quibblers.

◇◇◇◇◇◇◇◇◇◇◇◇◇◇◇◇◇◇◇◇◇◇◇◇◇◇◇◇◇◇

FOR DISCUSSION

1. *His Style:* Bacon is a remarkably modern writer. He knows how to use words with economy and he packs a world of meaning into a single sentence. He is a master of the terse, pithy sentence which makes for an epigrammatical style. His sentences are perfectly *balanced* in structure and in thought. Choose from the selection at least three epigrams and study them for their balanced structure.

2. Think over the opening sentence. Which studies that you are taking serve one or more of these uses of education?

3. In his essay Bacon is championing the cause of a *liberal* education, that is, an education which teaches us *how* to live, not necessarily how to make a living. Do you agree that a liberal education is a necessary preparation for life? Discuss.

4. To paraphrase means to reword a passage without changing its meaning. As a test of your understanding of the essay, try paraphrasing any three of sentences 2 to 10.

5. What does Bacon say about "digests"? Would he approve of all the "digests" on the market today? Discuss.

6. Give illustrations of the truth of the

[6] CURIOUSLY—With close attention.
[7] READ BY DEPUTY—"Read" through reviews or reports by others.
[8] FLASHY—Flat, tasteless.
[9] CONFERENCE A READY MAN—Conversation (or repartee) makes a man quick-witted.
[10] CONFER—Converse.
[11] *Abeunt studia in mores*—Studies pass into (or grow into) manners.
[12] NO STOND . . . WROUGHT OUT—No lack of mental ability but may be remedied.
[13] STONE AND REINS—Gallstones and similar affections.

statement that the chief use of studies "for delight is in privateness and retiring." Is it true, for instance, that an uneducated person is more at a loss for entertainment when he is alone than when he is with others? Do you think that the men in service appreciate the love of good reading which they acquired in school? Why?

7. Apply to the last part of the essay Bacon's precept that we should read "to weigh and consider." Do you think that a man lacking a logical mind can improve it by studying geometry? Or that a slow-witted person may become a clever conversationalist through much practice? Discuss.

WORDS

Be sure you understand the sense in which Bacon used the following words: *affectation, confute, discourse* (note pronunciation), *subtile, contend.* Distinguish between the synonyms: *taste, flavor, tang.*

PROJECTS

1. Memorize the sentences: "Reading maketh a full man; conference a ready man; and writing an exact man." "Some books are to be tasted, others to be swallowed, and some few to be chewed and digested."

2. Take one division of one of the above sentences as a topic sentence and expand it into a paragraph of at least one hundred words.

3. Prepare an oral debate or write a defense of either side of this question: Does a *liberally* educated man give a greater contribution to his age than a specialist without a liberal education? In other words, can an engineer without a liberal education give as great a contribution to society as an engineer with a liberal education?

RELATED READING

Read some other essays of Bacon; for example, "Of Truth" and "Of Friendship." Macaulay was a champion of everything Bacon stood for—especially "progress." Read Macaulay's *Essay on Bacon* and report to the class his general estimate of Bacon's character and his contribution to science.

THE DEVELOPMENT OF
ENGLISH DRAMA

We have already noted how popular drama had its beginnings in England with the miracle, mystery, and morality plays of Middle English times.

Toward the close of the fifteenth century, there developed another type of play, much shorter than the morality play, known as the *interlude*. The interlude was inserted between the acts of a longer play, or presented between the courses of a banquet. Later, interludes were given on any occasion that called for short entertainment. These playlets were frequently based on some life situation, and so led the way toward the appearance of realistic drama.

The British forerunner of modern drama is usually said to have been born in 1550, when a schoolmaster wrote a crude comedy entitled *Ralph Roister Doister*. In 1561 appeared what is called the first English tragedy, *Gorboduc*, written in blank verse; and in 1566 came another farcical comedy, *Gammer Gurton's Needle*, written by a bishop. These plays showed the influence of the Renaissance in their imitation of classic forms; but the scenes and characters were English, the situations lifelike, and the story with its action held the center of attention.

ELIZABETHAN DRAMA

The culmination toward which the English drama had been developing for centuries came in the days of Elizabeth. Plays became as popular as the movies are in our own. Strolling players armed with scripts and gay costumes set up their temporary stage in the quadrangular court of an inn. Rushes were strewn on the wooden scaffolding; juniper was burned in the yard to purify the air. At three o'clock the flag was run up to announce the beginning of the performance, trumpets blared, and the townsfolk flocked to the innyard. The common folk stood on the ground; the gentry, the burghers, and the dignitaries of the town occupied the galleries. Here the leading lady—whose chin often bristled with a new beard—squeaked her alarm at pasteboard dragons. Here armies had it out with wooden swords. Here "groundlings"—apprentices, serving men, soldiers, colliers, tinkers, and the like—drank ale, cracked nuts, jeered the villain, and hailed the hero.

Nowhere, of course, was the popularity of the play more to be marked than in London, where it early attracted the displeasure of the Puritans who were strong enough in 1574 to secure the enactment of an Order of the Common Council in Restraint of Dramatic Exhibitions. This order led to the building of the first playhouse, called *The Theater*, which was erected by James Burbage in 1576 on a site just north of the city limits where the Order did not apply. For a model he seems to have taken the innyard. It seems probable that the interior of *The Theater* was circular. In this open space, which was called the *pit* or *yard*, on the hard-packed earth stood the groundlings. About the inside walls on the three sides parallel and opposite to the stage were galleries, probably three tiers, after the

fashion of the innyards. The best seats were in the galleries. Here sat the "gallery-commoners"—the merchants and gentry. As the picture of *The Fortune* shows, there was also a gallery over the rear stage. This was the "Lords roome." In the "Lords roome" sat the more aristocratic patrons of the play, both men and women, the latter carefully masked. On the very edge of the stage itself sat the swaggering gallants of the day.

The stage was a raised platform projecting out into the pit. Over the "stage forward" was a "shadow or cover" supported by posts. At the rear and under the "Lords roome" was a kind of recess which might be cut off from the stage forward by a curtain or "arras." Rising above the gallery was a tower which was used for three purposes. Here was flown a flag giving the name of the theater, as *The Theater*, *The Swan*, or *The Globe*. On days when plays were to be given, a second flag announcing the fact was also hung out. From this tower also the trumpeter sounded the three blasts which announced that the play was about to begin.

There was no scenery such as we know on the Elizabethan stage. It is possible that the curtain or arras at the rear sometimes bore a crude painted picture. It is
STAGE SETTINGS probable, however, that the setting was generally indicated by no more than a placard or piece of cloth bearing a legend, such as *Macbeth's Castle*, or *A heath*. Although there was little or no scenery, considerable use was made of *properties*. A picture of *The Swan* shows a bench or settle on the stage, and other articles of furniture no doubt were used

when required. A document of the time mentions "engines, weapons, and powder used in plays."

One peculiarity of the Elizabethan stage was the absence of actresses. Women's parts were taken by boys, especially trained. This accounts for the fact that Shakespeare frequently has his women characters impersonate men and for the further fact that in all the plays men predominate. Elizabethan actors made little or no attempt to dress according to the time and setting of the play. "Costume," says one writer, "was a means of indicating rank and office more than time or place; it was meant to reveal the characters rather than the setting of the story." The Elizabethan age delighted in extravagant display, especially in clothes.

The actor's life was a strenuous one. Professor Adams in his *A Life of William Shakespeare* writes, "Elizabethan troupes . . . not only performed as a rule every week day, and often on Sundays, but also changed their plays from day to day in a most astonishing fashion. The forenoons of the actors were commonly spent in rehearsals. The afternoons, of course, were occupied with performances before the public, lasting from two or three o'clock until five or six. As to the evenings, not a small share of the time surely had to be devoted to learning new, or refreshing the memory on old plays."

In the reading of Elizabethan plays we are likely to overlook one of the chief attractions for the audience—the songs and incidental music. Elizabethans were fond of music. And the groundlings and gallants also loved "sound and fury" for its own sake. They liked hurly-burly and commotion. The reader should note the frequency of trumpet calls and fanfares, and other appeals to the ear indicated in the stage directions by *Flourish, Cry within, Thunder and lightning, Drum, Flourish and shout,* and the like. The frequency of *Alarums* in battle scenes no doubt served both to keep the audience on the alert and to stimulate its imagination.

SIDELIGHTS ON

THE THEATER

The audience itself was a turbulent and unruly one. Expressions of approval and disapproval were common through applause, noisy laughter, loud spitting, and a whole series of rude guffaws and curses. If the nobles were bored by the play, they interrupted or mimicked the actors or even jumped to the stage and engaged in combat with them.

There remains one thing to say about Elizabethan drama. The dialogue was written in verse. All of Shakespeare's plays—excepting a few comic scenes done in prose—are written in unrhymed iambic pentameter lines. Some scenes for emphasis close with a rhymed couplet. The remarkable thing is that although Shakespeare's characters talk like real men and women, they speak some of the greatest poetry the world has ever known. These mighty lines have power to grip the mind today just as they stilled the boisterous pit and gallery in the days of Elizabeth and James.

By 1616 there were in London at least seven well-established theaters in which plays were regularly given, not to mention certain great inns, such as the Boar's Head, where plays evidently continued.

So great was the demand for plays that not only professional literary men, but scholars and courtiers as well, tried their hand at playmaking. The first men who had taken up dramatic writing as a profession were the so-called "University Wits,"

"UNIVERSITY WITS" so named since they were all University men, who, instead of going into the church or teaching, turned to writing to earn their living. The most conspicuous of the "University Wits" was Christopher Marlowe, who, before his death at twenty-nine produced four remarkable dramas. Associated with Marlowe are the names of a number of other dramatists, all of whom worked feverishly, often in collaboration, to produce the greatest possible number of dramatic novelties for the stage. In their search for material, they ransacked the past. History, classic myth, legend, medieval romance, and folk tale were all grist to the mill. The situation much resembled that of our own day in which, to meet the insatiable demand for movies and television plays, the literature of the past has been freely used.

Then at the close of the sixteenth century came young William Shakespeare, destined to become the greatest dramatist of England, if not of all time. He raised English drama to heights never approached before or since. All the world was his stage, and his zest for life was so great that laughter and tears pulsate in every page of his work. His characters are always dynamic, energetic personalities, from kings like Macbeth to lovers like Romeo and Juliet. There are clowns and cut-purses and drunken porters and fairies and shrews and representatives of practically the whole Elizabethan world.

Perhaps one of the most tangible proofs of Shakespeare's greatness is the fact that after three centuries he is still a Broadway sell-out. The Old Vic Company from London performed *Henry* V, and seats were sold out six months in advance. Laurence Olivier's *Henry* V and *Hamlet* are hailed as the greatest movies of our times. Maurice Evans played *Hamlet* up and down the South Pacific and the soldiers liked it so much that he has since played the same version to enthusiastic American audiences. Will Shakespeare is the one playwright to whom all concede that final, ultimate adjective—*great!*

Macbeth

WILLIAM SHAKESPEARE

MACBETH tells a story from Scottish history. It was written soon after James VI of Scotland was crowned James I of England. Shakespeare could be sure of an interested audience because Englishmen would naturally be curious about the strange, picturesque country which was now joined to their own. The plot of MACBETH is from an old chronicle history of the British Isles written by Raphael Holinshed.

The play is a TRAGEDY, which means that the career of the central character ends in defeat. All plays contain a conflict or struggle of some kind, but in tragedies the struggle of the hero is unsuccessful. We first see him near the height of his fortune, and we follow the sequence of events that once begun leads inevitably to his downfall. In this play it is Macbeth's eagerness to become king of Scotland, and his willingness to commit murder to attain his desire, that starts him on his disastrous career. Alongside this outer conflict there is an inner conflict. Macbeth is not all bad, so we see good and bad struggling within him as he makes his first decisions. Later we see his increasing horror and desperation as he realizes where his evil deeds are leading him.

MACBETH is a POETIC DRAMA. By writing all his plays in poetic form, Shakespeare followed a stage tradition that had begun with the verse plays performed by the medieval guilds. Christopher Marlowe had also used verse in his colorful tragedies, and the other Elizabethan dramatists were proud to imitate Marlowe's "mighty line." However, in his less intense and dramatic scenes Shakespeare sometimes lets his characters speak in prose.

Probably many people in Shakespeare's audience did not understand the finer points of the tragedy of MACBETH or care for its poetry—but all of them could appreciate it as a roaring, blood-and-thunder tale of crime and punishment. Shakespeare gave them an eerie midnight murder; a blood-spattered ghost; villainy, cruelty, and terror; witches with their uncanny ceremonies and mysterious prophecies; and a fierce last battle in which the wicked Macbeth is brought to justice. On this simple, obvious level the story is as violent and melodramatic as a modern crime "thriller."

DRAMATIS PERSONÆ

DUNCAN, *king of Scotland*

MALCOLM } *his sons*
DONALBAIN }

MACBETH } *generals of the*
BANQUO } *king's army*

MACDUFF
LENNOX
ROSS } *noblemen of*
MENTEITH } *Scotland*
ANGUS
CAITHNESS

FLEANCE, *son to* BANQUO
SIWARD, *Earl of Northumberland, general of the English forces*
YOUNG SIWARD, *his son*
Boy, *son to* MACDUFF

SEYTON, *an officer attending on* MACBETH
An English Doctor
A Scotch Doctor
A Sergeant
A Porter
An Old Man

LADY MACBETH
LADY MACDUFF
Gentlewoman *attending on* LADY MACBETH
HECATE
Three Witches
Apparitions
Lords, Gentlemen, Officers, Soldiers, Murderers, Attendants, and Messengers

SCENE: *Scotland; England*

ACT I

One way to study MACBETH is to read it rapidly, with main emphasis on story and character—finishing the play in several class periods. Another way is to examine it in detail, with attention to the wording and to the poetic and dramatic quality of many specific passages. Whichever method is followed, you will not find it difficult to read an entire act at a time, giving closer consideration afterward to some of the great scenes and speeches.

For the day-by-day reading, it is important to get clearly in mind the central story of the whole act. Act I introduces all the principal characters —especially Macbeth himself, an honored nobleman in Duncan's kingdom who is now winning new military glory. Act I also presents the basic theme—Macbeth's temptation to become king by murdering Duncan. By the end of the act, we have found out what Lady Macbeth thinks of this idea.

The weird opening scene establishes an evil atmosphere that is appropriate to the whole play. The setting is "a desert place," that is, a deserted spot. With a crash of thunder, the three witches appear. For some reason, they are interested in meeting Macbeth.

SCENE 1. *A desert place.*

FIRST WITCH. When shall we three meet again
  In thunder, lightning, or in rain?
SECOND WITCH. When the hurly-burly's done,
  When the battle's lost and won.
THIRD WITCH. That will be ere the set of sun.   5
FIRST WITCH. Where the place?
SECOND WITCH.   Upon the heath.
THIRD WITCH. There to meet with Macbeth.
FIRST WITCH. I come, Graymalkin!
SECOND WITCH. Paddock calls.
THIRD WITCH. Anon!   10
ALL. Fair is foul, and foul is fair;
  Hover through the fog and filthy air.   [*Exeunt.*]

4. BATTLE—In the next scene we are to learn what battle is being fought.
8. GRAYMALKIN—Gray cat, old cat.
9. PADDOCK—Toad. Witches were supposed to be the servants of "familiar spirits" who gave them their power and often accompanied them in the shape of cats or toads. The witches are obeying the spirits who now summon them away.

SCENE 2. *A camp near Forres.**

[*Alarum within. Enter* DUNCAN, MALCOLM, DONALBAIN,
LENNOX, *with* Attendants, *meeting a bleeding* Sergeant.]

DUNCAN. What bloody man is that? He can report,
    As seemeth by his plight, of the revolt
    The newest state.
MALCOLM.   This is the sergeant
    Who like a good and hardy soldier fought
    'Gainst my captivity. Hail, brave friend!   5
    Say to the king the knowledge of the broil
    As thou didst leave it.
SERGEANT.   Doubtful it stood,
    As two spent swimmers that do cling together
    And choke their art. The merciless Macdonwald—
    Worthy to be a rebel, for to that   10
    The multiplying villainies of nature
    Do swarm upon him—from the western isles
    Of kerns and gallowglasses is supplied;
    And fortune, on his damnèd quarrel smiling,
    Showed like a rebel's whore. But all's too weak;   15
    For brave Macbeth—well he deserves that name—
    Disdaining fortune, with his brandished steel,
    Which smoked with bloody execution,
    Like valor's minion carvèd out his passage
    Till he faced the slave;   20
    Which ne'er shook hands, nor bade farewell to him,
    Till he unseamed him from the nave to the chaps,
    And fixed his head upon our battlements.
DUNCAN. O valiant cousin! worthy gentleman!
SERGEANT. As whence the sun 'gins his reflection   25
    Shipwrecking storms and direful thunders break,
    So from that spring whence comfort seemed to come
    Discomfort swells. Mark, king of Scotland, mark:
    No sooner justice had, with valor armed,
    Compelled these skipping kerns to trust their heels,   30
    But the Norweyan lord, surveying vantage,

* *Forres* (fŏr´ĭs)—A town in northern Scotland.
   2–3. OF THE REVOLT THE NEWEST STATE—The latest news of the battle. The purpose of
this rather tedious scene is to let us know that Macbeth has distinguished himself in helping to
put down the rebellion, and that he is to be rewarded by being made thane, or carl, of Cawdor.
   12. WESTERN ISLES—Ireland and the islands west of Scotland.
   13. KERNS AND GALLOWGLASSES—Light-armed and heavy-armed footsoldiers.
   22. FROM THE NAVE TO THE CHAPS—Macbeth "carved" him from the navel to the jaws.
   24. COUSIN—Macbeth is Duncan's cousin.
   25. 'GINS HIS REFLECTION—An allusion to the return of the sun at the spring equinox, a time
of storms. As the spring brings joy and also storms, Macbeth's victory is followed by a fresh assault on him by the Norwegian lord.

With furbished arms and new supplies of men,
Began a fresh assault.

DUNCAN.   Dismayed not this
Our captains, Macbeth and Banquo?

SERGEANT.   Yes;
As sparrows eagles, or the hare the lion.   35
If I say sooth, I must report they were
As cannons overcharged with double cracks, so they
Doubly redoubled strokes upon the foe.
Except they meant to bathe in reeking wounds,
Or memorize another Golgotha,   40
I cannot tell—
But I am faint, my gashes cry for help.

DUNCAN. So well thy words become thee as thy wounds;
They smack of honor both. Go get them surgeons.
Who comes here?   45

[*Exit* Sergeant, *attended.*]

[*Enter* ROSS.]

MALCOLM.   The worthy thane of Ross.

LENNOX. What a haste looks through his eyes! So should he look
That seems to speak things strange.

ROSS.   God save the king!

DUNCAN. Whence cam'st thou, worthy thane?

ROSS.   From Fife, great king;
Where the Norweyan banners flout the sky
And fan our people cold.   50
Norway himself, with terrible numbers,
Assisted by that most disloyal traitor,
The thane of Cawdor, began a dismal conflict;
Till that Bellona's bridegroom, lapped in proof,
Confronted him with self-comparisons,   55
Point against point rebellious, arm 'gainst arm,
Curbing his lavish spirit; and, to conclude,
The victory fell on us.

DUNCAN.   Great happiness!

ROSS.   That now
Sweno, the Norways' king, craves composition;
Nor would we deign him burial of his men   60
Till he disbursèd, at Saint Colme's inch,
Ten thousand dollars to our general use.

40. MEMORIZE ANOTHER GOLGOTHA—Make the place as memorable as another Golgotha, the scene of the crucifixion of Christ.
51. NORWAY HIMSELF—King of Norway.
54. BELLONA—Roman goddess of war. The "bridegroom" is Macbeth.
54. LAPPED IN PROOF—Clad in armor.
61. SAINT COLME'S INCH—The island of Inchcolm in the Firth of Forth.
62. DOLLARS—The word could mean either the German *thaler* or the Spanish *piece of eight.*

DUNCAN. No more that thane of Cawdor shall deceive
Our bosom interest. Go pronounce his present death,
And with his former title greet Macbeth. 65
ROSS. I'll see it done.
DUNCAN. What he hath lost, noble Macbeth hath won. [*Exeunt.*]

64. OUR BOSOM INTEREST—Trust and confidence.
64. PRONOUNCE HIS PRESENT DEATH—Sentence him to instant death.

SCENE 3. *A heath near Forres.*
[*Thunder. Enter the three* Witches.]

FIRST WITCH. Where hast thou been, sister?
SECOND WITCH. Killing swine.
THIRD WITCH. Sister, where thou?
FIRST WITCH. A sailor's wife had chestnuts in her lap,
And munched, and munched, and munched. "Give me," quoth I. 5
"Aroint thee, witch!" the rump-fed ronyon cries.
Her husband's to Aleppo gone, master o' the *Tiger:*
But in a sieve I'll thither sail,
And, like a rat without a tail,
I'll do, I'll do, and I'll do. 10
SECOND WITCH. I'll give thee a wind.
FIRST WITCH. Thou'rt kind.
THIRD WITCH. And I another.
FIRST WITCH. I myself have all the other;
And the very ports they blow, 15
All the quarters that they know
I' the shipman's card.
I'll drain him dry as hay.
Sleep shall neither night nor day
Hang upon his penthouse lid; 20
He shall live a man forbid:
Weary se'nnights nine times nine
Shall he dwindle, peak, and pine;
Though his bark cannot be lost,
Yet it shall be tempest-tost. 25
Look what I have.
SECOND WITCH. Show me, show me.
FIRST WITCH. Here I have a pilot's thumb,
Wrecked as homeward he did come. [*Drum within.*]

2. KILLING SWINE—Witches were supposed to kill livestock, blight the crops, and do other
malicious deeds.
6. AROINT THEE!—Get away!
6. RUMP-FED—Fat.
6. RONYON—Mangy creature.
9. LIKE A RAT—In the shape of a rat.
10. I'LL DO—Do something evil, such as gnaw a hole in the ship's bottom.
20. PENTHOUSE LID—Eyelid.
22. SE'NNIGHTS—Weeks.

THIRD WITCH. A drum, a drum!   30
    Macbeth doth come.

ALL. The weird sisters, hand in hand,
    Posters of the sea and land,
    Thus do go about, about;
    Thrice to thine, and thrice to mine,   35
    And thrice again, to make up nine.
    Peace! the charm's wound up.

                  [*Enter* MACBETH *and* BANQUO.]

MACBETH. So foul and fair a day I have not seen.

BANQUO. How far is 't called to Forres? What are these
    So withered, and so wild in their attire,   40
    That look not like the inhabitants o' the earth,
    And yet are on 't? Live you? Or are you aught
    That man may question? You seem to understand me,
    By each at once her choppy finger laying
    Upon her skinny lips. You should be women,   45
    And yet your beards forbid me to interpret
    That you are so.

MACBETH.   Speak, if you can: what are you?

FIRST WITCH. All hail, Macbeth! hail to thee, thane of Glamis!

SECOND WITCH. All hail, Macbeth! hail to thee, thane of Cawdor!

THIRD WITCH. All hail, Macbeth, that shall be king hereafter!   50

    32. WEIRD SISTERS—Fatal sisters.
    33. POSTERS—Travelers.

BANQUO. Good sir, why do you start, and seem to fear
    Things that do sound so fair? I' the name of truth,
    Are ye fantastical, or that indeed
    Which outwardly ye show? My noble partner
    You greet with present grace and great prediction   55
    Of noble having and of royal hope,
    That he seems rapt withal; to me you speak not.
    If you can look into the seeds of time,
    And say which grain will grow and which will not,
    Speak, then, to me, who neither beg nor fear   60
    Your favors nor your hate.
FIRST WITCH. Hail!
SECOND WITCH. Hail!
THIRD WITCH. Hail!
FIRST WITCH. Lesser than Macbeth, and greater.   65
SECOND WITCH. Not so happy, yet much happier.
THIRD WITCH. Thou shalt get kings, though thou be none;
    So all hail, Macbeth and Banquo!
FIRST WITCH. Banquo and Macbeth, all hail!
MACBETH. Stay, you imperfect speakers, tell me more.   70
    By Sinel's death I know I am thane of Glamis;
    But how of Cawdor? The thane of Cawdor lives,
    A prosperous gentleman, and to be king
    Stands not within the prospect of belief,
    No more than to be Cawdor. Say from whence   75
    You owe this strange intelligence? or why
    Upon this blasted heath you stop our way
    With such prophetic greeting? Speak, I charge you.

                                            [Witches *vanish*.]
BANQUO. The earth hath bubbles as the water has,
    And these are of them. Whither are they vanished?   80
MACBETH. Into the air; and what seemed corporal melted
    As breath into the wind. Would they had stayed!
BANQUO. Were such things here as we do speak about?
    Or have we eaten on the insane root
    That takes the reason prisoner?   85
MACBETH. Your children shall be kings.
BANQUO.   You shall be king.
MACBETH. And thane of Cawdor too: went it not so?
BANQUO. To the selfsame tune and words. Who's here?
                    [*Enter* ROSS *and* ANGUS.]
ROSS. The king hath happily received, Macbeth,
    The news of thy success; and, when he reads   90

67. GET—Beget.
71. SINEL—Macbeth's father.
81. CORPORAL—Corporeal, having body.

Thy personal venture in the rebels' fight,
His wonders and his praises do contend
Which should be thine or his. Silenced with that,
In viewing o'er the rest o' the selfsame day,
He finds thee in the stout Norweyan ranks, 95
Nothing afeard of what thyself didst make,
Strange images of death. As thick as hail
Came post with post; and every one did bear
Thy praises in his kingdom's great defense,
And poured them down before him.

ANGUS.   We are sent 100
To give thee from our royal master thanks;
Only to herald thee into his sight,
Not pay thee.

ROSS. And, for an earnest of a greater honor,
He bade me, from him, call thee thane of Cawdor; 105
In which addition, hail, most worthy thane!
For it is thine.

BANQUO.   [*Aside.*] What, can the devil speak true?

MACBETH.   The thane of Cawdor lives; why do you dress me
In borrowed robes?

ANGUS.   Who was the thane lives yet;
But under heavy judgment bears that life 110
Which he deserves to lose. Whether he was combined
With those of Norway, or did line the rebel
With hidden help and vantage, or that with both
He labored in his country's wreck, I know not;
But treasons capital, confessed and proved, 115
Have overthrown him.

MACBETH.   [*Aside.*] Glamis, and thane of Cawdor!
The greatest is behind. [*To* ROSS *and* ANGUS.] Thanks for your pains.
[*To* BANQUO.] Do you not hope your children shall be kings,
When those that gave the thane of Cawdor to me
Promised no less to them?

BANQUO.   That, trusted home, 120
Might yet enkindle you unto the crown,
Besides the thane of Cawdor. But 'tis strange;
And oftentimes, to win us to our harm,
The instruments of darkness tell us truths,
Win us with honest trifles, to betray 's 125
In deepest consequence.
Cousins, a word, I pray you.

98. POST WITH POST—Messenger after messenger.
104. EARNEST—Assurance.
112. LINE—Strengthen.
117. BEHIND—Yet to come.
127. COUSINS—A word applied to distant relatives, or sometimes to fellow noblemen.

MACBETH.   [*Aside.*]   Two truths are told,
    As happy prologues to the swelling act
    Of the imperial theme.—I thank you, gentlemen.
    [*Aside.*]   This supernatural soliciting   130
    Cannot be ill; cannot be good. If ill,
    Why hath it given me earnest of success,
    Commencing in a truth? I am thane of Cawdor.
    If good, why do I yield to that suggestion
    Whose horrid image doth unfix my hair   135
    And make my seated heart knock at my ribs,
    Against the use of nature? Present fears
    Are less than horrible imaginings.
    My thought, whose murder yet is but fantastical,
    Shakes so my single state of man that function   140
    Is smothered in surmise, and nothing is
    But what is not.
BANQUO.   Look, how our partner's rapt.
MACBETH. [*Aside.*] If chance will have me king, why, chance may crown me,
    Without my stir.
BANQUO.   New honors come upon him,
    Like our strange garments, cleave not to their mold   145
    But with the aid of use.
MACBETH.   [*Aside.*] Come what come may,
    Time and the hour runs through the roughest day.
BANQUO. Worthy Macbeth, we stay upon your leisure.
MACBETH. Give me your favor. My dull brain was wrought
    With things forgotten. Kind gentlemen, your pains   150
    Are registered where every day I turn
    The leaf to read them. Let us toward the king.
    [*To* BANQUO.] Think upon what hath chanced; and, at more time,
    The interim having weighed it, let us speak
    Our free hearts each to other.
BANQUO.   Very gladly.   155
MACBETH. Till then, enough. Come, friends.   [*Exeunt.*]

SCENE 4. *Forres. The palace.*
[*Flourish. Enter* DUNCAN, MALCOLM, DONALBAIN, LENNOX, *and* Attendants.]

DUNCAN. Is execution done on Cawdor? Are not
    Those in commission yet returned?
MALCOLM.   My liege,
    They are not yet come back. But I have spoke
    With one that saw him die; who did report
    That very frankly he confessed his treasons,   5
    Implored your highness' pardon, and set forth

A deep repentance. (Nothing in his life
Became him like the leaving it; he died
As one that had been studied in his death
To throw away the dearest thing he owed,   10
As 'twere a careless trifle.)

DUNCAN.   (There's no art
To find the mind's construction in the face;)
He was a gentleman on whom I built
An absolute trust.

             [*Enter* MACBETH, BANQUO, ROSS, *and* ANGUS.]
              O worthiest cousin!
The sin of my ingratitude even now   15
Was heavy on me. Thou art so far before,
That swiftest wing of recompense is slow
To overtake thee. Would thou hadst less deserved,
That the proportion both of thanks and payment
Might have been mine! Only I have left to say,   20
More is thy due than more than all can pay.

MACBETH. The service and the loyalty I owe,
In doing it, pays itself. Your highness' part
Is to receive our duties; and our duties
Are to your throne and state children and servants;   25
Which do but what they should, by doing everything
Safe toward your love and honor.

DUNCAN.   Welcome hither;
I have begun to plant thee, and will labor
To make thee full of growing. Noble Banquo,
That hast no less deserved, nor must be known   30
No less to have done so, let me infold thee
And hold thee to my heart.

BANQUO.   There if I grow,
The harvest is your own.

DUNCAN.   My plenteous joys,
Wanton in fullness, seek to hide themselves
In drops of sorrow. Sons, kinsmen, thanes,   35
And you whose places are the nearest, know,
We will establish our estate upon
Our eldest, Malcolm, whom we name hereafter
The Prince of Cumberland; which honor must
Not unaccompanied invest him only,   40
But signs of nobleness, like stars, shall shine
On all deservers. From hence to Inverness,

    10. OWED—Owned.
    35. DROPS OF SORROW—The meaning is tears of joy.
    39. PRINCE OF CUMBERLAND—The throne of Scotland was not hereditary, but Duncan by raising his eldest son to high office makes it very likely that he will some day be chosen king.
    42. INVERNESS—Macbeth's castle.

And bind us further to you.
MACBETH. The rest is labor, which is not used for you.
    I'll be myself the harbinger, and make joyful   45
    The hearing of my wife with your approach;
    So humbly take my leave.
DUNCAN.   My worthy Cawdor!
MACBETH. [*Aside.*] The Prince of Cumberland! That is a step
    On which I must fall down, or else o'erleap,
    For in my way it lies. Stars, hide your fires;   50
    Let not light see my black and deep desires;
    The eye wink at the hand; yet let that be
    Which the eye fears, when it is done, to see.   [*Exit.*]
DUNCAN. True, worthy Banquo; he is full so valiant,
    And in his commendations I am fed;   55
    It is a banquet to me. Let's after him,
    Whose care is gone before to bid us welcome.
    It is a peerless kinsman.   [*Flourish. Exeunt.*]

SCENE 5. *Inverness.* MACBETH's *castle.*
[*Enter* LADY MACBETH, *alone, with a letter.*]

LADY MACBETH. [*Reads.*] "They met me in the day of success; and I have learned
    by the perfectest report, they have more in them than mortal knowledge.
    When I burned in desire to question them further, they made themselves
    air, into which they vanished. Whiles I stood rapt in the wonder of it, came
    missives from the king, who all-hailed me 'Thane of Cawdor'; by   5
    which title, before, these weird sisters saluted me, and referred me to the
    coming on of time, with 'Hail, king that shalt be!' This have I thought good
    to deliver thee, my dearest partner of greatness, that thou mightst not lose
    the dues of rejoicing, by being ignorant of what greatness is promised thee.
    Lay it to thy heart, and farewell."   10

    Glamis thou art, and Cawdor, and shalt be
    What thou art promised. Yet do I fear thy nature;
    It is too full o' the milk of human kindness
    To catch the nearest way. Thou wouldst be great;
    Art not without ambition, but without   15
    The illness should attend it. What thou wouldst highly,
    That wouldst thou holily; wouldst not play false,
    And yet wouldst wrongly win. Thou 'ldst have, great Glamis,
    That which cries, "Thus thou must do, if thou have it";
    And that which rather thou dost fear to do   20
    Than wishest should be undone. Hie thee hither,
    That I may pour my spirits in thine ear,
    And chastise with the valor of my tongue

16. ILLNESS—Wickedness.

All that impedes thee from the golden round,
Which fate and metaphysical aid doth seem   25
To have thee crowned withal.)
> [*Enter a* Messenger.]
> What is your tidings?

MESSENGER.   The king comes here tonight.

LADY MACBETH.   Thou 'rt mad to say it!
Is not thy master with him? who, were 't so,
Would have informed for preparation.

MESSENGER.   So please you, it is true; our thane is coming.   30
One of my fellows had the speed of him,
Who, almost dead for breath, had scarcely more
Than would make up his message.

LADY MACBETH.   Give him tending;
He brings great news.   [*Exit* Messenger.]
                     The raven himself is hoarse
That croaks the fatal entrance of Duncan   35
Under my battlements. (Come, you spirits
That tend on mortal thoughts, unsex me here;
And fill me from the crown to the toe top-full
Of direst cruelty! make thick my blood;
Stop up the access and passage to remorse,   40
That no compunctious visitings of nature
Shake my fell purpose, nor keep peace between
The effect and it!   Come to my woman's breasts,
And take my milk for gall, you murdering ministers,
Wherever in your sightless substances   45
You wait on nature's mischief!   Come, thick night,
And pall thee in the dunnest smoke of hell,
That my keen knife see not the wound it makes,
Nor heaven peep through the blanket of the dark,
To cry, "Hold, hold!"
> [*Enter* MACBETH.]
>   Great Glamis! worthy Cawdor!   50
Greater than both, by the all-hail hereafter!
Thy letters have transported me beyond
This ignorant present, and I feel now
The future in the instant.

MACBETH.   My dearest love,
Duncan comes here tonight.

LADY MACBETH.   And when goes hence?   55

MACBETH.   Tomorrow, as he purposes.

LADY MACBETH.   O, never
Shall sun that morrow see!

24. GOLDEN ROUND—The crown.
25. METAPHYSICAL—Supernatural.

Your face, my thane, is as a book where men
May read strange matters. To beguile the time,
Look like the time; bear welcome in your eye, 60
Your hand, your tongue; look like the innocent flower
But be the serpent under 't. He that's coming
Must be provided for; and you shall put
This night's great business into my dispatch,
Which shall to all our nights and days to come 65
Give solely sovereign sway and masterdom.
MACBETH. We will speak further.
LADY MACBETH.   Only look up clear;
To alter favor ever is to fear.
Leave all the rest to me.   [*Exeunt.*]

SCENE 6. *Before* MACBETH'S *castle.*
[*Hautboys* * *and torches. Enter* DUNCAN, MALCOLM, DONALBAIN,
BANQUO, LENNOX, MACDUFF, ROSS, ANGUS, *and* Attendants.]

DUNCAN. This castle hath a pleasant seat; the air
Nimbly and sweetly recommends itself
Unto our gentle senses.
BANQUO.   This guest of summer,
The temple-haunting martlet, does approve,
By his loved mansionry, that the heaven's breath 5
Smells wooingly here; no jutty, frieze,
Buttress, nor coign of vantage, but this bird
Hath made his pendent bed and procreant cradle.
Where they most breed and haunt, I have observed
The air is delicate.
                    [*Enter* LADY MACBETH.]
DUNCAN.   See, see, our honored hostess! 10
The love that follows us sometime is our trouble,
Which still we thank as love. Herein I teach you
How you shall bid God 'ild us for your pains,
And thank us for your trouble.
LADY MACBETH.   All our service
In every point twice done and then done double 15
Were poor and single business to contend
Against those honors deep and broad wherewith
Your Majesty loads our house; for those of old,
And the late dignities heaped up to them,
We rest your hermits.

* HAUTBOYS (hō′boiz)—Oboes, sounded to announce the entrance of noble or royal persons.
4. MARTLET—An allusion to the martin, a bird which has built nests for its young in all convenient nooks about the castle.
20. HERMITS—Beadsmen; those who receive alms and are bound to pray for their benefactors.

DUNCAN. Where's the thane of Cawdor? 20
We coursed him at the heels, and had a purpose
To be his purveyor; but he rides well,
And his great love, sharp as his spur, hath holp him
To his home before us. Fair and noble hostess,
We are your guest tonight.

LADY MACBETH. Your servants ever 25
Have theirs, themselves, and what is theirs, in compt,
To make their audit at your Highness' pleasure,
Still to return your own.

DUNCAN. Give me your hand;
Conduct me to mine host. We love him highly,
And shall continue our graces towards him. 30
By your leave, hostess. [*Exeunt.*]

SCENE 7. MACBETH's *castle.*

[*Hautboys and torches. Enter a Sewer,* and divers* Servants *with
dishes and service, over the stage. Then enter* MACBETH.]

MACBETH. If it were done when 'tis done, then 'twere well
It were done quickly. If the assassination
Could trammel up the consequence, and catch
With his surcease success; that but this blow
Might be the be-all and the end-all here, 5
But here, upon this bank and shoal of time,
We 'ld jump the life to come. But in these cases
We still have judgment here, that we but teach
Bloody instructions, which, being taught, return
To plague the inventor. This even-handed justice 10
Commends the ingredients of our poisoned chalice
To our own lips. He's here in double trust:
First, as I am his kinsman and his subject,
Strong both against the deed; then, as his host,
Who should against his murderer shut the door, 15
Not bear the knife myself. Besides, this Duncan
Hath borne his faculties so meek, hath been
So clear in his great office, that his virtues
Will plead like angels, trumpet-tongued, against
The deep damnation of his taking-off; 20
And pity, like a naked newborn babe
Striding the blast, or heaven's cherubin horsed

* SEWER—The head servant who arranged dishes for a banquet.
3. TRAMMEL UP—Tangle up, and thus prevent the consequences from following.
21. PITY, LIKE A . . . BABE—Macbeth imagines pity for Duncan spreading swiftly over the
land as if a cherub, or spirit shaped like a child, flew everywhere to tell of the "horrid deed."

Upon the sightless couriers of the air,
Shall blow the horrid deed in every eye,
That tears shall drown the wind.) I have no spur 25
To prick the sides of my intent, but only
Vaulting ambition, which o'erleaps itself
And falls on the other.

[*Enter* LADY MACBETH.]
How now! what news?

LADY MACBETH. He has almost supped. Why have you left the chamber?
MACBETH. Hath he asked for me?
LADY MACBETH.   Know you not he has? 30
MACBETH. We will proceed no further in this business:
He hath honored me of late; and I have bought
Golden opinions from all sorts of people,
Which would be worn now in their newest gloss
Not cast aside so soon.
LADY MACBETH.   (Was the hope drunk 35
Wherein you dressed yourself?) Hath it slept since?
And wakes it now, to look so green and pale
At what it did so freely? From this time
Such I account thy love. Art thou afeard
To be the same in thine own act and valor 40
As thou art in desire? (Wouldst thou have that
Which thou esteem'st the ornament of life,
And live a coward in thine own esteem,
Letting "I dare not" wait upon "I would,")
Like the poor cat i' the adage?
MACBETH.   Prithee, Peace! 45
I dare do all that may become a man;
Who dares do more is none.
LADY MACBETH.   What beast was 't, then,
That made you break this enterprise to me?
When you durst do it, then you were a man;
And, to be more than what you were, you would 50
Be so much more the man. Nor time nor place
Did then adhere, and yet you would make both.
They have made themselves, and that their fitness now
Does unmake you. I have given suck, and know
How tender 'tis to love the babe that milks me; 55
I would, while it was smiling in my face,

23. SIGHTLESS . . . AIR—The invisible winds.
27. WHICH O'ERLEAPS ITSELF—Leaps too high, so that it falls disastrously on the other side of the obstacle.
35–38. WAS THE HOPE DRUNK . . . AT WHAT IT DID SO FREELY?—Macbeth's hope is like a drunken man who does bold things but awakens the next morning sick and pale, with all his courage gone.
45. THE ADAGE—The proverb which says, "The cat would eat fish, but she will not wet her feet."

Have plucked my nipple from his boneless gums,
And dashed the brains out, had I so sworn as you
Have done to this.

MACBETH.   If we should fail?

LADY MACBETH.   We fail!
But screw your courage to the sticking-place,   60
And we'll not fail. When Duncan is asleep—
Whereto the rather shall his day's hard journey
Soundly invite him—his two chamberlains
Will I with wine and wassail so convince,
That memory, the warder of the brain,   65
Shall be a fume, and the receipt of reason
A limbeck only. When in swinish sleep
Their drenchèd natures lie as in a death,
What cannot you and I perform upon
Th' unguarded Duncan? what not put upon   70
His spongy officers, who shall bear the guilt
Of our great quell?

MACBETH.   Bring forth men children only;
For thy undaunted mettle should compose
Nothing but males. Will it not be received,
When we have marked with blood those sleepy two   75
Of his own chamber and used their very daggers,
That they have done 't?

LADY MACBETH.   Who dares receive it other,
As we shall make our griefs and clamor roar
Upon his death?

MACBETH.   I am settled, and bend up
Each corporal agent to this terrible feat.   80
Away, and mock the time with fairest show;
False face must hide what the false heart doth know.   [*Exeunt.*]

FOR UNDERSTANDING OF ACT I

1. How is it made clear in Scene 3 that the witches are evil creatures?

2. Why does the fact that the witches have called Macbeth "thane of Cawdor" cause him to take more seriously their prophecy about becoming king? What favorable prediction do they make to Banquo?

3. Who gives the following advice, and what does it mean?

"Look like the innocent flower,
But be the serpent under 't."

4. As a nobleman of high rank who is also a brilliant soldier, Macbeth might expect to be chosen king some day—that is, if Duncan should happen to die. Find at least one passage in Scene 3 to show that he has already thought about murdering Duncan *before* he has an opportunity to discuss the matter with Lady Macbeth. How can we tell, in Scene 3, that he is reluctant to plan such a deed? On the other hand, how does his letter to Lady Macbeth (which she reads in Scene 5) suggest that he has made up his mind to commit murder?

5. In Scene 7, back in his own castle, Macbeth again has doubts about the murder. What arguments occur to him against killing Duncan? Explain why he is forced to make up his mind quickly.

6. Find one or more passages which show that Lady Macbeth feels no hesitation whatever. Explain her scheme for committing the crime and escaping detection.

7. The general impression which Shakespeare gives of Duncan is that, in contrast to the scheming Macbeths, he is an honorable and trusting person. Find at least two speeches by Duncan in Act I which give such an impression.

8. "Dramatic irony" is the name for a situation in a play which has a different meaning and more significance for the audience than for the speaker. Explain the irony of this speech by Duncan in Scene 6:

"This castle hath a pleasant seat; the air
Nimbly and sweetly recommends itself
Unto our gentle senses."

9. Shakespeare's plays contain frequent *soliloquies* and *asides*. A *soliloquy* is a speech in which a character "thinks aloud." An *aside* is the same thing, except that it is spoken while other persons are on stage. They cannot hear the remark—although the audience can. Give one example of a *soliloquy*, and one of an *aside*, in Act I.

SHAKESPEARE'S USE OF BLANK VERSE

Most of *Macbeth* is written in *blank verse*—that is, in unrhymed iambic pentameter. The term *iambic* refers to the particular kind of feet the line has. An iambic foot consists of two syllables with the accent falling on the second syllable. The word *cŏntén̄d* is an iambic foot. The term *pentameter* refers to the *meter*, or measure, of the line. *Penta* (from the Greek *pente*, meaning *five*) means that the line contains five feet, like this one:

Hĭs wón | dĕrs án̄d | hĭs práis | ĕs dó | cŏn
tén̄d.

Not all the lines are completely regular and exact, for perfectly regular verse would soon become monotonous to hear. Some of the lines are irregular in rhythm, like this one:

Glám ĭs | thóu árt, | ănd Cáw dŏr, | ănd
shált | bé.

There are still other variations, some lines containing extra syllables, some being shorter than the normal five-foot meter, and some being broken by pauses.

"Blank" verse is supposed to be unrhymed, but occasionally to make a more impressive close to a speech or a scene, Shakespeare rhymes the last two lines—or even the last four.

1. Analyze a short passage of blank verse in Act I. For instance, use a part of Lady Macbeth's speech near the end of Scene 5, "He that's coming/ Must be provided for." Start with the word "Must" and point out the stressed and unstressed syllables in each of the next four lines. (Don't expect that there will invariably be an unstressed syllable followed by a stressed syllable.) Then divide each line into feet.

2. Examine the concluding lines of Scenes 2, 3, 5, and 6. In which of these conclusions is *rhymed* verse used? Rhymed verse at the end gives a sense of finality or completeness.

GETTING A DRAMA UNDER WAY

A playwright is always faced with the problem of explaining who the characters are and what situation they are in, so that his audience can follow the story. In Scene 2 the lines spoken by the bleeding Sergeant and by Ross reveal that a great battle has just ended, and they give us necessary information as well. What line tells us exactly who Duncan is? Sum up the information that is given about Macbeth in the reports from the battlefield and Duncan's comments on them.

Since the entire play will portray the wicked career of Macbeth, Shakespeare wishes to get this career started as soon as possible. The witches predict that Macbeth will be king, but they do not say how this will come about. As Act I progresses Macbeth thinks seriously about murdering Duncan. What lines early in Scene 7 hint that this plan might eventually mean disaster to Macbeth? What lines near the end of the scene show that he has definitely made up his mind?

DAILY READING IN UNISON

Try reading Macbeth's famous soliloquy "Tomorrow, and tomorrow, and tomorrow" in unison each class period, beginning *before* you have actually reached Act V, Scene 5 where the lines occur. Immediately after every reading try it again without the book. After several times, with very little outside study most members of the class will be able to write or speak the passage from memory.

You may be surprised to find how much more vivid and interesting this bit of poetry will become after several readings. The class might consider briefly one particular aspect of the soliloquy each time before it is read. For example, before the first reading the class might discuss the

figures of speech: *how* is life like a candle, a player, a tale told by an idiot?

"MISUSED" WORDS

Several times in *Macbeth* the three witches are called "the weird sisters." The first time is in Scene 3, just before the entrance of Macbeth. In Old English the noun *wyrd* meant *fate*, and Englishmen used to refer to the three Fates of ancient mythology as "the weird sisters." Shakespeare's use of the same expression indicates that the witches have power over the destiny of men, or at least can foretell one's destiny. Shakespeare himself was probably responsible for the modern definition of *weird* because his "fatal" sisters were such mysterious, uncanny creatures. The original meaning of the word has almost disappeared.

A number of words in our language have a similar history. For instance, to the ancient Hebrews the word *talent* meant a money unit of about three thousand dollars. If you remember Jesus' parable of the talents (Matthew 25) you know how the word got into the English language. Because of the parable, *talent* came to be used figuratively for *ability* or *aptitude*— and this is now the principal meaning.

For still another "misused" word, look up the origin of the expression *forlorn hope.*

ACT II

This act might be entitled "The murder, and the first reactions afterward." Most of the action takes place in the dead of night, and Shakespeare puts all possible suspense and horror into the setting. The owl shrieks outside while Macbeth and his wife move about stealthily in the sleeping house-

hold. Then comes commotion and shouting when Duncan's body is discovered. In the final scene, which takes place next day, we learn who is blamed and who is to be the new king.

SCENE I. Inverness. Court of MACBETH'S castle.
[<i>Enter</i> BANQUO, <i>and</i> FLEANCE <i>with a torch before him.</i>]</div>

BANQUO. How goes the night, boy?
FLEANCE. The moon is down; I have not heard the clock.
BANQUO. And she goes down at twelve.
FLEANCE.   I take 't, 'tis later, sir.
BANQUO. Hold, take my sword. There's husbandry in heaven;
    Their candles are all out. Take thee that too.   5
    A heavy summons lies like lead upon me,
    And yet I would not sleep. Merciful powers,
    Restrain in me the cursèd thoughts that nature
    Gives way to in repose!
              [<i>Enter</i> MACBETH, <i>and a</i> Servant <i>with a torch.</i>]
              Give me my sword.
    Who's there?   10
MACBETH.   A friend.
BANQUO. What, sir, not yet at rest? The king's abed:
    He hath been in unusual pleasure, and
    Sent forth great largess to your offices.
    This diamond he greets your wife withal,   15
    By the name of most kind hostess; and shut up
    In measureless content.
MACBETH.   Being unprepared,
    Our will became the servant to defect;
    Which else should free have wrought.
BANQUO.   All's well.
    I dreamt last night of the three weird sisters: 20
    To you they have showed some truth.
MACBETH.   I think not of them;
    Yet, when we can entreat an hour to serve,
    We would spend it in some words upon that business,
    If you would grant the time.
BANQUO.   At your kind'st leisure.
MACBETH. If you shall cleave to my consent, when 'tis,   25
    It shall make honor for you.
BANQUO.   So I lose none
    In seeking to augment it, but still keep

---

    4. HUSBANDRY—Thrift.
    17–19. BEING UNPREPARED . . . HAVE WROUGHT—With more time to prepare, Macbeth would have entertained the king more nobly.

My bosom franchised and allegiance clear,
I shall be counseled.

MACBETH.   Good repose the while!

BANQUO. Thanks, sir; the like to you!   30

[*Exeunt* BANQUO *and* FLEANCE.]

MACBETH. Go bid thy mistress, when my drink is ready,
She strike upon the bell. Get thee to bed.   [*Exit* Servant.]
Is this a dagger which I see before me,
The handle toward my hand? Come, let me clutch thee.
I have thee not, and yet I see thee still.   35
Art thou not, fatal vision, sensible
To feeling as to sight? or art thou but
A dagger of the mind, a false creation,
Proceeding from the heat-oppressèd brain?
I see thee yet, in form as palpable   40
As this which now I draw.
Thou marshal'st me the way that I was going;
And such an instrument I was to use.
Mine eyes are made the fools o' the other senses,
Or else worth all the rest; I see thee still;   45
And on thy blade and dudgeon gouts of blood,
Which was not so before. There 's no such thing;
It is the bloody business which informs
Thus to mine eyes. Now o'er the one half-world
Nature seems dead, and wicked dreams abuse   50
The curtained sleep; witchcraft celebrates
Pale Hecate's offerings; and withered murder,
Alarumed by his sentinel, the wolf,
Whose howl's his watch, thus with his stealthy pace,
With Tarquin's ravishing strides, towards his design   55
Moves like a ghost. Thou sure and firm-set earth,
Hear not my steps, which way they walk, for fear
Thy very stones prate of my whereabout,
And take the present horror from the time,
Which now suits with it. Whiles I threat, he lives;   60
Words to the heat of deeds too cold breath gives.

[*A bell rings.*]

I go, and it is done; the bell invites me.
Hear it not, Duncan; for it is a knell
That summons thee to heaven or to hell.   [*Exit.*]

42. MARSHAL'ST ME—Leadest me.
46. DUDGEON—Haft or hilt.
52. HECATE'S (hĕk′ĭtz) OFFERINGS—Ceremonies offered to Hecate by witches. In Greek mythology Hecate was queen of Hades, the underworld.
55. TARQUIN (tär′kwĭn)—A wicked Roman king whose assault on Lucretia (lṳ·krē′shĭ·á), a
Roman matron, so aroused the people that they overthrew Tarquin's family and established a republic.

SCENE 2. *The same.*

[*Enter* LADY MACBETH.]

LADY MACBETH. That which hath made them drunk hath made me bold;
 What hath quenched them hath given me fire. Hark! Peace!
 It was the owl that shrieked, the fatal bellman,
 Which gives the stern'st good night. He is about it.
 The doors are open; and the surfeited grooms   5
 Do mock their charge with snores. I have drugged their possets,
 That death and nature do contend about them,
 Whether they live or die.

MACBETH.   [*Within.*] Who's there? what, ho!

LADY MACBETH. Alack, I am afraid they have awaked,
 And 'tis not done. The attempt and not the deed   10
 Confounds us. Hark! I laid their daggers ready;
 He could not miss 'em. Had he not resembled
 My father as he slept, I had done 't.

[*Enter* MACBETH.]

          My husband!

MACBETH. I have done the deed. Didst thou not hear a noise?

LADY MACBETH. I heard the owl scream and the crickets cry.   15
 Did not you speak?

MACBETH.   When?

LADY MACBETH.   Now.

MACBETH.   As I descended?

LADY MACBETH. Ay.

MACBETH. Hark!
 Who lies i' the second chamber?

LADY MACBETH.   Donalbain.

MACBETH. This is a sorry sight.   [*Looking on his hands.*]   20

LADY MACBETH. A foolish thought, to say a sorry sight.

MACBETH. There's one did laugh in 's sleep, and one cried "Murder!"
 That they did wake each other. I stood and heard them;
 But they did say their prayers, and addressed them
 Again to sleep.

LADY MACBETH.   There are two lodged together.   25

MACBETH. One cried "God bless us!" and "Amen" the other,
 As they had seen me with these hangman's hands.
 Listening their fear, I could not say "Amen,"
 When they did say "God bless us!"

LADY MACBETH.   Consider it not so deeply.

MACBETH. But wherefore could not I pronounce "Amen"?   30

 6. MOCK THEIR CHARGE—Make a mockery of their responsibility.
 6. THEIR POSSETS—Their going-to-bed drinks.
 11. CONFOUNDS—Ruins.
 25. TWO LODGED TOGETHER—Malcolm and Donalbain, in the second chamber.

I had most need of blessing, and "Amen"
Stuck in my throat.

LADY MACBETH.   These deeds must not be thought
After these ways; so, it will make us mad.

MACBETH. Methought I heard a voice cry "Sleep no more!   35
Macbeth does murder sleep"—the innocent sleep,
Sleep that knits up the raveled sleave of care,
The death of each day's life, sore labor's bath,
Balm of hurt minds, great nature's second course,
Chief nourisher in life's feast—

LADY MACBETH.   What do you mean?   40

MACBETH.   Still it cried "Sleep no more!" to all the house;
"Glamis hath murdered sleep, and therefore Cawdor
Shall sleep no more; Macbeth shall sleep no more!"

LADY MACBETH.   Who was it that thus cried?   Why, worthy thane,
You do unbend your noble strength, to think   45
So brainsickly of things. Go get some water,
And wash this filthy witness from your hand.
Why did you bring these daggers from the place?
They must lie there; go carry them, and smear
The sleepy grooms with blood.

37. SLEAVE—Floss-silk, slender filaments separated out of a thicker thread.
39. SECOND COURSE—The chief course, or meat course, at a dinner.

MACBETH. I'll go no more. 50
I am afraid to think what I have done;
Look on 't again I dare not.
LADY MACBETH. Infirm of purpose!
Give me the daggers: the sleeping and the dead
Are but as pictures; 'tis the eye of childhood
That fears a painted devil. If he do bleed, 55
I'll gild the faces of the grooms withal;
For it must seem their guilt. [*Exit. Knocking within.*]
MACBETH. Whence is that knocking?
How is 't with me, when every noise appalls me?
What hands are here? Ha! they pluck out mine eyes!
Will all great Neptune's ocean wash this blood 60
Clean from my hand? No; this my hand will rather
The multitudinous seas incarnadine,
Making the green one red.
[*Re-enter LADY MACBETH.*]
LADY MACBETH. My hands are of your color, but I shame
To wear a heart so white. [*Knocking within.*] I hear a knocking 65
At the south entry. Retire we to our chamber.
A little water clears us of this deed.
How easy is it, then! Your constancy
Hath left you unattended. [*Knocking within.*] Hark! more knocking.
Get on your nightgown, lest occasion call us, 70
And show us to be watchers. Be not lost
So poorly in your thoughts.
MACBETH. To know my deed, 'twere best not know myself.
[*Knocking within.*]
Wake Duncan with thy knocking! I would thou couldst!
[*Exeunt.*]

59. WHAT HANDS . . . MINE EYES—Macbeth's eyes bulge as he stares in horror at his bloody
hands.
68–69. YOUR CONSTANCY . . . UNATTENDED—Your firmness has deserted you.

SCENE 3. *The same.*
[*Enter a PORTER.* Knocking within.*]

PORTER. Here's a knocking indeed! If a man were porter of hell-gate, he should
have old turning the key. [*Knocking.*] Knock, knock, knock! Who's
there, i' the name of Beelzebub? Here's a farmer, that hanged himself on the expectation of plenty. Come in time; have napkins enough
about you; here you'll sweat for 't. [*Knocking.*] Knock, knock! 5

* PORTER—The Porter is drunk. As he fumbles to open the lock, he pretends he is porter
at hell-gate letting in the souls of the damned.
3. BEELZEBUB (bē·ĕl′zē·bŭb)—Prince of devils.

Who's there, in the other devil's name? Faith, here's an equivocator that could swear in both the scales against either scale; who committed treason enough for God's sake, yet could not equivocate to heaven. O, come in, equivocator. [*Knocking.*] Knock, knock, knock! Who's there? Faith, here's an English tailor come hither for stealing out of a French hose.   10 Come in, tailor; here you may roast your goose. [*Knocking.*] Knock, knock; never at quiet! What are you? But this place is too cold for hell. I'll devil-porter it no further. I had thought to have let in some of all professions that go the primrose way to the everlasting bonfire. [*Knocking.*] Anon, anon! I pray you, remember the porter.   [*Opens the gate.*]   15
[*Enter* MACDUFF *and* LENNOX.]

MACDUFF. Was it so late, friend, ere you went to bed,
  That you do lie so late?
PORTER. Faith, sir, we were carousing till the second cock.
MACDUFF. I believe drink gave thee the lie last night.
PORTER. That it did, sir, i' the very throat on me. But I requited him for   20
  his lie; and, I think, being too strong for him, though he took up my legs
  sometime, yet I made a shift to cast him.
MACDUFF. Is thy master stirring?
[*Enter* MACBETH.]

  Our knocking has awaked him; here he comes.
LENNOX. Good morrow, noble sir.
MACBETH.   Good morrow, both.   25
MACDUFF. Is the king stirring, worthy thane?
MACBETH.   Not yet.
MACDUFF. He did command me to call timely on him.
  I have almost slipped the hour.
MACBETH.   I'll bring you to him.
MACDUFF. I know this is a joyful trouble to you;
  But yet 'tis one.   30
MACBETH. The labor we delight in physics pain.
  This is the door.
MACDUFF.   I'll make so bold to call,
  For 'tis my limited service.   [*Exit.*]
LENNOX. Goes the king hence today?
MACBETH.   He does—he did appoint so.
LENNOX. The night has been unruly. Where we lay,   35
  Our chimneys were blown down; and, as they say,
  Lamentings heard i' the air, strange screams of death,
  And prophesying with accents terrible
  Of dire combustion and confused events

---

6. EQUIVOCATOR—One who tells the "truth," but by clever wording gives a false impression.
10. STEALING OUT OF A FRENCH HOSE—Stealing some of the cloth brought to him to be made into "hose," or breeches.
11. GOOSE—A tailor's pressing iron. The handle resembled the neck of a goose.
15. REMEMBER THE PORTER—Remember to tip the porter.

198

New hatched to the woeful time; the obscure bird   40
    Clamored the livelong night; some say, the earth
    Was feverous and did shake.
MACBETH.   'Twas a rough night.
LENNOX. My young remembrance cannot parallel
    A fellow to it.

                  [Re-enter MACDUFF.]

MACDUFF. O horror, horror, horror! Tongue nor heart   45
    Cannot conceive nor name thee!
MACBETH.
                              What's the matter?
LENNOX.
MACDUFF. Confusion now hath made his masterpiece!
    Most sacrilegious murder hath broke ope
    The Lord's anointed temple, and stole thence
    The life o' the building.
MACBETH.   What is 't you say? the life?   50
LENNOX. Mean you his Majesty?
MACDUFF. Approach the chamber, and destroy your sight
    With a new Gorgon. Do not bid me speak;
    See, and then speak yourselves.

                        [Exeunt MACBETH *and* LENNOX.]
                Awake, awake!
    Ring the alarum bell. Murder and treason!   55
    Banquo and Donalbain! Malcolm! awake!
    Shake off this downy sleep, death's counterfeit,
    And look on death itself! Up, up, and see
    The great doom's image! Malcolm! Banquo!
    As from your graves rise up, and walk like sprites,   60
    To countenance this horror. Ring the bell.   *[Bell rings.]*

                [Enter LADY MACBETH.]
LADY MACBETH. What's the business,
    That such a hideous trumpet calls to parley
    The sleepers of the house? Speak, speak!
MACDUFF.   O gentle lady,
    'Tis not for you to hear what I can speak;   65
    The repetition, in a woman's ear,
    Would murder as it fell.
                [Enter BANQUO.]
                O Banquo, Banquo,
    Our royal master's murdered!

40. OBSCURE BIRD—Bird of darkness, the owl.
    49. THE LORD'S ANOINTED TEMPLE—The body of the king; a reference to the idea that the king is chosen by God.
    53. GORGON—In Greek mythology, the Gorgons were three snaky-haired women whose appearance was so terrible that whoever saw them was turned to stone.

LADY MACBETH.   Woe, alas!
　　What, in our house?
BANQUO.   Too cruel anywhere.
　　Dear Duff, I prithee, contradict thyself,   70
　　And say it is not so.
　　　　　　　　　[*Re-enter* MACBETH *and* LENNOX, *with* ROSS.]
MACBETH. Had I but died an hour before this chance,
　　I had lived a blessed time; for, from this instant,
　　There's nothing serious in mortality.
　　All is but toys; renown and grace is dead;   75
　　The wine of life is drawn, and the mere lees
　　Is left this vault to brag of.
　　　　　　　　　[*Enter* MALCOLM *and* DONALBAIN.]
DONALBAIN. What is amiss?
MACBETH.   You are, and do not know 't.
　　The spring, the head, the fountain of your blood
　　Is stopped; the very source of it is stopped.   80
MACDUFF. Your royal father's murdered.
MALCOLM.   O! by whom?
LENNOX. Those of his chamber, as it seemed, had done 't:
　　Their hands and faces were all badged with blood;
　　So were their daggers, which unwiped we found
　　Upon their pillows.   85
　　They stared, and were distracted; no man's life
　　Was to be trusted with them.
MACBETH. O, yet I do repent me of my fury,
　　That I did kill them.
MACDUFF.   Wherefore did you so?
MACBETH. Who can be wise, amazed, temperate and furious,   90
　　Loyal and neutral, in a moment? No man.
　　The expedition of my violent love
　　Outrun the pauser, reason. Here lay Duncan,
　　His silver skin laced with his golden blood;
　　And his gashed stabs looked like a breach in nature   95
　　For ruin's wasteful entrance; there, the murderers,
　　Steeped in the colors of their trade, their daggers
　　Unmannerly breeched with gore. Who could refrain,
　　That had a heart to love, and in that heart
　　Courage to make 's love known?
LADY MACBETH.   Help me hence, ho!   100
MACDUFF. Look to the lady.
MALCOLM. [*Aside to* DONALBAIN.] Why do we hold our tongues,
　　That most may claim this argument for ours?

74. SERIOUS IN MORTALITY—Worth while in life.
76. LEES—Dregs.
92. EXPEDITION—Haste.
98. BREECHED—Covered.

DONALBAIN. [*Aside to* MALCOLM.] What should be spoken here, where our fate,
    Hid in an auger hole, may rush, and seize us?
    Let's away.   105
    Our tears are not yet brewed.
MALCOLM. [*Aside to* DONALBAIN.] Nor our strong sorrow
    Upon the foot of motion.
BANQUO.   Look to the lady;
                                 [LADY MACBETH *is carried out.*]
    And when we have our naked frailties hid,
    That suffer in exposure, let us meet
    And question this most bloody piece of work,   110
    To know it further. Fears and scruples shake us.
    In the great hand of God I stand, and thence
    Against the undivulged pretense I fight
    Of treasonous malice.
MACDUFF.   And so do I.
ALL.   So all.
MACBETH. Let's briefly put on manly readiness,   115
    And meet i' the hall together.
ALL.   Well contented.
                [*Exeunt all but* MALCOLM *and* DONALBAIN.]
MALCOLM. What will you do? Let's not consort with them;
    To show an unfelt sorrow is an office
    Which the false man does easy. I'll to England.
DONALBAIN. To Ireland, I; our separated fortune   120
    Shall keep us both the safer. Where we are,
    There's daggers in men's smiles; the near in blood,
    The nearer bloody.
MALCOLM.   This murderous shaft that's shot
    Hath not yet lighted, and our safest way
    Is to avoid the aim. Therefore, to horse;   125
    And let us not be dainty of leave-taking,
    But shift away. There's warrant in that theft
    Which steals itself, when there's no mercy left.   [*Exeunt.*]

107. FOOT OF MOTION—It is not yet time to express grief.
113. UNDIVULGED PRETENSE—Not-yet-known purpose.
115. MANLY READINESS—Armor and weapons.
123. THE NEARER BLOODY—Those closest to Duncan in relationship are those most likely to be murdered also.

SCENE 4. *Outside* MACBETH'S *castle.*
[*Enter* ROSS *and an* Old Man.]

OLD MAN. Threescore and ten I can remember well;
    Within the volume of which time I have seen
    Hours dreadful and things strange; but this sore night

Hath trifled former knowings.

ROSS.   Ah, good father,
Thou seest the heavens, as troubled with man's act,   5
Threatens his bloody stage. By the clock 'tis day,
And yet dark night strangles the traveling lamp.
Is 't night's predominance, or the day's shame
That darkness does the face of earth entomb,
When living light should kiss it?

OLD MAN.   'Tis unnatural,   10
Even like the deed that's done. On Tuesday last,
A falcon, tow'ring in her pride of place,
Was by a mousing owl hawked at and killed.

ROSS. And Duncan's horses—a thing most strange and certain—
Beauteous and swift, the minions of their race,   15
Turned wild in nature, broke their stalls, flung out,
Contending 'gainst obedience, as they would make
War with mankind.

OLD MAN.   'Tis said they eat each other.

ROSS. They did so, to the amazement of mine eyes,
That looked upon 't.

                    [*Enter* MACDUFF.]
                    Here comes the good Macduff.   20
How goes the world, sir, now?

MACDUFF.   Why, see you not?

ROSS. Is 't known who did this more than bloody deed?

MACDUFF. Those that Macbeth hath slain.

ROSS.   Alas, the day!
What good could they pretend?

MACDUFF.   They were suborned.
Malcolm and Donalbain, the king's two sons,   25
Are stolen away and fled; which puts upon them
Suspicion of the deed.

ROSS.   'Gainst nature still
Thriftless ambition, that will ravin up
Thine own life's means! Then 'tis most like
The sovereignty will fall upon Macbeth.   30

MACDUFF. He is already named; and gone to Scone
To be invested.

ROSS.   Where is Duncan's body?

MACDUFF. Carried to Colmekill,

---

   4. HATH TRIFLED FORMER KNOWINGS—Has made former experiences seem trifling.
   7. TRAVELING LAMP—The sun.
15. MINIONS—Favorites, most perfect specimens.
24. PRETEND—Expect to derive from the deed.
24. SUBORNED—Bribed.
28. RAVIN UP—Devour utterly.
31. SCONE (skōon)—The ancient royal city of Scotland, where Scottish kings were crowned.

The sacred storehouse of his predecessors,
And guardian of their bones.
ROSS.   Will you to Scone?   35
MACDUFF.   No, cousin, I'll to Fife.
ROSS.   Well, I will thither.
MACDUFF.   Well, may you see things well done there—adieu!—
Lest our old robes sit easier than our new!
ROSS.   Farewell, father.
OLD MAN.   God's benison go with you; and with those   40
That would make good of bad, and friends of foes!   [*Exeunt.*]

36. FIFE—Macduff's home. Macduff was Thane of Fife.
40. BENISON—Blessing.

◇◇

FOR UNDERSTANDING OF ACT II

1. What signal does Lady Macbeth give her husband when the moment has arrived for the murder? Macbeth's fear and his sense of guilt cause him to hear and see abnormal things. What are they?

2. The murder is made more terrible by the fact that it takes place in the dead of night. Point out three places in the opening scenes where the audience is reminded of the lateness of the hour.

3. Explain why Duncan's two grooms did not prevent the murder. How does Lady Macbeth make it appear that they are the ones who have killed Duncan?

4. What does Lady Macbeth's line, "A little water clears us of this deed," show about the way she feels and acts all during the murder? What proof do we have that Macbeth, in contrast, is horrified over having the murdered man's blood all over his hands?

5. Macbeth's great problem when the murder is discovered is to behave just as an innocent man would. Discuss his success or lack of success in this effort. Was Lady Macbeth's fainting real, or only a pretense for the purpose of diverting attention at a dangerous moment? Give reasons in support of each possibility.

6. Explain why Malcolm and Donalbain are afraid. How does their flight play into Macbeth's hands?

7. The drunken Porter in Scene 3 provides an example of the way Elizabethan dramatists sometimes introduced broadly comic situations into tragic plays. Point out as many details as you can in this scene that would raise a laugh. Does laughter at this time increase or decrease the feeling of horror developed in this act?

8. Shakespeare's plays are rich in figures of speech, especially metaphors. You remember that metaphors are comparisons made without using *like* or *as*. There are a number of metaphors in Macbeth's speech about sleep, lines 35–40 in Scene 2. What is meant by saying that sleep *knits up* the raveled sleave of care? Sleep is not *death*, but why could it be called the *death of each day's life*? What idea is conveyed by calling sleep a "bath"? Explain the remaining metaphors in the speech.

9. Study the metrical form of the first four lines of Scene 2. Divide the lines into feet. Point out the ones that are not regular iambic feet—that is, do not consist of one unstressed syllable followed by one stressed syllable. Point out which lines contain pauses; and explain how the halting, broken rhythm found in some lines is appropriate to the meaning of those lines.

10. At one of your choral readings of Macbeth's "Tomorrow, and tomorrow," Act V, Scene 5, try to define Macbeth's statement about life. Does he say that

life is long? that it is short? Are these complaints, or merely observations? With what important thought does he end his speech? Which of Macbeth's comments seem to express *his own* state of mind only and which ones seem *universally* true?

RISING ACTION IN A DRAMA

By the end of Act II Macbeth has committed his wicked deed and has won what he wanted. However, the action of the play is still rising toward a climax. We have yet to see Macbeth at the height of his power. We do not know what sort of career is in store for him as King of Scotland. A number of unanswered questions tell us that we are still in the early part of the story. For instance, at the moment of the murder Macbeth, in his overwrought state of mind, hears a voice cry, "Macbeth shall sleep no more!" Whether regarded as a prophecy or as Macbeth's own guess about the future, what different meanings could this have? And will it prove true or false? Will the people of Scotland, and Macbeth's fellow noblemen, accept him as their king? Both of Duncan's sons, Malcolm and Donalbain, have escaped out of the country. Have we heard the last of them? At the very end of Act II we learn that Macduff is not going to Scone to see Macbeth crowned. Does this mean that he intends to be Macbeth's enemy? As we read the story we hardly notice that these questions exist, but they are all waiting to be answered later on.

ACT III

Macbeth has attained success, but it is an uneasy triumph. In Act III we see his first murder leading to a second. The first royal banquet given by Macbeth and Lady Macbeth ends in disorder. Macbeth's efforts to increase his power and prestige are ineffective. Everywhere he turns, he sees difficulties.

SCENE 1. *Forres. The palace.*
[*Enter* BANQUO.]

BANQUO. Thou hast it now: king, Cawdor, Glamis, all
    As the weird women promised, and, I fear,
    Thou play'dst most foully for 't; yet it was said
    It should not stand in thy posterity,
    But that myself should be the root and father
    Of many kings. If there come truth from them,

5

As upon thee, Macbeth, their speeches shine—
Why, by the verities on thee made good,
May they not be my oracles as well,
And set me up in hope? But hush! no more.   10

[*Sennet * sounded. Enter* MACBETH, *as king;* LADY MACBETH, *as
queen;* LENNOX, ROSS, Lords, Ladies, *and* Attendants.]

MACBETH. Here's our chief guest.
LADY MACBETH.   If he had been forgotten,
It had been as a gap in our great feast,
And all-thing unbecoming.
MACBETH. Tonight we hold a solemn supper, sir,
And I'll request your presence.
BANQUO.   Let your Highness   15
Command upon me; to the which my duties
Are with a most indissoluble tie
Forever knit.
MACBETH. Ride you this afternoon?
BANQUO.   Ay, my good lord.
MACBETH. We should have else desired your good advice,   20
Which still hath been both grave and prosperous,
In this day's council; but we'll take tomorrow.
Is 't far you ride?
BANQUO. As far, my lord, as will fill up the time
'Twixt this and supper. Go not my horse the better,   25
I must become a borrower of the night
For a dark hour or twain.
MACBETH.   Fail not our feast.
BANQUO. My lord, I will not.
MACBETH. We hear our bloody cousins are bestowed
In England and in Ireland, not confessing   30
Their cruel parricide, filling their hearers
With strange invention. But of that tomorrow,
When therewithal we shall have cause of state
Craving us jointly. Hie you to horse; adieu,
Till you return at night. Goes Fleance with you?   35
BANQUO. Ay, my good lord. Our time does call upon 's.
MACBETH. I wish your horses swift and sure of foot;
And so I do commend you to their backs.
Farewell.   [*Exit* BANQUO.]
Let every man be master of his time   40
Till seven at night. To make society
The sweeter welcome, we will keep ourself

9. ORACLES—Prophets.
 * *Sennet*—A sound of trumpets.
29. BLOODY COUSINS—The sons of Duncan.
31. PARRICIDE—Murder of a parent.
32. INVENTION—Falsehood.

Till suppertime alone; while then, God be with you!

[*Exeunt all but* MACBETH, *and an* Attendant.]

Sirrah, a word with you. Attend those men

Our pleasure?   45

ATTENDANT. They are, my lord, without the palace gate.

MACBETH. Bring them before us.   [*Exit* Attendant.]

To be thus is nothing,

But to be safely thus. Our fears in Banquo

Stick deep; and in his royalty of nature

Reigns that which would be feared. 'Tis much he dares;   50

And, to that dauntless temper of his mind,

He hath a wisdom that doth guide his valor

To act in safety. There is none but he

Whose being I do fear; and, under him,

My Genius is rebuked, as, it is said,   55

Mark Antony's was by Caesar. He chid the sisters,

When first they put the name of king upon me,

And bade them speak to him; then prophetlike

They hailed him father to a line of kings.

Upon my head they placed a fruitless crown,   60

And put a barren scepter in my gripe,

Thence to be wrenched with an unlineal hand,

No son of mine succeeding. If 't be so,

For Banquo's issue have I filed my mind;

For them the gracious Duncan have I murdered;   65

Put rancors in the vessel of my peace

Only for them; and mine eternal jewel

Given to the common enemy of man,

To make them kings, the seed of Banquo kings!

Rather than so, come, fate, into the list,   70

And champion me to the utterance! Who's there?

[*Re-enter* Attendant, *with two* Murderers.]

Now go to the door, and stay there till we call.   [*Exit* Attendant.]

Was it not yesterday we spoke together?

FIRST MURDERER. It was, so please your Highness.

MACBETH.   Well then, now.

Have you considered of my speeches? Know   75

That it was he, in the times past, which held you

---

44. SIRRAH—A form commonly used in addressing a servant or child.

55–56. MY GENIUS . . . CAESAR—My guarding spirit; the spirit who presides over my destiny is inferior to that of Banquo, as Antony's fortune was inferior to Caesar's.

62. UNLINEAL HAND—By one not descended from me.

64. FILED—Defiled.

67–68. MINE ETERNAL JEWEL . . . ENEMY OF MAN—Given my immortal soul to Satan.

71. CHAMPION ME TO THE UTTERANCE—Fight with me to the death.

76. THAT IT WAS HE—"He" refers to Banquo. In this speech and the remainder of the scene, Macbeth tells the two men that all their misfortunes are Banquo's fault, and urges them to murder him.

So under fortune; which you thought had been
Our innocent self. This I made good to you
In our last conference, passed in probation with you,
How you were borne in hand, how crossed, the instruments,   80
Who wrought with them, and all things else that might
To half a soul and to a notion crazed
Say, "Thus did Banquo."
FIRST MURDERER.   You made it known to us.
MACBETH. I did so, and went further, which is now
Our point of second meeting. Do you find   85
Your patience so predominant in your nature
That you can let this go? Are you so gospeled,
To pray for this good man and for his issue,
Whose heavy hand hath bowed you to the grave
And beggared yours forever?
FIRST MURDERER.   We are men, my liege.   90
MACBETH. Ay, in the catalogue ye go for men;
As hounds and greyhounds, mongrels, spaniels, curs,
Shoughs, water rugs, and demiwolves, are clept
All by the name of dogs; the valued file
Distinguishes the swift, the slow, the subtle,   95
The housekeeper, the hunter, every one
According to the gift which bounteous nature
Hath in him closed; whereby he does receive
Particular addition, from the bill
That writes them all alike; and so of men.   100
Now, if you have a station in the file,
Not i' the worst rank of manhood, say 't;
And I will put that business in your bosoms,
Whose execution takes your enemy off,
Grapples you to the heart and love of us,   105
Who wear our health but sickly in his life,
Which in his death were perfect.
SECOND MURDERER.   I am one, my liege,
Whom the vile blows and buffets of the world
Hath so incensed, that I am reckless what
I do to spite the world.
FIRST MURDERER.   And I another   110
So weary with disasters, tugged with fortune,
That I would set my life on any chance,
To mend it, or be rid on 't.
MACBETH.   Both of you
Know Banquo was your enemy.
BOTH MURDERERS.   True, my lord.

79. PASSED IN PROBATION—Discussed point by point.
92-94. AS HOUNDS . . . DOGS—All breeds of dogs are called dogs.

MACBETH. So is he mine; and in such bloody distance,   115
    That every minute of his being thrusts
    Against my near'st of life; and though I could
    With barefaced power sweep him from my sight
    And bid my will avouch it, yet I must not,
    For certain friends that are both his and mine,   120
    Whose loves I may not drop, but wail his fall
    Who I myself struck down; and thence it is,
    That I to your assistance do make love,
    Masking the business from the common eye
    For sundry weighty reasons.
SECOND MURDERER.   We shall, my lord,   125
    Perform what you command us.
FIRST MURDERER.   Though our lives—
MACBETH. [Your spirits shine through you.] Within this hour at most
    I will advise you where to plant yourselves;
    Acquaint you with the perfect spy o' the time,
    The moment on 't; for 't must be done tonight,   130
    And something from the palace; always thought
    That I require a clearness; and with him—
    To leave no rubs nor botches in the work—
    Fleance his son, that keeps him company,
    Whose absence is no less material to me   135
    Than is his father's, must embrace the fate
    Of that dark hour. Resolve yourselves apart;
    I'll come to you anon.
BOTH MURDERERS.   We are resolved, my lord.
MACBETH. I'll call upon you straight; abide within.
                                  [*Exeunt* Murderers.]
    It is concluded. Banquo, thy soul's flight,   140
    If it find heaven, must find it out tonight.   [*Exit.*]

115. BLOODY DISTANCE—Within striking distance, as in a duel.
119. AVOUCH IT—Justify it; give no explanation except that it is my will or desire.
131. SOMETHING—At some distance.
131–2. ALWAYS THOUGHT . . . CLEARNESS—It being always remembered that I must be kept clear of suspicion.

SCENE 2. *The palace.*
[*Enter* LADY MACBETH *and a* Servant.]

LADY MACBETH. Is Banquo gone from court?
SERVANT. Ay, madam, but returns again tonight.
LADY MACBETH. Say to the king, I would attend his leisure
    For a few words.
SERVANT.   Madam, I will.

LADY MACBETH. Nought's had, all's spent,
    Where our desire is got without content. 5
    'Tis safer to be that which we destroy
    Than by destruction dwell in doubtful joy.
               [*Enter* MACBETH.]
    How now, my lord! why do you keep alone,
    Of sorriest fancies your companions making;
    Using those thoughts which should indeed have died 10
    With them they think on? Things without all remedy
    Should be without regard; what's done is done.
MACBETH. We have scotched the snake, not killed it;
    She'll close and be herself, whilst our poor malice
    Remains in danger of her former tooth. 15
    But let the frame of things disjoint, both the worlds suffer,
    Ere we will eat our meal in fear, and sleep
    In the affliction of these terrible dreams
    That shake us nightly. Better be with the dead,
    Whom we, to gain our peace, have sent to peace, 20
    Than on the torture of the mind to lie
    In restless ecstasy. Duncan is in his grave;
    After life's fitful fever he sleeps well;
    Treason has done his worst; nor steel, nor poison,
    Malice domestic, foreign levy, nothing, 25
    Can touch him further.
LADY MACBETH. Come on;
    Gentle my lord, sleek o'er your rugged looks;
    Be bright and jovial among your guests tonight.
MACBETH. So shall I, love; and so, I pray, be you.
    Let your remembrance apply to Banquo; 30
    Present him eminence, both with eye and tongue.
    Unsafe the while, that we
    Must lave our honors in these flattering streams,
    And make our faces vizards to our hearts,
    Disguising what they are.
LADY MACBETH. You must leave this. 35
MACBETH. O full of scorpions is my mind, dear wife!
    Thou know'st that Banquo, and his Fleance, lives.
LADY MACBETH. But in them nature's copy 's not eterne.
MACBETH. There's comfort yet; they are assailable;
    Then be thou jocund; ere the bat hath flown 40

13. SCOTCHED—Cut, slashed.
22. ECSTASY—Frenzy.
25. MALICE DOMESTIC—Rebellion, war from within the kingdom.
25. FOREIGN LEVY—War from without.
31. PRESENT HIM EMINENCE—Treat him with great respect.
34. VIZARDS—Masks.
38. IN THEM NATURE'S COPY'S NOT ETERNE—They will not live forever.

His cloistered flight; ere to black Hecate's summons
The shard-borne beetle with his drowsy hums
Hath rung night's yawning peal, there shall be done
A deed of dreadful note.

LADY MACBETH.   What's to be done?

MACBETH. Be innocent of the knowledge, dearest chuck,   45
    Till thou applaud the deed. Come, seeling night,
    Scarf up the tender eye of pitiful day,
    And with thy bloody and invisible hand
    Cancel and tear to pieces that great bond
    Which keeps me pale! Light thickens, and the crow   50
    Makes wing to the rooky wood;
    Good things of day begin to droop and drowse,
    Whiles night's black agents to their preys do rouse.
    Thou marvel'st at my words, but hold thee still;
    Things bad begun make strong themselves by ill.   55
    So, prithee, go with me.

                                                      [Exeunt.]

    42. SHARD-BORNE—Borne through the air on hard, shell-like wings.
    46. SEELING—Blindfolding. In falconry, seeling is closing up the eyes of a hawk until it is time to release him.
    49. THAT GREAT BOND—The prophecy that Banquo's heirs shall succeed to the throne.

SCENE 3. *A park near the palace.*
[*Enter three* Murderers.]

FIRST MURDERER. But who did bid thee join with us?

THIRD MURDERER.   Macbeth.

SECOND MURDERER. He needs not our mistrust; since he delivers
    Our offices, and what we have to do
    To the direction just.

FIRST MURDERER.   Then stand with us.
    The west yet glimmers with some streaks of day.   5
    Now spurs the lated traveler apace
    To gain the timely inn; and near approaches
    The subject of our watch.

THIRD MURDERER.   Hark! I hear horses.

BANQUO. [*Within.*] Give us a light there, ho!

SECOND MURDERER.   Then 'tis he: the rest
    That are within the note of expectation   10
    Already are i' the court.

FIRST MURDERER.   His horses go about.

THIRD MURDERER. Almost a mile; but he does usually,
    So all men do, from hence to the palace gate
    Make it their walk.

            [*Enter* BANQUO, *and* FLEANCE *with a torch.*]

SECOND MURDERER.　　　　A light, a light!
THIRD MURDERER.　　　　　　　　　'Tis he.
FIRST MURDERER. Stand to 't.　　　　　　　　　　　　　　15
BANQUO. It will be rain tonight.
FIRST MURDERER.　　　　　　Let it come down.

[They set upon BANQUO.]

BANQUO. O, treachery! Fly, good Fleance, fly, fly, fly!
　　Thou mayst revenge. O slave!　　　*[Dies. FLEANCE escapes.]*
THIRD MURDERER. Who did strike out the light?
FIRST MURDERER.　　　　　　　　　　Was 't not the way?
THIRD MURDERER. There's but one down; the son is fled.
SECOND MURDERER.　　　　　　　　　　We have lost　　　20
　　Best half of our affair.
FIRST MURDERER. Well, let's away, and say how much is done.　　　*[Exeunt.]*

SCENE 4. *The same. Hall in the palace.*
[*A banquet prepared. Enter* MACBETH, LADY MACBETH, ROSS, LENNOX,
LORDS, *and* Attendants.]

MACBETH. You know your own degrees; sit down. At first
　　And last the hearty welcome.

　1. DEGREES—Degrees of rank. The guests were seated according to rank.

211

LORDS.   Thanks to your Majesty.

MACBETH.   Ourself will mingle with society,
     And play the humble host.
     Our hostess keeps her state, but in best time   5
     We will require her welcome.

LADY MACBETH.   Pronounce it for me, sir, to all our friends,
     For my heart speaks they are welcome.

                 [*First* Murderer *appears at the door.*]

MACBETH.   See, they encounter thee with their hearts' thanks.
     Both sides are even: here I'll sit i' the midst.   10
     Be large in mirth; anon we'll drink a measure
     The table round. [*Approaching the door.*] There's blood upon thy face.

MURDERER.   'Tis Banquo's then.

MACBETH.   'Tis better thee without than he within.
     Is he dispatched?   15

MURDERER.   My lord, his throat is cut; that I did for him.

MACBETH.   Thou are the best o' the cutthroats; yet he's good
     That did the like for Fleance: if thou didst it,
     Thou art the nonpareil.

MURDERER.   Most royal sir,
     Fleance is 'scaped.   20

MACBETH.   Then comes my fit again: I had else been perfect,
     Whole as the marble, founded as the rock;
     As broad and general as the casing air;
     But now I am cabined, cribbed, confined, bound in
     To saucy doubts and fears. But Banquo's safe?   25

MURDERER.   Ay, my good lord; safe in a ditch he bides,
     With twenty trenchèd gashes on his head,
     The least a death to nature.

MACBETH.   Thanks for that.
     There the grown serpent lies; the worm that's fled
     Hath nature that in time will venom breed,   30
     No teeth for the present. Get thee gone; tomorrow
     We'll hear ourselves again.   [*Exit* Murderer.]

LADY MACBETH.   My royal lord,
     You do not give the cheer. The feast is sold
     That is not often vouched, while 'tis a-making,
     'Tis given with welcome. To feed were best at home;   35
     From thence the sauce to meat is ceremony;
     Meeting were bare without it.

         [*Enter the* Ghost of BANQUO, *and sits in* MACBETH's *place.*]

MACBETH.   Sweet remembrancer!

---

    14. 'TIS BETTER THEE WITHOUT THAN HE WITHIN—It is better on your face than in his veins.
    19. NONPAREIL (nŏn′pà·rĕl′)—One having no equal.
    33. THE FEAST IS SOLD—The feast is not better than a dinner at an inn.
    36–37. FROM THENCE . . . WITHOUT IT—Eating away from home is made more enjoyable by pleasant ceremonies.

Now, good digestion wait on appetite,
And health on both!

LENNOX.   May 't please your Highness sit.

MACBETH.   Here had we now our country's honor roofed,   40
    Were the graced person of our Banquo present;
    Who may I rather challenge for unkindness
    Than pity for mischance.

ROSS.   His absence, sir,
    Lays blame upon his promise. Please 't your Highness
    To grace us with your royal company.   45

MACBETH.   The table's full!

LENNOX.   Here is a place reserved, sir.

MACBETH.   Where?

LENNOX.   Here, my good lord. What is 't that moves your Highness?

MACBETH.   Which of you have done this?

LORDS.   What, my good lord?

MACBETH.   Thou canst not say I did it; never shake   50
    Thy gory locks at me.

ROSS.   Gentlemen, rise; his Highness is not well.

LADY MACBETH.   Sit, worthy friends; my lord is often thus,
    And hath been from his youth. Pray you, keep seat;
    The fit is momentary; upon a thought   55
    He will again be well. If much you note him,
    You shall offend him, and extend his passion.
    Feed, and regard him not. [*Aside to* MACBETH.]   Are you a man?

MACBETH.   Ay, and a bold one, that dare look on that
    Which might appall the devil.   60

LADY MACBETH.   [*Aside to* MACBETH.]   O proper stuff!
    This is the very painting of your fear;
    This is the air-drawn dagger which, you said,
    Led you to Duncan. O, these flaws and starts,
    Impostors to true fear, would well become
    A woman's story at a winter's fire,   65
    Authorized by her grandam. Shame itself!
    Why do you make such faces? When all's done,
    You look but on a stool.

MACBETH.   Prithee, see there! behold! look! lo! how say you?
    Why, what care I? If thou canst nod, speak too.   70
    If charnel houses and our graves must send
    Those that we bury back, our monuments
    Shall be the maws of kites.   [*Ghost vanishes.*]

LADY MACBETH.   [*Aside to* MACBETH.]   What, quite unmanned in folly?

MACBETH.   If I stand here, I saw him!

LADY MACBETH.   [*Aside to* MACBETH.]   Fie, for shame!

---

61. O PROPER STUFF!—Oh, nonsense!
73. MAWS OF KITES—Stomachs of hawks, or vultures.

MACBETH. Blood hath been shed ere now, i' the olden time,   75
    Ere humane statute purged the gentle weal;
    Ay, and since too, murders have been performed
    Too terrible for the ear. The time has been,
    That, when the brains were out, the man would die,
    And there an end; but now they rise again,   80
    With twenty mortal murders on their crowns,
    And push us from our stools. This is more strange
    Than such a murder is.
LADY MACBETH.   My worthy lord,
    Your noble friends do lack you.
MACBETH.   I do forget.
    Do not muse at me, my most worthy friends;   85
    I have a strange infirmity, which is nothing
    To those that know me. Come, love and health to all;
    Then I'll sit down. Give me some wine, fill full.

                    [*Re-enter the* Ghost.]

    I drink to the general joy o' the whole table,
    And to our dear friend Banquo, whom we miss;   90
    Would he were here! to all, and him, we thirst,
    And all to all.
LORDS.   Our duties, and the pledge.
MACBETH. Avaunt! and quit my sight! let the earth hide thee!
    Thy bones are marrowless, thy blood is cold;
    Thou hast no speculation in those eyes   95
    Which thou dost glare with!
LADY MACBETH.   Think of this, good peers,
    But as a thing of custom; 'tis no other;
    Only it spoils the pleasure of the time.
MACBETH. What man dare, I dare.
    Approach thou like the rugged Russian bear,   100
    The armed rhinoceros, or the Hyrcan tiger;
    Take any shape but that, and my firm nerves
    Shall never tremble. Or be alive again,
    And dare me to the desert with thy sword;
    If trembling I inhabit then, protest me   105
    The baby of a girl. Hence, horrible shadow!
    Unreal mockery, hence!   [Ghost *vanishes.*]
                    Why, so; being gone,
    I am a man again. Pray you, sit still.

76. ERE HUMANE . . . GENTLE WEAL—Before laws civilized the commonwealth.
81. MORTAL MURDERS—Fatal wounds.
85. MUSE—Wonder.
93. AVAUNT!—Away!
95. SPECULATION—Intelligence.
101. HYRCAN (hûr′kăn)—Referring to Hyrcania, a region south of the Caspian Sea.

LADY MACBETH.　You have displaced the mirth, broke the good meeting,
　　With most admired disorder.
MACBETH.　　　　　　　　　　Can such things be,　　　　　　110
　　And overcome us like a summer's cloud,
　　Without our special wonder?　You make me strange
　　Even to the disposition that I owe,
　　When now I think you can behold such sights,
　　And keep the natural ruby of your cheeks,　　　　　　115
　　When mine is blanched with fear.
ROSS.　　　　　　　　　　　　What sights, my lord?
LADY MACBETH.　I pray you, speak not; he grows worse and worse;
　　Question enrages him.　At once, good night.
　　Stand not upon the order of your going,
　　But go at once.
LENNOX.　　　　　　Good night; and better health　　　　120
　　Attend his Majesty!
LADY MACBETH.　　　　　A kind good night to all!
　　　　　　　　[*Exeunt all but* MACBETH *and* LADY MACBETH.]
MACBETH.　It will have blood; they say blood will have blood.
　　Stones have been known to move and trees to speak;
　　Augurs and understood relations have
　　By magot-pies and choughs and rooks brought forth　　125
　　The secret'st man of blood.　What is the night?
LADY MACBETH.　Almost at odds with morning, which is which.
MACBETH.　How say'st thou, that Macduff denies his person
　　At our great bidding?
LADY MACBETH.　　　　　Did you send to him, sir?
MACBETH.　I hear it by the way, but I will send.　　　　130
　　There's not a one of them but in his house
　　I keep a servant fee'd.　I will tomorrow,
　　And betimes I will, to the weird sisters:
　　More shall they speak; for now I am bent to know,
　　By the worst means, the worst.　For mine own good　135
　　All causes shall give way; I am in blood
　　Stepped in so far that, should I wade no more,
　　Returning were as tedious as go o'er.
　　Strange things I have in head, that will to hand,
　　Which must be acted ere they may be scanned.　　　140
LADY MACBETH.　You lack the season of all natures, sleep.
MACBETH.　Come, we'll to sleep.　My strange and self-abuse

110. ADMIRED—Strange.
124–126. AUGURS—Omens, signs.　The passage means that by watching the flight of magpies, etc., people who were able to read the omens have uncovered secret murders.
128. DENIES HIS PERSON—Refuses to come to the royal court.
132. I KEEP A SERVANT FEE'D—I have a servant in my pay, as a spy.
142–143. MY STRANGE . . . HARD USE—My strange self-delusion is the fear of a beginner, one not yet accustomed to killing.

Is the initiate fear that wants hard use;
We are yet but young in deed. [*Exeunt.*]

SCENE 5. A *heath.*
[*Thunder. Enter the three* Witches, *meeting* HECATE.]

FIRST WITCH. Why, how now, Hecate! you look angerly.
HECATE. Have I not reason, beldams as you are,
  Saucy and overbold? How did you dare
  To trade and traffic with Macbeth
  In riddles and affairs of death;   5
  And I, the mistress of your charms,
  The close contriver of all harms,
  Was never called to bear my part,
  Or show the glory of our art?
  And, which is worse, all you have done   10
  Hath been but for a wayward son,
  Spiteful and wrathful; who, as others do,
  Loves for his own ends, not for you.
  But make amends now: get you gone,
  And at the pit of Acheron   15
  Meet me i' the morning; thither he
  Will come to know his destiny.
  Your vessels and your spells provide,
  Your charms, and everything beside.
  I am for the air; this night I'll spend   20
  Unto a dismal and fatal end;
  Great business must be wrought ere noon.
  Upon the corner of the moon
  There hangs a vaporous drop profound;
  I'll catch it ere it come to ground;   25
  And that distilled by magic sleights
  Shall raise such artificial sprites
  As by the strength of their illusion
  Shall draw him on to his confusion.
  He shall spurn fate, scorn death, and bear   30
  His hopes 'bove wisdom, grace, and fear;
  And you all know security
  Is mortals' chiefest enemy.   [*Music, and a song.*]
  Hark! I am called; my little spirit, see,
  Sits in a foggy cloud, and stays for me.   [*Exit.*]   35
    [*Sing within:* "Come away, come away," etc.]

2. BELDAMS—Hags.
15. ACHERON (ăk'ĕr·ŏn)—A river in Hades.
27. SPRITES—Spirits.
32. SECURITY—Overconfidence.

FIRST WITCH. Come, let's make haste; she'll soon be back again.   [*Exeunt.*]

SCENE 6. *Forres. The palace.*
[*Enter* LENNOX *and another* LORD.]

LENNOX. My former speeches have but hit your thoughts,
          Which can interpret further; only, I say
          Things have been strangely borne. The gracious Duncan
          Was pitied of Macbeth; marry, he was dead;
          And the right-valiant Banquo walked too late;   5
          Whom, you may say, if 't please you, Fleance killed,
          For Fleance fled; men must not walk too late.
          Who cannot want the thought, how monstrous
          It was for Malcolm and for Donalbain
          To kill their gracious father? Damnèd fact!   10
          How it did grieve Macbeth! Did he not straight,
          In pious rage the two delinquents tear,
          That were the slaves of drink and thralls of sleep?
          Was not that nobly done? Ay, and wisely too;
          For 'twould have angered any heart alive   15
          To hear the men deny 't. So that, I say,
          He has borne all things well; and I do think
          That, had he Duncan's sons under his key—
          As, an 't please heaven, he shall not—they should find
          What 'twere to kill a father; so should Fleance.   20
          But, peace! for from broad words, and 'cause he failed
          His presence at the tyrant's feast, I hear,
          Macduff lives in disgrace. Sir, can you tell
          Where he bestows himself?
LORD.   The son of Duncan,
          From whom this tyrant holds the due of birth,   25
          Lives in the English court; and is received
          Of the most pious Edward with such grace
          That the malevolence of fortune nothing
          Takes from his high respect. Thither Macduff
          Is gone to pray the holy king, upon his aid   30
          To wake Northumberland and warlike Siward;
          That by the help of these, with Him above
          To ratify the work, we may again
          Give to our tables meat, sleep to our nights;
          Free from our feasts and banquets bloody knives,   35
          Do faithful homage and receive free honors;
          All which we pine for now; and this report

3. BORNE—Managed.
4. MARRY—"By St. Mary"; a mild oath meaning "indeed."
19. AN 'T—If it.
27. EDWARD—Edward the Confessor, King of England, 1042–1066.
28. MALEVOLENCE (ma·lĕv′ô·lĕns)—Malice.

Hath so exasperate the king that he
Prepares for some attempt of war.

LENNOX.   Sent he to Macduff?

LORD.   He did; and with an absolute "Sir, not I,"   40
      The cloudy messenger turns me his back,
      And hums, as who should say, "You'll rue the time
      That clogs me with this answer."

LENNOX.   And that well might
      Advise him to a caution, to hold what distance
      His wisdom can provide.   Some holy angel   45
      Fly to the court of England and unfold
      His message ere he come; that a swift blessing
      May soon return to this our suffering country
      Under a hand accursed!

LORD.   I'll send my prayers with him.   [*Exeunt.*]

40. "SIR, NOT I"—Macduff's reply to the messenger who brought Macbeth's command.
41. CLOUDY—Frowning.
43. CLOGS—Burdens. The messenger dislikes to bear the answer to Macbeth, who will be angry.

FOR UNDERSTANDING OF ACT III

1. Explain why Macbeth fears Banquo and wants to murder him. It will be helpful to read carefully the soliloquies by both men early in Scene 1. What does Banquo know that makes him suspect who killed Duncan? What characteristics of Banquo make him dangerous?

2. Explain why it would seem safer to Macbeth to hire murderers to kill Banquo than to do it himself.

3. Why is Macbeth disappointed that Fleance is not killed along with Banquo?

4. Do you think Shakespeare's audience was supposed to believe Banquo's ghost really appeared at the banquet? Or were they supposed to think the ghost was in Macbeth's imagination? Give reasons for each view.

5. Find a speech by Lady Macbeth which shows she does not believe Banquo's ghost is actually present. How does she try to "smooth over" Macbeth's strange behavior when he sees the ghost?

6. Explain why Ross's question (line 116) is such a dangerous one that Lady Macbeth decides the banquet must break up at once.

7. Near the end of Scene 5 Hecate tells the witches what their future purpose is to be in dealing with Macbeth. What is it? Why does Macbeth intend to visit the witches again?

8. In Scene 6 we learn where Macduff and Malcolm have gone. What do they hope to do there?

9. Turn back to Scene 2 and reread Macbeth's lines beginning "Duncan is in his grave." What does this speech reveal about how well Macbeth enjoys being king? Give reasons for the state of mind he is in.

10. Near the end of Scene 2 Macbeth hints to his wife that he has a pleasant surprise for her. "Then be thou jocund," he says, and adds:

"Be innocent of the knowledge, dearest
     chuck,
Till thou applaud the deed."

What is the surprise to be? Compare his

attitude here to his attitude toward the murder of Duncan. What change has taken place in his character? How do you account for the change?

11. At another of your class readings of Macbeth's "Tomorrow, and tomorrow," examine the passage as an example of blank verse. Find one line that is an example of completely regular iambic pentameter. Examine three others to see if there are variations either in number of feet or in stress.

THE TURNING POINT OF MACBETH'S FORTUNES

In Act III we can see that events are beginning to go against Macbeth. The failure to kill Fleance along with Banquo is a great setback—as the second Murderer realizes when he says, "We have lost best half of our affair." Find speeches by Macbeth which show that he places great importance on Fleance's death.

Macbeth's strange actions at the banquet, and the necessity of sending the guests home, mark another setback. Whether Banquo's ghost is real or imaginary, Macbeth's sight of it shows that he is unnerved by his sense of guilt and his fear of being found out. What will the guests think about Macbeth's conduct?

Macbeth shows also that he is afraid of all the Scottish nobility in the lines:

"There's not a one of them but in his house
I keep a servant fee'd."

How are we told that he is particularly afraid of Macduff? What makes him think Macduff may be his enemy?

The decision to seek advice from the witches, who are the servants of the Devil, is likewise important. Macbeth has determined to learn "By the worst means, the worst." He sees no way out of his troubles except further wickedness. How is this shown in lines 136–138 of Scene 4?

In Scene 5 immediately afterward, we learn that the witches will "draw him on to his confusion"—that is, to his downfall. And in Scene 6, the sarcastic remarks of Lennox show how much Macbeth is hated. The scene ends with the hope that there may be an invasion from England. From now on Macbeth's troubles will multiply.

ACT IV

In Act IV, Macbeth sinks deeper into crime. The confusing prophecies of the witches bolster up his confidence, but they also make him almost insanely cruel.

SCENE 1. *A cavern. In the middle, a boiling caldron.*
[*Thunder. Enter the three* Witches.]

FIRST WITCH. Thrice the brinded cat hath mewed.
SECOND WITCH. Thrice, and once the hedge pig whined.
THIRD WITCH. Harpier cries; " 'Tis time, 'tis time."
FIRST WITCH. Round about the caldron go;
    In the poisoned entrails throw.   5
    Toad, that under cold stone
    Days and nights has thirty-one
    Sweltered venom sleeping got,
    Boil thou first i' the charmed pot.
ALL. Double, double toil and trouble;   10
    Fire burn and caldron bubble.
SECOND WITCH. Fillet of a fenny snake,
    In the caldron boil and bake;
    Eye of newt and toe of frog,
    Wool of bat and tongue of dog,   15
    Adder's fork and blindworm's sting,
    Lizard's leg and howlet's wing,
    For a charm of powerful trouble,
    Like a hell-broth boil and bubble.
ALL. Double, double toil and trouble;   20
    Fire burn and caldron bubble.
THIRD WITCH. Scale of dragon, tooth of wolf,
    Witches' mummy, maw and gulf
    Of the ravined salt-sea shark;
    Root of hemlock digged i' the dark,   25
    Liver of blaspheming Jew,
    Gall of goat, and slips of yew
    Slivered in the moon's eclipse,
    Nose of Turk and Tartar's lips,
    Finger of birth-strangled babe   30
    Ditch-delivered by a drab,
    Make the gruel thick and slab:
    Add thereto a tiger's chaudron,
    For the ingredients of our caldron.
ALL. Double, double toil and trouble;   35
    Fire burn and caldron bubble.

---

1. BRINDED CAT—Brindled or streaked cat.
3. HARPIER—Harpy, a fabulous creature, half bird and half woman, that snatched away the food of its victims.
12. FENNY SNAKE—Marsh snake.
23. MAW AND GULF—Stomach and gullet.
24. RAVINED—Glutted with food, presumably human flesh.
26. BLASPHEMING—So called because not Christian.
27. GOAT—Formerly considered to represent wickedness, perhaps because of the heathen goat-god Pan.
29. TURK AND TARTAR—Non-Christians.
32. SLAB—Slimy.
33. CHAUDRON—Entrails.

SECOND WITCH.   Cool it with a baboon's blood,
    Then the charm is firm and good.
            [*Enter* HECATE *to the other three* Witches.]
HECATE.   O, well done! I commend your pains;
    And every one shall share i' the gains.   40
    And now about the caldron sing,
    Like elves and fairies in a ring,
    Enchanting all that you put in.

              [*Music, and a song,* "Black spirits," etc.]
                        [*Exit* HECATE.]
SECOND WITCH.   By the pricking of my thumbs,
    Something wicked this way comes.   45
    Open, locks,
    Whoever knocks!

             [*Enter* MACBETH.]
MACBETH.   How now, you secret, black, and midnight hags!
    What is 't you do?
ALL.   A deed without a name.
MACBETH.   I conjure you, by that which you profess,   50
    Howe'er you come to know it, answer me!
    Though you untie the winds and let them fight

Against the churches; though the yesty waves
Confound and swallow navigation up;
Though bladed corn be lodged, and trees blown down;   55
Though castles topple on their warders' heads;
Though palaces and pyramids do slope
Their heads to their foundations; though the treasure
Of nature's germens tumble all together,
Even till destruction sicken; answer me   60
To what I ask you.

FIRST WITCH.   Speak.

SECOND WITCH.   Demand.

THIRD WITCH.   We'll answer.

FIRST WITCH. Say, if thou 'dst rather hear it from our mouths,
Or from our masters?

MACBETH.   Call 'em, let me see 'em.

FIRST WITCH. Pour in sow's blood, that hath eaten
Her nine farrow; grease that's sweaten   65
From the murderer's gibbet throw
Into the flame!

ALL.   Come, high or low;
Thyself and office deftly show!

      [*Thunder.* First Apparition, *an armed Head.*]

MACBETH. Tell me, thou unknown power—

FIRST WITCH.   He knows thy thought.
Hear his speech, but say thou naught.   70

FIRST APPARITION. Macbeth! Macbeth! Macbeth! beware Macduff;
Beware the thane of Fife. Dismiss me. Enough.   [*Descends.*]

MACBETH. Whate'er thou art, for thy good caution, thanks;
Thou hast harped my fear aright. But one word more—

FIRST WITCH. He will not be commanded. Here's another,   75
More potent than the first.

      [*Thunder.* Second Apparition, *a bloody Child.*]

SECOND APPARITION. Macbeth! Macbeth! Macbeth!

MACBETH. Had I three ears, I'd hear thee.

SECOND APPARITION. Be bloody, bold, and resolute; laugh to scorn
The power of man, for none of woman born   80
Shall harm Macbeth.   [*Descends.*]

MACBETH. Then live, Macduff: what need I fear of thee?
But yet I'll make assurance double sure,
And take a bond of fate. Thou shalt not live;

53. YESTY—Foam-capped.
55. BLADED CORN—Corn, or grain, in the blade.
55. LODGED—Laid flat by the wind.
59. NATURE'S GERMENS—Seeds.
65. NINE FARROW—Litter of nine pigs.
68. OFFICE—Function.
74. HARPED MY FEAR ARIGHT—Struck the note of my fear.

That I may tell pale-hearted fear it lies,   85
  And sleep in spite of thunder.
[*Thunder.* Third Apparition, *a Child crowned, with a tree in his hand.*]
                        What is this,
  That rises like the issue of a king,
  And wears upon his baby brow the round
  And top of sovereignty?
ALL.   Listen, but speak not to 't.
THIRD APPARITION. Be lion-mettled, proud; and take no care   90
  Who chafes, who frets, or where conspirers are.
  Macbeth shall never vanquished be until
  Great Birnam wood to high Dunsinane hill
  Shall come against him.   [*Descends.*]
MACBETH.   That will never be.
  Who can impress the forest; bid the tree   95
  Unfix his earth-bound root? Sweet bodements! good!
  Rebellion's head, rise never till the wood
  Of Birnam rise, and our high-placed Macbeth
  Shall live the lease of nature, pay his breath
  To time and mortal custom. Yet my heart   100
  Throbs to know one thing: tell me, if your art
  Can tell so much—shall Banquo's issue ever
  Reign in this kingdom?
ALL.   Seek to know no more.
MACBETH. I will be satisfied: deny me this,
  And an eternal curse fall on you! Let me know.   105
  Why sinks that caldron? and what noise is this?

                            [*Hautboys.*]

FIRST WITCH. Show!
SECOND WITCH. Show!
THIRD WITCH. Show!
ALL. Show his eyes, and grieve his heart;   110
  Come like shadows, so depart!
     [*A show of eight* Kings,* *the last with a glass in his hand;*
                BANQUO's Ghost *following.*]
MACBETH. Thou art too like the spirit of Banquo; down!
  Thy crown does sear mine eyeballs. And thy hair,
  Thou other gold-bound brow, is like the first.

88. ROUND—Crown.
95. IMPRESS—Draft into military service.
99. LIVE THE LEASE . . . TIME AND MORTAL CUSTOM—Live a normal time and die a natural death.
  * *Eight* KINGS—The eight Stuart kings of Scotland, the last of whom, James VI, became also James I of England about three years before *Macbeth* was written. According to legend the Stuarts were Banquo's descendants. Fleance's son became Lord High Steward of Scotland, and from this office the Stuart family took its name.
112. TOO LIKE THE SPIRIT OF BANQUO—The first king, like the seven that follow, resembles his ancestor Banquo.

A third is like the former. Filthy hags! 115
Why do you show me this? A fourth! Start, eyes!
What, will the line stretch out to the crack of doom?
Another yet! A seventh! I'll see no more.
And yet the eighth appears, who bears a glass
Which shows me many more; and some I see 120
That twofold balls and treble scepters carry.
Horrible sight! Now I see 'tis true;
For the bloodboltered Banquo smiles upon me,
And points at them for his. [*Apparitions* vanish.]   What, is this so?
FIRST WITCH. Ay, sir, all this is so; but why 125
Stands Macbeth thus amazedly?
Come, sisters, cheer we up his sprites,
And show the best of our delights.
I'll charm the air to give a sound,
While you perform your antic round; 130
That this great king may kindly say,
Our duties did his welcome pay.
      [*Music. The* Witches *dance, and vanish with* HECATE.]
MACBETH. Where are they? Gone? Let this pernicious hour
Stand aye accursèd in the calendar!
Come in, without there!
               [*Enter* LENNOX.] 135
LENNOX.   What's your grace's will?
MACBETH. Saw you the weird sisters?
LENNOX.   No, my lord.
MACBETH. Came they not by you?
LENNOX.   No, indeed, my lord.
MACBETH. Infected be the air whereon they ride,
And damned all those that trust them! I did hear
The galloping of horse; who was 't came by? 140
LENNOX. 'Tis two or three, my lord, that bring you word
Macduff is fled to England.
MACBETH.   Fled to England!
LENNOX. Ay, my good lord.
MACBETH. [*Aside.*] Time, thou anticipat'st my dread exploits:
The flighty purpose never is o'ertook 145
Unless the deed go with it. From this moment
The very firstlings of my heart shall be
The firstlings of my hand. And even now,
To crown my thoughts with acts, be it thought and done.

119–120. THE EIGHTH . . . SHOWS ME MANY MORE—The glass (mirror) carried by the eighth king shows images of royal descendants of James I—who of course were still unborn when this play was written.
121. TWOFOLD BALLS AND TREBLE SCEPTERS—Another reference to James I, who united the two kingdoms of England and Scotland. "Treble scepters" refers to England, Scotland, and Ireland.

The castle of Macduff I will surprise;   150
Seize upon Fife; give to the edge o' the sword
His wife, his babes, and all unfortunate souls
That trace him in his line. No boasting like a fool;
This deed I'll do before this purpose cool.
But no more sights!—Where are these gentlemen?   155
Come, bring me where they are.   [*Exeunt.*]

SCENE 2. *Fife.* MACDUFF's *castle.*
[*Enter* LADY MACDUFF, *her* SON, *and* ROSS.]

LADY MACDUFF. What had he done, to make him fly the land?
ROSS. You must have patience, madam.
LADY MACDUFF.   He had none;
    His flight was madness. When our actions do not,
    Our fears do make us traitors.
ROSS.   You know not
    Whether it was his wisdom or his fear.   5
LADY MACDUFF. Wisdom! to leave his wife, to leave his babes,
    His mansion and his titles in a place
    From whence himself does fly? He loves us not;
    He wants the natural touch; for the poor wren,
    The most diminutive of birds, will fight,   10
    Her young ones in her nest, against the owl.
    All is the fear and nothing is the love;
    As little is the wisdom, where the flight
    So runs against all reason.
ROSS.   My dearest coz,
    I pray you, school yourself; but, for your husband,   15
    He is noble, wise, judicious, and best knows
    The fits o' the season. I dare not speak much further;
    But cruel are the times when we are traitors
    And do not know ourselves; when we hold rumor
    From what we fear, yet know not what we fear,   20
    But float upon a wild and violent sea
    Each way and move. I take my leave of you;
    Shall not be long but I'll be here again.
    Things at the worst will cease, or else climb upward
    To what they were before. My pretty cousin,   25
    Blessing upon you!
LADY MACDUFF. Fathered he is, and yet he's fatherless.
ROSS. I am so much a fool, should I stay longer,
    It would be my disgrace and your discomfort.
    I take my leave at once.   [*Exit.*]

19. DO NOT KNOW OURSELVES—Do not know it ourselves.

225

LADY MACDUFF. Sirrah, your father's dead; 30
And what will you do now? How will you live?

SON. As birds do, Mother.

LADY MACDUFF. What, with worms and flies?

SON. With what I get, I mean; and so do they.

LADY MACDUFF. Poor bird! thou'dst never fear the net nor lime,
The pitfall nor the gin. 35

SON. Why should I, Mother? Poor birds they are not set for.
My father is not dead, for all your saying.

LADY MACDUFF. Yes, he is dead. How wilt thou do for a father?

SON. Nay, how will you do for a husband?

LADY MACDUFF. Why, I can buy me twenty at any market. 40

SON. Then you'll buy 'em to sell again.

LADY MACDUFF. Thou speak'st with all thy wit; and yet, 'i faith,
With wit enough for thee.

SON. Was my father a traitor, Mother?

LADY MACDUFF. Ay, that he was.

SON. What is a traitor?

LADY MACDUFF. Why, one that swears and lies.

SON. And be all traitors that do so?

LADY MACDUFF. Everyone that does so is a traitor, and must be hanged.

SON. And must they all be hanged that swear and lie? 50

LADY MACDUFF. Every one.

SON. Who must hang them?

LADY MACDUFF. Why, the honest men.

SON. Then the liars and swearers are fools; for there are liars and swearers enow to
beat the honest men and hang up them. 55

LADY MACDUFF. Now, God help thee, poor monkey! But how wilt thou do for a
father?

SON. If he were dead, you'd weep for him; if you would not, it were a good sign
that I should quickly have a new father.

LADY MACDUFF. Poor prattler, how thou talk'st! 60

[*Enter a* Messenger.]

MESSENGER. Bless you, fair dame! I am not to you known,
Though in your state of honor I am perfect.
I doubt some danger does approach you nearly.
If you will take a homely man's advice,
Be not found here; hence, with your little ones. 65
To fright you thus, methinks I am too savage;
To do worse to you were fell cruelty,
Which is too nigh your person. Heaven preserve you!
I dare abide no longer. [*Exit.*]

34. LIME—Birdlime, a sticky substance smeared on twigs to catch birds.
35. PITFALL NOR THE GIN—Traps used to catch small birds, which were much used for food.
47. SWEARS AND LIES—Swears allegiance falsely.
62. IN YOUR STATE OF HONOR I AM PERFECT—I know all about who you are.
63. DOUBT—Fear.

LADY MACDUFF. Whither should I fly?
I have done no harm. But I remember now 70
I am in this earthly world; where to do harm
Is often laudable, to do good sometime
Accounted dangerous folly. Why then, alas,
Do I put up that womanly defense,
To say I have done no harm?
[*Enter* Murderers.]
What are these faces? 75
FIRST MURDERER. Where is your husband?
LADY MACDUFF. I hope, in no place so unsanctified
Where such as thou mayst find him.
FIRST MURDERER. He's a traitor.
SON. Thou liest, thou shag-eared villain!
FIRST MURDERER. [*Stabbing him.*] What, you egg!
Young fry of treachery!
SON. He has killed me, Mother: 80
Run away, I pray you! [*Dies.*]
[*Exit* LADY MACDUFF, *crying* "Murder!"]
[*Exeunt* Murderers, *following her.*]

SCENE 3. *England. Before the King's palace.*
[*Enter* MALCOLM *and* MACDUFF.]

MALCOLM. Let us seek out some desolate shade, and there
Weep our sad bosoms empty.
MACDUFF. Let us rather
Hold fast the mortal sword, and, like good men,
Bestride our down-fall'n birthdom. Each new morn
New widows howl, new orphans cry, new sorrows 5
Strike heaven on the face, that it resounds
As if it felt with Scotland, and yelled out
Like syllable of dolor.
MALCOLM. What I believe, I'll wail;
What know, believe; and what I can redress,
As I shall find the time to friend, I will. 10
What you have spoke, it may be so perchance.
This tyrant, whose sole name blisters our tongues,
Was once thought honest; you have loved him well;
He hath not touched you yet. I am young; but something
You may deserve of him through me, and wisdom 15

8–9. WHAT I BELIEVE . . . BELIEVE—Here and in the long conversation that follows, Malcolm is slow to trust Macduff. He fears that Macduff is a spy sent by Macbeth to trap him in some way.

To offer up a weak, poor, innocent lamb
To appease an angry god.

MACDUFF. I am not treacherous.

MALCOLM. But Macbeth is.
A good and virtuous nature may recoil
In an imperial charge. But I shall crave your pardon; 20
That which you are, my thoughts cannot transpose;
Angels are bright still, though the brightest fell.
Though all things foul would wear the brows of grace,
Yet grace must still look so.

MACDUFF. I have lost my hopes.

MALCOLM. Perchance even there where I did find my doubts. 25
Why in that rawness left you wife and child,
Those precious motives, those strong knots of love,
Without leave-taking? I pray you,
Let not my jealousies be your dishonors,
But mine own safeties. You may be rightly just, 30
Whatever I shall think.

MACDUFF. Bleed, bleed, poor country!
Great tyranny! lay thou thy basis sure,
For goodness dare not check thee; wear thou thy wrongs;
The title is affeered! Fare thee well, lord:
I would not be the villain that thou think'st 35
For the whole space that's in the tyrant's grasp,
And the rich East to boot.

MALCOLM. Be not offended;
I speak not as in absolute fear of you.
I think our country sinks beneath the yoke;
It weeps, it bleeds; and each new day a gash 40
Is added to her wounds. I think withal
There would be hands uplifted in my right;
And here from gracious England have I offer
Of goodly thousands. But, for all this,
When I shall tread upon the tyrant's head, 45
Or wear it on my sword, yet my poor country
Shall have more vices than it had before;
More suffer, and more sundry ways than ever,
By him that shall succeed.

MACDUFF. What should he be?

MALCOLM. It is myself I mean; in whom I know 50
All the particulars of vice so grafted,
That, when they shall be opened, black Macbeth
Will seem as pure as snow; and the poor state
Esteem him as a lamb, being compared

19. RECOIL—Reverse itself, turn bad.
34. AFFEERED—Confirmed. That is, there is no one to dispute Macbeth's title.

With my confineless harms.

MACDUFF.   Not in the legions   55
Of horrid hell can come a devil more damned
In evils to top Macbeth.

MALCOLM.   I grant him bloody,
Luxurious, avaricious, false, deceitful,
Sudden, malicious, smacking of every sin
That has a name; but there's no bottom, none,   60
In my voluptuousness. Your wives, your daughters,
Your matrons and your maids, could not fill up
The cistern of my lust, and my desire
All continent impediments would o'erbear,
That did oppose my will. Better Macbeth   65
Than such an one to reign.

MACDUFF.   Boundless intemperance
In nature is a tyranny; it hath been
The untimely emptying of the happy throne,
And fall of many kings. But fear not yet
To take upon you what is yours. You may   70
Convey your pleasures in a spacious plenty,
And yet seem cold, the time you may so hoodwink.
We have willing dames enough; there cannot be
That vulture in you, to devour so many
As will to greatness dedicate themselves,   75
Finding it so inclined.

MALCOLM.   With this there grows,
In my most ill-composed affection such
A stanchless avarice that, were I king,
I should cut off the nobles for their lands,
Desire his jewels and this other's house;   80
And my more-having would be as a sauce
To make me hunger more, that I should forge
Quarrels unjust against the good and loyal,
Destroying them for wealth.

MACDUFF.   This avarice
Sticks deeper, grows with more pernicious root   85
Than summer-seeming lust, and it hath been
The sword of our slain kings. Yet do not fear,
Scotland hath foisons to fill up your will
Of your mere own. All these are portable,

55. CONFINELESS HARMS—Unlimited vices.
58. LUXURIOUS—Licentious.
64. CONTINENT IMPEDIMENTS—Restraining motives.
71. CONVEY—Obtain.
87. SWORD—That which has slain our kings.
88. FOISONS—Abundance.
89. PORTABLE—Endurable.

With other graces weighed.   90

MALCOLM. But I have none; the king-becoming graces,
    As justice, verity, temperance, stableness,
    Bounty, perseverance, mercy, lowliness,
    Devotion, patience, courage, fortitude,
    I have no relish of them; but abound   95
    In the division of each several crime,
    Acting it many ways. Nay, had I power, I should
    Pour the sweet milk of concord into hell,
    Uproar the universal peace, confound
    All unity on earth.

MACDUFF.   O Scotland, Scotland!   100

MALCOLM. If such a one be fit to govern, speak.
    I am as I have spoken.

MACDUFF.   Fit to govern!
    No, not to live. O nation miserable,
    With an untitled tyrant bloody-sceptered,
    When shalt thou see thy wholesome days again,   105
    Since that the truest issue of thy throne
    By his own interdiction stands accursed,
    And does blaspheme his breed? Thy royal father
    Was a most sainted king; the queen that bore thee,
    Oftener upon her knees than on her feet,   110
    Died every day she lived. Fare thee well!
    These evils thou repeat'st upon thyself
    Have banished me from Scotland. O my breast,
    Thy hope ends here!

MALCOLM.   Macduff, this noble passion,
    Child of integrity, hath from my soul   115
    Wiped the black scruples, reconciled my thoughts
    To thy good truth and honor. Devilish Macbeth
    By many of these trains hath sought to win me
    Into his power; and modest wisdom plucks me
    From overcredulous haste; but God above   120
    Deal between thee and me! for even now
    I put myself to thy direction, and
    Unspeak mine own detraction; here abjure
    The taints and blames I laid upon myself,
    For strangers to my nature. I am yet   125
    Unknown to woman, never was forsworn,
    Scarcely have coveted what was mine own,
    At no time broke my faith, would not betray

---

108. BLASPHEME HIS BREED—Slander his family (by speaking so unfavorably of himself).
111. DIED EVERY DAY SHE LIVED—Each day of her holy life was a preparation for death.
118. TRAINS—Tricks.
123. ABJURE—Disavow, repudiate.

The devil to his fellow, and delight
No less in truth than life; my first false speaking   130
Was this upon myself. What I am truly,
Is thine and my poor country's to command;
Whither, indeed, before thy here-approach,
Old Siward, with ten thousand warlike men,
Already at a point, was setting forth.   135
Now we'll together; and the chance of goodness
Be like our warranted quarrel! Why are you silent?
MACDUFF. Such welcome and unwelcome things at once
    'Tis hard to reconcile.

                [*Enter a* Doctor.]

MALCOLM. Well; more anon.—Comes the king forth, I pray you?   140
DOCTOR. Ay, sir; there are a crew of wretched souls
    That stay his cure. Their malady convinces
    The great assay of art; but at his touch,
    Such sanctity hath Heaven given his hand,
    They presently amend.
MALCOLM.   I thank you, doctor.   [*Exit* Doctor.]   145
MACDUFF. What's the disease he means?
MALCOLM.   'Tis called the evil:
    A most miraculous work in this good king;
    Which often, since my here-remain in England,
    I have seen him do. How he solicits Heaven,
    Himself best knows; but strangely-visited people,   150
    All swoln and ulcerous, pitiful to the eye,
    The mere despair of surgery, he cures,
    Hanging a golden stamp about their necks,
    Put on with holy prayers; and 'tis spoken,
    To the succeeding royalty he leaves   155
    The healing benediction. With this strange virtue,
    He hath a heavenly gift of prophecy,
    And sundry blessings hang about his throne,
    That speak him full of grace.

                [*Enter* ROSS.]

MACDUFF.   See, who comes here?
MALCOLM. My countryman; but yet I know him not.   160
MACDUFF. My ever-gentle cousin, welcome hither.

135. AT A POINT—Armed, ready.
   142. STAY HIS CURE—Await his healing touch. Edward the Confessor, who is the king referred to, and other early kings of England were supposed to have had the gift of healing scrofula, a blood and skin disease, by "touching." This episode has nothing to do with the play. It is no doubt inserted because James I believed he had the same miraculous power.
   142–143. CONVINCES THE GREAT ASSAY OF ART—Baffles the best effort of professional skill.
   150. STRANGELY-VISITED—Strangely-afflicted.
   152. MERE—Complete.
   153. GOLDEN STAMP—Golden coin or medal.

MALCOLM. I know him now. Good God, betimes remove
    The means that makes us strangers!
ROSS.   Sir, amen.
MACDUFF. Stands Scotland where it did?
ROSS.   Alas, poor country,
    Almost afraid to know itself! It cannot   165
    Be called our mother, but our grave; where nothing,
    But who knows nothing, is once seen to smile;
    Where sighs and groans and shrieks that rend the air,
    Are made, not marked; where violent sorrow seems
    A modern ecstasy. The dead man's knell   170
    Is there scarce asked for who; and good men's lives
    Expire before the flowers in their caps,
    Dying or ere they sicken.
MACDUFF.   O, relation
    Too nice, and yet too true!
MALCOLM.   What's the newest grief?
ROSS. That of an hour's age doth hiss the speaker,   175
    Each minute teems a new one.
MACDUFF.   How does my wife?
ROSS. Why, well.
MACDUFF.   And all my children?
ROSS.   Well too.
MACDUFF. The tyrant has not battered at their peace?
ROSS. No; they were well at peace when I did leave 'em.
MACDUFF. Be not a niggard of your speech; how goes 't?   180
ROSS. When I came hither to transport the tidings
    Which I have heavily borne, there ran a rumor
    Of many worthy fellows that were out;
    Which was to my belief witnessed the rather,
    For that I saw the tyrant's power afoot.   185
    Now is the time of help; your eye in Scotland
    Would create soldiers, make our women fight,
    To doff their dire distresses.
MALCOLM.   Be't their comfort
    We are coming thither. Gracious England hath
    Lent us good Siward and ten thousand men;   190
    An older and a better soldier none
    That Christendom gives out.
ROSS.   Would I could answer

162. BETIMES—Soon.
169. NOT MARKED—Not even noticed.
174. TOO NICE—Too precise.
175. HISS THE SPEAKER—Because his news is already out of date.
176. TEEMS—Brings forth.
183. OUT—Up in arms, in rebellion.
188. DOFF—Throw off.

This comfort with the like! But I have words
That would be howled out in the desert air,
Where hearing should not latch them.   195
MACDUFF.   What concern they?
The general cause? or is it a fee-grief
Due to some single breast?
ROSS.   No mind that's honest
But in it shares some woe; though the main part
Pertains to you alone.
MACDUFF.   If it be mine,
Keep it not from me, quickly let me have it.   200
ROSS. Let not your ears despise my tongue for ever,
Which shall possess them with the heaviest sound
That ever yet they heard.
MACDUFF.   Hum! I guess at it.
ROSS. Your castle is surprised; your wife and babes
Savagely slaughtered. To relate the manner,   205
Were, on the quarry of these murdered deer,
To add the death of you.
MALCOLM.   Merciful Heaven!
What, man! ne'er pull your hat upon your brows;
Give sorrow words. The grief that does not speak
Whispers the o'er-fraught heart and bids it break.   210
MACDUFF. My children too?
ROSS.   Wife, children, servants, all
That could be found.
MACDUFF.   And I must be from thence!
My wife killed too?
ROSS.   I have said.
MALCOLM.   Be comforted.
Let's make us medicines of our great revenge,
To cure this deadly grief.   215
MACDUFF. He has no children.—All my pretty ones?
Did you say all? O hell-kite! All?
What, all my pretty chickens and their dam
At one fell swoop?
MALCOLM. Dispute it like a man.   220
MACDUFF.   I shall do so;
But I must also feel it as a man.
I cannot but remember such things were,
That were most precious to me. Did Heaven look on,
And would not take their part? Sinful Macduff,
They were all struck for thee! naught that I am,   225

195. LATCH—Catch.
196. FEE-GRIEF—Private grief.
206. QUARRY—A heap of the game killed during a hunt.

Not for their own demerits, but for mine,
Fell slaughter on their souls. Heaven rest them now!
MALCOLM. Be this the whetstone of your sword; let grief
    Convert to anger; blunt not the heart, enrage it.
MACDUFF. O, I could play the woman with mine eyes,   230
    And braggart with my tongue! But, gentle Heavens,
    Cut short all intermission; front to front
    Bring thou this fiend of Scotland and myself;
    Within my sword's length set him; if he scape,
    Heaven forgive him too!   235
MALCOLM.   This tune goes manly.
    Come, go we to the king; our power is ready;
    Our lack is nothing but our leave. Macbeth
    Is ripe for shaking, and the powers above
    Put on their instruments. Receive what cheer you may;
    The night is long that never finds the day.   [*Exeunt.*]   240

237. OUR LACK . . . LEAVE—All we lack is taking leave of the king.

◇◇

FOR UNDERSTANDING OF ACT IV

1. Reread the list of ingredients used by the witches in making their "hell-broth." Choose four of these and explain why they might be associated with fear, or with dread and loathing. Note that after each witch has recited her part of the chant, all three join in a refrain. Read this refrain aloud. It is an example of *onomatopoeia*—that is, it imitates in sound the idea it conveys. What sound does the refrain represent?

2. What two favorable pieces of information do the witches give Macbeth? What information do they give him concerning Banquo? Explain how it agrees with their earlier statement in Act I that Banquo was "Not so happy, yet much happier" than Macbeth.

3. One of Macbeth's chief reasons for visiting the witches is his fear of Macduff, who refused to attend Macbeth's coronation or come to the royal court. The First Apparition tells him, "Beware Macduff." Why does he think he need not fear Macduff after hearing the Second Ap-

parition? Find the words in which Macbeth decides to kill Macduff anyway, just to play safe. How do you interpret the line "And sleep in spite of thunder"?

4. What news at the end of Scene 1 makes Macbeth realize that he cannot kill Macduff, at least not immediately? What could be his motive for murdering Lady Macduff and her children? What does such a motive show about the further change in Macbeth's character? How does the first part of Scene 2, up to the entrance of the murderers, make us realize more fully the hideousness of this deed? What effect on public opinion will these murders have?

5. In Scene 3, why does Malcolm at first lie to Macduff, calling himself a wicked man who is unfit to be placed on the throne of Scotland? Explain what finally causes him to drop this pretense. Later in this scene, Ross enters with the latest news from Scotland. What is the public feeling toward Macbeth, according to his report? What special news does he have for Macduff? What do you think Macduff means by his remark in line 216,

"He has no children"? Whom does he mean?

6. Sum up the preparations that are being made to overthrow Macbeth. That is, where is the rebellion to begin, who are to be the leaders, where will the necessary troops be found, and whom are the rebels going to fight for as their rightful king?

7. At your next reading in unison of Macbeth's "Tomorrow, and tomorrow," pay special attention to vivid, expressive phrases. The titles of several books have been taken from these few lines of poetry. Even the simple words "Tomorrow, and tomorrow, and tomorrow" convey a feeling. What feeling? Notice the striking phrase Macbeth uses in referring to the past—"all our yesterdays." Point out two other brief phrases that you find very expressive.

FALLING ACTION IN A DRAMA

Most of the incidents in the fourth act show us that Macbeth is traveling downhill. Killing Macduff's wife and children is a senseless, hateful deed that cannot possibly do him any good. More important, this deed shows us the progress of the inner conflict of the play. Earlier, Macbeth could hardly bring himself to kill Duncan, but now the evil in his character has won out over the good.

Scene 3 makes us feel that Macbeth is doomed by stressing the preparations made against him in England, and the willingness of the Scottish people to help the invaders. However, Act IV would become tiresome if it merely repeated the news that the tide was turning against Macbeth. The favorable prophecies in the witch-scene provide some suspense. These prophecies encourage Macbeth and they puzzle the audience. How can Macbeth be beaten if the prophecies are true? Of course, Macbeth's very act of visiting the witches is itself an indication of how far he has fallen. Most people in an Elizabethan audience would regard this as a great sin—the equivalent of selling yourself to the Devil. Modern audiences, who do not believe in witches, are more likely to think that the ruler of a country must be in a bad way if he has to resort to fortune-tellers for advice.

ACT V

In this act the story jumps back and forth from Macbeth's castle to the Scottish countryside where the invading army is marching. We see Macbeth and Lady Macbeth tortured by guilt and desperation—while the army draws closer and closer. At last it arrives, and Macbeth must face his enemies.

SCENE 1. *Dunsinane. Anteroom in the Castle.*
[*Enter a* Doctor *of Physic and a* Waiting-Gentlewoman.]

DOCTOR. I have two nights watched with you, but can perceive no truth in your report. When was it she last walked?

GENTLEWOMAN. Since his Majesty went into the field, I have seen her rise from her bed, throw her nightgown upon her, unlock her closet, take forth paper, fold it, write upon 't, read it, afterwards seal it, and again return to   5 bed; yet all this while in a most fast sleep.

DOCTOR. A great perturbation in nature, to receive at once the benefit of sleep, and do the effects of watching! In this slumberly agitation, besides her walking and other actual performances, what, at any time, have you heard her say?

GENTLEWOMAN. That, sir, which I will not report after her.   10

DOCTOR. You may to me; and 'tis most meet you should.

GENTLEWOMAN. Neither to you nor anyone; having no witness to confirm my speech.

[*Enter* LADY MACBETH, *with a taper.*]

Lo, you, here she comes! This is her very guise; and, upon my life, fast asleep. Observe her; stand close.   15

DOCTOR. How came she by that light?

GENTLEWOMAN. Why, it stood by her. She has light by her continually; 'tis her command.

DOCTOR. You see, her eyes are open.

GENTLEWOMAN. Ay, but their sense is shut.   20

DOCTOR. What is it she does now? Look, how she rubs her hands.

GENTLEWOMAN. It is an accustomed action with her, to seem thus washing her hands; I have known her continue in this a quarter of an hour.

LADY MACBETH. Yet here's a spot.

DOCTOR. Hark! she speaks. I will set down what comes from her, to satisfy   25 my remembrance the more strongly.

LADY MACBETH. Out, damned spot! out, I say!—One, two; why, then 'tis time to do 't.—Hell is murky!—Fie, my lord, fie! a soldier, and afeard? What need we fear who knows it, when none can call our power to account?—Yet who would have thought the old man to have had so much blood in him?   30

DOCTOR. Do you mark that?

LADY MACBETH. The thane of Fife had a wife; where is she now?—What, will these hands ne'er be clean?—No more o' that, my lord, no more o' that; you mar all with this starting.

DOCTOR. Go to, go to; you have known what you should not.   35

GENTLEWOMAN. She has spoke what she should not, I am sure of that; Heaven knows what she has known.

LADY MACBETH. Here's the smell of the blood still; all the perfumes of Arabia will not sweeten this little hand. Oh, oh, oh!

DOCTOR. What a sigh is there! The heart is sorely charged.   40

GENTLEWOMAN. I would not have such a heart in my bosom for the dignity of the whole body.

---

3. WENT INTO THE FIELD—Led an army into the field to put down the rebels.
40. SORELY CHARGED—Heavily laden.

DOCTOR. Well, well, well—

GENTLEWOMAN. Pray God it be, sir.

DOCTOR. This disease is beyond my practice; yet I have known those which   45
   have walked in their sleep who have died holily in their beds.

LADY MACBETH. Wash your hands; put on your nightgown; look not so pale. I tell
   you yet again, Banquo's buried; he cannot come out on 's grave.

DOCTOR. Even so?

LADY MACBETH. To bed, to bed; there's knocking at the gate. Come, come,   50
   come, come, give me your hand. What's done cannot be undone. To bed,
   to bed, to bed.   [Exit.]

DOCTOR. Will she go now to bed?

GENTLEWOMAN. Directly.

DOCTOR. Foul whisperings are abroad; unnatural deeds   55
   Do breed unnatural troubles; infected minds
   To their deaf pillows will discharge their secrets.
   More needs she the divine than the physician.
   God, God forgive us all! Look after her;
   Remove from her the means of all annoyance,   60
   And still keep eyes upon her. So, good night!
   My mind she has mated, and amazed my sight.

62. MATED—Bewildered.

I think, but dare not speak.

GENTLEWOMAN. Good night, good doctor.

[Exeunt.]

SCENE 2. *The country near Dunsinane.*
[*Drum and colors. Enter* MENTEITH, CAITHNESS, ANGUS,
LENNOX, *and* Soldiers.]

MENTEITH. The English power is near, led on by Malcolm,
His uncle Siward, and the good Macduff.
Revenges burn in them; for their dear causes
Would to the bleeding and the grim alarm
Excite the mortified man. 5

ANGUS. Near Birnam wood
Shall we well meet them; that way are they coming.

CAITHNESS. Who knows if Donalbain be with his brother?

LENNOX. For certain, sir, he is not; I have a file
Of all the gentry. There is Siward's son,
And many unrough youths, that even now 10
Protest their first of manhood.

MENTEITH. What does the tyrant?

CAITHNESS. Great Dunsinane he strongly fortifies.
Some say he's mad; others, that lesser hate him,
Do call it valiant fury; but, for certain,
He cannot buckle his distempered cause 15
Within the belt of rule.

ANGUS. Now does he feel
His secret murders sticking on his hands;
Now minutely revolts upbraid his faith breach;
Those he commands move only in command,
Nothing in love. Now does he feel his title 20
Hang loose about him, like a giant's robe
Upon a dwarfish thief.

MENTEITH. Who then shall blame
His pestered senses to recoil and start,
When all that is within him does condemn
Itself for being there?

CAITHNESS. Well, march we on, 25
To give obedience where 'tis truly owed.
Meet we the medicine of the sickly weal;
And with him pour we in our country's purge

5. EXCITE THE MORTIFIED MAN—Excite even the holy or religious man.
10. UNROUGH—Beardless.
15–16. BUCKLE . . . RULE—Make his plans go right.
18. MINUTELY—Every minute.
27. MEDICINE OF THE SICKLY WEAL—Malcolm, who can cure the sick commonwealth.

Each drop of us.

LENNOX.   Or so much as it needs
To dew the sovereign flower and drown the weeds.   30
Make we our march towards Birnam.   *[Exeunt, marching.]*

30. DEW THE SOVEREIGN FLOWER—Revive the true king.

SCENE 3. *Dunsinane. A room in the castle.*
[Enter MACBETH, *the* Doctor, *and* Attendants.]

MACBETH. Bring me no more reports; let them fly all;
Till Birnam wood remove to Dunsinane
I cannot taint with fear. What's the boy Malcolm?
Was he not born of woman? The spirits that know
All mortal consequences have pronounced me thus: 5
"Fear not, Macbeth; no man that's born of woman
Shall e'er have power upon thee." Then fly, false thanes,
And mingle with the English epicures!
The mind I sway by and the heart I bear
Shall never sag with doubt nor shake with fear.   10
             [Enter a Servant.]
The devil damn thee black, thou cream-faced loon!
Where got'st thou that goose look?

SERVANT. There is ten thousand—

MACBETH.   Geese, villain?

SERVANT.   Soldiers, sir.

MACBETH. Go prick thy face, and over-red thy fear,
Thou lily-livered boy. What soldiers, patch?   15
Death of thy soul! those linen cheeks of thine
Are counselors to fear. What soldiers, whey face?

SERVANT. The English force, so please you.

MACBETH. Take thy face hence.   *[Exit* Servant.]
          Seyton! I am sick at heart,
When I behold—Seyton, I say!— This push   20
Will chair me ever, or disseat me now.
I have lived long enough. My way of life
Is fallen into the sear, the yellow leaf;
And that which should accompany old age,
As honor, love, obedience, troops of friends,   25
I must not look to have; but, in their stead,
Curses, not loud but deep, mouth-honor, breath
Which the poor heart would fain deny, and dare not.

8. EPICURES—People addicted to luxury. The Scots had few comforts in their barren land, and were contemptuous of the easier life led by the English.
15. PATCH—Fool.
20–21. THIS PUSH . . . NOW—This attack will make my seat permanently secure, or turn me out of it.

Seyton!

[Enter SEYTON.*]*

SEYTON.   What is your gracious pleasure?

MACBETH.   What news more?   30

SEYTON.   All is confirmed, my lord, which was reported.

MACBETH.   I'll fight, till from my bones my flesh be hacked.
     Give me my armor.

SEYTON.   'Tis not needed yet.

MACBETH.   I'll put it on.
     Send out moe horses, skirr the country round;   35
     Hang those that talk of fear.   Give me mine armor.
     How does your patient, doctor?

DOCTOR.   Not so sick, my lord,
     As she is troubled with thick-coming fancies,
     That keep her from her rest.

MACBETH.   Cure her of that.
     Canst thou not minister to a mind diseased,   40
     Pluck from the memory a rooted sorrow,
     Raze out the written troubles of the brain,
     And with some sweet oblivious antidote
     Cleanse the stuffed bosom of that perilous stuff
     Which weighs upon the heart?

DOCTOR.   Therein the patient   45
     Must minister to himself.

MACBETH.   Throw physic to the dogs, I'll none of it.
     Come, put mine armor on; give me my staff.
     Seyton, send out.   Doctor, the thanes fly from me.
     Come, sir, dispatch.   If thou couldst, doctor, cast   50
     The water of my land, find her disease,
     And purge it to a sound and pristine health,
     I would applaud thee to the very echo,
     That should applaud again.   Pull 't off, I say.
     What rhubarb, senna, or what purgative drug,   55
     Would scour these English hence?   Hear'st thou of them?

DOCTOR.   Ay, my good lord; your royal preparation
     Makes us hear something.

MACBETH.   Bring it after me.
     I will not be afraid of death and bane,
     Till Birnam forest come to Dunsinane.   60

DOCTOR.   [*Aside.*]   Were I from Dunsinane away and clear,
     Profit again should hardly draw me here.   *[Exeunt.]*

---

35. SKIRR—Scour.
47. PHYSIC—The whole practice of medicine.
51. HER DISEASE—The disease that ails the kingdom of Scotland.
54. PULL'T OFF—Macbeth in his agitation directs his armorer to pull off his armor, although
he has put it on only a moment before.

SCENE 4. *Country near Birnam wood.*
[*Drum and colors. Enter* MALCOLM, *old* SIWARD *and his* Son, MACDUFF, MENTEITH, CAITHNESS, ANGUS, LENNOX, ROSS, *and* Soldiers, *marching.*]

MALCOLM. Cousins, I hope the days are near at hand
    That chambers will be safe.
MENTEITH.   We doubt it nothing.
SIWARD. What wood is this before us?
MENTEITH.   The wood of Birnam.
MALCOLM. Let every soldier hew him down a bough,
    And bear 't before him: thereby shall we shadow   5
    The numbers of our host, and make discovery
    Err in report of us.
SOLDIERS.   It shall be done.
SIWARD. We learn no other but the confident tyrant
    Keeps still in Dunsinane, and will endure
    Our setting down before 't.
MALCOLM.   'Tis his main hope: 10
    For, where there is advantage to be given,
    Both more and less have given him the revolt,
    And none serve with him but constrainèd things,
    Whose hearts are absent too.
MACDUFF.   Let our just censures
    Attend the true event, and put we on   15
    Industrious soldiership.
SIWARD.   The time approaches
    That will with due decision make us know
    What we shall say we have and what we owe.
    Thoughts speculative their unsure hopes relate,
    But certain issue strokes must arbitrate;   20
    Toward which, advance the war.   [*Exeunt, marching.*]

5. SHADOW—Conceal.
12. MORE AND LESS—Great men and small.
19–20. THOUGHTS SPECULATIVE . . . ARBITRATE—Speculation leads to uncertain hopes; deeds will decide the outcome.

SCENE 5. *Dunsinane. Within the castle.*
[*Enter* MACBETH, SEYTON, *and* Soldiers, *with drum and colors.*]

MACBETH. Hang out our banners on the outward walls;
    The cry is still, "They come." Our castle's strength
    Will laugh a siege to scorn; here let them lie
    Till famine and the ague eat them up.
    Were they not forced with those that should be ours,   5
    We might have met them dareful, beard to beard,

5. FORCED—Reinforced.

And beat them backward home.   *[A cry of women within.]*

               What is that noise?

SEYTON. It is the cry of women, my good lord.   *[Exit.]*

MACBETH. I have almost forgot the taste of fears.

    The time has been, my senses would have cooled   10

    To hear a night-shriek, and my fell of hair

    Would at a dismal treatise rouse and stir

    As life were in 't: I have supped full with horrors;

    Direness, familiar to my slaughterous thoughts,

    Cannot once start me.

                 [Re-enter SEYTON.]

               Wherefore was that cry?   15

SEYTON. The queen, my lord, is dead.

MACBETH. She should have died hereafter;

    There would have been a time for such a word.

    Tomorrow, and tomorrow, and tomorrow,

    Creeps in this petty pace from day to day,   20

    To the last syllable of recorded time;

    And all our yesterdays have lighted fools

    The way to dusty death. Out, out, brief candle!

    Life's but a walking shadow; a poor player

    That struts and frets his hour upon the stage   25

    And then is heard no more. It is a tale

    Told by an idiot, full of sound and fury,

    Signifying nothing.

               [Enter a Messenger.]

    Thou comest to use thy tongue; thy story quickly.

MESSENGER. Gracious my lord,   30

    I should report that which I say I saw,

    But know not how to do 't.

MACBETH.   Well, say, sir.

MESSENGER. As I did stand my watch upon the hill,

    I looked toward Birnam, and anon, methought,

    The wood began to move.

MACBETH.   Liar and slave!   35

MESSENGER. Let me endure your wrath, if 't be not so.

    Within this three mile may you see it coming;

    I say, a moving grove.

MACBETH.   If thou speak'st false,

    Upon the next tree shalt thou hang alive,

    Till famine cling thee; if thy speech be sooth,   40

---

11. FELL OF HAIR—Scalp.
12. DISMAL TREATISE—Horrifying story, as a story of ghosts or supernatural events.
17. SHE SHOULD HAVE DIED HEREAFTER—She would have had to die some day.
40. SOOTH—Truth.

I care not if thou dost for me as much.
I pull in resolution, and begin
To doubt the equivocation of the fiend
That lies like truth: "Fear not, till Birnam wood
Do come to Dunsinane"; and now a wood   45
Comes toward Dunsinane. Arm, arm, and out!
If this which he avouches does appear,
There is nor flying hence nor tarrying here.
I 'gin to be aweary of the sun,
And wish the estate o' the world were now undone.   50
Ring the alarum bell! Blow, wind! come, wrack!
At least we'll die with harness on our back.   *[Exeunt.]*

51. WRACK—Ruin.
52. HARNESS—Armor.

SCENE 6. *Dunsinane. Before the castle.*
[Drum and colors. Enter MALCOLM, *old* SIWARD, MACDUFF, *and
their* Army, *with boughs.]*

MALCOLM. Now near enough; your leavy screens throw down,
  And show like those you are. You, worthy uncle,
  Shall, with my cousin, your right noble son,
  Lead our first battle; worthy Macduff and we
  Shall take upon 's what else remains to do,   5
  According to our order.
SIWARD.   Fare you well.
  Do we but find the tyrant's power tonight,
  Let us be beaten, if we cannot fight.
MACDUFF. Make all our trumpets speak; give them all breath,
  Those clamorous harbingers of blood and death.   *[Exeunt.]*   10
                                    [Alarums continued.]

SCENE 7. *Another part of the field.*
[Enter MACBETH.]

MACBETH. They have tied me to a stake; I cannot fly,
  But, bearlike, I must fight the course. What's he
  That was not born of woman? Such a one
  Am I to fear, or none.
                    [Enter young SIWARD.]
YOUNG SIWARD. What is thy name?
MACBETH.   Thou'lt be afraid to hear it.   5

1–2. TIED ME TO A STAKE . . . BEARLIKE—In the Elizabethan sport of bearbaiting, the
bear was tied to a stake and dogs were set on him.

YOUNG SIWARD. No; though thou call'st thyself a hotter name
    Than any is in hell.

MACBETH.   My name's Macbeth.

YOUNG SIWARD. The devil himself could not pronounce a title
    More hateful to mine ear.

MACBETH.   No, nor more fearful.

YOUNG SIWARD. Thou liest, abhorrèd tyrant; with my sword   10
    I'll prove the lie thou speak'st.
                            [*They fight, and young* SIWARD *is slain.*]

MACBETH.   Thou wast born of woman.
    But swords I smile at, weapons laugh to scorn,
    Brandished by man that's of a woman born.   [*Exit.*]
               [*Alarums. Enter* MACDUFF.]

MACDUFF. That way the noise is. Tyrant, show thy face!
    If thou be'st slain, and with no stroke of mine,   15
    My wife and children's ghosts will haunt me still.
    I cannot strike at wretched kerns, whose arms
    Are hired to bear their staves; either thou, Macbeth,
    Or else my sword, with an unbattered edge,
    I sheathe again undeeded. There thou shouldst be;   20
    By this great clatter, one of greatest note
    Seems bruited. Let me find him, fortune!
    And more I beg not.   [*Exit. Alarums.*]
             [*Enter* MALCOLM *and old* SIWARD.]

SIWARD. This way, my lord. The castle's gently rendered.
    The tyrant's people on both sides do fight;   25
    The noble thanes do bravely in the war;
    The day almost itself professes yours,
    And little is to do.

MALCOLM.   We have met with foes
    That strike beside us.

SIWARD.   Enter, sir, the castle.   [*Exeunt. Alarums.*]

    17. KERNS—Hired soldiers.
    22. SEEMS BRUITED—Seems indicated.
    24. GENTLY RENDERED—Surrendered with little resistance.
    29. STRIKE BESIDE US—Do not try to hit us.

            SCENE 8. *Another part of the field.*
               [*Enter* MACBETH.]

MACBETH. Why should I play the Roman fool, and die
    On mine own sword? whiles I see lives, the gashes
    Do better upon them.

    1. PLAY THE ROMAN FOOL—Kill myself, as was considered honorable for a Roman general to
do after being defeated.
    2. LIVES—Living foes.

[*Enter* MACDUFF.]

MACDUFF.   Turn, hell-hound, turn!

MACBETH.   Of all men else I have avoided thee.
But get thee back; my soul is too much charged   5
With blood of thine already.

MACDUFF.   I have no words;
My voice is in my sword, thou bloodier villain
Than terms can give thee out!   [*They fight.*]

MACBETH.   Thou losest labor;
As easy mayst thou the intrenchant air
With thy keen sword impress as make me bleed.   10
Let fall thy blade on vulnerable crests;
I bear a charmèd life, which must not yield
To one of woman born.

MACDUFF.   Despair thy charm;
And let the angel whom thou still hast served
Tell thee, Macduff was from his mother's womb   15
Untimely ripped.

MACBETH.   Accursèd be that tongue that tells me so,
For it hath cowed my better part of man!
And be these juggling fiends no more believed,
That palter with us in a double sense;   20
That keep the word of promise to our ear,
And break it to our hope.   I'll not fight with thee.

MACDUFF.   Then yield thee, coward,
And live to be the show and gaze o' the time.
We'll have thee, as our rarer monsters are,   25
Painted upon a pole, and underwrit,
"Here may you see the tyrant."

MACBETH.   I will not yield,
To kiss the ground before young Malcolm's feet,
And to be baited with the rabble's curse.
Though Birnam wood be come to Dunsinane,   30
And thou opposed, being of no woman born,
Yet I will try the last.   Before my body
I throw my warlike shield.   Lay on, Macduff;
And damned be him that first cries, "Hold, enough!"

[*Exeunt fighting.   Alarums.*]

[*Retreat.   Flourish.   Enter with drum and colors,* MALCOLM,
old SIWARD, ROSS, *the other* Thanes, *and* Soldiers.]

MALCOLM.   I would the friends we miss were safe arrived.   35

14. ANGEL—Spirit, in this case a spirit of evil.
15–16. MACDUFF . . . RIPPED—Macduff was not "born" in the ordinary sense of a natural birth, so Macbeth is not safe from him.
26. PAINTED UPON A POLE—Macbeth will be placed on exhibit, and advertised by a painted cloth hung on a pole.

SIWARD.   Some must go off; and yet, by these I see,
  So great a day as this is cheaply bought.
MALCOLM.   Macduff is missing, and your noble son.
ROSS.   Your son, my lord, has paid a soldier's debt.
  He only lived but till he was a man;   40
  The which no sooner had his prowess confirmed
  In the unshrinking station where he fought,
  But like a man he died.
SIWARD.   Then he is dead?
ROSS.   Ay, and brought off the field.   Your cause of sorrow
  Must not be measured by his worth, for then   45
  It hath no end.
SIWARD.   Had he his hurts before?
ROSS.   Ay, on the front.
SIWARD.   Why then, God's soldier be he!
  Had I as many sons as I have hairs,
  I would not wish them to a fairer death.
  And so his knell is knolled.   50
MALCOLM.   He's worth more sorrow,
  And that I'll spend for him.
SIWARD.   He's worth no more.
  They say he parted well, and paid his score;
  And so God be with him!   Here comes newer comfort.
    [Re-enter MACDUFF, with MACBETH's head.*]
MACDUFF.   Hail, king! for so thou art.   Behold, where stands
  The usurper's cursèd head.   The time is free.   55
  I see thee compassed with thy kingdom's pearl,
  That speak my salutation in their minds;
  Whose voices I desire aloud with mine:
  Hail, King of Scotland!
ALL.   Hail, King of Scotland! [Flourish.]
MALCOLM.   We shall not spend a large expense of time 60
  Before we reckon with your several loves,
  And make us even with you.   My thanes and kinsmen,
  Henceforth be earls, the first that ever Scotland
  In such an honor named.   What's more to do,
  Which would be planted newly with the time,   65
  As calling home our exiled friends abroad
  That fled the snares of watchful tyranny;
  Producing forth the cruel ministers
  Of this dead butcher and his fiendlike queen,
  Who, as 'tis thought, by self and violent hands 70

36. GO OFF—Die.
46. BEFORE—On the front.
* With MACBETH's head—The head was probably brought in on a pole or pike.
68. PRODUCING FORTH THE CRUEL MINISTERS—Hunting out the agents employed by Macbeth to do his murders.

Took off her life; this, and what needful else
That calls upon us, by the grace of Grace,
We will perform in measure, time, and place.
So, thanks to all at once and to each one,
Whom we invite to see us crowned at Scone.

75

[*Flourish.   Exeunt.*]

◇◆◇

FOR UNDERSTANDING OF ACT V

1. The almost pitiable mental condition of Lady Macbeth in Act V is in sharp contrast to her ruthless courage and decisiveness in the early part of the play. After Duncan was killed she calmly remarked, "A little water clears us of this deed." Can you prove from the sleepwalking scene that having her hands smeared with Duncan's blood made a deeper impression on her than she realized at the time? What other past events does she talk about during the sleepwalking scene? How does the change that has come over Lady Macbeth differ from the change that has come over Macbeth?

2. How is Macbeth's increasing desperation suggested by his manner toward his attendants in Scenes 3 and 5? Find evidence in either scene that some of his followers are escaping to join his enemies. Find evidence in Scene 3 that people are already saying he will be defeated.

3. Just before his death Macbeth says:

"And be these juggling fiends no more
   believed,
That palter with us in a double sense;
That keep the word of promise to our
   ear,
And break it to our hope."

He is referring to the two reassuring prophecies made by the witches. Explain how each has turned out to be "true," yet misleading.

4. When the story ends, what has become of Macbeth, of Macduff, of Young Siward, and of Banquo? If the character is dead, how did he die?

5. Some Shakespearean commentators have said that Macbeth's death is like that of a cornered rat. What circumstances of his last fight make his death ignoble rather than brave and honorable? If he was so completely at the end of his rope why didn't he refuse to fight at all—as for a moment he thought of doing?

6. Reread Macbeth's speech in Scene 3 in which the following passages occur. Then explain each.

"My way of life
Is fallen into the sear, the yellow leaf."

"Curses, not loud but deep, mouth-honor,
   breath
Which the poor heart would fain deny,
   and dare not."

7. At your last class reading of Macbeth's soliloquy, consider the events that have inspired his outburst. What announcement has just been made to him? Does the announcement appear to sadden him? Sum up the reasons Macbeth might have for being weary of life. You will find some of them given in the speech mentioned in Question 6. After you have read the soliloquy aloud this time, you may wish to see whether you can write or speak it without the book.

THE DENOUEMENT OR SOLU-
TION OF A DRAMA

The *denouement* (untying) of a plot has occurred when we are able to answer the question, "What is the outcome of the main story?" The defeat and death of Macbeth—after his miserable, desperate last days—is of course the denouement of this play. It is a convincing outcome because Shakespeare has been careful to show us the increasing wickedness of Macbeth, the increasing hatred people feel for him, and the growing number of his enemies.

A few odds and ends of plot remain to be cleared up. One matter—revenge for the murder of Lady Macduff and her children—is disposed of when Macbeth is killed. Why is this true? Who is now to be king of Scotland? Explain how the crowning of the new king will at least partly make up for the murder of Duncan. In Act IV it has already been explained how the murdered Banquo will eventually get his revenge. How? We learn indirectly about Lady Macbeth's final punishment. What is it? Notice that we are reminded of her death at the very end of the play, almost at the same moment that we are given proof Macbeth is dead. The new king speaks briefly of "this dead butcher and his fiendlike queen" and turns to a more pleasant subject—his coronation at Scone, marking the beginning of a happier time.

FOR UNDERSTANDING: THE PLAY AS A WHOLE

1. The events in a well-written tragedy should be inevitable. After the story is well begun, it should unfold so logically that there can be no escape for the main character. Does Macbeth's fear after his first crime lead inevitably to his later crimes and so to his downfall? Point out at least one case where his attempt to get out of a dangerous situation leads him into more danger. Is there any point at which he could have stopped after his first wrong decision?

2. When the play opens, Macbeth and Banquo are in somewhat parallel situations, but a difference between them appears when they are greeted by the witches. What is the difference in the way they respond? Which of these terms could correctly be used in describing Banquo—fearless, irresponsible, honest, easily excited, over-suspicious, easily frightened? Does Banquo's life and death represent tragedy and failure in the sense that Macbeth's does? What remains to Banquo even in death that Macbeth forfeited?

3. How does Shakespeare show that Macbeth would probably not have actually gone through with the crime if he had not been influenced by his wife? Does this make him any less guilty than Lady Macbeth? How would you sum up the difference in their characters?

4. The opening scene of Act I is a sort of prelude to the play. In it the witches mention Macbeth, and they chant, "Fair is foul, and foul is fair." Notice that Macbeth first appears on the stage, in Scene 3, with the remark, "So foul and fair a day I have not seen." In its more obvious meaning this speech refers to the unusual weather, but in a deeper sense it is a *foreboding* of the main action of the play. Explain how this day is both *foul* and *fair* for Macbeth.

5. The main theme of this tragedy is the terrible consequences, both to Macbeth's character and his career, that follow from his having made a wrong moral choice. However, interwoven with this theme are two others almost equally important to Elizabethans though not to modern readers.

a. Shakespeare believed in a strong, stable monarchy. Several of his plays show how disaster results from a dispute over a throne. Explain how the entire story of *Macbeth* might be interpreted as teaching allegiance to your king, and the importance of an orderly, legal passing of the crown from the king to his rightful heir.

b. Many Elizabethans sincerely believed in witchcraft. Show how an Elizabethan might interpret the play from beginning to end as a story teaching that you shouldn't have anything to do with witches. Don't fail to include Banquo's attitude toward the prophecies.

6. The cruel reign of Macbeth has been paralleled by dictatorships in the twentieth century. What would the modern name be for Malcolm, Macduff, and the others who fled from Scotland? Are there modern parallels to Macbeth's keeping "a servant fee'd" in the house of every nobleman, or to the killing of Lady Macduff after her husband had escaped? Have any modern dictators died as ignominiously as Macbeth did? Did some foreign country have a hand in their overthrow? What evidence can you find that Macbeth prevented freedom of speech as a modern dictator would? Why would he, or any dictator, do so? Why is any ruler who rises to power by violent methods almost forced to be more cruel and tyrannical than a king who has inherited his throne peacefully?

7. For full appreciation of Shakespeare, one must be able to understand his figurative language. Give the meaning of the following passages, and for each one explain how the figure of speech is appropriate.

a. "This murderous shaft that's shot
Hath not yet lighted."
(Malcolm to Donalbain,
Act II, Scene 3)

b. "After life's fitful fever he sleeps well."
(Macbeth's comment on Duncan,
Act III, Scene 2)

c. "Macbeth
Is ripe for shaking."
(Malcolm, at the end of Act IV)

d. "Now does he feel
His secret murders sticking on his hands;
. . . now does he feel his title
Hang loose about him, like a giant's robe
Upon a dwarfish thief."
(Angus, speaking of Macbeth
in Act V, Scene 2)

SHAKESPEAREAN AND MODERN DICTION

Shakespeare's diction, or choice of words, is obviously somewhat different from ours. This is partly because our language has changed in three centuries, and partly because Elizabethan poetry contained many words not heard in everyday life.

What proportion of words in a sample passage are not ordinarily used today, at least not in the same sense? To find out, make a list of such words in the first seven lines of Act I, Scene 2, of *Macbeth*. *Seemeth* is the first one. *Newest* is another. (We would say "latest.") Don't overlook *'gainst*—or do we sometimes hear the word pronounced like that? *Broil* seems familiar, but Shakespeare is not referring to a method of cooking. There are 54 words in the passage. Calculate the percentage of archaic words.

◇◇◇◇◇◇◇◇◇◇◇◇◇◇◇◇◇◇◇◇◇◇◇◇◇◇◇◇◇

PROJECTS

1. Draw a diagram or graph of the *rising* and *falling action* of the play. Insert into your graph an outline of the tragedy.

2. Compare and contrast in a written composition the tragic characters of Macbeth and Lady Macbeth.

3. Discuss Shakespeare as a great moral teacher.

4. Show the influence of the physical structure of the Elizabethan stage, the audience, contemporary history, and the condition of the actors upon Shakespeare's composition of *Macbeth*.

5. Imagine yourself to be Lady Macbeth (or any other character in the play) and write the story from your viewpoint.

RELATED READING

Do not fail to read *Hamlet*. Then compare Hamlet as a tragic hero with Macbeth. Compare and contrast the tragedies in plot development, dramatic conflict, and audience appeal.

Every high school senior should make an effort to read one of the following tragedies: *Othello, Romeo and Juliet, King Lear*.

Ben Jonson was a realist and a satirist. He shrewdly observed the human weaknesses of his time and made them the subject matter of his plays. He followed the classical dramatic theory (a) in presenting all the dramatic events at one place and in a short period of time, and (b) in considering the play as a means of reforming the audience by making vice look ridiculous. His best known drama, *Volpone*, has been acted several times both in England and the United States within recent years. You will want to read this story of "The Fox" who in his greed for money pretends to be dying in order to obtain more wealth from his equally greedy prospective heirs.

Read the beautifully illustrated articles on "Renaissance Man" in *Life*, March 3, 1947 and April 4, 1947.

SHAKESPEARE AND THE DRAMA

ADAMS, JOSEPH Q., *A Life of William Shakespeare; Shakespearean Playhouses*

CHUTE, MARCHETTE, *An Introduction to Shakespeare; Shakespeare of London; Ben Jonson of Westminster*

DEKKER, THOMAS, *The Shoemaker's Holiday* (play)

HARRISON, G. B., *On Reading Shakespeare* (Mentor Books Edition)

JONSON, BEN, *Volpone; The Alchemist* (plays)

MARLOWE, CHRISTOPHER, *Dr. Faustus* (play)

MASEFIELD, JOHN, *Shakespeare*

ROLFE, JOHN, *Shakespeare the Boy*

SHAKESPEARE, WILLIAM, *The Tempest* (play)

SMITH, LOGAN P., *On Reading Shakespeare*

WEBSTER, MARGARET, *Shakespeare without Tears*

Further Readings—The Renaissance and The Elizabethan Age

ANDERSON, MAXWELL, *Mary of Scotland; Elizabeth the Queen* (dramas)

* BARING, MAURICE, *In the End Is My Beginning* (Mary of Scotland)

* BELLOC, HILAIRE, *How the Reformation Happened; Wolsey; Cranmer; Characters of the Reformation; Elizabeth, Creature of Circumstance*

* BENSON, ROBERT HUGH, *The King's Achievement; The Queen's Tragedy; Come Rack! Come Rope!* (fiction)

* BRADY, CHARLES A., *Stage of Fools* (fictional biography of More)

* BREEN and SCHREIBE, *Who Ride on White Horses* (drama about Edmund Campion)

CHAMBERS, R. W., *Life of St. Thomas More*

* HOLLIS, CHRISTOPHER, *The Monstrous Regiment; Life of Thomas More*

JANELLE, PIERRE, *Robert Southwell* (critical study)

* KAYE-SMITH, SHEILA, *Superstition Corner* (fiction)

* MAYNARD, THEODORE, *Humanist As Hero* (life of More); *The Cross and the Crown* (biography of Thomas Cromwell)

* NOYES, ALFRED, *Tales of the Mermaid Tavern* (poetry)

OSGOOD, CHARLES G., *The Voice of England* (literary history)

PRESCOTT, H. F. M., *The Man on the Donkey* (historical fiction); *Mary Tudor*

* SARGENT, DANIEL, *Thomas More* (biography)

SABATINI, RAPHAEL, *The Sea Hawk* (fiction)

SCOTT, SIR WALTER, *Kenilworth* (fiction)

STRACHEY, LYTTON, *Elizabeth and Essex* (biographical study)

* WARD, MRS. WILFRID, *Tudor Sunset* (fiction)

* WAUGH, EVELYN, *Edmund Campion* (biographical study)

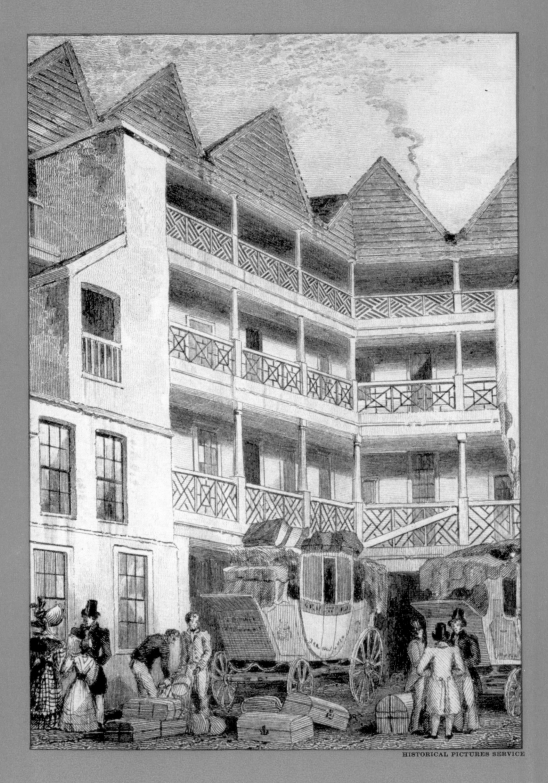

Mail coach and travelers at an old English inn.

THE SEVENTEENTH AND EIGHTEENTH CENTURIES

1 6 0 3 – 1 7 8 0

Elizabeth's death in 1603 was properly dramatic. The curtain came down on an ugly old woman in a henna wig calling piteously for a "true mirror" and begging for a good-luck charm to wear around her neck. The new century which she ushered in was to be a hectic one. It would embrace eight different administrations and four major revolutions of government. England would rise up against a king, indict and behead him; shift to a republican commonwealth; restore her monarch; rebel, and finally, without bloodshed, win another foothold in the march towards democracy—the Bill of Rights.

THE STUART INTERVAL (1603–1625)

In literature, the exuberance of Elizabeth's reign carried over into that of James, son of the tragic Queen of Scots, who followed Elizabeth to the throne. Shakespeare produced several of his later plays at James's court, and many of the other Elizabethan writers did some of their best work after the accession of the new monarch. James himself was a literary man and a much more generous patron of letters than his predecessor. The King James Version of the Bible, which was to have such a tremendous influence on the development of English prose, took its name from him. It was James who made Ben Jonson the first poet laureate of England.

The reign of James, however, did not fulfill either politically or in a literary way the national hopes that had sprung up in the days of Elizabeth. Mounting financial and religious difficulties that had been suppressed in her reign owing to the Spanish threat became of more and more concern under James. There were signs of conflict between Parliament and the king which in the next reign became an open revolt. The times were ripe for trouble.

THE PURITAN AGE (1625–1660)

At the death of James I in 1625, Charles I inherited a nightmare. Besides the eternal skirmishing with Scotland, there were unpleasant social conditions at home. The abject poverty of London slums cried out against the gross luxury of upstart lords, fat with the wealth of monastic houses. The newly rich thought nothing of hiring foreign mercenary troops to break up the revolts of the common people. But King Charles's worst headache was Parliament.

Wool, at this time, was the big money-making commodity. The new mercantile aristocracy, looking only toward prizes for itself, was not particular about methods. All sorts of high-pressure tactics were used, and small farms were ruthlessly seized to be turned into grazing lands. Unfortunately for Charles, the moneyed men had powerful representation in Parliament, and the Stuarts were more dependent upon Parliament for revenue than the Tudors had been. Charles had many debts. He was told that if he wanted money, he must grant to certain interests special rights affecting the control of commerce.

Charles was on tenterhooks. A firm believer in the "divine right of kings," he felt a personal responsibility for *all* his subjects. He knew that if he conceded the "rights of enclosure" to the wealthy land-grabbers, it would mean throwing countless poor off their farms and onto the highways as beggars. Hence he refused.

But this is not the whole story of the conflict. The religious situation was even more disturbing. English Protestantism had begun its inevitable process of division. A certain group, almost identical with the newly

PROTESTANTS

DIVIDED

rich merchant class, had subscribed to the cold, somber, joyless tenets of Calvinism. Though they were shrewd money-makers, they lived sober, abstemious lives. They believed that nature is inherently evil and totally depraved. They mistrusted pleasure; they disapproved of everything beautiful; they were especially opposed to the Catholic Church, which they called "the Scarlet Woman." As the Anglican state church was too "popish" for their taste, they wanted to "purify" it of its worldly formality. And so these straight-laced dissenters came to be known as Puritans.

The tension between Parliament and the king grew ever more serious. The Puritans were violently opposed to Charles on two scores: he refused to make their particular brand of Protestantism the state religion, and he refused to give them a free hand in the matter of enclosures.

There were men who came to the defense of Charles—some because the habit of loyalty is strong; some out of real devotion to their monarch. The king had an attractive personality. When he chose, he could be extremely gracious and generous. His followers—chiefly young men who enjoyed the gay life of the court—were called Cavaliers. The term originally meant "horsemen" or "knights"; but through the seventeenth century, it designated the party loyal to the king. After the fall of the Stuarts, it was replaced by the term Tory.

After three years of civil war, Charles and his Cavaliers were defeated at Naseby. Charles was imprisoned in the Tower of London, accused of high treason against his country, and sentenced to death. On a scaffold in 1649, with surprising dignity, he paid for his kingship with his life. Europe was aghast, and many of the English were horrified. Whatever the uprising meant, it did not mean a victory for democracy nor an emancipation of the poorer classes. There were many who felt that Charles had been their friend and the defender of their rights. Unlike the scenes of frenzied hatred that were to surround the guillotines of the French Revolution, here the silence was broken only by deep groans when the head of the Stuart king rolled in the dust.

KING CHARLES I PUT TO DEATH

A republican commonwealth was organized with Oliver Cromwell at its head. Its purpose was to secure civil freedom to the English people. But many of the leaders were themselves intolerant. The Parliamentary rule went to great extremes. Axes were applied to "idolatrous" statues, "popish pictures," and "the vain show of stained glass windows." But the rule of the Puritans was so confused and mismanaged that Cromwell in disgust finally dismissed Parliament, and with the support of a strong army ruled as absolute dictator. His position was ironic: he who had led the uprising to end the tyranny of the Stuart monarchs had himself become a tyrant.

Oliver Cromwell died in 1658. His son, Richard Cromwell, proved inadequate as a successor, and the Puritan power evaporated. Unrest stirred again. But the period from the accession of Charles in 1625 to the end of the commonwealth in 1660 was important in the field of literature.

CAVALIER POETS

Ben Jonson's influence upon the poets of the early seventeenth century was considerable. Chief among these poets, who because of their admiration and imitation of Jonson were styled "the Tribe of Ben," were Robert Herrick and Thomas

Carew. These two, together with Sir John Suckling and Richard Lovelace, have come to be known as "Cavalier Poets," since they were all close followers of King Charles. They wrote contemporaneously with the Metaphysical Group and at times felt that influence. Yet their verse is in a class by itself.

It is marked first by a practical, down-to-earth attitude toward "life and love and all things else." They seemed to be waging a "de-bunking" campaign in the field of poetry, especially love poetry. No Cavalier poet be- "GATHER YE lieved for one moment that his lady did "in herself con- ROSEBUDS" tain all this world's riches that may far be found." Beautiful she might be—but so what? Flowers fade and women grow old. One of two conclusions usually followed. The first was altogether worldly and materialistic—"Gather ye rosebuds while ye may!" Make the most of today, you can't escape wrinkles tomorrow! The second conclusion was— seek that loveliness which does not die, *beauty of mind and spirit*. Thus even the gayest Cavalier shows sometimes a serious nature.

There are other characteristics of Cavalier verse. It is keen, clever, sometimes flippant, sometimes delicately, sometimes indelicately sensual and voluptuous. Each poem has a theme and is carefully constructed around it. Sometimes the theme is idealistic, sometimes cynical. But it is there, and well inscribed in an attractive setting. These poets were good craftsmen, and they challenge our thought. Their work is a direct contrast to the Elizabethan lyrics which stir our hearts rather than our minds. Suckling, Herrick, Carew, and Lovelace were brilliant writers, and their verse has the polish and often the hardness of a well-cut gem.

◇◇◇◇◇

$\mathcal{A}$ $\mathcal{S}$ong

THOMAS CAREW

Carew's reputation as one of King Charles' cavaliers was not the most wholesome, but very little of his poetry reflects the excesses of his life at court. Many of his love poems are bitterly cynical, but his "A Song" is a faultless piece of lyrical composition.

Ask me no more where Jove bestows,
When June is past, the fading rose;
For in your beauty's orient deep
These flowers, as in their causes, sleep.

Ask me no more whither do stray   5
The golden atoms of the day;
For, in pure love, heaven did prepare
Those powders to enrich your hair.

Ask me no more whither doth haste
The nightingale, when May is past; 10
For in your sweet dividing throat
She winters, and keeps warm her note.

Ask me no more where those stars light
That downwards fall in dead of night;
For in your eyes they sit, and there 15
Fixèd become, as in their sphere.

Ask me no more if east or west
The Phoenix builds her spicy nest;
For unto you at last she flies,
And in your fragrant bosom dies. 20

11. DIVIDING—This was a musical term used in Carew's day and refers to singing in harmony or in parts.

18. PHOENIX—The Arabian bird of fable which alternately destroys itself and then rises from its own ashes.

FOR APPRECIATION

1. The subject of this poem is any lady of any time whose lover pays her five distinct compliments. He goes to nature, science, and myth to express these compliments. State the five questions he asks and give the five answers. What, then, is the theme of the poem? Do each of the five answers accentuate and develop the theme? Discuss.

2. Could there be any symbolism in the five stanzas, five compliments, and five fingers which one uses to compose a song on a musical instrument? Discuss.

3. Study the symmetry. Although the poem is written in the couplet form, it is divided into stanzas. Why?

4. In line 3, how many ideas does "orient deep" suggest to you? Show the relationship between "orient deep" and "flowers." Explain how the nightingales winter in "your sweet dividing throat." The poem ends with the word "dies." Is that word to be taken by itself or in connection with the Phoenix? Explain.

To Lucasta, on Going to the Wars

RICHARD LOVELACE

In 1645 Lovelace raised a regiment for service in France through which he hoped to restore Charles I to the throne. His departure to meet his regiment occasioned the following poem. In the poem, the poet is justifying his separation from his loved one. The eminent critic Mark Van Doren has called this poem "one of the briefest masterpieces in the world, and one of the best proofs that poetry can say what nothing else can."

Tell me not, sweet, I am unkind,
   That from the nunnery
Of thy chaste breast and quiet mind
   To war and arms I fly.

True, a new mistress now I chase,   5
   The first foe in the field;
And with a stronger faith embrace
   A sword, a horse, a shield.

    Yet this inconstancy is such
      As you, too, shall adore;   10
    I could not love thee, dear, so much,
      Loved I not honor more.

FOR APPRECIATION

1. How does the first line anticipate the problem to be met and the state of mind of the lady? Discuss. Does "Sweet" both soften the blow and indicate the poet's feeling?

2. In detail explain the beautiful imagery of lines 2 and 3. What does it tell us of the poet's estimate of his lady? Is there an apparent clash between "unkind" of the first line and the second and third lines?

3. Although he knows it would hurt his lady, is the poet honest when he says "a new mistress now I chase"? Explain your answer by carefully reading the rest of the poem. Why does he need a "stronger faith" to embrace "a sword, a horse, a shield"? Is there a clash in thought between "embrace" and the "first foe in the field"? Discuss.

4. Explain the meaning of the word "inconstancy" in line 9. Why must his lady adore this? Is he appealing to her intellect or to her emotions? Discuss.

5. Do you or do you not agree with the thought of the last two lines? Discuss.

To Althea, from Prison

RICHARD LOVELACE

At the age of twenty-four, Lovelace was imprisoned by the Puritans for petitioning the return of Charles. His most famous poem was written there. Although he produced less poetry than the other Cavalier Poets, much of it of inferior quality, Lovelace stands assured of lasting fame for the two or three lyrics in which he achieved virtual perfection. Few poems can rival TO ALTHEA, FROM PRISON for sheer beauty and expression.

When Love with unconfinèd wings
  Hovers within my gates,
And my divine Althea brings
  To whisper at the grates;
When I lie tangled in her hair   5
  And fettered to her eye,
The birds that wanton in the air
  Know no such liberty.

When flowing cups run swiftly round
  With no allaying Thames,   10
Our careless heads with roses bound,
  Our hearts with loyal flames;
When thirsty grief in wine we steep,
  When healths and drafts go free—
Fishes that tipple in the deep   15
  Know no such liberty.

When, like committed linnets, I
  With shriller throat shall sing
The sweetness, mercy, majesty
  And glories of my King;   20
When I shall voice aloud how good
  He is, how great should be,
Enlargèd winds, that curl the flood,
  Know no such liberty.

Stone walls do not a prison make,   25
  Nor iron bars a cage;
Minds innocent and quiet take
  That for an hermitage;
If I have freedom in my love
  And in my soul am free,   30
Angels alone, that soar above,
  Enjoy such liberty.

7. WANTON—To be extremely merry or gay.

10. ALLAYING THAMES—Not diluted by water.

17. COMMITTED LINNETS—Birds which are caged.

23. ENLARGÈD WINDS—Winds which are free.

FOR APPRECIATION

1. Enumerate the comparisons which the poet makes between the liberty of other creatures and his. Is stanza four a logical conclusion from the thought content of the first three? Explain. In stanza four, what two elements must be present if a prison is to be a pleasant hermitage?

2. From reading the poem, how would you know that Lovelace was a loyal Cavalier? What is the significance of "shriller notes" in line 17?

3. Discuss the connotation of such words as *hover, fettered, wanton, steep, tipple, committed linnets, curl the flood.*

Advice to Maidens

ROBERT HERRICK

Robert Herrick is one of the many paradoxes of this strange age. Although he spent over thirty-five years as an Anglican vicar in Devonshire, he is one of the most prolific love poets of the period. His often quoted "To the Virgins" can be interpreted either as a bit of practical advice to young women or as an expression of the "eat, drink, and be merry" attitude which is to be found in many of the songs of our own day.

Gather ye rosebuds while you may,
   Old Time is still a-flying;
And this same flower that smiles today,
   Tomorrow will be dying.

The glorious lamp of heaven, the sun,
   The higher he's a-getting, 6
The sooner will his race be run,
   And nearer he's to setting.

That age is best which is the first, 9
   When youth and blood are warmer;
But being spent, the worse and worst
   Times still succeed the former.

Then be not coy, but use your time;
   And while ye may, go marry;
For, having lost but once your prime,
   You may forever tarry. 16

FOR APPRECIATION

1. What images does the poet use to contrast youth and old age? Discuss their effectiveness.

2. Do you agree with the thought content of the third stanza? How does Herrick's attitude compare with that of Browning in "Rabbi Ben Ezra"?

3. How does the rhyme scheme and the meter produce a lightsome, singing quality in the poem? Does his choice of words also help produce this effect? Discuss.

4. Scan the poem with close attention to the initial and the final feet in each line.

◇◇◇◇◇

Why So Pale and Wan?

SIR JOHN SUCKLING

In this poem we have the typical Cavalier reaction to the love lyric of the Elizabethans. As a man, Suckling was of rather weak character; he avoided a duel involving his honor and fled from the battlefield during a war with Scotland. His gay and witty poetry, however, is highly rated.

Why so pale and wan, fond lover?
  Prithee, why so pale?
Will, when looking well can't move her,
  Looking ill prevail?
  Prithee, why so pale?   5

Why so dull and mute, young sinner?
  Prithee, why so mute?
Will, when speaking well can't win her,
  Saying nothing do't?
  Prithee, why so mute?   10

    Quit, quit for shame! This will not
      move;
      This cannot take her.
    If of herself she will not love,
      Nothing can make her:
      The devil take her!   15

◇◇

FOR APPRECIATION

1. Point out in detail the characteristics of Cavalier poetry as contained in this lyric. How does it differ from the poems of Lovelace? Discuss.

2. What purpose does the use of the question form serve? Does it make for unity? Do the questions carry the theme to a logical conclusion? Explain. Does the meter change with the abrupt change of thought in the last two lines? Explain.

METAPHYSICAL POETRY

In spite of their beautiful imagery and graceful expression, sonnets and love lyrics, the most popular types of poetry during the Renaissance, were really developing the anti-intellectual theories of the pagan Renaissance. The so-called Metaphysical poets made an effort to stem this pagan development, not primarily because it was pagan, but because it was the artificial product of an essentially Christian culture. They chose to treat the great concerns of man: God, love, sin, suffering, and death—seriously; and to satirize the prevailing ideals and practices. The result is an entirely new kind of lyric poetry. There are serious philosophical truths to be found in most of their poems. The themes are as great as any treated by the great Classical writers. The style attempts to create beauty not by the artificial heaping up of beautiful words or images, but by the perfect expression of man's deepest thoughts and emotions in a rhythm approaching that of natural speech.

The following are some of the elements to be looked for in the study of the Metaphysical poets: 1) dramatic speech; 2) colloquial words and expressions; 3) imagery from science which attempts to find points of similarity in widely differing things; 4) an argumentative approach to the poetic theme and a strict logical structure for the poem; 5) the use of religious imagery for sexual love, and sexual imagery for the expression of religious experience. Sometimes this is done shockingly. More often than not it represents a truer analogy than did the romantic goddesses and pagan myths of the earlier poetry.

The poetry of John Donne, Andrew Marvell, George Herbert, Richard Crashaw, and Henry Vaughan has exercised a tremendous influence upon modern poetry. These poets are much more modern in form and in thought than either the poets of the Renaissance or the Romantic or Victorian poets. Hopkins, T. S. Eliot, and W. H. Auden have written in their tradition. T. S. Eliot has written of Donne, the greatest of the Metaphysical group: "At any time Donne ought to be recognized as one of the few great reformers and preservers of the English tongue."

Repentance

JOHN DONNE

Modern poets like T. S. Eliot and W. H. Auden have reawakened interest in the poems of John Donne. Long considered a poet of mere fantastic "metaphysical conceits,"[1] in recent years he has been discovered as a poet not so much of the external world as of intensely vivid mental experiences. Eliot wrote in his SELECTED ESSAYS *that "a thought to Donne was an experience." His figures of speech were drawn more from his own learning than from sensuous experience. He had an ear for rugged rhythm which aptly expressed his mode of thought—highly intellectualized, yet suffused with emotion. His sonnet, "Repentance," is taken from his "Divine Poems," written during his years as an Anglican minister.*

> At the round earth's imagined corners, blow
> Your trumpets, Angels, and arise, arise
> From death, you numberless infinities
> Of souls, and to your scattered bodies go,
> All whom the flood did, and fire shall o'erthrow,   5
> All whom war, dearth, age, agues, tyrannies,
> Despair, law, chance, hath slain, and you whose eyes
> Shall behold God and never taste death's woe.
>
> But let them sleep, Lord, and me mourn a space,
> For if above all these my sins abound,   10
> 'Tis late to ask abundance of Thy grace
> When we are there; here on this lowly ground,
> Teach me how to repent; for that's as good
> As if Thou hadst seal'd my pardon with Thy blood.

FOR APPRECIATION

1. Why does the poet say the "round earth's imagined corners"? Is this an example of Johnson's definition of "metaphysical"? Explain.

2. The sonnet paints a picture of the Resurrection of the Dead in the octave and asks, in the sestet, for a longer span of life in which to repent. Is the personal application in the sestet effective?

3. What figure of speech is "numberless infinities"?

4. Explain the meaning of line 8. Is this correct theology?

[1] The word "metaphysical" was first used by William Drummond, a seventeenth-century Scottish poet, to describe Donne's poetry. Dr. Johnson describes such poetry as "a combination of dissimilar images, the discovery of resemblances in things apparently unlike." Johnson said that to write on the plan of the metaphysical poets, "it was necessary to read and think."

Batter My Heart

JOHN DONNE

The theme of this intense, at times violent, expression of the perpetual conflict between fallen human nature and the love of God is found throughout the Epistles of St. Paul, the writings of St. Augustine, and the spiritual autobiographies of the saints. As one reads this sonnet, it is impossible not to experience a sense of agonizing spiritual terror as we listen to the poet call from the depths of his captivity and ask God to break him completely. Here we have the refrain of the later poet Francis Thompson: "My harness piece by piece Thou hast hewn from me. And smitten me to my knee; I am defenseless utterly."

Batter my heart, three-personed God; for you
As yet but knock, breathe, shine, and seek to mend.
That I may rise and stand, o'erthrow me and bend
Your force to break, blow, burn, and make me new. 4
I, like an usurped town, to another due,
Labor to admit you, but, oh, to no end;
Reason, your viceroy in me, me should defend,
But is captived and proves weak or untrue.

Yet dearly I love you and would be loved fain,
But am betrothed unto your enemy; 10
Divorce me, untie or break that knot again,
Take me to you, imprison me, for I,
Except you enthrall me, never shall be free,
Nor ever chaste, except you ravish me.

◇◇

FOR APPRECIATION

1. Note the harsh, almost terrible, thought and diction of the poem, beginning with the opening word *batter*. Discuss the effectiveness of this diction. Contrast and discuss the effectiveness of the diction used in line 2 with that used in line 4.

2. Explain in detail the two metaphors employed in the poem. What is the complete spiritual significance of the phrase *usurped town?* In the light of thought content of this poem discuss the Scripture phrase: "The Kingdom of heaven is taken by violence and only the violent bear it away."

3. Note the use of marriage and love terminology. Is this an element of metaphysical poetry? Explain.

4. Explain the paradoxes in the last two lines. Here again we have an example of the metaphysical poet "discovering similarities in differences."

5. Select several other spiritual paradoxes from the Scriptures which express the same thought as that contained in lines 13 and 14.

(FROM) *On The Glorious Assumption of Our Blessed Lady*

RICHARD CRASHAW

Although the dogma of Our Lady's Assumption was not defined until 1950, it has been the subject of art and literature from earliest times. In the opening lines of Crashaw's beautiful tribute to the Blessed Mother, the poet places on the lips of the Holy Spirit a paraphrase of the words of the CANTICLE OF CANTICLES: *"Arise, make haste, my love, my dove, my beautiful one, and come. For winter is now past, the rain is over and gone."*

Hark! she is call'd, the parting hour is
    come;
Take thy farewell, poor World, Heaven
    must go home.
A piece of heavenly earth, purer and
    brighter
Than the chaste stars whose choice
    lamps come to light her,
While through the crystal orbs clearer
    than they   5
She climbs, and makes a far more Milky
    Way.
She's call'd! Hark, how the dear im-
    mortal Dove

Sighs to his silver mate: "Rise up, my
    love!
Rise up, my fair, my spotless one!
The Winter's past, the rain is gone: 10
The Spring is come, the flowers
    appear,
No sweets, but thou, are wanting
    here.
  Come away, my love!
  Come away, my dove!
    Cast off delay;   15
  The court of Heaven is come
  To wait upon thee home;
    Come, come away!"

FOR APPRECIATION

1. What is the dominant tone of the poem? Select the details which heighten this tone.

2. Explain the metaphor, the Scriptural allusion, and the Catholic theology implied in the phrase *immortal Dove sighs to his silver mate*. (See lines 7 and 8.)

3. Explain how the varying meter of the poem heightens the effect of the movement and conveys the idea of reluctance, swift ascension, joyful anticipation. For example, compare the meter and the thought expressed in line 2 with the meter and the thought in lines 4, 5, 6.

(FROM) The Flaming Heart

RICHARD CRASHAW

Saint Teresa (or Theresa) of Avila, who lived in Spain from 1515–1582, was one of the most remarkable saints of the Church. She was what is known as a mystic; that is, she possessed a rare knowledge of God, of future things, of heavenly joys, and particularly of God's tremendous love for man in all His works. This knowledge was given her by direct visitation of God and the story of these favors she wrote in a book of personal memoirs. Through this book the young English scholar, Richard Crashaw, came to know Saint Teresa, and by her guidance was brought, first into the Catholic Church, and then, to the altar of God as a priest. Father Crashaw wrote a poem in honor of the saint from which the following lines are taken:

O thou undaunted daughter of desires!
By all thy dower lights and fires;
By all the eagle in thee, all the dove;
By all thy lives and deaths of love;
By thy large draughts of intellectual
    day,   5
And by thy thirsts of love more large
    than they;
By all thy brim-fill'd bowls of fierce
    desire,

By thy last morning's draught of liquid
    fire;
By the full kingdom of that final kiss
That seized thy parting soul, and seal'd
    thee His;   10
By all the Heav'n thou hast in Him
(Fair sister of the seraphim!):
By all of Him we have in thee;
Leave nothing of myself in me.
Let me so read thy life, that I   15
Unto all life of mine may die!

◇◇

FOR APPRECIATION

1. If you were asked to write a brief outline of St. Teresa's character, what qualities, tightly packed into this poem, would you attribute to her?

2. Explain the figure and the meaning of lines 3, 8, 11. Is the imitation of the saints contained in line 15? Explain. Discuss the deep spiritual truth contained in lines 15–16.

3. If you wish to know more of one of the greatest of women saints, read *Teresa of Avila* by Thomas Walsh or *Teresa of Avila* by Kate O'Brien. Both authors have done an excellent piece of work.

The Pulley

GEORGE HERBERT

The title of the poem is a symbol of the restlessness which can draw man up to God. The key to the meaning of the poem is in the word "rest." As you read the poem, note the apparent conflict between "rest" and "restlessness," "dispersed" and "contract," "pulley" and "rest," "weariness" and "toss."

When God at first made man,
Having a glasse of blessings standing by,
"Let us," said He, "poure on him all we
    can;
Let the world's riches, which dispersèd
    lie,
Contract into a span."   5

So strength first made a way;
Then beautie flow'd, then wisdome,
    honour, pleasure;
When almost all was out, God made a
    stay,
Perceiving that, alone of all His treas-
    ure,
Rest in the bottome lay.   10

"For if I should," said He,
"Bestow this jewell also on My creature,
He would adore My gifts in stead of Me,
And rest in Nature, not the God of
    Nature:
So both should losers be.   15

"Yet let him keep the rest,
But keep them with repining restless-
    nesse;
Let him be rich and wearie, that at least,
If goodnesse leade him not, yet weari-
    nesse
May tosse him to My breast."   20

10. REST—Note the play on this word in lines 14 and 16.

◇◇

FOR APPRECIATION

1. Explain the logic of stanza three. Would you say the poem is merely a clever and amusing one, or does it contain a deep spiritual thought? Discuss.
2. Compare this poem in thought and structure with Herbert's "Collar."

RELATED READING

Read Henry Vaughan's "The World" and Andrew Marvell's "Dialogue Between Soul and Body."

PROJECTS

Compare and contrast two or more of the Cavalier poets with two or more of the Metaphysical poets. In a written or oral report discuss their attitude toward life, love, and religion, as well as their craftsmanship. Which group is more realistic?

Hold a discussion on the subject of "The Elizabethan versus the Metaphysical Poets." State your own preferences and give reasons for your choice. Do you find metaphysical poetry difficult?

PURITAN PROSE AND POETRY

The two outstanding literary figures of the seventeenth century who professed Puritanism in religion and politics were John Milton and John Bunyan.

John Milton, the greatest English poet next to Shakespeare, was born in London in 1608. His father was a Puritan who loved books and music and passed this love on to young John. He received his early education from private tutors and later attended St. Paul's School and Cambridge University.

Young Milton was an avid scholar who spent long hours with the Greek and Roman classics and in the study of several foreign languages. He deliberately chose

JOHN MILTON

literature for his vocation and was convinced that he had been called to be a great poet. For several years he lived in retirement with his father at Horton, near London, where he studied mathematics, music, history, and the classics. To this early period belong "L'Allegro," "Il Penseroso," "Hymn on the Morning of Christ's Nativity," and "Lycidas." These poems have little or nothing of the Puritan spirit; they breathe a deep love of the beauties of the classics and a deep love of nature.

After leaving retirement at Horton, Milton travelled in Europe. Upon his return he lived in London, where he took up tutoring and devoted himself to his studies.

During the reign of Cromwell, Milton became the warmest supporter of that dictator and served as Secretary to the Commonwealth. It was during this period that he engaged in controversial writing. In his *Areopagitica,* he opposed censorship of the press, although he denied freedom of press to Catholics. Because of his unhappy first marriage, he wrote a pamphlet advocating divorce.

After ten years of married life, Milton's first wife died. He married a second and a third time. His second wife died after fifteen months of married life.

With the Restoration of the Stuarts in 1660, Milton went into hiding. Although he had advocated regicide, or the killing of the Stuart kings, he was pardoned by Charles II. At forty-five Milton lost his sight because of the severe eyestrain involved in his work as Secretary of the Commonwealth. But with his youth and politics behind him, he entered upon his most productive literary period—the writing and completion of the great epics *Paradise Lost* and *Paradise Regained,* and his last long poem, *Samson Agonistes.*

John Bunyan

The most astonishingly successful prose piece of the period was *Pilgrim's Progress* by John Bunyan, a fervent evangelist of humble background and scant learning. Written in prison, where Bunyan had been thrown for refusing to submit to Anglicanism under Charles II, *Pilgrim's Progress* presents allegorically the life of a Christian. Containing and continuing the medieval theme of the religious allegory employed by the sermon writers of the Middle Ages and by the authors of the morality plays, *Pilgrim's Progress* is original only in this sense: it gives in a simple, dignified, forceful, dramatic, and concrete manner a Christian's personal religious experience along the stages of life "which lead a man marked out for faith, from the conviction of sin, through despair, temptations, to final peace and blessedness." It may well be called the Protestant lay Bible stripped of all that is not—to a Puritan conscience—the direct teaching of salvation. Perhaps no book in the English language, except the Bible, has been read more widely.

Izaak Walton

One other prose writer of the period deserves special mention—Izaak Walton (1593–1683) whose ninety years spanned the arc of the century. The book that has kept his name alive is his little treatise on fishermen and fishing—*The Compleat Angler.* Twentieth-century fishermen still turn its pages with an appreciative smile. It tells no "fish stories." The reader rambles along an English country road, meets a shepherd, hears a milkmaid singing, casts a fly, catches a trout or two, and speculates upon the world and all the pleasant things in it. To day-dreaming anglers, the book seems to have captured the charm of the sport that gives man a chance to "loaf and invite his soul." Walton was not a Puritan. He took no militant part in the struggles of his day. His books have the serenity and sweetness that marked the best prose of his puritanic age.

Many volumes of religious prose found an appreciative audience in the New World as well as the Old during the seventeenth century. Perhaps the most popular of these religious books were Browne's *Religion of a Physician* and Jeremy Taylor's *Holy Living and Holy Dying.*

On His Blindness

JOHN MILTON

From the days of his youth Milton had felt "called" to write a great religious poem. God had given him a talent which should be devoted to His service. In the mind of the poet there grew the plan of an epic retelling the story of the fall of man. It would explain the existence of sin in the world and "justify the ways of God to man." But at forty-five Milton found himself blind, his PARADISE LOST unwritten—apparently never to be written. After a period of profound dejection, he composed this meditation "On His Blindness."

> When I consider how my light is spent,
> Ere half my days in this dark world and wide,
> And that one talent which is death to hide
> Lodged with me useless, though my soul more bent
> To serve therewith my Maker, and present   5
> My true account, lest He returning chide—
> "Doth God exact day-labor, light denied?"
> I fondly ask.—But Patience, to prevent
> That murmur, soon replies, "God doth not need
> Either man's work, or His own gifts; who best   10
> Bear His mild yoke, they serve Him best. His state
> Is kingly; thousands at His bidding speed
> And post o'er land and ocean without rest;
> They also serve who only stand and wait."

1. LIGHT—His sight. IS SPENT—Used up.
3. TALENT—His power to write. Cf. the Parable of the Talents in Matthew 25.
4. BENT—Willing or desirous.
8. FONDLY—Foolishly.

◇◇

FOR APPRECIATION

1. Milton utters his complaint in the first seven and one-half lines. In a few simple words give the complete answer of "Patience."

2. Is the doctrine of Divine Providence expressed in the sestet? Explain.

3. Is this strictly an Italian sonnet? Explain. Give the rhyme scheme of the sonnet.

4. Discuss the connection between the words used in the sonnet and the movement of the poem. Does the poet use light, swiftly moving words, or does he use words which are largely monosyllabic, with long vowels? Is the movement of the poem solemn and dignified? Explain.

5. Are both the active and the contemplative life expressed in lines 12, 13, 14? Discuss.

6. Line 14 is famous in literature and

rich in suggestion. Do you think the Communist or the modern pagan would agree with the thought of that line? What is the attitude of the non-Christian toward pain and suffering? The Christian attitude? Do shut-ins, incurables, and invalids serve God, country, and fellow man? Discuss in detail.

7. Look up the origin of *post*. What do you mean by *posthaste*?

◇◇◇◇◇

(FROM) *Paradise Lost*

JOHN MILTON

Throughout Milton's mature years, the great work of his life, his epic, was his first concern. It filled his thoughts for more than twenty years, from its first conception as a possible drama to its completion and perfection as a narrative of epic proportions. He completed his work while the Plague was raging in 1665. Shortly after the outbreak of the Great Fire of 1666, he sent his manuscript to the printer. The payment he received for his masterpiece was a pittance of about ten pounds.

The construction of PARADISE LOST *is upon a vast scale and the result is a unified whole in which every part is logically related to every other part. The action of the twelve books of* PARADISE LOST, *with its setting in hell and in the Garden of Paradise, begins with the fall of Satan and ends with the banishment of Adam and Eve from Paradise. Equally heroic in stature are the characters of Adam and Eve—but Satan is Milton's masterpiece of character portrayal. Only the imagination of a great genius could conceive and execute such a titanic character.*

In some ways Satan seems to have run away with Milton. Perhaps in Satan's colossal spirit of defiance we see something of the poet's own rebellious nature. Satan is depicted with such grandeur that he is often looked upon as the hero of the epic. In this respect he is a typical Renaissance character whose "unconquerable will" rebelled against authority and made the creature the master of his own destiny.

PARADISE LOST *is more than "the dream of a Puritan fallen asleep over the first pages of the Bible." Milton was great despite his Puritanism.*

The glaring weakness of his epic is to be found in its Calvinistic theology with its emphasis upon predestination and its concept of God as drawn from the Old Testament exclusively. The greatness lies in the tremendous sweep of imaginative power, the stately and sonorous rhythms, the grandeur of epic architecture which Milton learned from Vergil and Dante. Many of his lines expressed in "the organ-music of his blank verse" are the essence of vast rich poetry. Like Shakespeare, he has built word-combinations of universal and immortal appeal.

There are pages in Milton which cannot be assimilated without help of an encyclopedia. But in spite of difficult allusions, long sentences, hard words, and extended metaphors, there is that in Milton's poetry which repays the study spent in reading it.

The following selection is taken from Book I of PARADISE LOST.

Of Man's first disobedience, and the fruit
Of that forbidden tree, whose mortal taste
Brought death into the world, and all our woe,
With loss of Eden, till one greater Man
Restore us, and regain the blissful seat,   5
Sing, heavenly Muse, that on the secret top
Of Oreb, or of Sinai, didst inspire
That shepherd who first taught the chosen seed
In the beginning how the heavens and earth
Rose out of chaos. Or, if Sión hill   10
Delight thee more, and Siloa's brook that flowed
Fast by the oracle of God, I thence
Invoke thy aid to my adventurous song,
That with no middle flight intends to soar
Above the Aonian mount, while it pursues   15
Things unattempted yet in prose or rime.
And chiefly thou, O Spirit, that dost prefer
Before all temples the upright heart and pure,
Instruct me, for thou know'st. Thou from the first
Wast present, and with mighty wings outspread,   20

6. HEAVENLY MUSE—Here not the Greek goddess of song, but the divine inspiration of Moses and the prophets.
7. OREB, SINAI—Twin peaks of mountain where Moses kept his flocks of sheep.
8. CHOSEN SEED—The Jewish people chosen by God in the Old Dispensation to be the nation of the Redeemer.
10. SION HILL—Zion, the city of Jerusalem; here King David sang the famous psalms.
12. ORACLE OF GOD—The temple in Jerusalem.
15. AONIAN MOUNT—Mount Helicon—represents Greek poetry. Milton means to write on a loftier theme.
17. SPIRIT—Here the Holy Spirit.

Dove-like sat'st brooding on the vast abyss,
And mad'st it pregnant. What in me is dark
Illumine, what is low raise and support;
That to the height of this great argument
I may assert Eternal Providence,   25
And justify the ways of God to men.

Say first—for heaven hides nothing from thy view,
Nor the deep tract of hell—say first what cause
Moved our grand parents in that happy state
Favored of heaven so highly, to fall off   30
From their Creator, and transgress his will
For one restraint, lords of the world besides.
Who first seduced them to that foul revolt?
The infernal serpent; he it was whose guile,
Stirred up with envy and revenge, deceived   35
The mother of mankind, what time his pride
Had cast him out from heaven, with all his host
Of rebel angels, by whose aid, aspiring
To set himself in glory above his peers,
He trusted to have equaled the Most High,   40
If he opposed; and with ambitious aim
Against the throne and monarchy of God
Raised impious war in heaven, and battle proud,
With vain attempt. Him the Almighty Power
Hurled headlong flaming from the ethereal sky,   45
With hideous ruin and combustion, down
To bottomless perdition; there to dwell
In adamantine chains and penal fire,
Who durst defy the Omnipotent to arms.

Nine times the space that measures day and night   50
To mortal men, he with his horrid crew
Lay vanquished, rolling in the fiery gulf,
Confounded, though immortal. But his doom
Reserved him to more wrath; for now the thought
Both of lost happiness and lasting pain   55
Torments him; round he throws his baleful eyes,
That witnessed huge affliction and dismay,
Mixed with obdurate pride and steadfast hate.
At once, as far as angels ken, he views
The dismal situation waste and wild.   60
A dungeon horrible on all sides round
As one great furnace flamed; yet from those flames

36. WHAT TIME—When.
59. KEN—Are able to see.

No light; but rather darkness visible
Served only to discover sights of woe,
Regions of sorrow, doleful shades, where peace   65
And rest can never dwell, hope never comes
That comes to all; but torture without end
Still surges, and a fiery deluge, fed
With ever-burning sulphur unconsumed.
Such place Eternal Justice had prepared   70
For those rebellious; here their prison ordained
In utter darkness, and their portion set,
As far removed from God and light of heaven
As from the center thrice to the utmost pole.
Oh, how unlike the place from whence they fell!   75
There the companions of his fall, o'erwhelmed
With floods and whirlwinds of tempestuous fire,
He soon discerns; and weltering by his side,
One next himself in power, and next in crime,
Long after known in Palestine, and named   80
Beëlzebub. To whom the arch-enemy,
And thence in heaven called Satan, with bold words

74. THE CENTER . . . UTMOST POLE—From the center of the earth to the most distant point
in the heavens. Milton here uses for poetic purpose the old theory that the earth was the center
of the universe.

Breaking the horrid silence, thus began:
"If thou beëst he—but oh, how fallen! how changed
From him who in the happy realms of light,   85
Clothed with transcendent brightness, didst outshine
Myriads, though bright!—if he whom mutual league,
United thoughts and counsels, equal hope
And hazard in the glorious enterprise,
Joined with me once, now misery hath joined   90
In equal ruin—into what pit thou seëst
From what height fallen. So much the stronger proved
He with his thunder; and till then who knew
The force of those dire arms? Yet not for those,
Nor what the potent Victor in his rage   95
Can else inflict, do I repent, or change,
Though changed in outward luster, that fixed mind,
And high disdain from sense of injured merit,
That with the Mightiest raised me to contend,
And to the fierce contention brought along   100
Innumerable force of spirits armed
That durst dislike his reign, and me preferring,
His utmost power with adverse power opposed
In dubious battle on the plains of heaven
And shook his throne. What though the field be lost?   105
All is not lost—the unconquerable will,
And study of revenge, immortal hate,
And courage never to submit or yield;
And what is else not to be overcome;
That glory never shall his wrath or might   110
Extort from me. To bow and sue for grace
With suppliant knee, and deify his power
Who, from the terror of this arm, so late
Doubted his empire—that were low indeed,
That were an ignominy and shame beneath   115
This downfall; since by fate the strength of gods
And this empyreal substance cannot fail;
Since, through experience of this great event
In arms not worse, in foresight much advanced,
We may with more successful hope resolve   120
To wage by force or guile eternal war,
Irreconcilable to our grand Foe,
Who now triumphs, and in the excess of joy
Sole reigning holds the tyranny of heaven."

So spake the apostate angel, though in pain,   125
Vaunting aloud, but racked with deep despair;

93. HE—God, the Victor.

And thus him answered soon his bold compeer:
"O Prince! O Chief of many thronèd powers
That led the embattled seraphim to war
Under thy conduct, and, in dreadful deeds   130
Fearless, endangered heaven's perpetual King,
And put to proof his high supremacy,
Whether upheld by strength, or chance, or fate!
Too well I see and rue the dire event
That with sad overthrow and foul defeat   135
Hath lost us heaven, and all this mighty host
In horrible destruction laid thus low,
As far as gods and heavenly essences
Can perish; for the mind and spirit remains
Invincible, and vigor soon returns,   140
Though all our glory extinct, and happy state
Here swallowed up in endless misery.
But what if he our Conqueror—whom I now
Of force believe almighty, since no less
Than such could have o'erpowered such force as ours—   145
Have left us this our spirit and strength entire,
Strongly to suffer and support our pains,
That we may so suffice his vengeful ire;
Or do him mightier service, as his thralls
By right of war, whate'er his business be,   150
Here in the heart of hell to work in fire,
Or do his errands in the gloomy deep?
What can it then avail, though yet we feel
Strength undiminished, or eternal being
To undergo eternal punishment?"   155

Whereto with speedy words the archfiend replied:
"Fallen Cherub, to be weak is miserable,
Doing or suffering; but of this be sure—
To do aught good never will be our task,
But ever to do ill our sole delight,   160
As being the contrary to his high will
Whom we resist. If then his providence
Out of our evil seek to bring forth good,
Our labor must be to pervert that end,
And out of good still to find means of evil;   165
Which ofttimes may succeed so as perhaps
Shall grieve him, if I fail not, and disturb
His inmost counsels from their destined aim.
But see! the angry Victor hath recalled
His ministers of vengeance and pursuit   170
Back to the gates of heaven; the sulphurous hail,

Shot after us in storm, o'erblown hath laid
The fiery surge that from the precipice
Of heaven received us falling; and the thunder,
Winged with red lightning and impetuous rage,   175
Perhaps hath spent his shafts, and ceases now
To bellow through the vast and boundless Deep.
Let us not slip the occasion, whether scorn
Or satiate fury yield it from our Foe.
Seest thou yon dreary plain, forlorn and wild,   180
The seat of desolation, void of light,
Save what the glimmering of these livid flames
Casts pale and dreadful? Thither let us tend
From off the tossing of these fiery waves;
There rest, if any rest can harbor there;   185
And, reassembling our afflicted powers
Consult how we may henceforth most offend
Our Enemy, our own loss how repair,
How overcome this dire calamity,
What re-inforcement we may gain from hope;   190
If not, what resolution from despair."

172. LAID—Calmed.

❖❖❖

FOR APPRECIATION

LINES 1–26—THE INVOCATION:

1. In the first five lines Milton states his theme. Recast the thought in your own words. What is the meaning of "mortal taste," "blissful seat"? Which line is most appealing to you? Does it have sweep and strength?

2. The call for guidance in lines 6–26 is in the classical manner, patterned after the invocations to the Muse in the *Iliad* and the *Aeneid*. To what two sources of inspiration does Milton appeal? Can you select any details which manifest Milton's knowledge of and affection for the Bible?

3. From the invocation, what do you judge the spirit and purpose of this epic to be? Can you identify the account of creation referred to in lines 8–10? Select certain phrases which manifest Milton's seriousness and his ambition to write great poetry. List five lines that you consider worthy of memory because of their happy expression of a worthy thought.

LINES 27–49—SUMMARY OF POEM:

1. What is the subject of the opening verb "say"? Discuss the full meaning of the phrase "lords of the world besides." What is Satan's sin expressed in line 39? Scan line 49; what force is added by the irregularity at the beginning of the line?

2. Why is it important for the author to offer changes from the iambic pentameter? Give a few examples where Milton's thought-phrases break up the over-all rhythm. Discuss what effect this has on the movement of the poem.

LINES 50–191—SCENE IN HELL:

1. Notice the manner in which Milton tells how long the devils have lain vanquished; does this add to the effect? What does Milton gain, in lines 57–58 by allowing us to view hell through Satan's "baleful eyes"? Lines 60–71 give a de-

scription of hell; list the details that form the picture. What does the utter simplicity of line 75 achieve? Is it especially powerful?

2. The opening of Satan's first speech might be compared to the soliloquies in *Macbeth*. Do lines 84–92 make a good sentence? Why or why not? Is the meaning clear? Discuss. How does Satan's mood change after line 92? What is the meaning of "What though the field be lost? All is not lost"? Is the remainder of his speech convincing? Do you think Satan is afraid?

3. What effect does Satan's speech have on Beëlzebub as evidenced in his reply? Is he as strong a character as Satan? What is the spirit of lines 141–42? Is there any trace of repentance in the remainder of his speech? Cite specific lines to prove your point.

4. Do you consider the opening lines of Satan's second speech great poetry? Discuss "to be weak is miserable, doing or suffering." Lines 163–68 give Satan's plan of renewed warfare; they have been applied to an individual case in *The Screwtape Letters* by C. S. Lewis. State this planned campaign simply in your own words.

5. Read aloud the description of the thunder in lines 174–77. How does the last line justify Milton's epithet of organ music? What is the spirit of the concluding lines? Select at least ten outstanding lines in this final section, and read them to the class.

SIGNIFICANT EXPRESSIONS

1. In lines 21–22 analyze "Dove-like sat'st brooding . . ." Compare this figure with that of Hopkins in "God's Grandeur."

2. Study these lines for (*a*) tone color, (*b*) diction, (*c*) thought:

Line 45: "Hurled headlong flaming from the ethereal sky."

Line 126: "Vaunting aloud, but racked with deep despair."

Lines 174–77: ". . . and the thunder
Winged with red lightning and impetuous rage,
Perhaps hath spent his shafts, and ceases now
To bellow through the vast and boundless Deep."

Lines 180–84: ". . . dreary plain, forlorn and wild . . . void of light,
Save what the glimmering of these livid flames
Casts pale and dreadful."

WORDS

Be sure you know the meaning of the following words: *baleful, obdurate, weltering, transcendent, ignominy, empyreal, apostate, compeer, rue, satiate, livid, dire.*

RELATED READING

Your teacher will give you extra credit for reading at least the rest of Book I and all of Book II of this great epic.

L'Allegro

JOHN MILTON

The most famous companion poems in English literature are Milton's "L'Allegro" and "Il Penseroso." The titles are translated as meaning "the cheerful man" and "the serious or thoughtful man." The poems describe a typical day in the lives of each. Both are pastoral poems written by Milton when he was but twenty-four years old.

The outline of both poems is the same. The poet begins by banishing the mood opposite to the one he wishes to create and gives a description of the mood he now wishes to enjoy. He then recounts the various pleasures of a typical day spent in that mood and concludes with the poet's attitude toward that mood. The poems, therefore, do not describe the day of two distinct individuals, but rather the alternating moods of one man, who happens to be Milton himself.

We shall study the poems as two parts of one unit. As you read them, follow the changes of scene and mood, and note the similarity of structure in both. Both poems are divided into thought units to help you in your comparison.

You should be warned that Milton's poetic language and his frequent allusions to classical mythology make the poems far from easy reading. But the satisfaction you can derive from what Dryden called Milton's "majesty" of expression and his "loftiness" of mind will well repay your efforts.

[*Melancholy banished.*]

Hence, loathèd Melancholy,
  Of Cerberus and blackest Midnight born
In Stygian cave forlorn
  'Mongst horrid shapes, and shrieks, and sights unholy!
Find out some uncouth cell,   5
  Where brooding Darkness spreads his jealous wings,
And the night-raven sings;

1. HENCE—Be gone!
2. CERBERUS (sŭr′bēr·ŭs)—The huge three-headed dog, with a serpent's tail, which in Greek mythology stood guard at the approach to Hades. The myth that Cerberus and Midnight were the parents of Melancholy is Milton's own invention.
3. STYGIAN (stĭj′ĭ·ăn)—That is, in the region of the Styx, the chief river of Hades.
5. UNCOUTH—Wild, mysterious.
6. JEALOUS WINGS—Because unwilling to let light enter.
7. NIGHT-RAVEN—The night-owl, night-heron.

There, under ebon shades and low-
    browed rocks,
As ragged as thy locks,   9
    In dark Cimmerian desert ever dwell.

[*Invitation to Mirth and her followers.*]

But come, thou Goddess fair and free,
In heaven yclept Euphrosyne,
And by men heart-easing Mirth;
Whom lovely Venus, at a birth,
With two sister Graces more,   15
To ivy-crownèd Bacchus bore:
Or whether (as some sager sing)
The frolic wind that breathes the spring,
Zephyr, with Aurora playing,
As he met her once a-Maying,   20
There, on beds of violets blue,
And fresh-blown roses washed in dew,
Filled her with thee, a daughter fair,
So buxom, blithe, and debonair.
Haste thee, Nymph, and bring with
    thee   25

Jest, and youthful Jollity,
Quips and Cranks and wanton Wiles,
Nods and Becks and wreathèd Smiles,
Such as hang on Hebe's cheek,
And love to live in dimple sleek;   30
Sport that wrinkled Care derides,
And Laughter holding both his sides.
Come, and trip it, as you go,
On the light fantastic toe;
And in thy right hand lead with thee   35
The mountain-nymph, sweet Liberty;
And, if I give thee honor due,
Mirth, admit me of thy crew,
To live with her, and live with thee,
In unreprovèd pleasures free;   40

[*The delights which the dawn and
early morning bring.*]

To hear the lark begin his flight,
And, singing, startle the dull night,
From his watch-tower in the skies,
Till the dapple dawn doth rise;
Then to come, in spite of sorrow,   45

10. CIMMERIAN—The land of the Cimmerians in classic mythology was a region of
mist and darkness across the stream Oceanus,
which surrounded the world of men. Beyond
the land of the Cimmerians was Hades.

12. YCLEPT—Called.

12. EUPHROSYNE (ū·frŏs'ĭ·nē)—One of the
three Graces, lesser deities, who as their designation indicates were the goddesses of gentility
and the polite amenities. Euphrosyne means
joy or cheerfulness. The other two were Aglaïa
(brightness) and Thalïa (bloom). They were
generally regarded as daughters of Zeus.

14. VENUS—The goddess of love and beauty.

16. BACCHUS—God of wine and revelry.
He was generally represented as wearing a
crown of ivy.

17. SOME SAGER—That is, some wiser poets.
That Mirth (Euphrosyne) is the child not of
Venus and Bacchus but of Zephyr and Aurora
is Milton's own invention.

19. ZEPHYR—The West Wind.

19. AURORA—The Dawn.

20. A-MAYING—The allusion is to the old
English custom of going out into the fields
early on May-day to celebrate the return of
spring and bring in the "may" or hawthorn.

24. BUXOM—In Milton's time the word
"buxom" meant blithesome.

25. NYMPH—That is, Euphrosyne or Mirth.

27. QUIPS—Flashes of wit.

27. CRANKS—Plays on words.

27. WANTON WILES—Sportive tricks.

28. BECKS—Bows, beckonings.

29. HEBE (hē'bē)—Goddess of youth, and
cupbearer to the gods.

31. CARE—Care is the object of derides.

34. FANTASTIC—The word as Milton uses
it here designates movements in the dance
made according to the fancy of those dancing.

36. MOUNTAIN-NYMPH, SWEET LIBERTY—
Here is another of Milton's inventions. The
idea of a mountain-nymph, Liberty, was suggested to Milton, it is safe to say, by the love
of freedom and hatred of tyranny which has
seemed peculiarly characteristic of mountain
dwellers, notably the Swiss.

39. HER—Liberty.

40. UNREPROVÈD—Innocent.

41. TO HEAR, etc.—Here begins the delineation of the "unreprovèd pleasures" which appeal to the cheerful mood.

41. TO HEAR THE LARK—The lark is a
small, brownish bird, which nests on the
ground. In flight it sings almost continuously,
soaring up until it becomes lost to sight and
then dropping to its nest.

45. THEN TO COME—The infinitive "to
come" is co-ordinate with "to hear." The
sense is: To hear the lark . . . [and] Then to
come . . .

And at my window bid good-morrow,
Through the sweet-briar or the vine,
Or the twisted eglantine;
While the cock, with lively din,
Scatters the rear of darkness thin;   50
And to the stack, or the barn-door,
Stoutly struts his dames before:
Oft listening how the hounds and horn
Cheerly rouse the slumbering Morn,
From the side of some hoar hill,   55
Through the high wood echoing shrill:
Sometime walking, not unseen,
By hedgerow elms, on hillocks green,
Right against the eastern gate
Where the great Sun begins his state,
Robed in flames and amber light,   61

48. TWISTED EGLANTINE—Honeysuckle.
55. HOAR—White with blossoming trees.
58. HEDGEROW ELMS—The elms which
grow along the lines of the hedges. In England
fields and lanes are bordered not by fences as
in America but generally by dense hedges.
60. SUN—Sun is personified and compared
to a great monarch setting out on a procession
of "state" richly robed and attended by a great
retinue of clouds in livery.

The clouds in thousand liveries dight;
While the ploughman, near at hand,
Whistles o'er the furrowed land,
And the milkmaid singeth blithe,   65
And the mower whets his scythe,
And every shepherd tells his tale
Under the hawthorn in the dale.

[*An ideal day in the country.*]

Straight mine eye hath caught new
      pleasures,
Whilst the landskip round it measures:
Russet lawns, and fallows gray,   71
Where the nibbling flocks do stray;
Mountains on whose barren breast
The laboring clouds do often rest;
Meadows trim, with daisies pied;   75

62. DIGHT—Dressed or garbed.
67. TELLS HIS TALE—Counts his sheep.
70. LANDSKIP—Landscape.
74. LABORING—Teeming, heavy with rain.
75. PIED—Variegated.   Pied   modifies
meadows, and alludes to the color effect which
the daisies produce. Have you ever looked
down from some hilltop on "meadows trim
with daisies pied"?

Shallow brooks, and rivers wide;
Towers and battlements it sees
Bosomed high in tufted trees,
Where perhaps some beauty lies,
The cynosure of neighboring eyes.   80
Hard by a cottage chimney smokes
From betwixt two aged oaks,
Where Corydon and Thyrsis met
Are at their savory dinner set
Of herbs and other country messes,   85
Which the neat-handed Phyllis dresses;
And then in haste her bower she leaves,
With Thestylis to bind the sheaves;
Or, if the earlier season lead,
To the tanned haycock in the mead.
Sometimes, with secure delight,   91
The upland hamlets will invite,
When the merry bells ring round,
And the jocund rebecks sound
To many a youth and many a maid   95
Dancing in the chequered shade,
And young and old come forth to play
On a sunshine holiday,
Till the livelong daylight fail:

[*The stories told at the social gathering.*]

Then to the spicy nut-brown ale,   100
With stories told of many a feat,

How Faery Mab the junkets eat.

This is Mab, the mistress fairy,
That doth nightly rob the dairy.

She that pinches country wenches
If they rub not clean their benches.

She was pinched and pulled, she said;
And he, by Friar's lantern led,
Tells how the drudging goblin sweat
To earn his cream-bowl duly set,   106
When in one night, ere glimpse of morn,
His shadowy flail hath threshed the corn
That ten day-laborers could not end;
Then lies him down, the lubber fiend,
And, stretched out all the chimney's length,   111
Basks at the fire his hairy strength,
And crop-full out of doors he flings,
Ere the first cock his matin rings.   114
Thus done the tales, to bed they creep,
By whispering winds soon lulled asleep.

[*Pleasures in the city: marriages, plays, music.*]

102. FAERY MAB, etc.—The allusion is best explained by quoting from Ben Jonson, a contemporary of Shakespeare.

102. JUNKETS—A dish made of curds mixed with cream.

102. EAT—This is the past tense of eat (ēt) —the form that Americans spell and pronounce *āte*.

103. SHE—One of the villagers, a country maid.

104. HE—Another of the villagers, a country fellow, or rustic.

104. FRIAR'S—Friar Rush. This was a Christmas game. Milton evidently refers to Will-o'-the-Wisp who led travelers astray.

105. DRUDGING GOBLIN—Robin Goodfellow, another fairy or brownie, who in return for a bowl of cream set out for him would do no end of work during the night.

110. LUBBER—Drudging. Note the description of Robin. He was a pretty husky brownie.

110. FIEND—Used here simply to designate a supernatural being, a demon, not necessarily evil.

113. CROP-FULL—That is, stomach-full, well fed.

114. ERE THE FIRST COCK HIS MATIN RINGS —Fairies and goblins had to return to their abodes before sunrise.

115. THEY—The villagers.

80. CYNOSURE—The center of attraction.

83. CORYDON AND THYRSIS (côr′y̆·dŏn, Thĕr′sĭs)—Shepherds in one of Vergil's poems of country life. Used here to indicate two English shepherds or rustics.

86. PHYLLIS—A shepherdess in one of Vergil's poems. Here used, of course, to designate an English maid.

87. BOWER—Cottage.

88. THESTYLIS (thĕs′tў̆·lĭs)—A shepherdess in one of Vergil's poems.

89. IF THE EARLIER SEASON LEAD—That is, if it is in the haying season which is earlier, of course, than the grain harvest.

92. INVITE—Appeal to the fancy.

93. RING ROUND—That is, ring one after another from the churches in the "upland hamlets." Milton is here describing a holiday, or holy-day, such as was celebrated in his day in every village.

94. REBECKS—An old-fashioned fiddle or violin.

Towered cities please us then,
And the busy hum of men,
Where throngs of knights and barons
    bold,   119
In weeds of peace, high triumphs hold,
With store of ladies, whose bright eyes
Rain influence, and judge the prize
Of wit or arms, while both contend
To win her grace whom all commend.
There let Hymen oft appear   125
In saffron robe, with taper clear,
And pomp, and feast, and revelry,
With mask and antique pageantry;
Such sights as youthful poets dream,
On summer eves by haunted stream.
Then to the well-trod stage anon,   131

If Jonson's learnèd sock be on,
Or sweetest Shakespeare, Fancy's child,
Warble his native wood-notes wild,
And ever, against eating cares,   135
Lap me in soft Lydian airs,
Married to immortal verse,
Such as the meeting soul may pierce,
In notes with many a winding bout
Of linkèd sweetness long drawn out   140
With wanton heed and giddy cunning,

132. IF JONSON'S LEARNÈD SOCK BE ON—
That is, to see if one of learnèd Ben Jonson's
comedies is playing. The "sock" was a term
used to designate comedy, and the "buskin" to
designate tragedy. The "sock" was a light shoe
worn by actors in comedy on the ancient stage,
and the "buskin," a laced boot, was worn by
tragic actors.

133. FANCY'S CHILD—Imagination's child.
Milton refers here to those lighter, gayer and
more fanciful products of Shakespeare's imagi-
nation—the comedies such as As You Like It,
Twelfth Night, and A Midsummer Night's
Dream.

134. HIS NATIVE WOOD-NOTES WILD—An oft
repeated distinction between Shakespeare and
Jonson is that Shakespeare had nature and
Jonson had art. The meaning is that the latter
taught himself to write drama by studying the
dramas of the ancients whose rules he followed,
whereas the former was a dramatist "by nature," so to speak, and was guided not by
learning but by native ability only.

135. EATING CARES—That is, cares that eat
the heart.

136. LAP—Enfold.

136. LYDIAN—A term designating one of the
ancient Greek "modes" or scales, of which
there were three: the Lydian, Dorian, and
Phrygian. The Lydian was "soft and effemi-
nate."

137. MARRIED TO IMMORTAL VERSE—He
would have immortal verse set to the Lydian
airs.

138. THE MEETING SOUL—That is, "the soul
which lends itself to the music."

139. BOUT—What in music is called a
"phrase."

141. WITH WANTON HEED AND GIDDY CUN-
NING—"Wanton heed" refers to playing that is
frolicsome and sportive, yet done with care and
accuracy. "Giddy cunning" refers to the rapidity of skill shown by the player. If you have
seen a violinist play a light, frolicsome piece
which called for almost lightning swift manipu-
lation of his instrument, you will know to what
Milton, who was himself an accomplished musician, refers.

119. WHERE THRONGS OF KNIGHTS . . . HIGH
TRIUMPHS HOLD—Tournaments, such as the
one described in Ivanhoe, had long since ceased
to be held by Milton's day. There survived,
however, a kind of mock tournament, known
as a "triumph" or "joust of peace," which was
the occasion for brilliant assemblage and courtly
ceremony. It is to such a "triumph" that Milton alludes.

120. WEEDS OF PEACE—Garments of peace,
there being no actual fighting to the death as
in the old tournaments.

123. OF WIT OR ARMS—In the days of Elizabeth, especially, both "wit," that is, speeches of
elaborate courtly compliment, and "arms,"
mimic contests with swords, lances, and pikes,
featured these triumphs.

124. HER GRACE—That is, the favor of the
Queen of Love and Beauty.

125. THERE—That is, at Court. Court
weddings were matters of elaborate ceremony
and display.

125. HYMEN—The god of marriage. Hymen
was represented as wearing a yellow robe and
bearing in his hand a torch.

128. MASK—A dramatic entertainment, generally written for some particular occasion.
Comus by Milton is a good example. The
mask, or masque, was a much favored form of
entertainment at court in the days of Milton.
One characteristic of its production was elaborate staging.

128. PAGEANTRY—Pageants were frequent
and extravagant in Elizabeth's day.

131. TO THE WELL-TROD STAGE—That is, to
the theater, well-trod, because in Milton's
youth London had a number of well-trained
companies of professional players.

The melting voice through mazes run-
   ning,
Untwisting all the chains that tie
The hidden soul of harmony;
That Orpheus' self may heave his head
From the golden slumber on a bed   146
Of heaped Elysian flowers, and hear
Such strains as would have won the ear

142. THE MELTING VOICE THROUGH MAZES
RUNNING—That is, while the voice blending
with the music accompanies it through its rapid
and intricate changes.
143–44. UNTWISTING ALL THE CHAINS THAT
TIE THE HIDDEN SOUL OF HARMONY—That is,
freeing the soul from the worries and cares of
life and restoring harmony to it.
145. ORPHEUS—Son of Apollo and Calliope,
the muse of epic poetry.
147. ELYSIAN—(ē·lĭzh'ăn)—The allusion is
to the Elysian fields, the abode of the blessed
or good, in Greek mythology.

Of Pluto to have quite set free
His half-regained Eurydice.   150

[*The poet's resolve to live with
Mirth.*]

These delights if thou canst give,
Mirth, with thee I mean to live.

149. PLUTO—God of Hades or the underworld.
150. EURYDICE (ū·rĭd'ĭ·sē)—A nymph, the
wife of Orpheus. Orpheus was inconsolable at
the death of Eurydice. Taking a lyre, given
him by Apollo, he made his way to Hades. His
music "drew iron tears down Pluto's cheek"
and so moved that god that he granted Orpheus's petition to let Eurydice return to the
upper world. One condition was attached to
this permission. Orpheus, who was to precede
Eurydice, was forbidden to look back; but as he
was about to leave Hades he turned to see if
Eurydice followed, whereupon she was carried
back and lost to him.

◇◇◇◇◇

Il Penseroso

JOHN MILTON

[*Folly and fickle Joys are banished.*]

Hence, vain deluding Joys,
   The brood of Folly without father
      bred!
How little you bested,
   Or fill the fixèd mind with all your
      toys!
Dwell in some idle brain,   5
   And fancies fond with gaudy shapes
      possess,
As thick and numberless
   As the gay motes that people the sun-
      beams,

3. BESTED—Help, profit.
4. TOYS—Trifles.
6. FOND—Foolish.

Or likest hovering dreams,
   The fickle pensioners of Morpheus'
      train.   10

[*Invitation to Melancholy.*]

But, hail! thou Goddess sage and holy!
Hail, divinest Melancholy!
Whose saintly visage is too bright
To hit the sense of human sight,
And therefore to our weaker view   15

9. LIKEST—Most like.
10. THE FICKLE . . . TRAIN—The unstable
dependents of the god of sleep.
12. MELANCHOLY—Pensive meditation, not
depression of spirits.
14. TO HIT . . . SIGHT—To be seen by the
naked eye.

O'erlaid with black, staid Wisdom's
 hue;
Black, but such as in esteem
Prince Memnon's sister might beseem,
Or that starred Ethiop queen that strove
To set her beauty's praise above   20
The Sea-Nymphs, and their powers of-
 fended.
Yet thou art higher far descended:
Thee bright-haired Vesta long of yore
To solitary Saturn bore;
His daughter she; in Saturn's reign   25
Such mixture was not held a stain.
Oft in glimmering bowers and glades
He met her, and in secret shades
Of woody Ida's inmost grove,   29
Whilst yet there was no fear of Jove.
Come, pensive Nun, devout and pure,
Sober, steadfast, and demure,
All in a robe of darkest grain,
Flowing with majestic train,
And sable stole of cypress lawn   35
Over thy decent shoulders drawn.
Come; but keep thy wonted state,
With even step, and musing gait,
And looks commercing with the skies,
Thy rapt soul sitting in thine eyes;   40
There, held in holy passion still,

Forget thyself to marble, till
With a sad leaden downward cast
Thou fix them on the earth as fast.
And join with thee calm Peace and
 Quiet,   45
Spare Fast, that oft with gods doth diet,
And hears the Muses in a ring
Aye round about Jove's altar sing;
And add to these retirèd Leisure,   49
That in trim gardens takes his pleasure;
But, first and chiefest, with thee bring
Him that yon soars on golden wing,
Guiding the fiery-wheelèd throne,
The Cherub Contemplation;
And the mute Silence hist along,   55
'Less Philomel will deign a song,
In her sweetest, saddest plight,
Smoothing the rugged brow of Night,
While Cynthia checks her dragon yoke
Gently o'er the accustomed oak.   60

[*The pleasures of evening: the thrill
of the nightingale and the moonlight
walk.*]

Sweet bird, that shunn'st the noise of
 folly,
Most musical, most melancholy!
Thee, chauntress, oft the woods among
I woo, to hear thy even-song;
And, missing thee, I walk unseen   65
On the dry smooth-shaven green,
To behold the wandering moon,
Riding near her highest noon,
Like one that had been led astray

 18. MEMNON'S SISTER—Memnon was a
dark Ethiopian prince, noted for his beauty.
The presumption is that his sister was dark and
beautiful.
 18. BESEEM—Suit.
 19. QUEEN—Cassiopeia.
 23–24. THEE . . . BORE — Here, Melancholy (pensive meditation) is the offspring of
Vesta (retirement) and Saturn (culture).
 23. VESTA—Vesta was the goddess of the
hearth; hence, light, fire, bright-haired.
 29. IDA'S INMOST GROVE—Mount Ida, in
Crete.
 33. GRAIN—Color, probably violet.
 35. CYPRESS LAWN—Crepe.
 36. DECENT—Beautiful.
 37. WONTED STATE—Habitual dignified attitude and conduct.
 38. MUSING—Thoughtful.
 39. COMMERCING WITH—Looking intently at.
 40. RAPT—Enraptured.

 42. TO MARBLE—To seem to become a
statue.
 43. SAD—Serious.
 44. FIX . . . FAST—Look intently on the
earth as you formerly did at the heavens.
 46. SPARE—Lean.
 50. TRIM GARDENS—Well-kept gardens
were the admiration of people in Milton's day
and during the Age of Classicism. Well-kept
meant, particularly, straight streams and geo-
metrical flower beds and shrubbery.
 55. SILENCE HIST—To call Silence by saying "Hist."
 61. SWEET BIRD—The nightingale.
 63. CHAUNTRESS—Singer.

Through the heaven's wide pathless way, 70
And oft, as if her head she bowed,
Stooping through a fleecy cloud.
Oft, on a plat of rising ground,
I hear the far-off curfew sound,
Over some wide-watered shore, 75
Swinging slow with sullen roar;
Or, if the air will not permit,
Some still removèd place will fit,
Where glowing embers through the room
Teach light to counterfeit a gloom, 80
Far from all resort of mirth,
Save the cricket on the hearth,
Or the bellman's drowsy charm
To bless the doors from nightly harm.

78. REMOVED—Remote.
80. WHERE . . . GLOOM—The smoldering remains of the fire cast shadows in the room.
83. BELLMAN'S—The town crier, going along the streets ringing a bell, announced the hour and the weather, and sometimes sang.
83. DROWSY CHARM—The song of the bellman lulled people to sleep.

[*Student's evening pleasures: astronomy, philosophy, drama, poetry.*]

Or let my lamp, at midnight hour, 85
Be seen in some high lonely tower,
Where I may oft outwatch the Bear,
With thrice great Hermes, or unsphere
The spirit of Plato, to unfold 89
What worlds or what vast regions hold
The immortal mind that hath forsook
Her mansion in this fleshly nook;
And of those demons that are found
In fire, air, flood, or underground,
Whose power hath a true consent 95

87. OUTWATCH THE BEAR—To stay up all night. The Bear, or "Big Dipper," never sets in England, but disappears with the dawn.
88. THRICE GREAT HERMES—Hermes Trismegistus, a fabled Egyptian, renowned as a king, priest, and philosopher or scientist.
89. UNSPHERE . . . PLATO—To discover the secrets of his philosophy, especially his teaching on the immortality of the soul, and on the demons who were supposed to inhabit the four elements, air, earth, fire, and water.
95. CONSENT—Sympathetic connection.

With planet or with element.
Sometime let gorgeous Tragedy
In sceptred pall come sweeping by,
Presenting Thebes, or Pelops' line,
Or the tale of Troy divine,   100
Or what (though rare) of later age
Ennobled hath the buskined stage.
But, O sad Virgin; that thy power
Might raise Musæus from his bower;
Or bid the soul of Orpheus sing   105
Such notes as, warbled to the string,
Drew iron tears down Pluto's cheek,
And made Hell grant what love did
     seek;
Or call up him that left half-told
The story of Cambuscan bold,   110
Of Camball, and of Algarsife,
And who had Canace to wife,
That owned the virtuous ring and glass,
And of the wondrous horse of brass
On which the Tartar king did ride;   115
And if aught else great bards beside
In sage and solemn tunes have sung,
Of turneys, and of trophies hung,
Of forests, and enchantments drear,
Where more is meant than meets the
     ear.   120

[*The pleasures of morning.*]

Thus, Night, oft see me in thy pale
     career,
Till civil-suited Morn appear,

Not tricked and frounced, as she was
     wont
With the Attic boy to hunt,
But kerchieft in a comely cloud,   125
While rocking winds are piping loud,
Or ushered with a shower still,
When the gust hath blown his fill,
Ending on the rustling leaves,   129
With minute drops from off the eaves.

[*A solitary walk in the woods.*]

And, when the sun begins to fling
His flaring beams, me, Goddess, bring
To archèd walks of twilight groves,
And shadows brown, that Sylvan loves,
Of pine, or monumental oak,   135
Where the rude axe with heavèd stroke
Was never heard the nymphs to daunt,
Or fright them from their hallowed
     haunt.
There, in close covert, by some brook,
Where no profaner eye may look,   140
Hide me from day's garish eye,
While the bee with honeyed thigh,
That at her flowery work doth sing,
And the waters murmuring,
With such consort as they keep,   145
Entice the dewy-feathered Sleep.
And let some strange mysterious dream
Wave at his wings, in airy stream
Of lively portraiture displayed,
Softly on my eyelids laid;   150

[*Pleasures of religious music, the cathedral.*]

And, as I wake, sweet music breathe
Above, about, or underneath,

98. SCEPTRED PALL—Kingly robes.
99–100. THEBES . . . DIVINE—These were mythical subjects of ancient classic tragedy.
101–102. WHAT . . . STAGE—Probably the great tragedies of Shakespeare.
104–105. MUSÆUS AND ORPHEUS—Mythical poets.
109. HIM—Chaucer.
110. STORY OF CAMBUSCAN—Milton is referring to the unfinished "Squire's Tale" in *The Canterbury Tales.* Camball and Algarsife were characters in the "Squire's Tale"; Canace is the heroine.
113. VIRTUOUS—Magical.
118. TURNEYS—Tournaments.
120. MORE . . . EAR—In allegories, like Spenser's "Faerie Queene."
122. CIVIL-SUITED—In civilian dress.

123. TRICKED AND FROUNCED—Fancifully dressed and adorned with curls.
124. ATTIC BOY—Cephalus. Aurora, the dawn, was in love with him.
125. KERCHIEFT . . . CLOUD—With a becoming cloud as a headdress.
127. STILL—Gentle.
134. BROWN—Dark.
134. SYLVAN—Roman god of the forests.
141. GARISH—Harsh and glaring.
145. CONSORT—Harmony.

Sent by some Spirit to mortals good,
Or the unseen Genius of the wood.
But let my due feet never fail   155
To walk the studious cloister's pale,
And love the high embowèd roof,
With antique pillars massy-proof,
And storied windows richly dight,
Casting a dim religious light.   160
There let the pealing organ blow,
To the full-voiced quire below,
In service high and anthems clear,
As may with sweetness, through mine
          ear,
Dissolve me into ecstasies,   165
And bring all Heaven before mine eyes.

[*Plans for old age.*]

And may at last my weary age
Find out the peaceful hermitage,
The hairy gown and mossy cell,
Where I may sit and rightly spell   170
Of every star that heaven doth shew,
And every herb that sips the dew,
Till old experience do attain
To something like prophetic strain.

[*Resolve to live with Melancholy.*]

These pleasures, Melancholy, give;   175
And I with thee will choose to live.

154. GENIUS—Guardian spirit.
155. DUE—Dutiful.
156. PALE—Enclosure.
157. EMBOWÈD—Arched.
158. MASSY-PROOF—Able to sustain great
weight.
159. DIGHT—Painted.
170. SPELL—Learn.

◇◇◇◇◇◇◇◇◇◇◇◇◇◇◇◇◇◇◇◇◇◇◇◇◇◇◇◇◇
COMPARATIVE STUDY

1. Enumerate the various delights in
the day and evening of the "light-hearted"
man. Compare and contrast these with
the choices of the "serious-minded" man.
Do the two have anything in common?
Discuss.

2. Show how the two poems are alike
in structure and development. Point out
the parallel passages.

3. Would you say that the pleasures of
both the "light-hearted" and "serious"
man in these poems are identical with
those which would occupy the lives of
men with similar temperaments today?
Discuss.

4. Both poems are *pastorals*. Select
passages which illustrate pastoral qualities.
How does pastoral poetry differ from
realistic farm poetry? Do you think
Milton knew much about a farm? Explain.

5. Milton has given us some beautiful
pictures of the English landscape. Select
and analyze these. In general are Englishmen more concerned with the care of
their landscapes than are Americans?
Discuss.

6. Some critics have expressed the
opinion that in "L'Allegro" Milton was
drawing a character sketch of the Cavaliers, and in "Il Penseroso" he was portraying the Puritan type. Do you find any
evidence of this? Discuss.

7. From what you know of Milton's
life, which poem is more typical of him?
From your study of the poems, which do
you think he preferred?

8. Which mood is more characteristic
of yourself? Is there a difference in the
prevalence of one mood over the other in
youth? in age?

POETIC IMAGERY

In lyric poetry, the poet is not merely
interested in giving us items of information. He wants to have us share with him
the emotion that arises from each particular situation he portrays. To achieve this,
he employs the poetic device of imagery—
a sense experience which the poet, through
the power of language, makes us seem to
see, hear, feel, taste, or smell, as the case
may be. In our understanding of the
poet's imagery we can awaken within our
own soul an experience similar to his, one
we have at some time felt but could not
so well express. Vividness of expression is
often heightened by the movement of the
verse.

Some of the most beautiful imagery in English poetry is contained in these two poems; for Milton, as he demonstrated in *Paradise Lost*, possessed the richest imagination in all of English literature. Study carefully the following passages.

L'ALLEGRO:

1. What is the predominant color in lines 1–10? Why? Select the words which create this color. What poetic effect does the use of sibilants convey in line 4? Study the image portrayed in line 6.

2. In lines 41–44, how does the lark startle the night? The lark is famous in English literature. Can you mention several other poems which celebrate it? Explain *dappled dawn*.

3. Analyze the imagery in lines 60–63. To whom is the sun compared? The clouds? Explain the imagery in lines 73–74.

IL PENSEROSO:

1. Note the difference in shading between the *deep* black of Melancholy in the opening lines of "L'Allegro" and the less dark shades in lines 15–36 of "Il Penseroso." Cite definite details and words in the passages to prove the point.

2. Explain the comparison between Melancholy and a nun in lines 31–32. Study the image in lines 33–34. Explain lines 74–76.

3. In line 80, how does "light counterfeit gloom"? Who chose a title for a book from line 82?

BOTH POEMS:

1. Point out passages from both the poems which appeal to the sense of sight; of taste; of hearing; of touch; of smell.

2. The first ten lines of each poem are written in the iambic measure. In the remainder of the poems the trochaic movement is principally employed. How does the variation of movement influence the thought expressed?

FAMOUS LINES

There are many famous lines in both poems which should be studied and even memorized. The following are a few from "L'Allegro": Lines 31–32—to what famous comic character in literature might line 32 apply? Could you write a good essay or editorial on the thought expressed in line 31? Explain. Reread lines 33–34; 95–99; 129–130. In "Il Penseroso" refer to line 120; 155; and lines 160–174.

THE RESTORATION (1660-1688)

England quickly tired of Cromwell and the Puritan regime. It was like having Ash Wednesday all year long. Lord Macaulay said that the Puritans objected to bearbaiting not because of the pain it caused the animals but because of the pleasure it gave the people. Just to see a play was made a criminal offense. The Londoners had had enough; they sighed for "the good old days," and dreamed romantically of "bonnie Prince Charlie" who had escaped to France.

The son of the dead monarch was living gaily in Paris, surrounded by the Cavaliers who had risked wealth and position, even their lives for him and his father. In 1660, two years after the death of Cromwell, the time seemed right for him to return to England. The people were wild with joy and crowned him Charles II. Witty, handsome, easy-going, he surrounded himself with a brilliant court. He was prepared to make whatever concessions were necessary for him to keep the throne.

His Catholic wife and his own secret Catholicism caused him no end of trouble and embarrassment, for England by this time had become solidly Protestant.

During the early years of his reign, two calamities struck London—the Plague of 1665, which raged up and down the narrow streets; and the Fire of 1666, which wiped out the heart of the city. Englishmen had to set about rebuilding London, and they were fortunate enough to have Sir Christopher Wren to do the architectural designing. The result may be seen in such magnificent structures as St. Paul's Cathedral and other religious and public buildings in London.

RESTORATION LITERATURE

To mark off and hold to sharp boundaries within short periods of literature is not possible nor advisable. John Dryden, for example, who was to become literary dictator of the Restoration period, began his writing while the Puritans were in control in England. John Milton and John Bunyan produced their greatest works after the Restoration. These discussions of seventeenth and eighteenth century literature, therefore, are based on feelings and attitudes rather than on historical dates. Because Milton and Bunyan reflected the Puritan mind, we call them writers of the Puritan Age. Because Dryden's mature sympathies were with the Restoration, and because his works show the trends of the later period, we think of him as a Restoration writer.

Indeed the works of Dryden reflect all the various phases of the Restoration period. His change from Puritanism to Anglicanism to Catholicism, and his satires describing and defending these changes reflect the conflicting currents of political and religious thought.

The French influence which had come to England with King Charles and his court set a new fashion in literature. It was a frivolous, sophisticated society, and it admired point and wit in letters. The closed couplet was perfectly suited to expressing flashes of irony and keen-edged comment. Dryden took up the form and used it so cleverly that for almost a hundred years it was the ruling verse form in England. His satires in verse are prophetic of the next period in which satire reigns supreme, and he also set the fashion for writing long allegories in verse. These allegories defended his views in politics and religion, ridiculed his opponents at court or his rivals in letters, and delighted or infuriated the social lights of London. Lesser poets adopted the style, and the stage and ballroom moved to the measure of iambic pentameter rhymes.

Dryden was also the most gifted of the Restoration playwrights; he was the first writer to do whole plays in closed couplets. In his position of playwright to the king, he wrote three plays a year for twenty years. His best play was a good comedy written in excellent blank verse—*All for Love*. But even Dryden, with his classical training, bowed to the taste of his audience and wrote scores of the trivial, cheaply immoral plays which were popular at the time.

Modern critics rate John Dryden's prose more important than his verse. One of them even goes so far as to say that Dryden is the "supreme stylist in English prose," possessing "strength, speed, music, continuity, and range." Like most of

JOHN DRYDEN

SAMUEL PEPYS

the interesting prose of the period, his too was written incidentally. In Dryden's case, we find it in the prefaces he wrote for collections of the works of earlier poets like Chaucer and Spenser. These prefaces are really critical essays in which Dryden gives his estimates of the writers and their works, besides expressing his own theories about art and literature. These essays display his strong expressive prose style at its best.

Of greater general interest to the modern reader are the diaries of two men who made no pretense of being writers. One, Samuel Pepys, was an energetic businessman. For his own satisfaction he kept a diary of the years from 1660–1669; but his pages are so filled with details of events large and small that the reader who samples them feels much at home in seventeenth-century England. It is all there—what people ate and drank, how they dressed, how the little old Queen and the Princesses looked, how business was transacted—everything very frankly and engagingly told.

John Evelyn wrote his diary more carefully and covered a much longer period of time—from 1640–1706. His record lacks the human-interest elements of Pepys's diary, yet makes extremely good reading. Evelyn tried to set down fairly and accurately the important events of the time. Like Pepys, he was a Royalist who rejoiced in the Restoration of the Stuarts. But he did not close his eyes to the shortcomings of his monarchs. In all matters he tries to weigh carefully both faults and virtues. Both Pepys's and Evelyn's diaries carry accounts of the coronation of Charles II, of the Plague, and of the Great Fire. Together, the works furnish a panoramic picture of England during the Restoration period.

Alexander's Feast, or The Power of Music

JOHN DRYDEN

AN ODE IN HONOR OF ST. CECILIA'S DAY

In 1697 the Saint Cecilia Society of London asked Poet Laureate Dryden to write its annual commemorative ode in honor of its patron saint. The result was "Alexander's Feast," which the poet composed in a single night.

Dryden took as his theme the power of music. The scene is the banquet that Alexander the Great gave to celebrate his conquest of Persia. Sitting beside him is the lovely Thais, the celebrated beauty of the day. The great musician Timotheus has been asked to play. Masterfully he excites within his hearers the elemental emotions as he sings of ambition, wine, pity, love, and revenge. Finally on the note of revenge, Alexander leaps up and in company with Thais and the rioting banqueters seizes torches from the walls to set fire to the city, Persepolis.

The final stanza which refers to the legend of the invention of the organ symbolizes the superiority of St. Cecilia and her music over that of the bard Timotheus who had swept Alexander from emotion to emotion as he willed.

Read the poem aloud with particular attention to the melody of the verse. This poem should be compared to "A Song for St. Cecilia's Day," written by Dryden ten years earlier.

I

'Twas at the royal feast for Persia won
   By Philip's warlike son:
  Aloft in awful state
  The godlike hero sate
   On his imperial throne: 5
His valiant peers were placed around,
Their brows with roses and with myrtles
   bound,
  (So should desert in arms be
   crowned);
The lovely Thais by his side,   9
Sate like a blooming Eastern bride
In flower of youth and beauty's pride.

2. PHILIP'S SON—Alexander the Great, son of Philip of Macedon.

292

Happy, happy, happy pair!
 None but the brave,
 None but the brave,
None but the brave deserves the
 fair.   15

CHORUS

Happy, happy, happy pair!
 None but the brave,
 None but the brave,
None but the brave deserves the
 fair.

II

Timotheus, placed on high,   20
 Amid the tuneful choir,
With flying fingers touched the
 lyre:
The trembling notes ascend the sky,
 And heavenly joys inspire.
The song began from Jove,   25
Who left his blissful seats above,
(Such is the power of mighty love).
A dragon's fiery form belied the god:
 Sublime on radiant spires he rode,
When he to fair Olympia pressed;
 And while he sought her snowy
  breast: 31
Then round her slender waist he curled,
And stamped an image of himself, a sov-
 ereign of the world.
The listening crowd admire the lofty
 sound,
"A present deity!" they shout around;
"A present deity!" the vaulted roofs
 rebound.   36
 With ravished ears
 The monarch hears,
  Assumes the god,
  Affects to nod,   40
And seems to shake the spheres.

III

The praise of Bacchus then the sweet
 musician sung,
Of Bacchus—ever fair and ever young:
 The jolly god in triumph comes;
 Sound the trumpets, beat the
  drums!   45
  Flushed with a purple grace
  He shows his honest face;
Now give the hautboys breath. He
 comes! He comes!
Bacchus, ever fair and young,
 Drinking joys did first ordain,   50
Bacchus' blessings are a treasure,
Drinking is the soldier's pleasure:
  Rich the treasure,
  Sweet the pleasure,
Sweet is pleasure after pain.   55

IV

Soothed with the sound the king grew
 vain;
 Fought all his battles o'er again;
And thrice he routed all his foes, and
 thrice he slew the slain.
 The master saw the madness rise,
 His glowing cheeks, his ardent eyes;
 And, while he heaven and earth de-
  fied,   61
Changed his hand, and checked his
 pride.
  He chose a mournful muse
  Soft pity to infuse:
He sung Darius, great and good,
 By too severe a fate,   66
Fallen, fallen, fallen, fallen,
Fallen from his high estate,
 And weltering in his blood;
Deserted at his utmost need   70
By those his former bounty fed:

20. TIMOTHEUS—Favorite musician of Alexander.
25. Alexander claimed to be a descendant of Jove, the king of the gods, so in his conquests he often pretended to be godlike.
30. OLYMPIA — Olympias, Alexander's mother.

42. BACCHUS—God of wine and revelry among the Greeks.
46. PURPLE GRACE—Wine.
48. HAUTBOYS—Wood-wind instruments; oboes.
65. DARIUS—King of Persia, conquered by Alexander.

On the bare earth exposed he lies,
With not a friend to close his eyes.
With downcast looks the joyless vic-
    tor sate,
      Revolving in his altered soul 75
        The various turns of chance
        below;
      And now and then a sigh he
        stole,
        And tears began to flow.   78

V

The mighty master smiled, to see
That love was in the next degree;
'Twas but a kindred sound to move,
For pity melts the mind to love.
    Softly sweet, in Lydian measures,
    Soon he soothed his soul to pleas-
    ures.   84
War, he sung, is toil and trouble,
    Honor but an empty bubble;

80. THE NEXT DEGREE—The feeling of love
was next to be aroused.
83. LYDIAN—Soft, sensual type of music
originating in Asia Minor. Lydia was famous
for luxury and music.

Never ending, still beginning,
Fighting still, and still destroying:
    If the world be worth thy win-
      ning,   89
    Think, oh, think it worth enjoying:
    Lovely Thais sits beside thee,
Take the good the gods provide thee.
The many rend the skies with loud ap-
    plause;
So Love was crowned, but Music won
    the cause.
    The prince, unable to conceal his
      pain,   95
      Gazed on the fair
      Who caused his care,
    And sighed and looked, sighed and
      looked,
    Sighed and looked, and sighed again:
At length, with love and wine at once
    oppressed,   100
The vanquished victor sunk upon her
    breast.

VI

Now strike the golden lyre again:
A louder yet, and yet a louder strain.

Break his bands of sleep asunder,
And rouse him like a rattling peal of
    thunder.   105
    Hark, hark, the horrid sound
      Has raised up his head:
      As awaked from the dead,
    And amazed, he stares around.
"Revenge! revenge!" Timotheus
    cries,   110
    "See the Furies arise!
  See the snakes that they rear,
  How they hiss in their hair,
And the sparkles that flash from their
  eyes!
Behold a ghastly band,   115
Each a torch in his hand!
Those are Grecian ghosts, that in battle
  were slain,
    And unburied remain,
    Inglorious on the plain:
  Give the vengeance due   120
  To the valiant crew.
Behold how they toss their torches on
  high,
How they point to the Persian abodes,
And glittering temples of their hostile
  gods!"
The princes applaud with a furious joy:
And the king seized a flambeau with
    zeal to destroy;   126
    Thais led the way,
    To light him to his prey,
And, like another Helen, fired another
    Troy!

VII

Thus long ago,   130
Ere heaving bellows learned to
    blow,
While organs yet were mute,

111. FURIES—The classic goddesses of vengeance. They are pictured as having coiled
serpents in their hair.
126. FLAMBEAU—Flaming torch.
129. HELEN—Troy was burned because
Helen, the beautiful wife of the Greek, Mene-
laus, had been stolen by the Trojan, Paris.

    Timotheus, to his breathing
      flute
    And sounding lyre,
Could swell the soul to rage, or kindle
  soft desire.   135
  At last divine Cecilia came,
  Inventress of the vocal frame,
The sweet enthusiast, from her sacred
  store,
  Enlarged the former narrow
    bounds,
  And added length to solemn
    sounds,   140
With nature's mother-wit, and arts un-
  known before.
  Let old Timotheus yield the prize,
  Or both divide the crown;
  He raised a mortal to the skies;
  She drew an angel down.   145

136. CECILIA—Saint Cecilia, patroness of
music and martyr, executed in A.D. 230. She is
represented in art as playing or singing with the
angels who have come down from heaven to
accompany her.
137. VOCAL FRAME—The organ, because of
its almost human tones.
140. ADDED LENGTH—Characteristic of the
organ are solemn, prolonged tones.

◇◇◇◇◇◇◇◇◇◇◇◇◇◇◇◇◇◇◇◇◇◇◇◇◇◇◇

FOR APPRECIATION

1. Study each stanza carefully. Then
indicate the particular emotion expressed
in that stanza. What poetic devices are
used to portray each emotion? Discuss.

2. Note the change of movement in
stanza IV. How is this accomplished?
Explain.

3. Discuss lines 85–90 and apply them
to the present world situation.

4. Study carefully the use of onomatopoeia in stanza VI.

5. Explain fully lines 128–129 and lines
144–145.

6. Select five significant figures of
speech and ten graphic and connotative
words.

7. This is one of the great odes of the
language. Why?

THE LONDON FIRE

SAMUEL PEPYS

Samuel Pepys, Secretary to the Admiralty and a "gentleman of worth and virtue of the days of the carefree Charles II," has left a record of his intimate thoughts during the years 1660–1669. Written in his own shorthand, his diary was meant only for his own eyes. It was decoded, however, in 1825, and publicly printed. In it he gives a frank account of his views on public affairs as well as his own virtues and failings. In the following excerpt we can share vividly the panic and fear of the people of London during the Great Fire of 1666.

September 2, 1666. (Lord's Day) Some of our maids sitting up late last night to get things ready against our feast today, Jane called us up[1] about three in the morning, to tell us of a great fire they saw in the city. So I rose and slipped on my nightgown, and went to her window, and thought it to be on the back side of Mark Lane at the farthest; but, being unused to such fires as followed, I thought it far enough off; and so went to bed again and to sleep. About seven rose again to dress myself, and there looked out at the window, and saw the fire not so much as it was and farther off. So to my closet to set things to rights after yesterday's cleaning. By and by Jane comes and tells me that she hears that above 300 houses have been burned down tonight by the fire we saw, and that it is now burning down all Fish Street, by London Bridge. So I made myself ready presently, and walked to the Tower, and there got up upon one of the high places, Sir J. Robinson's little son going up with me; and

there did I see the houses at the end of the bridge all on fire, and an infinite great fire on this and the other side the end of the bridge; which, among other people, did trouble me for poor little Michell and our Sarah on the bridge. So down, with my heart full of trouble, to the Lieutenant of the Tower, who tells me that it begun this morning in the King's baker's house in Pudding Lane, and that it hath burned St. Magnus Church and most part of Fish Street already. So I down to the waterside, and there got a boat and through bridge, and there saw a lamentable fire. Everybody endeavoring to remove their goods, and flinging into the river or bringing them into lighters[2] that lay off; poor people staying in their houses as long as till the very fire touched them, and then running into boats, or clambering from one pair of stairs by the waterside to another. And among other things, the poor pigeons, I perceive, were loath to leave their houses, but hovered about

[1] CALLED US UP—Awakened us.

[2] LIGHTERS—Large boats used to transport freight in a harbor or on a river.

the windows and balconies till they were some of them burned, their wings, and fell down. Having stayed, and in an hour's time seen the fire rage every way, and nobody, to my sight, endeavoring to quench it, but to remove their goods, and leave all to the fire, and having seen it get as far as the Steel Yard,[3] and the wind mighty high and driving it into the City;[4] and everything, after so long a drought, proving combustible, even the very stones of churches; I go to White Hall,[5] and there up to the King's [6] closet and the Chapel, where people come about me, and I did give

[3] THE STEEL YARD—Establishment for Hanse merchants on the north bank of the Thames above London Bridge.

[4] THE CITY—The commercial center of greater London. Most of the area known as the City was destroyed in the fire.

[5] WHITE HALL—The palace of the English kings.

[6] KING—King Charles II.

them an account dismayed them all, and word was carried in to the King. So I was called for, and did tell the King and Duke of York [7] what I saw, and that unless his Majesty did command houses to be pulled down nothing could stop the fire. They seemed much troubled, and the King commanded me to go to my Lord Mayor from him, and command him to spare no houses, but to pull down before the fire every way. The Duke of York bade me tell him that if he would have any more soldiers he shall; and so did my Lord Arlington afterward, as a great secret. Here meeting with Captain Cocke, I in his coach, which he lent me, and Creed with me to Paul's, and there walked along Watling Street, as well as I could, every creature coming away laden with goods to save,

[7] DUKE OF YORK—James, Duke of York and Pepys's political patron.

and here and there sick people carried away in beds. At last met my Lord Mayor in Canning Street, like a man spent, with a handkerchief about his neck. To the King's message he cried, like a fainting woman, "Lord! what can I do? I am spent: people will not obey me. I have been pulling down houses; but the fire overtakes us faster than we can do it." That he needed no more soldiers and that, for himself, he must go and refresh himself, having been up all night. So he left me, and I him, and walked home, seeing people all almost distracted, and no manner of means used to quench the fire. The houses, too, so very thick thereabouts, and full of matter for burning, as pitch and tar, in Thames Street; and warehouses of oil, and wines, and brandy, and other things. And to see the churches all filling with goods by people who themselves should have been quietly there at this time.

By this time it was about twelve o'clock; and so home, and there find my guests, which were Mr. Wood and his wife Barbary Sheldon, and also Mr. Moone: she mighty fine, and her husband, for aught I see, a likely man. But Mr. Moone's design and mine, which was to look over my closet and please him with a sight thereof, which he hath long desired, was wholly disappointed; for we were in great trouble and disturbance at this fire, not knowing what to think of it. However, we had an extraordinary good dinner, and as merry as at this time we could be. While at dinner Mrs. Batelier came over to inquire after Mr. Woolfe and Stanes (who, it seems, are related to them), whose houses in Fish Street are all burned, and they in a sad condition. She would not stay in the fright. Soon as dined, I and Moone away, and walked through the city, the streets full of nothing but people and horses and carts laden with goods, ready to run over one another. They now removing goods from one burned house to another. They now removing out of Canning Street, (which received goods in the morning) into Lombard Street, and farther; and among others I now saw my little goldsmith, Stokes, receiving some friend's goods, whose house itself was burned the day after. We parted at Pauls; he home, and I to Paul's Wharf, where I had appointed a boat to attend me and I took in Mr. Carcasse and his brother, whom I met in the street, and carried them below and above bridge to and again to see the fire, which was now got farther, both below and above, and no likehood of stopping it. Met the King and Duke of York in their barge, and with them to Queenhithe, and there called Sir Richard Browne to them. Their order was only to pull down houses apace, and so below bridge at the waterside; but little was or could be done, the fire coming upon them so fast. Good hopes there was of stopping it at the Three Cranes, above, and at Buttolph's Wharf below bridge, if care be used; but the wind carries it into the City, so as we know not by the waterside what it do there. River full of lighters and boats taking in goods, and good goods swimming in the water, and only I observed that hardly one lighter or boat in three that had the goods of a house in, but there was a pair of virginals [8] in it. Having seen as much as I could now, I away to White Hall by appointment, and there walked to St. James's Park, and there met my wife and Creed and Wood and his wife, and walked to my boat; and there upon

[8] PAIR OF VIRGINALS—The virginal was a musical instrument with a keyboard like that on the modern piano.

the water again, and to the fire up and down, it still increasing, and the wind great. So near the fire as we could for smoke; and all over the Thames, with one's face in the wind, you were almost burned with a shower of firedrops. This is very true; so as houses were burned by the drops and flakes of fire, three or four, nay five or six houses, one from another. When we could endure no more upon the water, we to a little alehouse on the Bankside, over against the Three Cranes, and there stayed till it was dark almost, and saw the fire grow; and, as it grew darker, appeared more and more, and in corners and upon steeples, and between churches and houses as far as we could see up the hill of the City, in a most horrid flame, not like the fine flame of an ordinary fire. Barbary and her husband away before us. We stayed till, it being darkish, we saw the fire as

only one entire arch of fire from this to the other side of the bridge and in a bow up the hill for an arch above a mile long: it made me weep to see it. The churches, houses, and all on fire and flaming at once; and a horrid noise the flames made, and the crackling of houses at their ruin.

So home with a sad heart, and there find everybody discoursing and lamenting the fire; and poor Tom Hater come with some of his goods saved out of his house, which is burned upon Fish Street Hill. I invited him to lie at my house, and did receive his goods, but was deceived by his lying there, the news coming every moment of the growth of the fire; so as we were forced to begin to pack up our own goods, and prepare for their removal; and did by moonshine (it being brave, dry, and moonshine and warm weather) carry much of my goods into the garden, and Mr. Hater and I did remove my money and iron chests into my cellar, as thinking that the safest place. And got my bags of gold into my office, ready to carry away, and my chief papers of accounts also there, and my tallies into a box by themselves.

3rd. About four o'clock in the morning my Lady Batten sent me a cart to carry away all my money, and plate, and best things, to Sir W. Rider's at Bednall Green. Which I did, riding myself in my nightgown in the cart; and, Lord! to see how the streets and the highways are crowded with people running and riding, and getting of carts at any rate to fetch away things. I find Sir W. Rider tired with being called up all night, and receiving things from several friends. His house full of goods, and much of Sir W. Batten's and Sir W. Pen's. I am eased at my heart to have my treasure so well secured. Then home, with much ado to find a way, nor any sleep all this night to me nor my poor wife.

FOR DISCUSSION

1. A diary is said to reveal in intimate detail the character of the author. Does this particular selection help you to understand the kind of person Pepys was? Do you consider him sympathetic or indifferent toward others? Is he light-hearted or worrisome? Is he wealthy? Find details to prove your points.

2. What details that Pepys uses would you consider exceptionally "good copy" for a newspaper account of the fire? Many successful columnists of the present day have adopted Pepys's style. Can you name any?

WORDS

Give the origin of *clambering*. Name at least three synonyms for *combustible*. What is the correct pronunciation of *lamentable?* What kind of vocabulary does Pepys employ? Discuss.

PROJECTS

1. Briefly write some personal experience or retell a news article from the daily newspaper in Pepys's manner. Remember that it is largely the personal point of view which creates and sustains interest.

2. Let a member of the class draw in broad outline on the blackboard a map of the London of 1666. Then trace the progress of the fire through the city.

RELATED READING

Read at least two or three excerpts from *Everybody's Pepys*, especially from the records of April, 1663. Compare Pepys's description of the fire with Defoe's *Journal of the Plague Year.*

THE AGE OF POPE (1689-1740)

On the death of Charles II in 1685, his brother, James II, took the throne. But James was not happy. Parliament continued to use the King's revenue as a sort of leash to keep His Majesty in check. Should he fail to play along with its leaders, they would simply curtail his allowance as with a naughty schoolboy. To make a delicate situation worse, James was a staunch Catholic and determined to re-establish the Faith in England even if it cost him the crown. And it did. After three years of rule, he had to seek refuge in France.

At the invitation of Parliament, Mary and William of Orange came from the Netherlands to become joint sovereigns of England. This was a triumph for Parliament. It made William sign a Declaration of Rights before he could be proclaimed king. The declaration was incorporated in a Bill of Rights passed by Parliament in 1689. Provisions of the Bill forbade the levying of taxes without the consent of Parliament. This meant that the ministers who constituted the Cabinet would henceforth be responsible, not to the king but to Parliament. Henceforth no minister and no cabinet could hold office if Parliament refused its support. It was the document which transformed England into a democratic monarchy.

The results of this change of government had a deep and lasting effect on the literature of the age. Two political parties sprang up, the Whigs and the Tories. In general they represent practically the same differences that have been pointed out between the Cavaliers and the Puritans. The Whigs were usually the dissenters from the Anglican Church, the rising merchant citizenry, and the city middle class led by some few aristocrats. The Tories were generally the landowners, the Anglican clergy, and the personal adherents of both. In the next two centuries the political history of England is the story of the ups and downs of these two parties; and the history of English literature is strongly colored by the conflict between them.

MERCHANTS VS.

LANDOWNERS

As a result of several victorious wars during this period, England acquired possessions in India, on the Mediterranean, and in America, which laid the foundation for the British Empire. These new possessions increased trade and enriched the merchant class tremendously, but the heavy war taxes impoverished the lower classes. The smuggling of tea, tobacco, and silk became a profitable enterprise. Buccaneering flourished about the West Indies, and Captain Kidd badgered the Spanish Main. Inside England, agriculture made no advance. Science and education seemed at a standstill. There was cold indifference toward religion. And though everyone talked about prosperity, there was great inequality in the distribution of wealth, and there were sharp distinctions in social classes. The age had a heavy, unventilated atmosphere.

Only the wealthy managed to relish life. The city had become the important center of living. Society flourished. Refinement and the ability to talk in innuendoes counted rather than virtue. Coffee was the favorite drink, and the Coffee

Houses became gathering places for writers, politicians, and dandies. Here men could learn the news, transact business, talk politics or art, or gossip. Different groups had their favorite clubs. The literary men gathered at Will's Coffee House where, a generation earlier, John Dryden had ruled.

Men and women donned elaborate dress to match their manners. Women wore extravagant, towering headdresses and billowing brocaded gowns. Men, too, wore powdered wigs, artificial moles, cocked hats, and satin waistcoats. Hogarth satirized the absurd styles and manners of the day in his paintings; while Handel caught the classic precision and formality in his music. As usual, the political and social background of the age determined the characteristics of its literature.

CLASSICISM AND NEO-CLASSICISM

During the years between the Restoration of Charles II and the death of Alexander Pope in 1744, there developed in England a group of writers who came to be known as the Neo-classic School. To understand the spirit of this movement and the literature of the period, one must first understand the meanings of classicism in its true sense.

For centuries the best Greek and Latin writings were known as *classics*, and the Greek and Latin languages as the *classical languages*. Today the term *classic*, or *classics*, may be applied in three different ways: (*a*) it may designate any piece of art, ancient or modern which is considered a masterpiece—like Dickens' *David Copperfield* or Vergil's *Aeneid*; (*b*) it may designate any Greek or Roman work because it is written in a classic language; (*c*) it may describe all writings that show the qualities that were considered fundamental in the literature of Greece and

JOSEPH ADDISON

RICHARD STEELE

Rome. It is in the last sense that we use the term *classicism* in distinction from *neo-classicism* and *romanticism*.

What are these qualities that mark real classicism? In general, they are balance and proportion, restraint, dignity, simplicity, and universality. Classic art tends to be objective and impersonal rather than subjective and personal. It expresses a restrained emotion. It is imaginative, but it does not go into flights of pure fancy. Rather, it uses the imagination to reveal the depth and significance of real experience.

In literature, classicism requires a suitable balance and proportion between expression or wording and the emotion to be expressed. Classic literature is far from lifeless; it does express emotion, but always emotion under control.

It was Aristotle in his famous *Poetics* who most clearly analyzed and formulated the principles of classic art. The Renaissance gave rise in Italy, France, and England to a restudy of the *Poetics* and to a restatement of classic principles. In Elizabethan times the learned Ben Jonson had come under this influence; and we find him and other playwrights writing new dramas according to the old rules.

A century later Dryden and Pope established the neo-classic style in England. This pseudo-classic movement grew out of a misinterpretation of Aristotle's teachings, particularly in respect to imitation. To the school of Dryden and Pope, classicism meant imitating older models of literature and

COPYING AND

IMITATION

following blindly well-established rules of writing. To Aristotle *imitation* did not mean copying. In the sense of the *Poetics*, to imitate meant to portray *universal* qualities by presenting *particular* objects, situations, and people. From the artistic portrayal of the joys, sorrows, and aspirations of one man, the reader can recognize in true

JONATHAN SWIFT   ALEXANDER POPE

303

classicism the joys, sorrows, and aspirations of all men. Through the selective portrayal of the emotion of pity in one particular person in one situation, there may arise the suggestion of the meaning of pity to all men in all times. This is what Aristotle means when he says that through the imitation (that is, *portrayal*) of nature, man expresses the quality of universal truth. To raise a work above the plane of mere photographic representation, to endow it with the power of expressing universal truth, is to express life in the authentically classic spirit.

Yet this is precisely what the pseudo- or neo-classicists failed to do. As we have said, they contented themselves with following rules and copying models. They appreciated the balance and proportion in the *form* of the classics, and these they copied to perfection. But they lacked emotional power and disregarded the importance of creative imagination. The chief doctrines of the neo-classic school may be expressed as follows:

1. Form was more significant than content; manner of expression more important than the truth expressed. It was better to follow tried rules than to attempt the expression of original genius.
2. Cleverness and wit should take the place of emotion, passion, or deep feeling. The poet should remain calm and critical. Display of personal feeling would offend good taste.
3. Poetry should not use commonplace words, but use a special dignified or ornamental vocabulary. Artificial elegance was to be admired.
4. The heroic couplet, with its precision and balance, should be the ideal form of poetic expression.

Although the writers of the Age of Pope are usually called the classic writers of English literature, it was really these neo-classic principles that they followed; and the term "The Classic Age" for the eighteenth century is an established misnomer.

In spite of all their faults, however, we can say that the one contribution of the neo-classic writers was the emphasis they placed on order and care in composition.

NEO-CLASSIC POETRY

In an era of "reason" and "common sense," lyric poetry was impossible. The best medium in which to express the cold literary ideal of the neo-classicists was the rhymed couplet.

Alexander Pope became the virtual dictator in this school of poetry. He was a Catholic poet born in 1688, the year of the "glorious" revolution when Mary and William moved in. He had to educate himself because the laws of the land barred Catholics from the universities. He imbibed all the confused ideas of his age to such an extent that one would never guess his Catholicity by reading his many satirical poems. He loved satire, and it is said of him that he purposely estranged his friends in order to have more people to ridicule. He has the distinction of being the first English writer to support himself by his pen alone.

Pope used the heroic couplet like a two-edged sword in his poetic satires. Perhaps the best known of his works is "The Rape of the Lock," a mock epic in which he holds up to ridicule the petty quarrels of court society. His "Dunciad"—the saga of the dunces—is a scathing criticism of the other poets of the time. Pope wrote even letters and essays in verse. His "Essay on Man" and "Essay on Criticism" present in quotable couplets his views on man's place in the world and his views of literary criticism. Pope's most ambitious undertaking was to translate the *Iliad* and the *Odyssey* into rhymed iambic pentameter lines. The venture did nothing to increase Homer's prestige as a poet, but it made a fortune for Mr. Pope.

The emphasis of the neo-classicists was on the importance of man. Pope put it this way, "The proper study of mankind is man." But without the Christian idea of the worth and dignity of each individual, some writers of the period presented a sorry picture of the human race. In his "Essay on Man," Pope emphasizes the puniness and insignificance of the human individual; and Jonathan Swift, the great prose satirist, in his last works reveals a terrible hatred for "that creature man."

◇◇◇◇◇

(FROM) *An Essay on Criticism*

ALEXANDER POPE

Pope's ESSAY ON CRITICISM *might well be called the commonplace book of eighteenth-century criticism. In his witty and pointed epigrams, Pope has expressed the current views of his day: follow "nature" (by which he means human conduct in the best cultivated society) ; model your writings on the classical authors; adhere closely to the standard rules; cultivate good taste and restraint.*

The subject matter of the poem seems to be better suited to prose than poetry, but Pope considered the function of verse to instruct the intellect rather than to arouse the emotions.

After reading the selection below we will understand how Pope's terse, epigrammatic couplets have made him the most often quoted source in the language, with the exception of the Bible and Shakespeare.

FROM PART I

'Tis hard to say, if greater want of skill
Appear in writing or in judging ill;
But, of the two, less dangerous is th' offence
To tire our patience, than mislead our sense.

Some few in that, but numbers err in this, 5
Ten censure wrong for one who writes amiss;
A fool might once himself alone expose,
Now one in verse makes many more in prose.
    'Tis with our judgments as our watches, none
Go just alike, yet each believes his own. 10
In poets as true genius is but rare,
True taste as seldom is the critic's share;
Both must alike from Heaven derive their light,
These born to judge, as well as those to write.
Let such teach others who themselves excel, 15
And censure freely who have written well.
Authors are partial to their wit, 'tis true,
But are not critics to their judgment too?

FROM PART II

    True wit is nature to advantage dressed,
What oft was thought, but ne'er so well expressed:
Something, whose truth convinced at sight we find.
That gives us back the image of our mind.
As shades more sweetly recommend the light, 5
So modest plainness sets off sprightly wit.
For works may have more wit than does 'em good,
As bodies perish through excess of blood.
    Others for language all their care express,
And value books, as women men, for dress; 10
Their praise is still—the style is excellent;
The sense they humbly take upon content.
Words are like leaves; where they most abound,
Much fruit of sense beneath is rarely found.
False eloquence, like the prismatic glass, 15
Its gaudy colors spreads on every place.
The face of nature we no more survey;
All glares alike, without distinction gay;
But true expression, like the unchanging sun,
Clears and improves whate'er it shines upon; 20
It gilds all objects, but it alters none.

5. SOME FEW IN THAT—Some few (err) in that.
8. NOW ONE IN VERSE, etc.—For one poor poet are many foolish critics.
11. IN POETS, etc.—True genius is rare among poets.
17. PARTIAL—Biased, in favor of.
17–18. AUTHORS ARE PARTIAL, etc.—The meaning is that authors have as much right to think their work is good as the critics have to think their criticisms are right.
1. WIT—Used in the meaning of writing.
9. LANGUAGE—Style.
12. CONTENT—Trust.

Expression is the dress of thought, and still
Appears more decent, as more suitable;
A vile conceit in pompous words expressed
Is like a clown in regal purple dressed;   25
For different styles with different subjects sort,
As several garbs with country, town and court.
Some by old words to fame have made pretense,
Ancients in phrase, mere moderns in their sense;
Such labored nothings, in so strange a style,   30
Amaze the unlearned, and make the learnèd smile.
Unlucky, as Fungoso in the play,
These sparks with awkward vanity display
What the fine gentleman wore yesterday;
And but so mimic ancients wits at best,   35
As apes our grandsires, in their doublets dressed.
In words, as fashions, the same rule will hold,
Alike fantastic, if too new, or old:
Be not the first by whom the new is tried,
Nor yet the last to lay the old aside.   40

. . . .

True ease in writing comes from art, not chance,
As those move easiest who have learned to dance.
'Tis not enough no harshness gives offense,
The sound must seem an echo to the sense.

23. DECENT—Attractive.
24. VILE CONCEIT—An unnatural expression.
32. FUNGOSO—A character in Ben Jonson's play, *Every Man Out of His Humour.*

FOR DISCUSSION

1. According to Pope what qualities should a critic possess? Do you agree with him? Discuss.

2. Interpret lines 1–6 of Part II in the light of what you have learned of the spirit of neo-classicism.

3. Do lines 13–25 express a sound theory of writing and speaking? Explain your answer.

4. Are lines 28–36 a criticism of the very things Pope stands for? Discuss.

5. Memorize at least three couplets which you consider worth remembering.

RELATED READING

If you like Pope's polished and sophisticated verse, you will enjoy reading "The Rape of the Lock."

NEO-CLASSIC PROSE

At its best classic prose is clear, forceful, and direct—lighted sometimes by wit but only occasionally mellow with humor. At its worst it is heavy, cumbersome, overloaded with long hard words and round-about expressions. It served as a vehicle for almost every possible kind of writing—satire, fantasy, argument, biography, letters, memoirs, essays, oratory, history, and fiction. Adequate mention cannot be made of all the kinds of writing turned out by the tireless scholars of the eighteenth century. And a disproportionately small number of works proved great enough to live. These we shall discuss briefly.

THE ESSAY

When the Frenchman, Montaigne, published the first two books of his *Essais* in 1580, a new kind of prose literature was born. *Essais* in French (*essays* in English) at that time meant *trials* or *attempts*. Montaigne had chosen the term as the title for his short prose pieces because they were attempts to present in no formal style his views on a variety of subjects.

In 1603 Florio translated Montaigne's essays into English, and immediately they became popular reading. Francis Bacon admired them greatly, and hastened to try out the new form. His essay, "Of Studies," which you have read, is an example of his success. To Bacon, an essay meant a first trial in the exposition of a subject; and so his works in the form seem like compact sentence outlines of thoughts that could be more fully developed. Later writers discovered many possibilities in the form.

Loosely, the essay may be defined as a piece of prose literature written to give a personal exposition of a subject. That is, in any essay the author is trying to explain his views or to express his thoughts and opinions. The viewpoint of the writer and the expression of his personality is of first importance. According to the author's special intention and method, essays are classified as (1) *formal*, and (2) *informal*, or *familiar*. In formal essays, like those written by Bacon, the personality of the writer is expressed indirectly. In the familiar essay, it is revealed more directly.

The primary purpose of the formal essay is to explain and instruct. Such an essay follows a unified plan in an orderly development of thought. It treats serious subjects in a serious and dignified manner. Formal essays may be *didactic* or *critical*. A didactic essay gives information on such matters as biography, history, science, politics, and philosophy. A *critical* essay presents a study and appraisal of some work in music or art or literature. We think of a formal essay as something to be read by a mature person or by an earnest student in search of enlightenment.

The informal or familiar essay may be compared in some respects to a lyric poem. Although it is written in prose, it is short; it presents an author's personal impressions; it draws the attention of the reader to the author's relation to his subject, rather than to the subject itself. The familiar essay is written for entertainment, primarily. But since one can never write much without expressing in some way his philosophy of life, even informal essays often serve a serious purpose. The subject matter may be deep or trivial; but the style is marked by originality of treatment, by geniality or humor, and by ease of manner. The informal essay allows great freedom in form. Whereas the formal essay may remind one of a structure in classical architecture, the familiar essay reminds one of a pleasant rambling dwelling. It is the sort of thing one reads lounging in a favorite chair beside a comfortable fire.

ESSAYS FOR ENTERTAINMENT

The first English essayists—Bacon, Jonson, and Dryden—were formal in style. It remained for Addison and Steele to introduce the informal essay. They did so in a new kind of periodical, a forerunner of the magazine.

As early as 1622 there had been weekly newspapers in England, but it was not until 1702 that there was a regular daily paper. Daniel Defoe was one of the earliest journalists, and one of the best. To him is given the credit for writing the first "interview" and of featuring the "leading editorial." Moreover, he contributed thousands of essays to his paper, the *Review*, over a nine-year period. Here was the germ of an idea upon which Richard Steele seized. Borrowing Swift's pen-name of "Isaac Bickerstaff" and Defoe's trick of dressing up a paper with literary contributions, Steele issued his *Tatler*.

The *Tatler* was a gossipy paper coming out three times a week. Each number featured a polished essay. But the paper was for entertainment rather than for spreading the news, and the essays became its most delightful feature. In that early day it served much the purpose of the modern magazine. It became immensely popular. Joseph Addison came in as a co-writer, and the paper ran for two years. After it was discontinued, the two friends issued a new publication, the *Spectator*, which became even more popular. Thereafter, the light periodical featuring a familiar essay became a habit of eighteenth-century English life. Nearly every writer tried his hand at writing one.

The essays were usually amusing rather than instructive. They presented serio-comic character studies, commented on fashions, or discussed in a semi-serious way philosophy and morals. The writers did not escape entirely the impersonal spirit of the age. In the essays of the *Tatler* and *Spectator* papers, the person who does the talking is the fictitious Mr. Bickerstaff. It is ostensibly his opinions—not Addison's or Steele's—that are expressed. Nonetheless, the essays proved so popular that many of them were collected and bound in book form. Those that enjoyed the widest reading were the *Spectator Papers*, and the special group from them called the *Sir Roger de Coverley Papers*.

THE SATIRES

Dryden and Pope had set a fashion for satire in verse which spilled over into prose. Individuals and institutions alike were victims. Education, history, government, religion—nothing was safe from the barbed words with double meaning.

Jonathan Swift was the most powerful of the prose satirists. In his hands satire became a political weapon. Pamphlets ridiculing leaders and policies were distributed like handbills about the streets of the city. Since Swift had a brilliant imagination and a kind of perverted genius, he was employed by the party in power, first by the Whigs and then by the Tories, to demolish their rivals. Two of his longer satires were allegories—*The Battle of the Books*, on the advantages of classic learning over "modern" learning; and *The Tale of a Tub*, intended to support the Church of England as opposed to the Dissenters and the Catholics. Swift overshot his mark and succeeded only in antagonizing all three churches.

The most surprising of all Swift's works was *Gulliver's Travels*, written to vent his spite against all men everywhere. It tells of Gulliver's adventures in four imaginary countries: Lilliput, or the land of tiny folk; Brobdingnag, or the land of the giants; Laputa, or the floating island of the scientists; and the land of the Houyhnhnms, where degraded human beings called Yahoos were the servants of fine, intelligent horses. Swift's venom grows devastating as the book progresses, so that the last two voyages prove unpleasant reading. But the direct, realistic style in which the first two voyages have been related has made them popular with young readers, who care nothing at all about the ironic purpose underlying them. They have become Swift's most enduring work.

The popular team of Joseph Addison and Sir Richard Steele used satire skillfully. Such essays as "The Coquette's Heart," "Fan Drill," and the "Sir Roger de Coverley" papers show English classic prose at its best. They deal with polite society; they reflect the polish and sophistication of the age; they are lightly satiric and delicately impersonal; they are gracefully written and smooth. There is an important difference between their kind of satire and that of Swift or Pope. The essays are pleasant reading because their fun is never aimed at individuals. They ridicule types and fashions but not some certain man or woman. When Pope's "The Rape of the Lock" came out, everyone knew the name of the girl and the incident that inspired it. Society tittered at the real Sir Plume of the "round, unthinking face." There was spite behind the work. But the Beau and Coquette of whom Steele and Addison wrote are no more nor less real than Skeezix and Nina of Gasoline Alley. The mark of a gentleman is kindness; and being gentlemen, Steele and Addison never stepped beyond the bounds of courtesy. One other point should be made about their work. It was their admitted intention, through satire, to make vice unattractive and virtue popular. Thus it is only the silly, trashy weaknesses of men that are held up to ridicule. And even in such an eccentric character as Sir Roger, there are fundamental human virtues of kindness and honor that endear him to the reader.

SIR ROGER AT CHURCH

JOSEPH ADDISON, WITH RICHARD STEELE

One of the most lovable figures moving through the pages of English literature is the country gentleman. He is always delightful, and somehow very typically British. But at no time is he more lovable than in the person of Sir Roger de Coverley—an eccentric, good-hearted eighteenth-century landlord.

Steele introduced him in the second number of the SPECTATOR, and he quickly became the feature of the paper. His ardent, if timorous, devotion to the widow was followed with as much eager suspense as are comic-strip love-adventures of modern heroes. When the co-author let him die, readers of the SPECTATOR protested their loss and were not at all consoled by the magnificence of his funeral.

But here is the good squire alive, and very much himself!

SIR ROGER HIMSELF

The first of our society is a gentleman of Worcestershire, of ancient descent, a baronet, his name Sir Roger de Coverley. His great grandfather was inventor of that famous country-dance which is called after him. All who know that shire, are very well acquainted with the parts and merits of Sir Roger. He is a gentleman that is very singular in his behavior, but his singularities proceed from his good sense, and are contradictions to the manners of the world, only as he thinks the world is in the wrong. However, this humor creates him no enemies, for he does nothing with sourness or obstinacy; and his being unconfined to modes and forms, makes him but the readier and more capable to please and oblige all who know him. When he is in town, he lives in Soho-square.[1] It is said, he keeps himself a bachelor by reason he was crossed in love by a perverse beautiful widow of the next county to him. Before this disappointment, Sir Roger was what you call a fine gentleman, had often supped with Lord Rochester and Sir George Etherege, fought a duel upon his first coming to town, and kicked Bully Dawson[2] in a public coffeehouse for calling him youngster. But being ill used by the above mentioned widow, he was very serious for a year and a half; and though, his temper being naturally jovial, he at last got over it, he grew careless of himself, and never dressed[3] afterwards. He continues to

[1] SOHO-SQUARE—A square in London.

[2] LORD ROCHESTER, SIR GEORGE ETHEREGE, BULLY DAWSON—The first, John Wilmot, an English poet and courtier of Charles II; the second, an English dramatist; the third, a notorious London sharper. These three are typical of the dissolute gentlemen prominent in London society in the closing years of the reign of Charles II.

[3] DRESSED—Dressed up.

wear a coat and doublet of the same cut that were in fashion at the time of his repulse, which, in his merry humors, he tells us, has been in and out [4] twelve times since he first wore it. He is now in his fifty-sixth year, cheerful, gay, and hearty; keeps a good house both in town and country; a great lover of mankind; but there is such a mirthful cast in his behavior, that he is rather beloved than esteemed; his tenants grow rich, his servants look satisfied; all the young women profess love to him, and the young men are glad of his company: when he comes into a house, he calls the servants by their names, and talks all the way upstairs to a visit. I must not omit, that Sir Roger is a justice of the quorum; [5] that he fills the chair at a quarter-session [6] with great abilities, and three months ago gained universal applause by explaining a passage in the game act.

SIR ROGER AT CHURCH

I am always very well pleased with a country Sunday, and think, if keeping holy the seventh day were only a human institution, it would be the best method that could have been thought of for the polishing and civilizing of mankind. It is certain the country people would soon degenerate into a kind of savages and barbarians, were there not such frequent returns of a stated time, in which the whole village meet together with their best faces, and in their cleanliest habits,[1] to converse with one another upon indifferent subjects, hear their duties explained to them, and join together in adoration of the Supreme Being. Sunday clears away the rust of the whole week, not only as it refreshes in their minds the notions of religion, but as it puts both the sexes upon appearing in their most agreeable forms, and exerting all such qualities as are apt to give them a figure in the eye of the village. A country fellow distinguishes himself as much in the churchyard, as a citizen does upon the 'Change, the whole parish-politics being generally discussed in that place either after sermon or before the bell rings.

My friend Sir Roger, being a good churchman, has beautified the inside of his church with several texts of his own choosing. He has likewise given a handsome pulpit-cloth, and railed in the communion-table at his own expense. He has often told me, that at his coming to his estate he found his parishioners very irregular; and that in order to make them kneel and join in the responses, he gave every one of them a hassock and a common prayer book; and at the same time employed an itinerant singing-master, who goes about the country for that purpose, to instruct them rightly in the tunes of the psalms: [2] upon which they now very much value themselves, and indeed outdo most of the country churches that I have ever heard.

As Sir Roger is landlord to the whole congregation, he keeps them in very good order, and will suffer nobody to sleep in it besides himself; for if by chance he has been surprised into a short nap at sermon, upon recovering out of it he stands up and looks about him, and if he sees anybody else nodding, either wakes them himself, or sends his servant to them. Several other of the old knight's peculiarities break out upon these occasions. Some-

---

[4] IN AND OUT—In and out of fashion.

[5] JUSTICE OF THE QUORUM—Justice of the peace.

[6] QUARTER-SESSION—A court held four times a year, trying many petty offences.

[1] HABITS—Clothes.

[2] PSALMS—The earliest church hymns were paraphrases of the Psalms set to music.

times he will be lengthening out a verse in the singing psalms, half a minute after the rest of the congregation have done with it; sometimes when he is pleased with the matter of his devotion, he pronounces Amen three or four times to the same prayer: and sometimes stands up when everybody else is upon their knees, to count the congregation, or see if any of his tenants are missing.

I was yesterday very much surprised to hear my old friend in the midst of the service calling out to one John Matthews to mind what he was about, and not disturb the congregation. This John Matthews it seems is remarkable for being an idle fellow, and at that time was kicking his heels for his diversion. This authority of the knight, though exerted in that odd manner which accompanies him in all circumstances of life, has a very good effect upon the parish, who are not polite [3] enough to see anything ridiculous in his behavior; besides that the general good sense and worthiness of his character make his friends observe these little singularities as foils that rather set off than blemish his good qualities.

As soon as the sermon is finished, nobody presumes to stir till Sir Roger is gone out of the church. The knight walks down from his seat in the chancel between a double row of his tenants, that stand bowing to him on each side: and every now and then inquires how such an one's wife, or mother, or son, or father do, whom he does not see at church; which is understood as a secret reprimand to the person that is absent.

The chaplain [4] has often told me, that upon a catechising day, when Sir Roger has been pleased with a boy that answers well, he has ordered a Bible to be given him next day for his encouragement; and sometimes accompanies it with a flitch of bacon to his mother. Sir Roger has likewise added five pounds a year to the clerk's place; and, that he may encourage the young fellows to make themselves perfect in the church service, has promised upon the death of the present incumbent, who is very old, to bestow it according to merit.

The fair understanding between Sir Roger and his chaplain, and their mutual concurrence in doing good, is the more remarkable, because the very next village is famous for the differences and contentions that rise between the parson and the squire, who live in a perpetual state of war. The parson is always preaching at the squire; and the squire, to be revenged on the parson, never comes to church. The squire has made all his tenants atheists and tithe-stealers; while the parson instructs them every Sunday in the dignity of his order, and insinuates to them almost in every sermon that he is a better man than his patron. In short, matters are come to such an extremity, that the squire has not said his prayers either in public or private this half year; and that the parson threatens him, if he does not mend his manners, to pray for him in the face of the whole congregation.

Feuds of this nature, though too frequent in the country, are very fatal to the ordinary people; who are so used to be dazzled with riches, that they pay as much deference to the understanding of a man of an estate, as of a man of learning; and are very hardly brought to regard any truth, how important soever it may be that is preached to them, when they know there are several men of five hundred a year [5] who do not believe it.

---

[3] POLITE—Here, sophisticated.
[4] CHAPLAIN—Here, a resident clergyman.

[5] FIVE HUNDRED A YEAR—Five hundred pounds a year, about $2,500.

FOR DISCUSSION

1. The *Tatler* and the *Spectator* might be called gossipy periodicals. Do you know any modern magazines similar to them? Addison and Steele were men-about-town in the eighteenth-century journalistic world. Mention some of their modern counterparts.

2. How do the styles of Bacon and Addison differ? Explain.

3. What sorts of people are likely to be "rather beloved than esteemed"? What kind of people may be both beloved and esteemed? Discuss, with illustrations.

4. Explain the meaning of the last sentence in the first paragraph of "Sir Roger at Church." Is the statement still true? Why or why not?

5. What parts of the essay are a satire on Sir Roger himself? Which parts are a satire on English society or upon any special classes of people? Discuss.

6. Does the reader feel scornful of Sir Roger in the end, or sympathetic towards him? Why?

7. Show that the two selections possess the qualities of an informal essay.

WORDS

From what sport is *foils* taken? Explain its usage in the sentence: "His friends observe these little singularities as foils that rather set off than blemish his good qualities." What is the difference in meaning between *itinerant* and *itinerary*? Look up the origin of the word, and explain why a man in office is called the present *incumbent*. Give the origin of *tithe*. What part of the church is the *chancel*? Give two synonyms for *insinuate*.

A PROJECT

One of the most interesting features of the *Reader's Digest* is the monthly portrayal of the "Most Interesting Character I Have Ever Met." Choose some interesting character you have known and try writing a pleasantly whimsical character sketch of him or her, modeled after the *Spectator* sketch of Sir Roger.

RELATED READING

Read other famous accounts of country squires such as those in Washington Irving's "Christmas Sketches" in *The Sketch Book* and in *Bracebridge Hall*, or the picture of Squire Cass in *Silas Marner*. Read "Sir Roger Goes A-Hunting" in the *Sir Roger de Coverley Papers*.

LIFE WITH THE GIANTS

JONATHAN SWIFT

Sometimes books written for children prove interesting to grown-ups, but the reverse is seldom true; children rarely enjoy a grown man's reading, particularly if it expresses views on politics, finance, customs or morals. There is one famous exception. GULLIVER'S TRAVELS was written to show the politicians and statesmen of England how much the writer despised them and their country. It amused or enraged a current generation and then, according to precedent, it should have found a place with other satires in the musty chambers of forgotten books. It should have, but it didn't. The children discovered it. The satire, you see, is masqueraded under the guise of fairy-tale adventures in four amazing countries.

Best known is the land of Lilliput where the tallest men are six inches high and everything else is in diminutive proportion. Equally interesting, though not so familiar, is the land of giants, Brobdingnag.[1] There a man may be sixty feet tall and a palace seven miles in circumference. The following selection contains enough of the fairy tale to recommend it to little brother or sister; it also has enough mockery to show the curious student how an embittered man took vengeance on his countrymen.

The King, who delighted in music, had frequent concerts at court, to which I was sometimes carried, and set in my box[2] on a table to hear them; but the noise was so great, that I could hardly distinguish the tunes. I am confident that all the drums and trumpets of a royal army, beating and sounding together just at your ears, could not equal it. My practice was to have my box removed from the places where the performers sat, as far as I could, then to shut the doors and windows of it, and draw the window curtains; after which I found their music not disagreeable.

I had learned in my youth to play a little upon the spinet. Glumdalclitch[3] kept one in her chamber, and a master attended twice a week to teach her: I

[1] BROBDINGNAG—The general name of the country. Swift locates the land on an undiscovered continent between California and Japan. Its capital was called "Lorbrulgrud" which Gulliver translates as "Pride of the Universe."

[2] BOX—Gulliver was kept in a box about twelve feet square and ten feet deep. It was lined with cloth and furnished with doll bed and chairs. When Gulliver accompanied the King and Queen of Brobdingnag on a progress through the realm, the box was strapped about the waist of "some grave or trusty servant."

[3] GLUMDALCLITCH—"Little Nurse," the name which Gulliver gave to the nine-year-old girl who became his caretaker. He describes her as "very good-natured, and not above forty feet high, being little for her age."

315

call it a spinet, because it somewhat resembled that instrument, and was played upon in the same manner. A fancy came into my head that I would entertain the King and Queen with an English tune upon this instrument. But this appeared extremely difficult; for the spinet was near sixty foot long, each key being almost a foot wide, so that, with my arms extended, I could not reach to above five keys, and to press them down required a good smart stroke with my fist, which would be too great a labor, and to no purpose. The method I contrived was this. I prepared two round sticks about the bigness of common cudgels; they were thicker at one end than the other, and I covered the thicker ends with a piece of a mouse's skin,[4] that by rapping on them I might neither damage the tops of the keys, nor interrupt the sound. Before the spinet a bench was placed, about four foot below the keys, and I was put upon the bench. I ran sideling upon it that way and this, as fast as I could, banging the proper keys with my two sticks, and made a shift to play a jig, to the great satisfaction of both their Majesties: but it was the most violent exercise I ever underwent, and yet I could not strike above sixteen keys, nor, consequently, play the bass and treble together, as other artists do; which was a great disadvantage to my performance.

The King, who, as I before observed, was a prince of excellent understanding, would frequently order that I should be brought in my box, and set upon the table in his closet. He would then command me to bring one of my chairs out of the box, and sit down within three yards' distance upon the top of the cabinet, which brought me almost to a level with his face. In this manner I had several conversations with him. I one day took the freedom to tell his Majesty, that the contempt he discovered towards Europe, and the rest of the world, did not seem answerable to those excellent qualities of mind he was master of. That, as inconsiderable as he took me to be, I hoped I might live to do his Majesty some signal service. The King heard me with attention, and began to conceive a much better opinion of me than he had ever before. He desired I would give him as exact an account of the government of England as I possibly could; because, as fond as princes commonly are of their own customs, he should be glad to hear of any thing that might deserve imitation.

Imagine with thyself, courteous reader, how often I then wished for the tongue of Demosthenes[5] or Cicero,[6] that might have enabled me to celebrate the praise of my own dear native country in a style equal to its merits and felicity.

I began my discourse by informing his Majesty that our dominions consisted of two islands, which composed three mighty kingdoms under one sovereign, besides our plantations in America. I dwelt long upon the fertility of our soil, and the temperature of our climate. I then spoke at large upon the constitution of an English Parliament, partly made up of an illustrious body called the House of Peers, persons of the noblest blood, and of the most ancient and ample patrimonies. I described that extraordinary care always taken of their education in arts and arms, to qualify them for being counselors born to the king and kingdom, to have a share in

---

[4] MOUSE'S SKIN—The mice were the size of large English dogs.

[5] DEMOSTHENES—An Athenian orator and patriot (384–322 B.C.).

[6] CICERO—A Roman orator and patriot (106–43 B.C.).

the legislature, to be members of the highest Court of Judicature, from whence there could be no appeal, and to be champions always ready for the defense of their prince and country, by their valor, conduct, and fidelity. That these were the ornament and bulwark of the kingdom, worthy followers of their most renowned ancestors, whose honor had been the reward of their virtue, from which their posterity were never once known to degenerate. To these were joined several holy persons, as part of that assembly, under the title of Bishops, whose peculiar business it is to take care of religion, and of those who instruct the people therein. These were searched and sought out through the whole nation, by the prince and his wisest counselors, among such of the priesthood as were most deservedly distinguished by the sanctity of their lives, and the depth of their erudition; who were indeed the spiritual fathers of the clergy and the people.

That the other part of the Parliament consisted of an assembly called the House of Commons, who were all principal gentlemen, freely picked and culled out by the people themselves, for their great abilities and love of their country, to represent the wisdom of the whole nation. And these two bodies make up the most august assembly in Europe, to whom, in conjunction with the prince, the whole legislature [7] is committed.

I then descended to the Courts of Justice, over which the Judges, those venerable sages and interpreters of the law, presided, for determining the disputed rights and properties of men, as well as for the punishment of vice, and protection of innocence. I mentioned the

[7] THE WHOLE LEGISLATURE—All legislation.

prudent management of our treasury; the valor and achievements of our forces by sea and land. I computed the number of our people, by reckoning how many millions there might be of each religious sect, or political party among us. I did not omit even our sports and pastimes, or any other particular which I thought might redound to the honor of my country. And I finished all with a brief historical account of affairs and events in England for about an hundred years past.

This conversation was not ended under five audiences, each of several hours, and the King heard the whole with great attention, frequently taking notes of what I spoke, as well as memorandums of several questions he intended to ask me.

When I had put an end to these long discourses, his Majesty, in a sixth audience, consulting his notes, proposed many doubts, queries, and objections, upon every article. He asked what methods were used to cultivate the minds and bodies of our young nobility, and in what kind of business they commonly spent the first and teachable part of their lives. What course was taken to supply that assembly when any noble family became extinct. What qualifications were necessary in those who were to be created new lords. Whether the humor of the prince, a sum of money to a court lady, or a prime minister, or a design of strengthening a party opposite to the public interest, ever happened to be motives in those advancements. What share of knowledge these lords had in the laws of their country, and how they came by it, so as to enable them to decide the properties of their fellow-subjects in the last resort. Whether they were always so free from avarice, partialities, or want, that a bribe, or some other sinister view, could have no place among them. Whether those holy lords I spoke of were always promoted to that rank upon account of their knowledge in religious matters, and the sanctity of their lives, had never been compliers with the times while they were common priests, or slavish prostitute chaplains to some nobleman, whose opinions they continued servilely to follow after they were admitted into that assembly.

He then desired to know what arts were practiced in electing those whom I called commoners: whether a stranger with a strong purse might not influence the vulgar voters to choose him before their own landlord, or the most considerable gentleman in the neighborhood. How it came to pass, that people were so violently bent upon getting into this assembly, which I allowed to be a great trouble and expense, often to the ruin of their families, without any salary or pension: because this appeared such an exalted strain of virtue and public spirit, that his Majesty seemed to doubt it might possibly not be always sincere: and he desired to know whether such zealous gentlemen could have any views of refunding themselves for the charges and trouble they were at, by sacrificing the public good to the designs of a weak and vicious prince in conjunction with a corrupted ministry. He multiplied his questions, and sifted me thoroughly upon every part of this head, proposing numberless inquiries and objections, which I think it not prudent or convenient to repeat.

Upon what I said in relation to our Courts of Justice, his Majesty desired to be satisfied in several points: and this I was the better able to do, having been formerly almost ruined by a long suit in chancery, which was decreed for me with costs. He asked, what time was usually spent in determining between right and wrong, and what degree of expense. Whether advocates and orators had liberty to plead in causes manifestly known to be unjust, vexatious, or oppressive. Whether party in religion or politics were observed to be of any weight in the scale of justice. Whether those pleading orators [8] were persons educated in the general knowledge of equity, or only in provincial, national, and other local customs. Whether they or their judges had any part in penning those laws which they assumed the liberty of interpreting and glossing upon at their pleasure. Whether they had ever at different times pleaded for and against the same cause, and cited precedents to prove contrary opinions. Whether they were a rich or a poor corporation. Whether they receive any pecuniary reward for pleading, whether they were ever admitted as members in the lower senate.

He fell next upon the management of our treasury; and said he thought my memory had failed me, because I computed our taxes at above five or six millions a year, and when I came to mention the issues,[9] he found they sometimes amounted to more than double; for the notes he had taken were very particular in this point, because he hoped, as he told me, that the knowledge of our conduct might be useful to him, and he could not be deceived in his calculations. But, if what I told him were true, he was still at a loss how a kingdom could run out of its estate [10] like a private person. He asked me, who were our creditors; and where we

[8] THOSE PLEADING ORATORS—Lawyers.
[9] ISSUES—Bonds of indebtedness for expenditures.
[10] RUN OUT OF ITS ESTATE—Live beyond its income.

should find money to pay them. He wondered to hear me talk of such chargeable and extensive wars; that certainly we must be a quarrelsome people, or live among very bad neighbors, and that our generals must needs be richer than our kings. He asked what business we had out of our own islands, unless upon the score of trade or treaty, or to defend the coasts with our fleet. Above all, he was amazed to hear me talk of a mercenary standing army in the midst of peace, and among a free people. He said, if we were governed by our own consent in the persons of our representatives, he could not imagine of whom we were afraid, or against whom we were to fight; and would hear my opinion, whether a private man's house might not better be defended by himself, his children, and family, than by half a dozen rascals picked up at a venture in the streets, for small wages, who might get an hundred times more by cutting their throats.

He was perfectly astonished with the historical account I gave him of our affairs during the last century, protesting it was only an heap of conspiracies, rebellions, murders, massacres, revolutions, banishments, the very worst effects that avarice, faction, hypocrisy, perfidiousness, cruelty, rage, madness, hatred, envy, lust, malice, or ambition could produce.

His Majesty in another audience was at the pains to recapitulate the sum of all I had spoken, compared the questions he made with the answers I had given, then taking me into his hands, and stroking me gently, delivered himself in these words, which I shall never forget nor the manner he spoke them in: My little friend Grildrig,[11] you have made a most admirable panegyric upon your country; you have clearly proved that ignorance, idleness, and vice, may be sometimes the only ingredients for qualifying a legislator; that laws are best explained, interpreted, and applied by

[11] GRILDRIG—The Brobdingnagians' name for Gulliver, signifying "mannikin," or "little man."

319

those whose interest and abilities lie in perverting, confounding, and eluding them. I observe among you some lines of an institution, which in its original might have been tolerable, but these half erased, and the rest wholly blurred and blotted by corruptions. It doth not appear from all you have said, how any one virtue is required towards the procurement of any one station among you; much less that men are ennobled on account of their virtue, that priests are advanced for their piety or learning, soldiers for their conduct or valor, judges for their integrity, senators for the love of their country, or counselors for their wisdom. As for yourself (continued the King) who have spent the greatest part of your life in travelling, I am well disposed to hope you may hitherto have escaped many vices of your country. But by what I have gathered from your own relation, and the answers I have with much pains wringed and extorted from you, I cannot but conclude the bulk of your natives to be the most pernicious race of little odious vermin that nature ever suffered to crawl upon the surface of the earth.

◇◇◇◇◇◇◇◇◇◇◇◇◇◇◇◇◇◇◇◇◇◇◇◇◇◇◇◇◇

FOR DISCUSSION

1. What evidence do you find in the first three paragraphs of Swift's carefulness about keeping all details in scale with the size of the people of Brobdingnag? Does he make any mistakes? Discuss.

2. To appreciate Gulliver's achievement in playing the spinet, try to imagine yourself playing a piano whose keys are a foot wide and whose keyboard is sixty feet long. Can you think of any better way of playing it than Gulliver devised? Do you think his scheme would work? Could he really play a jig tune on such a huge instrument? Discuss.

3. How does Swift prepare the reader to respect the judgment of the King? In describing the customs and government of England, does Gulliver seem to be praising his country or finding fault with it? Prove your point by referring to the text. Do you discover any traces of irony in Gulliver's words? If so, point them out.

4. What effect is gained by having the condemnations of England come from the King of Brobdingnag? What were some of the events that happened to England "during the last century"—that is, during the seventeenth century? Do you think that the King was justified in describing that period of English history as a "heap of conspiracies, rebellions, murders, massacres, revolutions," and so on? Discuss. Is there justice in any of the other condemnations of the King? If so, point out examples.

5. What do you discover in the life of Swift to account for his bitterness toward the Church and toward the Government? Discuss.

6. Does his condemnation of his country go beyond the limits of reason? Discuss.

WORDS

A man of integrity would certainly not be *perfidious, pernicious,* or *odious.* Why not? Give the differences in meaning among the adjectives. Is there a difference between a *panegyric* and a *eulogy?* Give synonyms for *recapitulate, procurement, servile. Pecuniary* and *mercenary* have a relationship to money. How do they differ in meaning? Trace the history of *vulgar.* Give the modern meaning of the word *patrimony.*

PROJECTS

1. Make a class report on Gulliver's voyage to Lilliput where everything had been on a tiny scale. Discuss the satire involved.

2. Prepare a list of the important events in English history from the death of Elizabeth in 1603 to the ascension of George III.

RELATED READING

Gilbert and Sullivan became immortal for their humorous operatic satires of English manners and government. Read their *Pinafore* and compare its style and content with that of Swift's stories of Gulliver. In recent years our American playwrights have satirized political life and government. Acquaint yourself with one of the following: *Of Thee I Sing*, *I'd Rather Be Right*, *The State of the Union*, *Call Me Madam*. They are witty, pointed, and very entertaining.

◇◇◇◇◇

THE AGE OF JOHNSON (1740-1780)

By 1745, classicism had almost played "its hour upon the stage"; the satyrs, fauns, goddesses were ready to retire to the musty regions where old literary props are stored. But then the great, uncouth, Falstaffian figure of Dr. Samuel Johnson waddled from the wings—the last and most celebrated of the classic Titans. He gathered about him a group of artists, essayists, and poets which included such outstanding figures as Sir Joshua Reynolds, David Garrick, Oliver Goldsmith, Edmund Burke, and Edward Gibbon, and founded the famous Literary Club. It was here that the great minds of the day drank in the sage wisdom of the greatest conversationalist of all time. Happily one of that group, James Boswell, was a born hero-worshipper, and his famous biography of Johnson has preserved for posterity the vigorous talk and wise comment of his hero.

Johnson's writings, which include his *Lives of the Poets* and the essays he wrote for his two magazines *The Rambler* and *The Idler*, show almost all the characteristics of eighteenth-century classicism: its wit, its interest in men and manners, its good sense, its love of the town, and its indifference to nature. It seems strange today that books of English literature usually contain more literature about Samuel Johnson than by him. The great literary dictator was ponderous in every respect: in body, in thought, in style. Few modern readers will have the patience to struggle with his Ciceronic sentences laden with heavy Latinisms and filled with erudite allusions to universal knowledge. His intimate friend and Club member, Goldsmith, once said of him that if Johnson wrote a fable about little fishes, he would have the fishes talk like whales. Johnson's great work is his *Dictionary*, upon which he spent seven years. Despite its real scholarship, the author frequently obscured rather than clarified the meanings of words by involved definitions. Thus he actually did define "network" as "any thing reticulated or decussated, at equal distances, with the interstices between the intersections." Also, in many instances he allowed his personal prejudices to color his definitions. With his traditional hatred of Scotland, he defined "oats" as "a grain which in England is generally given to horses, but in Scotland supports the people."

DR. JOHNSON'S

WRITING STYLE

Johnson, however, is more important for the inspiration and encouragement he gave others than for his writing. There is hardly a single contemporary writer who did not owe something to this dynamic man. Johnson was also remarkable for his simple and sincere piety in an age when religion was at a very low ebb.

His infectious vigor also effected a revival of interest in the theater. One of his circle was the madcap Irishman, Richard Sheridan, who, at twenty, fell in love with a singer, defied parental opposition, indulged in wild escapades, and fought two duels. His famous plays *The Rivals* and *The School for Scandal* are as dashing and spirited as himself. Oliver Goldsmith was a second friend of Johnson's to make history with a play—his famous comedy, *She Stoops to Conquer.*

Another writer of the Johnsonian school was the statesman, Edmund Burke. Though Americans know Burke chiefly through his speech, *On Conciliation with the American Colonies,* his collected works fill fourteen volumes. Well trained in the classics, he filled his speeches with references to the ancients. His style is rhetorical—filled with adjectives and dressed-up, round-about expressions. He used words precisely, and his orderly mind demanded logical development.

With the exception of Edward Gibbon, late eighteenth-century English prose writers composed in the heavy style of Johnson. But Gibbon, in his *Decline and Fall of the Roman Empire,* wrote flawless prose in the best neo-classic tradition. His history, however, is extremely bigoted and anti-Catholic.

THE NOVEL

There was one other important development in the literature of the period—the emergence of the novel. Our best sellers in their flaming jackets—our murder mysteries, our twentieth-century romances, our historical novels—all trace their genealogy back to this period. There had been long prose romances in English before this time, but it was this age which first produced stories with definite plot development.

To Samuel Richardson's *Pamela* is usually awarded the title of "the first English novel." Other well known novels of this period are: *Tom Jones* by Henry Fielding, *Peregrine Pickle* by Tobias Smollett, and *The Vicar of Wakefield* by Oliver Goldsmith. When Horace Walpole wrote his *Castle of Otranto* in 1764, he introduced the mystery story into the English novel.

(FROM) LIFE OF JOHNSON

JAMES BOSWELL

It is no exaggeration to say that Dr. Johnson, the most celebrated figure of the eighteenth century and the Great Dictator of London's literary circles, lives today not so much by what he wrote as by what James Boswell wrote of him. For almost twenty years this hero-worshipping little Scotsman carefully observed and made notes on what the "Great Bear of Literature" said and did. As a result we have the most famous and one of the most unprejudiced and readable biographies in the English language, written in a style both clear and flexible. John Kieran, of "Information Please" fame, has named Boswell's LIFE OF JOHNSON *as his third choice (after the Bible and Shakespeare) for a companion on a desert island. The excerpts below will give us a brief glimpse into the diverse characters of Johnson and his biographer.*

JOHNSON AT SCHOOL

He was first taught to read English by Dame Oliver, a widow, who kept a school for young children in Lichfield. He told me she could read black letter,[1] and asked him to borrow for her, from his father, a Bible in that character. When he was going to Oxford, she came to take leave of him, brought him, in the simplicity of her kindness, a present of gingerbread, and said he was the best scholar she ever had. He delighted in mentioning this early compliment: adding, with a smile, that "this was as high a proof of his merit as he could conceive." His next instructor in English was a master, whom, when he spoke of him to me, he familiarly called Tom Brown, who, said he, "published a spelling-book and dedicated it to the Universe; but I fear no copy of it can now be had."

He began to learn Latin with Mr. Hawkins, usher, or undermaster, of Lichfield school—"a man" (said he) "very skilful in his little way." With him he continued two years, and then rose to be under the care of Mr. Hunter, the head master, who according to his account, "was severe and wrong-headedly severe. He used" (said he) "to beat us unmercifully; and he did not distinguish between ignorance and negligence; for he would beat a boy equally for not knowing a thing, as for neglecting to know it. He would ask a boy a question, and if he did not answer it, he would beat him, without considering whether he had an opportunity of knowing how to answer it. For instance, he would call up a boy and ask him Latin for a candlestick, which the boy could not expect to be asked. Now, Sir, if a boy could answer every question, there would be no need of a master to teach him."

However, Johnson was very sensible how much he owed to Mr. Hunter. Mr. Langton[2] one day asked him how he had acquired so accurate a knowledge of Latin, in which I believe he was exceeded by no man of his time; he said, "My master whipped me very well. Without that, Sir, I should have done nothing." He told Mr. Langton that while Hunter was flogging his boys unmercifully, he used to say, "And this I do to save you from the gallows." Johnson, upon all occasions, expressed his approbation of enforcing instruction by means of the rod. "I would rather" (said he) "have the rod to be the general terror to all, to make them learn, than to tell a child, if you do thus, or thus, you will be more esteemed than your brothers or sisters. The rod produces an effect which terminates in itself. A child is afraid of being whipped, and gets his task, and there's an end on't: whereas, by exciting emulation and comparisons of superiority, you lay the foundation of lasting mischief; you

[1] BLACK LETTER—Old English letters.

[2] MR. LANGTON—Member of the Literary Club, famous Greek scholar.

make brothers and sisters hate each other."

That superiority over his fellows, which he maintained with so much dignity in his march through life, was not assumed from vanity and ostentation, but was the natural and constant effect of those extraordinary powers of mind, of which he could not but be conscious by comparison; the intellectual difference, which in other cases of comparison of characters, is often a matter of undecided contest, being as clear in his case as the superiority of stature in some men above others. Johnson did not strut or stand on tiptoe; he only did not stoop. From his earliest years, his superiority was perceived and acknowledged. He was from the beginning *anax andron*, a king of men. His schoolfellow, Mr. Hector, has obligingly furnished me with many particulars of his boyish days; and assured me that he never knew him corrected at school but for talking and diverting other boys from their business. He seemed to learn by intuition; for though indolence and procrastination were inherent in his constitution, whenever he made an exertion he did more than any one else. In short, he is a memorable instance of what has been observed, that the boy is the man in miniature; and that the distinguishing characteristics of each individual are the same through the whole course of life. His favourites used to receive very liberal assistance from him; and such was the submission and deference with which he was treated, such the desire to obtain his regard that three of the boys, of whom Mr. Hector was sometimes one, used to come in the morning as his humble attendants, and carry him to school. One in the middle stooped while he sat upon his back, and one on each side supported him, and thus he

was borne triumphant. Such a proof of the early predominance of intellectual vigour is very remarkable and does honour to human nature.

JOHNSON AND BOSWELL MEET

(1763) This is to me a memorable year; for in it I had the happiness to obtain the acquaintance of that extraordinary man whose memoirs I am now writing, an acquaintance which I shall ever esteem as one of the most fortunate circumstances in my life. Though then but two-and-twenty I had for several years read his works with delight and instruction, and had the reverence for their author, which had grown up in my fancy into a kind of mysterious veneration by figuring to myself a state of solemn, elevated abstraction, in which I supposed him to live in the immense metropolis of London. Mr. Gentleman, a native of Ireland, who passed some years in Scotland as a player, and as an instructor in the English language, a man whose talents and worth were depressed by misfortunes, had given me a representation of the figure and manner of "Dictionary Johnson," as he was then called; and during my first visit to London, which was for three months in 1760, Mr. Derrick, the poet, who was Gentleman's friend and countryman, flattered me with hopes that he would introduce me to Johnson. But he never found an opportunity, which made me doubt that he had promised to do what was not in his power; till Johnson some years afterwards told me, "Derrick, sir, might very well have introduced you. I had a kindness for Derrick, and am sorry he is dead."

Mr. Thomas Davies, the actor, who then kept a bookseller's shop in Russell Street, Covent Garden, told me that Johnson came frequently to his house, where he more than once invited me to meet him; but by some unlucky accident or other he was prevented from coming to us.

Mr. Davies recollected several of Johnson's remarkable sayings, and was one of the best of the many imitators of his voice and manner while relating them. He increased my impatience more and more to see the extraordinary man whose works I highly valued, and whose conversation was reported to be excellent.

At last, on Monday the 16th of May, when I was sitting in Mr. Davies' back parlor, after having drunk tea with him and Mrs. Davies, Johnson unexpectedly came into the shop; and Mr. Davies having perceived him through the glass door in the room in which we were sitting, advancing toward us—he announced his awful approach to me, somewhat in the manner of an actor in the part of Horatio when he addresses

Hamlet on the appearance of his father's ghost, "Look, my Lord, it comes." I found that I had a perfect idea of Johnson's figure, from the portrait of him painted by Sir Joshua Reynolds soon after he had published his *Dictionary*, in the attitude of sitting in his easy chair in deep meditation. Mr. Davies mentioned my name, and respectfully introduced me to him; I was much agitated, and recollecting his prejudice against the Scotch, of which I had heard much, I said to Davies, "Don't tell him where I come from."—"From Scotland," cried Davies, roguishly. "Mr. Johnson," said I, "I do indeed come from Scotland, but I cannot help it."

I am willing to flatter myself that I meant this as light pleasantry to soothe and conciliate him, and not as an humiliating abasement at the expense of my country. But however that might be, this speech was somewhat unlucky, for he seized the expression "come from

325

Scotland," and retorted, "That, sir, I find, is what a great many of your countrymen cannot help." This stroke stunned me a good deal, and when we had sat down, I felt myself not a little embarrassed, and apprehensive of what might come next. He then addressed himself to Davies: "What do you think of Garrick?[3] He refused me an order for the play for Miss Williams, because he knows the house will be full, and that an order would be worth three shillings." Eager to take any opening to get into the conversation with him, I ventured to say, "Oh, sir, I cannot think Mr. Garrick would grudge such a trifle to you." "Sir," said he, with a stern look, "I have known David Garrick longer than you have done, and I know no right you have to talk to me on the subject." Perhaps I deserved this check, for it was rather presumptuous in me, an entire stranger, to express any doubt of the justice of his animadversion upon his old acquaintance and pupil. I now felt myself much mortified, and began to think that the hope which I had long indulged of obtaining his acquaintance was blasted. And, in truth, had not my ardor been uncommonly strong, and my resolution uncommonly persevering, so rough a reception might have deferred me forever from making any further attempts. Fortunately, however, I remained upon the field not wholly discomfited, and was soon rewarded by hearing some of his conversation.

AN EVENING AT THE MITRE TAVERN

On Wednesday, July 6, he was engaged to sup with me at my lodgings in Downing Street, Westminster. But on the preceding night, my landlord having behaved very rudely to me and some company who were with me, I had resolved not to remain another night in his house. I was exceedingly uneasy at the awkward appearance I supposed I should make to Johnson and the other gentlemen whom I had invited, not being able to receive them at home, and being obliged to order supper at the Mitre, I went to Johnson in the morning, and talked of it as of a serious distress. He laughed and said, "Consider, sir, how insignificant this will appear a twelve-month hence. There is nothing," continued he, "in this mighty misfortune; nay, we shall be better at the Mitre." I told him that I had been at Sir John Fielding's[4] office, complaining of my landlord, and had been informed that though I had taken my lodgings for a year, I might upon proof of his bad behavior, quit them when I pleased, without being under an obligation to pay rent for any longer time than while I possessed them. The fertility of Johnson's mind could show itself even upon so small a matter as this. "Why, sir," said he, "I suppose this must be the law since you have been told so in Bow Street.[5] But if your landlord could hold you to your bargain, and the lodgings should be yours for a year, you may certainly use them as you think fit. So, sir, you may quarter two life-guardsmen upon him, or you may send the greatest scoundrel you can find into your apartments, or you may say that you want to make some experiments in natural phi-

---

[3] GARRICK—One of the greatest Shakespearean actors of all time and co-manager of the Drury Lane Theater in Covent Garden. A movie of some years ago, *The Great Garrick*, was well done.

[4] SIR JOHN FIELDING—A half-brother of Henry Fielding, classical novelist and author of *Tom Jones*.

[5] BOW STREET—The principal police court of London is situated there. A fashionable site in the eighteenth century where Will's Coffee House was situated.

losophy, and may burn a large quantity of asafetida [6] in his house."

I had as my guests, this evening at the Mitre Tavern, Dr. Johnson, Dr. Goldsmith, Mr. Thomas Davies, Mr. Eccles, an Irish gentleman, for whose agreeable company I was obliged to Mr. Davies, and the Reverend Mr. John Ogilvie.

Mr. Ogilvie was unlucky enough to choose for the topic of his conversation the praises of his native country. He began with saying that there was very rich land around Edinburgh. Goldsmith, who had studied physics there, contradicted this, very untruly, with a sneering laugh. Disconcerted a little by this, Mr. Ogilvie then took a new ground, where I suppose, he thought himself perfectly safe, for he observed that Scotland had a great many noble wild prospects. JOHNSON. "I believe, sir, you have a great many. Norway, too, has noble, wild prospects, and Lapland is remarkable for prodigious, noble, wild prospects. But sir, let me tell you, the noblest prospect which a Scotchman ever sees is the high road that leads him to England!" This unexpected and pointed sally produced a roar of applause. After all, however, those who admire the rude grandeur of nature cannot deny it to Caledonia.

On Saturday, July 9, I found Johnson surrounded with a numerous levee, but have not preserved any part of his conversation. On the 14th we had another evening by ourselves at the Mitre. It happening to be a very rainy night, I made some commonplace observations on the relaxation of nerves and depression of spirits which such weather occasioned, adding, however, that it was good for the vegetable creation. Johnson, who denied that the temperature of

[6] ASAFETIDA (ăs′á·fĕt′ĭ·dá)—A fetid smelling medicine.

the air had any influence on the human frame, answered, with a smile of ridicule, "Why, yes, sir, it is good for vegetables, and for the animals who eat those vegetables, and for the animals who eat those animals." This observation of his aptly enough introduced a good supper, and I soon forgot, in Johnson's company, the influence of a moist atmosphere.

FOR DISCUSSION

1. What traits of character are discovered in the selections just read? Is your impression of Johnson favorable?
2. Discuss Boswell's personality and character as revealed in the selections.
3. Explain what Boswell meant when he wrote: "The boy is the man in miniature." Wordsworth wrote that "the child is father of the man."
4. Boswell had lodgings in Downing Street. What English official resides at No. 10 Downing Street today?
5. Discuss the following quotations of Johnson:

"If man does not make new acquaintance as he advances through life, he will soon find himself left alone. A man, Sir, should keep his friendships in constant repair."

"What we read with inclination makes a much stronger impression. If we read without inclination half the mind is employed in fixing the attention; so there is but one half to be employed on what we read."

"A man of sense and education should meet a suitable companion in a wife. It is a miserable thing when the conversation can only be such as, whether the mutton should be broiled or roasted, and probably a dispute about that."

WORDS

By comparison, Boswell's diction is much lighter than that of Johnson; which makes for a much more flexible style. Remarkable for eighteenth-century prose, there are not more Latin words in his biography than one would find in a modern writer. Learn the definitions of *emulate, ostentatious, intuition, tremulous, lurking, impute, animadversion.* Rewrite the following in simple words: "procrastination was inherent in his constitution." Note that the English add a *u* to words ending in *-or*; for example, *favour, colour, honour,* and *dolour.*

PROJECTS

1. The Literary Club was founded by Johnson and Sir Joshua Reynolds in 1764. It met at Turk's Head Tavern every week and in later years numbered thirty-five members. Besides Johnson and Boswell, some of the famous members were Sir Joshua Reynolds, Oliver Goldsmith, David Garrick, Edmund Burke, and Richard Sheridan. Prepare a brief written or oral report on each of these men.

2. Select some outstanding twentieth-century Catholic writers for an imaginary Literary Club. From your knowledge of their interests and their views on certain subjects, write an imaginary conversation between them which could be used as a radio or television script.

3. Have the ghosts of the famous Club members return to life and comment on life and letters in this modern age.

RELATED READING

In the Victorian Age, Macaulay wrote a famous biographical essay on Johnson. Acquaint yourself with this essay. A hasty or a leisured reading of Boswell's *Johnson* in any abridged edition should be the ambition of every high school senior.

SAMUEL JOHNSON

JAMES BOSWELL

THE TRANSITION FROM CLASSICISM
TO ROMANTICISM (1780-1798)

As early as Pope's time a reaction against the neo-classic standards was evident among a group of poets living in isolated rural areas who wrote about nature, solitude, and death. Far removed from the sophistication of London life, they wrote about the things which surrounded them: about nature and the familiar objects of everyday life. They discarded satire and criticism and attempted ballads and simple tales. Convinced that by entirely suppressing their natural feelings and appealing only to cold, formal logic, they were missing a great deal in life, these poets began to use "the language of the heart" in odes, lyrics, and elegies. Some of these poems, which were written with sincerity and in good taste, possessed real literary merit. Others, however, reflected a morbid and almost unnatural interest in death; they contained long descriptions of cemeteries at night replete with phantoms, owls, newly dug graves, and crumbling ivy walls. So mawkish and melancholy were many of these poems that their authors were designated as the "Graveyard School."

A renewed interest in the poetry of the Elizabethans led the way to the adoption of new poetic interests and a return to a simpler diction. We see this influence partly at work in Gray's "Elegy," whose thought was definitely influenced by the "Graveyard School" and whose diction manifested a partial, though not complete, veering away from the stock diction of the neo-classic. The best examples of the work of this new school of "sentiment and return to nature" are Thomson's "Seasons," William Collins' "Ode to Evening," and Cowper's "Olney Hymns." Reflective poems of this type were written in blank verse, similar to Milton's, instead of in conventional couplets.

A reawakened interest in man as a human being and in democratic living found expression in Oliver Goldsmith's poem, "The Deserted Village" and in such poems of Robert Burns as "The Cotter's Saturday Night." Both voice a protest against the encroachments of a growing capitalistic economy and its oppression of the poor. In Burns, the purest lyricist of Scotland, with his incomparable songs of highland life and love, we find the most important forerunner of the Romantic Movement. The simple lyrics and mystical fancies of William Blake also show a complete turning away from the formality of eighteenth-century classicism.

Such a sweeping century of achievement proves in review to have left surprisingly little that is of intrinsic interest. The "classical" writers overestimated the value of their work. Much of it is of historic significance; little is still read. The student will remember it best for the vogue of classicism in literature; for the wit of Alexander Pope (one of the most quoted writers in the English tongue); for the satire of Swift; for the literary elegance and healthful influence of Addison and Steele; for the strange power wielded by Dr. Johnson; for a revival of the drama; for the emergence of three new literary forms: the newspaper, the magazine, and the novel.

Elegy Written in a Country Churchyard

THOMAS GRAY

A country burying-ground—especially an old one—has a curious fascination for anyone of imaginative mind. In England the churchyard cemeteries are very old. One knows that the people buried in them were humble; for according to European custom, persons of rank were buried within the churches, or in vaults or crypts beneath the floors.

At Stoke Poges in Buckinghamshire lies an old churchyard, once the haunt of a dreamy poet, Thomas Gray. Gray liked to wander among the graves, looking at the simple monuments and deciphering the inscriptions. Poorly worded, almost ludicrous in their awkwardness, the epitaphs told of the poverty of the neighborhood. As Gray tried to repicture the simple lives remembered there, he wondered what difference it might have made had these folks had the privileges of education and contact with public affairs. Did this spot hold the remains of some possible genius, forever hidden from the world? Fired by such fancies, Gray wrote an elegy to celebrate the "unhonored dead." His tribute has become one of the best known poems in the English language. To it, in conclusion, he added the lines that he chose for his own epitaph when he should be laid to rest in some such quiet spot.

> The curfew tolls the knell of parting day;
>   The lowing herd winds slowly o'er the lea;
> The plowman homeward plods his weary way,
>   And leaves the world to darkness and to me.
>
> Now fades the glimmering landscape on the sight,   5
>   And all the air a solemn stillness holds,
> Save where the beetle wheels his droning flight,
>   And drowsy tinklings lull the distant folds;

Save that from yonder ivy-mantled tow'r
    The moping owl does to the moon complain   10
Of such as, wandering near her secret bow'r,
    Molest her ancient solitary reign.

Beneath those rugged elms, that yew-tree's shade,
    Where heaves the turf in many a mold'ring heap,
Each in his narrow cell forever laid,   15
    The rude forefathers of the hamlet sleep.

The breezy call of incense-breathing Morn,
    The swallow twitt'ring from the straw-built shed,
The cock's shrill clarion, or the echoing horn,
    No more shall rouse them from their lowly bed.   20

For them no more the blazing hearth shall burn,
    Or busy housewife ply her evening care;
No children run to lisp their sire's return,
    Or climb his knees the envied kiss to share.

Oft did the harvest to their sickle yield,   25
    Their furrow oft the stubborn glebe has broke;
How jocund did they drive their team a-field!
    How bowed the woods beneath their sturdy stroke!

Let not Ambition mock their useful toil,
    Their homely joys and destiny obscure;   30
Nor Grandeur hear with a disdainful smile
    The short and simple annals of the poor.

The boast of heraldry, the pomp of pow'r,
    And all that beauty, all that wealth e'er gave,
Awaits alike the inevitable hour: 35
    The paths of glory lead but to the grave.

Nor you, ye proud, impute to these the fault,
    If Memory o'er their tomb no trophies raise,
Where, through the long-drawn aisle and fretted vault,
    The pealing anthem swells the note of praise.   40

26. GLEBE—Turf, sward.
29. AMBITION—Those who have made it their purpose to achieve power, fame, wealth, and the like. Similarly, *Grandeur*, in line 31, refers to those who have such wealth and power.
33. BOAST OF HERALDRY—Family pride; inherited rank, indicated by family coats-of-arms.

Can storied urn or animated bust
    Back to its mansion call the fleeting breath?
Can Honor's voice provoke the silent dust,
    Or Flatt'ry soothe the dull, cold ear of Death?

Perhaps in this neglected spot is laid   45
    Some heart once pregnant with celestial fire;
Hands that the rod of empire might have swayed,
    Or waked to ecstasy the living lyre.

But Knowledge to their eyes her ample page,
    Rich with the spoils of time, did ne'er unroll;   50
Chill Penury repressed their noble rage,
    And froze the genial current of their soul.

Full many a gem of purest ray serene
    The dark unfathomed caves of ocean bear;
Full many a flower is born to blush unseen,   55
    And waste its sweetness on the desert air.

Some village-Hampden that with dauntless breast
    The little tyrant of his fields withstood,
Some mute inglorious Milton, here may rest,
    Some Cromwell guiltless of his country's blood.   60

Th' applause of list'ning senates to command,
    The threats of pain and ruin to despise,
To scatter plenty o'er a smiling land,
    And read their hist'ry in a nation's eyes,

Their lot forbade: nor circumscribed alone,   65
    Their growing virtues, but their crimes confined;
Forbade to wade through slaughter to a throne,
    And shut the gates of mercy on mankind;

41. STORIED URN—Burial urns inscribed with records of achievements and honors.
41. ANIMATED—Lifelike.
43. PROVOKE—Arouse, awaken.
46. PREGNANT WITH CELESTIAL FIRE—Filled with heaven-sent genius.
51. PENURY REPRESSED THEIR NOBLE RAGE—Poverty stifled or smothered their talents.
52. FROZE THE GENIAL CURRENT OF THEIR SOUL—Prevented them from following their natural bents.
57. HAMPDEN—An English squire who refused to pay the "tax of ship money," thus starting the argument which led to the Puritan Revolution.
58. LITTLE TYRANT OF HIS FIELDS—His landlord.
61–64. Notice the punctuation in this stanza, which must be read together with the following stanza. *Lot* (l. 65) is the subject of the main clause; *forbade* is the verb; and the infinitives *to command, to despise, to scatter* and *read* are the objects.
65. CIRCUMSCRIBED—Set limits to. The thought is that if their lot prevented them from being benefactors of mankind, it may also have prevented them from causing widespread pain and suffering. It thus "confined their crimes."

The struggling pangs of conscious truth to hide,
    To quench the blushes of ingenuous shame,   70
Or heap the shrine of Luxury and Pride
    With incense kindled at the Muse's flame.

Far from the madding crowd's ignoble strife,
    Their sober wishes never learned to stray;
Along the cool sequestered vale of life   75
    They kept the noiseless tenor of their way.

Yet e'en these bones from insult to protect,
    Some frail memorial still erected nigh,
With uncouth rhymes and shapeless sculpture decked,
    Implores the passing tribute of a sigh.   80

Their name, their years, spelt by th' unlettered Muse,
    The place of fame and elegy supply;
And many a holy text around she strews,
    That teach the rustic moralist to die.

69–72. This stanza must be read in connection with the preceding one. The infinitives *to hide, to quench*, and *heap* are the objects of *forbade* in line 67. Gray is here referring to the practice of patronage under which an author would dedicate his work to a wealthy or influential person expecting to receive money or favors in return.

81. UNLETTERED MUSE—Uneducated poet or rhymster.

84. TEACH THE RUSTIC MORALIST TO DIE—Texts intended to give comfort in the face of death.

For who, to dumb Forgetfulness a prey,   85
    This pleasing, anxious being e'er resigned,
Left the warm precincts of the cheerful day,
    Nor cast one longing, ling'ring look behind?

On some fond breast the parting soul relies,
    Some pious drops the closing eye requires;   90
E'en from the tomb the voice of nature cries,
    E'en in our ashes live their wonted fires.

For thee who, mindful of th' unhonored dead,
    Dost in these lines their artless tale relate,
If chance, by lonely Contemplation led,   95
    Some kindred spirit shall inquire thy fate,

Haply some hoary-headed swain may say,
    "Oft have we seen him at the peep of dawn,
Brushing with hasty steps the dews away,
    To meet the sun upon the upland lawn.   100

"There, at the foot of yonder nodding beech
    That wreathes its old fantastic roots so high,
His listless length at noontide would he stretch,
    And pore upon the brook that babbles by.

"Hard by yon wood, now smiling as in scorn,   105
    Mutt'ring his wayward fancies, he would rove;
Now drooping, woeful—wan, like one forlorn
    Or crazed with care or crossed in hopeless love.

"One morn I missed him from the customed hill,
    Along the heath, and near his fav'rite tree.   110
Another came, nor yet beside the rill,
    Nor up the lawn, nor at the wood was he;

"The next, with dirges due, in sad array,
    Slow through the churchway path we saw him borne:
Approach and read (for thou canst read) the lay   115
    Graved on the stone beneath yon aged thorn."

THE EPITAPH

Here rests his head upon the lap of Earth,
    A youth to Fortune and to Fame unknown:
Fair Science frowned not on his humble birth,
    And Melancholy marked him for her own.   120

Large was his bounty, and his soul sincere;
  Heaven did a recompense as largely send:
He gave to Mis'ry (all he had) a tear,
  He gained from Heav'n ('twas all he wished) a friend.

No farther seek his merits to disclose,   125
  Or draw his frailties from their dread abode,
(There they alike in trembling hope repose),
  The bosom of his Father and his God.

FOR APPRECIATION

Although Gray has chosen a simple subject for his "Elegy," he has kept the long words of classic poetry. Yet so popular was the poem with our parents and grandparents that many of its lines have passed into common speech *in quotation*.

1. The first three stanzas are introductory, planned to set the mood for the poem. What things does the reader see? What does he hear? What does he feel? Choose three adjectives of your own to describe the kind of mood or feeling set by the first twelve lines.

2. Which stanza describes the cemetery? What kinds of trees grew there? What was the "narrow cell"?

3. Which three stanzas present imaginary scenes from the daily lives of those now lying in the churchyard? Are the pictures happy or sad?

4. What is the general thought of lines 29–36? What is the connection—expressed or implied—between the humble villagers of the churchyard and the "paths of glory"? Windsor Castle is situated just across the valley from Stoke Poges. Does this fact make the thought content of lines 33–44 more meaningful? Explain.

5. Quote the lines in the succeeding stanzas which express the following thoughts:

   a. The absence of suitable markers or memorials does not mean necessarily that the men were unworthy.

   b. Splendid monuments cannot alter the fact of death.

Quote the lines which indicate that England's "honored dead" are buried within the churches. Which English church holds the tombs of her greatest men? Where is it located?

6. Restate in simple prose the meaning of lines 45 and 46. Quote a later stanza which says that the same sort of thing happens often in the realm of nature.

7. In lines 45–60 what undeveloped talents does Gray suggest may have been buried in that "neglected spot"? Do you think that Gray approved or disapproved of the Puritan Revolution of the seventeenth century? How can you tell how he felt?

8. In which stanzas does Gray say that lack of opportunity may have prevented great misfortunes or unhappiness at the same time that it robbed men of fame and success? Do you think that Gray is right? In your discussion follow some of these thoughts to a conclusion:

   a. Name some men in history who "waded through a slaughter to a throne." Were they all men from privileged circumstances? Do you think they would have become famous no matter what their original circumstances were?

   b. Can you name some men or women of humble origin who have been the cause of great human suffering? How were they able to win or wield power?

9. Do you think Gray's ideas as presented in the first 72 lines are an argument for or against the principle that there should be equal opportunities for all persons? Discuss.

10. Which lines say that even these simple graves bear markers of some sort? Which lines say that it is a common trait of human nature to want to be missed and mourned?

11. How can the reader tell that Gray is writing of himself in lines 93–96? What do we learn about Gray's habits, in the stanzas that follow? What was he doing when he acted like one "crazed with care or crossed in hopeless love"? Was Gray excitable?

12. What does the parenthetical expression, "for thou canst read" imply about the educational status of the community?

13. It is customary in an epitaph to mention the virtues of the one remembered. What virtues does Gray claim in his epitaph?

14. How does the "Elegy" prove that Gray was interested in ordinary men and women? Which passages in it show the most effective use of poetic imagination?

15. Why do you think this poem became a favorite in Gray's time and for many succeeding generations? Make a list of lines or expressions from it which you have heard quoted. Which passages from it do you consider most worthy of memorization? Why?

◇◇◇◇◇

John Anderson, My Jo

ROBERT BURNS

Most of Robert Burns's poetry is written in Scotch brogue. The poet used dialect deliberately. It was not that he knew no better. You will notice that when it pleased him, he could turn out stanzas in pure English as polished and smooth as those of any classic poet.

Burns used dialect because—however well educated a Scotsman may be—when he is with those he loves and trusts, he drops naturally into brogue. It is the cozy, familiar speech of the home. John Muir, the Scottish-born American naturalist, has said that no matter how hot a Scotch argument waxed, so long as the men used dialect, you could know that all was friendly beneath; but if one man "put his English on"—then look out! Burns, writing for his neighbors and cronies, uses the daily speech, homelike and comfortable as their old clothes. He "puts his English on" only when he wants dignity for a dedication, as in the first stanza of "The Cotter's Saturday Night," or when he turns aside to moralize a bit.

Familiar songs like "*Auld Lang Syne*" and "*Comin' Through the Rye*" have given us some practice with Burns's speech. Try reading some of the following lines aloud until you can get them smoothly.

John Anderson, my jo, John,
  When we were first acquent,
Your locks were like the raven,
  Your bonie brow was brent;
But now your brow is beld, John,   5
  Your locks are like the snaw;
But blessings on your frosty pow,
  John Anderson, my jo!

John Anderson, my jo, John,
  We clamb the hill thegither;   10
And mony a canty day, John
  We've had wi' ane anither;
Now we maun totter down, John,
  And hand in hand we'll go,
And sleep thegither at the foot,   15
  John Anderson, my jo!

1. JO—Sweetheart.
4. BRENT—Smooth, unwrinkled.
5. BELD—Bald.
8. POW—Head.

11. CANTY—Happy.
13. MAUN—Must.

FOR APPRECIATION

1. Show how this poem is a beautiful "love lyric" of old age and a tribute to the fulfillment of marriage vows.

2. Find in the poem the secret of the old couple's happiness together.

3. Name at least two familiar American or English songs which express the same sentiment expressed in the poem. How many old couples do you know to whom this poem might be applied? Perhaps they can inspire you to write a lyric poem or prose tribute to one of them.

A Man's a Man for A' That

ROBERT BURNS

In the late years of the eighteenth century the British Isles hummed with democratic doctrines. Revolutions, first in America and then in France, had started Britishers thinking about "the rights of man." Ardent in his sympathies for poor men everywhere, Burns poured his articles of faith into what might be called the THEME-POEM of Democracy—"A Man's a Man for A' That." The "a' that" of the poem stands for all the external differences between men—dress, rank, manners, and the like. But for all that, says Burns, it's the Man himself that counts.

Is there for honest Poverty
 That hings his head, an' a' that;
The coward slave—we pass him by,
 We dare be poor for a' that!
For a' that, an' a' that,   5
 Our toils obscure an' a' that,
The rank is but the guinea's stamp,
 The Man's the gowd for a' that.

What though on hamely fare we dine,
 Wear hoddin greay, an' a' that; 10
Gie fools their silks, and knaves their
  wine,
A Man's a Man for a' that:
For a' that, and a' that,
 Their tinsel show, an' a' that;
The honest man, tho' e'er sae poor, 15
 Is king o' men for a' that.

Ye see yon birkie ca'd a lord,
 Wha struts, an' stares, an' a' that;
Tho' hundreds worship at his word,

He's but a coof for a' that: 20
For a' that, an' a' that,
 His ribband, star, an' a' that:
The man o' independent mind
 He looks an' laughs at a' that.

A prince can mak a belted knight, 25
 A marquis, duke, an' a' that;
But an honest man's aboon his might,
 Gude faith, he maunna fa' that!
For a' that, an' a' that,
 Their dignities an' a' that; 30
The pith o' sense, an' pride o' worth,
 Are higher rank than a' that.

Then let us pray that come it may,
 (As come it will for a' that,)
That Sense and Worth, o'er a' the earth,
 Shall bear the gree, an' a' that. 36
For a' that, an' a' that,
 It's coming yet for a' that,
That Man to Man, the world o'er,
 Shall brothers be for a' that. 40

2. HINGS—Hangs.
7. GUINEA—An English gold coin worth about $5.11.
8. GOWD—Gold. Burns meant that it is the gold, not the mark, or stamp, which makes the coin valuable.
9. HAMELY—Common; coarse.
10. HODDIN GREAY—Coarse grey woolen.
17. BIRKIE—Conceited fellow.

20. COOF—Dull fellow; dolt; ninny.
22. RIBBAND, STAR—Symbols of orders of nobility.
27. ABOON—Above.
28. MAUNNA FA'—Must not claim that.
36. BEAR THE GREE—Have the first place.

◇◇

FOR APPRECIATION

1. Does Burns mean in the first three lines that all poor men are "coward slaves"? Under what conditions dare a man be poor and proud?

2. Explain the meaning of the figure of speech which Burns uses in lines 7 and 8.

3. What kind of differences between men is the poet referring to in the second stanza? What are some of the things in life that might be classed as "tinsel show"?

4. What other poet, or poets, have expressed thoughts similar to the one in lines 15 and 16?

5. What kind of differences between men is the poet referring to in the third stanza? Do such distinctions exist even in America? Discuss.

6. Quote lines written by one of Burns's contemporaries which express a thought the same as that in lines 25–29. What does the poet say really indicates rank?

7. Since Burns wrote this poem there have been several civil wars and two world wars. Do you think the world is any closer today to the ideal expressed in the last stanza than it was in the poet's day? What nation or nations have come the closest to realizing these ideals?

8. Enumerate and discuss the definite Catholic principles which men and nations must follow if there is to be a universal brotherhood.

Flow Gently, Sweet Afton

ROBERT BURNS

In this romantic poem, Burns uses nature as the medium for expressing his theme. The Afton is a rivulet in Burns' native Ayrshire. The girl is, perhaps, his well-known sweetheart, Highland Mary. The poem has been put to music and has been sung by people the world over.

Flow gently, sweet Afton, among thy green braes;
Flow gently, I'll sing thee a song in thy praise;
My Mary's asleep by thy murmuring stream,
Flow gently, sweet Afton, disturb not her dream.

Thou stock dove whose echo resounds thro' the glen, 5
Ye wild whistling blackbirds, in yon thorny den,
Thou green crested lapwing thy screaming forbear—
I charge you, disturb not my slumbering Fair!

How lofty, sweet Afton, thy neighboring hills,
Far mark'd with the courses of clear, winding rills; 10
There daily I wander as noon rises high,
My flocks and my Mary's sweet cot in my eye.

How pleasant thy banks and green valleys below,
Where wild in the woodlands the primroses blow;
There oft, as mild ev'ning weeps over the lea, 15
The sweet-scented birk shades my Mary and me.

Thy crystal stream, Afton, how lovely it glides,
And winds by the cot where my Mary resides;
How wanton thy waters her snowy feet lave,
As, gathering sweet flowerets, she stems thy clear wave. 20

Flow gently, sweet Afton, among thy green braes,
Flow gently, sweet river, the theme of my lays;
My Mary's asleep by thy murmuring stream,
Flow gently, sweet Afton, disturb not her dream!

1. BRAES—Small hills.
5. STOCK DOVE—European wild pigeon.
7. LAPWING—Plover, a bird.
12. COT—Cottage.

FOR APPRECIATION

1. What lines in the poem tell us that "Mary's sleep" is natural sleep and not one of death?

2. Select the lines in the poem which have their primary appeal to the sense of a) sight b) sound c) touch.

3. Explain the meaning and the connotation of the following phrases: *weeps over the lea, wanton thy waters, the theme of my lays.*

⟡⟡⟡⟡⟡

I Love My Jean

ROBERT BURNS

Jean Armour, the girl Burns eventually married, is the subject of this love song, a lilting tribute to the young Scottish lass.

Of a' the airts the wind can blaw,
  I dearly like the west,
For there the bonnie lassie lives,
  The lassie I lo'e best:
There wild woods grow, and rivers row,
  And monie a hill between;   6
But day and night my fancy's flight
  Is ever wi' my Jean.

I see her in the dewy flowers,
  I see her sweet and fair;   10
I hear her in the tunefu' birds,
  I hear her charm the air:
There's not a bonnie flower that springs
  By fountain, shaw, or green,
There's not a bonnie bird that sings,
  But minds me o' my Jean.   16

1. AIRTS—Directions.
5. ROW—Roll.

14. SHAW—Wood.
16. MINDS—Reminds.

◇◇

FOR APPRECIATION

1. The subject of the poem is Jean Armour. What is the theme? What specific details did the poet choose to develop this theme? What is the mood of the poem? Do the meter and the rhythm develop this mood? Explain.

2. Is the thought content of the poem very deep? Discuss. Compare this love poem with Carew's "Song," Spenser's sonnet, and one of Shakespeare's sonnets.

(FROM) *Auguries of Innocence*

WILLIAM BLAKE

Can you do the things suggested in the four lines below? If so, you may count yourself wise. Blake says that they are "signs of innocence." Of course philosophers and poets have long said that the innocent are the truly wise, and that if we would understand the Kingdom of Heaven we must become as little children. Blake firmly believed this.

> To see a world in a grain of sand,
> And a heaven in a wild flower;
> Hold infinity in the palm of your hand,
> And eternity in an hour.

FOR APPRECIATION

1. Is there the same mystery involved in accounting for the existence of a single grain of sand that there is in accounting for the existence of a world? Discuss.

2. What element not present in sand or earth characterizes a plant or flower? What does a flower bear or produce? Why have flowers been used so often as the symbol of immortality? How can one "see a heaven in a wild flower"? Explain.

3. Is the bit of space that may be measured by the palm of one's hand *really* separated from the infinity of space that surrounds us? Discuss.

4. Are the limits that men set upon time *real*? Does time actually have a beginning and ending? In what respect is an "hour" a part of the eternity of time?

The Tiger

WILLIAM BLAKE

Man stands in bewilderment before the contrasts of nature. On the one hand we see the uplifting freshness of trees and flowers; on the other hand the destructive fury of the hurricane. There are volcanos; and there are snowflakes. And behind these paradoxes—what? What creative mind and force? "The Tiger" expresses man's bafflement over the problem.

341

Tiger! Tiger! burning bright
In the forests of the night,
What immortal hand or eye
Could frame thy fearful symmetry?

In what distant deeps or skies   5
Burnt the fire of thine eyes?
On what wings dare he aspire?
What the hand dare seize the fire?

And what shoulder, and what art,
Could twist the sinews of thy heart?   10
When thy heart began to beat,
What dread hand forged thy dread feet?

What the hammer?   What the chain?
In what furnace was thy brain?
What the anvil?   What dread grasp
Dared its deadly terrors clasp?   16

When the stars threw down their spears,
And watered heaven with their tears,
Did He smile His work to see?   19
Did He who made the Lamb make thee?

Tiger, Tiger, burning bright
In the forests of the night,
What immortal hand or eye
Dare frame thy fearful symmetry?

FOR APPRECIATION

1. Why do you think Blake chose the Tiger as especially symbolic of the mysteries of creation?   Discuss.   If you are not sure of the answer now, come back to it after you have considered the following questions.

2. Is there foundation in fact for Blake's poetic fancy which sees the tiger "*burning bright* in the forests of the *night*"?   Explain.

3. What does *symmetry* mean?   Is there symmetry in all living creatures?   Why is the tiger well described as a "fearful symmetry"?

4. What characteristics peculiar to the tiger are implied in the following expressions: (*a*) the fire of thine eyes? (*b*) the sinews of thy heart? (*c*) thy dread feet? (*d*) the deadly terrors of thy brain?

5. With what matching expressions does Blake suggest the Power that could create a tiger?   List at least four.

6. What do you think was Blake's intention in writing the first two lines of the fifth stanza?   What deeper question lies behind line 19?   What deeper question lies behind line 20?

7. Does Blake answer his questions in the last stanza?

8. What kind of thoughts or feelings does this poem excite in the reader?   Can you see any reasons why some critics have considered this short lyric to be the most truly poetic verse written in the eighteenth century?   Would you agree?   Why or why not?

The Little Black Boy

WILLIAM BLAKE

*In this childlike yet profound poem all the arguments against the inequal-
ity of races are swept away. The profundity of the arguments is clothed
in the sweet simplicity and innocence of a child retelling a lesson which
he learned at his mother's knee.*

My mother bore me in the southern wild,
And I am black, but O! my soul is white;
White as an angel is the English child,
But I am black, as if bereaved of light.

My mother taught me underneath a tree,   5
And, sitting down before the heat of day,
She took me in her lap and kissèd me,
And, pointing to the east, began to say:

"Look on the rising sun: there God does live,
And gives His light, and gives His heat away;   10
And flowers and trees and beasts and men receive
Comfort in morning, joy in the noonday.

"And we are put on earth a little space,
That we may learn to bear the beams of love;
And these black bodies and this sunburnt face   15
Is but a cloud, and like a shady grove.

"For when our souls have learned the heat to bear,
The cloud will vanish; we shall hear His voice,
Saying: 'Come out from the grove, my Love and care,
And round My golden tent like lambs rejoice.' "   20

Thus did my mother say, and kissèd me;
And thus I say to little English boy:
When I from black and he from white cloud free,
And round the tent of God like lambs we joy,

I'll shade him from the heat, till he can bear   25
To lean in joy upon our Father's knee;
And then I'll stand and stroke his silver hair,
And be like him, and he will then love me.

343

FOR APPRECIATION

1. What is the thought expressed in stanza 1? Is there implied in it both a sense of spiritual equality and social inferiority? Discuss.

2. Point out in detail how the mother teaches her son the important spiritual lesson of equality before God. Discuss the use of the image of the rising sun as referred to God. Is this image used throughout the poem? Of what advantage is the "cloud" of black upon earth? In heaven?

3. Discuss the thought content of stanza 3. Explain in detail the meaning of lines 19–20 and lines 25–26.

4. Would you say that the spiritual strength of the poem lies in this: the black boy will be able to stand the intense rays of God's love because while on earth he has borne the lack of understanding and sympathy from his white brothers? Discuss.

5. Scan line 12. Does this line break the iambic meter of the previous lines? Discuss the reason for this change.

Further Readings
The Seventeenth and Eighteenth Centuries

THE SEVENTEENTH CENTURY

* ATTERIDGE, HELEN, *At the Sign of the Silver Cup* (fiction)
* BELLOC, HILAIRE, *James I; Charles II; Milton; Cromwell* (biographical studies)
DEFOE, DANIEL, *Journal of the Plague Year*
* HOLLIS, CHRISTOPHER, *Dryden* (biographical study)
MACAULAY, THOMAS B., *Essay on Milton*
SABATINI, RAPHAEL, *Fortune's Fool* (fiction)
* YEO, MARGARET, *King of Shadows* (fiction)

THE AGE OF POPE

AITKEN, G. A., *Steele* (biography)
* CHESTERTON, G. K., *Essay on Pope*
DOBSON, AUSTIN, *Eighteenth Century Vignettes* (essays)
FITCH, CLYDE, *Beau Brummell* (drama)
* LESLIE, SHANE, *The Skull of Swift* (biographical study)
SCOTT, WALTER, *Rob Roy; Waverly* (fiction)
SHERIDAN, RICHARD BRINSLEY, *The Rivals; School for Scandal* (dramas)

TARKINGTON, BOOTH, *Monsieur Beaucaire* (fiction)
* THORNTON, FRANCIS B., *Alexander Pope* (biography)
THACKERAY, WILLIAM M., *Henry Esmond, Virginians* (fiction)
VAN DOREN, CARL, *Swift* (biographical study)

THE AGE OF JOHNSON

BALDERSTON, J. L. *Berkeley Square* (drama)
CARLYLE, THOMAS, *Essay on Burns*
* CHESTERTON, G. K., *The Judgment of Dr. Johnson* (biographical study)
DAICHIES, DAVID, *Robert Burns* (critical study)
DICKENS, CHARLES, *Barnaby Rudge* (fiction)
GOLDSMITH, OLIVER, *She Stoops to Conquer* (drama); *The Deserted Village* (poetry)
* HOLLIS, CHRISTOPHER, *Doctor Johnson* (biographical study)
KRUTCH, JOSEPH WOOD, *Samuel Johnson* (biography)
MOORE, L. L., *The Jessamy Bride* (fiction)
WILLIAMSON, CLAUDE, *Writers of Three Centuries*

GEORGE HERBERT

RICHARD LOVELACE

WILLIAM BLAKE

JOHN DONNE

345

COURTESY OF THE METROPOLITAN MUSEUM OF ART

"The Wise and Foolish Virgins," by William Blake.

THE AGE OF ROMANTICISM

1 7 8 0 – 1 8 4 0

There were many indications that the old formal world of classicism was "as dead as a coffin-nail." A new spirit was blowing through the land. England's complacency had been shaken by the American Revolution. In 1783, Sir William Pitt, a liberal, had become Prime Minister. Wisely he adopted a generous policy toward the remaining colonies of the Crown. And as English trade expanded, wealth increased and the country prospered.

But across the channel there was trouble. When the French Revolution broke out, Englishmen in general were in sympathy with the desperate peasant classes. Young idealists hurried abroad to do what they could to help. "Liberty! Fraternity! Equality!" was the war slogan of the day. Jean Jacques Rousseau proposed the idea that man left to himself is entirely good; that all evils to which flesh is heir have come from civilization; that "primitive man," the "noble savage," is naturally good. The idea of the French radicals was to destroy the artificial culture bred by the court and to start over.

But as the movement became more and more violent and the guillotine became the symbol of a Reign of Terror, English sympathy cooled. The terrorist measures of frenzied republican leaders alarmed the rest of Europe; and by 1793 English sympathy was no longer with the new Republic. The wild-eyed young Bonaparte had everyone on edge. Ambition was on the march, and no one knew where it would end. England was forced into defense. There was no peace until the Battle of Waterloo, fought in 1815 upon the fields of Belgium, disposed of Napoleon and his dreams of world conquest. Then the great powers met in Vienna to settle the peace of Europe. England emerged from the wars more powerful than before. She had gained new territory and new respect. The victory of Lord Nelson at Trafalgar in 1805 had reaffirmed her supremacy on the sea; and she was generally conceded to be the most powerful of existing empires.

THE DEFEAT

OF NAPOLEON

But Rousseau had made an impression. Men had grown tired of the classical ideal with its emphasis on reason. Perhaps the new philosophy of feeling and emotion might contribute more to the happiness they were seeking.

False as Rousseau's ideas were—he claimed that man was an *emotional animal* rather than a rational being—they did have several good effects on English literature. The suggestion that "primitive men" led a happier and nobler life than those "spoiled" by civilization prompted several poets to seek inspiration in humble people, instead of in urbane society. Nature, also, began to look good to them. Impelled by Rousseau's exaltation of the emotions, these poets became more interested in their own feelings and reactions to beauty than in the consecrated descriptions of classical authors. They looked at this magic planet, the earth, and at the wonder-change of seasons, as if they were seeing them for the first time. At times they approached the true Catholic attitude which sees the beauty of God shining forth from every corner of the universe. The fresh contact with nature and the new emphasis on emotion, imagination, and personal feeling created the right atmosphere for lyric poetry. At no other point in the history of English literature do we find such a joyous outburst of lyric melodies.

Renewed interest in the life and literature of the Middle Ages was also an important factor of the movement. A certain Bishop Percy had made a collection of medieval ballads and romances back in 1765. They had been read and imitated by a few writers at that time; but in this new century when THE REDISCOVERY young poets were rejecting the restrictions and rules of OF OLD BALLADS the classicists, the old ballads became immensely popular. The variety of verse forms and the sense of mystery and wonder that pervaded them became features of the new poetry. The ballads were the more eagerly taken over because the new writers preferred the simplicity of "primitive" medieval folk literature to the stiff, artificial forms of the classicists. And since these early nineteenth-century poets were trying to bring some of the freshness of the old romances into their own poetry, they came to be known as romanticists.

Romanticism stresses the personal feelings of the writer; therefore, no two romantic poets are alike. Wordsworth concerned himself with the simple, humble phases of nature which he met in the secluded Lake District. Coleridge gave voice to the mysterious and strange in such poems as "The Ancient Mariner." Keats captured the rich, sensuous beauty of nature and perpetuated it in his immortal odes. Byron and Shelley were in revolt against all law, not so much because they felt individual laws were unjust as because they believed that all law hampers personal liberty. This sense of rebellion is expressed passionately in their verse.

The accentuation of personal feeling also had its effect in the prose writing of the times. The personal essay, under the pen of Charles Lamb, achieved new charm. Addison and Steele had written delightful light essays. But Lamb added the personal note that made him the first great familiar essayist in our language. Under the influence of *Blackwood's Magazine* and the *London Magazine*, which furnished a ready market for the familiar essays of Lamb, Hazlitt, Hunt, and De Quincey, the personal essay attained a grace and perfection which have seldom been excelled. Few essayists have matched the charm of Lamb. He wrote not to instruct, but to share with his readers the humor, the pathos, and the beauty which he discovered in the common adventure of living.

ROMANTICISM AND EXAGGERATED ROMANTICISM

In any discussion of art, whether it be music, architecture, poetry, or literature, this question will always be asked—Is the work classical or romantic? Today, for example, we hear much about the preference, in music, for the classicism of Bach to the romanticism of Wagner.

The history of arts and letters has shown that the tempo and spirit of each age have emphasized either the romantic or the classical tradition. We say emphasized, since no age has seen the complete absence of either spirit. In fact, in the great masterpieces of world literature the two traditions have been fused harmoniously. Thus in Sophocles as in Vergil, in Shakespeare as in Milton, there is a wedding of the two spirits, with the classical element predominant in Vergil and the romantic triumphing in Shakespeare's dramas.

In our study of neo-classic literature we discussed the differences between real classicism and the exaggerated form of pseudo-classicists. Before beginning the study of the great romantic poets, we shall do well to understand what romanticism as opposed to classicism means, and to discuss the exaggerated romanticism which colored many of the writings of the romantic movement.

Someone has defined romanticism as "strangeness wedded to beauty." It is an attitude of the mind which views the world under the guise of the strange, the fanciful, the mysterious, and the wondrous. The artistic expression of this romantic spirit fills the beholder with awe and wonder. Romanticism symbolizes the restless pursuit of adventure, of the extraordinary, of the search for an ideal. This romantic spirit belongs to all ages. It is found in Homer's *Odyssey* and in Spenser's *Faerie Queene*. But in the Middle Age it was predominant. The Gothic cathedral—the contribution of the Middle Ages to architecture—symbolizes the fusion of the romantic spirit and Christianity. The gargoyles, the flying buttresses, the myriad details of its decorative devices all produce a sense of strangeness and wonder, the very opposite of the simplicity and repose of the classical temple. The arched columns and the Gothic spires reaching into the heavens represent the upward striving of man away from earth and his yearning for the *Summum Bonum*, God. In the medieval romances, especially those dealing with the quest of the Holy Grail, we have the perfect illustration of the romantic spirit in pursuit of idealistic adventure.

Strong as was the classical tradition in the writings of the great Elizabethans, the romantic elements triumphed. The romantic spirit was even kept alive throughout the neo-classical era; but it was in the Romantic Movement proper that the themes of extravagant love, heroism, and adventure came back into English literature. We have seen that the ballad literature was rediscovered and the Middle Ages explored, not for the faith which the Middle Ages possessed but for the romantic spirit which that faith had supernaturalized.

But with the dawn of the Romantic Movement a number of new qualities were added to the old spirit of romanticism. Hence the Romantic Movement, as an epoch in English art, is a mixture of old and new characteristics. Noteworthy among the new elements were a rebellion against the restraining influence of neo-classic rules and an insistence upon spontaneity in artistic expression; a rediscovery of the Middle Ages resulting in a renewal of interest in the themes of chivalrous love, heroism, and adventure; a rediscovery of the classical spirit as opposed to the neo-classical. Some of the poets looked beyond the Middle Ages to be influenced by the spirit of Greece and Rome. Hence we have in the

REVOLT AGAINST

ARTIFICIALITY

ROBERT BURNS

WILLIAM WORDSWORTH

SAMUEL COLERIDGE

WALTER SCOTT

LORD BYRON

PERCY BYSSHE SHELLEY

JOHN KEATS

CHARLES LAMB

odes of Keats a manifestation of a sane classicism—a suggestion of universal truth from particular images.

All the above tendencies were healthy and wholesome and of themselves would have produced masterpieces in the spirit of the medieval romances and of Shakespeare. But the great romantic poets, now almost completely cut off from the Catholic tradition and Christian philosophy, lost their way in the new and pagan doctrines of Rousseau. It is a far cry from the romantic poets of the Elizabethan era, who were consciously or unconsciously still fed upon the Christian orthodoxy of Thomas Aquinas, and the great romantic geniuses who inherited a Christianity stripped of the supernatural, the moral law stripped of everything but convention, and the human heart stripped of Divine Love and left alone to contemplate its morbidly sad, empty, and naked self.

It is little wonder that many dangerous elements entered into the authentic romantic spirit and created what we shall term an *exaggerated romanticism*. The most destructive of these elements were first, a contempt for restraint which led to the glorification of unrestrained emotions and the expression

NATURE AND

THE ETERNAL

of the poet's subjective feelings with an exaggerated intensity; and secondly, a misinterpretation of the place of nature in the eternal scheme of things; the romantics looked upon nature as an end rather than a stepping-stone to the Ultimate Good. For them nature was not a sacrament, a symbol of the beauty, power, and goodness of the Divine Creator, above and apart from the physical universe as it is for the Christian philosopher and poet. For the romanticists, nature constituted the ultimate with which they endeavored to become physically identified. Guided by a misty sort of pantheism, they wanted to come into an emotional communion with the "world soul." Religion for them became an emotional contemplation of the universe, and the poet became the high priest of a hazy nature worship. They failed to recognize the distinction between the natural and the supernatural and often confused the ideal with the real and the spiritual with the earthy.

Moreover, this extreme subjectivity led to an inevitable disillusionment and the disease of romantic melancholy. An unhealthy self-pity inspired the romanticists to picture themselves as sensitive and superior beings neglected and misunderstood by the common herd. This morbid brooding, this parading of the wounded, bleeding heart before the world intensified their egoism and made them revel in their own melancholy. Such exaggerated introspection influenced their poetry and greatly minimized the universal appeal and the objectivity which every truth artistically expressed should contain.

Hence the major weakness of the romantic poets was that they gave free rein to the expression of personal moods and distorted fancies rather than to the utterance of universal truths and emotions common to mankind.

This exaggerated romanticism paved the way for the naturalism and ultra-realism which have plagued English and American literature to the present day. Nor is it difficult to see the connection between modern surrealism [1] and that type of ro-

[1] SURREALISM—An artistic movement which tries to express subconscious mental activities in disconnected and dreamlike images.

manticism which overestimated the place of sensation, feeling, imagination, and emotion to the disregard of reason and objective truth; and which paraded for public dissection the intimate secrets of the poets' introspective selves.

◇◇◇◇◇

She Dwelt Among the Untrodden Ways

WILLIAM WORDSWORTH

When Wordsworth was twenty-nine years old, he wrote a group of five poems sometimes known as the "Lucy lyrics." There is no way of knowing who Lucy was. But the poems about her breathe a sense of reality. In the following "Lucy lyric," there is an authentic expression of the emotion of grief that avoids sentimentality. The poem tells its story so simply and clearly that it needs no explanation.

She dwelt among the untrodden ways
  Beside the springs of Dove;
A maid whom there were none to praise,
  And very few to love.

A violet by a mossy stone 5
  Half hidden from the eye;
Fair as a star, when only one
  Is shining in the sky.

    She lived unknown, and few could know
      When Lucy ceased to be; 10
    But she is in her grave, and oh
      The difference to me!

◇◇◇

FOR APPRECIATION

1. Point out the different ways in which the poet suggests that Lucy lived in a remote, lonely place. Do you have any idea where it was?

2. Discuss the aptness of the figures in stanza 2. What do they tell us of the character of Lucy? Is this the poetic, or artistic, way of expressing a reality? Discuss.

3. How does the third stanza convey the impression of sincere emotion? Would the feeling of grief be stronger if the poet said more about it? Why or why not?

She Was a Phantom of Delight

WILLIAM WORDSWORTH

The following lines are a beautiful tribute, "written from the heart," to Mrs. Wordsworth. Note the use of everyday language in the poem—an example of Wordsworth's theory that in treating of everyday realities commonplace and simple language should be used.

She was a phantom of delight
When first she gleamed upon my sight;
A lovely apparition, sent
To be a moment's ornament;
Her eyes as stars of twilight fair;   5
Like twilight's, too, her dusky hair;
But all things else about her drawn
From Maytime and the cheerful dawn;
A dancing shape, an image gay,
To haunt, to startle, and waylay.   10

I saw her upon nearer view,
A spirit, yet a woman too!
Her household motions light and free,
And steps of virgin liberty;
A countenance in which did meet   15
Sweet records, promises as sweet;

A creature not too bright or good
For human nature's daily food;
For transient sorrows, simple wiles,
Praise, blame, love, kisses, tears, and
    smiles.   20

And now I see with eye serene
The very pulse of the machine;
A being breathing thoughtful breath,
A traveler between life and death;
The reason firm, the temperate will,   25
Endurance, foresight, strength, and skill;
A perfect woman, nobly planned,
To warn, to comfort, and command;
And yet a spirit still, and bright
With something of angelic light.   30

22. MACHINE—Body.

FOR APPRECIATION

1. Sketch in a few sentences the character portrait of Mrs. Wordsworth as suggested by Wordsworth in the poem. Does the poet give us a picture of a person with one predominant characteristic, or is the portrait a series of equally important physical and spiritual qualities? Discuss.

2. Select various metaphors from the poem and state simply what physical or spiritual quality each metaphor describes. Discuss and memorize lines 27–28.

3. Compare and contrast this poem with any one or several of Elizabethan, Cavalier, or Metaphysical love poems. Which type do you prefer? Explain. Do not fail to compare and contrast both the diction and the imagery in the Romantics and the poets of the seventeenth century.

The Tables Turned

WILLIAM WORDSWORTH

The title of the poem indicates a rebuttal. And so it is. The poem is Wordsworth's answer to a critic who accused him of making nature his sole preoccupation to the neglect of formal study. The poem contains in germ what Wordsworth taught throughout his poetry: nature is a great moral teacher. We shall meet this theory again in "Tintern Abbey." In a certain sense nature can be a moral teacher, but not to the exclusion of those sacred and profane studies which contain the truths of Divine Wisdom made known to man through the light of reason and Revelation. The poem contains some truth, but exaggerates nature's importance.

Up! up! my Friend, and quit your books;
Or surely you'll grow double.
Up! up! my Friend, and clear your looks;
Why all this toil and trouble?

The sun, above the mountain's head,
A freshening lustre mellow   6
Through all the long green fields has
   spread,
His first sweet evening yellow.

Books! 'tis a dull and endless strife;
Come, hear the woodland linnet,   10
How sweet his music! on my life,
There's more of wisdom in it.

And hark! how blithe the throstle
   sings!
He, too, is no mean preacher;
Come forth into the light of things,   15
Let Nature be your teacher.

She has a world of ready wealth,
Our minds and hearts to bless—
Spontaneous wisdom breathed by
   health,
Truth breathed by cheerfulness.   20

One impulse from a vernal wood
May teach you more of man,
Of moral evil and of good,
Than all the sages can.

Sweet is the lore which Nature brings;
Our meddling intellect   26
Misshapes the beauteous forms of
   things—
We murder to dissect.

Enough of Science and of Art;
Close up those barren leaves;   30
Come forth, and bring with you a heart
That watches and receives.

<><><><><><><><><><><><><><><><><><><><><><><><><><><><><><><><><><><>

FOR APPRECIATION

1. Discuss in detail the meter and the rhyme of the poem in its relationship to

a) the poet's attitude toward his critic
b) the poet's attitude toward nature. Do you think that there is a disparity between the subject matter and the rhythm em-

ployed? Or do you think that the author deliberately varied his rhythms to express both his attitude toward the critic and his attitude toward nature? Compare, e.g., the thought and movement in stanza 3 with the thought and movement in stanza 6.

2. Would you consider the poem in its entirety to be a light and flippant reply to the critic, or do you think that at times Wordsworth is deadly serious when he says that Nature is more effective than study? Discuss.

3. Discuss the individual manifestations of Nature which the poet selects to contrast the place of Nature and of books in man's life.

4. Do you agree with the thought content of lines 25–29? Explain what the poet means in lines 29–32.

◇◇◇◇◇

Lines Written in Early Spring

WILLIAM WORDSWORTH

This poem illustrates both the subjectivism of lyric poetry and the heightened subjectivism of the poetry of the Romantics. A mood is created in this poem not by the objective consideration of nature in the springtime, but by the attitude or the mood which the poet brings to the subject. For Wordsworth the joyous manifestations of nature only intensify his lament of "what man has made of man." In the third and fourth lines he gives us the key to the mood of the poem in a typical expression of Romantic melancholy.

I heard a thousand blended notes
While in a grove I sate reclined,
In that sweet mood when pleasant thoughts
Bring sad thoughts to the mind.

To her fair works did Nature link   5
The human soul that through me ran;
And much it grieved my heart to think
What man has made of man.

Through primrose tufts, in that green bower,
The periwinkle trailed its wreaths;   10
And 'tis my faith that every flower
Enjoys the air it breathes.

The birds around me hopped and played,
Their thoughts I cannot measure:—
But the least motion which they made,
It seemed a thrill of pleasure.   16

The budding twigs spread out their fan,
To catch the breezy air;
And I must think, do all I can,
That there was pleasure there.   20

If this belief from heaven be sent,
If such be Nature's holy plan,
Have I not reason to lament
What man has made of man?

10. PERIWINKLE—A trailing evergreen herb with blue or white flowers.

FOR APPRECIATION

1. Discuss in detail how the poet develops the tone of "sweet mood" and "sad thoughts" throughout the poem.

2. Which is predominant in the poem, the intellectual or the emotional element?

Is the emotion expressed overdone? Do you think that it borders upon the sentimental? Discuss the meaning of "What man has made of man."

3. What is your opinion of both the intellectual and the poetic value of lines 11–12? Lines 19–20?

◇◇◇◇◇

The Solitary Reaper

WILLIAM WORDSWORTH

In this famous poem we have an illustration of how a chance line of casual reading can give birth to an immortal poem. It was while reading a sentence about a solitary girl in Wilkinson's TOUR OF SCOTLAND *that Wordsworth received the inspiration to write the poem. Wordsworth loved solitude, and perhaps the solitude of the girl had an immediate appeal to him. At any rate, solitude is the theme of the first stanza and the overtone of the entire poem. In the first stanza, which is by far the best, note how many words the poet uses to attain the effect of solitude.*

Behold her, single in the field,
Yon solitary highland lass!
Reaping and singing by herself;
Stop here, or gently pass!
Alone she cuts and binds the grain,   5
And sings a melancholy strain;
O listen! for the vale profound
Is overflowing with the sound.

No nightingale did ever chaunt
More welcome notes to weary bands
Of travelers in some shady haunt,   11
Among Arabian sands;
A voice so thrilling ne'er was heard
In springtime from the cuckoo-bird,
Breaking the silence of the seas   15
Among the farthest Hebrides.

Will no one tell me what she sings?
Perhaps the plaintive numbers flow
For old, unhappy, far-off things,
And battles long ago;   20
Or is it some more humble lay,
Familiar matter of today?
Some natural sorrow, loss, or pain,
That has been, and may be again!

Whate'er the theme, the maiden sang
As if her song could have no ending;
I saw her singing at her work,   27
And o'er the sickle bending—
I listened, motionless and still;
And, as I mounted up the hill,   30
The music in my heart I bore
Long after it was heard no more.

16. HEBRIDES (hĕb′rĭ·dēz)—A group of islands off the coast of Scotland.

FOR APPRECIATION

1. Explain the two figures of speech used in stanza 2 to suggest the quality of the girl's song. Explain the meaning of lines 15–16.

2. What kind of song is suggested in stanza 3? What would the mood of such a song be? Why? Discuss the place of the imagination in Romantic poetry as suggested by the stanza. Is it healthy?

3. How does this poem illustrate the meaning of Wordsworth's statement that "poetry is a powerful emotion recollected in tranquility"? Do lines 31–32 give the key to your answer? Explain.

4. Reread the poem and follow carefully the comparison between the girl and the bird. How does the song of the girl resemble the song of the birds?

◇◇◇◇◇

Composed Upon Westminster Bridge

WILLIAM WORDSWORTH

There is something about the silence of an unawakened city in the early morning hours that is awe-inspiring. From Westminster Bridge, Wordsworth watched London, born anew with the dawn, and saw the city almost as if it were some great object of nature.

Earth has not anything to show more
    fair:
Dull would he be of soul who could pass
    by
A sight so touching in its majesty:
This City now doth, like a garment, wear
The beauty of the morning; silent, bare,
Ships, towers, domes, theatres, and tem-
    ples lie   6
Open unto the fields, and to the sky;
All bright and glittering in the smoke-
    less air.
Never did sun more beautifully steep
In his first splendour, valley, rock, or
    hill;   10
Ne'er saw I, never felt, a calm so deep!
The river glideth at his own sweet
    will:
Dear God! the very houses seem asleep;
And all that mighty heart is lying still!

FOR APPRECIATION

1. The subject of this sonnet is a city at sunrise. Is this the ordinary subject matter of Wordsworth's poetry? What precise quality of the city so appealed to the poet that he was forced to state: "Dull would he be of soul, etc."? Do you think that Wordsworth proved his statement of line 1? Discuss.

2. State the central thought of the poem. What details did the poet select to develop this thought?

3. What is the predominant mood of the poem? Show how the meter and the choice of words help to attain this mood.

4. Discuss the effectiveness of the imagery; e.g., *wear the beauty of the morning; sun . . . steeps; mighty heart is lying still.*

5. Would Wordsworth's description be true of modern London? Of any modern city in early morning? Discuss.

PROJECTS

1. Read the interesting description of Westminster Bridge in E. V. Lucas' *Introducing London* and *London Afresh.*

2. Place yourself in reality or in imagination on some spot where you can view your city or town in panorama. Write a prose description or attempt a sonnet.

◇◇◇◇◇

The World Is Too Much With Us

WILLIAM WORDSWORTH

Since the Industrial Revolution ushered in the dawn of our mechanistic era, men have been tempted to think of success in terms of bank accounts, and to measure progress in the number of gadgets which clutter up our highways, offices, and homes. Men are so busy making a living that they have forgotten the art of how to live. The industrial world is so much with us that too often we have neither the time nor the inclination to enjoy the beauty of the universe or the beauty of the human mind. This is the lesson of Wordsworth's poem. But we need not be "a pagan suckled in a creed outworn" to appreciate God's handiwork. Christian philosophy gives the true perspective to time and eternity. As you read the poem, notice the special beauty of the sonnet form with its carefully woven rhyme scheme.

The world is too much with us; late and soon,
Getting and spending, we lay waste our powers;
Little we see in Nature that is ours;
We have given our hearts away, a sordid boon!
The sea that bares her bosom to the moon;   5
The winds that will be howling at all hours,
And are upgathered now like sleeping flowers;
For this, for everything, we are out of tune;
It moves us not.—Great God! I'd rather be
A pagan suckled in a creed outworn;   10
So might I, standing on this pleasant lea,
Have glimpses that would make me less forlorn;
Have sight of Proteus rising from the sea;
Or hear old Triton blow his wreathèd horn.

11. so might i—If then I might.
13. proteus—A lesser sea-god under Neptune who could transform himself into any shape that pleased him.
14. triton—The son of Poseidon or Neptune who blew upon a seashell trumpet to raise or calm the seas. Both gods are here used as symbolic of the great love of nature which the pagan Greeks and Romans had. Those who have studied the *Aeneid* are acquainted with both the sea-gods.

FOR APPRECIATION

1. Explain the meaning of "world" in line 1. Do lines 3 and 4 help us to obtain the right meaning? Explain fully line 4.

2. What is the figure of speech in lines 6 and 7?

3. Do you think that Wordsworth means literally that he would like to return to heathen beliefs? If not, what do the last six lines of his sonnet mean? Discuss.

A PROJECT

Write an editorial on the theme of this poem; or discuss in a written paper your reactions to the thoughts contained in the introduction to this poem.

The Virgin

WILLIAM WORDSWORTH

Many of the most perfect tributes to the Mother of God in English poetry were written, not by Catholics but by men of no pronounced religious beliefs. You may wonder why this should be, but perhaps the answer is a very simple one. England has been torn from the Catholic Faith for four centuries. The Protestantism of England has been a political, not a popular movement. The great body of Englishmen, among them her immortal poets, have unconsciously adhered to the Faith. They are at heart as Catholic as the Irish or the Italian people. They love the beautiful and noble features of the Church—such as devotion to the Mother of God.

> Mother! Whose virgin bosom was uncrost
> With the least shade of thought to sin allied;
> Woman! above all women glorified,
> Our tainted nature's solitary boast;
> Purer than foam on central ocean tost;   5
> Brighter than eastern skies at daybreak strewn
> With fancied roses, than the unblemished moon
> Before her wane begins on heaven's blue coast:
> Thy image falls to earth. Yet some, I ween,
> Not unforgiven, the suppliant knee might bend   10
> As to a visible power, in which did blend
> All that was mixed and reconciled in thee
> Of a mother's love with maiden purity,
> Of high with low, celestial with terrene.

9. WEEN—Think, believe.
14. TERRENE—Earthly, terrestrial.

◇◇

FOR APPRECIATION

1. Two great dogmas of our Catholic faith are implied in this poem: The Immaculate Conception and the Virgin Birth. Select the lines which treat of both and explain their meaning. What is the difference between the Immaculate Conception and the Virgin Birth?

2. Wordsworth uses three figures to express Mary's purity in lines 5–8. Analyze them closely.

3. What might be Wordsworth's meaning in the sentence: "Yet some I ween . . . visible power"? Does the author seem to be ignorant of Mary's place in Catholic worship? Explain and discuss.

Tintern Abbey

WILLIAM WORDSWORTH

LINES COMPOSED A FEW MILES ABOVE TINTERN ABBEY ON REVISITING THE
BANKS OF THE WYE, DURING A TOUR, JULY 13, 1798

In the summer of 1798, Wordsworth and his sister Dorothy went on a
walking tour through Scotland and Wales. Among the many places they
visited was Tintern Abbey, situated in the vicinity of the Wye River, a
tributary of the Severn in Wales. Five years before, at twenty-three, the
poet had visited this spot for the first time. In this descriptive lyric, written at the end of his tour, at Bristol, Wordsworth incorporates his romantic
concept of nature "as the guide and guardian of my heart and soul of my
moral being."

Read the poem for its imagery and for the stately cadence of its blank
verse; but also read it critically from the point of view of Catholic philosophy. Study carefully the outline and study questions at the end of the
poem.

> Five years have past; five summers, with the length
> Of five long winters! and again I hear
> These waters, rolling from their mountain springs
> With a soft inland murmur.—Once again
> Do I behold these steep and lofty cliffs,   5
> That on a wild secluded scene impress
> Thoughts of more deep seclusion; and connect
> The landscape with the quiet of the sky.
> The day is come when I again repose
> Here, under this dark sycamore, and view   10
> Those plots of cottage-ground, these orchard-tufts,
> Which at this season, with their unripe fruits,
> Are clad in one green hue, and lose themselves
> 'Mid groves and copses. Once again I see
> These hedge-rows, hardly hedge-rows, little lines   15
> Of sportive wood run wild; these pastoral farms
> Green to the very door; and wreaths of smoke
> Sent up, in silence, from among the trees!
> With some uncertain notice, as might seem

Of vagrant dwellers in the houseless woods,   20
Or of some hermit's cave, where by his fire
The hermit sits alone.

                These beauteous forms,
Through a long absence, have not been to me
As is a landscape to a blind man's eye;
But oft, in lonely rooms, and 'mid the din   25
Of towns and cities, I have owed to them,
In hours of weariness, sensations sweet,
Felt in the blood, and felt along the heart;
And passing even into my purer mind,
With tranquil restoration; feelings too   30
Of unremembered pleasure, such, perhaps,
As have no slight or trivial influence
On that best portion of a good man's life,
His little, nameless, unremembered acts
Of kindness and of love. Nor less, I trust,   35
To them I may have owed another gift,
Of aspect more sublime: that blessed mood,
In which the burthen of the mystery,
In which the heavy and the weary weight
Of all this unintelligible world,   40
Is lightened; that serene and blessed mood
In which the affections gently lead us on,
Until, the breath of this corporeal frame
And even the motion of our human blood
Almost suspended, we are laid asleep   45
In body, and become a living soul:
While with an eye made quiet by the power
Of harmony and the deep power of joy,
We see into the life of things.

                    If this
Be but a vain belief, yet, oh! how oft—   50
In darkness and amid the many shapes
Of joyless daylight; when the fretful stir
Unprofitable, and the fever of the world,
Have hung upon the beatings of my heart—
How oft, in spirit, have I turn'd to thee,   55
O sylvan Wye! thou wanderer through the woods,
How often has my spirit turned to thee!
    And now, with gleams of half-extinguished thought,
With many recognitions dim and faint,
And somewhat of a sad perplexity,   60
The picture of the mind revives again;

While here I stand, not only with the sense
Of present pleasure, but with pleasing thoughts
That in this moment there is life and food
For future years. And so I dare to hope,　　　　　　　65
Though changed, no doubt, from what I was when first
I came among these hills; when like a roe
I bounded o'er the mountains, by the sides
Of the deep rivers and the lonely streams,
Wherever nature led: more like a man　　　　　　　70
Flying from something that he dreads than one
Who sought the thing he loved. For nature then
(The coarser pleasures of my boyish days,
And their glad animal movements all gone by)
To me was all in all.—I cannot paint　　　　　　　75
What then I was. The sounding cataract
Haunted me like a passion; the tall rock,
The mountain, and the deep and gloomy wood,
Their colours and their forms, were then to me
An appetite, a feeling and a love,　　　　　　　80
That had no need of a remoter charm,
By thought supplied, nor any interest
Unborrowed from the eye.—That time is past,
And all its aching joys are now no more,
And all its dizzy raptures. Not for this　　　　　　　85
Faint I, nor mourn nor murmur; other gifts
Have followed, for such loss, I would believe,

Abundant recompense. For I have learned
To look on nature, not as in the hour
Of thoughtless youth; but hearing oftentimes   90
The still, sad music of humanity,
Nor harsh nor grating, though of ample power
To chasten and subdue. And I have felt
A presence that disturbs me with the joy
Of elevated thoughts; a sense sublime   95
Of something far more deeply interfused,
Whose dwelling is the light of setting suns,
And the round ocean and the living air,
And the blue sky, and in the mind of man;
A motion and a spirit, that impels   100
All thinking things, all objects of all thought,
And rolls through all things. Therefore am I still
A lover of the meadows and the woods,
And mountains; and of all that we behold
From this green earth; of all the mighty world   105
Of eye and ear, both what they half create,
And what perceive; well pleased to recognize
In nature and the language of the sense,
The anchor of my purest thoughts, the nurse,
The guide, the guardian of my heart, and soul   110
Of all my moral being.

                    Nor perchance,
If I were not thus taught, should I the more
Suffer my genial spirits to decay;
For thou art with me, here, upon the banks
Of this fair river; thou, my dearest friend,   115
My dear, dear friend; and in thy voice I catch
The language of my former heart, and read
My former pleasures in the shooting lights
Of thy wild eyes. Oh! yet a little while
May I behold in thee what I was once,   120
My dear, dear sister! and this prayer I make,
Knowing that nature never did betray
The heart that loved her; 'tis her privilege,
Through all the years of this our life, to lead
From joy to joy; for she can so inform   125
The mind that is within us, so impress
With quietness and beauty, and so feed
With lofty thoughts, that neither evil tongues,
Rash judgments, nor the sneers of selfish men,
Nor greetings where no kindness is, nor all   130
The dreary intercourse of daily life,

Shall e'er prevail against us, or disturb
Our cheerful faith, that all which we behold
Is full of blessings. Therefore let the moon
Shine on thee in thy solitary walk;   135
And let the misty mountain-winds be free
To blow against thee; and, in after years,
When these wild ecstasies shall be matured
Into a sober pleasure, when thy mind
Shall be a mansion for all lovely forms,   140
Thy memory be as a dwelling-place
For all sweet sounds and harmonies; oh! then,
If solitude, or fear, or pain, or grief,
Should be thy portion, with what healing thoughts
Of tender joy wilt thou remember me,   145
And these my exhortations! Nor, perchance—
If I should be where I no more can hear
Thy voice, nor catch from thy wild eyes these gleams
Of past existence—wilt thou then forget
That on the banks of this delightful stream   150
We stood together; and that I, so long
A worshipper of Nature, hither came
Unwearied in that service: rather say
With warmer love—oh! with far deeper zeal
Of holier love. Nor wilt thou then forget   155
That after many wanderings, many years
Of absence, these steep woods and lofty cliffs,
And this green pastoral landscape, were to me
More dear, both for themselves and for thy sake!

FOR APPRECIATION

LINES 1–22: THE POET'S RETURN TO
AN OLD SCENE:

1. Does the poet find the scene changed? What time of year is it?

2. If you were an artist and were to sketch the thought of lines 10–22, what precise details would you include?

LINES 22–57: THE PERSONAL MEAN-
ING OF FIRST VISIT DURING
INTERVENING YEARS:

1. Precisely what did the poet's first visit mean to him?

2. Explain how these lines illustrate Wordsworth's definition of poetry: "A powerful emotion recollected in tranquility."

3. Criticize lines 37–57. Do you think the "blessed mood" of Wordsworth is a *universal* emotion? Discuss. Is communion with nature the answer to this "unintelligible world"? What is the Catholic poet's answer?

LINES 58–65: WHAT THE POET
HOPES TO OBTAIN FROM
THIS VISIT:

Explain "life and food" in line 64. Is the thought contained in these lines a *universal* truth? Discuss.

LINES 66–83: WHAT NATURE MEANT
IN THE POET'S BOYHOOD:

Wordsworth later wrote a long poem in twelve books called *The Prelude* in which he gives descriptive biographical sketches of his love for nature. In lines 65–83 we have the germ of Book I of *The Prelude*. How did nature affect him as a boy?

LINES 83–111: WHAT NATURE MEANS
TO THE POET NOW:

1. Why should the same objective things of nature seem different to the poet now than they did when he was younger? Do we view the same things differently in the various stages of life? Explain.

2. Lines 88–91 are frequently quoted. Explain, in the light of the above questions and answers "The still, sad music of humanity." Is there a strain of *romantic melancholy* contained in this line? Explain.

3. In lines 94–102 just what is the "presence that disturbs me with joy, etc."? Is this an example of the romanticists' *pantheistic* tendency? Discuss. Would you say that the *imaginative* element is pronounced and the *intellectual* element vague and hazy? Discuss.

4. Would you say that lines 109–111 are highly exaggerated? Explain. Is this

same attitude toward nature held by many today? What American writers were influenced by Wordsworth to look upon nature in the same way?

LINES 111–159: AN EXPRESSION
OF LOVE AND ADMIRATION
FOR HIS SISTER:

1. Would you conclude from this passage that there was a deep intimacy between brother and sister?

2. Do you think the poet's attitude toward nature in lines 122–134 is exaggerated? Discuss.

3. In lines 134–154 we find many beautiful expressions. Read them carefully. Explain lines 139–142.

4. In the light of the above discussions criticize lines 155–159.

OVERVIEW

1. Read again the pages on the discussion of *romanticism*. Discuss the exaggerated elements of romanticism in "Tintern Abbey," such as extreme subjectivity, romantic melancholy, pantheistic tendency, emphasis on the imaginative and emotional element over the intellectual.

2. Explain the difference between the pantheistic and the Catholic "sacramental" approach to nature.

❖❖❖❖❖

Kubla Khan

SAMUEL TAYLOR COLERIDGE

In the summer of 1797 Coleridge, who was in ill health, went to a farm house near Porlock, England, hoping the rest would cure him. One morning as he sat reading PURCHAS'S PILGRIMAGE he fell asleep in his chair. The last words he read were: "In Xanadu did Cublai Can build a stately Palace, encompassing sixteene miles of plaine ground with a wall, wherein *are fertile Medowes, pleasant Springs, delightfull Streames, and all sorts of beasts of chase and game, and in the middest thereof a sumptuous house of pleasure." He said upon awakening that he had composed during his sleep about three hundred lines telling of magnificent scenes of oriental splendor. He immediately began writing them down and had completed fifty-four lines when he was interrupted by a visitor who stayed an hour. Coleridge was never able to remember any more of the dream.*

In Xanadu did Kubla Khan
A stately pleasure-dome decree,
Where Alph, the sacred river, ran
Through caverns measureless to man
    Down to a sunless sea.   5
So twice five miles of fertile ground
With walls and towers were girdled
    round;
And here were gardens bright with sinu-
    ous rills,
Where blossomed many an incense-
    bearing tree;
And here were forests ancient as the
    hills,   10
Enfolding sunny spots of greenery.

But O that deep romantic chasm which
    slanted
Down the green hill athwart a cedarn
    cover!
A savage place! as holy and enchanted
As e'er beneath a waning moon was
    haunted   15
By woman wailing for her demon-lover!
And from this chasm, with ceaseless tur-
    moil seething,

1. XANADU (zăn'á·dōō)—A region of Tartary.
1. KHAN—Khan means king or emperor. Kubla (or Kublai) Khan was the rich and powerful founder of the Mongol dynasty of China. He lived from 1216(?) to 1294. Medieval travelers have written of the splendors of his court.
3. ALPH—Probably an imaginary name suggested by the Alpheus, a river of southern Greece which plunges underground and flows under the sea, emerging in Sicily.

As if this earth in fast thick pants were
    breathing,
A mighty fountain momently was
    forced;
Amid whose swift half-intermitted
    burst,   20
Huge fragments vaulted like rebound-
    ing hail,
Or chaffy grain beneath the thresher's
    flail;
And 'mid these dancing rocks at once
    and ever
It flung up momently the sacred river.
Five miles meandering with a mazy mo-
    tion,   25
Through wood and dale the sacred river
    ran,
Then reached the caverns measureless
    to man,
And sank in tumult to a lifeless ocean;
And 'mid this tumult Kubla heard from
    far
Ancestral voices prophesying war!   30

The shadow of the dome of pleasure
Floated midway on the waves;
Where was heard the mingled meas-
    ure
From the fountain and the caves.
It was a miracle of rare device,   35
A sunny pleasure-dome with caves of
    ice!
A damsel with a dulcimer
In a vision once I saw;
It was an Abyssinian maid,
And on her dulcimer she played,   40

Singing of Mount Abora.
Could I revive within me
Her symphony and song,
To such a deep delight 't would win me,
That with music loud and long   45
I would build that dome in air,
That sunny dome! those caves of ice!

And all who heard should see them there,
And all should cry, "Beware! beware!
His flashing eyes, his floating hair!   50
Weave a circle round him thrice,
And close your eyes with holy dread,
For he on honey-dew hath fed,
And drunk the milk of Paradise."

41. MOUNT ABORA—There is a Mount Amara of fabled beauty in Abyssinia.

FOR APPRECIATION

1. The chief beauty of this uncompleted poem is in its music. Read aloud the poem, with a care for the cadences caused by the sentence structure. Can you suggest a reason for the changes in meter?

2. Where does the river have its source? How long does it run? Which is the better description of its end—"sunless sea" or "lifeless ocean"? Why?

3. Does line 30 give a hint as to how the thought might have been developed? Suggest a complete plot.

4. What does "the damsel with a dulcimer" have to do with the pleasure dome? What do lines 45–47 mean?

5. Who is the subject of the description in lines 50–55? What is suggested as the effect of feeding on *honey-dew* and drinking the *milk of Paradise?*

Ave Maria

WALTER SCOTT

To understand fully the sentiments expressed in this lovely song it is important to know its setting in the romantic tale, THE LADY OF THE LAKE. Ellen Douglas, a chieftain's daughter, is the heroine of the tale. Her home is in the midst of the wild Scottish highlands, far up in a mountain glade. Two powerful Scottish clansmen seek her hand in marriage; these two young warriors have met and quarrelled but have been suddenly called to gather their clans to defend Scotland. In the peril of the impending battle, Ellen's father, who must join in the fray, hides her away in a lonely, fearsome glen with only an old bard, Allan-Bane, for protector. As night falls the girl becomes frightened and lonely. Then it is that she turns like a little child to the Mother she had learned to love when she was but a baby.

Ave Maria! Maiden mild!
   Listen to a maiden's prayer!
Thou canst hear though from the wild,
   Thou canst save amid despair.
Safe may we sleep beneath thy care,   5
   Though banished, outcast and re-
     viled—
Maiden, hear a maiden's prayer;
   Mother, hear a suppliant child.
          Ave Maria!

Ave Maria! Undefiled!
   The flinty couch we now must share
Shall seem with down of eider piled,
   If thy protection hover there.   12
The murky cavern's heavy air
   Shall breathe of balm, if thou hast
     smiled;
Then, Maiden, hear a maiden's prayer;
   Mother, list a suppliant child!   16
          Ave Maria!

Ave Maria! Stainless styled!
   Foul demons of the earth and air,
From this their wonted haunt exiled,
   Shall flee before thy presence fair.
We bow us to our lot of care,   21
   Beneath thy guidance reconciled;
Hear for a maid a maiden's prayer;
   And for a father hear a child.
          Ave Maria!

FOR APPRECIATION

1. Which words of the song tell in what kind of place the maid is singing? What is her mood?

2. Is this really a prayer? Explain. Explain how Walter Scott, a non-Catholic, came to write a beautiful tribute to Mary.

3. Explain the meaning of the following phrases: *flinty couch; down of eider; breathe of balm; stainless styled; wonted haunt.*

4. What is the effect of the repeated invocation "Ave Maria"? What stanza do you like the best? Why?

5. If you have read *The Lady of the Lake*, recall the story and some of the characters.

(FROM) *CHILDE HAROLD'S PILGRIMAGE*

GEORGE GORDON, LORD BYRON

When Byron published the first two cantos of *Childe Harold's Pilgrimage* in 1812, he became famous overnight. In these cantos Byron takes "Harold" through Spain, Portugal, and Greece. The last two cantos, published later, cover his journey through Belgium, Switzerland, and Italy. In its entirety, the poem is a long descriptive narrative bound together by the endearing hero, "Childe Harold," who is Byron himself. In this indirect manner, Byron gave England a poetic personal travelogue in which he combines lyrical passages with romantic scenes and sentimental situations. Through the poem he also expresses his revolt against the conventions of English society, as well as his own enthusiasms, his disillusionments, and his romantic melancholy.

Poetry seems to have come more naturally to Byron than normal speech. Almost all of *Childe Harold* is written in the Spenserian stanza. Its best passages have always found an admiring audience.

◇◇◇◇◇

The Eve of Waterloo

A particularly vivid passage from the third canto of Byron's CHILDE HAROLD *is the description of the eve of Waterloo—a contrast of Brussels just before the battle, with the events that were to follow; carefree revelry, with horror and death. As you read, notice how effectively Byron has used the last line of each stanza to point out and emphasize the thought.*

It is true that there was a holiday spirit abroad in Brussels on the evening before the famous battle. Thackeray in his novel, VANITY FAIR, *has given us a similar picture in his description of Crawley's visit to Brussels, for the husbands of both Becky and Amelia were with the British forces. The same sort of scene has been enacted too often in human history, most notably—in recent times—when the Japanese during World War II stormed Singapore amidst the revelry in fashionable ball rooms, and when Rommel's German Army thundered at the back door of Alexandria while the gaiety of the night life in the city was at its height.*

There was a sound of revelry by night,
And Belgium's capital had gather'd then
Her Beauty and her Chivalry, and bright
The lamps shone o'er fair women and brave men;
A thousand hearts beat happily; and when   5
Music arose with its voluptuous swell,
Soft eyes looked love to eyes which spake again,
And all went merry as a marriage bell;
But hush! hark! a deep sound strikes like a rising knell!

Did ye not hear it?—No; 'twas but the wind,   10
Or the car rattling o'er the stony street;
On with the dance! Let joy be unconfined;
No sleep till morn, when Youth and Pleasure meet
To chase the glowing Hours with flying feet.—
But hark! that heavy sound breaks in once more,   15
As if the clouds its echo would repeat:
And nearer, clearer, deadlier than before!
Arm! Arm! it is—it is—the cannon's opening roar!

Within a window'd niche of that high hall
Sate Brunswick's fated chieftain; he did hear   20
That sound the first amidst the festival,
And caught its tone with Death's prophetic ear,
And when they smiled because he deemed it near,
His heart more truly knew that peal too well
Which stretched his father on a bloody bier,   25
And roused the vengeance blood alone could quell:
He rushed into the field, and, foremost fighting, fell.

Ah! then and there was hurrying to and fro,
And gathering tears, and tremblings of distress,
And cheeks all pale, which but an hour ago   30
Blush'd at the praise of their own loveliness;
And there were sudden partings, such as press
The life from out young hearts, and choking sighs
Which ne'er might be repeated: who could guess
If ever more should meet those mutual eyes,   35
Since upon night so sweet such awful morn could rise!

---

1. REVELRY BY NIGHT—On the evening of the Battle of Quatre Bras, which preceded the Battle of Waterloo, the Countess of Richmond gave a ball in Brussels.

20. BRUNSWICK'S FATED CHAMPION—The Duke of Brunswick, Frederick William, who was slain on the battlefield the next day.

And there was mounting in hot haste: the steed,
The mustering squadron, and the clattering car,
Went pouring forward with impetuous speed,
And swiftly forming in the ranks of war;   40
And the deep thunder, peal on peal afar;
And near, the beat of the alarming drum
Roused up the soldier ere the morning star;
While thronged the citizens with terror dumb,
Or whispering with white lips—"The foe! They come! they come!" 45

And wild and high the "Cameron's Gathering" rose!
The war-note of Lochiel, which Albyn's hills
Have heard, and heard, too, have her Saxon foes:—
How in the noon of night that pibroch thrills,
Savage and shrill! But with the breath which fills 50
Their mountain pipe, so fill the mountaineers
With the fierce native daring which instils
The stirring memory of a thousand years,
And Evan's, Donald's, fame rings in each clansman's ears!

The Ardennes waves above them her green leaves, 55
Dewy with Nature's tear-drops, as they pass,
Grieving, if aught inanimate e'er grieves,
Over the unreturning brave,—alas!
Ere evening to be trodden like the grass
Which now beneath them, but above shall grow 60
In its next verdure, when this fiery mass
Of living valour, rolling on the foe,
And burning with high hope, shall moulder cold and low.

Last noon beheld them full of lusty life,
Last eve in Beauty's circle proudly gay;   65
The midnight brought the signal-sound of strife,
The morn the marshalling in arms—the day
Battle's magnificently-stern array!
The thunder-clouds close o'er it, which when rent,
The earth is covered thick with other clay, 70
Which her own clay shall cover, heaped and pent,
Rider and horse—friend, foe—in one red burial blent!

49. PIBROCH (pē'brŏk)—A Scottish bagpipe.
54. EVAN'S . . . DONALD'S—The poet is here referring to Donald Cameron and his ancestor, Evan Cameron. In the preceding lines he describes the spirit of the Scottish soldiers in the English army.
55. THE ARDENNES—Situated in northern France. Byron is here using the wooded forests, associated with peace, for contrast with the marching army. These historic forests have been deluged with the blood of two World Wars. What part did they play in World War II?

FOR APPRECIATION

1. Select and study the passages which illustrate the contrast between the spirit of revelry and the spirit of war.

2. Line 12 is famous. What does it mean here in its context? Explain the figure in lines 13–14. The whole selection contains many famous lines. Make a list of those that you have heard quoted.

3. To how many kinds of sudden catastrophes could the description in stanza 4 apply? Discuss.

4. What differences in sound are indicated by stanzas six and seven?

5. Explain the meaning of the following phrases: *Death's prophetic ear; Albyn's hills* and *Saxon foes; noon of night; the stirring memory of a thousand years; covered thick with other clay.*

◇◇◇◇◇

The Coliseum

This selection is taken from Canto IV of CHILDE HAROLD. *Omitted from the selection are forty-five lines of Byron's introduction which contain some of the most boastful and arrogant passages in English literature. In the selection given below, Byron uses the ruins of the Coliseum as a medium for lyrical outburst of emotional eloquence. In it are contained his fierce pride and his hatred for, and resentment of, society.*

And here the buzz of eager nations ran,
In murmured pity or loud-roared applause,
As man was slaughtered by his fellow man.
And wherefore slaughtered? Wherefore, but because
Such were the bloody Circus' *genial* laws,   5
And the imperial pleasure.—Wherefore not?
What matters where we fall to fill the maws
Of worms—on battle-plains or listed spot?
Both are but theaters where the chief actors rot.

I see before me the Gladiator lie: 10
He leans upon his hand—his manly brow
Consents to death, but conquers agony,
And his drooped head sinks gradually low—
And through his side the last drops, ebbing slow
From the red gash, fall heavy, one by one,   15
Like the first of a thunder-shower; and now
The arena swims around him—he is gone,
Ere ceased the inhuman shout which hailed the wretch who won.

5. CIRCUS—The Roman amphitheatre. During the corruption of the last years of the Empire "bread and circuses" were given to the populace to keep them from revolting.

He heard it, but he heeded not—his eyes
Were with his heart, and that was far away;   20
He recked not of the life he lost, nor prize,
But where his rude hut by the Danube lay;
There were his young barbarians all at play,
There was their Dacian mother—he, their sire,
Butchered to make a Roman holiday—   25
All this rushed with his blood.—Shall he expire
And unavenged?—Arise! ye Goths, and glut your ire!

But here, where Murder breathed her bloody steam;
And here, where buzzing nations choked the ways,
And roared or murmured like a mountain stream   30
Dashing or winding as its torrent strays;
Here, where the Roman millions' blame or praise
Was death or life, the playthings of a crowd,
My voice sounds much, the fall the stars' faint rays
On the arena void—seats crushed—walls bowed—   35
And galleries, where my steps seem echoes strangely loud.

A ruin—yet what ruin! From its mass,
Walls, palaces, half-cities have been reared;
Yet oft the enormous skeleton ye pass,
And marvel where the spoil could have appeared.   40
Hath it indeed been plundered, or but cleared?
Alas! developed, opens the decay,
When the colossal fabric's form is neared.
It will not bear the brightness of the day,
Which streams too much on all years man have reft away.   45

But when the rising moon begins to climb
Its topmost arch, and gently pauses there;
When the stars twinkle through the loops of time,
And the low night-breeze waves along the air
The garland forest, which the gray walls wear   50
Like laurels on the bald first Caesar's head;
When the light shines serene but doth not glare,
Then in this magic circle raise the dead:
Heroes have trod this spot—'tis on their dust ye tread.

24. DACIAN—Dacia was a province of the Roman Empire.
27. GOTHS—The Goths together with the other Teutonic tribes eventually overran the Roman
Empire.

"While stands the Coliseum, Rome shall stand;   55
When falls the Coliseum, Rome shall fall;
And when Rome falls—the World!" From our own land
Thus spake the pilgrims o'er this mighty wall
In Saxon times, which we are wont to call
Ancient; and these three mortal things are still   60
On their foundations, and unaltered all;
Rome and her Ruin past Redemption's skill,
The World, the same wide den—of thieves, or what ye will.

55. These lines have been ascribed to Venerable Bede.

FOR APPRECIATION

1. Point out in detail how the selection lacks the objectivity of a narrative poem. Explain how it is a good example of Romantic poetry. Begin your study with an analysis of lines 10–27. In these lines, does Byron give the feelings of the gladiator, or his own feelings?

2. Study in detail the imagery of lines 46–54. Can you visualize it?

3. There is a great deal of objective truth in the entire passage. Discuss the Coliseum as a symbol of the decay of the Roman Empire.

4. Explain the meaning of lines 5–9; lines 60–64. Do you agree with the thought content of these lines? Explain. Does the place of Rome in the world today justify Byron's remark? Explain.

◇◇◇◇◇

The Destruction of Sennacherib

GEORGE GORDON, LORD BYRON

Remarkable for the swing of its rhythm and the vividness of its imagery, "The Destruction of Sennacherib" (sĕ·năk'ĕr·ĭb) is a descriptive version of the Old Testament story found in 4 Kings, 19. The scene is the besieging of Jerusalem by Sennacherib, king of the Assyrians, in 703 B.C.

The Assyrian came down like a wolf on the fold,
And his cohorts were gleaming in purple and gold;
And the sheen of their spears was like stars on the sea,
When the blue wave rolls nightly on deep Galilee.

2. HIS COHORTS—His troops of soldiers.

Like the leaves of the forest when Summer is green,   5
That host with their banners at sunset were seen:
Like the leaves of the forest when Autumn hath blown,
That host on the morrow lay withered and strown.

For the Angel of Death spread his wings on the blast,
And breathed in the face of the foe as he passed;   10
And the eyes of the sleepers waxed deadly and chill,
And their hearts but once heaved, and forever grew still!

And there lay the steed with his nostril all wide,
But through it there rolled not the breath of his pride,
And the foam of his gasping lay white on the turf,   15
And cold as the spray of the rock-beating surf.

And there lay the rider distorted and pale,
With the dew on his brow and the rust on his mail;
And the tents were all silent, the banners alone,
The lances unlifted, the trumpet unblown.   20

And the widows of Ashur are loud in their wail,
And the idols are broke in the temple of Baal;
And the might of the Gentile, unsmote by the sword,
Hath melted like snow in the glance of the Lord!

8. STROWN—Scattered.
21. ASHUR—Assyria.
22. BAAL—A heathen god which the Assyrians worshipped.
23. GENTILE—One not of the Jewish faith. Here, Sennacherib.

FOR APPRECIATION

1. Pick out the similes which describe the Assyrians in the first two stanzas.

2. What idea does the comparison in the first line give you about the Assyrians?

3. What two related comparisons does the poet use to contrast the Assryians in life with the Assyrians in death?

4. Was Sennacherib's army a large one? How do you know? Were they well equipped and clothed? Point out the lines which prove your answer.

5. Who or what was the Angel of Death?

6. Read the story in the last part of 4 Kings, 19, and point out what Byron omitted or added. On what particular verse in the Old Testament does this poem seem to be based?

⬦⬦⬦⬦⬦

She Walks in Beauty

GEORGE GORDON, LORD BYRON

It is a beautiful and charming woman whom Byron pictures here. She partakes of all the finest things of earth and yet is wound about with a soft, ethereal light that constitutes "the nameless grace which waves in every raven tress, or softly lightens o'er her face."

She walks in beauty, like the night
  Of cloudless climes and starry skies;
And all that's best of dark and bright
  Meet in her aspect and her eyes:
Thus mellowed to that tender light   5
  Which heaven to gaudy day denies.

One shade the more, one ray the less,
  Had half impaired the nameless grace
Which waves in every raven tress,
  Or softly lightens o'er her face;   10
Where thoughts serenely sweet express
  How pure, how dear, their dwelling-
      place.

And on that cheek, and o'er that brow,
  So soft, so calm, yet eloquent,
The smiles that win, the tints that glow,
  But tell of days in goodness spent,
A mind at peace with all below,   17
  A heart whose love is innocent!

FOR APPRECIATION

1. Although the poem appears in Byron's works under the heading "Hebrew Melodies," its inspiration is said to have been Mrs. Wilmot, the poet's cousin by marriage, who appeared at a ball in a black gown covered with spangles. What lines of the poem would lead you to suppose she wore that kind of dress?

2. In what sense is the term "beauty" used throughout the poem? Discuss. Could the lady described here be taken as an ideal of a lovely woman? Explain.

3. Could "aristocracy of character" be attributed to her? Enumerate the various qualities in the portrayal which you would desire in the ideal Catholic woman. Are there any qualities lacking? Discuss.

Ozymandias

PERCY BYSSHE SHELLEY

Shelley composed this well-known poem after he had read an account of a huge statue which had been found lying deserted in Egyptian sands. The inscription on the statue read: "I am Ozymandias, king of kings."

I met a traveler from an antique land
Who said: Two vast and trunkless legs of stone
Stand in the desert.   Near them, on the sand,
Half sunk, a shattered visage lies, whose frown,
And wrinkled lip, and sneer of cold command,   5
Tell that its sculptor well those passions read
Which yet survive, stamped on these lifeless things,
The hand that mocked them, and the heart that fed;
And on the pedestal these words appear:
"My name is Ozymandias, king of kings: 10
Look on my works, ye Mighty, and despair!"
Nothing beside remains.   Round the decay
Of that colossal wreck, boundless and bare
The lone and level sands stretch far away.

1. ANTIQUE LAND—Egypt.
7. YET SURVIVE—As seen in the face of the statue.
8. THEM—The passions.
8. HEART—The heart of the king.

FOR APPRECIATION

1. State in a sentence the theme of the poem.   Might the theme be contained in line 11?   Does it constitute a warning?

2. Discuss the effect of lines 12–14 in their relationship to the previous lines.

3. Discuss the structure of the poem.

The Cloud

PERCY BYSSHE SHELLEY

While boating on the Thames one afternoon, Shelley lay back in the boat to watch the constantly reshaping cloud masses and their gradual progress across the skies. The experience led him to compose the following poem which, because of the brilliancy of its individual pictures and the facile handling of its rhythm, has become one of his most popular.

A thoughtful reading of the poem discloses the fact that in it Shelley has his cloud take on all the shapes and forms that may ever be seen in the sky, at any time of day or night, in any season. He also suggests what the scientist would call the "function" of the cloud—that is, all the changes in weather and atmosphere that accompany various cloud formations. And last he touches upon the strange nature of the cloud—its unending cycle.

I bring fresh showers for the thirsting
    flowers,
  From the seas and the streams;
I bear light shade for the leaves when
    laid
  In their noonday dreams.
From my wings are shaken the dews
    that waken   5
  The sweet buds every one,
When rocked to rest on their mother's
    breast,
  As she dances about the sun.
I wield the flail of the lashing hail,
  And whiten the green plains under,
And then again I dissolve it in rain,   11
  And laugh as I pass in thunder.
I sift the snow on the mountains below,
  And their great pines groan aghast;
And all the night 'tis my pillow white,
  While I sleep in the arms of the blast.
Sublime on the towers of my skyey
    bowers,   17

  Lightning my pilot sits;
In a cavern under is fettered the thun-
    der,
  It struggles and howls at fits;   20
Over earth and ocean, with gentle mo-
    tion,
  This pilot is guiding me,
Lured by the love of the genii that move
  In the depths of the purple sea;
Over the rills, and the crags, and the
    hills,   25
  Over the lakes and the plains,
Wherever he dream, under mountain or
    stream,
  The Spirit he loves remains;
And I all the while bask in heaven's
    blue smile,
  Whilst he is dissolving in rains.   30

The sanguine Sunrise, with his meteor
    eyes,

31. SANGUINE—Red, like blood.

And his burning plumes outspread,
Leaps on the back of my sailing rack,
 When the morning star shines dead,
As on the jag of a mountain crag, 35
 Which an earthquake rocks and
 swings,
An eagle alit one moment may sit
 In the light of its golden wings.
And when sunset may breathe, from the
 lit sea beneath,
 Its ardors of rest and of love, 40
And the crimson pall of eve may fall
 From the depth of heaven above,
With wings folded I rest, on mine airy
 nest,
 As still as a brooding dove.

That orbèd maiden with white fire
 laden, 45
 Whom mortals call the Moon,
Glides glimmering o'er my fleece-like
 floor,
 By the midnight breezes strewn;
And wherever the beat of her unseen
 feet,
 Which only the angels hear, 50
May have broken the woof of my tent's
 thin roof,
 The stars peep behind her and peer;
And I laugh to see them whirl and flee,
 Like a swarm of golden bees,
When I widen the rent in my wind-
 built tent, 55
 Till the calm rivers, lakes, and seas,
Like strips of the sky fallen through me
 on high,
 Are each paved with the moon and
 these.

I bind the Sun's throne with a burning
 zone,
 And the Moon's with a girdle of
 pearl; 60
The volcanoes are dim, and the stars
 reel and swim,

33. RACK—Thin, floating, broken clouds.
59. ZONE—Girdle; belt.

 When the whirlwinds my banner un-
 furl.
From cape to cape, with a bridge-like
 shape,
 Over a torrent sea,
Sunbeam-proof, I hang like a roof—
 The mountains its columns be. 66
The triumphal arch through which I
 march
 With hurricane, fire, and snow,
When the Powers of the air are chained
 to my chair,
 Is the million-colored bow; 70
The sphere-fire above its soft colors
 wove,
 While the moist earth was laughing
 below.

I am the daughter of Earth and Water,
 And the nursling of the Sky;
I pass through the pores of the ocean
 and shores; 75
 I change, but I cannot die.
For after the rain when with never a
 stain
 The pavilion of heaven is bare,
And the winds and sunbeams with their
 convex gleams,
 Build up the blue dome of air, 80
I silently laugh at my own cenotaph,
 And out of the caverns of rain,
Like a child from the womb, like a
 ghost from the tomb,
 I arise and unbuild it again.

67. TRIUMPHAL ARCH—The rainbow.
81. CENOTAPH (sĕn′ô·tăf)—An empty
tomb.

<><><><><><><><><><><><><><><><><><><><><>

FOR APPRECIATION

1. What meters does Shelley employ to
achieve both the swift and majestic movement in the poem? Point out examples
of internal rhyme. What effect does the
habitual use of liquid sounds have upon
the movement of the poem? Explain.

2. What time of year does the first stanza suggest? What kind of clouds? What kind of weather? What is meant by "their mother's breast" (line 7)? How and when does she "dance about the sun"?

3. What time of year do lines 13–16 suggest? Does the rest of the stanza keep the same picture? How can you tell? Who is the *pilot* of the cloud? Through how many lines is this figure continued? What cloud shapes do you see as you read this second stanza? Describe them. If you have read Vergil's *Aeneid*, you will recall an expression similar to that of lines 19–20.

4. Which lines in the third stanza describe the effect of the sunrise on the cloud? Which lines describe the sunset? Explain the different meanings of the word *sanguine*. What is the meaning of the word in line 31? What does *pall* mean? What are the two sources of color for the cloud in lines 39–44? Describe the difference between the sunrise and the sunset clouds. A Homeric simile is a long simile in which a series of details are compared. Explain the Homeric simile in lines 31–38.

5. What time of year is suggested in the fourth stanza? Which words give that impression? What new and different picture does Shelley use for the moon? What does he call the cloud-form? Why? Draw a rough sketch of the picture described in the fourth stanza.

6. Does the fifth stanza present one picture or a series of pictures? Explain. What do you think is the "burning zone" of line 59? What is the meaning of the expression, "When the Powers of the *air are chained to my chair*"? Show how lines 71–72 describe the conditions that cause a rainbow.

7. In what sense is the cloud a "daughter of *earth* and *water*"? As a scientist, do you agree with Shelley's explanation of why the sky is *blue*? Show how the word *cenotaph* gives the key to the meaning of lines 81–84.

◇◇◇◇◇

To a Skylark

PERCY BYSSHE SHELLEY

Andre Maurois, the French biographer, wrote a life of Shelley entitled ARIEL—a name which has a two-fold connotation, both meanings being applicable to Shelley. In medieval folklore, Ariel was a light, graceful spirit of the air; in Milton's PARADISE LOST, Ariel was one of the rebel angels.

Shelley, in his subject matter as well as in his treatment of it, shows both natures. His works have an ethereal, intangible quality—an evidence of his yearning to escape from the conventional, earthy things in this material world. He shows himself also a rebel against the rules and shackles of society. He saw himself as a prophet, a liberator who would free mankind *from enslavement to a conventional morality and bring to the world a clear white vision of the "ideal"—an ideal which, sadly, had no counterpart in reality. Thus he wrote in his famous* Defence of Poetry, *"What were virtues of hope, love, . . . if Poetry did not ascend to bring light and fire from those eternal regions where the owl-winged faculty of calculation did not soar?"*

Hail to thee, blithe spirit!
  Bird thou never wert,
That from heaven, or near it,
  Pourest thy full heart
In profuse strains of unpremeditated
    art.   5

Higher still and higher
  From the earth thou springest
Like a cloud of fire;
  The blue deep thou wingest,
And singing still dost soar, and soaring
    ever singest.   10

In the golden lightning
  Of the sunken sun,
O'er which clouds are brightening,
  Thou dost float and run,
Like an unbodied joy whose race is just
    begun.   15

The pale purple even
  Melts around thy flight;
Like a star of heaven,
  In the broad daylight
Thou art unseen, but yet I hear thy
    shrill delight,   20

Keen as are the arrows
  Of that silver sphere,
Whose intense lamp narrows
  In the white dawn clear,
Until we hardly see, we feel that it is
    there.   25

All the earth and air
  With thy voice is loud,
As, when night is bare,

From one lonely cloud
The moon rains out her beams, and
    heaven is overflowed.   30

What thou art we know not;
  What is most like thee?
From rainbow clouds there flow not
  Drops so bright to see
As from thy presence showers a rain of
    melody.   35

Like a poet hidden
  In the light of thought,
Singing hymns unbidden,
  Till the world is wrought
To sympathy with hopes and fears it
    heeded not;   40

Like a high-born maiden
  In a palace tower,
Soothing her love-laden
  Soul in secret hour
With music sweet as love, which over-
    flows her bower;   45

Like a glowworm golden
  In a dell of dew,
Scattering unbeholden
  Its aërial hue
Among the flowers and grass, which
    screen it from the view;   50

Like a rose embowered
  In its own green leaves,
By warm winds deflowered,
  Till the scent it gives
Makes faint with too much sweet those
    heavy-winged thieves.   55

Sound of vernal showers
  On the twinkling grass,
Rain-awakened flowers,
  All that ever was
Joyous, and clear, and fresh, thy music
    doth surpass.   60

Teach us, sprite or bird,
  What sweet thoughts are thine;
I have never heard
  Praise of love or wine
That panted forth a flood of rapture so
    divine.   65

Chorus Hymeneal
  Or triumphal chaunt
Matched with thine, would be all
  But an empty vaunt—
A thing wherein we feel there is some
    hidden want.   70

What objects are the fountains
  Of thy happy strain?
What fields, or waves, or mountains?
  What shapes of sky or plain?
What love of thine own kind? what ig-
    norance of pain?   75

With thy clear keen joyance
  Languor cannot be;
Shadow of annoyance
  Never came near thee;
Thou lovest—but ne'er knew love's sad
    satiety.   80

Waking or asleep
  Thou of death must deem
Things more true and deep
  Than we mortals dream,
Or how could thy notes flow in such a
    crystal stream?   85

We look before and after,
  And pine for what is not;
Our sincerest laughter
  With some pain is fraught;
Our sweetest songs are those that tell of
    saddest thought.   90

Yet if we could scorn
  Hate, and pride, and fear;
If we were things born
  Not to shed a tear,
I know not how thy joy we ever should
    come near.   95

66. CHORUS HYMENEAL (hĭ′mĕ·nē′ăl)—Wedding music; from Hymen, the god of marriage.

Better than all measures
 Of delightful sound,
Better than all treasures
 That in books are found,
Thy skill to poet were, thou scorner of
  the ground!   100

Teach me half the gladness
 That thy brain must know,
Such harmonious madness
 From my lips would flow,
The world should listen then, as I am
  listening now.   105

◇◇◇◇◇◇◇◇◇◇◇◇◇◇◇◇◇◇◇◇◇◇◇◇◇◇◇◇◇◇

FOR APPRECIATION

1. Keeping in mind Shelley's theory about the function of the poet, we can see his skylark as a symbol of the poet-seer who ascends to the realm of the ideal to get his inspiration and then from those invisible realms sheds his music—and message—on the earth below. Exploring this point of view, re-read the poem, referring frequently to the following outline.

STANZA I:

An address to the lark as more than bird, as symbol of the poet's "unpremeditated art."

STANZAS II–VII:

A series of similes showing the lark's song as symbolic of the poet's song:
 (a) inspiring like fire
 (b) joyous
 (c) invisibly inspired
 (d) mysterious
 (e) poignant, keen, intense, moving
 (f) flooding all earth and air

STANZAS VIII–XII:

A series of similes showing that the source of inspiration is hidden:
 (a) like the source of a poet's song
 (b) like the light of a glowworm (sight)
 (c) like the fragrance of a rose (scent)

(d) like the sound and sight of raindrops on the grass

STANZAS XIII–XXI:

An apostrophe to the skylark as the spirit of inspiration, with the poet asking that his work may have the joyousness of the lark's song.

2. Show how the last phrase of line 100, "scorner of the ground" may be used to identify the skylark with the poet Shelley. Point out the passages in the poem which show the lark as a scorner of the ground. Point out examples from Shelley's poetry (his subjects and his treatment of them) that show the poet also as a scorner of the ground.

3. What is the meaning of the words, "love's sad satiety"? What were the circumstances in Shelley's life that make us feel that he had experienced that "sad satiety"? Select specific lines which express the strain of "romantic melancholy" running throughout the poem.

4. Quote the lines in stanza 8 that express the purpose and effect of a poet's work. Check the thought of this stanza with the explanation of the function of a poet as explained in the introduction to this poem.

5. Compare the thought of stanza 15 with Keats's "Ode on a Grecian Urn." Does any part of the ode express a similar thought? Is there any similarity in treatment? Discuss.

6. What lines of the poem imply Shelley's personal conviction that he is to bring a "new gospel" to the universe? Discuss. Compare these lines with the last stanza of the "Ode to the West Wind."

7. What modern English playwright took the title for one of his plays from the first line of the poem?

8. Do you or do you not agree with the thought content of stanza 17? Prove your answer from your knowledge of literature and music.

9. Select at least ten striking figures of speech and analyze their poetic imagery.

Ode to the West Wind

PERCY BYSSHE SHELLEY

Shelley has told us that his "Ode to the West Wind" was "conceived and chiefly written in a wood that skirts the Arno, near Florence, Italy." It was a day when the wind was gathering clouds for the beginning of the autumn rains. By sunset the rains came with a tempest of hail and with "that magnificent thunder and lightning peculiar to the . . . regions."

To appreciate the beauty of the poem, the reader should be aware of its design, which is based upon various sets of THREES. *The wind acts upon three things—the dead leaves of earth (Stanza I), the clouds of heaven (Stanza II), and the waves of the sea (Stanza III). The fourth stanza gathers together the three pictures; and in it and the last stanza the poet presents this "wild west wind" as a symbol of himself—"tameless and swift and proud." The stanzas, like sonnets, have fourteen lines, except that they are broken into sets of threes and a couplet, and that the interlocking rhyming words (all but the first group in each stanza) appear in sets of threes. As you read, notice the exquisite blending of thought and design.*

I

O wild West Wind, thou breath of Autumn's being,
Thou, from whose unseen presence the leaves dead
Are driven, like ghosts from an enchanter fleeing,

Yellow, and black, and pale, and hectic red,
Pestilence-stricken multitudes; O thou,   5
Who chariotest to their dark wintry bed

The wingèd seeds, where they lie cold and low,
Each like a corpse within its grave, until
Thine azure sister of the spring shall blow

Her clarion o'er the dreaming earth, and fill   10
(Driving sweet buds like flocks to feed in air)
With living hues and odors plain and hill;

Wild Spirit, which art moving everywhere;
Destroyer and preserver; hear, O hear!

9. AZURE SISTER—The mild west wind of spring as contrasted to the wild west wind of autumn.

II

Thou on whose stream, 'mid the steep sky's commotion,   15
Loose clouds like earth's decaying leaves are shed,
Shook from the tangled boughs of heaven and ocean,

Angels of rain and lightning; there are spread
On the blue surface of thine airy surge,
Like the bright hair uplifted from the head   20

Of some fierce Mænad, even from the dim verge
Of the horizon to the zenith's height,
The locks of the approaching storm.   Thou dirge

Of the dying year, to which the closing night
Will be the dome of a vast sepulcher,   25
Vaulted with all thy congregated might

Of vapors, from whose solid atmosphere
Black rain, and fire, and hail will burst; O hear!

III

Thou who didst waken from his summer dreams
The blue Mediterranean, where he lay,   30
Lulled by the coil of his crystalline streams,

Beside a pumice isle in Baiae's bay,
And saw in sleep old palaces and towers
Quivering within the wave's intenser day,

All overgrown with azure moss and flowers   35
So sweet, the sense faints picturing them! thou
For whose path the Atlantic's level powers

Cleave themselves into chasms, while far below
The sea-blooms and the oozy woods which wear
The sapless foliage of the ocean, know   40

Thy voice, and suddenly grow gray with fear,
And tremble and despoil themselves; O hear!

21. MÆNAD (mē'năd) --A frenzied priestess of Bacchus, the god of wine.
32. BAIAE (bī'ē)—A site of many ruins of ancient luxury near Naples.   The region is volcanic,
hence "pumice" or volcanic isle.
39–42. The explanation of these lines is to be found in Shelley's notes as follows: "The
phenomenon alluded to at the conclusion of the third stanza is well known to naturalists.   The
vegetation at the bottom of the sea, of rivers, and of lakes, sympathizes with that of the land in
the change of seasons, and is consequently influenced by the winds which announce it."

IV

If I were a dead leaf thou mightest bear;
If I were a swift cloud to fly with thee;
A wave to pant beneath thy power, and share   45

The impulse of thy strength, only less free
Than thou, O uncontrollable! If even
I were as in my boyhood, and could be

The comrade of thy wanderings over heaven,
As then, when to outstrip thy skyey speed   50
Scarce seemed a vision, I would ne'er have striven

As thus with thee in prayer in my sore need.
O lift me as a wave, a leaf, a cloud!
I fall upon the thorns of life! I bleed!

A heavy weight of hours has chained and bowed   55
One too like thee—tameless, and swift, and proud.

V

Make me thy lyre, even as the forest is;
What if my leaves are falling like its own!
The tumult of thy mighty harmonies

Will take from both a deep, autumnal tone,   60
Sweet though in sadness. Be thou, spirit fierce,
My spirit! Be thou me, impetuous one!

Drive my dead thoughts over the universe
Like withered leaves to quicken a new birth!
And, by the incantation of this verse,   65

Scatter, as from an unextinguished hearth
Ashes and sparks, my words among mankind!
Be through my lips to unawakened earth

The trumpet of a prophecy! O Wind,
If winter comes, can spring be far behind?   70

FOR APPRECIATION

1. In line 14 Shelley summarizes the twofold function of the west wind. Enumerate in detail how the west wind is both a destroyer and preserver.

2. Note the difference in tone quality, the harsh, staccato movement and the liquid cadence, between lines 1–8 and lines 9–12. Explain how the contrast is accomplished.

3. In stanza II Shelley uses at least four figurative representations of the cloud. Point out each of these four similes or metaphors. Which one links this stanza with the preceding one? Show how the last line of the second stanza describes part of the experience which inspired the poem.

4. What effect does the west wind of fall have on the Mediterranean? Explain the meaning of lines 33–34. Note carefully how, by the use of liquid sounds, Shelley achieves the languid movement in lines 29–31.

5. Show how the opening lines of the fourth stanza tie together the imagery of the first three stanzas. In what respects does Shelley resemble the west wind?

6. Reread carefully the introduction to Shelley's "To a Skylark." Then explain in detail the lines in this poem which portray Shelley's aspirations as a social reformer.

7. Shelley usually chose as the subject matter of his poetry the intangible and ethereal. Explain how "Ode to the West Wind" illustrates this fact.

8. Why are the last two lines of the poem famous in literature?

9. Explain the rich imagery of the following phrases: *ghosts from an enchanter fleeing; pestilence-striken multitudes; clarion o'er the dreaming earth; dirge of the dying year; incantation of this verse.*

PROJECTS

1. Some critics have found elements of exaggerated romanticism in this poem, such as intensity of subjective feelings, a suggestion of pantheism, an unhealthy self-pity, revolt against convention. Select the lines in the poem which might justify the claim of the critics.

2. Discuss in detail why or why not this poem is intellectually satisfying to a Catholic.

❖❖❖❖❖

On First Looking into Chapman's Homer

JOHN KEATS

Keats himself was not able to read Greek. A friend, however, brought him a copy of George Chapman's translation of Homer, and the two stayed up all night reading the book, "Keats shouting with delight as some passage of special energy struck his imagination." Fired by the splendors of the Greek culture thus opened to him, Keats composed the following sonnet after his friend had left, and presented it to him the next morning. It is considered one of the best sonnets in English literature.

Much have I traveled in the realms of gold
And many goodly states and kingdoms seen;
Round many western islands have I been
Which bards in fealty to Apollo hold.
Oft of one wide expanse had I been told   5
That deep-browed Homer ruled as his demesne;
Yet did I never breathe its pure serene
Till I heard Chapman speak out loud and bold.
Then felt I like some watcher of the skies
When a new planet swims into his ken;   10
Or like stout Cortez, when with eagle eyes
He stared at the Pacific—and all his men
Looked at each other with a wild surmise—
Silent, upon a peak in Darien.

1. REALMS OF GOLD—Great literature.
3–4. That is, I have read much poetry by English writers. "Western islands" refers to the British Isles. "Bards in fealty to Apollo" means "poets who have kept faith with Apollo, the god of song and music."
6. DEMESNE (dê·mān′)—Domain.
8. CHAPMAN—George Chapman (1559–1634), whose translation of Homer gives him a high place in English literature.
11. CORTEZ—Balboa, not Cortez, was discoverer of the Pacific Ocean.
14. DARIEN—A district covering the eastern part of the Isthmus of Panama joining Central and South America.

FOR APPRECIATION

1. Put the thought of the first four lines into a few simple prose sentences. Such an exercise will show you the difference between the approach of prose and poetry to a subject.

2. What is the wide expanse that Homer "ruled"? Mention several other great Greek writers.

3. The sestet summarizes Keats's reaction to his discovery of Greek literature. He gives us two figures to help make this experience real. Explain them. Try to appreciate his feelings. Perhaps you have had a similar experience in your own life. Portray your reactions in several similes.

4. Line 14 is very famous in English literature. Why? To what kind of human experiences can this line be applied?

5. What noun is understood after "serene" in line 7? Look up the origin of the words: *fealty; ken; demesne.*

6. Scan the sonnet. Is it Italian in form? Explain.

PROJECTS

1. Read Keats's sonnet, "When I Have Fears that I May Cease To Be."

2. Attempt a paper on the place of Greek culture in our present civilization.

Ode to a Nightingale

JOHN KEATS

In the spring of 1819 the spirits of John Keats were weighed down by the remembrance of the recent death of his brother, and by the knowledge that he himself had only a short time left to live. His contemplated marriage with Fanny Brawne, thus, would now be impossible. It was in this mood that Keats wrote his "Ode to a Nightingale." The poem opens with a description of Keats's experience of both joy and pain as he listens to the song of the nightingale. His desire to avoid pain leads him to dream about the pleasures of wine, but he finally determines to escape the pain of life by living in his imagination with the nightingale he hears singing. This imaginary life is found to carry with it great beauty as symbolized by the poet's description of the flowers surrounding him. In such beauty Keats finds that it would be pleasant to die. But the thought of death leads him to consider that the nightingale is, in a sense, deathless, and that the song of the nightingale has been present not only during his own sorrow but in the sorrow of all human beings as symbolized in the story of Ruth, a figure from the Old Testament. In Ruth, then, Keats sees that sorrow as well as joy is a thing of beauty, and he is led to accept without rebellion the human lot of pain as well as happiness. The use of the word "forlorn" serves to end the poet's musings on the pain of life, and with the flight of the nightingale he becomes uncertain whether his acceptance of the beauty of suffering was real or not. A Catholic, with his appreciation of suffering and pain derived from an understanding of Calvary, should be able to follow the poet's reasoning easily.

> My heart aches, and a drowsy numbness pains
>   My sense, as though of hemlock I had drunk,
> Or emptied some dull opiate to the drains
>   One minute past, and Lethe-wards had sunk;
> 'Tis not through envy of thy happy lot,   5
>   But being too happy in thine happiness—

2. HEMLOCK—A drug made from hemlock, a poisonous herb.
4. LETHE-WARDS –Lethe is a river in Hades, whose water when drunk would cause one to forget the past. "Lethe-wards" of course means "toward" or "in the direction of Lethe."

That thou, light-wingèd Dryad of the trees,
In some melodious plot
Of beechen green, and shadows numberless,
Singest of summer in full-throated ease.   10

O, for a draught of vintage! that hath been
Cooled a long age in the deep-delvèd earth,
Tasting of Flora and the country green,
Dance, and Provençal song, and sun-burnt mirth!
O for a beaker full of the warm South,   15
Full of the true, the blushful Hippocrene,
With beaded bubbles winking at the brim,
And purple-stainèd mouth;
That I might drink, and leave the world unseen,
And with thee fade away into the forest dim;   20

Fade far away, dissolve, and quite forget
What thou among the leaves hast never known,
The weariness, the fever, and the fret
Here, where men sit and hear each other groan;
Where palsy shakes a few, sad, last gray hairs;   25
Where youth grows pale, and specter-thin and dies
Where but to think is to be full of sorrow
And leaden-eyed despairs;
Where Beauty cannot keep her lustrous eyes
Or new Love pine at them beyond tomorrow.   30

Away! away! for I will fly to thee,
Not charioted by Bacchus and his pards,
But on the viewless wings of Poesy,
Though the dull brain perplexes and retards
Already with thee! tender is the night,   35
And haply the Queen-Moon is on her throne,
Clustered around by all her starry Fays;
But here there is no light,
Save what from heaven is with the breezes blown
Through verdurous glooms and winding mossy ways.   40

7. DRYAD—Wood nymph.
13. FLORA—Goddess of flowers and the spring.
14. PROVENÇAL SONG—Songs of the troubadours of Provençal in southern France.
16. HIPPOCRENE—A spring sacred to the goddesses who presided over poetry, art, and sciences (the Muses).
32. BACCHUS—God of wine. His chariot is often represented as being drawn by two leopards (pards).
37. FAYS—Fairies.

I cannot see what flowers are at my feet,
  Nor what soft incense hangs upon the boughs,
But, in embalmèd darkness, guess each sweet
  Wherewith the seasonable month endows
The grass, the thicket, and the fruit-tree wild;   45
    White hawthorne, and the pastoral eglantine;
      Fast fading violets covered up in leaves;
        And mid-May's eldest child,
    The coming musk-rose, full of dewy wine,
      The murmurous haunt of flies on summer eves.   50

Darkling I listen; and, for many a time
  I have been half in love with easeful Death,
Called him soft names in many a musèd rhyme,
  To take into the air my quiet breath;
Now more than ever seems it rich to die,   55
    To cease upon the midnight with no pain,
      While thou art pouring forth thy soul abroad
        In such an ecstasy!
    Still wouldst thou sing, and I have ears in vain—
      To thy high requiem become a sod.   60

Thou wast not born for death, immortal Bird!
  No hungry generations tread thee down;
The voice I hear this passing night was heard
  In ancient days by emperor and clown;
Perhaps the self-same song that found a path   65
    Through the sad heart of Ruth, when, sick for home,
      She stood in tears amid the alien corn;
        The same that oft-times hath
    Charmed magic casements, opening on the foam
      Of perilous seas, in faëry lands forlorn.   70

Forlorn! the very word is like a bell
  To toll me back from thee to my sole self!
Adieu! the fancy cannot cheat so well
  As she is famed to do, deceiving elf.
Adieu! adieu! thy plaintive anthem fades   75
    Past the near meadows, over the still stream,
      Up the hill-side; and now 'tis buried deep
        In the next valley-glades.
    Was it a vision, or a waking dream?
      Fled is that music:—Do I wake or sleep?   80

64. CLOWN—Peasant.
  66. RUTH—See the Book of Ruth in the Bible. With her mother-in-law, Naomi, Ruth left her home and went to Bethlehem.

FOR APPRECIATION

1. What mood does the song of the nightingale arouse in the poet? What words in the first stanza suggest the place and the time of year?

2. In the second stanza do you think that the poet really wants to be overcome with wine, or is he just daydreaming about the qualities associated with wine? Discuss. What connotation do you suppose "vintage" has that leds Keats to choose it rather than the word "wine"? What effect does the inclusion of the proper words *Flora, Provençal, Hippocrene* have? What associations do they carry with them to add to the effect of the stanza?

3. What word connects the thought of the third stanza with the thought of the second stanza? How is the poetic summary of the sorrows of life associated with the nightingale? Keep in mind that Keats himself was very ill.

4. The wish of the second stanza is now rejected. What new means of sharing the happiness of the nightingale is proposed? What common word would we use to express the idea "the viewless wings of Poesy"?

5. The impossibility of sight connects the fifth stanza with the previous one. Why does the poet use the phrase "embalmèd darkness"? Do you think line 50 is a successful line of poetry? Why or why not?

6. What words in the fifth stanza suggest the subject of death which the sixth stanza treats? What is the poet's attitude toward death in this stanza?

7. Why does Keats call the nightingale immortal? Is the nightingale's immortality similar to that implied by Shelley in the last stanza of "The Cloud"? Why did Keats refer to the story of Ruth in this passage? Lines 69, 70 are often chosen as two of the most poetical lines of English literature. Do you agree with such a selection? Why or why not?

8. How is the poet called back to actual life in the last stanza? What is the fault found with fancy in lines 73, 74? Explain the significance of the last half-line, "Do I wake or sleep?"

◇◇◇◇◇

Ode on a Grecian Urn

JOHN KEATS

The eternal freshness and the perennial quality of art—this might well summarize the theme of Keats's beautiful "Ode on a Grecian Urn." The poet's youthful life was dedicated to the search for beauty, an ideal beauty which would transcend the transient human joys and earthly beauties. He saw that art makes permanent what life destroys, another way of expressing the belief that runs throughout his poetry that "a thing of beauty is a joy forever."

One day Keats made a visit to the British Museum shortly after the famous collection of Elgin marbles had been brought from the Parthenon in Athens. One marble vase had a decorative band which showed a group of men and women going to offer a sacrifice. They were playing various instruments and dancing as they went—a happy scene. The vase inspired Keats to compose an ode which has made the beauty of one Greek vase in the British Museum full of meaning to readers of poetry all through the world.

> Thou still unravished bride of quietness,
>   Thou foster-child of silence and slow time,
> Sylvan historian, who canst thus express
>   A flowery tale more sweetly than our rhyme:
> What leaf-fringed legend haunts about thy shape   5
>   Of deities or mortals, or of both,
>   In Tempe or the dales of Arcady?
> What men or gods are these?   What maidens loth?
>   What mad pursuit?   What struggle to escape?
>   What pipes and timbrels?   What wild ecstasy?   10
>
> Heard melodies are sweet, but those unheard
>   Are sweeter; therefore, ye soft pipes, play on;
> Not to the sensual ear, but, more endeared,
>   Pipe to the spirit ditties of no tone.
> Fair youth, beneath the trees, thou canst not leave   15
>   Thy song, nor ever can those trees be bare;
>   Bold Lover, never, never canst thou kiss,
> Though winning near the goal—yet, do not grieve;
>   She cannot fade, though thou hast not thy bliss,
>   Forever wilt thou love, and she be fair!   20
>
> Ah, happy, happy boughs! that cannot shed
>   Your leaves, nor ever bid the Spring adieu;
> And, happy melodist, unwearièd,
>   Forever piping songs forever new;
> More happy love! more happy, happy love!   25
>   Forever warm and still to be enjoyed,
>   Forever panting, and forever young;
> All breathing human passion far above,
>   That leaves a heart high-sorrowful and cloyed,
>   A burning forehead, and a parching tongue.   30

1. Because undisturbed and unmolested, the urn has retained its original beauty and purity.
2. So-called because it has been preserved by silence and time.
3. SYLVAN HISTORIAN—Historian of rural scenes.
7. TEMPE—A valley in Greece, famed for its beauty and sacred to Apollo the sun god.
7. ARCADY—A district of Greece inhabited by simple, contented people. It has become a symbol of peace and happiness.

Who are these coming to the sacrifice?
　To what green altar, O mysterious priest,
Lead'st thou that heifer lowing at the skies,
　And all her silken flanks with garlands dressed?
What little town by river or sea shore,　　　　　　　　　　35
　Or mountain-built with peaceful citadel,
　　Is emptied of this folk, this pious morn?
And, little town, thy streets for evermore
　Will silent be; and not a soul to tell
　　Why thou art desolate, can e'er return.　　　　　　　　40

O Attic shape!　Fair attitude! with brede
　Of marble men and maidens overwrought,
With forest branches and the trodden weed;
　Thou, silent form, dost tease us out of thought
As doth eternity.　Cold Pastoral!　　　　　　　　　　　45
　When old age shall this generation waste,
　　Thou shalt remain, in midst of other woe
Than ours, a friend to man, to whom thou say'st,
　"Beauty is truth, truth beauty,"—that is all
　　Ye know on earth, and all ye need to know.　　　　　50

41. ATTIC SHAPE—The urn.　"Attic" means "Athenian."　Attic sculpture is marked by its
simplicity and purity.
41. BREDE—Decoration.
45. PASTORAL—That which pictures rural life and scenes.

◇◇◇

FOR APPRECIATION

1. Why is the vase called an "unrav-
ished bride," "a foster-child of silence and
slow time," "a sylvan historian"?

2. Do you think the vase really expresses a "flowery tale more sweetly" than
the poet's rhyme?　That is, do you think
you could read as much into the vase as
the poet did?　Discuss.

3. Explain fully the meaning of lines 11–14. Why will the key to your explanation be the power of the imagination? Discuss.

4. In the last lines of stanza 2 why does the poet say the fair youth will forever love and the maiden be forever fair? Is there a permanence about art? Explain.

5. Explain fully the meaning of line 24. Explain the moral truth contained in lines 29–30. Do they aptly express the difference between spiritual and purely sensual love? Discuss.

6. In stanza 4, why will the little town be forever empty? Is there something significant in the fact that the holiday is also a holy day? Explain.

7. In what sense is the word *attitude* used in line 41? What likeness is there in the thoughts inspired by this centuries-old vase and by eternity (lines 44–45)? What *generation* does Keats mean in line 46? Explain the meaning of the next four lines. Do you agree with them? Why or why not?

8. We have seen that the imagination played a great part in the poetic theory of the Romantic poets. Keats is *par excellence* the poet of the imagination. Show in detail how this statement is exemplified in the "Ode on a Grecian Urn."

◇◇◇◇◇

Bright Star! Would I Were Steadfast as Thou Art

JOHN KEATS

This last sonnet of Keats is a piercing cry of grief wrung from the young poet already dying of tuberculosis. While sailing from England to Italy in 1820, he was particularly struck one evening by the radiance of the evening star. He felt that he would never return to England nor see again his sweetheart, Fanny Brawne. In a moment of intense sadness he composed this beautiful lyric.

Bright Star! would I were steadfast as thou art—
Not in lone splendour hung aloft the night,
And watching, with eternal lids apart,
Like Nature's patient sleepless Eremite,
The moving waters at their priestlike task   5
Of pure ablution round earth's human shores,
Or gazing on the new soft fallen mask

4. EREMITE—Hermit.

Of snow upon the mountains and the moors:—
No—yet still steadfast, still unchangeable,
Pillow'd upon my fair love's ripening breast,   10
To feel forever its soft fall and swell,
Awake forever in a sweet unrest,
Still, still to hear her tender-taken breath,
And so live ever—or else swoon to death.

FOR APPRECIATION

1. Explain in detail the imagery in lines 3–6. What is the relationship between "priestlike task" and "ablution"? What is the precise meaning of "No" in line 9?

2. Explain the relationship between line 11 and the moving waters of line 5.

Discuss the emotion expressed in lines 12–14. Is it a pure or a mixed emotion? Explain the phrase *sweet unrest*.

PROJECTS

1. Write a paper or prepare an oral discussion comparing Keats and Shelley as Romantic poets. Which do you prefer and why? Which poet is more objective? What are the differences in their subject matters and their treatment of them? Are the elements of exaggerated romanticism present in one or the other, or both?

2. Compare and contrast the lyric poetry of the Romantic poets with that of the Elizabethan or seventeenth century poets.

RELATED READINGS

Wordsworth's "Ode on Intimations of Immortality" and "Michael"; Coleridge's "Christabel"; Byron's "Prisoner of Chillon"; Shelley's "Indian Serenade" and, for the very mature student, "Adonais"; Keats's "To Autumn" and "The Eve of St. Agnes."

WORD STUDY—ROMANTIC POETRY

The following words have been selected from the poems which you have studied. Endeavor to make them a part of your active vocabulary.

1. Give antonyms for: *transient; spontaneous; serene; sordid; unblemished; colossal; unpremeditated*.

2. What mood do the following words convey? *blithe; plaintive; fretful; hectic*.

3. What particular sensation is suggested by each of the following? *seething; meandering; sinuous; glut; satiety; fettered; sportive; meddling; lure*.

4. Make sure you know the meaning of: *recompense; matured; maws*.

◇◇◇◇◇

A DISSERTATION UPON ROAST PIG

CHARLES LAMB

Before the American Indian introduced wild turkey to the white man, the Englishman's favorite holiday dish was roast pig. Not roast pork, mind you, but young pig—from three to six weeks old—roasted whole with appropriate stuffing and served with a festive apple in its mouth! One who has enjoyed the tender sweetness of a crisply browned loin of pork can easily imagine the delicacy of its baby brother. 'Tis small wonder that Lamb was inspired to rhapsodize in its praise.

In the opening paragraphs, Lamb qualifies as a member of the "tall-

story club." We can see the twinkle in his eye as he gravely recounts the wasteful method by which man learned to cook his food. There's an idea to speculate upon! How DID man first get the idea of cooking his meat? There may be logical flaws in Lamb's explanation, but it makes a very amusing tale.

Mankind, says a Chinese manuscript, which my friend M—[1] was obliging enough to read and explain to me, for the first seventy thousand ages ate their meat raw, clawing or biting it from the living animal, just as they do in Abyssinia to this day. This period is not obscurely hinted at by their great Confucius[2] in the second chapter of his *Mundane Mutations*, where he designates a kind of golden age by the term *Cho-fang*, literally the Cook's holiday. The manuscript goes on to say that the art of roasting, or rather broiling (which I take to be the elder brother), was accidentally discovered in the manner following. The swineherd, Ho-ti, having gone out into the woods one morning, as his manner was, to collect mast[3] for his hogs, left his cottage in the care of his eldest son, Bo-bo, a great lubberly boy, who being fond of playing with fire, as younkers of his age commonly are, let some sparks escape into a bundle of straw which, kindling quickly, spread the conflagration over every part of their poor mansion, till it was reduced to ashes. Together with the cottage (a sorry antediluvian makeshift of a building, you may think it), what was of much more importance a fine litter of new-farrowed pigs, no less than nine in number, perished. China pigs have

been esteemed a luxury all over the East from the remotest periods that we read of. Bo-bo was in utmost consternation, as you may think, not so much for the sake of the tenement,[4] which his father and he could easily build up again with a few dry branches, and the labor of an hour or two, at any time, as for the loss of the pigs. While he was thinking what he should say to his father, and wringing his hands over the smoking remnants of one of these untimely sufferers, an odor assailed his nostrils, unlike any scent which he had before experienced. What could it proceed from?—not from the burnt cottage— he had smelt that smell before—indeed this was by no means the first accident of the kind which had occurred through the negligence of this unlucky young firebrand. Much less did it resemble that of any known herb, weed, or flower. A premonitory moistening at the same time overflowed his nether lip. He knew not what to think. He next stooped down to feel the pig, if there were any signs of life in it. He burnt his fingers, and to cool them he applied them in his booby fashion to his mouth. Some of the crumbs of the scorched skin had come away with his fingers, and for the first time in his life (in the world's life indeed, for before him no man had known it) he tasted —*crackling!* Again he felt and fumbled at the pig. It did not burn him so much now, still he licked his fingers

[1] M—Thomas Manning. The Chinese manuscript is, of course, purely imaginative.

[2] CONFUCIUS—Famous Chinese philosopher and teacher (551–478, B.C.). The allusion is used to give an air of authenticity to the tale.

[3] MAST—Acorns.

[4] TENEMENT—Here, merely "dwelling."

from a sort of habit. The truth at length broke into his slow understanding, that it was the pig that smelt so, and the pig that tasted so delicious; and, surrendering himself up to the newborn pleasure, he fell to tearing up whole handfuls of the scorched skin with the flesh next to it, and was cramming it down his throat in his beastly fashion, when his sire entered amid the smoking rafters, armed with retributory cudgel,[5] and finding how affairs stood, began to rain blows upon the young rogue's shoulders as thick as hailstones, which Bo-bo heeded not any more than if they had been flies. The tickling pleasure, which he experienced in his lower regions, had rendered him quite callous to any inconveniences he might feel in those remote quarters. His father might lay on, but he could not beat him from his pig, till he had fairly made an end of it, when, becoming a little more sensible of his situation, something like the following dialogue ensued.

"You graceless whelp, what have you got there devouring? Is it not enough that you have burnt me down three houses with your dog's tricks, and be hanged to you, but you must be eating fire, and I know not what—what have you got there, I say?"

"O, father, the pig, the pig, do come and taste how nice the burnt pig eats."

The ears of Ho-ti tingled with horror. He cursed his son, and he cursed himself that ever he should beget a son that should eat burnt pig.

Bo-bo, whose scent was wonderfully sharpened since morning, soon raked out another pig, and fairly rending it asunder, thrust the lesser half by main force into the fists of Ho-ti, still shouting out, "Eat, eat, eat the burnt pig,

father, only taste—O Lord,"—with such-like barbarous ejaculations, cramming all the while as if he would choke.

Ho-ti trembled in every joint while he grasped the abominable thing, wavering whether he should not put his son to death for an unnatural young monster, when the crackling scorching his fingers, as it had done his son's, and applying the same remedy to them, he in his turn tasted some of its flavor, which, make what sour mouths he would for a pretense, proved not altogether displeasing to him. In conclusion (for the manuscript here is a little tedious) both father and son fairly sat down to the mess, and never left till they had dispatched all that remained of the litter.

Bo-bo was strictly enjoined not to let the secret escape, for the neighbors would certainly have stoned them for a couple of abominable wretches, who could think of improving upon the good meat which God had sent them. It was observed that Ho-ti's cottage was burnt down now more frequently than ever. Nothing but fires from this time forward. Some would break out in broad day, others in the nighttime. As often as the sow farrowed, so sure was the house of Ho-ti to be in a blaze; and Ho-ti himself, which was the more remarkable, instead of chastising his son, seemed to grow more indulgent to him than ever. At length they were watched, the terrible mystery discovered, and father and son summoned to take their trial at Pekin,[6] then an inconsiderable assize town. Evidence was given, the obnoxious food itself produced in court, and verdict about to be pronounced, when the foreman of the jury begged that some of the burnt pig, of which the culprits stood accused,

---

[5] RETRIBUTORY CUDGEL—A club used for punishing.

[6] PEKIN—Now Peiping (bā'pǐng') a principal city of China.

might be handed into the box. He handled it, and they all handled it, and burning their fingers, as Bo-bo and his father had done before them, and Nature prompting to each of them the same remedy, against the face of all the facts, and the clearest charge which judge had ever given,—to the surprise of the whole court, townsfolk, strangers, reporters, and all present—without leaving the box, or any manner of consultation, whatever, they brought in a simultaneous verdict of Not Guilty.

The judge, who was a shrewd fellow, winked at the manifest iniquity of the decision; and, when the court was dismissed, went privily, and bought up all the pigs that could be had for love or money. In a few days his Lordship's town house was observed to be on fire. The thing took wing, and now there was nothing to be seen but fires in every direction. Fuel and pigs grew enormously dear all over the district. The insurance offices one and all shut up shop. People built slighter and slighter every day until it was feared that the very science of architecture would in no long time be lost to the world. Thus this custom of firing houses continued, till in process of time, says my manuscript, a sage arose, like our Locke,[7] who made a discovery, that the flesh of swine, or indeed of any other animal, might be cooked (*burnt*, as they called it) without the necessity of consuming a whole house to dress it. Then first began the rude form of a gridiron. Roasting by the string, or spit, came in a century or two later, I forget in whose dynasty. By such slow degrees, concludes the manuscript, do the most useful, and seemingly the most obvious arts, make their way among mankind.

Without placing too implicit faith in the account above given, it must be agreed that if a worthy pretext for so dangerous an experiment as setting houses on fire (especially in these days) could be assigned in favor of any culinary object, that pretext and excuse might be found in Roast Pig.

Of all the delicacies in the whole *mundus edibilis*,[8] I will maintain it to be the most delicate—*princeps obsoniorum*.[9]

I speak not of your grown porkers—things between pig and pork—those hobbydehoys—but a young and tender suckling—under a moon old—guiltless as yet of the sty—with no original speck of the *amor immunditiæ* [10] the hereditary failing of the first parent, yet manifest—his voice as yet not broken, but something between a childish treble, and a grumble—the mild forerunner or *præludium*, of a grunt.

He must be roasted. I am not ignorant that our ancestors ate them seethed, or boiled—but what a sacrifice of the exterior tegument!

There is no flavor comparable, I will contend, to that of the crisp, tawny, well-watched, not over-roasted, *crackling*, as it is well called—the very teeth are invited to their share of the pleasure at this banquet in overcoming the coy, brittle resistance—with the adhesive oleaginous—O call it not fat—but an indefinable sweetness growing up to it— the tender blossoming of fat—fat cropped in the bud—taken in the shoot —in the first innocence—the cream and quintessence of the child-pig's yet pure food—the lean, no lean, but a kind of animal manna—or, rather, fat and lean

---

[7] LOCKE—John Locke (1632–1704), an English philosopher.

[8] *Mundus edibilis* (mŭn′dŭs ĕ·dē′bĭl·ĭs)— World of food, eatables.

[9] *Princeps obsoniorum* (prĭn′kĕps ŏb·sōn′-ē·ō·rŭm)—Chief of dainties.

[10] *Amor immunditiæ* (ä·mōr′ ĭm·mŭn·dēt′sē·ä)—Love of dirt.

(if it must be so), so blended and running into each other, that both together make but one ambrosian result, or common substance.

Behold him, while he is doing—it seemed rather a refreshing warmth, than a scorching heat, that he is so passive to. How equably he twirleth round the string!—Now he is just done. To see the extreme sensibility of that tender age, he hath wept out his pretty eyes —radiant jellies—shooting stars—

See him in the dish, his second cradle, how meek he lieth!—wouldst thou have had this innocent grow up to the grossness and indocility which too often accompany maturer swinehood? Ten to one he would have proved a glutton, a sloven, an obstinate, disagreeable animal—wallowing in all manner of filthy conversation—from these sins he is happily snatched away—

> Ere sin could blight, or sorrow fade,
> Death came with timely care—[11]

his memory is odoriferous—no clown

[11] These lines are from Coleridge's "Epitaph on an Infant."

curseth, while his stomach half rejecteth, the rank bacon—no coal-heaver bolteth him in reeking sausages—he hath a fair sepulchre in the grateful stomach of the judicious epicure—and for such a tomb might be content to die.

He is the best of sapors.[12] Pineapple[13] is great. She is indeed almost too transcendent—a delight, if not sinful, yet so like to sinning, that really a tender-conscienced person would do well to pause—too ravishing for mortal taste, she woundeth and excoriateth the lips that approach her—like lovers' kisses, she biteth—she is a pleasure bordering on pain from the fierceness and insanity of her relish—but she stoppeth at the palate[14]—she meddleth not with the appetite—and the coarsest hunger might barter her consistently for a mutton chop.

Pig—let me speak his praise—is no less provocative of the appetite, than he

[12] SAPORS—Flavors, tastes.
[13] PINEAPPLE—A rare delicacy in nineteenth-century England.
[14] SHE STOPPETH AT THE PALATE—Pleases the taste without satisfying one's hunger.

is satisfactory to the criticalness of the censorious palate. The strong man may batten on him, and the weakling refuseth not his mild juices.

Unlike to mankind's mixed characters, a bundle of virtues and vices, inexplicably intertwisted, and not to be unraveled without hazard, he is good throughout. No part of him is better or worse than another. He helpeth, as far as his little means extend, all around. He is the least envious of banquets. He is all neighbors' fare.

I am one of those who freely and ungrudgingly impart a share of the good things of this life which fall to their lot (few as mine are in this kind) to a friend. I protest I take as great an interest in my friend's pleasures, his relishes, and proper satisfactions, as in mine own. "Presents," I often say, "endear Absents." Hares, pheasants, partridges, snipes, barndoor chickens (those "tame villatic fowl" [15]), capons, plovers, brawn, barrels of oysters, I dispense as freely as I receive them. I love to taste them, as it were, upon the tongue of my friend. But a stop must be put somewhere. One would not, like Lear,[16] "give everything." I make stand upon pig. Methinks it is an ingratitude to the Giver of all good flavors, to extra-domiciliate,[17] or send out of the house, slightingly (under pretext of friendship, or I know not what), a blessing so particularly adapted, predestined, I may say, to my individual palate—it argues an insensibility.

[15] "TAME VILLATIC FOWL"—From John Milton's *Samson Agonistes*. *Villatic* means rural, or pertaining to farm life.

[16] LEAR—The tragic hero of Shakespeare's *King Lear*, who gave up his kingdom to his children before his death.

[17] EXTRA-DOMICILIATE—Lamb uses an Anglicized expression in its literal Latin meaning, translating it for the reader in the following words.

I remember a touch of conscience in this kind at school. My good old aunt, who never parted from me at the end of a holiday without stuffing a sweetmeat, or some nice thing, into my pocket, had dismissed me one evening with a smoking plum-cake, fresh from the oven. On my way to school (it was over London Bridge) a gray-headed old beggar saluted me (I have no doubt at this time of day that he was a counterfeit.) I had no pence to console him with, and in the vanity of self-denial, and the very coxcombry of charity, schoolboy like, I made him a present of —the whole cake. I walked on a little, buoyed up, as one is on such occasions, with a sweet soothing of self-satisfaction; but before I had got to the end of the bridge, my better feelings returned, and I burst into tears, thinking how ungrateful I had been to my good aunt, to go and give her good gift away to a stranger, that I had never seen before, and who might be a bad man for aught I knew; and then I thought of the pleasure my aunt would be taking in thinking that I—I myself, and not another— would eat her nice cake—and what should I say to her the next time I saw her—how naughty I was to part with her pretty present—and the pleasure and the curiosity I had taken in seeing her make it, and her joy when she sent it to the oven, and how disappointed she would feel that I had never had a bit of it in my mouth at last—and I blamed my impertinent spirit of almsgiving, and out-of-place hypocrisy of goodness, and above all I wished never to see the face again of that insidious good-for-nothing, old gray imposter.

Our ancestors were nice in their method of sacrificing these tender victims. We read of pigs whipped to death with something of a shock, as we hear of any other obsolete custom. The age of discipline is gone by, or it would be curious to inquire (in a philosophical light merely) what effect this process might have towards intenerating and dulcifying [18] a substance, naturally so mild and dulcet as the flesh of young pigs. It looks like refining a violet. Yet we should be cautious, while we condemn the inhumanity, how we censure the wisdom of the practice. It might impart a gusto—

I remember an hypothesis, argued upon by the young students, when I was at St. Omer's,[19] and maintained with much learning and pleasantry on both sides, "Whether, supposing that the flavor of a pig who obtained his death by whipping (*per flagellationem extremam*) superadded a pleasure upon the palate of a man more intense than any possible suffering we can conceive in the animal, is man justified in using that method of putting the animal to death?" I forget the decision.

His sauce [20] should be considered. Decidedly, a few bread crumbs, done up with his liver and brains, and a dash of mild sage. But banish, dear Mrs. Cook, I beseech you, the whole onion tribe. Barbecue your whole hogs to your palate, steep them in shallots, stuff them out with plantations of the rank and guilty garlic; you cannot poison them, or make them stronger than they are— but consider, he is a weakling—a flower.

[18] INTENERATING AND DULCIFYING—Making tender and sweet.
[19] ST. OMER'S—An imaginative touch. Lamb attended a charity school not, by the way, "over London Bridge."
[20] HIS SAUCE—Dressing.

◇◇◇◇◇◇◇◇◇◇◇◇◇◇◇◇◇◇◇◇◇◇◇◇◇◇◇◇◇◇◇

FOR DISCUSSION

1. Most of Lamb's informal essays, like "Old China" and "Dream Children" are whimsical. His "Dissertation Upon Roast Pig" is definitely humorous; it is a burlesque of a high order. The learned manner, the Latin phrases, the poetic style are only a part of the fun. Discuss the humor and the elements of burlesque in the essay.

2. If you knew nothing of Lamb except what you might glimpse from the reading of this essay, how would you describe his personality?

3. From your knowledge of what constitutes a good informal essay, show that Lamb's essays fulfill these requirements.

4. The subject matter of Lamb's discussion on roast pig is clearly divided into two parts. Make a topical sentence outline of the first part.

5. So beautiful is the rhythm and structure of Lamb's prose that he ranks with the world's greatest essayists. Study a few of his sentences for structure and rhythm.

WORDS

Despite Lamb's informality in the treatment of his subject matter, his diction is heavy and, in some respects, is reminiscent of Samuel Johnson. There is no doubt, however, that he had an amazing vocabulary at his command.

What is the antonym for *mundane?* What does *antediluvian* mean historically and as a figure of speech? *Ambrosian* is classical in its origin. Why? The following words are connotative: *seethed, oleaginous, coxcombry.* Give the denotative word for each. Who is an *epicure?* Give the precise shade of meaning of *nice* in which Lamb has used the word in the third-from-the-last paragraph. What senses do the following words appeal to: *crackling, odoriferous, culinary, manna?* The following words are derived from the Latin. Make sure that you know their meaning: *obnoxious, premonitory, retributory, inexplicable* (note pronunciation), *provocative, insidious, intenerating, hypothesis.*

RELATED READINGS

Compare Lamb's "Roast Pig" with "Old China," "On Chimney Sweeps," or "Dream Children." Lamb is one of the most delightful and personable characters in English literature. You will want to know more about him, especially of his deep devotion to his sister Mary. You will want to read at least one chapter from *Lamb's Life* by the great English essayist, E. V. Lucas.

Further Readings—The Age of Romanticism

AUSTEN, JANE, *Pride and Prejudice; Sense and Sensibility* (fiction)

BOAS, L. S., *A Great Rich Man* (life of Scott)

DE QUINCEY, THOMAS, *The English Mail Coach; Flight of the Tartar Tribe* (essays)

ELIOT, GEORGE, *Adam Bede; Silas Marner* (fiction)

HAZLITT, THOMAS, *Essay on Byron*

* JULIAN, CONSTANCE, *Shadows Over English Literature* (critical study)

* KAYE-SMITH, SHEILA, *Speaking of Jane Austen* (essay)

LAMB, CHARLES, *Essays of Elia*

LOVELL, E. J., *Byron*

LUCAS, E. V., *Lamb* (biography)

MORE, PAUL ELMER, "Drift of Romanticism" in *Shelburne Essays*, Vol. VIII

PEARSON, HESKETH, *Sir Walter Scott* (biography)

READ, H. E., *Wordsworth* (critical study)

THACKERAY, WILLIAM M., *Vanity Fair* (fiction)

* THOMPSON, FRANCIS, *Essay on Shelley* (prose essay)

Brighton Beach, a resort town, in the Victorian Era.

THE VICTORIAN ERA

1 8 4 0 – 1 9 0 0

When the eighteen-year-old Victoria became Queen in 1837, England was confronted with the economic and social problems brought on by the industrial revolution. Feudalism was a thing of the past. The largely
agricultural economy of the sixteenth and seventeenth
centuries was being replaced by a new order. Cloth and
pottery making, once carried on in the home, were being
transferred to the factory. The family, as a closely bound social and economic
unit, was being disrupted by the necessity for finding work in the new industrial
centers.

CHANGING

ENGLAND

Within less than a century the whole pattern of English life was changed. The
invention of the steam engine, the flying shuttle, the spinning jenny, the spinning
mule, and the power loom untied the bonds of English energy. Industry moved
from the home; and hamlets, often within a generation, grew into cities. The resulting expansion of trade served to widen the gulf between the few rich and the
many poor. Factory production brought on an evil time of human exploitation,
child labor, and mass misery.

During this time of great industrial development, living and working conditions
were very bad for the many lowly paid workers. Women often worked fourteen
and sixteen hours a day in the coal mines, crawling on their hands and knees in the
narrow passages, like beasts of burden, drawing their loaded cars. The price of
food, kept high by a protective tariff on some staple products, attained levels almost
beyond the reach of many families. Living quarters were wretched and unsanitary,
as were the factories in which the people labored.

These were the first bitter fruits of the new industrial expansion. Times were
ripe for revolt, but unlike the French Revolution which had been a battle of
swords, the English revolution became a battle of books and legislation.

The social reforms which began in the middle years of the reign of Victoria have
been continuing under varying leadership through this twentieth century. Restrictions in voting and holding public office were removed from Roman Catholics in
1829 and from Jews in 1839. In 1846 the Corn Laws
were repealed. By 1833 slavery had been abolished in the
colonies of West India and in the same year was inaugurated the first important Factory Law, regulating child la-
bor. Trade unionism was legalized in 1864; in 1867 the vote was extended to laboring classes, and by 1885 the third Reform Bill gave complete manhood suffrage to
England. A post office system was adopted in 1839. Almost fifty years later—due
largely to the efforts of William Gladstone—a system of universal state education
was established, and religious tests were dropped from the entrance requirements of

DEMOCRACY

ON THE MARCH

Oxford and Cambridge. Tariff laws that had kept up the price of essential foods had been repealed. Little by little, at the insistence of an aroused public, conditions in charity schools, prisons, hospitals, and asylums were improved.

VICTORIAN WRITERS

The period was a prolific one for writers. Carlyle, Ruskin, Elizabeth Browning, Tennyson, Dickens, Thackeray—these were among the first Victorian writers to condemn the social injustices and the attendant moral degradation of their times. They threw the weight of their talents and prestige into the task of re-educating England to the rights and moral worth of every human individual, to the fact that these are higher values than those measured in terms of money. Carlyle rebuked the English for their smug materialism, crude tastes, and weekly genuflection condescending to God. Ruskin and Arnold urged their contemporaries to pick up once again the continuity of Western thought and culture which had been broken by the industrial revolution. But they relied on art, literature, and culture to produce virtuous living and felt that poetry was an adequate substitute for Grace and revealed truth. Dickens, Eliot, and Elizabeth Gaskell tried to make men conscious of the bond of brotherhood among the poor, while Thackeray held up to ridicule the follies and extravagances of the wealthy class. But prose and poetry alike reflected the spiritual uncertainty, the economic ills, the ethical and moral problems of the day.

While the non-fiction prose of Macaulay, Newman, Ruskin, Carlyle, and Huxley reached a new "high" in expression, Victorian England achieved its greatest distinction in the development of the novel. The men and women who walked out of the pages of the Victorian novel—Micawber, Becky Sharp, Madame DeFarge, Jane Eyre, Hetty Sorrel—have become as well known to the world as the great folks in history. The last years of the century also saw the short story make a beginning in Britain.

Tennyson and Browning were the two great poets of the period. Nothing ever seemed to cloud Browning's happy outlook on life or disturb his faith in the ultimate goodness of the world and its Maker. He was sincere, matter of fact, and healthily happy. Tennyson had his periods of distress and doubt, expressed in the poems written in the middle period of his life, but he worked them through to a triumphant assurance. He was sensitive to the changing conditions about him; thus his thoughtful work over a long lifetime reflects unusually well all that was most significant in the days of Queen Victoria.

OUTSTANDING

POETS

The works of the lesser poets reflect several varying phases or aspects of Victorian England. Elizabeth Barrett Browning began writing occasional verse, then became a crusader in the interests of social reform, and after her marriage produced her finest work in a cycle of love sonnets. The poetry of Matthew Arnold reveals moments of disillusionment and uncertainty about God and external reality. He constantly thought to find serenity but had to conclude that serenity was impossible in the Victorian life he saw about him with "its sick hurry, its divided aims." There was also the group, during the closing years of the century, known as the "Pre-Raphaelites"—men who found inspiration in the simple, imaginative, but primitive art of the days before Raphael. Their poetry was melodious, often medieval in subject, and symbolic rather than realistic. They glorified the ballad form, making of the once-simple folk song a highly artistic, though quite artificial, form of story telling. Their work may be studied in the poems of William Morris and the two Rossettis, Dante Gabriel and Christina. Algernon Charles Swinburne was greatly admired for the musical effects of his lyrics but is now seldom read because of the general lack of substance in his work. And there was the versatile Robert Louis Stevenson, whom some readers remember for his delightful *Child's Garden of Verses* and a few simple songs like "Requiem" rather than for his more pretentious works.

THE SHORT STORY APPEARS IN ENGLAND

The English short story may be said to have begun with Robert Louis Stevenson, when in 1877 he published "A Lodging for the Night." Stevenson was a born storyteller, and to give his talent proper expression he developed a polished style. He has described his method. He studied other great writers, and in self-imposed exercises he painstakingly imitated them. He was a close student of Hawthorne particularly, and most of his stories—like the American's—inquire into the moral nature of man. He was of course also familiar with Poe's technique and theories, with his emphasis upon tone and mood. But Stevenson had his own genius, too— a knack of telling an absorbing story, and a liking for adventure tempered by a knowledge of life and an understanding of people. This combination gives a sense of reality even to a story like "Markheim," removing it from the whimsical fantasy that Hawthorne delighted in and also from the exaggerated distortions of Poe. Stevenson, moreover, had a wide range of interests and a mastery of many styles so that he appeals to readers of various tastes. "Markheim" represents the peak of his work in the short story.

Almost at the same time that Stevenson's stories were winning readers, three other Englishmen began experimenting in the field—Kipling, Barrie, and Hardy; but because all three lived on well into the next century, it is customary to group them with the modern writers. Kipling did most of his work in his early years; and his Victorian period introduced a new scene to English letters—the scene of the British colonial empire, especially India. He sounded a vigorous new note; and his productivity, together with the promise of Hardy and Barrie, meant that the short story was at home in England by the end of the century.

VICTORIAN DRAMA

In the nineteenth century, the theater became so anemic that it was not until the last decade of the Victorian Era that one could be sure it was still breathing. Chief

ALFRED TENNYSON

ROBERT BROWNING

JOHN NEWMAN

MATTHEW ARNOLD

DANTE GABRIEL ROSSETTI

FRANCIS THOMPSON

ALICE MEYNELL

RUDYARD KIPLING

interest lay in revivals of earlier plays. This period has often been called the "age of actors." It was the name on the billboard that mattered, not the play.

In the last years of the century, there arose a new interest in light opera, awakened by the tuneful, hilariously satirical comedies of Sir Arthur Sullivan and Sir William S. Gilbert. Revivals of their operas *The Mikado, Trial by Jury*, and *The Pirates of Penzance* bring perennial delight to American and British audiences.

The three British playwrights chiefly responsible for bringing the English stage back into relationship with contemporary life were Pinero, Jones, and Wilde, who began to write social plays of truly dramatic power.

Sir Arthur Pinero (1855–1934) is probably best known for his tragedy, *The Second Mrs. Tanqueray*. Some of his other works are *The Magistrate, Trelawney of the Wells, Iris*, and *The Enchanted Cottage*.

Henry Arthur Jones (1851–1929), a contemporary of Pinero, first won recognition through *The Silver King*. Then a succession of plays including *The Liars, Mary Goes First*, and *Saints and Sinners* showed a developing power of characterization which placed him among the first-rank dramatists.

Oscar Wilde (1855–1900) also won consideration among the successful modern dramatists with his two plays, *The Importance of Being Earnest* and *Lady Windermere's Fan*. Both of these plays enjoy periodical revivals on the legitimate stages of England and the United States. *The Importance of Being Earnest* is considered by many critics to be the finest farce in the English language. With its crisp dialogue and its travesty on respectability, it conveys a dramatic protest against Victorian smugness.

◇◇◇◇◇

LONDON IN 1685

THOMAS BABINGTON MACAULAY

Writing of Macaulay the historian, a modern critic has said that "no one before had so well applied to literature the happy felicity of representing events in all details, time and circumstance." Concerning history, Macaulay himself once wrote, "It should invest with the reality of human flesh and blood, beings whom we are all too much inclined to consider as personified qualities in an allegory; call up our ancestors before us with all their peculiarities of language, manners, garb; show us over their houses, seat us at their tables, rummage their old fashioned wardrobes, explain the use of their ponderous furniture."

In an effort to meet that definition he wrote five volumes on sixteen years of English history, and the volumes became the best sellers of the day. The famous third chapter of his HISTORY OF ENGLAND, from which the selection below is taken, is representative of Macaulay's pictorial and classical English prose style at its best.

However, it would be untrue to call Macaulay an objective historian. An apostle of Victorian progress (which Carlyle, Arnold, Ruskin, and Newman criticized), Macaulay looked back with contempt from the golden summits of the industrial revolution upon the material crudities of the days of the Stuarts and Queen Anne. In his essay on Bacon, he clearly stated his platform of material progress: "The multiplying of human enjoyments and the mitigating of human sufferings." A rationalist in his thinking (he viewed Catholicism as "the most attractive of all superstitions") and a liberal Whig in politics, he often wrote prejudiced history. Chesterton has said of him "that his reason was one-sided and fanatical; it was his imagination that was well balanced and broad."

The position of London, relatively to the other towns of the empire, was, in the time of Charles the Second far higher than at present. For at present the population of London is little more than six times the population of Manchester or of Liverpool. In the days of Charles the Second the population of London was more than seventeen times the population of Bristol or of Norwich. It may be doubted whether any other instance can be mentioned of a great kingdom in which the first city was more than seventeen times as large as the second. There is reason to believe that, in 1685, London had been, during about half a century, the most populous capital in Europe. The inhabitants, who are now [1] at least nineteen hundred thousand, were then probably a little more than half a million. London had in the world only only one commercial rival, now long outstripped, the mighty and opulent Amsterdam.

Of the metropolis, the City, properly so called, was the most important division. At the time of the Restoration it had been built, for the most part, of wood and plaster; [2] the few bricks that were used were ill baked; the booths where goods were exposed to sale projected far into the streets, and were overhung by the upper stories. A few specimens of this architecture may still be seen in those districts which were not reached by the great fire. [3] That fire had, in a few days, covered a space of little less than a square mile with the ruins of eighty-nine churches and of thirteen thousand houses. But the city had risen again with a celerity which

[1] NOW—The first volume of the *History* was published in 1848. The estimated population in 1951 was 3,348,336 for London proper and 8,346,137 for London and its suburbs.

[2] BUILT OF WOOD AND PLASTER—For this reason the houses and buildings were infested with rats, spreaders of disease. It is interesting to note that after the great fire the city was never again the victim of a great plague such as that which raged in 1665.

[3] GREAT FIRE—The great fire of London in 1666.

had excited the admiration of neighboring countries. Unfortunately, the old lines of the streets had been to a great extent preserved; and those lines, originally traced in an age when even princesses performed their journeys on horseback, were often too narrow to allow wheeled carriages to pass each other with ease, and were therefore ill adapted for the residence of wealthy persons in an age when a coach and six was a fashionable luxury. The style of building was, however, far superior to that of the city which had perished. The ordinary material was brick, of much better quality than had formerly been used.

We should greatly err if we were to suppose that any of the streets and squares then bore the same aspect as at present. The great majority of the houses, indeed, have, since that time, been wholly or in great part rebuilt. If the most fashionable parts of the capital could be placed before us, such as they then were, we should be disgusted by their squalid appearance and poisoned by their noisome atmosphere. In Covent Garden a filthy and noisy market was held close to the dwellings of the great. Fruit women screamed, carters fought, cabbage stalks and rotten apples accumulated in heaps at the thresholds of the Countess of Berkshire and of the Bishop of Durham. The center of Lincoln's Inn Fields [4] was an open space where the rabble congregated every evening, within a few yards of Cardigan House and Winchester [5] House, to hear mountebanks harangue, to see bears dance, and to set dogs at oxen.

The houses were not numbered. There would indeed have been little advantage in numbering them; for of the

coachmen, chairmen, porters, and errand boys of London, a very small portion could read. It was necessary to use marks which the most ignorant could understand. The shops were therefore distinguished by painted signs, which gave a gay and grotesque aspect to the streets. The walk from Charing Cross to Whitechapel [6] lay through an endless succession of Saracen's Heads, Royal Oaks, Blue Bears, and Golden Lambs, which disappeared when they were no longer required for the direction of the common people.

When the evening closed in, the difficulty and danger of walking about London became serious indeed. The garret windows were opened, and pails were emptied, with little regard to those who were passing below. Falls, bruises, and broken bones were of constant occurrence. For, till the last year of the reign of Charles the Second, most of the streets were left in profound darkness. Thieves and robbers plied their trade with impunity; yet they were hardly so terrible to peaceable citizens as another class of ruffians. It was a favorite amusement of dissolute young gentlemen to swagger by night about the town, breaking windows, upsetting sedans, beating quiet men, and offering rude caresses to pretty women. The machinery for keeping the peace was utterly contemptible. There was an act of Common Council which provided that more than a thousand watchmen should be constantly on the alert in the city, from sunset to sunrise, and that every inhabitant should take his turn of duty. But the act was negligently executed. Few of those who were summoned left their homes; and those few generally found it more agreeable to tip-

[4] LINCOLN'S INN FIELDS—The largest square in London.

[5] CARDIGAN . . . WINCHESTER—Great residences.

[6] CHARING CROSS TO WHITECHAPEL—Across London.

ple in alehouses than to pace the streets.

It ought to be noticed that, in the last year of the reign of Charles the Second, began a great change in the police of London,—a change which has perhaps added as much to the happiness of the great body of the people as revolutions of much greater fame. An ingenious projector, named Edward Heming, obtained letters patent conveying to him, for a term of years, the exclusive right of lighting up London. He undertook, for a moderate consideration, to place a light before every tenth door, on moonless nights, from Michaelmas to Lady Day,[7] and from six to twelve of the clock. Those who now see the capital all the year round, from dusk to dawn, blazing with a splendor compared with which the illuminations for La Hogue[8] and Blenheim[9] would have looked pale, may perhaps smile to think of Heming's lanterns, which glimmered feebly before one house in ten during a small part of one night in three. But such was not the feeling of his contemporaries. His scheme was enthusiastically applauded and furiously attacked. The friends of improvement extolled him as the greatest of all the benefactors of his city. What, they asked, were the boasted inventions of Archimedes[10] when compared with the achievement of the man who had turned the nocturnal shades into noonday? In spite of these eloquent eulogies, the cause of

[7] MICHAELMAS TO LADY DAY— September 29 to the day of the Feast of the Annunciation, March 25.

[8] LA HOGUE—The English victory of La Hogue. This naval battle was fought between the English and the French in the war which Louis XIV brought against England in an attempt to put King James II back on the throne after the English had expelled him.

[9] BLENHEIM—The battle in which Marlborough defeated the French in 1704.

[10] ARCHIMEDES (är'kĭ·mē'dēz)—An ancient Greek scientist.

darkness was not left undefended. There were fools in that age who opposed the introduction of what was called the new light as strenuously as fools in our age have opposed the introduction of vaccination and railroads, as strenuously as the fools of an age anterior to the dawn of history doubtless opposed the introduction of the plough and of alphabetical writing. Many years after the date of Heming's patent, there were extensive districts in which no lamp was seen.

FOR DISCUSSION

1. Why are the streets of old London narrow and crooked? How were shops and inns distinguished in 1685? Why?

2. Which period has produced the greater changes—the 165 years between the death of Charles II and Macaulay's *History*, or the century which has elapsed since Macaulay's day? Illustrate by examples.

3. Do the older American cities present problems similar to those of London? Discuss.

WORDS

Give the origin of *squalid* (note pronunciation), and *rabble*. What might be the connection between *harangue* and *demagogue*? What is the difference between a *eulogy* and an *elegy*? Is there any distinction between a *mountebank* and a *charlatan*? Use *celerity* and *impunity* correctly in sentences.

PROJECTS

1. The most obvious characteristic of Macaulay's style is clearness. It has symmetry, proportion, unity, and a sense of value of parts. He does not use the periodic sentence, but a series of short sentences, never monotonous, built up into

a little paragraph. His style has been called "metallic." Select and study at lease five sentences which illustrate these qualities.

2. From your study of his style, discuss orally or in a written paper a comparison and contrast of Macaulay's style with that of Addison and Steele and Lamb and Hazlitt. Tell whether Macaulay writes in the classical or romantic tradition.

3. Locate on a map of London the limits of the City proper. Locate the parts of the city which you have read about in this and other selections: such places as Westminster, Covent Garden, Fleet Street, and Lincoln's Inn Fields.

4. Read Max Beerbohm's essay "On the Naming of Streets." In this essay Beerbohm protests against the rebuilding of some sections of London, with streets being widened, straightened, and renamed. Do you agree with Beerbohm, or do you think modern convenience should take precedence over respect for antiquity? Discuss. Discuss the same problem of retaining old landmarks in American cities.

RELATED READINGS

In the other sections of Chapter III of Macaulay's *History*, you will find interesting descriptions and discussions of the coffeehouses, highways, and transportation methods in the days of the Restoration.

◇◇◇◇◇

(FROM) RANKE'S HISTORY OF THE POPES

THOMAS BABINGTON MACAULAY

In 1840 Macaulay reviewed Ranke's HISTORY OF THE POPES *for the* EDINBURGH REVIEW. *In the introductory pages of this lengthy review, Macaulay wrote a tribute to the Catholic Church which has been quoted innumerable times since its publication. In this passage we see Macaulay's style at its best. Outside of its context in the Essay, his tribute to the Catholic Church is a glowing panegyric. Taken in its context, it is a fine example of how Macaulay, in spite of anti-Catholic prejudice, finds in the Church a splendid subject for his eloquent prose. The remainder of the Essay on Ranke's* HISTORY *evidences, in many places, both an ignorance and a lack of understanding of the history and position of the Catholic Church.*

The subject of this book has always appeared to us singularly interesting. How it was that Protestantism did so much, yet did no more, how it was that the Church of Rome, having lost a large part of Europe, not only ceased to lose, but actually regained nearly half of what she had lost, is certainly a most curious and important question; and on this question Professor Ranke has thrown far more light than any other person who has written on it.

There is not, and there never was on this earth, a work of human policy so well deserving of examination as the Roman Catholic Church. The history of that Church joins together the two great ages of human civilization. No other institution is left standing which carries the mind back to the times when the smoke of sacrifice rose from the Pantheon, and when camelopards and tigers bounded in the Flavian amphitheatre. The proudest royal houses are but of yesterday, when compared with the line of the Supreme Pontiffs. That line we trace back in an unbroken series, from the Pope who crowned Napoleon in the nineteenth century to the Pope who crowned Pepin in the eighth; and far beyond the time of Pepin the august dynasty extends, till it is lost in the twilight of fable. The republic of Venice came next in antiquity. But the republic of Venice was modern when compared with the Papacy; and the republic of Venice is gone, and the Papacy remains. The Papacy remains, not in decay, not a mere antique, but full of life and youthful vigor. The Catholic Church is still sending forth to the farthest ends of the world, missionaries as zealous as those who landed in Kent with Augustine, and still confronting hostile kings with the same spirit with which she confronted Attila. The number of her children is greater than in any former age. Her acquisitions in the New World have more than compensated her for what she has lost in the Old. Her spiritual ascendency extends over the vast countries which lie between the plains of the Missouri and Cape Horn, countries which, a century hence, may not improbably contain a population as large as that which now inhabits Europe. The members of her communion are certainly not fewer than a hundred and fifty millions; and it will be difficult to show that all other Christian sects united amount to a hundred and twenty millions. Nor do we see any sign which indicates that the term of her long dominion is approaching. She saw the commencement of all the governments and of all the ecclesiastical establishments that now exist in the world; and we feel no assurance that she is not destined to see the end of them all. She was great and respected before the Saxon had set foot on Britain, before the Frank had passed the Rhine, when Grecian eloquence still flourished in Antioch, when idols were still worshipped in the temple of Mecca. And she may still exist in undiminished vigor when some traveller from New Zealand shall, in the midst of a vast solitude, take his stand on a broken arch of London Bridge to sketch the ruins of St. Paul's.

We often hear it said that the world is constantly becoming more and more enlightened, and that this enlightening must be favorable to Protestantism and unfavorable to Catholicism. We wish that we could think so. But we see great reason to doubt whether this be a well-founded expectation. We see that during the last two hundred and fifty years the human mind has been in the highest degree active, that it has made great advances in every branch of natural philosophy, that it has produced innumerable inventions tending to promote the convenience of life, that medicine, surgery, chemistry, engineering, have been very greatly improved, though not to so great an extent as the physical sciences. Yet we see that, during these two hundred and fifty years, Protestantism has made no conquests worth speaking of. Nay, we believe that, as far as there has been a change, that change has, on the whole, been in favor of the Church of Rome. We cannot, therefore, feel confident that the progress of knowledge will necessarily be fatal to a system which has, to say the least, stood its ground in spite of the immense progress made by the human race in knowledge since the days of Queen Elizabeth.

◇◇◇◇◇◇◇◇◇◇◇◇◇◇◇◇◇◇◇◇◇◇◇◇◇◇◇◇◇

FOR DISCUSSION

1. Select and analyze two or more sentences of the essay for 1) their perfectly balanced structure, 2) their pictorial appeal, 3) their historical allusions.

2. In what definite sense was this passage from Macaulay prophetic? Discuss. Discuss the thought expressed in the last sentence.

PROJECTS

Make an oral report or hold a class discussion on the growth of the Catholic Church in the United States since 1840.

In Macaulay's time it was the popular notion that all progress, cultural, scientific, or economic, was a result of the Reformation. In such books as *Europe and the Faith, Survivals and New Arrivals* by Hilaire Belloc, and *Progress and Religion* by Christopher Dawson this thesis has been challenged. You may want to read selections from these books and hold a class discussion on the subject of the relationship between Western civilization and Catholicism.

◇◇◇◇◇

THE STORMING OF THE BASTILLE

THOMAS CARLYLE

In this exciting selection, Carlyle reminds us of a twentieth century news reporter as he pours forth his almost incoherent account of the French Revolution. He is a glorified radio announcer, standing, as it were, at the ringside of the battle of the century—the tumultuous eighteenth century. Though the battle was fought and won six years before Carlyle was born, it comes to us hot from his pages as if, instead, he were being borne by the crowd through the streets of Paris, microphone to his lips, shouting to the world the blow-by-blow description of the fall of the Bastille.

"And now, friends, we switch you over to our announcer, Mr. Thomas Carlyle, who will pick up the story. Here we are—"

The Bastille [1] is besieged!

On, then, all Frenchmen that have hearts in your bodies! Roar with all your throats of cartilage and metal, ye sons of liberty; stir spasmodically whatsoever of utmost faculty is in you, soul, body, or spirit, for it is the hour! Smite thou, Louis Tournay, cartwright of the Marais, old soldier of the Regiment Dauphine; [2] smite at that outer drawbridge chain, though the fiery hail whistles around thee! Never, over nave or felloe, [3] did thy axe strike such a stroke. Down with it, man; down with it to Orcus; [4] let the whole accursed edifice sink thither, and tyranny be swallowed up forever. Mounted, some say, on the roof of the guard-room, some "on bayonets stuck into joints of the wall," Louis Tournay smites, brave Aubin Bonnemère (also an old soldier) seconding him. The chain yields, breaks; the huge drawbridge slams down, thundering. Glorious! and yet, alas! it is still but the outworks. The eight grim towers with their invalide musketry, [5] their paving-stone and cannon-mouths still soar aloft intact; ditch yawning impassable, stone-faced; the inner drawbridge with its back toward us; the Bastille is still to take!

To describe this siege of the Bastille (thought to be one of the most important in history) perhaps transcends the talent of mortals. . . . Paris, wholly, [6] has got to the acme of its frenzy, whirled all ways by panic madness. At every street-barricade there whirls, simmering a minor whirlpool, strengthening the barricade, since God knows what is coming; and all minor whirlpools play distractedly into that grand fire-maelstrom which is lashing round the Bastille.

And so it lashes and roars. Cholat, the wine-merchant, has become an impromptu cannoneer. See Georget, of the marine service, fresh from Brest, [7] play the King of Siam's cannon. Singular (if we were not used to the like). Georget lay last night taking his ease at his inn; the King of Siam's cannon also lay, knowing nothing of him for a hundred years; yet now, at the right instant, they have got together, and discourse eloquent music; for, hearing what was toward, Georget sprang from the Brest diligence, [8] and ran. Gardes Francaises, [9] also, will be here with real artillery. Were not the walls so thick! Upward from the esplanade, horizontally from all neighboring roofs and windows, flashes one irregular deluge of musketry, without effect. The invalides lie flat, firing comparatively at their ease from behind stone; hardly through port-holes show the tip of a nose. We fall, shot, and make no impression!

Let conflagration rage of whatsoever is combustible! Guard rooms are burnt, invalides mess-rooms. A distracted "peruke-maker with two fiery torches" is burning "the saltpeters of the arsenal," had not a woman run screaming, had

[1] BASTILLE (băs·tēl')—The former state-prison of France, begun in 1370, one of the strongest fortresses and most dreaded prisons of Europe. On July 14, 1789, the mobs of Paris stormed the fortress and demanded its surrender. The governor of the prison pretended to comply, then had his soldiers fire into the mob and the fight was on.

[2] REGIMENT DAUPHINE—Regiment of the prince.

[3] NAVE OR FELLOE—Parts of a wooden wheel.

[4] ORCUS—In Roman mythology, the underworld, the abode of the dead.

[5] INVALIDE MUSKETRY—The handful of soldiers defending the Bastille; invalide meaning originally a wounded soldier, later, any veteran.

[6] PARIS, WHOLLY—A mob of about 12,000 citizens, armed with whatever they could lay hands on.

[7] BREST—A French seaport.

[8] DILIGENCE—A stagecoach.

[9] GARDES FRANCAISES—French guards.

not a patriot, with some tincture of natural philosophy, instantly struck the wind out of him (butt of musket on pit of stomach), overturned barrels, and stayed the devouring element. A young, beautiful lady seized, escaping, in these outer courts, and thought, falsely, to be De Launay's [10] daughter, shall be burnt in De Launay's sight; she lies, swooned, on a paillasse; [11] but, again, a patriot—it is brave Aubin Bonnemère, the old soldier—dashes in, and rescues her. Straw is burnt; three cartloads of it, hauled hither, go up in white smoke, almost to the choking of patriotism itself; so that Elie had, with singed brows, to drag back one cart, and Rèole, the "gigantic haberdasher," another. Smoke as of Tophet,[12] confusion as of Babel,[13] noise as of the crack of doom!

Blood flows, the aliment of new madness. The wounded are carried into houses of the Rue Cerisaie,[14] the dying leave their last mandate not to yield till the accursed stronghold fall. And yet, alas! how fall? The walls are so thick! Deputations, three in number, arrive from the Hôtel-de-Ville.[15] . . . These wave their town flag in the arched gateway, and stand, rolling their drum, but to no purpose. In such crack of doom De Launay cannot hear them, dare not believe them; they return, with justified rage, the whew of lead still singing in their ears. What to do? The firemen are here, squirting with their fire-pumps on the invalides cannon to wet the touch-holes; they unfortunately cannot squirt so high, but produce only clouds

[10] DE LAUNAY—The governor of the prison. He was killed by the mob.

[11] PAILLASSE—Bed of straw.

[12] TOPHET (tō'fĕt)—Part of a valley near Jerusalem, used for burning refuse; hence, hell.

[13] BABEL (bā'bĕl)—The tower described in Genesis 11:9; hence, confusion of sound, tumult.

[14] RUE CERISAIE—A neighboring street.

[15] HÔTEL-DE-VILLE—Town-house, guild-hall.

of spray. Individuals of classical knowledge propose *catapults*. Santerre, the sonorous brewer of the suburb Saint-Antoine, advises rather that the place be fired by "a mixture of phosphorous and oil of turpentine spouted up through forcing-pumps." O Spinola-Santerre,[16] hast thou the mixture *ready?* Every man his own engineer! And still the fire-deluge abates not; even women are firing, and Turks—at least one woman (with her sweetheart) and one Turk. Gardes Francaises have come; real cannon, real cannoneers. Usher Maillard is busy; half-pay Elie, half-pay Hulin, rage in the midst of thousands.

How the great Bastille clock ticks (inaudible) to its inner court, there, at its ease, hour after hour; as if nothing special, for it or the world, were passing! It tolled one when the firing began, and is now pointing toward five, and still the firing slakes not. Far down in their vaults, the seven prisoners hear muffled din as of earthquakes; their turnkeys answer vaguely.

Woe to thee, De Launay, with thy poor hundred invalides! . . .

What shall De Launay do? One thing only De Launay could have done —what he said he would do. Fancy him sitting, from the first, with lighted taper, within arm's-length of the powder-magazine; motionless, like an old Roman senator, or bronze lamp-holder; coldly apprising Thuriot,[17] and all men, by a slight motion of his eye, what his resolution was. Harmless he sat there, while unharmed; but the king's fortress, meanwhile, could, might, would, or should in nowise be surrendered, save to the king's messenger; one old man's life

is worthless, so it be lost with honor; but think, ye brawling *canaille*,[18] how will it be when a whole Bastille springs skyward? In such statuesque, taper-holding attitude, one fancies De Launay might have left Thuriot, the red clerks of the Basoche,[19] cure of St. Stephen, and all the tagrag and bobtail of the world, to work their will.

And yet, withal, he could not do it. Hast thou considered how each man's heart is so tremulously responsive to the hearts of all men? Hast thou noted how omnipotent is the very sound of many men? How their shriek of indignation palsies the strong soul? Their howl of contumely withers with unfelt pangs? . . . Great is the combined voice of men, the utterance of their *instincts*, which are truer than their *thoughts*; it is the greatest a man encounters, among the sounds and shadows which make up this world of time. He who can resist that, has his footing somewhere *beyond* time. Distracted he hovers between two—hopes in the middle of despair; surrenders not his fortress; declares that he will blow it up, seizes torches to blow it up, and does not blow it. Unhappy old De Launay, it is the death agony of the Bastille and thee! Jail, jailoring, and jailor, all three, such as they may have been, must finish.

For four hours now has the world-bedlam roared; call it the world-chimera,[20] blowing fire! The poor invalides have sunk under their battlements, or rise only with reversed muskets; they have made a white flag of napkins, go beating the chamade,[21] or seeming to beat, for one can hear nothing. The

---

[16] SPINOLA-SANTERRE—Santerre was a leader of the mob; Spinola was an Italian general in the early seventeenth century.

[17] THURIOT—A revolutionary leader.

[18] *Canaille*—Mob.

[19] RED CLERKS OF BASOCHE—The revolutionists.

[20] CHIMERA—One of the mythical fire-breathing monsters.

[21] CHAMADE—Drum signal for a conference.

very Swiss [22] at the portcullis look weary of firing, disheartened in the fire-deluge; a port-hole at the drawbridge is opened, as by one that would speak. See Huissier Maillard, the shifty man! On his plank, swinging over the abyss of that stoned ditch, plank resting on parapet, balanced by weight of patriots, he hovers perilous—such a dove toward such an ark! Deftly, thou shifty ushers; one man already fell and lies smashed, far down there against the masonry! Usher Maillard falls not; deftly, unerringly, he walks, with outspread palm. The Swiss holds a paper through the port-hole; the shifty usher snatches it and returns. Terms of surrender: Pardon, immunity to all! Are they accepted? *"Foi d' officier* (on the word of an officer)," answers half-pay Hulin, or half-pay Elie —for men do not agree on it—"they are!" Sinks the drawbridge, Usher Maillard bolting it when down; rushes in the living deluge; the Bastille is fallen! *Victoire! La Bastille est prise!* [23]

[22] SWISS—Swiss mercenary soldiers hired by the French government.
[23] *Victoire! La Bastille est prise*—Victory! The Bastille is taken.

◇◇◇◇◇◇◇◇◇◇◇◇◇◇◇◇◇◇◇◇◇◇◇◇◇◇◇◇◇

FOR DISCUSSION

1. How would you summarize Carlyle's style? Compare it with that of Macaulay. Which do you prefer? Why? Do you think reading Carlyle might grow monotonous after a while? Explain.

2. Note the scarcity of adjectives and adverbs in the narrative. Why? List ten vivid nouns and ten expressive verbs from the passage.

3. Where do Carlyle's sympathies lie —with the mob or with the defenders of the prison? How do you know? Should De Launay have blown up the prison?

WORDS

Many French words are used in the passage. If there are pupils in the class who have studied French, let them list all the French names and words on the blackboard, give the correct pronunciation and, if possible, translate them. Carlyle also uses a number of words used in war terminology. Make a list of them. Give the word history of *maelstrom, bedlam, chimera*. Be sure you know the meaning of *esplanade, aliment, portcullis*. Give synonyms for *slake* and *immunity*.

PROJECTS

1. Consult a standard encyclopedia for a short history of the Bastille to be given before the class.

2. Charles Dickens used *The French Revolution* as a principal source for *A Tale of Two Cities*. Compare his description of the storming of the Bastille with that of Carlyle. Which do you prefer? Why?

3. Write an editorial on the significance of July 14 in present-day France.

RELATED READINGS

Carlyle has written a biographical and critical essay on his fellow countryman, Robert Burns, which you may use for a book report.

MAN'S USE AND FUNCTION

JOHN RUSKIN

Most of Ruskin's earlier writings contain his theories on painting and architecture. In his MODERN PAINTERS he encouraged the artist to go directly to nature for his inspiration rather than to the studied imitation of other artists. In his two great books on architecture, THE SEVEN LAMPS OF ARCHITECTURE and THE STONES OF VENICE, he extolled the beauties of the Middle Ages and encouraged the construction of Gothic churches and other buildings throughout England.

In his middle years, after reading Carlyle's PAST AND PRESENT, he became a prophet of social reform and joined other Victorian critics in decrying the materialism of the Industrial Revolution. He spent the last forty years of his life lecturing to working men, forming labor guilds, proposing housing projects, and in general endeavoring to make England conscious of something more than material progress. In none of these undertakings was he successful. His contemporaries admired the beauty of his prose rhythms which passionately expressed his zeal for reform, but they turned a deaf ear to his proposals.

It is a strange coincidence of history that while Ruskin was ineffectually crying out against the abuses of the Industrial Revolution, just a short distance from his house a young man named Karl Marx was penning a pamphlet which was to revolutionize the world. Ruskin was too prejudiced in his hatred for railroads, factories, and industrial commerce, which were destroying the beauty of the English countryside and the cities, and at the same time making economic slaves of the English people. He was also too vague in his social reforms to awaken a sympathetic understanding of those social conditions which ultimately led to the Marxist revolution.

However, in SESAME AND LILIES, FORS CLAVIGERA, UNTO THIS LAST, and THE CROWN OF WILD OLIVES, books which developed Ruskin's social ideas, can be found the germ of many of the social reforms which the modern capitalistic world has adopted.

The following passage is a good example of both the strength and the weakness of Ruskin's prose style. His strength lies in his animated and balanced cadences and in his rich imagination; his weaknesses are a too abundant use of words and a piling up of impassioned phrases and clauses.

Man's use and function (and let him who will not grant me this follow me no further, for this I propose always to assume) are, to be the witness of the glory of God, and to advance that glory by his reasonable obedience and resultant happiness.

Whatever enables us to fulfil this function is, in the pure and first sense of the word, useful to us; preeminently, therefore, whatever sets the glory of God more brightly before us. But things that only help us to exist are, in a secondary and mean sense, useful; or rather, if they be looked for alone, they are useless, and worse, for it would be better that we should not exist, than that we should guiltily disappoint the purposes of existence.

And yet people speak in this working age, when they speak from their hearts, as if houses and lands, and food and raiment, were alone useful, and as if sight, thought, and admiration were all profitless, so that men insolently call themselves utilitarians, who would turn, if they had their way, themselves and their race into vegetables; men who think, as far as such can be said to think, that the meat is more than the life, and the raiment than the body, who look to the earth as a stable, and to its fruit as fodder; vine-dressers and husbandmen, who love the corn they grind, and the grapes they crush, better than the gardens of the angels upon the slopes of Eden; hewers of wood and drawers of water, who think that it is to give them wood to hew, and water to draw, that the pine-forests cover the mountains like the shadow of God, and the great rivers move like His eternity. And so come upon us that woe of the preacher, that though God "hath made everything beautiful in his time, also He hath set the world in their heart, so that no man can find out the work that God maketh from the beginning to the end."

This Nebuchadnezzar curse,[1] that sends men to grass like oxen, seems to follow but too closely on the excess or continuance of national power and peace. In the perplexities of nations, in their struggles for existence, in their infancy, their impotence, or even their disorganization, they have higher hopes and nobler passions. Out of the suffering comes the serious mind; out of the salvation, the grateful heart; out of endurance, fortitude; out of deliverance, faith; but when they have learned to live under providence of laws, and the decency and justice of regard for each other, and when they have done away with violent and external sources of suffering, worse evils seem to arise out of their rest; evils that vex less and mortify more, that suck the blood though they do not shed it, and ossify the heart though they do not torture it. And deep though the causes of thankfulness must be to every people at peace with others and at unity in itself, there are

[1] NEBUCHADNEZZAR CURSE—Cf. *The Book of Daniel*, Chapter 4. Nabuchadonosor, King of the Babylonians, was punished by God with the loss of reason; and he was cast out among beasts to eat grass as an ox, because he refused to recognize God as the Supreme Ruler.

causes of fear, also, a fear greater than of sword and sedition: that dependence on God may be forgotten, because the bread is given and the water sure; that gratitude to Him may cease, because His constancy of protection has taken the semblance of a natural law; that heavenly hope may grow faint amidst the full fruition of the world; that selfishness may take the place of un-demanded devotion, compassion be lost in vain-glory, and love in dissimulation; that enervation may succeed to strength, apathy to patience, and the noise of jesting words and foulness of dark thoughts, to the earnest purity of the girded loins and the burning lamp. About the river of human life there is a wintry wind, though a heavenly sun-shine; the iris colors its agitation, the frost fixes upon its repose. Let us be-ware that our rest become not the rest of stones, which so long as they are torrent tossed and thunder stricken maintain their majesty, but when the stream is silent, and the storm passed, suffer the grass to cover them and the lichen to feed on them, and are ploughed down into dust.

And though I believe that we have salt enough of ardent and holy mind amongst us to keep us in some measure from this moral decay, yet the signs of it must be watched with anxiety, in all matter however trivial, in all directions however distant. And at this time, when the iron roads are tearing up the surface of Europe, as grapeshot do the sea, when their great net is drawing and twitching the ancient frame and strength together, contracting all its various life, its rocky arms and rural heart, into a narrow, finite, calculating metropolis of manufactures; when there is not a mon-ument throughout the cities of Europe that speaks of old years and mighty people, but it is being swept away to build cafes and gaming-houses; when the honor of God is thought to consist in the poverty of His temple, and the column is shortened and the pinnacle shattered, the color denied to the case-ment and the marble to the altar, while exchequers are exhausted in luxury of boudoirs and pride of reception-rooms; when we ravage without a pause all the loveliness of creation which God in giv-ing pronounced good, and destroy with-out a thought all those labors which men have given their lives and their sons' sons' lives to complete, and have left for a legacy to all their kind, a leg-acy of more than their hearts' blood, for it is of their souls' travail; there is need, bitter need, to bring back into men's minds, that to live is nothing, unless to live be to know Him by whom we live; and that He is not to be known by mar-ring His fair works, and blotting out the evidence of His influences upon His creatures; not amidst the hurry of crowds and crash of innovation, but in solitary places, and out of the glowing intelligences which He gave to men of old. He did not teach them how to build for glory and for beauty, He did not give them the fearless, faithful, in-herited energies that worked on and down from death to death, generation after generation, that we might give the work of their poured-out spirit to the axe and the hammer; He has not cloven the earth with rivers, that their white wild waves might turn wheels and push paddles, nor turned it up under, as it were fire, that it might heat wells and cure diseases; He brings not up His quails by the east wind, only to let them fall in flesh about the camp of men; He has not heaped the rocks of the moun-tain only for the quarry, nor clothed the grass of the field only for the oxen.

WORD STUDY AND STYLE

Ruskin is a master in the use of figures of speech. Study carefully and explain the meaning of the following: "About the river of human life there is a wintry wind, though a heavenly sunshine; the iris colors its agitation, the frost fixes upon its repose." Select and give the literal meaning of five other figurative expressions.

Do the long sentences which Ruskin uses appeal to you? Why or why not?

Select and study one sentence which exemplifies Ruskin's prose rhythm. In general does Ruskin employ the loose, the balanced, or the periodic sentence? Explain.

Give antonyms for the following: *impotent*; *dissimulation*; *travail*; *enervation*. Give both the literal and the figurative meaning of *ossify*. Is there any relationship between *sedition* and *treason*?

FOR DISCUSSION

1. State in a sentence the theme of the essay. Do you agree with Ruskin's general conclusions? Discuss. Did Ruskin have more reason to write as he did in 1860 than he would were he alive today?

2. What are the reasons which Ruskin gives for his fear that a continuance of national power and peace can lead to moral decay and to the neglect of God? Did Ruskin write this passage during a time of peace? Would the reasons he puts forward be valid today? Discuss.

3. Discuss the thought content of the last paragraph. In what way could it be applied to our own age?

◇◇◇◇◇

Break, Break, Break

ALFRED TENNYSON

When Tennyson was in Trinity College, Cambridge, he formed a deep and sincere friendship with a fellow student, Arthur Hallam. During college and in later years the men were constantly together, and Hallam's sudden death in 1833 left Tennyson heartbroken. "Break, Break, Break" was Tennyson's first cry of sadness at the loss of his friend.

Break, break, break,
  On thy cold gray stones, O Sea!
And I would that my tongue could utter
  The thoughts that arise in me.

O, well for the fisherman's boy,   5
  That he shouts with his sister at
    play!
O, well for the sailor lad,
  That he sings in his boat on the bay!

And the stately ships go on
  To their haven under the hill;   10
But O for the touch of a vanish'd hand,
  And the sound of a voice that is still!

Break, break, break,
  At the foot of thy crags, O Sea!
But the tender grace of a day that is
    dead   15
  Will never come back to me.

1. Can this simple lyric be called an elegy? If so, why?

2. What universal emotion does it express? What details does the poet use to express it? Enumerate. Is the emotion intensified by the use of contrast? Explain. Would you say the author displays a *classical restraint* in the expression of the emotion? Discuss.

3. Lines 11 and 12 are frequently quoted. Can you suggest why? Explain the meaning of "haven under the hill." What is the thought of the last two lines?

4. The rhythm plays an important part in the poem. Why? Scan the first stanza carefully.

◇◇◇◇◇

(FROM) *In Memoriam*

ALFRED TENNYSON

Arthur Hallam, the friend and confidant of Tennyson's young manhood, died in 1833. The event made an unusual impression on the poet because, added to the sense of personal grief, came perplexing questions concerning what had been his fundamental faiths. Why, if there was Divine justice, should a gifted and good young man die? Were the new philosophers right who denied a God with any personal interest in human beings? Was there indeed a human immortality? For years Tennyson wrestled with these and similar questions. And throughout that time he wrote down his thoughts in lyrics—some very short, others of many stanzas. Those that were in any way the outgrowth of his affection for Hallam, he kept together, using for them a special stanza form.

In 1850 there were one hundred and thirty lyrics which he published together under the title of IN MEMORIAM. They show a growth in vision and understanding. The early poems reflect mostly the bewilderment of his grief—

> "O life as futile, then, as frail!
> O for thy voice to soothe and bless!
> What hope of answer, or redress?
> Behind the veil, behind the veil."

In the later ones, he sets his personal experience against the background of universal life and of eternity. And in the end there grows within him a faith larger and stronger than that of his youth, a belief in

"That God, which ever lives and loves,
One God, one law, one element,
And one far-off divine event,
To which the whole creation moves."

The separate lyrics are designated merely by number. They are of many moods, and concern many incidental themes. The following selections will introduce you to some of the finest thoughtful poetry of the last century.

LYRIC 27

If you had to be a prisoner, would you wish that you had never known freedom? Is the animal better off than man because it has no sense of right or wrong? Is it better never to love than to have to suffer separation from a dear one? Tennyson gives his answers to these questions in the following stanzas.

I envy not in any moods
  The captive void of noble rage,
  The linnet born within the cage,
That never knew the summer woods;

I envy not the beast that takes   5
  His license in the field of time,
  Unfetter'd by the sense of crime,
To whom a conscience never wakes;

Nor, what may count itself as blest,
  The heart that never plighted troth
  But stagnates in the weeds of sloth;
Nor any want-begotten rest.   12

I hold it true, whate'er befall;
  I feel it, when I sorrow most;
  'T is better to have loved and lost   15
Than never to have loved at all.

3. LINNET—A singing bird, caged in England as we cage canaries.

12. NOR ANY WANT-BEGOTTEN REST—Rest or contentedness which is the result of never having known a high desire.

LYRIC 54

Is there really a divine and growing purpose guiding the destiny of the ages? Is there a meaning to the sin and the waste and the losses of life? When the following lines were written, the poet HOPED, but he was not confident in his hope.

O, yet we trust that somehow good
  Will be the final goal of ill,
  To pangs of nature, sins of will,
Defects of doubt, and taints of blood;

That nothing walks with aimless feet;
  That not one life shall be destroy'd,
  Or cast as rubbish to the void,   7
When God hath made the pile complete;

That not a worm is cloven in vain;
  That not a moth with vain desire   10
  Is shrivell'd in a fruitless fire,
Or but subserves another's gain.

Behold, we know not anything;
  I can but trust that good shall fall
  At last—far off—at last, to all,   15
And every winter change to spring.

So runs my dream; but what am I?
  An infant crying in the night;
  An infant crying for the light,
And with no language but a cry.   20

LYRICS 126 AND 127

Again Tennyson shows himself to have a touch of prophetic insight. In lyrics 126 and 127, which really belong together, it is almost as if he were seeing through a crystal ball the fury of two world wars and their accompanying changes. Some of the thrones did topple in World War I. But "social justice" was by no means established. Is ours the great æon that must "sink in blood"? Was World War II the predicted conflict? Is there comfort in the faith that believes the outcome will be a new order in which "All is well"?

The first of these two lyrics serves merely as an introduction to the stanzas of the second. Tennyson pictures the spirit of his friend as now "living in God" and thus being able to see human affairs with the understanding of eternal values.

LYRIC 126

Love is and was my lord and king,
  And in his presence I attend
  To hear the tidings of my friend,
Which every hour his couriers bring.

Love is and was my king and lord,   5
  And will be, tho' as yet I keep
  Within the court on earth, and sleep
Encompass'd by his faithful guard,

  And hear at times a sentinel
    Who moves about from place to
      place,   10
    And whispers to the worlds of space,
  In the deep night that all is well.

---

1. LOVE—Tennyson's faith is in a God of love. He made love a guiding principle of his life. This lyric expresses the poet's belief that his friend's spirit lives and forms a bond between this world and eternity.

LYRIC 127

And all is well, tho' faith and form
　Be sunder'd in the night of fear;
　Well roars the storm to those that
　　hear　　　　　　　　　　15
A deeper voice across the storm,

Proclaiming social truth shall spread,
　And justice, even tho' thrice again
　The red fool-fury of the Seine　19
Should pile her barricades with dead.

But ill for him that wears a crown,
　And him, the lazar, in his rags!
　They tremble, the sustaining crags;
The spires of ice are toppled down,

And molten up, and roar in flood;　25
　The fortress crashes from on high,
　The brute earth lightens to the sky,
And the great Æon sinks in blood

And compass'd by the fires of hell;
　While thou, dear spirit, happy star,
　O'erlook'st the tumult from afar,　31
And smilest, knowing all is well.

16. STORM—The social disturbances of Tennyson's day.

22. LAZAR—Beggar. The two extremes of social injustice are represented by the crowned head on one hand and the beggar on the other.

24. SPIRES OF ICE—The artificial distinctions of society—of class, of caste, of race, etc. —which allow a small proportion of men to enrich themselves at the cost of the impoverished masses.

◇◇

FOR APPRECIATION

LYRIC 27

1. How would you answer the first question in the introduction to this lyric? Would the bird hatched in a cage be happier than the one caught and brought from the woods to captivity? Is a pet singing canary *really* happy? Discuss.

2. Do you agree with the poet that it is better to be a man knowing what *good* is, though often falling short of it, than to be like a beast with no sense of right and wrong? Why or why not?

3. In what respect is the man who has seen and lost his eyesight *richer* than the man who has never seen at all? What things can the person born deaf not even *imagine?* In what sense was Tennyson's life richer after Hallam's death than if he had never known the man? Do you agree with the poet in the thought of the closing lines of the lyric?

LYRIC 54

1. Is it true that a long view of events *often* shows that what looked like misfortunes proved to be blessings? Cite at least one example from history. Cite one example, if possible, from your own life or from the life of someone you know. Is the reverse situation sometimes true?

2. Express in your own words the theme of the first three stanzas. Quote, if you can, a sentence from some other book or piece of literature which expresses the same thought.

3. Lines 14–16 echo a thought expressed by what other poet whose works you have recently studied? What feeling does the poet suggest in lines 13–20?

LYRICS 126 AND 127

1. To understand the meaning of these three stanzas one must study the metaphor in which it is expressed. The key is contained in the first line. Who or *what* is

the king? Who "waits in the presence" of the king? Why? What do you think could be meant by the *couriers* of the king? What is meant by keeping "within the court on earth"? Who is the *faithful guard*? Who do you think is the *sentinel*?

2. Explain the relationship in thought between the third stanza of lyric 126 and the last stanza of lyric 127.

3. Mention briefly some of the political, economic, and social disturbances in England during the nineteenth century.

4. At what times before 1850 had heaps of dead reddened the waters of the Seine? To which occasion do you think Tennyson is referring in his "red fool-fury" (1. 19)? How many times since 1850 has the Seine been the scene of war?

5. What reforms does the poet say need to be accomplished? Why does the beggar need to tremble? How does Tennyson think those reforms will come about? Quote the lines with which the poet says the reforms will come.

6. To what extent has history in the last one hundred years proved the poet correct in his prophecies? For example, what *crowns* have fallen since 1850? When did most of them go? Are we any closer to achieving *social justice* today?

7. Why does the "spirit" over-looking the conflict *smile*? How does the underlying thought of this lyric differ in spirit from lyric 54, which was written years earlier? Do you see any indication of growth or maturity in the poet? Discuss.

◇◇◇◇◇

Ulysses

ALFRED TENNYSON

The average reader lays aside the ODYSSEY of Homer with some misgivings at its conclusion. Could Ulysses after twenty years of warfare and of wandering settle down to peaceful domesticity? Would the faithful Penelope remain so charming after all those years of waiting? Somehow the usually accepted "happily-ever-after" ending is threatened in this instance with a number of possible snags. Tennyson, with poetic insight, saw the greatest hazard to retirement in the restless nature of Ulysses. And so this more realistic poet has written a new ending to an old story— or rather he carries on where the older poet stopped. Ulysses is speaking as the poem opens.

> It little profits that an idle king,
> By this still hearth, among these barren crags,
> Matched with an aged wife, I mete and dole
> Unequal laws unto a savage race,

3. METE AND DOLE—Measure and give out.

That hoard, and sleep, and feed, and know not me.   5
I cannot rest from travel; I will drink
Life to the lees. All times I have enjoyed
Greatly, have suffered greatly, both with those
That loved me, and alone; on shore, and when
Through scudding drifts the rainy Hyades   10
Vext the dim sea. I am become a name;
For always roaming with a hungry heart,
Much have I seen and known; cities of men
And manners, climates, councils, governments,
Myself not least, but honored of them all;   15
And drunk delight of battle with my peers,
Far on the ringing plains of windy Troy.
I am a part of all that I have met;
Yet all experience is an arch wherethrough
Gleams that untraveled world whose margin fades   20
Forever and forever when I move.
How dull it is to pause, to make an end,
To rust unburnished, not to shine in use!
As though to breathe were life! Life piled on life
Were all too little, and of one to me   25
Little remains; but every hour is saved
From that eternal silence, something more,
A bringer of new things; and vile it were
For some three suns to store and hoard myself,
And this gray spirit yearning in desire   30
To follow knowledge like a sinking star,
Beyond the utmost bound of human thought.

     This is my son, my own Telemachus,
To whom I leave the scepter and the isle—
Well-loved of me, discerning to fulfill   35
This labor, by slow prudence to make mild
A rugged people, and through soft degrees
Subdue them to the useful and the good.
Most blameless is he, centered in the sphere
Of common duties, decent not to fail   40
In offices of tenderness, and pay
Meet adoration to my household gods,
When I am gone. He works his work, I mine.

There lies the port; the vessel puffs her sail;
There gloom the dark, broad seas. My mariners,   45
Souls that have toiled, and wrought, and thought with me—
That ever with a frolic welcome took

10. HYADES (hī′a·dēz)—Rain nymphs, placed in the sky by Jupiter.
33. TELEMACHUS—Pronounced tĕ·lĕm′a·kŭs.

The thunder and the sunshine, and opposed
Free hearts, free foreheads—you and I are old;
Old age hath yet his honor and his toil.   50
Death closes all; but something ere the end,
Some work of noble note, may yet be done,
Not unbecoming men that strove with gods.
The lights begin to twinkle from the rocks;
The long day wanes; the slow moon climbs; the deep   55
Moans round with many voices. Come, my friends,
'Tis not too late to seek a newer world.
Push off, and sitting well in order smite
The sounding furrows; for my purpose holds
To sail beyond the sunset, and the baths   60
Of all the western stars, until I die.
It may be that the gulfs will wash us down;
It may be we shall touch the Happy Isles,
And see the great Achilles, whom we knew.
Though much is taken, much abides; and though   65
We are not now that strength which in old days
Moved earth and heaven, that which we are, we are—
One equal temper of heroic hearts,
Made weak by time and fate, but strong in will
To strive, to seek, to find, and not to yield.   70

58–59. SMITE THE SOUNDING FURROWS—Row.
63. HAPPY ISLES—The Islands of the Blest, sometimes confused with the Elysian Fields, the home of heroes after death.

FOR APPRECIATION

1. Tennyson said that the poem "was written sometime after Hallam's death and gave my feeling about going forward in the struggle of life more simply perhaps than anything in *In Memoriam*." In the light of this statement, can the poem be looked upon as an *allegory* depicting life as a great adventure? Discuss.

2. Tennyson was a young man when he wrote this poem. Do you think the poet has interpreted old age from a young man's viewpoint? Discuss your opinion.

3. According to Tennyson, what has Ulysses been doing since his return? Is he fitted for this kind of work? Explain. With what feelings does he look back on his years of wandering? Read aloud the lines that give the answer.

4. How does Ulysses think old age should be spent? What lines tell what he hoped to do?

5. To whom is Ulysses speaking from line 45 to the end of the poem? What picture of declining years does he present? Quote the lines with which Ulysses expresses his purpose. Does he have some definite goal in mind? Discuss. With what lines does the poet sum up the spirit of Ulysses? Do you think Ulysses has an admirable character?

6. What do you think is the theme of the poem? Can you find the line or lines that state it?

7. Explain the figures and the imagery

in lines 6–7; lines 15–16; lines 18–21; lines 22–23; lines 50–53; lines 60–61; line 70.

8. Select the lines which have been fre-quently quoted and that could serve as mottoes. Discuss some venerable old men of our present age who hold high positions and carry on in the spirit of "Ulysses."

◇◇◇◇◇

Locksley Hall

ALFRED TENNYSON

"Locksley Hall," one of the earlier poems of Tennyson, is well-known today for the startling prophecies it contains about the scientific, social, and political progress of a future age. Tennyson puts on the lips of a young man—who is disappointed in love and has turned for inspiration to "the large excitement that the coming years will yield"—his own convictions of a better and braver world.

The excerpt given below was often quoted by ex-President Truman during those days when the United Nations Assembly was being established and the vision of peace in "One World" seemed to be a reality.

Men, my brothers, men the workers, ever reaping something new:
That which they have done but earnest of the things that they shall do.

For I dipt into the future, far as human eye could see,
Saw the Vision of the world, and all the wonder that would be;

Saw the heavens fill with commerce, argosies of magic sails,   5
Pilots of the purple twilight, dropping down with costly bales;

Heard the heavens fill with shouting, and there rain'd a ghastly dew
From the nations' airy navies grappling in the central blue;

Far along the world-wide whisper of the south-wind rushing warm,
With the standards of the peoples plunging thro' the thunder-storm;   10

Till the war-drum throbb'd no longer, and the battle-flags were furl'd
In the Parliament of man, the Federation of the world.

There the common sense of most shall hold a fretful realm in awe,
And the kindly earth shall slumber, lapt in universal law.

5. ARGOSIES—Fleets of ships filled with great riches.
14. LAPT—Wrapped.

1. Enumerate and discuss the prophecies in the poem which have become realities.

2. Discuss the thought expressed in lines 11–14 and apply them to the situation of our own world.

3. Scan the poem for its meter and rhyme scheme.

❖❖❖❖❖

The Year's at the Spring

ROBERT BROWNING

In his dramatic poem, "Pippa Passes," Browning presents a little Italian girl from a silk factory, singing as she enjoys her one holiday of the year. Her path crosses those of four persons, each facing a great crisis; and each is helped by the unknowing singer. "The Year's at the Spring" is the song with which Pippa began her day.

The year's at the spring,
And day's at the morn;
Morning's at seven;
The hillside's dew-pearled;
The lark's on the wing;　　　　5
The snail's on the thorn;
God's in His heaven—
All's right with the world.

FOR APPRECIATION

1. What is the dominant mood of the poem? Select the details which show it.

2. Scan the poem. What is the effect of the change of meter within each line?

3. The last two lines sum up Browning's spirit of optimism. They are famous. In what sense are they true and in what sense false? Explain.

❖❖❖❖❖

Home Thoughts from Abroad

ROBERT BROWNING

Homesickness strikes suddenly sometimes. A sudden fragrance on the wind, a hint of rain in the air—and our hearts are miles away! Browning found rare happiness in Italy and in another poem, "De Gustibus," expresses a preference for his southern home. But once on an April day, his thoughts flew to England—England in the spring!

Oh, to be in England
Now that April's there,
And whoever wakes in England
Sees, some morning, unaware,
That the lowest boughs and the brushwood sheaf   5
Round the elm tree bole are in tiny leaf,
While the chaffinch sings on the orchard bough
In England—now!

And after April, when May follows,
And the whitethroat builds, and all the swallows!   10
Hark, where my blossomed pear tree in the hedge
Leans to the field and scatters on the clover
Blossoms and dewdrops—at the bent spray's edge—
That's the wise thrush; he sings each song twice over,
Lest you should think he never could recapture   15
The first fine careless rapture!
And though the fields look rough with hoary dew,
All will be gay when noontide wakes anew
The buttercups, the little children's dower
—Far brighter than this gaudy melon flower!   20

FOR APPRECIATION

1. It is the little details in a picture—whether on canvas or in the memory—that give the touch of reality. Mention the details that make Browning's description of spring in England sound real. What birds does he name? What trees? What flowers? What unexpected bits of detail?

2. What makes the blossoming pear tree lean to the edge of the field with one bent spray? What do you learn in lines 14–16 about the way a thrush sings?

3. How does spring in England compare with spring in your home state? Discuss.

4. With what feelings would an English soldier on duty in Africa or Australia read this poem? Discuss.

(FROM) *Rabbi Ben Ezra*

ROBERT BROWNING

What is failure? How do you gauge it or success? You will find the answers in your Catholic philosophy. This poem of Browning's, put into the mouth of a famous Jewish philosopher and poet of the twelfth century, contains some of the most often quoted expressions of Browning's faith in life and in immortality. The poem is full of a healthy optimism; its central theme is: Look forward triumphantly, for aspiration means more than accomplishment, and the apparent failure may be really high success. The most striking feature of the poem, however, is its estimate of old age; the human soul is immortal, and the climax and fruition of this life on earth are reached not in youth or middle age but in old age. Read Browning slowly, and you will find his expression not too difficult and his thought inspiring.

Grow old along with me!
The best is yet to be,
The last of life, for which the first was
    made;
Our times are in His hand
Who saith, "A whole I planned;   5
Youth shows but half; trust God, see all,
    nor be afraid!". . .

Then, welcome each rebuff
That turns earth's smoothness rough,
Each sting that bids nor sit nor stand
    but go!
Be our joys three parts pain!   10
Strive, and hold cheap the strain;
Learn, nor account the pang; dare, never
    grudge the throe! . . .

Fool! All that is, at all,
Lasts ever, past recall;
Earth changes, but thy soul and God
    stand sure;
What entered into thee,
THAT was, is, and shall be;
Time's wheel runs back or stops; Potter
    and clay endure. . . .

So, take and use Thy work;
Amend what flaws may lurk,   20
What strain o' the stuff, what warpings
    past the aim!
My times be in Thy hand!
Perfect the cup as planned!
Let age approve of youth, and death
complete the same!

FOR APPRECIATION

1. How would you scan the first stanza? What is the rhyme scheme?

2. In the first three lines what relationship is expressed between youth and old age?

3. To whom does the pronoun "His" in the fourth line refer? What is the tenor of His message?

4. What attitude towards difficulties and trouble does Browning express in the second stanza? What is the value of these "rebuffs," these strivings, in their effect upon character?

5. Browning has developed at some length the metaphor of the Potter's wheel: man, affixed to the wheel of Life, is the clay which God molds to his designs. Explain in your own words the poet's message in this third stanza. How are the experiences we undergo, the "things that enter us," given a kind of immortality?

6. In the next to the last stanza, the poet has addressed himself to God, stating his own need of Him "Who moldest men." In the concluding stanza, as given here, what is the poet's prayer? What lines express the poet's yielding to God's will?

Prospice (Look Ahead!)

ROBERT BROWNING

"Faces front!" The crisp command suggests Browning's attitude toward death. His thoughts about it were expressed in the following poem written in the first year after Mrs. Browning had died. The poet admits the instinctive fear men have of this last experience; but he finds in it a challenge, to be met face forward, strongly, gladly, in expectation of what lies ahead.

Twenty-five years passed before Browning's call came. He met it just as he had looked forward to it—a momentary paying of "glad life's arrears."

Fear death?—to feel the fog in my throat,
   The mist in my face,
When the snows begin, and the blasts denote
   I am nearing the place,
The power of the night, the press of the storm,   5
   The post of the foe;
Where he stands, the Arch Fear in a visible form,
   Yet the strong man must go:
For the journey is done and the summit attained,
   And the barriers fall,   10
Though a battle's to fight ere the guerdon be gained,
   The reward of it all.
I was ever a fighter, so—one fight more,
   The best and the last!
I would hate that death bandaged my eyes, and forbore,   15
   And bade me creep past.
No! let me taste the whole of it, fare like my peers
   The heroes of old,
Bear the brunt, in a minute pay glad life's arrears
   Of pain, darkness and cold.   20
For sudden, the worst turns the best to the brave,
   The black minute's at end,
And the elements' rage, the fiend-voices that rave,
   Shall dwindle, shall blend,
Shall change, shall become first a peace out of pain,   25
   Then a light, then thy breast,
O thou soul of my soul! I shall clasp thee again,
   And with God be the rest!

FOR APPRECIATION

1. Browning compares the experience of dying to a mountain citadel to be stormed. Enumerate each detail which develops this metaphor.

2. Is the "guerdon" to be gained in line 11 described in lines 27–28? Explain. Discuss the meaning of lines 15 and 16.

3. Explain fully "glad life's arrears" in line 19. Would you conclude from these words that Browning's life had been a happy one? Explain. Can you cite any examples where the "worst" may turn into the "best" for someone not afraid to face an experience?

4. Note the change of movement in lines 24–25 and 26–27. By the use of what poetical devices is this change brought about? Does the change in movement correspond to the change in thought? Discuss.

5. What lines express Browning's love for his wife? Compare the conclusion of this poem with the conclusion of Mrs. Browning's "How Do I Love Thee."

❖❖❖❖❖

My Last Duchess

ROBERT BROWNING

This poem is a dramatic monologue. The speaker is the Duke of Ferrara. The setting is his ducal palace in Italy during the Renaissance. Read the poem aloud in a conversational tone of voice, as if you were the Duke himself; pay careful attention to the punctuation marks, for the ends of the sentences seldom coincide with the line-endings. The business negotiations for a marriage between the Duke and the daughter of a neighboring Count have just been concluded. Now, about to descend the stairs with the ambassador, the Duke pauses to draw aside the curtain which hangs before the portrait of his latest wife, the last Duchess of Ferrara.

> That's my last Duchess painted on the wall,
> Looking as if she were alive. I call
> That piece a wonder, now: Frà Pandolf's hands
> Worked busily a day, and there she stands.
> Will 't please you sit and look at her? I said   5
> "Frà Pandolf" by design, for never read

3. FRÀ—Italian for brother. Many of the Italian painters of the Renaissance were friars.
5. The Duke offers the ambassador a chair.
6. BY DESIGN—That is, for the purpose of concealing the name of the real painter. Frà Pandolf is evidently a fictitious name.

Strangers like you that pictured countenance,
The depth and passion of its earnest glance,
But to myself they turned (since none puts by
The curtain I have drawn for you, but I)   10
And seemed as they would ask me, if they durst,
How such a glance came there; so, not the first
Are you to turn and ask thus. Sir, 'twas not
Her husband's presence only, called that spot
Of joy into the Duchess' cheek: perhaps   15
Frà Pandolf chanced to say, "Her mantle laps
Over my lady's wrist too much," or "Paint
Must never hope to reproduce the faint
Half flush that dies along her throat"; such stuff
Was courtesy, she thought, and cause enough   20
For calling up that spot of joy. She had
A heart—how shall I say?—too soon made glad,
Too easily impressed: she liked whate'er
She looked on, and her looks went everywhere.
Sir, 'twas all one! My favor at her breast,   25
The dropping of the daylight in the west,
The bough of cherries some officious fool

16–19. The Duke throws out as an explanation for the "spot of joy" the tactful compliments to the Duchess' beauty in the remarks of the painter. He implies his contempt for a woman in the Duchess' position who would be affected by the compliments of such an ordinary person as a portrait painter. See lines 19–20.
23–31. The Duke describes an eager soul that delighted in life.
27. OFFICIOUS—Impertinent, one who should have minded his own business.

Broke in the orchard for her, the white mule
She rode with round the terrace—all and each
Would draw from her alike the approving speech,   30
Or blush, at least. ⌈She thanked men—good! but thanked
Somehow—I know not how—as if she ranked
My gift of a nine-hundred-years-old name
With anybody's gift. Who'd stoop to blame
This sort of trifling? Even had you skill   35
In speech—(which I have not)—to make your will
Quite clear to such an one, and say, "Just this
Or that in you disgusts me; here you miss,
Or there exceed the mark"—and if she let
Herself be lessoned so, nor plainly set   40
Her wits to yours, forsooth, and made excuse
—E'en then would be some stooping; and I choose
Never to stoop.⌋ Oh, sir, she smiled, no doubt,
Whene'er I passed her; but who passed without
Much the same smile? This grew; I gave commands;   45
Then all smiles stopped together. There she stands
As if alive. Will 't please you rise? We'll meet
The company below, then⌋ I repeat,
The Count your master's known munificence
Is ample warrant that no just pretence   50
Of mine for dowry will be disallowed;
Though his fair daughter's self, as I avowed
At starting, is my object. Nay, we'll go
Together down, sir. Notice Neptune, though,
Taming a sea horse, thought a rarity,   55
Which Claus of Innsbruck cast in bronze for me!

34. WHO'D . . . TRIFLING—That is, who would lower himself to explain to such a person that her conduct was vulgar?

41. SET HER WITS—That is, argued.

45. I GAVE COMMANDS—Hiram Corson once asked Browning if he meant that the Duke gave commands that the Duchess be put to death. "Yes," Browning said, "I meant that the commands were that she should be put to death," and then he added after a pause, "or he might have had her shut up in a convent."

47. The Duke intimates that the ambassador has looked at the picture long enough.

48–51. The Duke says that knowing the Count's reputation for doing things in a magnificent way, he has no fear that the latter will refuse the dowry which he, the Duke, wishes, and then he adds that it is, of course, not the wedding gift which he wants but the Count's fair daughter. Do you believe him?

53. The ambassador has stepped back to let the Duke precede him, but the latter condescends to treat him as an equal.

54. NEPTUNE—That is, a statue of Neptune, the ancient god of the sea.

56. CLAUS OF INNSBRUCK—An imaginary artist.

◇◇

FOR APPRECIATION

1. No description of the Duke is given us, yet in his speech his character is com-pletely revealed. What general notion did you receive?

2. What is the outstanding quality of the picture which causes comment?

What feeling on the part of the Duke is suggested in lines 14–15?

3. List the qualities of the Duchess which are commented upon in lines 22–23, 29–34. Does his attitude towards these qualities also characterize the Duke?

4. What do you learn of the Duke in lines 22–26, 43–46, 48–53?

5. The section of Italy known as Ferrara produces a famous marble. Can you now attach any significance to the word "Ferrara" used in connection with the title of the poem?

6. Explain the meaning of the following expressions: *thought a rarity, too soon made glad, let herself be lessoned so.*

7. Throughout the poem Browning has implied that there was a contrast of wills between the proud Duke of Ferrara and his young wife. Unable to dominate her while alive, his sense of possessive tyranny is satisfied by placing her portrait among his collections. In the light of the above statement, can you explain the almost casual remark at the conclusion of the poem: "Notice Neptune, . . ."?

◇◇◇◇◇

How Do I Love Thee

ELIZABETH BARRETT BROWNING

"The face of all the world is changed, I think,
Since first I heard the footsteps of thy soul
Move still, oh still, beside me as they stole
Betwixt me and the dreadful outer brink
Of obvious death, where I, who thought to sink,
Was caught up into love, and taught the whole
Of life in a new rhythm."

There is no over-statement in these lines from the seventh of the "Sonnets from the Portuguese." When Robert Browning first came to see her, Elizabeth Barrett had been given only a few months to live. She had almost stopped writing, and had reconciled all her thoughts to death. Forty-four sonnets tell the story of the transformation that Browning's love brought into her life. The poems were intended for him alone to read. But he believed that they were truly great and should be published. It was a gesture toward disguising their personal meaning that gave them the printed title, "Sonnets from the Portuguese."

One needs to read the whole cycle to learn the story. But one sonnet —the forty-third—is a perfect summing-up of Elizabeth's love. Indeed it is a question whether anything in literature has surpassed these fourteen lines in defining the love that may exist between man and woman.

How do I love thee? Let me count the ways.
I love thee to the depth and breadth and height
My soul can reach, when feeling out of sight
For the ends of being and ideal Grace.
I love thee to the level of every day's   5
Most quiet need, by sun and candlelight.
I love thee freely, as men strive for right;
I love thee purely, as they turn from praise,
I love thee with the passion put to use
In my old griefs, and with my childhood's faith.   10
I love thee with a love I seemed to lose
With my lost saints—I love thee with the breath,
Smiles, tears, of all my life! and, if God choose,
I shall but love thee better after death.

◇◇

FOR APPRECIATION

1. In order to see the full meaning of the sonnet, you must be sure to understand some of the expressions in it, considering it first line by line. What is the meaning implied in the expression, "when feeling out of sight for the *ends of being* and *ideal Grace*"? What word usually covers this human experience? Why is the word *freely* good to use in connection with men's striving for *right*? What is the thought suggested in the line, "I love thee *purely*, as they *turn from praise*"? Do all men and women turn away from praise? What kind of motives do we usually find in people who are not interested in winning honor or praise? Are the emotions of children usually more intense than those of grown-ups? What kind of faith do children give to their beliefs? Is it a true and strong faith?

2. Considering the sonnet as a whole, which lines express the *idealism* that is a part of true love? Which lines express love's kindness and consideration in everyday living? Which lines express the intensity of love? The unquestioning assurance of love? Which lines sum up the range of Elizabeth's love? Which lines express the deathlessness of love?

3. Reread Shakespeare's Sonnet CXVI beginning "Let me not to the marriage of true minds." Note that Mrs. Browning's sonnet appeals to the emotional sense; Shakespeare's has a reasoning appeal. Which do you prefer?

4. For further study of the romance between the Brownings, read *Flush* by Virginia Woolf and *The Barretts of Wimpole Street* by Rudolph Besier.

Dover Beach

MATTHEW ARNOLD

In "Dover Beach" we have an example of the reflective or meditative lyric
—a poem in which the writer presents a chain of thoughts that have come
to him while contemplating some familiar object, some natural scene.   In
this instance, the scene shows a strip of moonlit beach and beyond it the
sea.   The sound of the waves breaking upon the sands has brought in "an
eternal note of sadness" which sets the mood of the poem.   The sea, at
ebb tide, turns the thought of the poet from a contemplation of its own
melancholy beauty to a consideration of the "sea of faith" which was "once
too at the full," and this in turn leads him to reflections on the condition
of the world and his own relationships with it.

The lyric is typical of Arnold's poetry, which is touched with romantic
melancholy.   Such melancholy, when not morbid, may be beautifully expressed; and there is much beauty in this poem.   The emotion here is
one of almost universal sadness, wrung from the depth of a human heart.
It is not a dramatic show of feeling like that—for instance—of Byron,
whom Arnold characterized as bearing through Europe "the PAGEANT of a
bleeding heart."   In "Dover Beach" Arnold is voicing the cry of every
person—Victorian or modern—who has lost his way in the profound
gloom of spiritual confusion, doubt, and flight from reality.   It is the
agonizing cry of one who has lost the key to the riddle of human existence
and whose heart cannot be satisfied until it discovers the End of all living.

The sea is calm tonight.
The tide is full, the moon lies fair
Upon the straits; on the French coast
   the light
Gleams and is gone; the cliffs of Eng-
   land stand,
Glimmering and vast, out in the tran-
   quil bay.   5
Come to the window, sweet is the night-
   air!

Only, from the long line of spray
Where the sea meets the moon-blanched
   land,
Listen! you hear the grating roar
Of pebbles which the waves draw back,
   and fling,   10
At their return, up the high strand,
Begin, and cease, and then again begin,
With tremulous cadence slow, and bring
The eternal note of sadness in.

Sophocles long ago   15
Heard it on the Ægean, and it brought
Into his mind the turbid ebb and flow
Of human misery; we
Find also in the sound a thought,
Hearing it by this distant northern sea.
The sea of faith   21
Was once, too, at the full, and round
   earth's shore
Lay like the folds of a bright girdle
   furled.
But now I only hear
Its melancholy, long, withdrawing roar,
Retreating, to the breath   26

15. SOPHOCLES (sŏf'ȯ·klēz)—One of the great tragic poets of Greece.
16. ÆGEAN (ē·jē'ăn)—The sea lying between Greece and Asia Minor.

Of the night-wind, down the vast edges
   drear
And naked shingles of the world.

Ah, love, let us be true
To one another! for the world which
   seems   30
To lie before us like a land of dreams,
So various, so beautiful, so new,
Hath really neither joy, nor love, nor
   light,
Nor certitude, nor peace, nor help for
   pain;
And we are here as on a darkling plain
Swept with confused alarms of struggle
   and flight,   36
Where ignorant armies clash by night.

28. SHINGLES—Pebbled shores.

◇◇

FOR APPRECIATION

1. Lines 1–6 paint a vivid picture. From what position is the poet viewing the scene? If you were to use this section for a scene in a movie, give the details of the setting.

2. How do the rhythm and the sense pauses in lines 7–14 convey the movement of the sea and the mood of the poem? Have you ever had a similar experience as you stood by the seashore? How did it affect you?

3. Compare the thought expressed in line 14 with Wordsworth's "still, sad music of humanity" in "Tintern Abbey."

4. In what lines are we told that the sea had a similar effect on Sophocles?

5. Lines 21–23 contain a beautiful simile. Explain it. At what precise age in history was "the sea of faith" full? Why and how was the "bright girdle" broken?

6. Lines 25–28 contain a fine example of poetic imagination. Why? Does the opinion poetically expressed there describe the condition of faith in the Victorian era? Discuss.

7. Is devoted love the only solution for lack of faith? What is the attitude of Arnold in lines 30–34? What is the reason for the contrast of "the world which seems" and the actual? Criticize the thought expressed in these lines.

8. Could lines 35–37 be applied in any sense to the historical events of the past twenty years? Discuss.

9. Explain fully the meaning of the following phrases: *moon-blanched land; line of spray; tremulous cadence; turbid ebb and flow; vast edges drear; darkling plain.*

Lost Days

DANTE GABRIEL ROSSETTI

Time is a table of measurement by which we gauge the glory of life really lived, or by which we are judged before the grim accusation of life lived in vain. Our poet faces the specters of lost days as they spring up suddenly before him . . .

The lost days of my life until today,
What were they, could I see them on the street
Lie as they fell? Would they be ears of wheat
Sown once for food but trodden into clay?
Or golden coins squandered and still to pay? 5
Or drops of blood dabbling the guilty feet?
Or such spilt water as in dreams must cheat
The undying throats of Hell, athirst alway?
I do not see them here: but after death
God knows I know the faces I shall see, 10
Each one a murdered self, with low last breath.
"I am thyself,—what hast thou done to me?"
"And I—and I—thyself" (lo! each one saith),
"And thou thyself to all eternity!"

FOR APPRECIATION

1. What different ways of wasting or misusing time are suggested in the first eight lines by:
   a. The trampled ears of wheat?
   b. The squandered coins?
   c. The drops of blood on *guilty* feet?
   d. The spilt water?
From what you know about Rossetti's life, did he *lose* some of his days?

2. In what sense is it true that each wasted day is a "murdered self"? What, on the other hand, may be said of past days that have been wisely used? Can you think of a good figure for a poet to use in representing such days?

3. What, according to Rossetti, will be the saddest reproach for wasted time as each soul reaches eternity? Do you waste much time yourself?

4. Compare the thought content of this poem with that of Edna Carbery's "Mea Culpa."

Up-Hill

CHRISTINA ROSSETTI

Christina Rossetti's "Up-Hill" is a question-and-answer poem. We hear each swift question, then listen to the steady reply. Isn't it always true that the beginner is eager, though fearful, and that the one who has found the way is confident?

Does the road wind up-hill all the
    way?
  Yes, to the very end.
Will the day's journey take the whole
    long day?
  From morn to night, my friend.

But is there for the night a resting-place?
  A roof for when the slow dark hours
    begin.   6
May not the darkness hide it from my
    face?
  You cannot miss that inn.

Shall I meet other wayfarers at night?
  Those who have gone before.   10
Then must I knock, or call when just in
    sight?
  They will not keep you standing at
    that door.

Shall I find comfort, travel-sore and
    weak?
  Of labour you shall find the sum.
Will there be beds for me and all who
    seek?   15
  Yea, beds for all who come.

FOR APPRECIATION

1. What is the full meaning of "up-hill" as it is used in this poem? What is the "road"? Are the words here used in a universal sense? Explain.

2. What is the traveler really asking? What gives us the impression that it is a young traveler who asks the questions? What does Experience—or Knowledge— reply? Try to express the theme or central thought of this beautiful poem in your own words.

3. Show how the dialogue of the poem might be applied to a young Catholic graduate about to start out in his new life. Of whom might he be asking his questions? How might it be applied to a prospective convert seeking the Faith? Discuss.

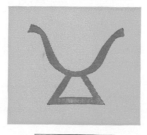

If you lock the door

how am I # Gunga Din

RUDYARD KIPLING

A veteran British soldier, who has seen service in India, tells, or possibly sings this ballad to a group of buddies gathered in the barracks at Aldershot, a famous military camp near London. The dialect is cockney.

You may talk o' gin and beer
When you're quartered safe out 'ere,
An' you're sent to penny-fights an' Aldershot it;
But when it comes to slaughter
You will do your work on water, 5
An' you'll lick the bloomin' boots of 'im
   that's got it.
Now in Injia's sunny clime,
Where I used to spend my time
A-servin' of 'Er Majesty the Queen,
Of all them blackfaced crew 10
The finest man I knew
Was our regimental *bhisti*, Gunga Din.
  He was "Din! Din! Din!
  You limping lump o' brick-dust,
    Gunga Din!
  Hi! *slippy hitherao!* 15
  Water! get it! *Panee lao!*
  You squidgy-nosed old idol, Gunga
    Din."

The uniform 'e wore
Was nothin' much before,

"Gunga Din" from *Departmental Ditties and Ballads and Barrack-Room Ballads*, by Rudyard Kipling, reprinted by permission of Mrs. George Bambridge and Doubleday & Company, Inc.; also by permission of A. P. Watt & Son, London, and The Macmillan Company of Canada Ltd., Toronto.

    2. QUARTERED SAFE OUT 'ERE—Quartered at Aldershot, near London.
    3. PENNY-FIGHTS—Sham battles.
    6. IT—Water. That is, you will do anything, no matter how servile, for a drink of water.
    12. *Bhisti*—Water-carrier.
    15. *Slippy hitherao*—Slide here quickly.
    16. *Panee lao*—Bring water swiftly.

An' rather less than 'arf o' that be'ind,
For a piece o' twisty rag 21
An' a goatskin water-bag
Was all the field-equipment 'e could
  find.
When the sweatin' troop-train lay
In a sidin' through the day, 25
Where the 'eat would make your
  bloomin' eyebrows crawl,
We shouted "*Harry By!*"
Till our throats were bricky-dry,
Then wopped 'im cause 'e couldn't serve
  us all.
  It was "Din! Din! Din!
  You 'eathen, where the mischief 'ave
    you been?
  You put some *juldee* in it
  Or I'll *marrow* you this minute
  If you don't fill up my helmet, Gunga
    Din!"

'E would dot an' carry one 35
Till the longest day was done;
An' 'e didn't seem to know the use o'
  fear.
If we charged or broke or cut,
You could bet your bloomin' nut,
'E'd be waitin' fifty paces right flank
  rear. 40
With 'is *mussick* on 'is back
'E would skip with our attack,

    27. "*Harry By*"—"Oh, brother!"
    32. *Juldee*—Speed.
    33. *Marrow*—Hit.
    41. *Mussick*—Water bag made of skin.

An' watch us till the bugles made "Re-
tire,"
An' for all 'is dirty 'ide
'E was white, clear white, inside   45
When 'e went to tend the wounded un-
der fire!
  It was "Din! Din! Din!"
  With the bullets kickin' dust-spots on
  the green,
  When the cartridges ran out,   49
  You could hear the front-files shout,
  "Hi! ammunition-mules an' Gunga
  Din!"

I shan't forgit the night
When I dropped be'ind the fight
With a bullet where my belt-plate
should 'a' been.
I was chokin', mad with thirst,   55
An' the man that spied me first
Was our good old grinnin', gruntin'
Gunga Din.
'E lifted up my 'ead,
An' he plugged me where I bled,

An' 'e guv me 'arf-a-pint o' water—
green;   60
It was crawlin' and it stunk,
But of all the drinks I've drunk,
I'm gratefullest to one from Gunga Din.
  It was "Din! Din! Din!"
  'Ere's a beggar with a bullet through
  'is spleen,   65
  'E's chawin' up the ground,
  An' 'e's kickin' all around:
  For Gawd's sake git the water, Gunga
  Din!"

'E carried me away
To where a *dooli* lay,   70
An' a bullet come an' drilled the beggar
clean.
'E put me safe inside,
An' just before 'e died:
"I hope you liked your drink," sez
Gunga Din.
So I'll meet 'im later on
At the place where 'e is gone—
    70. *Dooli*—A litter for the wounded.

449

Where it's always double drill and no
  canteen;
'E'll be squattin' on the coals,
Givin' drink to poor damned souls,
An' I'll get a swig in hell from Gunga
  Din!   80
  Yes, Din! Din! Din!
  You Lazarushian-leather Gunga Din!
Though I've belted you and flayed you,
By the livin' Gawd that made you,
You're a better man than I am, Gunga
  Din!

82. LAZARUSHIAN—From Lazarus, a kindly
beggar.

◇◇◇◇◇◇◇◇◇◇◇◇◇◇◇◇◇◇◇◇◇◇◇◇◇◇◇

FOR APPRECIATION

1. What line indicates the subject of
the soldiers' talk before this poem begins?
What contrast is brought out in line 5?

2. Who is the "blackfaced crew"?
What is the figure of speech in line 26?
Is it a good one? Does the comparison
in line 28 convey the idea of thirst?
What does line 45 mean?

3. What were the virtues of Gunga
Din? Did the soldiers like him? How
do you know? What do you think of the
way they talked to him?

4. Do you think the soldier really
means what he says in the last stanza, or
do you think it is just a way an old soldier
would talk?

5. Why is Gunga Din a better man
than the soldier? Do you think so? Why
or why not?

6. What is the principal emotion of
this poem?

7. This poem is a barrack-room ballad.
Can you discover any ballad characteristics
in it? Compare it with some of the old
ballads. Which do you prefer? Why?

◇◇◇◇◇

Recessional

RUDYARD KIPLING

The Diamond Jubilee which marked Queen Victoria's sixty years of sovereignty was held in England in 1897. The power of England, her imperial possessions, her wealth were all subjects of song and story. It remained for Kipling in his now famous "Recessional" to write a prayer for moderation and humility. The two-line refrain at the conclusion of each stanza has become immortal. The poem has been set to music and is frequently heard today.

God of our fathers, known of old,
  Lord of our far-flung battle-line,

Beneath whose awful hand we hold
  Dominion over palm and pine—
Lord God of Hosts, be with us yet,   5
Lest we forget—lest we forget!

4. PALM AND PINE—Representative of the
extent of the British colonies.

The tumult and the shouting dies;
  The Captains and the Kings depart:
Still stands Thine ancient sacrifice,
  An humble and a contrite heart.   10
Lord God of Hosts, be with us yet,
Lest we forget—lest we forget!

Far-called our navies melt away;
  On dune and headland sinks the fire;
Lo, all our pomp of yesterday   15
  Is one with Nineveh and Tyre!
Judge of the nations, spare us yet,
Lest we forget—lest we forget!

If, drunk with sight of power, we loose
  Wild tongues that have not Thee in
    awe,   20
Such boasting as the Gentiles use
  Or lesser breeds without the Law—
Lord God of Hosts, be with us yet,
Lest we forget—lest we forget!

For heathen heart that puts her trust
  In reeking tube and iron shard,   26
All valiant dust that builds on dust,
  And guarding calls not Thee to guard,
For frantic boast and foolish word—
Thy mercy on Thy people, Lord!   30

16. NINEVEH (nĭn'ĕ·vĕ) AND TYRE (tīr)—
The Assyrian empire, after existing as a great
power for more than twelve centuries, came to
an end with the fall of Nineveh. Tyre was a
splendid Phoenician city which was captured by
Alexander the Great in 332 B.C. and never recovered its greatness.

21. GENTILES—Kipling thinks of the English as being God's chosen people of modern
times—the Israelites. Hence, the Gentiles
would be other nations, outside or "without"
God's law.

26. TUBE AND IRON SHARD—Cannon and
bombshell.

FOR APPRECIATION

1. As Chesterton has pointed out, there
is definitely a note of "jingoism" or exaggerated nationalism in the poem. This is
developed by borrowing from Old Testament terminology. Point out specific examples of exaggerated nationalism in the
poem.

2. In stanza 1 what figures does Kipling
use to tell us the extent of the British Empire? In stanzas 2 and 3 how does he tell
us the celebration is over? Explain fully.

3. In lines 9 and 10 there is a reference
to the Psalm "Miserere." What sentiment does Kipling wish to express in the
midst of national exaltation? Discuss.

4. To what leaders of today and the
past decade could lines 19 and 20 be applied? Has World War II verified the
deep truth of lines 25–29? Discuss.

5. Could every American make the refrain of the poem a real prayer? Discuss
your answer.

THE OXFORD MOVEMENT
AND THE CATHOLIC REVIVAL

It was natural that for many unthinking persons, the Victorian era with its numerous reform bills, national prosperity, scientific discoveries, expansion of trade, and gradual development of the English imperialistic policy, should seem to mark the "golden age" of progress. It was largely through the influence of such optimistic rationalists as James Mill and T. R. Malthus that there grew up the belief that every day in every way man was getting better and better. This belief was reinforced by the "findings" of Darwin and the theory of evolutionary perfectibility.

Most of the great writers of the period realized what was amiss—the loss of a spiritual basis for life. Instead of prescribing the only remedy that would be effective, however, they seemed willing to accept any other substitute. But, as Maritain says:

> "Poetry is a spiritual nourishment, but the savour of it is created and insufficient. There is only one eternal nourishment. Unhappy you who think yourselves ambitious, if you whet your appetites for anything less than the three divine Persons and the humanity of Christ."—*Art and Scholasticism*

Man, who had unwisely sought to repair the seamless Robe of Christ by cutting it, now found that he no longer possessed a robe but countless unassorted pieces of cloth. One by one the great doctrines of Revelation had become vague, or had been discarded altogether. Outside of Catholicism and the devoted followers of Wesley's Methodism, the Deism of the eighteenth century had left very little faith in England. It was typical of the "Victorian Compromise" that it was possible to be a Deist with no belief in the supernatural and an Anglican in good standing. The Fundamentalists, the religious group who based their beliefs on the literal interpretation of the Bible, had, in their sincere zeal for reform in government and personal life, done much to awaken men to the need of God in their lives. The "broad churchmen" or Latitudinarians, following the *laissez faire* theory in religious thought, held conflicting opinions but were one in maintaining that what one believed was not so important as how one lived. Finally, the Established Church or "high church" Anglicanism had itself tended to become a tool of the government.

THE "VICTORIAN COMPROMISE"

To some, this decline of Anglicanism was a matter of grave concern. One such individual was John Henry Newman, who in 1833 sailed back from Sicily where he had barely escaped death from the fever. He was convinced that God had spared him to fight the dry rot of liberalism and rationalism that was eating away the heart of the Church of England. So obsessed was he with his mission that even his close friends Keble, Froude, and Pusey, failed to recognize the shy don they had known at Oxford. Newman's zeal was infectious and soon all three were writing against those who wanted to whittle down revealed truths to pure naturalism. Convinced

452

that the Anglican Church was the reformed stock of Christ's Apostolic Community, the Oxford group set out to restate the doctrinal content of early Christianity. A feeling of almost unbearable nostalgia filled the souls of these men when they contrasted the religion and life of the Primitive Church with the church of nineteenth-century England. It was their conviction that these glories might be resurrected and used as a kind of spiritual blood transfusion for the languishing faith.

John Keble's sermon on "National Apostasy" was the match that set off enough spiritual fireworks to startle even the complaisant Victorian conscience. The preaching of this rousing indictment on July 14, 1833, was considered the beginning of the Oxford Movement. The immediate occasion was

THE CHURCH the famous Reform Bill and its aftermath. The Whigs,

CHALLENGED or Liberal Party, were riding roughshod over religion.

BY THE STATE Their latest venture had been abolishing of the ten Anglican bishoprics in Ireland. This was the state of things Keble opposed, protesting that the Anglican Church derived authority not from the secular state but from the Apostles. Here is the recurrence of that age-old battle between church and state which cost the lives of Thomas à Becket, Thomas More, John Fisher, and Edmund Campion.

In a series of famous tracts, the leaders of the movement endeavored to show that "authority" was not in the individual nor in the Bible, but in the "undivided Catholic Church" of the early centuries of Christianity. They claimed that since the Anglican Church enjoyed "apostolic succession" it should be Catholic as well as Protestant. They called their position the *via media*.

But for some, like Newman, this "middle way" was hard to find and keep, and after ten years of leadership, he abandoned the Oxford Movement. It was while engaged in the study of the heretical Arians of the fourth century that the brilliant Oxford scholar came to believe that the Anglican Church stood in the same heretical position towards Rome as had the Arians of the fourth century. He saw that a rebirth of religion in England was not primarily a matter of renewing contact with the past at all. It was primarily a matter of re-establishing contact with the authentic source *in the present*. There was no other road left for him to take but the road that leads to Rome. In his famous *Apologia pro Vita Sua*, he tells how on a rainy night at Littlemore, in 1845, he was received into the Catholic Church. Years later he was to become one of her Princes.

John Henry Newman's acceptance of the ancient Faith of Britain marks the "second spring" of Catholic letters. His conversion was the beginning of an era of great converts to Catholicism, foremost of whom were Henry Manning, later to become Archbishop of Westminster and Primate of England; William George Ward; and Frederick William Faber. Although Newman did not consciously form a literary movement, he did supply the impetus and inspiration to other artist-converts like DeVere, Patmore, Hopkins, and Alice Meynell to turn their search for beauty and truth towards the English Catholic heritage.

Victorian Catholic letters reached its impressive renaissance under the influence and leadership of the brilliant Alice Meynell. She brought together and inspired such Catholic writers as Francis Thompson, "the poet of the return to God"; Coventry Patmore, the poet of wedded love; Lionel Johnson; and Katharine Tynan. Of Mrs. Meynell, Calvert Alexander writes in his *Catholic Literary Revival*, "In her vision the Catholic tradition stood not apart, but in the center of things, in intimate contact with the glories of the European past and the really valuable tendencies of the present, engaged in the work of carrying forward the main stream of Catholic letters. This mark of hers may be seen in the Revival today."

◇◇◇◇◇

(FROM) APOLOGIA PRO VITA SUA

JOHN HENRY NEWMAN

Newman's APOLOGIA *is one of the greatest autobiographies in the English language; and, next to St. Augustine's* CONFESSIONS, *one of the best known spiritual autobiographies of world literature.*

All but the last chapter of the APOLOGIA *are concerned with a detailed history of Newman's mind during his long journey from Anglicanism to Roman Catholicism in 1845. In the last chapter, Newman answers the difficulties to some of the Catholic dogmas misunderstood by his contemporaries. In the passage which you will read, he endeavors to prove from reason that only a religious body invested with the prerogative of infallibility could save Christianity from the deluge of agnosticism, atheism, and moral decay. With prophetic vision he predicted the almost total collapse of the religious and moral structure of the modern world.*

From the time that I became a Catholic, of course I have no further history of my religious opinions to narrate. In saying this, I do not mean to say that my mind has been idle, or that I have given up thinking on theological subjects; but that I have had no variations to record, and have had no anxiety of heart whatever. I have been in perfect peace and contentment; I never have had one doubt. I was not conscious to myself, on my conversion, of any change, intellectual or moral, wrought in my mind. I was not conscious of firmer faith in the fundamental truths of Revelation, or of more self-command; I had not more fervour; but it was like coming into port after a rough sea; and my happiness on that score remains to this day without interruption.

Nor had I any trouble about receiving those additional articles, which are not found in the Anglican Creed. Some of them I believed already, but not any one of them was a trial to me. I made a profession of them upon my reception with the greatest ease, and I have the same ease in believing them now. I am far of course from denying that every article of the Christian Creed, whether as held by Catholics or by Protestants, is beset with intellectual difficulties; and it is simple fact, that, for myself, I cannot answer those difficulties. Many persons are very sensitive of the difficulties of Religion: I am as sensitive of them as any one; but I have never been able to see a connexion between apprehending those difficulties, however keenly, and multiplying them to any extent, and on the other hand doubting the doctrines to which they are attached. Ten thousand difficulties do not make one doubt, as I understand the subject; difficulty and doubt are incommensurate. A man may be annoyed that he cannot work out a mathematical problem, of which the answer is or is not given to him, without doubting that it admits of an answer, or that a certain particular answer is the true one.

People say that the doctrine of Transubstantiation is difficult to believe; I did not believe the doctrine till I was a Catholic. I had no difficulty in believing it, as soon as I believed that the Catholic Roman Church was the oracle of God, and that she had declared this doctrine to be part of the original revelation. It is difficult, impossible, to imagine, I grant;—but how is it difficult to believe? Yet Macaulay thought it so difficult to believe, that he had need of a believer in it of talents as eminent as Sir Thomas More, before he could bring himself to conceive that the Catholics of an enlightened age could resist "the overwhelming force of the argument against it." "Sir Thomas More," he says, "is one of the choice specimens of wisdom and virtue; and the doctrine of Transubstantiation is a kind of proof charge. A faith which stands that test, will stand any test." But for myself, I cannot indeed prove it, I cannot tell *how* it is; but I say, "Why should it not be? What's to hinder it? And, in like manner, of that majestic Article of the Anglican as well as of the Catholic Creed,—the doctrine of the Trinity in Unity. What do I know of the Essence of the Divine Being? I know that my abstract idea of three is simply incompatible with my idea of one; but when I come to the question of concrete fact, I have no means of proving that there is not a sense in which one and three can equally be predicated of the Incommunicable God.

Starting then with the being of a God (which, as I have said, is as certain to me as the certainty of my own existence, though when I try to put the grounds of that certainty into logical shape I find a difficulty in doing so in mood and figure to my satisfaction,) I look out of myself into the world of men, and there I see a sight which fills me with unspeakable distress. The world seems simply to give the lie to that great truth, of which my whole being is so full; and the effect upon me is, in consequence, as a matter of necessity, as confusing as if it denied that I am in existence myself. If I looked into a mirror, and did not see my face, I should have the sort of feeling which actually comes upon me, when I look into this living busy world, and see no reflexion of its Creator. This is, to me, one of those great difficulties of this absolute primary truth, to which I referred just now.

To consider the world in its length

and breadth, its various history, the many races of man, their starts, their fortunes, their mutual alienation, their conflicts; the greatness and littleness of man, his far-reaching aims, his short duration, the curtain hung over his futurity, the disappointments of life, the defeat of good, the success of evil, physical pain, mental anguish, the prevalence and intensity of sin, the pervading idolatries, the corruptions, the dreary hopeless irreligion, that condition of the whole race, so fearfully yet exactly described in the Apostle's words, "having no hope and without God in the world," —all this is a vision to dizzy and appal: and inflicts upon the mind the sense of a profound mystery, which is absolutely beyond human solution.

And in these latter days, in like manner, outside the Catholic Church things are tending,—with far greater rapidity than in that old time from the circumstance of the age,—to atheism in one shape or other. What a scene, what a prospect, does the whole of Europe present at this day! and not only Europe, but every government and every civilization through the world, which is under the influence of the European mind! Especially, for it most concerns us, how sorrowful, in the view of religion, even taken in its most elementary, most attenuated form, is the spectacle presented to us by the educated intellect of England, France, and Germany!

What shall be said to this heart-piercing, reason-bewildering fact? I can only answer, that either there is no Creator, or this living society of men is in a true sense discarded from His presence. Did I see a boy of good make and mind, with the tokens on him of a refined nature, cast upon the world without provision, unable to say whence he came, his birthplace or his family connexions, I should conclude that there was some mystery connected with his history, and that he was one, of whom, from one cause or other, his parents were ashamed. Thus

only should I be able to account for the contrast between the promise and the condition of his being. And so I argue about the world;—*if* there be a God, *since* there is a God, the human race is implicated in some terrible aboriginal calamity. It is out of joint with the purposes of its Creator. This is a fact, a fact as true as the fact of its existence; and thus the doctrine of what is theologically called original sin becomes to me almost as certain as that the world exists, and as the existence of God.

And now, supposing it were the blessed and loving will of the Creator to interfere in this anarchical condition of things, what are we to suppose would be the methods which might be necessarily or naturally involved in His purpose of mercy? Since the world is in so abnormal a state, surely it would be no surprise to me, if the interposition were of necessity equally extraordinary—or what is called miraculous. The necessity of some form of religion for the interests of humanity, has been generally acknowledged; but where was the concrete representative of things invisible, which would have the force and the toughness necessary to be a breakwater against the deluge? Three centuries ago the establishment of religion, material, legal, and social, was generally adopted as the best expedient for the purpose, in those countries which separated from the Catholic Church; and for a long time it was successful; but now the crevices of those establishments are admitting the enemy. Thirty years ago, education was relied upon: ten years ago there was a hope that wars would cease for ever, under the influence of commercial enterprise and the reign of the useful and fine arts; but will any one venture to say that there is any thing any where on this earth, which will afford a fulcrum for us,

whereby to keep the earth from moving onwards?

Supposing then it to be the Will of the Creator to interfere in human affairs, and to make provisions for retaining in the world a knowledge of Himself, so definite and distinct as to be proof against the energy of human scepticism, in such a case,—I am far from saying that there was no other way,—but there is nothing to surprise the mind, if He should think fit to introduce a power into the world, invested with the prerogative of infallibility in religious matters. Such a provision would be a direct, immediate, active, and prompt means of withstanding the difficulty; it would be an instrument suited to the need; and, when I find that this is the very claim of the Catholic Church, not only do I feel no difficulty in admitting the idea, but there is a fitness in it, which recommends it to my mind. And thus I am brought to speak of the Church's infallibility, as a provision, adapted by the mercy of the Creator, to preserve religion in the world, and to restrain that freedom of thought, which of course in itself is one of the greatest of our natural gifts, and to rescue it from its own suicidal excesses.

◇◇◇◇◇◇◇◇◇◇◇◇◇◇◇◇◇◇◇◇◇◇◇◇◇◇◇◇◇

WORD STUDY AND STYLE

Is the diction used by Newman predominantly of Latin or Anglo-Saxon origin? Could you explain the reason for Newman's choice of words? Are the words, for the most part, denotative or connotative? Again, can you defend Newman's choice?

Give the definition of *incompatible* and *attenuated*. Also, define *prerogative* and *infallibility*.

Give three adjectives which would best describe Newman's style. Illustrate your choice of adjectives from one passage of the autobiography.

FOR DISCUSSION

1. What were Newman's reactions upon becoming a Roman Catholic? Would his reactions differ, perhaps, from those of a converted atheist? Discuss.

2. Discuss Newman's statement: "Ten thousand difficulties do not make a doubt. . . . Difficulty and doubt are incommensurate." Discuss the application of the above statement to his treatment of the difficulty of Transubstantiation.

3. Outline the points which Newman puts forward to prove the fact of "some terrible aboriginal calamity," or original sin.

4. Outline the arguments which he proposes to prove the necessity of a "power invested with the prerogative of infallibility in religious matters."

5. Could the thoughts expressed in paragraph 6 be well applied to our present day world? Explain.

(FROM) *THE IDEA OF A UNIVERSITY*

Newman's *The Idea of a University* belongs "to the literature of all time." In his lucidly logical style of liquid rhythms and stately balanced expressions, Newman proposed his theory of education which, in his own day, was an answer to the growing utilitarian concept of education; which was to serve as the ideal of the Catholic University of Ireland which he was invited to establish; and which, in our own day, still serves as a blueprint for a liberal education.

His *Idea* is expressed in the published lectures given at the Irish university. Newman's ambition was to produce an intelligent Irish laity, such as he had outlined on a previous occasion in his *The Present Position of Catholics in England*. He said: "I want a laity, not arrogant, not rash in speech, not disputatious, but men who know their religion, who enter into it, who know just where they stand, who know what they hold, and what they do not, who know their creed so well, that they can give an account of it, who know so much of history that they can defend it. I want an intelligent, well-instructed laity."

Newman could not envisage a university in which religion, science, and literature did not flourish side by side. He insisted that a university was not a university which did not teach theology and religion. Since a university is supposed to teach universal knowledge, its curriculum must include theology, because theology gives "unity and coherence to all our knowledge in the light of ultimate ends." Newman was opposed to purely secular education for the simple fact that it was not complete education. Knowledge of the whole truth is the primary aim of education, but we cannot know the *whole* truth unless we also know revealed truths.

Newman, however, was certainly opposed to making a university into a "glorified theological school" or seminary. He insisted that all his students be acquainted with secular literature and science for, as he states in his essay on "Literature and Life," "we educate . . . to prepare for the world."

Newman's concept of education differs radically from that of educators who see little value in the mental discipline of the traditional subjects, and who would make the primary end of education *social adjustment* or the direct preparation for life. Newman would certainly deny that the prime object of education is "educating for freedom" or "making enlightened citizens for Democracy." He certainly held that "good citizenship" would be a natural by-product of any sound program of liberal education.

For Newman, education was not "the loading of the memory with a mass of undigested facts"; it was not "a smattering in a dozen branches of study"; it was not "learning without exertion, without attention, and without toil." Education was not "dancing and fencing," "stuffing birds or playing string instruments." In the final analysis, Newman held that, although education can help, its prime purpose is not the making of saints. An education is not "a guarantee of sanctity . . . it makes not the Christian, not the Catholic, but the gentleman."

Excerpts from *The Idea of a University* are given below: the first is taken from his lecture "Knowledge and Professional Skill" and the second from "Duties of the Church Towards Knowledge."

◇◆◇◆◇

THE PURPOSE OF
A LIBERAL EDUCATION

JOHN HENRY NEWMAN

Today I have confined myself to saying that that training of the intellect, which is best for the individual himself, best enables him to discharge his duties to society. The Philosopher, indeed, and the man of the world differ in their very notion, but the methods, by which they are respectively formed, are pretty much the same. The Philosopher has the same command of matters of thought, which the true citizen and gentleman has of matters of business and conduct. If then a practical end must be assigned to a University course, I say it is that of training good members of society. Its art is the art of social life, and its end is fitness for the world. It neither confines its views to particular professions on the one hand, nor creates heroes or inspires genius on the other. Works indeed of genius fall under no art; heroic minds come under no rule; a University is not a birthplace of poets or of immortal authors, of founders of schools, leaders of colonies, or conquerors of nations. It does not promise a generation of Aristotles or Newtons, or Napoleons or Washingtons, of Raphaels or Shakespeares, though such miracles of nature it has before now contained within its precincts. Nor is it content on the other hand with forming the critic or the experimentalist, the economist or the engineer, though such too it includes within its scope. [But a University training is the great ordinary means to a great but ordinary end;] it aims at raising the intellectual tone of society, at cultivating the public mind, at purifying the national taste, at supplying true principles to popular enthusiasm and fixed aims to popular aspiration, at giving enlargement and sobriety to the ideas of the age, at facilitating the exercise of political power, and refining the intercourse of private life. It is the education which gives a man a clear conscious view of his own opinions and judgments, a truth in developing them, an eloquence in expressing them, and a force in urging them. It teaches him to see things as they are, to go right to the point, to disentangle a skein of thought, to detect what is sophistical, and to discard what is irrelevant. It prepares him to fill any post with credit, and to master any subject with facility. It shows him how to accommodate himself to others, how to throw himself into their state of mind, how to bring before them his own, how to influence them, how to come to an understanding with them, how to bear with them. He is at home in any society, he has common ground with every class; he knows when to speak and when to be silent; he is able to converse, he is able to listen; he can ask a question pertinently, and gain a lesson seasonably, when he has noth-

ing to impart himself; he is ever ready, yet never in the way; he is a pleasant companion, and a comrade you can depend upon; he knows when to be serious and when to trifle, and he has a sure tact which enables him to trifle with gracefulness and to be serious with effect. He has the repose of a mind which lives in itself, while it lives in the world, and which has resources for its happiness at home when it cannot go abroad. He has a gift which serves him in public, and supports him in retirement, without which good fortune is but vulgar, and with which failure and disappointment have a charm. The art which tends to make a man all this, is in the object which it pursues as useful as the art of wealth or the art of health, though it is less susceptible of method, and less tangible, less certain, less complete in its result.

◇◇◇◇◇◇◇◇◇◇◇◇◇◇◇◇◇◇◇◇◇◇◇◇◇◇◇◇◇◇◇

FOR DISCUSSION

1. According to Newman, what is the practical end of a liberal education? Enumerate the specific advantages of a liberal education as given by Newman to develop this statement: "A university training is the great ordinary means to a great but ordinary end."

2. Do you agree with any or all of these purposes? Discuss. Do you think that they are important in the world today?

LITERATURE AND LIFE

JOHN HENRY NEWMAN

Literature stands related to Man as Science stands to Nature; it is his history. Man is a being of genius, passion, intellect, conscience, power. He exercises these various gifts in various ways, in great deeds, in great thoughts, in heroic acts, in hateful crimes. He founds states, he fights battles, he builds cities, he ploughs the forest, he subdues the elements, he rules his kind. He creates vast ideas, and influences many generations. Literature records them all.

He pours out his fervid soul in poetry; he soars, he dives in his restless speculations; he touches the canvas and it glows with beauty; he sweeps the strings, and they thrill with ecstatic meaning. He looks back into himself, and he reads his own thoughts, and notes them down. All this constitutes his life; of all this Literature is the expression; so that Literature is to man in some sort what autobiography is to the individual; it is his Life and Remains.

Man will never continue in a mere state of innocence; he is sure to sin, and his literature will be the expression of his sin, and this whether he be heathen or Christian. It is a contradiction in terms to attempt a sinless Literature of sinful man. You may gather together something very great and very high; something higher than any Literature ever was; and when you have done so, you will find that it is not Literature at all. You will simply have left the delineation of man, as such, and have substituted for it, as far as you have had anything to substitute, that of man, as

he is or might be, under certain special advantages. Not till the whole human race is made new will its literature be pure and true. Possible of course it is in idea, for nature, inspired by heavenly grace, to exhibit itself on a large scale, in an originality of thought or action, even far beyond what the world's literature has recorded or exemplified; but, if you would in fact have a literature of saints, first of all have a nation of them. If then by Literature is meant the manifestation of human nature in human language, you will seek for it in vain except in the world. Put up with it, as it is, or do not pretend to cultivate it; take things as they are, not as you could wish them.

Nay, I am obliged to go further still; even if we could, still we should be shrinking from our plain duty, Gentlemen, did we leave out Literature from Education. For why do we educate, except to prepare for the world? Why do we cultivate the intellect of the many beyond the first elements of knowledge, except for this world? Will it be much matter in the world to come whether our bodily health or whether our intellectual strength was more or less, except of course as this world is in all its circumstances a trial for the next? If then a University is a direct preparation for this world, let it be what it professes. It is not a Convent, it is not a Seminary; it is a place to fit men of the world for the world. We cannot possibly keep them from plunging into the world, with all its ways and principles and maxims, when their time comes; but we can prepare them against what is inevitable; and it is not the way to learn to swim in troubled waters, never to have gone into them. Proscribe (I do not merely say particular authors, particular works, particular passages) but Secular Literature as such; cut out from your class books all broad manifestations of the natural man; and those manifestations are waiting for your pupil's benefit at the very doors of your lecture room in living and breathing substance. They will meet him there in all the charm of novelty, and all the fascination of genius or of amiableness. Today a pupil, tomorrow a member of the great world: today confined to the Lives of the Saints, tomorrow thrown upon Babel;—thrown on Babel, without the honest indulgence of wit and humour and imagination having ever been permitted to him, without any fastidiousness of taste wrought into him, without any rule given him for discriminating "the precious from the vile," beauty from sin, the truth from the sophistry of nature, what is innocent from what is poison. You have refused him the masters of human thought who would in some sense have educated him, because of their incidental corruption: you have shut up from him those whose thoughts strike home to our hearts, whose words are proverbs, whose names are indigenous to all the world, who are the standard of their mother tongue, and the pride and boast of their countrymen, Homer, Ariosto, Cervantes, Shakespeare, because the old Adam smelt rank in them; and for what have you reserved him? You have given him "a liberty unto" the multitudinous blasphemy of his day; you have made him free of its newspapers, its reviews, its magazines, its novels, its controversial pamphlets, of its Parliamentary debates, its law proceedings, its platform speeches, its songs, its drama, its theatre, of its enveloping, stifling atmosphere of death. You have succeeded but in this,—in making the world his University.

FOR DISCUSSION

1. In what specific ways is Literature man's "Life and Remains"? Could we have civilization without literature? Or literature without civilization?

2. What reasons does Newman give to prove that you cannot have a "sinless Literature of sinful man"? Do you think the human race will ever be free of sin?

3. Outline Newman's arguments for the necessity of the study of Secular Literature in a Catholic school. Do you think his arguments are valid ones? Explain.

4. What is your opinion of studying Catholic authors and works exclusively in a Catholic High School? Would it give you a balanced education?

WORD STUDY AND STYLE

Does the style in Newman's *Idea of a University* differ from that of the *Apologia*? Discuss in detail.

What kind of diction does Newman use in his lectures? Are the words denotative or connotative? Abstract or concrete? Illustrate by examples.

By selecting examples from the two essays show that Newman's style is "lucidly logical with liquid rhythms and stately balanced expressions."

Give the origin of the following words: *tangible; sophisticated; sobriety.* Could you select one *maxim* from Newman's writing? What is the difference between *proscribe* and *prescribe*? Describe a *fastidious* person. Define *indigenous.*

PROJECTS

1. Hold a class discussion on the basic differences between Newman's theory of a liberal education and those proposed by many modern educators, such as: progressive education, education for life adjustment, education for Democracy, education for practical utility, etc.

2. Reread Bacon's Essay "On Studies" and compare his ideas with Newman's.

RELATED READING

Read Newman's great sermon, "The Second Spring." You will find it clear and stimulating.

◇◇◇◇◇

A General Communion

ALICE MEYNELL

Alice Meynell, the wife of the energetic Catholic journalist, Wilfrid Meynell, and the mother of eight children, wrote sparingly but exquisitely. Both her prose and poetry have a perfection of form and a rich Catholic thought. But perhaps more important than her finely chiseled and polished literary works was her influence upon the literary artists of her generation and upon those young men who were to become the Catholic literary giants of the twentieth century.

We cannot fully appreciate the Catholic Literary Revival without knowing Alice Meynell. Such writers as Meredith, Patmore, Lionel Johnson, and Francis Thompson respected her almost to veneration and presented to her, as to a literary dictator, the works that make that period stand out in our minds today. Her home became the meeting place of such young Catholic writers as Belloc, Chesterton, Kilmer, Katherine Tynan, and Alfred Noyes. Her intimates included writers like Max Beerbohm, Oscar Wilde, W. B. Yeats, John Ruskin and many others. The first appearance in print of such Catholic writers as Johnson, Thompson, Belloc, Patmore, Tynan, and Wilfrid Ward appeared in her husband's MERRIE ENGLAND, a monthly magazine which she helped to edit.

Alice Meynell once said, "If I had been a man and large, I should have been Chesterton." And glancing over the splendid career of this truly great Catholic woman, we can scarcely doubt it. Her death in 1923 brought to a close the life of a woman who did almost as much for Catholic literature indirectly as the robust Chesterton did for it directly.

All of Alice Meynell's poetry is Catholic in thought and in tone. It is noted for its compactness and compression, its intellectual appeal, its understanding of the inner depth of Catholic life and doctrine. In the poem "A General Communion," the theme is the Mystical Body of Christ—the unity and individuality of the human soul and the universality of all Christians united in Christ as their Head.

I saw the throng, so deeply separate,
    Fed at only one board—
The devout people, moved, intent, elate,
    And the devoted Lord.

O struck apart! not side from human side,   5
    But soul from human soul,
As each asunder absorbed the multiplied,
    The ever unparted, whole.

I saw this people as a field of flowers,
    Each grown at such a price   10
The sum of unimaginable powers
    Did no more than suffice.

A thousand single central daisies they,
    A thousand of the one;   14
For each, the entire monopoly of day;
    For each the whole of the devoted sun.

FOR APPRECIATION

1. Select and discuss those lines which develop the theme of the Christian paradox of the Mystical Body—individuality and universality combined.

2. Analyze the figures of speech in stanzas 3 and 4 which develop the theme of the poem. Explain the expressions: *the entire monopoly of day.*

RELATED READING

Select and read from Mrs. Meynell's *Prose and Poetry* "To a Daisy" and "Christ in the Universe." A fine example of her prose writing is her essay, "Spirit of Place."

Viola Meynell has written a beautiful biography of her mother in her *Alice Meynell—A Memoir.*

The Young Neophyte

ALICE MEYNELL

"The three greatest sonnets ever written by a woman are 'Renunciation,' 'Thoughts in Separation,' and 'The Young Neophyte.' More than this, the last two are greater than the first, and ascend to heights that have been

"The Young Neophyte" by Alice Meynell, reprinted by permission of Charles Scribner's Sons.

touched very rarely in the history of literature." This indeed is high praise coming from the poet Alfred Noyes, but it only re-echoes tributes to Mrs. Meynell's literary genius by other prominent Victorian writers.

Written on the occasion of her conversion to Catholicism at the age of twenty, Alice Meynell's "Neophyte" presents in perspective her whole Catholic life. How clearly she sees in the dedication of her youth the dedication of her old age! Indeed she goes beyond time, since she considers her baptismal vow as something eternal which death will only seal.

> Who knows what days I answer for today?
>   Giving the bud I give the flower. I bow
>   This yet unfaded and a faded brow;
> Bending these knees and feeble knees, I pray.
>
> Thoughts yet unripe in me I bend one way,   5
>   Give one repose to pain I know not now,
>   One check to joy that comes, I guess not how.
> I dedicate my fields when Spring is grey.
>
> O rash! (I smile) to pledge my hidden wheat.
>   I fold today at altars far apart   10
> Hands trembling with what toils?   In their retreat
>
> I seal my love to-be, my folded art.
> I light the tapers at my head and feet,
> And lay the crucifix on this silent heart.

FOR APPRECIATION

1. What is the central thought of the poem? Show how it ties in with the title.

2. This main thought is expressed poetically by a series of metaphors: (a) "Giving the bud, I give the flower." (b) "I light the tapers at my head and feet. . . ." Discuss the effectiveness of the imagery in these expressions. Paraphrase each in a simple prose sentence. Such an exercise will demonstrate the effectiveness of poetry, its suggestive richness, its mental discipline.

3. What is the source of the figure in lines 13 and 14?

4. What is the mood expressed: melancholy, restrained joy, solemnity? Discuss.

5. Can the message of this poem be applied to the young bride, to the nun or the religious on taking vows, to the priest at ordination? Explain.

6. In what lines does the author indicate that she faces the future with humility?

7. Fully explain lines 13 and 14. In what lines is the sacrificial aspect of life treated? Explain.

8. Noyes writes that "no poem in any tongue has so completely foretold and symbolized its author's own life, or has been so deliberately and serenely fulfilled in life and death."

The Kingdom of God

FRANCIS THOMPSON

*The poet of "the return—not to nature—but to God" did nature no in-
justice. Other poets may have re-awakened man's enjoyment of natural
beauties; Thompson offered to the thinking man a much deeper appreciation of those beauties. For Thompson viewed nature under this "sacramental" aspect: God is continually mirrored in the wonders of His creation; all of nature is an object that should lift man to love his God. In
the poet's eyes, this world of ours is "The Kingdom of God." Yet in the
world of sense, so engaged as we are with the things we see and touch and
feel, the eyes of our faith may grow dim. We creatures of spirit and flesh
may lose our appreciation of the world of the spirit; we may forget that our
God continually conserves us and all beings in existence, and that His
grace is ever leading us.*

O world invisible, we view thee,
O world intangible, we touch thee,
O world unknowable, we know thee,
Inapprehensible, we clutch thee!

Does the fish soar to find the ocean,   5
The eagle plunge to find the air—
That we ask of the stars in motion
If they have rumour of thee there?

Not where the wheeling systems darken,
And our benumbed conceiving soars!   10
The drift of pinions, would we hearken,
Beats at our own clay-shuttered doors.

The angels keep their ancient places;—
Turn but a stone, and start a wing!

'Tis ye, 'tis your estrangèd faces,   15
That miss the many-splendoured thing.

But (when so sad thou canst not sad-
   der)
Cry,—and upon thy so sore loss
Shall shine the traffic of Jacob's ladder
Pitched betwixt Heaven and Charing
   Cross.   20

Yea, in the night, my Soul, my daughter,
Cry,—clinging Heaven by the hems;
And lo, Christ walking on the water
Not of Gennesareth, but Thames.

19. JACOB'S LADDER—The ladder seen by
Jacob in a dream, stretching from earth to
heaven. Cf. Genesis 28.
20. CHARING CROSS—A public square in
London.
24. GENNESARETH—Sea of Galilee.

FOR APPRECIATION

1. In the first stanza the poet states his theme four times. What contrast is heightened by this repetition? Does the reader naturally expect this apparent contradiction to be explained in the remainder of the poem?

2. The "ocean" water is the natural habitat of the fish; there it comes into existence, and there all the demands of its nature can be satisfied. So too, the eagle has the air continually about it. What contrasting picture is offered of man's seeking for the God that his complete human nature demands? What figure of speech is used in lines 7 and 8? Is it abstract, or concrete?

3. The first two lines of the third stanza refer to the "drift of pinions," not off in such vast distances that we can hardly conceive them, but right in our own natural surroundings and in our own human nature. Explain the meaning of the highly imaginative expression, *clay-shuttered doors*. Does the poet hint at man's lack of concern and interest in such things? Where?

4. You have observed the kind of insect life that is uncovered when you turn over an old stone. Does Thompson mean literally what he says in line 14, or is he attempting to picture the close contact we have with the spirit world? Then, instead of saying that mankind has become too much engrossed in material things to realize the spiritual forces about him, the poet uses the word "faces" and follows out the figure. What is the meaning of "estranged"?

5. What is the meaning of line 17? What is the subject of "cry" in line 18? The helping angels are pictured as coming and going between heaven and—not the ancient and far-off Biblical lands—but the busy heart of modern London. What comfort is there in this? How shall this "shine" upon or lessen man's grief?

6. How does "in the night" make a connection of feeling or emotion with the previous stanza? What is the picture of supplication given in line 22? Why is such a comparison used in lines 23–24; to whom did Christ walk on the Lake of Gennesareth, and in what respect is this modern person like to them? What does the poet actually mean when he says that Christ will walk on the Thames?

❖❖❖❖❖

The Hound of Heaven

FRANCIS THOMPSON

This is the story of Thompson's life. And yet each of us can see in it the story of his own life. Like Thompson, we have searched our world seeking happiness in the various beautiful things about us. Like Thompson, we have fled from God, afraid of His rule, and have tried to escape to creatures for laughter and peace and love. Yet disappointment awaited us in each attempt; and always we could sense God wanting us, pursuing us. We have been fortunate if, like Thompson, we have realized that the

God who tracks us by His grace wants to shower us with blessings, not to injure or restrict us. This poem is worth all our study, for it will help us realize what our faith and our experiences teach us—that only in God is the complete answer to our desires and longings. In the richness of Thompson's imagery is beautifully expressed the strong and uplifting truths of Christian reality.

[*The flight from God at all times, in all moods*]

I fled Him, down the nights and down the days;
I fled Him, down the arches of the years;
I fled Him, down the labyrinthine ways
    Of my own mind; and in the mist of tears
I hid from Him, and under running laughter.   5
    Up vistaed hopes I sped;
    And shot, precipitated;
Adown Titanic glooms of chasmed fears,
    From those strong Feet that followed, followed after.
    But with unhurrying chase,
    And unperturbèd pace,   11
    Deliberate speed, majestic instancy,
    They beat—and a Voice beat
More instant than the Feet—
"All things betray thee, who betrayest Me."   15

[*The flight to fellow-man for love*]

I pleaded, outlaw-wise,

By many a hearted casement, curtained red,
    Trellised with intertwining charities;
(For, though I knew His love Who followed,
    Yet was I sore adread   20
Lest, having Him, I must have naught beside.)
But, if one little casement parted wide,
    The gust of His approach would clash it to:
Fear wist not to evade, as Love wist to pursue.

[*The flight to the Heavens for a hiding place*]

Across the margent of the world I fled,
    And troubled the gold gateways of the stars,   26
    Smiting for shelter on their clangèd bars;
    Fretted to dulcet jars
And silvern chatter the pale ports o' the moon.
I said to Dawn: Be sudden—to Eve: Be soon;   30

"The Hound of Heaven" by Francis Thompson. Reprinted by permission of Sir Francis Meynell.

8. TITANIC GLOOMS OF CHASMED FEARS—Periods of frightful despondency that came upon him from time to time.

14. INSTANT—Urgent.

16. I PLEADED, OUTLAW-WISE, ETC.—Here the sinner pleading for the love of his fellow man is compared to an outlaw pleading at a latticed window, the human heart being the window which is curtained in red, the symbol of love.

24. WIST—Knew, past of wit, to know or learn. God in His love knew of more ways to pursue than the sinner in his fear knew to escape.

25. MARGENT—Limit, boundary.

28. FRETTED TO DULCET JARS, ETC.—I fretted to dulcet jars; that is, the sinner beat against the gates of the moon until their vibrations set up a kind of sweet music—dulcet jars and silvern chatter.

30. I SAID TO DAWN: BE SUDDEN—TO EVE: BE SOON—The natural desire of a fugitive criminal, the speedy passing of time.

With thy young skiey blossoms heap
  me over
From this tremendous Lover—
Float thy vague veil about me, lest He
  see!
I tempted all His servitors, but to find
My own betrayal in their constancy, 35
In faith to Him their fickleness to me,
    Their traitorous trueness, and their
    loyal deceit.
To all swift things for swiftness did I
  sue;
  Clung to the whistling mane of every
    wind.
    But whether they swept, smoothly
    fleet,   40
The long savannahs of the blue;
    Or whether, Thunder-driven,
They clanged His chariot 'thwart a
  heaven,
Plashy with flying lightnings round the
  spurn o' their feet:—
Fear wist not to evade as Love wist to
    pursue.   45
    Still with unhurrying chase,
    And unperturbèd pace,
Deliberate speed, majestic instancy,
    Came on the following Feet,
    And a Voice above their beat—
"Naught shelters thee, who wilt not
  shelter Me."   51

[*The flight to little children for affection*]

I sought no more that after which I
  strayed
  In face of man or maid;
But still within the little children's
  eyes

Seems something, something that
  replies,   55
They at least are for me, surely for me!
I turned me to them very wistfully;
But just as their young eyes grew sud-
  den fair
  With dawning answers there,
Their angel plucked them from me by
  the hair.   60

[*The flight to Nature for companionship*]

"Come then, ye other children, Na-
  ture's—share
With me" (said I) "your delicate fel-
  lowship;
  Let me greet you lip to lip,
  Let me twine with you caresses,
    Wantoning   65
  With our Lady-Mother's vagrant
    tresses,
    Banqueting
  With her in her wind-walled pal-
  ace,
  Underneath her azured daïs,
  Quaffing, as your taintless way is,
    From a chalice   71
Lucent-weeping out of the dayspring."
    So it was done:
I in their delicate fellowship was one—
Drew the bolt of Nature's secrecies. 75
  I knew all the swift importings
  On the wilful face of skies;
  I knew how the clouds arise,
  Spumed of the wild sea-snortings;
  All that's born or dies   80
  Rose and drooped with; made them
  shapers

31. SKIEY BLOSSOMS—The stars.
37. LOYAL DECEIT—Everything in which
the sinner seeks a selfish happiness becomes a
traitor to him in so far as it refuses to be an end
in itself. By the Creator it was meant to reflect His beauty, thus leading men to God.
Therefore the sinner cannot accept it as something beautiful in itself without at the same
time accepting its maker—God.

60. THEIR (GUARDIAN) ANGEL PLUCKED—
They died suddenly.
69. AZURED DAÏS—The blue sky.
72. LUCENT-WEEPING—A chalice pouring
out streams of light.
72. DAYSPRING—Day at its source, that is,
early dawn.
75. NATURE'S SECRECIES—A thorough
knowledge of Nature.

Of mine own moods, or wailful or di-
vine;
With them joyed and was bereaven.
I was heavy with the even,   84
When she lit her glimmering tapers
Round the day's dead sanctities.
I laughed in the morning's eyes.
I triumphed and I saddened with all
weather,
Heaven and I wept together,
And its sweet tears were salt with
mortal mine;   90
Against the red throb of its sunset-
heart
I laid my own to beat,
And share commingling heat;
But not by that, by that, was eased
my human smart.
In vain my tears were wet on Heav-
en's grey cheek.   95
For ah! we know not what each other
says,
These things and I; in sound I
speak—
Their sound is but their stir, they
speak by silences.
Nature, poor stepdame, cannot slake
my drought;
Let her, if she would owe me,
Drop yon blue bosom-veil of sky, and
show me   101
The breasts o' her tenderness:
Never did any milk of hers once bless
My thirsting mouth.   104
Nigh and nigh draws the chase,
With unperturbèd pace,
Deliberate speed, majestic instancy;
And past those noisèd Feet
A Voice comes yet more fleet—

"Lo! naught contents thee, who content'st not Me."   110

[*The poet ceases to flee; makes a sorry
review of himself and of God's love as
he misunderstands it*]

Naked I wait Thy Love's uplifted
stroke!
My harness piece by piece Thou hast
hewn from me,
And smitten me to my knee;
I am defenseless utterly.
I slept, methinks, and woke,
And, slowly gazing, find me stripped
in sleep.   116
In the rash lustihead of my young
powers,
I shook the pillaring hours
And pulled my life upon me; grimed
with smears,
I stand amid the dust o' the mounded
years—   120
My mangled youth lies dead beneath
the heap.
My days have crackled and gone up in
smoke,
Have puffed and burst as sun-starts on
a stream.
Yea, faileth now even dream
The dreamer, and the lute the luta-
nist;   125
Even the linked fantasies, in whose
blossomy twist

82. SHAPERS OF MINE OWN MOODS—
Thompson knew Nature so well that he could
find in it a parallel for every mood, be it joyful or sad.
91. AGAINST THE RED THROB—From this
line down to "My thirsting mouth" the relation between Nature and the fugitive is that
of mother and child.
99. SLAKE—Satisfy.

115. I SLEPT, METHINKS, AND WOKE—He is
giving a picture of his wasted life in the past.
118. I SHOOK THE PILLARING HOURS—A reference to Samson, the strong man of the Old
Testament (Judges 16, 30) who, by shaking
the pillars of the house in which the Philistines
were banqueting, pulled down the building,
destroying all within, including himself.
123. SUN-STARTS—Sun-lit bubbles that appear on the water.
126. EVEN THE LINKED FANTASIES . . . ARE
YIELDING . . . The soul has woven strands of
poetry around the world and in poetic fancy
has toyed with it. Now the world has grown
heavy with grief and the lovely but fragile
strands of poetry can no longer support it.

I swung the earth a trinket at my
    wrist,
Are yielding; cords of all too weak ac-
    count
For earth with heavy griefs so over-
    plussed.
      Ah! is Thy love indeed   130
A weed, albeit an amaranthine weed,
Suffering no flowers except its own to
      mount?
      Ah! must—
      Designer infinite!—
Ah! must Thou char the wood ere
    Thou canst limn with it?   135
My freshness spent its wavering
    shower i' the dust;
And now my heart is as a broken
    fount,

131. AMARANTHINE WEED—Imaginary plant
which absorbed all the moisture around it,
thus killing all the other plants in the vicinity.
135. CHAR THE WOOD—As the artist must
burn the wood before he can draw with it, so
must God purify the soul by suffering and trial?

Wherein tear-drippings stagnate, spilt
    down ever
    From the dank thoughts that
      shiver
Upon the sighful branches of my
    mind.   140
    Such is; what is to be?
The pulp so bitter, how shall taste the
    rind?
I dimly guess what Time in mists con-
    founds:
Yet ever and anon a trumpet sounds
From the hid battlements of Eter-
    nity: 145
Those shaken mists a space unsettle,
    then
Round the half-glimpsèd turrets
    slowly wash again.
    But not ere him who summoneth
    I first have seen, enwound
With glooming robes purpureal,
    cypress-crowned;   150
148. HIM WHO SUMMONETH—Death.

His name I know, and what his trumpet saith.
Whether man's heart or life it be
which yields
Thee harvest, must Thy harvest-
fields
Be dunged with rotten death?

[God, *the pursuer, draws near and ex-*
plains His love and pursuit]

Now of that long pursuit
Comes on at hand the bruit;
That Voice is round me like a burst-
ing sea: 157
"And is thy earth so marred,
Shattered in shard on shard?
Lo, all things fly thee, for thou fliest
Me!   160
Strange, piteous, futile thing!
Wherefore should any set thee love
apart?
Seeing none but I makes much of
naught" (He said),
"And human love needs human mer-
iting:
How hast thou merited—
Of all man's clotted clay the dingiest
clot?   166
Alack, thou knowest not
How little worthy of any love thou
art!
Whom wilt thou find to love ignoble
thee,
Save Me, save only Me?   170
All which I took from thee I did but
take,
Not for thy harms,
But just that thou might'st seek it in
my arms.
All which thy child's mistake

154. ROTTEN DEATH—In his natural fear of
death Thompson asks why it is that the joys
or sorrow of eternity must be approached only
through the avenue of death.
156. BRUIT—Archaic word for sound, clamor,
din.
159. SHARD—Piece of broken pottery.

Fancies as lost, I have stored for thee
at home: 175
Rise, clasp my hand, and come!"
Halts by me that footfall:
Is my gloom, after all,
Shade of His hand, outstretched ca-
ressingly?   179
"Ah, fondest, blindest, weakest,
I am He Whom thou seekest!
Thou dravest love from thee, who
dravest Me."

182. DRAVEST—Old form of the verb to
drive.

◇◇◇◇◇◇◇◇◇◇◇◇◇◇◇◇◇◇◇◇◇◇◇◇

FOR APPRECIATION

SECTION I:

1. What is the effect of the repetition
of the first three words and the varied expressions of time? What picture do you
see in "the arches of the years" and "the
labyrinthine ways"?

2. What are the two moods contrasted
in "mist of tears" and "running laughter"? What is the thought contrast in
the next three lines?

3. How does the meter change in lines
10–15? Is it consistent with the change
in thought? These lines with gradual
variations will serve as a refrain through
the poem.

SECTION II:

1. Can you explain the "charities" that
intertwine the heart?

2. What reason does the poet offer for
fleeing from God's love?

3. Discuss the figurative meaning of
line 23.

SECTION III:

1. How is the meaning of "troubled"
clarified in line 27? What is the figure
of speech used in line 30? Do you regard
this line as being especially worthy of
memory?

2. Line up the terms used in lines 35–
37 explaining the one idea.

3. Explain the use of the figure of speech in line 38. How does the rhythm help convey the thought in lines 42–44?

4. Why are the refrain and measured rhythm inserted again in lines 46–51? What variation is there from the previous refrain?

SECTION IV:

1. The theme of the entire poem is stated in line 52. What is your explanation of "that"?

2. Give the meaning in the context of lines 58–59. Is the development consistent with the "children's eyes" of lines 54–55?

SECTION V:

1. Instead of simple narration, the poet now uses direct address in lines 61–72. Can you offer any reason for this?

2. Does the melody of these lines make the invitation more appealing?

3. What is the subject of "drew" in line 75? Explain the figure of speech used in this line. What knowledge is thus gained?

4. "With them joyed and was bereaven"—what pictures of shared sorrow and joy are given in the following lines?

5. Does the poet explain nature's failure to ease "my human smart"?

6. The measured beat of the refrain is again introduced. In your own words give the meaning of line 110.

SECTION VI:

1. A series of word-pictures here describes the poet's feelings as he awaits "Love's uplifted stroke." Show how the introductory picture (lines 112–114) makes the connection with line 111.

2. What are the other two pictures, illustrative of the poet's position, given in lines 115–123?

3. How does the general statement (lines 124–125) reject the sources of imaginary joy and happiness? Why is the poetic outlook and enjoyment found now unsatisfactory?

4. Again the poet states his faulty attitude towards God's love. Why is this figurative statement better than a repetition of "lest having Him I must have naught besides"?

5. List the various details given in the highly artistic picture of lines 137–140.

6. Explain in your own words the poet's attitude towards God even in his surrender.

7. In line 143 the poet starts the build-up towards his most bitter complaint. Man must give glory to God; by the simple fact that he has "life," he mirrors forth the power and other perfections of God; but by his "heart," by the morality of his free actions, he can give a much greater "harvest" of glory. Do you believe that Thompson's complaint against death is mitigated by his belief in immortality?

SECTION VII:

1. What reason is God imagined as giving for the poet's failure to win real love from the things of creation?

2. What is the contrast implied between human love and God's love? "Human love needs human meriting" and you have only sought for your own selfish good.

3. What is the Catholic explanation of human suffering and loss and pain given in lines 171–179? Give your interpretation line for line.

4. God has been pictured as standing off a few paces, giving His explanation of the poet's search and suffering. Describe the movement then in lines 176–177.

5. Does the answer here offered satisfy all the questionings of the poet and of ourselves?

PROJECTS

1. Read Thompson's "Orient Ode." Then compare and contrast his treatment of nature with that of Wordsworth or Shelley.

2. Discuss in class Thompson's diction and poetic imagination. What adjectives would you use to describe them? Do you think his diction and figures are overdone? Give reasons for your answers.

Cadgwith

LIONEL JOHNSON

Grand thoughts sometimes come to us in the evening as we look out at the vast dome of the heavens dotted with myriad stars and great, steady planets. So, one sleepless night, the poet was carried away by the majesty of his vision and left us a memorial of his ecstasy in these lines:

My windows open to the autumn night,
In vain I watched for sleep to visit me:
How should sleep dull mine ears, and
   dim my sight,
Who saw the stars, and listened to the
   sea?

Ah, how the City of our God is fair!
If, without sea, and starless though
   it be,
For joy of the majestic beauty there,
Men shall not miss the stars, nor mourn
   the sea.

FOR APPRECIATION

1. The title refers to the seaside English village where Johnson was inspired to write the poem. What is the setting of the poem as given in the first two lines?

2. Line 5 explains the connection between the two stanzas. What is the difference in theme between them?

3. In the "City of God" why shall men "not miss the stars, nor mourn the sea"? How would you explain the "City of God" to a non-Christian? What is the essence of heaven?

4. What emotion does the poem leave with you? Does it help in the enjoyment of nature?

5. Is this poem one of the many examples in this book of the Christian treatment of nature? Why, do you think, did God make the world so beautiful?

"Cadgwith" from *Poems* by Lionel Johnson. Reprinted by permission of George Allen & Unwin Ltd., London, publishers.

◇◇◇◇◇

God's Grandeur

GERARD MANLEY HOPKINS, S.J.

Intensity, at white-heat, is the dominant characteristic of Hopkins' poetry —an emotional intensity which attempts to express his several moods simultaneously; an intellectual intensity which endeavors to recognize and explain the unity and multiplicity of the universe; an intensity of expression which forces the poet to use complex and compound words where other poets would use phrases and clauses; an intense insight into details of the physical universe as well as into the inner consciousness of man's mind and heart. Such intensity has produced poems which a modern critic has summarized as "continual shocks of beauty and strength."

Such a poem is the sonnet, "God's Grandeur." It is the poet's intense utterance of the grandeur of God as reflected in nature, ever fresh and never spent despite the efforts of materialism to make it ugly and to exhaust the storehouse of its wealth.

In your study of the poem, note the modernity of its diction, the ruggedness of its movement, the graphic realism of its expression. Written over sixty years ago, this poem, like most of Hopkins' poetry, is prophetic both in its portrayal of the modern industrial world and in its foreshadowing of the new poetry which would one day reveal and criticize the spirit of that world.

> The world is charged with the grandeur of God.
>   It will flame out, like shining from shook foil;
>   It gathers to a greatness, like the ooze of oil
> Crushed. Why do men then now not reck his rod?
> Generations have trod, have trod, have trod;   5
>   And all is seared with trade; bleared, smeared with toil;
>   And wears man's smudge and shares man's smell: the soil
> Is bare now, nor can foot feel, being shod.
>
> And for all this, nature is never spent;
>   There lives the dearest freshness deep down things;   10
> And though the last lights off the black West went
>   Oh, morning, at the brown brink eastward, springs—
> Because the Holy Ghost over the bent
>   World broods with warm breast and with ah! bright wings.

FOR APPRECIATION

1. Note the words in the poem which are all symbolic of the Holy Ghost: *fire, oil, dove, sun.*

2. The pause after "springs" in line 12 is suggestive of the pause before sunrise. Then the sun breaks over the earth. The long vowels in "ah," "broods," "warm," etc. suggest the sunlight spreading. Note that the sun and dove both suggest the productive and life-giving power of the Holy Ghost—"Come, Holy Ghost, *replenish . . .* and *kindle."*

3. We have noted that the poet's diction is intensely charged with meaning.

Select at least ten words to illustrate this fact and explain their use in the context of the poem.

4. In the tradition of Langland, Milton, and Browning, Hopkins makes frequent use of alliteration and assonance. Select and analyze for their effectiveness at least four examples.

5. What is Hopkins' attitude toward man's use of nature? What is his solution? How does Hopkins' attitude toward nature differ from that of the Romantic poets? Discuss. Compare this poem with Wordsworth's "The World Is Too Much With Us."

6. What social conditions of Hopkins' day and, in a greater measure, of our own, are described in lines 6–7? Discuss.

7. What is the rhyme scheme of the sonnet? Do not attempt to give the meter unless you wish to study the "counterpointed or sprung rhythm" of Hopkins. You will find a simple but enlightening explanation of this in Father Lahey's *Gerard Manley Hopkins*.

RELATED READING

Now that you have been introduced to a more difficult poem of Hopkins, read "The Starlight Night" and, if you are very brave, "The Windhover." A serious and patient study of the latter will repay the efforts of any mature student.

Explanations of some of the poetry of Hopkins, including "The Windhover," may be found in *Immortal Diamond*, edited by Norman Weyand and in *Gerard Manley Hopkins*, edited by the Kenyon Critics.

Spring

GERARD MANLEY HOPKINS, S.J.

The beauty of spring, always fresh after the long winter, reminds us of the beauty God intended the world to have always—the beauty of the Garden of Eden before death touched it. And it reminds Hopkins of a greater beauty, the beauty of the human soul before sin has touched it. The poet prays to Christ to take and guard those pure young souls, fresh as the month of May, like the Son of the Maid of Nazareth. Christ chose these little ones once, "Suffer the little ones to come unto me," and they are worth the sacrifice He has made to have and keep them.

Nothing is so beautiful as spring—
    When weeds, in wheels, shoot long and lovely and lush;
    Thrush's eggs look little low heavens, and thrush
Through the echoing timber does so rinse and wring
The ear, it strikes like lightnings to hear him sing;   5
    The glassy peartree leaves and blooms, they brush
    The descending blue; that blue is all in a rush
With richness; the racing lambs too have fair their fling.

What is all this juice and all this joy?
    A strain of the earth's sweet being in the beginning   10
In Eden garden.—Have, get, before it cloy,
    Before it cloud, Christ, lord, and sour with sinning,
Innocent mind and Mayday in girl and boy,
    Most, O maid's child, thy choice and worthy the winning.

2. IN WHEELS—Perhaps Hopkins refers to the circular unwinding of some types of fern and of other wild plants.

7–8. Compare these lines with lines 73 ff. in "Blessed Virgin Mary Compared to the Air We Breathe."

10. STRAIN—A musical strain or theme.

FOR APPRECIATION

1. The subject of the poem is spring. Select the details which the poet uses to develop this subject.

2. What is the theme of the poem? Is the theme developed in the sestet of the sonnet? Discuss, pointing out examples.

3. Discuss the effectiveness of the constant use of alliteration in the poem.

4. Explain in detail the meaning of the following: *rinse and wring the ear; they brush the descending blue; have, get, before it cloy; Mayday in girl and boy.*

The Blessed Virgin Mary Compared to the Air We Breathe

GERARD MANLEY HOPKINS, S.J.

The Motherhood of Mary is the basis for all her privileges. She is not the mother of a body merely, but of a person, like all other mothers. But she alone is the mother of a divine Person; she alone is the Mother of God.

She brings God to us in His human nature, and hence brings us the source of divine grace. She continues to bring forth Christ in our souls, as mediatrix of all grace. This is the first great Marian privilege of which Hopkins treats in this poem.

Mary also reveals the mystery of the great and fearful majesty of God in a way suited to our human weakness, by bringing forth her divine Child. This Hopkins discusses in the second part of the poem.

The poem first discusses the mothering qualities of air and then applies those to Mary. As the air brings us the elements we need to live naturally, so Mary brings us the grace we need to live supernaturally. As the air carries off the poisons in our blood which would kill us, so Mary carries off the supernatural poisons and leaves behind Christ.

Again, as the air diffuses the light to suit our vision, so Mary brings us God's revelation of Himself in the Word-made-Flesh, suited to our human vision. The poem ends with a prayer to Mary, the living air, who is the Mother of our Savior and our God.

Wild air, world-mothering air,
Nestling me everywhere,
That each eyelash or hair
Girdles; goes home betwixt
The fleeciest, frailest-flixed   5

1. WILD—Here means natural, such as "a wild flower."
5. FLIXED—Furred—*flix* is the soft fur on the breast of a rabbit or similar animal.

Snowflake; that's fairly mixed
With, riddles, and is rife
In every least thing's life;
This needful, never spent,
And nursing element;   10
My more than meat and drink,
My meal at every wink;
This air, which, by life's law,
My lung must draw and draw

Now but to breathe its praise, 15
Minds me in many ways
Of her who not only
Gave God's infinity
Dwindled to infancy
Welcome in womb and breast, 20
Birth, milk, and all the rest
But mothers each new grace
That does now reach our race—
Mary Immaculate,
Merely a woman, yet 25
Whose presence, power is
Great as no goddess's
Was deemèd, dreamèd; who
This one work has to do—
Let all God's glory through, 30
God's glory which would go
Through her and from her flow
Off, and no way but so.

I say that we are wound
With mercy round and round 35
As if with air: the same
Is Mary, more by name.
She, wild web, wondrous robe,
Mantles the guilty globe,
Since God has let dispense 40
Her prayers his providence:
Nay, more than almoner,
The sweet alms' self is her
And men are meant to share
Her life as life does air. 45

If I have understood,
She holds high motherhood
Towards all our ghostly good
And plays in grace her part
About man's beating heart, 50
Laying, like air's fine flood,
The deathdance in his blood;
Yet no part but what will
Be Christ our Saviour still.
Of her flesh he took flesh: 55
He does take fresh and fresh,
Though much the mystery how,
Not flesh but spirit now
And makes, O marvellous!
New Nazareths in us, 60
Where she shall yet conceive
Him, morning, noon, and eve;
New Bethlems, and he born
There, evening, noon, and morn—
Bethlem or Nazareth, 65
Men here may draw like breath
More Christ and baffle death;
Who, born so, comes to be
New self and nobler me
In each one and each one 70
More makes, when all is done,
Both God's and Mary's Son.

Again, look overhead
How air is azurèd;
O how! nay do but stand 75
Where you can lift your hand

16. MINDS—Reminds.
37. MORE BY NAME—That "mercy" which surrounds us is more properly called by the name "Mary."
38. WILD WEB—Web is a word denoting spun cloth, and connoting something mystical or preternatural, as the web woven by the Lady of Shalott. "Wild web" here indicates that the web, in the case of air, is woven by nature; in Mary's case, it is woven by grace.
43. THE SWEET ALM'S SELF IS HER—Mary gives her own life to us, as she gave her life to Christ. When a mother gives her life to her child, the result is that the child has his or her own life, not the mother's. Hopkins develops this analogy between natural and supernatural birth in the next section (lines 46–72).

51. LAYING—Here means to banish.
52. DEATHDANCE—Deathdance is suggestive both of the physical motion of the poisonous gases in the moving blood and of the destructive forces dangerous to the supernatural life of the soul.
55. Cf. St. John, Chap. I, "The Word was made Flesh."
58. NOT FLESH BUT SPIRIT NOW—In all of Hopkins' poetry the idea of the Mystical Body persists. He is here emphasizing the marvelous union of the soul with Christ through grace and is poetically expressing the words of St. Paul: "I live now not I, but Christ lives in me."
76–77. LIFT YOUR HAND SKYWARDS—An artist's trick, which by contrast brings out the vivid shades of blue in the sky.

Skywards: rich, rich it laps
Round the four fingergaps.
Yet such a sapphire-shot,
Charged, steepèd sky will not   80
Stain light. Yea, mark you this:
It does no prejudice.
The glass-blue days are those
When every colour glows,
Each shape and shadow shows.   85
Blue be it: this blue heaven
The seven or seven times seven
Hued sunbeam will transmit
Perfect, not alter it.
Or if there does some soft,   90
On things aloof, aloft,
Bloom breathe, that one breath more
Earth is the fairer for.
Whereas did air not make
This bath of blue and slake   95
His fire, the sun would shake,
A blear and blinding ball
With blackness bound, and all
The thick stars round him roll
Flashing like flecks of coal,   100
Quartz-fret, or sparks of salt,
In grimy vasty vault.

So God was god of old:
A mother came to mould
Those limbs like ours which are   105
What must make our daystar
Much dearer to mankind;

80. CHARGED—STEEPED—Charged as with electricity, full. Steeped here means saturated.
87. This line refers to the seven primary colors and the forty or fifty shades of those.
91. ON THINGS ALOOF, ALOFT—For example, snow-capped mountains which sometimes reflect a soft halo of blue. Note the effect which Hopkins gets by inserting between the adjective and noun "soft bloom"—a suspension which suggests tenuousness of the thing he is talking about.
94. WHEREAS DID AIR NOT MAKE—An exact physical picture of what the heavens would look like if there were no air to reflect and diffuse the light.
103. GOD OF OLD—i.e., in the Old Testament.
106. DAYSTAR—The sun—the symbol of Christ.

Whose glory bare would blind
Or less would win man's mind.
Through her we may see him   110
Made sweeter, not made dim,
And her hand leaves his light
Sifted to suit our sight.

Be thou then, O thou dear
Mother, my atmosphere;   115
My happier world, wherein
To wend and meet no sin;
Above me, round me lie
Fronting my froward eye
With sweet and scarless sky;   120
Stir in my ears, speak there
Of God's love, O live air,
Of patience, penance, prayer:
World-mothering air, air wild,
Wound with thee, in thee isled,   125
Fold home, fast fold thy child.

112. HER HAND—A veiled reference back to line 76—"lift your hand skywards." Through Mary, the Word was made flesh, and we see his glory. (Cf. line 30.)
113. TO SUIT OUR SIGHT—The sun is blinding without air; God is blinding without Mary.
119. FROWARD—Bold, rash.

◇◇◇◇◇◇◇◇◇◇◇◇◇◇◇◇◇◇◇◇◇◇◇◇◇◇◇◇

WORD STUDY

Give the meaning and study the connotation of the following: *rife*, *dwindled*, *deem*, *slake*, *grimy*, *wend*. Explain *sapphire-shot* and *quartz-fret*.

FOR APPRECIATION

1. Give the main idea in one sentence of the following passages: lines 1–15; lines 16–33; lines 34–45; lines 46–72; lines 73–103; lines 104–113; lines 114–126.
2. Explain in detail the meaning of the following: line 13; line 39; lines 60–67; lines 110–114.
3. In lines 49–52, Hopkins deals with the activity of air in the lungs. Check on the accuracy of his comparisons in the light of the modern scientific view of the activity of air in the body.
4. Check the physics of the passage beginning with line 94.

PROJECTS

Write a paper or hold an oral discussion of the poet's treatment of the doctrines of the Mystical Body and Mary as the Mediatrix of All Graces.

Compile a list of ten great Marian poems written by English authors.

RELATED READING

Read Coventry Patmore's great Marian poem "The Child's Purchase."

Further Readings—The Nineteenth Century

* ALEXANDER, CALVERT, The Catholic Literary Revival (critical study)

ARNOLD, MATTHEW, Culture and Anarchy (essays)

BARRIE, JAMES M., "R. L. S." (essay on Stevenson)

BENSON, E. F., As We Were (historical study)

BESIER, RUDOLPH, The Barretts of Wimpole Street (drama)

BOAS, LOUIS, Elizabeth Barrett Browning (biography)

* BRAYBROOKE, PATRICK, Some Georgian Catholics (short biographies)

* BREGY, KATHERINE, Poets' Chantry (essays on Victorian Catholic writers)

BRONTË, CHARLOTTE, Jane Eyre (novel)

BRONTË, EMILY, Wuthering Heights (novel)

BROWNING, ELIZABETH BARRETT, Sonnets from the Portuguese (poetry)

* CHESTERTON, G. K., The Victorian Age in Literature (critical study); Charles Dickens (critical study)

* CONNOLLY, TERENCE, Francis Thompson: In His Paths (critical study)

* DE LA GORCE, AGNES, Francis Thompson and His Circle (critical study)

DICKENS, CHARLES, Oliver Twist, David Copperfield, Nicholas Nickelby, A Tale of Two Cities, Dombey and Son, Great Expectations (novels)

ELIOT, GEORGE, The Mill on the Floss (novel)

GILBERT and SULLIVAN: The Mikado, H.M.S. Pinafore, The Pirates of Penzance (dramas)

HARDY, THOMAS, Far from the Madding Crowd, The Return of the Native (novels)

HOUSMAN, LAURENCE, Victoria Regina (drama)

* LAHEY, G. H., Gerard Manley Hopkins (critical study)

* MADELEVA, SISTER, Chaucer's Nuns and Other Essays (essay on Thompson)

* MAYNARD, THEODORE, Our Best Poets (essays)

MEREDITH, GEORGE, The Egoist (novel)

* MEYNELL, EVERARD, Francis Thompson (biography)

* MOODY, JOHN, John Henry Newman (biography)

* NOYES, ALFRED, Pageant of Letters (essays on Victorian Catholics)

* PATMORE, DEREK, The Life and Times of Coventry Patmore (critical study)

PEARSON, HESKETH, Gilbert and Sullivan (biography); Charles Dickens (biography)

* SHUSTER, GEORGE, The Catholic Spirit in Modern Literature (critical study)

STEVENSON, ROBERT LOUIS, Travels with a Donkey (essays); New Arabian Nights (short stories)

THACKERAY, WILLIAM M., Henry Esmond, Vanity Fair (novels)

* TUELL, ANNE K., Mrs. Meynell and Her Literary Generation (critical study)

* WARD, MAISIE, The Wilfrid Wards and the Transition (critical study); The Young Mister Newman (biography)

WOOLF, VIRGINIA, Flush (biography of the Brownings)

An aerial view of Trafalgar Square and the National Gallery.

THE TWENTIETH CENTURY

The diamond Jubilee of Queen Victoria in 1897 symbolized the full tide of English glory. It marked the occasion when the world paid homage to England as the wealthiest, the most secure, the most liberal, and the most powerful nation of the world. At the turn of the century, the ordinary middle-class Victorian, steeped in the heritage of material well-being which the liberal reforms of the democratic Gladstone and the confident imperialism of Disraeli had bequeathed him, considered himself a part of an integral and fixed society. Amidst the rumblings of international, political, social, and industrial unrest, the horizons of the new-born twentieth century heralded the vision of "a brave, new world" which would far surpass the "golden age" of Victoria.

The England of today is a far cry from the birth of "the brave, new world" of 1900. Within the space of a half-century, two colossal World Wars, political upheaval, national strikes, and a paralyzing depression have left England deeply in debt, her vast Empire disintegrating, and her world leadership in question, as she faces the intricately complex problems of the Atomic Age.

POLITICAL AND SOCIAL CHANGES

By the time of Queen Victoria's death in 1901 it was apparent that Parliament, much more than the king or queen, was the real ruler of the English people. The English monarch now has no direct power, but stands above and outside political parties as a symbol of national unity. In the first decades of the twentieth century Parliament became more completely representative of the people. The English have kept their House of Lords just as they have kept their monarch, but the Parliament Bill of 1911 took away the Lords' power of veto. The supreme governmental power is the House of Commons, which is an elected body. Electoral reforms finally extended the vote to nearly all male adults in England. In 1918, women won the right to vote. Both Parliament and the municipal governments made strenuous efforts to help the poorer classes and to provide equal opportunities for all members of society. Free public education was improved and extended, and unemployment insurance, health insurance, and old age pensions were established.

During the past twenty years a new party has emerged powerfully upon the English political scene. The Labor Party, under the guidance of labor union officials, was strong enough at the conclusion of World War II to dethrone Winston

THE RISE OF THE

LABOR PARTY

Churchill and his liberal Conservatives by winning a sweeping victory in the general elections. The new administration enacted a series of laws designed to benefit the small wage-earners, at the same time laying heavier taxes on merchants and manufacturers. Among the more controversial measures were free medical care for the entire population and the taking over of the coal mining industry by the government. The Labor Party aroused much antagonism.

It was charged with being too extreme and with being destructive of private initiative. It was defended with equal vigor, but by 1951 public opinion had shifted sufficiently to bring Churchill, Anthony Eden, and his liberal Conservatives back to office. At present the two parties seem to be almost exactly equal in strength.

England is no longer the proprietor of a vast empire. Canada, Australia and New Zealand, which were formerly colonial possessions, have long been self-governing nations. India and Pakistan have had the same status since 1947. All these nations are members of the loosely organized "British Commonwealth." No doubt some of these nations would come to the aid of the mother country in case of war —but the days of England's military superiority over the rest of the world are gone.

In World War I (1914–1918) England came dangerously near being defeated by Germany under Kaiser Wilhelm II. She was saved when, angered by German submarine attacks on neutral ships, America entered the war with fresh troops in 1917.

ENGLAND SUFFERED FROM WORLD WARS

In World War II (1939–45) England faced a still greater ordeal. Again the chief enemy was Germany, this time under the Nazi regime of Adolf Hitler. Hitler and his generals were confident of victory. In the second year of the war the Nazis swept over France and drove the British troops off the continent. During the next few months there was mass bombing of London and other English cities. This "Battle of Britain" was halted only by heroic attacks on German planes by the outnumbered Royal Air Force. The United States was brought into the war in 1941 by Japan's bombing of Pearl Harbor. American troops and equipment were sent to England until the whole island was one great fortress. American and British armies together invaded the continent in 1944, and after a year of bitter fighting Germany surrendered.

England suffered terribly from both World Wars. The weapons of war developed by modern science devastated her cities and industrial plants; and while England was busy fighting, she lost her foreign markets. The country also suffered peacetime reverses. The world depression of the 1930's drained her of her wealth. Today she finds it difficult to compete with America in most kinds of manufacturing; and nations all over the world are building up their own industries rather than buying from Britain. For a nation that must sell in order to eat, the outlook is far from bright. Like her European allies, England must live under threat of an annihilating attack by Communist Russia, the most powerful nation of Europe.

But "there will ever be an England." And England still stands, the last fortress and the hope of Western Civilization in Europe against the menace of Communism. England has survived and will survive because there is inherent in the British character that insatiable love of the homeland and the British soil, and that indomitable fire of liberty and thirst for freedom. In the English character there is a conservatism which has effected revolutions without bloodshed, and a strong faith in the stability and enduring quality of her centuries-old Christian culture. English reverence for the past showed itself again in the pageantry of Queen Elizabeth's coronation in 1953, when the nation was thrilled by ceremonies and traditions which had their roots in the Catholic Middle Ages.

LITERATURE REFLECTS COMPLEXITY OF THE AGE

As is to be expected, the literature of the twentieth century is as complex and diverse as the age that produces it. It varies in its interpretation of life in proportion to the writers' reaction to the "Victorian Compromise," and to the twentieth century upheaval in which they live.

Writers of the generation before and shortly after World War I rebelled against the "Victorian Compromise." They noted with cynical eyes the contradiction of Church attendance on Sunday with the widespread injustices against the laboring classes, and with the adoration and service of materialism six days a week. The result was a loss of faith in tradition, an intellectual and spiritual decline, a lowering of moral standards, and a general attitude of world-weariness and disillusionment. Some of the writers of the age simply mirrored this despair. Others, with a strong social and religious consciousness, attempted to expose the social injustices and the absence of traditional values. Some others attempted an escape from reality by losing themselves in the substitution of the subconscious and the experience of sex for moral and religious values.

THE CATHOLIC REVIVAL

The revival of Catholic letters and life, which began over a century ago with the conversion of Newman and other leaders of the Oxford Movement to the Faith, has grown steadily during the twentieth century. It is no exaggeration to say that Catholic men and women of letters have and are contributing works of distinction to every field of English literature. The contemporary intellectual and literary leadership of Catholicism in England was due largely to two men, Hilaire Belloc and G. K. Chesterton. The plan of these two men was to reawaken England to the glories of the Catholic heritage and to redirect English life and letters into the main stream of English Catholic culture, with a re-emphasis on man's free will and his supernatural destiny.

In the wake, and oftentimes under the influence of Belloc and Chesterton, there emerged many other Catholic writers, mostly converts: writers like Christopher Dawson, with his erudition and precise scholarship; Monsignor Ronald Knox, a leader of British thought for both Catholic and non-Catholic youth; Arnold Lunn and Christopher Hollis, who continued the work of Belloc in the revaluation of English history; and the brilliant fiction writers, Sheila Kaye-Smith, Bruce Marshall, Evelyn Waugh, and Graham Greene.

Closely allied to the Catholic resurgence in England, there has risen an Anglo-Catholic literary awakening under the leadership of T. S. Eliot and C. S. Lewis. Both have exerted a profound influence on contemporary England and have helped in the redirection of English thought toward a complete Christian thinking. Eliot has traveled far from his early unbelief to his firm belief in Anglo-Catholic theology. C. S. Lewis, in his skillful allegories, deals frankly with the doctrines of grace, hell, the Trinity, and the spiritual life of the soul. W. H. Auden, who began his literary career as an intellectual radical with Leftist leanings, within recent

JOHN MASEFIELD

WILLIAM BUTLER YEATS

T. S. ELIOT

PORTRAIT BY AUGUSTUS JOHN, COURTESY NEW DIRECTIONS

DYLAN THOMAS

EVELYN WAUGH

GRAHAM GREENE

G. K. CHESTERTON

HILAIRE BELLOC

years has aligned himself with Belloc, Dawson, and the great French philosopher, Maritain, in diagnosing the decline of culture and predicting the death of Western Civilization unless the world returns to the true sources of life. Auden is now an American citizen.

THE SHORT STORY

In the accelerated tempo of the twentieth century, it is not surprising that there has been a rich development of the short story. But the traditional pattern of Poe's short story structure has lost favor. Poe with his insistence upon "a certain unique or single effect" was the first to make a distinction between the short story and the novel. In 1885, Brander Matthews pointed out that "a true short story differs from the novel chiefly in its essential unity of impression . . . A short story deals with a single character, a single event, a single emotion, or the series of emotions called forth by a single situation . . . Thus the short story has what the novel cannot have, the effect of 'totality' as Poe called it, the unity of impression." In the old type of short story, the author must introduce his characters and set his scene briefly, vividly. In the body of the story, the reader sees the characters perform and the plot rise step by step to a climax. This climax has to come near the end of the story with the untangling of the problem.

During the past thirty years, partly because of the influence of the brilliant Russian writer, Anton Chekhov, the rules governing short story writing have been much relaxed. Perhaps the only requirement for writing a short story is that there must be some opposition or struggle involved (external or internal) and that the story leave one definite impression. The modern technique is usually terse and direct, and the subject matter is limited to what the character sees, hears, feels, and does. There is little description, and the reader must supply the details of time, place, and situation. We judge the character indirectly—by what he says and does.

SHORT STORIES OF TODAY

Many present day stories might be called "narrative essays"—portraying some seemingly ordinary situation, but doing it in such a way as to express an idea or a mood of the author's, or to reveal some interesting character trait. Outwardly nothing remarkable happens in the story.

Both the older and the newer types of short stories are written in great numbers today. Both kinds, at their best, are more subtle and penetrating than the stories created by earlier writers. They are fine works of literary art in which every sentence, almost every word, plays its part in creating the effect the author wants to achieve.

Most of the twentieth century English novelists have succeeded in writing good short stories. Among these we can number Joseph Conrad, John Galsworthy, Conan Doyle, Somerset Maugham, Elizabeth Bowen, E. M. Forster and the great Catholic writers G. K. Chesterton, Bruce Marshall, Evelyn Waugh and Graham Greene.

Among the best exponents of the modern technique is Katherine Mansfield. Eric Knight, Llewelyn Rhys, and H. H. Munro (who wrote under the pen name of "Saki") have all successfully written in her tradition.

Perhaps the best short story writing of the present day is being done by Irish Catholic writers. Oustanding among this group are Bryan MacMahon, Michael McLaverty, and Sean O'Faolain.

◇◇◇◇◇

QUALITY

JOHN GALSWORTHY

John Galsworthy grew to manhood before machines and quick, cheap manufacture became a prominent feature of our civilization. To him, it seems that something fine and valuable is disappearing from the world. In the following story Galsworthy gives us a glimpse of what we are losing. It is a simple story—just a series of purchases from a shoemaker.

I knew him from the days of my extreme youth, because he made my father's boots;[1] inhabiting with his elder brother two little shops let into one, in a small bystreet—now no more, but then most fashionably placed in the West End.

That tenement had a certain quiet distinction; there was no sign upon its face that he made for any of the Royal Family[2]—merely his own German name of Gessler Brothers, and in the window a few pairs of boots. I remember that it always troubled me to account for those unvarying boots in the window, for he made only what was ordered, reaching nothing down, and it seemed so inconceivable that what he made could ever have failed to fit. Had he bought them to put there? That, too, seemed inconceivable. He would never have tolerated in the house, leather on which he had not worked himself. Besides, they were too beautiful—the pair of pumps, so inexpressibly slim, the patent leathers with cloth tops, making water come into one's mouth, the tall brown riding boots with marvelous sooty glow, as if, though new, they had been worn a hundred years. Those pairs could only have been made by one who saw before him the Soul of Boot—so truly were they prototypes incarnating the very spirit of all footgear. These thoughts, of course, came to me

---

[1] BOOTS—In England "boots" means simply "shoes."

[2] FOR ANY OF THE ROYAL FAMILY—English shopkeepers who had sold something to a member of the royal family, no matter how long ago, mentioned this fact in their advertising. The shoemaker in this story refuses to put up such a sign.

later, though even when I was promoted to him, at the age of perhaps fourteen, some inkling haunted me of the dignity of himself and brother. For to make boots—such boots as he made—seemed to me then, and still seems to me, mysterious and wonderful.

I remember well my shy remark, one day, while stretching out to him my youthful foot:

"Isn't it awfully hard to do, Mr. Gessler?"

And his answer, given with a sudden smile from out of the sardonic redness of his beard: "Id is an Ardt!" [3]

Himself, he was a little as if made from leather, with his yellow crinkly face, and crinkly reddish hair and beard, and neat folds slanting down his cheeks to the corners of his mouth, and his guttural and one-toned voice, for leather is a sardonic substance, and stiff and slow of purpose. And that was the character of his face, save that his eyes, which were gray-blue, had in them the simple gravity of one secretly possessed by the Ideal. His elder brother was so very like him—though watery, paler in every way, with a great industry—that sometimes in early days I was not quite sure of him until the interview was over. Then I knew that it was he, if the words, "I will ask my brudder," had not been spoken; and that, if they had, it was his elder brother.

When one grew old and wild and ran up bills, one somehow never ran them up with Gessler Brothers. It would not have seemed becoming to go in there and stretch out one's foot to that blue iron-spectacled glance, owing him for more than—say—two pairs, just the comfortable reassurance that one was still his client.

For it was not possible to go to him very often—his boots lasted terribly, hav-

ing something beyond the temporary—some, as it were, essence of boot stitched into them.

One went in, not as into most shops, in the mood of: "Please serve me, and let me go!" but restfully, as one enters a church; and, sitting on the single wooden chair, waited—for there was never anybody there. Soon, over the top edge of that sort of well—rather dark, and smelling soothingly of leather—which formed the shop, there would be seen his face, or that of his elder brother, peering down. A guttural sound, and the tip-tap of bast [4] slippers beating the narrow wooden stairs, and he would stand before one without coat, a little bent, in leather apron, with sleeves turned back, blinking—as if awakened from some dream of boots, or like an owl surprised in daylight and annoyed at this interruption.

And I would say: "How do you do, Mr. Gessler? Could you make me a pair of Russia leather boots?"

Without a word he would leave me, retiring whence he came, or into the other portion of the shop, and I would continue to rest in the wooden chair, inhaling the incense of his trade. Soon he would come back, holding in his thin, veined hand a piece of gold-brown leather. With eyes fixed on it, he would remark: "What a beaudiful biece!" When I, too, had admired it, he would speak again. "When do you wand dem?" And I would answer: "Oh! As soon as you conveniently can." And he would say: "Tomorrow fordnighd?" Or if he were his elder brother: "I will ask my brudder!"

Then I would murmur: "Thank you! Good morning, Mr. Gessler." "Goot morning!" he would reply, still looking at the leather in his hand. And as I moved to the door, I would hear the tip-tap of

[3] "ID IS AN ARDT!"—"It is an art!"

[4] BAST—Ropelike material.

his bast slippers restoring him, up the stairs, to his dream of boots. But if it were some new kind of footgear that he had not yet made me, then indeed he would observe ceremony—divesting me of my boot and holding it long in his hand, looking at it with eyes at once critical and loving, as if recalling the glow with which he had created it, and rebuking the way in which one had disorganized this masterpiece. Then, placing my foot on a piece of paper, he would two or three times tickle the outer edges with a pencil and pass his nervous fingers over my toes, feeling himself into the heart of my requirements.

I cannot forget that day on which I had occasion to say to him: "Mr. Gessler, that last pair of town walking boots creaked, you know."

He looked at me for a time without replying, as if expecting me to withdraw or qualify the statement, then said:

"Id shouldn'd 'ave greaked."

"It did, I'm afraid."

"You goddem wed before dey found demselves?"

"I don't think so."

At that he lowered his eyes, as if hunting for memory of those boots, and I felt sorry I had mentioned this grave thing.

"Zend dem back!" he said; "I will look at dem."

A feeling of compassion for my creaking boots surged up in me, so well could I imagine the sorrowful long curiosity of regard which he would bend on them.

"Zome boods," he said slowly, "are bad from birdt.[5] If I can do noding wid dem, I dake dem off your bill."

Once (once only) I went absent-mindedly into his shop in a pair of boots bought in an emergency at some large firm's. He took my order without showing me any leather, and I could feel his

⁵ birdt—Birth.

eyes penetrating the inferior integument of my foot. At last he said:

"Dose are nod my boods."

The tone was not one of anger, nor of sorrow, not even of contempt, but there was in it something quiet that froze the blood. He put his hand down and pressed a finger on the place where the left boot, endeavoring to be fashionable, was not quite comfortable.

"Id 'urds you dere," he said. "Dose big virms[6] 'ave no self-respect. Drash!" And then, as if something had given way within him, he spoke long and bitterly. It was the only time I ever heard him discuss the conditions and hardships of his trade.

"Dey ged id all," he said, "dey ged id by adverdisement, nod by work. Dey dake id away from us, who lofe our boods. Id gomes to this—bresently I haf no work. Every year id gets less—you will see." And looking at his lined face I saw things I had never noticed before, bitter things and bitter struggle—and what a lot of gray hairs there seemed suddenly in his red beard!

As best I could, I explained the circumstances of the purchase of those ill-omened boots. But his face and voice made so deep an impression that during the next few minutes I ordered many pairs. Nemesis fell![7] They lasted more terribly than ever. And I was not able conscientiously to go to him for nearly two years.

When at last I went I was surprised to find that outside one of the two little windows of his shop another name was painted, also that of a bootmaker—making, of course, for the Royal Family. The

⁶ virms—Firms.
⁷ nemesis (nĕm′ē·sĭs) fell—The ancient Greeks believed that the goddess Nemesis pursued, and struck down, mortals who had committed crimes or who were overconfident of success.

old familiar boots, no longer in dignified isolation, were huddled in the single window. Inside, the now contracted well of the one little shop was more scented and darker than ever. And it was longer than usual, too, before a face peered down, and the tip-tap of the bast slippers began. At last he stood before me, and, gazing through those rusty iron spectacles, said:

"Mr. ——, isn'd it?"

"Ah! Mr. Gessler," I stammered, "but your boots are really *too* good, you know! See, these are quite decent still!" And I stretched out to him my foot. He looked at it.

"Yes," he said, "beople do nod wand good boods, id seems."

To get away from his reproachful eyes and voice I hastily remarked: "What have you done to your shop?"

He answered quietly: "Id was too exbensif. Do you wand some boods?"

I ordered three pairs, though I had only wanted two, and quickly left. I had, I do not know quite what feeling of being part, in his mind, of a conspiracy against him; or not perhaps so much against him as against his idea of boot. One does not, I suppose, care to feel like that; for it was again many months before my next visit to his shop, paid I remember, with the feeling: "Oh! well, I can't leave the old boy—so here goes! Perhaps it'll be his elder brother!"

For his elder brother, I knew, had not character enough to reproach me, even dumbly.

And, to my relief, in the shop there did appear to be his elder brother, handling a piece of leather.

"Well, Mr. Gessler," I said, "how are you?"

He came close, and peered at me.

"I am breddy well," he said slowly, "but my elder brudder is dead."

And I saw that it was indeed himself—but how aged and wan! And never before had I heard him mention his brother.

Much shocked, I murmured: "Oh! I am sorry!"

"Yes," he answered, "he was a good man, he made a good bood; but he is dead." And he touched the top of his head, where the hair had suddenly gone as thin as it had been on that of his poor brother, to indicate, I suppose, the cause of death. "He could nod ged over losing de oder shop. Do you wand any boods?" And he held up the leather in his hand: "Id's a beaudiful biece."

I ordered several pairs. It was very long before they came—but they were better than ever. One simply could not wear them out. And soon after that I went abroad.

It was over a year before I was again in London. And the first shop I went to was my old friend's. I had left a man of sixty, I came back to one of seventy-five, pinched and worn and tremulous, who genuinely, this time, did not at first know me.

"Oh! Mr. Gessler," I said, sick at heart; "how splendid your boots are! See, I've been wearing this pair nearly all the time I've been abroad; and they're not half worn out, are they?"

He looked long at my boots—a pair of Russia leather, and his face seemed to regain steadiness. Putting his hand on my instep, he said:

"Do dey vid you here? I 'ad drouble wid dat bair, I remember." I assured him that they had fitted beautifully.

"Do you wand any boods?" he said. "I can make dem quickly; id is a slack dime."

I answered: "Please, please! I want boots all around—every kind!"

"I will make a vresh model. Your food must be bigger." And with utter slowness, he traced round my foot, and felt my toes, only once looking up to say:

"Did I dell you my brudder was dead?"

To watch him was painful, so feeble had he grown; I was glad to get away.

I had given those boots up, when one evening they came. Opening the parcel, I set the four pairs out in a row. Then one by one I tried them on. There was no doubt about it. In shape and fit, in finish and quality of leather, they were the best he had ever made me. And in the mouth of one of the town walking boots I found his bill. The amount was the same as usual, but it gave me quite a shock. He had never before sent it in till quarter day. I flew downstairs, and wrote a cheque, and posted it at once with my own hand.

A week later, passing the little street, I thought I would go in and tell him how splendidly the new boots fitted. But when I came to where his shop had been, his name was gone. Still there, in the window, were the slim pumps, the patent leathers with cloth tops, the sooty riding boots.

I went in, very much disturbed. In the two little shops—again made into one— was a young man with an English face.

"Mr. Gessler in?" I said.

He gave me a strange, ingratiating look.[8]

"No, sir," he said, "no. But we can attend to anything with pleasure. We've taken the shop over. You've seen our name, no doubt, next door. We make for some very good people."

"Yes, yes," I said, "but Mr. Gessler?"

"Oh!" he answered; "dead."

"Dead! But I only received these boots from him last Wednesday week."

"Ah!" he said; "a shockin' go. Poor old man starved 'imself."

"Good God!"

"Slow starvation, the doctor called it! You see he went to work in such a way!

[8] INGRATIATING LOOK—A look which it is hoped will win favor.

Would keep the shop on; wouldn't have a soul touch his boots except himself. When he got an order, it took him such a time. People won't wait. He lost everybody. And there he'd sit, goin' on and on—I will say that for him—not a man in London made a better boot! But look at the competition! He never advertised! Would 'ave the best leather, too, and do it all 'imself. Well, there it is. What could you expect with his ideas?"

"But starvation—"

"That may be a bit flowery, as the sayin' is—but I know myself he was sittin' over his boots day and night, to the very last. You see I used to watch him. Never gave 'imself time to eat; never had a penny in the house. All went in rent and leather. How he lived so long I don't know. He regular let his fire go out. He was a character. But he made good boots."

"Yes," I said, "he made good boots."

And I turned and went out quickly, for I did not want that youth to know that I could hardly see.

⟡⟡⟡⟡⟡⟡⟡⟡⟡⟡⟡⟡⟡⟡⟡⟡⟡⟡⟡⟡⟡⟡⟡⟡

FOR DISCUSSION

1. "Quality" is a short story of theme. State the theme in a sentence.

2. Would you say that the conflict in the story is staged "on or off stage"? Explain your answer.

3. What historical industrial movement brought about the catastrophe in the lives of the Gesslers? How does mass production affect the individual craftsman today? Do you think most workmen still take pride in their craftsmanship? Why or why not?

4. Do you agree with Galsworthy's implied criticism of mass production? Defend your answer.

5. Select and discuss four passages which portray Gessler's attitude towards his work. Would it be true to say that Gessler's life was a complete failure?

6. It is said that the chief attribute of the Devonshire man is "a surface softness under which lie the grimmest obstinacies —the velvet glove on the marble hand." Do you find any of these traits in "Quality"? Discuss.

WORD STUDY

Reread the description of Gessler in paragraph 6. Study the effectiveness of the following descriptive adjectives: *crinkly reddish hair*; *guttural and one-toned* voice; *simple gravity* of one possessed by an Ideal. How does the *sardonic substance* of leather summarize the character of Gessler?

In what sense is God the eternal *Prototype* of all things?

RELATED READING

Read Galsworthy's short story, "The Apple Tree," in *The Modern Library's* edition of *Great Modern Short Stories*.

THE BLUE CROSS

GILBERT KEITH CHESTERTON

In the field of detective fiction, Chesterton was eminently successful; and in his four volume series of the FATHER BROWN *stories, he has created a literary character as appealing as the immortal Sherlock Holmes. Many of his Father Brown stories have been made into movies.*

The Chestertonian detective story is a type in itself. In them we find no mass of perverted criminal acts; nor do we find fate, superstition, magic, insanity, and cold-blooded murder—elements so common in the machinery of detective thrillers. Father Brown is a Catholic priest who knows crime because he knows repentant criminals. The plots he sets out to unravel are not intricate; but intelligence is required to follow the clues which Father Brown follows.

Between the silver ribbon of morning and the green glittering ribbon of sea, the boat touched Harwich[1] and let loose a swarm of folk like flies, among whom the man we must follow was by no means conspicuous—nor wished to be. There was nothing notable about him, except a slight contrast between the holiday gaiety of his clothes and the official gravity of his face. His clothes included a slight, pale grey jacket, a white waistcoat, and a silver straw hat with a grey-blue ribbon. His lean face was dark by contrast, and ended in a curt black beard that looked Spanish and suggested an Elizabethan ruff. He was smoking a cigarette with the seriousness of an idler. There was nothing about him to indicate the fact that the grey jacket covered a loaded revolver, that the white waistcoat covered a police card, or that the straw hat covered one of the most powerful intellects in Europe. For this was Valentin himself, the head of the Paris police and the most famous investigator of the world; and he was coming from Brussels to London to make the greatest arrest of the century.

Flambeau was in England. The police of three countries had tracked the great criminal at last from Ghent to Brussels, from Brussels to the Hook of Holland; and it was conjectured that he would take some advantage of the unfamiliarity and confusion of the Eucharistic Congress, then taking place in London. Probably he would travel as some minor clerk or secretary connected with it; but, of course, Valentin could not be certain; nobody could be certain about Flambeau.

It is many years now since this colossus of crime suddenly ceased keeping

[1] HARWICH—A seaport and a resort in Essex, England.

the world in a turmoil; and when he ceased, as they said after the death of Roland,[2] there was a great quiet upon the earth. But in his best days (I mean, of course, his worst) Flambeau was a figure as statuesque and international as the Kaiser. Almost every morning the daily paper announced that he had escaped the consequences of one extraordinary crime by committing another. He was a Gascon[3] of gigantic stature and bodily daring; and the wildest tales were told of his outbursts of athletic humor; how he turned the *juge d'instruction* upside down and stood him on his head, "to clear his mind"; how he ran down the Rue de Rivoli with a policeman under each arm. It is due to him to say that his fantastic physical strength was generally employed in such bloodless though undignified scenes; his real crimes were chiefly those of ingenious and wholesale robbery. But each of his thefts was almost a new sin, and would make a story by itself. It was he who ran the great Tyrolean Dairy Company in London, with no dairies, no cows, no carts, no milk, but with some thousand subscribers. These he served by the simple operation of moving the little milk cans outside people's doors to the doors of his own customers. It was he who had kept up an unaccountable and close correspondence with a young lady whose whole letter-bag was intercepted, by the extraordinary trick of photographing his messages infinitesimally small upon the slides of a microscope. A sweeping simplicity, however, marked many of his experiments. It is said that he once repainted all the numbers in a street in the dead of night merely to divert one traveller into a trap. It is quite certain that he invented a portable pillar-box,[4] which he put up at corners in quiet suburbs on the chance of strangers' dropping postal orders into it. Lastly, he was known to be a startling acrobat; despite his huge figure, he could leap like a grasshopper and melt into the tree-tops like a monkey. Hence the great Valentin, when he set out to find Flambeau, was perfectly aware that his adventures would not end when he had found him.

But how was he to find him? On this the great Valentin's ideas were still in process of settlement.

There was one thing which Flambeau, with all his dexterity of disguise, could not cover, and that was his singular height. If Valentin's quick eye had caught a tall apple-woman, a tall grenadier, or even a tolerably tall duchess, he might have arrested them on the spot. But all along his train there was nobody that could be a disguised Flambeau, any more than a cat could be a disguised giraffe. About the people on the boat he had already satisfied himself; and the people picked up at Harwich or on the journey limited themselves with certainty to six. There was a short railway official traveling up to the terminus, three fairly short market gardeners picked up two stations afterwards, one very short widow lady going up from a small Essex town, and a very short Roman Catholic priest going up from a small Essex village. When it came to the last case, Valentin gave it up and almost laughed. The little priest was so much the essence of those Eastern flats; he had a face as round and dull as a Norfolk dumpling; he had eyes as empty as the North Sea; he had several brown

---

[2] ROLAND—A French hero comparable to King Arthur. He lived at the time of Charlemagne and was killed by the Gascons at Roncesvalles in 778.

[3] GASCON—A native of the province of Gascony in France.

[4] PILLAR-BOX—Mail box.

paper parcels, which he was quite incapable of collecting. The Eucharistic Congress had doubtless sucked out of their local stagnation many such creatures, blind and helpless, like moles disinterred. Valentin was a skeptic in the severe style of France, and could have no love for priests. But he could have pity for them, and this one might have provoked pity in anybody. He had a large, shabby umbrella, which constantly fell on the floor. He did not seem to know which was the right end of his return ticket. He explained with a moon-calf simplicity to everybody in the carriage that he had to be careful, because he had something made of real silver "with blue stones" in one of his brown-paper parcels. His quaint blending of Essex flatness with saintly simplicity continuously amused the Frenchman till the priest arrived (somehow) at Tottenham with all his parcels, and came back for his umbrella. When he did the last, Valentin even had the good nature to warn him not to take care of the silver by telling everybody about it. But to whomever he talked, Valentin kept his eye open for someone else; he looked out steadily for anyone, rich or poor, male or female, who was well up to six feet; for Flambeau was four inches above it.

He alighted at Liverpool Street, however, quite conscientiously secure that he had not missed the criminal so far. He then went to Scotland Yard to regularize his position and arrange for help in case of need; he then lit another cigarette and went for a long stroll in the streets of London. As he was walking in the streets and squares beyond Victoria, he paused suddenly and stood. It was a quaint, quiet square, very typical of London, full of an accidental stillness. The tall, flat houses round looked at once prosperous and uninhabited; the square of shrubbery in the center looked as deserted as a green Pacific islet. One of the four sides was much higher than the rest, like a dais; and the line of this side was broken by one of London's admirable accidents—a restaurant that looked as if it had strayed from Soho.[5] It was an unreasonably attractive object, with dwarf plants in pots and long, striped blinds of lemon yellow and white. It stood specially high above the street, and in the usual patchwork way of London, a flight of steps from the street ran up to meet the front door almost as a fire-escape might run up to a first-floor window. Valentin stood and smoked in front of the yellow-white blinds and considered them long.

The most incredible thing about miracles is that they happen. A few clouds in heaven do come together into the staring shape of one human eye. A tree does stand up in the landscape of a doubtful journey in the exact and elaborate shape of a note of interrogation. I have seen both these things myself within the last few days. Nelson does die in the instant of victory; and a man named Williams does quite accidentally murder a man named Williamson; it sounds like a sort of infanticide. In short, there is in life an element of elfin coincidence which people reckoning on the prosaic may perpetually miss. As it has been well expressed in the paradox of Poe, wisdom should reckon on the unforeseen.

Aristide Valentin was unfathomably French; and the French intelligence is intelligence specially and solely. He was not "a thinking machine"; for that is a brainless phrase of modern fatalism and materialism. A machine only *is* a

machine because it cannot think. But he was a thinking man, and a plain man at the same time. All his wonderful successes, that looked like conjuring, had been gained by plodding logic, by clear and commonplace French thought. The French electrify the world not by starting any paradox, they electrify it by carrying out a truism. They carry a truism so far—as in the French Revolution. But exactly because Valentin understood reason, he understood the limits of reason. Only a man who knows nothing of motors talks of motoring without petrol; only a man who knows nothing of reason talks of reasoning without strong, undisputed first principles. Here he had no strong first principles. Flambeau had been missed at Harwich; and if he was in London at all, he might be anything from a tall tramp on Wimbledon Common to a tall toastmaster at the Hotel Metropole. In such a naked state of nescience, Valentin had a view and a method of his own.

In such cases he reckoned on the unforeseen. In such cases, when he could not follow the train of the reasonable, he coldly and carefully followed the train of the unreasonable. Instead of going to the right places—banks, police stations, rendezvous—he systematically went to the wrong places; knocked at every empty house, turned down every *cul de sac*,[6] went up every lane blocked with rubbish, went round every crescent that led him uselessly out of the way. He defended this crazy course quite logically. He said that if one had a clue this was the worst way; but if one had no clue at all it was the best, because there was just the chance that any oddity that caught the eye of the pursuer might be the same that had caught the

---

[5] SOHO—A famous fashionable square in London.

[6] *Cul de sac*—A passage open only at one end; a blind alley; a trap.

eye of the pursued. Somewhere a man must begin, and it had better be just where another man might stop. Something about that flight of steps up to the shop, something about the quietude and quaintness of the restaurant, roused all the detective's rare romantic fancy and made him resolve to strike at random. He went up the steps, and sitting down at a table by the window, asked for a cup of black coffee.

It was half-way through the morning, and he had not breakfasted; the slight litter of other breakfasts stood about on the table to remind him of his hunger; and adding a poached egg to his order, he proceeded musingly to shake some white sugar into his coffee, thinking all the time about Flambeau. He remembered how Flambeau had escaped, once by a pair of nail scissors, and once by a house on fire; once by having to pay for an unstamped letter, and once by getting people to look through a telescope at a comet that might destroy the world. He thought his detective brain as good as the criminal's, which was true. But he fully realized the disadvantage. "The criminal is the creative artist; the detective only the critic," he said with a sour smile, and lifted his coffee cup to his lips slowly, and put it down very quickly. He had put salt in it.

He looked at the vessel from which the silvery powder had come; it was certainly a sugar-basin; as unmistakably meant for sugar as a champagne-bottle for champagne. He wondered why they should keep salt in it. He looked to see if there were any more orthodox vessels. Yes; there were two salt-cellars quite full. Perhaps there was some specialty in the condiment in the salt-cellars. He tasted it; it was sugar. Then he looked round at the restaurant with a refreshed air of interest, to see if there were any other traces of that singular artistic taste which puts the sugar in the salt-cellars and the salt in the sugar-basin. Except for an odd splash of some dark fluid on one of the white-papered walls, the whole place appeared neat, cheerful and ordinary. He rang the bell for the waiter.

When that official hurried up, fuzzy-haired and somewhat blear-eyed at that early hour, the detective (who was not without an appreciation of the simpler forms of humor) asked him to taste the sugar and see if it was up to the high reputation of the hotel. The result was that the waiter yawned suddenly and woke up.

"Do you play this delicate joke on your customers every morning?" inquired Valentin. "Does changing the salt and sugar never pall on you as a jest?"

The waiter, when this irony grew clearer, stammeringly assured him that the establishment had certainly no such intention; it must be a most curious mistake. He picked up the sugar-basin and looked at it; he picked up the salt-cellar and looked at that, his face growing more and more bewildered. At last he abruptly excused himself, and hurrying away, returned in a few seconds with the proprietor. The proprietor also examined the sugar-basin and then the salt-cellar; the proprietor also looked bewildered.

Suddenly the waiter seemed to grow inarticulate with a rush of words.

"I zink," he stuttered eagerly, "it is those two clergymen."

"What two clergymen?"

"The two clergymen," said the waiter "that threw soup at the wall."

"Threw soup at the wall?" repeated Valentin, feeling sure this must be some singular Italian metaphor.

"Yes, yes," said the attendant excitedly, and pointing at the dark splash on the white paper; "threw it over there on the wall."

Valentin looked his query at the proprietor, who came to his rescue with fuller reports.

"Yes, sir," he said, "it's quite true, though I don't suppose it has anything to do with the sugar and salt. Two clergymen came in and drank soup here very early, as soon as the shutters were taken down. They were both very quiet, respectable people; one of them paid the bill and went out; the other, who seemed a slower coach altogether, was some minutes longer getting his things together. But he went at last. Only, the instant before he stepped into the street he deliberately picked up his cup, which he had only half emptied, and threw the soup slap on the wall. I was in the back room myself, and so was the waiter; so I could only rush out in time to find the wall splashed and the shop empty. It don't do any particular damage, but it was confounded cheek; and I tried to catch the men in the street. They were too far off though; I only noticed they went round the next corner into Carstairs Street."

The detective was on his feet, hat settled and stick in hand. He had already decided that in the universal darkness of his mind he could only follow the first odd finger that pointed; and this finger was odd enough. Paying his bill and clashing the glass doors behind him, he was soon swinging round into the other street.

It was fortunate that even in such fevered moments his eye was cool and quick. Something in a shop-front went by him like a mere flash; yet he went back to look at it. The shop was a popular greengrocer and fruiterer's, an array of goods set out in the open air and plainly ticketed with their names and prices. In the two most prominent compartments were two heaps, of oranges and of nuts respectively. On the heap of nuts lay a scrap of cardboard, on which was written in bold, blue chalk, "Best tangerine oranges, two a penny." On the oranges was the equally clear and exact description, "Finest Brazil nuts, 4d. a lb." M. Valentin looked at these two placards and fancied he had met this highly subtle form of humor before, and that somewhat recently. He drew the attention of the red-faced fruiterer, who was looking rather sullenly up and down the street, to this inaccuracy in his advertisements. The fruiterer said nothing, but sharply put each card into its proper place. The detective, leaning elegantly on his walking-cane, continued to scrutinize the shop. At last he said, "Pray excuse my apparent irrelevance, my good sir, but I should like to ask you a question in experimental psychology and the association of ideas."

The red-faced shopman regarded him with an eye of menace; but he continued gaily, swinging his cane, "Why," he pursued, "why are two tickets wrongly placed in a greengrocer's shop like a shovel hat that has come to London for a holiday? Or, in case I do not make myself clear, what is the mystical association which connects the idea of nuts marked as oranges with the idea of two clergymen, one tall and the other short?"

The eyes of the tradesman stood out of his head like a snail's; he really seemed for an instant likely to fling himself upon the stranger. At last he stammered angrily: "I don't know what you 'ave to do with it, but if you're one of their friends, you can tell 'em from me that I'll knock their silly 'eads off, parsons or no parsons, if they upset my apples again."

"Indeed?" asked the detective, with great sympathy. "Did they upset your apples?"

"One of 'em did," said the heated shopman; "rolled 'em all over the street. I'd 'ave caught the fool but for havin' to pick 'em up."

"Which way did these parsons go?" asked Valentin.

"Up that second road on the left-hand side, and then across the square," said the other promptly.

"Thanks," replied Valentin, and vanished like a fairy. On the other side of the second square he found a policeman, and said: "This is urgent, constable; have you seen two clergymen in shovel hats?"

The policeman began to chuckle heavily. "I 'ave, sir; and if you arst me, one of 'em was drunk. He stood in the middle of the road that bewildered that—"

"Which way did they go?" snapped Valentin.

"They took one of them yellow buses over there," answered the man; "them that go to Hampstead."

Valentin produced his official card and said very rapidly: "Call up two of your men to come with me in pursuit," and crossed the road with such contagious energy that the ponderous policeman was moved to almost agile obedience. In a minute and a half the French detective was joined on the opposite pavement by an inspector and a man in plain clothes.

"Well, sir," began the former, with smiling importance, "and what may—?"

Valentin pointed suddenly with his cane. "I'll tell you on the top of that omnibus," he said, and was darting and dodging across the tangle of the traffic. When all three sank panting on the top seats of the yellow vehicle, the inspector said: "We could go four times as quick in a taxi."

"Quite true," replied their leader placidly, "if we only had an idea of where we were going."

"Well, where *are* you going?" asked the other, staring.

Valentin smoked frowningly for a few seconds; then, removing his cigarette, he said: "If you *know* what a man's doing, get in front of him; but if you want to guess what he's doing, keep behind him. Stray when he strays; stop when he stops; travel as slowly as he. Then you may see what he saw and may act as he acted. All we can do is to keep our eyes skinned for a queer thing."

"What sort of queer thing do you mean?" asked the inspector.

"Any sort of queer thing," answered Valentin, and relapsed into obstinate silence.

The yellow omnibus crawled up the northern roads for what seemed like hours on end; the great detective would not explain further, and perhaps his assistants felt a silent and growing doubt of his errand. Perhaps, also, they felt a silent and growing desire for lunch, for the hours crept long past the normal luncheon hour, and the long roads of the North London suburbs seemed to shoot out into length after length like an infernal telescope. It was one of those journeys on which a man perpetually feels that now at last he must have come to the end of the universe, and then finds he has only come to the beginning of Tufnell Park. London died away in draggled taverns and dreary scrubs, and then was unaccountably born again in blazing high streets and blatant hotels. It was like passing

through thirteen separate vulgar cities all just touching each other. But though the winter twilight was already threatening the road ahead of them, the Parisian detective still sat silent and watchful, eyeing the frontage of the streets that slid by on either side. By the time they had left Camden Town behind, the policemen were nearly asleep; at least, they gave something like a jump as Valentin leaped erect, struck a hand on each man's shoulder, and shouted to the driver to stop.

They tumbled down the steps into the road without realizing why they had been dislodged; when they looked round for enlightenment they found Valentin triumphantly pointing his finger towards a window on the left side of the road. It was a large window, forming part of the long façade of a gilt and palatial public-house; it was the part reserved for respectable dining, and labelled "Restaurant." This window, like all the rest along the frontage of the hotel, was of frosted and figured glass; but in the middle of it was a big, black smash, like a star in the ice.

"Our cue at last," cried Valentin, waving his stick; "the place with the broken window."

"What window? What cue?" asked his principal assistant. "Why, what proof is there that this has anything to do with them?"

Valentin almost broke his bamboo stick with rage.

"Proof!" he cried. "Good night! the man is looking for proof! Why, of course, the chances are twenty to one that it has *nothing* to do with them. But what else can we do? Don't you see we must either follow one wild possibility or else go home to bed?" He banged his way into the restaurant, followed by his companions, and they were soon seated at a late luncheon at a little table, and looking at the star of smashed glass from the inside. Not that it was very informative to them even then.

"Got your window broken, I see," said Valentin to the waiter as he paid the bill.

"Yes, sir," answered the attendant, bending busily over the change, to which Valentin silently added an enormous tip. The waiter straightened himself with mild but unmistakable animation.

"Ah, yes, sir," he said. "Very odd thing, that sir."

"Indeed? Tell us about it," said the detective with careless curiosity.

"Well, two gents in black came in," said the waiter; "two of those foreign parsons that are running about. They had a cheap and quiet little lunch, and one of them paid for it and went out. The other was just going out to join him when I looked at my change again and found he'd paid me more than three times too much. 'Here,' I says to the chap who was nearly out of the door, 'you've paid too much.' 'Oh,' he says, very cool, 'have we?' 'Yes,' I says, and picks up the bill to show him. Well, that was a knock-out."

"What do you mean?" asked his interlocutor.

"Well, I'd have sworn on seven Bibles that I'd put 4s. on that bill. But now I saw I'd put 14s., as plain as paint."

"Well?" cried Valentin, moving slowly, but with burning eyes, "and then?"

"The parson at the door he says all serene, 'Sorry to confuse your accounts, but it'll pay for the window.' 'What window?' I says. 'The one I'm going to break,' he says, and smashed that blessed pane with his umbrella."

All three inquirers made an exclamation; and the inspector said under his breath, "Are we after escaped lunatics?" The waiter went on with some relish for the ridiculous story:

"I was so knocked silly for a second, I couldn't do anything. The man marched out of the place and joined his friend just round the corner. Then they went so quick up Bullock Street that I couldn't catch them, though I ran round the bars to do it."

"Bullock Street," said the detective, and shot up that thoroughfare as quickly as the strange couple he pursued.

Their journey now took them through bare brick ways like tunnels; streets with few lights and even with few windows; streets that seemed built out of the blank backs of everything and everywhere. Dusk was deepening, and it was not easy even for the London policemen to guess in what direction they were treading. The inspector, however, was pretty certain that they would eventually strike some part of Hampstead Heath. Abruptly one bulging gas-lit window broke the blue twilight like a bull's-eye lantern; and Valentin stopped an instant before a little garish sweet-stuff shop. After an instant's hesitation he went in; he stood amid the gaudy colours of the confectionery with entire gravity and bought thirteen chocolate cigars with a certain care. He was clearly preparing an opening; but he did not need one.

An angular, elderly young woman in the shop had regarded his elegant appearance with a merely automatic inquiry; but when she saw the door behind him blocked with the blue uniform of the inspector, her eyes seemed to wake up.

"Oh," she said, "if you've come about

that parcel, I've sent it off already."

"Parcel!" repeated Valentin; and it was his turn to look inquiring.

"I mean the parcel the gentleman left—the clergyman gentleman."

"For goodness' sake," said Valentin, leaning forward with his first real confession of eagerness, "for Heaven's sake tell us what happened exactly."

"Well," said the woman a little doubtfully, "the clergymen came in about half an hour ago and bought some peppermints and talked a bit, and then went off towards the Heath. But a second after, one of them runs back into the shop and says, 'Have I left a parcel?' Well, I looked everywhere and couldn't see one; so he says, 'Never mind; but if it should turn up, please post it to this address,' and he left me the address and a shilling for my trouble. And sure enough, though I thought I'd looked everywhere, I found he'd left a brown paper parcel, so I posted it to the place he said. I can't remember the address now; it was somewhere in Westminster. But as the thing seemed so important, I thought perhaps the police had come about it."

"So they have," said Valentin shortly. "Is Hampstead Heath near here?"

"Straight on for fifteen minues," said the woman, "and you'll come right out on the open." Valentin sprang out of the shop and began to run. The other detectives followed him at a reluctant trot.

The street they threaded was so narrow and shut in by shadows that when they came out unexpectedly into the void common and vast sky they were startled to find the evening still so light and clear. A perfect dome of peacock-green sank into gold amid the blackening trees and the dark violet distances. The glowing green tint was just deep enough to pick out in points of crystal one or two stars. All that was left of the daylight lay in a golden glitter across the edge of Hampstead and that popular hollow which is called the Vale of Health. The holiday makers who roam this region had not wholly dispersed; a few couples sat shapelessly on benches; and here and there a distant girl still shrieked in one of the swings. The glory of heaven deepened and darkened around the sublime vulgarity of man; and standing on the slope and looking across the valley, Valentin beheld the thing which he sought.

Among the black and breaking groups in that distance was one especially black which did not break—a group of two figures clerically clad. Though they seemed as small as insects, Valentin could see that one of them was much smaller than the other. Though the other had a student's stoop and an inconspicuous manner, he could see that the man was well over six feet high. He shut his teeth and went forward, whirling his stick impatiently. By the time he had substantially diminished the distance and magnified the two black figures as in a vast microscope, he had perceived something else; something which startled him, and yet which he had somehow expected. Whoever was the tall priest, there could be no doubt about the identity of the short one. It was his friend of the Harwich train, the stumpy little *curé* of Essex whom he had warned about his brown paper parcels.

Now, so far as this went, everything fitted in finally and rationally enough. Valentin had learned by his inquiries that morning that a Father Brown from Essex was bringing up a silver cross with sapphires, a relic of considerable value, to show some of the foreign priests at the congress. This undoubtedly was the "silver with blue stones"; and Father Brown undoubtedly was the little greenhorn in the train. Now there was nothing wonderful about the fact that what Valentin had found out Flambeau had also found out; Flambeau found out everything. Also there was nothing wonderful in the fact that when Flambeau heard of a sapphire cross he should try to steal it; that was the most natural thing in all natural history. And most certainly there was nothing wonderful about the fact that Flambeau should have it all his own way with such a silly sheep as the man with the umbrella and the parcels. He was the sort of man whom anybody could lead on a string to the North Pole; it was not surprising that an actor like Flambeau, dressed as another priest, could lead him to Hampstead Heath. So far the crime seemed clear enough; and while the detective pitied the priest for his helplessness, he almost despised Flambeau for condescending to so gullible a victim. But when Valentin thought of all that had happened in between, of all that had led him to his triumph, he racked his brains for the smallest rhyme or reason in it. What had the stealing of a blue-and-silver cross from a priest from Essex to do with chucking soup at wall paper? What had it to do with calling nuts oranges, or with paying for windows first and breaking them afterwards? He had come to the end of his chase; yet somehow he had missed the middle of it. When he failed (which was seldom), he had usually grasped the clue, but nevertheless missed the criminal. Here he had grasped the criminal, but still he could not grasp the clue.

The two figures that they followed were crawling like black flies across the huge green contour of a hill. They were evidently sunk in conversation and perhaps did not notice where they were going; but they were certainly going to the wilder and more silent heights of the Heath. As their pursuers gained on them, the latter had to use the undignified attitudes of the deer-stalker, to crouch behind clumps of trees and even to crawl prostrate in deep grass. By these ungainly ingenuities the hunters even came close enough to the quarry to hear the murmur of the discussion, but no word could be distinguished except the word "reason" recurring frequently in a high and almost childish voice. Once over an abrupt dip of land and a dense tangle of thickets, the detectives actually lost the two figures they were following. They did not find the trail again for an agonizing ten minutes, and then it led round the brow of a great dome of hill overlooking an amphitheatre of rich and desolate sunset scenery. Under a tree in this commanding yet neglected spot was an old ramshackle wooden seat. On this seat sat the two priests still in serious speech together. The gorgeous green and gold still clung to the darkening horizon; but the dome above was turning slowly from peacock-green to peacock-blue, and the stars detached themselves more and more like solid jewels. Mutely motioning to his followers, Valentin contrived to creep up behind the big branching tree, and, standing there in deathly silence, heard the words of the strange priests for the first time.

After he had listened for a minute and a half, he was gripped by a devilish doubt. Perhaps he had dragged the two English policemen to the wastes of a nocturnal heath on an errand no saner than seeking figs on its thistles. For the two priests were talking exactly like priests, piously, with learning and leisure, about the most aërial enigmas of theology. The little Essex priest spoke the more simply, with his round face turned to the strengthening stars; the other talked with his head bowed, as if he were not even worthy to look at them. But no more innocently clerical conversation could have been heard in any white Italian cloister or black Spanish cathedral.

The first he heard was the tail of one of Father Brown's sentences, which ended: ". . . what they really meant in the Middle Ages by the heavens' being incorruptible."

The taller priest nodded his bowed head and said:

"Ah, yes, these modern infidels appeal to their reason; but who can look at those millions of worlds and not feel that there may well be wonderful universes above us where reason is utterly unreasonable?"

"No," said the other priest; "reason is always reasonable, even in the last limbo, in the lost borderland of things. I know that people charge the Church with lowering reason, but it is just the other way. Alone on earth, the Church makes reason really supreme. Alone on earth, the Church affirms that God himself is bound by reason."

The other priest raised his austere face to the spangled sky and said:

"Yet who knows if in that infinite universe—?"

"Only infinite physically," said the little priest, turning sharply in his seat, "not infinite in the sense of escaping from the laws of truth."

Valentin behind his tree was tearing his fingernails with silent fury. He seemed almost to hear the sniggers of the English detectives whom he had brought so far on a fantastic guess only to listen to the metaphysical gossip of two mild old parsons. In his impatience he lost the equally elaborate answer of the tall cleric, and when he listened again it was again Father Brown who was speaking:

"Reason and justice grip the remotest and the loneliest star. Look at those stars. Don't they look as if they were single diamonds and sapphires? Well, you can imagine any mad botany or geology you please. Think of forests of adamant with leaves of brilliants. Think the moon is a blue moon, a single elephantine sapphire. But don't fancy that all that frantic astronomy would make the smallest difference to the reason and justice of conduct. On plains of opal, under cliffs cut out of pearl, you would still find a notice-board, 'Thou shalt not steal.' "

Valentin was just in the act of rising from his rigid and crouching attitude and creeping away as softly as might be, felled by the one great folly of his life. But something in the very silence of the tall priest made him stop until the latter spoke. When at last he did speak, he said simply, his head bowed and his hands on his knees:

"Well, I still think that other worlds may perhaps rise higher than our reason. The mystery of heaven is unfathomable, and I for one can only bow my head."

Then, with brow yet bent and without changing by the faintest shade his attitude or voice, he added:

"Just hand over that sapphire cross of yours, will you? We're all alone here, and I could pull you to pieces like a straw doll."

The utterly unaltered voice and attitude added a strange violence to that shocking change of speech. But the guarder of the relic only seemed to turn his head by the smallest section of the compass. He seemed still to have a somewhat foolish face turned to the stars. Perhaps he had not understood. Or, perhaps, he had understood and sat rigid with terror.

"Yes," said the tall priest, in the same low voice and in the same still posture, "yes, I am Flambeau."

Then, after a pause, he said:

"Come, will you give me that cross?"

"No," said the other, and the monosyllable had an odd sound.

Flambeau suddenly flung off all his pontifical pretensions. The great robber leaned back in his seat and laughed low but long.

"No," he cried, "you won't give it me, you proud prelate. You won't give it me, you little celibate simpleton. Shall I tell you why you won't give it me? Because I've got it already in my own breast-pocket."

The small man from Essex turned what seemed to be a dazed face in the dusk, and said, with the timid eagerness of "The Private Secretary":

"Are—are you sure?"

Flambeau yelled with delight.

"Really, you're as good as a three-act farce," he cried. "Yes, you turnip, I am quite sure. I had the sense to make a duplicate of the right parcel, and now, my friend, you've got the duplicate and I've got the jewels. An old dodge, Father Brown—a very old dodge."

"Yes," said Father Brown, and passed his hand through his hair with the same strange vagueness of manner. "Yes, I've heard of it before."

The colossus of crime leaned over to the little rustic priest with a sort of sudden interest.

"*You* have heard of it?" he asked. "Where have *you* heard of it?"

"Well, I mustn't tell you his name, of course," said the little man simply. "He was a penitent, you know. He had

lived prosperously for about twenty years entirely on duplicate brown paper parcels. And so, you see, when I began to suspect you, I thought of this poor chap's way of doing it at once."

"Began to suspect me?" repeated the outlaw with increased intensity. "Did you really have the gumption to suspect me just because I brought you up to this bare part of the heath?"

"No, no," said Brown with an air of apology. "You see, I suspected you when we first met. It's that little bulge up the sleeve where you people have the spiked bracelet."

"How in Tartarus," [7] cried Flambeau, "did you ever hear of the spiked bracelet?"

"Oh, one's little flock, you know!" said Father Brown, arching his eyebrows rather blankly. "When I was a curate in Hartlepool, there were three of them with spiked bracelets. So, as I suspected you from the first, don't you see, I made sure that the cross should go safe, anyhow. I'm afraid I watched you, you know. So at last I saw you change the parcels. Then, don't you see, I changed them back again. And then I left the right one."

"Left it behind?" repeated Flambeau, and for the first time there was another note in his voice beside his triumph.

"Well, it was like this," said the little priest, speaking in the same unaffected way. "I went back to that sweet-shop and asked if I'd left a parcel, and gave them a particular address if it turned up. Well, I knew I hadn't; but when I went away again I did. So, instead of running after me with that valuable parcel, they have sent it flying to a friend of mine in Westminster." Then he added rather sadly: "I learnt that, too, from a

[7] TARTARUS—The place of punishment for the wicked in classical mythology.

poor fellow in Hartlepool. He used to do it with handbags he stole at railway stations, but he's in a monastery now. Oh, one gets to know, you know, you know," he added, rubbing his head again with the same sort of desperate apology. "We can't help being priests. People come and tell us these things."

Flambeau tore a brown-paper parcel out of his inner pocket and rent it in pieces. There was nothing but paper and sticks of lead inside it. He sprang to his feet with a gigantic gesture, and cried:

"I don't believe you. I don't believe a bumpkin like you could manage all that. I believe you've still got the stuff on you, and if you don't give it up— why, we're all alone, and I'll take it by force!"

"No," said Father Brown simply, and stood up also, "you won't take it by force. First, because I really haven't still got it. And, second, because we are not alone."

Flambeau stopped in his stride forward.

"Behind that tree," said Father Brown, pointing, "are two strong policemen and the greatest detective alive. How did they come here, do you ask? Why, I brought them, of course! How did I do it? Why, I'll tell you if you like! Lord bless you, we have to know twenty such things when we work among the criminal classes! Well, I wasn't sure you were a thief, and it would never do to make a scandal against one of your own clergy. So I just tested you to see if anything would make you show yourself. A man generally makes a small scene if he finds salt in his coffee; if he doesn't, he has some reason for keeping quiet. I changed the salt and sugar, and *you* kept quiet. A man generally objects if his bill is three times too big. If he pays it, he has some motive for passing unnoticed. I altered your bill, and *you* paid it."

The world seemed waiting for Flambeau to leap like a tiger. But he was held back as by a spell; he was stunned with the utmost curiosity.

"Well," went on Father Brown, with lumbering lucidity, "as you wouldn't leave any tracks for the police, of course somebody had to. At every place we went to, I took care to do something that would get us talked about for the rest of the day. I didn't do much harm —a splashed wall, spilt apples, a broken window; but I saved the cross, as the cross will always be saved. It is at Westminster by now. I rather wonder you didn't stop it with the Donkey's Whistle."

"With the what?" asked Flambeau.

"I'm glad you've never heard of it," said the priest, making a face. "It's a foul thing. I'm sure you're too good a man for a Whistler. I couldn't have countered it even with the Spots myself; I'm not strong enough in the legs."

"What on earth are you talking about?" asked the other.

"Well, I did think you'd know the Spots," said Father Brown, agreeably surprised. "Oh, you can't have gone so very wrong yet!"

"How in blazes do you know all these horrors?" cried Flambeau.

The shadow of a smile crossed the round, simple face of his clerical opponent.

"Oh, by being a celibate simpleton, I suppose," he said. "Has it never struck you that a man who does next to nothing but hear men's real sins is not likely to be wholly unaware of human evil? But, as a matter of fact, another part of my trade, too, made me sure you weren't a priest."

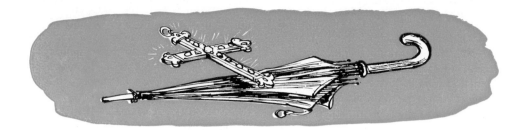

"What?" asked the thief, almost gaping.

"You attacked reason," said Father Brown. "It's bad theology."

And even as he turned away to collect his property, the three policemen came out from under the twilight trees. Flambeau was an artist and a sportsman. He stepped back and swept Valentin a great bow.

"Do not bow to me, *mon ami*," said Valentin with silver clearness. "Let us both bow to our master."

And they both stood an instant uncovered while the little Essex priest blinked about for his umbrella.

FOR DISCUSSION

1. Is this a short story of plot, character, or setting? Defend your answer from your knowledge of the story.

2. How are the opening paragraphs designed to catch your attention at once? Are you conscious of being roughly introduced to "plot, setting, and character"? Explain. What is your first reaction to Flambeau?

3. Why did Chesterton introduce Father Brown through the eyes of Valentin? What is your first reaction to Father Brown?

4. Enumerate the startling series of "accidents" by which Father Brown deliberately led Valentin to discover the criminal.

5. What were the two tests which Father Brown applied to be sure his "clerical" companion was not a priest? How did he outwit the thief in the matter of the Blue Cross?

6. Do you or do you not prefer this story to other detective stories which you have read? Discuss your answer.

WORDS

Chesterton applied much of his knowledge of painting to the art of composition. His appeal to the sense of color is unusual. He refers to at least six different colors in the first paragraph. Write out at least ten color adjectives which are used in the remainder of the story. It will help you to use more color adjectives yourself.

Chesterton's diction is not simple, but it is graphic, precise, and richly connotative. Words taken out of their context may lose their delicate precision of meaning which arises partly from their right association with other words. It demands real artistry to choose the right word in the right context. Analyze the following words in their context: The boat *touched* Harwich; *curt* black beard; *colossus* of crime; a figure as *statuesque* and *international* as the Kaiser; *dexterity* of disguise; *essence* of those Norfolk flats; *sucked out* of their local *stagnation*; naked state of *nescience*; crossed the road with such *contagious* energy that the *ponderous* policeman moved to almost *agile* obedience;

raised his *austere* face to the *spangled* sky; the *metaphysical* gossip of two mild old parsons; followed at a *reluctant* trot; the *sublime vulgarity* of man; a blue moon, a single *elephantine* sapphire; *flung off his pontifical* pretensions; *lumbering lucidity.*

Brilliantly handled, the sharply-phrased paradox became Chesterton's keen sword against sham and shallow thinking. Select three sentences which are paradoxical in style.

PROJECTS

1. Enumerate at least five instances where Chesterton uses his story as a medium to express a correct philosophy.

2. Discuss, both in and out of their context, the following statements. Choose at least one of them as a subject for a written editorial or a short expository paper.

a. "The most incredible thing about miracles is that they happen."

b. "There is in life an element of elfin coincidence which people reckoning on the prosaic may perpetually miss."

c. "The French electrify the world not by starting a paradox, they electrify it by carrying out a truism. They carry a truism so far—as in the French Revolution."

d. "Alone on earth, the Church affirms that God is bound by reason."

e. "On plains of opal, under cliffs cut out of pearl, you would still find a notice-board, 'Thou shalt not steal.'"

RELATED READING

You are already acquainted with the *Father Brown Omnibus,* the collection of Chesterton's Father Brown stories. Read "The Hammer of God" in this collection.

❖❖❖❖❖

TAKING THE VEIL

KATHERINE MANSFIELD

This story takes us inside the mind of a very emotional, very imaginative eighteen-year-old girl. She is pretty, she wears pretty clothes, she is engaged to be married—but now, all of a sudden, she thinks she can never be happy again. Ah, what will ever become of her? In her mind she goes over her present life, her future—

It seemed impossible that anyone should be unhappy on such a beautiful morning. Nobody was, decided Edna, except herself. The windows were flung wide in the houses. From within there came the sound of pianos, little hands chased after each other and ran away from each other, practicing scales. The trees fluttered in the sunny gardens, all bright with spring flowers. Street boys whistled, a little dog barked; people passed by, walking so lightly, so swiftly, they looked as though they wanted to break into a run. Now she actually saw in the distance a parasol, peach-colored, the first parasol of the year.

Perhaps even Edna did not look quite as unhappy as she felt. It is not easy to look tragic at eighteen, when you are extremely pretty, with the cheeks and lips and shining eyes of perfect health. Above all, when you are wearing a French blue frock, and your new spring hat trimmed with cornflowers. True, she carried under her arm a book bound in horrid black leather. Perhaps the book provided a gloomy note, but only by accident; it was the ordinary library binding. For Edna had made going to the library an excuse for getting out of the house to think, to realize what had happened, to decide somehow what was to be done now.

An awful thing had happened. Quite suddenly, at the theater last night, when she and Jimmy were seated side by side in the dress circle, without a moment's warning—in fact, she had just finished a chocolate almond and passed the box to him again—she had fallen in love with an actor. But—fallen—in—love. . . .

The feeling was unlike anything she had ever imagined. It wasn't in the least pleasant. It was hardly thrilling. Unless you call the most dreadful sensation of misery, despair, agony, and wretchedness thrilling. Combined with the certainty that if that actor met her on the pavement after, while Jimmy was fetching their cab, she would follow him to the ends of the earth, at a nod, at a sign, without giving another thought to Jimmy or her father and mother or her happy home and countless friends again.

The play had begun fairly cheerfully. That was at the chocolate almond stage.

Then the hero had gone blind. Terrible moment! Edna had cried so much she had to borrow Jimmy's folded, smooth-feeling handkerchief as well. Not that crying mattered. Whole rows were in tears. Even the men blew their noses with a loud trumpeting noise and tried to peer at the program instead of looking at the stage. Jimmy, most mercifully dry-eyed—for what would she have done without his handkerchief?—squeezed her free hand, and whispered "Cheer up, darling girl!" And it was then she had taken a last chocolate almond to please him and passed the box again. Then, there had been that ghastly scene with the hero alone on the stage in a deserted room at twilight, with a band playing outside and the sound of cheering coming from the street. He had tried—ah! how painfully, how pitifully—to grope his way to the window. He had succeeded at last. There he stood holding the curtain while one beam of light, just one beam, shone full on his raised sightless face, and the band faded away into the distance.

It was—really, it was absolutely—oh, the most—it was simply—in fact, from that moment Edna knew that life could never be the same. She drew her hand away from Jimmy's, leaned back, and shut the chocolate box forever. This at last was love.

Edna and Jimmy were engaged. She had had her hair up for a year and a half; they had been publicly engaged for a year. But they had known they were going to marry each other ever since they walked in the Botanical Gardens with their nurses, and sat on the grass with a wine biscuit and a piece of barley-sugar each for their tea. It was so much an accepted thing that Edna had worn a wonderfully good imitation of an engagement ring out of a cracker [1] all the time she was at

[1] A CRACKER—A package of candy.

school. And up till now they had been devoted to each other.

But now it was over. It was so completely over that Edna found it difficult to believe that Jimmy did not realize it too. She smiled wisely, sadly, as she turned into the gardens of the Convent of the Sacred Heart and mounted the path that led through them to Hill Street. How much better to know it now than to wait until after they were married! Now it was possible that Jimmy would get over it. No, it was no use deceiving herself; he would never get over it! His life was wrecked, was ruined; that was inevitable. But he was young. Time, people said, Time might make a little, just a little difference. In forty years when he was an old man, he might be able to think of her calmly—perhaps. But she— what did the future hold for her?

Edna had reached the top of the path.

There under a new-leafed tree, hung with little bunches of white flowers, she sat down on a green bench and looked over the Convent flower beds. In the one nearest to her there grew tender stocks, with a border of blue, shell-like pansies, with at one corner a clump of creamy freesias, their light spears of green crisscrossed over the flowers. The Convent pigeons were tumbling high in the air, and she could hear the voice of Sister Agnes who was giving a singing lesson. *Ah-me*, sounded the deep tones of the nun, and *ah-me*, they were echoed.

If she did not marry Jimmy, of course she would marry nobody. The man she was in love with, the famous actor—Edna had far too much common sense not to realize that would never be. It was very odd. She didn't even want it to be. Her love was too intense for that. It had to be endured, silently; it had to torment her. It was, she supposed, simply that kind of love.

"But, Edna!" cried Jimmy.[2] "Can you never change? Can I never hope again?"

Oh, what sorrow to have to say it, but it must be said. "No, Jimmy, I will never change."

Edna bowed her head; and a little flower fell on her lap, and the voice of Sister Agnes cried suddenly *ah-no*, and the echo came, *ah-no*. . . .

At that moment the future was revealed. Edna saw it all. She was astonished; it took her breath away at first. But, after all, what could be more natural? She would go into a convent. Her father and mother would do everything to dissuade her, in vain. As for Jimmy, his state of mind hardly bears thinking about. Why can't they understand? How can they add to her suffering like this? The world is cruel, terribly cruel! After a last scene when she gives away her jewelry and so on to her best friends—she so calm, they so brokenhearted—into a convent she goes. No, one moment. The very evening of her going is the actor's last evening at Port Willin. He receives by a strange messenger a box. It is full of white flowers. But there is no name, no card. Nothing? Yes, under the roses, wrapped in a white handkerchief, Edna's last photograph with, written underneath:

The world forgetting, by the world forgot.[3]

Edna sat very still under the trees; she clasped the black book in her fingers as

[2] "BUT, EDNA!" CRIED JIMMY—This conversation is only in the girl's imagination.
[3] THE WORLD . . . FORGOT—This line from Alexander Pope's "Eloïsa to Abelard" expresses the peace and seclusion of a life as a nun.

though it were her missal. She takes the name of Sister Angela. Snip! Snip! All her lovely hair is cut off. Will she be allowed to send one curl to Jimmy? It is contrived somehow. And in a blue gown with a white headband Sister Angela goes from the convent to the chapel, from the chapel to the convent with something unearthly in her look, in her sorrowful eyes, and in the gentle smile with which they greet the little children who run to her. A saint! She hears it whispered as she paces the chill, wax-smelling corridors. A saint! And visitors to the chapel are told of the nun whose voice is heard above the other voices, of her youth, her beauty, of her tragic, tragic love, "There is a man in this town whose life is ruined. . . ."

A big bee, a golden furry fellow, crept into a freesia, and the delicate flower leaned over, swung, shook; and when the bee flew away it fluttered still as though it were laughing. Happy, careless flower.

Sister Angela looked at it and said, "Now it is winter." One night, lying in her icy cell she hears a cry. Some stray animal is out there in the garden, a kitten or a lamb or—well, whatever little animal might be there. Up rises the sleepless nun. All in white, shivering but fearless, she goes and brings it in. But next morning when the bell rings for matins, she is found tossing in high fever . . . in delirium . . . and she never recovers. In three days all is over. The service has been said in the chapel, and she is buried in the corner of the cemetery reserved for the nuns, where there are plain little crosses of wood. *Rest in Peace, Sister Angela.*

Now it is evening. Two old people leaning on each other come slowly to the grave and kneel down sobbing, "Our daughter! Our only daughter!" Now there comes another. He is all in black;

he comes slowly. But when he is there and lifts his black hat, Edna sees to her horror his hair is snow-white. Jimmy! Too late, too late! The tears are running down his face; he is crying *now*. Too late, too late! The wind shakes the leafless trees in the churchyard. He gives one awful bitter cry.

Edna's black book fell with a thud to the garden path. She jumped up, her heart beating. My darling! No, it's not too late. It's all been a mistake, a terrible dream. Oh, that white hair! How could she have done it? She has not done it. Oh, heavens! Oh, what happiness! She is free, young, and nobody knows her secret. Everything is still pos-

sible for her and Jimmy. The house they have planned may still be built, the little solemn boy with his hands behind his back watching them plant the standard roses may still be born. His baby sister . . . But when Edna got as far as baby sister, she stretched out her arms as though the little love came flying through the air to her, and gazing at the garden, at the white sprays on the tree, at those darling pigeons blue against the blue, and the Convent with its narrow windows, she realized that now at last for the first time in her life—she had never imagined any feeling like it before—she knew what it was to be in love, but—in —love!

FOR UNDERSTANDING

1. Was Edna really in love with the actor?

2. Edna does not seem to have a genuine religious vocation, and therefore is not a suitable person to become a nun. To her, entering a convent is only a romantic notion which comes because she imagines her life is "over." How did she happen to think of *this particular* way of spending the future?

3. Edna's vivid daydreaming centers closely on herself—how she will send a good-by message to the actor, how she will look, where she will be buried, how sad her parents will be. Of course, since it is only a daydream, some of the details are vague —as when she gives away her jewelry "*and so on*." What detail is equally vague in her mental picture of *what she finds* on the wintry night she goes out into the garden?

4. Which imaginary event finally makes Edna realize that she is still in love with Jimmy after all? How does it resemble the event in the play which caused her to fall in love with the actor?

5. How might Edna's age, and the conditions of her life, help to make her a kind of person likely to have daydreams?

THE HINT OF AN EXPLANATION

GRAHAM GREENE

*In his essay, "The Lost Childhood," Graham Greene discussed the in-
fluence of his childhood reading upon his life and writings. Speaking of
Marjorie Bowen's* VIPER OF MILAN, *he wrote: "Anyway she had given me
my pattern— perfect evil walking the world where perfect goodness can
never walk again, and only the pendulum ensures that after all in the end
justice will be done . . . Goodness has only once found a perfect incarnation in a human body and never will again, but evil can always find a
home there. Human nature is not black and white but black and grey."*

*Throughout Greene's works we find the constant theme of the problem
of evil and grace. The visible world of external events is not the great
reality but the symbol of the internal struggle of characters who have souls
to be saved or lost. If sin is an obsession with Greene, he sees it as the
frightful calamity resulting from man's free refusal to accept Love.*

*With that classical economy of style which has made him the outstand-
ing master craftsman of modern English prose, Greene gives us in "The
Hint of an Explanation" a short story of incarnate evil—starkly realistic
and almost terrifying in its emotional impact. Here is Catholic literature
at its very best.*

A long train journey on a late December evening, in this new version of
peace, is a dreary experience. I suppose
that my fellow traveller and I could consider ourselves lucky to have a compartment to ourselves, even though the
heating apparatus was not working,
even though the lights went out entirely

"The Hint of an Explanation" from *Nineteen
Stories* by Graham Greene, copyright, 1949, by
Graham Greene, reprinted by permission of The
Viking Press, Inc., New York, and Pearn, Pollinger &
Higham, Ltd., London.

in the frequent Pennine tunnels and
were too dim anyway for us to read our
books without straining our eyes, and
though there was no restaurant car to
give at least a change of scene. It was
when we were trying simultaneously to
chew the same kind of dry bun bought
at the same station buffet that my companion and I came together. Before
that we had sat at opposite ends of the
carriage, both muffled to the chin in
overcoats, both bent low over type we

could barely make out, but as I threw the remains of my cake under the seat our eyes met, and he laid his book down.

By the time we were half-way to Bedwell Junction we had found an enormous range of subjects for discussion; starting with buns and the weather, we had gone on to politics, the government, foreign affairs, the atom bomb, and, by an inevitable progression, God. We had not, however, become either shrill or acid. My companion, who now sat opposite me, leaning a little forward, so that our knees nearly touched, gave such an impression of serenity that it would have been impossible to quarrel with him, however much our views differed, and differ they did profoundly.

I had soon realized I was speaking to a Catholic, to someone who believed—how do they put it?—in an omnipotent and omniscient Diety, while I was what is loosely called an Agnostic. I have a certain intuition (which I do not trust, founded as it may well be on childish experiences and needs) that a God exists, and I am surprised occasionally into belief by the extraordinary coincidences that beset our path like the traps set for leopards in the jungle, but intellectually I am revolted at the whole notion of such a God who can so abandon his creatures to enormities of Free Will. I found myself expressing this view to my companion, who listened quietly and with respect. He made no attempt to interrupt: he showed none of the impatience or the intellectual arrogance I have grown to expect from Catholics; when the lights of a wayside station flashed across his face that had escaped hitherto the rays of the one globe working in the compartment, I caught a glimpse suddenly of—what? I stopped speaking, so strong was the impression.

I was carried back ten years, to the other side of the great useless conflict, to a small town, Gisors in Normandy. I was again, for a moment, walking on the ancient battlements and looking down across the grey roofs, until my eyes for some reason lit on one grey stony "back" out of the many, where the face of a middle-aged man was pressed against a windowpane (I suppose that face has ceased to exist now, just as I believe the whole town with its medieval memories has been reduced to rubble). I remember saying to myself with astonishment, "That man is happy—completely happy." I looked across the compartment at my fellow traveller, but his face was already again in shadow. I said weakly, "When you think what God—if there is a God—allows. It's not merely the physical agonies, but think of the corruption, even of children . . ."

He said, "Our view is so limited," and I was disappointed at the conventionality of his reply. He must have been aware of my disappointment (it was as though our thoughts were huddled as closely as ourselves for warmth), for he went on, "Of course there is no answer here. We catch hints . . ." and then the train roared into another tunnel and the lights again went out. It was the longest tunnel yet; we went rocking down it, and the cold seemed to become more intense with the darkness like an icy fog (perhaps when one sense—of sight—is robbed of sensation, the others grow more sensitive). When we emerged into the mere grey of night and the globe lit up once more, I could see that my companion was leaning back on his seat.

I repeated his last words as a question, "Hints?"

"Oh, they mean very little in cold

print—or cold speech," he said, shivering in his overcoat. "And they mean nothing at all to a human being other than the man who catches them. They are not scientific evidence—or evidence at all for that matter. Events that don't, somehow, turn out as they were intended—by the human actors I mean, or by the thing behind the human actors."

"The thing?"

"The word Satan is so anthropomorphic." [1]

I had to lean forward now: I wanted to hear what he had to say. I am—I really am, God knows—open to conviction.

He said, "One's words are so crude, but I sometimes feel pity for that thing. It is so continually finding the right weapon to use against its Enemy and the weapon breaks in its own breast. It sometimes seems to me so—powerless. You said something just now about the corruption of children. It reminded me of something in my own childhood. You are the first person—except for one —that I have thought of telling it to, perhaps because you are anonymous. It's not a very long story, and in a way it's relevant."

I said, "I'd like to hear it."

"You mustn't expect too much meaning. But to me there seems to be a hint. That's all. A hint."

He went slowly on, turning his face to the pane, though he could have seen nothing real in the whirling world outside except an occasional signal lamp, a light in a window, a small country station torn backwards by our rush, picking

[1] ANTHROPOMORPHIC (ăn′thrô·pô·môr′fĭc) —From two Greek words meaning to represent a non-mortal with human attributes. The narrator's companion says that "The Thing" is a better expression than "Satan," since the word "Satan" makes him too much like a human being.

his words with precision. He said, "When I was a child they taught me to serve at Mass. The church was a small one, for there were very few Catholics where I lived. It was a market town in East Anglia, surrounded by flat, chalky fields and ditches—so many ditches. I don't suppose there were fifty Catholics all told, and for some reason there was a tradition of hostility to us. Perhaps it went back to the burning of a Protestant martyr in the sixteenth century—there was a stone marking the place near where the meat stalls stood on Wednesdays. I was only half aware of the enmity, though I knew that my school nickname of Popey Martin had something to do with my religion, and I had heard that my father was nearly excluded from the Constitutional Club when he first came to the town.

"Every Sunday I had to dress up in my surplice and serve Mass. I hated it—I have always hated dressing up in any way (which is funny when you come to think of it), and I never ceased to be afraid of losing my place in the service and doing something which would put me to ridicule. Our services were at a different hour from the Anglican, and as our small, far-from-select band trudged out of the hideous chapel the whole of the townsfolk seemed to be on the way past to the proper church —I always thought of it as the proper church. We had to pass the parade of their eyes, indifferent, supercilious, mocking; you can't imagine how seriously religion can be taken in a small town, if only for social reasons.

"There was one man in particular; he was one of the two bakers in the town, the one my family did not patronize. I don't think any of the Catholics patronized him because he was called a freethinker—an odd title, for, poor man, no one's thoughts were less free than his. He was hemmed in by his hatred—his hatred of us. He was very ugly to look at, with one wall-eye and a head the shape of a turnip, with the hair gone on the crown, and he was unmarried. He had no interests, apparently, but his baking and his hatred, though now that I am older I begin to see other sides to his nature—it did contain, perhaps, a certain furtive love. One would come across him suddenly sometimes on a country walk, especially if one were alone and it was Sunday. It was as if he rose from the ditches, and the smear of chalk on his clothes reminded one of the flour on his working overalls. He would have a stick in his hand and stab at the hedges, and if his mood were very black he would call out after one strange abrupt words like a foreign tongue—I know the meaning of those words, of course, now. Once the police went to his house because of what a boy said he'd seen, but nothing came of it except that the hate shackled him closer. His name was Blacker and he terrified me.

"I think he had a particular hatred of my father—I don't know why. My father was manager of the Midland Bank, and it's possible that at sometime Blacker may have had unsatisfactory dealings with the bank; my father was a very cautious man who suffered all his life from anxiety about money—his own and other people's. If I try and picture Blacker now I see him walking along a narrowing path between high window-less walls, and at the end of the path stands a small boy of ten—me. I don't know whether it's a symbolic picture or the memory of one of our encounters— our encounters somehow got more and more frequent. You talked just now about the corruption of children. That

poor man was preparing to revenge himself on everything he hated—my father, the Catholics, the God whom people persisted in crediting—and that by corrupting me. He had evolved a horrible and ingenious plan.

"I remember the first time I had a friendly word from him. I was passing his shop as rapidly as I could when I heard his voice call out with a kind of sly subservience as though he were an under servant. 'Master David,' he called, 'Master David,' and I hurried on. But the next time I passed that way he was at his door (he must have seen me coming) with one of those curly cakes in his hand that we called Chelsea buns. I didn't want to take it, but he made me, and then I couldn't be other than polite when he asked me to come into his parlour behind the shop and see something very special.

"It was a small electric railway—a rare sight in those days, and he insisted on showing me how it worked. He made me turn the switches and stop and start it, and he told me that I could come in any morning and have a game with it. He used the word 'game' as though it were something secret, and it's true that I never told my family of this invitation and of how, perhaps twice a week those holidays, the desire to control that little railway became overpowering, and looking up and down the street to see if I were observed, I would dive into the shop."

Our larger, dirtier, adult train drove into a tunnel and the light went out. We sat in darkness and silence, with the noise of the train blocking our ears like wax. When we were through we didn't speak at once and I had to prick him into continuing. "An elaborate seduction," I said.

"Don't think his plans were as sim-

ple as that," my companion said, "or as crude. There was much more hate than love, poor man, in his make-up. Can you hate something you don't believe in? And yet he called himself a free-thinker. What an impossible paradox, to be free and to be so obsessed. Day by day all through those holidays his obsession must have grown, but he kept a grip; he bided his time. Perhaps that thing I spoke of gave him the strength and the wisdom. It was only a week from the end of the holidays that he spoke to me on what concerned him so deeply.

"I heard him behind me as I knelt on the floor, coupling two coaches. He said, 'You won't be able to do this, Master David, when school starts.' It wasn't a sentence that needed any comment from me any more than the one that followed. 'You ought to have it for your own, you ought,' but how skill-fully and unemphatically he had sowed the longing, the idea of a possibility. . . . I was coming to his parlour every day now; you see, I had to cram every opportunity in before the hated term started again, and I suppose I was becoming accustomed to Blacker, to that wall-eye, that turnip head, that nauseating subservience. The Pope, you know, describes himself as 'the servant of the servants of God,' and Blacker—I sometimes think that Blacker was 'The servant of the servants of . . . ,' well, let it be.

"The very next day, standing in the doorway watching me play, he began to talk to me about religion. He said, with what untruth even I recognized, how much he admired the Catholics; he wished he could believe like that, but how could a baker believe? He accented 'a baker' as one might say a biologist, and the tiny train spun round the gauge o track. He said, 'I can bake the things you eat just as well as any Catholic can,' and disappeared into his shop. I hadn't the faintest idea what he meant. Presently he emerged again, holding in his hand a little wafer. 'Here,' he said, 'eat that and tell me . . .' When I put it in my mouth I could tell that it was made in the same way as our wafers for communion—he had got the shape a little wrong, that was all—and I felt guilty and irrationally scared. 'Tell me,' he said, 'what's the difference?'

" 'Difference?' I asked.

" 'Isn't that just the same as you eat in church?'

"I said smugly, 'It hasn't been consecrated.'

"He said, 'Do you think, if I put the two of them under a microscope, you could tell the difference?'

"But even at ten I had the answer to that question. 'No,' I said, 'the—accidents don't change,' stumbling a little on the word 'accidents' which had suddenly conveyed to me the idea of death and wounds.

"Blacker said with sudden intensity, 'How I'd like to get one of your ones in my mouth—just to see. . . .'

"It may seem odd to you, but this was the first time that the idea of transubstantiation really lodged in my mind. I had learned it all by rote; I had grown up with the idea. The Mass was as lifeless to me as the sentences in *De Bello Gallico*; communion a routine like drill in the school-yard, but here suddenly I was in the presence of a man who took it seriously, as seriously as the priest whom naturally one didn't count—it was his job. I felt more scared than ever.

"He said, 'It's all nonsense, but I'd just like to have it in my mouth.'

"You could if you were a Catholic,' I said naively.

"He gazed at me with his one good eye, like a Cyclops.[2] He said, 'You serve at Mass, don't you? It would be easy for you to get at one of those things. I tell you what I'd do—I'd swap this electric train for one of your wafers—consecrated, mind. It's got to be consecrated.'

" 'I could get you one out of the box,' I said. I think I still imagined that his interest was a baker's interest—to see how they were made.

" 'Oh, no,' he said, 'I want to see what your God tastes like.'

" 'I couldn't do that.'

" 'Not for a whole electric train, just for yourself? You wouldn't have any trouble at home. I'd pack it up and put a label inside that your dad could see: "For my bank manager's little boy from a grateful client." He'd be pleased as punch with that.'

"Now that we are grown men it seems a trivial temptation, doesn't it? But try to think back to your own childhood. There was a whole circuit of rails there on the floor at our feet, straight rails and curved, and a little station with porters and passengers, a tunnel, a footbridge, a level crossing, two signals, buffers, of course—and, above all, a turntable. The tears of longing came into my eyes when I looked at the turntable. It was my favorite piece—it looked so ugly and practical and true. I said weakly, 'I wouldn't know how.'

"How carefully he had been studying the ground! He must have slipped several times into Mass at the back of the church. It would have been no good, you understand, in a little town like that, presenting himself for communion. Everybody there knew him for

[2] CYCLOPS (sī′klŏps)—One-eyed giant of Grecian mythology.

what he was. He said to me, 'When you've been given communion you could just put it under your tongue a moment. He serves you and the other boy first, and I saw you once go out behind the curtain straight afterwards. You'd forgotten one of those little bottles.'

" 'The cruet,' I said.

" 'Pepper and salt.' He grinned at me jovially, and I—well, I looked at the little railway which I could no longer come and play with when term started. I said, 'You'd just swallow it, wouldn't you?'

" 'Oh, yes,' he said, 'I'd just swallow it.'

"Somehow I didn't want to play with the train any more that day. I got up and made for the door, but he detained me, gripping my lapel. He said, 'This will be a secret between you and me. Tomorrow's Sunday. You come along here in the afternoon. Put it in an envelope and post it to me. Monday morning the train will be delivered bright and early.'

" 'Not tomorrow,' I implored him.

" 'I'm not interested in any other Sunday,' he said. 'It's your only chance.' He shook me gently backwards and forwards. 'It will always have to be a secret between you and me,' he said. 'Why, if anyone knew they'd take away the train and there'd be me to reckon with. I'd bleed you something awful. You know how I'm always about on Sunday walks. You can't avoid a man like me. I crop up. You wouldn't ever be safe in your own house. I know ways to get into houses when people are asleep.' He pulled me into the shop after him and opened a drawer. In the drawer was an odd looking key and a cut-throat razor. He said, 'That's a master key that opens all locks and that

—that's what I bleed people with.' Then he patted my cheek with his plump floury fingers and said, 'Forget it. You and me are friends.'

"That Sunday Mass stays in my head, every detail of it, as though it had happened only a week ago. From the moment of the Confession to the moment of Consecration it had a terrible importance; only one other Mass has ever been so important to me—perhaps not even one, for this was a solitary Mass which would never happen again. It seemed as final as the last Sacrament when the priest bent down and put the wafer in my mouth where I knelt before the altar with my fellow server.

"I suppose I had made up my mind to commit this awful act—for, you know, to us it must always seem an awful act—from the moment when I saw Blacker watching from the back of the church. He had put on his best black Sunday clothes, and, as though he could never quite escape the smear of his profession, he had a dab of dried talcum on his cheek, which he had presumably applied after using that cut-throat of his. He was watching me closely all the time, and I think it was fear—fear of that terrible undefined thing called bleeding— as much as covetousness that drove me to carry out my instructions.

"My fellow server got briskly up and, taking the paten preceded Father Carey to the altar rail where the other communicants knelt. I had the Host lodged under my tongue; it felt like a blister. I got up and made for the curtain to get the cruet that I had purposely left in the sacristy. When I was there I looked quickly round for a hiding place and saw an old copy of the *Universe* lying on a chair. I took the Host from my mouth and inserted it between two sheets—a little damp mess of pulp.

Then I thought: perhaps Father Carey has put out the paper for a particular purpose and he will find the Host before I have time to remove it, and the enormity of my act began to come home to me when I tried to imagine what punishment I should incur. Murder is sufficiently trivial to have its appropriate punishment, but for this act the mind boggled at the thought of any retribution at all. I tried to remove the Host, but it stuck clammily between the pages, and in desperation I tore out a piece of the newspaper and, screwing the whole thing up, stuck it in my trousers pocket. When I came back through the curtain carrying the cruet my eyes met Blacker's. He gave me a grin of encouragement and unhappiness —yes, I am sure, unhappiness. Was it perhaps that the poor man was all the time seeking something incorruptible?

"I can remember little more of that day. I think my mind was shocked and stunned, and I was caught up too in the family bustle of Sunday. Sunday in a provincial town is the day for relations. All the family are at home, and unfamiliar cousins and uncles are apt to arrive, packed in the back seats of other people's cars. I remember that some crowd of the kind descended on us and pushed Blacker temporarily out of the foreground of my mind. There was somebody called Aunt Lucy, with a loud hollow laugh that filled the house with mechanical merriment like the sound of recorded laughter from inside a hall of mirrors, and I had no opportunity to go out alone even if I had wished to. When six o'clock came and Aunt Lucy and the cousins departed and peace returned, it was too late to go to Blacker's, and at eight it was my own bed-time.

"I think I had half forgotten what I had in my pocket. As I emptied my pocket the little screw of newspaper brought quickly back the Mass, the priest bending over me, Blacker's grin. I laid the packet on the chair by my bed and tried to go to sleep, but I was haunted by the shadows on the wall where the curtains blew, the squeak of furniture, the rustle in the chimney, haunted by the presence of God there on the chair. The Host had always been to me—well the Host. I knew theoretically, as I have said, what I had to believe, but suddenly, as someone whistled in the road outside, whistled secretively, knowingly, to me, I knew that this which I had beside my bed was something of infinite value—something a man would pay for with his whole peace of mind, something that was so hated one could love it as one loves an outcast or a bullied child. These are adult words, and it was a child of ten who lay scared in bed, listening to the whistle from the road, Blacker's whistle, but I think he felt fairly clearly what I am describing now. That is what I meant when I said this Thing, whatever it is, that seizes every possible weapon against God, is always, everywhere, disappointed at the moment of success. It must have felt as certain of me as Blacker did. It must have felt certain too of Blacker. But I wonder, if one knew what happened later to that poor man, whether one would not find again that the weapon had been turned against its own breast.

"At last I couldn't bear that whistle any more and got out of bed. I opened the curtains a little way, and there right under my window, the moonlight on his face, was Blacker. If I had stretched my hand down, his fingers reaching up could almost have touched mine. He looked up at me, flashing the one good eye, with hunger—I realize

now that near-success must have developed his obsession almost to the point of madness. Desperation had driven him to the house. He whispered up at me. 'David, where is it?'

"I jerked my head back at the room. 'Give it me,' he said. 'Quick. You shall have the train in the morning.'

"I shook my head. He said, 'I've got the bleeder here, and the key. You'd better toss it down.'

" 'Go away,' I said, but I could hardly speak for fear.

" 'I'll bleed you first and then I'll have it just the same.'

" 'Oh, no, you won't,' I said. I went to the chair and picked it—Him—up. There was only one place where He was safe. I couldn't separate the Host from the paper, so I swallowed both. The newsprint stuck like a prune skin to the back of my throat, but I rinsed it down with water from the ewer. Then I went back to the window and looked down at Blacker. He began to wheedle me. 'What have you done with it, David? What's the fuss? It's only a bit of bread,' looking so longingly and pleadingly up at me that even as a child I wondered whether he could really think that, and yet desire it so much.

" 'I swallowed it,' I said.

" 'Swallowed it?'

" 'Yes,' I said. 'Go away.'

"Then something happened which seems to me now more terrible than his desire to corrupt or my thoughtless act: he began to weep—the tears ran lopsidedly out of the one good eye and his shoulders shook. I only saw his face for a moment before he bent his head and strode off, the bald turnip head shaking, into the dark. When I think of it now, it's almost as if I had seen that Thing weeping for its inevitable defeat. It had tried to use me as a weapon, and now I had broken in its hands and it wept its hopeless tears through one of Blacker's eyes."

The black furnaces of Bedwell Junction gathered around the line. The points switched and we were tossed from one set of rails to another. A spray of sparks, a signal light changing to red, tall chimneys jetting into the gray night sky, the fumes of steam from stationary engines—half the cold journey was over, and now remained the long wait for the slow cross-country train. I said, "It's an interesting story. I think I should have given Blacker what he wanted. I wonder what he would have done with it."

"I really believe," my companion said, "that he would first of all have put it under his microscope—before he did all the other things I expect he had planned."

"And the hints," I said, "I don't quite see what you mean by that."

"Oh, well," he said vaguely, "you know for me it was an odd beginning, that affair, when you come to think of it," but I never should have known what he meant had not his coat, when he rose to take his bag from the rack, come open and disclosed the collar of a priest.

I said, "I suppose you think you owe a lot to Blacker."

"Yes," he said, "you see, I am a very happy man."

◇◇◇◇◇◇◇◇◇◇◇◇◇◇◇◇◇◇◇◇◇◇◇◇◇◇◇◇◇

WORD STUDY AND STYLE

Does Greene's style appeal primarily to the imagination or to the intellect? Select examples from the story to prove your point.

Some or all of the following adjectives might characterize Greene's style. List these adjectives in the order of their importance and select at least one sentence which each adjective might describe: *compact, concise, controlled, restrained, economical, austere, classical, graphic.*

Is there any difference between *intuition* and *reasoning*? When is some fact *relevant* to an argument? What kind of glance would a *furtive* glance be? Describe a *supercilious smirk.*

FOR DISCUSSION

1. Which is greater in the story—the external or internal action? Could this story be called a psychological study? Discuss in detail.

2. Show in detail how the word "Hint" in the title carries the theme throughout the story. Just what is "hinted"?

3. "Serenity" is the key word to describe the character of the narrator's companion. Discuss in detail how the narrator's companion arrived at this "serenity." Explain the relationship between "serenity," "the thing," "the hint," and Blacker.

4. Enumerate the details of the "elaborate seduction" of the child. What particular human weaknesses of the child and what external circumstances made him so susceptible to the temptation of Blacker? Are these temptations described realistically? Is there a great deal of "Satanic psychology" contained in them? Explain.

5. Describe in a few words the climax of the story. What is the predominant effect which the short story produces upon the reader? Explain.

6. Briefly describe the physical appearance of Blacker. Why is his name an appropriate one?

7. What was the narrator's great obstacle to a belief in a personal God? Does this argument introduce the story proper? Explain.

8. Do you consider this story to be a good piece of Christian propaganda? Why or why not?

9. Reread the statements of Greene quoted in the introduction to this story. Apply these statements to the short story.

10. Explain: 1) the general meaning of the following statements; 2) their meaning in their context in the story:
   a. "Intellectual arrogance I have grown to expect from Catholics."
   b. "I sometimes feel pity for this thing. It is continually finding the right weapon to use against its Enemy and the weapon breaks in its own breast."
   c. "Can you hate something you don't believe in? And yet he called himself a free-thinker. What an impossible paradox to be free and to be so obsessed."
   d. "The Mass was as lifeless to me as the sentences in *De Bello Gallico*; Communion a routine like a drill in the school-yard."
   e. "This Thing . . . . that seizes every sensible weapon against God is always, everywhere disappointed at the moment of success."

RELATED READING

Read another short story by Greene in his collection, *Nineteen Stories*.

Read Section II of Book 3 of Greene's *Heart of the Matter*, which describes the sacrilegious communion of Scobie.

Read Evelyn Waugh's "Bella Fleace Gave a Party," and Caryll Houselander's "The Father" in *Stories of Our Century By Catholic Authors*, edited by John Gilland Brunini and Francis X. Connolly.

◇◇◇◇◇

BY THE SEA

BRYAN MacMAHON

The following story from MacMahon's THE LION-TAMER *is modern prose fiction at its refreshing best. It is also proof that some of the best modern prose is being written by Irishmen. MacMahon weaves into prose fiction the magic of a Gaelic imagination attuned to a delicate perception of the beauty of the physical universe as symbolical of the mind and the mood of man.*

Once on the gravelled path of the village the Boy Scouts squinted up at the bus-top. But the summer sun was a sudden splash of limewash in their eyes and their screwed faces faltered and fell. Down the broken gapped village street drove a wind tinctured with the sea, and immediately the boys began to laugh and twitter and twinkle like a flock of sparrows bathing in a deep well of road-dust.

Canvas, poles, tinware utensils, rucksacks and boxes came perilously down from the bus-top. Little hands clawed chattels safely home. Finally, all the gear was piled on the pathway; the conductor offered them his absolutely final company smile; a woman in the rear seat of the bus fisted a clear circle in the

glass; the exhaust jetted blue-purple and the bus churned away. It left a huddle of blue-clad boys tangled in a medley of mostly green gear.

They trudged up to the higher end of the village. When they saw the sea they cheered. Between them and the sea, the sandhills below the village held creamy flanks lipped with generous shocks of emerald bent-grass. Out on the ocean there were no waves. There was little sound except the half-imagined, half-audible whisper of the inshore ripples, repeating "Lipsss, lipsss." To the right were the sun-drenched cliffs; to the left, the long, attenuating scimitar of red sand. From their place of vantage at the end of the village the boys halted to appreciate the sea, the squirming and crawling of it, the slithering and sidling of it, the terror and delight of it. Capricious highways of green ink wandered in its spurious blueness. Under a short cliff to the right floated a dirty blanket of unmoving foam which seemed independent of submarine movement. The sun, swinging ponderously above the cloudy mountain damps across the bay, threw its royal image along the sea even to the strand below. Seeing, hearing, smelling, tasting and touching became luxuries. Luxuries, indeed, since there was nothing worth seeing but the sea; nothing worth hearing but the soft inshore "lipsss, lipsss"; nothing worth smelling or tasting but that which came to nostrils and palate in wild salinity; nothing fit for the body's touch but the velvet stroking of the waves.

Christy Hickey roused them. They turned from the sea and dragged themselves up to the Castle gates: the gates were set in a high corner of the green above the ocean. Over the gapped demesne [1] wall they saw the great hulk of the burning building—its battlements cut clearly out of the cooler northern sky. To the right of the Castle they noticed the wing which had not suffered in the conflagration—its sashes and windows and verandah shone very white in the sunlight. The boys began to marvel at the gateway—they had never seen such a gateway before. It was actually a dwelling-house, and out of this fairy-tale portal walked a fairy-tale old woman to laugh with them and at them, to welcome them and to wonder at them, to feel the texture of the blue cloth on their tunics, to finger their golden-coloured crosses, and now and again to stoop to discover what particular sample of sweating imp lurked beneath the blue toadstool of a hat. The old lady caught Christy Hickey's hand but showed no eagerness to release it as she talked of

[1] DEMESNE (dê·mān')—Here meaning the manor or castle wall.

soda-bread and butter-scotch and mushrooms on the coals, and eggs as brown as . . . as brown as . . . here she tried heaven and earth and ocean for a suitable comparison and failed to find one. When at last the astonished youngsters estimated that there was a period to her clucking, she began her incoherencies over again just to show her delight at this, her new family. Afterwards the white gates that showed blotches of rust screamed open; the boys began to shout, "Where? Where?" and to answer, "Over there! Over there!" They streamed across the grassy lawn and dumped their possessions beside the wall adjoining the road. Beyond the road was a short field that sloped down to a cliff above the sea. Above them the field lifted in gentle acclivity to the Castle. Below them stretched the fine span of the bay.

Bell-tents and bivouacs up, latrines, grease-traps and hip-hollows dug, flag hoisted; water-carriers, couriers and cooks appointed—all the dismal chores performed with new zest. The owner of the Castle came down to greet them. He was enormous, Irish and friendly. He stood smiling at this ant-hill of activity on his land. He asked the Scout-master to bring the boys up to help him pick his gooseberries. He had many things that would interest them, he said.

The rest of the day was a great rush hither and thither in an effort to experience everything at the same time. They swam before dinner; after the swim they rushed here and there on the long strand marvelling at new wonders. They found three green glass balls and some huge chunks of cork. Also a battered wickerwork lobster pot. They walked along the tide's lip for the most of a mile and found things eloquent of the sea's mystery. On the high-water mark,

clothed in sea-weed, they saw the body of a marmoset [2]—at least Jimmy Stephens said it was a marmoset, though the others considered it a plain monkey. Then there was the skeleton of what someone suggested was a bottle-nosed shark.

On the way back to the Castle they met the old parish priest—he examined them unbelievingly over his breviary before he addressed them. One of the younger Scouts stood on his hands to amuse the old man: the boy held his balance for a short time before sprawling backwards into the fuchsia.[3] When they went up to the Castle they found marvel piled on marvel. The gooseberries were of two kinds, the red and hairy, and the amber and hairless. The man who owned the Castle had a trick gooseberry. It was as big as a small apple. He had grown it by removing all but one of the immature fruits on a branch. By allowing this single gooseberry to droop into a cup of water he had produced a freak fruit. He also had a hawk chained to a perch: when the youngsters threw pieces of stick to it the bird pounced on them ferociously. There was a fig tree growing in the open air near the garden door. As a final titbit their host made his Alsatian leap high to pull a bell-rope. Towards evening, with bulging pockets, the Scouts ambled down the lawn.

Night came upon the Scouts and heightened their sense of adventure. True, they sang around the fire, more to justify a cardinal principle in Scout literature than from motives of inward urgency, but they were more than satisfied with this simulacrum [4] of enjoyment—they enjoyed the singing and the

[2] MARMOSET—A species of monkey.
[3] FUCHSIA (fū′sha)—Shrubs of the primrose family.

[4] SIMULACRUM (sĭm′ū·lā′krŭm)—A mock appearance; sham.

527

firelight because it would be a type of blasphemy to admit that they did not enjoy it. But the strongest perceptible emotion amongst the boys was a type of inarticulate fear which the lusty singing did its share to dispel. Afterwards a great beast of a moon clambered up the blue velvet sky—the boys struggled to the top of the mossy wall and saw what wonders it could work on the ball-room floor of the ocean. As the day-light seeped out of the heavens the reiterated complaint of the tide-edge impinged more and more upon the conscious ear. Insignificant sounds increased in portentousness; the violent bugling of a cow from the shelter belt behind the Castle rocked the world; a spurt of laughter from the village almost approximated to rifle fire; a light flickering on the hills was a thing of great mystery. The boys crowded in on the dying fire. What remnants of cold the summer night held fastened its hooks in their backs. Christy Hickey watched them narrowly and was quick to recognize the sense of dwarfishness in their faces. The boys continued to shrill loudly in order to compensate for their inner cowardice.

Then the camp bugler stood up beyond the firelight and sounded "Taps." His instrument flung the separate notes out into the shining night sea. On leaving the bugle each note seemed to become a small silver globe that went bounding beautifully out to seek its fortune in a blue world. When he had finished, the echo of the music took a while to die.

Christy Hickey opened the end wall of his own white sleeping-tent and hung a large black crucifix within on the pole of the opposite tent-wall. Under the crucifix he suspended a lighting storm lantern. As he did so, he kept repeating softly to himself, "The tents of Israel, the tents of Israel." The boys crowded in on the mouth of the white tent, the surplus spilling out into the grassy dark. Then the Scoutmaster knelt beneath the crucifix and gave out the Rosary. Prayers never seemed so delightful before; all the old appellations flashed new lights from unsuspected facets of grandeur. The praying fused them warmly into one another, as if indeed this single act of communal moonlight prayer had the power to make them blood brothers. The drone of the praying made them sleepy, too; when the Rosary and Litany were ended each small head was fully loaded with sleep.

Eight boys in each bell-tent—seven and a patrol leader. Christy Hickey and Jimmy Stephens were to sleep in the white sleeping-tent. Christy walked around, warning the boys not to put their hand to the canvas if it rained and impressing on the patrol leaders the necessity for loosening the guy ropes in a shower. Before long he blew the whistle for lights out. Afterwards he stayed at the wall for a while. He was looking out over the sea. He released breath through his nostrils in easy hisses of satisfaction. Now that the boys had retired and were safe, he found the knapsack of responsibility slipping from his shoulders. This was his first outing of this nature since his appointment as Scoutmaster, and, as the group was a new one, all but two of the boys had never been under canvas before. He looked across his shoulder. Just then Jimmy Stephens put his head out of the sleeping-tent that he and the Scoutmaster were to share, and looked expectantly towards the figure by the moonlit wall. Christy padded softly around the bell-tents. A snatch of eager narrative filtered through the canvas—". . . a weeny rabbit that a weasel killed—an', man, he was hot!" He walked to the triangular doors of the tents and threw back the canvas so as to give the boys air. Within, the boys were lying like the spokes of a wheel, the recumbent bodies radiating from the tent-pole. As he rustled away he found the dammed-up tittering break softly behind him. He smiled contentedly at the sound. Then he blessed himself, slipped into the tent and stripped speedily. Jimmy Stephens and himself conversed softly for a while before they bade each other good night.

Christy found it difficult to sleep. The excitement of the day, more or less dormant during dusk, now began to gnaw in him as a wary mouse gnaws in a house that has grown silent. Tittering began in one of the tents—the patrol leader's voice was raised in muffled reproval. An inquisitive cow began to lumber down the lawn. With his ear to the ground Christy could hear the animal tearing at the grass as if it were paper. The noise became more determined as the cow approached the tent. Finally the animal's shadow lunged across the canvas. He could hear her breathing and snuffling close to his face but he made no movement; he tautened his body and hoped that she would not become entangled in the tent-ropes. Jimmy Stephens was breathing easily in sleep. Then the cow, satisfied with her scrutiny, bore away to the left and soon he heard the soft plopping of falling cow-dung. Christy smiled and dropped down into uneasy sleep.

It was two-fifty-five by the phosphorescent face of his wrist-watch when the patrol leader of one of the bell-tents roused him. "Christy! Christy!" he called agitatedly, shaking the Scoutmaster's shoulder. "Christy!" the boy said,

"Richie Maloney is retching off his stomach all the time." Christy slipped on his shoes and scrambled into his overcoat. He felt in the pocket of his overcoat for his torch. Outside, the night was possessed of a surpassing brightness. The sky above the sea that was previously powder-blue had now become suffused with a delightful apple-green. He had scarcely time to appreciate its curiousness when the night-air tentatively laid its keen blade across his skin. He flashed his torch through the tent doorway, picked out the patrol leader and another boy holding the sick scout upright in a sitting position. He stepped carefully among the still forms and put his arm around the sick lad's shoulder. He flashed the light full into the pale face, and the boy's reaction to the light seemed so unusual that he immediately switched off the torch. "What is it, Richie?" he wheedled. Then, "Lift him up!" he whispered to the other two. "Perhaps he'd be better off out in the air." The boy made no effort to put his legs under him, so Christy carried him in his arms.

Out in the air the sick boy brightened momentarily; then his head lolled heavily. The Scoutmaster slipped off his overcoat and threw it across Richie Maloney's shoulders. He helped him to a sitting position on a little mound near the wall. "Richie! Richie!" he whispered again. Then to the other two, "Call Jimmy Stephens and ask him to get the drop of brandy out of my case." One of the boys raced towards the white tent.

Christy began to speak softly to the sick lad; once again came the weary effort to raise the heavy head. The other Scout was whimpering with cold; Christy told him to put on some clothes. The boy went away into the bell-tent.

When he was alone with the sick lad Christy slewed [5] him around until the moon was shining into the wan face. Suddenly the Scoutmaster noticed that the boy's weak bulbous [6] tongue was ballooning out through the opening of his mouth. Before the cold significance of this could reach Christy's consciousness, the boy had begun to snore stertorously.[7] Christy cupped his mouth against the boy's ear and clearly crooned out the Act of Contrition. His maternal eyes kept holding the boy's profile as if seeking, by the power of animal fascination alone, to pin the soul to life. But Richie Maloney suddenly added two terrifying inches to his size, deflated all the air that was in him in the ultimate throe, squeaked like a wet palm on a bannister-rail, and died.

Christy held the boy for an unmoving minute after he knew that he had passed out. The moon froze the pair to a piece of statuary, the sight of which chilled the two returning Scouts. "What is it, Christy?" Jimmy Stephens began anxiously, crouching down to the moonlit pair. The other boy was just beyond Jimmy's shoulder. Christy let the body sag a little. "He's dead!" he said. "Sweet God above!" said Jimmy, "How could he be dead? Why do you say that? He might only have fainted!" Jimmy put his hand against the inert head—it was now the head of a broken doll. In the background the patrol leader began to blubber. It was a chittering type of blubber. Jimmy Stephens began to cross himself over and over again. "But what'll we do, Christy? How'll we face home with him? Didn't his mother warn you to watch him carefully? We watched him, Christy, didn't we? The two of us watched him, Christy, didn't we?"

The morning was thrusting its great green fist into the sky. The inshore wavelets kept repeating "lipsss—lipsss —lipsss." A cock crowed from the fowl-runs behind the Castle.

Christy spoke to the patrol leader. "Val," he said, "get Tom Donnell's bike and ride for the priest. Ask the priest where the doctor lives and bring him too. Not that it's any use now, but . . . Hurry, Val, like a good boy."

Afterwards the affair became nightmarish. Christy carried the body into his own tent and covered it with a sheet. Jimmy Stephens and he took their clothes out into the dew-wet grass and dressed themselves. By now it was clear that the tragedy had communicated itself to the other Scouts. Heads appeared in the doorways of the bell-tents; a chorus of whispering broke out. It was difficult to know how the news of death had spread. Perhaps the subconscious is always sharpening its ear to hear it, senses are sharpened to apprehend it, a further dole of smell is kept in reserve to sniff new-made clay even through sleep, an extra access of sight is held in reserve to visualize (even through two canvas walls) a taut blue face and the final grimace of stripped teeth.

The Scouts were up and dressed and about without reprimand. They huddled in little frightened schools well away from the tent where the dead boy lay. A light twinkled in one of the windows of the Castle. The inquisitive cow munched nearer and nearer to the tent of death. No one raised a hand to frighten her away. The animal put a truculent [8] head against the canvas and snuffed loudly. Christy took a step or

---

[5] SLEWED—Twisted.

[6] BULBOUS—An enlarged, swollen, or massy tongue.

[7] STERTOROUSLY—Breathing hoarsely.

[8] TRUCULENT—Fierce or savage.

two in her direction and stamped suddenly on the grass. The cow heaved out with astonishing agility. A figure with a lighted candle in its hand came to the window of the Castle. Then the lights of the priest's car were shining through the bars of the gateway. The gate clanged open and the tires roared on the gravel.

Morning was upon them almost before they realized it. The owner of the Castle came down with his wife and led away the boys for a phantom meal. When later they emerged into the strengthening sunlight the old woman of the gateway was walking around in the dew-wet grass. She was tying and untying her fingers and calling out the Holy Name. People began to knot outside the white-barred gate. Two vivid young women strolled past the road.

Each was swinging a blue bathing costume. When they learned the news from the people at the gateway the pair were pricked of their splendour and became ordinary frightened people. The boys looked up at the sun mounting behind the sandhills. The holiday was over. They set about taking down the bell-tents and piling their belongings. The little white bivouac was left standing, and the disconsolate lads sat dismally on their gear. The sea had a great sleekness to it. The thin mist of morning was vanishing; the long revolving lip of the tide was increasing in whiteness. The boys looked wistfully at the sea, at the faint mountaincamps of the south, at the creamy flanks of the sandhills, at the long, attenuating scimitar of sand. Then they looked at the tent of death.

FOR DISCUSSION

1. Every short story should leave the reader with one definite impression. Discuss the single effect produced by this story.

2. This is neither a story of plot nor of character, but of mood. What is the predominant mood of the first seven paragraphs? Enumerate the details which the author chooses to convey this mood. In paragraph 8 is there any indication of a change of mood? Select those details which develop this change.

3. In paragraphs 9, 10, 11, and 12 does the atmosphere of well-being return? Again discuss those details which develop this atmosphere.

4. Is possible disaster hinted at in paragraph 13? Explain.

5. Discuss in detail how the author uses descriptions of nature to heighten the

sense of catastrophe in paragraphs 14, 15, 16, 17, 18.

6. Are we prepared for the final tragedy, or does it come upon us by surprise? Explain.

7. What is the significance of the Scoutmaster's repetition of the phrase "The tents of Israel"? Read the last line of the story for your answer. Explain the Biblical meaning of the phrase.

THE AUTHOR'S STYLE

1. Almost every sentence of the story contains an original and striking image. At one time or another he uses figures which appeal to every sense. Select and study at least ten sentences which contain fresh imagery. Select one sentence in which the primary appeal is to each of the five senses.

2. Analyze in detail the description in paragraph 3. What is the point of view of the description? What is the basic image? Enumerate the details which the author chose to develop this basic image. Select the key words of the paragraph which accentuate the mood.

WORD STUDY

Perhaps while reading the story you ran across many words whose meaning you did not know. Study the following words, first for their general meaning; then study them for their connotation in the context of the phrase: "wind *tinctured* with sea"; "tangled in a *medley* of mostly green gear"; "*attenuating scimitar* of red sand"; "*capricious* highways"; "the field lifted in gentle *acclivity* to the castle"; "*simulacrum* of enjoyment"; "*inarticulate* fear"; "a moon *clambered* up the blue-velvet sky"; "the *reiterated* complaint of the tide-edge *impinged* upon the conscious ear"; "all the old *appellations* flashed new lights from unsuspected *facets* of grandeur"; "a taut blue face and the final *grimace* of stripped teeth."

RELATED READING

Sister Mariella Gable, O.S.B. has edited three volumes of Catholic short stories: *Great Modern Catholic Short Stories, Our Father's House,* and *Many Colored Fleece.* Select one or more stories from each of these collections for your outside reading. In particular, read "Yung Mari Li" by Bryan MacMahon and "The Road to One Shore" by Michael McLaverty. Both of these stories can be found in *Many Colored Fleece.* Also read "The Trout" by Sean O'Faolin, which can be found in his fine collection, *The Man Who Invented Sin.*

Bryan MacMahon's *The Red Petticoat* is a collection of short stories published in 1954. These stories have been acclaimed by the critics as his best writing to date. Read from this collection "Evening in Ireland."

THE MODERN NOVEL

Because of its multiplicity and variety, the twentieth century novel is extremely difficult to classify. In the years before and shortly after World War I, such names as Conrad, H. G. Wells, Galsworthy, and Arnold Bennett loomed large in the field of fiction.

Joseph Conrad, a Pole by birth, did not learn English until he was twenty-one; yet he lived to become one of the great masters of English prose. In a preface to his *The Nigger of the Narcissus*, which he regarded as his best literary work, he wrote: "My task which I am trying to achieve is, by the power of the written word, to make you hear, to make you feel—above all, to make you *see*." There is no doubt that Conrad succeeded in his aim. As a novelist who spent more than twenty years at sea, he portrayed individuals who must fight the forces of nature. *Lord Jim* is typical of his brooding tales about men and ships in lonely tropical seas. Conrad specialized in exploring the inner workings of his characters' minds. But he did not isolate character from the outside world. For him "the perfection of individual conduct" was the theme of all his novels; but this conduct resulted from following objective moral standards.

JOSEPH CONRAD: WRITER OF MEN AND THE SEA

Because science fiction is so extremely popular today, we might falsely conclude that this kind of writing is something very new. But at the beginning of the century, H. G. Wells was writing about mechanical devices that would carry man into the future as far ahead as the year 802,701, and of the invasion of the earth by the Martians. These possibilities he discussed in *The Time Machine* and *The War of the Worlds*.

Later, Wells turned from the study of physical science to the study of human society. *Tono-Bungay* he regarded as his masterpiece. Tono-Bungay was a worthless patent medicine which the hero of the novel and his uncle manufactured, and which they sold to the public through high-pressure advertising. Wells used this patent medicine as a symbol of a disintegrating society.

War, religion, and education formed the themes of Wells' other works. In *Mr. Britling Sees It Through*, a novel of World War I, he announced his discovery of God. But the God which Wells described was a very vague and finite god—the captain of those great souls who fight for a better world. A modern critic has said that the typical Wells hero is either a scientist or a man of affairs who is determined to better the world in which he lives; however, such a hero is liable to succumb at any time to the temptation of private profit. The pet theories of Wells about social reform, religion, and history—all of which excluded the spiritual and absolute moral concepts—were the frequent targets for the literary barbs of such men as Chesterton and Belloc.

Arnold Bennett is famous for the *Old Wives' Tale* and *The Clayhanger Trilogy*, a series of novels about the people who lived in Staffordshire, the pottery-manufacturing center of England. Bennett gave infinite care to the physical details of his stories—clothes, food, dwellings—and traced the effects of economic and social trends in his characters' personal lives. He describes his characters through environment. Bennett's basic weakness was that his realism focused attention on the lowest elements of life. He failed to describe the good man from within.

One year before he died in 1933, John Galsworthy was awarded the Nobel Prize for literature. Galsworthy is most famous for his *Forsyte Saga*, a trilogy. It is a family novel with Soames Forsyte as the hero. In picturing the "Forsyte age and the Forsyte way of life," Galsworthy viewed the transformation that was taking place in every aspect of English life in the first years of the century, changes in the concept of property, manners, and morals. As a somewhat detached critic of life, Galsworthy was not too reliable. He rejected all religious authority and believed that "life was a mess and that we should be kind." Summing up his own philosophy, he wrote: "Life for those who still have vital instinct in them is good enough in itself even if it lead to nothing, and we have only ourselves to blame if we, alone among animals, so live that we lose the love of life for *itself*."

CHANGING TIMES
AS SEEN BY
JOHN GALSWORTHY

In the 1920's James Joyce, the rebellious, ex-Catholic Irishman, and Virginia Woolf gave impetus to the stream of consciousness technique. Miss Woolf turned her attention away from the outside world to the mind of man as it *knows* and *feels* the outside world. She recorded the involuntary movements of the mind, and portrayed character through the description of impressions which are fragmentary and disconnected. Her descriptions of sensations as they flow through the mind were sensitive. She turned her prose into a lyrical instrument which recorded sensations in the process of change. As a result, she did not portray a complete personality, but only the sum total of disconnected sensations. *To the Lighthouse, Mrs. Dalloway,* and *The Waves* brilliantly exemplify this type of writing.

Joyce explored the vague and chaotic area of the subconscious mind in his *Ulysses*, a novel that exhausts seven hundred pages about the events of a single day in Dublin. In the novels of Joyce, D. H. Lawrence, and Somerset Maugham, we have realism which has degenerated into naturalism and, at times, pure animalism. In too many of their novels, hatred, lust, and the uninhibited and unprincipled activity of the imagination are all described with minute fidelity. In Maugham, Aldous Huxley and other realistic novelists, we have competent writing and a fine technique; but all their writings are suffused with a materialism which finds no lasting significance in life.

Most of the realism of the twentieth century non-Catholic novelists is, paradoxically, not realism at all, but an escape from reality. Viewing man as a helpless victim of social environment or blind fate is not realism. Nor is morbid self-analysis, or the portrayal of the objective world through disconnected and subconscious images, true realism. A return to primitive animalism in which the exaltation of sex is substituted for religion and objective morality can hardly be called viewing life realistically. All of these novelists have failed artistically be-

NON-CATHOLIC
"REALISM"

cause they have not re-created life in its *totality*. They have been lacking in an understanding of man's *total nature* because they have deliberately cut themselves off from the spiritual, moral, and cultural traditions of the past.

Although it is not the purpose of fiction to deal with philosophy or the causes of things, but only with things themselves, still it is impossible to know life and artistically re-create it unless one can see the relationships between life and the ultimate meaning of life. Unfortunately, many modern novelists tell only half-truths; or they mistake disordered and chaotic impressions for reality. They consciously or unconsciously fail to portray man as a moral and religious creature. All great literature is profoundly religious. It is ever haunted by the memory of a lost paradise and a deep sense of humility which represents man neither as an animal nor as a god—but as a rational being ever conscious of his tremendous freedom. This freedom, which implies a moral responsibility to himself and to society, man can abuse and thus become the tragic hero; or he can, against all odds, accept his responsibility and his place in the scheme of Divine Providence, and thus play a superb role in the Divine Comedy.

The twentieth century Catholic novelists have helped to preserve the human and supernatural values in a world dedicated to materialism and imbued with a sense of disillusionment. Aware of man's insecurity and the ease with which he falls prey to the naturalistic viewpoint, the Catholic fiction writer has provided a means by which an ordinary man may see life in its totality.

In many ways this task is being accomplished today, whether it be through the subtle and indirect approach of the satires of Evelyn Waugh and Bruce Marshall; or through the stark and, at times, startling presentation of the conflict between man's lower nature and grace in the realistic novels of Graham Greene; or in the more subdued character study of the historical novels of Sheila Kaye-Smith. Writing in the Catholic tradition (although not a Catholic) is H. F. M. Prescott, whose historical chronicle, *The Man on the Donkey*, is unquestionably one of the classics of the twentieth century. Prescott's *The Unhurrying Chase* was published in 1955.

No survey of English Catholic novelists would be complete that did not include such names as: A. J. Cronin, Compton MacKenzie, Philip Gibbs, Maurice Baring, Robert Spaight, and the Irish Catholic fiction writers Kate O'Brien and Michael McLaverty.

(FROM) SUPERSTITION CORNER

SHEILA KAYE-SMITH

In 1923, Sheila Kaye-Smith published THE END OF THE HOUSE OF ALARD, which recorded the extinction of the Alard family. In SUPERSTITION CORNER and GALLYBIRD, she returned to the early history of that family in the sixteenth and seventeenth centuries. In both of these novels the author paints a realistic picture of the moral and intellectual degeneration of a family which has rejected the Faith.

Miss Kaye-Smith has called SUPERSTITION CORNER her first Catholic novel. It takes its name from a Sussex crossroads a short distance from the home of the Alards.

The time and setting of SUPERSTITION CORNER is in Elizabethan England very shortly after the defeat of the Spanish Armada. Catholicism is at its lowest ebb. Into this setting comes Catherine Alard, a young lady in her late twenties, devotedly and zealously Catholic. Catherine's father, the Squire of Conster Manor, has already conformed to the new Protestant religion, but her twin brother, Simon, is studying for the priesthood on the Continent.

In the opening chapters of the novel we find Catherine spending much of her time at Fuggesbroke visiting the Tuktones, the only thoroughly Catholic family in the neighborhood. She is also endeavoring to reclaim to the Old Faith Nicholas Pecksall, an ex-priest turned Protestant, and Thomas Harman, the rich old Squire of Holly Crouch. Catherine does not realize that Pecksall is very much in love with her and that he secretly wishes that she would turn Protestant.

News that a secret Mass is going to be celebrated at Fuggesbroke is sent to Catherine. In her great joy she communicates this knowledge to Pecksall and Harman with the plea that they come to the early morning Mass and be reconciled to the Faith. At the Tuktones she meets the priest, who has just arrived from Rheims bringing a personal message and a letter from Simon, who has recently been ordained and is on his way to Chichester.

Catherine then quickly returns to the Alard Manor to retire early so she can be refreshed for the glorious experience of the midnight Mass. A few hours later she is rudely awakened with the tragic news that the Tuktone Manor is in flames and completely destroyed by the agents of the Queen. Nicholas Pecksall confesses to Catherine that he is guilty of betraying the secret of the priest's visit. He had turned informer because in his love for Catherine he wished to spare her from possible capture and death. As a result of the catastrophe, the Tuktones give up their faith.

Another blow befalls Catherine when her father is killed in a scuffle with the steward of Conster Manor over her mother's affections. Catherine herself had been interested in the steward. Disillusioned with her mother and bereaved of her father, she sets out to find Simon. Disguised as a man, who could be taken for her brother's twin, she rides to Chichester. There Catherine finds Simon and his priest companions. She informs him of their father's death and of the other tragedies of the past years. Simon tries to persuade her to return to Conster Manor, but she refuses. He urges her to become a nun on the Continent, where she could do in the cloister for Christ and the Church what he must do in certain martyrdom. The novel then concludes with the following:

XIII

It was quite dark all the time they rode across the downs, and sometimes they had to make their way slowly over steep, uncertain ground. They would probably have lost the track but for Peter Smith,[1] who had already more than once made the journey from Chichester[2] to West Rooting. The sky was black with a high mist that hid the stars. There was a smell of darkness, of night, of heaviness, and never at any time the faintest sound, except for the beating of their horses' hoofs on the turf and the murmur of their voices.

At last a pale rift showed in the east, and at the same time they came off the downs and rode through the silent village of Bury. Thence they had a well-marked road to Pulborough, where they turned into a mass of little twisting lanes, which Smith seemed to know as well as he knew the downs. The sun was rising as they came to Warminghurst, in the midst of an agricultural country, with farms and their enclosures of fields dotted about the common land. Then after Thakeham it was all forest, but a forest unthreatened by iron.[3]

Catherine was beginning to feel tired at last, and the dawn had brought her a little chill. She found that her head ached, and that her joy in motion was growing less. She would be glad to slide from her horse's back, and to lay her head on some cool pillow. Simon, seeing that his sister was tired, suggested

[1] PETER SMITH—In reality, a priest named Father Amyas in disguise, with Simon, known as James Philips.

[2] CHICHESTER—(chĭch'ĭs·tĕr) A city in West Sussex.

[3] UNTHREATENED BY IRON—The growing smelting industry was beginning to invade the Sussex forests.

Selection from *Superstition Corner* by Sheila Kaye-Smith, reprinted by permission of A. D. Peters, London.

that they should stop at an inn and refresh themselves with a drink of ale; but Peter Smith disparaged the idea. It would be dangerous, he said, to halt at an inn they did not know, and there was no inn kept by Catholics between Halfnakede and Kent. She must take heart, for their journey's end was not far off—only a few more miles.

Catherine was ashamed to find herself defaulting now that she was in the company of heroes. She did her best to hold up her head, and listen to the tales that Smith had to tell of his adventures in England two years ago. The cool, moving leaves of the forest kept the sun from her head, and once they halted by a brook side, and all three lay down and drank deep of the cold, earth-tasting water. After that she felt better, and able to face the last three miles of her journey.

It was nearly noon when they came to the ancient clearing which hundreds of years ago the Saxons had made in the forest for their hogs. Here now was all the steading of a village—the thatched huts and cottages of the peasantry, a decent house or two, a Saxon-built church, and a little way off among the trees the roofs of a Manor.

This was Tabeler Hall, home of the Beyntons, and centre of the most important Mission in the South of England. Scarcely a priest who landed at Hulkesmouth or at Littlehampton but came to say Mass at West Rooting, and the family had enjoyed an immunity which was rare, but possible in such times of personal favour and arbitrary administration.

The Beyntons were known and beloved throughout the neighbourhood, both by the Squires and Magistrates, and by the common folk, among whom otherwise the hope of gain might have made informers. They lived with discretion, but so securely that for weeks at a time they had been able to keep the Blessed Sacrament in their home. Here at last Catherine was to find English Catholics whose faith was not starved, and she took heart again as she heard Peter Smith tell their story. It would be good to rest at Tabeler Hall, even if afterwards she must leave it, like Simon Peter, to be carried whither she would not go. . . .

She was so tired that she had almost fallen asleep by the time she reached the house, and was conscious only of a hurry and stir about her as she sat nodding on her saddle. Then Simon came up, leading an elderly lady dressed in black and followed by a thick-set young man, to both of whom he introduced her as his sister. She was relieved to find that she would not have to maintain her disguise, for she had scarcely the wits for it now. Soon she found that all disguises were unneeded here, and Peter Smith and James Philips were openly Father Amyas and Father Alard.

For the first time in her life Catherine found herself in a Catholic household; from the lowest scullion [4] to the dowager head of the family, all held the Faith and practised it according to opportunity. She dismounted stiffly from her horse, and entered the hall on her brother's arm. She was aware of many people about her—she saw two young boys kneeling to receive Father Amyas's blessing—servants came forward with trays of food and wine—she was led to a seat by the fire and found herself shivering.

"What will you take, child?" asked Lady Beynton. "Here is some lamb pasty, some soused eels, and some salad

[4] SCULLION—A kitchen servant.

—or will you have marchpane?[5] Ralphe, pour out some wine."

But Catherine found that she could not eat; she could only sip a little wine, and then feel glad to go upstairs, where her ladyship's own woman took her to a guest-chamber and helped her to undress. Soon she was asleep.

XIV

She did not sleep well. Every now and then she would wake, feeling terrified till she remembered where she was; and when at last she managed to sleep for a few hours she woke with memories of many dreams, to find her body covered with sweat that clogged her shift and the sheets.

After that she did not sleep again, but lay awake thinking. She heard a clock strike five, and thought that someone would be sure to call her soon to supper, so that it was not worth while trying to go to sleep. The sunlight came like a red sword between the heavy curtains. She watched it move across the room till it lay upon her bed; then it moved till it touched her heart—it looked as if the sunset pierced her with a sword.

The sun was a jealous lover, running her through the heart, because she was going to leave him, to shut herself out of his power, though surely the sun would not be quite shut out of the cloisters at Bruges[6]. . . No, but he would touch her only respectfully, his kisses would never again burn her face and

[5] MARCHPANE—A dessert made of almonds and sugar.

[6] BRUGES (broozh)—A city in western Belgium.

neck as brown as a field of hay; she would grow pale as hemlock . . . She had never seen a nun, but she knew that nuns were pale.

"Then, O, then, O, then, O, my true
   love said:
   Till this time come again I cannot
      live a maid . . ."

No, I cannot, I cannot, I cannot—but I must. I am condemned to an eternal maidenhood . . . I who want love, even Protestant love . . . No, no, no, I do not—not now. He was terrible—he killed both my father and my mother. Oh, what am I thinking . . . ?

Her head was hot and swimming with thoughts, and she raised herself on her pillows that she might clear them. This nunnery—she would have to face it. If she would not go into a nunnery, where else could she go? Could she go back to Conster and live with her uncle? She would live in shame and dependence because all her uncle's family would know why she did not live with her mother. Could she live with her mother? No, she could never do that. Could she live with Simon? No, for he would have no home and probably soon would lose his life as well. Oh, Simon, Simon . . . tears oozed from under her eyelids, and seemed to dry at once on her hot cheeks. Why couldn't she and Simon live together as brothers and sisters do? Why must religion take him from her to wander about the world until he left it? When a woman does not marry . . . Oh, why couldn't she marry? Why must religion make it impossible for her to find a mate? Religion had breathed over her like a hot wind from the desert, withering up its flower.

She must not think such thoughts. They were wicked and blasphemous. A demon was surely whispering to her—*libera nos a malo*. The Lord is my fir-

mament, my God is my helper. I would die for my religion. She thought of how she had wanted to die with Simon, feeling that she could even bear to see him mangled if they might share the joy of martyrdom together. Simon wanted her to go into a nunnery—he had no wish to see her with him on the scaffold, the sight of her sufferings would weaken him. If she were somewhere happy and safe he would feel stronger to die. That was why he wanted her to go into a convent—he knew she would be safe and he thought she would be happy. She would have the substance of religion—all the holy privileges she had never known: Mass even every day and constant prayer with those of her own faith. She would sit down to a banquet after years of starvation.

But banquets do not always tempt those who are used to eating under hedges. All her life she had been a gipsy in religion and now she felt herself shrinking from the thought of settled ways. It was wrong, she knew, but she could not help it. A sudden wild idea came to her to put on her man's attire again, and ride out into the country, and from henceforward be an adventurer. She would rather wear a man's doublet and side-slops than a nun's trailing robes . . . though years ago she used to think and sometimes say what a sin it was that there were no convents in England for a woman to go to . . . But she had no vocation—she wanted to be married . . . Simon said there was such a thing as a vocation of circumstances. What else could she do if she did not go into a nunnery? She could not really ride away as a man. She could not take the roads as a vagabond—not for any length of time. She had not quite the stuff in her for that.

She had told Nicholas Pecksall that

her religion was the dearest thing to her in life (or she might have married a dancing Parson). Then she ought to love it better than her freedom. Religion was something more than plots and risks and contrivances. It was life and death. She wished it could be death, but it was not expedient for her to die . . . expedient, expedient—that was a word of Nicholas Pecksall's. She did not like expediency. But Simon did not wish her to die—oh, how her head ached!—he wished her to live and pray for him. By prayers and blood . . . and he had said it would not be the blood of armadas—nor only the blood of martyrs. If she poured out her soul in suffering she might bring back the Faith to England, even though she did not pour out her blood, as she would so much rather do. She mustn't weaken Simon, and the cause that was his and hers. If only her head didn't ache so, she would get this clearer. Thousands of priests, marching from Rome, from Rheims, from Douai, to be hanged in England, and a poor nun praying in Bruges who would rather be hanged— and the Faith is back again.

XV

There was a knock at her door, and Lady Beynton's woman came in, carrying an armful of her mistress's clothes. Supper would be served in half an hour, she said, and she helped Catherine to dress. The clothes were stiff and rich, such as Catherine was not used to, and for the first time in her life she had to wear a ruff,[7] instead of the partlet[8] that had left her neck free and sunburnt.

7 RUFF—Wheel-shaped collar of starched muslin worn in sixteenth century.
8 PARTLET—Sixteenth century covering for neck and shoulders.

The ruff scratched her chin, and made her headache worse; but she endured it as good practice for the days when her head and neck would be bound up together in a nun's coif.

Supper was laid in the great hall, and was a well-cooked, bountiful meal eaten with solemnity. Sir Ralphe Beynton, virtual head of the house, sat at the head of the table, with his mother, the actual and effectual head, at his left hand. Catherine sat on his right, and below her and Lady Beynton came the two priests, and afterwards other members of the family, none of whom yet was married. The men and women of the household sat down with their masters. It all reminded Catherine a little of Fuggesbroke, except that the food and table furniture were of the best, and the atmosphere was both less fearful and less gay.

Catherine could eat only a little, to the concern of her hostess. She was ashamed of feeling tired and languid, but told herself she would be well again after a night's rest. Neither did she feel able to join much in the conversation, though she enjoyed listening to the tales of Rome and foreign parts. It appeared that Lady Beynton had a son in the new college at Douai as well as a daughter in the nunnery at Bruges, also that at one time she had been to Flanders to see them both. Catherine was puzzled to think how she could have contrived it.

It was not till they had left table that she heard there would be Mass the next morning. At first she thought this meant the end of her night's rest at one or two o'clock, but she was told that these things did not have to be done so desperately at Tabeler Hall. Father Amyas would say Mass at six o'clock, before setting out again on his journey. Simon, she learned to her inexpressible joy, would stay a day or two longer at West Rooting.

"Then I am to join Amyas at Rochester—and I shall travel by way of Leasan and Vinehall."

"Shall you go to Conster?"

He shook his head. "There is nothing now to take me to Conster. But I shall go to Fuggesbroke and to Holly Crouch."

"Shall you see Thomas Harman?" [9]

"That's my chief purpose."

"To reconcile him?"

"Aye, to finish your work."

"My work?—it was none of my work —my mischief, rather." But she was comforted to hear Simon speak of the reconciliation of Thomas Harman as her work.

She was also comforted to find that her talk with Lady Beynton about the future was not to happen that night. She would far sooner go upstairs to her room and creep into bed again, though she had been out of it barely three hours. She thought now that she must have caught some kind of sickness in Chichester; for she was certain that she had a fever—her head ached and her pulses throbbed, and her skin felt hot and burning. Doubtless there were many fevers about in the city and she remembered having heard that in October the decline of the Sign of Virgo [10] made for fevers and sweats.

All she hoped was that she would not be too sick and heavy for Mass tomorrow morning. She would have liked to ask for some remedy, such as a lavender poultice or an infusion of ragwort.[11]

[9] THOMAS HARMAN—Master of the Manor of Holly Crouch, who conformed to the new religion outwardly, but who still wished to die a Catholic.

[10] SIGN OF VIRGO—In Astrology, the sixth sign of the zodiac, represented as feminine, melancholy, and cold.

[11] RAGWORT—An herb.

But she did not want anyone to take alarm at her state and maybe forbid her to come to Mass. At all costs, in spite of herself and in spite of anyone, she would be there. The cup should not be snatched from her lips a second time.

Her resolution grew with her illness, as she lay in the great bed, sleeping lightly and fitfully, and always chased by dreams. Once she dreamed that she had overslept, that no one had waked her, that Mass was over and both the priests were gone. She set out after them—riding—riding—she would hear Mass at Fuggesbroke. She could see it far off, but she came no nearer, though she beat and urged on Ball; [12] and then suddenly flames rose up out of the roof, and she could feel the heat of them, though they were ten miles away.

Another time she dreamed that she was riding dressed in a nun's habit. Riding in her dreams was never the rest and release it was in her waking hours, rather it was something that wore her out, that seemed part of a useless struggle . . . She was riding and she met Nicholas Pecksall, and for some reason Richard Tuktone was there too. They were in the Parsonage garden, and she could see great roses growing up a kind of frame that towered against the sky. Pecksall put his arms round her and kissed her—she could feel his kisses in her dream—and all the time Richard Tuktone stood by them and would not go. Then she woke, feeling the dream still about her, and knowing that the frame up which the roses climbed was a gallows. "Gallows-garden," she heard herself saying aloud; "Gallows-garden."

She prayed desperately, because she thought her wits were leaving her. But after a while she was able to reassure herself that it was only a dream. She

[12] BALL—Catherine's horse.

was not used to illness, but she knew that in a fever dreams have a strange intensity. As soon as Mass was over she would ask for medicine.

XVI

Mass was over . . . or had she dreamed it? No, for she could remember it so clearly. The altar stood like an island among the mists that were gathering round her—an island that burned at each end. She could see it there even when she closed her eyes, and the household kneeling round it, and Simon standing before it, with Father Amyas at his side to serve the heavenly table. She could hear her brother's voice: *introibo ad altare Deo.* She had gone up to the altar of God after two years. That was why she did not feel afraid now, though she knew she must be very ill. She did not fear anything, even death itself, now that she was sure the Mass was not a dream. She was quite, quite sure, for she could remember how a long ray of light had slanted down from the window to touch the chalice. She could remember the colours of the clothes the family wore—black for Lady Beynton, purple for Sir Ralphe, watchet [13] for Joyce and green for Margery . . . and she could remember how at the end of Mass she had fallen backwards against Humphrey's shoulder. That proved it. She would never have dreamed that.

But how was it that Nicholas Pecksall could have said the Mass?—how had he managed to come as far as West Rooting? She must ask Father Amyas, for she could see his face above her, clear among the shadows. But instead she

[13] WATCHET—A pale blue or light blue cloth.

found herself telling him that the decline of the Sign of Virgo often brings fevers and sweats.

"They've sent for a physician," he said, and she was glad to find that she could hear his voice quite clearly, and that it sounded cool and rational. Her own did not seem quite so rational as she heard it say:

"It should be a conjurer, for all these things are in the stars."

"Nay, Mistress, our sicknesses have not such a dignity. Rather they come from the dust of the earth than the stars of heaven . . . The physicians of the Jesuit order . . . travelling . . . inns . . . lice and vermin . . . contagion . . . good hope . . ."

His voice seemed to come from very far away, which was strange, because his face was still quite close to hers. His voice seemed to ebb and flow like the sea waves. She suddenly felt scared, and called: "Simon! Simon!"

"I'm here."

There was a hand in hers. She held it, and clung to it.

"Where's Father Amyas?"

"He hath been gone two hours."

"Simon, you wön't go—you wön't leave me—"

"No, dear Kate."

She could hear voices murmuring, men's and women's, ebbing and flowing and sighing. Then she felt a prick, and a kind of languor. She could hear something being poured into a bowl.

"Simon, when you get to Holly Crouch, will you let them know at Fuggesbroke?" She was feeling much clearer, though very weak. She could see the room and the people in it without mistiness, and she could feel the bed and the pillows under her instead of floating in a treacherous void. Simon sat at the foot of the bed, watching her.

"Yes, I shall go to Fuggesbroke. Are you better now?"

"Aye, I am clearer in my head."

"The doctor hath just bled you. He took two ounces of blood from your foot."

"My feet feel cold."

"That is the fever leaving you."

Lady Beynton came forward with a cup of milk, but Catherine found she could take very little of it.

"How much longer will you stay here?" she asked her brother.

"I shall stay until you're better."

"Have I the sweat?"

"The physician thinks you have some sort of putrid fever. He doth not think it is the sweat."

"Then I pray none of you catches it from me. Simon, you mun take care."

"I always take care," he said, smiling at her.

Her pillow was growing hot, and she tried to turn it over, but found she was too weak. Lady Beynton turned it and Catherine's head fell back. The pillow seemed to stand out round her like a nun's coif.

XVII

Mass was over . . . no, she hadn't dreamed it. She could remember it so clearly. Or had she dreamed it,—for there was nothing now, only a void beneath her and above her and a great darkness. Ah, now she remembered—there was to have been Mass at Fuggesbroke, and on her way to it Thomas Harman had met her and told her that the soldiers had come and beaten up Tuktone . . . She had run away disguised as a pedlar . . . She was trying to find Simon. He was in Rome, at the English College, and she was trying to find him, though she had lost her horse

and all her money, and had the plague . . . miserere mei . . . she was in a ship burning at both ends . . . oh, Simon! Simon! . . .

"I'm here, darling Kate. Don't you know me?"

. . . Simon by her side in the darkness, waiting for the first light, so that they could slide down the wall together and run away to Leasan . . . no, they were in the dark forest of Wogenmarye, so very dark—the trees were hiding the stars. Simon, can you see the stars? O, God my firmament . . . Go forth, Christian soul, from this world . . . Squire Tuktone said "We shall meet in Paradise". . . Simon would die on the gallows—no, no in the prison . . . in the name of Christ, Son of the living God who suffered for thee . . . Who's that playing a lute? I like not the music —let me go! let me go!—he is treading on the lute . . . mother! mother! . . . let thine habitation to-day be in peace, and thine abode in Sion.

She was lying with her knees raised, and a crucifix was propped against them. Simon was kneeling beside her; she felt as if she had wakened between two sleeps.

"Brother, how long have I been ill?"

"Around five days."

It seemed more like five minutes—or five years.

"Then how much longer can you stay with me?"

"I shall stay as long as you need me."

"That won't be much longer now," she said, and knew that she was dying.

She was not afraid, but she would have liked to keep her head clear. She wanted to speak to Simon—to ask him to say Mass for her soul; but the words would not come. Then she knew that he would say it without her asking.

Her mind was slipping back into

darkness . . . she groped for her brother's hand and touched the wood of the cross. It was time to start, or Nicholas Pecksall would have begun Mass. Why didn't they light the candles? . . . gallows-garden . . . who said that? . . . I want my horse—I want my horse . . . O, God, my firmament . . . I cannot be a nun . . . a gittern and a recorder [14] . . . then, O, then, O, then, O, my true love said . . . may the choir of angels receive thee, and mayest thou have eternal rest with Lazarus who once was poor . . .

An altar with a candle burning at each end . . . she and Simon were kneeling before it . . . there was no darkness now . . . she could see the light, and it seemed as she watched it to increase and surge up like sunrise . . . *introibo ad altare Deo* . . . the light swept towards her and blazed about her and then became a sound . . . a Name . . . A Name that was on her lips. Then the sound once more became light and the light darkness, but a darkness without fear. She knew that she had only to look up to see the sky blaze with stars—stars that were no longer the distant arbitrators of man's fate but the tokens of God's unchanging mercy towards him. So she closed her eyes in sleep and gave herself to the darkness.

[14] GITTERN AND RECORDER—A wire musical instrument like a guitar and a flute. Both are medieval musical instruments.

FOR DISCUSSION

1. Briefly describe the physical aspects of the countryside through which Catherine and Simon journeyed. What were the conditions under which Catholics lived in this section of England? Did Catherine find a different atmosphere here from that of her own locality? Explain.

2. Select those passages where the external physical details are symbolic of her own internal feelings. Show how the author effectively describes, through brief and apparently unconnected statements, the internal struggle of Catherine's mind: the conflict between marriage and the life of a nun; between love and marriage with a Protestant.

3. Is the stream of consciousness technique employed here? What artistic device does the author use to connect Catherine's semi-conscious dreams with the outside world? Are the liturgy of the Mass and the prayers for the dying effectively used in the death bed scene? Discuss.

4. Now that you have been introduced to *Superstition Corner*, you will want to read the entire book. Perhaps you will then see why this novel has been chosen as one of the *Thomas More Books to Live* series.

NONFICTION: BIOGRAPHY

A new trend in the writing of biographies appeared in the 1920's. A modern biographer sets himself the task of *interpreting and explaining* the man he is writing about; of re-creating him as a complex and interesting human being.

The older biographers, following a strict chronological order, plodded along through a mass of fact, until they concluded with their subject's death and burial. They did not distinguish between important and less important facts, and failed to emphasize the personality of the subject about whom they were writing. The modern biographer will record his hero's weaknesses and prejudices along with his achievements. He sifts all his source material in such a way as to present a sharply defined character-portrait or a dramatic life story. This kind of biography at its best rivals fiction in vividness, color, and drama. But in the hands of cynical writers intent on finding all bad and no good in the record of a human life it is dangerous and destructive of objective truth.

Outstanding among the English non-Catholic biographers of this new school are Lytton Strachey, Philip Guedalla, and Hesketh Pearson. Any enumeration of British Catholic biographers must include Hilaire Belloc, G. K. Chesterton, Christopher Hollis, and Evelyn Waugh. All of these use the new biographical techniques to present vivid analytical and dramatic interpretations of important historic and literary personages. In another sense, however, they are biographical essayists, since they utilize both the subject of the biography and the period background as mediums for reinterpreting an historical age and for restating the Catholic position.

Under the impetus and the influence of the great French Catholic writer, Henri Gheon, much has been done by modern biographers of saints to present them as human beings of flesh and blood. Father C. C. Martindale was one of the first who succeeded in making hagiography, or the biographies of saintly people, both a literary accomplishment and an inspiration to the average Christian. This method has been enthusiastically followed by Margaret Yeo and Christopher Hollis. Father James Brodrick should be mentioned as an historical biographer of the first rank, who satisfies the high demand of both art and scholarship.

QUEEN VICTORIA'S MARRIAGE

LYTTON STRACHEY

The queen was twenty years old—high time, according to the ideas of a century ago, for a girl to be married. However, she was not certain she was in love with her cousin Albert. There was the additional difficulty that no well-mannered young man would be brash enough to propose marriage to the ruler of a great nation.

The following selection from QUEEN VICTORIA *tells how Victoria met these and later problems. It pictures the strange situation of a young wife and mother who was also Queen of the United Kingdom of Great Britain and Ireland, mistress of several palaces, and consultant of Prime Ministers. At the same time it shows, by Victoria's words and actions, what kind of person she was.*

Any change would be for the worse; and the worst change of all . . . no, she would not hear of it; it would be quite intolerable, it would upset everything, if she were to marry. And yet everyone seemed to want her to—the general public, the Ministers, her Saxe-Coburg relations—it was always the same story. Of course, she knew very well that there were excellent reasons for it. For one thing, if she remained childless, and were to die, her uncle Cumberland, who was now the King of Hanover,[1] would succeed to the throne of England. That, no doubt,

[1] HANOVER—A former province of Prussia. Cumberland was the fifth son of George III. He inherited the throne of Hanover in 1837. A political reactionary, Cumberland was extremely unpopular in England.

would be a most unpleasant event; and she entirely sympathized with everybody who wished to avoid it. But there was no hurry; naturally, she would marry in the end—but not just yet—not for three or four years. What was tiresome was that her uncle Leopold [2] had apparently determined, not only that she ought to marry, but that her cousin Albert [3] ought to be her husband. That was very like her uncle Leopold, who wanted to have a finger in every pie; and it was true that long ago, in far-off days, before her accession even, she had written to him in a way which might well have encouraged him in such a notion. She had told him then that Albert possessed "every quality that could be desired to render her perfectly happy," and had begged her "dearest uncle to take care of the health of one, now *so dear* to me, and to take him under *your special* protection," adding, "I hope and trust all will go on prosperously and well on this subject of so much importance to me." But that had been years ago, when she was a mere child; perhaps, indeed, to judge from the language, the letter had been dictated by Lehzen; [4] at any rate, her feelings, and all the circumstances, had now entirely changed. Albert hardly interested her at all.

In later life the Queen declared that she had never for a moment dreamt of marrying anyone but her cousin; her letters and diaries tell a very different story. On August 26, 1837, she wrote in her journal: "Today is my *dearest* cousin Albert's eighteenth birthday, and I pray Heaven to pour its choicest blessings on his beloved head!" In the subsequent years, however, the date passes unnoticed. It had been arranged that Stockmar [5] should accompany the Prince to Italy, and the faithful Baron left her side for that purpose. He wrote to her more than once with sympathetic descriptions of his young companion; but her mind was by this time made up. She liked and admired Albert very much, but she did not want to marry him. "At present," she told Lord Melbourne [6] in April, 1839, "*my* feeling is quite against ever marrying." When her cousin's Italian tour came to an end, she began to grow nervous; she knew that, according to a long-standing engagement, his next journey would be to England. He would probably arrive in the autumn, and by July her uneasiness was intense. She determined to write to her uncle, in order to make her position clear. It must be understood she said, that "there is *no engagement* between us." If she should like Albert, she could "*make no final promise this year*, for, at the *very earliest*, any such event could not take place till *two or three years hence*." She had, she said, "a *great* repugnance" to change her present position; and, if she should not like him, she was "*very* anxious that it should be understood that she would *not* be guilty of any breach of promise, for she *never gave any*." To Lord Melbourne she was more explicit. She told him that she "had no great wish to see Albert, as the whole subject was an odious one"; she hated to have to decide about it; and she repeated once again that seeing Albert would be "a disagreeable thing." But there was no escaping the horrid business; the visit must be made, and she must see him.

[2] HER UNCLE LEOPOLD—Leopold I, king of the Belgians.

[3] HER COUSIN ALBERT—Second son of the duke of Saxe-Coburg-Gotha, in Germany.

[4] LEHZEN—Louise Lehzen, from Germany, had been Victoria's governess. For her service to the English royal family she was made a baroness.

[5] STOCKMAR—Baron von Stockmar of Coburg was confidential adviser both to Victoria and her cousin Albert.

[6] LORD MELBOURNE—Prime Minister and head of the Whig party.

The summer slipped by and was over; it was the autumn already; on the evening of October 10 Albert, accompanied by his brother Ernest, arrived at Windsor.

Albert arrived; and the whole structure of her existence crumbled into nothingness like a house of cards. He was beautiful—she gasped—she knew no more. Then, in a flash, a thousand mysteries were revealed to her; the past, the present, rushed upon her with a new significance; the delusions of years were abolished, and an extraordinary, an irresistible certitude leaped into being in the light of those blue eyes, the smile of that lovely mouth. The succeeding hours passed in a rapture. She was able to observe a few more details—the "exquisite nose," the "delicate moustachios and slight but very slight whiskers," the "beautiful figure, broad in the shoulders and a fine waist." She rode with him, danced with him, talked with him, and it was all perfection. She had no shadow of a doubt. He had come on a Thursday evening, and on the following Sunday morning she told Lord Melbourne that she had "a good deal changed her opinion as to marrying." Next morning, she told him that she had made up her mind to marry Albert. The morning after that, she sent for her cousin. She received him alone, and "after a few minutes I said to him that I thought he must be aware *why* I wished them to come here—and that it would make me *too happy* if he would consent to what I wished (to marry me)." Then "we embraced each other, and he was *so kind, so* affectionate." She said that she was quite unworthy of him, while he murmured that he would be very happy *"Das Leben mit dir zu zubringen."* [7] They parted, and she felt "the happiest of human beings," when Lord M. came in. At first she beat about the bush, and talked of the weather and indifferent subjects. Somehow or other she felt a little nervous with her old friend. At last, summoning up her courage, she said, "I have got well through this with Albert." "Oh! you have," said Lord M. . . .

He was not in love with her. Affection, gratitude, the natural reactions to the unqualified devotion of a lively young cousin who was also a queen—such feelings possessed him, but the ardors of reciprocal passion [8] were not his. Though he found that he liked Victoria very much, what immediately interested him in his curious position was less her than himself. Dazzled and delighted, riding, dancing, singing, laughing, amid the splendors of Windsor, he was aware of a new sensation—the stirrings of ambition in his breast. His place would indeed be a high, an enviable one! And then, on the instant, came another thought. The teachings of religion, the admonitions of Stockmar, his own inmost convictions, all spoke with the same utterance. He would not be there to please himself, but for a very different purpose—to do good. He must be "noble, manly, and princely in all things," he would have "to live and to sacrifice himself for the benefit of his new country"; to "use his powers and endeavors for a great object—that of promoting the welfare of multitudes of his fellowmen." One serious thought led on to another. The wealth and the bustle of the English Court might be delightful for the moment, but, after all, it was Coburg that had his heart. "While I shall be untiring," he wrote to his grandmother, "in my efforts and labors for the country to which I shall in future belong,

[7] *Das Leben mit dir zu zubringen* (däs lä'bǎn mǐt dēr tsōō tsōō'brǐng·ǎn)—To spend life with you.

[8] RECIPROCAL PASSION—Emotion felt in response to or equal to that of another.

and where I am called to so high a position, I shall never cease *ein treuer Deutscher, Coburger, Gothaner zu sein.*" [9] And now he must part from Coburg forever! Sobered and sad, he sought relief in his brother Ernest's company; the two young men would shut themselves up together, and, sitting down at the pianoforte, would escape from the present and the future in the sweet familiar gaiety of a Haydn [10] duet.

They returned to Germany; and while Albert, for a few farewell months, enjoyed, for the last time, the happiness of home, Victoria, for the last time, resumed her old life in London and Windsor. She corresponded daily with her future husband in a mingled flow of German and English; but the accustomed routine reasserted itself; the business and the pleasures of the day would brook no interruption; Lord M. was once more constantly beside her; and the Tories [11] were as intolerable as ever. Indeed, they were more so. For now, in these final moments, the old feud burst out with redoubled fury. The impetuous sovereign found, to her chagrin, that there might be disadvantages in being the declared enemy of one of the great parties in the State. On two occasions, the Tories directly thwarted her in a matter on which she had set her heart. She wished her husband's rank to be fixed by statute, and their opposition prevented it. She wished her husband to receive a settlement from the nation of £50,000 a year; and, again owing to the Tories, he was only allowed £30,000. It was too bad. When the question was discussed in Parliament, it

[9] *Ein treuer Deutscher, Coburger, Gothaner zu sein* (ĭn troi′ĕr doich′ĕr kō′bŭr·gĕr gō′tä·nĕr tsoō zĭn). To be a true citizen of Germany, Coburg, Gotha.

[10] HAYDN (hī′d′n)—Franz Joseph Haydn, famous Austrian composer.

[11] THE TORIES WERE AS INTOLERABLE AS EVER—The Tory, or conservative, party was not now in power but held many seats in Parliament.

had been pointed out that the bulk of the population was suffering from great poverty, and that £30,000 was the whole revenue of Coburg; but her uncle Leopold had been given £50,000,[12] and it would be monstrous to give Albert less. Sir Robert Peel—it might have been expected—had had the effrontery to speak and vote for the smaller sum. She was very angry and determined to revenge herself by omitting to invite a single Tory to her wedding. She would make an exception in favor of old Lord Liverpool,[13] but even the Duke of Wellington[14] she refused to ask. When it was represented to her that it would amount to a national scandal if the Duke were absent from her wedding, she was angrier than ever. "What! That old rebel![15] I won't have him," she was reported to have said. Eventually she was induced to send him an invitation; but she made no attempt to conceal the bitterness of her feelings, and the Duke himself was only too well aware of all that had passed. . . .

Albert had foreseen that his married life would not be all plain sailing; but he had by no means realized the gravity and the complication of the difficulties which he would have to face. Politically, he was a cipher. Lord Melbourne was not only Prime Minister, he was in effect the Private Secretary of the Queen, and thus controlled the whole of the political existence of the sovereign. A queen's husband was an entity unknown to the British Constitution. In State affairs there seemed to be no place for him; nor was Victoria herself at all unwilling that this should be so. "The English," she had told the Prince when, during their engagement, a proposal had been made to give him a peerage, "are very jealous of any foreigner interfering in the government of this country, and have already in some of the papers expressed a hope that you would not interfere. Now, though I know you never would, still if you were a Peer, they would all say, the Prince meant to play a political part." "I know you never would!" In reality, she was not quite so certain, but she wished Albert to understand her views. He would, she hoped, make a perfect husband; but, as for governing the country, he would see that she and Lord M. between them could manage that very well, without his help.

But it was not only in politics that the Prince discovered that the part cut out for him was a negligible one. Even as a husband, he found, his functions were to be of an extremely limited kind. Over the whole of Victoria's private life the Baroness reigned supreme; and she had not the slightest intention of allowing that supremacy to be diminished by one iota. Since the accession, her power had greatly increased. Besides the undefined and enormous influence which she exercised through her management of the Queen's private correspondence, she was now the superintendent of the royal establishment and controlled the important office of Privy Purse.[16] Albert very soon perceived that he was not master in his own house. Every detail of his own and his wife's existence was supervised by a third person: nothing could be done until the consent of Lehzen had first been ob-

[12] £50,000—Leopold was given this sum when he married Princess Charlotte.

[13] LORD LIVERPOOL—Former Prime Minister.

[14] DUKE OF WELLINGTON—The famous general who defeated Napoleon in the Battle of Waterloo.

[15] THAT OLD REBEL!—English readers of this biography would be much amused by the thought of Wellington as a "rebel." He was the most conservative of the Tory leaders.

[16] OFFICE OF PRIVY PURSE—The office of supervising the handling of the allowance granted the monarch for private expenses.

tained. And Victoria, who adored Lehzen with unabated intensity, saw nothing
in all this that was wrong.

Nor was the Prince happier in his social surroundings. A shy young foreigner,
awkward in ladies' company, unexpansive
and self-opinionated, it was improbable
that, in any circumstances, he would have
been a society success. His appearance,
too, was against him. Though in the eyes
of Victoria he was the mirror of manly
beauty, her subjects, whose eyes were of
a less Teutonic cast, did not agree with
her. To them—and particularly to the
highborn ladies and gentlemen who naturally saw him most—what was immediately and distressingly striking in Albert's
face and figure and whole demeanor was
his un-English look. His features were
regular, no doubt, but there was something smooth and smug about them; he
was tall, but he was clumsily put together,
and he walked with a slight slouch.
Really, they thought, this youth was more
like some kind of foreign tenor than anything else. These were serious disadvantages; but the line of conduct which the
Prince adopted from the first moment of
his arrival was far from calculated to dispel them. Owing partly to a natural
awkwardness, partly to a fear of undue
familiarity, and partly to a desire to be
absolutely correct, his manners were infused with an extraordinary stiffness and
formality. Whenever he appeared in
company, he seemed to be surrounded by
a thick hedge of prickly etiquette. He
never went out into ordinary society; he
never walked in the streets of London; he
was invariably accompanied by an equerry [17] when he rode or drove. He
wanted to be irreproachable and, if that
involved friendlessness, it could not be
helped. Besides, he had no very high

[17] AN EQUERRY—A personal attendant of
noblemen when riding.

opinion of the English. So far as he
could see, they cared for nothing but fox
hunting and Sunday observances; they
oscillated between an undue frivolity and
an undue gloom; if you spoke to them of
friendly joyousness they stared; and they
did not understand either the Laws of
Thought or the wit of a German University. Since it was clear that with such
people he could have very little in common, there was no reason whatever for
relaxing in their favor the rules of etiquette. In strict privacy, he could be natural and charming; Seymour and Anson [18]
were devoted to him, and he returned
their affection; but they were subordi-
nates—the receivers of his confidences
and the agents of his will. From the
support and the solace of true companionship he was utterly cut off. . . .

Minor disagreements made matters
worse. The royal couple differed in their
tastes. Albert, brought up in a régime of
Spartan simplicity and early hours, found
the great Court functions intolerably
wearisome, and was invariably observed
to be nodding on the sofa at half past
ten; while the Queen's favorite form of
enjoyment was to dance through the
night, and then, going out into the por-
tico of the Palace, watch the sun rise
behind St. Paul's and the towers of Westminster. She loved London and he detested it. It was only in Windsor that
he felt he could really breathe; but Windsor too had its terrors: though during the
day there he could paint and walk and
play on the piano, after dinner black
tedium descended like a pall.[19] He would

[18] SEYMOUR AND ANSON—Lieutenant Francis
Seymour was a young Englishman who had
been assigned to accompany Albert on his tour
of Italy. George Anson was Albert's private
secretary.
[19] TEDIUM DESCENDED LIKE A PALL—Bore-
dom descended like a gloomy cloud.

have liked to summon distinguished scientific and literary men to his presence, and after ascertaining their views upon various points of art and learning, to set forth his own; but unfortunately Victoria "had no fancy to encourage such people"; knowing that she was unequal to taking a part in their conversation, she insisted that the evening routine should remain unaltered; the regulation interchange of platitudes [20] with official persons was followed as usual by the round table and the books of engravings, while the Prince, with one of his attendants, played game after game of double chess.

It was only natural that in so peculiar a situation, in which the elements of power, passion, and pride were so strangely apportioned, there should have been occasionally something more than mere irritation—a struggle of angry wills. Victoria, no more than Albert, was in the habit of playing second fiddle. Her arbitrary temper flashed out. Her vitality, her obstinacy, her overweening sense of her own position, might well have beaten down before them his superiorities and his rights. But she fought at a disadvantage; she was, in very truth, no longer her own mistress; a profound preoccupation dominated her, seizing upon her inmost purposes for its own extraordinary ends. She was madly in love. The details of those curious battles are unknown to us; but Prince Ernest, who remained in England with his brother for some months, noted them with a friendly and startled eye. One story, indeed, survives, ill-authenticated [21] and perhaps mythical, yet summing up, as such stories often do, the central facts of the case. When, in wrath, the Prince one day had locked himself into his room, Victoria, no less furious,

[20] PLATITUDES—Dull, commonplace remarks.
[21] ILL-AUTHENTICATED—Not well supported by evidence.

knocked on the door to be admitted. "Who is there?" he asked. "The Queen of England" was the answer. He did not move, and again there was a hail of knocks. The question and the answer were repeated many times; but at last there was a pause, and then a gentler knocking. "Who is there?" came once more the relentless question. But this time the reply was different. "Your wife, Albert." And the door was immediately opened. . . .

The early discords had passed away completely—resolved into the absolute harmony of married life. Victoria, overcome by a new, an unimagined revelation, had surrendered her whole soul to her husband. The beauty and the charm which so suddenly had made her his at first were, she now saw, no more than but the outward manifestation of the true Albert. There was an inward beauty, an inward glory which, blind that she was, she had then but dimly apprehended, but of which now she was aware in every fiber of her being—he was good—he was great! How could she ever have dreamt of setting up her will against his wisdom, her ignorance against his knowledge, her fancies against his perfect taste? Had she really once loved London and late hours and dissipation? She who now was only happy in the country, she who jumped out of bed every morning—oh, so early!—with Albert, to take a walk, before breakfast, with Albert alone! How wonderful it was to be taught by him! To be told by him which trees were which; and to learn all about the bees! And then to sit doing cross-stitch while he read aloud to her Hallam's Constitutional History of England! Or to listen to him playing on his new organ ("The organ is the first of instruments," he said); or to sing to him a song by Mendelssohn,[22] with a great deal of care over the time and the breathing, and only a very occasional false note! And, after dinner, too—oh, how good of him! He had given up his double chess! And so there could be round games at the round table, or everyone could spend the evening in the most amusing way imaginable —spinning counters [23] and rings. When the babies came it was still more wonderful. Pussy was such a clever little girl ("I am not Pussy! I am the Princess Royal!" she had angrily exclaimed on one occasion); and Bertie—well, she could only pray *most* fervently that the little Prince of Wales would grow up to "resemble his angelic dearest Father in *every*, *every* respect, both in body and mind." [24] Her dear Mamma, too, had been drawn once more into the family circle, for Albert had brought about a reconciliation, and the departure of Lehzen had helped to obliterate the past. In Victoria's eyes, life had become an idyll,[25] and, if the essential elements of an idyll are happiness, love, and simplicity, an idyll it was; though, indeed, it was of a kind that might have disconcerted Theocritus.[26] "Albert brought in dearest little Pussy," wrote Her Majesty in her journal, "in such a smart white merino dress trimmed with blue, which Mamma had given her,

and a pretty cap, and placed her on my bed, seating himself next to her, and she was very dear and good. And, as my precious, invaluable Albert sat there, and our little Love between us, I felt quite moved with happiness and gratitude to God."

The past—the past of only three years since—when she looked back upon it, seemed a thing so remote and alien that she could explain it to herself in no other way than as some kind of delusion—an unfortunate mistake. Turning over an old volume of her diary, she came upon this sentence—"As for 'the confidence of the Crown,' God knows! No *Minister*, *no friend* EVER possessed it so entirely as this truly excellent Lord Melbourne possesses mine!" A pang shot through her— she seized a pen, and wrote upon the margin—"Reading this again, I cannot forbear remarking what an artificial sort of happiness *mine* was *then*, and what a blessing it is I have now in my beloved Husband *real* and solid happiness, which no Politics, no worldly reverses *can* change; it could not have lasted long as it was then, for after all, kind and excellent as Lord M. is, and kind as he was to me, it was but in Society that I had amusement, and I was only living on that superficial resource, which I *then fancied* was happiness! Thank God! for *me* and others, this is changed, and I *know what* REAL *happiness* is—V. R." [27] How did she know? What is the distinction between happiness that is real and happiness that is felt? So a philosopher— Lord M. himself perhaps—might have inquired. But she was no philosopher, and Lord M. was a phantom, and Albert was beside her, and that was enough.

Happy, certainly, she was; and she wanted everyone to know it. Her letters

[22] MENDELSSOHN (měn'děl·s'n)—Felix Mendelssohn, German pianist and composer.

[23] COUNTERS—Circular, coin-like disks used for computing— like the "chips" used in gambling.

[24] TO RESEMBLE . . . IN BODY AND MIND— Instead, the prince grew up to be a worldly, pleasure-loving man. As King Edward VII, he encouraged the reaction against Victorianism.

[25] AN IDYLL—A simple, beautiful existence like that of the peasants described by the ancient Greek poet, Theocritus (thē·ŏk'rĭ·tŭs).

[26] THOUGH, INDEED, IT . . . THEOCRITUS—By referring to Theocritus, whose name we associate with classic dignity, the author makes fun of Victoria's way of gushing over "dearest little Pussy."

[27] V.R.—Victoria Regina; that is, Victoria the Queen.

to King Leopold are sprinkled thick with raptures. "Oh! my dearest uncle, I am sure if you knew *how* happy, how blessed I feel, and how *proud* I feel in possessing *such* a perfect being as my husband . . ." such ecstasies seemed to gush from her pen unceasingly and almost of their own accord. When, one day, without thinking, Lady Lyttelton described someone to her as being "as happy as a queen," and then grew a little confused, "Don't correct yourself, Lady Lyttelton," said Her Majesty. "A queen *is* a very happy woman."

But this new happiness was no lotus dream.[28] On the contrary, it was bracing, rather than relaxing. Never before had she felt so acutely the necessity for doing her duty. She worked more methodically than ever at the business of State; she watched over her children with untiring vigilance. She carried on a large correspondence; she was occupied with her farm—her dairy—a whole multitude of household avocations—from morning till night. Her active, eager little body hurrying with quick steps after the long strides of Albert down the corridors and avenues of Windsor, seemed the very expression of her spirit. Amid all the softness, the deliciousness of unmixed joy, all the liquescence, the overflowings of inexhaustible sentiment, her native rigidity remained. "A vein of iron," said Lady Lyttelton, who, as royal governess, had good means of observation, "runs through her most extraordinary character.". . .

The next task upon which the Prince embarked was a more arduous one: he determined to reform the organization of the royal household. This reform had

been long overdue. For years past the confusion, discomfort, and extravagance in the royal residences, and in Buckingham Palace particularly, had been scandalous; no reform had been practicable under the rule of the Baroness; but her functions had now devolved upon the Prince, and in 1844, he boldly attacked the problem. Three years earlier, Stockmar, after careful enquiry, had revealed in an elaborate memorandum an extraordinary state of affairs. The control of the household, it appeared, was divided in the strangest manner between a number of authorities, each independent of the other, each possessed of vague and fluctuating powers, without responsibility, and without co-ordination. Of these authorities, the most prominent were the Lord Steward and the Lord Chamberlain—noblemen of high rank and political importance, who changed office with every administration, who did not reside with the Court, and had no effective representatives attached to it. The distribution of their respective functions was uncertain and peculiar. In Buckingham Palace, it was believed that the Lord Chamberlain had charge of the whole of the rooms, with the exception of the kitchen, sculleries, and pantries, which were claimed by the Lord Steward. At the same time, the outside of the Palace was under the control of neither of these functionaries—but of the Office of Woods and Forests; and thus, while the insides of the windows were cleaned by the Department of the Lord Chamberlain—or possibly, in certain cases, of the Lord Steward—the Office of Woods and Forests cleaned their outsides. Of the servants, the housekeepers, the pages, and the housemaids were under the authority of the Lord Chamberlain; the clerk of the kitchen, the cooks, and the porters were under that of the Lord Steward; but the

[28] LOTUS DREAM—Greek legend tells of a land where the people lived on lotus fruit, which kept them in a state of dreamy, lazy contentment.

footmen, the livery-porters, and the underbutlers took their orders from yet another official—the Master of the Horse. Naturally, in these circumstances the service was extremely defective and the lack of discipline among the servants disgraceful. They absented themselves for as long as they pleased and whenever the fancy took them; "and if," as the Baron put it, "smoking, drinking, and other irregularities occur in the dormitories, where footmen, etc., sleep ten and twelve in each room, no one can help it." As for Her Majesty's guests, there was nobody to show them to their rooms, and they were often left, having utterly lost their way in the complicated passages, to wander helpless by the hour. The strange divisions of authority extended not only to persons but to things. The Queen observed that there was never a fire in the dining room. She inquired why. The answer was "the Lord Steward lays the fire, and the Lord Chamberlain lights it"; the underlings of those two great noblemen having failed to come to an accommodation, there was no help for it—the Queen must eat in the cold.

A surprising incident opened everyone's eyes to the confusion and negligence that reigned in the Palace. A fortnight after the birth of the Princess Royal the nurse heard a suspicious noise in the room next to the Queen's bedroom. She called to one of the pages, who, looking under a large sofa, perceived there a crouching figure "with a most repulsive appearance." It was "the boy Jones." This enigmatical [29] personage, whose escapades dominated the newspapers for several ensuing months, and whose motives and character remained to the end ambiguous,[30] was an undersized lad of seventeen, the son of a tailor, who had apparently gained admittance to the Palace by climbing over the garden wall and walking in through an open window. Two years before he had paid a similar visit in the guise of a chimney sweep. He now declared that he had spent three days in the Palace, hiding under various beds, that he had "helped himself to soup and other eatables," and that he had "sat upon the throne, seen the Queen, and heard the Princess Royal squall." Every detail of the strange affair was eagerly canvassed. *The Times* reported that the boy Jones had "from his infancy been fond of reading," but that "his countenance is exceedingly sullen." It added: "The sofa under which the boy Jones was discovered, we understand, is one of the most costly and magnificent material and workmanship, and ordered expressly for the accommodation of the royal and illustrious visitors who call to pay their respects to Her Majesty." The culprit was sent for three months to the "House of Correction.". . .

But discomfort and alarm were not the only results of the mismanagement of the household; the waste, extravagance, and peculation [31] that also flowed from it were immeasurable. There were preposterous perquisites and malpractices [32] of every kind. It was, for instance, an ancient and immutable rule that a candle that had once been lighted should never be lighted again; what happened to the old candles, nobody knew. Again, the Prince, examining the accounts, was puzzled by a weekly expenditure of thirty-five shillings on "Red Room Wine." He inquired into the matter, and after great difficulty discovered that in the time of George III a room in Windsor Castle with red hangings had once been used as a guardroom, and that five shillings a day had been al-

---

[29] ENIGMATICAL—Mysterious or puzzling.
[30] AMBIGUOUS—Unclear.

[31] PECULATION—Theft or embezzlement.
[32] PERQUISITES AND MALPRACTICES—Excessive profits, and cases of misconduct.

lowed to provide wine for the officers. The guard had long since been moved elsewhere, but the payment for wine in the Red Room continued, the money being received by a half-pay officer who held the sinecure position [33] of underbutler.

After much laborious investigation, and a stiff struggle with the multitude of vested interests which had been brought into being by long years of neglect, the Prince succeeded in effecting a complete reform. The various conflicting authorities were induced to resign their powers into the hands of a single official, the Master of the Household, who became responsible for the entire management of the royal palaces. Great economies were made, and the whole crowd of venerable abuses was swept away. Among others, the unlucky half-pay officer of the Red Room was, much to his surprise, given the choice of relinquishing his weekly emolument or of performing the duties of an underbutler. Even the irregularities among the footmen, etc., were greatly diminished. There were outcries and complaints; the Prince was accused of med-

dling, of injustice, and of saving candle-ends; but he held on his course, and before long the admirable administration of the royal household was recognized as a convincing proof of his perseverance and capacity.

At the same time his activity was increasing enormously in a more important sphere. He had become the Queen's Private Secretary, her confidential adviser, her second self. He was now always present at her interviews with Ministers. He took, like the Queen, a special interest in foreign policy; but there was no public question in which his influence was not felt. A double process was at work; while Victoria fell more and more absolutely under his intellectual predominance, he, simultaneously, grew more and more completely absorbed by the machinery of high politics—the incessant and multifarious business of a great State. Nobody any more could call him a dilettante; [34] he was a worker, a public personage, a man of affairs. Stockmar noted the change with exultation. "The Prince," he wrote, "has improved very much lately. He has evidently a head for politics. He has become, too, far more in-

[33] SINECURE POSITION—A position "without care"; that is, a job that pays a salary but requires little or no work.

[34] A DILETTANTE—A superficial dabbler.

dependent. His mental activity is constantly on the increase, and he gives the greater part of his time to business, without complaining." "The relations between husband and wife," added the Baron, "are all one could desire." [35]

Long before Peel's ministry [36] came to an end, there had been a complete change in Victoria's attitude towards him. His appreciation of the Prince had softened her heart; the sincerity and warmth of his nature, which, in private intercourse with those whom he wished to please, had the power of gradually dissipating the awkwardness of his manners, did the rest. She came in time to regard him with intense feelings of respect and attachment. She spoke of "our worthy Peel," for whom, she said, she had "an *extreme* admiration" and who had shown himself "a man of unbounded *loyalty, courage,* patriotism, and *high-mindedness,* and his conduct towards me has been *chivalrous* almost, I might say." She dreaded his removal from office almost as frantically as she had once dreaded that of Lord M. It would be, she declared, a *great calamity.* Six years before, what would she have said, if a prophet had told her that the day would come when she would be horrified by the triumph of the Whigs? Yet there was no escaping it; she had to face the return of her old friends. In the ministerial crises of 1845 and 1846, the Prince played a dominating part. Everybody recognized that he was the real center of the negotiations—the actual controller of the forces and the functions of the Crown. The process by which this result was reached had been

so gradual as to be almost imperceptible; but it may be said with certainty that, by the close of Peel's administration, Albert had become, in effect, the King of England.

◇◇◇◇◇◇◇◇◇◇◇◇◇◇◇◇◇◇◇◇◇◇◇◇◇◇◇◇

FOR UNDERSTANDING

1. At first, did Victoria seem favorable or unfavorable toward marrying her cousin? What was her attitude at the time the engagement was settled? Who made the actual proposal of marriage? When she looked back three years afterward, what was Victoria's opinion of the happiness she had felt when she was single?

2. Give several reasons why Albert felt ill at ease in his new position as the Queen's husband. As time went on, did his situation improve or get worse? Explain.

3. After Victoria's marriage we see her changing quickly from a girl who loved nothing better than games and dances to a busy, almost overearnest young woman. What evidence can you give that she was adapting herself to *Albert's attitudes and tastes?*

4. Victoria's admiration of her husband was so extreme that modern readers find it amusing. Albert was serious and high-minded—but to our taste he seems a little stuffy, even absurd. How did Victoria's confidence in him lead to his becoming an important figure in the British government?

5. The remarks made by Victoria herself are not imaginary ones—as they would be in some popular biographies. The author follows the practice of scholarly writers by frequently quoting the exact words of his source—in this case Victoria's private journal. Usually he does this to support what he has just been saying about Victoria's thoughts; if readers wish, they can even look up the journals for themselves and find out whether the author has reported accurately. Point out two quotations that show Victoria as a rather childish or oversentimental person. What impression of

---

[35] THE RELATIONS . . . ARE ALL ONE COULD DESIRE—The Baron is pleased because his protégé Albert has assumed leadership over the Queen.

[36] PEEL'S MINISTRY—Under the leadership of Sir Robert Peel, the Tory party had come into power for several years.

her do we get from her frequent underlining of words and phrases? On the other hand, what admirable characteristics of Victoria are shown in this selection?

6. At best, a great royal household would be cumbersome to manage. It was made worse by the fact that responsibilities were divided among different government offices. Give examples of waste or mismanagement that resulted from such an arrangement. How were matters improved?

WORDS

1. In paragraph 3, study the effectiveness of the diction. What literal facts are suggested in the following expressions: *a thousand mysteries were revealed to her; the delusions of the years were abolished; an irresistible certitude leaped into being?*

2. In paragraph 8, select those adjectives which most forcibly portray the character of Albert as seen by his English associates. What insight into his personality do the following expressions give: *unexpansive and self-opinionated; something smooth and smug* (about his features); *seemed to be surrounded by a hedge of prickly etiquette?* Explain the meaning of the expression: *they oscillated between undue frivolity and undue gloom.*

PROJECTS

Report on the article on Strachey in the April, 1932 issue of the *Catholic World*.

An interesting study would be the comparison of Strachey's treatment of Queen Victoria with that of Laurence Housman in his play *Victoria Regina*.

RELATED READING

The strange story of "the boy Jones" who for three days prowled around Buckingham Palace is told in the recent novel *The Mudlark*, by Theodore Bonnet. Perhaps you have seen the movie version of this novel.

◇◇◇◇◇

(FROM) EDMUND CAMPION

EVELYN WAUGH

The publication of any book by Evelyn Waugh is a literary landmark. It was not surprising, then, that TIME magazine and the SATURDAY REVIEW OF LITERATURE gave generous space to their reviews of his CAMPION when the American edition appeared in 1946. CAMPION, written in the sparkling brilliance of the purest modern prose, first appeared in England in 1935 as Waugh's tribute to the English faith and to Father Martin D'Arcy, gifted Jesuit and Master of Campion House at Oxford, who converted Waugh to Catholicism. The biography won for Waugh the Hawthornden Prize in 1936.

Selection from *Edmund Campion* by Evelyn Waugh, copyright, 1946, by Evelyn Waugh, reprinted by permission of Little, Brown & Company and A. D. Peters, London, by arrangement with the author and Messrs. Hollis & Carter, publishers of the British Empire edition.

The word "fabulous" has been attributed to Campion by both his biographer and recent reviewers, and the epithet best summarizes the underground of the bloody and tragic days of Elizabethan persecution.

As a young Oxford scholar, Campion caught the fancy of Queen Elizabeth by his learning and his charm. He might have enjoyed a rich career as an ecclesiastic in the Church of England but clear logic and a correct conscience persuaded him from playing the hypocrite. He left England for Douai to study for the priesthood and shortly afterward joined the new Jesuit Order. After spending several years as a brilliant orator and professor at Prague, in 1580 he received the summons to return to England and martyrdom; for Elizabeth's government had made it high treason to act as a Roman Catholic priest in England. For a full year Campion journeyed up and down England, eluding Topcliffe and his pursuivants, saying Mass in "priest-holes," instructing, inspiring, and consoling English Catholics whose hopes for their beloved religion were slowly dying. He issued his famous BRAG which he had published for distribution in the event of his arrest, but which was circulated by fellow Catholics immediately. In the following selection, Waugh gives us an account of his reception and his labors in England following the publication of the BRAG.

Campion was eventually arrested, imprisoned, racked, and finally dragged through the rain to Tyburn where he was hanged and quartered. After you have been introduced to Campion the Hero in the following selection, you will want to complete this brilliant book about a brilliant martyr, written by a brilliant Catholic.

The result, both for good and ill, was a vast augmentation of Campion's fame. This, obscured now by his long absence abroad, had, even in the old days before his exile, been local and limited; he was known at the Universities and at Court, among scholars, men of affairs and men of fashion, but it is improbable that his name had ever reached the market towns and remote manors, where now it became fabulous.

Both sides now looked upon him as the leader and spokesman of the new mission; his membership in the Society of Jesus cast over him a peculiar glamour, for, it must be remembered, the Society had, so far, no place in the English tradition. Many Englishmen could remember the day when the great estates were religious property; when friars tramped the roads from village to village, and monks, tonsured and habited, drove their animals to market and dispensed alms and hospitality to the destitute; many had had their earliest lessons from Dominican or Benedictine in the drowsy village schools; the desolate monuments of the old orders stood in every county; their names were familiar and their memory still sweet with the gentleness and dignity of a lost age. But "Jesuit" was a new word, alien and modern.

To the Protestants it meant conspiracy. The countryman knew for himself the virtues and defects of the old monks; he had seen the methods by which the Royal Commissioners obtained their evidence, and he understood their motives perfectly; but of the Jesuits he knew nothing, except distorted and monstrous reports; that their founder was a Spaniard [1] and they were sworn to another allegiance than the Queen's. Stories of Spanish atrocities were eagerly devoured; the Jesuits were the vanguard of Spanish invasion; their business was to murder the Queen and the Council, and set the country in anarchy so that Philip [2] could march in with the tortures of the Inquisition. Preposterous tales obtained credence of the Jesuits' rule and training and the enormous crimes daily committed behind their walls. The news that disguised Jesuits were now at large in the English countryside caused indignation and alarm, and those who had been apathetic in helping the authorities when the quarry was a Marian [3] priest, now joined fiercely in the hunt.

To the Catholics, too, it meant something new, the restless, uncompromising zeal of the Counter-Reformation.[4] The

[1] SPANIARD — Ignatius of Loyola, who founded the Jesuits.

[2] PHILIP—Philip II of Spain who sent the Armada of 1588 against the English.

[3] MARIAN—The native English clergyman who served under Queen Mary Tudor, 1553–58.

[4] COUNTER-REFORMATION—The bold counter movement of the Catholic Church against the Reformers, planned by the Council of Trent and assisted by the activities of the new Jesuit Order.

Queen's Government had taken away from them the priest that their fathers had known; the simple, unambitious figure who had pottered about the parish, lived among his flock, christened them and married them and buried them; prayed for their souls and blessed their crops; whose attainments were to sacrifice and absolve and apply a few rule-of-thumb precepts of canon law; whose occasional lapses from virtue were expected and condoned; with whom they squabbled over their tithes, about whom they grumbled and gossiped; whom they consulted on every occasion; who had seemed, a generation back, something inalienable from the soil of England, as much a part of their lives as the succession of the seasons—he had been stolen from them, and in his place the Holy Father was sending them, in their dark hour, men of new light, equipped in every Continental art, armed against every frailty, bringing a new kind of intellect, new knowledge, new holiness. Campion and Persons found themselves travelling in a world that was already tremulous with expectation.

We have few details of this expedition. The two priests separated at Hoxton and met again three months later at Uxbridge; in the intervening time Persons had passed through Gloucester, Hereford, Worcester, and up into Derbyshire; Campion had been in Berkshire, Oxfordshire, and Northamptonshire. Both they and their hosts were careful to leave no record of their visits, and the letters in which the Jesuits reported progress to their superiors maintain strict anonymity for their converts; edifying anecdotes are related of "*a certain noble lady*" who was offered her liberty on the condition of once walking through a Protestant church, but indignantly refused; of *"a young lady of six-teen"* who was flung into the public prison for prostitutes on account of her courageous answers to the *"sham Bishop of London"*; of a *"boy of, I believe, twelve years"* who was inveigled into acting as page at a Protestant wedding, was inconsolable with shame until he was able to make his confession to a priest—but nothing is said to identify the protagonists. The only names that can be given with any certainty as Campion's hosts during this journey are Sir William Catesby of Ashby St. Leger, Lord Vaux of Harrowden, and Sir Thomas Tresham, a man of exceptional character, eventually brought to ruin for his faith, whose singular and brilliant taste in architecture may still be seen in the exquisite, unfinished mansion at Lyveden and the unique, triangular pavilion, planned and intricately decorated in honour of the Trinity, which stands, concealed and forlorn, among the trees that border the park at Rushton. It is possible, however, to form a tolerably clear, general impression of the journey from the letters already mentioned and the numerous sources of information about Elizabethan conditions.

He travelled in fair comfort, mounted and equipped as befitted a gentleman of moderate means. He was attended by his servant, and more often than not by one or more of the younger members of the household where he had last stayed, but it was his habit for the most of the way to ride in silence at some little distance from his companions, praying and meditating as he had done on the road to Rheims. Changes of horse and clothing were provided for him at different stages; he was constantly on the move, rarely, for fear of the pursuivants, stopping anywhere for more than one night. He must in this way have visited fifty or more houses during the three months.

Along the road the scenes were familiar enough, but he was seeing them with new eyes; the scars of the Tudor revolution [5] were still fresh and livid; the great houses of the new ruling class were building, and in sharp contrast to their magnificence stood the empty homesteads of the yeomen, evicted to make way for the "grey-faced sheep" or degraded to day-labour on what had once been their common land; the village churches were empty shells, their altars torn out and their ornaments defaced; while here and there throughout his journey he passed, as with a different heart, he had often passed before, the buildings of the old monasteries, their roofs stripped of lead and their walls a quarry for the new contractors. [6] The ruins were not yet picturesque; moss and ivy had barely begun their work, and age had not softened the stark lines of change. Many generations of orderly living, much gentle association, were needed before, under another Queen, the State Church should assume the venerable style of *Barchester Towers*. [7] But if the emotions of the Journey were shame and regret, hope and pride waited for him at the end of the day. Wher-

[5] TUDOR REVOLUTION—The destruction of the Catholic monasteries, churches and Catholic estates begun by Henry VIII.

[6] THE GREAT HOUSES . . . QUARRY FOR THE NEW CONTRACTORS—Here the author refers to the historical fact that the "new rich" became so through the enclosures of the common lands when wool-growing became a monopoly; through the destruction of the Church and monasteries, the precious metals of which were given to those who supported Henry in his revolt against Rome. Shakespeare is apparently summarizing this condition when he writes in his sonnet: "Bare ruined choirs where late the sweet birds sang."

[7] *Barchester Towers*—Made famous in Trollope's Victorian novel, *Barchester Towers*.

ever they went the priests found an eager reception. Sometimes they stayed in houses where only a few were Catholic. There was constant coming and going in the vast ramshackle households of the day, and an elaborate hierarchy in the great retinues; there were galleries where the master never penetrated. It was natural enough that any respectable wayfarer should put up there for the night, whether or no he had any acquaintance with his host. . . .

At Catholic houses they found themselves guests of the highest honour, and there they sometimes prolonged their stay for a few days, until the inevitable warning of the pursuivants' approach drove them once more on to the road. In recent years most of the houses had been furnished with secret cupboards where were stored the Mass vestments, altar stones, sacred vessels and books; these "priest-holes" were usually large enough to provide a hiding-place for the missionaries in case of a sudden raid; in some cases there were complete chapels with confessionals and priest's room. Many houses sheltered one of the old Marian priests who had left his cure at Elizabeth's succession, and now lived in nominal employment as secretary and butler. At this early date these seculars had no quarrel with the Fathers of the Society. The Jesuits, fresh from Rome and Continental schools, were as welcome to them as to their flocks; cut off, as they were, from episcopal control, from their reading and from intercourse with other clerics, they constantly found themselves confronted with problems to which their simple training afforded no solution; all these were brought to Campion and Persons. Their prayers were always for more Jesuits. . . .

Campion found his Catholic hosts impoverished to the verge of ruin by the recusancy fines;[8] often the household were in mourning for one or more of their number who had been removed to prison. "No other talk but of death, flight, prison, or spoil of friends," yet everywhere he was amazed at the constancy and devotion which he found. The listless, yawning days were over, the half-hour's duty perfunctorily accorded on days of obligation. Catholics no longer chose their chaplain for his speed in saying Mass, or kept Boccaccio[9] bound in the covers of their missals. Driven back to the life of the catacombs, the Church was recovering their temper. No one now complained of the length of the services, a priest reported to Father Agazzari; if a Mass did not last nearly an hour they were discontented, and if, as occasionally happened, several priests were together, the congregation would assist at five or six Masses in one morning.

Word would go round the countryside that Campion had arrived, and throughout the evening Catholics of every degree, squire and labourer and deposed cleric, would stealthily assemble. He would sit up half the night receiving each in turn, hearing their confessions and resolving their difficulties. Then before dawn a room would be prepared for Mass. Watches were set in case of alarm. The congregation knelt on the rushstrewn floor. Mass was said, communion was given. Then Campion would preach.

It needs little fancy to reconstruct the scene; the audience hushed and intent, every member of whom was risking lib-

[8] RECUSANCY FINES—Those who refused to conform to the new religion and attend the Anglican Church were fined heavily. Practicing his faith in those days cost a man several thousand pounds a year.

[9] BOCCACCIO—Writer of the Italian Renaissance, famed for his *Decameron*.

erty and fortune, perhaps his life, by attendance. The dusk lightened and the candles paled on the improvised altar, the tree tops outside the window took fire, as Campion spoke. The thrilling tones, the profusion of imagery, the polish and precision, the balanced, pointed argument, the whole structure and rich ornament of rhetoric which had stirred the lecture halls and collegiate chapels of Oxford and Douai, Rome, Prague, and Rheims,[10] inspired now with more than human artistry, rang through the summer dawn. And when the discourse had mounted to its peroration and the fiery voice had dropped to the quiet, traditional words of the blessing, a long silence while the priest disrobed and assumed once more his secular disguise; a hurried packing away of the altar furni-

[10] OXFORD, DOUAI, ROME, PRAGUE, RHEIMS —These were the various places where Campion studied, taught, and preached.

ture, a few words of leave taking, and then the horses' hooves clattered once more in the cobbled yard; Campion was on his way, and the Catholics dispersed to their homes.

The danger was increasingly great. *"I cannot long escape the hands of the heretics,"* said Campion, in the letter quoted above, *"The enemy have so many eyes, so many tongues, so many scouts and crafts. I am in apparel to myself very ridiculous; I often change my name also. I read letters sometimes myself that in the first front tell news that Campion is taken. . . . Threatening edicts come forth against us daily. . . . I find many neglecting their own security to have only care of my safety."*

More than once while Campion was sitting at dinner strangers would be heard at the outer doors. *"Like deer when they hear the huntsmen"* the company would leap to their feet and Campion would be rushed into hiding. Sometimes it proved to be a false alarm; sometimes the pursuivants would enter, question the inmates, and depart satisfied. The party would resume their meal and the interrupted conversation. Events of this kind were now a part of his life, but by the loyalty and discretion of his friends, and by his own resources, he escaped unmolested through the three-month journey, and his report ends in a triumphant mood. *"There will never want in England men that will have care of their own salvation, nor such as shall advance other men's; neither shall this Church here ever fail so long as priests and pastors shall be found for their sheep, rage man or devil never so much."*

◇◇◇◇◇◇◇◇◇◇◇◇◇◇◇◇◇◇◇◇◇◇◇◇◇◇◇◇◇

FOR DISCUSSION

1. Discuss in detail the different reactions of the English Catholics and the Protestants to Campion's return to England. Explain the reasons for these reactions.

2. Describe the manner in which Campion traveled, as well as the countryside through which he passed.

3. Contrast the material and the spiritual condition of Campion's hosts. Discuss their attitude toward the Mass as contrasted with that of former years.

4. Explain what Waugh means, in the second paragraph, when he says that "the Society, so far, had no place in English tradition."

5. Discuss at some length the ninth paragraph and the sixth footnote.

6. Waugh's description of Campion's preaching is a splendid example of modern English prose at its best. Analyze it carefully.

7. Has Campion's thrilling prophecy of the last sentence of this selection been fulfilled? Explain.

8. Waugh has given us several quotations from Campion's own writings. Do you think that Campion was a good writer in his own right?

WORDS

1. What is the relationship between the words *apathetic, pathos,* and *sympathetic?* What is the difference between *credence* and personal experience? Give several synonyms for *pottered. Livid* describes what color?

2. Discuss the rich meaning of the following expressions: *tremulous expectation; age had not yet softened the stark lines of change.*

PROJECTS

1. Trace on a map of England the journeys of Campion.

2. Could you mention some of the prominent leaders of the Counter-Reformation in England?

3. Attempt a radio or television script in which you describe the martyrdom of Campion. Base your text on the passage of Waugh's *Campion,* pp. 150–161.

RELATED READING

Richard Breen and Harry Schnibbe have written a modern drama which has as its theme the heroism of Campion. This drama can be found in *Theatre for Tomorrow.*

Many Catholic novels have been written about the persecution of Catholics during the days of Henry and Elizabeth. Among them are Monsignor Hugh Benson's *The King's Achievement, The Queen's Tragedy, Come Rack, Come Rope;* Mrs. Wilfrid Ward's *Tudor Sunset;* and *The Mass of Brother Michel* by Michael Kent.

SIR WALTER SCOTT

HESKETH PEARSON

Sir Walter Scott was one of the most appealingly human characters in English literature. In almost every respect he was outstanding—as a man of genius, of modesty, of physical and moral courage, of tremendous energy.

The story of how Scott overcame his youthful physical handicap of lameness; how he turned from the legal profession, which his father had chosen for him, to professional writing; how he became enormously wealthy and famous as a ballad collector and as a writer of narrative poetry and romantic fiction; how in middle age he became bankrupt and paid off the last farthing of the debt by continuous writing even though in ill health—all these facts and many more are presented by Hesketh Pearson in a fascinating manner in his life of Walter Scott.

In the selection which you are to study, you are given a picture of Scott the man, his physical appearance, and his captivating personality.

It is worth our while to pause here and look at the Laird [1] of Abbotsford, who was about to exchange the national fame of a poet for the international fame of a novelist. He was six feet tall. The upper part of his body was bulky but not corpulent; the chest, arms and shoulders were those of a Hercules; and if it had not been for a shrunken leg, his build, muscular development and carriage would have been extremely impressive. As it was, the foot of his right limb only touched ground at the toes, which made him rock from side to side as he walked, his thick stick moving along with his short leg and coming to earth with it. His head was tall and cylindrical, the part below the eyes being quite an inch and a half less in measurement than the part above. The eyes were light grey, small and shrewd, with humorous diverging lines about them. When he was amused, they seemed to close as much from below as above. The eyebrows were shaggy and prominent, completely shrouding the eyes while he was reading or writing. In early life his hair, usually unkempt, was of a pale sandy-brown colour, but it thinned and became grey before he was fifty. His nose and chin were commonplace, his mouth was straight, his lips

[1] LAIRD OF ABBOTSFORD—A laird is a landed proprietor in Scotland. Abbotsford was the palatial, castle-like home which Scott built for himself and his family. It was situated among the beautiful Eldon Hills in Scotland.

were thin. Between the nose and mouth was a considerable space intersected by a hollow. His cheeks were firm but heavy, and when walking alone or sitting in court his expression was vacant, dull, and even repellent. But under the stimulus of conversation his countenance was transformed; his eyes lit up, his mouth twitched with humour, his face beamed good nature. Along with the benevolence which irradiated his features in society, people sometimes caught a foxy penetrating look, as if he were meditating mischief; but in an instant this would be banished by a beatific smile, as if there were nothing but friendliness and trustfulness in the man.

As might be expected from one of his physique, there was not much fastidiousness in his habits and tastes. He indulged in large breakfasts and small dinners, a round of beef, a cold sheep's head and a huge brown loaf being the main dishes of the former. Having satisfied the craving of a famished farmer at this early meal, he had little appetite for the rest of the day, taking food as sparingly at dinner as he had eaten voraciously at breakfast. The evenings at home were passed in conversation or singing or reading. He liked to read aloud, preferably Shakespeare, Dryden's Fables and Johnson's Satires. Of his contemporaries his favourites were Joanna Baillie, Crabbe, Burns, Byron, Wordsworth and Southey. He read with great effect, characterising the figures in a drama by changes of intonation, his face alive with intelligence and expressive of his own feelings.

The outstanding feature of his character, attested by all who knew him well, was benevolence. Scarcely anyone appealed to him for help in vain. People wholly unknown to him were befriended. A single example must suffice. To a young fellow at Trinity College, Cambridge, who wished to devote his life to a specal form of study, he sent £20, entreating him to consider it as his own 'until better fortunes shall enable you with convenience to accommodate in the same manner any young man of genius in temporary distress.' Advice was as much in demand as money, and he gave it ungrudgingly. Two instances reveal his common sense, which was as much a part of his nature as kindliness. A youthful correspondent complained of depression and wanted a cure. 'The fiend which haunts you is one who, if resisted, will flee from you,' wrote Scott. 'Plunge into active study, diversified by agreeable company and regular exercise; ride, walk, dance or shoot, or hunt, or break stones on the highway rather than despond about your health, which is the surest way in the world to bring about the catastrophe which you are apprehensive of. . . . If you would not laugh at me, I would recommend you to fall heartily in love with the best and prettiest girl in your neighbourhood. The committing the power of teasing us to another, is very apt to prevent us from exercising that irritability of feeling upon ourselves.'

Next to benevolence his most marked characteristic was humility, perhaps the offspring of benevolence. He was great enough to be humble without pretence, though it seems remarkable to us that he could truthfully have considered the poetry of Campbell, Southey and Joanna Baillie[2] as greatly superior to his own. 'Envy of superior talents, I thank God, is unknown to my disposition,' he once told Southey, but the strange thing

[2] CAMPBELL, SOUTHEY, AND JOANNA BAILLIE —These were contemporary poets of Scott. They are now considered minor poets in English literature.

is that he did not envy the successful exploitation of any talent, and he overestimated the works of nearly everyone except his own. When Byron displaced him as a popular poet, he honestly joined in the chorus of praise for his supplanter, and turned to the writing of novels. Had anyone ousted him as a novelist, he would have been equally frank in his admiration and equally adaptable in changing his medium of expression. He could not sympathise with the vanity of writers: 'I believe many dilettanti authors do cocker[3] themselves up into a great jealousy of anything that interferes with what they are pleased to call their fame, but I should as soon think of nursing one of my own fingers into a whitlow[4] for my private amusement as encouraging such a feeling.' He had no conceit, and as he had managed to overcome his vanity he could regard his contemporaries without envy, hatred, jealousy or malice, but with charity, admiration, affection and toleration.

Having no self-importance he enjoyed the passing hour, and though 'by nature a very lonely animal' he liked the company of his fellow-creatures. He could even put up with bores, partly from kindliness and partly because he found them amusing or instructive. Ill-natured jokes at other people's expense were not heard from him, and whenever an acrimonious argument started in his company he invariably managed to make the disputants laugh and forget their differences. 'I am always vexed at myself when I give way even to a shade of ill-humour,' he declared, 'and can truly say it is not my general fault, however many I may have besides.'

His dislike of extreme attitudes in religion, politics and social life was due to the fact that his own feelings were guided by reflection rather than impulse; for which reason he was a better helper than consoler. He could endure so much himself that he found it difficult to sympathise with those who succumbed to distress. Nature had given him a buoyancy of spirit that enabled him to rise above his deepest afflictions and gloomiest hours, and his imagination, coupled with a wonderful memory, saved him from prolonged periods of melancholy or pessimism. He could have built castles in the clouds and kept himself amused if he had been in prison. 'I have worn a wishing-cap,' he wrote in his *Journal*, 'the power of which has been to divert present griefs by a touch of the wand of imagination, and gild over the future prospect by prospects more fair than can ever be realised.' Nowadays the popular form of escape, to use the cant[5] term of the hour, is either into the mental home of economics or into the lunatic asylum of politics. Scott lived in the sane world of his imagination, which produced happiness for himself and his readers. His memory, too, was a constant source of comfort. It was abnormal. At the age of fifty-four he said that he could repeat every letter he had written since the age of fifteen if someone would quote the opening line of each. He heard a poem by Hogg[6] in eighty-eight stanzas, and some weeks later recited it verbatim. He could repeat the whole of an English translation of Corneille's *Le Cid*[7] after

[3] COCKER—To pamper.
[4] WHITLOW—An inflammation of the finger which generally comes from an infected cuticle.

[5] CANT—Here meaning insincere or affected.
[6] HOGG—An English poet now considered of minor importance.
[7] CORNEILLE'S *Le Cid*—Corneille (kôr′nā′) was a great French dramatist of the seventeenth century. His most famous drama was *Le Cid*.

it had been read aloud to him. He recited Coleridge's *Christabel* to Byron having heard it on a single occasion. Many of Wordsworth's poems he knew by heart after one hearing. A number of the poetic pieces that head the chapters in his novels were remembered from early youth. His is perhaps the only example in history of a phenomenal memory joined to a fertile imagination.

The foxy look that sometimes appeared on his face had its counterpart in his spiritual make-up: he never outgrew the recalcitrance and secrecy of his boyhood, which remained with him along with his chivalric dreams. Just as, when a youth, he was unreasonably stubborn over the destination of his walks and rides, so in manhood he was always anxious to escape an imposed or appointed task. If he were told that he had to do something, or if he knew that it ought to be done, he instantly wished to do something else. For preference he would work at a dozen things together, his idea of recreation being an increase of occupations, but the desire to leave a prescribed task was often irresistible. His obstinacy was also aroused by hostility. He strove against this all his life, but never quite succeeded in maintaining his normal equanimity when treated with coldness or rudeness.

The chivalric dreams of his youth, nourished by the stories of the Border barons which he had heard in his childhood, stayed with him to the end, and resulted in the exceptional deference he paid to rank. His attitude to the aristocracy of the age was roughly the same as the modern attitude to the bureaucracy. In his day the ruling class existed more or less by descent, whereas now it is largely recruited by ascent; and the main difference between the two viewpoints is that he had a romantic respect for tradition while the modern world has a realistic respect for tyranny. There was nothing in him of the snob; that is, one who apes gentility and pretends to a nodding acquaintance with half the peerage. He paid far more respect to a poor Scottish chieftain than to a modern English lord. He loved, not the title, but its historic associations. He was proud of his family, and thought nothing of his fame as a writer compared with his place as the cadet of Harden [8] and clansman of Buccleuch.[9] He and his family always kept Christmas with the immediate head of his race, Scott of Harden, in acknowledgment of his vassalage. This was all part of the romantic feeling which inspired his poems and novels. But he could have given lessons in democracy to a modern socialist. He never felt that, as a man, he was essentially superior to any living creature, or that he was essentially inferior to anyone. He treated his own servants like his blood relations and talked to them as equals; and though he shared Dr. Johnson's belief in the distinctions of society, and gave formal deference in speech and writing to those who were above him in rank, he held strong views on such as were unworthy of their order. In short he was willing to honour those who stood above him in the social world, just as he honoured those who, in his opinion, stood above him in the literary world. It was part of his romance and of his humility. But he knew that the sterling qualities in man were not to be found in one class, nor only among those known to fame.

His novels best illustrate his true

[8] HARDEN—The name of the clan and the locality from which some of Scott's ancestors sprang.

[9] BUCCLEUCH—The name of another clan from which the Scotts descended.

feelings about people; for the paradox of Scott as a writer is that, though in outlook a romancist, his primary achievement was the realistic portrayal of common people without an ounce of romance in them, not the romantic creation of knightly figures. 'I am a bad hand at depicting a hero, properly so called,' he told Morritt, 'and have an unfortunate propensity for the dubious characters of borderers, buccaneers, highland robbers, and all others of a Robin Hood description.' But he was a still better hand at depicting a beggar, a baillie,[10] a cowman, a servant; and this dual aspect of the romantic-realistic author was manifested in the man by his friendship on the one hand with the Duke of Buccleuch, on the other with Tom Purdie,[11] by his lairdship of Abbotsford and his clerkship in Edinburgh.[12]

[10] BAILLIE—An alderman.

[11] TOM PURDIE—Tom Purdie was the foreman of Scott's estate and his life-long, intimate friend.

[12] CLERKSHIP IN EDINBURGH—Scott spent several months every year serving as a clerk in the Edinburgh courts.

◇◇◇◇◇◇◇◇◇◇◇◇◇◇◇◇◇◇◇◇◇◇◇◇◇◇◇◇◇◇◇◇

FOR DISCUSSION

1. Analyze very closely the physical description of Scott in paragraph one. Select what you consider to be the *key* adjectives in the description of Scott's a) body b) head c) eyes, hair, nose, and cheeks. What three adjectives would you choose to paint a general impression of Scott?

2. What were Scott's reading and eating habits?

3. What examples does the author give to show that Scott's character trait was "benevolence"? Would you agree with Scott's remedy for mental depression?

4. In what concrete ways did Scott manifest humility? What part did imagination play in his life? Discuss. Does this give a key to his success as a writer of romantic fiction? Discuss.

5. Enumerate some of the faults or eccentricities in his character. What was his attitude toward the higher and lower classes of society? Give examples to prove your answer.

6. Most of Scott's novels have an appeal for high school students. Enumerate the novels of Scott which you have read. Make a list of four of Scott's novels which you would recommend to high school students.

WORDS

What is the difference between a *recalcitrant* and an obedient student? Would a debater who resorted to *acrimony* in his rebuttal be likely to win the debate? Explain. Could a *voracious* eater be a *fastidious* person? Why or why not?

TWENTIETH CENTURY POETRY

The first years of the twentieth century inaugurated no revolution in poetry. The big names of the late nineteenth century continued to be the big names of the early twentieth. Poets such as Thomas Hardy, A. E. Housman, Rudyard Kipling, and W. B. Yeats dominated the poetic scene.

The first two new poets arrived in 1902: Walter de la Mare, the poet of childhood and magic dreamland; and John Masefield, who poured new life into English narrative poetry with his realistic themes of the sea and the common man. W. W. Gibson discarded his earlier tendency to follow the style of Tennyson and began to write simply and realistically of miners, engineers, and shepherds.

The Catholic poets, Belloc, G. K. Chesterton, and Alfred Noyes belong to this earlier generation. Chesterton will always be remembered for his stirring narrative, *The Ballad of the White Horse*, and his *Lepanto*. Belloc rivalled Kipling in praise of his native Sussex; his sonnets and epigrams will be long remembered.

FIRST WORLD WAR YEARS

The First World War brought forth the muse of many young soldiers. Outstanding among these young poets were Wilfred Owen, Siegfried Sassoon, and Rupert Brooke. Like most of the soldiers in the First War, Sassoon entered the conflict with youthful idealism, but that idealism soon turned to horror and indignation. Both Owen and Brooke were killed in the bloody conflict. A Catholic and a true poet who survived front-line action in the war was Maurice Baring, intimate friend of Belloc and Chesterton.

The generation of post-war poets revolted against what they called the emotionalism and anti-intellectualism of Romantic and Victorian poetry. However, their revolt was more than poetic. It was a revolt against the man-centered view of life which had supplanted the God-centered view of the Middle Ages. The leaders of the revolt, following the philosophical and historical findings of Catholic and non-Catholic scholars, maintained that Western Europe had taken a wrong turn at the time of the Renaissance, which made Man, not God, the center of all things. Europe had finally and fatally gone astray at the time of the French Revolution. Under the influence of Rousseau, who denied Original Sin and wanted man to go back to the pure state of nature, the culture of Europe had broken its final link with the ancient Faith.

These young poets of revolt were not only against the spirit of Romantic poetry, but against its form and its diction. The two great exponents of the new school were T. S. Eliot and Miss Edith Sitwell. Miss Sitwell did not discard traditional meter and rhyme, but experimented in the mental effects of assonance and alliteration. Much of her early poetry was obscured imagery—but she did teach us to see things we never saw before, and she helped to freshen the diction of the English language. Her later poems have a definite Christian tone and flavor.

In 1922 T. S. Eliot's *Waste Land* was heralded as a landmark in English poetry as important as Wordsworth's *Lyrical Ballads*. Its main attraction lay in the manner in which it mirrored the disillusionment of his age and its bold innovation in versification and style. It is the voice of one crying in the wilderness of a Godless world. Eliot took the symbol of the Waste Land from the Grail legend. Despite its elaborately obscure and conventionally simple style, the lesson of the *Waste Land* is a powerful one: our culture will never bloom again until the Holy Vessel of the Grail is found. Eliot's forthcoming conversion to Anglo-Catholicism is implied in this poem. In 1928 he declared himself a classicist in literature and an Anglo-Catholic in religion. His other well known poems include: *The Love Song of J. Alfred Prufrock, Ash Wednesday, The Rock, Four Quartets,* and his dramatic poetry, *Murder in a Cathedral, The Cocktail Party* and *The Confidential Clerk*.

SEARCH FOR THE

HOLY GRAIL

The twentieth century witnessed the birth of a poetic movement in Ireland. Its major poets, W. B. Yeats, G. W. Russell (A.E.), and John M. Synge, did not go to the traditional Catholic faith of Ireland for their themes, but to the pagan mythology of the ancient Gaels. As a result, their poetry lacks strength and virility and constitutes a sort of beautiful escapism into the twilight world of pagan legend. The Irish Catholic tradition has been kept alive in the poetry of Katherine Tynan, James Stephens, and Padraic Colum.

THE NEW GENERATION

A new generation of poets began to arrive in 1930 in the persons of W. H. Auden, Stephen Spender, and Cecil Lewis. In their earlier poetry they copied Eliot's and Gerard Manley Hopkins' techniques, but not their doctrines. All three of these poets had Leftist leanings at one time. But Auden, now an American citizen, discarded his radicalism many years ago and today he is championing the cause of the Christian tradition.

Dylan Thomas, the great Welsh poet, was first caught up in the poetic imagery of the stream of consciousness and surrealistic schools. But in his later poems he became much more distinct and understandable. He gave concrete evidence in such a poem as "Vision and Prayer" of his growing interest in Christian themes.

Roy Campbell, the most notable British Catholic poet living today, is a traditionalist in form and in content. The Spanish Civil War marked a crisis in his life. He fought valiantly on the side of Franco against the Loyalists when all the other young British poets were espousing the cause of the Republicans and the Communists. So convinced was Campbell that Franco and Spain had saved Europe from Communism that he became a citizen of Spain. He is at present engaged in writing a history of the Spanish Civil War. No British poet has ever had a more thrilling and varied career. The first part of his autobiography appeared in 1953 under the title *Light on a Dark Horse*. There is sublimity and "a lyre of savage thunder" in his poetry, published under the titles *The Flaming Terrapin, The Georgiad,* and *Mithraic Emblems*.

ROY CAMPBELL'S

EXCITING CAREER

Eileen Duggan, New Zealand's poet Laureate, is the twentieth-century replica of the great woman poet, Alice Meynell. Her *Poems* of 1937 won for her a place in the King of England's Honours List, and the Order of the British Empire was conferred upon her in 1940. Miss Duggan wrote *New Zealand Poems* in 1940 to celebrate the centenary of New Zealand.

◇◇◇◇◇

The Man He Killed

THOMAS HARDY

How can mankind EN MASSE *commit brutal, bloody acts which as an individual one would consider unthinkable? This is a question which has been asked since the beginning of time.*

"Had he and I but met
    By some old ancient inn,
We should have sat us down to wet
    Right many a nipperkin!

"But ranged as infantry,   5
    And staring face to face,
I shot at him as he at me,
    And killed him in his place.

"I shot him dead because—
    Because he was my foe,   10

Just so: my foe of course he was;
    That's clear enough; although

"He thought he'd 'list, perhaps,
    Off-hand like—just as I—
Was out of work—had sold his traps—
    No other reason why.   16

"Yes; quaint and curious war is!
    You shoot a fellow down
You'd treat, if met where any bar is,
    Or help to half-a-crown."   20

4. NIPPERKIN—A small drink.
13. 'LIST—Enlist.
15. TRAPS—Personal belongings.
20. OR HELP TO HALF-A-CROWN—Give, in charity, half a crown—a coin worth about fifty cents.

◇◇

FOR APPRECIATION

1. If the two men of the poem had met during times of peace, what would have happened?

2. Can you explain the pause at the end of line 9? Is the narrator sure of the reason he offers in the next three lines?

3. What autobiographical notes are offered in the fourth stanza?

4. What condemnation of war by the ordinary people of the world is offered in this poem?

Reveille

A. E. HOUSMAN

In army terms, "reveille" is the bugle call to awaken soldiers at the appointed morning hour. In Housman's poem, "Reveille" is the call to awaken sleepers to the beauties of nature and to the joy of living.

Wake: the silver dusk returning
  Up the beach of darkness brims,
And the ship of sunrise burning
  Strands upon the eastern rims.

Wake: the vaulted shadow shatters,   5
  Trampled to the floor it spanned,
And the tent of night in tatters
  Straws the sky-pavilioned land.

Up, lad, up, 'tis late for lying;
  Hear the drums of morning play;   10
Hark, the empty highways crying
  "Who'll beyond the hills away?"

Towns and countries woo together,
  Forelands beacon, belfries call;
Never lad that trod on leather   15
  Lived to feast his heart with all.

Up, lad: thews that lie and cumber
  Sunlit pallets never thrive;
Morns abed and daylight slumber
  Were not meant for man alive.   20

Clay lies still, but blood's a rover;
  Breath's a ware that will not keep.
Up, lad: when the journey's over
  There'll be time enough to sleep.

"Reveille" from *A Shropshire Lad* by A. E. Housman, reprinted by permission of Henry Holt and Company, Inc., also by permission of The Society of Authors, London, as the Literary Representative of the Trustees of the Estate of the late A. E. Housman, and Messrs. Jonathan Cape Ltd., publishers of A. E. Housman's *Collected Poems*.

1. SILVER DUSK—Moonlight.
4. STRANDS—A verb meaning "drifts ashore." The "ship of sunrise" has drifted to the eastern shore of the world.
8. STRAWS—Strews.
17. THEWS—Muscles.
18. PALLETS—Beds.

FOR APPRECIATION

1. There is exquisite imagery in this poem. Paint a word picture of the dawn as the poet sees it. What are some of the morning sounds?

2. The poet expresses regret at the passing of youth. Which lines express that feeling?

3. How does the rhythm of the poem suggest a bugle call? Explain the following figures: *ship of sunrise; tent of night . . . sky-pavilioned land; thews that lie and cumber sunlit pallets; blood's a rover.*

4. Is there a practical application here for the city boy or girl who makes it a custom to sleep late into the morning?

To an Athlete Dying Young

A. E. HOUSMAN

A very pathetic figure is the aged and forgotten athlete as he pages through yellowed and time-worn scrapbooks which speak of his former fame. In this poem, Housman intimates that fame is less fleeting to those who die at the height of their athletic prowess.

The time you won your town the race
We chaired you through the market-
    place;
Man and boy stood cheering by,
And home we brought you shoulder-
    high.

Today, the road all runners come,   5
Shoulder-high we bring you home,
And set you at your threshold down,
Townsman of a stiller town.

Smart lad, to slip betimes away
From fields where glory does not stay,
And early though the laurel grows   11
It withers quicker than the rose.

Eyes the shady night has shut
Cannot see the record cut,
And silence sounds no worse than cheers
After earth has stopped the ears;   16

Now you will not swell the rout
Of lads that wore their honors out,
Runners whom renown outran
And the name died before the man.   20

So set, before its echoes fade,
The fleet foot on the sill of shade,
And hold to the low lintel up
The still-defended challenge-cup.

And round that early-laureled head   25
Will flock to gaze the strengthless dead,
And find unwithered on its curls
The garland briefer than a girl's.

FOR APPRECIATION
    1. Select the details by which the poet contrasts the victory procession with the funeral procession. Explain the meaning of: *chaired you; road all runners run; stiller town.*
    2. Why is the athlete called "smart lad"? What connotation has "the laurel"? Explain the meaning of lines 19–20. Can you mention any famous athletes to whom these lines might apply? To set you thinking, we will name Jim Thorpe.
    3. Can you mention some modern athletes who died young and to whom the poem as a whole can be applied? Again to set you thinking, we mention the immortal Gipp of Notre Dame.
    4. Does the poem appeal to you? Why or why not?

The Lake Isle of Innisfree

WILLIAM BUTLER YEATS

Homesickness, and the sound of water, inspired this poem. Mr. Yeats has told how in his teens he formed the ambition of going to live in solitude on Innisfree, a small island in Lough Gill. Years later, ". . . when walking through Fleet Street, very homesick, I heard a little tinkle of water and saw a fountain in a shop window which balanced a little ball upon its jet, and began to remember lake water. From the sudden remembrance came my poem 'Innisfree.' "

I will arise and go now, and go to Innisfree,
And a small cabin build there, of clay and wattles made;
Nine bean rows will I have there, a hive for the honey bee,
And live alone in the bee-loud glade.

And I shall have some peace there, for peace comes dropping slow,   5
Dropping from the veils of the morning to where the cricket sings;
There midnight's all a-glimmer, and noon a purple glow,
And evening full of the linnet's wings.

I will arise and go now, for always night and day
I hear lake water lapping with low sounds by the shore;   10
While I stand on the roadway, or on the pavements gray,
I hear it in the deep heart's core.

2. WATTLES—Twigs; flexible withes.

◇◇◇

FOR APPRECIATION

1. At the beginning of the poem, all in an instant the vision of a secluded Robinson Crusoe life on Innisfree flashes into the speaker's mind. What details suggest the rural simplicity of the home he dreams of? What is a *glade*, and why does this word fit the atmosphere of the poem better than "woods" or "among the trees"?

2. The second stanza is more vague, giving a general impression of quiet contentment. How does it suggest that the speaker would like to spend the entire twenty-four hours of each day drinking in the beauty of the scene around him?

3. The last stanza returns to actuality —to the wistful poet instead of his dream. How can we tell that he is in the city? How can we guess that he has to stay there

instead of going to Innisfree? What line do you think best expresses his longing?

4. Try to think of a childhood scene or experience that sometimes flashes vividly into your memory. What single thing—a sound or perhaps a scent—sets off the recollection? List the other details that instantly come to mind when this "flashback" occurs.

OF FORM AND STYLE

1. Thinking of the whole poem, see if you can explain how the beginning, "I will arise and go now," adds to its effectiveness even though the poet does not expect us to believe that he will actually "go."

2. What examples of *alliteration* can you find in the line about lake water in stanza 3? Notice the *a* sounds in this line, followed by *o* sounds. This repetition of vowel sounds in a sort of semi-rhyme is called *assonance*. What words in the following lines echo the same two vowels?

◇◇◇◇◇

When You Are Old

WILLIAM BUTLER YEATS

Here is a message addressed by a young poet to the woman he loves. It is meant to be read many years later, perhaps even after the poet is dead. It will remind the woman of her former youth and loveliness, and of the man who understood and loved her best.

When you are old and gray and full of sleep,
And nodding by the fire, take down this book,
And slowly read, and dream of the soft look
Your eyes had once, and of their shadows deep;

How many loved your moments of glad grace,   5
And loved your beauty with love false or true,
But one man loved the pilgrim soul in you,
And loved the sorrows of your changing face;

And bending down beside the glowing bars,
Murmur, a little sadly, how Love fled   10
And paced upon the mountains overhead
And hid his face amid a crowd of stars.

FOR APPRECIATION

1. The poet shows that he has valued the woman's grace and beauty, just as many others have. Explain how his love was deeper and more valuable than theirs.

2. In the last stanza, what are the "glowing bars"? How does the vivid final phrase, "a crowd of stars," show us something about the sky that we might not notice for ourselves?

3. Reread the last stanza and see if you can decide what is meant by saying that love "fled." Notice particularly *where* the poet says love has gone. The stanza could mean that intense personal love has been transformed into something else, such as religious idealism, love of art, or love of humanity. In that case, what would be the reason for mentioning mountains and stars? How does this stanza suggest that the feeling of two young lovers toward each other is also a very fine and precious thing?

4. When the woman mentioned in the poem looks at "this book," she will literally receive a message written long before. All through history, men have been fascinated by the fact that something written down a long time ago is still read and understood—as if the dead author still had the power to talk to us. Give one example of a "message from the past" which has come down to us in the Bible. Then give examples of (*a*) a saying from Shakespeare which is often repeated; (*b*) an old proverbial expression; (*c*) a statement by some former American leader which we still use as a slogan in our national life. Members of the class who are Latin students may be able to think of an idea or phrase which was known to the ancient Romans and which we still repeat, in translation.

◇◇◇◇◇

The Second Coming

WILLIAM BUTLER YEATS

Frankly, this is a difficult poem. But it well illustrates the second phase in the development of Yeats' poetry. In his later years, Yeats turned away from romantic and fanciful themes and the use of colorful symbols and sensuous language. Instead, he wrote in a language almost bare of ornament; used sharp and harsh words; and an almost conversational tone. He did not discard the use of symbols, but gave them a deeper intellectual significance.

The poem is written in blank verse and is divided into two sections: lines 1–8 and lines 9–22.

In the first section we are told that the world is in disorder; it is out of joint and a change is overdue. This thought is symbolized poetically by the image of the falcon going so far away from the falconer that it has lost contact with its master. The world has lost its center of gravity, all things which should be bound together by its center have fallen apart, and anarchy is turned loose. It is plainly evident that the poet is symbolizing the rejection of God, the absolute moral order, and traditional Christianity —the rejection of which has resulted in the present world chaos. The bloody tide of war, of strife, and of disillusionment has drowned out the innocence which comes from faith. Even the best men lack conviction of the truth, and the worst are passionately intent on destroying the world.

In the second section, the poet utters the cry that surely Christ and His Revelation will be born anew. But SPIRITUS MUNDI, the Spirit of the World, haunts the poet's sight and makes him fearful. The poet sees in the desert wasteland (the world without God) the head of a man (his rational nature) and the body of a lion (his lower nature turned ferocious) as if ready to move. Perhaps this beast who has rejected his Christian inheritance is ready for a change for the better. But desert birds or false prophets indignantly reel about him. Darkness comes again (is it the darkness of Communism?) and perhaps it is too late. But then the poet remembers. Was not mankind which was asleep to the light of Christianity for twenty centuries before the First Coming, aroused to the paradoxical nightmare of the Christian Revelation by the rocking cradle of the Infant Savior? In the last lines the poet poses the tremendous question: Is it possible that modern mankind, laden with the Spirit of the World, is slowly creeping back to Christ?

Turning and turning in the widening
  gyre
The falcon cannot hear the falconer;
Things fall apart; the centre cannot
  hold;
Mere anarchy is loosed upon the
  world,
The blood-dimmed tide is loosed, and
  everywhere   5
The ceremony of innocence is drowned;
The best lack all conviction, while the
  worst
Are full of passionate intensity.

Surely some revelation is at hand;
Surely the Second Coming is at hand.
The Second Coming! Hardly are those
  words out   11
When a vast image out of *Spiritus*
  Mundi
Troubles my sight: somewhere in sands
  of the desert
A shape with lion body and the head of
  a man,
A gaze blank and pitiless as the sun,
Is moving its slow thighs, while all
  about it   16

1. GYRE (jīr)—A circle described by a moving body.

Reel shadows of the indignant desert
   birds.
The darkness drops again; but now I
   know
That twenty centuries of stony sleep

Were vexed to nightmare by a rocking
   cradle,   20
And what rough beast, its hour come
   round at last,
Slouches towards Bethlehem to be born?

FOR APPRECIATION

Discuss in detail the economy of statement; the stark, unadorned, yet thought-packed symbols which the poet uses. Do these symbols appeal primarily to the intellect, or to the senses? Illustrate your answer by examples. Do the symbols merely suggest and imply meanings, or do they directly state the thought intended? Illustrate by examples.

2. Do you or do you not agree with the interpretation of the poem as given in the introduction? Discuss. Why could not any prose paraphrase of the poem do justice to its meaning or its striking interpretations?

3. Study carefully the meter and the rhythm of the poem. The rhythm of the iambic measure is frequently broken with a counter rhythm. Select lines where this occurs, and give reasons for this change in movement. Study, for example, lines 6, 15, 17, and 19.

A Consecration

JOHN MASEFIELD

The present poet laureate of England prefixed "A Consecration" to his collected poems. In this particular poem as well as in the majority of his other poems he fulfills his promise of speaking for "the scorned and the rejected," "the man with too weighty a burden, too weary a load." In this respect, he has something in common with the medieval poet of the common people, William Langland.

Not of the princes and prelates with periwigged charioteers
Riding triumphantly laurelled to lap the fat of the years,—
Rather the scorned—the rejected—the men hemmed in with the spears;

The men of the tattered battalion which fights till it dies,
Dazed with the dust of the battle, the din and the cries.   5
The men with the broken heads and the blood running into their eyes.

A CONSECRATION

Not the be-medaled Commander, beloved of the throne,
Riding cock-horse to parade when the bugles are blown,
But the lads who carried the koppie and cannot be known.

Not the ruler for me, but the ranker, the tramp of the road,   10
The slave with the sack on his shoulders pricked on with the goad,
The man with too weighty a burden, too weary a load.

The sailor, the stoker of steamers, the man with the clout,
The chantyman bent at the halliards putting a tune to the shout,
The drowsy man at the wheel and the tired look-out.   15

Others may sing of the wine and the wealth and the mirth,
The portly presence of potentates goodly in girth;—
Mine be the dirt and the dross, the dust and scum of the earth!

Theirs be the music, the colour, the glory, the gold;
Mine be a handful of ashes, a mouthful of mold.   20
Of the maimed, of the halt and the blind in the rain and the cold—
Of these shall my songs be fashioned, my tales be told.

9. KOPPIE—A word used in South Africa to mean kop, or small hill. The reference is to the
Boer War.
13. CLOUT—Cloth or rag.
14. CHANTYMAN—The sailor who leads in the singing as the men work at the halliards (sails).

FOR APPRECIATION

1. Writers commonly speak of a "dedication" of their works to someone they wish to honor. What added meaning is there in the word "consecration" as Masefield used it in the title of his poem?

2. The poem is a series of comparisons between the powerful and the weak, the successful and the scorned, the rich and the poor. What is the comparison of the first stanza? What picture do you see? What is the meaning of the "fat of the years"?

3. In your own words describe the picture in the second stanza; in the third stanza.

4. In the fourth stanza, how does the "ranker" offer contrast to the "ruler"? What is the meaning of "pricked on with the goad"?

5. What would Masefield think of the men mentioned in the fifth stanza? Was there anything in Masefield's own life which would lead him to sing of the toiling and suffering types of humanity? Or anything to lead him to enumerate the various seamen's jobs?

6. What is the figure of speech used in line 17? To whom does the "Theirs" of the last stanza refer? Explain the meaning of the figure of speech in line 20.

7. Which stanza presents to you the most vivid picture? Which lines best express the poet's sympathy for the workers of the world?

Spanish Waters

JOHN MASEFIELD

Here Masefield carries us back to the seventeenth-century buccaneering days when English pirates robbed treasure ships in the Caribbean Sea. Los Muertos (lōs mwĕr′tōs) is an island off Puerto Rico; the speaker remembers the time he and his shipmates went ashore there and buried their gold. As we follow his thoughts, we too can imagine what the old pirate days were like.

Spanish waters, Spanish waters, you are ringing in my ears,
Like a slow sweet piece of music from the gray forgotten years;
Telling tales, and beating tunes, and bringing weary thoughts to me
Of the sandy beach at Muertos, where I would that I could be.

There's a surf breaks on Los Muertos, and it never stops to roar, 5
And it's there we came to anchor, and it's there we went ashore,
Where the blue lagoon is silent amid snags of rotting trees,
Dropping like the clothes of corpses cast up by the seas.

We anchored at Los Muertos when the dipping sun was red,
We left her half-a-mile to sea, to west of Nigger Head; 10
And before the mist was on the Cay, before the day was done,
We were all ashore on Muertos with the gold that we had won.

We bore it through the marshes in a half-score battered chests,
Sinking, in the sucking quagmires, to the sunburn on our breasts,
Heaving over tree trunks, gasping, damning at the flies and heat, 15
Longing for a long drink, out of silver, in the ship's cool lazareet.

The moon came white and ghostly as we laid the treasure down,
There was gear there'd make a beggarman as rich as Lima Town,
Copper charms and silver trinkets from the chests of Spanish crews,
Gold doubloons and double moidores, louis d'ors and portagues, 20

10. NIGGER HEAD—Probably the sailors' name for a promontory which was a nearby landmark.
11. THE CAY—The "island"—that is, Los Muertos. From this word, pronounced "kā" or "kē," comes our name for the "keys" off the Florida coast.
16. LAZAREET—Lazaretto, a provision room between decks of a ship.
20. MOIDORES—Gold coins of Portugal.

Clumsy yellow-metal earrings from the Indians of Brazil,
Uncut emeralds out of Rio, bezoar stones from Guayaquil;
Silver, in the crude and fashioned, pots of old Arica bronze,
Jewels from the bones of Incas desecrated by the Dons.

We smoothed the place with mattocks, and we took and blazed the tree,   25
Which marks yon where the gear is hid that none will ever see,
And we laid aboard the ship again, and south away we steers,
Through the loud surf of Los Muertos which is beating in my ears.

I'm the last alive that knows it. All the rest have gone their ways—
Killed, or died, or come to anchor in the old Mulatas Cays,   30
And I go singing, fiddling, old and starved and in despair,
And I know where all that gold is hid, if I were only there.

22. BEZOAR . . . GUAYAQUIL (gwä′yä·kēl)—Stones valued as a supposed remedy for poison-
ing, found in Guayaquil, a seaport of Ecuador, on the western coast of South America.
23. ARICA (ä·rē′kä)—A region in Chile.
30. MULATAS (mū·lä′täs) CAYS—Probably the Mulatas Archipelago off the eastern coast of
Panama.

It's not the way to end it all. I'm old, and nearly blind,
And an old man's past's a strange thing, for it never leaves his mind.
And I see in dreams, awhiles, the beach, the sun's disk dipping red,   35
And the tall ship, under topsails, swaying in past Nigger Head.

I'd be glad to step ashore there. Glad to take a pick and go
To the lone blazed coco-palm tree in the place no others know,
And lift the gold and silver that has moldered there for years
By the loud surf of Los Muertos which is beating in my ears.   40

FOR APPRECIATION

1. This is a poem which expresses nostalgia—that is, recollection and longing—as do "The West Wind," Yeats's "Innisfree," and Kipling's "Mandalay." In what ways does it resemble "Mandalay" more closely than it does the others? How many of its ten stanzas build up the atmosphere of foreignness by mentioning *names of specific places*? Point out other words besides place names that contribute to such an atmosphere. Do you like descriptive poetry of this type?

2. In stanza 4 the speaker recalls how he helped carry the treasure chests inland. Point out two phrases in the stanza which add especially vivid details to the picture. What line later in the poem shows that

the treasure was buried? What eventually became of it?

3. Stanzas 5 and 6 give an impression of great riches heaped up helter-skelter. The doubloons are from Spain and the moidores are from Portugal. From what lands do you suppose the "louis d'ors" came? the "portagues"? What city is meant by "Rio," and where is it? In what country did the fabulously rich Inca civilization once flourish? Of what country were the "Dons" who conquered it? What reference to that country is made earlier?

4. Why is "Spanish Waters" a more appropriate title than "Spanish Treasure" would be? Before answering, look over the poem again to notice what the old man remembers besides all the lost wealth.

Silver

WALTER DE LA MARE

There is a magical quality in the poetry of Walter de la Mare. The following poem makes us realize what a magical change can come over ordinary things at night—and in doing so reminds us that the commonplace is often marvelous if we have eyes to see.

Slowly, silently, now the moon
Walks the night in her silver shoon;
This way, and that, she peers, and sees
Silver fruit upon silver trees;
One by one the casements catch   5
Her beams beneath the silvery thatch;
Couched in his kennel, like a log,

With paws of silver sleeps the dog;
From their shadowy cote the white breasts peep
Of doves in a silver-feathered sleep;   10
A harvest mouse goes scampering by,
With silver claws and a silver eye;
And moveless fish in the water gleam,
By silver reeds in a silver stream.

FOR APPRECIATION

1. Describe the picture suggested by the first six lines of the poem. If you were an artist, what sort of illustration would you make for those six lines? Describe now a companion illustration for the rest of the poem. Perhaps you would like to paint a real picture.

2. Do you think the poet may have written the poem after being outside in a moonlight night? Or do you think he made it up in his imagination? Give the reasons for your answer.

3. What kind of place or scene is suggested by the details in the picture? What is there in the poem that suggests movement as well as moonlight? Discuss.

4. What is the meter of the poem? Explain how the use of assonance and alliteration helps emphasize mood and meaning.

In Memory of G. K. Chesterton

WALTER DE LA MARE

In many ways De la Mare is poetically akin to Chesterton, to whom he pays tribute in this thought-crammed quatrain. Like Chesterton, he revels in the innocency of childhood, in the unspeakable beauty of the world. Again, like Chesterton, there is always a serious undertone in the playfulness of his fancy, and an intense reality comes from his realization that this is "a world where sin and beauty whisper Home."

Knight of the Holy Ghost, he goes his way,
Wisdom his motley, Truth his loving jest;
The mills of Satan keep his lance in play,
Pity and innocence his heart at rest.

"In Memory of G. K. Chesterton" by Walter de la Mare, reprinted by permission of Faber and Faber Limited, London, and the author.

FOR APPRECIATION

From your knowledge of Chesterton's life and work, explain each line of the poem. Show that it is a perfect summing up of what G. K. was. Explain "a world where sin and beauty whisper Home."

✧✧✧✧✧

The Soldier

RUPERT BROOKE

This is one of the more famous poems inspired by World War I. Rupert Brooke, who lost his life shortly after he wrote these lines, has expressed the patriotic sentiment of millions of young Britons and Americans who fought in foreign fields.

If I should die, think only this of me;
That there's some corner of a foreign field
That is forever England. There shall be
In that rich earth a richer dust concealed;
A dust whom England bore, shaped, made aware, 5
Gave, once, her flowers to love, her ways to roam,
A body of England's, breathing English air,
Washed by the rivers, blest by suns of home.

And think, this heart, all evil shed away,
A pulse in the eternal mind, no less 10
Gives somewhere back the thoughts by England given;
Her sights and sounds; dreams happy as her day
And laughter, learnt of friends; and gentleness,
In hearts at peace, under an English heaven.

✧✧✧

FOR APPRECIATION

1. Explain the meaning of the first three lines. What is the "richer dust" of line 4? Has the soldier returned home?

2. What meaning does Brooke give to immortality in lines 9–14? Is this Catholic or Christian? Explain.

3. What are the things about England he has appreciated most? Might one of today's servicemen think these same thoughts, substituting America and American for England and English? Discuss.

4. Is there an echo of Browning's "Home Thoughts from Abroad" in the poem? Discuss.

5. Mention some modern war poets who wrote about World War II.

Sight

W. W. GIBSON

For some years Wilfrid Gibson lived in the East End, the slum district of London. His poems arouse sympathy for the man with the lunch pail, for the underprivileged and the unfortunate. He has been called "the twentieth-century Thomas Hood." In "Sight," he demonstrates how even a vegetable market, under the magic of a poet's inspiration, takes on a new and surprising significance. He uncovers the fires of Krakatao in a tomato and a Tyrean sunset in an orange. But there is further a stab of sympathy for the one who cannot see such beauty.

By the lamplit stall I loitered, feasting my eyes
On colors ripe and rich for the heart's desire—
Tomatoes, redder than Krakatao's fire,
Oranges like old sunsets over Tyre,
And apples golden-green as the glades of Paradise.   5

And as I lingered, lost in divine delight,
My heart thanked God for the goodly gift of sight
And all youth's lively senses keen and quick . . .
When suddenly, behind me in the night,
I heard the tapping of a blind man's stick.

3. KRAKATAO—Island volcano in Dutch East Indies; its eruption in 1883 has been the most tremendous in recent centuries.
4. TYRE—Famous maritime city of antiquity, in Phoenicia.

"Sight" from Collected Poems by Wilfrid Wilson Gibson, used with his permission and that of The Macmillan Company of Canada Limited, Toronto.

◇◇

FOR APPRECIATION

1. In the first stanza, the poet uses the colors of a tomato, orange, and apple as a basis for suggesting three very dramatic and historic pictures. Explain.

2. How does the last line of the poem reinforce the effect of the whole poem? Discuss.

3. Read Gibson's sonnet "Color."

Aftermath

SIEGFRIED SASSOON

During the actual conflict of World War I and a few years after it, many a young English poet wrote idealistically of the heroic spirit of those who fought and those who fell. Among these were Rupert Brooke and Edmund Blunden. But as the vision of "a world safe for democracy" faded and the terrible disillusionment of the futility of that war was seen in its stark reality, other poets began to portray the physical horrors, the brutality, the mockery, and the black despair of world carnage. These qualities are especially dominant in the poetry of Wilfrid Owen and Siegfried Sassoon. The reaction of contemporary poets to World War II and Korea is yet to be seen as a complete picture.

Have you forgotten yet? . . .
For the world's events have rumbled on since those gagged days,
Like traffic checked a while at the crossing of city ways:
And the haunted gap in your mind has filled with thoughts that flow
Like the clouds in the lit heavens of life; and you're a man reprieved to go,   5
Taking your peaceful share of Time, with joy to spare.
But the past is just the same,—and War's a bloody game. . . .
Have you forgotten yet? . . .
Look down, and swear by the slain of the War that you'll never forget.

Do you remember the dark months you held the sector at Mametz,—   10
The nights you watched and wired and dug and piled sand-bags on parapets?
Do you remember the rats; and the stench
Of corpses rotting in front of the front-line trench,—
And dawn coming, dirty-white, and chill with a hopeless rain?
Do you ever stop and ask, "Is it all going to happen again?"   15

10. MAMETZ—A village along the Somme River in France where a decisive battle in World War I occurred in 1916.

"Aftermath" by Siegfried Sassoon, reprinted by permission of the author.

Do you remember that hour of din before the attack,—
And the anger, the blind compassion that seized and shook you then
As you peered at the doomed and haggard faces of your men?
Do you remember the stretcher-cases lurching back
With dying eyes and lolling heads, those ashen-gray   20
Masks of the lads who once were keen and gay?

Have you forgotten yet? . . .
Look up, and swear by the green of the Spring that you'll never forget.

FOR APPRECIATION

1. What simile does Sassoon employ to illustrate the speedy passage of events since the war days? Discuss the meaning of *game* in line 7.

2. Why would Sassoon be not likely to forget? Discuss.

3. Why does the poet fill his picture of war experiences with such sharply distressing details? What does he fear will happen? Were his fears realized? Explain. Do you think World War II was any more successful than World War I? Discuss. Is it necessary to be mindful of war in time of peace?

4. What does the word "Aftermath" mean? Explain why it is an appropriate title for the poem.

5. Explain: *haunted gap in your mind; man reprieved to go . . . with joy to spare.*

◇◇◇◇

SIEGFRIED SASSOON

Sassoon bitterly protested against the false glorification of war. He was a soldier and knew the anguish and misery which are far removed from the romantic gestures of flying flags and beating drums. "Dreamers" is a vivid picture of what the soldier feels.

Soldiers are citizens of death's gray land,
Drawing no dividend from time's tomorrows.
In the great hour of destiny they stand,
Each with his feuds, and jealousies, and sorrows.
Soldiers are sworn to action; they must win   5
Some flaming, fatal climax with their lives.
Soldiers are dreamers; when the guns begin
They think of firelit homes, clean beds, and wives.

"Dreamers" by Siegfried Sassoon, reprinted by permission of the author.

I see them in foul dug-outs, gnawed by rats,
And in the ruined trenches, lashed with rain,   10
Dreaming of things they did with balls and bats,
And mocked by hopeless longing to regain
Bank-holidays, and picture shows, and spats,
And going to the office in the train.

FOR APPRECIATION

1. What does the first line of the poem say about the lot of a soldier? In what sense is it true? What is the meaning of the second line? What is the aim or purpose of the soldier as Sassoon sees it?

2. When do soldiers become dreamers? Why? What do they dream about? Why these particular things?

3. Mention some modern movies, stories, and dramas which give a realistic picture of war.

PROJECTS

1. Write two graphic prose sketches or vignettes which you may call "A Study in Contrast." In the first portray the dreams of home of one particular serviceman during the lull of some major military engagement. In the other paint him in the environment of a confused world a few weeks after his return to civilian life.

2. Attempt a sonnet on the subject: "Soldier's Return." Talking to a war veteran first might help you.

The Express

STEPHEN SPENDER

The ordinary sights of our mechanized civilization seem strange and exciting to Stephen Spender. Here he tries to show us the beauty of an express train—not the kind of beauty a flower or a peaceful stream has, but a wilder, more powerful, and disturbing kind of beauty.

After the first powerful plain manifesto
The black statement of pistons, without more fuss
But gliding like a queen, she leaves the station.
Without bowing and with restrained unconcern
She passes the houses which humbly crowd outside,   5
The gasworks and at last the heavy page

1. MANIFESTO—Declaration; announcement.

Of death, printed by gravestones in the cemetery.
Beyond the town there lies the open country
Where, gathering speed, she acquires mystery,
The luminous self-possession of ships on ocean.　　　　　10
It is now she begins to sing—at first quite low
Then loud, and at last with a jazzy madness—
The song of her whistle screaming at curves,
Of deafening tunnels, brakes, innumerable bolts.
And always light, aerial, underneath　　　　　15
Goes the elate meter of her wheels.
Steaming through metal landscape on her lines
She plunges new eras of wild happiness
Where speed throws up strange shapes, broad curves
And parallels clean like the steel of guns.　　　　　20
At last, further than Edinburgh or Rome,
Beyond the crest of the world she reaches night
Where only a low streamline brightness
Of phosphorus on the tossing hills is white.
Ah, like a comet through flame she moves entranced　　　　　25
Wrapped in her music no bird song, no, nor bough
Breaking with honey buds, shall ever equal.

16. ELATE—Elated; joyous.

◇◆◇

FOR APPRECIATION

1. At the beginning of the poem, the express train is slowly moving away from the depot toward the edge of town. "Powerful plain manifesto" and "black statement of pistons" suggest a vigorous outburst of some kind at the moment the train starts. What details of the train is the poet describing? Explain why a moment later the train is "gliding like a queen."

2. What realistic detail about the outskirts of a city is supplied by "the houses which *humbly* crowd outside"? Why is the cemetery mentioned *after* the gasworks?

3. What phrases suggest that the truly important characteristics of the express train begin to appear only after it has moved well into the country? What are the various sounds the poet has in mind when he says "she begins to sing"? Why does he speak of the *meter* of the wheels?

4. What are the "parallels" in line 20? What keeps them "clean like the steel of guns"? Just as the train passes out of sight over the horizon the poet compares it to a flaming comet. The "flame" may be a figurative expression for the noise or "music" that surrounds the speeding train. What literal flame may also be seen around a steam locomotive at night?

5. What general feeling toward the environment we live in is implied in the last two lines? Explain how this poem might serve as a reply to Masefield's "Cargoes."

6. Decide what typical spectacle of our machine age seems most impressive or thrilling to you. If you were to write a poem in praise of it, what specific details would you include?

The Unknown Citizen

W. H. AUDEN

Many modern writers have protested that in our day each human being's life is controlled by the newspapers, by advertisements, by various organizations, and by government. Swept along in the current like a soldier in an army, he can hardly make his own choices or have any individuality. Such a thought is suggested by the very title of this poem. The epitaph at the beginning suggests two things: that the man is such a nobody that he has a number rather than a name; and that he is exactly the kind of person modern society honors.

TO JS/07/M/378
THIS MARBLE MONUMENT IS
ERECTED BY THE STATE

He was found by the Bureau of Statistics to be
One against whom there was no official complaint,
And all the reports on his conduct agree
That, in the modern sense of an old-fashioned word, he was a saint,
For in everything he did he served the Greater Community.   5
Except for the War till the day he retired
He worked in a factory and never got fired,
But satisfied his employers, Fudge Motors Inc.
Yet he wasn't a scab or odd in his views,
For his Union reports that he paid his dues,   10
(Our report on his Union shows it was sound)
And our Social Psychology workers found
That he was popular with his mates and liked a drink.
The Press are convinced that he bought a paper every day
And that his reactions to advertisements were normal in every way.   15
Policies taken out in his name prove that he was fully insured,
And his Health-card shows he was once in a hospital but left it cured.
Both Producers Research and High-Grade-Living declare
He was fully sensible to the advantages of the Installment Plan.
And had everything necessary to the Modern Man,   20

A phonograph, a radio, a car, and a frigidaire.
Our researchers into Public Opinion are content
That he held the proper opinions for the time of year;
When there was peace, he was for peace; when there was war, he went.
He was married and added five children to the population,   25
Which our Eugenist says was the right number for a parent of his generation,
And our teachers report that he never interfered with their education.
Was he free? Was he happy? The question is absurd:
Had anything been wrong, we should certainly have heard.

FOR APPRECIATION

1. This is a satirical poem about conformity. Notice that the citizen conformed to what his employers expected —and at the same time conformed to what his labor union expected. Point out two other statements that show him doing as he was told. What is satirical about ". . . held the proper opinions for the time of year"? What is satirical about the line just following this one?

2. Why do you think the poet capitalizes so many words?

3. For fun, the poet has made the epitaph rhyme. What word rhymes with "State"? Within the poem itself, find the earlier word that rhymes with "drink."

4. Read several lines aloud, noticing how the absence of regular meter creates the effect of conversation rather than the effect we usually expect in poetry. Point out three phrases resembling prose more than traditional poetic language.

5. The poem implies that JS/o7/M/378 never really thought or acted for himself, but merely followed the dictates of one group or another. What do you think about the accuracy of this idea as applied to citizens of our own country? Give an example of a person doing something just because "everybody else does." Then give an example proving that some citizens, at least, make up their minds independently of group opinion.

6. Read the concluding two lines again. What feeling do they leave in your mind about whether the citizen was or was not free and happy? Much evidence is given in the poem that he was not *free*. Explain your own opinion on whether or not such a person could be *happy*.

◇◇◇◇◇

(FROM) *Chorus No. 1 of "The Rock"*

T. S. ELIOT

"The Rock" is a pageant on the church, men's neglect of it, and the place it has held and should hold in the life of the nation. Chorus No. 1 is a lament over the present unreligious state of mankind.

The Eagle soars in the summit of Heaven,
The Hunter with his dogs pursues his circuit.
O perpetual revolution of configured stars,
O perpetual recurrence of determined seasons,
O world of spring and autumn, birth and dying!   5
The endless cycle of idea and action,
Endless invention, endless experiment,
Brings knowledge of motion, but not of stillness;
Knowledge of speech, but not of silence;
Knowledge of words, and ignorance of the Word.   10
All our knowledge brings us nearer to our ignorance,
All our ignorance brings us nearer to death,
But nearness to death no nearer to God.
Where is the Life we have lost in living!
Where is the wisdom we have lost in knowledge?   15
Where is the knowledge we have lost in information?
The cycles of Heaven in twenty centuries
Bring us farther from God and nearer to the Dust.

　I journeyed to London, to the timekept City,
Where the River flows, with foreign flotations.   20
There I was told: we have too many churches,
And too few chophouses. There I was told:
Let the vicars retire. Men do not need the Church
In the place where they work, but where they spend their Sundays.
In the City, we need no bells: 25
Let them waken the suburbs.
I journeyed to the suburbs, and there I was told:
We toil for six days, on the seventh we must motor
To Hindhead, or Maidenhead.
If the weather is foul we stay at home and read the papers.   30
In industrial districts, there I was told
Of economic laws.
In the pleasant countryside, there it seemed
That the country now is only fit for picnics.
And the Church does not seem to be wanted   35
In country or in suburbs; and in the town
Only for important weddings.

　　1–2. EAGLE . . . HUNTER WITH HIS DOGS—The constellations Aquila, Orion, and Canis Major and Canis Minor. The rotation of the earth causes these and the other stars to appear to travel a circuit around it.
　　29. HINDHEAD . . . MAIDENHEAD—A hill and a city, both near London.

◇◇◇

FOR APPRECIATION

1. The beginning of the poem introduces the idea of "perpetual recurrence" of seasons and of birth and death. Then it is suggested that history, too, is only an endless cycle that is leading to no greater wisdom and no nearer to God. What

does the poet mean by saying that we have "Knowledge of words, and ignorance of the Word"? Judging from this line, what does he mean by contrasting "stillness" and "silence" in the two preceding lines?

2. What do you think is the difference between "Life" and "living" in line 14? Reread lines 15–16, and explain the difference between wisdom and knowledge; also between knowledge and information.

3. All through the second part of the poem there runs the idea that there are not very many churches in England, and also the deeper idea that there is not enough interest in religion. By its expression of both these ideas simultaneously, the poem is satirical and witty. For instance, when the city people say they have too many churches and too few chop-houses, the deeper meaning is that they think prosperity—making a living—is more important than religion. Explain the deeper meaning of their belief expressed in lines 23–24.

4. What passage suggests that religion is becoming a mere social custom?

5. In every community there can be found earnestly religious people, and also those who are indifferent to religion. In your opinion, can Eliot's comments be applied to American life in general?

❖❖❖❖❖

Journey of the Magi

T. S. ELIOT

Long after the event, one of the Magi ponders the significance of their journey to Bethlehem. The Magi went to witness a Birth, but their rebirth in Christ spelled death to their old way of life. Upon returning to their homeland, the Magi feel as aliens among a people who know not Christ, and they would gladly die.

Eliot takes his introductory lines from a sermon of Lancelot Andrewes, a seventeenth century Anglican sermon-writer.

The description of the difficulties of the journey outwardly symbolizes the internal conflict of the Magi and suggests events to come in the life of Christ. As you read, notice the contrast between the plain, matter-of-fact account of the journey, which ends with the understatement: "it was (you may say) satisfactory"; and the spiritually transforming effect of that journey.

'A cold coming we had of it,
Just the worst time of the year
For a journey, and such a long journey:
The ways deep and the weather sharp,
The very dead of winter.'   5
And the camels galled, sore-footed, re-
    fractory,
Lying down in the melting snow,
There were times we regretted
The summer palaces on slopes, the ter-
    races,   9
And the silken girls bringing sherbet.
Then the camel men cursing and grum-
    bling
And running away, and wanting their
    liquor and women,
And the night-fires going out, and the
    lack of shelters,
And the cities hostile and the towns un-
    friendly
And the villages dirty and charging high
    prices: 15
A hard time we had of it.
At the end we preferred to travel all
    night,
Sleeping in snatches,
With the voices singing in our ears, say-
    ing
That this was all folly.   20

Then at dawn we came down to a tem-
    perate valley,
Wet, below the snow line, smelling of
    vegetation;
With a running stream and a water-mill
    beating the darkness,
And three trees on the low sky,
And an old white horse galloped away
    in the meadow.   25
Then we came to a tavern with vine-
    leaves over the lintel,
Six hands at an open door dicing for
    pieces of silver,
And feet kicking the empty wine-skins.

6. GALLED—Irritated.
6. REFRACTORY—Obstinate.

But there was no information, and so
    we continued
And arrived at evening, not a moment
    too soon   30
Finding the place; it was (you may say)
    satisfactory.

All this was a long time ago, I remember,
And I would do it again, but set down
This set down
This: were we led all that way for   35
Birth or Death? There was a Birth, cer-
    tainly,
We had evidence and no doubt. I had
    seen birth and death,
But had thought they were different;
    this Birth was
Hard and bitter agony for us, like Death,
    our death.
We returned to our places, these King-
    doms,   40
But no longer at ease here, in the old
    dispensation,
With an alien people clutching their
    gods.
I should be glad of another death.

◇◇◇◇◇◇◇◇◇◇◇◇◇◇◇◇◇◇◇◇◇◇◇◇◇◇◇◇◇◇◇◇◇◇

FOR APPRECIATION

1. Point out the contrast in mood between lines 1–8 and lines 9–10. Show
how these lines suggest the sacrifice of the
Magi.

2. In lines 11–20 enumerate the particular hardships they encountered. Line
21 indicates that they have traveled a long
way and have at last come into a warm climate. What precise details are chosen to
develop this thought?

3. Explain the prophetic symbolism of
lines 24 and 27. Explain the Biblical reference in line 29.

4. In what sense was the visit of the
Magi a "Birth"? In what sense was it a
"Death"? Discuss the deep spiritual
meaning of these lines. Do they sum up

what Christ said, "He who loses his life shall find it"? Explain.

5. Why were the Magi ill at ease on their return home? Can a Christian ever be perfectly at home in a pagan world? Discuss. Explain the meaning of the last line.

6. The poem is written in a conversational tone, suggesting a series of loosely connected statements. Is this typical of Eliot's technique? Discuss. Explain why this is a poem and not a piece of prose. Does the poem appeal primarily to the intellect, or to the emotions? Explain.

The Barrel Organ

ALFRED NOYES

The scene is London— -or any large city—in the late spring. It is the end of the day and people are hurrying home. A street musician is grinding out tunes on his hand organ—once a familiar feature of city life. The season and the hour contrive to give the music more than its natural charm, for it awakens in each listener his own memories and dreams.

As you read the poem, notice the changes in rhythm and length of line. They correspond to the different kinds of tunes the barrel organ grinds out. Between tunes, in long swinging lines the poet tells of the effect of the music on different passers-by.

> There's a barrel organ caroling across a golden street
> In the City as the sun sinks low;
> And the music's not immortal; but the world has made it sweet
> And fulfilled it with the sunset glow;
> And it pulses through the pleasures of the City and the pain   5
> That surrounds the singing organ like a large eternal light;
> And they've given it a glory and a part to play again
> In the Symphony that rules the day and night.
>
> And now it's marching onward through the realms of old romance,
> And trolling out a fond familiar tune,   10
> And now it's roaring cannon down to fight the King of France,
> And now it's prattling softly to the moon.

2. THE CITY—The main business section of London.

And all around the organ there's a sea without a shore
  Of human joys and wonders and regrets;
To remember and to recompense the music evermore   15
  For what the cold machinery forgets . . .

      Yes; as the music changes,
        Like a prismatic glass,
      It takes the light and ranges
        Through all the moods that pass;   20
      Dissects the common carnival
        Of passions and regrets,
      And gives the world a glimpse of all
        The colors it forgets.

      And there *La Traviata* sighs   25
        Another sadder song;
      And there *Il Trovatore* cries
        A tale of deeper wrong;
      And bolder knights to battle go
        With sword and shield and lance,   30
      Than ever here on earth below
        Have whirled into—*a dance!*—

Go down to Kew in lilac time, in lilac time, in lilac time;
  Go down to Kew in lilac time (it isn't far from London!)
And you shall wander hand in hand with love in summer's wonderland;   35
  Go down to Kew in lilac time (it isn't far from London!)

The cherry trees are seas of bloom and soft perfume and sweet perfume,
  The cherry trees are seas of bloom (and oh, so near to London!)
And there they say, when dawn is high and all the world's a blaze of sky
  The cuckoo, though he's very shy, will sing a song for London.   40

The Dorian nightingale is rare, and yet they say you'll hear him there
  At Kew, at Kew in lilac time (and oh, so near to London!)
The linnet and the throstle, too, and after dark the long halloo
  And golden-eyed *tu-whit, to-whoo* of owls that ogle London.

For Noah hardly knew a bird of any kind that isn't heard   45
  At Kew, at Kew in lilac time (and oh, so near to London!)
And when the rose begins to pout, and all the chestnut spires are out,
  You'll hear the rest without a doubt, all chorusing for London—

25. *La Traviata* (lä trä·vyä′tä)—An opera by the Italian composer Verdi.
27. *Il Trovatore* (êl trō′vä·tō′rä)—Another opera by Verdi.
    33. KEW—A village and park near London much visited by city-dwellers during spring and
summer.

Come down to Kew in lilac time, in lilac time, in lilac time;
 Come down to Kew in lilac time (it isn't far from London!) 50
And you shall wander hand in hand with love in summer's wonderland;
 Come down to Kew in lilac time (it isn't far from London!)

And then the troubadour begins to thrill the golden street,
 In the City as the sun sinks low;
And in all the gaudy busses there are scores of weary feet 55
Marking time, sweet time, with a dull mechanic beat,
And a thousand hearts are plunging to a love they'll never meet,
Through the meadows of the sunset, through the poppies and the wheat,
 In the land where the dead dreams go.

Verdi, Verdi, when you wrote *Il Trovatore* did you dream 60
 Of the City when the sun sinks low,
Of the organ and the monkey and the many-colored stream
On the Piccadilly pavement, of the myriad eyes that seem
To be litten for a moment with a wild Italian gleam
As *Ah che la morte* parodies the world's eternal theme 65
 And pulses with the sunset glow?

There's a thief, perhaps, that listens with a face of frozen stone
 In the City as the sun sinks low,
There's a portly man of business with a balance of his own,
There's a clerk and there's a butcher of a soft reposeful tone, 70
And they're all of them returning to the heavens they have known;
They are crammed and jammed in busses and—they're each of them alone
 In the land where the dead dreams go.

There's a very modish woman, and her smile is very bland
 In the City as the sun sinks low; 75
And her hansom jingles onward, but her little jeweled hand
Is clenched a little tighter, and she cannot understand
What she wants or why she wanders to that undiscovered land,
For the parties there are not at all the sort of thing she planned,
 In the land where the dead dreams go. 80

There's an Oxford man that listens, and his heart is crying out
 In the City as the sun sinks low,
For the barge, the eight, the Isis, and the coach's whoop and shout,

53. TROUBADOUR— *Il Trovatore* means "The Troubadour"—the hero of the opera.
 62. MONKEY—The organ player's trained monkey would pass the tin cup among the crowd for pennies.
 63. PICCADILLY—One of the famous streets of London.
 65. *Ah che la morte* (ä kā lä mōr′tä)—The first words of one of the chief songs from *Il Trovatore,* meaning "To whom death."
 83. THE EIGHT, THE ISIS—The Oxford or Cambridge crew of eight oarsmen, and the part of the Thames where races between the two universities are held.

THE TWENTIETH CENTURY

For the minute gun, the counting, and the long disheveled rout,
For the howl along the towpath and a fate that's still in doubt,   85
For a roughened oar to handle and a race to think about
    In the land where the dead dreams go.

There's a laborer that listens to the voices of the dead
    In the City as the sun sinks low;
And his hand begins to tremble and his face is rather red   90
As he sees a loafer watching him and—there he turns his head
And stares into the sunset where his April love is fled,
For he hears her softly singing, and his lonely soul is led
    Through the land where the dead dreams go.

There's an old and haggard demirep, it's ringing in her ears,   95
    In the City as the sun sinks low;
With the wild and empty sorrow of the love that blights and sears,
Oh, and if she hurries onward, then be sure, be sure she hears,
Hears and bears the bitter burden of the unforgotten years,
And her laugh's a little harsher and her eyes are brimmed with tears   100
    For the land where the dead dreams go.

There's a barrel organ caroling across a golden street
    In the City as the sun sinks low;
Though the music's only Verdi there's a world to make it sweet,
Just as yonder yellow sunset where the earth and heaven meet   105
Mellows all the sooty City! Hark, a hundred thousand feet
Are marching on to glory through the poppies and the wheat
    In the land where the dead dreams go.

        So it's Jeremiah, Jeremiah,
           What have you to say   110
       When you meet the garland girls
           Tripping on their way?

       All round my gala hat
           I wear a wreath of roses;
       (A long and lonely year it is   115
           I've waited for the May!)

       If anyone should ask you,
           The reason why I wear it is—
       My own love, my true love
           Is coming home today.   120

And it's buy a bunch of violets for the lady
    (*It's lilac time in London; it's lilac time in London!*)
95. DEMIREP—A woman of doubtful character.

_____

Buy a bunch of violets for the lady,
  While the sky burns blue above:

On the other side of the street you'll find it shady   125
  (*It's lilac time in London; it's lilac time in London!*)
But buy a bunch of violets for the lady,
  And tell her she's your own true love.

There's a barrel organ caroling across a golden street
  In the City as the sun sinks glittering and slow;   130
And the music's not immortal; but the world has made it sweet
And enriched it with the harmonies that make a song complete
In the deeper heavens of music where the night and morning meet,
  As it dies into the sunset glow;

And it pulses through the pleasures of the City and the pain   135
  That surround the singing organ like a large eternal light,
And they've given it a glory and a part to play again
  In the Symphony that rules the day and night.

      And there, as the music changes,
        The song runs round again.   140
      Once more it turns and ranges
        Through all its joy and pain,
      Dissects the common carnival
        Of passions and regrets;
      And the wheeling world remembers all   145
        The wheeling song forgets.

      Once more *La Traviata* sighs
        Another sadder song;
      Once more *Il Trovatore* cries
        A tale of deeper wrong;   150
      Once more the knights to battle go
        With sword and shield and lance
      Till once, once more, the shattered foe
        Has whirled into—*a dance!*

Come down to Kew in lilac time, in lilac time, in lilac time;   155
  Come down to Kew in lilac time (it isn't far from London!)
And you shall wander hand in hand with love in summer's wonderland;
  Come down to Kew in lilac time (it isn't far from London!)

FOR UNDERSTANDING

1. Each person in this street scene is affected in a different way by the music. What former moment of excitement is the "Oxford man" reminded of? What memory comes to the mind of the laborer?

When the "modish" rich woman hears the music she is momentarily dissatisfied with her glittering, empty existence. What precious things do you think may be lacking in her life?

2. Which parts of the poem imitate the rhythm of a dance? Which part shows by rhythm and words that the barrel organ is now playing a sprightly love tune? Lines 9, 10, and 11 are intended to suggest three different kinds of tunes played by the organ. What kind of tune is represented by each of these lines?

3. The barrel organ does not produce fine music, but at the beginning of the poem we are told that the world has "made it sweet" and has "fulfilled it." Near the end, the same idea is expressed in almost the same words. Reread this later passage, and then explain how "the world" can be said to enrich or to fulfill the music. In both passages, the word "symphony" is a figurative expression for people's thoughts, hopes, and memories. Can you explain how these are like a symphony?

OF FORM AND STYLE

1. This poem is in some ways the opposite of Yeats's "The Lake Isle of Innisfree." The speaker in "The Barrel Organ" is not thinking of escaping from the city, but reflecting on the hum and activity around him. What effect does this difference have on the number of sights and sounds presented in each poem? In which poem is the rhythm quiet and unobtrusive, and in which is it strong and obvious? Which poem seems crowded, as if the poet wished to take a sweeping view of all life? Which one is centered on a single easily defined mood? Mention some words in both poems which suggest the sounds they describe.

2. Point out three lines in "The Barrel Organ" in which the use of alliteration is especially noticeable.

◇◇◇◇◇

Lepanto

GILBERT K. CHESTERTON

In the great naval battle of Lepanto, fought on October 7, 1571, the combined fleets of Venice, Spain, and the Papal States, which had been formed into a Holy League by Pius V, were ranged against a powerful Turkish Armada. The immediate cause of the battle was the determination of Sultan Selim II to wrest Cyprus from Venice. The engagement took place in the Gulf of Corinth off the coast of Greece. The allied Christian fleet, consisting of 250 ships, was commanded by Don John of Austria, natural brother of King Philip II of Spain, but the illegitimate son

of his father, Charles V. The engagement resulted in a victory for the
Christian fleet. About 8000 Christians were killed, while the Turks were
believed to have lost 20,000. Twelve thousand Christian galley slaves
were liberated by the victory.

Chesterton's "Lepanto" is an excellent example of how a poet can take
an historical event, select a hero, and breathe into that event the stuff of
which high adventure and romance are made. Chesterton paints Don John
as the last of the chivalrous knights and troubadours who, in this outburst
of the spirit of the Crusades, counted no price too great to pay for the
privilege of answering the call of the Cross.

To be fully appreciated, this poem must be read aloud. Here is music
with a meaning; a story that is a message, told in great song. The narrative is given by scenes, each scene ending with the martial music of its
central figure.

SECTION I

[*The Turks and the Christians*]

White founts falling in the Courts of the Sun,
And the Soldan of Byzantium is smiling as they run;
There is laughter like the fountains in that face of all men feared,
It stirs the forest darkness, the darkness of his beard;
It curls the blood-red crescent, the crescent of his lips;   5
For the inmost sea of all the earth is shaken with his ships.
They have dared the white republics on the capes of Italy,
They have dashed the Adriatic round the Lion of the Sea,
And the Pope has cast his arms abroad for agony and loss,
And called the kings of Christendom for swords about the Cross.   10
The cold queen of England is looking in the glass;
The shadow of the Valois is yawning at the Mass;
From evening isles fantastical rings faint the Spanish gun,
And the Lord upon the Golden Horn is laughing in the sun.

2. SOLDAN OF BYZANTIUM—Sultan of Constantinople.
6. INMOST SEA—The Mediterranean.
8. LION OF THE SEA—The free city of Venice, which had for its emblem the winged lion of
St. Mark.
9. THE POPE—Pope Pius V, who called for help to save Europe.
11. COLD QUEEN—Elizabeth of England who took no part in the Crusade.
12. SHADOW OF THE VALOIS—Charles IX, only the nominal King of France.
14. THE GOLDEN HORN—The Sultan's palace overlooked an arm of the Bosporus called the
Golden Horn.

603

SECTION II

[Don John prepares for war]

Dim drums throbbing, in the hills half heard,   15
Where only on a nameless throne a crownless prince has stirred,
Where, risen from a doubtful seat and half-attained stall,
The last knight of Europe takes weapons from the wall,
The last and lingering troubadour to whom the bird has sung,
That once went singing southward when all the world was young.   20
In that enormous silence, tiny and unafraid,
Comes up along a winding road the noise of the Crusade.
Strong gongs groaning as the guns boom far,
Don John of Austria is going to the war;
Stiff flags straining in the night blasts cold   25
In the gloom black-purple, in the glint old-gold,
Torchlight crimson on the copper kettledrums,
Then the tuckets, then the trumpets, then the cannon, and he comes.
Don John laughing in the brave beard curled,
Spurning of his stirrups like the thrones of all the world,   30
Holding his head up for a flag of all the free.
Love light of Spain—hurrah!
Death light of Africa!
Don John of Austria
Is riding to the sea.   35

SECTION III

[The Turkish powers prepare]

Mahound is in his paradise above the evening star;
(Don John of Austria is going to the war.)
He moves a mighty turban on the timeless houri's knees,
His turban that is woven of the sunsets and the seas.
He shakes the peacock gardens as he rises from his ease,   40
And he strides among the treetops and is taller than the trees;
And his voice through all the garden is a thunder sent to bring
Black Azrael and Ariel and Ammon on the wing.
Giants and the Genii,
Multiplex of wing and eye,   45

16. CROWNLESS PRINCE—Don John of Austria.
19. THE BIRD—The spirit of Catholic courage which gave rise to the military movement called the Crusades.
28. TUCKETS—Flourish of trumpets.
36. MAHOUND (má·hound')—Mohammed.
38. TIMELESS HOURI (hōō'rĭ)—The Mohammedans believed that they would be rewarded in paradise with the eternal company of beautiful women.
43. AZRAEL (ăz'rá·ĕl)—Angel of death; ARIEL—Spirit of air; AMMON—God of the Egyptians.

Whose strong obedience broke the sky
When Solomon was king.

They rush in red and purple from the red clouds of the morn,
From the temples where the yellow gods shut up their eyes in scorn;
They rise in green robes roaring from the green hells of the sea   50
Where fallen skies and evil hues and eyeless creatures be,
On them the sea valves cluster and the gray sea forests curl,
Splashed with a splendid sickness, the sickness of the pearl;
They swell in sapphire smoke out of the blue cracks of the ground—
They gather and they wonder and give worship to Mahound.   55
And he saith, "Break up the mountains where the hermit-folk can hide,
And sift the red and silver sands lest bone of saint abide,
And chase the Giaours flying night and day, not giving rest,
For that which was our trouble comes again out of the west.
We have set the seal of Solomon on all things under sun,   60
Of knowledge and of sorrow and endurance of things done.
But a noise is in the mountains, in the mountains, and I know
The voice that shook our palaces—four hundred years ago:
It is he that saith not 'Kismet'; it is he that knows not Fate;
It is Richard, it is Raymond, it is Godfrey at the gate!   65
It is he whose loss is laughter when he counts the wager worth,
Put down your feet upon him, that our peace be on the earth."
For he heard drums groaning and he heard guns jar,
(*Don John of Austria is going to the war.*)
Sudden and still—hurrah!   70
Bolt from Iberia!
Don John of Austria
Is gone by Alcalar.

SECTION IV

[North Europe will not answer the call]

St. Michael's on his Mountain in the sea roads of the north
(*Don John of Austria is girt and going forth.*)   75
Where the gray seas glitter and the sharp tides shift
And the seafolk labor and the red sails lift.
He shakes his lance of iron and he claps his wings of stone;
The noise is gone through Normandy; the noise is gone alone;

47. SOLOMON—Mohammedans believed that Solomon possessed power over the genii by virtue of a ring on which God's name was written.
58. GIAOURS (jours)—Infidels. In this case, those not of Mohammedan faith.
63. FOUR HUNDRED YEARS AGO—The time of the first Crusades.
64. KISMET—Fate, or "it is fate, so I surrender."
65. RICHARD, RAYMOND, GODFREY—Gallant Christian Crusaders who defeated the Turks at different times.
71. IBERIA—Spain
74. ST. MICHAEL—Patron of holy warriors, for whom the rocky island off the coast of Normandy is named.

The North is full of tangled things and texts and aching eyes,   80
And dead is all the innocence of anger and surprise,
And Christian killeth Christian in a narrow dusty room,
And Christian dreadeth Christ that hath a newer face of doom,
And Christian hateth Mary that God kissed in Galilee—
But Don John of Austria is riding to the sea.   85
Don John calling through the blast and the eclipse
Crying with the trumpet, with the trumpet of his lips,
Trumpet that sayeth *ha!*
Domino gloria!
Don John of Austria   90
Is shouting to the ships.

[*Spain does not answer the call*]

King Philip's in his closet with the Fleece about his neck
(*Don John of Austria is armed upon the deck.*)
The walls are hung with velvet that is black and soft as sin,
And little dwarfs creep out of it and little dwarfs creep in.   95
He holds a crystal phial that has colors like the moon,
He touches, and it tingles, and he trembles very soon,
And his face is as a fungus of a leprous white and gray
Like plants in the high houses that are shuttered from the day,
And death is in the phial, and the end of noble work,   100
But Don John of Austria has fired upon the Turk.
Don John's hunting, and his hounds have bayed—
Booms away past Italy the rumor of his raid
Gun upon gun, ha! ha!
Gun upon gun, hurrah!   105
Don John of Austria
Has loosed the cannonade.

SECTION V

[*The vision of the battle*]

The Pope was in his chapel before day or battle broke,
(*Don John of Austria is hidden in the smoke.*)
The hidden room in man's house where God sits all the year,   110

80–84. The Reformation infected the North of Europe. It set Christian men to fighting one another. Preachers of the new sects taught fear of God and hell, instead of love for God, Christ, and His Blessed Mother.

89. *Domino gloria*—Glory be to God!

92. In the following lines, Chesterton appears to be unfair to Philip II of Spain. He did join the Holy League organized by Pius V to resist the Turks. *The Catholic Encyclopedia* writes of him: "he was industrious, tenacious, serious, simple-minded . . . a dutiful son, a loving husband . . . the courage with which he endured the sufferings of his last illness are worthy of admiration. . . . On the other hand, he was cold, suspicious, secretive, scrupulous, indecisive, little disposed to clemency or forgetfulness of wrong."

110. HIDDEN ROOM—The tabernacle from which Christ in the Blessed Sacrament views the world.

The secret window whence the world looks small and very dear.
He sees as in a mirror on the monstrous twilight sea
The crescent of his cruel ships whose name is mystery;
They fling great shadows foe-wards, making Cross and Castle dark,
They veil the plumèd lions on the galleys of St. Mark;   115
And above the ships are palaces of brown, black-bearded chiefs,
And below the ships are prisons, where with multitudinous griefs,
Christian captives sick and sunless, all a laboring race repines
Like a race in sunken cities, like a nation in the mines.
They are lost like slaves that swat, and in the skies of morning hung   120
The stairways of the tallest gods when tyranny was young.
They are countless, voiceless, hopeless as those fallen or fleeing on
Before the high Kings' horses in the granite of Babylon.
And many a one grows witless in his quiet room in hell
Where a yellow face looks inward through the lattice of his cell,   125
And he finds his God forgotten, and he seeks no more a sign—
(*But Don John of Austria has burst the battle line!*)
Don John pounding from the slaughter-painted poop,
Purpling all the ocean like a bloody pirate's sloop,

114. CROSS AND CASTLE—The emblems of the Spanish Christians from Aragon and Castile.
115. GALLEYS OF ST. MARK—Venetian ships. St. Mark was patron of Venice.
118. CHRISTIAN CAPTIVES—Galley slaves in the Turkish fleet.
120. SWAT—Sweat, past tense. This is an old form.

Scarlet running over on the silvers and the golds,   130
Breaking of the hatches up and bursting of the holds,
Thronging of the thousands up that labor under sea
White for bliss and blind for sun and stunned for liberty.
Vivat Hispania!
Domino gloria!   135
Don John of Austria
Has set his people free!
Cervantes on his galley sets the sword back in the sheath
(*Don John of Austria rides homeward with a wreath.*)
And he sees across a weary land a straggling road in Spain,   140
Up which a lean and foolish knight forever rides in vain,
And he smiles, but not as Sultans smile, and settles back the blade. . . .
(*But Don John of Austria rides home from the Crusade.*)

138. CERVANTES—Author of *Don Quixote,* great Spanish satire on the medieval romance. Cervantes was a member of this Crusade. Perhaps his smile signifies that his hero, Don Quixote, apparently a simpleton, was not so foolish after all.

FOR APPRECIATION

Section I—How does line 2 tie together with lines 1 and 3? List the color adjectives used in the first fourteen lines. By what method does Chesterton portray the advance of the Turks? . . . The reaction of the Christian leaders to the call for a Crusade?

Section II—What figure of speech is used in line 15? Is the lengthening of the meter in lines 16–20 consistent with the thought? Notice the martial music in lines 23–25. Read aloud lines 25–28 which serve as an introduction to the fanfare for Don John. Here, too, list the colors given.

Section III—What is the meter change in line 36? Is it natural? What attributes are given to Mahound? What specific figures are used to portray these attributes? Whom does he command, and from whence do they come? Briefly summarize the message of Mahound. What reason has Mahound for fearing the "noise in the mountains"? Interpret line 66.

Section IV—Interpret each line in which we learn the reasons why St. Michael's call to arms has gone unheeded. What heresies are implied in these lines?

Section V—What specific details of the battle are seen in the Pope's vision? Is this an effective manner of portraying the battle? Explain. How many figures of speech are used in lines 117–126? Read aloud the action-rhythm in lines 128–137. What is the attitude implicitly contrasted in the smile of Cervantes and the Sultan? Is there an implied relationship between Don Quixote and Don John? Explain fully.

PROJECT

Choose from the poem at least ten onomatopoetic and alliterative lines. Write out fifteen rich connotative epithets.

RELATED READING

Margaret Yeo has written a colorful, romantic life, *Don John of Austria,* and Frank Spearman has made Don John the hero of his novel, *Spanish Lover.*

To Dives

HILAIRE BELLOC

D. B. Wyndham Lewis, a modern Catholic satirist and biographer, once wrote that "if the pill is sufficiently gilded with humor and nonsense, the public will swallow anything—even the truth!" In prose and in satirical verse, such Catholic satirists as Chesterton, Belloc, J. B. Morton, Douglas Woodruff, Ronald Knox, and Anglo-Catholic C. S. Lewis have been giving the "Catholic attitude," the truth about contemporary society, and the English public have swallowed the pill with delight.

In Belloc's "To Dives" we have an example of Catholic humor with a sting, a controlled but biting contempt for the modern, self-made millionaire who has chosen Wealth as a way of life.

Dives, when you and I go down to Hell,
Where scribblers end and millionaires as well,
We shall be carrying on our separate backs
Two very large but very different packs;
And as you stagger under yours, my friend,   5
Down the dull shore where all our journeys end,
And go before me (as your rank demands)
Towards the infinite flat underlands,
And that dear river of forgetfulness—

Charon, a man of exquisite address   10
(For, as your wife's progenitors could tell,
They're very strict on etiquette in Hell),
Will, since you are a lord, observe, "My lord,
We cannot take these weighty things aboard!"
Then down they go, my wretched Dives, down—   15
The fifteen sorts of boots you kept for town;
The hat to meet the Devil in; the plain
But costly ties; the cases of champagne;
The solid watch, and seal, and chain, and charm;   19
The working model of a Burning Form
(To give the little Belials); all the three
Biscuits for Cerberus; the guarantee
From Lambeth that the Rich can never burn,

---

1. DIVES—Pronounced dī'vēz.

1. HELL—The hell of Greek mythology known as Hades was a dreary place where the ghosts of the dead led a vague, unsubstantial life. A few fortunate ones escaped to Elysium, while those who had offended the gods were removed to Tartarus for punishment. Hades was separated from the land of the living by the river Styx; and it was Charon's job to ferry the dead across the river. The three-headed watch-dog, Cerberus, stood guard at the entrance to Hades to prevent any of the dead from going out again. The Cocytus was another river of the infernal region.

22. GUARANTEE FROM LAMBETH—Lambeth is the official London residence of the Anglican Archbishop of Canterbury. Here Belloc is satirizing the official teaching of the Archbishop that, perhaps, there is no hell and certainly it is not eternal.

"To Dives" by Hilaire Belloc, reprinted by permission of A. D. Peters, London.

And even promising a safe return;
The admirable overcoat, designed   25
To cross Cocytus—very warmly lined:
Sweet Dives, you will leave them all behind
And enter Hell as tattered and as bare
As was your father when he took the air
Behind a barrow-load in Leicester Square.   30
Then turned to me, and noting one that brings
With careless step a mist of shadowy things:
Laughter and memories, and a few regrets,
Some honour, and a quantity of debts,
A doubt or two of sorts, a trust in God,

26. COCYTUS (kō·sī'tŭs)—In Greek mythology, one of the rivers of Hades.

And (what will seem to you extremely odd)   36
His father's granfer's father's father's name,
Unspoilt, untitled, even spelt the same;
Charon, who twenty thousand times before
Has ferried Poets to the ulterior shore,
Will estimate the weight I bear, and cry—   41
"Comrade" (He has himself been known to try
His hand at Latin and Italian verse,
Much in the style of Virgil—only worse)
"We let such vain imaginaries pass!"
Then tell me, Dives, which will look the ass—   46
You, or myself? Or Charon? Who can tell?
They order things so damnably in Hell.

FOR APPRECIATION

1. Explain in detail the two different packs which the scribbler and the millionaire will carry. Which would you rather be: a millionaire or a scribbler?

2. What indications are there in the poem that Belloc is satirizing the "new rich" and the "newly titled"? Explain lines 36–38.

3. Does Belloc soften the satire in the last three lines? Discuss.

4. How does this famous line of Chesterton's express the same attitude: "I do not mind the swindle, but deprecate the swank"?

On a Dead Hostess

HILAIRE BELLOC

Do not be fooled into judging the merits of this poem by its length. An epigram, like a cameo, requires exquisite perfection, and this couplet of Belloc's has been acclaimed one of the few "great" epigrams in the language.

Of this bad world the loveliest and the best
Has smiled and said "Good Night," and gone to rest.

"On a Dead Hostess" by Hilaire Belloc, reprinted by permission of A. D. Peters, London.

Pilgrimage

EILEEN DUGGAN

Bells seem to have an especial appeal for the poet; Alice Meynell has her beautiful lyric "The Chimes"; Poe rings delightful onomatopoetic changes with "The Bells"; Tennyson contributes "Ring Out, Wild Bells." Now Eileen Duggan comes forward to acclaim the bells of the Universal Church as they make their pilgrimage to the Easter tomb at Jerusalem.

Now are the bells unlimbered from their spires
In every steeple-loft from pole to pole:
The four winds wheel and blow into this gate,
And every wind is wet with carillons.
The two Americas at eagle-height,   5
The pure, abstracted Himalayan chimes,
Great ghosts of Clappers from the Russian fries,
And sweet, wind-sextoned tremblers from Cathay;
The bells of Ireland, jesting all the way,
The English bells, slowbosomed as a swan,   10
The queenly, weary din of Notre Dame,
And the Low Countries ringing back the sea.
Then Spain, the Moor still moaning through the saint,
The frosty, fiery bells of Germany,
And on before them, baying, sweeping down,   15
The heavy, joyful pack of thunder-jowls
That tongue hosannas from the Leash of Rome—
All float untethered over Jaffa Gate
To fling one peal when angels cheat the stone.
But if one little gaping country bell,   20
Blown from its weather-boarding in the south,
Should be too lost to keep its covenant,
Or lift its heart and reins up to the hour,
Know that its dumbness riots more than sound.

7. FRIES—Belfries.

FOR APPRECIATION

1. In this poem the author attributes qualities to the bells of each country. Enumerate the various countries and explain the peculiar quality of the bells—for example, the jesting bells of Ireland.

2. In line 1 what image is implied in

unlimbered? Analyze the following expressions: *wet with carillons; Russian fries; tongue hosannas; float untethered.* Find other striking expressions in the poem.

3. In line 19 we have a beautiful picture of the bells gathering at the tomb on Easter morning, like the holy women in the Gospel story, to witness the angels roll back the stone and thus "cheat" the tomb. Why does the poet use the phrase "one peal"? Could all the bells sound at once?

4. Read the Gospel narrative of Christ's Resurrection. What symbolism of Peter's effort to keep up with St. John in his race for the Easter tomb can you find in lines 20–24? Explain fully the rich connotation of line 25.

5. Compare the tone and spirit of this poem with Alice Meynell's essay, "The Spirit of Place."

EILEEN DUGGAN

This poem demonstrates the Gaelic penchant for spiritual reference. Any and every aspect of nature is able to send the Irish soul spiraling heavenwards. Here it is the sight of autumn paying its royal devoir that lifts the poet's thoughts to another royal welcome . . . and its ironic consequence.

Ah royal, surely royal, I concede you.
What else this rush of homage on their part?
But all these hot salutes, these dusty honours,
I see them with a wary, brooding heart.
If multitudes of fruits come forth to greet you,   5
If flowers and clouds give you a king's estate,
What is it but a justice, a fulfillment?
Why should I sadden that they shout you great?
The trees have spread their garments down before you.
Larks lead you in, a living haze of cries,   10
Thrones and dominions in the hills avow you,
The winds and the mid-winds unto you arise.
It is not long, God knows, you do the monarch.
This ardent irony that is the land
Sends you upon an ass into your winter   15
That drives a nail of sleet through either hand.

FOR APPRECIATION

1. Explain in detail how the poem gives the Catholic approach to nature.

2. What is the meaning of line 7? In line 8 the poet implies that autumn's royal acclaim saddens her. Why do you suppose she feels that way?

3. Explain the Biblical allusion in lines 9–16.

4. Explain and analyze these phrases: *rush of homage; hot salutes; wary, brooding heart; this ardent irony.*

5. Re-read Chesterton's poem, "The Donkey," and Plunkett's verse, "I See His Blood upon the Rose."

❖❖❖❖❖

To the Sun

ROY CAMPBELL

Since the early ages of the Church, poets have been using symbols drawn from nature to represent Christ. At various times, Our Lord has been represented as a Lamb, a Fish, a Pelican. To Joseph Mary Plunkett, the Irish poet, the whole of nature was a symbol of Our Lord. In the following poem, Roy Campbell has exquisitely drawn subtle relationships between the colors of the sun and Christ.

Oh let your shining orb grow dim,
Of Christ the mirror and the shield,
That I may gaze through you to Him,
See half the miracle revealed,
And in your seven hues behold   5
The Blue Man walking on the Sea,
The Green, beneath the summer tree,
Who called the children; then the Gold,

With palms; the Orange, flaring bold
With scourges: Purple in the garden
(As Greco saw): and then the Red   11
Torero (Him who took the toss
And rode the black horns of the cross—
But rose snow-silver from the dead!)

11. GRECO—Theotocopuli, a Spanish painter of the sixteenth century. The reference is to a painting, "Christ in the Garden," done in heavy red and purple. "As Greco saw" means "as the artist conceived it."

12. TORERO—A Spanish bullfighter on foot.

"To the Sun" from *Collected Poems* by Roy Campbell, reprinted by permission of John Lane The Bodley Head Limited, London, and Henry Regnery Company.

❖❖❖

FOR APPRECIATION

1. Examine carefully the implied metaphor of the white light of the sun broken into its prismatic rays. Is there any relationship between such a figure and the Liturgical year which "breaks down" Christ, the Way, the Truth, and the Life into the various mysteries of His life?

2. Is it natural to make such comparisons between those we love and external objects? Give some examples from modern song writers.

3. Compare Campbell's use of color with that of W. W. Gibson in "Sight."

4. Explain the implied figure in lines 12–14.

5. For other religiously beautiful comparisons, read the opening stanzas of Thompson's "Ode to the Setting Sun."

ESSAYS

If broadly defined as "any short piece of nonfiction," the essay is the most prominent form of modern prose writing. This is because the definition includes the articles that fill our magazines. Modern articles, of course, do not pretend to the literary merits of essays by Bacon or Addison. They differ also in subject matter, being more full of specific information. They consist of recently gathered facts about places, people, and events. A sound, well-written article can supersede all earlier articles on its topic—but may be out of date within weeks or months.

Side by side with factual articles, present day magazines continue to carry the type of essay that makes judgments, expresses personal tastes or opinions, or recollects and describes personal experiences. Editorials, book reviews, and historical and cultural studies are examples of this form. Oftentimes these articles are given permanence when their authors publish them in book form.

Virginia Woolf's *The Common Reader* contains some of the finest essays in literary criticism that have appeared in our century. E. V. Lucas is a modern follower of Lamb's personal, whimsical style of writing. Among many other non-Catholic British writers who have produced brilliant essays are George Orwell, Rebecca West, E. M. Forster, and Dylan Thomas. On any list of Catholic twentieth century essayists and prose writers must be included: G. K. Chesterton, Hilaire Belloc, Monsignor Ronald Knox, Arnold Lunn, Eric Gill, Caryll Houselander, Douglas Woodruff, Frank Sheed, Martin D'Arcy, S.J., and the two Dominicans, Bede Jarrett and Vincent McNabb.

A very frequent type of the modern essay is the humorous sketch. A. P. Herbert, J. B. Priestley, and Stephen Leacock are three of the best known humorous essayists. Short humorous pieces find a constant market in newspapers and in magazines like the famous English weekly, *Punch.*

Christopher Dawson is England's greatest Catholic historian of culture. Barbara Ward, in her *Faith and Freedom,* has given a penetrating analysis of the great ideas and movements which have made Western culture. Winston Churchill, who was as skillful a master of English prose as he was a statesman, has written an outstanding example of the *eye-witness* historical account in his *The Second World War.*

THE PATH TO ROME

HILAIRE BELLOC

Hilaire Belloc's literary reputation can rest secure upon his travel essays, The Cruise of the Nona, The Four Men, Hills and the Sea, *and* The Path to Rome. *In all of these we have some of the loveliest lyrical prose in all English letters. In these works Belloc views the universe as a thoroughly Catholic universe. He sees physical nature as something good to be reverenced, but not to be worshipped for its own sake. He loved the sea and the hills and the mountains because he saw in them the seal of God's power, and he beheld in them a great sacrament symbolizing the beauty and majesty of the Creator.*

Belloc's The Path to Rome *is the best of all travel books. It breathes the refreshing spirit of a Catholic at home in Christendom. Belloc tramps through the Alps down into the Italian plains, and his heart expands under the graciousness of Catholic skies. The book abounds in his adventure and in good humor. He exults in existence and manifests a zest for living, as he lyrically expresses his love of the mountains, good companionship, wine, and all the other great gifts of God.*

Two passages from The Path to Rome *have been selected for our study: The first is a description of the Alps as seen from the Jura mountains; the second is a description of dawn as he sees the plains of Tuscany from a mountain ridge.*

DESCRIPTION OF ALPS

The wood went up darkly and the path branched here and there so that I was soon uncertain of my way, but I followed generally what seemed to me the most southerly course, and so came at last up steeply through a dip or ravine that ended high on the crest of the ridge.

Just as I came to the end of the rise, after perhaps an hour, perhaps two, of that great curtain of forest which had held the mountain side, the trees fell away to brushwood, there was a gate, and then the path was lost upon a fine

Selections from *The Path to Rome* by Hilaire Belloc, reprinted by permission of Henry Regnery Company.

open sward which was the very top of the Jura and the coping of that multiple wall which defends the Swiss Plain. I had crossed it straight from edge to edge, never turning out of my way.

It was too marshy to lie down on it, so I stood a moment to breathe and look about me.

It was evident that nothing higher remained, for though a new line of wood —firs and beeches—stood before me, yet nothing appeared above them, and I knew that they must be the fringe of the descent. I approached this edge of wood, and saw that it had a rough fence of post and rails bounding it, and as I was looking for the entry of a path (for my original path was lost, as such tracks are, in the damp grass of the little down) there came to me one of those great revelations which betray to us suddenly the higher things and stand afterwards firm in our minds.

There, on this upper meadow, where so far I had felt nothing but the ordinary gladness of The Summit, I had a vision.

What was it I saw? If you think I saw this or that, and if you think I am inventing the words, you know nothing of men.

I saw between the branches of the trees in front of me a sight in the sky that made me stop breathing, just as great danger at sea, or great surprise in love, or a great deliverance will make a man stop breathing. I saw something I had known in the West as a boy, something I had never seen so grandly discovered as was this. In between the branches of the trees was a great promise of unexpected lights beyond.

I pushed left and right along that edge of the forest and along the fence that bound it, until I found a place where the pine-trees stopped, leaving a gap, and where on the right, beyond the gap, was a tree whose leaves had failed; there the ground broke away steeply below me, and the beeches fell, one below the other, like a vast cascade, towards the limestone cliffs that dipped down still further, beyond my sight. I looked through this framing hollow and praised God. For there below me, thousands of feet below me, was what seemed an illimitable plain; at the end of that world was an horizon, and the dim bluish sky that overhangs an horizon.

There was brume [1] in it and thickness. One saw the sky beyond the edge of the world getting purer as the vault rose. But right up—a belt in that empyrean—ran peak and field and needle of intense ice, remote, remote from the world. Sky beneath them and sky above them, a steadfast legion, they glittered as though with the armour of the immovable armies of Heaven. Two days' march, three days' march away, they stood up like the walls of Eden. I say it again, they stopped my breath. I had seen them.

So little are we, we men: so much are we immersed in our muddy and immediate interests that we think, by numbers and recitals, to comprehend distance or time, or any of our limiting infinities. Here were these magnificent creatures of God, I mean the Alps, which now for the first time I saw from the height of the Jura; and because they were fifty or sixty miles away, and because they were a mile or two high, they were become something different from us others, and could strike one motionless with the awe of supernatural things. Up there in the sky, to which only clouds belong and birds and the last trembling colours of pure light, they stood fast and hard; not moving as do

[1] BRUME—Mist or fog.

the things of the sky. They were as distant as the little upper clouds of summer, as fine and tenuous; but in their reflection and in their quality as it were of weapons (like spears and shields of an unknown array) they occupied the sky with a sublime invasion: and the things proper to the sky were forgotten by me in their presence as I gazed.

To what emotion shall I compare this astonishment? So, in first love one finds that *this* can belong to *me*.

Their sharp steadfastness and their clean uplifted lines compelled my adoration. Up there, the sky above and below them, part of the sky, but part of us, the great peaks made communion between that homing creeping part of me which loves vineyards and dances and a slow movement among pastures, and that other part which is only properly at home in Heaven. I say that this kind of description is useless, and that it is better to address prayers to such things than to attempt to interpret them for others.

These, the great Alps, seen thus, link one in some way to one's immortality. Nor is it possible to convey, or even to suggest, those few fifty miles, and those few thousand feet; there is something more. Let me put it thus: that from the height of Weissenstein [2] I saw, as it were, my religion. I mean, humility, the fear of death, the terror of height and of distance, the glory of God, the infinite potentiality of reception whence springs that divine thirst of the soul; my aspiration also towards completion, and my confidence in the dual destiny. For I know that we laughers have a gross cousinship with the most high, and it is this contrast and perpetual quarrel which feeds a spring of merriment in the soul of a sane man.

[2] WEISSENSTEIN—A Ridge of the Jura mountains.

617

Since I could now see such a wonder and it could work such things in my mind, therefore, some day I should be part of it. That is what I felt.

DESCRIPTION OF SUNRISE

I have waited for the dawn a hundred times, attended by that mournful, colourless spirit which haunts the last hours of darkness; and influenced especially by the great timeless apathy that hangs round the first uncertain promise of increasing light. For there is an hour before daylight when men die, and when there is nothing above the soul or around it, when even the stars fail. And this long and dreadful expectation I had thought to be worst when one was alone at sea in a small boat without wind; drifting beyond one's harbour in the ebb of the outer channel tide, and sogging back at the first flow on the broad, confused movement of a sea without any waves. In such lonely mornings I have watched the Owers light turning, and I have counted up my gulf of time, and wondered that moments could be so stretched out in the clueless mind. I have prayed for the morning or for a little draught of wind, and this I have thought, I say, the extreme of absorption into emptiness and longing. .

But now, on this ridge, dragging myself on to the main road, I found a deeper abyss of isolation and despairing fatigue than I had ever known, and I came near to turning eastward and imploring the hastening of light, as men pray continually without reason for things that can but come in a due order. I still went forward a little, because when I sat down my loneliness oppressed me like a misfortune; and because my feet, going painfully and slowly, yet gave a little balance and rhythm to the movement of my mind.

I heard no sound of animals or birds. I passed several fields, deserted in the half-darkness; and in some I felt the hay, but always found it wringing wet with dew, nor could I discover a good shelter from the wind that blew off the upper snow of the summits. For a little space of time there fell upon me, as I crept along the road, that shadow of sleep which numbs the mind, but it could not compel me to lie down, and I accepted it only as a partial and beneficent oblivion which covered my desolation and suffering as a thin, transparent cloud may cover an evil moon.

Then suddenly the sky grew lighter upon every side. That cheating gloom (which I think the clouds in purgatory must reflect) lifted from the valley as though to a slow order given by some calm and good influence that was marshalling in the day. Their colours came back to things; the trees recovered their shape, life, and trembling; here and there, on the face of the mountain opposite, the mists by their movement took part in the new life, and I thought I heard for the first time the tumbling water far below me in the ravine. That subtle barrier was drawn which marks to-day from yesterday; all the night and its despondency became the past and entered memory. The road before me, the pass on my left (my last ridge, and the entry into Tuscany), the mass of the great hills, had become mixed into the increasing light, that is, into the familiar and invigorating Present which I have always found capable of opening the doors of the future with a gesture of victory.

My pain either left me, or I ceased to notice it, and seeing a little way before me a bank above the road, and a fine grove of sparse and dominant chestnuts,

I climbed up thither and turned, standing to the east.

There, without any warning of colours, or of the heraldry that we have in the north, the sky was a great field of pure light, and without doubt it was all woven through, as was my mind watching it, with security and gladness. Into this field, as I watched it, rose the sun.

The air became warmer almost suddenly. The splendour and health of the new day left me all in repose, and persuaded or compelled me to immediate sleep.

I found therefore in the short grass, and on the scented earth beneath one of my trees, a place for lying down; I stretched myself out upon it, and lapsed into a profound slumber, which nothing but a vague and tenuous delight separated from complete forgetfulness. If the last confusion of thought, before sleep possessed me, was a kind of prayer —and certainly I was in the mood of gratitude and of adoration—this prayer was of course to God, from whom every good proceeds, but partly (idolatrously) to the Sun, which, of all the things He has made, seems, of what we at least can discover, the most complete and glorious.

◇◇◇◇◇◇◇◇◇◇◇◇◇◇◇◇◇◇◇◇◇◇◇◇◇◇◇◇

FOR APPRECIATION

DESCRIPTION OF ALPS

1. Describe in detail the *point of view* from which Belloc describes the Alps.

2. Explain in your own words Belloc's first reaction to this "vision."

3. What physical details of the Alps did Belloc select to describe the immensity and beauty of the scene? What was Belloc's emotional reaction to the scene? What was his personal religious reaction? Explain in detail.

4. Study the imagery contained in these expressions: *they occupied the sky with a sublime invasion.* Is this expression consistent with the other figures, *steadfast legion, armour of the immovable armies, spears and shields,* previously used in this description? Explain.

DESCRIPTION OF SUNRISE

1. The *mood* expressed in paragraphs 1, 2 and 3 is entirely different from that of paragraphs 4, 5 and 6. What are these predominant moods? Select those details which Belloc uses to describe these moods.

2. Would you say that Belloc gives us description through the use of many individual *concrete physical* details of the sunrise, or does he try to convey a particular *impression* suggesting an intangible and indescribable atmosphere? Discuss.

3. Would you say that word-painting is much more difficult than painting with oils or water color? Explain. What are the tools which a literary artist must employ in word painting? Would you say that no one who had not seen what Belloc saw could describe the scene which he paints? Explain. Does he effectively capture the fugitive effects of fleeting loveliness in the scene? Explain your answer by selecting phrases and sentences from the descriptive passages.

WORDS

Explain the meaning of the expression *beneficent oblivion.* Give three synonyms for *tenuous.* Give the origin of *sward.* Discuss the connotation of *cheating gloom.*

RELATED READING

Everything that Belloc stands for is contained in his essay "A Remaining Christmas," which may be found in his *Conversation with a Cat.*

The mature student who would understand Belloc, the man and his work, should read Frederick Wilhelmsen's brief but brilliant analysis in his *Hilaire Belloc.*

REMINISCENCES OF CHILDHOOD

DYLAN THOMAS

Dylan Thomas tells us in his "Reminiscences of Childhood" that "the memories of childhood have no order and no end."   As you read the essay, you will see how convincingly he has written of many things shared by all in that world of childhood where trifles are tremendous and tragedies are frequent but fleeting; where the physical confines of home and neighborhood take on, at times the aspect of a magic world of high adventure; and, at other times, become the twilight borderland between the unexplainable adult world and the world of childhood reality with its swift succession of apparently unrelated moments and events.

I like very much people telling me about their childhood, but they'll have to be quick or else I'll be telling them about mine.

I was born in a large Welsh town at the beginning of the Great War [1]—an ugly, lovely town (or so it was and is to me), crawling, sprawling by a long and splendid curving shore where truant boys and sandfield boys and old men from nowhere, beachcombed, idled and paddled, watched the dock-bound ships or the ships steaming away into wonder and India, magic and China, countries bright with oranges and loud with lions; threw stones into the sea for the barking outcast dogs; made castles and forts and harbours and race tracks in the sand;

[1] GREAT WAR—The author is here referring to World War I.

"Reminiscences of Childhood" from *Quite Early One Morning* by Dylan Thomas, copyright, 1954, by New Directions.

and on Saturday summer afternoons listened to the brass band, watched the Punch and Judy, or hung about on the fringes of the crowd to hear the fierce religious speakers who shouted at the sea, as though it were wicked and wrong to roll in and out like that, white-horsed and full of fishes.

One man, I remember, used to take off his hat and set fire to his hair every now and then, but I do not remember what it proved, if it proved anything at all, except that he was a very interesting man.

This sea-town was my world; outside a strange Wales, coal-pitted, mountained, river-run, full, so far as I knew, of choirs and football teams and sheep and storybook tall hats and red flannel petticoats, moved about its business which was none of mine.

Beyond that unknown Wales with its

wild names like peals of bells in the darkness, and its mountain men clothed in the skins of animals perhaps and always singing, lay England which was London and the country called the Front, from which many of our neighbours never came back. It was a country to which only young men travelled.

At the beginning, the only "front" I knew was the little lobby before our front door. I could not understand how so many people never returned from there, but later I grew to know more, though still without understanding, and carried a wooden rifle in the park and shot down the invisible unknown enemy like a flock of wild birds. And the park itself was a world within the world of the sea-town. Quite near where I lived, so near that on summer evenings I could listen in my bed to the voices of older children playing ball on the sloping paper-littered bank, the park was full of terrors and treasures. Though it was only a little park, it held within its borders of old tall trees, notched with our names and shabby from our climbing, as many secret places, caverns and forests, prairies and deserts, as a country somewhere at the end of the sea.

And though we would explore it one day, armed and desperate, from end to end, from the robbers' den to the pirates' cabin, the highwayman's inn to the cattle ranch, or the hidden room in the undergrowth, where we held beetle races, and lit the wood fires and roasted potatoes and talked about Africa, and the makes of motor cars, yet still the next day, it remained as unexplored as the Poles—a country just born and always changing.

There were many secret societies but you could belong only to one; and in blood or red ink, and a rusty pocket-knife, with, of course, an instrument to remove stones from horses' feet, you signed your name at the foot of a terrible document, swore death to all the other societies, crossed your heart that you would divulge no secret and that if you did, you would consent to torture by slow fire, and undertook to carry out by yourself a feat of either daring or endurance. You could take your choice: would you climb to the top of the tallest and most dangerous tree, and from there hurl stones and insults at grown-up passers-by, especially postmen, or any other men in uniform? Or would you ring every doorbell in the terrace, not forgetting the doorbell of the man with the red face who kept dogs and ran fast? Or would you swim in the reservoir, which was forbidden and had angry swans, or would you eat a whole old jam jar full of mud?

There were many more alternatives. I chose one of endurance and for half an hour, it may have been longer or shorter, held up off the ground a very heavy broken pram we had found in a bush. I thought my back would break and the half hour felt like a day, but I preferred it to braving the red face and the dogs, or to swallowing tadpoles.

We knew every inhabitant of the park, every regular visitor, every nurse-maid, every gardener, every old man. We knew the hour when the alarming retired policeman came in to look at the dahlias and the hour when the old lady arrived in the Bath chair with six Pekinese, and a pale girl to read aloud to her. I think she read the newspaper, but we always said she read the *Wizard*. The face of the old man who sat summer and winter on the bench looking over the reservoir, I can see clearly now and I wrote a poem long long after I'd left the park and the sea-town called: "The Hunchback in the Park."

And that park grew up with me; that small world widened as I learned its secrets and boundaries, as I discovered new refuges and ambushes in its woods and jungles; hidden homes and lairs for the multitudes of imagination, for cowboys and Indians, and the tall terrible half-people who rode on nightmares through my bedroom. But it was not the only world—that world of rockery, gravel path, playbank, bowling green, bandstands, reservoir, dahlia garden, where an ancient keeper, known as Smoky, was the whiskered snake in the grass one must keep off. There was another world where with my friends I used to dawdle on half holidays along the bent and Devon-facing seashore, hoping for gold watches or the skull of a sheep or a message in a bottle to be washed up with the tide; and another where we used to wander whistling through the packed streets, stale as station sandwiches, round the impressive gasworks and the slaughter house, past by the blackened monuments and the museum that should have been in a museum. Or we scratched at a kind of cricket on the bald and cindery surface of the recreation ground, or we took a tram that shook like an iron jelly down to the gaunt pier, there to clamber under the pier, hanging perilously on to its skeleton legs or to run along to the end where patient men with the seaward eyes of the dockside unemployed capped and mufflered, dangling from their mouths pipes that had long gone out, angled over the edge for unpleasant tasting fish.

Never was there such a town as ours, I thought, as we fought on the sandhills with rough boys or dared each other to climb up the scaffolding of half-built houses soon to be called Laburnum Beaches. Never was there such a town,

I thought, for the smell of fish and chips on Saturday evenings; for the Saturday afternoon cinema matinees where we shouted and hissed our threepences away; for the crowds in the streets with leeks in their hats on international nights; for the park, the inexhaustible and mysterious, bushy red-Indian hiding park where the hunchback sat alone and the groves were blue with sailors. The memories of childhood have no order, and so I remember that never was there such a dame school as ours, so firm and kind and smelling of galoshes, with the sweet and fumbled music of the piano lessons drifting down from up-stairs to the lonely schoolroom, where only the sometimes tearful wicked sat over un-done sums, or to repeat a little crime— the pulling of a girl's hair during geog-raphy, the sly shin kick under the table during English literature. Behind the school was a narrow lane where only the oldest and boldest threw pebbles at win-dows, scuffled and boasted, fibbed about their relations—

"My father's got a chauffeur."

"What's he want a chauffeur for? He hasn't got a car."

"My father's the richest man in the town."

"My father's the richest man in Wales."

"My father owns the world."

And swapped gob-stoppers for slings, old knives for marbles, kite strings for foreign stamps.

The lane was always the place to tell your secrets; if you did not have any, you invented them. Occasionally now I dream that I am turning out of school into the lane of confidences when I say to the boys of my class, "At last, I have a real secret."

"What is it—what is it?"

"I can fly."

And when they do not believe me, I flap my arms and slowly leave the ground only a few inches at first, then gaining air until I fly waving my cap level with the upper windows of the school, peering in until the mistress at the piano screams and the metronome falls to the ground and stops, and there is no more time.

And I fly over the trees and chimneys of my town, over the dockyards skim-ming the masts and funnels, over Inker-man Street, Sebastopol Street, and the street where all the women wear men's caps, over the trees of the everlasting park, where a brass band shakes the leaves and sends them showering down on to the nurses and the children, the cripples and the idlers, and the garden-ers, and the shouting boys: over the yel-low seashore, and the stone-chasing dogs, and the old men, and the singing sea.

The memories of childhood have no order, and no end.

◇◇◇◇◇◇◇◇◇◇◇◇◇◇◇◇◇◇◇◇◇◇◇◇◇◇◇◇◇◇◇

FOR DISCUSSION

1. Thomas writes that the town of his birth was "an *ugly*, *lovely* town." Does he stress the "ugly" or the "lovely" aspect of the town? Explain.

2. Precisely what did the outside world of Wales mean to the author? What was his childhood "front"? Enumerate the "terrors and the treasures" of the park. Describe some of the daily visitors to the park.

3. What were some of the ordeals a young boy had to undergo to be initiated into the secret societies? What particular ordeal did the author choose?

4. What particular experiences does the author describe which have something in common with the experiences of every young boy?

5. In what particular way does the au-

thor connect the events of his childhood with the dreams of manhood? Is it true that childhood memories often form the substance of later dreams? Discuss.

FOR APPRECIATION

1. Select and study those passages from the essay which effectively show that a child views the world as touched with magic.

2. Read aloud two or three paragraphs. Try to capture the rhythm and the singing quality of his prose.

3. By his use of imagery Thomas *suggests* reality; he does not describe it *literally*. Study the following expressions for their power of suggestion and state to what particular sense they appeal: the sea is *white-horsed and full of fishes; storybook tall hats and red flannel petticoats; Wales with its wild names like peals of bells in the darkness; I think she read the newspaper, but we always said she read the Wizard; tall terrible half-people who rode on nightmares through my bedroom; I used to dawdle on half holidays along the bent and Devon-facing shore; tram that shook like iron jelly; gaunt pier (with its) skeleton legs; the groves were blue with sailors; the sweet and fumbled music of the piano lesson.*

❖❖❖❖❖

THE ROMANCE OF ORTHODOXY

GILBERT K. CHESTERTON

Chesterton's ORTHODOXY is a mature book, but it is also an important book. The selection given below must "be chewed and digested"; but it will well repay study, for it is one of the finest passages Chesterton has written and one of the best in modern prose. Chesterton has a way of compressing a whole movement, an entire century, in one sentence. Here we have the fine gold of Chesterton's thought and style; a brief but brilliant synthesis of the balance and romance of Orthodoxy as the sane and permanent ideal in a fickle and changing universe.

The thesis of Chesterton's ORTHODOXY, written ten years before his conversion to Catholicism, is that "the central Christian theology (sufficiently expressed in the Apostles' Creed) is the best root and energy of sound ethics." Christianity represents a new balance that constitutes a liberation. The idea of the pagan balance, as expressed by the best Greeks and Romans, was to enforce moderation by getting rid of extremes. Christianity combined in a perfect balance furious opposites. "The more

I considered Christianity," writes G. K., "the more I felt that while it had established a law and order, the chief aim of that order was to give room for good things to run wild."

This was the big fact about Christian ethics; the discovery of the new balance. Paganism had been like a pillar of marble, upright because proportioned with symmetry. Christianity was like a huge and ragged and romantic rock, which, though it sways on its pedestal at a touch, yet, because its exaggerated excrescences exactly balance each other, is enthroned there for a thousand years. In a Gothic cathedral the columns were all different, but they were all necessary. Every support seemed an accidental and fantastic support; every buttress was a flying buttress. So in Christendom apparent accidents balanced. Becket[1] wore a hair shirt under his gold and crimson, and there is much to be said for the combination; for Becket got the benefit of the hair shirt while the people in the street got the benefit of the crimson and gold. It is at least better than the manner of the modern millionaire, who has the black and the drab outwardly for others, and the gold next his heart. But the balance was not always in one man's body as in Becket's; the balance was often distributed over the whole body of Christendom. Because a man prayed and fasted on the Northern snows, flowers could be flung at his festival in the Southern cities; and because fanatics drank water on the sands of Syria, men could still drink cider in the orchards of England. This is what makes Christendom at once so much more perplexing and so much more interesting than the Pagan empire; just as Amiens Cathedral is not better but more interesting than the Parthenon.[2] If anyone wants a modern proof of all this, let him consider the curious fact that, under Christianity, Europe (while remaining a unity) has broken up into individual nations. Patriotism is a perfect example of this deliberate balancing of one emphasis against another emphasis. The instinct of the Pagan empire would have said, "You shall all be Roman citizens, and grow alike; let the German grow less slow and reverent; the Frenchman less experimental and swift." But the instinct of Christian Europe says, "Let the German remain slow and reverent, that the Frenchman may the more safely be swift and experimental. We will make an equipoise out of these excesses. The absurdity called Germany shall correct the insanity called France."

Last and most important, it is exactly this which explains what is so inexplicable to all the modern critics of the history of Christianity. I mean the monstrous wars about small points of theology, the earthquakes of emotion about a gesture or a word. It was only a matter of an inch; but an inch is everything when you are balancing. The Church

[1] BECKET—St. Thomas à Becket was both the Chancellor of the realm and later Archbishop of Canterbury under Henry II. He was murdered in his Cathedral by four retainers of the King because he consistently opposed Henry's encroachments upon the rights of the Church. See *The Canterbury Tales* of Chaucer and T. S. Eliot's *Murder in the Cathedral*.

"The Romance of Orthodoxy" from *Orthodoxy* by G. K. Chesterton, copyright, 1908, 1935, by G. K. Chesterton, reprinted by permission of Dodd, Mead & Company, Inc., and John Lane The Bodley Head Limited, London.

[2] PARTHENON—The Doric temple of Athena, perfect product of Greek architecture.

could not afford to swerve a hair's breadth on some things if she was to continue her great and daring experiment of the irregular equilibrium. Once let one idea become less powerful and some other idea would become too powerful. It was no flock of sheep the Christian shepherd was leading, but a herd of bulls and tigers, of terrible ideals and devouring doctrines, each one of them strong enough to turn to a false religion and lay waste the world. Remember that the Church went in specifically for dangerous ideas; she was a lion tamer. The idea of birth through a Holy Spirit, of the death of a divine being, of the forgiveness of sins, or the fulfillment of prophecies, are ideas which, anyone can see, need but a touch to turn them into something blasphemous or ferocious. The smallest link was let drop by the artificers of the Mediterranean, and the lion of ancestral pessimism burst his chain in the forgotten forests of the north.[3] Of these theological equalisations I have to speak afterwards. Here it is enough to notice that if some small mistake were made in doctrine, huge blunders might be made in human happiness. A sentence phrased wrong about the nature of symbolism would have broken all the best statues in Europe.[4] A slip in the definitions might stop all the dances; might wither all the Christmas trees or break all the Easter eggs. Doctrines had to be defined within strict limits, even in order that man might enjoy general human liberties. The Church had to be careful, if only that the world might be careless.

This is the thrilling romance of Orthodoxy. People have fallen into a foolish habit of speaking of orthodoxy as something heavy, humdrum, and safe. There never was anything so perilous or so exciting as orthodoxy. It was sanity: and to be sane is more dramatic than to be mad. It was the equilibrium of a man behind madly rushing horses, seeming to stoop this way and to sway that, yet in every attitude having the grace of statuary and the accuracy of arithmetic. The Church in its early days went fierce and fast with any warhorse; yet it is utterly unhistoric to say that she merely went mad along one idea, like a vulgar fanaticism. She swerved to left and right, so exactly as to avoid enormous obstacles. She left on one hand the huge bulk of Arianism,[5] buttressed by all the worldly powers to make Christianity too worldly. The next instant she was swerving to avoid an orientalism,[6] which would have made it too unworldly. The orthodox Church never took the tame course or accepted the conventions; the orthodox Church was never respectable. It would have been easier to have accepted the earthly power of the Arians. It would have been easy, in the Calvinistic seventeenth century, to fall into the bottomless pit of predestination. It is easy to be a madman; it is easy to be a heretic. It is

[3] THE SMALLEST LINK . . . FORGOTTEN FORESTS OF THE NORTH—Chesterton is referring here to the doctrines of Calvin and Knox. The southern peoples of Europe are by nature light-hearted; the Nordics rather somber and gloomy.

[4] BROKEN ALL THE BEST STATUES IN EUROPE—A reference to the Iconoclast heresy of the eighth and ninth centuries which rejected the use and veneration of images.

[5] ARIANISM—The first great heresy in the Church. It denied the Divinity of Christ and was condemned at the Council of Nicea in 325. It had the support of most of the rulers in Christendom.

[6] ORIENTALISM—No doubt Chesterton has reference here to the Monophysite heresy which taught there was one nature in Christ, the Divine Nature. The Orientals, in general, tend toward the mystical, the hidden, the other-worldly, and the occult. The Western mind is more practical.

always easy to let the age have its head; the difficult thing is to keep one's own. It is always easy to be a modernist; as it is easy to be a snob. To have fallen into any of those open traps of error and exaggeration which fashion after fashion and sect after sect set along the historic path of Christendom—that would indeed have been simple. It is always simple to fall; there are an infinity of angles at which one falls; only one at which one stands. To have fallen into any one of the fads from Gnosticism to Christian Science[7] would indeed have been obvious and tame. But to have avoided them all has been one whirling adventure; and in my vision the heavenly chariot flies thundering through the ages, the dull heresies sprawling and prostrate, the wild truth reeling but erect.

[7] GNOSTICISM TO CHRISTIAN SCIENCE—The Gnostics were the first heretics to deny the Divinity of Christ. St. John's Gospel was written to prove them wrong. Christian Science denies the existence of cause and effect outside the mind. Hence Christian Scientists argue that all organic sickness is imaginary.

◇◇◇◇◇◇◇◇◇◇◇◇◇◇◇◇◇◇◇◇◇◇◇◇◇◇◇◇◇◇◇

FOR DISCUSSION

1. In his G. K. Chesterton, Maurice Evans analyzes Chesterton's style and discovers that he is: (a) a writer of brilliant epigrams; (b) a master of the paradox; (c) an artist in the use of vivid imagery and alliteration; (d) a writer with a deep love for solid and concrete things; (e) an author capable of packing into a single sentence an historical movement, a life of a man, or an entire book. Keeping the above elements in mind, choose sentences from the passage which clearly illustrate each of these qualities.

2. Chesterton has defined a paradox as "a truth standing on its head to attract attention." Discuss this definition and apply some of Chesterton's paradoxes to it.

3. G. K. gives us example after example to prove his point that Christianity is the discovery of a new balance. Enumerate some of these examples.

4. What are the differences between classical and Gothic architecture? Do you think the Gothic better expresses the Catholic ideal? Explain. What is a flying buttress?

5. Discuss these statements: (a) "It is at least better than the manner of the modern millionaire, who has the black and drab outwardly for others, and the gold next his heart." (b) "To be sane is more dramatic than to be mad."

6. Study carefully the figure which Chesterton uses to illustrate the romance of Orthodoxy. Is it vivid, striking, graphic, powerful, convincing? Why?

7. In the passage Chesterton refers to St. Thomas à Becket. Is there any similarity between Thomas à Becket and Thomas More? Explain.

PROJECTS

1. Make an outline and write a formal essay on the topic: "To be a Christian is more thrilling than to be a pagan."

2. Read Chesterton's essays "On Lying in Bed" and "Laughter." Discuss their humor and satire.

RELATED READING

Read at least the first chapter of Chesterton's Autobiography. An interesting introduction to Chesterton, Belloc, and Maurice Baring is given in Calvert Alexander's The Catholic Literary Revival.

MODERN DRAMA

After languishing for almost a century—except for the sparkling operettas of Gilbert and Sullivan—English drama began to revive in the 1890's. The daring challenges to unjust social conditions and existing moral standards, which were presented in Ibsen's realistic dramas, served as models for the social criticisms of Galsworthy and G. B. Shaw. In his *Strife, Justice,* and *The Silver Snuff-box,* Galsworthy re-echoed some of the thinking of the Norwegian dramatist's *The Doll's House, Hedda Gabler,* and *The Idiot.* On the other hand, disapproval of the realistic themes of Ibsen were expressed in the romantic fantasies of James M. Barrie.

Ibsen introduced the intellectual discussion to the stage, and G. B. Shaw seized upon this device to preach his own social doctrines. Shaw had been a prominent leader of the Fabian Society, a group of English Socialists who advanced their own ideas on social and economic problems. But soon Shaw evolved his own theory of man and society, and with wit, satire, and prejudice pronounced judgment on all things under the sun. He satirized war in *Arms and the Man;* made fun of medical science in *The Doctor's Dilemma;* and suggested in *Pygmalion* that the "higher" classes in England were superior to the "lower" only in their pronunciation of words. One of his finest plays, *St. Joan,* has as its theme the justification of Protestant individualism.

Shaw was a brilliant technician, an egotist whose wit was sparkling and whose satire was biting, trenchant and, at times, uproariously funny. But he substituted for revealed religion the religion of the Superman,[1] with himself as its prophet and high priest. Graham Greene has written of Shaw that "he plays the fool at enormous length. . . . Ideas are adopted for the sake of their own paradoxes and are discarded as soon as they cease to startle. He gives his audience a sense of intellectual activity—but they often imagine they have exercised their brains when they had really done no more than strain their eyes at the startling convolutions of a tumbler."

SIR JAMES BARRIE

In the early years of the century, Sir James Barrie was a popular fiction writer who used his native Scotland as a background for realistic stories with a tragic undertone. His *Sentimental Tommy* and his sensitive biography of his mother, *Margaret Ogilvy,* are the best of his prose works. But Barrie is known today for his dramas. He openly protested against the realism of the Ibsen imitators and was prompted to write plays with fancy and romance as their theme. Barrie will always remain immortal as the creator of *Peter Pan* with its Never-Never Land. The best of his longer dramas are *Dear Brutus* and *Quality Street.* These plays, as well as his one-act plays, have been frequently presented in the movies and on television.

[1] SUPERMAN—Shaw conceived God as a growing Life Force, an imperfect power striving to become perfect. As the instrument of the Life Force, man must help God perfect Himself. Shaw said that man should so live that when he dies God is in man's debt.

THE IRISH THEATER MOVEMENT

One of the most interesting movements in the history of twentieth century drama has been the rise and success of the Irish National Theater. Stirred by the political nationalistic movement and by the activities of "little theater" groups throughout the world, several writers of Irish nationality undertook to preserve Irish folklore and the traditional legends through the medium of the drama. Led by William B. Yeats and Lady Gregory, they took over the Abbey Theater, from which have come some of the finest plays and actors of our century.

John M. Synge, who died at the early age of thirty-eight, has been the most successful in capturing the real spirit of the Irish peasant. He took realistic material and clothed it in a language which expressed verbal beauty, irony, and satire. In his best known one-act play, *Riders to the Sea*, he wrote of the humble folk whose daily battle is with the sea. Because he lived among them, Synge caught that blending of stark realism and mysticism which belongs to those who spend their days close to the beauty and despair of the sea.

The realism of the English and continental drama influenced the Abbey Group in 1910, and the poetic and imaginative dramas of Yeats were heard less and less. Other Irish playwrights were discovered, the most conspicuous of whom was Sean O'Casey. His *Juno and The Paycock* brought him international fame, as did his *Plough and the Stars*. These tragicomedies present the seamiest side of London tenement life in alternating scenes of sparkling comedy and stark tragedy. Contrary to what one might expect, O'Casey is not a Catholic nor a Christian, but an atheist. According to his biography, published in 1954, he appeared to have deep sympathies for the Reds and a deep hatred for the traditional Faith of his homeland.

Other well-known Irish dramatists whose plays have been witnessed in recent years by the Abbey Theater audience are: George Shields, Frank O'Connor, Lord Dunsany, Daniel Corkery, Paul Vincent Carroll, Lennox Robinson, and Bryan MacMahon.

THE POETS IN THE THEATER

Poetry, the traditional medium of expression in the fifteenth, sixteenth, seventeenth, and eighteenth centuries, returned to the drama in the 1930's, when the theater ceased to be the exclusive hunting ground for the realists. The poetic movement was stimulated with the publication of T. S. Eliot's *Murder in the Cathedral*. The drama is an old Greek tragedy transplanted into medieval Canterbury. Eliot wrote the play to aid restoration of Canterbury Cathedral in England, where the murder of St. Thomas à Becket actually occurred in 1170. Eliot opens the play with Thomas' return to England. The women of Canterbury, in the manner of the old Greek chorus, chant a warning of death and destruction which will follow his homecoming. Uncertain about the course he will follow, Thomas listens to four tempters who offer him in turn: easy living and good times; temporal authority, which he had once enjoyed as Chancellor before he was forced to flee from

England; leadership of a titled group out to overthrow the throne; and finally, martyrdom. The climax of the play is the dramatic murder scene at the high altar. As in the Elizabethan play, the poetry builds a unique atmosphere, much more effective than lights and setting.

In 1932 the *Group Theater* was formed for the express purpose of reviving poetry in drama, especially through the expression of religious themes. Recalling the days when the Church and dramatic art were on friendly terms, English Churchmen (mostly Anglican) encouraged the poet-dramatist by commissioning plays for performance under Church sponsorship. It might be said that the stage followed where the Church led. Christopher Fry, like Eliot, wrote his earliest plays for religious festivals, as did other poetic dramatists such as Ronald Duncan, Norman Nicholson, Anne Ridler, and James Birdie. It is important to note that such impressive religious plays as Fry's A *Sleep of Prisoners* and *The Boy with a Cart* have been frequently and successfully staged by amateur dramatic groups, and by college and high school dramatic clubs in the United States—evidence that poetic drama is appreciated by youthful actors and audiences.

Fry's *The Lady's Not for Burning* was made famous by the acting of John Gielgud, Britain's outstanding actor. In this play Fry demonstrated a talent for pouring out phrases like liquid silver. His poetic imagination, like a rocket, illuminates a galaxy of words and metaphors which recall the great Elizabethans. The play combines the piety as well as the raucous realism of the medieval morality and mystery play—but throughout it all there is the breath of spiritual sensitivity.

Two noted playwrights of more recent years are Noel Coward and a much younger author, Terence Rattigan. Perhaps Noel Coward is the best craftsman in modern drama. *Journey's End* by R. C. Sherriff is one of the most powerful plays ever written on the theme of war.

◇◇◇◇◇

THIS WAY TO THE TOMB

RONALD DUNCAN

Ronald Duncan's THIS WAY TO THE TOMB *is an excellent example of religious poetic drama which connects the twentieth century with the age of the miracle and morality play. It is written in the form of a masque and an anti-masque. The masque is a study of the fasting and temptations of St. Antony of Ferrata. The anti-masque is a twentieth century satire on materialism in which a set of "hot-gospellers" invade the scene of the saint's death and tomb and assault him as an impostor when he appears to them by means of a miracle. The action of the masque is static; that is, characters are presented, tableau-like, through dialogue,* lighting, and musical accompaniment. The choir presents the theme music which is symbolic of the internal struggle of the main character.

The following selection has been taken from the Masque with some portions of the drama synopsized and others given in the original. As you read, be aware that the characters are not portrayed for their own sake but as symbols of some abstract quality or vice. The theme of this spiritual drama is that pride is the root of all evil and self-deception, and constitutes the greatest stumbling block to sanctity.

The setting of the Masque is on the Island of Zante, off the coast of Greece. The time is the fourteenth century. Antony, recently Abbot of Santa Ferrata, has voluntarily resigned his position; and with three novices, Marcus, the peasant; Julian, the poet; and Bernard, the scholar, has retired to the Island of Zante, vowing to fast and meditate until he can find the complete peace of Christ. Antony and the novices have already been on the Island for three years as the following scene opens:

MARCUS. Bernard, how long do you think we will be here?

BERNARD. Are you homesick, too? Why don't you and Julian return? I can look after Father Antony.

MARCUS. Oh no! I don't want to leave here. And besides how could you look after him? He needs more than arguments which you give him, he needs food which I prepare; and songs and poems which Julian sings and recites. I don't want to leave here. I was only frightened that Father Antony might be returning soon.

BERNARD. Why, what makes you think that?

MARCUS. The way Father Antony stays up on the hill under that dead tree and sits for hours and hours; and looks at everything as if he were saying good-bye to it and will never see it again. I am sure that he must be thinking of going back to be the great Abbot of St. Ferrata again, with the endless proces-

sion of coaches and important portfolios.[1]

BERNARD. No! he will not do that; he has more pride than to give in, you needn't worry, he'll not return.

MARCUS. I am glad of that, for if he were to return, it would not do him good. Too many banquets, too much worry, endless worry. And I'd see little of him then, he in the study, I in the kitchen.

BERNARD. He won't return. Leave that to me.

MARCUS. Yes, he listens to you. It is strange, he'll listen to you and nobody else. But I can't understand how a man can spend his life reaching such a proud position, the most influential abbot in the whole state and such luxury, and leave it all to become the hermit of Zante. He was used to a busy life, a grand life. Now he sits on an old board

[1] PORTFOLIOS—Here meaning important functions.

Condensation of *This Way to the Tomb* by Ronald Duncan, published 1946 by Faber and Faber Limited, London, reprinted by their permission and that of the author.

under a dead tree and doesn't even read.
I cannot understand it.

BERNARD. Can't you? Why the
whole Church is talking about his renunciation, his sacrifice, and already
calling him a saint.

MARCUS. But what does he do up
there forever, sitting, not even reading
or writing, just staring at something I
cannot see.

BERNARD. He is meditating, thinking.

MARCUS. But if it does not make him
happy, why does he do it?

BERNARD. You must ask him that at
supper. Shall I light the candles?

MARCUS. No, not till Father Antony
comes. We are short of them. I wonder what has happened to him and
where's Julian?

BERNARD. He's coming now, alone.

[Enter JULIAN.]

JULIAN. Oh it's cold out. I can't
find him.

MARCUS. Have you been down to the
beach?

JULIAN. I have been everywhere, to
all the usual places, and called and
called but there's no answer.

MARCUS. I think I know where he
might be: up on the hill by the waterfall. For the other day, yesterday, when
we were walking back, he stopped there
a long time just looking into the water.
I asked him what he could see. And he
said he could see a proud old man full of
fear and full of desire. That's where
he'll be. Let's go and see if he's there
for it's getting dark and cold; and he
may have fallen asleep or is sick. He's
had nothing to eat since breakfast.
Throw a log on the fire, Julian, so that
the cell is warm when we come in again.

[They walk across the darkening
stage.]

BERNARD. You lead the way, Marcus.

JULIAN. Is it far?

MARCUS. Just up by the waterfall.
Listen!

BERNARD. I can't hear anything.

JULIAN. Nor I.

MARCUS. Listen.

JULIAN. Well, what do you hear?

MARCUS. A voice. Father Antony's
voice. Let's hurry: perhaps there is
something wrong. I'll call. Father Antony!

[They go off back stage calling. Light
picks out FATHER ANTONY seated on
rock back stage centre.]

VOICE. Father Antony.

ANTONY. Yes, I am coming. Agnus
Dei, qui tollis peccata mundi: miserere
nobis. Yes, yes, yes.
Lord, pity me, for with imperfect faith
I am full of fear.
I have gleaned the dry stubble of sixty
years,
And have gathered up my faith like a
hungry widow;
And stored each grain of Thy Love in
repeated prayer;
Yet I have nothing, but myself talking
to myself
And the fear.
Dear Christ, how fear's hurricane
threshes my heart hollow
And winnows my faith till it is lost with
the waste
The grain swept away with the straws of
doubt.
And now they are coming to call me to
supper.
And the sun drops like a coin
Into the hands of those who have
begged another day, another to-mor-
row.
For me, another night nearer. Nearer?
Thy Love to enfold me, as closely as the
finch's wings
Fit the finch's body as it alights;
Or nearer the greedy earth's slow diges-
tion?

Yes, I am coming.
Coming from birth going to death.
My mind wandering and my breath
Failing, as the leaves fall, are falling,
    have fallen . . .
[*Enter* MARCUS.]
MARCUS. Father Antony!
ANTONY. Yes, my son.
MARCUS. It's time for supper, and it's
getting dark. You will get a cold sitting
here by the water. Is there nobody with
you?
ANTONY. No.
MARCUS. We thought we heard
voices and so we called to you. Here's
Bernard, and Julian. We all thought
something might be wrong.
ANTONY. No, nobody was here
It was I you heard talking.
I speak my thoughts aloud.
For I find that in silent meditation
The agile mind conjures an awkward
    conclusion
Into a comfortable cushion

On which the soul sits like a lap dog
And dreams. Dreams the frantic hare is
    caught
Then barks and wakes to disappoint-
    ment.
As a poet, Julian, you'll have found that
    pleasant dreams
Often make unpleasant poetry.
And Bernard will agree, too,
That though dreams and prophecy
Contribute to theology,
Their drunken logic will not mix
With strict philosophy.
And who'd drive a straight furrow, Mar-
    cus,
With one eye on his fame and the other
    on his glory?
Dreams mirror our self-esteem,
    behind the glass—is another story.
MARCUS. Father, the sun has set.
ANTONY. Let us pray.
[*They kneel and pray. Then they rise
    and chant Gregorian.*]
MARCUS. Father.

ANTONY   (*as if in a trance*)
"Tandem mente serenatus
Latitat ergastulo." [2]
Which is what I have sought.
It is what we all seek
Each according to his own perception
Seeks his idea of God.
I, in my cloister, my brother, in uniform;
Some seek it in power
Some seek it in prayer
Some think it is plenty
Some think it is poverty.
If it were in power, I should have
    found it.
For an Abbot is powerful, but I did not
    find it:
For me it was not in power.
If it were in plenty, I should have
    found it
For I was rich but I did not find it:
For me it was not in riches.
If it were in poverty, I should have
    found it
For I have nothing but I have not
    found it:
For me, it is not in poverty.
In power there is the desire to be more
    powerful
And the fear of being disobeyed.
In wealth there is the desire to be more
    wealthy
And the fear of being cheated.
And in poverty there is the pride of pov-
    erty
And in prayer the pride of prayer.
Only he who has found God
Can believe in God.
Only he who has belief can find.
Perhaps He is not in power or plenty
Neither in poverty nor in prayer.
Perhaps God has no permanent reality [3]

[2] Loosely translated these lines mean: At
last the mind has found serenity as it is lost in
meditation.
[3] NO PERMANENT REALITY—The author
does not mean here that God has no objective
existence; but that man, rightly or wrongly, can
conceive God in various ways.

But exists as and when we create Him.
Through the labor of humility
He is born in the death of pride.
Marcus, you look sad. I did not mean
    to make you miserable. And even
    our lively Julian is half asleep. So get
    along, the three of you, and have a
    hot supper.

(*The novices entreat him to return to
his cell and take some food, but he replies:*)

ANTONY. No, Marcus, I shall eat no
    more.
I will stay alone, here by the water
Till death relieves me
Or Christ receives me;
This, my soul's resolved upon.
    Oh my sons, how can I tell you
What I have known forever
And yet not known before;
Known in my heart and known in my
    bone
As an indissoluble certainty:
But to my mind, that was not fact
    enough.
Age makes us slow-witted and this is an
    advantage;
For then, our heart's sure beat can com-
    pete
With the mind's argument
And give the soul back its first dumb
    certainty. . . .
You see, Marcus, as old men we face
    death
With our souls in pawn to our business
And none of our business accomplished.
For living is an endless chain of inter-
    locking actions,
Distractions disguised as important ac-
    tions.
I will do this, when I have done that.
I will do that, when I have done this.
And so on and so on and so on.
The Abbot's wealth was the Abbot's dis-
    traction.

The Hermit's poverty is the Hermit's
    distraction.
For here on Zante, our poverty and sim-
    plicity
Can be made a distraction also. . . .
And this, Bernard, this I do: to find my
    first certainty and final faith.
By fasting with no attachment to life,
I pray I may lose my fear of death.
By contemplating the object of my
    dreams
I hope to shed my desire.
By meditating on my intentions
I hope to achieve my object
Which is the comfort of His Compas-
    sion
And the simple peace within the tumult
    of the mystery.
It may well be that it is a sin to seek so
    high.
That may well be: Yes, certainly.
But I do not think either the love of
    woman or the love of God
Comes to a man like an unexpected let-
    ter.
Love must be dredged out of our own
    souls
    By our own effort:
And this is the only love we know
Though it may not be the only love we
    receive.
And I believe Christ lies in my heart
    like a green leaf in an old book
Revealed, if only I could find my heart,
    open it and look.

*(Antony announces that he wishes to
be left entirely alone for a week. Marcus is sad at Antony's decision to fast,
since he can only serve him by cooking.
Julian, after singing to Father Antony,
leaves him. Bernard and Julian see
Marcus climbing across a hill with hot
soup. They follow Marcus and dissuade him from tempting Antony to eat.*

*Bernard says that he is glad that Antony
has made his vow, for now he is a saint.
Marcus, Julian, and Bernard move to
the front of the stage and kneel. The
light moves from them to the rock on
which Antony is sitting.)*

ANTONY. . . . What are my fears?
Of all my fears it is loneliness which
    wears
The worst mask, with lips bitten and
    bleeding, and its eyes red with tears.
Loneliness is the soul's wilderness and I
Am alone, Jesu, unless in Thy Company,
Which I have known—when you had
    left me,
For when you were with me, I was not
    lonely;
But then I, full of the strength of you,
    denied I needed you; and I
Blind fool and prig and called a saint
Am lonely now, and cry of this com-
    plaint.
SOPRANO SOLO. *(sings off stage)*
*Oh proud heart take pity on that part
of me*
Which lies in you as your own lost heart.
ANTONY. . . .
How I fear Time: which is all change.
Oh, where is there a fair face found to
    challenge
Advancing age, with his full equipage
    and cortege,[4] and not surrender?
I have pressed my lips upon
Helen's[5] mouth and kissed a skele-
    ton . . .
. . . so I've put off this introspection[6]
On my lean soul, which I have fed

    [4] EQUIPAGE AND CORTEGE—Its laden car-
riage and train of attendants. Here these
words meaning long years of experience,
memories, and recollections.
    [5] HELEN'S MOUTH—Helen of Troy who
stands for the beauty, youth, and vitality of
young womanhood. It means here figuratively
that nothing remains of the bloom of youth
but shrivelled vitality.
    [6] INTROSPECTION—Self-analysis.

Worse than a dog, fattened it on flattery instead
Of starving it, thrown it whole joints of
vanity, and taken it to bed,
And suckled it on the cream of self-
deception
—Which for any soul or dog spells indigestion. . . .
I have described myself and fears
Because the one is made up of the
other;
And because clarity towards one's conscience is a kind of prayer.

(*While a chorus off stage is singing
Latin verses, the light leaves Antony and
shines on the three novices. Kneeling,
Marcus and Julian express their own
concern about Antony. The light now
shines on the rock where Antony prays
to be released from all desires. The
light is taken off the rock and three
figures are lit.*)

JULIAN. Marcus, wake up Marcus.
It's Sunday today. The week's past.
We can go and see Father Antony this
morning.

MARCUS. I cannot go.

JULIAN. Why? Bernard and I are
going.

MARCUS. I am too weak to go.

JULIAN. We'll carry you.

MARCUS. No. Julian you are not well
enough.

JULIAN. But Bernard can—there is
nothing wrong with Bernard. He's
strong enough. Bernard, help me to
carry Marcus. (*They move off to center of stage, carrying* MARCUS.)

BERNARD. We should not take Marcus up to see Father Antony.

JULIAN. Why, you know how he has
looked forward to going and how he has
worried. What do you mean?

BERNARD. If Father Antony sees him
so ill and weak he may feel obliged to
break his fast on account of Marcus.

JULIAN. And that might upset your
plan of writing the Account of the Fast
of St. Antony. Is that it?

MARCUS. No, Julian; Bernard is right.
It would be unfair to go. I will stay
here. Put me down. I'll stay here in
the shade. (*They put him down tenderly.*)

JULIAN. Shall I stay with you?

MARCUS. No. Father Antony is sure
to ask you to sing to him. It is the body
he punishes; but he will enjoy a song.

JULIAN. I will come back here. Bernard, wait for me, I am too weak to
climb alone.

[*They go off stage and re-enter behind
the rock.*]

ANTONY. Julian, why what is wrong
with you?

JULIAN. I am not well and the hill is
steep.

ANTONY. And where is Marcus?

JULIAN. He is too ill to come.

ANTONY. What is wrong with you
both? You are not eating enough. It is
I who fast, not you. Look at Bernard,
here; he's fit and well.

(*Antony asks Julian to sing a song,
which he does. Bernard then tells
Julian to return to Marcus. Antony approves this.*)

JULIAN. Father, shall I go?

ANTONY. If Marcus is unwell, Julian.
You must be with him; for you two were
always close together. (*Exit* JULIAN.)
It is strange that they are ill.

BERNARD. They do not understand.

ANTONY. Perhaps I should break my
vow for their sake.

BERNARD. Many seed are sown for
one to germinate. It would be a pity to
turn back for their sake.

ANTONY. Yes, it is even possible to

use Mercy to hide our weakness. I am tired, how tired.

BERNARD. Then I will leave you alone to sleep awhile.

ANTONY. I am not alone. Only God can be alone, His Soul
The Sentinel guarding the fragile tent
Of creation against the dark waves of chaos, which bent with inarticulate power roll back spent,
Into a calm nothingness, smoothed by the stroke of His last sacrament.[7]

BERNARD. And yet you are alone; for you have rinsed your heart
of fear and of desire, and therefore are free of time;
For by desire and fear we're chained to time, and by time locked within each other's hearts.
You are as the stone is to the water, within yet apart
From the endless river, which flows forever; For you, within Time
Perceive the continuity of Time;
And in that, find tranquillity, climb to the bank, apart.

ANTONY. Tranquillity? I have not found tranquillity.
And I am weary. I have turned over my heart
Like a coin in my pocket. I now know my nature.
But to know oneself is not to change one's nature.
It is to discover extreme disparity,[8]
And the dishonesty of a Prince's court
Where vanity's the fashion and flattery's an art.
The soul's a state in miniature;
In each of us all: king, slave, both rich and poor. . . .
(In this exhausted condition, Antony is now tempted by Gluttony and Lechery or Lust. He has no difficulty in overcoming the temptation of both because, as he says, they have no subtlety; their temptations are too obvious. Then Lechery says:)

LECHERY. I'll go St. Antony
But there is one to follow me
Who has your own subtlety.
[She takes up a statuesque position front stage near Gluttony. Enter MARCUS from back stage.]

ANTONY. You, Marcus?
Not my own Marcus.

MARCUS. Yes, Father.

ANTONY. Why, you were like a son from my own body.

MARCUS. I am your own body.
Pity me or what is left of me.
And eat for my sake which is your sake.

ANTONY. Would you, too, tempt me?

MARCUS. Not to Gluttony, nor to Lechery.
I speak for moderation, and balance, poise.
What evil was there in your ascetic[9] life?
Was it not a modest sacrament?
Now by fasting you feed your mind to gluttony;
Eat this and revive me, your body's agony.

BERNARD. (who is standing in the shadow)
Moderation is a word, Father:
Compromise is its meaning.

MARCUS. Unless you eat, I must die
For I am your body, Antony.

ANTONY. I will not eat.
[MARCUS lies down as dead.]
(A young woman, SIGHT, now enters and asks why Antony is starving his

[7] SACRAMENT—Here it signifies the power and presence of the omnipotent God.
[8] DISPARITY—Inequality; differences in character and kind.

[9] ASCETIC LIFE—A life of strict discipline and self-denial.

*senses to the beauties of the universe.
Antony rejects her and becomes blind.
Julian enters, and when Antony asks
him to sing, Julian replies that he is too
weak, and that Antony could not hear
anyway, for Antony is deaf. Then Julian
lies near Marcus. Now that his external
senses are dead, Antony feels that he
may hear his soul's unanswered question. Next enters a beautiful young
woman to whom Antony would now
give his heart. But the young woman,
TIME, replies that it is too late. She re-
moves her mask and shows the face of
an old crone. She moves off to the
other figures.)*

ANTONY. Well, now all's said. Our
    rime's run out
To the last grain, the last hour. And
    who's power or strength
Can add a second to a minute's length
    and fill this glass again?
Even the sea's vanquished by little
    waves leading the tide in and out.
Over and over; the mower every blade
    devours. But with strength
I would not add to my life's length for
    life's preface is all pain
The plot disappointment: the end, pity,
    self-pity.
From that: free! At last I'm out of
    fear's tight halter
And desire's short tether, both are bro-
    ken behind me.
They cannot retie me, for by my own
    effort, I am free.
From the tangle of teasing distractions
    which blinded me
Hid Christ from me. Now my will is
    my protection
And Christ alone my Master to Whose
    sweet tyranny
I will submit, and can submit, for I am
    free!

*[The figure of Bernard comes from
    the shadows.]*

BERNARD. Except, Antony, from me.
From me you are not free.
    ANTONY. What horror now invades
my hollow heart
And parades the vacant cities of my
    brain?
    BERNARD. Antony, don't you recog-
nize me?
I, Bernard, your nearest, closest friend?
With whom you've shared the secrets of
    your soul
And to whom your mind's intricate cir-
    cuit
Is as a garden maze to the gardener?
And Antony, have I not always walked
Before you, beside you and behind you
As your retinue, your substantial
    shadow
For you to lean upon and lead you on?
Was it not Bernard who made you Ab-
    bot
And did I not lead you from there, to
    here?
And have I not stood by you in your
    fast?
Why, your whole life's a pilgrimage
    to me:
By way of meditation you approached
    me
And by privation you have fed me.
Marcus, the peasant, was your own body
    and your sight
And Julian, the poet, your sensual appe-
    tite.
They weakened as you starved, and died.
But look, Antony, I, Bernard, thrived.
And stand still, the shadow at your side,
For Antony, I am your own Pride.
    ANTONY. Must a man crawl to God?
    BERNARD. Pride is self-respect
By your own effort, your own thought,
    you have reached here, where
There is no fear and no desire, the
    whole earth floats upon your reason.

ANTONY. But where's the peace of
God? It is all loneliness except
In Him whom I have sought,
Within this loneliness of thought and
    by this fire
Which has burnt out my heart and my
    desire—and left self-love and reason.
Now blind and deaf and weak to death,
    I cannot struggle more
And therefore I am free, without liberty
Imprisoned in my sad soul's captivity:
    my own mind, a tomb for me;
My own pride the punctual jailer of my
    pride's own tyranny.
Dear Christ, Who stands above me and
    beyond me, restore
My sight before I die, that I may see
    your sweet humility
And know you love me. Dear Christ,
    I sink in my own misery.
For pity's sake lift me into your Mercy,
    Mercy!
    [At this word MERCY, Bernard falls by
        Marcus and Julian.]
VOICE. Come, Antony, you are weak
and tired.
Put down your burden of pride.
Kneel humbly, rise gladly.
    [Antony kneels, then stands.]
ANTONY. Father!
VOICE. My son.
ANTONY. Father, I have found you.
VOICE. My son, I had not lost you.

ANTONY. Is this death, Father?
VOICE. There is no death, my son.
ANTONY. Nor is there fear in you
Nor desire in you.
VOICE. Soon you will be free in me.
ANTONY. Soon Father?
VOICE. Soon as you have renounced
all pride
And eaten of humility.
ANTONY. That I will do gladly.
VOICE. Then go back to your body
and eat what your poor servants brought
to you. Then follow me.
ANTONY. Marcus, wake up, my son,
Give me the food you brought me.
MARCUS. Praise be to God, Father,
we thought you were dead.
ANTONY. There is no death, my son.
[ANTONY takes the cup, drinks, then
    stands.]
Jesu, I come.

⟨⟩⟨⟩⟨⟩⟨⟩⟨⟩⟨⟩⟨⟩⟨⟩⟨⟩⟨⟩⟨⟩⟨⟩⟨⟩⟨⟩⟨⟩⟨⟩

FOR DISCUSSION

1. Reread the play and study those lines
and situations which indicate that Bernard
stands for the vice of Pride. By what
means does Bernard try to persuade Antony to break his fast? Why do Marcus
and Julian sicken and die while Bernard
grows strong? What ultimately causes
Bernard to die?

2. When did you first discover that Marcus stood for Antony's body and Julian for his senses? Why did not Antony find God in poverty, in power, in plenty?

3. The two great obstacles to Antony's peace with Christ *seemed* to be fear and desires. Enumerate these fears and desires. Why did not Antony find Christ when he had rid himself of fear and desires? Explain. What finally gave him the peace of Christ?

4. As a Christian, would you say that a person should despise his body and his senses? Or should he see them as something blessed by God to lead him to God? Discuss.

5. Explain the deep spiritual significance of the following passages: "We face death with our souls in pawn to our business and none of our business accomplished." "The soul's a state in miniature: king, slave, both rich and poor." (I, Bernard) "always walked before you, beside you and behind you as your retinue, your substantial shadow for you to lean upon and lead you on." "Must a man crawl to God?" "There is no death, my son."

FOR APPRECIATION

1. There are many beautiful figures of speech and symbols in the poem. Select several of these and study their meaning. For example, consider the following: *I have gleaned the dry stubble of sixty years, and have gathered up my faith like a hungry widow; fear's hurricane threshes my heart hollow and winnows my faith . . . the grain's swept away with the straws of doubt; the silent mind conjures awkward conclusions into a comfortable cushion; Christ lies in my heart like a green leaf in an old book.*

2. Give the literal meaning of the following figurative expressions: *earth's slow digestion; dreams are our self-esteem; behind the glass is another story; life's preface is all pain, the plot disappointment: the end, self-pity; my own mind a tomb for me.*

PROJECT

Read the anti-masque of *This Way to the Tomb.* Note its biting satire, its sophisticated expression so different from the beautiful imagery of the masque, and the portrayal of the breezy, superficial attitude toward religion and all things. Try to understand how the author pictures Pride as the greatest sin of the modern age, as it is of all ages.

RELATED READING

Many excellent religious poetic plays have been written. Among them are Christopher Fry's *The Boy with a Cart* and W. H. Auden's *For the Time Being.*

THE WINSLOW BOY

TERENCE RATTIGAN

This play tells with warm sympathy about a fight to clear the name of a young boy who has been charged with theft. He has already been expelled from school, and the case is supposedly closed. The action centers not so much on the boy himself as on the older members of the family. The question arises as to whether the father is justified in using the family savings for costly legal proceedings. There is the further question of whether or not Ronnie is guilty after all. And guilty or not, with all their effort and sacrifice his family may not be able to prove his innocence.

Aside from the main plot, there is much of interest to be looked for in The Winslow Boy. The time of the play is set just before World War I (1914–1918) when great social unrest was gripping England and other democratic nations of the western world. Women were demanding suffrage (the privilege to vote) with men, and the members of their movement were hence called Suffragettes.

Catherine Winslow is active in the Suffragette cause. She represents modern woman, in that she is alert, intelligent, and well-informed. Keenly interested in the political and economic problems of her country, she is at the same time thoroughly warm-hearted and feminine, as her relationships with her family and with John Watherstone and Desmond Curry attest.

Oddly enough, the man who best realizes Catherine's great abilities and the impending success of the Suffragette cause is Sir Robert Morton, the proud and aristocratic lawyer for the Winslow family. As a strict conservative, he is opposed to everything Catherine stands for, yet between the two there exists a bond of understanding—a deep interest in humanity and justice for the unprotected.

The play is based on a famous actual happening—the Archer-Shee case at the Royal Navy College at Osborne. It retells a story that Englishmen recall with pride—the demand made by decent people that "Right be done."

SCENE: *The drawing room of a house in Courtfield Gardens, South Kensington, on a morning in July, at some period not long before the war of 1914–1918.*

The furnishings betoken solid but not undecorative upper middle-class comfort.

A glass door at back leads, down a few iron steps, into a tiny, rectangular garden. Through this door and the windows on either side of it, we can see the back of a row of exactly similar houses, with exactly similar glass doors leading, down exactly similar iron steps, into exactly similar gardens. In the center of the wall L. is a door which leads to the hall and front door. In the opposite wall, downstage, another door leads into the dining room. There is a fireplace R.C., concealed at the moment by a very ornate fire screen.

On the rise of the curtain A BOY of about fourteen, dressed in the uniform of an Osborne naval cadet, is discovered perched on an arm of the sofa, staring, with wide, unblinking eyes, at his neatly polished boots. There is something rigid and tense in his attitude, and his face is blank and without expression.

There is the sound of someone in the hall. THE BOY is on his feet at once, swiveled to face the hall door. As the sound comes nearer, he looks despairingly round, as if contemplating flight. An elderly maid VIOLET comes in, with dustpan and brush, and stops in astonishment at sight of him.

VIOLET. Master Ronnie!

RONNIE (*with ill-managed sang-froid [1]*). Hello, Violet.

VIOLET. Why, good gracious! We weren't expecting you back till Thursday.

RONNIE. Yes, I know.

VIOLET. Why ever didn't you let us

[1] SANG-FROID (sän' frwä')—Literally "cold blood," this expression means "nonchalant manner."

know you were coming, you silly boy? Your mother should have been at the station to meet you. The idea of a child like you wandering all over London by yourself! I never did. And where's your trunk and your tuck box?

RONNIE. Upstairs. The taximan carried them up—

VIOLET. Taximan? You took a taxi? [RONNIE *nods.*] All by yourself? Well, I don't know what little boys are coming to, I'm sure. What your father and mother will say, I don't know—

RONNIE. Where are they, Violet?

VIOLET. Church, of course.

RONNIE (*vacantly*). Oh, yes. It's Sunday, isn't it?

VIOLET. What's the matter with you? What have they been doing to you at Osborne?

RONNIE (*sharply*). What do you mean?

VIOLET. They seem to have made you a bit soft in the head, or something. Well—I suppose I'd better get your unpacking done—Mr. Dickie's been using your chest of drawers for all his dress clothes and things. I'll just clear 'em out and put 'em on his bed—that's what I'll do. He can find room for 'em somewhere else.

RONNIE. Shall I help you?

VIOLET (*scornfully*). I know *your* help. With *your* help I'll be at it all day. No, you just wait down here for your mother and father. They'll be back in a minute.

[RONNIE *nods and turns hopelessly away.* VIOLET *looks at his retreating back, puzzled.*]

Well?

RONNIE (*turning*). Yes?

VIOLET. Don't I get a kiss or are you too grown-up for that now?

RONNIE. Sorry, Violet. (*He goes up to her and is enveloped in her ample bosom.*)

VIOLET. That's better. My, what a big boy you're getting! (*She holds him at arm's length and inspects him.*) Quite the little naval officer, aren't you?

RONNIE (*smiling forlornly*). Yes. That's right.

VIOLET. Well, well—I must be getting on—(*She goes out.*)

[RONNIE, *left alone, resumes his attitude of utter dejection. He takes out of his pocket a letter in a sealed envelope. After a second's hesitation, he opens it, and reads contents. The perusal appears to increase his misery. Again as if acting on some obscure impulse, he takes a fountain pen from his breast pocket, and appears, for a moment, to be about to write something on the letter. Then he shakes his head, hopelessly, and puts pen back in his pocket.*]

The sound of church bells, coming from quite close, suddenly breaks the silence. RONNIE *looks up and hurriedly puts letter back into envelope. He makes for a moment as if to tear it up; then changes his mind again, and puts it back in his pocket. He gets up and takes two or three quick steps toward hall door. Then he stops, uncertainly. The church bells continue their dismal clanging.* RONNIE *is evidently near tears. He sits down again, suddenly,*

as if his knees failed to support him.

There is the sound of voices in the hall. RONNIE *jumps to his feet; then, with a strangled sob, runs to garden door, and down the iron steps into the garden.*

The hall door opens and the rest of the Winslow family file in. They are ARTHUR *and* GRACE—*Ronnie's father and mother—and* DICKIE *and* CATHERINE—*his brother and sister. All are carrying prayer books, and wear that faintly unctuous, after-church air.* ARTHUR *leans heavily on a stick. He is a man of about sixty, with a rather deliberately cultured patriarchal air.* GRACE *is about ten years younger, with the faded remnants of prettiness.* DICKIE *is an Oxford undergraduate, large, noisy, and cheerful.* CATHERINE, *approaching thirty, has an air of masculinity about her which is at odd variance with her mother's intense femininity.*]

GRACE (*as she enters*)—But he's so old, dear. From the back of the church you really can't hear a word he says—

ARTHUR. He's a good man, Grace.

GRACE. But what's the use of being good, if you're inaudible?

CATHERINE. A problem in ethics for you, Father.

[ARTHUR *has sat down heavily, in what is evidently his favorite armchair. He looks round at the open garden door.*]

ARTHUR. There's a draft, Grace.

[GRACE *goes to door and closes it.*]

GRACE. Oh, dear—it's coming on to rain. I hoped we could have had our coffee in the garden.

DICKIE. I'm on Mother's side. The old boy's so doddery now he can hardly finish the course at all. I timed him to-day. It took him seventy-five seconds dead from a flying start to reach the pulpit, and then he needed the whip coming round the bend. I call that pretty bad going.

ARTHUR. I'm afraid I don't think that's very funny, Richard.

DICKIE. Oh, don't you, Father?

ARTHUR. Doddery though Mr. Jackson may seem now, I very much doubt if when he was at Oxford he failed in his pass mods.[2]

DICKIE (aggrieved). Dash it—Father—you promised not to mention that again this vac—

GRACE. You did, you know, Arthur.

ARTHUR. There was a condition to my promise—if you remember—that Dickie should provide me with reasonable evidence of his intentions to remedy his lapse—

DICKIE. Well, haven't I, Father? Didn't I stay in all last night—a Saturday night—and work?

ARTHUR. You stayed in, Dickie. I would be the last to deny that.

GRACE. You *were* making rather a noise, dear, with that old gramophone of yours. I really can't believe you could have been doing much work with that going on all the time—

DICKIE. Funnily enough, Mother, it helps me to concentrate—

ARTHUR. Concentrate on what?

DICKIE. Work, of course.

ARTHUR. That wasn't exactly what you appeared to be concentrating on when I came down to fetch a book—sleep, may I say—having been rendered out of the question, by the hideous sounds emanating from this room.

DICKIE. Edwina and her father had just looked in on their way to the Grantchesters' dance—they only stayed a minute.

GRACE. What an idiotic girl that is!

2 PASS MODS—Examinations.

Oh, sorry, Dickie—I was forgetting. You're rather keen on her, aren't you?

ARTHUR. You would have had ample proof of that fact, Grace, if you had seen them in the attitude in which I found them last night.

DICKIE. We were practicing the Bunny Hug.

GRACE. The what, dear?

DICKIE. The Bunny Hug. It's the new dance.

CATHERINE (helpfully). It's like the Turkey Trot—only more dignified.

GRACE. Oh, I thought that was the Tango?

DICKIE. No. More like a Fox Trot, really. Something between a Boston Glide and a Kangaroo Hop.

ARTHUR. We appear to be straying from the point. Whatever animal was responsible for the posture I found you in with Edwina Gunn has little to do with the fact that to my certain knowledge you have not yet done one single stroke of work so far this vacation.

DICKIE. Oh. Well, I do work awfully fast, you know—once I get down to it.

ARTHUR. Indeed? That assumption can hardly be based on experience, I take it?

DICKIE. Dash it, Father! You are laying in to me this morning.

ARTHUR. I think it's time you found out, Dickie, that I'm not spending two hundred pounds a year keeping you at Oxford, merely that you may make a lot of useless friends and learn to dance the Bunny Hop.

DICKIE. Hug, Father.

ARTHUR. The exact description of the obscenity is immaterial.

GRACE. Father's quite right, you know, dear. You really have been going the pace a bit, this vac.

DICKIE. Yes, I know, Mother—but the season's nearly over now—

GRACE (*with a sigh*). I wish you were as good about work as Ronnie.

DICKIE (*hotly*). I like that! That's a bit thick, I must say! All Ronnie ever has to do with his footling little homework is to add two and two, while I—

ARTHUR. Ronnie, may I remind you, is at least proving a good deal more successful in adding two and two than you were at his age.

DICKIE (*now furious*). Oh, yes! I know. *I* know. *He* got into Osborne and *I* failed. That's going to be brought up again—

GRACE. Nobody's bringing it up, dear—

DICKIE. Oh, yes, they are. It's going to be brought up against me all my life. Ronnie's the good little boy, I'm the bad little boy. You've just stuck a couple of labels on us that nothing on earth is ever going to change.

GRACE. Don't be so absurd, dear—

DICKIE. It's not absurd. It's quite true. Isn't it, Kate?

[CATHERINE *looks up from a book, she has been reading in the corner.*]

CATHERINE. I'm sorry, Dickie. I haven't been listening. Isn't what quite true?

DICKIE. That in the eyes of Mother and Father nothing that Ronnie does is ever wrong, and nothing that I do is ever right?

CATHERINE (*after a pause*). If I were you, Dickie dear, I'd go and have a nice lie-down before lunch.

DICKIE (*after a further pause*). Perhaps you're right. (*He goes toward hall door.*)

ARTHUR. If you're going to your room I suggest you take that object with you. (*He points to a gramophone—1912 model, with horn—lying on a table.*) It's out of place in a drawing room.

[DICKIE, *with an air of hauteur, picks up gramophone and carries it to door.*] It might help you to concentrate on the work you're going to do this afternoon.

[DICKIE *stops at door, then turns slowly.*]

DICKIE (*with dignity*). That is out of the question, I'm afraid.

ARTHUR. Indeed? Why?

DICKIE. I have an engagement with Miss Gunn.

ARTHUR. On a Sunday afternoon? You're escorting her to the National Gallery, no doubt?

DICKIE. No. The Victoria and Albert Museum. (*He goes out with as much dignity as is consistent with the carrying of a very bulky gramophone.*)

GRACE. How stupid of him to say that about labels! There's no truth in it at all —is there, Kate?

CATHERINE (*deep in her book*). No, Mother.

GRACE (*noticing rain outside*). Oh, dear, it's simply pelting. What are you reading, Kate?

CATHERINE. Len Rogers' Memoirs.

GRACE. Who's Len Rogers?

CATHERINE. A Trades Union leader.

GRACE. Does John know you're a Radical?

CATHERINE. Oh, yes.

GRACE. And a Suffragette? [3]

CATHERINE. Certainly.

GRACE (*with a smile*). And he still wants to marry you?

CATHERINE. He seems to.

GRACE. Oh, by the way, I've told him to come early for lunch—so that he can have a few words with Father first.

CATHERINE. Good idea. I hope you've been primed, have you, Father?

[3] SUFFRAGETTE—A Suffragette demanded *woman suffrage*—the right of women to vote. Some of them created public disturbances, either in mobs or individually, to help advertise their campaign.

ARTHUR (*who has been nearly asleep*). What's that?

CATHERINE. You know what you're going to say to John, don't you? You're not going to let me down and forbid the match, or anything, are you? Because I warn you, if you do, I shall elope— (*Behind his chair, she kisses top of his head.*)

ARTHUR (*taking her hand*). Never fear, my dear. I'm far too delighted at the prospect of getting you off our hands at last.

CATHERINE (*smiling*). I'm not sure I like that "at last."

GRACE. Do you love him, dear?

CATHERINE. John? Yes, I do.

GRACE. You're such a funny girl. You never show your feelings much, do you? You don't behave as if you were in love.

CATHERINE. How does one behave as if one is in love?

ARTHUR. One doesn't read Len Rogers. One reads Byron.

CATHERINE. I do both.

ARTHUR. An odd combination.

CATHERINE. A satisfying one.

GRACE. I meant—you don't talk about him much, do you?

CATHERINE. No. I suppose I don't.

GRACE (*sighing*). I don't think you modern girls have the feelings our generation did. It's this New Woman attitude.

CATHERINE. Very well, Mother. I love John in every way that a woman can love a man, and far, far more than he loves me. Does that satisfy you?

GRACE (*embarrassed*). Well, really, Kate darling—I didn't ask for anything quite like that— (*To* ARTHUR.) What are you laughing at, Arthur?

ARTHUR (*chuckling*). One up to the New Woman.

GRACE. Nonsense. She misunderstood me, that's all. (*At window.*) Just look at the rain! (*Turning to* CATHERINE.) Kate, darling, does Desmond know about you and John?

CATHERINE. I haven't told him. On the other hand, if he hasn't guessed, he must be very dense.

ARTHUR. He *is* very dense.

GRACE. Oh, no. He's quite clever, if you really get under his skin.

ARTHUR. Oddly enough I've never had that inclination.

GRACE. I think he's a dear. Kate, darling, you *will* be kind to him, won't you?

CATHERINE (*patiently*). Yes, Mother. Of course, I will.

GRACE. Poor Desmond! He's really a very good sort— (*She breaks off suddenly and stares out of window.*) Hullo! There's someone in our garden.

CATHERINE (*coming to look*). Where?

GRACE (*pointing*). Over there, do you see?

CATHERINE. No.

GRACE. He's just gone behind that bush. It was a boy, I think. Probably Mrs. Williamson's awful little Dennis.

CATHERINE (*leaving window*). Well, whoever it is must be getting terribly wet.

GRACE. Why can't he stick to his own garden?

[*There is a ring of a bell outside in hall.*]

Was that the front door?

CATHERINE. It sounded like it.

GRACE (*after listening*). Yes. It's John. (*To* CATHERINE.) Quick! In the dining room!

CATHERINE. All right. (*She dashes across to dining-room door.*)

GRACE. Here! You've forgotten your bag. (*She darts to table and picks it up.*)

ARTHUR (*startled*). What on earth is going on?

GRACE (*in a stage whisper*). We're leaving you alone with John. When you've finished, cough or something.

ARTHUR (*testily*). What do you mean, or something?

GRACE. I know. Knock on the floor with your stick—three times. Then we'll come in.

ARTHUR. You don't think that might look a trifle coincidental?

GRACE. Sh!

[*She disappears from view as hall door opens and* VIOLET *comes in.*]

VIOLET (*announcing*). Mr. Watherstone.

[JOHN WATHERSTONE *comes in. He is a man of about thirty, dressed in an extremely well-cut morning coat and striped trousers, an attire which, though excused by church parade, we may well feel has been donned for this occasion.*]

ARTHUR. How are you, John? I'm very glad to see you.

JOHN. How do you do, sir?

ARTHUR. Will you forgive me not getting up? My arthritis has been troubling me rather a lot lately.

JOHN. I'm very sorry to hear that, sir. Catherine told me it was better.

ARTHUR. It was, for a time. Now it's worse again. Do you smoke? (*He indicates cigarette box.*)

JOHN. Yes, sir. I do. Thank you. (*He takes cigarette, adding hastily.*) In moderation, of course.

ARTHUR (*with a faint smile*). Of course.

[*Pause, while* JOHN *lights his cigarette and* ARTHUR *watches him.*]

Well, now, I understand you wish to marry my daughter?

JOHN. Yes, sir. That's to say, I've proposed to her and she's done me the honor of accepting me.

ARTHUR. I see. I trust when you corrected yourself, your second statement

647

wasn't a denial of your first? [JOHN *looks puzzled.*] I mean, you do *really* wish to marry her?

JOHN. Of course, sir.

ARTHUR. Why, of course? There are plenty of people about who don't wish to marry her.

JOHN. I mean, of course, because I proposed to her.

ARTHUR. That, too, doesn't necessarily follow. However, we don't need to quibble. We'll take the sentimental side of the project for granted. As regards the more practical aspect, perhaps you won't mind if I ask you a few rather personal questions?

JOHN. Naturally not, sir. It's your duty.

ARTHUR. Quite so. Now your income, I take it, is derived chiefly from your army pay?

JOHN. Yes, sir. With an allowance from my father.

ARTHUR. Exactly. Now, as a subaltern in the West Berkshires, you would be earning something, I gather, in the neighborhood of two hundred and sixty-three pounds a year, plus sundry allowances?

JOHN (*surprised*). Yes, sir. That's exactly right—

ARTHUR. And your father's allowance would be roughly, I imagine, about twenty-four pounds a month?

JOHN (*more surprised*). Again, exactly the figure.

ARTHUR. Quite so. So, in all—what with your army pay and your father's allowance your total income is, at a vague computation, not far off five hundred and fifty-one pounds a year.

JOHN. Er—yes, sir. Not far off.

ARTHUR. Well, well. It all seems perfectly satisfactory. I really don't think I need delay my congratulations any longer. (*He extends his hand, which* JOHN *gratefully takes.*)

JOHN. Thank you, sir, very much.

ARTHUR. I must say, it was very good of you to be so frank and informative.

JOHN. Not at all.

ARTHUR. Your answers to my questions deserve an equal frankness from me about Catherine's own affairs. I'm afraid she's not—just in case you thought otherwise—the daughter of a rich man.

JOHN. I didn't think otherwise, sir.

ARTHUR. Good. Well, now— (*He suddenly cocks his head on one side and listens. There is the sound of a gramophone playing "You Made Me Love You" from somewhere upstairs.*) Would you be so good as to touch the bell? [JOHN *does so.*] Thank you. Well, now, continuing about my own financial affairs. The Westminster Bank pays me a small pension—three hundred and fifty, to be precise—and my wife has about two hundred a year of her own. Apart from that we have nothing, except such savings as I've been able to make during my career at the bank. The interest from which raises my total income to about nine hundred and fifty pounds per annum.

[VIOLET *comes in.*]

VIOLET. You rang, sir?

ARTHUR. Yes, Violet. My compliments to Mr. Dickie and if he doesn't stop that cacophonous[4] hullaballoo at once, I'll throw him and his infernal machine into the street.

VIOLET. Yes, sir. What was that word again? Cac—something—

ARTHUR. Never mind. Say anything you like, only stop him.

VIOLET. Very good, sir. (*She goes out.*)

ARTHUR. Now, in addition to the ordinary expenses of life in Courtfield Gardens, I have to maintain two sons—one

---

[4] CACOPHONOUS (kă·kŏf′ô nŭs)—Discordant.

at Osborne, and the other at Oxford—neither of whom, I'm afraid, will be in a position to support themselves for some time to come—one, because of his extreme youth and the other because of—er—other reasons. [*Gramophone stops suddenly.*] So, you see, I am not in a position to be very lavish as regards Catherine's dowry.

JOHN. No, sir. I quite see that.

ARTHUR. I propose to settle on her twelve hundred and fifty pounds, which represents precisely one sixth of my total capital.

JOHN. I call that very generous, sir.

ARTHUR. Not as generous as I would have liked, I'm afraid. However—as my wife would say—beggars can't be choosers.

JOHN. Exactly, sir.

ARTHUR. Well, then, if you're agreeable to that arrangement, I don't think there's anything more we need discuss.

JOHN. No, sir.

ARTHUR. Splendid. (*Pause.* ARTHUR *takes his stick and raps it with an air of studied unconcern, three times on floor. Nothing happens.*)

JOHN. Pretty rotten weather, isn't it?

ARTHUR. Yes. Vile. (*He raps again. Again nothing happens.*) Would you care for another cigarette?

JOHN. No, thank you, sir. I'm still smoking.

[ARTHUR *takes up his stick to rap again, then thinks better of it. He begins to struggle out of his chair.*]

ARTHUR. Would you mind?

[JOHN *goes to his assistance.*]

Thank you so much.

[ARTHUR *goes slowly but firmly to dining-room door, which he throws open—in apparent surprise.*]

Well, imagine that! My wife and daughter are in here, of all places. Come in, Grace. Come in, Catherine. John's here.

[GRACE *comes in, with* CATHERINE *behind.*]

GRACE. Why, John—how nice! (*She shakes hands.*) My, you do look a swell! Doesn't he, Kate darling?

CATHERINE. Quite one of the Knuts.

[*Pause.* GRACE *is unable to repress herself.*]

GRACE (*coyly*). Well?

ARTHUR. Well, what?

GRACE. How did your little talk go?

ARTHUR (*testily*). I understood you weren't supposed to know we were having a little talk?

GRACE. Oh, you are infuriating! Is everything all right, John?

[JOHN *nods, smiling.*]

GRACE. Oh, I'm so glad. I really am.

JOHN. Thank you, Mrs. Winslow.

GRACE. May I kiss you? After all, I'm practically your mother now.

JOHN. Yes. Of course. (*He allows himself to be kissed.*)

ARTHUR. While I, by the same token, am practically your father, but if you will forgive me—

JOHN (*smiling*). Certainly, sir.

ARTHUR. Grace, I think we might allow ourselves a little modest celebration at luncheon. Will you find me the key of the cellars? (*He goes out through hall door.*)

GRACE. Yes, dear. (*She turns at door. Coyly.*) I don't suppose you two will mind being left alone for a few minutes, will you? (*She follows* ARTHUR *out.*)

[JOHN *goes to* CATHERINE *and kisses her.*]

CATHERINE. Was it an ordeal?

JOHN. I was scared to death.

CATHERINE. My poor darling—

JOHN. The annoying thing was that I had a whole lot of neatly turned phrases ready for him and he wouldn't let me use them.

CATHERINE. Such as—?

JOHN. Oh—how proud and honored I was by your acceptance of me, and how determined I was to make you a loyal and devoted husband—and to maintain you in the state to which you were accustomed—all that sort of thing. All very sincerely meant.

CATHERINE. Anything about loving me a little?

JOHN (*lightly*). That I thought we could take for granted. So did your father, incidentally.

CATHERINE. I see. (*She gazes at him.*) Goodness, you do look smart!

JOHN. Not bad, is it? Poole's.

CATHERINE. What about *your* father? How did he take it?

JOHN. All right.

CATHERINE. I bet he didn't.

JOHN. Oh, yes. He's been wanting me to get married for years. Getting worried about grandchildren, I suppose.

CATHERINE. He disapproves of me, doesn't he?

JOHN. Oh, no. Whatever makes you think that?

CATHERINE. He has a way of looking at me through his monocle that shrivels me up.

JOHN. He's just being a colonel, darling, that's all. All colonels look at you like that. Anyway, what about the way your father looks at me! Tell me, are all your family as scared of him as I am?

CATHERINE. Dickie is, of course; and Ronnie, though he doesn't need to be. Father worships him. I don't know about Mother being scared of him. Sometimes, perhaps. I'm not—ever.

JOHN. You're not scared of anything, are you?

CATHERINE. Oh, yes. Heaps of things.

JOHN. Such as?

CATHERINE (*with a smile*). Oh— they're nearly all concerned with you.

[RONNIE *looks cautiously in at window door. He now presents a very bedraggled and woebegone appearance, with his uniform wringing wet, and his damp hair over his eyes.*]

JOHN. You might be a little more explicit—

RONNIE (*in a low voice*). Kate!

[CATHERINE *turns and sees him.*]

CATHERINE (*amazed*). Ronnie! What on earth—?

RONNIE. Where's Father?

CATHERINE. In the cellar. I'll go and tell him—

RONNIE (*urgently*). No, don't. Please, Kate, don't!

[CATHERINE, *halfway to door, stops, puzzled.*]

CATHERINE. What's the trouble, Ronnie?

[RONNIE *trembling on the edge of tears, does not answer her.*] (*She approaches him.*) You're wet through. You'd better go and change.

RONNIE. No.

CATHERINE (*gently*). What's the trouble, darling? You can tell me. [RONNIE *looks at* JOHN.] You know John Watherstone, Ronnie? You met him last holidays, don't you remember?

[RONNIE *remains silent, obviously reluctant to talk in front of a comparative stranger.*]

JOHN (*tactfully*). I'll disappear.

CATHERINE (*pointing to dining room*). In there, do you mind?

[JOHN *goes out quietly.* CATHERINE *gently leads* RONNIE *into the room.*] Now, darling, tell me. What is it? Have you run away?

[RONNIE *shakes his head, evidently not trusting himself to speak.*] What is it then?

[RONNIE *pulls out the document from his pocket which we have seen him reading earlier, and slowly hands it to her.* CATHERINE *reads it quietly.*]

CATHERINE. Oh!

RONNIE. I didn't do it.

[CATHERINE *rereads the letter in silence.*]

Kate, I didn't. Really, I didn't.

CATHERINE (*abstractedly*). No, darling. (*She seems uncertain of what to do.*) This letter is addressed to Father. Did you open it?

RONNIE. Yes.

CATHERINE. You shouldn't have done that—

RONNIE. I was going to see if I could alter it. Then I was going to tear it up. Then I heard you come in from church and ran into the garden—I didn't know what to do—

CATHERINE (*still distracted*). How brutal of them to send you up alone!

RONNIE. They sent a petty officer up with me. He was supposed to wait and see Father, but I sent him away. (*Indicating letter.*) Kate—shall we tear it up, now?

CATHERINE. No, darling.

RONNIE. We could tell Father term had ended two days sooner—?

CATHERINE. No, darling.

RONNIE. It's all lies, Kate. It's all lies. I didn't do it—really I didn't—

[DICKIE *comes in from hall. He does not seem surprised to see* RONNIE.]

DICKIE (*cheerfully*). Hullo, Ronnie, old lad. How's everything?

[RONNIE *turns away from him.*]

CATHERINE. You knew he was here?

DICKIE. Oh, yes. His trunks and things are all over our room. Trouble?

CATHERINE. Yes.

DICKIE. I'm sorry.

CATHERINE. You stay here with him. I'll find Mother.

DICKIE. All right.

[CATHERINE *goes out by hall door. There is a pause.*]

DICKIE. What's up, old chap?

RONNIE. Nothing.

DICKIE. Come on—tell me.

RONNIE. It's all right.

DICKIE. Have you been sacked? [RONNIE *nods.*] Bad luck. What for?

RONNIE. I didn't do it!

DICKIE (*reassuringly*). No, of course, you didn't.

RONNIE. Honestly, I didn't.

DICKIE. That's all right, old chap. No need to go on about it. I believe you.

RONNIE. You don't.

DICKIE. Well, I don't know what it is they've sacked you for, yet—

RONNIE (*in a low voice*). Stealing.

DICKIE (*evidently relieved*). Oh, is that all? Good heavens! I didn't know they sacked chaps for *that*, these days.

RONNIE. I didn't do it.

DICKIE. Why, good heavens, at Repton we used to pinch everything we could jolly well lay our hands on.[5] All of us. I remember there was one chap—Carstairs his name was—captain of cricket, believe it or not—absolutely nothing was safe with him—nothing at all. Pinched a squash racket of mine once, I remember— (*He has quietly approached* RONNIE, *and now puts his arm on his shoulder.*) Believe me, old chap, pinching's nothing. Nothing at all. I say—you're a bit damp, aren't you?

RONNIE. I've been out in the rain—

DICKIE. You're shivering a bit, too, aren't you? Oughtn't you to go and change? I mean, we don't want you catching pneumonia—

RONNIE. I'm all right.

[GRACE *comes in, with* CATHERINE *following.* GRACE *comes quickly to* RONNIE, *who, as he sees her, turns away*

[5] WE USED TO . . . HANDS ON. Dickie does not yet realize what his brother is accused of. He remembers that at boarding school the boys helped themselves to each other's belongings— and quarreled over it—as if they were members of the same family.

from DICKIE *and runs into her arms.*]

GRACE. There, darling! It's all right, now.

[RONNIE *begins to cry quietly, his head buried in her dress.*]

RONNIE (*his voice muffled*). I didn't do it, Mother.

GRACE. No, darling. Of course you didn't. We'll go upstairs now, shall we, and get out of these nasty wet clothes.

RONNIE. Don't tell Father.

GRACE. No, darling. Not yet. I promise. Come along, now. (*She leads him towards door held open by* CATHERINE.) Your new uniform, too. What a shame! (*She goes out with him.*)

DICKIE. I'd better go and keep "cave" [6] for them. Ward off the old man if he looks like going upstairs. [CATHERINE *nods.*] (*At door.*) I say—who's going to break the news to him eventually? I mean, someone'll have to.

CATHERINE. Don't let's worry about that now.

DICKIE. Well, you can count me out. In fact, I don't want to be within a thousand miles of that explosion. (*He goes out.*)

[CATHERINE *comes to dining-room door, which she opens.* JOHN *comes out.*]

JOHN. Bad news?

[CATHERINE *nods. She is plainly upset, and dabs her eyes with her handkerchief.*]

That's rotten for you. I'm awfully sorry.

CATHERINE (*violently*). How can people be so cruel!

JOHN (*uncomfortably*). Expelled, I suppose?

[*He gets his answer from her silence, while she recovers herself.*]

CATHERINE. How little imagination some people have! Why should they

---

6 KEEP "CAVE"—This is school slang for "keep watch." The Latin word *cave* means *beware*.

---

torture a child of that age, John, darling? What's the point of it?

JOHN. What's he supposed to have done?

CATHERINE. Stolen some money.

JOHN. Oh.

CATHERINE. Ten days ago, it said in the letter. Why on earth didn't they let us know? Just think what that poor little brat has been going through these last ten days up there, entirely alone, without anyone to look after him, knowing what he had to face at the end of it! And then, finally, they send him up to London with a petty officer— Is it any wonder he's nearly out of his mind?

JOHN. It does seem pretty heartless, I know—

CATHERINE. Heartless? It's cold, calculated inhumanity. How I'd love to have that Commanding Officer here for just two minutes! I'd—I'd—

JOHN (*gently*). Darling, it's quite natural you should feel angry about it, but you must remember, he's not really at school. He's in the Service.

CATHERINE. What difference does that make?

JOHN. Well, they have ways of doing things in the Service which may seem to an outsider horribly brutal—and probably are, come to that—but at least they're always scrupulously fair. You can take it from me that there must have been a very full inquiry before they'd take a step of this sort. What's more, if there's been a delay of ten days, it would only have been in order to give the boy a better chance to clear himself—

[*Pause.* CATHERINE *is silent.*]

I'm sorry, Catherine darling. I'd have done better to keep my mouth shut.

CATHERINE. No. What you said was perfectly true—

JOHN. It was idiotically tactless of me to say it, though. I'm sorry.

CATHERINE (*lightly*). That's all right.

JOHN. Forgive me? (*He lays his arm on her shoulder.*)

CATHERINE (*taking his hand*). Nothing to forgive.

JOHN. Believe me, I'm awfully sorry. (*After a pause.*) How will your father take it?

CATHERINE (*simply*). It might kill him—

[*There is the sound of a ring at front door.*]

Oh, heavens! We've got Desmond to lunch. I'd forgotten—

JOHN. Who?

CATHERINE. Desmond Curry—our family solicitor. Oh! (*In a hasty whisper.*) Darling—be polite to him, won't you?

JOHN. Why? Am I usually so rude to your guests?

CATHERINE. No, but he doesn't know about us yet—

JOHN. Who does?

CATHERINE (*still in a whisper*). Yes, but he's been in love with me for years—it's a family joke—

[VIOLET *comes in.*]

VIOLET (*announcing*). Mr. Curry.

[DESMOND CURRY *comes in. He is a man of about forty-five, with a drooping moustache, and the figure of an athlete gone to seed. He has a mildly furtive manner, rather as if he had just absconded with his firm's petty cash, but hopes no one is going to be too angry about it.* JOHN, *when he sees him, cannot repress a faint smile at the thought of his loving Catherine.*]

CATHERINE. Hullo, Desmond. I don't think you know John Watherstone—

DESMOND. No—but, of course, I've heard a lot about him—

JOHN. How do you do? [*He wipes the smile off his face, as he meets*

Catherine's glance. There is a pause.]

DESMOND. Well, well, well. I trust I'm not early?

CATHERINE. No. Dead on time, Desmond—as always.

DESMOND. Capital. Capital.

[*There is another pause, broken by* CATHERINE *and* JOHN *both speaking suddenly at once.*]

CATHERINE. Tell me, Desmond— } (*Simultaneously.*)

JOHN. Pretty ghastly this rain— }

JOHN. I'm so sorry—

CATHERINE. It's quite all right. I was only going to ask how you did in your cricket match yesterday, Desmond?

DESMOND. Not too well, I'm afraid. My shoulder's still giving me trouble— (*There is another pause. At length.*) Well, well. I hear I'm to congratulate you both—

CATHERINE. Desmond—you know?

DESMOND. Violet told me, just now—in the hall. Yes—I must congratulate you both.

CATHERINE. Thank you so much, Desmond.

JOHN. Thank you.

DESMOND. Of course, it's quite expected, I know. Quite expected. Still it was rather a surprise, hearing it like that —from Violet in the hall—

CATHERINE. We were going to tell you, Desmond dear. It was only official this morning, you know. In fact, you're the first person to hear it.

DESMOND. Am I? Am I, indeed? Well, I'm sure you'll both be very happy.

CATHERINE. Thank you, Desmond. } (*Murmuring together.*)

JOHN. Thank you. }

DESMOND. Only this morning? Fancy.

[GRACE *comes in.*]

GRACE. Hullo, Desmond, dear.

DESMOND. Hullo, Mrs. Winslow.

GRACE (*to* CATHERINE). I've got him to bed—

CATHERINE. Good.

DESMOND. Nobody ill, I hope?

GRACE. No, no. Nothing wrong at all—

[ARTHUR *comes in, with two wine bottles under his arm. He rings bell.*]

ARTHUR. Grace, when did we last have the cellars seen to?

GRACE. I can't remember, dear.

ARTHUR. Well, they're in a shocking condition. Hullo, Desmond. How are you? You're not looking well.

DESMOND. Am I not? I've strained my shoulder, you know—

ARTHUR. Well, why do you play these ridiculous games of yours? Resign yourself to the onrush of middle age, and abandon them, my dear Desmond.

DESMOND. Oh, I could never do that. Not give up cricket. Not altogether.

JOHN (*making conversation*). Are you any relation of D. W. H. Curry who used to play for Middlesex?

DESMOND (*whose moment has come*). I *am* D. W. H. Curry.

GRACE. Didn't you know we had a great man in the room?

JOHN. Gosh! Curry of Curry's match?

DESMOND. That's right.

JOHN. Hat trick against the players in —what year was it?

DESMOND. 1895. At Lord's. Twenty-six overs, nine maidens, thirty-seven runs, eight wickets.

JOHN. Gosh! Do you know you used to be a schoolboy hero of mine?

DESMOND. Did I? Did I, indeed?

JOHN. Yes. I had a signed photograph of you.

DESMOND. Yes. I used to sign a lot once, for schoolboys, I remember.

ARTHUR. Only for schoolboys, Desmond?

DESMOND. I fear so—yes. Girls took no interest in cricket in those days.

JOHN. Gosh! D. W. H. Curry—in person. Well, I'd never have thought it.

DESMOND (*sadly*). I know. Very few people would nowadays—

CATHERINE (*quickly*). Oh, John didn't mean that, Desmond—

DESMOND. I fear he did. (*He pats his protuberant stomach.*) This is the main trouble. Too much office work and too little exercise, I fear.

ARTHUR. Nonsense. Too much exercise and too little office work.

[VIOLET *comes in.*]

VIOLET. You rang, sir?

ARTHUR. Yes, Violet. Bring some glasses, would you?

VIOLET. Very good, sir. (*She goes out.*)

ARTHUR. I thought we'd try a little of the Madeira before luncheon—we're celebrating, you know, Desmond—

[GRACE *jogs his arm furtively, indicating Desmond.*]

(*Adding hastily*)—my wife's *fifty-fourth* birthday—

GRACE. Arthur! Really!

CATHERINE. It's all right, Father, Desmond knows—

DESMOND. Yes, indeed. It's wonderful news, isn't it? I'll most gladly drink a toast to the—er—to the—

ARTHUR (*politely*). Happy pair, I think, is the phrase that is eluding you—

DESMOND. Well, as a matter of fact, I was looking for something new to say—

ARTHUR (*murmuring*). A forlorn quest, my dear Desmond.

GRACE (*protestingly*). Arthur, really! You mustn't be so rude.

ARTHUR. I meant, naturally, that no one—with the possible exception of Voltaire—could find anything new to say about an engaged couple—

[DICKIE *comes in.*]

Ah, my dear Dickie—just in time for a

glass of Madeira in celebration of Kate's engagement to John—

[VIOLET *comes in with tray of glasses.*
ARTHUR begins to pour out wine.]

DICKIE. Oh, is that all finally spliced up now? Kate definitely being withdrawn to raise a family? Good egg!

ARTHUR. Quite so. I should have added just now—with the possible exception of Voltaire and Dickie Winslow. (*To* VIOLET.) Take these round, will you, Violet?

[VIOLET *goes first to* GRACE, *then to* CATHERINE, *then to* JOHN, DESMOND, DICKIE *and finally* ARTHUR.]

CATHERINE. Are we allowed to drink our own healths?

ARTHUR. I think it's permissible.

GRACE. No. It's bad luck.

JOHN. We defy augury.[7] Don't we, Kate?

GRACE. You mustn't say that, John dear. I know. You can drink each other's healths. That's all right.

ARTHUR. Are my wife's superstitious terrors finally allayed? Good.

[*Drinks have now been handed round. Toasting.*]

Catherine and John!

[ALL *drink*—CATHERINE *and* JOHN *to each other.* VIOLET *lingers, smiling, in doorway.*]

ARTHUR (*seeing* VIOLET). Ah, Violet. We mustn't leave you out. You must join this toast.

VIOLET. Well—thank you sir.

[*He pours her out a glass.*]

Not too much, sir, please. Just a sip.

ARTHUR. Quite so. Your reluctance would be more convincing if I hadn't noticed you'd brought an extra glass—

VIOLET (*taking glass from* ARTHUR). Oh, I didn't bring it for myself, sir. I brought it for Master Ronnie— (*She extends her glass.*) Miss Kate and Mr.

John. (*She takes a sip, makes a wry face and hands glass back to* ARTHUR.)

ARTHUR. You brought an extra glass for Master Ronnie, Violet?

VIOLET (*mistaking his bewilderment*). Well—I thought you might allow him just a sip, sir. Just to drink the toast. He's that grown-up these days.

[*She turns to go. The others, with the exception of* DESMOND *who is staring gloomily into his glass, are frozen with apprehension.*]

ARTHUR. Master Ronnie isn't due back from Osborne until Thursday, Violet.

VIOLET (*turning*). Oh, no, sir. He's back already. Came back unexpected this morning, all by himself.

ARTHUR. No, Violet. That isn't true. Someone has been playing a joke—

VIOLET. Well, I saw him with my own two eyes, sir, as large as life, sitting on that there sofa, just before you come in from church—and then I heard Mrs. Winslow talking to him in his room—

ARTHUR. Grace—what does this mean?

CATHERINE (*quietly taking charge*). All right, Violet. You can go—

VIOLET. Yes, Miss. (*She goes out.*)

ARTHUR (*to* CATHERINE). Did *you* know Ronnie was back?

CATHERINE. Yes—

ARTHUR. And you, Dickie? [DICKIE *nods.*] Grace?

GRACE (*helplessly*). We thought it best you shouldn't know—for the time being. Only for the time being, Arthur.

ARTHUR (*slowly*). Is the boy very ill? (*No one answers.* ARTHUR *looks from one face to another in bewilderment.*) Answer me, someone! Is the boy very ill? Why must I be cozened[8] like this? Surely I have the right to know. If he's ill I must be with him—

CATHERINE (*steadily*). No, Father. He's not ill.

[7] AUGURY—Signs and omens; superstition.

[8] COZENED—Deceived.

[ARTHUR *suddenly realizes the truth from her tone of voice. Leaning heavily on his stick he sinks on to the arm of a chair.*]

ARTHUR. Will someone tell me what has happened, please?

[GRACE *looks at* CATHERINE *with helpless inquiry.* CATHERINE *nods.* GRACE *takes letter from her dress.*]

GRACE (*timidly*). He brought this letter for you—Arthur.

ARTHUR. Read it to me, please—

GRACE. Arthur—not in front of—

ARTHUR. Read it to me, please.

[GRACE *again looks at* CATHERINE *for advice, and again receives a nod.* ARTHUR *is sitting with his head bowed.* GRACE *begins to read.*]

GRACE (*reading*). "Confidential. I am commanded by My Lords Commissioners of the Admiralty [9] to inform you that they have received a communication

⁹ MY LORDS COMMISSIONERS OF THE ADMIRALTY—The heads of the Royal Navy.

from the Commanding Officer of the Royal Naval College at Osborne, reporting the theft of a five-shilling postal order at the College on the 7th instant, which was afterwards cashed at the post office. Investigation of the circumstances of the case leaves no other conclusion possible than that the postal order was taken by your son, Cadet Ronald Arthur Winslow. My Lords deeply regret that they must therefore request you to withdraw your son from the College." It's signed by someone—I can't quite read his name—

[*She turns away quickly to hide her tears.* CATHERINE *puts a comforting arm on her shoulder.* ARTHUR *has not changed his attitude. There is a pause, during which we can hear sound of a gong in the hall outside.*]

ARTHUR (*at length*). Desmond—be so good as to touch the bell.

[DESMOND *does so. There is another pause, until* VIOLET *comes in.*]

ARTHUR. Violet, will you ask Master

Ronnie to come down and see me, please?

GRACE. Arthur—he's in bed.

ARTHUR. You told me he wasn't ill?

GRACE. He's not at all well.

ARTHUR. Do as I say, please, Violet.

VIOLET. Very good, sir. (*She goes out.*)

ARTHUR. Perhaps the rest of you would go in to luncheon? Grace, would you take them in?

GRACE (*hovering*). Arthur—don't you think—?

ARTHUR (*ignoring her*). Dickie, will you decant that bottle of claret I brought up from the cellar?

DICKIE. Right-o.

ARTHUR. I put the bottle on the table in the hall.

DICKIE. I know. (*He goes out.*)

ARTHUR. Will you go in, Desmond? And John?

[*The* TWO MEN *go out into dining room, in silence.* GRACE *still hovers.*]

GRACE. Arthur?

ARTHUR. Yes, Grace?

GRACE. Please don't—please don't— (*She stops, uncertainly.*)

ARTHUR. What mustn't I do?

GRACE. Please don't forget he's only a child—

[ARTHUR *does not answer her.* CATHERINE *takes* GRACE'S *arm.*]

CATHERINE. Come on, Mother. (*She leads* GRACE *to dining-room door.*)

[*At door* GRACE *looks back at* ARTHUR. *He has still not altered his position and is ignoring her. She goes into dining room, followed by* CATHERINE. ARTHUR *does not move after they are gone, but his hands take a convulsive hold of the handle of his stick. After an appreciable pause there comes a timid knock on door.*]

ARTHUR. Come in.

[RONNIE *appears in doorway. He is in a dressing gown. He stands on threshold.*]

Come in and shut the door.

[RONNIE *closes door behind him.*]

Come over here.

[RONNIE *walks slowly up to* ARTHUR. ARTHUR *gazes at him steadily for some time, without speaking. At length.*]

Why aren't you in your uniform?

RONNIE (*murmuring*). It got wet.

ARTHUR. How did it get wet?

RONNIE. I was out in the garden in the rain.

ARTHUR. Why?

RONNIE (*reluctantly*). I was hiding.

ARTHUR. From me?

[RONNIE *nods.*]

Do you remember once, you promised me that if ever you were in trouble of any sort you would come to me first?

RONNIE. Yes, Father.

ARTHUR. Why didn't you come to me now? Why did you have to go and hide in the garden?

RONNIE. I don't know, Father.

ARTHUR. Are you so frightened of me?

[RONNIE *does not reply.* ARTHUR *gazes at him for a moment, then picks up letter, which is on his lap.*]

In this letter it says you stole a postal order.

[RONNIE *opens his mouth to speak.* ARTHUR *stops him.*]

Now I don't want you to say a word until you've heard what *I've* got to say. If you did it, you must tell me. I shan't be angry with you, Ronnie—provided you tell me the truth. But if you tell me a lie, I shall know it, because a lie between son and father can't be hidden. I shall know it, Ronnie—so remember that before you speak. (*Pause.*) Did you steal this postal order?

RONNIE (*without hesitation*). No, Father. I didn't.

[ARTHUR *takes him by the arms and pulls him violently towards him.*]

ARTHUR (*staring into his eyes*). Did you steal this postal order?

RONNIE. No, Father. I didn't.

[ARTHUR *continues to stare into his eyes for a second, then relaxes and pushes him gently away.*]

ARTHUR. Go on back to bed.

[RONNIE *goes gratefully to door.*]

And in future I trust that a son of mine will at least show enough sense to come in out of the rain.

RONNIE. Yes, Father. (*He disappears.*)

[ARTHUR *gets up quite briskly and goes to telephone in corner of room.*]

ARTHUR (*at telephone*). Hullo. Are you there? (*Speaking very distinctly.*) I want to put a trunk call through, please. A trunk call . . . Yes . . . The Royal Naval College, Osborne . . . That's right . . . Replace receiver? Certainly, dear lady. (*He replaces receiver and then, after a moment's meditation, turns and walks briskly into dining room.*)

ACT II

SCENE: *The same, six months later. It is about six o'clock of a winter evening.*

DICKIE *is winding up his gramophone which, somehow or other, appears to have found its way back into the drawing room. A pile of books and an opened notebook on the table provide evidence of interrupted labors.*

The gramophone, once started, emits a scratchy and muffled rendering of an early ragtime. DICKIE *listens for a few seconds with evident appreciation, then essays a little "pas seul."* [10]

CATHERINE *comes in. She is in evening dress.* DICKIE *switches off gramophone.*

DICKIE. Hullo. Do you think the old man can hear this upstairs?

CATHERINE. I shouldn't think so. I couldn't.

[10] *Essays a little "pas seul"* (pä sûl)—Tries a little solo dancing step.

DICKIE. Soft needle and an old pair of flannel bags down the horn. Is the doctor still with him? [CATHERINE *nods.*] What's the verdict, do you know?

CATHERINE. I heard him say he needed a complete rest.

DICKIE. Don't we all?

CATHERINE (*indicating books*). It doesn't look as if *you* did. He said he ought to go to the country and forget all his worries—

DICKIE. Fat chance there is of that, I'd say.

CATHERINE. I know.

DICKIE. I say, you look a treat. New dress?

CATHERINE. Is it likely? No, it's an old one I've had done up.

DICKIE. Where are you going to?

CATHERINE. Daly's. Dinner first—at Criterion.

DICKIE. Nice. You wouldn't care to take me along with you, I suppose?

CATHERINE. You suppose quite correctly.

DICKIE. John wouldn't mind.

CATHERINE. I dare say not. I would.

DICKIE. I wish I had someone to take me out. In your new Feminist world do you suppose women will be allowed to do some of the paying?

CATHERINE. Certainly.

DICKIE. Really? Then the next time you're looking for someone to chain themselves to Mr. Asquith [11] you can jolly well call on me—

CATHERINE (*laughing*). Edwina might take you out if you gave her the hint. She's very rich—

DICKIE. If I gave Edwina a hint of that sort I wouldn't see her this side of doomsday.

CATHERINE. You sound a little bitter, Dickie dear.

DICKIE. Oh no. Not bitter. Just realistic.

[VIOLET *comes in with an evening paper on a salver.*]

Good egg! *The Star!*

[CATHERINE *makes a grab for it and gets it before* DICKIE.]

VIOLET. You won't throw it away, will you, Miss? If there's anything in it again, Cook and I would like to read it, after you.

[CATHERINE *is hastily turning over the pages, with* DICKIE *craning his head over her shoulder.*]

CATHERINE. No. That's all right, Violet.

[VIOLET *goes out.*]

Here it is. (*Reading.*) "The Osborne Cadet." There are two more letters.

DICKIE. Read them out.

CATHERINE (*reading*). "Sir. I am entirely in agreement with your correspondent, Democrat, concerning the scandalously high-handed treatment by the Admiralty of the case of the Osborne Cadet. The efforts of Mr. Arthur Winslow to secure a fair trial for his son have evidently been thwarted at every turn by a soulless oligarchy—" [12]

DICKIE. "Soulless oligarchy." That's rather good—

CATHERINE. "It is high time private and peaceful citizens of this country awoke to the increasing encroachment——"

DICKIE. "Increasing encroachment"— not so good—

CATHERINE. "Encroachment of their ancient freedom by the new despotism of Whitehall. [13] The compulsory filling in of forms and the enforced adhesion of stamps to Insurance Cards and suchlike

[11] CHAIN THEMSELVES TO MR. ASQUITH — Some Suffragettes attracted attention by handcuffing themselves to lampposts, or to public officials. Herbert Asquith was prime minister from 1908 to 1916.

[12] OLIGARCHY (ŏl'ĭ·gär'kĭ)—Government by a few men.

[13] WHITEHALL—The street where several government offices are located.

bare-faced interferences with our personal liberties—" (*Breaking off.*) Idiot! Social legislation's a different thing altogether—

DICKIE. Only to Socialists. Go on.

CATHERINE (*reading*). "—are, in all conscience, bad enough but may, perhaps, be excused by social necessity"— Sucks, Dickie—"but arbitrary condemnation without trial is another matter. The Englishman's home was once said to be his castle. It seems it is rapidly becoming his prison. Your obedient servant, Liberatatis Amator." [14]

DICKIE. Good for old Amator!

CATHERINE. The other's from "Perplexed." (*Reading.*) "Dear sir. I cannot understand what all the fuss is about in the case of the Osborne Cadet. Surely we have more important matters to get ourselves worked up about than a fourteen-year-old boy and a five-shilling postal order." Silly old fool!

DICKIE. How do you know he's old?

CATHERINE. Isn't it obvious? (*Reading.*) "With the present troubles in the Balkans and a certain major European Power rapidly outbuilding our navy, the Admiralty might be forgiven if it stated that it had rather more urgent affairs to deal with than Master Ronnie Winslow's little troubles. But, on the other hand, the First Lord's answer in the House last Wednesday to the member for Kensington shows that his department has behaved with scrupulous fairness throughout. A further inquiry before the judge advocate of the Fleet has now fully confirmed the original findings that the boy was guilty, and in addition has wasted valuable time and the taxpayer's money. I sincerely trust that this will finally end this ridiculous and sordid little storm in a teacup. I am, sir, etc. Perplexed."

[14] LIBERATATIS AMATOR (lē′bĕr·ȧ·tä′tĭs ă·mä′tōr)—Lover of liberty.

[*Pause.*]

DICKIE (*reading over her shoulder*). "This correspondence must now cease. Editor."

CATHERINE. Oh, dear! How hopeless it seems, sometimes!

DICKIE. Yes, it does, doesn't it? (*Thoughtfully, after a pause.*) You know, old girl—don't give me away to the old man, will you—but the awful thing is, if it hadn't been my own brother, I think I might quite likely have seen "Perplexed's" point.

CATHERINE. Might you?

DICKIE. Well, I mean—looking at it from every angle and all that—it does seem rather a much ado about all. I mean to say—a mere matter of pinching. (*Bitterly.*) And it's all so beastly expensive— Let's cheer ourselves up with some music. (*He sets gramophone going.*)

CATHERINE (*listening to record*). Is that what it's called?

DICKIE. Come and practice a few steps. [CATHERINE *joins him and they dance, in the manner of the period, with arms fully outstretched and working up and down, pump-handle style.*] (*Surprised.*) I say! Jolly good!

CATHERINE. Thank you, Dickie.

DICKIE. Who taught you? John, I suppose?

CATHERINE. No. I taught John, as it happens—

DICKIE. Feminism—even in love? [CATHERINE *nods, smiling. Pause, while they continue to dance.*] When's the happy date now?

CATHERINE. Postponed again.

DICKIE. Oh, no. Why?

CATHERINE. His father's gone abroad for six months.

DICKIE. Why pay any attention to that old— (*He substitutes word.*) gentleman?

CATHERINE. I wouldn't—but John does—so I have to.

[*Something in her tone makes* DICKIE *stop dancing and gaze at her seriously.*]

DICKIE. I say, old girl—nothing wrong, is there?

[CATHERINE *shakes head, smiling, but not too emphatically.*]

I mean—you're not going to be left on the altar rails or anything, are you?

CATHERINE. Oh, no. I'll get him to the altar rails, if I have to drag him there.

DICKIE (*as they resume their dance*). Do you think you might have to?

CATHERINE. Quite frankly, yes.

DICKIE. Competition?

CATHERINE. Not yet. Only—differences of opinion.

DICKIE. I see. Well, take some advice from an old hand, will you?

CATHERINE. Yes, Dickie.

DICKIE. Suppress your opinions. Men don't like 'em in their lady friends, even if they agree with 'em. And if they don't—it's fatal. Pretend to be half-witted, like Edwina, then he'll adore you.

CATHERINE. I know. I do, sometimes, and then I forget. Still, you needn't worry. If there's ever a clash between what I believe and what I feel, there's not much doubt about which will win.

DICKIE. That's the girl. Of course I don't know why you didn't fall in love with Ramsay Macdonald—[15]

[ARTHUR *comes in. He is walking with more difficulty than when we last saw him.* DICKIE *and* CATHERINE *hastily stop dancing, and* DICKIE *turns off gramophone.*]

CATHERINE (*quickly*). It was entirely my fault, Father. I enticed Dickie from his work to show me a few dance steps.

[15] RAMSAY MACDONALD—The leader of the Labor Party, which the Suffragettes supported.

ARTHUR. Oh? I must admit I am surprised you succeeded.

DICKIE (*getting off subject*). What did the doctor say, Father?

ARTHUR (*sitting very painfully*). He said, if I remember his exact words, that we weren't quite as well as when we last saw each other. That information seems expensive at a guinea. (*Seeing evening paper.*) Oh, is that the *Star*? Let me see it, please.

[CATHERINE *brings it over to him.*]

John will be calling for you here, I take it?

CATHERINE. Yes, Father.

ARTHUR. It might be better, perhaps, if you didn't ask him in. This room will shortly be a clutter of journalists, solicitors, barristers, and other impedimenta.[16]

CATHERINE. Is Sir Robert Morton coming to see you here?

ARTHUR (*deep in the "Star"*). Certainly. I could hardly go and see him, could I?

[DICKIE, *in deference to his father's presence, has returned to his books.* ARTHUR *reads "Star."* CATHERINE *glances at herself in mirror, and then wanders to door.*]

CATHERINE. I must go and do something about my hair.

DICKIE. What's the matter with your hair?

CATHERINE. Nothing, except I don't like it very much. (*She goes out.*)

[DICKIE *opens two more books with a busy air and chews his pencil.* ARTHUR *finishes reading paper and stares moodily into space.*]

ARTHUR (*at length*). I wonder if I could sue "Perplexed"?

DICKIE. It might be a way of getting the case into court.

ARTHUR. On the other hand, he has not been libelous. Merely base.

[16] IMPEDIMENTA—Obstructions.

[*He throws paper away and regards* DICKIE *thoughtfully.* DICKIE, *feeling his father's eye on him, is elaborately industrious— At length, politely.*] Do you mind if I disturb you for a moment?

DICKIE (*pushing books away*). No, Father.

ARTHUR. I want to ask you a question.

DICKIE. Fire away.

ARTHUR. I must impress on you the urgent necessity for an absolutely truthful answer.

DICKIE. Naturally.

ARTHUR. "Naturally" means by nature, and I'm afraid I have not yet noticed that it has invariably been your nature to answer my questions truthfully.

DICKIE. Oh. Well, I will, this one, Father, I promise.

ARTHUR. Very well. (*He stares at him a moment.*) What do you suppose one of your bookmaker friends would lay in the way of odds against your getting a degree?

[*Pause.*]

DICKIE. Oh. Well, let's think. Say—about evens.

ARTHUR. Hm. I rather doubt if at that price your friend would find many takers.

DICKIE. Well—perhaps seven to four against.

ARTHUR. I see. And what about the odds against your eventually becoming a civil servant?

DICKIE. Well—a bit steeper, I suppose.

ARTHUR. Exactly. Quite a bit steeper.

[*Pause.*]

DICKIE. You don't want to have a bet, do you?

ARTHUR. No, Dickie. I'm not a gambler. And that's exactly the trouble.

DICKIE. What's exactly the trouble, Father?

ARTHUR. That I'm afraid I'm no longer in a position to gamble two hundred pounds a year on what you yourself admit is an outside chance.

DICKIE. Not an outside chance, Father. A good chance.

ARTHUR. Not good enough, Dickie, I'm afraid—with things as they are at the moment. Definitely not good enough. I fear my mind is finally made up.

[*There is a long pause.*]

DICKIE. You want me to leave Oxford —is that it?

ARTHUR. I'm very much afraid so, Dickie.

DICKIE. Oh. Straightaway?

ARTHUR. No. You can finish your second year.

DICKIE. And what then?

ARTHUR. I can get you a job in the bank.

DICKIE (*quietly*). Oh, no!

[*Pause.*]

ARTHUR (*rather apologetically*). It'll be quite a good job, you know. Luckily, my influence in the bank still counts for something.

[DICKIE *gets up and wanders about, slightly in a daze.*]

DICKIE. Father—if I promised you—I mean, *really* promised you—that from now on I'll work like a Trojan—

[ARTHUR *shakes his head slowly.*] It's the case, I suppose?

ARTHUR. It's costing me a lot of money.

DICKIE. I know. It must be. Still, couldn't you—I mean, isn't there any way—?

[ARTHUR *again shakes his head.*]

ARTHUR. I'm afraid this is rather a shock for you. I'm sorry.

DICKIE. What? No. No, it isn't, really. I've been rather expecting it, as a matter of fact—especially since I heard you'd briefed Morton. Still, I can't say but what it isn't a bit of a slap in the face with a wet haddock—

ARTHUR (*sincerely*). I can only tell you, Dickie, that I am genuinely sorry to have been forced to administer it.

[*There is a ring at front door.*]

There is a journalist coming to see me. Do you mind if we talk about this some other time?

DICKIE. No. That's all right. (DICKIE *begins forlornly to gather his books.*)

ARTHUR (*with a half-smile*). I should leave those there, if I were you.

DICKIE. Yes. I will. Good idea. (*He goes to door.*)

ARTHUR (*politely*). Tell me—how is your nice friend, Miss Gunn, these days?

DICKIE. Very well, thanks awfully.

ARTHUR. You don't suppose she might like you to take her to the theater—or buy her a little present perhaps?

DICKIE. Well, I do. Yes.

[ARTHUR *has taken out his wallet and now extracts two pound notes.*
DICKIE *comes and takes them.*]

Thanks awfully, Father.

ARTHUR. With what's left over you can always buy something for yourself.

DICKIE. Oh. Well, as a matter of fact, I don't suppose there will be an awful lot left over. Still, it's jolly decent of you— I say, Father—I think I could do with a little spot of something. Would you mind?

ARTHUR. Of course not. You'll find the decanter in the dining room.

DICKIE. Thanks awfully. (*He goes to dining-room door.*)

ARTHUR. I must thank you, Dickie, for bearing what must have been a very unpleasant blow with some fortitude.

DICKIE (*uncomfortably*). Oh. Rot! (*He goes out.*)

[ARTHUR *sighs deeply.* VIOLET *comes in at hall door.*]

VIOLET (*announcing proudly*). The Daily Mirror!

[MISS BARNES *comes in. She is a rather untidily dressed woman of about forty, with a gushing manner.*]

MISS BARNES. Mr. Winslow? So good of you to see me.

ARTHUR. How do you do? Will you forgive me for not getting up? I have arthritis—

MISS BARNES. Oh, but of course—

ARTHUR (*eyeing her with surprise and some distaste*). If I'd known it was a lady I was going to receive I would have made arrangements to have myself hoisted to a standing position—

MISS BARNES (*simpering*). You're surprised to see a lady reporter? I know. Everyone is. And yet why not? What could be more natural?

ARTHUR. What, indeed? Pray sit down—

MISS BARNES. My paper usually sends me out on stories which have a special appeal to women—stories with a little heart, you know, like this one—a father's fight for his little boy's honor—

[ARTHUR *visibly winces.*]

ARTHUR. I venture to think this case has rather wider implications than that—

MISS BARNES. Oh, yes. The political angle. I know. Very interesting but not quite my line of country. Now what I'd really like to do—is to get a nice picture of you and your little boy together. I've brought my assistant and camera. They're in the hall. Where is your little boy?

ARTHUR. My son is arriving from school in a few minutes. His mother has gone to the station to meet him.

MISS BARNES (*making a note*). From school? How interesting! So you got a school to take him? I mean, they didn't mind the unpleasantness?

ARTHUR. No.

MISS BARNES. And why is he coming back this time?

ARTHUR. He hasn't been expelled again, if that is what you're implying. He is coming to London to be examined by Sir Robert Morton, whom we are hoping to brief—[17]

MISS BARNES. Sir Robert Morton! (*She whistles appreciatively.*) Well!

ARTHUR. Exactly.

MISS BARNES (*doubtingly*). But do you *really* think he'll take a little case like this?

ARTHUR (*explosively*). It is *not* a little case, madam—

MISS BARNES. No, no. Of course not. But still—Sir Robert Morton!

ARTHUR. I understand that he is the best advocate in the country. He is certainly the most expensive—

[17] TO BRIEF—To employ—here, as Ronnie's lawyer.

MISS BARNES. Oh, yes. I suppose if one is prepared to pay his fee, one can get him for almost *any* case.

ARTHUR. Once more, madam—this is *not* almost any case—

MISS BARNES. No, no. Of course not. Well, now, perhaps you wouldn't mind giving me a few details? When did it all start?

ARTHUR. Six months ago. My son was expelled from Osborne as a thief and a forger without any trial. During the preliminary so-called investigation, which lasted ten days, I was not informed that anything was amiss. The first I knew of the charge was when my son arrived home with a letter from the Admiralty informing me of his expulsion. I telephoned Osborne to protest and was referred by them to their Lordships. My solicitors then took the matter up, and demanded from the Admiralty the fullest possible inquiry. For weeks we were ignored, then met with a blank refusal, and only finally got reluctant permission to view the evidence.

MISS BARNES (*indifferently*). Really?

[*During* ARTHUR'S *speech she has been looking round the room, making notes on its appearance and furnishings.*]

ARTHUR. My solicitors decided that the evidence was highly unsatisfactory, and fully justified the re-opening of proceedings. We applied to the Admiralty for a Court Martial. They ignored us. We applied for a civil brief. They ignored us again. Are you listening to me, madam?

MISS BARNES (*still viewing room*). Oh, yes, indeed. They ignored you, you were saying—

ARTHUR. Exactly. So far, the Admiralty could, possibly, be excused for their behavior by the usual inertia and incompetence of any government department. But what follows will seem to you incredible. After tremendous pressure had been brought to bear—letters to the papers, questions in the House, and other means open to private citizens of this country—the Admiralty eventually agreed to what they called an independent inquiry.

MISS BARNES (*vaguely*). Oh, good!

ARTHUR. It was not good, madam. At that independent inquiry, conducted by the judge advocate of the Fleet—against whom I am saying nothing, mind you— my son—a child of fourteen, was not represented by counsel, solicitors, or friends. What do you think of that?

MISS BARNES. Fancy!

ARTHUR. You may well say "fancy."

MISS BARNES (*jerking her attention back to* ARTHUR). And what happened at the inquiry?

ARTHUR. What do you think happened? Inevitably he was found guilty

again, and thus branded for the second time before the world as a thief and a forger—

MISS BARNES (*her attention wandering again*). What a shame! (*She gets up and goes purposefully to window.*)

ARTHUR. I need hardly tell you, madam, that I am not prepared to let the matter rest there. I shall continue to fight this monstrous injustice with every weapon and every means at my disposal. Now it happens I have a plan—

MISS BARNES. Oh, what charming curtains! What are they made of?

[ARTHUR *sits for a moment in paralyzed silence.*]

ARTHUR (*at length*). Madam—I fear I have no idea.

[*There is the sound of voices in hall.*]

MISS BARNES. Ah. Do I hear the poor little chap himself?

[*Hall door opens and* RONNIE *comes in boisterously, followed by* GRACE. *He is evidently in the highest of spirits.*]

RONNIE. Hullo, Father! (*He runs to him.*)

ARTHUR. Hullo, Ronnie.

RONNIE. I say, how long am I supposed to stay up, because Mr. Moore said I was to tell you he'd like me back by Saturday, because that's the day the house colts [18] are playing Parkin's, and I'm scrum half [19] but it doesn't matter because we'll beat them anyway and I'd jolly well rather be here, I can tell you—

ARTHUR. Mind my leg! (*He kisses his forehead.*) How are you, my boy?

RONNIE. Oh, I'm absolutely tophole, Father. Mother says I've grown an inch—

[18] HOUSE COLTS—The younger students in the dormitory.

[19] SCRUM HALF—In Rugby football, the *scrum* or *scrummage* is the line-up of players on both sides of the scrimmage line when a play is to begin. One halfback, who stands close to the scrummage, is called the *scrum half.*

MISS BARNES. Ah! Now that's exactly the way I'd like to take my picture. Would you hold it, Mr. Winslow? (*She goes to hall door and calls.*) Fred! Come in now, will you?

RONNIE (*in a sibilant whisper*). Who's she?

[FRED *appears. He is a listless photographer, complete with apparatus.*]

FRED (*gloomily*). Afternoon, all.

MISS BARNES. That's the pose I suggest.

FRED. Yes. It'll do.

[*He begins to set up his apparatus.* ARTHUR, *holding* RONNIE *close against him in pose suggested, turns his head to* GRACE.]

ARTHUR. Grace, dear, this lady is from the *Daily Mirror.* She is extremely interested in your curtains.

GRACE (*delighted*). Oh, really? How nice!

MISS BARNES. Yes, indeed. I was wondering what they were made of?

GRACE. Well, it's an entirely new material, you know. I'm afraid I don't know what it's called, but I got them at Peter Jones's. Apparently it's a sort of mixture of wild silk and—

MISS BARNES (*now genuinely busy with pencil and pad*). Just a second, Mrs. Winslow. I'm afraid my shorthand isn't very good. I must just get that down—

RONNIE (*to* ARTHUR). Father, are we going to be in the *Daily Mirror?*

ARTHUR. It appears so—

RONNIE. Oh, good! They get the *Daily Mirror* in the school library and everyone's bound to see it—

FRED. Quite still, please— (*He takes his photograph.*) All right, Miss Barnes.

MISS BARNES (*engrossed with* GRACE). Thank you, Fred. (*To* GRACE, *effusively.*) Well, it was very good of you to tell me all that, Mrs. Winslow. I'm sure our readers will be most interested. (*To* ARTHUR.) Good-by, Mr. Winslow, and

the very best of good fortune in your inspiring fight. (*Turning to* RONNIE.) Good-by, little chap. Remember. The darkest hour is just before the dawn. (*She goes out, followed by* FRED.)

RONNIE (*before she has gone, to* ARTHUR). What's she talking about?

GRACE. What a charming woman, Arthur!

ARTHUR. Charming! I trust you gave her full details about our curtains?

GRACE. Oh, yes. I told her everything.

ARTHUR (*wearily*). I'm so glad.

GRACE. I do think women reporters are a good idea—

RONNIE (*excitedly*). I say, Father—I was top in history at half-term, and I was only second by three marks in French and Mr. Markham says if I keep it up they'll give me a double remove—[20] (*He jogs his father's leg again.*)

ARTHUR. Mind my leg!

RONNIE. Oh, sorry, Father. Is it bad?

ARTHUR. Yes, it is. I'm glad to hear of your successes, Ronnie. (*To* GRACE.) Grace, take him upstairs and clean him up a bit. Sir Robert will be here in a few minutes.

GRACE (*to* RONNIE). Come on, darling.

RONNIE. All right. (*On his way to door with his mother.*) I say, do you know how long the train took? 123 miles in two hours and fifty-two minutes. That's an average of 46.73 miles an hour—I worked it out— (*He disappears, still chattering shrilly.*)

ARTHUR (*calling*). Grace!

[GRACE *reappears.*]

GRACE. Yes?

ARTHUR. That ridiculous doctor you foisted on me has left some brew or other with which you are supposed to massage

[20] DOUBLE REMOVE—A promotion of two forms, or grades, at the end of the school term instead of one.

my leg, four times a day. I think you'd better do one now—

[GRACE *goes to his assistance as he struggles out of his chair.*]

GRACE. Have we time, dear?

ARTHUR (*looking at his watch*). Ten minutes.

[CATHERINE *comes in.*]

CATHERINE. Ronnie's back, judging by the noise—

GRACE (*examining her*). I must say that old frock has come out very well. John'll never know it isn't brand new—

CATHERINE. He's late, curse him.

ARTHUR. Grace, go on up and attend to Ronnie. I'll go to my room and prepare for your ministrations—

GRACE. Very well, dear. (*To* CATHERINE.) Yes, that does look good. I must say Mme. Dupont's a treasure. (*She goes out.*)

ARTHUR (*wearily*). Oh, Kate, Kate! Are we both mad, you and I?

CATHERINE. What's the matter, Father?

ARTHUR. I don't know. I suddenly feel suicidally inclined. (*Bitterly.*) A father's fight for his little boy's honor. Special appeal to all women. Photo inset of Mrs. Winslow's pink curtains— Is there any hope for the world?

CATHERINE (*smiling*). I think so, Father.

ARTHUR. Shall we drop the whole thing, Kate? The whole, shabby business?

CATHERINE. It's not a shabby business, Father—and you know it.

ARTHUR. You wouldn't have said that if you'd been here five minutes ago. (*He sighs deeply.*) You really think we should go on, Kate?

CATHERINE. I don't consider that a serious question, Father.

ARTHUR (*slowly*). You realize that if we do, your dowry must go?

CATHERINE (*lightly*). Oh, yes. I gave that up for lost weeks ago.

ARTHUR. Things are all right between you and John, aren't they?

CATHERINE. Oh, yes, Father, of course. Everything's perfect.

ARTHUR. I mean—it won't make any difference between you, will it?

CATHERINE. Good heavens, no!

ARTHUR. Very well, then. Let us pin our faith to Sir Robert Morton.

[CATHERINE *is silent.* ARTHUR *looks at her as if he had expected an answer, then nods.*]

I see I'm speaking only for myself in saying that.

CATHERINE (*lightly*). You know what I think of Sir Robert Morton,[21] Father. Don't let's go into it again, now. It's too late, anyway.

ARTHUR. It's not too late. He hasn't accepted the brief yet.

CATHERINE (*shortly*). Then I'm rather afraid I hope he never does. And that has nothing to do with my dowry, either.

[*Pause.* ARTHUR *looks angry for a second, then subsides.*]

ARTHUR (*mildly*). I made inquiries about that fellow you suggested—I am told he is not nearly as good an advocate as Morton—

CATHERINE. He's not nearly so fashionable.

ARTHUR (*doubtfully*). I want the best—

CATHERINE. The best in this case certainly isn't Morton.

ARTHUR. Then why does everyone say he is?

CATHERINE (*roused*). Because if one happens to be a large monopoly attacking a Trade Union or a Tory paper libeling a Labor leader, he *is* the best. But it

[21] YOU KNOW . . . SIR ROBERT MORTON— Sir Robert belongs to the Tory, or Conservative, Party, which the Suffragettes despise.

utterly defeats me how you or anyone else could expect a man of his record to have even a tenth of his heart in a case where the boot is entirely on the other foot—

ARTHUR. Well, I imagine, if his heart isn't in it, he won't accept the brief.

CATHERINE. He might still. It depends what there is in it for him. Luckily there isn't much—

ARTHUR (*bitterly*). There is a fairly substantial check—

CATHERINE. He doesn't want money. He must be a very rich man.

ARTHUR. What does he want, then?

CATHERINE. Anything that advances his interests.

[ARTHUR *shrugs his shoulders. Pause.*]

ARTHUR. I believe you are prejudiced because he spoke against Women's Suffrage.

CATHERINE. I am. I'm prejudiced because he is always speaking against what is right and just. Did you read his speech in the House on the Trades Disputes Bill?

[*Pause.*]

ARTHUR (*smiling*). Oh, well—in the words of the Prime Minister—let us wait and see.

[*He turns to door.* CATHERINE, *to recover her loss of composure, takes a cigarette from silver box and lights it.* ARTHUR *turns at door.*]

You're my only ally, Kate. Without you I believe I should have given up long ago.

CATHERINE. Rubbish.

ARTHUR. It's true. Still, you must sometimes allow me to make my own decisions. I have an instinct about Morton. [CATHERINE *does not reply.*] (*Doubtfully.*) We'll see which is right —my instinct or your reason, eh? (*He goes out.*)

CATHERINE (*half to herself*). I'm afraid we will.

[DICKIE *comes out of dining-room door.*]

DICKIE (*bitterly*). Hullo, Kate.

CATHERINE. Hullo, Dickie.

[DICKIE *crosses mournfully to other door.*]

What's the matter? Edwina jilted you or something?

DICKIE. Haven't you heard? [CATHERINE *shakes her head.*] I'm being scratched from the Oxford Stakes at the end of the year—

CATHERINE. Oh, Dickie! I'm awfully sorry—

DICKIE. Did you know it was in the wind?

CATHERINE. I knew there was a risk—

DICKIE. You might have warned a fellow. I fell plumb into the old man's trap. My gosh, I could just about murder that little brother of mine. (*Bitterly.*) What's he have to go about pinching postal orders for? And why does he have to get himself nabbed doing it? Silly little blighter! (*He goes out gloomily.*)

[*There is a ring at front door.* CATHERINE, *obviously believing it is* JOHN, *picks up her cloak and goes to hall door.*]

CATHERINE (*calling*). All right, Violet. It's only Mr. Watherstone. I'll answer it. (*She goes out.*)

[*The sound of voices in hall, and then* CATHERINE *reappears, leading in* DESMOND *and* SIR ROBERT MORTON. SIR ROBERT *is a man in the early forties, tall, thin, cadaverous and immensely elegant. He wears a long overcoat, and carries his hat and stick. He looks rather a fop, and his supercilious expression bears out this view.*] (*As she re-enters.*) I'm so sorry. I was expecting a friend. Won't you sit down, Sir Robert? My father won't be long.

[SIR ROBERT *bows slightly, and sits down on a hard chair, still in his overcoat.*]

Won't you sit here? It's far more comfortable.

SIR ROBERT. No, thank you.

DESMOND (*fussing*). Sir Robert has a most important dinner engagement, so we came a little early.

CATHERINE. I see.

DESMOND. I'm afraid he can only spare us a very few minutes of his most valuable time this evening. Of course it's a long way for him to come—so far from his chambers—and very good of him to do it, too, if I may say so—(*He bows to* SIR ROBERT, *who bows slightly back.*)

CATHERINE. I know. I can assure you we're very conscious of the honor he is doing us.

[SIR ROBERT *gives her a quick look, and a faint smile.*]

DESMOND. Perhaps I had better advise your father of our presence—?

CATHERINE. Yes, do, Desmond. You'll find him in his bedroom—having his leg rubbed.

DESMOND. Oh. I see. (*He goes out.*)

[*A pause.*]

CATHERINE. Is there anything I can get you, Sir Robert? A whiskey and soda or a brandy?

SIR ROBERT. No, thank you.

CATHERINE. Will you smoke?

SIR ROBERT. No, thank you.

CATHERINE (*holding her cigarette*). I hope you don't mind me smoking?

SIR ROBERT. Why should I?

CATHERINE. Some people find it shocking.

SIR ROBERT (*indifferently*). A lady in her own home is surely entitled to behave as she wishes.

[*Pause.*]

CATHERINE. Won't you take your coat off, Sir Robert?

SIR ROBERT. No, thank you.

CATHERINE. You find it cold in here? I'm sorry.

SIR ROBERT. It's perfectly all right.

[*Conversation languishes again.* SIR ROBERT *looks at his watch.*]

CATHERINE. What time are you dining?

SIR ROBERT. Eight o'clock.

CATHERINE. Far from here?

SIR ROBERT. Devonshire House.

CATHERINE. Oh. Then of course you mustn't on any account be late.

SIR ROBERT. No.

[*Another pause.*]

CATHERINE. I suppose you know the history of this case, do you, Sir Robert?

SIR ROBERT (*examining his nails*). I believe I have seen most of the relevant documents.

CATHERINE. Do you think we can bring the case into court by a collusive action? [22]

SIR ROBERT. I really have no idea—

CATHERINE. Curry and Curry seem to think that might hold—

SIR ROBERT. Do they? They are a very reliable firm.

[*Pause.* CATHERINE *is on verge of losing her temper.*]

CATHERINE. I'm rather surprised that a case of this sort should interest you, Sir Robert.

SIR ROBERT. Are you?

CATHERINE. It seems such a very trivial affair, compared to most of your great forensic triumphs. [23]

[SIR ROBERT, *staring languidly at ceiling, does not reply.*]

I was in court during your cross-examination of Len Rogers, in the Trades Union embezzlement case.

SIR ROBERT. Really?

CATHERINE. It was masterly.

[22] A COLLUSIVE ACTION—A charge of a secret agreement with intent to defraud.
[23] FORENSIC TRIUMPHS—Victories in public debate, as in a law court.

SIR ROBERT. Thank you.

CATHERINE. I suppose you heard that he committed suicide a few months ago?

SIR ROBERT. Yes. I had heard.

CATHERINE. Many people believed him innocent, you know.

SIR ROBERT. So I understand. (*After a faint pause.*) As it happens, however, he was guilty.

[GRACE *comes in hastily.*]

GRACE. Sir Robert? My husband's so sorry to have kept you, but he's just coming.

SIR ROBERT. It's perfectly all right. How do you do?

CATHERINE. Sir Robert is dining at Devonshire House, Mother.

GRACE. Oh, really? Oh, then, you have to be punctual, of course, I do see that. It's the politeness of princes, isn't it?

SIR ROBERT. So they say.

GRACE. In this case the other way round, of course. Ah, I think I hear my husband on the stairs. I hope Catherine entertained you all right?

SIR ROBERT (*with a faint bow to* CATHERINE). Very much indeed, thank you.

[ARTHUR *comes in, followed by* DESMOND.]

ARTHUR. Sir Robert? I am Arthur Winslow.

SIR ROBERT. How do you do?

ARTHUR. I understand you are rather pressed for time?

GRACE. Yes. He's dining at Devonshire House—

ARTHUR. Are you indeed? My son should be down in a minute. I expect you will wish to examine him.

SIR ROBERT (*indifferently*). Just a few questions. I fear that is all I will have time for this evening—

ARTHUR. I am rather sorry to hear that. He has made the journey specially from school for this interview—

DESMOND (*pacifically*). Well, perhaps Sir Robert would consent to finish his examination some other time?

SIR ROBERT. It might be arranged.

ARTHUR. Tomorrow?

SIR ROBERT. Tomorrow is impossible. I am in court all the morning and in the House of Commons for the rest of the day. (*Carelessly.*) If a further examination should prove necessary it will have to be sometime next week.

ARTHUR. I see. Will you forgive me if I sit down? (*He sits in his usual chair.*) Desmond has been telling me you think it might be possible to proceed by Petition of Right?

CATHERINE. What's a Petition of Right?

DESMOND. Well—granting the assumption that the Admiralty, as the Crown, can do no wrong—

CATHERINE (*murmuring*). I thought that was exactly the assumption we refused to grant?

DESMOND. In law, I mean. Now, a subject can sue the Crown nevertheless, by Petition of Right, redress being granted as a matter of grace—and the custom is for the Attorney-General—on behalf of the King—to endorse the Petition, and allow the case to come to court.

SIR ROBERT. It is interesting to note that the exact words he uses on such occasions are: "Let Right be done."

ARTHUR. "Let Right be done"? I like that phrase, sir.

SIR ROBERT. It has a certain ring about it—has it not? (*Languidly.*) "Let Right be done."

[RONNIE *comes in. He is in an Eton suit,[24] looking very spick and span.*]

ARTHUR. This is my son, Ronald. Ronnie, this is Sir Robert Morton.

[24] *Eton suit*—A suit having a short coat, worn with a large, stiff, turnover collar.

RONNIE. How do you do, sir?

ARTHUR. He is going to ask you a few questions. You must answer them all truthfully—as you always have. (*He begins to struggle out of his chair.*) I expect you would like us to leave—

SIR ROBERT. No. I would like you all to remain, provided, of course, that you don't interrupt. (*To* CATHERINE.) Miss Winslow, will you sit down, please?

[CATHERINE *takes a seat abruptly.*]

DESMOND (*to* CATHERINE). Courtroom atmosphere, you see—

SIR ROBERT (*to* RONNIE). Will you stand at the table, facing me?

[RONNIE *does so.*]

That's right.

[SIR ROBERT *and* RONNIE *now face each other across table,* SIR ROBERT *with his hands on the lapels of his overcoat, towering over the boy. He begins his examination very quietly.*]

Now, Ronald, how old are you?

RONNIE. Fourteen and three months.

SIR ROBERT. You were, then, thirteen and ten months old when you left Osborne: is that right?

RONNIE. Yes, sir.

SIR ROBERT. Now I would like you to cast your mind back to July 7th of last year. Will you tell me in your own words exactly what happened to you on that day?

RONNIE. All right. Well, it was a half-hol, so we didn't have any work after lunch—at least until prep at seven. Just before lunch I went to the Chief Petty Officer and asked him to let mc have sixteen bob out of what I had in the school bank—

SIR ROBERT. Why did you do that?

RONNIE. I wanted to buy an air pistol.

SIR ROBERT. How much was the air pistol?

RONNIE. Fifteen and six.

SIR ROBERT. And how much money did you have in the school bank at the time?

RONNIE. Two pounds three shillings.

ARTHUR. So you see, sir, what incentive could there possibly be for him to steal five shillings?

SIR ROBERT (*coldly*). I must ask you to be good enough not to interrupt me, sir. (*To* RONNIE.) After you had withdrawn the sixteen shillings, what did you do?

RONNIE. I had lunch.

SIR ROBERT. Then what?

RONNIE. I went to the locker room and put the sixteen shillings in my locker.

SIR ROBERT. Yes. Then?

RONNIE. I went to get permission to go down to the post office. Then I went to the locker room again, got out my money, and went down to the post office.

SIR ROBERT. What time was that?

RONNIE. About a quarter past three.

SIR ROBERT. I see. Go on.

RONNIE. I bought my postal order—

SIR ROBERT. For fifteen and six?

RONNIE. Yes. Then I went back to college. Then I met Elliot minor,[25] and he said: "I say, isn't it rot? Someone's broken into my locker and pinched a postal order. I've reported it to the P.O."

SIR ROBERT. Those were Elliot minor's exact words?

RONNIE. He might have used another word for rot—

SIR ROBERT. I see. Continue—

RONNIE. Well, then, just before prep I was told to go along and see Commander Flower. The woman from the post office was there, and the Com-

[25] ELLIOT MINOR—The expression *minor* means that this boy is second in age or in school standing to another boy of the same last name, Elliot *major*.

mander said: "Is this the boy?" and she said: "It might be. I can't be sure. They all look so much alike."

ARTHUR. You see? She couldn't identify him.

[SIR ROBERT *glares at him.*]

SIR ROBERT (*to* RONNIE). Go on.

RONNIE. Then she said: "I only know that the boy who bought a postal order for fifteen and six was the same boy that cashed one for five shillings." So the Commander said: "Did you buy a postal order for fifteen and six?" And I said: "Yes," and then they made me write Elliot minor's name on an envelope, and compared it to the signature on the back of the postal order—then they sent me to the sanatorium and ten days later I was sacked—I mean—expelled.

SIR ROBERT. I see. (*Quietly.*) Did you cash a postal order belonging to Elliot minor for five shillings?

RONNIE. No, sir.

SIR ROBERT. Did you break into his locker and steal it?

RONNIE. No, sir.

SIR ROBERT. And that is the truth, the whole truth, and nothing but the truth?

RONNIE. Yes, sir.

[DICKIE *has come in during this, and is standing furtively in doorway, not knowing whether to come in or go out.* SIR ROBERT *waves him impatiently to a seat.*]

SIR ROBERT. Right. Now, Ronald, when the Commander asked you to write Elliot's name on an envelope, how did you write it? With Christian name or initials?

RONNIE. I wrote Joseph K. Elliot.

SIR ROBERT. And how was his name written on the back of the postal order?

RONNIE. The same.

SIR ROBERT. The same? Joseph K. Elliot?

RONNIE. Yes, sir.

SIR ROBERT. What made you choose that particular form?

RONNIE. That was the way he usually signed his name—

SIR ROBERT. How did you know?

RONNIE. Well—he was a great friend of mine—

SIR ROBERT. That is no answer. How did you know?

RONNIE. I'd seen him sign things.

SIR ROBERT. What things?

RONNIE. Oh—ordinary things.

SIR ROBERT. I repeat: what things?

RONNIE (*reluctantly*). Bits of paper.

SIR ROBERT. Bits of paper? And why did he sign his name on bits of paper?

RONNIE. I don't know.

SIR ROBERT. You do know. Why did he sign his name on bits of paper?

RONNIE. He was practicing his signature.

SIR ROBERT. And you saw him?

RONNIE. Yes.

SIR ROBERT. Did he know you saw him?

RONNIE. Well—yes—

SIR ROBERT. In other words, he showed you exactly how he wrote his signature?

RONNIE. Yes. I suppose he did.

SIR ROBERT. Did you practice writing it yourself?

RONNIE. I might have done.

SIR ROBERT. What do you mean you might have done? Did you, or did you not?

RONNIE. Yes—

ARTHUR (*sharply*). Ronnie! You never told me that.

RONNIE. It was only for a joke—

SIR ROBERT. Never mind whether it was for a joke or not. The fact is you practiced forging Elliot's signature—

RONNIE. It wasn't forging—

SIR ROBERT. What do you call it then?

RONNIE. Writing.

SIR ROBERT. Very well. Writing.

Whoever stole the postal order and cashed it also *wrote* Elliot's signature, didn't he?

RONNIE. Yes.

SIR ROBERT. And, oddly enough, in the exact form in which you had earlier been practicing *writing* his signature—

RONNIE (*indignantly*). I say. Which side are you on?

SIR ROBERT (*snarling*). Don't be impertinent! You know that the Admiralty sent up the forged postal order to Mr. Williams—the greatest handwriting expert in England?

RONNIE. Yes.

SIR ROBERT. And you know that he said that there was no doubt that the signature on the postal order and the signature you wrote on the envelope were by one and the same hand?

RONNIE. Yes.

SIR ROBERT. And you still say that you didn't forge that signature?

RONNIE. Yes, I do.

SIR ROBERT. In other words, Mr. Williams doesn't know his job?

RONNIE. Well, he's wrong anyway.

SIR ROBERT. When you went into the locker room after lunch, were you alone?

RONNIE. I don't remember.

SIR ROBERT. I think you do. Were you alone in the locker room?

RONNIE. Yes.

SIR ROBERT. And you knew which Elliot's locker was?

RONNIE. Yes. Of course.

SIR ROBERT. Why did you go in there at all?

RONNIE. I've told you. To put my sixteen shillings away.

SIR ROBERT. Why?

RONNIE. I thought it would be safer.

SIR ROBERT. Why safer than your pocket?

RONNIE. I don't know.

SIR ROBERT. You had it in your pocket

at lunchtime. Why this sudden fear for its safety?

RONNIE (*plainly rattled*). I tell you, I don't know—

SIR ROBERT. It was rather an odd thing to do, wasn't it? The money was perfectly safe in your pocket. Why did you suddenly feel yourself impelled to put it away in your locker?

RONNIE (*almost shouting*). I don't know.

SIR ROBERT. Was it because you knew you would be alone in the locker room at the time?

RONNIE. No.

SIR ROBERT. Where was Elliot's locker in relation to yours?

RONNIE. Next to it, but one.

SIR ROBERT. Next, but one. What time did Elliot put his postal order in his locker?

RONNIE. I don't know. I didn't even know he had a postal order in his locker. I didn't know he had a postal order at all.

SIR ROBERT. Yet you say he was a great friend of yours—

RONNIE. He didn't tell me.

SIR ROBERT. How very secretive of him! What time did you go to the locker room?

RONNIE. I don't remember.

SIR ROBERT. Was it directly after lunch?

RONNIE. Yes. I think so.

SIR ROBERT. What did you do after leaving the locker room?

RONNIE. I've told you. I went for permission to go to the post office.

SIR ROBERT. What time was that?

RONNIE. About a quarter past two.

SIR ROBERT. Lunch is over at one forty-five. What were you doing in the locker room for half an hour?

RONNIE. I wasn't there all that time—

SIR ROBERT. You've just said you were.

RONNIE. Well—you're muddling me—

SIR ROBERT. How long were you there?

RONNIE. About five minutes.

SIR ROBERT. What were you doing for the other twenty-five?

RONNIE. I don't remember.

SIR ROBERT. It's odd that your memory is so good about some things and so bad about others—

RONNIE. Perhaps I waited outside the C.O.'s office!

SIR ROBERT (*with searing sarcasm*). Perhaps you waited outside the C.O.'s office! And perhaps no one saw you there, either?

RONNIE. No. I don't think they did.

SIR ROBERT. What were you thinking about outside the C.O.'s office for twenty-five minutes?

RONNIE (*wildly*). I don't even know if I was there. I can't remember. Perhaps I wasn't there at all.

SIR ROBERT. No. Perhaps you were still in the locker room, rifling Elliot's locker—?

ARTHUR (*indignantly*). Sir Robert, I must ask you—

SIR ROBERT. Quiet!

RONNIE. I remember now. I remember. Someone did see me outside the C.O.'s office. A chap called Casey. I remember I spoke to him.

SIR ROBERT. What did you say?

RONNIE. I said: "Come down to the post office with me. I'm going to cash a postal order."

SIR ROBERT (*triumphantly*). Cash a postal order.

RONNIE. I mean get.

SIR ROBERT. You said "cash." Why did you say "cash" if you meant get?

RONNIE. I don't know. I didn't mean it.

SIR ROBERT. I suggest "cash" was the truth.

RONNIE. No, no. It wasn't, really. You're muddling me.

SIR ROBERT. You seem easily muddled. Why did you lie about the time you went to the post office?

RONNIE. I didn't.

SIR ROBERT. You told the Commander two-thirty. You told me three-fifteen.

RONNIE. I was muddled, with the Commander.

SIR ROBERT. Muddled again? How many other lies have you told?

RONNIE. None. Really, I haven't—

SIR ROBERT (*bending forward malevolently*). I suggest your whole testimony is a lie—

RONNIE. No! It's the truth—

SIR ROBERT. I suggest there is barely one single word of truth in anything you have said either to me, or to the judge advocate or to the Commander. I suggest that you did break into Elliot's locker, that you did steal the postal order, that you did cash it and forge his name—

RONNIE (*wailing*). I didn't. I didn't. I didn't need the money—

SIR ROBERT. I suggest that you did it for a joke, meaning to give Elliot the five shillings back, but that when you met him and he said he had reported the matter that you got frightened and decided to keep quiet—

RONNIE. No, no, no. It isn't true—

SIR ROBERT. I suggest that by continuing to deny your guilt you are causing great hardship to your own family, and considerable annoyance to high and important persons in this country—

CATHERINE (*on her feet*). That's a disgraceful thing to say!

ARTHUR. I agree.

SIR ROBERT (*leaning forward and glaring at* RONNIE *with the utmost venom*). I suggest, boy, that the time has at last come for you to undo some of the misery you have caused by confessing to us all now that you are a forger, a liar, and a thief!

RONNIE (*in tears*). I'm not! I'm not! I'm not! I didn't do it—

[GRACE *has flown to his side and now envelops him.*]

GRACE. There, darling! Never mind, now! Never mind—

ARTHUR. This is outrageous, sir—

[JOHN *appears at door, dressed in evening clothes.*]

JOHN. Kate, dear, I'm most terribly sorry—

[*He stops short as he takes in the scene, with* RONNIE *sobbing hysterically on his mother's breast, and* ARTHUR *and* CATHERINE *glaring indignantly at* SIR ROBERT, *who is engaged in putting his papers together.*]

SIR ROBERT (*to* DESMOND). Can I drop you anywhere? My car is at the door.

DESMOND. Er—no—I thank you—

SIR ROBERT (*carelessly*). Well, send all this stuff round to my chambers tomorrow morning, will you?

DESMOND. But—but will you need it now?

SIR ROBERT. Oh, yes. The boy is plainly innocent. I accept the brief.

[*He bows to* ARTHUR *and* CATHERINE *and walks languidly to door past the bewildered* JOHN, *to whom he gives a polite nod as he goes out.* RONNIE *continues to sob hysterically.*]

ACT III

SCENE: *The same. Nine months later. The time is about ten-thirty* P.M.

ARTHUR *is sitting in his favorite armchair, reading aloud from an evening paper, whose wide headline:* "WINSLOW DEBATE: FIRST LORD REPLIES," *we can read on the front page. Listening to him are* RONNIE *and* GRACE, *though neither of them seems to be doing so with much concentration.* RONNIE, *on sofa, is finding it hard to keep his eyes open, and* GRACE, *darning socks in other armchair, has evidently other and, to her, more important matters on her mind.*

ARTHUR (*reading*). "—The Admiralty, during the whole of this long drawn-out dispute, have at no time acted hastily or ill-advisedly, and it is a matter of mere histrionic hyperbole [26] for the right honorable and learned gentleman opposite to characterize the conduct of my department as that of callousness so inhuman as to amount to deliberate malice towards the boy Winslow. (Ministerial cheers and opposition cries of 'Oh!') Such unfounded accusations I can well choose to ignore. (An honorable member: 'You can't.') Honorable members opposite may interrupt as much as they please, but I repeat—there is nothing whatever that the Admiralty has done, or failed to do, in the case of this cadet for which I, as First Lord, need to apologize. (Further opposition interruptions.)" (*He stops reading and looks up.*) I must say it looks as if the First Lord's having rather a rough passage—(*He breaks off, noticing* RONNIE's *head has fallen back on cushions, and he is asleep.*) I trust my reading isn't keeping you awake. (*There is no answer.*) I say I trust my reading

isn't keeping you awake! (*Again there is no answer. Helplessly.*) Grace!

GRACE. My poor sleepy little lamb! It's long past his bedtime, Arthur.

ARTHUR. Grace, dear—at this very moment your poor sleepy little lamb is the subject of a very violent and heated debate in the House of Commons. I should have thought, in the circumstances, it might have been possible for him to contrive to stay awake for a few minutes past his bedtime—

GRACE. I expect he's overexcited.

[ARTHUR *and* GRACE *both look at the tranquilly oblivious form on sofa.*]

ARTHUR. A picture of overexcitement. (*Sharply.*) Ronnie! (*No answer.*) Ronnie!

RONNIE (*opening his eyes*). Yes, Father?

ARTHUR. I am reading the account of the debate. Would you like to listen, or would you rather go to bed?

RONNIE. Oh, I'd like to listen, of course, Father. I was listening too, only I had my eyes shut—

ARTHUR. I see. That, no doubt, was why your attitude was barely distinguishable from a heavy doze—

RONNIE. Oh no, Father. It's jolly interesting. Go on—do.

ARTHUR. Very well. (*Reading.*) "The First Lord continued amid further interruptions: The chief point of criticism against the Admiralty appears to center in the purely legal question of the Petition of Right brought by Mr. Arthur Winslow and the Admiralty's demurrer [27] thereto. I am very ready to admit that this has raised a constitutional issue of the first importance, but the implications must be viewed from every angle. The right honorable and learned gentleman

---

[26] HISTRIONIC HYPERBOLE (hī·pûr′bô·lē)— Dramatic exaggeration.

[27] DEMURRER—In legal proceedings, a plea made by the defendant to have the case dropped for technical reasons.

has made great play with his eloquent reference to the liberty of the individual menaced, as he puts it, by the new despotism of bureaucracy [28]—and I was as moved as any honorable member opposite by his resonant use of the words: 'Let Right be Done'—the time-honored phrase with which, in his opinion, the Attorney-General should without question have endorsed Mr. Winslow's Petition of Right. Nevertheless, the matter is not nearly as simple as the right honorable and learned gentleman appears to imagine. The Admiralty, it is true, in instructing the Attorney-General to reject this Petition, have relied upon an ancient prerogative [29] of the Crown. But it must be remembered that in this twentieth century the prerogatives of the Crown are no longer exercised on behalf of a despotic monarch, but on behalf of a free and democratically protected people. (Ministerial cheers and further opposition interruptions.) Cadet Ronald Winslow is a servant of the Crown, and has therefore no right whatever—no more right than any other member of His Majesty's forces—to sue the Crown in open court. To allow him to do so—whether through legal quibble of a claim for breach of contract by his father or by any other means his legal advisers may hit upon, would undoubtedly raise the most dangerous precedents. (Honorable members: Dangerous to whom?) There is no doubt whatever in my mind that in certain cases —and this is one of them—private rights may have to be sacrificed for the public good—(Opposition laughter and ministerial counter cheers.)" (He looks up.)

And what other excuse, pray, did Charles I make for ship money [30] and—?

[RONNIE, after a manful attempt to keep his eyes open by self-pinchings and other devices, has once more succumbed to oblivion.]

(Sharply.) Ronnie! Ronnie!

[RONNIE stirs, turns over, and slides more comfortably into cushions.]

Would you believe it!

GRACE. He's dead tired. I'd better take him up to his bed—

ARTHUR. No. If he must sleep, let him sleep there.

GRACE. Oh, but he'd be much more comfy in his little bed—

ARTHUR. I dare say; but the debate continues and until it's ended the cause of it all will certainly not make himself comfy in his little bed.

[VIOLET comes in.]

VIOLET. There are three more reporters in the hall, sir. Want to see you very urgently. Shall I let them in?

ARTHUR. No. Certainly not. I issued a statement yesterday. Until the debate is over I have nothing more to say.

VIOLET. Yes, sir. That's what I told them, but they wouldn't go.

ARTHUR. Well, make them. Use force, if necessary.

VIOLET. Yes, sir. And shall I cut some sandwiches for Miss Catherine, as she missed her dinner?

GRACE. Yes, Violet. Good idea.

[VIOLET goes out.]

VIOLET (off stage). Mr. Winslow made a statement yesterday. He has nothing more to say.

[Voices answer her, fading at length into silence. GRACE puts a rug over RONNIE, now sleeping very soundly.]

[28] THE NEW DESPOTISM OF BUREAUCRACY— The meaning is that in modern times, large and powerful government bureaus may become as heedless of the people's rights as the despots (tyrants) of earlier centuries.

[29] PREROGATIVE—A special right, one that takes priority over the rights of other people.

[30] CHARLES I . . . SHIP MONEY—The "ship money" tax levied by Charles I, which was considered unfair by many people, helped bring about the quarrel with Parliament which led to his downfall.

ARTHUR. Grace, dear—

GRACE. Yes?

ARTHUR. I fancy this might be a good opportunity of talking to Violet?

GRACE (*quite firmly*). No, dear.

ARTHUR. Meaning that it isn't a good opportunity? Or meaning that you have no intention at all of ever talking to Violet?

GRACE. I'll do it one day, Arthur. To-morrow, perhaps. Not now.

ARTHUR. I believe you'd do better to grasp the nettle. Delay only adds to your worries—

GRACE (*bitterly*). My worries! What do you know about my worries?

ARTHUR. A good deal, Grace. But I feel they would be a lot lessened if you faced the situation squarely.

GRACE. It's easy for you to talk, Arthur. You don't have to do it.

ARTHUR. I will, if you like.

GRACE. No, dear.

ARTHUR. If you explain the dilemma to her carefully—if you even show her the figures I jotted down for you yesterday—I venture to think you won't find her unreasonable.

GRACE. She's nearly seventy, Arthur. It won't be easy for her to find another place. I don't mind how many figures she's shown, it's a brutal thing to do.

ARTHUR. Facts are brutal things.

GRACE (*a shade hysterically*). Facts? I don't think I know what facts are any more—

ARTHUR. The facts, at this moment, are that we have a half of the income we had a year ago and we're living at nearly the same rate. However you look at it that's bad economics—

GRACE. I'm not talking about economics, Arthur. I know about those facts as well as you. Probably better, as I have to deal with them. I'm talking about ordinary, common, or garden facts—things

we took for granted a year ago and which now don't seem to matter any more.

ARTHUR. Such as?

GRACE (*with rising voice*). Such as a happy home and peace and quiet and an ordinary respectable life, and some sort of future for us and our children. In the last year you've thrown all that overboard, Arthur. There's your return for it, I suppose, (*She indicates headline in paper.*) and it's all very exciting and important, I'm sure, but it doesn't bring back any of the things that we've lost. I can only pray to God that you know what you're doing.

[RONNIE *stirs in his sleep.* GRACE *automatically pulls rug over him and lowers her voice at end of her speech. A pause.*]

ARTHUR (*quietly*). I do know what I'm doing, Grace.

GRACE. Do you? I'm not so sure. I sometimes think you're just marching blindly ahead without knowing where you're going.

ARTHUR. I know exactly where I'm going, Grace. I'm going to publish my son's innocence before the world, and for that end I am not prepared to weigh the cost.

GRACE. But the cost may be out of all proportion—

ARTHUR. It may be. That doesn't concern me. I hate heroics, Grace, but you force me to say this. An injustice has been done. I am going to set it right, and there is no sacrifice in the world I am not prepared to make in order to do so.

GRACE (*with sudden violence*). Oh, I wish I could see the sense of it all! (*Pointing to* RONNIE.) He's perfectly happy, at a good school, doing very well. No one need ever have known about Osborne, if you hadn't gone and shouted it out to the whole world. As it is, whatever happens now, he'll go through the rest of his life as the boy in that Winslow case—the boy that stole that postal order.

ARTHUR (*grimly*). The boy that didn't steal that postal order.

GRACE (*wearily*). What's the difference? When millions are talking and gossiping about him, a *did* or a *didn't* hardly matters. The Winslow boy is bad enough. You talk about sacrificing everything for him: but when he's grown up he won't thank you for it, Arthur—even though you've given your life to—publish his innocence, as you call it. [ARTHUR *makes impatient gesture.*] Yes, Arthur—your life. You talk gaily about arthritis and a touch of gout and old age and the rest of it, but you know as well as any of the doctors what really is the matter with you and how vital it is for you to have some rest and quiet. (*Nearly in tears.*) You're destroying yourself, Arthur, and me and your family besides—and for what? For what, I'd like to know? I've asked you and Kate to tell me a hundred times—but you can't. You never can—For what, Arthur? For what?

[ARTHUR *has struggled painfully out of his seat and now approaches her.*]

ARTHUR (*quietly*). For justice, Grace.

GRACE. Justice? That sounds very noble. Are you sure it's true? Are you sure it's true? Are you sure it isn't just plain pride and self-importance and sheer brute stubbornness? You and Kate can't bear the thought of anyone ever getting the better of you. Isn't it just plain selfishness in you both that stops you saying: "All right. I'll give up. They've *won*"?

ARTHUR (*putting a hand out*). No, Grace. I don't think it is. I really don't think it is—

GRACE (*shaking off his hand*). No. This time I'm not going to cry and say I'm sorry, and make it all up again. It's past that now, Arthur. I can't stand it any more. If there was a reason I could stand anything. Anything. But for no reason at all, it's unfair to ask so much of me. It's unfair—

[*She breaks down. As* ARTHUR *puts a comforting arm around her she pushes him off and runs out of door.* RONNIE *has meanwhile opened his eyes.*]

RONNIE. What's the matter, Father?

ARTHUR (*turning from door*). Your mother is a little upset—

RONNIE (*drowsily*). Why? Aren't things going well?

ARTHUR. Oh, yes. (*Murmuring.*) Very well. (*He sits with more than his usual difficulty, as if he were utterly exhausted.*) Very well indeed.

[RONNIE *contentedly closes his eyes again.* ARTHUR, *for a long time, stares broodingly into space, laying his stick methodically beside him. Then he turns his head to sofa. Gently.*]

You'd better go to bed now, Ronnie. You'll be more comfortable.

[*He sees* RONNIE *is asleep again. He struggles out of his chair and goes over to sofa, where he stands looking down at his sleeping son, barely visible under the rug. He makes as if to wake him, then shrugs his shoulders and turns away.* VIOLET *comes in with sandwiches on a plate, and a letter on a salver.*]

Thank you, Violet.

[VIOLET *puts sandwiches on table and hands* ARTHUR *letter.* ARTHUR *puts it down on table beside him without opening it.* VIOLET *turns to go out.*]

Oh, Violet—

VIOLET (*turning placidly*). Yes, sir?

ARTHUR. How long have you been with us?

VIOLET. Twenty-four years next April, sir.

ARTHUR. As long as that?

VIOLET. Yes, sir. Miss Kate was that high when I first came (*She indicates a small child.*) and Mr. Dickie hadn't even been thought of—

ARTHUR. I remember you coming to us now. I remember it well. What do you think of this case, Violet?

VIOLET. A fine old rumpus that is, and no mistake.

ARTHUR. It is, isn't it? A fine old rumpus.

VIOLET. There was a leading article in the *Evening News*. Did you read it, sir?

ARTHUR. No. What did it say?

VIOLET. Oh, about how it was a fuss about nothing and a shocking waste of the Government's time, but how it was a good thing all the same because it could only happen in England—

ARTHUR. There seems to be a certain lack of logic in that argument—

VIOLET. Well, perhaps they put it a bit different, sir. Still, that's what it said all right. And when you think it's all because of that little mite over there on the sofa—I have to laugh about it sometimes, I really do. Wasting the Government's time at his age! I never did. Well, wonders will never cease.

ARTHUR. I know. Wonders will never cease.

VIOLET. Well—would that be all, sir?

[*Slight pause.*]

ARTHUR. Yes, Violet. That'll be all.

[VIOLET *goes out; we can hear her greeting* CATHERINE *in hall with the news that Mr. Winslow's in drawing room.* CATHERINE *comes in.*]

CATHERINE. Hullo, Father. (*She kisses him. Indicating* RONNIE.) An honorable member described *that* this evening as a piteous little figure, crying aloud to humanity for justice and redress. I wish he could see him now.

ARTHUR (*testily*). It's long past his

bedtime. What's happened? Is the debate over?

CATHERINE. As good as. When I left all excitement had gone out of it. The First Lord gave an assurance that in future there would be no inquiry at Osborne or Dartmouth without informing the parents first. That seemed to satisfy most members—

ARTHUR. But what about *this* case? Is he going to allow us a fair trial? [31]

CATHERINE. Apparently not.

ARTHUR. But that's iniquitous.[32] I thought he would be forced to—

CATHERINE. I thought so, too. The House evidently thought otherwise.

ARTHUR. Will there be a division? [33]

CATHERINE. There may be. If there is, the Government will win.

ARTHUR. What is the motion?

CATHERINE. To reduce the First Lord's salary by a hundred pounds. (*With a faint smile.*) Naturally, no one really wants to do that. (*Indicating sandwiches.*) Are these for me?

ARTHUR. Yes.

[CATHERINE *starts to eat sandwiches.*] So we're back where we started, then?

CATHERINE. It looks like it.

ARTHUR. The debate has done us no good at all?

CATHERINE. It's aired the case a little, perhaps. A few more thousand people will say to each other at breakfast tomorrow: "That boy ought to be allowed a fair trial."

ARTHUR. What's the good of that,

[31] FAIR TRIAL—The Prime Minister has reported on Ronnie's case to the House of Commons, at the same time denying the request for a regular jury trial in a civilian court.

[32] INIQUITOUS (ĭ·nĭk′wĭ·tŭs)—Wicked.

[33] A DIVISION—A vote. Because of the Prime Minister's refusal, some member of Parliament may make a motion to reduce his salary. The debate on the motion would, in effect, turn the House of Commons into a court to decide Ronnie's guilt or innocence.

if they can't make themselves heard?

CATHERINE. I think they can—given time.

ARTHUR. Given time? (*Pause.*) But didn't Sir Robert make any protest when the First Lord refused a trial?

CATHERINE. Not a verbal protest: something far more spectacular and dramatic. He uncoiled those long legs of his—he'd had his feet on the Treasury table and his hat over his eyes, during most of the First Lord's speech—and got up very deliberately. Then he glared at the First Lord, threw a whole bundle of notes on the floor, and stalked out of the House. It made a magnificent effect. If I hadn't known I could have sworn he was genuinely indignant—

ARTHUR. Of course he was genuinely indignant. So would any man of feeling be—

CATHERINE. Sir Robert, Father dear, is not a man of feeling. I don't think any emotion at all can stir that fishy heart—

ARTHUR. Except perhaps a single-minded love of justice.

CATHERINE. Nonsense. A single-minded love of Sir Robert Morton.

ARTHUR. You're very ungrateful to him, considering all he's done for us these last months—

CATHERINE. I'm not ungrateful, Father. He's been wonderful—I admit it freely. No one could have fought a harder fight.

ARTHUR. Well, then—?

CATHERINE. It's only his motives I question. At least I *don't* question them at all. I know them.

ARTHUR. What are they?

CATHERINE. First—publicity—you know—look at me, the staunch defender of the little man—and then second—a nice popular stick to beat the Government with. Both very useful to an ambitious man. Luckily for him, we've provided them.

ARTHUR. Luckily for us, too, Kate.

CATHERINE. Oh, granted. But don't fool yourself about him, Father, for all that. The man is a fish, a hard, cold-blooded, supercilious, sneering fish.

[VIOLET *enters.*]

VIOLET (*announcing*). Sir Robert Morton.

[CATHERINE *chokes over her sandwich.*
SIR ROBERT *comes in.*]

SIR ROBERT. Good evening.

CATHERINE (*still choking*). Good evening.

SIR ROBERT. Something gone down the wrong way?

CATHERINE. Yes.

SIR ROBERT. May I assist? (*He pats her on back.*)

CATHERINE. Thank you.

SIR ROBERT (*to* ARTHUR). Good evening, sir. I thought I would call and give you an account of the day's proceedings, but I see your daughter has forestalled me.

CATHERINE. Did you know I was in the gallery?

SIR ROBERT (*gallantly*). With such a charming hat, how could I have missed you?

ARTHUR. It was very good of you to call, sir, nevertheless—

SIR ROBERT (*seeing* RONNIE). Ah. The *casus belli* [34]—dormant—

ARTHUR. Kate—wake him up.

SIR ROBERT. No, no. I beg of you. He is a delightful boy, but a little rampageous. I imply no disparagement. [35] All youngsters are, at that age, of course. But I think, none the less, that I prefer him—asleep.

ARTHUR. My daughter has told me of

[34] *Casus belli* (kä′sŏŏs bĕl′lē)—The reason for the war.

[35] DISPARAGEMENT—Unfavorable criticism.

your demonstration during the First Lord's speech. She described it as—magnificent.

SIR ROBERT (*with a glance at* CATHERINE). Did she? That was good of her. It's a very old trick, you know. I've done it a hundred times in the courts. It's nearly always surprisingly effective—

[CATHERINE *catches her father's eye and nods triumphantly.*]

(*To* CATHERINE.) Was the First Lord at all put out by it—did you notice?

CATHERINE. How could he have failed to be? (*To* ARTHUR *approaching his chair.*) I wish you could have seen it, Father—It was—(*She notices letter on table beside* ARTHUR, *and snatches it up with a sudden gesture. She examines envelope.*) When did this come?

ARTHUR. A few minutes ago. Do you know the writing?

CATHERINE. Yes. (*She puts letter back on table.*)

ARTHUR. Whose is it?

CATHERINE. I shouldn't bother to read it, if I were you.

[ARTHUR *looks at her, puzzled, then takes up letter.*]

ARTHUR (*to* SIR ROBERT). Will you forgive me?

SIR ROBERT. Of course.

[ARTHUR *opens letter and begins to read.* CATHERINE *watches him for a moment, then turns with a certain forced liveliness to* SIR ROBERT.]

CATHERINE. Well, what do you think the next step should be?

SIR ROBERT. I have already been considering that, Miss Winslow. I believe that perhaps the best plan would be to renew our efforts to get the Director of Public Prosecutions to act.

CATHERINE (*with one eye on her father*). But do you think there's any chance of that?

SIR ROBERT. Oh, yes. In the main, it will chiefly be a question of making ourselves a confounded nuisance—

CATHERINE. We've certainly done that quite successfully so far—thanks to you—Sir Robert.

SIR ROBERT (*suavely*). Ah. That is perhaps the only quality I was born with—the ability to make myself a confounded nuisance. (*He, too, has his eye on* ARTHUR, *sensing something amiss.*)

[ARTHUR *finishes reading letter and lays it slowly on his lap.*]

CATHERINE (*with false vivacity*). Father—Sir Robert thinks we might get the Director of Public Prosecutions to act—

ARTHUR. What?

SIR ROBERT. We were discussing how to proceed with the case—

ARTHUR. The case? (*He stares, a little blankly, from one to the other.*) Yes. We must think of that, mustn't we? (*Pause.*) How to proceed with the case? (*To* SIR ROBERT, *abruptly.*) I'm afraid I don't think, all things considered, that much purpose would be served by going on—

[SIR ROBERT *and* CATHERINE *stare at him blankly.* CATHERINE *goes quickly to him and snatches letter from his lap. She begins to read.*]

SIR ROBERT (*with sudden change of tone*). Of course we must go on.

ARTHUR (*in a low voice*). It is not for you to choose, sir. The choice is mine.

SIR ROBERT (*harshly*). Then you must reconsider it. To give up now would be insane.

ARTHUR. Insane? My sanity has already been called in question tonight—for carrying the case as far as I have.

SIR ROBERT. Whatever the contents of that letter, sir—or whatever has happened to make you lose heart, I insist that we continue the fight—

ARTHUR. Insist? We? It is my fight, sir—my fight alone—and it is for me alone to judge when the time has come to give up.

SIR ROBERT (*violently*). But why give up? Why? In heaven's name, man, why give up?

ARTHUR (*slowly*). I have made many sacrifices for this case. Some of them I had no right to make, but I made them, none the less. But there is a limit and I have reached it. I am sorry, Sir Robert. More sorry, perhaps, than you are, but the Winslow case is now closed.

SIR ROBERT. Balderdash!

[ARTHUR *looks surprised at this unparliamentary expression.* CATHERINE *has read and reread letter, and now breaks silence in a calm methodical voice.*]

CATHERINE. My father doesn't mean what he says, Sir Robert.

SIR ROBERT. I am glad to hear it.

CATHERINE. Perhaps I should explain this letter—

ARTHUR. No, Kate.

CATHERINE. Sir Robert knows so much about our family affairs, Father, I don't see it will matter much if he learns a little more. (*To* SIR ROBERT.) This letter is from a certain Colonel Watherstone, who is the father of the man I'm engaged to. We've always known he was opposed to the case, so it really comes as no surprise. In it he says that our efforts to discredit the Admiralty in the House of Commons today have resulted merely in our making the name of Winslow a nation-wide laughingstock. I think that's his phrase. (*She consults letter.*) Yes. That's right. A nation-wide laughingstock.

SIR ROBERT. I don't care for his English.

CATHERINE. It's not very good, is it? He goes on to say that unless my father will give him a firm understanding to drop this—this (*She consults letter*

again.) whining and reckless agitation—I suppose he means the case—he will exert every bit of influence he has over his son to prevent him marrying me.

SIR ROBERT. I see. An ultimatum.

CATHERINE. Yes—but a pointless one.

SIR ROBERT. He has no influence over his son?

CATHERINE. Oh, yes. A little, naturally. But his son is of age, and his own master—

SIR ROBERT. Is he dependent on his father for money?

CATHERINE. He gets an allowance. But he can live perfectly well—we both can live perfectly well without it.

[*Pause.* SIR ROBERT *stares hard at her, then turns abruptly to* ARTHUR.]

SIR ROBERT. Well, sir?

ARTHUR. I'm afraid I can't go back on what I have already said. I will give you a decision in a few days—

SIR ROBERT. Your daughter seems prepared to take the risk—

ARTHUR. I am not. Not, at least, until I know how great a risk it is—

SIR ROBERT. How do you estimate the risk, Miss Winslow?

[*Pause.* CATHERINE, *for all her bravado, is plainly scared. She is engaged in lighting a cigarette as* SIR ROBERT *asks his question.*]

CATHERINE (*at length*). Negligible.

[SIR ROBERT *stares at her again. Feeling his eyes on her, she returns his glance defiantly. Pause.*]

SIR ROBERT (*returning abruptly to his languid manner*). I see. May I take a cigarette, too?

CATHERINE. Yes, of course. I thought you didn't smoke?

SIR ROBERT. Only occasionally—in moments of stress. (*To* ARTHUR.) I really must apologize to you, sir, for speaking to you as I did. It was unforgivable.

ARTHUR. Not at all, sir. You were upset at giving up the case—and, to be frank, I liked you for it—

SIR ROBERT (*with a deprecating gesture*). It was more, I fear, a matter of overstrained nerves. It has been rather a tiring day. The House of Commons is a peculiarly exhausting place, you know. Too little ventilation, and far too much hot air—I really am most truly sorry, sir—

ARTHUR. Please—

SIR ROBERT (*carelessly*). Of course, you must decide about the case as you wish. That really is a most charming hat, Miss Winslow—

CATHERINE. I'm glad you like it.

SIR ROBERT. It seems decidedly wrong to me that a lady of your political persuasion should be allowed to adorn herself with such a very feminine allurement. It really looks so awfully like trying to have the best of both worlds—

CATHERINE. I'm not a militant, you know, Sir Robert. I don't go about breaking shop windows with a hammer or pouring acid down pillar boxes.[36]

SIR ROBERT (*languidly*). I am truly glad to hear it. Both those activities would be highly unsuitable in that hat—

[CATHERINE *glares at him, but suppresses an angry retort.*]

I have never yet fully grasped what active steps you do take to propagate your cause, Miss Winslow.

CATHERINE (*shortly*). I'm an organizing secretary at the West London Branch of the Woman's Suffrage Association.

SIR ROBERT. Indeed? Is the work hard?

CATHERINE. Very.

SIR ROBERT. But not, I should imagine, particularly lucrative?

CATHERINE. The work is voluntary and unpaid.

[36] PILLAR BOXES—Public collection boxes for mail.

SIR ROBERT (*murmuring*). Dear me! What sacrifices you young ladies seem prepared to make for your convictions—

[VIOLET *enters.*]

VIOLET (*to* CATHERINE). Mr. Watherstone is in the hall, Miss. Says he would like to have a word with you in private—most particular—

[*Pause.*]

CATHERINE. Oh. I'll come out to him—

ARTHUR. No. See him in here. (*He begins to struggle out of his chair.* SIR ROBERT *assists him.*) You wouldn't mind coming to the dining room, would you, Sir Robert, for a moment?

[VIOLET, *at a nod from* CATHERINE, *goes out.*]

SIR ROBERT. Not in the least.

[JOHN *comes in. He is looking depressed and anxious.* CATHERINE *greets him with a smile, which he returns only halfheartedly. This exchange is lost on* ARTHUR, *who has his back to them, but not on* SIR ROBERT.]

CATHERINE. Hullo, John.

JOHN. Hullo. (*To* ARTHUR.) Good evening, sir.

ARTHUR. Good evening. (*He goes on towards dining room.*)

CATHERINE. I don't think you've met Sir Robert Morton?

JOHN. No, I haven't. How do you do, sir?

SIR ROBERT. How do you do? (*He sizes him up quickly.*) May I offer my very belated congratulations?

JOHN. Congratulations? Oh, yes. Thank you, sir.

ARTHUR (*at door*). Can I get you a whiskey and soda, Sir Robert?

SIR ROBERT. Thank you, yes. That would be most welcome.

[ARTHUR *and* SIR ROBERT *go into dining*

room. There is a pause. CATHERINE *is watching* JOHN *with an anxious expression.*]

JOHN (*indicating* RONNIE). Is he asleep?

CATHERINE. Yes.

JOHN. Sure he's not shamming?

CATHERINE. Yes.

JOHN (*after a pause*). My father's written your father a letter.

CATHERINE. I know. I've read it.

JOHN. Oh.

CATHERINE. Did you?

JOHN. Yes. He showed it to me. [*Pause.* JOHN *is carefully not looking at her.*] (*At length.*) Well, what's his answer?

CATHERINE. My father? I don't suppose he'll send one.

JOHN. You think that he'll ignore it?

CATHERINE. Isn't that the best answer to blackmail?

JOHN (*muttering*). It was highhanded of the old man, I admit.

CATHERINE. Highhanded?

JOHN. I tried to get him not to send it—

CATHERINE. I'm glad.

JOHN. The trouble is—he's perfectly serious.

CATHERINE. I never thought he wasn't.

JOHN. If your father does decide to go on with the case, I'm very much afraid he'll do everything he threatens.

CATHERINE. Forbid the match?

JOHN. Yes.

CATHERINE (*almost pleadingly*). Isn't that rather an empty threat, John?

JOHN (*slowly*). Well, there's always the allowance—

CATHERINE (*dully*). Yes, I see. There's always the allowance.

JOHN. I tell you, Kate darling, this is going to need careful handling; otherwise we'll find ourselves in the soup.

CATHERINE. Without your allowance would we be in the soup?

JOHN. And without your dowry? My dear old girl, of course we would. Dash it all, I can't even live on my pay as it is, but with two of us—

CATHERINE. I've heard it said that two can live as cheaply as one.

JOHN. Don't you believe it. Two can live as cheaply as two, and that's all there is to it.

CATHERINE. Yes, I see. I didn't know.

JOHN. Unlike you, I have a practical mind, Kate. I'm sorry, but it's no good dashing blindly ahead without thinking of these things first. The problem has got to be faced.

CATHERINE. I'm ready to face it, John. What do you suggest?

JOHN (*cautiously*). Well—I think you should consider very carefully before you take the next step—

CATHERINE. I can assure you we will, John. The question is—what *is* the next step?

JOHN. Well—this is the way I see it. I'm going to be honest now. I hope you don't mind—

CATHERINE. No. I should welcome it.

JOHN. Your kid brother over there pinches, or doesn't pinch, a five-bob postal order. For over a year you and your father fight a magnificent fight on his behalf, and I'm sure everyone admires you for it—

CATHERINE. Your father hardly seems to—?

JOHN. Well, he's a die-hard. He's like the type you've been up against at the Admiralty. I meant ordinary reasonable people, like myself. But now look —you've had two inquiries, the Petition of Right case which the Admiralty had thrown out of Court, and the Appeal. And now, good heavens, you've had the whole House of Commons getting them-

selves worked up into a frenzy about it. Surely, darling, that's enough for you? Surely the case can end there?

CATHERINE (*slowly*). Yes. I suppose the case can end there.

JOHN (*pointing to* RONNIE). *He* won't mind.

CATHERINE. No. I know he won't.

JOHN. Look at him! Perfectly happy and content. Not a care in the world. How do you know what's going on in his mind? How can you be so sure he didn't do it?

CATHERINE (*also gazing down at* RONNIE). I'm not so sure he didn't do it.

JOHN (*appalled*). Then why in heaven's name have you and your father spent all this time and money trying to prove his innocence?

CATHERINE (*quietly*). His innocence or guilt aren't important to me. They are to my father. Not to me. I believe he didn't do it: but I may be wrong. All that I care about is that people should know that a government department has ignored a fundamental human right, and that people should force it to acknowledge it. That's all that's important to me, John, but it *is* terribly important.

JOHN. But, darling, after all those long noble words, it does really resolve itself to a question of a fourteen-year-old kid and a five-bob postal order, doesn't it?

CATHERINE. Yes, it does.

JOHN (*reasonably*). Well now, look. There's a European war blowing up, there's a coal strike on, there's a fair chance of civil war in Ireland, and there's a hundred and one other things on the horizon at the moment that I think you genuinely could call *important*. And yet, with all that on its mind, the House of Commons takes a whole day to discuss him, (*Pointing to sofa.*) and his beastly postal order. Surely you must see that's a little out of proportion—?

[*Pause.* CATHERINE *raises her head slowly.*]

CATHERINE (*with some spirit*). All I know is, John, that if ever the time comes that the House of Commons has so much on its mind that it can't find time to discuss a Ronnie Winslow and his beastly postal order, this country will be a far poorer place than it is now. (*Wearily.*) But you needn't go on, John dear. You've said quite enough. I entirely see your point of view.

JOHN. Well, perhaps there is just one thing I ought to mention. I haven't said anything about it up to now because I didn't want to upset you. But it's this. I don't know whether you realize that all this publicity you're getting is making the name of Winslow a bit of a—well—

CATHERINE (*steadily*). A nation-wide laughingstock, your father said.

JOHN. Well, that's putting it a bit steep. But people do find the case a bit ridiculous, you know. I mean, I got chaps coming up to me in the mess all the time and saying: "I say, is it true you're going to marry the Winslow girl? By gosh, old man, you'd better be careful. You'll find yourself up in front of the House of Lords for pinching the Adjutant's bath." Things like that. They're not awfully funny—

CATHERINE. That's nothing. They're singing a verse about us at the Alhambra—

Winslow one day went to Heaven
And found a poor fellow in quod.[37]
The fellow said I didn't do it,
So naturally Winslow sued God.

JOHN. Well, darling—you see—

CATHERINE. Yes. I see. (*Quietly.*) Do you want to marry me, John?

JOHN. What?

[37] QUOD—Slang for *prison.*

CATHERINE. I said: do you want to marry me?

JOHN. Well, of course I do. You know I do. We've been engaged a year now. Have I ever wavered before?

CATHERINE. No. Never before.

JOHN (*correcting himself*). I'm not wavering now. Not a bit—I'm only telling you what I think is the best course for us to take.

CATHERINE. But isn't it already too late? Even if we gave up the case, would you still want to marry—the Winslow girl?

JOHN. All that would die down in a couple of weeks.

CATHERINE (*slowly*). And we'd have the allowance—

JOHN. Yes. We would.

CATHERINE. And that's so important—

JOHN (*quietly*). It is, darling. I'm sorry, but you can't shame me into saying it isn't.

CATHERINE. I didn't mean to shame you—

JOHN. Oh yes, you did. I know that tone of voice.

CATHERINE (*humbly*). I'm sorry.

JOHN (*confidently*). Well, now— what's the answer?

CATHERINE (*slowly*). The answer? You know quite well what the answer is, John. I've told it to you often enough. I love you and want to be your wife. Do you need another answer?

JOHN. No. That's quite good enough for me. Quite good enough. Darling! I was sure nothing so stupid and trivial could possibly come between us.

[*He kisses her. She responds wearily. Telephone rings. After a pause she releases herself and picks up receiver.*]

CATHERINE. Hullo . . . Yes . . . Will you hold on? (*She goes to dining-room door and calls.*) Sir Robert! Sir Robert!

Someone wants you on the telephone—

[SIR ROBERT *comes out of dining room.*]

SIR ROBERT. Thank you. I'm so sorry to interrupt.

CATHERINE. You didn't. We'd finished our talk.

[SIR ROBERT *looks at her inquiringly. She gives him no sign. He walks to telephone.*]

SIR ROBERT (*noticing sandwiches*). How delicious. May I help myself?

CATHERINE. Do.

SIR ROBERT (*into receiver*). Hullo . . . Yes, Michael . . . F. E.? I didn't know he was going to speak . . . I see . . . Go on . . .

[*The man at other end of line speaks for some time.* SIR ROBERT *listens with closed eyelids, munching a sandwich, meanwhile. At length.*]

Thank you, Michael. (*He rings off.* ARTHUR *has appeared in dining-room doorway. To* ARTHUR.) There has been a most interesting development in the House, sir.

ARTHUR. What?

SIR ROBERT. It appears that a barrister friend of mine who, quite unknown to me, was interested in the case, got on his feet shortly after nine-thirty and delivered one of the most scathing denunciations of a government department ever heard in the House. (*To* CATHERINE.) What a shame we missed it. His style is quite superb—I am one of his most ardent admirers—

ARTHUR. Never mind that, sir. What happened?

SIR ROBERT. The debate revived, of course, and the First Lord, who must have felt himself fairly safe, suddenly found himself under attack from all parts of the House. My secretary tells me that rather than risk a division [38] he has this moment given an undertaking that he will instruct the Attorney-General to endorse our Petition of Right. The case of Winslow versus Rex [39] can now therefore come to court.

[*There is a pause.* ARTHUR *and* CATHERINE *stare at him unbelievingly. At length.*]

Well, sir. What are my instructions?

ARTHUR (*slowly*). The decision is no longer mine, sir. You must ask my daughter.

SIR ROBERT. What are my instructions, Miss Winslow?

[CATHERINE *goes slowly to sofa and looks down at the sleeping* RONNIE. ARTHUR *is at the other end of the sofa, watching her intensely.* SIR ROBERT, *in the middle, munching sandwiches, is also looking at her.*]

CATHERINE (*in a flat voice*). Do you need any instructions, Sir Robert? Aren't they already on the Petition? Doesn't it say: Let Right be done?

[JOHN *makes a move of protest toward her. She does not look at him. He turns abruptly to door.*]

JOHN (*furiously*). Good night, Kate.

[*He goes out.* SIR ROBERT, *with languid speculation, watches him go.*]

SIR ROBERT (*his mouth full*). Well, then—we must endeavor to see that it is.

[38] RATHER THAN RISK A DIVISION—The Prime Minister is afraid that his side will be defeated if Parliament votes on the stand he has taken. Therefore, yielding to public opinion, he has granted Ronnie permission to sue the government in court.

[39] WINSLOW VERSUS REX—Winslow against the King.

ACT IV

SCENE: *The same, about eight months later. It is a stiflingly hot June day— nearly two years, less one month, since Ronnie's dismissal from Osborne. The glass door to the garden stands open, and a Bath chair,*[40] *unoccupied, has been placed nearby.*

On the rise of the curtain the stage is empty and the telephone is ringing insistently.

DICKIE *comes in from hall carrying a suitcase, evidently very hot, his straw hat pushed onto the back of his head and panting from his exertions. He is wearing a neat blue suit, a sober tie, and a stiff collar. He puts suitcase down and mops his face with his handkerchief. Then he goes to hall door and calls:*

DICKIE. Mother! (*There is no reply.*) Violet! (*Again no reply.*) Anyone about? (*He closes door, shrugs his shoulders, and goes to telephone—taking off receiver.*) Hullo . . . No, not Senior— Junior . . . I don't know where he is . . . *Daily Mail?* . . . No, I'm the brother . . . Elder brother—that's right . . . Well—I'm in the banking business . . . That's right. Following in Father's footsteps . . . My views on the case?

Well—I—er—I don't know I have any, except, I mean, I hope we win and all that . . . No, I haven't been in court. I've only just arrived from Reading . . . Reading . . . Yes. That's where I work . . . Yes, I've come up for the last two days of the trial. Verdict's expected to-morrow, isn't it? . . . Twenty-two, last March . . . *Seven* years older . . . No. He was thirteen when it happened, but now he's fifteen[41]. . . Well, I suppose, if I'm anything I'm a sort of Liberal-Conservative . . . Single . . . No. No immediate prospects. I say, is this at all interesting to you? . . . Well, a perfectly ordinary kid, just like any other— makes a noise, does fretwork, doesn't wash and all that . . . Doesn't wash . . . (*Alarmed.*) I say, don't take that too literally. I mean he does, sometimes . . . Yes. All right. Good-by . . .

[*He rings off and is just going to sit down when telephone rings again. He gets up to answer it, when* GRACE, *dressed for going out, comes out of dining room.*]

GRACE. Oh, hullo, darling. When did you get here? (*On her way to him she picks up telephone receiver. Into receiver.*) Everyone out. (*She rings off*

[40] *Bath chair*—A wheel chair with a hood or cover, such as is used by invalids at the town of Bath.

[41] *Seven* YEARS OLDER . . . NOW HE'S FIF-TEEN—The newspaper reporter has confused Dickie's age with Ronnie's, and has jumped to the conclusion that the case has been going on for seven years.

and embraces DICKIE.) You're thinner. I like your new suit.

DICKIE. Straight from Reading's Savile Row.[42] Off the peg [43] at three and a half guineas. (*Pointing to telephone.*) I say —does that go on all the time?

GRACE. All the blessed day. The last four days it simply hasn't stopped.

DICKIE. I had to fight my way in through an army of reporters and people—

GRACE. Yes, I know. You didn't say anything, I hope, Dickie dear? It's better not to say a word—

DICKIE. I don't think I said anything much . . . (*Carelessly.*) Oh, yes. I did say that I personally thought he did it—

GRACE (*horrified*). Dickie! You didn't. [*He is smiling at her.*] Oh, I see. It's a joke. You mustn't say things like that, even in fun, Dickie dear—

DICKIE. How's it all going?

GRACE. I don't know. I've been there all four days now and I've hardly understood a word that's going on. Kate says the judge is against us, but he seems a charming old gentleman to me. (*Faintly shocked.*) Sir Robert's so rude to him— (*Telephone rings,* GRACE *answers it automatically.*) Nobody in. (*She rings off and turns to garden door—calling.*) Arthur! Lunch! I'll come straight down. Dickie's here. (*To* DICKIE.) Kate takes the morning session, then she comes and relieves me with Arthur, and I go in the afternoons, so you can come with me as soon as she's in.

DICKIE. Will there be room for me?

GRACE. Oh, yes. They reserve places for the family. You never saw such crowds in all your life. And such excite-

[42] SAVILE ROW—A fashionable street in London on which are located some exclusive tailor shops. Dickie is making fun of the inferior shops in Reading where he now lives.
[43] OFF THE PEG—The suit is ready-made, taken just as it comes off the clothes rack.

ment! Cheers and applause and people being turned out. It's thrilling—you'll love it, Dickie.

DICKIE. Well—if I don't understand a word—

GRACE. Oh, that doesn't matter. They all get so terribly worked up, you find yourself getting worked up yourself. Sir Robert and the Attorney-General go at each other hammer and tongs—you wait and hear them—all about petitions and demurrers and prerogatives and things. Nothing to do with Ronnie at all—seems to me—

DICKIE. How did Ronnie get on in the witness box?

GRACE. Two days he was cross-examined. Two whole days. Imagine it, the poor little pet! I must say he didn't seem to mind much. He said two days with the Attorney-General wasn't nearly as bad as two minutes with Sir Robert. Kate says he made a very good impression with the jury—

DICKIE. How is Kate, Mother?

GRACE. Oh, all right. You heard about John, I suppose—?

DICKIE. Yes. That's what I meant. How has she taken it?

GRACE. You can never tell with Kate. She never lets you know what she's feeling. We all think he's behaved very badly—

[ARTHUR *appears at garden door, walking very groggily.*]

Arthur! You shouldn't have come up the stairs by yourself.

ARTHUR. I had little alternative.

GRACE. I'm sorry, dear. I was talking to Dickie. (GRACE *helps* ARTHUR *into Bath chair.*)

ARTHUR. How are you, Dickie?

DICKIE (*shaking hands*). Very well, thank you, Father.

ARTHUR. I've been forced to adopt this ludicrous form of propulsion. I apologize. (*He wheels himself into room and examines* DICKIE.) You look very well. A trifle thinner, perhaps—

DICKIE. Hard work, Father.

ARTHUR. Or late hours?

DICKIE. You can't keep late hours in Reading.

ARTHUR. I should have thought you could keep late hours anywhere. I've had quite a good report about you from Mr. Lamb.

DICKIE. Good egg! He's a decent old stick, the old baa-lamb. I took him racing last Saturday. Had the time of his life and lost his shirt.

ARTHUR. Quite so. I have no doubt that, given the chance, you'll succeed in converting the entire Reading branch of the Westminster Bank into a bookmaking establishment. Mr. Lamb says you've joined the Territorials? [44]

DICKIE. Yes, Father.

ARTHUR. Why have you done that?

DICKIE. Well, from all accounts there's a fair chance of a bit of a scrap quite soon. If there is, I don't want it to be all over before I can get in on it—

ARTHUR. If there is what you call a scrap, you'll do far better to stay in the bank—

DICKIE. Oh no, Father. I mean, the bank's all right—but still—a chap can't help looking forward to a bit of a change —I can always go back to the bank afterwards—

[*Telephone rings.* GRACE *answers it.*]

GRACE. Hullo! . . . Sorry. Everyone's out. (*She rings off.*)

ARTHUR. Why don't you disconnect that thing? Look. (ARTHUR *wheels himself over and takes receiver off.*)

GRACE. Oh, no, dear. You can't do that.

ARTHUR. Why not?

GRACE. It annoys the exchange.

ARTHUR. I prefer to annoy the exchange than have the exchange annoy me. (*To* GRACE.) Catherine's late. She was in at half past yesterday.

GRACE. Perhaps they're taking the lunch interval later today?

ARTHUR. Lunch interval? This isn't a cricket match. (*Looking at her.*) Nor, may I say, is it a matinee at the Gaiety. Why are you wearing that highly unsuitable get-up?

GRACE. Don't you like it, dear? I think it's Mme. Dupont's best.

ARTHUR. Grace—your son is facing a charge of theft and forgery—

GRACE. Oh, dear! It's so difficult! I simply can't be seen in the same old dress, day after day. (*A thought strikes her.*) I tell you what, Arthur. I'll wear my black coat and skirt tomorrow—for the verdict.

[ARTHUR *glares at her, helplessly, then turns his chair to dining room.*]

ARTHUR. Did you say my lunch was ready?

GRACE. Yes, dear. It's only cold. I did the salad myself. Violet and Cook are at the trial.

DICKIE. Is Violet still with you? She was under sentence last time I saw you—?

GRACE. She's been under sentence for the last six months, poor thing—only she doesn't know it. Neither Arthur nor I have the courage to tell her—

ARTHUR (*stopping at door*). I have the courage to tell her.

GRACE. It's funny that you don't, then, dear.

ARTHUR. I will.

GRACE (*hastily*). No, no, you mustn't. When it's to be done, I'll do it.

ARTHUR. You see, Dickie? These taunts of cowardice are daily flung at my head; but should I take them up I'm for-

---

[44] TERRITORIALS—The Territorial Reserve, a branch of the army organized primarily for the defense of foreign possessions.

bidden to move. Such is the logic of women.

[*He goes into dining room.* DICKIE, *who has been holding door open, closes it after him.*]

DICKIE (*seriously*). How *is* he?

[GRACE *shakes her head quietly.*]

Will you take him away after the trial?

GRACE. He's promised to go into a home.

DICKIE. Do you think he will?

GRACE. How do I know? He'll probably find some new excuse—

DICKIE. But surely, if he loses this time, he's lost for good, hasn't he?

GRACE (*slowly*). So they say, Dickie dear—I can only hope it's true.

DICKIE. How did you keep him away from the trial?

GRACE. Kate and Sir Robert together. He wouldn't listen to me or the doctor.

DICKIE. Poor old Mother! You must have been having a pretty rotten time of it, one way and another—

GRACE. I've said my say, Dickie. He knows what I think. Not that he cares. He never has—all his life. Anyway, I've given up worrying. He's always said he knew what he was doing. It's my job to try and pick up the pieces, I suppose.

[CATHERINE *comes in.*]

CATHERINE. Heavens! The heat! Mother, can't you get rid of those reporters—? Hullo, Dickie.

DICKIE (*embracing her*). Hullo, Kate.

CATHERINE. Come to be in at the death?

DICKIE. Is that what it's going to be?

CATHERINE. Looks like it. I could cheerfully strangle that old brute of a judge, Mother. He's dead against us.

GRACE (*fixing her hat in mirror*). Oh, dear! Do I look all right, Kate?

CATHERINE. Yes, Mother. You look extremely smart. Sir Robert's very worried. He said the Attorney-General's speech made a great impression on the jury.

GRACE. Such a fine-looking man, the Attorney-General, don't you think, Kate?

CATHERINE. Yes, Mother. Very fine-looking. Also, I'm afraid, very eloquent. To listen to him yesterday you would have thought that a verdict for Ronnie would simultaneously cause a mutiny in the Royal Navy and triumphant jubilation in Berlin. Very clever.

[ARTHUR *appears in his chair, at dining-room door.*]

ARTHUR. You're late, Catherine.

CATHERINE. I know, Father. I'm sorry. There was such a huge crowd outside as well as inside the court that I couldn't get a cab. And I stayed to talk to Sir Robert.

GRACE (*pleased*). Is there a bigger crowd even than yesterday, Kate?

CATHERINE. Yes, Mother. Far bigger.

ARTHUR. How did it go this morning?

CATHERINE. Sir Robert finished his cross-examination of the post mistress. I thought he'd demolished her completely. She admitted she couldn't identify Ronnie in the Commander's office. She admitted she couldn't be sure of the time he came in. She admitted that she was called away to the telephone while he was buying his fifteen-and-six postal order, and that all Osborne cadets looked alike to her in their uniforms, so that it might quite easily have been another cadet who cashed the five shillings. It was a brilliant cross-examination. So gentle and quiet. He didn't bully her, or frighten her—he just coaxed her into tying herself into knots. Then when he finished the Attorney-General asked her again whether she was absolutely positive that the same boy that bought the fifteen-and-six postal order also cashed the five shilling one. She said yes. She was quite, quite sure because Ronnie was such a good-looking little boy that she had specially noticed him. She hadn't said that in her examination-in-chief. I could see those twelve good men and true nodding to each other. I believe it undid the whole of that magnificent cross-examination.

ARTHUR. If she thought him so especially good-looking, why couldn't she identify him the same evening?

CATHERINE. Don't ask me, Father. Ask the Attorney-General. I'm sure he has a beautifully reasonable answer.

DICKIE. Ronnie good-looking! What utter rot! She must be lying, that woman.

GRACE. Nonsense, Dickie! I thought he looked very well in the box yesterday, didn't you, Kate?

CATHERINE. Yes, Mother.

ARTHUR. Who else gave evidence for the other side?

CATHERINE. The Commander, the Chief Petty Officer, and one of the boys at the College.

ARTHUR. Anything very damaging?

CATHERINE. Nothing that we didn't expect. The boy showed obviously he hated Ronnie and was torn to shreds by Sir Robert. The Commander scored, though. He's an honest man and genuinely believes Ronnie did it.

GRACE. Did you see anybody interesting in court, dear?

CATHERINE. Yes, Mother. John Watherstone.

GRACE. John? I hope you didn't speak to him, Kate?

CATHERINE. Of course I did.

GRACE. Kate, how could you! What did he say?

CATHERINE. He wished us luck.

GRACE. What impertinence!

CATHERINE. He said some fellows in his battalion had been having quite heated arguments lately about the rights and wrongs of the case. He was surprised, he said. People didn't seem to be finding it a joke any more. Some people, even—quite intelligent fellows, too—seemed to be finding it rather important. That was why he had come to court—

ARTHUR. Did he find it important?

CATHERINE. No. He pretended to, politely, for my benefit—of course—

GRACE. I should hope so—

CATHERINE. But to him it's still a five-bob postal order and a fifteen-year-old kid.

DICKIE. Sorry for being dense, but what else is it?

CATHERINE. Quite a lot, Dickie. I'll explain to you some time.

ARTHUR. You will be wasting your breath if you do.

GRACE. The idea of John Watherstone coming calmly up in court to wish you luck—I think it's the most disgraceful, cold-blooded—

ARTHUR. Grace—you will be late for the resumption.

GRACE. Oh, will I? Are you ready, Dickie?

DICKIE. Yes, Mother.

GRACE. You don't think that nice, gray suit of yours you paid so much money for—?

ARTHUR. What time are they resuming, Kate?

CATHERINE. Two o'clock.

ARTHUR. It's twenty past two now.

GRACE. Oh, dear! We'll be terribly late. Kate—that's your fault. Arthur, you must finish your lunch—

ARTHUR. Yes, Grace.

GRACE. Promise now.

ARTHUR. I promise.

GRACE (to herself). I wonder if Violet will remember to pick up those onions? Perhaps I'd better do it on the way back from the court. (As she passes CATHERINE.) Kate, dear, I'm so sorry—

CATHERINE. What for, Mother?

GRACE. John proving such a bad hat. I never did like him very much, you know.

CATHERINE. I know.

GRACE. Has Desmond been in to see you at all lately?

CATHERINE. No, Mother.

GRACE. Funny. Oh, well. I expect he's so busy on the case. (*To* DICKIE.) Now, Dickie, when you get to the front door put your head down, like me, and just charge through them all.

ARTHUR. Why don't you go out by the garden into the mews? [45]

GRACE. I wouldn't like to risk tearing this dress getting through that hedge. Come on, Dickie. I always shout: "I'm the maid and don't know nothing," so don't be surprised.

DICKIE. Right-o, Mother.

[GRACE *goes out.* DICKIE *follows her to door.*]

CATHERINE. What's happened to Edwina, Dickie?

DICKIE. Engaged to a chap I used to know. Stockbroker. You wouldn't expect her to look at a mere bank clerk, would you?

CATHERINE. Bad luck.

DICKIE. Oh, I don't know. On a long view I suppose you might say it's about the only good thing that's come out of this case—Well—good-by-ee! (*He goes out.*)

ARTHUR. Good-by-ee! Where does he pick up these loathsome expressions?

CATHERINE. I think it comes from a song.

[*There is a pause.*]

ARTHUR. Are we going to lose this case, Kate?

[CATHERINE *quietly shrugs her shoulders.*]

[45] INTO THE MEWS—By way of the stables—that is, the back way.

It's our last chance.

CATHERINE. I know.

ARTHUR (*with sudden violence*). We've got to win it.

[CATHERINE *does not reply.*]

What does Sir Robert think?

CATHERINE. He's very worried.

ARTHUR (*thoughtfully*). I wonder if you were right, Kate? I wonder if we could have had a better man?

CATHERINE. No, Father. We couldn't have had a better man.

ARTHUR. You admit that now, do you?

CATHERINE. Only that he's the best advocate in England and for some reason —prestige, I suppose—he seems genuinely anxious to win this case. I don't go back on anything else I've ever said about him.

ARTHUR. The papers said that he began today by telling the judge he felt ill and might have to ask for an adjournment. I trust he won't collapse—

CATHERINE. He won't. It was just another of those brilliant tricks of his that he's always boasting about. It got him the sympathy of the court and possibly— no, I won't say that—

ARTHUR. Say it.

CATHERINE (*slowly*). Possibly provided him with an excuse if beaten.

ARTHUR. You don't like him, do you?

CATHERINE (*indifferently*). There's nothing in him to like or dislike, Father. I admire him.

[DESMOND *appears at garden door. Standing inside the room, he knocks diffidently.* CATHERINE *and* ARTHUR *turn and see him.*]

DESMOND. I trust you do not object to me employing this rather furtive entrance? The crowds at the front door are most alarming—

ARTHUR. Come in, Desmond. Why have you left the court?

DESMOND. I have not returned there

since the lunch adjournment. My partner will be holding the fort. He is perfectly competent, I promise you—as competent in some aspects of the case, as I myself.

ARTHUR. That is truly reassuring.

DESMOND. I wonder if I might see Catherine alone? I have a matter of some urgency to communicate to her—

ARTHUR. Oh. Do you wish to hear this urgent matter, Kate?

CATHERINE. Yes, Father.

ARTHUR. Very well. I shall go and finish my lunch.

[*He wheels his chair to dining-room door.* DESMOND *flies to help.*]

Thank you. I can manage this vehicle without assistance. (*He goes out.*)

DESMOND. I fear I should have warned you of my visit this afternoon. Perhaps I have interrupted—?

CATHERINE. No, Desmond. Please sit down.

DESMOND. Thank you. I'm afraid I have only a very short time. A very short time. I must get back to court for the cross-examination of the Judge-Advocate. My partner is, I can confess to you, Kate, not really so well-versed in this case as I am. Not his fault, of course, poor fellow. It just so happens that I have been involved in the battle from the beginning. From the very beginning, in fact. Do you remember that day?

CATHERINE. Yes, Desmond. Well.

DESMOND. Of course you do. Who better? I have a taxicab waiting at the end of the street.

CATHERINE (*smiling*). How very extravagant of you, Desmond!

DESMOND (*also smiling*). Is it not? But it shows you how rushed this visit must necessarily be. The fact of the matter is—it suddenly occurred to me during the lunch recess that I had far better see

you today than tomorrow, and if today, why not this very minute?

CATHERINE (*her thoughts far distant*). Why not, indeed?

DESMOND. I have a question to put to you, Kate, which, if I had postponed putting until after the verdict, you might —who knows—have thought had been prompted by pity—if we had lost. Or— if we had won, your reply might—again who knows?—have been influenced by gratitude. Do you follow me, Kate?

CATHERINE. Yes, Desmond. I think I do.

DESMOND. Ah. Then possibly you have some inkling of what the question is I have to put to you?

CATHERINE. Yes. I think I have.

DESMOND (*a trifle disconcerted*). Oh.

CATHERINE. I'm sorry, Desmond. I ought, I know, to have followed the usual practice in such cases, and told you I had no inkling whatever.

DESMOND. No, no. Your directness and honesty are two of the qualities I so much admire in you. I am glad you have guessed. It makes my task the easier—

CATHERINE (*in a matter-of-fact voice*). Will you give me a few days to think it over?

DESMOND. Of course. Of course.

CATHERINE. I need hardly tell you how flattered I feel, Desmond.

DESMOND (*a trifle bewildered*). There is no need, Kate. No need at all—

[CATHERINE *has risen brusquely.*]

CATHERINE. You mustn't keep your taxi waiting—

DESMOND. Oh, bother my taxi! (*He glares at her almost fiercely.*) I know perfectly well you are pining to get rid of me and be alone with your thoughts of the man you really love. Oh, yes, I saw you talking to him this morning in court. I saw the way you looked at him. Nevertheless, I am determined to say my say.

CATHERINE (*subsiding into a chair*). I'm sorry, Desmond.

DESMOND. It is this. I am entirely aware of what you really feel about me. If I proved the most devoted and adoring husband that ever lived—which, I may say, if you give me the chance, I intend to be—I know that you could never, never feel anything for me except a faintly affectionate but nevertheless contemptuous pity. I know you think—you and your father both—that I'm a middle-aged nonentity living on the memory of a past athletic eminence.

CATHERINE. Desmond!

DESMOND. It's no good saying "Desmond!" like that. I know that's what you both think of me and worst of all, I know that it's true. [CATHERINE, *this time, is silent, looking at him surprised.*] However, that is beside the point. The points germane to the issue [46] are that you don't love me and that you never can: that I love you, always have, and always will. That is the situation—and it is a situation which—after most careful consideration of all the relevant pros and cons—I am fully prepared to accept. I reached this decision some months ago, but thought at first it would be better to wait until this case, which is so much on all our minds, should be over. Then at lunch today I determined, as I told you, to anticipate the verdict tomorrow, and acquaint you with my decision forthwith. No matter what you feel or don't feel for me—no matter what you feel for anyone else—I want you to be my wife, Kate.

[*Pause.*]

CATHERINE (*at length*). I see. Thank you, Desmond. That makes everything much clearer.

DESMOND. There is much more that I had meant to say, but your directness in

coming to the point has a little disconcerted me. I shall put it in a letter.

CATHERINE. Yes, Desmond. Do.

DESMOND. Then I may expect your answer in a few days?

CATHERINE. Yes, Desmond.

DESMOND. Can you give me any hint at all now as to what that answer might be?

CATHERINE. No. No hint at all, I'm afraid. Like you, I shall have to give very careful consideration to all the relevant pros and cons.

DESMOND. That is most hopeful. Most hopeful. I don't mind telling you I had feared an instant and furious rebuttal.

CATHERINE. Then you don't know me, Desmond, as well as you think you do.

DESMOND. I say I feared it. I didn't say I expected it. (*Looking at his watch.*) I must get back to court. (*He collects his hat, stick, and gloves.*) How did you think it went this morning?

CATHERINE. I thought the postmistress restored the Admiralty's case with that point about Ronnie's looks—

DESMOND. Oh, no, no. Not at all. There is still the overwhelming fact that she couldn't identify him. What a brilliant cross-examination, was it not?

CATHERINE. Brilliant.

DESMOND. He is a strange man, Sir Robert. At times, so cold and distant and—and—

CATHERINE. Fishlike.

DESMOND. Fishlike, exactly. And yet he has a real passion about this case. A real passion. I happen to know—of course this must on no account go any further—but I happen to know that he has made a very, very great personal sacrifice in order to bring it to court.

CATHERINE. Sacrifice? What? Of another brief?

DESMOND. No, no. Of course not. That is no sacrifice to him. No—he was

[46] POINTS GERMANE TO THE ISSUE—The points that have some bearing on the matter.

offered—you really promise to keep this to yourself?

CATHERINE (*impatiently*). Yes, yes. I promise.

DESMOND (*tenderly*). The first secret —of many—let us hope.

CATHERINE. What was he offered, Desmond?

DESMOND. The post of Lord Chief Justice. He turned it down, simply in order to be able to carry on with the case of Winslow versus Rex.[47] Strange are the ways of men, are they not? Good-by, my dear. I shall await your reply in all eagerness.

CATHERINE. Good-by, Desmond.

[DESMOND *goes.* CATHERINE *turns from window, deep in thought. She has a puzzled, strained expression. It does not look as though it were* DESMOND *she was thinking of. There is a peremptory knock on dining-room door. She goes to open it.* ARTHUR *wheels his chair in.*]

(*Slowly.*) I've been a fool, Father.

ARTHUR. Have you, my dear?

CATHERINE. An utter fool.

[ARTHUR *waits for* CATHERINE *to make herself plain. She does not do so.*]

ARTHUR. In default of further information, I can only repeat, have you, my dear?

CATHERINE. There's no further information. I'm under a pledge of secrecy.

ARTHUR. Oh. What did Desmond want?

CATHERINE. To marry me.

ARTHUR. I trust the folly you were referring to wasn't your acceptance of him?

CATHERINE (*smiling*). No, Father. (*She comes and sits on arm of his chair.*) Would it be such folly, though?

[47] HE TURNED IT DOWN . . . WINSLOW VERSUS REX—Because Sir Robert would not drop the Winslow case, which was a lawsuit against the present political administration, he could not accept office under the same administration.

ARTHUR. Lunacy.

CATHERINE. Oh, I don't know. He's a nice old thing and he's doing very well as a solicitor.

ARTHUR. Neither very compelling reasons for marrying him.

CATHERINE. Seriously—I shall have to think it over.

ARTHUR. Think it over, by all means. But decide against it.

CATHERINE. I'm nearly thirty, you know.

ARTHUR. Thirty isn't the end of life.

CATHERINE. It might be—for an unmarried woman, with not much looks and no charm.

ARTHUR. Rubbish. [CATHERINE *shakes her head.*] Better far to live and die an old maid than to marry Desmond.

CATHERINE. Even an old maid must eat.

[*Pause.*]

ARTHUR. I am leaving you and Grace everything, you know.

CATHERINE (*quietly*). Everything?

ARTHUR. There is still a little left. (*Pause.*) Did you take my suggestion as regards your Suffrage Association?

CATHERINE. Yes, Father.

ARTHUR. You demanded a salary?

CATHERINE. I asked for one.

ARTHUR. And they're going to give it to you, I trust?

CATHERINE. Yes, Father. Two pounds a week.

ARTHUR (*angrily*). That's insulting.

CATHERINE. No. It's very generous. It's all they can afford. We're not a very rich organization—you know.

ARTHUR. You'll have to think of something else.

CATHERINE. What else? Darning socks? That's about my only other accomplishment.

ARTHUR. There must be something useful you can do.

CATHERINE. You don't think the work I am doing at the W.S.A. is useful. [ARTHUR *is silent*.] You may be right. But it's the only work I'm fitted for, all the same. (*Pause*.) No, Father. The choice is quite simple. Either I marry Desmond and settle down into quite a comfortable and not really useless existence—or I go on for the rest of my life earning two pounds a week in the service of a hopeless cause.

ARTHUR. A hopeless cause? I've never heard you say that before.

CATHERINE. I've never felt it before. [ARTHUR *is silent*.] (CATHERINE *leans her head against his chair*.) John's going to get married next month.

ARTHUR. Did he tell you?

CATHERINE. Yes. He was very apologetic.

ARTHUR. Apologetic!

CATHERINE. He didn't need to be. It's a girl I know slightly. She'll make him a good wife.

ARTHUR. Is he in love with her?

CATHERINE. No more than he was with me. Perhaps, even, a little less.

ARTHUR. Why is he marrying her so soon after—after—?

CATHERINE. After jilting me? Because he thinks there's going to be a war. If there is, his regiment will be among the first to go overseas. Besides, his father approves strongly. She's a general's daughter. Very, very suitable.

ARTHUR. Poor Kate! (*Pause. He takes her hand slowly*.) How I've messed up your life, haven't I?

CATHERINE. No, Father. Any messing-up that's been done has been done by me.

ARTHUR. I'm so sorry, Kate. I'm so sorry.

CATHERINE. Don't be, Father. We both knew what we were doing.

ARTHUR. Did we?

CATHERINE. I think we did.

ARTHUR. Yet our motives seem to have been different all along—yours and mine, Kate? Can we both have been right?

CATHERINE. I believe we can. I believe we have been.

ARTHUR. And yet they've always been so infernally logical, our opponents, haven't they?

CATHERINE. I'm afraid logic has never been on our side.

ARTHUR. Brute stubbornness—a selfish refusal to admit defeat. That's what your mother thinks have been our motives—

CATHERINE. Perhaps she's right. Perhaps that's all they've been.

ARTHUR. But perhaps brute stubbornness isn't such a bad quality in the face of injustice?

CATHERINE. Or in the face of tyranny. (*Pause*.) If you could go back, Father, and choose again—would your choice be different?

ARTHUR. Perhaps.

CATHERINE. I don't think so.

ARTHUR. I don't think so, either.

CATHERINE. I still say we both knew what we were doing. And we were right to do it.

[ARTHUR *kisses the top of her head*.]

ARTHUR. Dear Kate. Thank you.

[*There is a silence. A* NEWSBOY *can be heard dimly shouting from the street outside*.] You aren't going to marry Desmond, are you?

CATHERINE (*with a smile*). In the words of the Prime Minister, Father—let us wait and see.

[*He squeezes her hand.* NEWSBOY *can still be heard—now a little louder*.]

ARTHUR. What's the boy shouting, Kate?

CATHERINE. Only—Winslow case—Latest.

ARTHUR. It didn't sound to me like "Latest."

[CATHERINE *gets up to listen at window. Suddenly we hear it quite plainly: "Winslow Case Result! Winslow Case Result!"*]

Result?

CATHERINE. There must be some mistake.

[*There is a very loud knocking at front door.* ARTHUR *is struggling out of his chair.*]

Stay there, Father! Stay there!

[*Knocking continues, growing louder and more incessant.* CATHERINE *runs out of room.* ARTHUR *stays still in his chair, clutching its sides with a convulsive grip. There is a sudden babel of voices and cheers as the front door is opened, ceasing again as we hear it being slammed.* CATHERINE *reappears, walking quite slowly. She is reading in the stop-press column.[48] She slips onto floor beside* ARTHUR *and begins to read with a voice in which emotion is at war with a desperate attempt to keep her tones flat and level.*]

(*Reading.*) "Winslow Case Result. Immediately on court reassembling after adjournment Attorney-General, after consultation Sir. R. Morton, announced on point fact Admiralty now prepared accept R. Winslow's statement he did not steal postal order. Scenes of tremendous enthusiasm greeted judge's—" (*Her voice breaks. She repeats.*) "scenes of tremendous enthusiasm greeted judge's announcement. Case now closed with complete vindication R. Winslow and Mr. A. Winslow's action in bringing Petition of Right." (*She pauses to control her voice before going on.* ARTHUR *is listening without a sign of emotion.*) "Cheering

[48] *Stop-press column*—The "flash" news items that were inserted at the last minute.

lasted several minutes and was taken up in street outside. Neither R. Winslow nor Mr. A. Winslow nor any member of Winslow family in court to hear verdict which not expected until tomorrow. Reports say demonstrations still continue"— (*She finishes reading.*) That's all, Father.

ARTHUR. It would seem, then, that we've won.

CATHERINE. Yes. It would seem that we've won.

[*She rests her head in his lap and cries quietly.* ARTHUR *strokes her head.*]

ARTHUR. I would have liked to have been there.

[*There is another sudden outburst of noise from hall as front door is opened. It subsides again.* VIOLET *comes in quickly with a broad smile.*]

VIOLET. Oh, sir! Oh, sir! (*She shakes hands with* ARTHUR.)

ARTHUR. Thank you, Violet.

VIOLET. Oh, Miss Kate, what a shame you missed it! Just after they come back from lunch, and Mrs. Winslow she wasn't there neither, nor Master Ronnie. The cheering and the shouting and the carrying-on—you never heard anything like it in all your life—and Sir Robert standing there at the table with his wig on crooked and the tears running down his face and not able to speak because of the noise. Cook and me did a bit of crying, too; we just couldn't help it—you couldn't, you know. Oh, we did enjoy ourselves! And then outside—the street it was just the same—the cheering and the shouting— you couldn't move for the crowd and when Sir Robert came out and got in his car they sang "For he's a jolly good fellow," and he asked us to get in—fancy, Miss—a great big Rolls Royce, and he drove us away through the crowd all singing and cheering still, and some of them even climbing on the car—

CATHERINE. Sir Robert drove you home?

VIOLET. Oh yes, Miss. We sat on the back seat, one on either side of him. You would have laughed—Cook said—

CATHERINE. Where is he now?

VIOLET. Oh, those reporters caught him at the door, Miss. You know what they're like. I just slipped him the key and went on in. (*To* ARTHUR.) Well, sir—you must be feeling nice and pleased, now it's all over?

ARTHUR. Yes, Violet. I am.

VIOLET. That's right. I always said it would come all right in the end, didn't I?

ARTHUR. Yes. You did.

VIOLET. Two years all but one month it's been now, since Master Ronnie come back that day. Fancy.

ARTHUR. Yes.

VIOLET. I don't mind telling you, sir, I wondered sometimes whether you and Miss Kate weren't just wasting your time carrying on the way you have all the time. Still—you couldn't have felt that if you'd been in court today— (*She turns to go and stops.*) Oh, sir, Mrs. Winslow asked me to remember most particular to pick up some onions from the green-grocer, but seeing as I was in a Rolls Royce car—

CATHERINE. That's all right, Violet. I think Mrs. Winslow is picking them up herself, on her way back—

VIOLET. I see, Miss. Poor Madam! What a sell for her when she gets to the court and finds it's all over. Well, sir— congratulations, I'm sure.

ARTHUR. Thank you, Violet.

[VIOLET *is about to go out, when* SIR ROBERT *walks in.*]

VIOLET. Oh, sir—thank you so much for the ride—

SIR ROBERT. Not at all. Glad to have been of service.

[VIOLET *goes out.* SIR ROBERT *walks calmly and methodically into the* room. *He looks as spruce and neat as ever, and Violet's description of him in court does not seem to tally with his composed features.*]

I thought you might like to hear the actual terms of the Attorney-General's statement— (*He pulls out a scrap of paper.*) So I jotted it down for you. (*Reading.*) "I say now, on behalf of the Admiralty, that I accept the declaration of Ronald Arthur Winslow that he did not write the name on the postal order, that he did not take it, and that he did not cash it, and that consequently he was innocent of the charge which was brought against him two years ago. I make that statement without any reservation of any description, intending it to be a complete acceptance of the boy's statements." (*He folds paper up and hands it to* ARTHUR.)

ARTHUR. Thank you, sir. It is rather hard for me to find the words I should speak to you.

SIR ROBERT. Pray do not trouble yourself to search for them, sir. Let us take these rather tiresome and conventional expressions of gratitude for granted, shall we? Now, on the question of damages and costs. I fear we shall find the Admiralty rather niggardly. You are likely still to be left considerably out of pocket. However, doubtless we can apply a slight spur to the First Lord's posterior in the House of Commons—

ARTHUR. Please, sir—no more trouble —I beg. Let the matter rest here. (*He shows piece of paper.*) This is all I have ever asked for.

SIR ROBERT. Well, we shall see. (*Turning to* CATHERINE.) A pity you were not in court, Miss Winslow. The verdict appeared to cause quite a sensible stir.

CATHERINE. So I heard. Why did the Admiralty throw up the case?

SIR ROBERT (*carelessly*). Oh, it was a foregone conclusion. No jury in the world would have convicted on the post-mistress's evidence.

CATHERINE. But this morning you seemed so depressed?

SIR ROBERT. Did I? The heat in the courtroom was very trying, you know. Perhaps I was a little fatigued— (*There is, again, a loud knocking at front door— To* ARTHUR.) Ah, yes. The gentlemen at the front door are rather anxious that you should make a statement to them—

ARTHUR. Yes? What shall I say?

SIR ROBERT (*indifferently*). I hardly think it matters. Whatever you say will have little bearing on what they write.

ARTHUR. What shall I say, Kate?

CATHERINE. You'll think of something, Father. (*She begins to wheel his chair toward door.*)

ARTHUR (*sharply*). No! I refuse to meet the Press in this ridiculous convey-ance. (*To* CATHERINE.) Get me my stick!

CATHERINE (*protestingly*). Father— you know what the doctor—

ARTHUR. Get me my stick!

[CATHERINE *without more ado gets his stick for him. She and* SIR ROBERT *help him out of his chair.*]

How is this? "I am happy to have lived long enough to have seen justice done to my son—"

CATHERINE. It's a little gloomy, Father. You're going to live for ages yet—

ARTHUR. Am I? In the words of the Prime Minister, my dear—let us wait and see. I could say: "This victory is not mine. It is the people who have tri-umphed—as they always will triumph— over despotism." How does that strike you, sir? A trifle pretentious, perhaps?

SIR ROBERT. Perhaps, sir. I should say it, none the less. It will be very popular.

ARTHUR. Hm! Perhaps I had better say what I really feel, which is merely:

"Thank God we beat 'em." (*He goes out.*)

[SIR ROBERT *turns abruptly to* CATHER-INE.]

SIR ROBERT. Miss Winslow—might I be rude enough to ask you for a little of your excellent whiskey?

CATHERINE. Of course. (*She goes into dining room.*)

[SIR ROBERT, *left alone, droops his shoulders wearily. He subsides into a chair. When* CATHERINE *comes back with whiskey he straightens his shoulders instinctively, but does not rise.*]

SIR ROBERT. That is very kind. Per-haps you would forgive me not getting up? The heat in that courtroom was really so infernal. (*He takes glass from her and drains it quickly. She notices his hand is trembling slightly.*)

CATHERINE. Would you like me to get a doctor, Sir Robert?

SIR ROBERT. No, no. Certainly not. There is nothing the matter with me. Just a slight nervous reaction—that's all. Besides, I have not been feeling myself all day. I told the judge so, this morn-ing, if you remember, but I doubt if he believed me. He thought it was a trick. What suspicious minds people have, have they not?

CATHERINE. Yes.

SIR ROBERT (*handing her back the glass*). Thank you.

[CATHERINE *puts glass down, then turns slowly back to face him as if nerving herself for an ordeal.*]

CATHERINE. Sir Robert—I'm afraid I have a confession and an apology to make to you.

SIR ROBERT (*sensing what is coming*). Dear lady—I am sure the one is rash and the other superfluous. I would far rather hear neither—

CATHERINE (*with a smile*). I am afraid you must. This is probably the last time I shall see you, and it is a better penance for me to say this than to write it. I have entirely misjudged your attitude to this case, and if in doing so I have ever seemed to you either rude or ungrateful, I am sincerely and humbly sorry.

SIR ROBERT (*indifferently*). My dear Miss Winslow, you have never seemed to me either rude or ungrateful. And my attitude to this case has been the same as yours—to win it at all costs. Only— when you talk of gratitude—you must remember that those costs were not mine, but yours.

CATHERINE. Weren't they also yours, Sir Robert?

SIR ROBERT. I beg your pardon?

CATHERINE. Haven't you too made a certain sacrifice for the case?

[*Pause.*]

SIR ROBERT. The robes of that office would not have suited me.

CATHERINE. Wouldn't they?

SIR ROBERT. No. (*With venom.*) And what is more, I fully intend to have Curry expelled from the Law Society.

CATHERINE. Please don't. He did me a great service by telling me—

SIR ROBERT. I must ask you never to divulge it to another living soul, and even to forget it yourself.

CATHERINE. I shall never divulge it. I'm afraid I can't promise to forget it myself.

SIR ROBERT. Very well. If you choose to give an unimportant incident a romantic significance, you are perfectly at liberty to do so. I must go. (*He gets up.*)

CATHERINE. Why are you always at such pains to prevent people knowing the truth about you, Sir Robert?

SIR ROBERT. Am I, indeed?

CATHERINE. You know you are. Why?

SIR ROBERT. Perhaps because I do not know the truth about myself.

CATHERINE. That is no answer.

SIR ROBERT. My dear Miss Winslow, are you cross-examining me?

CATHERINE. On this point, yes. Why are you so ashamed of your emotions?

SIR ROBERT. Because, as a lawyer, I must necessarily distrust them.

CATHERINE. Why?

SIR ROBERT. To fight a case on emotional grounds is the surest way I know of losing it. Emotions muddy the issue. Cold, clear logic—and buckets of it— should be the lawyer's only equipment.

CATHERINE. Was it cold, clear logic that made you weep today at the verdict?

[*Pause.*]

SIR ROBERT. Your maid, of course, told you that? It doesn't matter. It will be in the papers tomorrow, anyway. (*Fiercely.*) Very well, then, young lady, if you must have it, here it is, in all its high-falutin repulsiveness. I wept today because Right had been done.

CATHERINE. Not justice?

SIR ROBERT. No. Not justice. Right. It is easy to do justice—very hard to do right. Unfortunately, while the appeal of justice is intellectual, the appeal of right appears for some odd reason to induce tears in court. That is my answer and my excuse. And now, may I leave the witness box?

CATHERINE. No. One last question. How can you reconcile your support of Winslow against the Crown with your political beliefs?

SIR ROBERT. Very easily. No one party has a monopoly of concern for individual liberty. On that issue, all parties are united.

CATHERINE. I don't think so.

SIR ROBERT. You don't?

CATHERINE. No. Not all parties. Only some people from all parties.

SIR ROBERT. That—oddly enough—is quite a wise remark. We can only hope, then, that those same people will always prove enough people. And now, may I go?

CATHERINE. Yes, Sir Robert. Please forgive me for being impertinent.

SIR ROBERT. Not at all. It was an interesting experience to get a little of my own medicine. You would make a good advocate.

CATHERINE. Would I?

SIR ROBERT. Yes. It is a pity your leanings are more political than forensic. (*Playfully*.) Why do you not canalize [49] your feministic impulses towards the law courts, Miss Winslow, and abandon the lost cause of Women's Suffrage?

CATHERINE. Because I don't believe it *is* a lost cause.

SIR ROBERT. No? Are you going to continue to pursue it?

CATHERINE. Certainly.

SIR ROBERT. You will be wasting your time.

CATHERINE. I don't think so.

SIR ROBERT. A pity. Well. Good-by, Miss Winslow.

CATHERINE. Good-by, Sir Robert.

SIR ROBERT. In the House of Commons in days to come I shall make a

[49] CANALIZE—Guide into channels.

point of looking up at the Gallery in the hope of catching a glimpse of you in that provocative hat.

[RONNIE *comes in. He is fifteen now, and there are distinct signs of an incipient man about town. He is very smartly dressed in lounge suit and homburg hat.*]

RONNIE. I say, Sir Robert, I'm most awfully sorry. I didn't know anything was going to happen.

SIR ROBERT. Where were you?

RONNIE. At the flicks.

SIR ROBERT. Flicks. What is that?

CATHERINE. Cinematograph show.

RONNIE. You see, there's one just near the Courts and there was the *Trial of Madame X* on and I thought it would be rather fun to have a squint at it, as I'd been sitting in a court myself for four days. I'm most awfully sorry. I say— we won, didn't we?

SIR ROBERT. Yes. We won. Now that it's all over, tell me something, Ronald.

RONNIE. Right-o.

SIR ROBERT. What were you really doing in the locker room all that time?

RONNIE. I was smoking.

SIR ROBERT. That's just what I thought. (*He brings his stick down with some force on* RONNIE'S *backside.*)

RONNIE. Ow!

SIR ROBERT. Good-by, Miss Winslow. Shall I see you in the House then, one day?

CATHERINE (*with a smile*). Yes, Sir Robert. One day. But not in the Gallery. Across the floor.[50]

SIR ROBERT (*with a faint smile*). Perhaps. Good-by. (*He turns to go.*)

[50] ACROSS THE FLOOR—Catherine means that some day she may be a member of Parliament herself—after women have won a voice in politics. In other words, "I'm still a Suffragette, and I'm still opposed to the political party you belong to."

◇◇◇◇◇◇◇◇◇◇◇◇◇◇◇◇◇◇◇◇◇◇◇◇◇◇◇◇◇◇

FOR UNDERSTANDING

1. What is the exact crime Ronnie is charged with? Explain why it looks as if he is guilty.

2. How are we shown Ronnie's great reluctance to break the news of his disgrace to his family—especially his father? Being very young, after he finds that he has his father's support he soon begins to forget the whole thing. How are we shown that this is true? What is he doing at the time the jury announces its verdict? Do you think it would have made any difference to him in later years if the false accusation had been allowed to stand?

3. Ronnie's brother and sister are typical young people of the period just before 1914. What seem to be Dickie's main interests? Catherine's? What reason do we have for thinking she is an attractive young lady in spite of her assertive, know-it-all manner?

4. A dramatist sometimes avoids *showing* some things that happen in his story. He arranges for certain events—usually the ones that would be hard to perform—to "happen" off stage, and arranges for messengers to come in and describe them. This trick, which was already known to Greek dramatists more than two thousand years ago, is used in *The Winslow Boy*. Catherine and Violet, the maid, come on stage to report how the case is progressing; and Mr. Winslow reads about it in the newspapers. Why would it be difficult to stage the House of Commons and courtroom scenes? Do you think a series of such scenes, covering a period of two years, would be interesting to an audience? What is the author's excuse for keeping Mr. Winslow *at home*, so that the news must be brought to him (and to the audience)? How do we get a vivid impression of the excitement and cheering at the end of the trial?

MOMENTS OF CLIMAX

1. The great moment of the play—what the audience has been waiting for—comes in Act IV when Violet bursts in with news of the jury's decision. In the *denouement*, or "untying" of the plot, which follows, we are given brief glimpses of how the outcome of the trial affects several people. How can we tell that Mr. Winslow's happiness is great enough to make the ordeal worth while? What apology does Catherine wish to make to Sir Robert? How has his attitude toward her changed—or has it? Who seems least affected by the victory?

2. The verdict of "not guilty" might be called the *emotional climax* of the play, and a slightly earlier moment in Act IV might be called the *artistic climax*. In a very important sense the story is complete by the time Mr. Winslow and Catherine end their conversation. What decision do they come to about the long struggle they have been through—a decision that will not be altered by the outcome of the trial?

3. Each of the earlier acts has its own climax, just before the curtain falls. In Act I, suspense is built up as to how Mr. Winslow will take the news of Ronnie's expulsion. The family naturally try to postpone telling him while guests are present. In spite of their efforts, how does he suddenly discover that Ronnie has come home? The tension increases when Mr. Winslow sends for Ronnie and questions him. He has still not revealed what he is thinking. Explain how the tension is finally broken

by Mr. Winslow's long distance call.

4. Act II comes to a more powerful climax than Act I. Explain how the entire future action of the play depends on the outcome of Sir Robert's questioning of Ronnie. What would be the emotions of the audience during the questioning? Why would Sir Robert's final remark in Act II come as a surprise?

5. Act III ends with a double climax. In the first place, there is the question of whether Ronnie will be given the opportunity to be tried in court. This question is answered when Sir Robert receives an unexpected telephone call. In the second place, a crisis has arisen between Catherine and John. What demand has John's father made? What will he do if his demand is refused? Explain why Catherine's decision, after she learns that a court trial will be granted, is a very important one in her life. What is her decision? How does John show what his future action will be?

6. In your opinion, what incident in the first two acts first convinces the reader that Ronnie is innocent? Give your reasons.

A FAMILY'S SACRIFICES

In considering the sacrifices made by Ronnie's family, it is important to remember that without them—that is, without long-continued and costly effort—the case would never have been reopened.

1. The heaviest burden falls on Mr. Winslow because he is responsible for the welfare of others. He realizes that he is harming them by carrying on the fight. For instance, he can no longer afford to send Dickie to Oxford. Even though Mr. Winslow has a legal right to use his money as he sees fit, he feels that this is not living up to his obligations to his oldest son. On the other hand, Mr. Winslow need not feel totally responsible for the breakup of Catherine's engagement. Why not? He may have some doubts about whether he is doing the best thing for Ronnie. Why will Ronnie be worse off, if unable to prove his innocence, than if Mr. Winslow had al-

lowed the case to remain closed? Explain how Mr. Winslow is endangering his own life by the fight he is carrying on.

2. Dickie is a rather thoughtless fellow who doesn't even seem to think an accusation of theft makes much difference. Still, he has good qualities. How does he show them when his father tells him he can't continue at Oxford? What kind of work does he take up after leaving the university? What do you think his career at Oxford would have been like?

3. Mrs. Winslow says ". . . the cost may be out of all proportion" to what will be gained by the struggle. We should realize that a great many people would agree with her opinion. However, the author clearly wants us to think that she is wrong and Mr. Winslow is right. Later on, she begins to enjoy the excitement ("It's thrilling—you'll love it, Dickie"), and dresses up for the court sessions as if going to the theater. This further lowers our opinion of her. She shows better qualities when she is distressed over the necessity of discharging the maid. Explain how her concern is more for Violet's sake than for her own. When the play ends, has Violet been discharged?

4. Catherine loses her fiancé. Do you think she will regret losing him, looking back afterward at her own life? Explain why she will probably live a satisfying life even if she never marries. How would Desmond's proposal to her—even though she has no wish to marry him—make the audience feel better about her situation?

THE CHARACTER OF
SIR ROBERT MORTON

We naturally dislike Sir Robert's aristocratic, haughty manner. It is the accepted manner of a "fine gentleman" of the period —especially a public man whose life is spent in debate and in efforts to overawe and beat down determined opponents. Sir Robert has the intellectual arrogance of a brilliant Oxford or Cambridge graduate who has gone on to dazzling success in his profession, and who can expect to become a leading figure in government. We are to assume that the "Sir" was conferred in recognition of his high achievements.

1. Explain why Catherine calls Sir Robert "fishlike." According to her, what is his reason for accepting the Winslow case? In Act IV, what does she say about his request that the trial be temporarily adjourned because of his illness?

2. What excuses could be offered for Sir Robert's treatment of Ronnie in Act II?

3. Toward the end of the play, what incidents show us that Sir Robert is human after all? How are we convinced that he is sincerely concerned over proving Ronnie's innocence?

4. When Catherine apologizes for her former attitude, at first Sir Robert is indifferent—almost rude. How does he feel about having wept when the verdict was announced? Point out at least one speech in which he shows a warmer attitude toward Catherine. In reading their conversation, we suspect that their new friendship *might* develop into romance. They respect each other, and both are intelligent people of high ideals. On the other hand, what opposite views do they have which may hold them apart?

"LET RIGHT BE DONE"

At first, Mr. Winslow and Catherine have different reasons for insisting that "Right be done." Mr. Winslow thinks only of defending his son, who he believes is innocent. To Catherine, the fight for Ronnie is in a sense the same thing as the fight for Woman Suffrage. In both cases, she wants to make the government more heedful of the rights of individuals. In Act III she sums up her attitude as follows: ". . . a government department has ignored a fundamental human right and . . . people should force it to acknowledge it." By this time Mr. Winslow also thinks of Ronnie's case in broader terms, much like Catherine's. *Indignation for Ronnie's sake*, and a more general *insistence on the principle of justice*, are the two motives that create the action of the play.

1. In the conversation that ends the play, Sir Robert tells Catherine, "No one party has a monopoly of concern for individual liberty. On that issue, all parties are united." Does she seem to agree?

2. In Act III a newspaper editorial is quoted as saying that so much concern over a minor incident "could only happen in England." In Act IV, Mr. Winslow says, "Perhaps brute stubbornness isn't such a bad quality in the face of injustice." The English are rightly proud that stubborn resistance to tyranny or injustice is deeply ingrained in their culture. The custom of trial by jury goes back at least to medieval times, and perhaps to Anglo-Saxon times. Can you think of events in history in which the common people of England showed their quality of stubbornness? American culture and American laws are to a large extent based on those of England. Explain how the Revolutionary War was an example of "stubbornness in the face of injustice."

3. In a strict legal sense Ronnie had no right to a court trial. This was because he was under Navy discipline—and the Admiralty, or Navy, had the right to conduct its own affairs as it saw fit. However, there was so much indignation over the case that there was even a threat that the House of Commons might stop all other business to settle the matter. Do you believe the legislative branch of the government, directly responsible to the people, should ever interfere with the actions of particular departments? Explain your reasons. Why, to many people, would it seem absurd for a national legislature to concern itself with such a case as Ronnie's? The opposite point of view is expressed by Catherine: ". . . if ever the time comes that the House of Commons . . . can't find time to discuss a Ronnie Winslow and his beastly postal order, this country will be a far poorer place than it is now." What evils might result in a nation where most people felt, as Mrs. Winslow did, that justice or injustice in such a matter was not of great importance?

4. In Act IV, Catherine has become so downhearted about her work for the Woman Suffrage Association that she even calls it "a hopeless cause." Yet soon afterward, in her final speech in the play, she prophesies that some day women will be elected to Parliament. Explain why her attitude toward the possibility of reform has become more optimistic.

FOR DRAMATIZATION

Sir Robert Morton's cross-questioning of Ronnie is an effective scene for class presentation. Use the books, as in a radio play. The actor who represents Sir Robert should be merciless and overbearing. The actor who reads Ronnie's lines should speak in a low, quiet voice without trying to show Ronnie's emotions or imitate his crying. Appoint a third actor to read all the other lines—Arthur's, Catherine's, etc. Begin the scene with the line, "Now I would like you to cast your mind back to July 7th of last year."

WORDS FROM LATIN

1. Twice, Sir Robert is called *supercilious* (proud, scornful). What is the literal meaning of the two Latin words from which *supercilious* comes? Name at least three additional English words beginning with the prefix *super-*. For each word, explain briefly and clearly how the prefix fits the meaning.

2. Sir Robert is *cadaverous* in appearance. What is a *cadaver*? In what field of science would this word be most often heard? What more common word, also beginning with *c*, means the same as *cadaver*? From what Latin word is it derived? What does *corporal* mean?

3. Seeing Ronnie stretched out on the sofa, Sir Robert describes him as *dormant*. What does he mean? The word comes, by way of the French language, from Latin *dormire*. When might we speak of a volcano as *dormant*? When is a plant or tree *dormant*? What is a *dormitory*? Have you ever been inside one?

Further Readings in the Twentieth Century

NOVELS

BENNETT, ARNOLD. *Tales of Five Towns*

BOWEN, ELIZABETH. *The Heat of the Day*

* CHESTERTON, G. K. *The Flying Inn*

CONRAD, JAMES. *Lord Jim; Typhoon*

* CRONIN, A. J. *The Citadel*

* GREENE, GRAHAM. *Brighton Rock; The Ministry of Fear*

HILTON, JAMES. *Random Harvest; Good-Bye, Mr. Chips; Lost Horizon*

* KAYE-SMITH, SHEILA. *The End of the House of Alard*

KIPLING, RUDYARD. *Kim*

KNIGHT, ERIC. *This Above All*

LEWIS, C. S. *Perelandra; Out of the Secret Planet*

ORWELL, GEORGE. *Animal Farm*

PATON, ALAN. *Cry, The Beloved Country; Too Late the Phalarope*

PRIESTLEY, J. B. *Festival*

* McLAVERTY, MICHAEL. *School for Hope*

* MacMAHON, BRYAN. *Children of the Rainbow*

* MARSHALL, BRUCE. *Father Malachy's Miracle; The White Rabbit*

* WAUGH, EVELYN. *The Loved One; Helena*

WODEHOUSE, P. G. *Jeeves; Leave It to Smith*

SHORT STORY

BOWEN, ELIZABETH. *Ivy Gripped the Steps* (collection)

* BRUNINI, JOHN AND CONNOLLY, F. X., editors. *Stories of Our Century by Catholic Authors*

CARTMELL, VAN H. AND GRAYSON, CHARLES, editors. *The Golden Argosy* (collection)

* CHESTERTON, G. K. *The Father Brown Omnibus*

CONRAD, JOSEPH. *The Portable Conrad* (Viking Press)

DOYLE, A. CONAN. *The Adventures of Sherlock Holmes*

* GABLE, SISTER MARIELLA, O.S.B., ed. *Great Modern Catholic Short Stories; Our Father's House; Many Colored Fleece*

* MacMAHON, BRYAN. *The Red Petticoat* (collection)

MANSFIELD, KATHERINE. *The Garden Party* (collection)

MUNRO, H. H. ("Saki"). *Complete Short Stories of Saki*

BIOGRAPHY AND AUTOBIOGRAPHY

* BARING, MAURICE. *The Puppet Show of Memory*

* BELLOC, HILAIRE. *Marie Antoinette; Cranmer*

* BRODRICK, JAMES, S.J. *St. Francis Xavier; A Procession of Saints* (collection)

* CAMPBELL, ROY. *Light on a Dark Horse*

* CHESTERTON, G. K. *Autobiography; Stevenson; Thomas Aquinas*

* CURTAYNE, ALICE. *St. Catherine of Siena*

* KAYE-SMITH, SHEILA. *Three Ways Home*

* LEEN, EDWARD, C. S. Sp. *In the Likeness of Christ*

* LUNN, ARNOLD. *Now I See; Saint Among the Slave Trade*

* MacMANUS, SEUMAS. *The Rocky Road to Dublin*

MASEFIELD, JOHN. *Autobiography*

* MARTINDALE, C. C., S.J. *The Vocation of St. Aloysius*

* NOYES, ALFRED. *Two Worlds for Meaning*

* O'BRIEN, KATE. *Teresa of Avila*

PEARSON, HESKETH. *Charles Dickens; Gilbert and Sullivan*

* SHEED, F. J., ed. *The English Way; Saints Are Not Sad; Born Catholics* (collections)
* YEO, MARGARET. *These Three Hearts*

SHERRIFF, R. C. *Journey's End*
WILLIAMS, EMLYN. *The Corn Is Green*
YEATS, W. B. *Cathleen ni Hoolihan*

ESSAYS

* BELLOC, HILAIRE, *Selected Essays*
* CHESTERTON, G. K. *The Man Who Was Chesterton*
* CROSS, RAPHAEL, C.P.P.S. *A Century of the Catholic Essay*
* DAWSON, CHRISTOPHER. *The Making of Europe; Understanding Europe*
* HOUSELANDER, CARYLL. *The Reed of God; The Flowering Tree*
* KNOX, MSGR. RONALD. *Essays in Satire; The Hidden Stream*
ORWELL, GEORGE. *Dickens and Others*
* PAKENHAM, LADY, ed. *Catholic Approaches*
PRIESTLEY, J. B. *English Journey; The Other Places and Other Stories*
WEST, REBECCA. *A Train of Powder*
* WILHELMSEN, FREDERIC. *Hilaire Belloc*
WOOLF, VIRGINIA. *The Common Reader*

DRAMA

BARRIE, JAMES M. *Dear Brutus; Quality Street; Peter Pan; Half Hours*
BESIER, RUDOLPH. *The Barretts of Wimpole Street*
COWARD, NOEL. *Cavalcade*
DRINKWATER, JOHN. *Abraham Lincoln*
DUNSANY, LORD. *A Night at the Inn*
FRY, CHRISTOPHER. *A Sleep of Prisoners*
GREGORY, LADY. *Seven Short Plays*
HOUSMAN, LAURENCE. *Victoria Regina*
MORGAN, CHARLES. *The Burning Glass*
RIDLER, ANN. *The Show Factory* (modern Nativity Play)
SHAW, G. B. *Pygmalion; Arms and the Man*

POETRY

ARLINGTON, RICHARD, ed. *The Viking Book of Poetry*
* CAMPBELL, ROY. *Collected Poems*
* NOYES, ALFRED. *The Golden Book of Catholic Poetry*
* SHEED, F. J., ed. *Poetry and Life*
UNTERMEYER, LOUIS, ed. *Modern British Poetry; A Treasury of Great Poems*
YEATS, W. B., ed. *Oxford Book of Modern Verse*

GENERAL BACKGROUND AND CRITICISM

* ALEXANDER, CALVERT. *The Catholic Literary Revival*
BOYD, ERNEST. *Ireland's Literary Renaissance*
CHENEY, SHELDON. *The Theatre*
CUNLIFFE, J. W. *England in Picture, Song, and Story*
* GARDINER, HAROLD, S.J. *Norms for the Novel*
* GIBBS, SIR PHILIP. *The Life and Times of George V*
HARVEY, PAUL. *The Oxford Companion to English Literature*
KAVANAUGH, PETER. *The Story of the Abbey Theatre*
MONROE, N. ELIZABETH. *The Novel and Society*
ROUGHHEAD, W. N., ed., *Hilaire Belloc.* (collection)
WAGENKNECHT, EDWARD. *Cavalcade of the Novel*
* WARD, BARBARA. *Faith and Freedom*
* WARD, MAISIE. *Return to Chesterton*
WILLIAMSON, AUDREY. *Theater of Two Decades*
WILLIAMSON, GEORGE. *A Reader's Guide to T. S. Eliot*
* WEYAND, NORMAN, S.J., ed. *The Catholic Renascence*

Meet the Authors

JOSEPH ADDISON (1672–1719) epitomizes the eighteenth century. Meticulously bewigged and beruffled, he was a thoroughly respectable and respected gentleman. He was a competent scholar, a politician and a statesman, a conversationalist and a coffee drinker. His sense of humor, satiric in the eighteenth-century manner, was tempered with much good nature and some kindliness; here he parts company with many of the other leading writers of his day.

From his early school days Addison was marked for fame. At fifteen he went to Oxford where his skill in Latin versifying brought him favor after favor. He won a pension, traveled abroad for three years, came forth with polished little verses at the proper times, and began his political rise. Ultimately he became Secretary of Ireland, then Secretary of State. In his leisure he wrote pamphlets, verses, opera, formal tragedy and—what is most important—copy for the *Tatler* and *Spectator* with Richard Steele.

MATTHEW ARNOLD (1822–1888) was a busy Inspector of Schools who, besides improving the British school system, wrote poetry and attacked with books and essays the priggish *status quo* of Victorianism. His father, whom he honors in the poem "Rugby Chapel," was Thomas Arnold, an author and the famous headmaster at Rugby. Matthew took honors at Rugby and at Balliol College, Oxford, and then traveled widely in France.

Appointed Inspector of Schools after his return to England, he fulfilled his onerous duties with diligence; he married well and happily. For recreation he wrote poetry, as he had at Oxford. His best verse includes the Homeric narrative, "Sohrab and Rustum"; the elegy, "Thyrsis," written in memory of his friend, H. Clough; and the melancholic lyric, "Dover Beach."

WYSTAN HUGH AUDEN (1907–) is one of the three or four best known and most influential poets of his generation. Born in York, England, young Auden first doted on photography, engineering, motorcycles, and whales. But during his years at Oxford, he turned to poetry as a serious career. By the early 1930's, he was a leader of Britain's famed Leftist "Auden Circle," composed of Stephen Spender, Cecil Day Lewis, Louis MacNiece, and Auden. Like most original poets, Auden experimented constantly with the styles and techniques of his predecessors—Donne, Blake, Byron, Housman, Yeats, and Rilke. His early poems were written under the influence of Freud and Marx. In 1935, he married Erika, the daughter of the famed German novelist, Thomas Mann.

In collaboration with Christopher Isherwood, he wrote a series of verse-prose dramas, *The Dog Beneath the Skin*, *The Ascent of F. 6*, and *On the Frontier*. In 1937, he received the King George Gold Medal for poetry. In 1946, Auden became a citizen of the United States. His later poems, *Another Time*, *The Double Man*, and *The Age of Anxiety*, are chiefly concerned with the problems of philosophy and religion. *For the Time Being* is an intense declaration of the poet's new found religious faith and a rejection of the more radical and self-centered aspects of his past. He was awarded the Pulitzer Prize for his *Age of Anxiety*.

Auden has taught at numerous American colleges and universities.

FRANCIS BACON (1561–1626). Were one to read the works of Francis Bacon without knowing anything of his life and personality, one might well ask, "What manner of man is this?" The mirror of his works reflects the portrait of a courtier —brilliant, keen, clear-headed, cold, unscrupulous, and hard.

Born the son of the Lord Keeper of the Seal, Francis Bacon found the finest educational facilities of the age open to him. There was private instruction under tutors, followed by college work at Cambridge, and travel with study abroad.

Finding himself without income at the death of his father, the eighteen-year-old youth turned to the practice of law for his living, and his rise was rapid. Within ten years he was Counsel-Extraordinary to Elizabeth. After the Queen's death in 1603, Bacon's rise was even more rapid. He was at once knighted by James I. In succeeding years he rose from post to post, until in 1618 he became Lord High Chancellor of England.

That very year he was accused of having accepted bribes. Bacon made a complete confession, exonerating his associates— some of them of higher rank than himself. Punishment was severe but left him his life.

From his nineteenth year Bacon had been writing more or less steadily—chiefly scientific, political, and economic discussions in Latin and English. Now he gave himself over to scientific studies. It is a matter of common knowledge that he contracted the bronchitis which caused his death while he was trying an initial experiment in the modern principle of cold storage. He wanted to see whether packing a chicken with snow would preserve it.

HILAIRE BELLOC (1870–1953). When Hilaire Belloc died in 1953, an old man of over eighty years, a chorus of appreciation hard to parallel was heard in every newspaper and magazine. It would have astonished the old man, so sure was he that he was a failure and mainly forgotten. Secluded in his Sussex home, he had lived the last years of his life a lonely and tired old warrior.

But Belloc can never be forgotten by the English speaking Catholic world, for he was its champion for over fifty years. Nor can the world of letters ever forget him for his pure, limpid prose, a prose which Lord Tweedsmuir praised when he wrote: "No man has written purer and nobler prose in the great tradition of classical English."

When Belloc left Oxford in his late twenties, the English world had little regard for Catholic intelligence. It had little habit of listening to Catholics; and English Catholicism, being a segregated minority, accepted the situation. Belloc changed all of that. With his wit, humor, intellectual power and eloquence, he succeeded in making the world listen to him and in stimulating Catholics to challenge the world.

Perhaps Belloc's apologetic writing may not endure. But his reputation as a man of letters, justly earned by his poetry and essays, must endure. As a poet his appeal is to the very young as well as the more mature. His reverence for children is seen in his delightful *Cautionary Tales* and *Bad Child's Book of Beasts*, delightful children's verse. His mature poetry manifests a love for the land, for the simple, elemental things of life: laughter, song, wine, and humor. His mastery of the personal essay illuminates the pages of such works as *Conversations with a Cat* and *Conversations with an Angel*.

The Path to Rome and *The Four Men* are delightful travelogues which offer the very best introduction to Belloc's great and earnest soul.

WILLIAM BLAKE (1757–1827). There seems little in the dull facts of the life of William Blake—second son of a London hosier, apprentice at fifteen to an engraver, underpaid magazine illustrator —that would explain the excellence of his work. Even in his lifetime he was almost a legend. Charles Lamb once said of him, "Blake is a real name, I assure you, and a most extraordinary man if he be still living. He paints in watercolors marvelous strange pictures, visions of his brain. . . . His poems have been sold hitherto only in manuscript. I never read them . . . but there is one to a tiger which I have heard recited which is glorious. But alas! I have not the book; for the man is flown, whither I know not—to Hades or a Mad House." But Blake had gone to neither place. He was quietly laboring at his second-rate engraving job to earn enough to support himself and his family. At night he and his wife would work on his own engravings that he loved to do and that no one wanted to buy. During his sleep he would be wakened by strange visions and he would get up to write long mystical poems that no one bought and few read. He and his wife invented a new method of engraving called "illuminated printing," but the exquisite volumes went unsold. Most people thought Blake quite mad; only a few realized his genius and encouraged him. Not until the early nineteenth century was it agreed that the strange William Blake, between his twelfth and twentieth years, had written some of the most beautiful lyrics in the English language, and that his engravings and watercolors entitled him to first rank among all artists.

JAMES BOSWELL (1740–1795). The man who was to give the world a book possessing "more of life than any work ever yet appeared" began humbly enough as a Scotch lawyer who found clients hard to get. James Boswell was really much less interested in his legal cases than he was in his hobby of celebrity-hunting. The book that has made him famous was not at all an accident. He had evidently early made up his mind to search out the most likely man in London, study him closely, and write a book about him. Samuel Johnson was the subject that he selected; and when he finally achieved an introduction to the Doctor, he attached himself to the man like a shadow. Johnson was big and Boswell small, and the couple were often likened to a lumbering bear with a devoted little terrier frisking about him.

It took Boswell seven years after the death of Johnson to arrange and edit the mass of notes in which he had recorded the very words and gestures of his master. When the *Life of Samuel Johnson* finally appeared, it presented not only the portrait of one man but an encyclopedic fund of information about eighteenth-century life. The little Scotch lawyer had insured immortality not only for himself, but for the curious lion of classic letters—Samuel Johnson.

RUPERT BROOKE (1887–1915). What would you think if the captain of your football team had won prizes for poetry, honors in scholarship, and fostered revivals of Elizabethan plays? And, if in addition, he was tall, handsome, vivacious, and charming? You'd remember him, wouldn't you, especially if later he went into military service and died as a soldier at the age of twenty-eight?

And so it is with Britishers of the first-war generation. Rupert Brooke is well remembered, not only for his poetry but for the brilliant promise of his life.

At Cambridge, Brooke dabbled in radical campus politics, college theatricals, and journalism. His brilliant writing even then won him the friendship of other poets, De la Mare, Gosse, and Drinkwater. His unusual academic standing earned him a fellowship at Cambridge and with the publication of his *Poems* in 1911 he seemed assured of success. He wrote and lectured until 1914, but with the outbreak of war he immediately enlisted and received a commission in the Royal Naval

Division. On his way to the Dardanelles after a winter's training he died on board ship of an infection following sunstroke. "The Soldier" was written only a few months before his death. The shock of his death touched all who knew him. His work, although excellent, still showed more promise than achievement. We can only speculate as to the verse and man England might have had if Brooke had lived.

ELIZABETH BARRETT BROWNING

(1806–1861). It is one of the vagaries of fickle popularity that a woman, who after the death of Wordsworth was seriously considered for the poet laureateship, should today be remembered for a handful of love sonnets and because she became Mrs. Robert Browning. The sentimental appeal of Elizabeth Barrett's life will never lose its charm for youthful romantics. The eldest of a family of eleven, she was hailed as a prodigy when she read Greek at eight and wrote an epic at twelve. Father and family doted on the frail, tiny child. A fall from her pony at fifteen resulted in a spinal injury; the tryannical devotion of her father, her grief at the death of her mother and a favorite brother forced upon her an invalid's life.

At this time she began corresponding with an impetuous young poet, quite unknown, but whose verses pleased her. At last the poet came to call, Robert Browning—yellow-gloved, bewhiskered and dashing. The rest of the story is familiar history—the father's displeasure, Robert's insistence, her own growing love, and their final elopement. The years in Italy where they went to live saw her health recovered; she walked, rode horseback, and became almost robust. After their son's birth, Mrs. Browning was less well. She still wrote—some of her *Sonnets from the Portuguese*, her most beautiful lyrics, belong to this period—but Robert's fame was overshadowing hers. Her death in 1861 ended one of the happiest marriages in all literature.

ROBERT BROWNING (1812–1889).

It is impossible to imagine Robert Browning as an old man, warming his rheumatic knees in the sun. He is forever young, forever boisterous, and forever charming. With him and of him we can chant, "How good is man's life, the mere living!"

Browning was a struggling young author when he began writing fan mail to the invalid poetess, Elizabeth Barrett. Through a mutual friend, meetings were arranged despite the vigilance of Miss Barrett's father and the animosity of Miss Barrett's dog, Flush. In 1846 the two eloped, sailed for Italy, and remained there for sixteen years, ideally happy. Elizabeth and Italy matured Browning's genius; he wrote rapidly and brilliantly. In Italy and England he was hailed as one of the greatest poets.

After his wife's death he returned to London, continued his writing with rare courage, and even aided in the editing of his wife's works; but he refused ever again to return to Florence where they had spent their life together. To the end Browning himself retained his optimism and his boyishness; his interest in painting, in music, in people, and in life.

ROBERT BURNS (1759–1796). The

simple, tender lyrics that poured their good Scotch burr from the tongue of Robert Burns are far removed from the tinkling elegance of the eighteenth century. As a person he was equally distant from his contemporaries. Robert Burns was a Scotch peasant to whom song came as naturally as thought; the only things he knew well were Scotland and his own heart and of them he wrote, sometimes with tenderness, often with humor, but always with truthfulness. He might have belonged to any century, but he belongs to all centuries and to all men.

As a child Burns knew the simple peasant life, long hours of work brightened with a few simple pleasures. His father, from whom Burns modeled the father in "The Cotter's Saturday Night," wanted an education for his children, but there was always too little money and too much work. At fifteen Burns was the principal laborer on the farm, his only reading snatched over the plow or at his lunch. Later, he decided to emigrate to Jamaica. To earn passage money he sold his first book of poetry; it was immediately popular. Edinburgh society demanded acquaintance with the "rustic prodigy"; Burns was feted and toasted, but more as a strange exhibit than as a brilliant writer. Bewildered and disillusioned, he began to drink and to cultivate companions who seemed to him more sincere than the socialites he had met.

Early in 1788 he returned to his boyhood home where he married Jean Armour, the sweetheart he had left when he planned on Jamaica. "To give the rest of my story in brief," he wrote, "I have married 'my Jean' and taken a farm." The poet was accustomed to say that the most happy period of his life was the first winter he spent on this farm. But his happiness was short-lived. Although he wrote furiously and passionately for the next seven years, poverty and unrest remained his lot. He died at thirty-seven, old and broken before his time, not suspecting the lasting fame that would be his.

GEORGE GORDON, LORD BYRON

(1788–1824). "I have not loved the world nor the world me," despaired Byron when, as a young man he left England forever. The words were partly truth and partly pose. The world had showered favors at his feet; London society and London letters proclaimed him the greatest genius of the century. Europe agreed. But the handsome lord of the shrewish temper and maimed foot flouted fame and favor to become, by his own choice, "a wandering outlaw of his own dark mind."

Byron's character developed early a combination of passionate temper, pride, and sensitivity. His father was an unprincipled spendthrift who fled to France, leaving behind a tempestuous Scotch wife, a beautiful child with a crippled foot, and a stack of unpaid bills. At ten the child inherited the title of "Lord Byron" and the estate of Newstead Abbey, to which he and his mother moved. Lady Byron tried one scheme after another to cure her son's limp, succeeding only in making him unhappily conscious of his defect.

In school at Harrow and then at Cambridge Byron excelled in boxing and swimming—and fits of temper. He was intelligent and loved to read—not a bad student when left to his own bent—but impatient of discipline, and "touchy."

Soon after his graduation, Byron set out on a tour of Europe. Travel gave a touch of maturity to his poetry, and he really worked at the first two cantos of *Childe Harold's Pilgrimage*. Published upon his return, it became immediately popular— tremendously so.

After an unhappy marriage, Byron left England. In Switzerland he met Shelley, also an outcast, and the two rambled and talked for days. In Greece and Italy Byron was as happy as his own disposition could make him. He wrote two more cantos for *Childe Harold*. These and his other works continued to find enthusiastic sale in England, Europe, and America.

In Greece he became absorbed in the Greek dreams of independence. He organized a force to meet the Turks, furnishing it with his own funds. And he gave tirelessly of himself to the cause. Before he could see battle, he contracted rheumatic fever and died in camp at Missolonghi on April 19, 1824—an embittered man, "old" at thirty-six, but destined, strangely enough, to become a hero in a land not his own. Greece still honors him as a truly great man.

ROY CAMPBELL (1902–   ). "A

poetic tornado" aptly suits both Campbell's life and his poetry. He was brought up in the wilds of South Africa, was arrested when fifteen for leaving high school to join the infantry, was married in England in 1922, eked out a living on the shores of Wales and later as a fisherman along the Mediterranean, took up bull-fighting and won the steer-throwing championship of Provence in 1932–33. Campbell joined Franco in the Spanish War, and became a war correspondent for the London *Tablet*. Dissatisfied with his life as a free-thinker, he became a Catholic about 1935.

His first poetic work, "The Flaming Terrapin," was a sensation. He was recognized as a gifted craftsman. Most of his subsequent works, "Georgiad," "Mithraic Emblems," and "Flowering Reeds," are considered inferior to his first work, although "Flowering Rifle," a satiric narrative of the Spanish Civil War, received wide attention.

EDMUND CAMPION, S.J. (1540–1581). One of the best scholars in England in 1566 when Elizabeth visited Oxford University, Edmund Campion delighted the royal party with his delicate Ciceronian language and exquisite taste. He was presented to the Queen and was favored by the patronage of two of the most influential earls in the domain. Why, then, with everything a young scholar could desire, did Edmund Campion finish his work at Oxford and on August 1, 1569—but three years later—give up all his preferments and retire to Dublin, thence to France? The answer is the story of his whole courageous life. Edmund Campion became convinced that Catholicism was the true faith and to follow it he surrendered all, even his life.

After a brief time in Dublin, Campion studied in the seminary at Douai in France. Here again his great learning and distinguished position offered him a life full of honor as a teacher and student of theology. But he grew restless. He had given up everything. It seemed that this scholarly life was too easy. Accordingly, on January 21, 1573, he left Douai for Rome, to enter, if he might, the Society of Jesus. He was received as a novice in the Austrian province of the new Society and spent the next six years of his life in Prague, where he was ordained a priest in 1578.

The same courage that characterized these successive moves brought him back to England, the land of sure martyrdom. The Jesuits were called by the Pope to aid the priests of Douai in their work for persecuted England. First to be chosen was the heroic Father Campion. He returned to England joyfully. The march from Prague to Rome and from Rome to Calais was a triumphant procession. There Father Campion waited for the letter which called him to his death.

In the busy ministerial work of the next eighteen months Father Campion had to live a hunted life, disguised in ever-differing costumes, traveling steadily, and saying Mass in secret rooms and caves. He never doubted that the outcome would be death. He simply took all precautions that he might do a full life's work before his capture. In this he succeeded. No one helped more to restore the faith and courage of the persecuted English Catholics than this heroic, scholarly, kindly martyr who moved among them so calmly. His death was preceded by terrible rackings and tortures, but through them all Father Campion proclaimed the doctrines of Christ to the confusion of the Queen's satellites. Campion's "Brag" is an eloquent speech, full of fire and deep religious feeling, a clarion call to his co-religionists to hold fast.

THOMAS CAREW (1595–1645), one of the earliest of the Cavalier song writers, was also the only one fortunate enough to live out his life before the execution of Charles I and the ensuing misfortunes which came to the followers of that unhappy King. Born of wealthy parents, Carew went to Oxford at thirteen. His court career began as a secretary to an ambassador whom he accompanied on missions to France and The Hague. Rising rapidly through services to the Crown, he became, in 1630, server (taster-in-ordinary) to Charles I and one of the

King's close confidants. Although his busy court life left him little leisure, Carew often wrote verses modeled after those of Ben Jonson. He was a respected member of both literary and court circles.

THOMAS CARLYLE (1795–1881). Not unlike the dour, rugged country from which he came was Thomas Carlyle. He had the rather common Scotch combination of a crusty exterior and a sweet, sound core.

There are four important settings in the drama of Carlyle's life. The first is a farmer's cottage at Ecclefechan, near Dumfries in Scotland. Thomas himself is a peasant lad—sturdy, ruddy-cheeked, accustomed to hard work. He is the oldest child and his parents have decided that he is to be a Presbyterian minister. At fourteen, therefore, he sets off on foot for the University of Edinburgh, eighty miles away.

The second scene is a poor student's lodgings at college. Carlyle is friendless and miserable. The indigestion which tormented him the rest of his days has begun—undoubtedly the result of privation.

The third scene is not a parsonage, but a farmhouse. Carlyle has become a writer instead of a minister. In 1826 he had married Jane Welsh, a beautiful girl who owned a farm at Craigenputtock; here the couple decided to live while Thomas was getting established. It was a lonely place, and life was hard—especially for Jane, who baked bread, scrubbed floors, washed clothes, and wheedled her husband. Carlyle responded by writing *The Life of Burns* and *Sartor Resartus* (reflective of his interest in German philosophy).

For the next forty-seven years a house in Cheyne Row, Chelsea, in London is the setting. It was here that fame came to Thomas; it was here that he and Jane entertained the wise and great of England. Carlyle's books had always commanded readers, but it took *The French Revolution* with its unusual style and vigor to make him famous. The book was published in 1837.

From the appearance of *The French Revolution* until the death of Mrs. Carlyle in 1866, the author was busy lecturing and writing. His house became a Mecca for everyone interested in books and philosophy. But when Jane Carlyle died, Thomas was a broken man. His last fifteen years were sadly lonely.

GEOFFREY CHAUCER (1340–1400). We know little of Chaucer's life except that he was a busy man of affairs, happy now and then at "having balanced his ledgers and gone back to his books." His father was a wine merchant, rather well-to-do, and as was the custom his son was placed as a page in the home of a nobleman. As a young squire, Chaucer saw service in the army of Edward III in France, was captured and later released through ransom paid by the king. It seems likely that his career as a secret agent and diplomat had already begun.

Chaucer's duties in the service of three kings had put him in touch with literary movements, especially in Italy, and had given him an opportunity to observe at first hand the life of the fourteenth century. His power to depict life, to make his characters live, can be seen in *The Canterbury Tales*. Today, after six centuries, the prioress almost fingers the amulet on her rosary and the moonstruck squire lifts huge sighs to heaven and his lady.

The Canterbury Tales established Chaucer as one of the three great English poets. *Troilus and Criseyde*, also in verse, was one of the first sustained narratives in English and has been called a forerunner of the modern novel.

GILBERT KEITH CHESTERTON (1874–1936), often known by his initials, G. K. C., was one of the most outstanding personalities in modern England. He was born at Campden Hill, Kensington, and in his early years studied at the famous Slade School of Art. But literature was in his blood; with his publication of the *Wild Knight* in 1900, he was prompted to abandon art as a profession and devote himself entirely to journalism and letters. From his facile pen came a constant stream of witty essays, controversial writing, delightful verse, mystery stories, biographical and historical studies, and sound literary criticism.

Although Chesterton wrote like a Catholic and championed the fundamental truths of Christianity throughout his life, he did not enter the Church until 1922. Perhaps his most important works in the field of prose are: *Orthodoxy, The Everlasting Man, Charles Dickens, St. Thomas Aquinas,* and his *Autobiography.* His *Lepanto* and *Ballad of the White Horse* are truly great poems, but even his comic and satiric verse is not negligible. In Don John of Austria, the hero of *Lepanto* flinging back the destructive force of Islam; and in noble Alfred, the hero of *Ballad of the White Horse,* struggling to preserve Catholic England from the inroads of the heathen Danes, we catch glimpses of another knight of Christendom flinging all the forces of his mind and pen against the ranks of modern paganism.

SAMUEL TAYLOR COLERIDGE

(1772–1834) had a brilliant mind. He read easily before he was four and entertained his father's friends with intelligent conversation when he was seven. The son of a vicar, he was to be educated for the ministry as were his three older brothers; but Samuel had other plans. In Cambridge at fifteen, he showed little interest in the church.

Unconcerned about his studies, Coleridge left school and enlisted in the Dragoons, but was rescued from a military career by his family. In the interlude, he met Robert Southey and the two dreamers, captivated by the French Revolution and its promises of democracy, decided that

they, too, would found a new order on the banks of the Susquehanna in America. They married two sisters and planned their ideal community—only to realize that they had no money to take them to America.

Coleridge turned to writing, lecturing, journalism, and even to preaching in a Unitarian church. He always captivated his audience, but was careless about keeping appointments and collecting his fees. He had published a small volume of poems for which he was well paid, but which had little sale. Then he met Wordsworth, the stronger character who was to influence the rest of his life. The publication of *Lyrical Ballads* gave him the chance to express his revolutionary ideas about poetry and to exemplify them with some notable verse —especially with his fanciful tale, "The Rime of the Ancient Mariner."

The rest of his life was spent quietly in writing, dreaming, visiting his friends—especially the Wordsworths—and fighting ill health and drugs, which he had begun taking to relieve intense neuralgia. He grew torpid and fat, but remained an amazing conversationalist, exerting an influence equal perhaps to that of Samuel Johnson. Unfortunately, there was no Boswell to write down his words. His poetry was fragmentary. Unconscious of fame, he dreamed away the last years of his life in the company and care of a friendly physician. Like his "Kubla Khan," his life seems an unfinished tale.

RICHARD CRASHAW (1613?–1649).

To the ever-growing list of converts who have written fine Catholic literature in England must be added the name of Richard Crashaw.

During the years he spent at Cambridge (1634–1642) he rejected his father's Puritanism and became a devout high-church Anglican. In fact, he went further than Anglicans generally went in the practice of Catholic asceticism, seeking through devout prayer, retreats, and penance a true and deep union with God.

Some time in 1645 Crashaw was received into the Catholic Church, and later he became a priest.

His poems, *Delights of the Muses*, were first published after he had become a Catholic, in 1646. Through them we learn of his great devotion to St. Theresa of Avila, which led him into the Church. His poetry is largely devotional and includes some of the best sacred lyrics of the seventeenth century.

WALTER DE LA MARE (1873–   ) has been called "a shadowy Pied Piper." Surely he turns as bewitching a tune with his delicate rhythms as the Piper ever blew, and his following is equally devoted and blind. In the prosaic post of bookkeeper for the Standard Oil Company, De la Mare took refuge in long hair, velvet coat, and his writing world of fantasy. For several years he published verse in magazines under the pseudonym of Walter Ramal, and drudged daily over figures as Walter de la Mare. In 1908 a government grant and pension won him release from his desk; the success of his poems, appealing as they do to the child in every adult, gradually lessened the necessity for book reviewing which he detested. His novel, *Memoirs of a Midget*, has been equally popular, and today he ranks as one of the better known twentieth-century English poets.

JOHN DONNE (1573–1631), the leader of the metaphysical school of poets, might well be called the father of such modern poets as T. S. Eliot and W. H. Auden. A man of immense learning, he clothed his poetry in learned and abstract metaphors and similes. He had a contempt for outworn literary ornaments and expressed his poetic feelings in personal, virile, realistic, and dramatic language.

John Donne came from a family which combined literary genius and a great religious faith. He was a grandson of the poet John Heywood and a descendant of St. Thomas More. When he was forty-three Donne became a minister of the Anglican Church, Dean of St. Paul's, and the most popular preacher of his day. After the death of his wife in 1617, he became intensely religious. He died in poverty and ill health.

As a poet, Donne had a range which included sensual elegies, biting satires, and holy sonnets. Some of his love poems are frankly sensual. In others Donne expresses a very pure concept of love, passionate and tender. In his *Holy Sonnets*, we have some of the most sublime religious poetry which has been written in the English language.

JOHN DRYDEN (1631–1700), who contributed much to English poetry and more to the formation of modern English prose, mirrors much of the time during which he lived. Born among Puritan sympathizers during the reign of Charles I, he lived through the Cromwell interlude, through the restoration of the last two Stuarts, and on into the period of William and Mary. He was a Puritan under Cromwell, an Episcopalian under Charles, and a Catholic under James II.

Like Ben Jonson before him and Samuel Johnson after, Dryden was a literary dictator around whom many disciples gathered. His reputation as a poet was established in 1666 with *Annus Mirabilis*. He wrote nearly thirty plays which brought him a handsome income but contained little of merit. His poetry which has endured includes his satires and the two odes on music, "A Song for Saint Cecilia's Day" and "Alexander's Feast."

We are most indebted to Dryden for his contribution to the development of prose. This new prose was mostly criticism and is chiefly found in the prefaces to his works.

EILEEN DUGGAN, New Zealand's poet laureate, is considered by some to be the outstanding living poet and the twentieth-century replica of the great Catholic woman poet, Alice Meynell. Although born and educated in New Zealand, her parents came from Ireland, and the Irish influence is most pronounced in her literary works.

Her *Poems* of 1937 won for her a place on the King of England's Honours List, and the Order of the British Empire has been conferred upon her. To celebrate the centenary of New Zealand, Miss Duggan wrote and published *New Zealand Poems* in 1940. She has written many prose pieces for *Sign*, *America*, and *Commonweal*, and her prose is as distinguished as her poetry.

RONALD DUNCAN (1914–   ).

One of England's leading dramatists today, Duncan was educated in Switzerland and at Cambridge. Among his more recent plays are *Nothing Up My Sleeve* and *Our Lady's Tumbler*, the latter produced at Salisbury Cathedral in 1951. He has also published a volume of poetry. For recreation, Duncan breeds Arab horses.

THOMAS STEARNS ELIOT (1888–   ),

an important figure in English letters since 1920, was born in St. Louis. He belongs to the distinguished Boston family which included solid merchants, ministers, famous presidents of Harvard, and the founder of Washington University in St. Louis. After graduating from Harvard in 1910, Eliot continued his education by travel in Europe and further studies at the Sorbonne, Harvard, and Oxford. He remained in London after his marriage in 1915, becoming a British subject in 1927.

Eliot's poem, "The Waste Land," brought him the $2,000 Dial Award in 1922 and world-wide recognition. The poem graphically portrays the barrenness of the disillusioned post-war civilization.

Eliot found a way out of "the waste land" about 1928 when he forsook a vague Unitarian Protestantism to become an Anglo-Catholic. His subsequent dramatic and poetic writing like "Ash Wednesday," "The Rock," *Murder in the Cathedral*, *Family Reunion*, and *Four Quartets* mirror his conversion. The tradition of the divine in the Eliot family has reasserted itself in T. S. Eliot's *The Idea of a Christian Society* in which he claims that Christian society is the only hope for the world. He was awarded the 1948 Nobel prize for literature.

Eliot's more recent poetic dramatic achievements are *The Cocktail Party* and *The Confidential Clerk*.

JOHN GALSWORTHY (1867–1933).

The Galsworthys have been in Devonshire, England, "since the flood—of Saxons, at all events," as the writer once put it. John was born at Coombe, in Surrey, in 1867, and his works are typical of good English birth and breeding.

After his schooling at Harrow and Oxford, he made an attempt at the practice of law, his father's profession. But it proved uncongenial. "I read," he said, "in various chambers, practiced almost not at all, and disliked my profession thoroughly." His father's wealth and generosity enabled the young man to close his office and go vagabonding. He traveled for two years, visiting most of the out-of-the-way places of the world. On one of his voyages he made the acquaintance of Joseph Conrad, then still a sailor. John Galsworthy encouraged Conrad to begin writing, and was soon turning out novels, essays, and plays himself. His most notable work is the history of three generations of the Forsyte family, the nucleus of which has been gathered into one thick volume, *The Forsyte Saga*.

In 1906, Mr. Galsworthy became very much interested in the stage, and for the next twelve years wrote chiefly plays. About two thirds of his work are novels and dramas, the rest including short stories, sketches, essays, and a few poems.

WILFRID WILSON GIBSON (1878–   ).

From a home in the spare country of Northumberland, Wilfrid Gibson made his way as a young man to London.

Though he had had little education, he was eager to write. Before he was thirty he had tasted some success, and with the years he has gained mastery in his writing. He has written of the shepherds of the north country, of the city people with whom he works, and of soldiers and battles. He has an easy lyric style and a bright imagination. His war poetry is convincingly right in thought and feeling.

THOMAS GRAY (1716–1771). Most of Gray's tranquil life was spent at Cambridge, first as a student and later as professor of history and modern languages. He wrote little but wrote carefully and thoughtfully, with much revision. The "Elegy Written in a Country Churchyard" was published after seven years of revision, when Gray was thirty-five. His poetry was much what the man was—quiet, somewhat somber, neat, and intellectual rather than impassioned.

GRAHAM GREENE (1904–   ) was the son of the headmaster of Birkhamsted School in Hertfordshire, England. After completing his education at Balliol College, Oxford, he worked on the staff of the London *Times*; and from 1935–1939, he was film critic for the *Spectator*. His travels have taken him through Europe, to Mexico and to Africa. During the war his work for the British foreign office included a year of duty in Freetown on the west coast of Africa.

Greene has written novels, travel books, short stories, critical essays, drama, and film scripts. In addition to *The Third Man*, written originally for the screen, several of his novels and short stories have been made into movies. In 1949 Greene published his collection of short stories under the title of *Nineteen Stories*. His *Lost Childhood*, a collection of essays, gives us an important insight into his literary background and the religious theme which runs throughout his serious works. Greene became a Catholic in 1926.

He is married and has two children, a son and a daughter. It is interesting to know that he is a cousin of Robert Louis Stevenson.

Greene holds an eminently high place in contemporary writing; and he is without doubt the leading English Catholic fiction writer.

THOMAS HARDY (1840–1928), the son of a prosperous stone mason, was early destined for his father's trade. At sixteen he was apprenticed to a local ecclesiastical architect, sympathetic enough to let him read more Greek stories than architecture texts. At twenty-seven he was ready to set up business for himself; but he found it a dull livelihood at best.

Hardy had already begun writing poetry, but no one would have it. It was not until his career as a novelist was finished that any was published. When finally Hardy's genius matured, his novels acquired wider reputation until with the publication of his two most famous stories, *Tess of the D'Urbervilles* and *Jude the Obscure*, a storm of abuse was heaped upon him. The Victorians resented, bitterly, his boldness in disclosing the hearts of men and women. Exhausted from his long struggle, he vowed never to write fiction again and returned to his first interest, poetry. Belatedly the world realized his great gifts; he was showered with honors, the Order of Merit only one among them.

GEORGE HERBERT (1593–1633). At a period when the excesses of Renaissance England were often too evident, the quiet, scholarly life of George Herbert was as welcome as were his graceful lyrics. Born in Wales, George Herbert early distinguished himself as a scholar and orator at Cambridge, and was appointed public orator there for eight years. Like Spenser he was hopeful of a position at court, but when none came he resigned himself to a quiet life in the Anglican Church.

His little church held services twice a

day; many of the hymns he wrote himself. His poetry was filled with sincere religious feeling. As a model for other young clerics, he wrote A *Priest to the Temple*, a sort of handbook of useful rules for a country parson. He and his parish grew fond of each other, but after only three years Herbert died of tuberculosis.

ROBERT HERRICK (1591–1674) was the most famous of "the Tribe of Ben," that group of poets who listened with admiration to Ben Jonson as he discussed literature in the Devil Tavern in London. Herrick was born in London and it was in London that he spent his happiest years.

But the greater part of Herrick's life was spent as an Anglican minister in a village far from his beloved London. By nature Herrick was not a country pastor but a light-hearted singer. During his long years in the country he wrote some twelve hundred lyrics.

GERARD MANLEY HOPKINS (1844–1889). "The only honors the Society has to bestow,—and they are posthumous," says Father James Daly in *The Jesuit in Focus*, "are those won by sanctity of life . . . all else is secondary and even negligible." The Jesuit poet, Gerard Manley Hopkins, exemplified this statement to a remarkable degree. Though he possessed rare poetic genius, he completely subordinated his artistic talent to the higher calling of holiness, and the product of his art became the finer for his sanctity.

Even as a young boy, Gerard gave evidence of a keen intellect, rare sensitivity to beauty, and the practice of taking his religion (Anglican) seriously. Oxford made Hopkins. Here he mastered the classics, developed his talent for poetry, read and relived Newman's *Apologia*, and finally became a convert and a Catholic priest.

Putting first the exacting duties of his life, whether in the pulpit at Farmstreet, the classroom at Stonyhurst, the slums of Liverpool, or the Catholic University in Ireland, Father Hopkins still found time to leave a slender volume, an exquisite legacy, hardly surpassed in literature, of "the world charged with the grandeur of God," of Mary, "world-mothering air," and of "God's better beauty, grace."

A. E. HOUSMAN (1859–1936) has done for Shropshire what Thomas Hardy did for Wessex and Arnold Bennett for the pottery towns—he has presented it to the world. Yet he did it quite unwillingly and with the utmost difficulty. According to his own confession, writing poetry was something of a fever, which he had strength to endure during just a few brief periods. He wrote almost continually from the time he was twenty, yet published only two slim volumes: *A Shropshire Lad* and *Last Poems*, both jewel-like in their perfection.

LIONEL JOHNSON (1867–1902). This slight, frail young man, "too pale and delicate even for speech" as Alice Meynell described him, possessed one of the keenest and best-trained minds in England at his time. He had been sent to Winchester, one of the famed English "public" schools, founded in the Catholic past and handing down through its "half-a-thousand years" all the traditions of classical education. Here Lionel Johnson acquired a splendid knowledge of Latin and Greek, a fine English style, and a close acquaintance with literary affairs in England and on the continent.

In his keen interest in literary affairs he naturally became acquainted with the Catholic trend called the Oxford Movement, which had led John Henry Newman into the Church, and which under his guidance was bringing many of the finest minds in England to realize that Catholicism was the one religion founded by Christ. Johnson could not fail to recognize its cogent proofs, and he too entered the Catholic Church.

BEN JONSON (1573?–1637). "Literary dictator" of the brilliant circle of dramatists at the court of James I was the versatile Ben Jonson—poet, actor, dramatist, critic, and song writer. As prolific a writer as Shakespeare, Jonson wrote more exclusively for his own time; his elaborate masques, comedies of manners, and classical tragedies have gone out of fashion, but in his own lifetime he was famous.

Unlike Shakespeare and Marlowe, Jonson was convinced that truly great drama must be ordered and stately, following the rules set down by Greek and Roman critics. He was not afraid to criticize the extravagance and lack of unity in the English drama and by the use of satire and ridicule, he set out to improve the manners and morals of his countrymen. On the accession of James I in 1603 he was named the first poet laureate.

SHEILA KAYE-SMITH (1888–   ). In her autobiography, *Three Ways Home*, which records her own and her husband's conversion to Catholicism in 1929, Sheila Kaye-Smith wrote that she had three childhood ambitions: to live in the country, to be a celebrated novelist, and to be extremely high church. Today Sheila Kaye-Smith is one of England's most distinguished woman novelists. The countryside of Sussex has been both her continual home and the locale of all her novels. And she has found "an extremely high church" in Roman Catholicism.

Some of her better known novels, other than *Superstition Corner* and the *End of the House of Alard*, are *Susan Spray* and *Shepherds in Sackcloth*. Miss Kaye-Smith has written a delightful and thoroughly Catholic book of essays entitled *Kitchen Fugue*.

JOHN KEATS (1795–1821) was born in London, where his father kept a large stable. As a boy, John helped out about the stable and attended school at Enfield. He was an eager student; but the great schools of Eton, Harrow, Oxford, or Cambridge were not for boys like him. He was orphaned at fifteen and apprenticed to a surgeon. For nearly seven years he tried to like his profession, but books and writing were much more real to him.

When Keats was twenty-three he fell in love with Fanny Brawne, a girl of eighteen. For a time the poet was overwhelmingly happy; and in the next year and a half produced his greatest poems. But in the meantime his brother Tom had died; and the dread consumptive disease had fastened itself upon John. Knowing his heritage and his poverty, he refused to consider marriage. In September, 1820, he went to Italy in an attempt to save his life; but there in February he died, four months after his twenty-fifth birthday. He was the third and youngest of a tragic group of young romanticists; but among his poems, written in less than four years' time, are some that take their place with the masterpieces of our literature.

RUDYARD KIPLING (1865–1936) was born in Bombay, India, of English parents; learned Hindustani as soon as English, and listened wide-eyed to the tales of the natives. At six he was sent back to England to be educated, then returned to India to become a newspaperman.

As fillers for the paper, Kipling wrote rollicking sketches of three British Tommies in India or human verses in cockney dialect. Letters came from all over India asking that the poems and stories be published. *Departmental Ditties* and *Plain Tales from the Hills* were the result.

Kipling's popularity in India led him to want to try his hand in England. A period of travel to Japan and America followed, and then came the *Jungle Books* and *Captains Courageous*. In 1901 the publication of *Kim* saw him truly famous. He retired to a large country estate in Sussex, settled down to politics, and the celebrating of England and her glory. In 1907 he won the Nobel Prize, and all England rejoiced. During the first World War he lost his only son; yet he bravely continued his lecturing and writing for the Allied cause.

Mr. Kipling died when just past seventy, beloved by a truly tremendous reading public.

RONALD A. KNOX (1888–   ). The exuberant Monsignor Ronald Knox, the son of an Anglican Bishop and brother of the editor of *Punch*, has fulfilled the promise of a literary career which began when as a boy of ten he wrote Latin and Greek epigrams. After completing his courses at Oxford with brilliance, he took holy orders and became Anglican chaplain at Trinity College. Converted to Catholicism in 1917, he was ordained priest two years later and returned to Oxford in 1925 to be chaplain for the Catholic undergraduates.

His translation of the New Testament, written since 1939 during his retirement from Oxford, is in the words of a leading Catholic critic, "marked by the purity and delicacy of Monsignor Knox's own ear for the rhythm and sonorousness of our modern English speech." His translation of the Old Testament was published in 1948.

CHARLES LAMB (1775–1834). It does not take a large man to make a hero; it does take courage. Charles Lamb was a small man, shabby and insignificant looking. He did nothing sensational, but he was heroic just the same. He had the courage to accept the support of himself, his sister, his father, and—at times—other dependents. Though he loved deeply, he was strong enough not to consider a marriage that would have been selfish and perhaps unwise. And he was brave enough to care for his insane sister Mary in the periods of temporary relief and to walk with her to the asylum when a fit of violence was coming on.

There was heroism, too, in Lamb's smiling acceptance of everyday hardships. The family had always been poor. For seven years Charles was a charity student in the Bluecoat School of Christ's Hospital. Most English boys found little but suffering in the charity schools. Lamb absorbed an excellent education and made one good friend, Samuel Coleridge. For thirty-three years he was a clerk in the India House.

Lamb showed an early interest in writing, but his first works were poems and plays, now little remembered. He had always been interested in Elizabethan drama, and his first successful works grew out of this field. In 1807 he and Mary published their *Tales from Shakespeare*—short, easily read synopses of the important plays of the poet. Lamb was almost forty-five when he began contributing to the *London Magazine* little sketches which he signed "Elia." Thus began the famous *Essays of Elia*. Addison and Steele a century before had made the essay entertaining; Lamb made it personal. The *Essays of Elia* and its successors are as self-revealing as an autobiography.

RICHARD LOVELACE (1618–1658), devoted to the Royalist cause, lost his fortune, his fiancée, his health, and his freedom to the Parliamentarians—but not without a valiant struggle. Wealthy, handsome, and clever, Lovelace was popular among the circle of Charles I's court. After the break between the King and Parliament, Lovelace sponsored and presented to Parliament a petition defending the King. He was promptly thrown in prison. It was during this two years' imprisonment that he wrote his lyric, "To Althea." Later he was captured and held as a prisoner on parole throughout the Civil War. Generous to musicians and scholars, as long as he had money, he died in near poverty.

THOMAS BABINGTON MACAULAY (1800–1859). An ardor and appetite for great books, great battles, great cities, and great men made the champion of Victorianism, Lord Macaulay, a writer of colorful, interesting, and, at times, unsound history.

Macaulay had a rare combination of natural gifts. His mind was phenomenally quick and retentive. He could read at three years of age, was studying serious books at five, had written a compendium of universal history at ten. In maturity he could read like lightning and he seemed to remember, literally, everything that he had ever read. He could recite at will from *Paradise Lost*, from novels or histories or newspapers.

He had excellent health and a happy disposition. Everyone liked and respected him. He was thoroughly honest and conscientious in his business and political life. In Parliament, besides being its most eloquent speaker, he was a trustworthy leader. He accepted some high offices—such as a cabinet position—and refused others. Two years before his death he was made Baron Macaulay of Rothley.

The success that Macaulay enjoyed in other things came to him also as a writer. In fact, the sale of his works contributed largely to his fortune. When he was twenty-five, his "Essay on Milton" appeared in the *Edinburgh Review*. It was a sensational success. For the next twenty years he contributed essays on literary and historical themes to magazines. Then he began the *History of England* on which he worked until his death. He finished five volumes. The sales of this *History* were so successful that he once received a check of £100,000 from his publisher.

BRYAN MacMAHON (1909–   ) was born and continues to live and work in Listowel, County Kerry, Ireland. He received his higher education at St. Patrick's College in Dublin, but immediately returned to his own town to teach and to write. His wide literary activities include high success in the short story, drama, poetry, and radio-script writing. He is at present master of Listowel's National School.

MacMahon published his collection of short stories under the title of *The Lion-Tamer* in 1949. In March of that same year, his play, *The Bugle in the Blood*, was presented at the Abbey Theater. The opening night audience clamored for the author at the conclusion of the play. In 1952 appeared *Children of the Rainbow*, a novel which strengthened his position as a writer of the first rank. His latest collection of short stories, *The Red Petticoat*, has been acclaimed as his best literary contribution to that rapidly growing and brilliantly written literary heritage which contemporary Catholic Irish writers are bequeathing to English literature.

KATHERINE MANSFIELD (1888–1923) was born in New Zealand. Her father was a banker, and she was given a good education in the schools near her home. Later she attended Queen's College in London. There her gift for writing was recognized, and she edited the college magazine. She married the literary editor and critic, J. Middleton Murry, who encouraged her literary efforts. She became a critic and reviewer for the British *Athenaeum*. Her health, though, was poor and she traveled on the continent looking for a more suitable climate. She was still a young woman when she died in Paris in 1923.

CHRISTOPHER MARLOWE (1564–1593), of all the Elizabethans who flung cape over shoulder, was perhaps the most dashing, the most tempestuous, and the most appealing. Born the same year as Shakespeare, he had much of Shakespeare's power, many of his poetic gifts, but none of his stability. Marlowe's early work shows as much promise as Shakespeare's, but Marlowe was dead at twenty-nine, his only bequest to the world four tragedies, full of greatness and littleness.

Marlowe, who was the son of a poor shoemaker, managed to spend some years at Cambridge, absorbing some knowledge and a lot of life. He attached himself to the tawdry fringe of society connected with the theater. He probably began by acting, but later turned to writing for the Earl of Nottingham's companies. His first play, *Tamburlaine*, with an ambition-maddened hero, took the theaters by storm. His second play, *Dr. Faustus*, was equally popular. Its theme of a man selling his soul for the price of *all knowledge* held a strange fascination for grasping, superstitious Elizabethans. His two other plays were *The Jew of Malta*, a drama centered about thirst for wealth, and *Edward II*, an early historical play. Both repeated his earlier successes.

JOHN MASEFIELD (1878–   ) has led a life as colorful and as varied as his poetry. He has known the sea and the fields, laborers and statesmen, hospital ships and country estates, nonentity and fame. Today he is poet laureate of England; holder of the Order of Merit, the most coveted honor England can bestow; former member of the British Council of World War II, and the acknowledged dean of English letters.

Masefield's early life was colored by his experiences sailing before the mast on a windjammer. His formal schooling ended at thirteen when he was placed by his guardian on the training ship *Convoy*. From then on, life and the sea took over his education.

In 1897 he returned to London, his mind set on a career in letters. For five years he struggled with editors and at last was named literary editor of the *Manchester Guardian*. His volume, *Salt Water Ballads*, was successful. His rapid, racy style, the humble origin of his characters and the brisk pattern of his rhythms made him a popular writer. During World War I he served on a hospital ship in Gallipoli. After the war his reputation as England's most popular poet was secure.

ALICE MEYNELL (1847–1922). One of the best ways of understanding the important literary movement of the last century known as the "Catholic Literary Revival" is to appreciate the life of Alice Thompson Meynell.

All literary periods and movements are gradual changes, carried on through many decades, led by a few moving spirits with more or less definite ideals, and intermingled with very many differing tendencies and tastes. In tracing the life of Alice Meynell one may see this growth of literature all the way from the Romantic poets to twentieth century authors like Belloc, Chesterton, Noyes, Max Beerbohm and Oscar Wilde. All the literary people of the second half of the nineteenth and early part of the twentieth centuries were friends of Alice Meynell.

Alice Meynell was born in 1847 into a very literary and artistic family. Her early life was spent chiefly in traveling in Europe, cultivating literary and artistic tastes, and pursuing her general education under her father's guidance. The family was not Catholic at the time, but one by one, Alice, her mother, and her sister Elizabeth embraced the Faith. Alice was twenty when she became a Catholic.

In 1877 Alice married Wilfrid Meynell, an energetic young Catholic journalist, and from then on these two formed a perfect unity, raising a splendid Catholic family and publishing the best of Catholic writing. Their busy home became the *salon* of advanced literature in England. Here, in these parlor conversations, we may see all the trends, but particularly the Catholic trend in literature, take shape and grow.

Mrs. Meynell was never lost in the narrow confines of her own home, but her truly Catholic vision extended to all worthwhile social endeavors—to works of charity, to woman suffrage, to the encouragement of youthful literary talents and, above all, to the rehabilitation and inspiration of Francis Thompson.

When Alice Meynell died in 1922, she left behind the literary legacy of six published volumes of poetry and thirteen volumes of prose essays. Outstanding among her prose works are *The Rhythm of Life,* the *Color of Life,* and *The Spirit of Place.*

JOHN MILTON (1608–1674). It is easy to imagine young Will Shakespeare cutting classes, flunking a quiz now and then, playing a good game at shortstop. John Milton was of a different sort. He was a frail studious child, the son of a well-to-do banker and lawyer.

After finishing the course at St. Paul's School, he entered Christ College, Cambridge. There, like Bacon, he found little that was challenging. Once, in utter disgust he described the curriculum as an "asinine feast of soused thistles and brambles."

For five years Milton retired to his father's country house at Horton; reading in English, Latin, Greek, French, Italian, and Hebrew; writing some and meditating. A period of travel in Italy followed. He returned to set up a small school for boys where his strictness and impatience with failure must have made him respected but unloved.

Milton continued his teaching and writing until the Puritan-Cavalier disputes flamed into Civil War. For the next twenty years he gave his time to politics. Because of his ability as a writer and scholar, he entered the disputes as a pamphleteer, his violence enraging the Royalists and delighting the Puritans. With Cromwell's rise as "Protector," Milton became his secretary under the title of Latin Secretary to the Council of State. Part of his task was to carry on all the correspondence with foreign countries—in Latin. Warned by his physician that continued writing meant blindness, Milton remained at his post: handling the records, writing state documents, and defending the new government by pamphlets.

The last years of Milton's life have been called his period of "defeat," but a glorious defeat it was. At forty-five he was totally blind; he thus retired from active life and set himself to his great work, *Paradise Lost,* dictating the chapters to his three daughters who chafed at his severity and at having to read long hours to him in languages of which they understood not a word. In 1667 the poem was published; Milton received about twenty pounds for his years of labor. Its popularity, however, resulted in the sale of 1,200 copies within three months of publication. *Paradise Regained* and *Samson Agonistes* followed.

Had Milton died at thirty-four he would have been famous as one of the great lyricists. Had he died at forty-four he would have been revered as a great statesman and pamphleteer. Living to be sixty-six he added to both of these his best claim to fame, that of the greatest epic poet in English literature.

THOMAS MORE (1478–1535), like Christ his Lord, did all things well. He made a success of his profession, his family, his writing, and his life. The son of a barrister who later rose to be a justice of the King's Bench, Thomas was trained in the household of Cardinal Morton, the Archbishop of Canterbury, educated at Oxford under the new Humanists, Colet, Grocyn, and Linacre, and then transferred to Lincoln's Inn to follow his father's profession, law.

His rise in public life was remarkable. He became under-sheriff of London in 1510, was Ambassador to Flanders in 1515, became a Privy Councillor three years later, and was knighted in 1521. After another series of rapid advancements Sir Thomas More became in 1529 the first layman to hold the office of Lord Chancellor, the highest office in the realm. "The King's good servant, but God's first," More resigned the Great Seal in disapproval of Henry VIII's projected divorce from the Queen, Catherine of Aragon.

In 1505 Thomas More married Jane Colt. They had one son and three daughters. After his wife's death More married Alice Middleton. The More home was a happy one, for Sir Thomas was an excellent father who knew how to train his children. When he found them discouraged or sad about the hard things in their lives, he gently reminded them that they should not expect to fare better than Christ, their Lord, adding, "We may not look at our pleasure to go to heaven in fether beddes, it is not the way." His children's loyalty to the Faith in the future persecution gave evidence of this training.

The Humanistic training at Oxford bore rich results. More was recognized by the leading scholars of Europe. Erasmus in the Netherlands, Vives in Spain, and Budee in France were personal friends. More's *Utopia*, England's first significant contribution to Renaissance literature, may still be found among the works composing the "world's greatest literature." With his *History of King Richard III*, English historical writing took on significance and distinction. A voluminous apologist, More was about the only writer who battled in the vernacular against heresy. His prophetic *Dialogue of Comfort in Tribulation* shows him to be a spiritual writer of note.

More's greatest achievement was his saintly life and heroic death. Daily prayers, Mass, and meditation on the Passion joined to penitential exercises, known only to himself, were part of his entire life. His death is beautifully told by William Roper. St. Thomas More, canonized in 1935, says G. K. Chesterton, "may come to be counted the greatest Englishman, or at least the greatest historical character in English history."

JOHN HENRY NEWMAN (1801–1890), herald, symbol, and triumph of the Second Spring, was a religious teacher of tremendous significance. As a leader of the Oxford movement, he spearheaded the first, most rational, and most devastating attack on the shapeless creeds of Victorian Utilitarianism.

At Trinity College, Oxford, Newman became associated with a brilliant group of Anglicans who were keenly interested in restoring consistency and vitality to their religion. Beset with inborn prejudice against Rome, Newman, studying, thinking, praying, tried for years to find a *via media* between Anglicanism and the Catholic Church. Failing to do so, he embraced the true Faith and became a priest.

In 1852 Newman went to Dublin where he delivered the lectures afterward embodied in *The Idea of a University*. Two years later he was installed as rector of the new Catholic University at Dublin.

Then in 1863 the novelist Charles Kingsley stated in Macmillan's Magazine: "The truth for its own sake has never been a virtue with the Roman clergy. Father Newman informs us that it need not be." Newman protested. Kingsley answered with a denunciatory pamphlet, "What, Then, Does Dr. Newman Mean?" Aroused to the full meaning of the issue, Father Newman riddled the pamphlet and in a series of articles written at white heat over a period of eight weeks, told the story of his conversion, the *Apologia Pro Vita Sua*. Newman's victory was complete.

In his last years Newman's prestige returned. Oxford elected him as an honorary fellow of Trinity College, the first in the history of the college. The Church paid him a high, richly deserved recognition in 1879 when Pope Leo XIII created him Cardinal of St. George in Velabro. Newman's motto which he took on becoming a Cardinal—COR AD COR LOQUITUR —"heart speaks to heart" gives the key to his personality, as his epitaph epitomized his life—EX UMBRIS ET IMAGINIBUS IN VERITATEM—"Out of shadows and representations into the full light of the truth."

ALFRED NOYES (1880–   ), whose autobiography, *Two Worlds for Meaning*, appeared in 1953, calmly recounts the story of a very normal, very happy, and very full and busy life writing poetry. Noyes told the story of his conversion to Catholicism in 1925 in *The Unknown God*. Catholicism soon became a profound influence in his life. This is especially noteworthy in his poetic trilogy, *The Torch Bearers*, an epic of Science which he began in 1924 and completed in 1930. His epic ends in an act of adoration before the Sacramental Christ, the sign and reality of the unity of "our sundered truth."

He has written several books of criticism, including *The Pageant of Letters*. But Noyes will always be remembered for his lilting, singing poems: "The Highwayman," "Forty Singing Seamen," and "The Barrel Organ."

HESKETH PEARSON (1887–   ) has often been called the successor of Lytton Strachey in the field of the new biography. Until 1930, however, he did not write for publication; for during the years 1911–1931, except for a brief interval of service in World War I, he was busily engaged as a professional actor.

In 1930 he published a life of Erasmus Darwin, a maternal ancestor. This book was the beginning of a long series of excellent biographies, all of which were received enthusiastically by his readers. Pearson has written lives of Oscar Wilde, Benjamin Disraeli, Charles Dickens, Gilbert and Sullivan, and Whistler.

SAMUEL PEPYS (1633–1703) might very well be styled a self-made man, for he began life humbly as clerk in a government office in London and advanced until he became Secretary to the Admiralty. He was alert and politic; he knew what friends to make and how to keep them. He also managed to have a busy, entertaining time. For nine years he kept a diary, and as he wished it to be private, he wrote it in a special shorthand with a code of his own. He wrote freely all the gossipy details of his life and the life about him. He used real names and exact figures, for he supposed that no one else would ever read it. No one did during his lifetime.

More than a hundred years after his death, the books were discovered. The code was deciphered and the entries transcribed. The result was a unique record of a section of one man's life and personal glimpses of hundreds of others.

Samuel Pepys perhaps congratulated himself on amassing a considerable fortune, on being elected president of the Royal Society, and on having a speaking acquaintance at Court; but if his Diary had proved undecipherable, the twentieth century would never have heard of him.

ALEXANDER POPE (1688–1744) is the chief representative of classicism in English literature. His outstanding characteristic is formal correctness. He brought the heroic couplet to a high degree of perfection, and his verse is written with precision and exactness.

Pope was a strange mixture of incongruity in nature, for in spite of acknowledged disagreeable traits which he had, he was a leader in literature, a man of tremendous intellect, and probably, next to Shakespeare, the most often quoted of the English poets. His *Essay on Criticism* gives the principles of writing poetry. This was followed by "The Rape of the Lock," the *Dunciad*, and the *Essay on Man*.

Pope was witty and his verse was melodious. In form, finish, and compactness, he stands alone. His deficiencies are lack of emotional power and force. His appeal is almost wholly to the intellect. Pope was a Catholic, but his Catholicism had very little influence on his poetry.

SIR WALTER RALEIGH (1552–1618) is best known to the average American student as the adventurous explorer who attempted to found a colony in America, which he called Virginia.

A close friend of Spenser and Marlowe, Raleigh was ambitious and sometimes unscrupulous. Hot-tempered by nature, he was alternately in and out of favor with Queen Elizabeth. While imprisoned in the Tower of London for thirteen years, Raleigh wrote his celebrated *History of the World*. He was finally sentenced to death and died under the executioner's axe.

TERENCE RATTIGAN (1911–   ) began writing plays while he was a student at Oxford. Today he is one of England's most popular dramatists, with numerous stage and screen plays to his credit. His first successes were light, hilarious comedies—except for *Flare Path*, a war play which he wrote while on active duty as a gunner in the Royal Air Force.

Other entertaining comedies followed, establishing Rattigan as a seasoned playwright. However, their great box office success caused him to be considered only as a writer of high-spirited nonsense. One producer told him, "What's so nice about your doing your plays in my theater is that their profits pay for the good ones." Mr. Rattigan did not have to wait long to get revenge. Within a few years critics were enthusiastically proclaiming the excellence of his more serious plays, *The Winslow Boy* and *The Browning Version*.

The Winslow Boy won the Ellen Terry Award as the best play of 1946, and the New York Critics' Award as the best foreign play of the season.

WILLIAM ROPER (1496–1578) was St. Thomas More's son-in-law, the husband of his daughter Margaret. He had lived in the More's household for sixteen years and always remained a close associate of More. After his father-in-law's advice and prayers saved him from the heresy into which he had lapsed for several years, Roper remained loyal to the Faith during the subsequent persecution. His *Life of More*, written during Queen Mary's reign, is among the best prose works of the time and is one of the first biographies in the English language.

CHRISTINA ROSSETTI (1830–1894), sister of Gabriel, found life nearly as uncompromising in its severity as her brother. Educated like him at home, she early showed great poetic promise. She was a beautiful girl, slim and nun-like; her brothers and their friends loved to paint the stillness of her face, a stillness that covered deep and often melancholy emotion. After an unhappy romance ended because of a difference in religion, Christina turned entirely to poetry and religion.

DANTE GABRIEL ROSSETTI (1828–1882). Although his own life was full of tragedy, Rossetti's influence on his own and succeeding ages was completely wholesome and good. Not since the time of the strange William Blake had art and poetry fused to such brilliance in a single artist.

More Italian than English, Gabriel Rossetti was the son of an exiled Italian, a professor at the University of London, and a half-Italian mother. At school the nervous little boy learned little; at home the household was filled with the music of Italy. Gabriel, his sister, and brother drew and wrote, learned literature from their father and religion from their mother. At fourteen, he left school to prepare to be a painter. Thoroughly disgusted with the teaching methods of the Royal Academy of Art, he soon began experimenting with his own theories. With other young artists, he organized a group called the Pre-Raphaelites, who denounced the still prettiness of the paintings then fashionable, and substituted realistic detail and actual form. A few distinguished critics—Ruskin among them—befriended the shabby group. Along with his painting, Rossetti wrote poetry. The same results brightened both: color and form and reality.

Success came at last to both poetry and painting, but the prosperity had come too late for Rossetti's enjoyment. His health and mind had failed under repeated criticism and his last years were spent wandering and friendless.

JOHN RUSKIN (1819–1900). It is refreshing to read of a reformer sincere enough to try putting his theories into practice and sensible enough to have practical ideas. Such a man was John Ruskin, the famous Victorian writer and critic.

When only twenty-one, Ruskin published the introductory volume to *Modern Painters*, in which he warmly defended nineteenth-century art, especially the work of the landscape painter, William Turner. The book created something like a revolution in taste, and within the next ten years Ruskin became the art dictator of England. Besides *Modern Painters*, he had written *The Seven Lamps of Architecture* and *The Stones of Venice*.

It was at this time that his love for art led him to realize the need for changes in the living and working conditions in England. He did not think of art as a pleasure to be reserved for the wealthy few. He thought of it as something to enrich the lives of everyone. What use was there in writing about the glories of Gothic architecture in Venice when a million Londoners were living in tenement slums?

His writings, from 1860 on, all reveal this new interest. Many of them were lectures to schools or clubs for working men. Several volumes of letters addressed to the laboring classes were published under the title of *Fors Clavigera*. *Unto This Last* was a bold challenge to the industrialism of Victorian England and the ugliness of a mechanized world which Ruskin hated.

SIEGFRIED SASSOON (1886–   ) is one of the few war poets of World War I fortunate to live through that violent debacle in which many of England's young men were lost. Since then, he has never ceased to write with brutal realism of war. At Cambridge in the early nineteen-hundreds Sassoon was more interested in poetry, hunting, and tennis than in studies; and was "sent down" before graduation. The war turned Sassoon into a pacifist and a true poet. After his enlistment and commission he served four years, was wounded twice, won the Military Cross, and emerged a captain. Utter desolation was his only personal reaction.

After the war and its subsequent glorifying of peace, Sassoon's bitter exposure of the horror of trench warfare was accepted. In 1928 he published anonymously the *Memoirs of a Fox-Hunting Man*, which was eventually recognized as his own fictionalized autobiography.

SIR WALTER SCOTT (1771–1832). Born of an old Scottish Border family, Scott grew up amid the ballads and legends of the Highland clans. His lameness forced him to rely on books and stories for amusement rather than sports. At ten he had already collected a large store of ballads and tales. During his vacations from school he would ramble over the country, collecting the folklore and landscape he later popularized. Parental influence led him to the study of law at the University of Edinburgh, but he practiced only desultorily, closing up shop in good weather to set out on his beloved rambles. Appointed to the post of sheriff of Selkirkshire where the light duties and good salary pleased him, he began writing poetry in earnest.

Unfortunately, the forty-year-old Scott was a far better poet than businessman. Entangled with a publishing firm, he lost his entire fortune by its failure and incurred debts of over five hundred thousand dollars. The last years of his life were spent in a desperate attempt to pay back every penny. With great difficulty he kept the splendid castle he had built in the Highland country. The death of his wife and his own weakened health only added to his determination. Anonymously, to earn money speedily, he published his novel, *Waverley*, the first of a series of twenty-nine historical novels all written after he was forty-three. The novel was tremendously successful; more stories poured from the pen of "The Great Unknown." Readers snatched at each new volume offered for sale. At the time of his death Scott had almost completely cleared himself of his debts, but the strain had been too great on his never-robust health.

WILLIAM SHAKESPEARE (1564–1616), greatest of all the Elizabethans and greatest of all dramatists, grew up in Stratford-on-Avon, a busy trading village. Will was a typical Elizabethan boy. He punted (boated) on the river, played the sixteenth-century version of cops and robbers in the meadows across the Avon, and growled about his lessons. As a youngster he must have stood more than once, mouth gaping, to see the traveling theatrical companies parade over Clopton bridge and up to the marketplace—banners flying, drums beating, costumes gaudy in the breeze, the trumpeters' blasts calling the villagers to the afternoon performance. Perhaps when he was twelve, he saw Queen Elizabeth herself passing through Stratford with her splendid retinue on her "progress" to a near-by nobleman's castle. Until he was eighteen, Shakespeare knew only the little town of Stratford; but it was full of the bustle and color of Elizabethan days.

In 1582 Shakespeare married Anne Hathaway, and three children were born to them, Susannah, Hamnet, and Judith. From boyhood Shakespeare had been interested in amateur dramatics and in working with traveling troupes of players that came to Stratford. About 1588 or 1589 he went to London to try his luck at playing. Meager records indicate that he acted in various capacities from stagehand to callboy and eventually as an actor, "and did acte exceeding well." The fortunate company of players with whom he became associated was the Earl of Pembroke's Men, and for this company he wrote his earlier plays, most of which are revisions or adaptations of older plays which had long been favorites with the public.

In 1592 and 1593 outbreaks of the plague caused the closing of the theaters in London. Pembroke's Men went on a tour in the country, but meeting with no success, they returned to the city, sold their stock of plays and disbanded. From the time the company went on tour until 1594, Shakespeare was apparently connected with no theater. He wrote *Venus and Adonis*, and *Lucrece*, and began the *Sonnets*. These poems were well received and raised their author to a place of eminence in the literary world.

In 1594, the famous company of players, The Lord Chamberlain's Men, later known as The King's Men, was organized. It numbered among its members the most able and popular actors of the day, and it is significant of Shakespeare's reputation that he was taken in as full sharer apparently from the outset. With this company Shakespeare was actively associated as actor and as playwright for nearly twenty years. For it he wrote thirty-two of the thirty-seven plays which have come down to us in the *Folio of 1623*, and he had without doubt a hand in the writing and revision of many more.

Shakespeare's death occurred in April, 1616. He was buried simply in the church at Stratford. Although he deserved a place in Westminster Abbey with England's great, his body was never removed there. Tradition has it that local superstition accounts for this, for the inscription on his tombstone, said to have been written "by himselfe a little before his death," reads as follows:

GOOD FREND FOR JESUS SAKE FORBEARE,
TO DIGG THE DUST ENCLOASED HEARE.
BLESTE BE YE MAN WHO SPARES THESE
    STONES,
AND CURST BE HE WHO MOVES MY BONES.

PERCY BYSSHE SHELLEY (1792–1822) was born in Field Place, Sussex. Shelley was a sensitive, nervous child of unusual beauty, but he was never a coward. On the contrary, he always stood out against oppression and was called "mad Shelley" at school. At Eton and Oxford, he was constantly in trouble with the masters, for he continued to express his revolutionary ideas.

Shelley's field of poetry is the lyric. No greater lyric poet has ever lived. True it is that one must enjoy flights of fancy into infinite spaces to really appreciate Shelley, but his lyrics contain some of the sweetest and most liquid harmonies ever written. His notes are as clear as a flute, now high, now low, but always in a minor key. Shelley is at his best in "To a Skylark," "The Cloud," and "Ode to the West Wind."

Shelley was drowned in the Gulf of Lerici off the Italian coast when he was only thirty years old.

PHILIP SIDNEY (1554–1586), when only thirty-two years old, died for his country from wounds received in the battle of Zutphen. It is said that during the battle he passed on a cup of water to another wounded soldier, saying, "Thy necessity is greater than mine."

Sir Philip was the son of the high-born Sir Henry Sidney. His early training was received at Shrewsbury and Oxford. As a member of the Areopagus, an English literary academy, he strove with the other members to naturalize the classic meters into English verse. His *Defense of Poesie* marks the beginning of literary criticism, while *Arcadia* is the first long prose-verse pastoral romance in English.

ROBERT SOUTHWELL, S.J. (1561?–1595). "I would willingly tear up many of my works to be the author of 'The Burning Babe.'" So spoke Ben Jonson in criticism of Robert Southwell as a poet.

Robert Southwell was born in Norfolk and was sent to school at Douai in France because his loyal Catholic parents would not expose him to the Protestant schools of the Queen. He continued his education in Paris, and when barely seventeen entered the Society of Jesus. He was ordained in 1584 after distinguishing himself as a poet during his studies. In spite of the law which fixed a death penalty upon him for doing so, he took up his lifework in the English mission.

Inevitably, in his work for souls, he drew the suspicion and the hatred of the priest-hunters. He was captured in a raid and held prisoner for three years. During this time he was repeatedly tortured in order that information about the activities of his fellow priests in England, and the names of English Catholics might be wrested from him. But with the utmost heroism Father Southwell steadfastly refused to make any disclosures whatsoever. For this, and for his constancy in the Faith, he was falsely charged with treason and unjustly condemned to die. He was hanged in 1595, a martyr to the Faith.

STEPHEN SPENDER (1909–   ). Like W. H. Auden, whom he knew at Oxford, Spender started out as an earnest young writer determined to do battle against conventional poetry and conservative politics. However, his poetry is less satirical than Auden's, less intellectual, and more lyrical. Spender has lived much in Germany and is something of a globetrotter. He is a critic as well as a poet, and was one of the editors of the distinguished but now defunct literary magazine *Horizon*. He helped to found the new magazine *Encounter* in 1953.

Spender was at one time closely associated with Auden and C. Day Lewis in espousing Left Wing causes. Auden has since become a conservative and more traditional in his views of society. Spender, however, continues his Leftist political leanings. As a poet, he is much better when he steers clear of satire and simply lifts his voice in lyrical song.

EDMUND SPENSER (1552–1599) had all the attributes of a successful courtier but never attained the success. The son of a cloth maker, he worked his way through Cambridge by serving as a sizar or waiter. Soon after he left college he published "The Shepherd's Calendar," a long poem in allegorical form about the then popular shepherds and shepherdesses. The poem brought him immediate success. He hoped for a court appointment, but was given a post in Ireland instead. During his years in Ireland he wrote his best work, *The Faerie Queene*, which although presented by Sir Walter Raleigh to the Queen and popular with the reading public, failed to bring him either a new job or the Queen's smile.

Spenser started the "escapist" school of literature. He preferred the pageantry of life as he liked to dream it—all the edges softened and blurred with color, beauty, and the delicacy of rhyme.

RICHARD STEELE (1672–1729) was a rollicking Irishman who became an English writer. Whatever his failings, and he had many, two achievements stand to his credit—the production of the first popular magazine and the creation of Sir Roger de Coverley.

Steele was a student in the Charterhouse charity school, where he first met Joseph Addison, and later in Queen's College, Oxford. After leaving school he drifted from one job to another, taking a turn at journalism, at soldiering, and at politics. Always he managed to write—sketches, articles, pamphlets, comedies—whatever the public wanted.

In 1709 there appeared a little four-page paper, the *Tatler*, which was designed for pleasant entertainment and so may rightly be termed the first English magazine. It became exceedingly popular and many speculations were made as to the author. Joseph Addison was the first to guess that it was Steele. After that he became a contributor to the periodical, which continued to appear until 1711 when it was replaced by the *Spectator*. The second magazine was the work of Addison and Steele jointly.

LYTTON STRACHEY (1880–1932) had a background which fitted him to be the creator of the *new* biography. His father, Sir Richard Strachey, a British general and an Indian administrator, provided an income that left him free for scholarly pursuits at Trinity College, Cambridge.

At first Strachey tried verse, but was unsuccessful. His gift for vivid historical biography developed slowly. He was thirty-two before he published his first book. Though generally sociable, Strachey, all beard and spectacles, would bury himself in Berkshire whenever he had a book in the making. *Eminent Victorians* in 1918 was his first successful book. Said a reviewer: "At every word a reputation dies." Other works were *Queen Victoria* (1921), *Pope* (1925), *Elizabeth and Essex* (1928), and *Portraits in Miniature* (1931).

SIR JOHN SUCKLING (1609–1642) was the gayest of the whole crowd of Cavalier poets who danced and sang and bowled at the court of Charles I. At eighteen he inherited huge estates left by his father, who had been Secretary of State under James I.

With the rise of the Puritan Party and the death of Charles I, Suckling's life was changed overnight. As a trusted friend of the King, he had to flee the country to save his life. Disconsolate and afraid to face poverty and banishment, he took poison shortly after reaching France.

JONATHAN SWIFT (1667–1745). The tragedy in the life of Jonathan Swift is reflected in his characterization of his countrymen as "the most pernicious race of little odious vermin that nature ever suffered to crawl upon the surface of the earth." Behind the bitterness of that sentence lies a lifetime of disappointment and disillusionment.

Swift came from a good Irish family and was educated at Trinity in Dublin and later at Oxford. But he was poor. It was a time of general snobbishness and bitter prejudices. Intelligence and learning were respected, but poverty was a personal disgrace. Swift was impelled to take a position as secretary to Sir William Temple, a wealthy relative who treated him with condescending contempt. In an attempt to become independent he took orders in the Church and was assigned to Ireland.

An able man, Swift hoped to secure advancement, but one of his earliest satires had offended the Queen and the appointments he hoped for never came. However, in the years between 1700 and 1713 he divided his time between London and Ireland. In London he became the most powerful writer of political pamphlets. For three years he enjoyed prosperity and fame. When Queen Anne died, he hoped to be made bishop of an English diocese. His appointment was to the deanship of St. Patrick's Cathedral in Dublin. Thoroughly embittered, Dean Swift went to Ireland to remain the rest of his life.

ALFRED, LORD TENNYSON (1809–1892)

ALFRED, LORD TENNYSON (1809–1892) was a minister's son, the fourth of twelve children. The father, a man of intelligence and understanding, was proud to recognize signs of poetic ability in several of his offspring.

Tennyson was educated by his father and at Cambridge. He disliked college, but there he won a prize for his poem "Timbuctoo"; and there he made friends with his talented fellow student, Arthur Hallam.

The death of his father in 1830 left Alfred as the eldest son at the head of a large and demanding family. The next fourteen years during which he wrote continually were exacting. The death of his beloved college friend, Hallam, left Tennyson unhappy and confused. He continued to write, but published nothing for almost ten years. However, in 1842, a volume called *Poems by Alfred Tennyson* was kindly received, and he was granted a government pension.

In 1850, Tennyson was finally named poet laureate. From that time his fame and happiness increased yearly. Queen Victoria and Prince Albert admired and welcomed him; the *Idylls of the King* and *In Memoriam* were brilliantly successful. In 1884 the Queen conferred on him the title of Lord Tennyson.

DYLAN THOMAS (1914–1953)

When Dylan Thomas died at the early age of thirty-nine, there ended abruptly the career of one of our great contemporary men of letters. Many had known him as the greatest lyric poet of the younger generation. But, with the publication of *Quite Early One Morning*, the literary world discovered that his prose equally matched his poetry in verbal imagery. Already Thomas' "A Child's Christmas in Wales" is challenging the place of Dickens' *Christmas Carol* as an English classic.

Thomas was born in Carmarthenshire, Wales. Aside from attending Swansea Grammar School, he had no formal education. His deep rich voice won him a job with the British Broadcasting Corporation, and he later toured the United States, reading his poetry to college students. Some of his selections were recorded, and they are enjoyed by poetry lovers throughout the English-speaking world today.

FRANCIS THOMPSON (1859–1907)

One morning's mail in the winter of 1888 brought to the desk of Wilfrid Meynell, the Catholic editor of *Merrie England*, a literary periodical, one of the most sorry-looking manuscripts he had ever seen. Odds and ends of greasy and dog-eared paper, mere scraps, were shuffled together and on them written an essay called "Paganism, Old and New" and two poems, "Passion of Mary" and "Dream Tryst." The laconic note that accompanied them simply said, "Kindly address your rejection of these works to the Charing Cross Post Office." They were signed, "Francis Thompson," and their author, Meynell found out when he later published them enthusiastically, was as ragged and sorry looking as his parcel had been.

One thing was held in common by the forlorn beggar of London, the author of mystic poems like "The Hound of Heaven," and the youth who had set out in 1870 to begin his education at Ushaw College. This was his Catholic faith. His mother and father had been fervent converts to Catholicism, and when eleven-year-old Francis set out to learn Latin at Ushaw College it was with the idea of one day becoming a priest. But he dreamed too much. He could not follow the strict discipline necessary for a priest's life. In the end he had to give it up, and his teachers sent him home to seek some new vocation.

The new vocation was one chosen by his father. Since he himself was a doctor, he willed Francis to take up the study of medicine. Obediently Francis set out again, this time to Owens College in Manchester. But he failed his examinations, returned home, and was met with the just anger of his father. During a sickness while at medical school, laudanum had been given him, and already the habit was upon him. To stay at home was no longer possible, it seemed to him, so with Aeschylus' *Plays* and Blake's *Poems* as his only treasures, he set out on foot to be a writer in London. How he succeeded we have already seen.

In the years between 1890 and his death in 1907, Francis Thompson wrote and published the works which have since made him one of the first poets of the age. Part of the time he lived with the Meynells and part of the time at a Capuchin monastery in Wales. These were the years of his success. They were also years of great spiritual growth. With him, to be a poet and to be a saint were one and the same thing, for he was a "poet of the return to God."

EVELYN WAUGH (1903–   ) was born in London and educated at Lancing School and at Oxford. He studied painting, became a teacher, and finally a journalist before he chose writing as an exclusive career.

Waugh published his first novel in 1928. There quickly followed a series of other social satires, including *A Handful of Dust*, a vicious satire on the society set of London who confused lust for love.

In 1930 Waugh joined the Catholic Church. As a tribute to his new-found Faith and to Father Martin D'Arcy, the brilliant English Jesuit who converted him, he wrote *Edmund Campion*. With the appearance of *Brideshead Revisited*, he was given top-rank as a novelist.

In 1952 Waugh wrote *Men at Arms*, followed by *Officers and Gentlemen* in 1955. Both deal with World War II.

WILLIAM WORDSWORTH (1770–1850) was born in a small village in Cumberland and grew up as a boy in the beautiful Lake District of England.

He attended Cambridge University and after his graduation spent two years in continental travel. In France he came into contact with the ideas which produced the French Revolution, and as a young man his sympathies were wholly with the revolutionists. The excesses of the Revolution resulted in disillusionment, and he returned to England somewhat despondent.

After three years of rather unhappy, unsettled life, he received a small legacy which enabled him to take a cottage in the country, and here he established himself and his sister Dorothy and devoted himself to writing poetry. The rest of his life was simple and an example of "plain living and high thinking." In the preface to a book, *Lyrical Ballads*, produced in collaboration with Coleridge, Wordsworth took his stand against the classicists, declaring that poetry is "the spontaneous overflow of powerful feelings" and is not to be encased in hard and fast rules. Recognition of Wordsworth's ability as a poet was slow, but in 1843 he was appointed poet laureate.

WILLIAM BUTLER YEATS (1865–1939). Someone once wrote of Yeats that he fell in love with Ireland and with literature and the affair lasted his life. Ireland never had a greater nor a more sincere champion; nearly all his life was willingly spent there, and any stay in London found him lonesome for County Sligo. After grammar school, Yeats at eighteen began studying painting only to discover that he was a poet. Following a brief and not too successful fling in London literary society, he returned to Dublin to take a leading part, with Lady Gregory's aid, in the Celtic revival, the Irish literary renaissance. Together they founded the Irish Literary Theater (later called the Abbey Theater) and the Irish Academy. In 1917 Yeats married and settled in a tower on the seacoast of Ireland. He served in the Irish Senate for six years, but his heart was always in his poetry for which he won the Nobel Prize in 1923.

GLOSSARY

A

abasement (*à*·bās′měnt). Humiliation; loss of self-respect.

abhorred (ăb·hôrd′). Hateful.

abject (ăb′jěkt). Wretched and miserable.

ablution (ăb·lū′shŭn). The act of washing or cleansing.

abominable (*à*·bŏm′ĭ·n*à*·b'l). Hateful.

aboriginal (ăb·ô·rĭj′ĭ·n*ă*l). First; original.

abound (*à*·bound′). To have plenty of.

abscond (ăb·skŏnd′). To secretly run away; usually to avoid punishment.

abstract (ăb′străkt). A term or idea considered apart from practical or actual conditions.

abundant (*à*·bŭn′d*à*nt). Plentiful.

access (ăk′sěs). An entrance.

accession (ăk·sěsh′ŭn). Taking the throne; rising to the rule of a country.

acclivity (*à*·klĭv′ĭ·tĭ). An upward slope.

acquisition (ăk′wĭ·zĭsh′ŭn). That which is gained.

acrimonious (ăk′rĭ·mō′nĭ·ŭs). Bitter.

adamantine (ăd′*à*·măn′tĭn). Unbreakable; unyielding.

addled (ăd′ 'ld). Confused; muddled.

addressed (*à*·drěst′). Directed or applied.

adhere (ăd·hēr′). To agree; to hold together in agreement.

admonition (ăd′mô·nĭsh′ŭn). A warning.

adversary (ăd′věr·sĕr′ĭ). An opponent.

adverse (ăd·vûrs′). That which acts against or in a contrary direction.

adversity (ăd·vûr′sĭ·tĭ). Bad luck; misfortune.

affectation (ăf′ěk·tā′shŭn). A false show of knowledge or manners.

agile (ăj′ĭl). Deftly nimble; active.

agitation (ăj′ĭ·tā′shŭn). Restlessness.

ague (ā′gū). Chills and fever accompanied by violent shaking.

alchemy (ăl′kě·mĭ). The medieval chemical science and philosophy whose chief aim was to change base metal to gold.

alienation (āl′yěn·ā′shŭn). 1. Estrangement. 2. Withdrawal.

aliment (ăl′ĭ·měnt). 1. That which nourishes. 2. Means of support.

allege (*à*·lěj′). To state positively without proof.

allegory (ăl′ê·gō′rĭ). A description of one thing under the image of another.

alliteration (*à*·lĭt′ĕr·ā′shŭn). The repetition of the same beginning sound in two or more words which are next to, or near each other.

allude (*à*·lūd′). To refer to.

allusion (*à*·lū′zhŭn). Indirect reference.

amble (ăm′b'l). To go at an easy gait.

ambrosia (ăm·brō′zhĭ·*à*). Food fit for the gods.

amend (*à*·měnd′). 1. To become better; to recover. 2. To correct.

analogy (*à*·năl′ô·jĭ). A likeness between things.

anarchical (ăn·är′kĭ·k*ă*l). Without rule or order.

animadversion (ăn′ĭ·măd·vûr′shŭn). A remark by way of criticism.

annihilating (*à*·nī′ĭ·lāt′ĭng). Destroying entirely.

antagonism (ăn·tăg′ô·nĭz′m). Active opposition.

antediluvian (ăn′tě·dĭ·lū′vĭ·*ă*n). Before the flood.

anticipate (ăn·tĭs′ĭ·pāt). To prevent; to stop.

antidote (ăn′tĭ·dōt). That which makes a poison ineffective; a remedy.

apathy (ăp′*à*·thĭ). Lack of passion or emotion.

aphorism (ăf′ô·rĭz′m). A short, pithy sentence stating a general doctrine or truth.

apoplexy (ăp′ô·plěk′sĭ). A brain hemorrhage or stroke.

apostasy (*à*·pŏs′t*à*·sĭ). The act by which a person forsakes his former religion or beliefs.

appall (*à*·pôl′). To horrify; to fill with terror.

apparition (ăp′*à*·rĭsh′ŭn). A ghost or spirit.

appease (*à*·pēz′). To soothe or calm.

apportioned (*à*·pōr′shŭnd). Proportioned; divided.

apprehend (ăp′rê·hěnd′). To understand.

approbation (ăp′rô·bā′shŭn). Approval.

arbitrary (är′bĭ·trĕr′ĭ). Emphatic; decisive.

arduous (är′dụ·ŭs). Difficult; exhausting.

armada (är·mā′d*à*). A fleet of armed ships.

arrear (*à*·rēr′). That which is overdue.

ascertain (ăs′ēr·tān′). To make certain; to find out.

aspect (ăs′pěkt). Appearance.

assail (*à*·sāl′). To attack.

assimilation (*à*·sĭm′ĭ·lā′shŭn). The act of absorbing.

athwart (*à*·thwôrt′). Across.

attenuate (*à*·těn′ụ·āt). 1. To make thin or slender. 2. To weaken.

attuned (*à*·tūnd′). Brought into harmony.

audit (ô′dĭt). Report of accounts or actions.

auger (ô′gēr). A tool used for boring holes.

augmentation (ôg′měn·tā′shŭn). Increase.

augury (ô′gụ·rĭ). An indication; sign or omen.

august (ô·gŭst′). Of majestic dignity and grandeur.

austere (ôs·tēr′). Harsh; severe.

authorized (ô′thēr·īzd). Guaranteed to be true.

āte, châotic, dâre, ădd, *ă*ccuse, bär, căsk, *à*far; ēat, dẽar, ělude, ěgg, quĭet, cẽntēr; īdle, ĭf; actĭvĭty; ōpen, ôbey, ôr, ŏrange, ôffer, ŏccur.

avarice (ăv′a·ris). Excessive desire of gain; greediness.

avid (ăv′ĭd). Keenly eager.

avocation (ăv′ô·kā′shŭn). A hobby or secondary occupation.

avouch (a·vouch′). To confirm; to state positively.

azure (ăzh′ēr). The blue color of the clear sky.

B

badge (băj). To mark or smear.

baleful (bāl′fool). Evil; harmful.

bane (bān). Ruin.

bark (bärk). A boat; a ship.

barrister (băr′ĭs·tēr). A lawyer.

base (bās). Low down; unworthy.

batten (băt′ 'n). 1. To grow fat. 2. To fertilize.

beatific (bē′a·tĭf′ĭk). Blessed; blissful.

bedlam (bĕd′lăm). Any place of uproar and confusion.

beguile (bê·gīl′). To deceive or mislead.

bellman (bĕl′măn). A crier who warned prisoners who were to be executed.

beneficent (bê·nĕf′ĭ·sĕnt). Doing or producing good.

bestow (bê·stō′). 1. To reside; to live. 2. To give.

bier (bēr). A coffin and the stand on which it is placed.

blanch (blånch). To become pale; to whiten.

blatant (blā′tănt). Vulgar and noisy.

bob (bŏb). Slang for shilling; worth about twenty-five cents.

bole (bōl). A tree trunk.

bombastic (bŏm·băs′tĭk). High-sounding; pretentious.

bower (bou′ēr). 1. A rustic house. 2. A bedroom. 3. An arbor.

brandish (brăn′dĭsh). To shake or wave; to flourish.

bravado (bra·vä′dō). A great show of boldness without much real courage.

brawn (brôn). 1. Animal flesh. 2. Muscular strength.

breach (brēch). A break; an opening.

broil (broil). A fight or struggle.

buckle (bŭk′ 'l). To keep under control; to hold together.

buffet (bŭf′ĕt). A knocking about; a blow.

buffoonery (bŭ·fōōn′ēr·ĭ). Vulgar clowning.

burlesque (bŭr·lĕsk′). Ludicrous or broadly humorous caricature.

buttress (bŭt′rĕs). A support or prop for a building.

C

cadence (kā′dĕns). A regular rise and fall.

caldron (kôl′drŭn). A large iron cooking pot.

capricious (ka·prĭsh′ŭs). Fanciful.

carnage (kär′nĭj). Mass destruction of human life, calling to mind the heaped up bodies of the dead.

cast (kåst). To turn; to direct.

catacomb (kăt′a·kōm). Underground passages in Rome used as hiding places by early Christians.

catapult (kăt′a·pŭlt). A mechanical device, using recoil of spring, for hurling bombs, grenades, and the like.

catastrophe (ka·tăs′trô·fe). A sudden calamity; a great misfortune.

cedarn (sē′dĕrn). Made of cedar.

celerity (sê·lĕr′ĭ·tĭ). Rapidity of motion; swiftness.

celibate (sĕl′ĭ·bāt). Unmarried.

censorious (sĕn·sō′rĭ·ŭs). Severely critical.

censure (sĕn′shēr). Opinion; placing the blame; fault finding.

certitude (sûr′tĭ·tūd). Certainty.

chaffy (chăf′ĭ). Full of chaff or the husks of grain.

chagrin (sha·grĭn′). Extreme embarrassment.

chalice (chăl′ĭs). A cup.

chamade (sha·mäd′). A signal made for a parley by beat of drum or sound of trumpet.

chancel (chàn′sĕl). The space around the altar of a church, used by clergy and choir.

charlatan (shär′la·tăn). A quack; a pretender to knowledge and ability.

charnel house (chär′nĕl hous). A place where the bones of the dead are kept.

chastising (chăs·tīz′ĭng). Correcting; punishing.

cheek (chēk). Cool confidence; audacity.

chide (chīd). To scold.

cistern (sĭs′tērn). 1. A pool. 2. A reservoir or tank for holding water.

citadel (sĭt′a·dĕl). A fortress.

clamorous (klăm′ēr·ŭs). Urgently demanding; noisy.

cleave (klēv). 1. To separate; to split. 2. To stick or cling to.

clept (klĕpt). Called, named.

cloyed (kloid). Filled to overflowing; having had too much.

coign (koin). A corner.

colloquial (kŏ·lō′kwĭ·al). Language used in common talk but not used in formal speech or writing.

colossus (kŏ·lŏs′ŭs). Anything of gigantic size.

comber (kōm′ēr). A long, curling wave.

combustion (kŏm·bŭs′chŭn). Violent tumult and disorder.

comeliest (kŭm′lĭ·ĕst). Most pleasing.

commemorate (kŏ·mĕm′ô·rāt). To preserve or honor the memory of.

commend (kŏ·mĕnd′). To deliver.

commingling (kŏ·mĭng′glĭng). Blending together.

compassed (kŭm′påst). Surrounded.

compeer (kŏm·pēr′). A companion.

compose (kŏm·pōz′). To put together or to fashion.

composition (kŏm′pô·zĭsh′ŭn). An agreement to settle differences.

compt (kŏmpt). Count.

compunctious (kŏm·pŭngk′shŭs). Regretful; full of sorrow for what one has done.

cool, cook; our, boil; cūte, ûnite, bûrn, cŭt, ŭnless, menü; chĕck; goat, sing, ~~this~~, thick, scripture, verdure.

conciliate (kŏn·sĭl′ĭ·āt). To gain good will; to win over.

concord (kŏn′kôrd). Harmony; order.

concurrence (kŏn·kûr′ĕns). Agreement; meeting together of thought.

condone (kŏn·dōn′). To pardon or forgive.

configured (kŏn·fĭg′ûrd). Arranged in a pattern as, for instance, some constellations seem to be in the shape of a man or animal.

conflagration (kŏn′flå·grā′shŭn). A fire.

confute (kŏn·fūt′). To overcome by argument.

conjecture (kŏn·jĕk′tŭr). To guess.

conjure (kŏn·jōōr′). 1. To appeal; beg. 2. (kŭn′jẽr) To call up, as if by magic, imaginative scenes.

connotation (kŏn′ô·tā′shŭn). That which is suggested by a word apart from its actual meaning.

consort (kŏn·sôrt′). To mingle; to be a part of.

contemn (kŏn·tĕm′). To treat with contempt; to despise.

contend (kŏn·tĕnd′). 1. To struggle or fight. 2. To argue.

contradistinction (kŏn′trå·dĭs·tĭngk′shŭn). Distinction by opposition or contrast. *Today we cross the continent by fast airplanes in contradistinction to the slow covered wagons of our ancestors.*

controversial (kŏn′trô·vûr′shăl). That which is subject to argument or disagreement.

contumely (kŏn′tû·mē′lĭ). Rude language or treatment arising from contempt.

convex (kŏn′vĕks). Curved or rounded.

convolution (kŏn·vô·lū′shŭn). A coiling, winding, or twisting together.

corporeal (kôr·pō′rê·ăl). Bodily; material; tangible.

corpulent (kôr′pú·lĕnt). Bulky; fat.

corruption (kŏ·rŭp′shŭn). Pollution; defilement.

cote (kōt). A shelter.

countenance (koun′tê·năns). To face; to look upon.

covert (kŭv′ẽrt). A hide-away.

coxcombry (kŏks′cōm′rĭ). Vanity.

coy (koi). Bashful; demure.

credence (krē′dĕns). Belief.

crest (krĕst). Headpiece.

cribbed (krĭbd). Hemmed in; surrounded.

crudities (krōō′dĭ·tĭz). Harshness; roughness.

culled (kŭld). Selected.

culmination (kŭl′mĭ·nā′shŭn). Climax.

cumber (kŭm′bẽr). To trouble, embarrass, or burden.

cumbersome (kŭm′bẽr·sŭm). Clumsy and awkward.

cure (kūr). Spiritual charge; care of souls.

curt (kûrt). Short; rudely brief; abrupt.

curtail (kûr·tāl′). To shorten.

cynical (sĭn′ĭ·kăl). Distrustful of human nature; sneering and sarcastic.

cynosure (sī′nô·shōōr). A center of attraction.

D

dabbler (dăb′lẽr). One who dips slightly into anything; a dilettante.

dank (dăngk). Disagreeably moist.

darkling (därk′lĭng). Being in darkness; sometimes also darkly or gloomily.

daunt (dônt). To frighten; to make timid.

debonair (dĕb′ô·nâr′). Lighthearted; polished in manner.

decry (dê·krī′). To lessen the value of something publicly; to condemn or discredit it.

deem (dēm). To suppose; to think.

definitive (dê·fĭn′ĭ·tĭv). That which is conclusive; final.

degenerate (dê·jĕn′ẽr·āt). To lower in value; to sink.

deign (dān). 1. To stoop to; to condescend. 2. To grant or permit.

delineation (dê·lĭn′ê·ā′shŭn). The act of describing clearly pictures to the mind by the use of words.

deluding (dê·lūd′ĭng). False and tricky; deceptive.

demagogue (dĕm′å·gŏg). A popular leader who stirs up the people by appealing to their prejudices and emotions.

demure (dê·mūr′). Modest and shy; proper.

denotation (dē′nô·tā′shŭn). The actual meaning of a word.

depose (dê·pōz′). To remove from office.

deprecate (dĕp′rê·kāt). Express strong disapproval of.

deride (dê·rīd′). To ridicule; to laugh at with scorn.

desecrate (dĕs′ê·krāt). To violate that which is holy.

design (dê·zīn′). 1. A plan or scheme. 2. An aim or objective.

despoil (dê·spoil′). To strip of possessions

devastated (dĕv′ăs·tāt′ĕd). Plundered; demolished.

devoir (dê·vwär′). Duty.

dialect (dī′å·lĕkt). A local form of language.

dicing (dīs′ĭng). Gambling.

diffuse (dĭ·fūz′). Poured or spread out on all sides.

diligence (dĭl′ĭ·jĕns). Attention and hard work.

dire (dīr). Dreadful.

dirge (dûrj). A mournful song.

disburse (dĭs·bûrs′). To give in payment.

discern (dĭ·zûrn′). Perceive; distinguish; recognize.

discomfit (dĭs·kŭm′fĭt). To embarrass greatly.

disconcert (dĭs′kŏn·sûrt′). To disturb.

discord (dĭs′kôrd). Disagreement; contention; strife.

discreet (dĭs·krēt′). Showing good judgment in conduct and especially in speech.

disdain (dĭs·dān′). Scorn.

disillusionment (dĭs′ĭ·lū′zhŭn·mĕnt). The state of having lost faith in something.

disintegration (dĭs·ĭn′tê·grā′shŭn). Breaking up.

āte, chảotic, dâre, ădd, ăccuse, bär, càsk, åfar; ēat, dẹar, êlude, ĕgg, quiĕt, centēr; īdle, ĭf, activĭty; ōpen, ȯbey, ȯr, ȯrange, ȯffer, ȯccur.

disjoint (dĭs·joint'). Become twisted out of proper shape.

disparage (dĭs·păr'ĭj). To discredit or speak slightingly of.

disparity (dĭs·păr'ĭ·tĭ). Difference in character.

dispel (dĭs·pĕl'). To drive away.

disputatious (dĭs·pū·tā'shŭs). Quarrelsome.

disseat (dĭs·sēt'). To remove from the chair of authority.

dissimulation (dĭ·sĭm'ū·lā'shŭn). False pretension.

dissipation (dĭs'ĭ·pā'shŭn). Wasteful living.

dissolute (dĭs'ŏ·lūt). Unrestrained; reckless and wild.

distempered (dĭs·tĕm'pĕrd). Diseased.

distracted (dĭs·trăkt'ĕd). Insane; in a confused state.

diversified (dĭ·vûr'sĭ·fīd). Full of variety.

divest (dĭ·vĕst'). To take off, as of wearing apparel.

divine (dĭ·vīn'). 1. n-. A minister. 2. v-. To draw a mental picture; to imagine; to detect.

dolour (dō'lēr). Sadness; grief.

dormant (dôr'mănt). Sleeping; quiet as if as asleep.

dower (dou'ēr). 1. Gift. 2. Endowment.

dross (drŏs). Worthless matter; refuse.

dulcimer (dŭl'sĭ·mēr). A stringed musical instrument.

dunnest (dŭn'ĕst). Gloomiest and darkest.

dwindle (dwĭn'd'l). To diminish; to become less.

E

eerie (ē'rĭ). Weird; dismal.

effigy (ĕf'ĭ·jĭ). An image of a person.

effrontery (ĕ·frŭn'tēr·ĭ). Boldness; rudeness.

effusive (ĕ·fū'sĭv). Gushing; over-demonstrative.

ejaculation (ĕ·jăk'ū·lā'shŭn). An exclamation.

elegy (ĕl'ē·jĭ). A song of mourning; a lament.

eloquence (ĕl'ô·kwĕns). Talk or discussion characterized by strong force and sincerity.

elude (ê·lūd'). To avoid or escape by quickness or cleverness.

emanating (ĕm'á·nat'ĭng). Issuing from a source.

emolument (ê·mŏl'û·mĕnt). Salary or wage.

empyreal (ĕm·pĭr'ê·ăl). Pertaining to that which is celestial or sublime.

emulation (ĕm'û·lā'shŭn). Ambition or the endeavor to equal or excel.

encroachment (ĕn·krōch'mĕnt). Trespassing on the property or rights of another.

endow (ĕn·dou'). To give a gift; to present.

enervation (ĕn'ēr·vă'shŭn). Weakness.

engendering (ĕn·jĕn'dēr·ĭng). Bringing forth; producing.

enhanced (ĕn·hånst'). Made greater.

enigma (ê·nĭg'má). A puzzle; something difficult to understand.

enjoin (ĕn·join'). To order or command.

enow (ê·nou'). Enough.

entice (ĕn·tīs'). To tempt.

entity (ĕn'tĭ·tĭ). Being; existence.

entrails (ĕn'trĕlz). Intestines.

envisage (ĕn·vĭz'ĭj). To view with the mind's eye.

epicure (ĕp'ĭ·kūr). A person who cares much about food and drink.

epigram (ĕp'ĭ·grăm). A short saying or poem ending in a witty or clever thought.

equanimity (ē'kwá·nĭm'ĭ·tĭ). Calm temper; serenity.

equipoise (ē'kwĭ·poiz). Equality of weight; balance.

equity (ĕk'wĭ·tĭ). Law; rights.

equivocation (ê·kwĭv'ô·kā'shŭn). Deceit through double meaning.

erudition (ĕr'ōō·dĭsh'ŭn). Learning; scholarship.

eschew (ĕs·chōō'). Avoid; shun.

esplanade (ĕs'plá·nād'). A clear level space, especially along a shore, used for public walks or drives.

espouse (ĕs·pouz'). Support.

essence (ĕs'ĕns). The purest, most perfect form.

estrange (ĕs·trānj'). To turn from attachment to enmity or indifference.

ethereal (ê·thēr'ê·ăl). That which has to do with the regions beyond the earth.

eulogy (ū'lô·jĭ). An oration in praise of someone or something.

ewer (ū'ēr). A wide-mouthed jug.

exchequer (ĕks·chĕk'ēr). A national treasury.

excoriate (ĕks·kō'rĭ·āt). To strip or wear off the skin of; to flay.

exhortation (ĕg'zôr·tā'shŭn). Strong urging; earnest advice or warning.

exorbitant (ĕg·zôr'bĭ·tănt). Excessive.

expediency (ĕks·pē'dĭ·ĕn·sĭ). That which is practical and efficient rather than universally right.

expeditious (ĕks'pê·dĭsh'ŭs). Rapid and efficient.

exploit (ĕks'ploit). A heroic act; a deed of renown.

exploitation (ĕks'ploi·tā'shŭn). Use, usually for selfish purposes.

exponent (ĕks·pō'nĕnt). 1. Explainer; interpreter. 2. A representative type of something.

exposition (ĕks'pô·zĭsh'ŭn). A speech or writing explaining a process, thing, or idea.

extoll (ĕks·tŏl'). To praise.

extort (ĕks·tôrt'). To obtain (money, promises, etc.) from a person by force, threat or wrong use of authority.

F

facet (făs'ĕt). Any of numerous sharply defined views of one subject or object.

facilitating (fá·sĭl'ĭ·tāt'ĭng). Assisting.

faculty (făk'ŭl·tĭ). An ability.

fain (fān). Eager and willing.

faithbreach (fāth'brēch). A break with faith; a disloyalty.

fastidious (făs·tĭd'ĭ·ŭs). Extremely delicate and particular in manner.

cōol, cŏŏk; our, boil; cūte, ūnite, bûrn, cŭt, ŭnless, menū; check; goat, sing, ~~th~~is, thick, scriptŭre, verdŭre.

felicity (fê·lǐs′ǐ·tǐ). A state of perfect joy; happiness.
fell (fĕl). Bad or wicked.
fettered (fĕt′ẽrd). Enchained; shackled.
fickle (fǐk′'l). Unsettled; likely to change.
fie (fī). An exclamation expressing disgust.
fillet (fǐl′ĕt, fǐl′ā). A slice of meat which does not contain bones.
finite (fī′nīt). Having bounds or limits.
flagon (flăg′ŭn). A container for liquids.
flail (flāl). 1. n-. An instrument for threshing or beating grain by hand. 2. v-. To thrash or flog.
flotation (flô·tā′shŭn). The act of floating; figuratively, the act of financing a business or commercial venture.
flout (flout). To mock.
fold (fōld). An enclosure or pen for cattle or sheep.
fond (fŏnd). Foolish.
fop (fŏp). A man very fond of clothes; a dandy.
foray (fŏr′å). Raid; battle.
forsook (fŏr·sŏŏk′). Took leave of; abandoned.
fortitude (fôr′tǐ·tūd). Firmness; endurance; courage.
franchised (frăn′chīzd). 1. Freed; set at liberty. 2. Granted a right or privilege, as the right to vote.
fraught (frôt). Laden; burdened.
freebooter (frē′bŏŏt′ẽr). One who goes about plundering; a pirate.
fretted (frĕt′ĕd). That which is decorated with ornamental openwork or carving.
frieze (frēz). An ornamental band of trimming on a building.
fulcrum (fŭl′krŭm). A support on which a lever turns or is supported in moving or lifting something.
fume (fūm). A vapor or smoke.
furbish (fûr′bǐsh). To polish; to scour.
furtive (fûr′tǐv). Sly; secret.
fusion (fū′zhŭn). A blending.

G

gainsay (gān′sā′). To contradict; to dispute.
gall (gôl). A bitter liquid.
gallant (găl′ănt). 1. n-. A gay fashionable man. 2. adj-. Polite and chivalrous to women.
garrulous (găr′ŭ·lŭs). Talkative.
gaunt (gônt). 1. Grim; forbidding. 2. Lean; haggard.
germinate (jûr′mǐ·nāt). To begin to grow and develop.
gild (gǐld). Overlay or smear.
gin (jǐn). A snare or trap.
girt (gûrt). Equipped for war.
goad (gōd). A pointed rod used to urge on a beast.
gout (gout). 1. A disease in which the joints are affected. Excessive eating and drinking sometimes brings it on. 2. A clot of blood.
grafted (gráf′tĕd). Closely joined; united.
grandam (grăn′dăm). Grandmother.
grapple (grăp′'l). To struggle.

grimace (grǐ·mās′). A twisting of the face.
grimy (grīm′ǐ). Dirty; also swarthy.
gross (grōs). That which is coarse or vulgar; not sensitive in feeling or understanding.
grotesque (grô·tĕsk′). Fantastic; odd or unnatural in shape, appearance, manner, etc.
guerdon (gûr′dŭn). A reward.
guile (gīl). Treachery and deceit.
guinea (gǐn′ǐ). A gold coin, now discontinued, worth about five dollars.
guise (gīz). Disguise.
gullible (gŭl′ǐ·b'l). Easily deceived or cheated.
gusto (gŭs′tō). Keen, zestful appreciation.
guttural (gŭt′ẽr·ål). A harsh sound formed in the throat.

H

habitat (hăb′ǐ·tăt). The place where anything is commonly found; an environment.
haggard (hăg′ẽrd). Thin and suffering.
harangue (há·răng′). A noisy ranting speech.
harbinger (här′bǐn·jẽr). One sent ahead to prepare for those who follow him.
harness (här′nĕs). Armor.
harry (hăr′ǐ). To make a destructive raid upon property; to persecute.
hauteur (hô·tûr′). Extreme dignity and pride.
heather (hĕth′ẽr). A purple shrub covering wastelands and plains.
hedgepig (hĕj′pǐg′). The hedgehog, a small, prickly, insect-eating mammal.
henchman (hĕnch′măn). An active follower and supporter, interested in personal gain.
heretic (hĕr′ĕ·tǐk). One who deliberately upholds a belief that differs from his church; one who rejects orthodox opinions and beliefs.
hew (hū). To cut or chop.
hoary (hōr′ǐ). White or gray with age.
howlet (hou′lĕt). An owlet.
hypothesis (hī·pŏth′ĕ·sǐs). A theory; supposition.

I

idiom (ǐd′ǐ·ŭm). A people's way of expressing itself; a language proper to a region.
ignoble (ǐg·nō′b'l). Dishonorable; contemptible.
ignominy (ǐg′nô·mǐn·ǐ). Disgrace or dishonor.
imbue (ǐm·bū′). To tinge deeply; saturate.
immunity (ǐ·mū′nǐ·tǐ). Freedom; exemption.
imperceptible (ǐm′pēr·sĕp′tǐ·b'l). Gradual; slight.
impetuous (ǐm·pĕt′ụ·ŭs). Acting without thought; on the spur of the moment.
impinge (ǐm·pǐnj′). 1. To hit or strike. 2. Encroach.
importunate (ǐm·pôr′tụ·nǐt). Troublesome; urgent; burdensome.
impotence (ǐm′pô·tĕns). A lack of strength or power.
impunity (ǐm·pū′nǐ·tǐ). Freedom from punishment.
impute (ǐm·put′). Consider as belonging; charge (a fault, mistake, etc.) to a person; blame.

āte, châotic, dâre, ădd, åccuse, bär, càsk, åfar; ēat, dẹar, ĕlude, ĕgg, quiĕt, centēr; īdle, ǐf, activǐty; ōpen, ôbey, ôr, ŏrange, ôffer, ŏccur.

inanimate (ĭn·ăn'ĭ·māt). Lifeless; dull.

inapprehensible (ĭn'ăp·rê·hĕn'sĭ·b'l). That which is unthinkable; impossible to understand.

inarticulate (ĭn'är·tĭk'ů·lāt). 1. Indistinct. 2. Dumb.

incantation (ĭn'kăn·tā'shŭn). Use of a magic spell, spoken or sung.

incarnadine (ĭn·kär'nà·dĭn). To make red.

incarnation (ĭn'kär·nā'shŭn). An idea made flesh.

incensed (ĭn·sĕnst'). Angered.

incipient (ĭn·sĭp'ĭ·ent). Commencing; beginning to show itself.

incoherencies (ĭn'kô·hēr'ĕn·sĭz). Disconnected or rambling thoughts or words.

incommensurate (ĭn'kŏ·mĕn'shŏo·rĭt). Unequal; that cannot be compared.

incompatible (ĭn'kŏm·păt'ĭ·b'l). Inharmonious; opposed in character.

indigenous (ĭn·dĭj'ê·nŭs). Native.

indissoluble (ĭn·dĭs'ô·lû·b'l). Unable to be dissolved or separated; indestructible.

indomitable (ĭn·dŏm'ĭ·tà·b'l). Unconquerable; unyielding.

inevitable (ĭn·ĕv'ĭ·tà·b'l). Unavoidable.

inexplicable (ĭn·ĕks'plĭ·kà·b'l). That which cannot be explained.

infanticide (ĭn·făn'tĭ·sīd). Child murder.

inflection (ĭn·flĕk'shŭn). A change in the pitch or tone of a voice.

infuse (ĭn·fūz'). To introduce or insinuate; to inspire.

ingenious (ĭn·jēn'yŭs). Clever; inventive.

ingenuous (ĭn·jĕn'ů·ŭs). Unreserved; artless and frank.

inherent (ĭn·hēr'ĕnt). Indwelling; belonging to a person or thing as a quality or attribute.

iniquitous (ĭn·ĭk'wĭ·tŭs). Extremely unjust; wicked.

initiate (ĭ·nĭsh'ĭ·āt). Beginning; new; young.

initiative (ĭ·nĭsh'ĭ·ā'tĭv). The ability to act or think for one's self without help of others.

innovation (ĭn'ô·vā'shŭn). The introduction of something new.

innuendo (ĭn'ů·ĕn'dō). An indirect hint or reference; a veiled slur against someone.

insatiable (ĭn·sā'shĭ·à·b'l). Incapable of being satisfied.

insidious (ĭn·sĭd'ĭ·ŭs). 1. Deceitful. 2. Working secretly or subtly.

insinuate (ĭn·sĭn'ů·āt). Hint; suggest indirectly.

insolent (ĭn'sô·lĕnt). Boldly rude; proud and overbearing.

intangible (ĭn·tăn'jĭ·b'l). That which has no substance.

integrity (ĭn·tĕg'rĭ·tĭ). Truthfulness; honesty; sincerity.

intense (ĭn·tĕns'). Powerful; vivid.

inter (ĭn·tûr'). Bury.

interfuse (ĭn'tĕr·fūz'). To mingle.

interim (ĭn'tĕr·ĭm). In the meantime; meanwhile.

interlocutor (ĭn'tĕr·lok'ů·tēr). A talker, interpreter or questioner.

interposition (ĭn'tĕr·pô·zĭsh'ŭn). Mediation; intervention.

intrenchant (ĭn·trĕn'chănt). Unable to be cut.

intrinsic (ĭn·trĭn'sĭk). Inner; belonging to the nature or essence of a thing. Example: *The intrinsic value of a keepsake may be very small, but it is treasured for other, outer reasons.*

introspection (ĭn'trô·spĕk'shŭn). The examination of one's own thoughts and feelings.

intuition (ĭn'tů·ĭsh'ŭn). Perception of facts or truths without reasoning; insight.

inveigled (ĭn·vē'g'ld). Led on or astray; won over by guile.

invest (ĭn·vĕst'). 1. To surround. 2. To put in office; to be given the robes or vestments of public office. 3. To clothe.

involuntary (ĭn·vŏl'ŭn·tĕr'ĭ). Not done by choice or an act of will.

ire (īr). Anger.

irony (ī'rô·nĭ). 1. Light sarcasm. 2. A state of affairs which is the reverse of what was expected.

irradiated (ĭ·rā'dĭ·āt'ĕd). Surrounded by rays of light.

irrelevance (ĭr·rĕl'ê·văns). A remark that has no bearing on the subject at hand.

issue (ĭsh'ū). 1. Children; offspring. 2. The outcome.

itinerant (ī·tĭn'ēr·ănt). Wandering.

J

javelin (jăv'lĭn). A light spear, to be thrown or cast, used as a weapon of war and for hunting.

jeopardy (jĕp'ēr·dĭ). Danger.

jet (jĕt). Lustrous black.

jocund (jŏk'ŭnd). Happy and gay.

judicious (jŏo·dĭsh'ŭs). Showing good and careful judgment.

jutty (jŭt'ĭ). A projecting piece of a building.

K

ken (kĕn). That which is within the range of sight or within the range of knowledge.

kindred (kĭn'drĕd). Having and understanding the same feelings as another; to be kin or related to another.

knave (nāv). 1. A servant; a man of humble birth or position. 2. A tricky, deceitful fellow.

L

labyrinthine (lăb'ĭ·rĭn'thĭn). Intricate; involved.

languidly (lăng'gwĭd·lĭ). Sluggishly; without interest or show of energy.

languor (lăng'gēr). Sadness; listlessness.

largess (lär'jĕs). Generosity; openhandedness.

laudable (lôd'à·b'l). Worthy of praise.

lave (lāv). To bathe or to wash.

lees (lēz). Dregs.

levee (lĕv'ê). 1. A morning reception. 2. Any miscellaneous gathering of guests.

cōol, cŏok; our, boil; cūte, ûnite, bûrn, cŭt, ŭnless, menü; check; goat, sing, ~~this~~, thick, scriptŭre, verdŭre.

lichen (lī′kĕn). A dry-looking plant that grows on rocks, trees, and other surfaces.

limbeck (lĭm′bĕk). A glass vessel used for distilling.

limn (lĭm). 1. To paint (a picture). 2. To portray in words.

lintel (lĭn′tĕl). A horizontal supporting beam above a door or window.

liquescence (lĭ·kwĕs′ĕns). State of melting.

list (lĭst). The area of battle.

livery (lĭv′ēr·ĭ). Special clothing chosen by an association or household to distinguish it from others.

livid (lĭv′ĭd). 1. Ashy pale. 2. Discolored.

loathe (lōth). To detest; to hate.

lore (lōr). 1. The facts and legends about a certain subject. 2. Learning; knowledge.

loth (lōth). Reluctant; unwilling.

lucid (lū′sĭd). That which is easily understood; clear.

lucrative (lū′krȧ·tĭv). Profitable.

ludicrous (lū′dĭ·krŭs). Ridiculous; causing laughter.

lurch (lûrch). To roll suddenly to the side.

lurking (lûrk′ĭng). To stay in or about a place secretly or furtively.

lustrous (lŭs′trŭs). Shining.

M

mail (māl). Armor.

main (mān). The sea.

malady (mǎl′ȧ·dĭ). A sickness or illness.

malevolently (mȧ·lĕv′ō·lĕnt·lĭ). With evil intention.

mandate (mǎn′dāt). A command.

manifestation (mǎn′ĭ·fĕs·tā′shŭn). An act that shows or proves something.

marauder (mȧ·rôd′ēr). A rover in quest of booty or plunder.

material (mȧ·tēr′ĭ·ǎl). Necessary.

maw (mô). A stomach, mouth or throat.

maxim (mǎk′sĭm). A general truth or a rule of conduct.

mean (mēn). That which is of little value or account; contemptible.

meandering (mē·ǎn′dēr·ĭng). Winding; turning.

medium (mē′dĭ·ŭm). A means of communication.

medley (mĕd′lĭ). A mixture.

melancholy (mĕl′ǎn·kŏl′ĭ). Gloomy; depressed.

menacing (mĕn′ĭ·sĭng). Threatening.

mercantile (mûr′kǎn·tĭl). Having to do with or engaged in trade.

mercenary (mûr′sĕ·nĕr′ĭ). 1. n-. A soldier serving for pay in a foreign army. 2. adj-. One who is moved by consideration of money or profit.

metaphor (mĕt′ȧ·fēr). Use of a word or phrase in place of another to suggest resemblance between them.

mettle (mĕt′'l). Courage; brave spirit.

minimize (mĭn′ĭ·mīz). Reduce to the least possible amount or degree.

minion (mĭn′yŭn). A servant; a dependent.

minister (mĭn′ĭs·tēr). 1. n-. Clergyman serving a church. 2. v-. To attend; to give aid to.

ministration (mĭn′ĭs·trā′shŭn). Help; aid, as *ministrations* to an invalid.

minutely (mĭn′ĭt·lĭ). By minutes; continual.

misnomer (mĭs·nō′mēr). A wrong name; an incorrect designation or term.

mitigate (mĭt′ĭ·gāt). To moderate; to become less severe.

monologue (mŏn′ō·lŏg). A long speech uttered by one person.

moulder (mōl′dēr). To turn to dust.

morbid (môr′bĭd). Unhealthy; unwholesome.

motive (mō′tĭv). A personal feeling or idea that inspires an individual's actions.

motley (mŏt′lĭ). A fabric of mixed colors worn by a medieval jester.

mountebank (moun′tē·bǎngk). Any boastful and unscrupulous pretender.

multifarious (mŭl′tĭ·fâr′ĭ·ŭs). Many and varied.

multiplex (mŭl′tĭ·plĕks). Multiple.

mundane (mŭn′dān). That which pertains to worldly rather than spiritual affairs.

munificence (mū·nĭf′ĭ·sĕns). Lavish generosity.

murky (mûr′kĭ). Dark and gloomy.

myriad (mĭr′ĭ·ǎd). An indefinitely large number.

N

naïve (nä·ēv′). Simple in nature; artless.

negligence (nĕg′lĭ·jĕns). Omission of duty; neglect.

nescience (nĕsh′ĭ·ĕns). Lack of knowledge; complete ignorance.

nether (nĕth′ēr). Lower.

nicety (nī′sĕ·tĭ). Exactness; excessive delicacy.

niggard (nĭg′ērd). A miser.

nocturnal (nŏk·tûr′nǎl). Nightly.

noisome (noi′sŭm). Disgusting; offensive.

nominal (nŏm′ĭ·nǎl). 1. Existing in name only. 2. Too small to be considered.

O

obdurate (ŏb′dū·rȧt). Stubborn and unyielding.

obliquely (ŏb·lēk′lĭ). On a slant.

obliterate (ŏb·lĭt′ēr·āt). To blot out.

oblivious (ŏb·lĭv′ĭ·ŭs). To be unaware of surroundings; without memory.

obnoxious (ŏb·nŏk′shŭs). Disliked; hateful.

obscure (ŏb·skūr′). Hidden.

obsolete (ŏb′sŏ·lēt). No longer in use; out of date.

odious (ō′dĭ·ŭs). Hateful; offensive.

odoriferous (ō′dēr·ĭf′ēr·ŭs). Yielding an odor.

office (ŏf′ĭs). 1. Function. 2. An order or direction.

officious (ŏ·fĭsh′ŭs). Full of a feeling of self-importance; commanding.

oleaginous (ō′lē·ǎj′ĭ·nŭs). Oily.

omnipotent (ŏm·nĭp′ō·tĕnt). All-powerful.

omniscient (ŏm·nĭsh′ĕnt). Knowing all things; infinitely wise.

opiate (ō′pĭ·āt). A drug; a narcotic.

āte, châotic, dâre, ǎdd, ȧccuse, bär, cȧsk, ȧfar; ēat, dẹar, ēlude, ĕgg, quiĕt, centēr; īdle, ĭf, activĭty; ōpen, ȯbey, ôr, ŏrange, ôffer, ŏccur.

opulent (ŏp'ů·lĕnt) Powerful; wealthy; plenti-
fully provided.
orthodoxy (ôr'thô·dŏk'sĭ). The holding of correct or generally accepted beliefs.
oscillate (ŏs'ĭ·lāt). To waver; to switch back
and forth from one side to the other.
ossify (ŏs'ĭ·fī). 1. To harden or become callous.
2. To become set in a conventional form.
ostentatious (ŏs'tĕn·tā'shŭs). That which is
done for display; showy.
overcredulous (ō'vēr·krĕd'ů·lŭs). Too easily
trusting or believing.
overplussed (ō'vēr·plŭst). Over-supplied.
overweening (ō'vēr·wēn'ĭng). Full of a feeling
of self-importance.

P

pacifically pȧ·sĭf'ĭ·kȧl·lĭ). In a calm or soothing manner.
packmen (păk'mĕn). Peddlers.
palfrey (pôl'frĭ). A saddle horse.
pall (pôl). 1. n-. A gloomy, overspreading mass.
2. n-. A cloak or covering. 3. v-. To pale; to
wrap in a covering.
palpable (păl'pȧ·b'l). Able to be felt or
touched.
palsy (pôl'zĭ). A trembling affliction; also a
paralyzing affliction.
palter (pôl'tēr). To use trickery; to act without
sincerity.
panegyric (păn'ê·jĭr'ĭk). A formal speech or
writing in terms of enthusiastic praise.
pantheism (păn'thê·ĭz'm). The belief that
there is no God but the forces of nature.
paradox (păr'ȧ·dŏks). A person or thing that
seems to be full of contradictions.
parapet (păr'ȧ·pĕt). A low wall such as a rail-
ing to protect soldiers fighting from a fortress
tower or roof.
parody (păr'ô·dĭ). An imitation of the form
and style of someone or something, usually
to provoke laughter.
pathos (pā'thŏs). The quality in speech, writing, music, etc. that arouses a feeling of pity
or sadness.
patricide (păt'rĭ·sīd). The murder of one's
father.
patrimony (păt'rĭ·mō'nĭ). An estate inherited
from one's father or ancestors.
peaked (pēk'ĕd). Thin and sickly.
pecuniary (pê·kū'nĭ·ĕr'ĭ). Relating to money.
peer (pēr). Match; equal.
penchant (pĕn'chȧnt). A strong attraction.
pendent (pĕn'dĕnt). Hanging; suspended in
air.
perchance (pēr·chȧns'). Perhaps; maybe.
perfidious (pēr·fĭd'ĭ·ŭs). Treacherous or faith-
less.
perfunctorily (pēr·fŭngk'tô·rĭ·lĭ). That which
is done in a mechanical or off-hand manner.
periwig (pĕr'ĭ·wĭg). A wig, often of white or
powdered hair.
permeate (pûr'mê·āt). To spread through;
penetrate.

pernicious (pēr·nĭsh'ŭs). Highly destructive in
character; deadly.
peroration (pĕr'ô·rā'shŭn). The concluding
part of a discourse; a final summing-up of an
argument.
perspective (pēr·spĕk'tĭv). Viewpoint.
perturbation (pûr'tēr·bā'shŭn). Unrest; tumult, violent tossing.
peruke (pê·rook'). A wig.
perusal (pê·rooz'ȧl). A careful reading; an
examination.
pervert (pēr·vûrt'). To cause to turn aside
from the right, true or regular course; to
corrupt.
phenomenal (fê·nŏm'ê·nȧl). Unusual in its
kind, order, etc.
phial (fī'ȧl). A small bottle.
pillage (pĭl'ĭj). To rob or plunder.
pinion (pĭn'yŭn). 1. A wing. 2. Flight feathers
of a bird.
pithy (pĭth'ĭ). Having substance and pointed-
ness of expression.
pittance (pĭt'ȧns). A meager compensation.
pivotal (pĭv'ŭt·ȧl). Central.
plaintive (plān'tĭv). Sad and melancholy.
poignant (poin'yȧnt). Keen; painfully moving
or touching.
portcullis (pōrt·kŭl'ĭs). A sliding, protective
door in a fort or castle, capable of being
lowered to prevent entry.
portent (pōr'tĕnt). An omen.
posterity (pŏs·tĕr'ĭ·tĭ). Future generations.
potent (pō'tĕnt). Strong and powerful.
potentate (pō'tĕn·tāt). A ruler or prince.
potentiality (pô·tĕn'shĭ·ăl'ĭ·tĭ). A possibility
or capacity.
prate (prāt). To talk; chatter.
precedence (prê·sēd'ĕns). Place of honor
given to one of superior rank.
precept (prē'sĕpt). A rule or command.
precipitated (prê·sĭp'ĭ·tāt'ĕd). Hurled downward.
predestination (prê·dĕs'tĭ·nā'shŭn). The belief that man's fate has been determined in
advance by the Creator.
predicated (prĕd'ĭ·kāt'ĕd). Proclaimed; affirmed or preached.
predominance (prê·dŏm'ĭ·nȧns). Superior
power.
prefiguration (prê·fĭg·û·rā'shŭn). Act of fore-
telling; to foreshadow.
prelate (prĕl'ĭt). A church dignitary.
premonitory (prê·mŏn'ĭ·tō'rĭ). Giving warning beforehand.
preoccupation (prê·ŏk'û·pā'shŭn). State of
being lost in thought.
prep (prĕp). A study hour or period. (Short
for preparation).
prerogative (prê·rŏg'ȧ·tĭv). Exclusive privilege.
presumptuous (prê·zŭmp'tû·ŭs). Taking undue liberties; bold.
pretentious (prê·tĕn'shŭs). Making claims to
excellence or importance.
preternatural (prē'tēr·năt'û·rȧl). That which
is strange or irregular.

cōōl, cŏŏk; our, boil; cūte, ûnite, bûrn, cŭt, ŭnless, menü; check; goat, sing, this, thick, scriptŭre,
verdŭre.

prig (prĭg). An irritatingly self-sufficient or overly-mannered person.

prim (prĭm). Formally neat and stiff.

prioress (prī′ēr·ĕs). A nun who is in charge of a convent.

prismatic (prĭz·măt′ĭk). Highly colored; brilliant.

pristine (prĭs′tēn). Original; former; uncorrupted.

privily (prĭv′ĭ·lĭ). Secretly.

procrastination (prô·krăs′tĭ·nā′shŭn). Delay.

procreant (prō′krē·ănt). Bringing forth young.

procurement (prô·kūr′mĕnt). The act of obtaining.

prodigious (prô·dĭj′ŭs). Enormous; amazing.

profaner (prō·fān′ēr). One who violates a holy place.

profusion (prô·fū′zhŭn). An abundance.

progenitor (prô·jĕn′ĭ·tēr). A forefather.

projector (prô·jĕk′tēr). One who forms schemes.

prolific (prô·lĭf′ĭk). Highly productive.

prologue (prō′lŏg). An introduction to an action which is to follow.

propagate (prŏp′a·gāt). To increase; to spread or extend.

propensity (prô·pĕn′sĭ·tĭ). A natural inclination.

prosaic (prô·zā′ĭk). Unimaginative; matter-of-fact.

proscribe (prô·skrīb′). To prohibit.

prostrate (prŏs′trāt). In a prone position.

protagonist (prô·tăg′ô·nĭst). 1. The leading character in a story. 2. The spokesman for a cause.

prototype (prô′tô·tīp). An original pattern used as a model for others.

protuberant (prô·tū′bēr·ănt). Bulging.

provocative (prô·vŏk′a·tĭv). Likely to stir up controversy.

prowess (prou′ĕs). Power; strength.

prudent (prōō′dĕnt). Careful and wise.

pulsate (pŭl′sāt). To throb; to vibrate with feeling.

purge (pŭrj). To cleanse; to clear away.

purpureal (pŭr·pū′rē·ăl). Purple.

pursuivant (pŭr′swĭ·vănt). An attendant on the king.

purveyor (pŭr·vā′ēr). One who arrives before the rest to provide for or make things ready for them.

push (pōōsh). An attack.

pyre (pīr). A combustible heap of wood for burning a dead body as a funeral rite.

Q

quagmire (kwăg′mīr). Quicksand; a bog.

quell (kwĕl). 1. n-. Slaughter. 2. v-. To finish or put a stop to; to put down.

quintessence (kwĭnt·ĕs′ĕns). 1. Pure essence; purest form. 2. The most perfect example of something.

quittance (kwĭt′ăns). Discharge from a debt or an obligation; recompense.

R

rabble (răb′ 'l). The lowest classes; a mob.

raiment (rā′mĕnt). Clothing.

rancour (răng′kēr). Bitterness; hatred.

rapt (răpt). In a dream-like state.

ratify (răt′ĭ·fī). To give approval.

rational (răsh′ŭn·ăl). 1. Having reason or understanding. 2. Intelligent; sensible.

raucous (rô′kŭs). Disagreeably harsh and strident.

ravage (răv′ĭj). To lay waste; to sack; plunder.

ravishing (răv′ĭsh·ĭng). Full of the purpose of robbing and plundering.

raze (rāz). To tear down; to destroy.

rebuff (rē·bŭf′). A blow; a snub.

recalcitrant (rē·kăl′sĭ·trănt). Obstinate; stubbornly rebellious.

recapitulate (rē′ka·pĭt′ủ·lāt). To repeat briefly the principal parts in an argument.

recompense (rĕk′ŏm·pĕns). Fair return for anything lost, damage done, or hurt received; payment for services done.

reconciliation (rĕk′ŏn·sĭl′ĭ·ā′shŭn). Return to agreeable terms.

recreant (rĕk′rē·ănt). A coward.

redound (rê·dound′). Come back as a result; contribute.

redress (rê·drĕs′). 1. n-. Amends for wrong. 2. v-. To right a wrong.

reeking (rēk′ĭng). Having a disagreeable odor.

refute (rê·fūt′). Disprove.

regenerated (rê·jĕn′ēr·āt′ĕd). To cause to be spiritually born again.

reiterate (rê·ĭt′ēr·āt). To repeat.

relevant (rĕl′ê·vănt). That which has bearing on the matter at hand.

render (rĕn′dēr). To surrender; to give up.

repellent (rê·pĕl′ĕnt). Unattractive; disagreeable.

requital (rê·kwīt′ăl). Reward.

resolution (rĕz′ô·lū′shŭn). 1. Certainty. 2. Decided action.

resonant (rĕz′ô·nănt). Loud and of a rich tone; vibrant.

respite (rĕs′pĭt). Pause or rest.

resurgence (rê·sûr′jĕns). A rising again into life.

retainer (rê·tān′ēr). A person attached to, or owing service to a household.

retinue (rĕt′ĭ·nū). A train of attendants.

retributory (rê·trĭb′ủ·tō′rĭ). Punishing.

revelry (rĕv′ĕl·rĭ). Boisterous merry-making.

revile (rê·vīl′). To despise; to subject to abuse.

revitalize (rê·vī′tăl·īz). To give new life to.

rife (rīf). Abounding.

rill (rĭl). A small brook.

rooky (rōōk′ĭ). Full of rooks, birds resembling crows.

rout (rout). To defeat; to crush.

rude (rōōd). Unpolished or untaught in manners or customs.

rue (rōō). To be sorry for; repent; regret.

rug (rŭg). A woolen blanket.

āte, châotic, dâre, ădd, ăccuse, bär, càsk, afar; ēat, dēar, ĕlude, ĕgg, quĭet, centēr; īdle, ĭf, actĭvĭty; ōpen, ôbey, ôr, ŏrange, ŏffer, ŏccur.

GLOSSARY

S

sable (sā′b'l). Black.

saffron (săf′rŭn). A deep yellow color.

sally (săl′ĭ). A witty remark.

sardonic (sär·dŏn′ĭk). Bitterly scornful; mocking.

satiate (sā′shĭ·āt). To satisfy one's desires completely.

satire (săt′īr). Ridicule of human follies and vices.

savannah (sȧ·văn′ȧ). A treeless plain.

savory (sā′vẽr·ĭ). Appetizing.

scan (skăn). To examine.

scarf (skärf). To wrap or cover, as with a scarf.

scathing (skāth′ĭng). Withering; causing great damage.

school (skōol). To learn self-control or self-discipline.

scourge (skûrj). To beat, or whip.

scruple (skrōō′p'l). Doubt or uncertainty.

scrutinize (skrōō′tĭ·nīz). To examine closely.

scullery (skŭl′ẽr·ĭ). The room where dishes are washed.

sear (sēr). To burn or scorch.

seat (sēt). Location; site.

seethed (sēthd). 1. Boiled. 2. Bubbled and foamed.

sensuous (sĕn′shōo·ŭs). That which appeals to the senses rather than to the mind.

sequestered (sê·kwĕs′tẽrd). Withdrawn; retired and secluded.

servile (sûr′vĭl). Slavish; dependent and submissive.

shallot (shȧ·lŏt′). An onionlike plant.

shrew (shrōō). A scolding or brawling woman.

sibilant (sĭb′ĭ·lȧnt). Hissing.

sickle (sĭk′'l). A short-handled cutting tool with a curved blade.

simulacrum (sĭm′ū·lā′krŭm). A shadowy likeness of something; a sham.

simultaneous (sī′mŭl·tā′nê·ŭs). Happening at the same time.

singular (sĭng′gụ·lẽr). Extraordinary.

sinuous (sĭn′ụ·ŭs). Winding, as a serpent moves.

skeptic (skĕp′tĭk). Unbeliever; doubter.

slake (slāk). 1. To relax; moderate. 2. To quench; to satisfy.

sloth (slōth). Laziness.

smite (smīt). To strike a heavy blow.

smug (smŭg). Highly self-satisfied.

snipe (snīp). A marsh bird.

solace (sŏl′ĭs). Diversion.

solicit (sô·lĭs′ĭt). To obtain aid; to call upon for help.

soliciting (sô·lĭs′ĭt·ĭng). Urging.

solicitude (sô·lĭs′ĭ·tūd). Anxiety; expression of concern.

soliloquies (sô·lĭl′ô·kwĭz). Discourses made by one in solitude.

sonorous (sô·nō′rŭs). Full and rich in sound.

sophistry (sŏf′ĭs·trĭ). A clever but misleading argument.

sordid (sôr′dĭd). Base; worthy of being despised.

sovereign (sŏv′ẽr·ĭn). A gold coin worth a pound (about five dollars).

spasmodic (spăz·mŏd′ĭk). Occurring very irregularly.

speculative (spĕk′ụ·lā′tĭv). Still in the guessing stage.

spontaneous (spŏn·tā′nê·ŭs). A natural feeling without restraint.

sportive (spōr′tĭv). Gay and playful.

spurious (spū′rĭ·ŭs). That which is not genuine; false.

spurn (spûrn). To ignore; to cast aside; to scorn.

squalid (skwŏl′ĭd). Dirty through neglect; poverty-stricken.

stagnate (stăg′nāt). 1. To become inactive or dull. 2. To become foul from lack of motion, as standing water.

staid (stād). Stiff and proper; strait-laced.

stalwart (stôl′wẽrt). 1. n.- A strong and trusted man. 2. adj.- Firm and steadfast.

stanchless (stänch′lĕs). A flow which cannot be stopped.

stark (stärk). Unadorned; harsh and desolate.

stave (stāv). A wooden staff or pike.

steep (stēp). To stand and soak in.

sterling (stûr′lĭng). Genuine.

strand (strănd). The beach.

studied (stŭd′ĭd). Full of thought and knowledge about a subject.

suave (swäv). Worldly; sophisticated.

subjugate (sŭb′jōo·gāt). To conquer by force.

subsequent (sŭb′sê·kwĕnt). Coming after something else; later; following.

subserve (sŭb·sûrv′). To be useful in an inferior capacity.

subservience (sŭb·sûr′vĭ·ĕns). Slavish politeness and obedience.

subtile (sŭb′tĭl). Keenly perceptive; mentally alert.

succor (sŭk′ẽr). Aid.

succumb (sŭ·kŭm′). To sink down; to give in.

suffer (sŭf′ẽr). To allow.

suffice (sŭ·fīs′). To meet or satisfy a need.

suffuse (sŭ·fūz′). To overspread; to tinge.

sullen (sŭl′ĕn). Dark and gloomy.

sumptuous (sŭmp′tụ·ŭs). Luxurious.

sunder (sŭn′dẽr). Divided.

sundry (sŭn′drĭ). Several and varied.

supercilious (sū′pẽr·sĭl′ĭ·ŭs). Haughtily contemptuous.

superfluous (sụ·pûr′flōo·ŭs). Unnecessary.

supplanter (sụ·plăn′tẽr). One who takes the place of another.

suppliant (sŭp′lĭ·ȧnt). One who beseeches.

surcease (sûr·sēs′). Stop or cease.

surfeited (sûr′fĭt·ĕd). Completely filled; full to the brim.

surmise (sûr·mīz′). A guess or imagining.

swain (swān). A country lover; an admirer.

swashbuckling (swŏsh′bŭk′lĭng). Boasting; bragging.

swathe (swāth). Wrap up closely; surround like a wrapping.

---

cōol, cŏŏk; our, boil; cūte, ûnite, bûrn, cŭt, ŭnless, menü; check; goat, sing, this, thick, scriptụre, verdụre.

745

swelter (swĕl′tēr). 1. To ooze or to give off a moisture. 2. To be oppressed by heat.

symmetry (sĭm′ê·trĭ). Well balanced form or arrangement.

synthesis (sĭn′thê·sĭs). Combination of parts or elements into a whole.

T

taper (tā′pēr). A candle.

targe (tärj). A shield or target; a protection.

tedious (tē′dĭ·ŭs). Wearisome; boring and time-consuming.

tegument (tĕg′û·mĕnt). A covering; skin.

temperate (tĕm′pēr·ĭt). Moderate and restrained.

temporal (tĕm′pô·rắl). Earthly.

tenement (tĕn′ê·mĕnt). An apartment; a shop.

tenet (tĕn′ĕt). Any principal or doctrine held as true by an organization.

tenterhook (tĕn′tēr·hŏŏk). A nail or spike on which cloth is fastened on a tenter. Hence, "On tenterhooks" denotes a feeling of strain, as if by stretching; suspense.

terrene (tĕ·rēn′). Pertaining to the earth.

terse (tûrs). That which is free of unnecessary words; pithy.

thrall (thrôl). A slave; a bondman.

throe (thrō). A struggle or effort.

tincture (tĭngk′tûr). A trace; tinge.

tipple (tĭp′ 'l). To sip; to drink.

titanic (tī·tăn′ĭk). Of enormous magnitude.

tranquil (trăng′kwĭl). Calm; peaceful.

transcendent (trăn·sĕn′dĕnt). Surpassing; superior; extraordinary.

transient (trăn′shĕnt). Changing; always moving.

transitory (trăn′sĭ·tō′rĭ). Fleeting.

transpose (trăns·pōz′). To exchange places.

travesty (trăv′ĕs·tĭ). A ridiculous imitation.

tremulous (trĕm′û·lŭs). Fearful; quivering.

trenchant (trĕn′chănt). Keen; mentally energetic.

trenched (trĕncht). Like a trench or ditch.

trencher (trĕn′chēr). That which pertains to eating or carving at meals.

tribulation (trĭb′û·lā′shŭn). Distress or suffering.

troth (trŏth). Faith; loyalty.

truism (trōō′ĭz'm). A self-evident truth.

tumultuous (tû·mŭl′tû·ŭs). Violent; very noisy and disorderly.

turbid (tûr′bĭd). Clouded; muddled.

turmoil (tûr′moil). Commotion; disturbance.

U

ulterior (ŭl·tēr′ĭ·ēr). Further.

ultimate (ŭl′tĭ·mĭt). The last; final.

unblemished (ŭn·blĕm′ĭsht). Spotless; flawless.

unintelligible (ŭn′ĭn·tĕl′ĭ·jĭ·b'l). That which cannot be understood.

unkempt (ŭn·kĕmpt′). Not combed; disheveled.

unmanned (ŭn·mand′). Without manly strength and courage.

unpremeditated (ŭn′prê·mĕd′ĭ·tāt′ĕd). Occurring without thought; unplanned.

unreproved (ŭn′rê·prōōved′). Unpunished; free from reproof.

unsmote (ŭn·smōt′). Not struck.

upbraid (ŭp·brād′). To scold or rebuke; to punish.

urbane (ûr·bān′). Refined; elegant and smoothly polite.

usurper (ů·zûr′pēr). One who steals the place of another.

V

vanguard (văn′gärd′). The foremost or leading position.

vantage (văn′tĭj). Opportunity.

vault (vôlt). 1. n-. A storage place. 2. v-. To leap.

vaunt (vônt). Boast.

verbatim (vûr·bā′tĭm). Word for word.

verdurous (vûr′dûr·ŭs). Freshly green, as plants are in springtime.

verities (vĕr′ĭ·tĭz). Truths.

vernacular (vēr·năk′û·lēr). The everyday language of the people.

vernal (vûr′nắl). Springlike.

viceroy (vīs′roi). A representative of a king or sovereign.

vicissitude (vĭ·sĭs′ĭ·tūd). Change of fortune.

visage (vĭz′ĭj). The face or countenance.

voluptuous (vô·lŭp′tû·ŭs). Luxurious and exotic.

voracious (vô·rā′shŭs). Greedy.

vouch, avouch (vouch). To recognize; to call attention to.

vouchsafe (vouch·sāf′). To be willing to grant or give.

vulnerable (vŭl′nēr·ă·b'l). Able to be wounded; open to attack.

W

wane (wān). To fade or grow smaller.

wanton (wŏn′tŭn). 1. Merry and gay. 2. Luxuriant in growth.

wary (wâr′ĭ). Cautious.

wassail (wŏs′ 'l). A festive occasion with much drinking and good cheer.

weal (wēl). Prosperity and well being.

ween (wēn). To suppose; to expect.

weltering (wĕl′tēr·ĭng). Wallowing.

wend (wĕnd). To proceed on one's way.

whelp (hwĕlp). 1. A young animal. 2. A contemptuous word for a youth.

whet (hwĕt). To sharpen.

whetstone (hwĕt′stōn′). An implement for sharpening steel.

whimsical (hwĭm′zĭ·kắl). Fanciful.

winnow (wĭn′ō). To disperse or scatter.

winsome (wĭn′sŭm). Charming and attractive.

woof (wōŏf). The cross thread in a woven fabric.

wrack (răk). Ruin; destruction.

wrought (rôt). 1. Fashioned or constructed. 2. Pertaining to metal work produced by hammering into shape.

Y

younker (yŭng′kēr). A youngster; a child.

āte, châotic, dâre, ădd, ắccuse, bär, càsk, ȧfar; ēat, dẽar, êlude, ĕgg, quiĕt, centēr; īdle, ĭf, activĭty; ōpen, ôbey, ôr, ŏrange, ŏffer, ŏccur.

INDEX

John O'Dwyer
4E
150 Idora Avenue
S. F.
Lo. 4-0287